MW00992764

Alaska Politics and Public Policy

The Dynamics of Beliefs, Institutions, Personalities, and Power

EDITED BY
Clive S. Thomas

WITH
Laura C. Savatgy
and Kristina Klimovich

Published by
University of Alaska Press
P.O. Box 756240
Fairbanks, AK 99775-6240

Cover and interior design by Jen Gunderson, 590 Design, fiveninetydesign.com

Cover photo credits (from back cover to front):

Pipeline: © Heather Nicaise
Small Port City: iStockphoto
Sow and Cub: © HILDEBRAND photography
Capitol Building: Shutterstock
Anchorage in the Fall: © Jonathan Nafzger
Alaska Flag: iStockphoto

Indigenous Peoples and Languages of Alaska Map: Indigenous Peoples and Languages of Alaska map, copyright 2011 Michael Krauss, Gary Holton, Jim Kerr and Colin T. West. Published by the Alaska Native Language Center in collaboration with the UAA Institute of Social and Economic Research. Printed with permission from the ANLC.

Library of Congress Cataloging-in-Publication Data

Names: Thomas, Clive S., editor. | Savatgy, Laura C., editor. | Klimovich, Kristina, editor.
Title: Alaska politics and public policy : the dynamics of beliefs, institutions, personalities and power / Clive S. Thomas, editor ; with Laura C. Savatgy, and Kristina Klimovich.
Description: Fairbanks, AK : University of Alaska Press, [2016] | Includes bibliographical references and index.
Identifiers: LCCN 2015022970| ISBN 9781602232891 (lithocase : acid-free paper) | ISBN 9781602232907 (e-book)
Subjects: LCSH: Alaska--Politics and government--1959- | Political planning—Alaska. | Alaska--Economic policy. | Power (Social sciences)—Alaska.
Classification: LCC JK9541 .A56 2015 | DDC 320.609798—dc23
LC record available at http://lccn.loc.gov/2015022970

This book is dedicated to the memory of
Thomas B. Stewart
(1920-2007)

Life-long Alaskan, Secretary to the Alaska Constitutional Convention, Alaska Superior Court judge, patron of the arts, mentor to those of us studying Alaska politics, and friend to so many

Images of Alaska Native culture
by
Jarell Eastman of Tatitlek, Alaska

CONTENTS

PART III

DEVELOPING AND IMPLEMENTING PUBLIC POLICY: THE INTERACTION OF BELIEFS, INSTITUTIONS, PERSONALITIES, AND POWER

PART IV

ISSUES AND POLICIES GENERATED BY THE POLITICAL ECONOMY OF THE OWNER STATE

PART V

ISSUES AND POLICIES REGARDING STATE SERVICES DELIVERY

PART VI

POLITICS, ISSUES, POLICIES, AND POLITICAL POWER IN ALASKA: PAST, PRESENT, AND FUTURE PERSPECTIVES

EXTENDED CHAPTER CONTENTS

PART I: ALASKA POLITICS AND PUBLIC POLICY: AN INTRODUCTION

Chapter 1: Understanding Alaska and Its Political Environment

Chapter 2: The Fundamentals of Alaska Politics: Influences, Characteristics, Issues, and Power

Chapter 3: Making Public Policy in Alaska: An Overview of the Process and Its Political Dynamics

PART II: MAJOR INFLUENCES SHAPING ALASKA'S POLITICS AND ITS POLICY ENVIRONMENT

Chapter 4: Alaska's Constitution: Shaping the Foundations and Development of Politics, Government, and Public Policy

Chapter 5: Alaska's Political Culture: The Confluence of Individualism, Dependence, and Pragmatism

Chapter 14: Campaigns and Elections: The Interaction of Weak Partisanship, Ideology, Personality, and Pragmatism

Chapter 15: Interest Groups, Lobbying, and Lobbyists, and Their Effects on Democracy in Alaska

Chapter 16: The Legislature, the Governor, and the Bureaucracy: Conflict, Cooperation, Personalities, and Power

Chapter 22: The Politics of Alaska's Environment: Reconciling Conflicts

Chapter 23: Fisheries Politics and Policy Making: The Move from General to Restricted Access

Chapter 24: Oil and Gas Issues and Policies: The Risks and Rewards of Being an Energy-Producing State

Chapter 25: The Alaska Permanent Fund and the Permanent Fund Dividend: The Owner State's Experiment in Managing Petroleum Wealth

PART V: ISSUES AND POLICIES REGARDING STATE SERVICES DELIVERY

Chapter 26: Education—K–12 and the University: Meeting the Needs of all Alaska Students?

LIST OF MAPS, TABLES, FIGURES, AND BOXES

MAPS

TABLES

FIGURES

BOXES

FOREWORD

Alaska has changed tremendously during its nearly sixty years as a state. A small, natural resource–based economy dependent on fishing, mining, and timber in its early years underwent a major transformation when oil became the state's principal income generator in the late 1970s. Although federal dominance over many policy issues waned with statehood, government—federal, state, and local—remains a major player in Alaska as employer, as landowner, as regulator, and as a funding source for education, health, social programs, and transportation. Alaska Natives (the state's indigenous population), little involved in public affairs before statehood, have emerged as a powerful economic force, service provider, and participant on the political stage. And even though the boom-and-bust cycle is still an aspect of the state's natural resource economy, almost sixty years of developments have given state policy makers more choices in dealing with the challenges that the state faces.

This book provides extensive coverage of these and other developments in its comprehensive, up-to-date, probing, and original analysis of Alaska's contemporary politics and public policy. Written in a readable style, the book covers a broad range of subjects, integrating them through effective structuring and formatting of chapters, case studies, comparisons with other states, and insightful and thought-provoking balanced perspectives on political developments, incidents, controversies, issues, and policies. Of particular note is that the book combines technical explanations by social scientists and other academics with the day-to-day understanding of state politics through contributions by politicians, legislative staffers, appointed public officials, political party leaders, journalists, lobbyists, and interest group leaders, among others.

The invaluable information and insights that the book provides make it of great value not only to teachers, students, and those engaged in the practice of government and politics, but also for the general public within and outside the state. It will be particularly useful to Alaskans who want to know more about their state's politics and government and how it really works. As one who has been close to Alaska politics and public policy for more than sixty years, I have always felt that it is the responsibility of every citizen in a democracy to be informed about their government and to participate in the governance of their state and local community. This book will help Alaskans become better citizens and more effectively discharge their responsibilities under the Alaska Constitution.

Victor Fischer
Delegate to Alaska's Constitutional Convention,
1955–56, and former Alaska State Senator
March 31, 2014

PREFACE

This book has two major purposes. One is indicated in the book's subtitle: to explain *The Dynamics of Beliefs, Institutions, Personalities, and Power* that shape Alaska politics and public policies. Understanding how these elements interact in the political arena helps to explain why and how some issues are dealt with by government in Alaska, why others get little attention, why some are tackled but cannot be resolved, and why others are not addressed at all. Combining the human element with the interrelationship of the parts of the political system gets to the root of what politics is all about.

The second purpose is to provide a wide range of information and analysis that will be of value to a broad readership—from those with very little knowledge of Alaska politics to Alaska politics junkies. To this end, the book ranges from covering the basics of Alaska politics to providing detailed treatments of the factors shaping politics and the operation of government in the state to providing in-depth analysis of issues and policies.

To facilitate ease of use and learning, each chapter is divided into distinct sections, with the first part of the chapter setting out the basics and the latter part providing a more in-depth analysis.

MAJOR ASPECTS OF THE APPROACH AND TIPS ON USING THE BOOK

To achieve the book's two purposes, we have combined several elements: (1) drawing on three diverse information sources; (2) explaining terms, concepts, and acronyms; (3) setting the scene in Chapters 1, 2, and 3; and (4) building most chapters around a theme or argument.

Three Diverse Information Sources

Throughout the book we have combined: (1) research from political science, other social sciences, and history; (2) the perspectives of past and present state elected and appointed officials, as well as other political practitioners and observers such as lobbyists and journalists; and (3) information from other states and regions, particularly the American West, in order to place Alaska's politics in a comparative framework. This combination of sources enables us to utilize a theoretical and comparative perspective as well as explain the practical realities of Alaska politics.

Explaining Terms, Concepts, and Acronyms

The book contains over 250 terms, concepts, and acronyms, which are explained in one of four places in the book. First, terms that are used in more than one chapter (often in several chapters) are briefly defined in the glossary at the end of the book. Second, some chapters include short definitions of additional terms, concepts, and acronyms used specifically in that chapter. Third, terms and concepts that need fuller treatment are explained in detail in the body of the chapters. Fourth, Chapters 1, 2, and 3 explain many of the terms and concepts used throughout the book (or refer the reader to the glossary for their definitions), including the local parlance of Alaska politics and political geography and the language of the policy process.

Setting the Scene in Chapters 1, 2, and 3

The first three chapters set the scene for the rest of the book in several ways. Besides defining and explaining several terms and concepts, the three chapters present a discussion about the myths and realities of Alaska state politics in order to move readers beyond facts and figures and to get them thinking analytically. These chapters also explore comparisons with other states, particularly those in the American West. Comparisons provide initial insights into the strengths and weaknesses of Alaska's political system and what reforms might be advantageous. To provide a foundation for the analysis that threads through the book, Chapter 2 identifies twelve prominent characteristics of Alaska politics. Chapter 3 provides an overview of the public policy-making process, and, drawing on the first two chapters, explains the particulars of Alaska's state policy process.

A Specific Theme or Argument for Most Chapters

Chapters 4 through 28 address a wide range of topics relating to Alaska politics and public policy issues, while Chapters 29 and 30 take a look at the past performance of state government generally and offer an assessment of the future of Alaska's politics and public policy. A quick review of the table of contents and the extended table of contents shows that each chapter contains a lot of information. So, developing a specific theme or argument for each chapter provides a focus and a way to manage this information and present it in an understandable way. In most chapters, the theme is encapsulated in its title or subtitle, such as the subtitle of Chapter 14, "Campaigns and Elections: The Interaction of Weak Partisanship, Ideology, Personality, and Pragmatism." Using a theme approach also provides a thought-provoking way to aid discussion, pro and con, in analyzing the chapter and considering which of the twelve characteristics of Alaska politics best fits the chapter topic.

Those interested in further exploring a topic can refer to the notes and sources provided at the end of each chapter as well as the Further Reading and Research Resources section at the end of the book.

A NOTE ON VARIATIONS IN STATISTICS

This book is based upon the latest available research and information on Alaska politics and public policy as gathered by its contributors. As with any book of this type, however, there are minor problems with statistical sources.

Depending on whether federal, state, local government, or private sources are used, there are often differences in the figures obtained on the same subject. For instance, there are different figures available for the number of people employed in government in Alaska, the percentage of state revenues coming from oil, and how much the state receives in federal funds. These inconsistencies often arise because different items or factors are included in the statistic. Where significant differences do occur we bring them to the reader's attention and, where possible, provide an explanation. In general, however, minor variations in statistics do not affect the arguments in the book.

Another problem is obtaining up-to-date statistics. There is often a time lag, sometimes as long as three or four years, in the publication of statistical and other information by federal and state governments and private agencies like the Council of State Governments. Besides this, budget cuts since the mid-2000s at the state and federal level have reduced funding for agencies and units providing statistical information. As a result, some data that had been gathered for decades is no longer available. When the authors encountered such problems, they have provided an explanation and discussed how it might affect their analysis, if at all.

ACKNOWLEDGMENTS

In a book project involving so many people and requiring a major exercise in organization and management, there are many people to thank. At the top of the list are the sixty-seven contributors. Of these, thirty-one were chapter authors or co-authors and thirty-six wrote or provided information for the boxes that appear in various chapters, including many past and present Alaska political practitioners and political observers. Laura "Lola" Savatgy deserves special thanks. She aided with the editing of the book and co-authored several chapters. Kristina Klimovich was a first-rate researcher, particularly in rooting out hard to find statistics, as well as a skillful editor and resourceful chapter co-author. Without Lola's and Kristina's help this book would not have been completed. I also thank Anthony "Tony" Nakazawa for recruiting contributors, reviewing some chapters, conducting research, and co-authoring chapters. George Ascott also helped with research on the project and provided valuable insights. At our many lunches over the years, Dave Donaldson, former Alaska Public Radio Network (APRN) political reporter, was an indispensable sounding board for ideas and a valuable source of information. He is also a contributor to the book. Fran Ulmer, currently the chair of the U.S. Arctic Research Commission, former chancellor at the University of Alaska Anchorage, and former lieutenant governor (among many other public positions she has held), provided encouragement and insightful advice. Arliss Sturgelewski, former state senator and twice candidate for governor, also provided much encouragement. Amber Granados was a wizard at producing the graphics, box inserts, and tables. Six people at the University of Alaska Press were also very helpful: former directors Robert Mandel and Joan Braddock; Amy Simpson, the UA Press manager; Elisabeth Dabney, former acquisitions editor; James Engelhardt, also a former acquisitions editor; and Krista West, production editor. Lindsey Doctorman of Western Governors University and Glenn Wright at the University of Alaska Southeast reviewed the manuscript and made several valuable suggestions for which I thank them very much.

In addition, this book would not have been possible, particularly its hands-on practical dimension, without the insights of close to three hundred public officials (elected and appointed), lobbyists, journalists, and others who gave freely of their time. The more than two hundred students who were interns in the University of Alaska's Legislative Internship Program during the twenty-five years that I ran the program, plus the students who took my Alaska politics classes, also helped tremendously. Each year I gained new insights into Alaska politics by teaching them.

Finally, and most importantly, I thank my wife, Susan Burke, for her extensive editing, encouragement, and realistic assessment of what needed to be done when things weren't working out quite the way I'd planned. Our four cats, Dinsdale, Toby, Chesterton, and Cromwell (as well as our late cats, Hamilton, Ernesto, and Wellington), also deserve a mention for their constant companionship, love, and affection.

Clive S. Thomas

Juneau, Alaska, and Pullman, Washington

April 1, 2016

★ PART I ★

Alaska Politics and Public Policy: An Introduction

About Part I

As indicated by its Table of Contents, this book contains a massive amount of information on Alaska politics and the public policies that the state enacts and implements. This amount of information can be daunting for the novice and a challenge even to the informed observer in making sense of the many factors involved in politics and policy making in the state. However, as with other subjects, we can explain the essence of Alaska politics and policy making in an encapsulated form. The purpose of the three chapters in the first part of the book is to provide a basic political and policy road map for navigating the rest of the book. In sum, the three chapters are intended to do six things.

First, they explain many terms and concepts, some common to politics and government in general, others specific to Alaska, necessary for understanding the arguments and information throughout the book.

Second, in each of the three chapters there is an attempt to separate the myths and misconceptions about Alaska, its politics, and public policy-making process from the reality. One of these myths is that Alaska is vastly different from other places in many aspects, including its politics.

Third, the three chapters show the link between the academic study of politics and public policy and its practical day-to-day operation. This is particularly important because throughout the book there are references to both the concept and the exercise of political power to explain many actions and inactions of government.

Fourth, in combination, the three chapters provide an overview of the economic, social, cultural, geographical, and other factors shaping Alaska's political environment. This environment in turn shapes the way politics are conducted and the policies that result.

Fifth, in Chapter 2, twelve characteristics of Alaska politics are identified. These provide a shorthand explanation for much of what happens in the state politically. The characteristics appear in various forms and combinations throughout the book as they relate to the various aspects of Alaska politics, government, and public policy.

And sixth, this first part of the book places Alaska within the context of politics and policy making in other states, particularly the American West. This comparative approach facilitates an understanding of how similar or different Alaska is from other states and is a valuable exercise in itself. But it also provides perspectives for assessing the experience of other states in working to improve the effectiveness of Alaska's democratic system of politics and its policy process.

In reading these three chapters, the newcomer to Alaska politics will become less intimidated by the scope of the book and will find many ideas and circumstances that are familiar. The informed observer should find different ways of looking at Alaska politics, its government and policy process and, it is hoped, gain new insights. After completing Part I, both the novice and the seasoned reader will be well equipped to approach any of the chapters or topics in the rest of the book.

★ CHAPTER 1 ★

Understanding Alaska and Its Political Environment

Clive S. Thomas and Laura C. Savatgy

Hundreds of thousands of Americans and people from all over the world visit Alaska each year. Among the questions some visitors ask are: What currency do Alaskans use? What country do they belong to? Is it dark for half the year? Other common images of Alaska among those from "Outside" (as Alaskans refer to the rest of the country and the world) are outrageously high prices for most goods and services, rugged individualists battling against the elements on the "Last American Frontier," the romance of the Iditarod sled-dog race, the yearly "giveaway payment" to the state's citizens from the Alaska Permanent Fund, and the "idyllic" life of Eskimos in their igloos. Even as recently as 2006 a survey revealed that many Americans felt that Alaska was different, still manifesting much of the frontier spirit, and that Alaskans were "different" too.[1]

More recent images of Alaska among Outsiders include the political corruption scandals involving Alaska's state and federal politicians of 2006 through 2008, including the late U.S. Senator Ted Stevens. Then there is the flamboyant figure of the hockey mom, Governor Sarah Palin, the 2008 vice presidential candidate who resigned as governor unexpectedly in July 2009 with nearly eighteen months of her term left, and her continuing place in the national spotlight. And Alaska's 2010 U.S. Senate race received national attention when the incumbent Republican, Lisa Murkowski, was beaten in the primary election by a Tea Party–backed candidate, Joe Miller. Murkowski then ran the first successful U.S. Senate general election write-in campaign since 1954.

However, it is not only Outsiders from Maine, California, Japan, England, and Brazil, among a host of other places, who hold mixed, distorted, or blinkered views of Alaska. Many Alaskans, among them politicians and other public officials, view their state as an intricate mix of myth, misconception, wishful thinking, and reality. This mix includes beliefs such as Alaskans are individualists and would be much better off with less government; Alaska has boundless economic potential if only Outside forces would not block the state from developing them; and that the federal government has a stranglehold on Alaska. This mix of beliefs often translates into a range of negative attitudes toward government in general as epitomized by the support for Joe Miller, who ran on an essentially antigovernment platform in 2010 and again in 2014.

One of the purposes of this book is to separate the myths, misconceptions, and misunderstandings from the realities of Alaska politics. This involves addressing such questions as: Are the oil companies running Alaska? Is, in fact, the federal government choking the state's economic and political potential? Is there a solution to the state's chronic revenue instability? Is Alaska unique from other places or, at least, exceptional in its politics? What is the role of Alaska's indigenous population (Indians, Eskimos, and Aleuts) in state politics? This segment of Alaska's population is referred to collectively as "Alaska Natives" or simply as "Natives." Do the political corruption scandals exposed during 2006–2008 mean that Alaska is one of the more corrupt states in the nation?

The first three chapters in the book provide the background for tackling these questions. This chapter provides essential information for studying Alaska politics and for understanding Alaska's political environment. Chapter 2 builds on this and explains the essence of Alaska politics, partly by placing it in context with other states, particularly the American West. Chapter 3 provides an overview of public policy making in general and draws on the first two chapters to explain the specifics of Alaska's state policy-making process. The three chapters include explanations of many terms, concepts, and acronyms used in other chapters in the book. In addition, there is an extensive glossary at the end of the book that includes short explanations of more than 250 terms, concepts, acronyms, events, court cases, and Alaska-specific parlance that are used in various chapters throughout the book.

Specifically, this chapter has five goals. The first is to explain the approach to analyzing Alaska politics used in the book. The second is to explore some basic but key concepts to enhance this analytical approach, which emphasizes politics as first and foremost a human activity. Goal three is to explain the essentials of the state's political geography and the local parlance associated with it. The fourth is to raise the issue of Alaska's exceptionalism as a frame of reference to question common beliefs about the state and, in particular, attitudes toward Alaska politics. And fifth, the key events in Alaska's political history and development are outlined.

1. ANALYZING ALASKA POLITICS: A FOCUS ON THE BEHAVIORAL PERSPECTIVE

There are a number of generally recognized approaches to explaining and understanding politics. These include three that were used extensively up until the 1960s: the historical perspective (viewing current policy making as the product of historical forces); the institutional approach (primarily describing the structure and powers of government institutions); and the political economy approach (which views politics as being driven primarily by economic forces). Since the 1960s a fourth perspective has become the most prominent one—the so-called behavioral approach, which emphasizes human behavior and attitudes. The behavioral approach focuses on: (1) political culture, which emphasizes the importance of peoples' beliefs and values in shaping political actions and policies; (2) the political process, which concentrates on the policy-making process and sees it as a set of interrelated stages forming a policy cycle; and (3) the realist perspective, which emphasizes human self-interest, pragmatism, and power as a way of explaining political action and inaction.

While all approaches have insights to offer, none by itself tells the whole story, and we should be wary of those who say there is a single, exclusive, comprehensive approach to explaining politics. The most enlightening analysis uses elements of all of the various approaches, emphasizing some as major explanations and using others as supplementary. Our primary emphasis is on the behavioral approach, combining political culture, political process, and the realist perspective. This combination provides an in-depth understanding of the dynamic nature of Alaska politics and policy making.

2. POLITICS, GOVERNMENT, PUBLIC POLICY, AND RELATED TERMS AND CONCEPTS

For many of us, our high school civics classes focused on the contents of the U.S. Constitution and the structure and power of governmental institutions, such as Congress and the powers of the president. At its root, however, politics results from clashes over issues that emerge from the needs and desires of the citizenry and is shaped by historical experiences (particularly economic and social factors); geography (physical location, terrain, and resources or lack thereof); contact with Outside forces (particularly close neighbors); and the values and beliefs of the citizenry as well as the beliefs and personalities of public officials elected and appointed to various positions in government. All of these factors shape the power structure of a political system. Above all, in Alaska as elsewhere, it is, in fact, political power that determines which policies will be enacted and which ones will not.

So to provide a foundation for studying Alaska politics and public policy, we first explain the concepts that are central to this book and how they are interrelated. These are: (1) politics; (2) power, authority, and political compromise; (3) government; (4) political issues; (5) public policies; and (6) political leadership.

Politics

While many Americans, including Alaskans, have a negative perception of politics (associating it with politicians, bureaucratic controls, wasteful government, benefits to special interests, and so on), politics is actually among the most common of all human activities. Politics occurs in almost all situations where two or more people get together, not just in government. Politics occurs in families, clubs, and the workplace (office politics), as well as at the city, state, national, and international level.

If we accept the pluralist perspective of politics (that many forces compete to get public policies enacted or defeated), political activity results from three human characteristics: (1) a strong social tendency and the desire to live with other human beings as opposed to being hermits; (2) an essentially selfish nature and the desire to benefit oneself, one's close kin, and friends; and (3) a variety of different goals that sometimes clash with the goals of others. When we combine these three elements, the result is conflict between and among people—one of the most common aspects of human existence. For example, some people might want to develop a piece of land for houses while others may want to turn the land into a park.

Conflict requires some form of resolution, whether this is movement to a new situation, such as using the land to build houses, turning the land into a park, or a compromise in which some of the land is used for houses and some is set aside for a park. Or the resolution could be to do nothing and maintain the status quo. Doing nothing is often the resolution to a political conflict because the status quo is very difficult to change, particularly in the U.S. political system and in Alaska. This emergence of conflict, and the process of resolving it, is the core of the activity of politics or what is often called the political process.

Power and Influence, Authority, and Political Compromise

A common mistake often made by those not attuned to politics is to assume that the organizational chart represents the power structure in that organization. What an organizational chart represents is the authority structure. The power structure is best described in terms of who actually determines what gets done or, to use political parlance, who has the political clout or the political juice.

While the authority structure in most cases approximates the power structure, there are usually variations between the two, and the reality is usually much more complex. Authority is *the vested right to exercise power given to an official by a constitution or law.* But to turn authority into power, which we define as *the ability to influence behavior and make someone do something they would not otherwise do*, requires many factors in addition to authority, including personal intercommunication skills. Some people are good at exercising political skill and acumen and others are not, regardless of whether they are in a high position on an organizational chart. Individuals lower down the chart may be much more effective in getting things done. For example, one of the most effective and powerful politicians in Alaska was the late Senator Frank Ferguson of Kotzebue, whose highest legislative position was as chair of a senate committee. He never held the top job of president of the twenty-member senate. Also, for many years, his chief aide, Mike Scott, was also very powerful and often referred to as Alaska's twenty-first senator. Both men were powerful because they had extensive political skills that many who had much more authority lacked.

What determines how close a person or group gets to what they want in a political conflict is not so much whether they are right or wrong, good or bad, or are known to be fair or unfair, though these factors may come into play, but how much *political power* they wield. That is, how much pressure, clout, or "juice" they can bring to bear on the situation, which in turn is based upon their control over resources, such as information and money.

Some people, including some scholars, differentiate between the degree of pressure exerted in politics and the level of effectiveness of individuals and organizations by distinguishing between power and influence. While some see influence as less extensive and decisive than power, others see it as more extensive and more subtle in its operation. Thus, the exact difference between influence and power has yet to be satisfactorily determined. Consequently, in this book the terms power and influence are used synonymously and interchangeably.

In pluralist democracies such as the United States, including Alaska, power is not concentrated in one source, as it is in a dictatorship. Power is fragmented into many locations—the legislature, the executive, the courts, political parties, interest groups, the media, prominent individuals, and so on. Thus, resolving an issue usually requires compromise when the various power forces clash. Compromise, then, is one of the major characteristics of democratic politics, including politics in Alaska.

Government

Political conflicts in families and small groups can often be resolved, and the resolution enforced, in informal ways among the parties. For instance, this would be the case when, after a discussion, a group of friends decide to go to the same movie even though originally some of the group wanted to go to a different one. When the organization gets to a certain size, however, like a club, a workplace, or a town, state, or nation, more formal rules to resolve conflict and to apply and enforce the resolution are needed. Institutions—legislatures, executive departments, courts, boards and commissions, and so on—created to formalize this process of conflict resolution, to formalize the resolution in laws and regulations, and enforce them, are what constitute government. The basic structure of government is usually set out in a constitution, but the details of its day-to-day operation are found in statutes, regulations, court rulings, and so on.

Obviously, politics and government are inextricably linked. For some purposes, however, it is useful to see politics as mainly a product of human nature and to view government as mainly a human creation, originating from human choice and decisions, even though many of these choices are shaped by political influences. Keeping this distinction in mind enables us to understand why politics is the way it is in Alaska and how politics may have shaped the structures and processes of government in terms of their strengths and weaknesses.

Political Issues

People turn to government to deal with concerns that they cannot resolve themselves or that the private sector cannot or will not handle. These include public safety, defense, regulation of environmental quality, and building and maintaining infrastructure. Some people also want government to perform tasks for philosophical reasons: for the common good, including securing a fair distribution of benefits to all citizens as in social democracies like Sweden, and to create a sense of community and increased human self-worth. Others strongly oppose this perspective and question whether these are legitimate roles for government.

In essence, then, a political issue is a problem that an individual, a group, or a segment of society expects government to solve. The issue could be anything from what to do about bears raiding trashcans in an Anchorage neighborhood, to what to do with revenue surpluses in Alaska, to what the United States should do about international terrorism. These and a myriad of other issues become subjects of public debate because a conflict develops among some individuals, groups, or segments of society about how to resolve them. Conflict develops for one or more of the following reasons: whether the problem is in fact a problem, and if so, whether government should deal with it; if government is to deal with it, how it should do so; and if dealt with, whether the result has had the desired effect.

Some political issues, though very few, are easily resolved and never appear again. These are usually simple, technical issues, such as the color and shape of a stop sign, or the date for filing income taxes. Most issues, however, are less easily dealt with and often have only a short-term solution, if any solution at all. Three major reasons underlie the inability to permanently solve most political issues.

First, any issue based upon a value—a person's or group's beliefs of what is right or wrong, good or bad, fair or unfair, and so on—will likely be contentious, even on such a seemingly simple subject as how best to educate children. Not only that, over time people's values undergo change and adaptation and this often causes issues to resurface, even after they appear to have been permanently resolved, such as use of the death penalty.

Second, policy solutions apply to future events and circumstances, and no one can predict those future developments with certainty. In addition, some policies may have unforeseen consequences, and others that may be appropriate for a while lose their relevancy or are no longer workable when conditions change. For this reason, today's solutions are often tomorrow's problems. This is certainly the case with the push to develop biofuel from corn and other cereals as a substitute for oil. It now appears that diverting corn production from food to fuel has contributed to worldwide food shortages and increased costs.

Third, an issue may be beyond government's ability to resolve. This could be because the issue is so contentious that no long-term compromise is possible, as with the issue of abortion in the United States. Or it could be because the issue is beyond the ability or the political capacity of government to handle. A good example is Alaska's inability to stabilize state revenues. With the bulk of state revenues coming from oil production, there is little public support for imposing taxes on individual Alaskans, particularly when the price of oil is high. This lack of public support translates into a lack of political capacity on this issue—the inability to muster support within Alaska society necessary to form a political consensus to deal with the problem.

Public Policies

A public policy is *the course of action taken by government to deal with a political issue resulting from a short- or long-term resolution of conflicting perspectives of various groups and individuals on that issue.* As noted earlier, a political conflict can be resolved by establishing a new course of action or by doing nothing for the moment (thus maintaining the status quo), either out of choice or the inability to muster support. If the resolution is a new course of action, it is usually accomplished by the enactment of that policy into law. Once a policy is enacted, and its rules and regulations are drawn up, it is usually implemented by one or more agencies of the executive branch of government and enforced by the courts. Examples of relatively simple issues dealt with through policies are limiting bar hours, prohibiting the sale of cigarettes to minors, and determining who is and who is not eligible to receive an Alaska Permanent Fund Dividend (PFD). More complex and challenging policy issues include determining and enforcing water quality standards, improving Alaska high school graduation rates, and deciding on the rate at which to tax the oil industry to maximize state revenue but not discourage oil exploration and production.

It would be a mistake, however, to assume that all new policies or the revision of existing ones are clear in their intent, are diligently implemented by the executive, and once dealt with are solved for all time. As there is rarely one force, group, or interest powerful enough to get everything they want in resolving an issue, the need for compromise sometimes leads to policies that lack clarity because they are so general. Furthermore, if a policy is passed over the objection of the executive branch, the agency concerned may drag its feet in implementing the policy or try to avoid implementing it at all. Plus, because many political issues are never permanently resolved, the original policies developed to deal with them are often revisited and amended or completely rewritten. So policy making through the policy process is an intermittent but continual policy cycle as attempts are made to reform many policies. Chapter 3 provides an overview of the policy process and its political dynamics in Alaska.

Political Leadership

In the rough-and-tumble of everyday politics, some people are better at the political game than others. Particularly among elected officials, but also among senior appointed officials and political party and interest group leaders, the more adept individuals usually move into leadership positions and often become household names in the nation, state, or community.

But just because a person is a skillful politician and holds a formal and high-profile leadership position, it does not necessarily follow that he or she has good political leadership skills. Such skills are central to politics in a democracy (in fact, in all political systems). They are needed to bring people together to make things happen, to resolve clashes of values, beliefs, and issues, and to navigate diverse power points, personalities, and egos involved in politics and the policy process. So what is political leadership? Box 1.1 explores the concept and shows that it involves more than high office or popularity.

With these general concepts in mind, we begin our examination of Alaska politics by looking at the state's political geography. Then, we raise the question of Alaska's exceptionalism followed by a brief historical outline of Alaska's political development.

3. ALASKA'S POLITICAL GEOGRAPHY

In essence, political geography includes the political issues that geography—what geographers call the spatial environment—generates in a particular place. Geographical factors such as location, neighbors, and physical features (including climate and natural resources) often produce political issues, some long-standing, some short-term. For example, the lack of water in deserts in the American West means that acquiring, controlling, and allocating water is a hot issue that continues to be part of the political geography of the region. And the dominant factor that shapes the political geography of Israel is that nation's establishment in 1948 against the will of many of its Middle East Arab neighbors. Box 1.2 explains important geographical terms used in Alaska, including some of the parlance of Alaska politics, and raises awareness of the imprecise terms "bush" and "rural."

BOX 1.1

Political Leadership: A Complex Phenomenon

Political leadership is a complex phenomenon. Good leaders are not always high-profile, charismatic politicians. They do, however, share some common attributes.

At a basic level, leadership is the ability to guide, direct, or influence people toward achieving a goal. In the case of politics, this means a political or policy goal. To be a leader a politician needs followers. The fact that they get elected to office is evidence that they have some followers in the electorate and some measure of persuasive ability. Beyond this basic attribute, the quality, extent, and level of leadership skills depend on personal traits, political style, and political circumstances and events.

Regarding personal traits, good leaders tend to have three qualities. First is courage—the courage to take chances, at times even go against the wishes of their constituents, and the courage to admit when they are wrong and pursue a new course of action when circumstances require it. Second is judgment or intuition, what some call "political smarts"—the ability to see a situation in its various political facets, make calculated judgments about the consequences of various courses of action, and recognize when it is appropriate to act or not to act. Third is will power—a combination of determination and self-discipline that enables a politician to persevere despite the difficulties involved. Finally, while many good political leaders possess charisma in varying degrees, charisma is not in itself essential to good leadership.

Political style refers to whether a politician tends to be outgoing or more of a behind-the-scenes type. Everyone who seeks elective office needs to be extroverted to some extent in order to get elected. Once in office, however, some are more inclined to seek publicity and the limelight. Others are more introverted deal-makers, political managers, or technical types. The same is true for high-level appointed officials.

Opportunity also plays a role in the making of a political leader. Political circumstances and events may present some politicians with opportunities to exercise their leadership skills and be viewed as great leaders. George Washington had the War of Independence and the founding of the new nation, Abraham Lincoln the Civil War, and Franklin Roosevelt the Great Depression and World War II. All of them rose to the occasion and ultimately became some of the most prominent leaders in the nation's history. Other politicians do not get such opportunities. It seems unfair to label certain politicians as poor leaders solely because they did not have the opportunity to rise to the occasion in a major crisis. It is impossible to know, for instance, whether President Hayes (1877–81) or President Taft (1905–13) might now be considered a great president if he had had an opportunity to deal successfully with a major crisis during his presidency.

Finally, values, particularly partisanship and ideology, have a lot to do with popular views of good or great leaders. Conservatives and Republicans are less likely to consider a liberal or a Democrat as a good or great leader, and vice versa. For example, partisanship and ideology very much separate those who disagree about the leadership qualities of President Barack Obama and former Alaska Governor Sarah Palin. Plus, it is sometimes hard to assess a politician's leadership skills in the present moment. Both Lincoln and Roosevelt were very divisive characters and were dismissed and despised as leaders by many Americans during their presidencies. Unbiased assessments of leadership qualities often need the distance of time, perhaps forty or fifty years or even longer.

Source: Developed by the authors.

There are four geographic factors that have far-reaching effects on politics and public policy in Alaska: the state's relatively remote location, the size of the state, its physical environment, and the size and distribution of the population. Maps 1.1 and 1.2 (on pages 50 and 51) illustrate these four factors and help explain their political consequences.

BOX 1.2

The Parlance of Alaska's Political Geography

The Bush: An imprecise term to designate parts of the state in which communities are mostly inaccessible by road (only by air and sometimes by water), have a predominantly Alaska Native population, and subsistence (hunting, fishing, and gathering) plays a very important part in their economy. Naknek and King Salmon in Southwest Alaska and Ambler and Kobuk in Northwest Alaska are examples. See rural and rural-bush below for a further amplification of this term and its use in this book.

The Aleutian Chain or The Chain: The Aleutian chain in Southwest Alaska that crosses the international dateline at its far end.

"Down south": Used to refer to the Lower 48 states or the continental United States (usually not including Hawaii). Thus, it does not mean the southern states (the old Confederacy), as "down South" means in the Lower 48.

Lower Kuskokwim: Part of Southwest Alaska; the area centered around Bethel.

The Interior: The term is an imprecise one. It generally refers to the vast central part of the state, with Fairbanks as the major city.

Mat-Su: Shorthand for the Matanuska-Susitna valley, which extends about thirty-five miles north and east of Anchorage and includes the cities of Palmer, Willow, and Wasilla. The Mat-Su has seen a major population increase since the early 1980s and is one of the most conservative areas of the state.

The North Slope: The part of the state north of the Brooks Range that slopes down to the Arctic Ocean. Its major town is Barrow, and its major local government is the North Slope Borough (NSB). The North Slope includes the Prudhoe Bay oil field, the Arctic National Wildlife Refuge (ANWR), and the National Petroleum Reserve-Alaska (NPR-A).

Northwest or Northwest Alaska: This is the area south and west of the North Slope; Kotzebue is the major city.

Outside: Everywhere outside of Alaska. Implicit in this parlance is the notion that Alaska is separate, isolated, and to some extent different or exceptional.

The Railbelt: The area served by the Alaska Railroad from Seward on the southern Kenai Peninsula, through Anchorage to Fairbanks. Over 70 percent of the state's population resides along the Railbelt, the middle and southern portions of which are part of Southcentral Alaska.

Rural: This term, like "the bush," is broadly and imprecisely used to designate parts of Alaska, usually small, Caucasian/non-Native communities outside of the major urban areas that are on the road system and have a cash economy. Haines and Skagway in Southeast Alaska, Anderson southwest of Fairbanks on the road to Anchorage, and Delta Junction, southeast of Fairbanks on the Alaska Highway, are examples. See also bush and rural-bush.

Rural-bush: The term used in this book to designate areas outside of major urban centers both on and off the road system. There has never been a clear distinction made between urban, rural, and bush Alaska, so there is no consensus on their use in the state. This vagueness is at the root of several problems in state policy making, including the issue of subsistence. What is particularly confusing is that the terms "rural" and "bush" are often used synonymously in everyday speech in Alaska as well as by writers and academics.

Southcentral or Southcentral Alaska: The greater Anchorage metropolitan area including the northern Kenai Peninsula and the Mat-Su valley.

Southeast or Southeast Alaska: The mountainous region bordering the Yukon and British Columbia is shaped like a panhandle (though it is rarely referred to as the panhandle by Alaskans, but rather as "Southeast"). Its three major cities are Juneau, Sitka, and Ketchikan, all of which are inaccessible by road.

Southwest or Southwest Alaska: The region that includes Bethel in the Lower Kuskokwim and the Bristol Bay and Dillingham areas.

Source: Developed by the authors.

A Noncontiguous State of the Union

Alaska's remote location from the Lower 48 states means that it costs more to ship goods to and from the state. This pushes up the cost of doing business and makes many business ventures not feasible, particularly manufacturing. These and other factors translate into political issues by exacerbating Alaska's constant search for economic development, as well as political issues such as whether or not the major airlines and barge companies are taking advantage of their often monopoly positions to charge Alaskans more for their services than they could in more competitive markets. Its location also means that Alaska is dependent on Seattle, Washington, as a shipping port, particularly for goods coming into the state, though whether Alaska is a "colony" of Seattle is very debatable (see Box 1.3 on page 53).

The State's Size, Physical Environment, and Population Distribution

The sheer size of Alaska, 663,267 square miles (571,951 land and 91,316 water) or about one-sixth the size of the continental United States and more than twice the size of Texas (258,581 square miles), is often represented by placing a map of Alaska on an outline of the Lower 48 states (see the inset in Map 1.1). Then there is the climate, with heavy snowfalls and frozen ground in much of the state for at least six months of the year and rain and a lack of sunshine in Southeast Alaska and along the Aleutian chain. Plus, the terrain varies from high mountain ranges to tundra, making the building of roads very expensive and difficult in some places. But under this terrain lies some of the world's most extensive deposits of natural resources, including oil and gas, copper, gold, and many other minerals. And there are more than 6,600 miles of coastline and an ocean teeming with marine life.[2]

But this vast state has only a small population. It stood at 710,231 in 2010 (estimated at 732,000 in 2013 and projected to be about 800,000 by 2020). In 2013 this ranked Alaska forty-seventh in the Union (just above Vermont, North Dakota, and Wyoming at fiftieth). Alaska had less than one-quarter of 1 percent of the 309 million total U.S. population in 2010 and the estimated 316 million in 2013 (California has 12 percent and Washington State about 2 percent). In 2010 Alaska had the fewest inhabitants per square mile of any state at 1.2 (New Jersey ranks highest at 1,195 and Wyoming forty-ninth at 5.8). However, Alaska's population is highly concentrated in four or five urban areas, with Anchorage and its nearby communities dwarfing them all. Anchorage has 41 percent of the state's population and is the only city in Alaska with more than 100,000 people (California has 71 such cities).

As to its ethnic and racial composition, Alaska Natives are by far the largest minority group, with about 15 percent of the population or just under 105,000 in 2010, about half of whom live in rural-bush Alaska. Nationwide, American Indians and Alaska Natives

MAP 1.1

Map of Alaska

Source: Developed by the authors.

MAP 1.2

The Physical Geography of Alaska

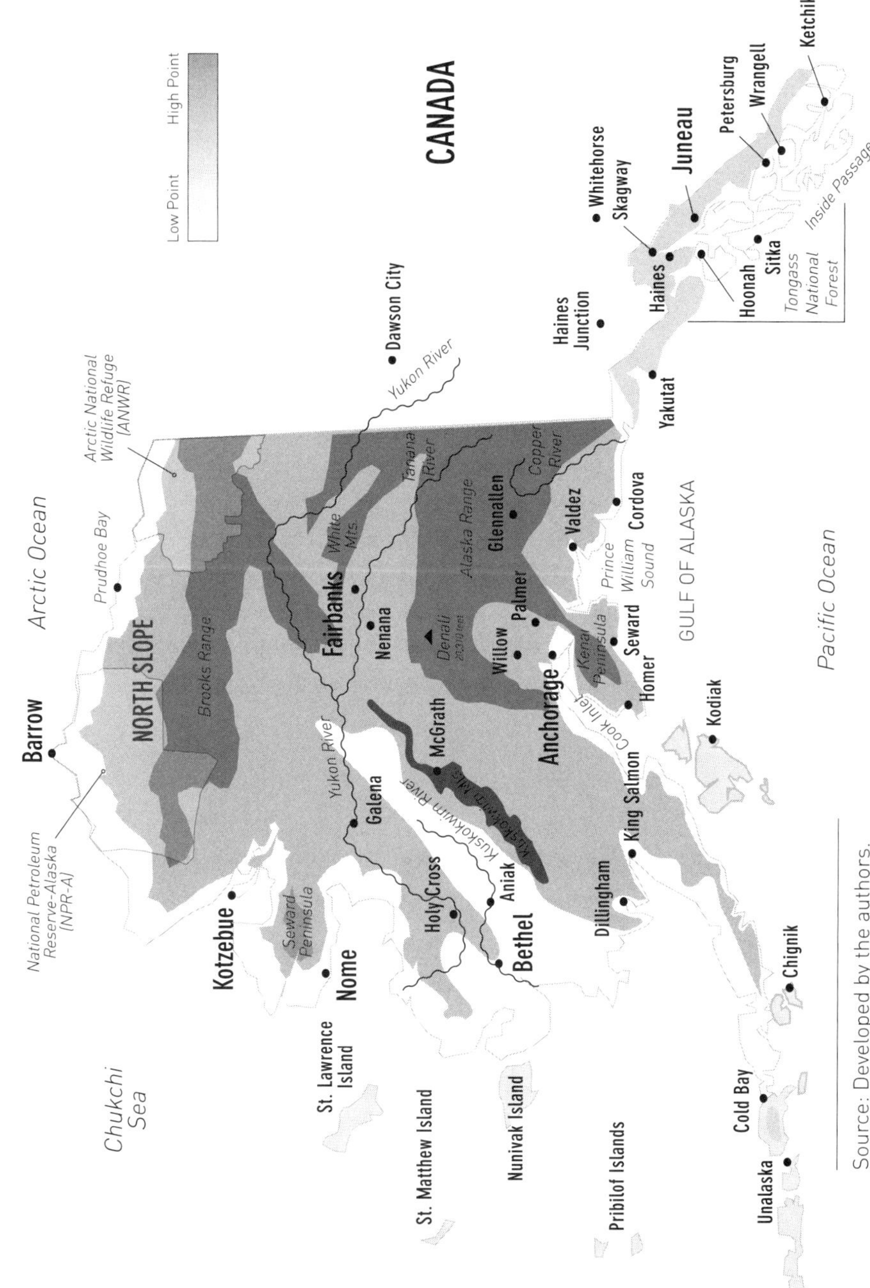

Source: Developed by the authors.

make up only 0.95 percent of the population. Those of Latino and Asian origin each make up about 5 percent of Alaska's population, but constitute 16.3 and 4.8 percent respectively of the U.S. population. African Americans make up just over 3 percent of Alaska's population, but 12.6 percent nationwide. Allowing for other small minority groups, about 66 percent of Alaskans are white or Caucasian, about 4 percent above the national average of 62 percent in both 2010 and the estimates for 2014.

Taken together, these spatial or geographical factors (including human geography), particularly those internal to the state, produce a political geography manifesting certain long-standing elements of Alaska politics and a range of political issues. These issues include the high cost of providing infrastructure, such as roads and airports, especially in rural-bush Alaska; the minimal role of agriculture and the central role of resource extraction; and the often intense conflict between those who want to develop the state for economic benefit and those who want to preserve or conserve it for its natural beauty.

Two aspects of Alaska's political geography provide particular insights into the political conflicts and the processes by which they are resolved. The first is regionalism and the related issue of conflict between urban and rural-bush areas. The second is the concept of "friends and neighbors" politics. These concepts are explained in detail in Chapter 2.

4. ALASKA'S EXCEPTIONALISM: AN INITIAL EXPLORATION

There is a belief among many Alaskans and many outside the state that Alaska is unique or exceptional in a number of ways. Several scholars have also argued the case for Alaska exceptionalism both past and present.[3] But is contemporary Alaska exceptional or unique and, if so, in what ways?

Certainly, when it comes to easily measurable characteristics such as land area, miles of coastline, inhabitants per square mile, and so on, Alaska is exceptional. When we turn to the realms of its socio-economic, political, and governmental characteristics, however, Alaska exceptionalism is subject to considerable debate. Scholars and informed observers disagree about the degree of exceptionalism, as we will see in many chapters in this book. Furthermore, to return to a point made earlier, many aspects of Alaska life are subject to myths and misunderstandings that tend to get perpetuated down the years. For instance, there is a belief among many Alaskans and some scholars that Alaska has unique features because it is still a colony of the Lower 48 states, the federal government, and international interests.[4] This view, however, is subject to a strong counterargument. Box 1.3 provides a closer look at the extent to which Alaska is or is not a colony.

Specifically, a question that we tackle in this book is the extent to which Alaska politics, government, political issues, and public policies are unique or exceptional. As with the issue of Alaska as a colony, informed observers disagree on this, depending on what

BOX 1.3

Is Alaska a Colony of the Lower 48 and International Economic Interests?

In the days of the British, French, and Spanish empires (from around 1500 to after World War II), what might be called traditional colonialism or imperialism was characterized by military conquest and control by the colonial power, including: (1) rule of the colony by the imperial country and exclusion of the colony's inhabitants from politics, including voting and forming political organizations; (2) a military presence by the imperial power for internal security and to ward off imperial rivals; (3) economic exploitation of the colony with little benefit to the local people; and (4) a very low standard of living and often extensive poverty among the colony's inhabitants.

Modern forms of colonialism are far less overt. They are often spearheaded by strong national governments, such as the United States since the turn of the twentieth century, or by multinational corporations (MNCs), often aided by national governments. This new imperialism involves the "colonial power" and/or the MNCs gaining indirect control of the economies of countries by being a major purchaser of their products. Furthermore, these "contemporary colonies" have little control over the prices of these products, which are determined by world markets. The natural resource and one-crop economies of many developing countries are often seen as victims of this new imperialism.

Given these perspectives, to what extent is Alaska a colony? By any stretch of logic Alaska is not a colony in the traditional sense. Like all states in the Union, Alaska is politically semi-sovereign, with its own government and freedom of political association. There is no military occupation by a foreign power. It is also hard to argue that major economic exploitation of Alaska occurs, given the close to $190 billion in revenues it generated from oil and gas taxes and royalties by 2014, and given a Permanent Fund with assets of over $52 billion at the end of fiscal year 2015 (June 30, 2015), four times the state budget that fiscal year. Plus, overall, Alaskans are not poor. Their median household income in 2012 was $66,521 (compared with a national average of $51,371), putting Alaska third among the fifty states that year, with Maryland first and New Jersey second.[1] Even given the higher cost of living in Alaska (which is much lower than it was in the 1980s) Alaskans are still among the most affluent people in the world.

As to the modern form of economic imperialism, Alaska is, more or less, a one-crop economy—oil—and is also highly dependent on the federal government for funding for many programs and on Seattle and its various businesses for shipping goods to the state. So, if one defines a colony narrowly in this economic dependency sense, Alaska is a colony. Even here, however, Alaska is far from politically and economically powerless. It has the wherewithal—with the Permanent Fund—to become independent of dictates by MNCs and could even become less dependent on the federal government if it chose to do so.

Generally, however, Alaskans choose not to do so, and they tax themselves as little as possible. So a good case can be made that Alaska has imposed "colonial status" upon itself as a result of fiscal conservatism and internal political divisions. For example, in 1990 Alaska lost the right to manage subsistence hunting and fishing on federal lands because it could not deal with the subsistence issue. Furthermore, almost all economies are dependent on Outside forces to some extent. Agricultural economies, like those in the Midwest, are affected by unpredictable weather as well as market prices over which the farmers have little control. Even industrial states like Michigan depend on people buying U.S. instead of foreign products.

---

[1]U.S. Census, Household Income: 2012, retrieved July 27, 2014, from http://www.census.gov/prod/2013pubs/acsbr12-02.pdf.

Source: Developed by the authors.

BOX 1.4

Alaska Historical Timeline

THE PRE-ALASKA PURCHASE PERIOD—TO 1867

10,000-3,000 years ago Humans inhabit the Bering Sea coast.

1741 Russian seafarers Vitus Bering and Alexei Cherikov sight Alaska.

1799 Alexander Baranov establishes the Russian post of Old Sitka. Trade charter given to Russian-American Company.

1853 Russians find the first oil seeps in Cook Inlet (near present-day Anchorage).

1867 Under President Andrew Johnson and Secretary of State William Seward, the United States purchases Alaska from Russia for $7.2 million. The purchase was often referred to at the time as "Seward's folly." After the formal transfer took place on October 18, at Sitka, the U.S. Army was given jurisdiction over what was called the Department of Alaska.

FROM THE PURCHASE TO TERRITORIAL STATUS—1967–1912

1872 Gold discovered near Sitka.

1878 First salmon canneries established in Southeast Alaska at Klawock and Old Sitka.

1884 An Organic Act gives Alaska its first civil government.

1891 First oil claims staked in Cook Inlet in Southcentral Alaska.

1897-1900 Klondike gold rush in the Yukon Territory; heavy traffic through Alaska on the way to the gold fields.

1898 Gold discovered on Nome beaches in western Alaska.

1906 Peak gold production year.

Alaska is granted a nonvoting delegate to Congress.

Governor's office moves from Sitka to Juneau.

1912 Territorial status granted by Congress for Alaska.

FROM TERRITORY TO STATEHOOD—1912–59

1913 First territorial Legislature convened in Juneau.

1914 President Woodrow Wilson authorizes construction of the Alaska Railroad.

1916 First bill proposing Alaska statehood introduced in Congress.

1920 Jones Act passed by Congress. Shipping goods between U.S. ports must be in U.S.-built vessels with U.S. crews.

1923 President Warren Harding drives spike completing the Alaska Railroad.

1935 Matanuska Valley Project, which moves farming families to Alaska, begins.

1942 Alaska Highway built—first overland connection to Lower 48.

NOV.-FEB. 1955-56 Alaska Constitutional Convention of fifty-five delegates held on the University of Alaska Fairbanks campus.

1956 In April, Alaska voters ratify the Constitution by a 2–1 margin.

1957 Oil discovered at Swanson River on the Kenai Peninsula, marking the start of Cook Inlet oil and gas production.

1958 Congress passes Alaska statehood measure.

1959 Statehood is officially proclaimed on January 3, 1959.

FROM STATEHOOD TO THE ALASKA PIPELINE—1959–77

1963 State ferry service begins between Seattle and Southeast Alaska.

1966 Alaska Federation of Natives (AFN) established.

1968 Oil and gas discovered at Prudhoe Bay on the North Slope.

1969 Lease sale on state selected lands totaling $900 million for Prudhoe Bay oil field.

1971 Congress enacts Alaska Native Claims Settlement Act (ANCSA), granting title to 44 million acres of land and providing $962.5 million in payment to Alaska Natives.

1972 Federal passage of the Coastal Zone Management Act and the Marine Mammal Protection Act.

State constitutional amendment institutes limited entry in the Alaska fishery.

1973 Congress passes the Endangered Species Act.

1974 Trans-Alaska pipeline system (TAPS) receives final approval; construction build-up begins.

1975 Alaska's population and labor force soar with construction of the pipeline. Alaska gross domestic product (GDP) hits $5.8 billion—double the 1973 figure.

1976 Creation of the Alaska Permanent Fund by constitutional amendment.

The *Molly Hootch* settlement. The state agrees to build high schools in most Alaska villages. Before this, Native students had to attend regional boarding schools for high school.

1977 Completion of TAPS from Prudhoe Bay to Valdez; shipment of first oil by tanker from Valdez to Puget Sound in Washington State.

FROM THE PIPELINE TO THE PRESENT

1978 A 200-mile offshore fishing zone goes into effect.

President Jimmy Carter withdraws fifty-six million acres of federal lands in Alaska to create seventeen new national monuments.

1979 State of Alaska files suit to halt withdrawal of the fifty-six million acres. The suit was unsuccessful.

1980 Alaska repeals the personal state income tax.

U.S. Census shows Alaska's population grew by 32.4 percent during the 1970s, to more than 400,000.

The Alaska National Interest Lands Conservation Act (ANILCA) enacted by the federal government.

1982 First Permanent Fund dividend checks mailed to all qualified residents of Alaska.

1984 State of Alaska purchases the Alaska Railroad from the federal government.

1985 Failed attempt by the Alaska Legislature to impeach Governor Bill Sheffield.

1986 Price of oil drops to under $10 a barrel (usual price was around $30) causing major budget crisis, job layoffs, mortgage foreclosures, and the exodus of tens of thousands from Alaska.

1989 Worst oil spill to date in U.S. history occurs in Prince William Sound when the *Exxon Valdez* runs aground.

1994 Exxon is found liable for actual and punitive damages in litigation over the 1989 oil spill in Prince William Sound.

2002 The U.S. Congress defeats an amendment to open the Arctic National Wildlife Refuge (ANWR) to oil development. Alaska's congressional delegation vows to continue the fight to access the oil.

2005 Oil prices reach all-time high of nearly $70 per barrel.

2006 Alaska voters elect the state's first woman governor, Sarah Palin.

Federal corruption investigation begins into Alaska state and federal politicians, lobbyists, and oil service company VECO's executives. Several convictions follow in the next two years.

2008 Oil reaches close to $150 a barrel. State projects a $12 billion–plus surplus by 2009—twice the annual state budget at that time.

July Alaska U.S. Senator Ted Stevens indicted on federal charges of failing to disclose gifts from oil service company VECO.

August Governor Palin chosen as vice presidential running mate by Republican presidential nominee John McCain.

October Senator Stevens found guilty by a Washington, D.C., jury on all counts for failing to disclose gifts.

November The McCain and Palin Republican ticket defeated in the presidential election.

Senator Stevens defeated by Democrat Mark Begich in the U.S. Senate race.

2009 In April, Stevens's conviction overturned and charges dismissed because of prosecutorial misconduct.

On July 3, Sarah Palin resigns as governor; Lieutenant Governor Sean Parnell sworn in as governor.

2010 Former Senator Ted Stevens killed in plane crash.

U.S. Senator Lisa Murkowski defeated in primary election by Joe Miller, who was supported by the Tea Party Express, but she wins write-in campaign for the seat in the fall election.

Sean Parnell elected as governor in his own right.

2011 Governor Parnell proposes tax break for the oil companies to encourage exploration. State Senate majority, the Bipartisan Working Group (BWG) of Republicans and Democrats, oppose the governor's proposal.

2012 Governor's oil tax proposal defeated. But BWG suffers losses in the November election and it falls apart.

2013 Republican-dominated legislature in both houses passes oil company tax break (Senate Bill 21—the More Alaska Production Act [MAPA]), prompting a citizen referendum to repeal it. The legislature also introduces several conservative proposals, including a constitutional amendment to allow state funds to go to private and religious schools.

2014 Tax referendum—Proposition 1—defeated in August primary—MAPA remains in force.

June–Dec. Oil prices drop almost 50 percent, from more than $100 to less than $60 per barrel. A major budget crisis ensues.

In the November general election:

Governor Parnell defeated for a second term by nonpartisan candidate Bill Walker.

Democrat Mark Begich defeated for reelection to the U.S. Senate by former Alaska Attorney General Dan Sullivan.

Use of marijuana legalized by initiative—Ballot Measure 2.

2015 The 2015 legislative session was dominated by the need for budget cuts due to low oil prices. Disagreements between Governor Walker and the Republican majority in each house over the gas pipeline and Medicaid expansion were also prominent.

Oil prices gradually declined from the mid-$60s range per barrel in July 2014 to the mid- to high-$40s range per barrel by July 2015.

By June 30 the Alaska Permanent Fund had passed the $52 billion mark.

Late summer: President Obama visits Alaska to highlight dealing with climate change.

September: Royal Dutch Shell pulls out of drilling for oil and gas in the Arctic.

December: Oil prices hover in the mid-$40s a barrel and then drop to the low-$30s.
Governor Walker proposes major restructuring of the Permanent Fund and a state individual income tax to help fund the state's budget shortfall.

Source: Developed by the authors.

aspects of Alaska politics and government are under discussion. In general, however, the most balanced answer to this question is to view Alaska's exceptionalism on a spectrum. At one end there are some undeniably unique characteristics or features, such as the role of Alaska Natives, the local government system, and the fact that the state owns and in some cases manages vast quantities of natural resources (the so-called Owner State). At the other end of the spectrum, Alaska has many elements in common with other states, such as the separation of powers in its governmental structure, similar components of the policy process, and semi-sovereign status within the federal system. Between these two points of the spectrum there are a combination of similarities and differences, such as the role and influence of political parties and interest groups, and the role of political ideology in shaping politics and policy making.

An exploration of the extent of Alaska's political and governmental exceptionalism and how this is intertwined with the myths, misunderstandings, and realities of politics, threads throughout the book. This is one aspect of placing Alaska in a comparative context. Chapter 2 provides a foundation for this comparative aspect of the book by offering insights on the degree to which Alaska's politics, government, and public policy are exceptional.

5. FROM THE PAST TO THE PRESENT: ALASKA'S POLITICAL DEVELOPMENT

It is certainly true that understanding the past can teach us a lot about the present, but an initial understanding of contemporary Alaska politics does not require extensive historical details and explanations. Those interested in the details of Alaska history can consult the Further Reading and Research Sources section at the end of the book. Plus, background on historical developments as they relate to specific aspects of Alaska politics, issues, policies, and political and governmental institutions are provided in the individual chapters. Much more useful than a detailed historical review is the identification of the major events and broad phases of Alaska's political, social, economic, and political development. These major events and phases are set out in Box 1.4.

6. CONCLUSION: MOVING FROM THE GENERAL POLITICAL ENVIRONMENT TO THE SPECIFICS OF ALASKA POLITICS

This general background on Alaska's past and present political environment provides a basis for understanding the specifics of Alaska's contemporary politics and public policy and for placing these in a broader regional, national, and international context. So we are now equipped to explore the specific factors that shape the characteristics of Alaska politics, the issues that face the state, and the particulars of the policy process for addressing these issues. And we have a foundation for delving into the factors that shape the power relationships in Alaska and how these play out to advance or block various policy proposals to deal with the short- and long-term problems facing the state.

ENDNOTES

[1] Dittman Research Corporation, *How the U.S. Views Us* (Anchorage: Dittman Research, 2006).

[2] These and other statistics on Alaska and comparisons with other states are taken mainly from *Almanac of the 50 States: Basic Date Profiles with Comparative Tables* (Woodside, CA: Information Publications, 2010); *The Book of the States*, volume 43 (Lexington, KY: Council of State Governments, 2012); and U.S. Census Bureau, 2010 Census: Population Distribution and Change 2000 to 2010, Table 1, retrieved April 15, 2011, from http://www.census.gov/prod/cen2010/briefs/c2010br-01.pdf; U.S. Census Bureau, 2010 Census: Population Density, retrieved April 15, 2011, from http://2010.census.gov/2010census/data/apportionment-dens-text.php; U.S. Census Bureau, American FactFinder Fact Sheet: Race and Hispanic or Latino, 2010, retrieved April 15, 2014, from http://factfinder2.census.gov/faces/tableservices/jsf/pages/productview.xhtml?pid=DEC_10_PL_GCTPL1.ST13&prodType=table; and U.S. Census Bureau, Population Estimates for 2013, retrieved August 2, 2014, from http://quickfacts.census.gov/qfd/states/00000.html.

[3] See Stephen Haycox, *Alaska: An American Colony* (Seattle: University of Washington Press, 2002) and his *Frigid Embrace: Politics, Economics and Environment in Alaska* (Corvallis: Oregon State University Press, 2002); Stephen W. Haycox and Mary Childers Mangusso, eds., *An Alaska Anthology: Interpreting the Past* (Seattle: University of Washington Press, 1994); and Peter Coates, "The Crude and the Pure: Oil and Environmental Politics in Alaska," in Richard Lowitt, ed., *Politics in the Postwar American West* (Norman: University of Oklahoma Press, 1995).

[4] See Haycox, *Alaska: An American Colony*, esp. Chapters 1 and 13.

★ CHAPTER 2 ★

The Fundamentals of Alaska Politics: Influences, Characteristics, Issues, and Power

Clive S. Thomas and Mary Sattler

Building on the initial insights into Alaska politics presented in Chapter 1, this chapter provides a more in-depth exploration. It does so by identifying the fundamental characteristics of Alaska politics, the influences that shape them, the issues they generate, and the power dynamics that work to deal with them or not deal with them, as the case may be. Explanation of the fundamental factors that make Alaska politics what they are (and what they are not) is essential to understanding the topics treated in the rest of the book. In exploring these topics, we will not be looking at Alaska in isolation but will compare it with other states, principally those in the American West.

The chapter is set out as follows. First, we distinguish between characteristics and influences. Then, after explaining why Alaska should be considered a "western" state, we review the traditional influences that have shaped both Alaska politics and those in other western states. This is followed by examining some recent trends and influences in the region and in Alaska. With an understanding of these influences and trends, we move to identify the contemporary characteristics of Alaska politics. Next we review the major issues in Alaska, both past and present. Finally, we turn to the question of where power lies in Alaska—a question that will be addressed throughout the book in the context of a variety of policies and issues.

1. DEFINING CHARACTERISTICS AND INFLUENCES

By *characteristic* we mean a distinguishing feature of politics. The political characteristics of a city, state, or nation incorporate three elements that shape political action: (1) the prevailing political values and attitudes; (2) the organization of the political and governmental institutions and the power relationships between and among them; and (3) the current issues and concerns. Some characteristics are unique to Alaska, such as the role of Alaska Natives in Alaska politics. Others, while not unique to the state, have a particular Alaskan or western bent to them, such as regionalism.

On the other hand, *influences* are the factors that shape or determine the political characteristics of a place. Influences are part of the larger environment and include a multitude of factors, many of which were identified in Chapter 1. These include historical developments; geography; social and economic factors such as religion, race, and ethnicity; economic opportunity or lack thereof; and, in some cases, international conditions.

So while political characteristics are by definition political, influences are often not political. For example, it is the vastness of many states in the American West and often the distinct economies in different parts of these states that have produced the political characteristic of regionalism.

2. ALASKA AS A WESTERN STATE

While the politics and government of all fifty states share much in common, Alaska differs most from the states of the Northeast (such as Maine, Massachusetts, New York, and New Jersey) and the Upper Midwest (Michigan, Minnesota, and Wisconsin), as will be explained in various chapters in the book. Alaska's similarities to and differences from the southern states will also be explored. Alaska is most similar to other states in the American West, particularly the Mountain West, and not just for geographical reasons. With regard to its economy, social makeup, political traditions, and its recent and contemporary politics, Alaska is a western state. Plus, for reasons of geography and common political issues, it has more interaction with states in the West than with those in other regions.

The way we define the American West is different from the images of the "Old West" or "Wild West" that come to mind from hundreds of Hollywood westerns and thousands of books. While one can still find areas of the American West that resemble those images, the boundaries are hard to precisely identify and for the most part they cannot be defined in political terms. In this book we define the West strictly in terms of geography. As arbitrary as this may sound, there is a political logic to it as states in the West share many common characteristics and influences.

The American West in this book includes the thirteen states west of the Great Plains: Alaska, Arizona, California, Colorado, Hawaii, Idaho, Montana, Nevada, New Mexico, Oregon, Utah, Washington, and Wyoming. Sometimes we need to make a distinction between the subregions of the West, such as the Pacific states, Mountain states, the Pacific Northwest, and the Southwest. The exact extent of these subregions varies, however, depending on who is using them and the purpose for their use. For example, the Pacific states usually include Washington, Oregon, and California. In some ways, however, Alaska can also be viewed as a Pacific state, particularly in regard to fisheries issues. Similarly, Arizona is sometimes regarded as part of the Southwest, but both Arizona and Alaska share some characteristics and political issues with the Mountain states, particularly in regard to mining issues. To avoid misunderstanding, we specify the boundaries of a subregion when referring to it.

3. THE TRADITIONAL INFLUENCES ON WESTERN AND ALASKA POLITICS

Box 2.1 briefly explains the traditional influences on western politics and the extent to which they apply to Alaska.[1] They are labeled as "traditional" because they are the influences that have worked to shape the characteristics of western politics over many years—in some cases since the days of the Wild West. In reviewing Box 2.1, it is important to bear in mind that there are always exceptions to generalizations, and this is true of the influences on western politics. California, as a giant in the region with one of the largest and most balanced economies in the nation (it would be the eighth largest in the world if it were a separate country), is an exception to some of the generalizations we make. Also, there are some major differences between the economies of most Mountain states and the Pacific states (Pacific in this case excludes Alaska). Nevertheless, all thirteen states have several influences on their politics in common.[2]

It is clear from Box 2.1 that in some way all the traditional influences on western politics apply to Alaska and produce similar characteristics of politics. As with all states in the West, though, specifics of Alaska history, economy, social structure, and geography, among other factors, result in variations in these influences that produce characteristics of politics particular to Alaska. Two are especially important. One is Alaska's demographics, which, as outlined in Box 2.1, includes a significant number of Alaska Natives and the bulk of the population living in Southcentral Alaska. The other influence is Alaska's late admission into the Union, an influence it shares only with Hawaii.

Two consequences of this late admission are particularly significant.

First, the authors of Alaska's Constitution had the experience of the other forty-eight states to draw upon in designing the state's governmental system, and they tried to avoid some of the mistakes made in the Lower 48. Second, by the time Alaska became a state, America was beginning to reconsider its treatment of Native Americans, and an age of atonement was dawning. Alaska Natives were the beneficiaries of this new era. This, together with a large percentage of them living in rural-bush areas and often electing Native legislators, helps explain their prominence in Alaska politics since statehood.

BOX 2.1

Influences on Western Politics and Their Relevance to Alaska

1. NATIONAL INFLUENCES—PAST AND PRESENT

Despite some distinctive features of the West, most westerners have always seen themselves as Americans first and citizens of their states second. Those who came west brought American values and the American system of government.

This, for the most part, is the case in Alaska. National influences are particularly strong because most of Alaska's population migrated from the Lower 48, Alaska was one of the last states admitted to the Union, it is dependent on federal funds, and it is considered by many to be "the Last American Frontier."

2. THE PHYSICAL ENVIRONMENT

The size of a state, its terrain, and its climate all produce factors such as regional identities within a state and the high cost of providing infrastructure (roads, bridges, and aqueducts), which in turn generate political issues.

This influence certainly applies to Alaska. Because of Alaska's physical beauty and its vast and unspoiled wilderness, within a decade after statehood, many Americans began to view Alaska as the poster child for a host of environmental issues.

3. THE DEPENDENCE OF THE WEST ON EXTERNAL FORCES

Western states have long been dependent in varying degrees on external forces, such as the federal government, world markets, and U.S. and foreign business corporations. This dependence often generates political antipathy, and sometimes an overt populist (anti–big business and big government) reaction from the public and politicians.

Probably no state is more subject to external influences over its politics than Alaska. Its economic well-being is determined in large part by world markets, the influence of national and international businesses, and the actions of the federal government, as well as national and international interest groups.

4. THE BOOM AND BUST ECONOMY

In the past, most western state economies were based on primary production—agriculture and natural resource extraction—timber, precious metals, coal, and oil and gas. The price of primary products is determined by national and world markets, and prices fluctuate with changes in supply and demand. When major price fluctuations occur, employment and state revenues can rise and fall, sometimes abruptly, leading to economic booms and busts. These booms and busts have generated many issues and policy proposals, such as the constant search for economic development and diversification.

Alaska's economy has long been dependent on natural resource extraction, federal aid, and government employment. The state has little manufacturing industry and virtually no agriculture. In fact, Alaska has the most unbalanced economy and state revenue sources of all fifty states. Between 80 and 90 percent of state revenues come from oil and gas production. But these oil revenues can and have fluctuated widely, making the state chronically vulnerable to the boom and bust cycle.

5. THE DOMINANT PRESENCE OF GOVERNMENT, PARTICULARLY THE FEDERAL GOVERNMENT

In twelve of the thirteen western states, government is the largest employer, and seven of the top ten states in the nation where government is the major employer are in the West. This situation influences politics in many ways, such as cutbacks in government employment negatively affecting the economy. Plus, no region in the nation has had more of a federal presence. Today, the federal government is a large landowner (from 85 percent of Nevada to 63 percent in Idaho to 19 percent in Hawaii), and a major funding source for many services and programs from infrastructure to welfare.

Few states are more dependent on government—federal, state, and local—than Alaska. Rural-bush areas are particularly dependent upon federal and state spending and employment as it has few other sources of income and employment.

6. DEMOGRAPHIC FACTORS, INCLUDING THE PRESENCE OF MINORITY GROUPS

States with large urban areas, particularly California, have urban issues prominent in state politics, such as crime, social service needs, and demands for public transportation. The presence of large minority populations, such as Hispanics, can lead to particular issues, such as English-only movements that are, in part, a reaction to bilingual education. In states with small populations, such as Idaho, Montana, and Wyoming, an atmosphere of friends and neighbors politics exists where it is easy for politicians to get to know many of their constituents.

With its small population, Alaska is a good example of a friends and neighbors state in regard to politics. And it is certainly subject to the influence of a significant minority group—Alaska Natives. However, the population of many parts of rural-bush Alaska being well over 50 percent Natives and the dominance of one metropolitan area, Anchorage in Southcentral Alaska, make for some different influences on state politics than in most western states,.

7. STATE CONSTITUTIONS

Constitutions not only shape the framework of governments but also influence politics and generate issues. The content of a state's constitution is very much a product of the era in which the state entered the Union. Nine of the thirteen western states joined the Union during the populist and progressive (largely anti-political party and pro-clean government) eras from the 1870s through 1920. As a consequence, the populist and progressive tradition lives on today in many western states. For instance, these traditions produced a predilection for nonpartisanship, separately elected top executive branch officials in many states, and provisions for direct democracy—the initiative, referendum, and recall.

Although Alaska's constitution includes provisions similar to those of other western states, particularly those of direct democracy, it is streamlined and avoids many of the problems with other state constitutions. As such, its constitution influences the nature of politics, particularly regarding the three strong and often conflicting branches of government and the state's unique local government system.

8. THE FRONTIER ETHOS

American values that were brought west were adapted in response to the physical and economic environment and conflicts with Native Americans. This produced the frontier ethos, which manifests progress, optimism, pragmatism, qualified egalitarianism (it did not apply to minorities like Chinese laborers or Native Americans), laissez-faire, and rugged individualism—American individualism enhanced by courage, tenacity, and endurance.

Early Alaska pioneers manifested many elements of the frontier ethos, though its major dependence on government from the beginning made the much-touted Alaska trait of individualism more of a myth than a reality.

9. WESTERN POLITICAL CULTURE AND SUBCULTURES

The frontier ethos contributed to the development of political culture in the West. Political cultures and subcultures are key to shaping the actions of government and public reactions to them. While the overall culture of the West is individualistic, the degree of individualism varies widely from state to state and within states, from the communal attitudes of western Washington to the strong individualism of eastern Montana. Moreover, as most states are dependent on government, a significant element of western political culture is the so-called western political paradox: the contradiction of touting individualism while depending on government. This is an indication that one of the major elements of western political culture is political pragmatism.

Overall, Alaska very much reflects the more individualist political culture of the West, including the western political paradox.

10. POLITICAL IDEOLOGY

Political ideology in the West has been shaped by both the frontier ethos and the political culture. Whereas political culture is a set of general attitudes to politics and government, political ideology is more specific in including preferred policies and particularly a perspective on the role of government in society. Political ideologies range across the political spectrum from conservative to moderate to liberal.

The three Pacific states of California, Oregon, and Washington tend to be moderate to liberal in their western regions and northern California and conservative in their eastern regions and in southern California. Most Mountain states, as well as Alaska, tend to be right-of-center conservative politically, with pockets of liberalism in some urban areas, such as Denver and Juneau.

Source: Developed by the authors.

4. RECENT DEVELOPMENTS IN WESTERN AND ALASKA POLITICS

Since the mid-1970s, forces have been at work that have modified, and in some cases wrought major changes to, the nature of the politics of the West overall and its individual states.[3] The new dynamics of politics not only shapes issues and public policies in the thirteen western states but also how they operate in their dealings with Washington, D.C. Box 2.2 explains these recent developments as they have affected the West in general. The developments discussed in this section have had particular effects on Alaska politics.

Increased In-Migration and Urbanization

Alaska is becoming more urbanized with the gravitational pull toward Anchorage and its surrounding area. Most people live there when they first come to the state, and it is a major destination for many Alaska Natives when they leave bush villages. In 2010 there were ninety-two language groups in the Anchorage School District.[4] Consequently, as John Katz's quip in Box 2.2 indicates, Anchorage has become more like urban America and less like other parts of the state and particularly different from rural-bush Alaska.

Alaska's Continued Dependence on Government

Increased urbanization throughout the West and increased demand on government, particularly for social programs, partly explains the continued significant role of government. Today, in fact, all western states are as dependent on government—federal, state, and local—as at any time in the past, and in some cases more so. For instance, from 1995 to 2009 federal spending in Montana increased from $1.6 billion to $10.9 billion per year, a 573 percent increase, with per capita federal expenditures climbing sharply from less than $2,000 to around $11,000. In addition, total federal funds in the state budget rose from 26.6 to 43 percent.[5] Across the western states federal Medicaid funding (medical assistance for the poor) increased by 98 percent from 2005 to 2009.[6]

During 2000–2009, Alaska, Wyoming, Montana, and New Mexico were among the top six states regarding per capita federal funds received.[7] Alaska and Wyoming alternated between the first and second position in this ranking. As for employment, in 2009, 30 percent of Alaska's workforce was employed by federal, state, or local government, the highest percentage in the nation, with the average across the states at 18 percent government employment.[8] A good case can be made that Alaska is now more dependent on government, particularly the federal government, than at any time in its history.

Alaska's Public Lands Are No Longer Just for Economic Development

The Federal Land Policy and Management Act of 1976 heralded a new era in western land policy. It repealed dozens of public land laws, including virtually all statutes that authorized land entry without a permit. The enactment in 1959 of the Alaska Statehood

BOX 2.2

The American West: Changing Issues and Alliances and New Advocacy Techniques in Washington, D.C.

Throughout the American West, attitudes toward the federal government and natural resource development are changing, as is the way that western states operate in Washington, D.C.

In some cases the adversarial relationship between the federal government and the western public land states is being replaced by wary cooperation and improved communication as all levels of government contend with common problems, such as scarce supplies of water and energy. Furthermore, certain bedrock underpinnings of western life, like rugged individualism and the use of public lands primarily for economic development purposes, are changing. Reasons for these changes include demographic shifts, such as in-migration from other states and abroad; cultural attitudes, some of which result from in-migration; urbanization; and recent federal laws implemented by a new generation of land managers. Consequently, even the mythology of strong, individualistic people living off the land no longer exists in many areas. Instead, most westerners live in cities with the same problems and opportunities experienced by the rest of the country.

So, although California, Oregon, and Washington are western public land states, they hardly meet the traditional conceptions implied by this terminology. States such as Alaska, Wyoming, and Idaho satisfy the customary definition, but even they are confronting the problems of urban locales as they also struggle with natural resource and public land issues more reminiscent of times past. This dichotomy is exemplified by an oft-heard quip in Alaska that the nicest thing about Anchorage is that it's only twenty minutes from Alaska.

These changes have helped shape a new approach to advocacy in the nation's capital. The western states can no longer rely on their dominance of relevant congressional committees with members who share traditional western values. Accordingly, these states have become more sophisticated in their advocacy techniques, utilizing many lobbying strategies familiar to their sometime opponents, such as national environmental organizations. Many western states have opened offices in D.C. and also rely more heavily on the collective advocacy of the Western Governors Association (WGA) and on contract lobbyists.

In particular, the relationship between the western states and the U.S. Department of the Interior, which oversees millions of acres of public lands in the West, has become more competitive and more sophisticated. The Department now hears from a diverse array of interest groups with varying, often highly conflicting, perspectives regarding natural resource extraction and the use of public lands. Adjusting their advocacy approach to this and other federal agencies has enabled the western states to become major players in a range of issues such as the national debate on climate change and the development and transportation of domestic energy resources.

On another level, the West's, and particularly the Mountain West's, relationship to the federal government is rather schizophrenic. On the one hand, the region is still reliant on federal largesse in the form of expenditures for state programs and, in many cases, the money pumped into their economies by national defense expenditures. On the other, there are many points of conflict as states like Nevada, Wyoming, and Idaho seek to develop their natural resources in the face of environmental laws and other federally imposed constraints.

Source: Authored by John W. Katz, former Director of State-Federal Relations and Special Counsel to the Governor.

Act reflected an earlier conception of public land use. At that time, Congress was concerned that Alaska should not be a ward of the federal government, which was expressed in the state's authorization to select more than 102 million acres of federal land in the hope that it could generate enough income to enable the state to take care of itself. Congressional approval of construction of the trans-Alaska pipeline system (TAPS, commonly known as the Alaska pipeline) also helped implement the promise of the Statehood Act.

Since the late 1960s, however, with the rise of the environmental movement nationwide and Alaska's status as the Last Frontier, there has been an attempt to balance development and environmentalism. A major step in this direction was the Alaska National Interest Lands Conservation Act (ANILCA) of 1980, which shifted the political balance toward conservation, establishing more than one hundred million acres of new parks, wildlife refuges, and other conservation units.

Changing Attitudes to the Federal Government

Like the West in general, since the mid-1970s, Alaska's attitude and relationship to the federal government have changed and become more complex. Early statehood concerns about the need to develop the state still exist among many Alaskans, but today increasing numbers of people are concerned about environmental issues, often in alliance with political forces in the Lower 48 and internationally. Consequently, many Alaskans, including some conservatives, have developed a more positive attitude toward the federal government because they see the benefit of federal funds and actions and of working in harmony with Washington, D.C.

Increased Ideological Conservatism Tempered by Pragmatism

The late 1980s and early 1990s saw a rise in support for conservatism across the nation. Particularly in the Mountain West, this was in part a reaction to the rise of the environmental movement, which placed constraints on development, plus reaction to the increasing presence of the federal government. This rise of conservatism also included the increasing prominence of the ideological wing of the Republican Party, which pushed such issues as the right to life, family values, and reduced government spending and regulation in many policy areas.

Generally, however, the pragmatic conservatives have been able to control policy and continue to use government as a major source of employment and economic stimulus. This has certainly been the case in Alaska. The rise of the Republicans in Alaska in the late 1980s and beyond was less ideological than an attempt to control the political agenda. Their goal was to allocate government funds in a different direction than Democrats had done—toward business and development projects and away from social programs.

Weak Political Parties, but Their Increasing Strength in the Mid-1980s and Beyond

Political parties in the western states have generally been weak and ineffectual policy initiators and promoters compared with parties in many states in the Northeast and Upper Midwest. Beginning in the mid-1980s, however, political parties in the West, particularly the Republicans, became more cohesive and effective in setting the policy agenda and ensuring enactment of its preferred policies. This also occurred in Alaska, although political parties have never been strong as organizations in the state nor has the identification of voters with parties.

Increased Professionalism in State Government

Increased professionalism of both elected and appointed officials has been a phenomenon of state politics across the United States since the late 1960s. And even though legislatures in a number of western states, such as Wyoming and New Mexico, are still part-time and have relatively small numbers of support staff, other legislatures such as California, Washington, and even Alaska are becoming increasingly professionalized. Western state governors are no longer the "good old boys" of the past and generally bring business or professional experience to the job. With the increasing size of state government, governors have to be managers as well as politicians.

In addition, since the 1970s, the enactment of public disclosure, ethics, campaign finance, and lobby laws has made government decision making more transparent and has likely reduced corruption in politics. For instance, today's lobbyists are a much more professional bunch than their back-slapping, cigar-chomping, "good old boy" counterparts of the past.

Alaska reflects all these developments and is constantly seeking to improve the performance of government, though its success in this regard is mixed.

Expansion in Pluralism—More Political Forces at Work

During the first half of the twentieth century, and even later in some states, the politics of the West (including territorial Alaska) was dominated by business. Often this was a single business interest such as the Seattle-based fishing industry in territorial Alaska, the mining industry in the Mountain states, and the railroads in the Pacific states. As the result of the recent developments outlined in this section, however, both western and Alaska politics include many more political interests of all types.

In Alaska the range of interest groups includes minority and public interests that were not active in the early years of statehood, such as Alaska Natives, women's groups, environmentalists, and numerous social issue groups, such as pro-choice and anti-abortion, gay rights, and family-values groups. In short, Alaska's political system has become much more pluralistic, with an increasing number of interests and interest groups competing to promote their causes.

5. THE CONTEMPORARY CHARACTERISTICS OF ALASKA POLITICS

In combination, traditional and recent influences have shaped a set of contemporary political characteristics across the West and in Alaska that have much in common. Here we focus on those manifested in Alaska politics.[9] Twelve characteristics are particularly apparent, many of which are interrelated. They are as follows:

1. A political culture of pragmatic dependent individualism
2. A strong strain of self-proclaimed fiscal conservatism
3. The all-pervasive importance of government
4. The myths and contradictions of Alaska political discourse
5. The significant role of external economic and political forces
6. Economic development versus conservation and environmentalism
7. Friends and neighbors politics
8. The prominent role of Alaska Natives in state politics
9. Regionalism and conflicts between urban and rural-bush areas
10. Weak political parties versus strong interest groups
11. Influential legislative party caucuses (a grouping within the legislature) often coupled with bipartisanship
12. Three strong contending branches of state government, sometimes resulting in a stymied or deadlocked policy process

1. A Political Culture of Pragmatic Dependent Individualism

While many Alaskans view themselves as individualists, the Alaska political culture is actually much more pragmatic because of Alaskans' dependence on government to achieve and maintain the lifestyle they desire. Thus, Alaska's political culture manifests dependent individualism, an individualist spirit that is coupled with a heavy dependence on government aid and support of all types.[10] Some dependent individualists recognize their dependence on government, but many deny it vociferously, which often translates into general antigovernment rhetoric, particularly against the federal government (see characteristic 4 below).

Political pragmatism combined with friends and neighbors politics (see characteristic 5) undermines both political ideology as well as strong, cohesive political parties (see characteristic 10). For most Alaskans and their politicians, ideology is subordinate to whatever goal has been set, resulting in ideological inconsistencies, such as the pursuit of government funds and subsidies while professing an antigovernment attitude.

2. A Strong Strain of Self-Proclaimed Fiscal Conservatism

Individualism often goes hand-in-hand with fiscal conservatism, an antipathy to paying taxes and to the government services they fund. Most people around the world dislike paying taxes, but many governments are able to impose taxes, sometimes at extremely high rates, in order to provide the services that the citizens of those countries demand. In contrast, the existence of high oil revenues in most years has enabled Alaskans to keep personal taxes at a minimum. Consequently, the connection that traditional conservatives draw between big government and the imposition of high personal taxes needed to fund it simply does not exist in Alaska.

This lack of connection between spending and taxes, coupled with pragmatism, helps to explain why many Alaskan politicians who claim to be fiscally conservative nonetheless seek to include in the state budget large capital projects for their districts to spur economic development. Moreover, many Alaskans, conservatives as well as liberals, lobby the federal and state governments to provide funds for a wide array of projects and services.

The Tea Party, which emerged across the nation after 2008 with support in Alaska, is more consistent in its fiscal conservatism. It would end many federal benefits and other government programs, although, given Alaska's major dependence on government, this would seriously affect the quality of life of many Alaskans.

3. The All-Pervasive Importance of Government

The pervasiveness of government manifests itself in a host of ways in everyday politics in Alaska and in policy making. These include federal ownership of 55 percent of Alaska's land area and the issues and conflicts that this often produces in land and resource use; dependence on Washington, D.C., for funding of all types, from infrastructure to social services; and, in the absence of an industrial and agricultural sector, the importance of government employment at the federal, state, and local levels, particularly in rural-bush Alaska, and its importance in maintaining economic stability in the state.

In addition, using the term coined by the late Governor Walter (Wally) Hickel, Alaska is an "Owner State": it owns and controls extensive land and natural resources and regulates their use. Certainly, many western states have large holdings of state lands. But Alaska owns more than 95 percent of the land from which substantial quantities of oil and gas have been extracted since the late 1970s. By contrast, in other oil- and gas-rich states, such as Texas, New Mexico, and Wyoming, these resources are largely located under privately owned land. The existence of the Owner State produces a particular political dynamic in Alaska, especially in regard to state revenues and natural resource policy.

4. The Myths and Contradictions of Alaska Political Discourse

The first three characteristics reflect a somewhat mythical view of Alaska: that of individualism, fiscal conservatism, and negative attitudes toward the role of the federal government. Such myths, however, are very much part of Alaska's political discourse among large segments of the electorate and politicians. These myths are clearly evident in the political rhetoric of many election campaigns and in day-to-day political debate, and often are translated into policy proposals. They are particularly evident in cries to cut the state budget when, in fact, most legislators are working to increase spending for their causes and constituents.

In Alaska the perpetuation of these myths produces a version of the western political paradox: a contradiction between the myth and reality of the Alaska situation.[11] For instance, the myth of economic conservatism is prevalent in the Mat-Su Valley, which over the years has had many legislators who are very conservative, while at the same time securing major state funds for this rapidly developing area.

5. Significant Role of External Economic and Political Forces

Particularly important in Alaska politics are four external forces. One is the federal government. Alaska's noncontiguous status with the Lower 48 states, its extensive size, distribution of population, large Alaska Native population, federal ownership of 55 percent of the state's lands, and location of its natural resources, make dealing with the federal government a prominent aspect of Alaska politics.

Second is national public opinion and interests often manifested through congressional action. Particularly evident here is the ability of these national forces to prevent or impede Alaskan development of resources in the face of national desires to preserve the natural environment of the Last Frontier. Third are national and multinational corporations (MNCs), particularly those engaged in natural resource development (minerals, oil, and gas). And fourth are global economic forces, particularly those that determine the price of Alaska natural resources, including the crude oil that provides the overwhelming majority of state revenues.

Directly or indirectly, and for better or for worse, these external forces shape many political actions and policies in Alaska. Because Alaskans lack control over these forces, they can have the effect of undermining Alaska's ability to control its own affairs and reduce its political and governmental capacity—that is, the ability to address and solve the issues facing it.

6. Economic Development versus Conservation and Environmentalism

Economic development and economic diversity are prominent issues in Alaska in part because of the obvious need for jobs and economic well-being. But economic development and diversity are also seen as a solution to Alaska's budgetary instability, which is a result of Alaska's heavy dependence on oil revenues and their volatility, over which Alaska has no control.

The policy shift to include public uses for lands and natural resources as well as private ones often adds a dimension of conflict to the pursuit of economic development in Alaska. This stems from the rise of the conservation movement and environmental interest groups both within and outside of Alaska. It is probably this aspect of Alaska politics that generates the most active expressions of concern from Outsiders, both in the Lower 48 and internationally. This includes the conflict over opening the Arctic National Wildlife Refuge (ANWR) to oil and gas development, aerial wolf hunts, and protecting endangered species.

7. Friends and Neighbors Politics

The notion of friends and neighbors politics in a state the size of Alaska seems paradoxical at first. How can a state over twice the size of Texas have a friends and neighbors atmosphere? The answer lies in Alaska's small population—one that is concentrated in four or five major urban areas, with Anchorage being the transportation hub for most of the state, and most of the rest spread out in more than two hundred small towns and villages across the state. In this environment, people get to know each other in all aspects of their lives, including politics. So Alaska is akin to a village of types. Or as one lobbyist and former legislative staffer, Dennis DeWitt, put it: "Alaska is the biggest little state in the nation."[12] It was political scientist V. O. Key Jr. who coined the term "friends and neighbors" politics, and it accurately describes the atmosphere of most parts of Alaska.[13]

This type of politics is characteristic of small towns, and also of states with small populations, regardless of their geographic size, including some in the West as well as Vermont, Maine, and North and South Dakota, among others. With the social intimacy of a village, the public can easily access their elected and appointed government officials. Personal relationships are key to the way people vote, support particular political candidates, or work together on issues. Such personalism is often as important, and sometimes more so, than party affiliation and political ideology.

Excluding the unicameral Nebraska legislature with forty-nine seats, Alaska has the smallest number of legislative seats of any state (forty in the House of Representatives and twenty in the Senate). After the 2010 census the population was only 18,000 per house district and only 36,000 per senate district. This means that Alaska legislators, even those from urban areas such as Anchorage, Fairbanks, and Juneau, know many of their constituents on a first-name basis and often run into them at the grocery store or dry cleaners. Compare this situation with California, with house and senate districts of 405,000 and 910,000 respectively. The latter figure is 200,000 more than the entire population of Alaska—710,000—in 2010. Even a medium-sized state like Indiana has house and senate districts of 63,000 and 126,000, respectively.

In Alaska, friends and neighbors politics is reflected in state politics in several ways. One is that elections are most often oriented to a candidate and his or her personality, as opposed to party affiliation or partisan ideology. Election campaign signs, for example, usually feature the candidate's name in large letters and the party affiliation in very small ones, if at all. Compare this with eastern states such as New Jersey, Massachusetts, and Connecticut, where campaign signs have the name of the party in the same size or even larger print than the candidate's.

Second, friends and neighbors politics contributes to the organizational weakness of political parties. The emphasis on a candidate's personality tends to undermine political ideology, making political pragmatism more the rule than it is in states with more distinct ideological divisions, such as those in the Northeast. In Alaska's pragmatic political atmosphere, politicians often work across party lines and even change parties from time to time. This is evidenced by several bipartisan coalitions in both houses over the years. Another consequence of friends and neighbors politics is that many Alaskans seem to have a greater feeling of political efficacy—the sense that they can influence political decisions—than most other Americans do.

However, some would argue that Alaska's political intimacy, in terms of the effects listed above, may be detrimental. Weak ideology and weak political parties arguably deny Alaska important forces to develop and enforce policy, particularly planning efforts that may provide solutions to pressing problems.

8. The Prominent Role of Alaska Natives in State Politics

The prominent role of the indigenous population in Alaska's politics is unique among all Native American groups in the fifty states. This prominence stems from several sources. First, because of Native dominance in the population in bush Alaska, many Alaska Natives are elected to the state legislature. Also, some of the most skillful and powerful politicians in Alaska have been Alaska Natives. In addition, a number of the more prominent issues in Alaska affect Alaska Natives, including the cost of providing services to the rural-bush areas, conflicts over subsistence hunting and fishing rights, and Native sovereignty. While Alaska Natives continue to be a force in Alaska politics, the shift of population toward urban areas has resulted in a decline in rural-bush and Native political power compared with what it was in the 1980s.

9. Regionalism and Conflicts between Urban and Rural-Bush Areas

Alaska follows the pattern of the American West in its regionalism (Hawaii excepted). Regional conflicts, as in most western states, are based primarily on economic differences, such as between the service economy of Southcentral Alaska and the resource and subsistence economy of rural-bush communities. Alaska also reflects the situation across the states regarding urban and rural-bush tensions, and sometimes deep conflicts. The conflicts that arise between urban and rural-bush areas in Alaska, however, are different in origin from urban and rural conflicts in most other states, primarily because of the state's large Alaska Native population.

Regionalism

Alaska is, in many ways, a number of separate "states," with the vast majority of the population located in three of them: Southeast Alaska, Southcentral, and the Interior. Each of these three largest "states" has its own university campus, which has a measure of administrative autonomy. The North Slope, Northwest Alaska, and Southwest Alaska are smaller Alaska "states" in population, though they are large in area. One manifestation of regionalism is the dominant status of Anchorage and Southcentral Alaska in population, which translates into a majority of seats in the legislature and thus the region's increasing political clout. Anchorage's increasing influence since statehood is reflected in regional conflict over moving the capital from Juneau to Southcentral Alaska, explained in Box 2.3.

Urban versus Rural-Bush Conflict

As John Katz points out in Box 2.2, urban Alaska is much like any other urban area in the nation. However, bush Alaska and some rural areas of the state are quite different from rural areas in other states, and in many ways are unique. The three major differences are: (1) commercial agriculture in rural-bush Alaska is negligible; (2) indigenous people, in this case Alaska Natives, are in the majority in most bush areas and in some rural areas; and (3) there is a combined cash and non-cash—mainly subsistence—economy. Over the years, including currently, this urban versus rural-bush split has been as much a product of racism and cultural misunderstanding as economics.

State government and its public policy makers have long grappled with the challenge of addressing the needs and aspirations of people in these two very different kinds of places. This is one of the major challenges facing the state today and will be a major challenge in the future as urban versus rural-bush conflicts continue, sometimes overtly and sometimes politically less obvious.[14]

10. Weak Political Parties versus Strong Interest Groups

Political parties and interest groups are major links between the government and the governed in a democracy, and there is an interesting power relationship between them. A strong political party possesses the following three attributes: (1) it can determine who its candidates will be (and exclude those it does not want); (2) it is a major source of funding for candidates' campaigns and thus has a "hold" over the party members who are elected; and (3) it can use its "hold" to enforce discipline in the legislature. In such circumstances, parties control the political agenda and what policies do and do not get enacted. But when parties are weak, the power vacuum is filled by other forces, particularly interest groups. As indicated in Box 2.1, most states in the American West have a history of weak parties and policy systems that are dominated by strong interest groups, such as the Union Pacific Railroad in Wyoming and the Anaconda Copper Company in Montana.

BOX 2.3

The Recurring Issue of Moving Alaska's State Capital

A recurring issue in Alaska is whether to move the state capital from Juneau, in Southeast Alaska, to Southcentral Alaska. Proponents argue that Juneau is inaccessible by road, often hard to fly into because of inclement weather, and 600 miles from the Anchorage area, where 60 percent of the state population lives. Others, particularly the business community and developers, see a major economic bonanza in relocating the capital and many of its state workers.

Alaska was only a year old when the first major call came to move the capital. Its champion was Bob Atwood, owner of the *Anchorage Daily Times* (renamed the *Anchorage Times* in 1976 but ceased publication in 1992). He continued to be a strong advocate of the move until his death in 1997. In 1976, the electorate chose Willow, 35 miles north of Anchorage, as the location of the new capital; but in a 1982 referendum voters rejected a proposal to fund the move.

Proponents and opponents of the move have sparred off at the ballot box on several occasions since then. This includes a 1994 initiative adopted by the voters, requiring that, before the state can spend money to move the capital or the legislature, the voters must know and approve all costs of the move. The issue reappeared again in 2006 with the election of Sarah Palin to the governorship. A resident of the Mat-Su Valley and a populist of sorts, she occasionally made statements that the capital should be "nearer to the people." No formal capital move proposals, however, have been seriously considered since the late 1990s.

The population numbers are stacked in the Railbelt's favor, there have been some influential and committed crusaders for the move, and the logic of democracy argues in favor of it. Why, then, is the capital still in Juneau? Part of the reason is simply the force of the status quo in politics—it requires concerted action to get all forces in political sync to approve the move. Another reason is Alaskans' aversion to paying the costs for the move, as evidenced in the 1982 and 1994 votes. In addition, Juneau has worked hard to make itself a "user-friendly" capital city. Probably the main reason, however, is rooted in regional rivalries and fears in other parts of the state that Anchorage will become the vortex of state political power. Most of the rest of the state has, up until now at least, united against Anchorage to prevent the move. In various and subtle ways, this fear of Anchorage and its potential power is one element that makes up the mosaic of power relationships and alliances in Alaska politics.

So while economic and political power in the state is centered in Anchorage, the capital remains in Juneau. But with more and more people moving to Southcentral Alaska and its political representation becoming increasingly dominant in the legislature and other parts of state government, it is likely that one day the capital will move. Given past obstacles to its official relocation, the capital is more likely to move through a process of "capital creep"—moving the capital incrementally and unofficially. This can be achieved, and in some ways it is already happening, by holding cabinet meetings in Anchorage and allowing commissioners (heads of executive departments) and other senior state officials to live there and visit Juneau only when necessary. Given this situation, the legislature would also likely increase its meetings held in Anchorage, as it has done occasionally since 2008. The court system has been headquartered in Anchorage since statehood in 1959.

Source: Developed by the authors with reference to Clive S. Thomas, "Alaska," in *The Political Encyclopedia of U.S. States and Regions* (Washington, D.C.: Congressional Quarterly Press, 2008).

Over the years, including today, Alaska's political parties have been organizationally weak in contrast to many states in the Northeast and Upper Midwest. The Alaska situation results from a combination of factors: downplaying ideology and emphasizing political pragmatism and individualism; plus, for many years, Alaska had a blanket or open primary election system (where any voter could vote for any candidate, regardless of party affiliation). The weakness of parties in Alaska is reflected in the numbers. In August 2015, almost 54 percent of Alaska's voters were not affiliated with any party—the highest percentage in the nation.[15] To a degree, the victory in the 2014 governor's race of nonpartisan Bill Walker over Republican Governor Sean Parnell was a manifestation of weak parties and to some extent bipartisanship among the Alaska electorate. Walker headed the Alaska First Unity ticket, a post-primary election fusion of his independent candidacy with the Democratic, gubernatorial candidate Byron Mallott, who took the lieutenant governor's slot.

The existence of relatively weak parties has led to the formation of strong interest groups over the years, from the canneries and mining interests in the period before statehood to the oil companies and certain unions and government interests today. Interest groups in Alaska, however, are not as dominant as they are in other states, such as Nevada and Florida.[16] Part of the reason for this lesser degree of dominance lies in the next characteristic.

11. Influential Legislative Party Caucuses, often Coupled with Bipartisanship

While Alaska parties have been organizationally weak, since the mid-1990s the Republican caucuses in the legislature, particularly in the House of Representatives, have tended to provide cohesiveness by enforcing discipline on caucus members, primarily demanding unified support for the budget. To some extent, these caucuses have shared and promoted a conservative ideology, which has tended to undermine the importance and influence of some interest groups.

Strong caucus discipline has not, however, totally done away with the long-standing practice in Alaska of bipartisanship, not just in terms of legislators crossing party lines on individual votes, but also in joining bipartisan coalitions. This has occurred in both the House and the Senate a number of times, particularly since the 1980s. The most recent example is a senate coalition that was in place between 2007 and 2012, the so-called Bipartisan Working Group (BWG). Moreover, even when the legislature is controlled by strong one-party caucuses and the governor and legislature are of the same party, factors such as regional loyalties may trump party loyalty in policy making on some issues.

12. Three Strong Contending Branches of State Government, Sometimes Resulting in a Stymied and Deadlocked Policy Process

With memories of a federally appointed territorial governor as a dominant political force, Alaska's founders evened-up the balance by incorporating into the state constitution a strong legislature and a strong governor. The governor was given extensive authority with a view to streamlining government operations and avoiding the problems of fragmented policy making and implementation that were characteristic of many states in the mid-1950s. The founders also created a strong centralized judicial system and attempted to insulate it from politics.

However, Alaska's so-called model constitution does not always translate into a strong, efficient policy-making process. In fact, because of the strong contending legislative and executive forces (along with political pragmatism, regionalism, and weak political parties), Alaska often exhibits a stymied and deadlocked policy process and has problems with policy implementation. Sometimes the courts are asked to break these deadlocks through the filing of lawsuits. On other occasions the courts make far-reaching policy decisions.

6. MAJOR ALASKA ISSUES AND PUBLIC POLICIES AND THEIR INCREASING INTERRELATIONSHIP

The influences and characteristics considered in this chapter produce a range of issues that form the raw material for developing the public policies that may ultimately be adopted. Table 2.1 lists by category the issues that have been before Alaska state government over the years and the ones currently occupying the attention of government (with some issues prominent in more than one category). Some of these issues are particular to Alaska, such as subsistence. Others have an Alaska complexion to them, as in the case of the debate over the quality of rural-bush schools. Still others are common issues across the United States and, indeed, across the world, such as protecting endangered species and climate change.

The traditional way to classify issues and policies is by broad general categories, such as education, economic development, and health. Traditional classifications also include subcategories within a general policy area, such as funding K–12 education within education policy or mass transit policy within transportation. Increasingly, however, and particularly since the big surge in federal and state government activity of the mid-1960s, it is a mistake to see issues and policies as compartmentalized into totally separate categories. Many issues overlap and affect other issues. The same is true for policies after they have been adopted. For example, a seemingly straightforward plan to upgrade the track and roadbed of the Alaska Railroad, reroute some of its track, and build additional branch lines, may

TABLE 2.1

Major Contemporary Political Issues in Alaska
(Listed in Eight Categories)

1 ECONOMIC AND FISCAL ISSUES

Issues Concerning the Economy

- Economic development and diversity
- Use of the Permanent Fund for economic development/diversity
- Continued state support of agriculture
- Dealing with economic fluctuations
- Developing international trade
- Local hire of Alaskans
- Unemployment, especially in rural-bush Alaska
- Foreign ownership of Alaska resources/businesses
- Long-range economic planning

Fiscal Issues

- Extent of oil and gas taxes
- Is there really a fiscal gap?
- Declining state revenues
- Reducing state spending:
  - Which programs to cut?
  - Criteria for reductions
- Developing alternative revenue sources:
  - Reinstituting the personal income tax
  - Imposing a state sales tax
  - Increasing corporate taxes
  - Imposing and increasing user fees for roads, bridges, airports, etc.
  - Dedicating funds for services from user fees, e.g., roads, airports, docks.
  - Use of Permanent Fund earnings to supplement state budget
  - Liquidating the Permanent Fund
  - Capping the PFD–Permanent Fund Dividend
  - Developing additional oil, gas and other taxable resources, e.g., Arctic National Wildlife Refuge (ANWR)
  - Gas pipeline to Lower 48 or Southcentral Alaska
- State vs. local revenue sources
- Long-range fiscal planning
- Revenue surplus
  - To save or spend the funds or a combination of both?
  - If for services, which ones? Who benefits, who loses?

2 EDUCATION, HEALTH, SOCIAL, AND CRIMINAL JUSTICE ISSUES

- State residency requirements for receiving services and benefits

Education Issues—K-12

- The Foundation Funding Formula
- Forward funding for education/special budget account for education
- Constitutional amendment to use state funds for private and religious schools
- Improving graduation rates and scores on national scholastic tests
- Quality in rural-bush schools
- Teacher tenure

Higher Education Issues

- Rising student costs of higher education
- Reforming the student loan program
- Future of rural-bush campuses
- Retention of Native students at U of A campuses

Health Issues

- Universal access for all Alaskans and implementation of the Affordable Care Act (ACA—Obamacare)
- Access to health services in rural-bush areas
- Medicaid funding
- Air/water quality

Social Issues

- Welfare/public assistance reform
- Alcohol and drug abuse
- Domestic violence/child abuse
- Senior citizen services
- Day care
- Abortion
- Gay rights and same-sex marriage
- Extent of state support of the arts

Criminal Justice Issues

- Purpose of incarceration: rehabilitation or punishment?
- Dealing with soaring prison costs:
  - Addressing high recidivism rates
  - Revisiting mandatory sentencing policy for nonviolent crimes
  - State use of private prisons
- Reinstating the death penalty
- Regulating marijuana use
- State trooper vs. city police jurisdiction

3 TRANSPORTATION, UTILITY, AND COMMUNICATIONS ISSUES

Transportation

- Funding the Federal Highway Trust Fund (FHTF)
- Extending the road system: e.g., connecting Juneau by road, roads in the Interior
- Mass transit vs. highways
- Alaska Railroad relations with the state
- Future of Marine Highway System
- Dedication of user fees
- The statewide transportation plan—*Let's Get Moving 2030*
- Regional differences—Marine Highways vs. surface transportation
- Equality of transportation funding—urban surface vs. rural-bush air facilities

Utilities

- Electric power cost equalization (PCE) for rural-bush communities
- Extending broadband Internet to the rural-bush areas
- Conflicts between the state's long-distance telephone companies

Communications

- Extent of state support of public broadcasting
- Funding of Alaska Rural-Bush Communications System (ARCS), formerly Rural Alaska TV Network (RATNet)
- State Telecommunication and Information Technology Plan

4 LAND, NATURAL RESOURCES, AND ENVIRONMENTAL ISSUES

Developers vs. Conservationists/Environmentalists

- Drilling in ANWR
- Use of National Petroleum Reserve-Alaska (NPR-A)—conservation or leasing for oil and gas extraction?
- Timber harvesting in the Tongass
- Mining development
- Mining activity and water quality as it affects salmon
- Mass transit vs. highways as it affects air quality
- Corridors across federal lands e.g., Denali National Park
- Hunting and trapping practices

User Group Conflicts

- Commercial vs. sports fishing
- Subsistence vs. sports hunting and fishing
- Access to lands by developers vs. recreational interests
- Wolf management
- Aquaculture/salmon farming/genetically produced salmon

State Trust Lands

- Mental Health Lands Trust and the use of their revenues
- University of Alaska trust lands

Global Warming/Climate Change

- State government approach for dealing with the issue
- User group disagreements over the seriousness of the issue

Table 2.1/ Continued...

5 ISSUES CONCERNING THE POLITICAL AND GOVERNMENTAL SYSTEM	6 NATIVE ISSUES AND URBAN VERSUS RURAL-BUSH CONFLICTS	7 FEDERAL-STATE RELATIONS/STATE-FEDERAL-FOREIGN RELATIONS	8 RELATIONS WITH OTHER STATES, FOREIGN COUNTRIES, AND INTERNATIONAL ORGANIZATIONS
Public vs. private provision of services Additional campaign finance reform Extend public official ethics provisions More stringent lobbying regulations Extend open meetings provisions in the conduct of legislative business Election of the attorney general Institute 50% +1 of popular vote for electing the governor Capital move Establish unicameral legislature Expand seats in legislature to comply with U.S. Justice Department's reapportionment rules Modified closed primary vs. other forms of primary election Should Alaska create a cabinet-level Department of Energy? Local government reforms: Extending the borough system Unified vs. non-unified boroughs Appropriateness of Alaska's local government structure to rural-bush communities Local revenue sources	Subsistence International restrictions on whale hunting Native sovereignty Municipal incorporation/ dissolution of villages Sewer and waste in the villages Native poverty Electric power cost equalization (PCE) Success/failures of Native corporations Rural-bush economic development Unemployment in rural-bush Alaska Cost of urban vs. rural-bush services Native educational performance K–12 and higher education Bush justice and jurisdiction of tribal courts Continued support for Alaska Rural Communications System (ARCS), formerly the Rural Alaska TV Network (RATNet) Equality of transportation funding—urban surface vs. rural-bush air facilities	**Federal-State Relations** Oil-drilling particularly in the Arctic Fisheries jurisdictional conflicts State-federal share of royalty payments from resources taken from federal lands State management of fish and game under federal laws Designating species as endangered Managing the Tongass **State-Federal-Foreign Relations** Development of the Arctic Taiwanese/Japanese/South Korean interception of Alaska bound salmon Alaskan-Canadian Issues: Interception of salmon Management of migrating wildlife Canadian attitudes to opening ANWR British Columbia mining and pollution of Southeast Alaska rivers Policies of the International Whaling Commission (IWC) Endangered species issues, e.g. agreement between U.S. and Russia on Chukchi/ Bering Sea polar bears Cooperation on global warming	**Alaska–Other 49 State Relations** Membership in national and regional associations of states, e.g., National Council of State Legislatures (NCSL), Western Governors Assoc. (WGA) Cooperating with other states, especially for lobbying in Washington, D.C. Use of national and regional organizations for lobbying in Washington, D.C. **Alaska-Foreign Country Relations** In which countries to set up trade offices/hire promotional contractors Informal political relations with: Canada, Pacific Rim, Arctic countries, etc. **Relations between Alaska and International Organizations** International Whaling Commission (IWC) Inuit Circumpolar Council (ICC) Northern Forum Arctic Council Arctic Circle

Source: Developed by the authors.

raise environmental issues, such as protection of habitat and animal life, as well as the labor issue of whether to hire people from outside the state or from Alaska to do the work.

7. WHERE DOES POLITICAL POWER LIE IN ALASKA?

In Chapter 1 we examined the concept of power and also stated that a main focus of the approach in this book is the behavioral and realist's perspective that the use of power is the underlying element in politics and government, particularly in public policy making. After the overview of the essence of Alaska politics and what shapes it covered in these first two chapters, we can make some initial observations about where political power lies in the state. The location of power can be viewed at three levels: (1) the political system in general; (2) particular policy areas; and (3) individual issues that come up for consideration.

The material in this chapter, particularly in regard to the characteristics of Alaska politics, makes it clear that at the level of the political system overall, power is fragmented in the state. Alaska has a pluralist system in which power is shared and exercised among many power centers with no single dominating force. So even though they may have considerable sway from time to time on particular issues, neither the oil companies nor the federal government runs Alaska. There is an executive branch with considerable influence but also a strong legislature and judiciary—three strong contending branches. State and national public opinion can also shape policy. And because political parties are less significant in Alaska, there is a different power dynamic in its political system than in many other states.

Examining political power at the system level provides the big picture of the dynamics of the process and is useful for comparing Alaska with other states, evaluating its performance, and identifying possible reforms. But it is examining policy areas and particular individual policy proposals, and actions taken on them, that are most instructive for understanding the day-to-day operation of power at work in Alaska politics.

Regarding particular policy areas, a power relationship is often developed over time among organizations and individuals who have a stake in the area. These groups are often called policy communities. In K–12 education, for instance, the policy community includes the state Department of Education, teachers and school boards and their respective organizations, parent groups, vendors who supply materials and services, interested legislators, the governor, and so on. The power dynamics within the policy community will change from time to time, depending on the personalities and leadership skills of individual members, the issues at hand, and the available funds, among other factors. Several chapters in this book examine specific policy areas and, in many cases, explain the past and present distribution of power within the policy community.

Individual policy proposals come in a variety of forms, including, for example, a bill introduced in the legislature, a governor's policy initiative, or the inclusion of a particular item in a budget bill. The final outcome of these proposals depends on the particular power relationships in play concerning any given proposal. More important, however, is the current political environment. This includes: the makeup and power dynamics in the legislature and executive branches and the relations between them, whether the person making the proposal is in a position of power, the mix of personalities involved, the needs and goals of these individuals, and the strength of any interest groups that might be involved in the proposal. Several case studies and examples of the exercise of power in individual circumstances are provided throughout the book.

Chapter 3 provides insights into the way that power operates in the policy process and in state politics in general.

8. CONCLUSION: HOW THE DYNAMICS OF BELIEFS, INSTITUTIONS, PERSONALITIES, AND POWER SHAPE ALASKA POLITICS

This book is subtitled *The Dynamics of Beliefs, Institutions, Personalities, and Power* because it is the dynamic interaction of various factors and influences that best explains Alaska politics and policy making. Each of these factors plays a role. People's *beliefs* and values are at the root of the political clashes that occur. Their political ideology and political culture have a lot to do with their attitudes toward politics and government, how they deal with government, and how they react to its policies. Add to this the *personalities* involved in politics, with all their likes, dislikes, foibles, needs, goals, and egos. Then add the element of *power*, the major and motive force in resolving a political conflict. The three together provide the essence of the human-centered approach used in this book to explain Alaska politics and public policy.

This is not to say that *institutions* are not important. They are, indeed, an integral part of politics and policy making. In a pluralist democracy like Alaska, institutions, including the three branches of government, political parties, and interest groups, and the interaction of these institutions in a political process within the broader political environment, constitute both the formal constitutional and legal framework and the informal relationships and networks for resolving conflict. However, political institutions and the processes involving them are not the dominant forces in politics and policy making. Politics is first and foremost about human beings and the relationships between them. This will become particularly evident when we explore Alaska's public policy-making process in the next chapter.

ENDNOTES

[1] Some information on the traditional influences on western and Alaska politics is taken from Clive S. Thomas, ed., *Politics and Public Policy in the Contemporary American West* (Albuquerque: University of New Mexico Press, 1991), Chapter 2, "Influences on Western Political Culture"; and Clive S. Thomas, ed., *Alaska Public Policy Issues: Background and Perspectives* (Juneau: Denali Press, 1999), Chapter 1, "Understanding and Evaluating Alaska Issues and Public Policies."

[2] Statistics on Alaska's economy and revenues and comparisons with other states over the years are taken from Bureau of Economic Analysis, Bureau of Labor Statistics, National Agricultural Statistics Service, National Center for Health Statistics, U.S. Census Bureau, www.fedstats.gov revised April 14, 2010; State Export-Related Employment Project, International Trade Administration and Bureau of the Census, November 2010, http://www.ita.doc.gov/td/industry/otea/state%5Freports/; State of Alaska Department of Revenue, *Annual Report 2010,* retrieved on April 15, 2011, from

http://www.tax.alaska.gov/programs/sourcebook/index.aspx; and interview by Clive Thomas with Patrick Galvin, former commissioner, Alaska Department of Revenue, May 4, 2009.

[3] Information on the recent influences on western and on Alaska politics is taken from Thomas, *Politics and Public Policy in the Contemporary American West*, Chapter 20, "Conclusion: Continuity, Change and Future Directions in Western Politics and Public Policy"; Thomas, with Susan A. Burke, *Alaska Public Policy Issues*, Chapter 21, "Alaska Public Policy Issues and Policy-Making Process: Reflections and Prospects"; and an interview by Clive Thomas with John W. Katz, former director of state/federal relations and Special Counsel to the Governor of Alaska, in Washington, D.C., October 17, 2011.

[4] Interview by Tony Nakazawa with Matthew Crow, Department of Multicultural Education, Anchorage School District, October 6, 2010.

[5] U.S. Census Bureau (1995), Consolidated Federal Funds Report for FY 1995 (updated 2004), retrieved on June 26, 2011, from http://www.census.gov/prod/2/gov/cffr/cffr95.pdf; Consolidated Federal Funds Report for FY 2009, retrieved on June 26, 2011, from http://www.census.gov/prod/2010pubs/cffr-09.pdf; and U.S. Census Bureau, State Government Finances: 2009, Montana, retrieved on June 25, 2011, from http://www.census.gov/govs/state/0927mtst.html and U.S. Census Bureau, State GovernmentFinances: 1995, Montana, retrieved on June 25, 2011, from http://www2.census.gov/govs/state/95stmt.txt.

[6] U.S. Census Bureau, Federal Aid to States for Fiscal Year 2009, retrieved on June 25, 2011, from http://www.census.gov/prod/2010pubs/fas-09.pdf; and U.S. Census Bureau, Federal Aid to States for Fiscal Year 2005, retrieved on June 25, 2011, from http://www.census.gov/prod/2007pubs/fas-05.pdf. For a detailed table see appendix on this website.

[7] U.S. Census Bureau, Federal Aid to States Reports, retrieved on June 25, 2011, from http://www.census.gov/prod/www/abs/fas.html.

[8] U.S. Bureau of Economic Analysis, "Full-time and Part-time Wage and Salary Employment by NAICS Industry (1990–2009), retrieved June 25, 2011, from www.bea.gov/regional/spi/default.cfm?selTable=SA27N&selSeries=NAICS.

[9] For an explanation of the political characteristics of western politics, see Thomas, *Politics and Public Policy in the Contemporary American West*, Chapter 1, "The Western Brand of Politics"; and Thomas, *Alaska Public Policy Issues*, Chapter 1.

[10] Thomas A. Morehouse, "Alaska's Political and Economic Future" (Lecture Notes and Illustrations), a lecture delivered to the faculty at the University of Alaska Anchorage on his retirement, April 28, 1994. See Chapter 5 for a detailed consideration of Alaska's political culture.

[11] Thomas, *Politics and Public Policy in the Contemporary American West*, 15.

[12] Interview by Clive Thomas with Dennis L. DeWitt, Alaska lobbyist for the National Federation of Independent Business, February 21, 2012.

[13] V. O. Key Jr., *Southern Politics in State and Natio*n, new edition, first published 1949 (Knoxville: University of Tennessee Press, 1984).

[14] Gunnar Knapp, "Four Alaska Innovations," a Presentation to the Board of Directors of the Federal Reserve Bank of San Francisco and Its Seattle Branch, Anchorage, July 11, 2007.

[15] State of Alaska, Division of Elections as of August 3, 2014, at http://www.elections.alaska.gov/statistics/vi_vrs_stats_party_2014.08.03.htm.

[16] Anthony J. Nownes, Clive S. Thomas, and Ronald J. Hrebenar, "Interest Groups in the States," in Virginia Gray and Russell L. Hanson, eds., *Politics in the American States: A Comparative Analysis*, 9th ed. (Washington, D.C.: Congressional Quarterly Press, 2008), Table 4.3, p. 121.

⋆ CHAPTER 3 ⋆

Making Public Policy in Alaska: An Overview of the Process and Its Political Dynamics

Fran Ulmer and Clive S. Thomas

Why do political needs and demands that benefit a small group sometimes get dealt with in Alaska while others get little, if any, attention even though they would benefit Alaskans as a whole? On other occasions, why does the majority, sometimes a large majority in the state, not get what it wants politically?

This chapter offers insights into these and other questions in an overview of Alaska's public policy-making process. As the process is fundamental to understanding Alaska politics and all the chapters that follow, this chapter uses as its theme the subtitle of the book—the *Dynamics of Beliefs, Institutions, Personalities, and Power* as they relate to the policy-making process. What all these elements boil down to is that policy making is a political process involving various institutions and personalities, with power as the juice that makes things happen. Underlying the dynamics of institutions and personalities are the beliefs and values as expressed through Alaska's political culture. Several aspects of this culture will be referred to here, but an in-depth aspect of Alaska's political culture is presented in Chapter 5.

This chapter begins by explaining four theoretical perspectives on the policy process and their practical applications. Then we consider the Alaska policy-making environment and the specifics of the policy process. The next two sections identify the policy makers, both individuals and organizations, involved in the process and what influences their decisions. Following this we explain the elements that go into policy making by presenting two case studies—one successful and the other unsuccessful. This is followed by a short section comparing Alaska's public policy process with that of other places. The conclusion sets the scene for the rest of the book.

1. UNDERSTANDING THE POLICY-MAKING PROCESS: FOUR THEORETICAL PERSPECTIVES AND THEIR PRACTICAL VALUE

Many academic books, chapters, and articles have been written to explain various aspects of public policy making at the federal, state, and local levels in the United States.[1] Four perspectives are sufficient as a foundation for understanding Alaska's public policy-making process and its consequences for specific areas of policy. These are: (1) theories of the policy process; (2) practical perspectives on policies; (3) the concept of policy capacity; and (4) policy evaluation—the overall analysis of public policies. As we will see, there is an interrelationship between all four.

Theories of the Public Policy-Making Process

Theories of policy making attempt to explain what factors and forces shape the process. In some cases they also explain the consequences of the process for various groups and individuals, and for society as a whole. Five theories have emerged as the major explanations of the process. They are briefly explained in Box 3.1.

None of these theories tells the whole story of public policy making, but each has important contributions to make. So in explaining Alaska's public policy process in the next section, we draw on the most useful elements of the five theories listed in Box 3.1. This provides a comprehensive composite explanation of public policy making in the state.

Practical Perspectives on Issues and Policies

A second enlightening approach to issues and public policy making is to categorize them from a practical perspective. Here we consider three important aspects and realities of the day-to-day policy process: the extent of the visibility of the policy; policy communities and their variations; and who wins and who loses from particular policies.

High-Profile versus Low-Profile Issues

A high-profile issue (sometimes referred to as a high-salience issue) is one that is much publicized in the media, is likely well-known among the public, and is of concern to most, if not all, elected and many appointed public officials. High-profile issues are sometimes very controversial, such as opening the Arctic National Wildlife Refuge (ANWR) for oil and gas exploration, or using Permanent Fund earnings to supplement the state budget. A low-profile (low-salience) issue is one that receives little, if any publicity, is likely not well-known by the public, and is of interest to only a few public officials. These issues are also often noncontroversial, such as the rules about who should be licensed as a dentist and changing the rules in the state's procurement code for purchasing goods and services.

BOX 3.1

Theories of the Public Policy-Making Process

ELITE THEORY

This argues that the needs and preferences of various social, economic, and political elites are more influential in determining public policy than those of the general public. But it does not argue that there is a united national elite. There are many elites in various fields—business, the professions, the media, and politics, for example. Sometimes these elites are themselves in conflict. For instance, liberal elites may be in opposition to business elites over environmental protection. And sometimes there are conflicts within a particular elite group, such as between large and small businesses.

GROUP THEORY

Here policy making is seen as a struggle between numerous groups and interests, both formal (organized interest groups like the American Medical Association for doctors and the National Education Association for teachers) and informal interests (for instance, a street demonstration against closing a school). Unlike the elitist perspective theorists, group theory emphasizes pluralism, with some groups counterbalancing others, such as labor opposing business, so that no one group or interest dominates the policy process.

INSTITUTIONAL THEORY

This theory emphasizes the formal institutions of government (particularly the legislature, executive and government departments, and the judiciary), their formal and informal rules and procedures, and the power distribution among them, as the major forces that shape policy. For instance, this theory helps explain why U.S. Senator Ted Stevens got large amounts of money for Alaska even though he was from a state with a small population, a small congressional delegation, and an economy dwarfed by states like California, Florida, and New York.

RATIONAL CHOICE THEORY

Sometimes called public choice theory, rational choice uses economic theory and mathematical models to explain policy decisions. Based on the assumption that human beings are rational and will work to maximize their preference or their self-interest, the theory seeks to explain and predict how those involved in the policy process, from politicians to lobbyists to the electorate, will act under a variety of conditions.

POLITICAL SYSTEMS THEORY

Unlike the previous four theories, this looks at the actual process, the various stages through which a policy goes as it is adopted or rejected. It is more general than the other theories and is concerned with the various ways that the process responds to demands from the entire policy environment, including the public, interest groups, political elites, and so on. In this regard, the policy process is seen as a kind of living organism that responds—adapts, changes, or offers resistance—to its environment.

Sources: Developed by the authors with reference to Kraft and Furlong, *Public Policy*, esp. Chapter 3; and Birkland, *An Introduction to the Policy Process*, esp. Chapter 9.

The distinction between high- and low-profile policy issues is important for three reasons. First, much of government policy making—perhaps as much as 80 percent or more—is low-profile. This may seem surprisingly high, but not when one considers that the media tends to report only the high-profile and controversial issues and those that affect a large segment of the nation or state. Second, policy makers approach high-profile and low-profile issues in different ways. In essence, they tend to be more partisan, and seek more media coverage on high-profile issues than on low-profile ones, all of which likely affects the policy outcome. Third, just because an issue is low-profile does not mean that it is insignificant in terms of the resources involved or the effect on the public or the interests concerned. The two examples used above illustrate this point. Limiting the number of people who can be licensed as dentists can raise dental costs for the public but increase the income of dentists. And if the state awards a contract for computer services to a company without using a competitive bidding process, this can mean millions of dollars for the company receiving the contract, but it might cost the state (and thus the public) more than if the bidding had been competitive.

Policy Communities, Policy Networks, Ad Hoc Policy Coalitions, and Policy Entrepreneurs

All issue areas, from K–12 education to mental health to economic development, involve the political activities of several interests that have a stake in the outcome of public policies to deal with their particular issues. This so-called policy community and two related policy groupings drive most public policy making. In some circumstances, however, policy can be driven by an individual in or out of government.

Policy Communities: These consist of all the groups, organizations, government agencies, and individuals, including members of the public, lobbyists, elected and appointed officials, and sometimes segments of the media, concerned with an area of policy, such as the environment or transportation. A policy community can be defined narrowly or broadly largely because the interests involved vary on particular issues. From the narrow perspective, the community always includes those interests that are continually affected by an issue area, such as teachers and school boards in K–12 education. More broadly, on particular issues, such as school safety, the K–12 education policy community may include other interests, such as local or state public safety agencies.

Moreover, although it is traditional to categorize policies by subject area—health, transportation, economic development, and so on (see Chapter 2, Table 2.1)—since the 1960s, policies in one area increasingly affect those in other areas. As a result, policy making is becoming more and more interrelated, which in turn affects the behavior of policy makers, both public officials and others involved in the policy process. Those promoting economic development, for example, must be aware of how this affects land use, the environment, and transportation, among other issue areas, and work to accommodate them.

Policy Networks and Ad Hoc Policy Coalitions: As we noted, a *policy community* is a generic term covering all those interests involved in a particular policy area, many of which may never engage in concerted action or even have any interaction with other members of that policy community. Policy networks and ad hoc coalitions, by contrast, involve direct interaction and usually political activity. A *policy network* is an active interrelationship of the various interests involved in a particular policy area or with interconnected issues. The interested parties can create an active interrelationship formally by setting up a new organization or using an existing one (such as the Alaska Municipal League on local government issues) or informally by simply exchanging information, both technical and political, for mutual benefit (such as a group of parents networking with public officials in order to obtain more state funding for gifted children in public schools). Unlike ad hoc coalitions, policy networks tend to exist long term to deal with recurring issues of common concern.

In contrast to policy networks, *ad hoc policy coalitions* tend to form around a single issue and disband once the issue has been resolved. The politics and politicking of ad hoc policy coalitions can be quite complex and convoluted and lead to a coalition of groups that are often political opponents forming a temporary political alliance. A recent example at the national level and in many states are ad hoc coalitions created to deal with increasing health care costs. This issue has brought together business groups, particularly small business, such as the National Federation of Independent Business (NFIB), traditional labor unions (blue collar), and public and private universities, among other groups.

Policy entrepreneur: Some issues are low priority and are not addressed by the major forces that are usually behind public policy making, such as political parties, legislative caucuses, the executive branch, interest groups, and the media. The low priority could be because they are unpopular issues, such as gay rights and same-sex marriage have been in Alaska, because they are issues that affect a group with little power, such as the poor or prisoners, because they are seen as unessential in times of budget crises, as with the arts, or for other reasons.

In these cases, often an elected or appointed public official, but sometimes a prominent private citizen, champions an issue and attempts to get policy enacted, such as educational services for disabled children. These individuals are entrepreneurs exercising policy leadership. For instance, this has recently been the case with several individuals across the country and in Alaska regarding the issue of sentencing reform for convicted felons, particularly for nonviolent crimes. The actions of policy entrepreneurs may turn an issue into a high-priority policy concern for government, as is the case with sentencing reform. Often, though, the policy entrepreneur's efforts fall on deaf political ears.

Those Who Benefit and Those Who May Lose from Certain Policies

It is also useful to consider how certain types of policies affect society as a whole, or segments of it, in terms of who wins and who loses. The classic categories for this analysis were developed by Theodore Lowi.[2] Lowi argues that the actions of government in regard to policy can be divided into three categories: distributive, redistributive, and regulatory policies. Box 3.2 explains these categories and the particulars of the political interactions that they involve. Several chapters throughout the book use this classification for explaining aspects of Alaska politics, government, and public policy.

The Concept of Policy Capacity and Alaska's Varying Levels of Capacity

In Chapter 1 we noted that political capacity is an important factor because it determines the society's ability to address an issue or problem. Policy capacity is a similar though narrower concept. It is the ability of the public policy process in a country, state, or local government to address an issue or problem with the political, economic, and other resources it has available (this, in turn, is related to but differs from governmental capacity, which is the ability of government to carry out its various functions on a daily basis). Whether or not the policy is successful is a separate matter, if it is determined that positive action is warranted.

Obviously, dealing with many issues is beyond a government's capacity even if it has extensive resources. For example, a government might not have legal jurisdiction over an issue, such as local governments not having the authority to deal with foreign affairs. Or it might be because a problem is beyond the control of any government, such as influencing fluctuations in world commodity prices or preventing the global economic meltdown of 2008. That said, governments, particularly in advanced democracies including the United States, have extensive resources at their disposal to deal with issues and problems.

Apart from resources, another determining factor of policy capacity is the institutional arrangement of a government and its political institutional strength, particularly that of political parties. In parliamentary democracies such as Australia and Finland, the executive (the prime minister and cabinet) is drawn from the majority party or coalition in the parliament. Since the executive controls the parliament, parties tend to be strong and disciplined on votes. As a consequence, well over 90 percent of the policies of the majority party or coalition get enacted. In other words, parliamentary democracies have a very high level of policy capacity. The institutional arrangements are less cohesive and integrated in the United States and in its fifty states. In fact, in many ways there is a fragmented policy process, largely because of the separation of powers among the three branches of government and often a lack of cohesiveness in political parties.

When the U.S. founding fathers put together the U.S. Constitution back in 1787, part of their goal was to deal with the weak central government formed under the Articles of Confederation. However, the memory of the perceived abuses of England's King George III was stronger than concerns over the shortcomings of the Articles of Confederation. So their overriding goal was to prevent one branch of government, particularly the executive, from dominating the others. To achieve this, they established three separate branches (legislative, executive, and judicial) with the three branches sharing

BOX 3.2

Theodore Lowi's Types of Public Policies

DISTRIBUTIVE POLICY

These are programs or grants that government provides directly to a group, a particular constituency, or a political jurisdiction that are not the result of competition in the policy process. No one group or constituency is denied a benefit—directly loses—as the result of such policies. Examples include: grants of funding to local governments for new buildings or to buy equipment; research grants to universities; agricultural subsidies; and awarding contracts without any bidding (a sole-source contract), such as for janitorial services.

Distributive policy making largely describes the tendency of lawmakers to provide programs and benefits to their constituents. These are often known as pork barrel projects in which lawmakers "bring home the bacon." They are rarely publicized through committee hearings and debates in either house of the legislature. Plus, they are usually noncontroversial, as one legislator does not want to oppose another's project for fear that their own will not be funded. A master at this type of policy making was Alaska's late U.S. Senator Ted Stevens, who got hundreds of such policies passed, ranging from money for the company that makes salmon-based dog treats (Yummy Chummies) to major ongoing funding for the Denali Commission to promote economic development in rural-bush Alaska.

REDISTRIBUTIVE POLICY

In contrast to distributive policies, redistributive policies involve conflict—often major conflict—because there are winners and losers as government resources are redistributed (or reallocated). These benefits may be financial (such as shifting higher tax burdens to the wealthy), a nonmonetary benefit (such as affirmative action in admitting students to college), or some special service (such as reducing funds for school art programs to provide more money for other educational programs).

Such policy conflicts are great fodder for the media and are usually highly publicized. Often the political debate and emotion is so intense that it causes deadlock on the issue.

REGULATORY POLICY

This is policy that restricts or controls actions by individuals, groups, or organizations in society to prevent activities that are deemed dangerous or unacceptable. Regulatory policy includes both *competitive* and *protective* regulation. The former mainly involves the regulation of specific businesses and their practices, such as utilities and car manufacturers. The latter includes protecting the public from certain activities including regulating the drinking age and bar hours and various types of environmental laws, such as regulating marine discharges from cruise ships.

Regulatory policies can also be conflict-ridden as the two sides try to promote, modify, or kill the proposal. On the one side are public officials who support the policy, often aided by public interest groups; on the other are officials who oppose the laws, usually aided by the lobbyists and organizations representing those to be regulated, who likely oppose the proposal because it will increase their cost of doing business.

Source: Developed by the authors with reference to Lowi, "American Business"; Kraft and Furlong, *Public Policy*, esp. Chapter 3; and Birkland, *An Introduction to the Policy Process*, esp. Chapter 6.

power and particularly sharing the power to make policy. The result is a system that often makes it difficult for government to achieve a cohesive set of policies and gives enormous advantage in the policy process to the forces of the status quo. This is often referred to as the "advantage of the defense," a situation that persists to this day despite over two hundred years of political developments in the United States.

This "advantage of the defense" is reinforced by the fact that strong, disciplined political parties based on deep-rooted ideologies did not develop in the United States, partly because there were not the economic and social cleavages in the American "land of opportunity" and socialism was not a major force as it was in Europe. All fifty states adopted the same constitutional arrangement as the federal government and more or less reflect the same relative weakness of parties. Separation of powers and the situation with parties create political and governmental barriers to policy making. Furthermore, when parties tend to be less than united, interest groups fill the power vacuum and have more leeway to operate and more influence over the outcome of policy proposals. All these factors in combination favor the political and policy status quo and undermine the policy capacity of the federal government and the states, including Alaska.

Certainly, both federal and state policy makers can move with alacrity if they wish to and if circumstances require it, and bipartisanship can be part of this process. For example, the U.S. Patriot Act (2001) passed rapidly by Congress with overwhelming Republican and Democratic support in response to the 9/11 terrorist attacks on the United States. Similarly, the Alaska Gasline Inducement Act (AGIA) passed in the summer of 2007 with much bipartisan support. Speed and agreement among policy makers is usually not the norm in federal or state politics, however. This is particularly the case where there is little sense of urgency among politicians, when political parties are in conflict over the issue, there is dissent within a party over the solution perhaps because of regional loyalties or perspectives, or one or more strong interest groups are against the policy. All these circumstances undermine the capacity of the policy-making system. This was the case, for instance, with President Clinton's attempt to enact a national health policy in 1993–1994. It was also very much in evidence during President Obama's presidency, particularly after the 2010 midterm Congressional elections when the Republicans gained control of the House of Representatives and after the 2014 midterms when they also gained control of the Senate. Insufficient policy capacity is also evident in Alaska's inability to deal with the subsistence hunting and fishing issue.

Several other factors also undermine the capacity of Alaska's policy-making process and its policy makers. One is the prevalence of pragmatic dependent individualism in the state's political culture, explored in Chapter 5. Others include regionalism, the populist perspective among many Alaskans, and contending co-equal branches of government, discussed in various chapters throughout the book.

The upshot is that Alaska's policy capacity is often reduced and policy making may be stymied on some issues and even deadlocked in some instances.

Policy Evaluation

A fourth informative perspective on public policy is to follow a policy from its origin as an issue through its formulation and enactment (including the politics of its passage) and finally an evaluation of its success or shortcomings after implementation. Policy evaluation, as it is termed by political scientists and public administration specialists, is an important aspect of studying public policy making. The methods can be complex, involving quantitative and qualitative techniques and often a combination of the two.[3] Plus, to some scholars policy evaluation refers only to assessing the effects of the policy. Here we use a broad definition of the concept that will enable us to understand the factors that go into making a policy, and list some key questions regarding its effects and consequences. This exercise provides an assessment of whether or not the policy needs to be changed and placed back on the policy agenda. Box 3.3 sets out points and questions to bear in mind in evaluating Alaska's public policies.

In addition, combining what we have learned in this section about theories of the policy process, policies in practice, and policy capacity also aids in evaluating policies. For example, policy capacity is likely to be increased considerably if the issue is both low-profile and distributive in contrast to a high-profile redistributive policy, though the degree of policy capacity depends on several factors.

2. ALASKA'S POLICY ENVIRONMENT AND PUBLIC POLICY-MAKING PROCESS: INTERNAL AND EXTERNAL FORCES, FORMAL AND INFORMAL INFLUENCES

Next we explain the general policy environment and the specifics of the Alaska policy process. Many of the factors that shape policy are formal as they are part of the state constitution (the legislature, for example) or official bodies (such as executive departments). Others are informal, including interest groups, the media, and various outside forces.

The General Alaska Policy Environment

Alaska may be physically isolated from the Lower 48, far from world population centers, and have a much smaller government than many places, but when it comes to public policy making, the forces that shape its policy environment are very similar to those in other states and political jurisdictions. Figure 3.1 shows the international, national, and Alaska forces that shape the state's public policy environment.

The major forces are explained in detail in later chapters, including national and intergovernmental (IGR) forces in Chapter 10 and Alaska, national, and international economic forces in Chapters 6, 7, and 11. The five major forces that shape this environment and determine specific policies on a year-to-year basis are: (1) state revenues, largely determined by the world price of oil; (2) federal policy and federal funding; (3) the policy

BOX 3.3

Analyzing and Evaluating Public Policies

THE VALUE-BASED NATURE OF ISSUES AND POLICIES

Because most issues and policies are based on values and are permeated by political considerations, there is no definitive way to evaluate them in terms of being right or wrong, good or bad, fair or unfair. A policy that may be considered wrong, bad, or unfair to one individual or group may be seen as right, good, and fair by another individual or group.

INSIGHTS FROM SPECIFIC QUESTIONS

While we cannot arrive at any definitive assessment about issues and policies, we can acquire greater insights into particular issues and policies—their impetus, substance, impact, pros and cons, and so on—by asking specific questions, such as:

1. Who are the players in this policy area—the interest groups, individual politicians, government departments (federal and state)? Are they all in-state or are some from out-of-state?
2. Who has won and who has lost among these players in past and present policy arrangements? Who is likely to win and lose in the future and why?
3. Is there a proposed policy solution to the issue? If so, is it based on technical expertise, ideology, pragmatism, or a combination of these? What might be the consequences of these methods of resolution for the success or failure of the policy?

THE POLICY CONSTITUENCY PERSPECTIVE

This could include: an ideological constituency (conservative, liberal, libertarian, etc.); the point of view of an interest group; the politician's or bureaucrat's perspective; and the realist's or the idealist's perspective. One particularly useful perspective is that of the geographical constituency—the Alaskan, national, or international perspective. This way of evaluating a policy can also be stated best in a series of questions:

1. How does this policy benefit or adversely affect Alaskans as a whole? Does it benefit one region of the state over another, say Southeast over the Interior or Southcentral, or over the rest of the state?
2. Does it benefit urban Alaska at the expense of rural-bush areas, or vice versa? How might a resident of the bush, particularly an Alaska Native or a resident of Anchorage, view this policy?
3. How might this issue or policy be viewed by someone in the Lower 48, by general American public opinion, or by members of a branch of the federal government?
4. How might some international constituency affected by an issue, such as a country like Canada or a region like the Pacific Rim, view the policy action?

Source: Developed by the authors.

agenda of the governor and executive branch; (4) the policy agenda of the legislative leadership; and (5) the health or weakness of the industries that shape Alaska's economy (such as oil and gas, fishing, and mining).

All these formal and informal factors, external and internal to Alaska, affect the state public policy-making process—sometimes on a continual basis and sometimes intermittently.

The Alaska Public Policy-Making Process

The public policy-making process in Alaska, as in most of the United States, involves a series of stages through which a policy proposal goes from formulation and enactment to implementation and evaluation. This process involves the interaction of policy makers both formally (for example, in legislative hearings) and informally (such as private social functions and a chance encounter in a local restaurant). From a practical perspective, the outcome of the policy process is determined by power and personalities operating within the bounds of institutional constraints and partly shaped by values, especially political culture. A practical way to view the day-to-day operation of this process is as a cycle—the policy cycle. This is represented in Figure 3.2.

The six stages of the process are not entirely self-contained, which is why they are separated in Figure 3.2 by a dotted line. In some cases, adjacent stages overlap, but for

FIGURE 3.1

The Alaska Public Policy-Making Environment

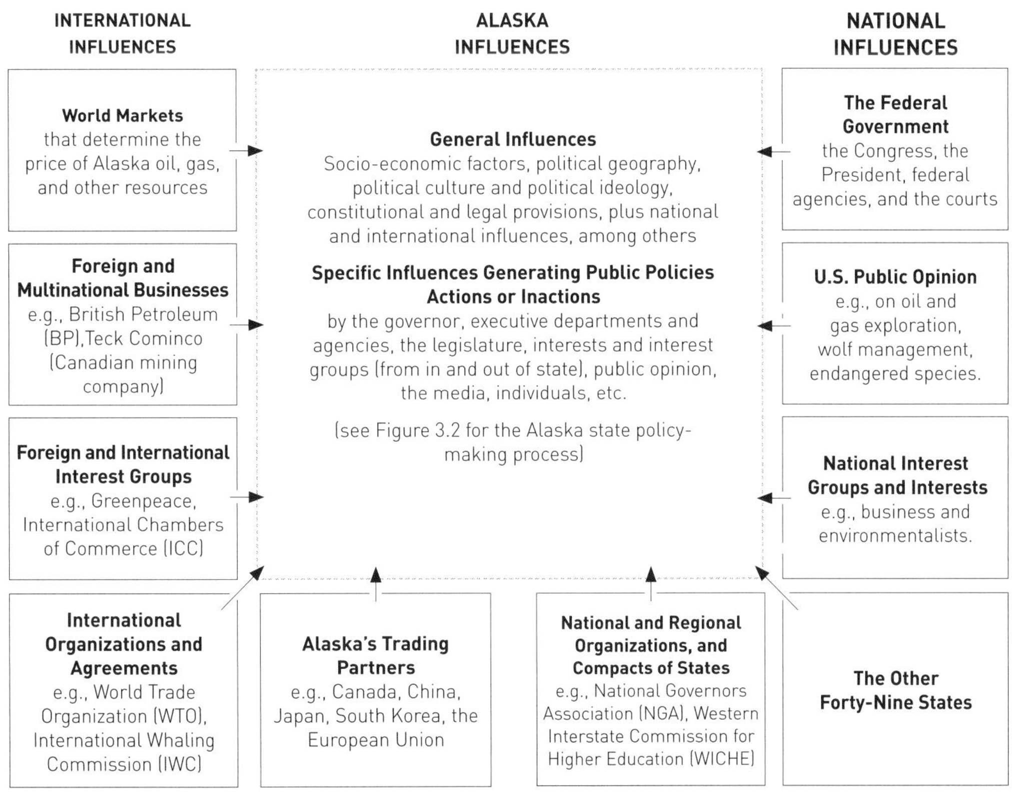

Source: Developed by the authors.

explanatory purposes it is useful to see them as separate. The stages and operation of this process are also fairly self-explanatory from the diagram, but a few supplemental comments will provide a more thorough understanding of each stage.

Phase 1: Getting an Issue on the Policy Agenda

The policy agenda is the array of issues being dealt with by government or that government is trying to avoid addressing. In reality, there is no actual list, and different policy makers, such as the governor and various legislators, have different agendas. The concept of a policy agenda or agendas is useful, however, for explaining the policy process.

Getting an issue on the policy agenda can be difficult and often has less to do with the urgency or necessity of the issue than with the political clout of those behind it. This is why some organizations hire lobbyists with major access to key policy makers who will help get their issue before government. However, just because something is placed on the policy agenda and a bill is written does not mean it will get serious consideration. Unless supported by key policy makers, such as majority caucus members, committee chairs, and the governor, it is not likely to go anywhere (see the case study of the soda pop bill in Box 3.6). Moreover, legislators often introduce bills for their constituents or supporters but sometimes do not put much effort into getting them passed.

Phase 2: Government Considering the Issue—the Proposed Law and Its Enactment

The rough-and-tumble phase of the process involves the drafting of a bill and its introduction into the legislature; committee hearings; lobbying; cutting of political deals; floor action in the legislature; and, in most cases, involvement of the governor and the governor's staff, the affected state agencies, and their senior personnel. Most items on the policy agenda never get past the introduction stage—perhaps as many as 75 percent. And while on the surface this second stage is an open process, in reality the majority legislative caucuses and the governor have, in most cases, decided beforehand which proposals will pass and which ones will be blocked or left to die. Also, the state's revenue picture—whether it is in surplus, facing a deficit, or stable—will be a major factor affecting the success or failure of many policy proposals (see Chapter 8).

Phase 3: Fleshing Out the Law—Preparing It for Implementation

Novices heave a sigh of relief when they see a policy enacted into law and often head off for a celebration. Far from being the end of the process, this may only be the beginning in getting the policy effectively implemented. Often politicians' and the media's interest in a policy wanes after it is passed and the law is turned over to an executive department for implementation and possible regulation writing. Department heads and interest groups can both work to delay implementation or minimize the effectiveness of a policy if the law was passed over their objections.

FIGURE 3.2

The Alaska State Public Policy-Making Process

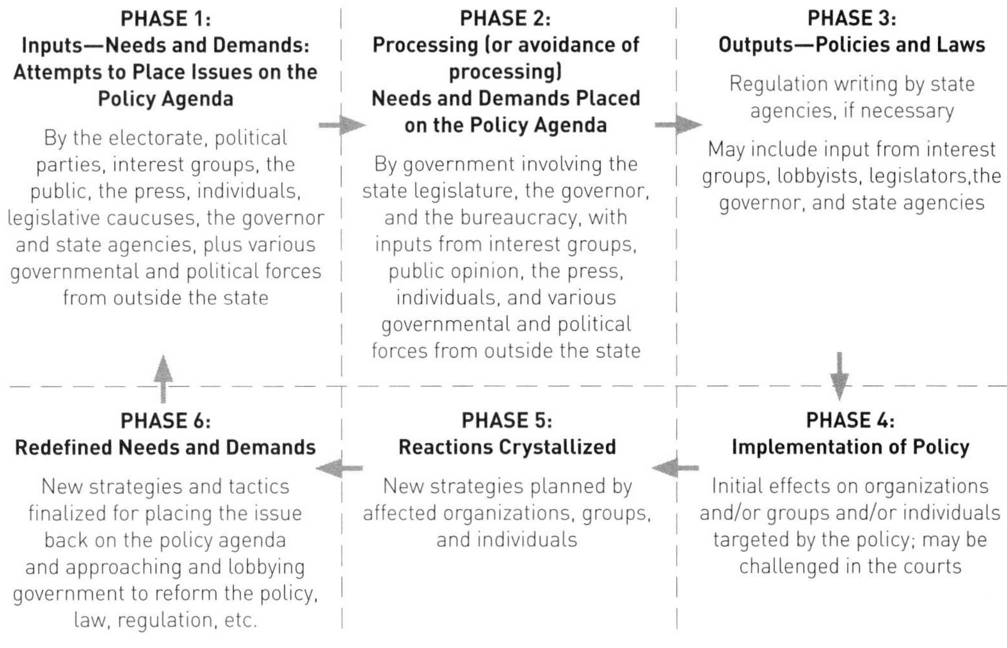

Source: Developed by the authors.

Phase 4: Initial Implementation

Some laws are implemented and produce little initial concern or reaction. Others may generate major reactions. For example, when those supporting a policy get less than they wanted in the final form of the policy, they may seek further change, and those who opposed the policy from the start may work to have it repealed. Phase 4 of the policy process may even involve a challenge in the courts (see Chapter 17).

Phase 5: Reactions to the Policy Crystallized

In contrast to Phase 4, Phase 5 involves the forces, both pro and con, formulating their plans over a longer period of time to change or protect the policy. These plans might include a court challenge or an attempt to put the policy before the public in an initiative or referendum.

Phase 6: Redefined Needs and Demands

At this stage, those who want to see a policy changed or repealed will work to get it back on the policy agenda (Phase 1). If they are successful, the policy process begins all over again.

Another Policy-Making Dimension in Alaska: The Initiative, Referendum, and Recall

In the tradition of the Progressive Movement and in line with many states in the American West, Article XI of the Alaska Constitution includes provisions for direct democracy—the initiative, referendum, and recall.[4] The recall is a blunt policy instrument used to remove an elected official from office. The initiative and referendum are more finely tuned.

An initiative is a proposed law placed on the ballot by a citizen petition. A referendum involves a citizen petition that places on the ballot the proposed repeal of a law recently enacted by the legislature. An initiative may not be used to amend the Alaska Constitution, and there are additional constitutional restrictions on both the initiative and the referendum, including a prohibition against their use with respect to enacting or repealing appropriations. Both the initiative and the referendum were intended as political safety valves. They are a way to bypass the regular policy process when the legislature or governor is perceived as being unresponsive or unwise on an issue.

The legislature occasionally directs the lieutenant governor to include an advisory vote on the ballot with respect to an issue. An advisory vote is neither an initiative nor a referendum as those processes are defined in Article XI of the Constitution. Rather, advisory votes are a means of enabling the legislature to assess the will of the people on issues of major concern. For instance, they have been used concerning the use of Permanent Fund earnings to balance the state budget. These votes can be seen as positive by providing policy makers with public opinion on an issue through a majority vote. Or they can be seen as a populist political escape hatch for policy makers to avoid taking a position on a controversial issue, saying in effect: "It's not for me to decide, let's leave it up to the voters."[5]

3. THE POLICY MAKERS: THEIR MOTIVES AND GOALS

Who exactly are the people and organizations that make policy in Alaska or work to block it? And what drives them—what are their motives and goals and what shapes their specific decisions on policies? In answering these questions, we move away from institutions and processes and focus on the human element in politics and policy making.

Because their goals and motives and what determines their specific decisions may vary, we divide policy makers into two categories. The first includes those who have been elected, appointed, or hired to work in the legislative and executive branches of state government. In practice, members of the third branch of government, the judiciary, sometimes make policy. But because their role in policy is reactive and involves different circumstances from the other two branches, we do not include them here but leave their policy role until Chapter 17. The second category includes policy makers and institutions external to the three branches. Depending on the issue and circumstances, external policy makers are often major influences, sometimes more so than policy makers in state government.

Policy Makers in the Legislative and Executive Branches

These include legislators and their staff, legislative caucuses, the governor and his or her staff, and departmental personnel. Before looking at each individually, we offer general perspectives on the motives of all key policy makers in the legislative and executive branches.

General Perspectives on Motives

The general perspectives can be stated in three questions: (1) What motivates policy makers; (2) Do they see themselves as delegates or representatives; and (3) What is their particular interest in politics and policy?

Motivation: Most, if not all, elected and appointed officials claim to be in public office first and foremost for the betterment of the people and for the state. This may certainly be an important motive and many government officials are committed to the public good. Additionally, many people seek public office because it gives them personal satisfaction. They are usually personable people who like dealing with others and solving problems. Some are political junkies who enjoy the rough-and-tumble of politics, the deal making, and the challenge of getting things done in a very fluid situation. Others may be more inclined to pursue their goals in a quieter, behind-the-scenes approach. Most office holders also enjoy the recognition and status of being a governor, legislator, or department head and in a position to wield some power. In the case of elected officials, it takes a particular type of person to run for office and be in a fishbowl for their time in office. This is evidenced by the fact that fewer than 1 percent of Americans ever run for any type of public office.[6] Very few people are willing to campaign and be exposed to public scrutiny every two or four years and, in effect, ask, "Hey, am I popular?"

Do They See Themselves as Delegates or Representatives? With extensive pressure on them from the public and their colleagues, elected officials of all types alternate between the so-called *delegate* and *representative* theories of elected office.

Under the delegate theory, they see themselves as pursuing what their constituents want more or less to the letter (assuming that what their constituents want can be determined). As such, they are essentially "clones" of their constituents, or at least the more vocal constituents, including those who fill out surveys, write letters, call their representatives' offices, or send e-mails.

The representative theory holds that public officials should be free to develop their own positions on issues because, by virtue of their offices, they have access to more and better information about issues than their constituents. Thus, "representative" officials will make reasoned judgments based upon available information and what they consider to be in their constituents' or the state's interest, even if their position on an issue is not reflected in the majority will of their constituents. A legislator might respond to a critical constituent, "You didn't elect me to be a rubber stamp, did you? You elected me to think and do what I believe is in your best interest." Most politicians practice the representative theory most of the time, but use the delegate theory when it is convenient to say they went with the "majority will" of their constituents or public opinion in the state.

The Focus of Their Interests: Elected state officials have to deal with a broad range of issues. Even for governors, with their large staff, and certainly for legislators, time does not permit them to become conversant with all issues. Legislators tend to specialize in the issues that interest them and benefit their constituents. Some legislators are interested in and informed about many policy issues, while others are interested in fewer issues. Still other legislators are more interested in the wheeling and dealing of politics, relying on their staff, trusted fellow legislators, and sometimes lobbyists, for information and direction on many issues. Obviously, state department officials will primarily be interested in their department's area of policy unless the governor directs them otherwise or they see a connection between one of their policy areas or issues and that of another department.

Legislators

Legislators have one of the broadest job descriptions in society. They are called upon to "represent" their constituents, the "public interest," and "the interests of the state." The problem is that it is impossible to find universal agreement on what constitutes "representation" and what might be in the public's and the state's best interests. This is because all of these are based on values, personal perspective, and interpretation. As a result, legislators have a job with few boundaries and they can use this flexibility to avoid issues—alternating between the delegate and representative position as convenient—and claim that they are doing their jobs even if many people disagree with their decisions.

Most legislators also want to be reelected, and this is a powerful motivating force. Pleasing their constituents is of paramount importance, and trying to balance that goal with the desire to create good public policy may create a dilemma. Moreover, legislators must deal with shortages that also influence their actions in the policy process. These are a shortage of: (1) power to get things done—every time they bring pressure to bear to get something done, they use up some of their limited supply of power (that is, political capital is not infinite); (2) information necessary to determine what is the "right thing" to do, which is why they often turn to their staff and to lobbyists; and (3) the time to do all they want to do.

Legislative Caucuses

These are groupings of legislators within the House and Senate (sometimes including members from both houses) who come together on an issue or range of issues in which they have a common interest. Most important of these are the majority caucuses in both houses as they essentially run the show and have the most influence on policy. Each house also has a minority caucus. There are also caucuses based on geography and on policy issues. For instance, the bush caucus (rural-bush legislators from both parties) was extremely influential in the 1970s and 1980s, but is less so today. Regional cross-party caucuses (such as the Southeast and Interior caucus) can exert influence on regional issues as long as the majority caucuses give tacit approval. An example of a specific policy issue caucus is the children's caucus.

Legislative Staff—Legislative Aides

The major job description for legislative staff (often referred to as legislative aides) is to carry out the instructions of the legislator for whom they work. In a real sense, their major goal is "to make their boss look good." This is particularly important because legislative staff hold their jobs at the pleasure of their legislator who can hire and fire them at will. So they have no job security even though some staffers have worked for their legislator for years.

Legislative aides are not equal in their role or influence. Some are simply gofers for their bosses. Others have important advisory roles and are a major influence on their legislator's decisions. Some, particularly those working for majority caucus members, especially the leadership, are often more of an influence on policy than many legislators in both the majority and minority.

The Governor

Unlike legislators, who are elected from a particular legislative district or region, the governor has a statewide responsibility, as he or she and the lieutenant governor are the only state officials elected statewide. The governor's job description is more or less set out in Article III of the state constitution. It involves a host of responsibilities, including running the executive branch of government, appointing judges, and exercising veto power over legislation. The motives of those who run for governor are probably very similar to those who run for the legislature. The governor's goals and needs are also probably similar.

The Governor's Staff

Like legislative staff, the governor's staff works hard to make the boss look good partly because they are also employees at will. They also likely have similar motives to legislative staff and similar needs and goals. Many members of the governor's staff worked on the governor's campaign or were professional associates or personal friends before the governor was elected.

Department Personnel—Bureaucrats

At the top level are the commissioners and deputy commissioners and other political appointees who are also at-will employees (with the exception, in theory but not in practice, of the commissioners of education and of fish and game). These political appointees have a range of motives much like any political official, though many of them are career people in fields such as labor, finance, and the environment.

At a lower level, but with much less turnover, are the midlevel bureaucrats: those who head divisions within a department or work as specialists, such as finance or personnel officers. These are the career bureaucrats. They likely have qualifications or extensive training in their particular profession and sometimes managerial training as well. Their job description is usually very clear and much narrower than any elected official or staffer for the legislature or the governor. While many of them are well aware of the political aspects of government and may deal with the legislature, the governor's office, and other government departments from time to time in a political capacity, most are primarily concerned with performing their jobs as professionals or as semiprofessionals.

Policy Makers and Forces External to the Legislature and the Executive Branch

The major external policy makers and forces briefly explained here are the state's congressional delegation, political parties, interest groups and lobbyists, federal government personnel, the media and public opinion, and other political forces.

The Three Members of Alaska's Congressional Delegation

The motives and goals of Alaska's two U.S. senators and sole representative are likely similar to other politicians in terms of public service and seeking reelection. However, they may also be mindful of the ambitions of state politicians who might want to run against them. All three members have the task of balancing the regional interests within the state and that of the state's interest with the national interest. The congressional delegation can have considerable influence on state public policy when it involves federal lands, federal funds, and regulations or political forces outside the state.

Political Parties

One of the characteristics of Alaska politics is that the state's parties are organizationally weak. So even though virtually all elected officials are either Democrats or Republicans, the party platform has little influence on policy. The majority caucuses in the Alaska legislature, particularly the House of Representatives, often include at least a few members of the minority. Nevertheless, some elected officials who are strong partisans do use party positions to shape policy.

Interest Groups and Lobbyists

What all lobbyists have in common in their job description is that they promote the cause and goals of their interest group or organization to try to influence government policy in their favor. The tools of their trade are: contacts and relationships with key public officials; trust and credibility, which often includes confidentiality; gathering and presenting information; planning and replanning their strategy and tactics; and in some cases, assisting politicians with election and reelection efforts.

Federal Government Personnel

Career bureaucrats in the various federal departments and agencies deal with Alaska on a daily basis, such as those in the Department of the Interior and the Forest Service. Their motives are very similar to Alaska's career bureaucrats. These federal employees seek to implement their agency's mission, which may involve influencing state policy makers and those who implement state policy to comply with federal laws and regulations.

The Media and Public Opinion

The main role of the media is to report the news, to sell newspapers, or to secure high ratings on the radio, TV, or website. Public radio and TV reporters, however, are less pressured to sell their products than those who work for commercial enterprises. The media's influence on the policy process is largely indirect: few issues can be said to have been directly shaped or strongly influenced by the media. What influence they do have on policy comes primarily from being a sort of political information clearinghouse between policy makers and the public by reporting on the opinion of the public and the actions of policy makers in the image-conscious world of politics. At the same time, the media can turn low-profile issues into high-profile ones, and increase the intensity of attention to, and possibly action on, an issue.

Other than voting, citizens have no specified role in the political process, but they are often an integral part of it. However, discovering the motives, needs, and goals of the public regarding public policy in general, and especially on particular issues, and deciding how this should be translated into policy, if at all, is extremely problematic. One reason is that it is difficult to define exactly what constitutes "the public." Is it the entire population, only those who vote, only those interested in the issue at hand, or some other segment of the population? Should more weight be given to what the majority thinks or more weight to the intensity of feelings of a minority very much concerned with or affected by an issue? Yet another problem is determining the accuracy of the public message being delivered to government. The accuracy may depend on the form of the message, whether it is delivered, for example, through public opinion polls, the media, through letters or e-mails to public officials, social media, major interest groups, or other means.

Chapter 20 deals with the role of the media and public opinion, and attempts to answer some of these questions. For the moment, we can simply say that the public's motives, goals, and needs are complex, often mixed, and sometimes contradictory. However, despite this lack of clarity of expression and despite what a cynical public may often believe, policy makers, particularly elected officials, are very concerned about gauging what the public thinks. It is often the most important factor that shapes their policy decisions.

Other Political Forces

Less prominent but sometimes of influence are other states, through state compacts or state organizations, and foreign governments, such as Canada and Japan, on various economic issues, particularly fisheries.

4. THE POLICY MAKERS: WHAT SHAPES THEIR SPECIFIC CHOICES ON POLICY PREFERENCES?

What are the factors that influence policy makers' decisions on specific policies? That is, faced with an issue, such as funding K–12 education for the disabled, dealing with a state budget deficit, or public pressure to reinstate the death penalty, what influences a public official's actions? There are three major forces: (1) institutional influences; (2) ideological and partisan influences; and (3) the forces of political necessity. All three will affect an official's policy decision, but the exact combination will depend on the particular issue and the political circumstances surrounding its development.

Institutional Influences

Institutional influences result from elected or appointed officials being part of an organization, such as a legislative caucus or the executive branch of government. These influences can both constrain and enhance the options available to a policy maker. The various institutional circumstances that influence the policy decisions of Alaska's elected and appointed officials are set out in Box 3.4.

Ideological and Partisan Influences

All politicians have a belief system, a political philosophy, or ideology, and this is a large part of what they market to the voters when they run for office. As elsewhere in the United States, in Alaska these beliefs range from right-wing conservative to left-wing

BOX 3.4

Factors Influencing Policy Makers' Choices to Pursue or Block Specific Policy Actions

There are three circumstances that shape the approach of elected and appointed state officials in pursuing certain courses of action: (1) the unique position of the governor; (2) when the decision is a collective one; and (3) freedom to decide the course of action. There is overlap between these categories, but the distinctions are important.

1. THE UNIQUE POSITION OF THE GOVERNOR

Governors are in a unique position as policy makers. The governor's policy approaches are partly determined by: the mandate on which he or she was elected; the need to represent the interest of the state as a whole (if they see this as important); paying back, in direct or indirect ways, those who helped win the election; his or her own philosophy (liberal, conservative, populist, etc.); issues that are particularly important to the governor; and perhaps an eye to reelection if it is the governor's first term.

As the head of the executive branch and with extensive formal constitutional authority, governors have the most flexibility of all policy makers in terms of what courses of action to follow. Nonetheless, they are constrained by the need to get legislative support and the support of certain interest groups for their budgets and high-priority issues.

2. WHEN THERE IS A COLLECTIVE DECISION ON POLICY ACTION

Collective decisions include those made by the majority caucuses in the legislature, particularly supporting the budget; a regional caucus that has agreed on a course of action for obtaining funds and how these might be allocated among the members; and the governor's staff and senior department personnel, on the governor's policy approaches. In these circumstances the policy maker risks being castigated, including being expelled from the caucus or fired from their appointed position, if they do not go along with this collective decision.

3. WHEN POLICY MAKERS ARE FREE TO DECIDE ON SPECIFIC ACTION

Three different circumstances influence the policy approach when the policy maker is free to choose a position on a particular issue.

When the Issue is High-Profile

On high-profile issues, such as whether to limit or eliminate the Permanent Fund Dividend (PFD), reinstating the personal income tax, opening ANWR, and abortion, among other issues, policy makers need to take a position. The particular position taken will be shaped by their philosophy, the views of their constituents, and the benefit to their district, by interest groups, and so on.

When the Issue Is Low-Profile but of Major Concern

When a policy maker has a major stake in a policy outcome, perhaps because of personal philosophy or the benefit to their district, but the issue is not high-profile, their course of action is most likely determined by those who can help secure a policy or help block one they oppose. Even if they are influential legislators or executive branch officials, including the governor, this involves building alliances and coalitions with other public officials, lobbyists, and interest groups. For many it may involve trading future favors or votes.

When the Issue Is of Minor, if any, Concern

Even when an issue is of minor interest to a policy maker, the governor and legislators may be required to pass judgment on it—in the governor's case by signing or vetoing a bill or letting it become law without signature, and in the case of legislators, by voting. Governors and legislators often do not take their own stance on issues that are of little or no concern to them. Instead, they often rely on their personal staff, interest groups, executive branch personnel, their constituents, and other sources for information. In terms of policy approach, this is likely the situation in which public officials are most open to persuasion. In the case of legislators, they may rely on trusted colleagues to decide how to vote, a situation known as cueing, or taking direction from others on how to vote.

Source: Developed by the authors.

liberal. Ideology usually leads a candidate to run as a Republican or a Democrat, and also leads those elected to office to argue for certain types of solutions to problems. For example, a liberal may be against the death penalty whereas some conservatives favor it. Many conservatives want to use the free enterprise system to help solve many problems, such as dealing with health care coverage for the uninsured, whereas liberals believe government should provide universal health care to citizens.

However, many elected officials downplay ideology and emphasize pragmatism and, in certain circumstances, bipartisanship. This is partly because of the friends and neighbors politics in Alaska and partly because of Alaska's pragmatic dependent individualistic political culture. Political pragmatism is a particular characteristic of rural-bush legislators.

The Forces of Political Necessity

Political necessity often leads politicians to make compromises to get their bills passed or to kill proposals they oppose. Political necessity may include paying back political obligations to campaign contributors, including interest groups, to a legislative colleague for their support in the past, or even to the governor. Or it might involve building up political capital to cash in at some point in the future. Political necessity involves the rough-and-tumble of politics and the exercise of political power, whether overtly or covertly expressed. In Alaska it often leads to bipartisanship and the prominence of political pragmatism.

5. SUCCESS AND FAILURE IN POLICY MAKING: TWO CASE STUDIES AND DEALING WITH A POWER DEFICIT

To give practical meaning to the points made in this chapter, we turn to two case studies of policy making in Alaska. In Lowi's terms, both were attempts at regulatory policy, and in presenting them the two legislators who provide the studies present a policy evaluation of types, at least to the point where they were passed or defeated. Both were medium-profile public issues, but nevertheless had some intense supporters and opponents in a pluralist policy-making environment as opposed to an elitist one. The first illustrates a success in policy making. It is the Real ID bill, introduced by Senator Bill Wielechowski of Anchorage to prevent the implementation of a federal law in Alaska requiring a personal ID in addition to a driver's license. The other, which did not pass, was introduced by then-Representative Mary Nelson of Bethel. It would have banned the sale of soda pop in schools during school hours.

The contrast between the respective success and failure of these policy issues illustrates two fundamental and related points about the policy process that are central to our explanation in this chapter. The first is the dynamics of the process and the need to marshal certain political forces. The second is what constitutes political power in the process and the challenges that face those policy makers, groups, and individuals who have a power deficit, or the lack of sufficient elements of power to enact policies they support or to defeat policies they oppose.

The Practical Lessons for Policy Making

The Real ID bill (see Box 3.5) illustrates the involvement of many groups and organizations, the federal government, and Alaska's executive branch. It shows the necessity of coalition building, having major interest groups support the measure, garnering public support and bipartisan support if it can be enlisted. In particular, it is a textbook example of ad hoc coalition building. It also helped considerably that Senator Wielechowski was in the majority coalition in the Senate.

In contrast, former Representative Nelson's effort lacked many of these political assets (see Box 3.6). She had major interest groups against her, one powerful group in particular that had much to lose if her bill passed. She had an unsupportive—in fact, a strongly opposed—key committee chair, and some public opposition. Added to all this, Representative Nelson was in the House Democratic minority. Whether in the House or the Senate, minority bills are often dead on arrival at their first hearing, unless an unusual set of circumstances prevails. Most of all, as she points out, the failure illustrates that sometimes a public policy that benefits a large segment of Alaska's population and maybe all of it does not get considered on its merits. It falls victim to narrow group interests that would be adversely affected by the bill and have the power to kill it.

Dealing with a Power Deficit: Is It Possible in Alaska Politics?

The lessons from these case studies and from this chapter are that organizations, groups, and individuals, including some legislators and other politicians, who have been unsuccessful in their policy quests must deal with their power deficit. How is this to be done? Is it practically feasible for all groups and individuals to be influential in a democracy like Alaska's?

The short answer to the first question is to understand the elements of power. There are no secrets about what constitutes power and how to acquire it, but securing it in practice and keeping it is quite another matter. Acquiring power requires a politician to have political know-how and also enough political incentives to offer the power brokers and other key players who can affect that politician's goals in the policy process to persuade them to help his or her cause.

The short answer to the second question is that the acquisition of power by groups and individuals depends on the nature of the group, its resources, and the issue at hand.

BOX 3.5

The Politics of Successful Policy Making: Senator Bill Wielechowski's Real ID Bill

Senate Bill 202, which I introduced in 2007 and became law in 2008, is a good example of how political coalitions, bipartisanship and the art of compromise can be used to overcome major political opposition.

This legislation forbids the state from spending funds to implement a federal law known as the Real ID Act of 2005, which was intended to enhance national security by making state driver's licenses national ID cards. This law would have been costly as the states were required to implement it almost entirely at their own expense. Plus privacy and personal information would be less secure than before. My bill was Alaska's response in a nationwide grassroots effort to oppose this ill-conceived plan.

Two crucial factors in SB 202's success were strong bipartisan support in the legislature and support by an unusual coalition of conservative and liberal organizations. Across the nation, over 600 groups opposed Real ID, ranging from the American Conservative Union, Catholic Social Services, Citizens Against Government Waste, the John Birch Society, the National Center on Domestic and Sexual Violence, the National Taxpayers Union, the Privacy Rights Clearinghouse, and the National Rifle Association (NRA). In Alaska the effort was aided by many private individuals, including liberal and conservative activists who organized a statewide network to testify against Real ID.

My bill had no easy ride, however. It met powerful opposition, particularly from high-level officials with strong misgivings about opposing the federal law, including Kevin Brooks, Deputy Commissioner of the Department of Administration. He testified that SB 202 could prevent the Division of Motor Vehicles (DMV) from conducting what they considered to be "best practices." Yet, many of the requirements of the Real ID Act, such as fraud identification training for staff and the use of digital technology, were already in place through DMV regulations. Mr. Brooks was also concerned because the U.S. Department of Homeland Security threatened to deny air travel to those who could not present a Real ID—a frightening prospect for a state dependent on flying for transportation. Despite these concerns, SB 202 moved smoothly through the Senate, with the only opposition coming from several members of the Republican minority.

Then SB 202 went to the House side. Even though it had strong bipartisan support, it hit a roadblock with the Chair of the House State Affairs Committee, who was concerned that the bill would negatively impact attempts to curtail illegal immigration. I worked with the committee chair and Deputy Commissioner Brooks to craft a compromise. We made it clear that SB 202 would not prevent the state from implementing and conducting best practices that would help curtail illegal immigration.

Upon clearing this major obstacle, the new version of SB 202 moved through its remaining committees of referral and ultimately passed the State House 39–1 with the State Senate concurring 19–1. On May 28, 2008, Governor Palin, who had not taken a clear position on SB 202, allowed the bill to become law without her signature.

Source: Authored by Senator Bill Wielechowski, Democrat of Anchorage.

BOX 3.6

The Politics of Failed Policy Making: Representative Mary Nelson's Soda Pop Bill

In November 2002, I read in the book *Fast Food Nation* about a school district in Colorado facing revenue shortfalls that brokered a ten-year deal giving Coca-Cola exclusive beverage supplier rights. This scheme was replicated by school districts across the nation, contributing to excessive soda consumption by children with accompanying health hazards. Coupled with my concerns about health challenges facing Alaska Natives—soaring obesity rates and other preventable ills—the book motivated me to try to prevent beverage manufacturers from cutting similar deals with Alaska's schools.

So for the first time I sponsored a bill that was not championed by a constituent or an interest group. In four years as a legislator, I had sponsored several bills. A school safety bill (suggested by one of the school districts I represent) flew through the legislative process after the 1999 Columbine school shooting tragedy in Colorado. Another bill (suggested by fishermen in Bristol Bay) created a loan fund for fishermen who owed money to the Internal Revenue Service (IRS).

But House Bill 80, "An Act Prohibiting Sales of Certain Soft Drinks in Public Schools," was solely mine to promote. It prohibited the sale of all carbonated soft drinks and drinks with more than 42 grams of sugar per 20-ounce serving from 8 a.m. to 5 p.m. on school days, leaving the option open to sell sodas during evening events.

As a Democratic minority member, I recruited a Republican majority member, a retired dentist, to co-sponsor the bill. I felt he would lend credibility to the cause. The bill seemed to me like a no-brainer: it was obviously the right thing to do for the health of Alaska's young people. I was soon to learn that bills don't pass merely because they would make good public policy.

The bill was introduced in the House on February 5, 2003. Soon after, I met with a lobbyist for a soda manufacturer. He pointedly told me that if I did not pull the bill, they would find someone to run against me in the next election. I was shocked but decided not to cower beneath such a threat. I didn't pull the bill.

My bill was referred to two committees: Labor and Commerce and Health, Education, and Social Services (HESS). The Chair of Labor and Commerce was freshman Representative Tom Anderson, a former Executive Director of CHARR (the Alaska Cabaret, Hotel, Restaurant and Retailers Association). CHARR lobbies for Alaska's hospitality industry and was against the bill. The entire first year Representative Anderson refused to allow the bill a single hearing. The second year he held a cursory fifteen-minute hearing on HB 80, after which it lingered and eventually died because he refused to let it out of his committee.

While the bill did not see much daylight in the legislature, it spurred considerable statewide debate pro and con. School districts were largely opposed because vending machines generate considerable revenues. On the other hand, many health professionals favored the bill for health reasons; but there was no organized cohesive support to overcome CHARR's and Representative Anderson's opposition.

The moral of this story: as a legislator, you can't be too far out ahead of the public, as I was in this case. Plus, committee chairs wield near dictatorial power, as do some interest groups, and being a minority member often has serious drawbacks in terms of exercising power.

Source: Authored by former Representative Mary Nelson, Democrat of Bethel, now Mary Sattler.

Not all organizations, groups, and individuals have sufficient resources or the ability to acquire them, and not all issues have sufficiently broad appeal to get the attention of policy makers. This is the case even in a democracy and even in the friends and neighbors political atmosphere of Alaska. Furthermore, even referendum or initiative campaigns take major resources. Across the states, only about 20 percent of ballot proposition elections are won by "underdog" groups, which spend considerably less than the typical well-funded interests. This means that in most cases money is a major determining factor in these elections.[7] Clear evidence of this in Alaska was a 2014 proposition on the ballot—the result of a grassroots, populist groundswell—to repeal a tax break to the oil industry passed by the legislature in 2013. The oil industry and its supporters outspent those favoring repeal by almost 18 to 1 and defeated the challenge by a 52–48 percent margin.

In essence, then, the fundamental right of citizen and group representation and participation is one thing, but turning that right into power is quite another. While democratic constitutions and laws can promote equality of representation, no theory of democracy advocates equal power for all groups and interests. Even if such a right were advocated, it could not be made to work in practice. It is a stark fact of political life that political power is unevenly distributed in any political system. In fact, pluralist democracy is geared to make power uneven, with groups and organizations working to acquire more power than their opponents and, in many cases, scheming to deprive their opponents of power.

6. HOW DIFFERENT IS ALASKA'S PUBLIC POLICY-MAKING PROCESS?

The answer to this question can be summarized in the same way we approached Alaska's exceptionalism in Chapter 1—by dividing it into three broad areas of similarity, distinguishing characteristics, and uniqueness.

First, the role that personality and motives play in the policy process, as well as the policy cycle itself, is virtually the same in Alaska as in other states and very similar to most democracies worldwide. There are characteristics that distinguish Alaska from some states but not from others. For example, Alaska has a unified executive branch in which the governor appoints the members of the cabinet, while some states, like California, have a plural executive branch in which several top executive officials are elected and have their own power bases. Distinguishing characteristics also include: the role of legislative staff in Alaska compared with most states in the nation where there are few such staff; the relative weakness of political parties and of political ideology, particularly when compared with states in the Northeast; and Alaska's limits on the use of the initiative and referendum.

There are some characteristics of Alaska's policy process that, while in some cases are not unique, are in considerable contrast to other states. The role of Alaska Natives, combined with urban versus rural-bush tensions, is one of them. Another is the tradition, even if an intermittent one, of bipartisan legislative coalitions. A third is the major dependence of the state budget, and thus the funding of policies, on one source of revenue—oil and gas taxes. In sum, these and other factors make Alaska's policy process different overall from most of the states in the West and particularly the Mountain West, a region with which Alaska otherwise has much in common politically.

7. CONCLUSIONS: BELIEFS, INSTITUTIONS, PERSONALITIES, AND POWER, AND ALASKA'S PUBLIC POLICY PROCESS

This chapter began by asking two questions: Why do political needs and demands that benefit a small group sometimes get dealt with in Alaska while others get little, if any, attention even though they would benefit Alaskans as a whole? And on other occasions, why do the majority, sometimes a large majority in the state, not get what they want politically?

The argument presented here is that the answer to both questions revolves around harnessing and exercising political power. The ability to do this successfully varies depending on the issue, who controls political and other resources, and the general political environment. More broadly, power is a key factor in understanding the dynamics of Alaska's public policy process. The essence of these dynamics is the interaction of beliefs, institutions, personalities, and power within Alaska's political environment, shaped by various influences and manifesting particular characteristics as explained in Chapters 1 and 2.

This chapter provides the background for understanding several aspects of Alaska politics covered in the rest of the book, particularly the way in which various factors in Alaska's political environment, institutions, and processes affect, and are in turn affected by, the policy process. This background will also be helpful in understanding the specific policy issues dealt with later on, as well as the assessment of the performance of Alaska's political system since statehood, possible reforms, and the future for Alaska politics.

ENDNOTES

[1] Two comprehensive texts on public policy making in the United States are: Michael E. Kraft and Scott R. Furlong, *Public Policy: Politics, Analysis and Alternatives*, 4th ed. (Washington, D.C.: Congressional Quarterly Press, 2012); and Thomas A. Birkland, *An Introduction to the Policy Process: Theories, Concepts and Models of Public Policy Making*, 4th ed. (New York: Routledge/Taylor & Francis, 2015). Both use good practical examples to illustrate the academic theories of the policy process.

[2] Theodore J. Lowi, "American Business, Public Policy, Case Studies, and Political Theory," *World Politics*, volume 16 (1964): 667–715.

[3] For fuller details on policy evaluation, see Kraft and Furlong, *Public Policy*, esp. Chapter 3; and Birkland, *An Introduction to the Policy Process*, esp. Chapter 8.

[4] Gordon Harrison, *Alaska's Constitution; A Citizen's Guide*, 5th ed. (Juneau: Alaska Legislative Affairs Agency, 2012), 179–80.

[5] See Chapter 4, Alaska's constitution, and Chapter 14, campaigns and elections, for more discussion of direct democracy.

[6] Thomas R. Dye and Susan A. McManus, *Politics in States and Communities*, 14th ed. (Upper Saddle River, N.J.: Pearson/Prentice Hall, 2012), 108.

[7] Thomas E. Cronin, *Direct Democracy: The Politics of Initiative, Referendum and Recall* (Cambridge, MA: Harvard University Press, 1999), 113.

★ PART II ★

Major Influences Shaping Alaska's Politics and its Policy Environment

About Part II

This second part of the book provides an in-depth look at several key factors, touched on in Part I, that both influence and characterize Alaska politics and shape the state's governmental system and its policy-making environment. Each chapter illustrates the various aspects of Alaska politics identified in Chapter 2 and throws some light on all the chapters in the rest of the book.

Chapter 4 considers the legal foundation of Alaska's democratic political and governmental system—the state constitution. However, it considers this less from a formal, legal angle and more from a political and policy perspective by asking: How has the constitution influenced politics and public policy? Alaska's so-called "model constitution" has been an important influence. But, as we will see, in some ways it has had political impacts not intended or foreseen by Alaska's founders.

Chapter 5 explains Alaska's political culture, which is the very foundation of what shapes politics and public policy in the state. The chapter provides insights into all twelve of the characteristics of state politics set out in Chapter 2. For instance, Chapter 5 helps explain the apparent contradiction inherent in the dependent individualism of the state's political culture, Alaska's friends and neighbors politics, weak political parties, and the role of bipartisanship in Alaska politics.

Together with political culture, of the key factors that influence politics in a democracy, none is more important than the economy. The interaction of political culture, aspects of the economy, and various elements of politics and government, including prominent issues, the power structure, and the nature of the policy process, all shape the so-called political economy of a place. The political economy of a nation, state, or locality provides insights into its politics and the distribution of political power. It also presents policy makers with both opportunities and constraints. Chapters 6, 7, 8, and 9 deal with four aspects of Alaska's political economy.

Chapter 6 provides an overview of Alaska's economy and its effects on the power dynamics within the state's political sphere. Chapter 7 examines the relationship of Alaska's economy with the economies of the other 49 states and other countries. This chapter also explains how both external and internal economic forces affect Alaska politics, especially the economic policy options open to the state's public officials. Drawing on the analysis in Chapters 6 and 7, Chapter 8 explains the political economy of Alaska's unbalanced revenue sources for funding state and local government. Then, in Chapter 9, a particularly Alaskan aspect of the state's political economy is examined—the role and significance of Alaska Natives in state politics and the Alaska economy. This chapter includes an explanation of conflicts between urban and rural-bush areas, and explores the special relationship between Alaska Natives and the federal government.

A major aspect of Alaska's political economy is the central role of government as an economic force as well as a provider of law and order, and various services. The three remaining chapters of Part II deal with the role of government in Alaska. Chapter 10 explores the significance of the role of the federal government and intergovernmental relations (IGR), both generally and as they affect specific political constituencies, such as Alaska Natives, Alaskans favoring economic development and those emphasizing environmental protection. Chapter 11 looks at Alaska's international interactions over the years. Whereas Chapter 7 focuses on the Outside economy and, in part, Alaska's international trade, Chapter 11 takes a broader perspective and examines how state policy makers and private individuals and organizations have approached Alaska's involvement in an increasingly globalized world.

The final chapter, Chapter 12, takes a holistic look at many of the particular aspects of the role of government as they relate to the major characteristics of Alaska politics discussed in the first eleven chapters of the book. For instance, Chapter 12 sheds light on the all-pervasive importance of government in Alaska in contrast to the often negative attitudes toward it. The chapter also identifies some of the myths and contradictions in Alaska's political discourse associated with the role of government, and discusses the way that the characteristic of fiscal conservatism plays out in everyday politics in relation to the state's heavy dependence on government.

⋆ CHAPTER 4 ⋆

Alaska's Constitution: Shaping the Foundations and Development of Politics, Government, and Public Policy

Gordon S. Harrison with Clive S. Thomas

Since statehood, in certain situations Alaska's constitution has been an active influence on politics and government and on several key and sometimes very controversial policy issues. Given this influence, we can state the theme of this chapter as a question: In what circumstances and in what ways has Alaska's constitution had an influence on politics, government, and public policy, past and present? The answer lies in explaining the political forces that have shaped the evolution of the document and the way it has been interpreted and in providing perspectives on the connection between the constitution and key political issues.[1]

This chapter is organized as follows. First come some preliminaries for understanding the major analysis in the chapter, including a brief explanation of the constitution's contents and some comparisons with other state constitutions. This is followed by a section outlining the writing and development of the constitution and one covering the major amendments to the document and their implications for Alaska politics. Next is a perspective on the relationship of the constitution to several major state issues. Then we briefly consider the extent to which the constitution itself has contributed to Alaska's more contentious political issues. The conclusion points to chapters in the rest of the book that contain more detailed discussions of the interactions between particular state policies and some of the constitutional provisions explained in this chapter.

Other than the short section detailing the major content of the document, this chapter does not provide a comprehensive article-by-article, section-by-section review of the constitution. That can be acquired by reading the document itself.[2] In fact, we recommend browsing the Alaska Constitution before reading this chapter.

1. THE MAJOR CONTENT OF ALASKA'S CONSTITUTION: HOW DIFFERENT IS IT?

A constitution is a document containing the basic laws and principles by which a country or state is to be governed. It sets out the authority of institutions of government—legislature, executive, and judiciary—how they are to be constituted and how they relate, plus provisions regarding elections, finance and taxation, local government, and individual rights. Constitutions also often include special provisions that reflect the history, experiences, and needs of that country or state. The provisions of Alaska's constitution very much reflect Alaska's historical experiences and many contemporary concerns.

As to basic structure and powers, all state constitutions follow the general pattern of the U.S. Constitution: they enumerate individual rights, create three branches of government, provide for checks and balances among the branches, authorize creation of local government, and grant taxing authority, among other powers. Alaska's constitution both follows this basic structure and grants these general powers.

When it comes to specifics, however, state constitutions vary widely, and some variations have a major effect on political processes and policy making. For example, constitutions vary in the size of the legislatures they establish. The New Hampshire Constitution creates a House of Representatives of 400 members; the Alaska Constitution creates a House of Representatives of 40 members. In fact, Alaska's legislature, with its 40 representatives and 20 senators, is the smallest state legislature apart from Nebraska's unicameral body of 49 members. Delaware with 61 members and Nevada with 62 are close to Alaska's. But across the country the average state legislature has about 150 members with an average of 39 senators and 110 representatives.[3]

Constitutions also vary in the way they specify how senior members of the executive branch are chosen. In some states, such as California, top executive officials are elected separately, including the lieutenant governor. As a result, the governor and lieutenant governor may be members of different political parties. Some state constitutions include use of the initiative, referendum, and recall, while others do not, and those that do often have different rules for the use of these provisions of direct democracy. State constitutions also vary in the way they can be amended. Several allow amendment by voter initiative, while others do not. These and many other differences in constitutional provisions affect the politics of the individual states and thus the particulars of the public policy process and even the issues that arise.[4]

Like the U.S. and other state constitutions, the Alaska Constitution begins with a preamble:

> We the people of Alaska, grateful to God and to those who founded our nation and pioneered this great land, in order to secure and transmit to succeeding generations our heritage of political, civil and religious

> liberty within the Union of States, do ordain and establish this constitution for the State of Alaska.

Beyond this, the document manifests the similarities with, and differences from, other state constitutions as outlined above. Alaska's constitution has been viewed as a "model," and among the most modern and progressive of the fifty state constitutions. A list of the titles of the constitution's fifteen Articles and its major amendments is set out in Box 4.1.

2. HISTORICAL BACKGROUND AND THE PROVISIONS OF THE ORIGINAL "MODEL" CONSTITUTION

This section examines the origins of the constitution and the historical forces that shaped the provisions creating strong legislative and executive branches of state government. It also explains why Alaska's constitution is regarded as a model among the fifty states, though later in the chapter we question this accolade.

The Convention

Alaska's constitution was written between November 1955 and February 1956, three years before Alaska became a state, at a convention assembled at the University of Alaska in Fairbanks.[5] The call for a constitutional convention came from the territorial legislature early in 1955, when there was momentum building in Congress for a statehood bill. Advocates for statehood saw the drafting of a constitution as a means of promoting their cause at home and in Washington, D.C. Hawaii, also in the pursuit of statehood, had drafted a constitution some years before. Statehood bills pending in Congress required Alaska to have an acceptable constitution. While this legislation also dictated the process by which it would be written, Alaskans chose not to wait for congressional action and initiated their own process for convening a constitutional convention.

Having a constitutional convention that was called by Alaskans on their own terms proved a masterful stroke in the fight for statehood. The final document and the convention itself demonstrated to Congress the political wisdom and maturity of Alaskans. Moreover, a well-crafted constitution and the pageantry of a convention served to publicize the statehood movement across Alaska and helped win over skeptics at home. Some wondered if this approach was a little too gimmicky, but the zeal of statehood advocates looking for ways to maintain positive momentum in the movement brought the plan to fruition.

The document, the process, and the publicity were exactly what statehood advocates hoped for. Several factors account for this success. Experts were recruited from Alaska and around the United States to provide background information and advice on the range of issues that the delegates dealt with. The convention president, William A. Egan, kept

BOX 4.1

Articles and Major Amendments of the Alaska Constitution as of 2016

ARTICLES

Article I: Declaration of Rights

Article II: The Legislature

Article III: The Executive

Article IV: The Judiciary

Article V: Suffrage and Elections

Article VI: Legislative Apportionment

Article VII: Health, Education, and Welfare

Article VIII: Natural Resources

Article IX: Finance and Taxation

Article X: Local Government

Article XI: The Initiative, Referendum, and Recall

Article XII: General Provisions

Article XIII: Amendment and Revision

Article XIV: Apportionment Schedule

Article XV: Schedule of Transitional Measures

MAJOR AMENDMENTS

There have been twenty-eight amendments since 1959, with twelve measures rejected by the voters. The major amendments are:

1970: Secretary of State designated as Lieutenant Governor

1972: Limited entry provision for commercial fishing

The right to privacy

1976: Creation of the Alaska Permanent Fund

1982: State appropriation limit

1984: Legislative session limited to 120 days

1990: Constitutional Budget Reserve (CBR) created

1998: Authority to redistrict the legislature by the governor transferred to an independent board

Marriage defined as a union between a man and a woman (such provisions held unconstitutional in June 2015 by the U.S. Supreme Court)

2004: Requirements made more stringent for an initiative to qualify for the ballot

Source: Compiled by the authors.

the delegates working amicably together as a cohesive body. Meeting in Fairbanks in the middle of winter, the delegates had the benefit of the contemplative surroundings of the university, the absence of distractions, and distance from the "politics as usual" ambience of Juneau, the territorial capital. In addition, the fifty-five elected delegates were diverse and broadly representative of the socio-economic interests and geographical regions of the state. The convention was "the most representative group of popularly elected officials in Alaska," which contributed to "the ultimate acceptance of the constitution by the voters."[6]

Under terms set out in statehood bills before Congress at the time, the stipulation was that a constitutional convention be held in Juneau with twenty-seven delegates elected from four districts. It is clear that a constitution written by such a convention would have produced a far less commendable document than the one crafted in Fairbanks and far less likely to garner support among Alaskans for the statehood movement.

A Model Constitution

Alaska's Constitution is hailed as a model of modern constitutional draftsmanship. This is largely because the mid-1950s produced a national groundswell of interest in reforming state constitutions. Explosive economic growth and urbanization in post–World War II America placed new demands on state governments. Many states struggled to respond to these demands. Most legislatures were dominated by rural interests, which resulted in weak and fragmented state administrative structures and state constitutions containing many roadblocks to governmental action. Federal commissions, national civic organizations, scholars, and practitioners of government were calling for states to undertake major constitutional reforms, to reorganize and rationalize the executive branch, and to reapportion state legislatures. When the fifty-five Alaskans gathered in Fairbanks to draft a new constitution, they had extensive documentation of the failings of state governments and state constitutions elsewhere.

The length of these older constitutions was often the beginning of their problems. Constitutions are often made long by including details and minutiae of government that rapidly become obsolete and so must be amended regularly.[7] But because the amendment process is often complicated and uncertain, states with long, detailed constitutions frequently resort to evasive maneuvers that may result in a tangle of obscure governmental practices. A short constitution, on the other hand, assigns authority to formulate the details of government to specific branches and agencies of government. It does not need frequent amendment. Alaska's new constitution was written, in part, to be responsive to changing circumstances. The convention delegates were not only witnessing dramatic changes in Alaska, but were also engaged in a quest for statehood precisely as a stimulus to more and greater change. Consequently, at the outset of the convention the delegates formally declared: "It is the intent of this convention that the Constitution should be a document of fundamental principles of basic government, and contain only the framework for state government."[8]

Key Provisions of the Constitution: The Three Branches of Government

The delegates understood that a strong legislature was the key to effective self-government. They also understood that a strong executive branch was essential to efficient government and that protecting the judiciary from political pressure was imperative to an effective democracy.

The Alaska Legislature

The legislature is the primary beneficiary of the state's short constitution. The document leaves the details of government mainly to the legislature, and for this reason that body has a great deal of power. Furthermore, the constitution lets the legislature exercise its power as it sees fit by allowing it to adopt its own rules of procedure. It authorizes sessions every year, in contrast to biennial sessions (every other year) imposed on the territorial legislature and on a few but dwindling number of state legislatures. Originally, there was no limit on the length of its sessions, unlike the sixty-day limit imposed on the biennial territorial sessions.[9] The constitution also allows the legislature to call itself into special session to deal with problems that arise between regular sessions. And the legislature can hire staff, and its members are paid a salary.

The constitution creates a bicameral legislature of a Senate and House of Representatives. A unicameral legislature had several proponents among the delegates, and the concept interested others. It was discussed at some length on the floor of the convention. But with some members of Congress questioning the political "maturity" of Alaskans, the convention was not about to abandon the time-honored bicameral legislative structure.[10] However, the constitution requires the legislature to meet in joint session as one body for a number of actions, such as overriding a governor's veto (Article II, Section 16) and confirming appointees of the governor (Article III, Section 25).[11]

Even with only twenty senators and forty representatives, Alaska's state legislature has twenty more seats than its territorial predecessor (it had sixteen senators and twenty-four representatives). The delegates wanted a larger legislature to assure broader representation of regions and interests, but they kept the number of members small, in large part because the challenging fiscal prospects for the new state demanded frugality.

The Governor and the Executive Branch

As is the case with all U.S. territories, Alaska's territorial governor was not elected by Alaskans but appointed by the U.S. president. Consequently, the governor's primary allegiance was to the federal agencies that held sway over the natural resources of Alaska. This allegiance was the source of constant conflict with the popularly elected territorial legislature. Over the years, the territorial legislature contrived to diminish the governor's influence by dispersing executive power among a network of elected offices and appointed boards and commissions. At the time of statehood the territorial administration was:

> .... a multi-headed mass of uncoordinated, disorganized, overlapped and sometimes misnamed departments, offices, bureaus, divisions, boards, commissions, councils and committees under the nominal headship of an appointed federal employee, guided by the general policies set forth by a popularly elected territorial legislature, three independent elected officials, and a scattering of independent agencies.[12]

This chaotic situation was similar to that in many of the older states, which had their own tradition of hostility to the governor, and was a major impetus of the national movement to rationalize the administration of state government.[13]

The remedy prescribed by the nation's reformers was for agencies to be consolidated by function into a comparatively small number of departments organized in a hierarchical structure with the governor at its apex. There was no place in this modern concept of administrative organization for authority independent of the governor, such as directly elected department heads and agencies run by appointed boards with fixed terms. In order to avoid the lack of policy coordination inherent in that degree of departmental independence, the model for executive branch organization called for all department heads to be appointed by the governor and serve at his or her pleasure. Only with complete control over the administrative agencies could the governor be held accountable for their performance.

The Alaska convention delegates adopted this model of executive organization. The constitution stipulates that there shall be no more than twenty departments (in 2015 there were fourteen, and there have never been more than fifteen) and that the governor shall appoint department heads, subject to legislative confirmation. Surprisingly few other state constitutions provide for such a streamlined, unified executive branch of government. So-called plural executives (multiple, separately elected department heads) are commonplace in other states.[14]

However, the delegates left a loophole for the legislature to establish a board at the head of a department. Article II, Section 25 says "the head of each principal department shall be a single executive unless otherwise provided by law." This is because the convention delegates were under great pressure to put boards in charge of education and fish and game management. The fish and game lobby wanted the constitution to stipulate a board for commercial fishing and another one for sport fishing and hunting. The delegates bowed to this pressure to some extent by authorizing the legislature to designate a board, rather than an individual, to be the head of a department. But they resisted the demands that specific boards be created in the constitution (except for the board of regents to head the University of Alaska, which was universally considered a good idea).

Today there is only one executive department headed by a board, the Department of Education and Early Development. The boards of fisheries and game do not head the Department of Fish and Game, although they have unusual statutory authority in determining the head of the department, namely to require the governor to make the appointment from a list of names provided jointly by the two boards. From time to time a proposal is advanced to amend the constitution to make the attorney general (head of the Department of Law) an elected office. The primary point of this change is to weaken the governor, and it would be a major departure from the original constitutional scheme of a unified executive branch. So far, such an amendment has not been placed before the electorate.[15]

The Judiciary

Alaska's judiciary article is widely lauded as exemplary because it creates a statewide, centrally administered system of courts, and it fills the bench with judges selected by a process that emphasizes their professional qualifications and not their political connections. This selection process contrasts sharply with selecting judges by popular election, which is still the method used to recruit the judiciary in many states.[16] This is yet another reason Alaska is credited with having a model constitution.

3. CONSTITUTIONAL AMENDMENTS

The convention delegates drafted a short constitution that they hoped would not require frequent amendment. Nonetheless, as Box 4.1 points out, as of 2016, it has been amended twenty-eight times since 1959, with twelve proposed amendments rejected by the voters.[17] This section focuses on the most noteworthy amendments—those that reflect changing socio-economic and political circumstances in Alaska, plus those that have had important political and policy implications.

All constitutional amendments must be ratified by the electorate. Proposed amendments can come from two sources only: the legislature or a constitutional convention. Sixteen state constitutions allow amendment by the initiative process, but not Alaska's. A proposed amendment from the legislature must be passed by a two-thirds majority of each house. From time to time the legislature has called for advisory votes to gauge popular opinion on possible amendments. Such calls for advisory votes require only a simple majority in each house. Alaskans have consistently declined to call another constitutional convention at each ten-year interval (most recently in 2012 and next in 2022) when the question is placed on the ballot (as required by the constitution). This suggests either general public satisfaction with the constitution or lack of interest, or perhaps a combination of both. It may also indicate voter apprehension about the kinds of revisions that might be proposed by a convention, as well as the feeling that it is best to change the constitution piecemeal as specific problems arise.

Technical and Fine-Tuning Amendments

Comparatively few of the twenty-eight amendments fundamentally alter the document. The majority of changes were either required by federal law or "fine-tuned" the work of the founders. Amendments required by federal law (or made in anticipation of changes in federal law) concern mainly the qualification of voters found in Article V, Section 1 and elimination of the requirement that voters be able to read or speak the English language.[18] Rulings by the U.S. Supreme Court also required various changes, including that state senates should be apportioned on the basis of population.

Amendments that fine-tune the constitution include four changes made to Article IV, the judiciary article. These amendments refined the Commission on Judicial Conduct, specified that the chief justice be elected by fellow justices rather than appointed by the governor, and made the administrative director of the court system accountable to the entire Supreme Court rather than to the chief justice alone. Overall, however, no amendments have been placed before the voters that would upset the basic design of Alaska's judicial system.

Major Amendments

Some amendments have made substantive changes to the constitution. Two have had far-reaching effects on public policy: one authorizing limited entry in the state's commercial fisheries, the other authorizing the Permanent Fund. Both are exceptions to constitutional principles that the delegates held dear.

Limited Entry

The limited entry amendment modifies the principle of "common use" in Article VIII (the natural resources article), which declares the right of all citizens to have equal access to the natural resources of the state. Section 15 states unambiguously: "No exclusive right or special privilege of fishery shall be created or authorized in the natural waters of the State." At the time of statehood, Alaska's commercial salmon fisheries were in serious decline and worsened in the 1960s. There were too many fishermen chasing too few fish, and each year there were more and more boats on the water.

The only solution was to prevent more people from entering the distressed fisheries. This required a complex licensing system that limited the number of people who could engage in commercial fisheries by creating exclusive rights and special privileges in the fishery. It required a constitutional amendment. The limited entry system was ratified by the voters in 1972, amid bitter controversy (the details are explained in Chapter 23).

The Alaska Permanent Fund

An amendment to create the Alaska Permanent Fund was needed because of the prohibition in Section 7 of Article IX against dedicated funds. Such funds receive the stream of revenue from a specific source that would otherwise go into the general fund (the state's major budget operating account) and limit the expenditures of the dedicated fund to a specified program. The delegates prohibited dedicated funds (with a few exceptions involving federal programs) because they wanted all state programs to compete equally for annual funding. This gave the legislature maximum control over state finances. However, had they foreseen the wealth accruing to the state from oil production, they may well have authorized something similar to the Permanent Fund (details about the Permanent Fund can be found in Chapter 25).

Article IX—Finance and Taxation

More doubtful perhaps is how the delegates might have viewed two other amendments that have been made to Article IX. One established a cap on annual appropriations (Section 16); the other created a fund called the Constitutional Budget Reserve (CBR; Section 17). Both of these rather wordy amendments violate the delegates' resolve to state only basic principles of government in the constitution. They also seem to signal the inability of the legislature to manage the fiscal affairs of the state without explicit constitutional constraints.

The Appropriation Limit. The cap on annual appropriations was adopted in 1982 when state revenue from North Slope oil vastly exceeded the annual state operating expenses.[19] Multimillion-dollar projects were added to the budget with little or no review of their technical feasibility or of their relevance to state and local facility development plans. Pressure for restraint, coming from both the public and from Governor Jay Hammond, resulted in the proposed amendment to limit appropriations, which was readily adopted by the voters. The amendment prohibits appropriations above a base of $2.5 billion, adjusted annually for the growth of population and inflation (so real per capita spending would remain constant). The intended cap on appropriations, however, proved to be a dead letter: appropriations were never actually restricted by the amendment because the population and inflation adjustments outpaced the growth of revenues.

The Constitutional Budget Reserve. An even longer, more complex, and clumsier amendment to Article IX created the budget reserve fund in 1990. At the time, the state was poised to receive billions of dollars in lump-sum payments from oil companies as settlements in disputes about the underpayment of past taxes and royalties. The amendment was championed by Governor Steve Cowper, in part to thwart more restrictive proposals being crafted by some legislators. It was designed to channel all "windfall" settlement payments into a budget reserve fund that would be tapped only when there is a shortfall in annual revenues. Appropriations from the fund would be limited to the amount necessary to cover the shortfall from the previous year's appropriation. When revenues rebound the fund would have to be repaid.

This simple and appealing concept has not worked as designed. Several billion dollars have been set aside in the CBR, but the money has been reached by the legislature through an escape clause that allows money in the fund to be appropriated "for any public purpose upon affirmative vote of three-fourths of each house of the legislature," set out in Article IX, Section 17(c). Also, evasion of the requirement to repay the fund has complicated and obscured the negotiations on annual budget bills. In addition, in most years through 2015, the legislative minority has, of necessity, been included in the negotiations over the budget bill in order to secure the supermajority necessary to use money from the CBR. This cooperation has altered the dynamics of the budget process, and it has encouraged even higher levels of spending. By 2007 the "debt" to the CBR was approximately $5 billion. Not until the second session of the Twenty-Fifth Legislature in 2008, when record-high oil prices and a new oil tax law combined to produce a substantial revenue surplus, was an effort made to repay the fund with a $4 billion deposit. With high oil prices through mid-2014, the value of the CBR had risen to more than $11.5 billion.[20] The fiscal problems brought on by the major fall in oil prices beginning in the summer of 2014, however, make it doubtful that a high balance in the CBR can be sustained. In fact, the CBR stands a high risk of being depleted.

Limits on the Length of the Legislative Session

The delegates would likely have been genuinely surprised and disappointed by the 1984 constitutional amendment that limits the length of regular legislative sessions to 120 days. In the early years of statehood, legislative sessions lasted from about sixty-five to eighty-five days. By the early 1980s, however, sessions lasted nearly twice that long, in large part because of complicated wrangling over the enormous capital appropriation bills made possible by massive oil revenues. As a result, legislators could not seem to bring the sessions to a close in a timely manner.

Many legislators were as unhappy as the general public was about this situation, resulting in the constitutional amendment of 1984. Following the change, however, the legislature increasingly relied on special sessions to complete its work after the 120-day deadline had expired. The reliance on special sessions was made even greater by a statutory amendment adopted by voter initiative in 2006 limiting the regular sessions to ninety days. In 2008, the first regular session to be constrained by this limit successfully concluded on the ninetieth day, but the governor immediately called a special session to deal with a major issue the legislature had not taken up. Other special sessions have been called since then, including one in 2012 to deal with oil and gas taxes, and three in 2015 due to disagreements between the governor and the legislature over the state budget, Medicaid expansion, and the natural gas pipeline.

Several legislators, including former Senate President Gary Stevens, have called for reconsideration of the ninety-day session.[21] It remains to be seen whether the legislature will continue to accommodate the new limit (with more special sessions), extend the regular session as they did in 2014, or repeal the limitation (which the legislature can do with an initiative two years or more after its adoption). There is, however, always a political risk attending the repeal of a voter-initiated statute.

Reapportionment and Redistricting

Another amendment ratified in 1998 changes the method of redrawing legislative districts. The original apportionment provisions of Article VI were progressive and visionary in light of the malapportioned legislatures that existed in many states at the time. For many years, the courts would not hear lawsuits on the matter, saying that the equitability of legislative representation was a political issue, not a judicial one. This reluctance changed in 1962 when the U.S. Supreme Court held in *Baker v. Carr* that legislative apportionment issues could be determined by the courts.

Alaska's constitutional convention delegates sought to forestall malapportionment by requiring house districts to be redrawn after each federal decennial census. It gave responsibility for redistricting to the governor rather than the legislature and by authorizing citizens to sue to force the government to act and to correct "errors" in redistricting plans. Furthermore, it required the governor to empanel a redistricting board to prepare the redistricting plan, from which he or she could not deviate without an explanation.

It is clear that the delegates intended the governor's redistricting board to act in an independent and non-partisan fashion. Nonetheless, redistricting was always a partisan affair controlled by the governor. The opposition party invariably took redistricting plans to court, which delayed or otherwise complicated their implementation. In 1972 and in 1982 the state superior court was forced to promulgate its own interim plan for the forthcoming elections because the governor's redistricting board failed to produce a plan that would pass constitutional muster. In fact, it was 1987 before there was a final judicial resolution of challenges to the redistricting plan of 1982 following the 1980 census.

In 1998 the Republican-controlled legislature proposed that Article VI be amended to remove authority for redistricting from the governor's office and pass it to an independent, constitutionally created, five-member redistricting board. Although the change was promoted as a means of obtaining nonpartisan redistricting plans, it was actually a strategy to create an opportunity for the Republicans to control the process in the likely event that the Democratic governor, Tony Knowles, would be reelected in 1998 (he was). Democrats opposed the amendment, although it was likely that they would hold (and, in fact, did secure) a majority on the board controlling the first redistricting process, which took place in 2002.

Under the 1998 amendment, two members of the Alaska Redistricting Board are appointed by the governor, one by the speaker of the House of Representatives, and one by the president of the Senate. The fifth member is appointed by the chief justice of the state supreme court. While theoretically the new process should preclude domination of the restricting process by one party, the reality is quite the opposite. For example, if the majority of one house of the legislature is of the same party as the governor, that party will have a majority on the board, regardless of who the chief justice appoints. Also, the person appointed by the chief justice can be affiliated with either party (that is, the fifth member is not required to function in a nonpartisan capacity). As a result, if the governor's party is different from both houses of the legislature (as was the case following the federal census in 2000), the partisan alignment of the fifth member will determine which party controls the process. Thus, although the constitution has a new redistricting process, Alaska's legislative districts will continue to be drawn by one party or the other.[22] This was certainly the case following the 2010 federal census, when Republicans controlled the board and its plan was challenged from several quarters and not finalized until mid-2013, after court action and a revised plan was developed.

Amendments to Article I

Article I of the constitution enumerates the personal liberties of Alaska citizens, much the way the Bill of Rights in the first ten amendments of the U.S. Constitution does for American citizens. Alaska's Article I has been amended six times. One of these amendments added a right to privacy, which touches social issues that have stirred the political passions of Alaskans. The following section discusses several of these issues.

4. THE CONSTITUTION AND CONTEMPORARY POLITICAL ISSUES

To further illustrate how the constitution directly touches the lives of Alaskans today, this section discusses major political issues generated by the inclusion in Article I of the right to privacy. The section also briefly discusses effects of the Alaska Constitution on the issues of the rural subsistence priority, and the formation of local governments.

The Right to Privacy

In 1972, Section 22 was added to Article I of the constitution by an amendment that states:

> The right of the people to privacy is recognized and shall not be infringed.
> The legislature shall implement this section.

This is a novel constitutional right, one that is found in only a few state constitutions and is not stated explicitly in the federal constitution. The Alaska Supreme Court has said that it establishes a higher level of protection than the federal constitution, or else it would be meaningless. Furthermore, the court has said that its application should not be limited to the concern that prompted it originally, which was government databanks of personal information. The court has found in it protections that were unanticipated at the time it was adopted, some of which involve intense social and political controversies.

Possession of Marijuana

The first ruling came in 1975, when the court held that the right to privacy prevented prosecution of an adult who possessed a small amount of marijuana for personal use in his or her own home.[23] Although the court did not extend this protection to persons caught in public with marijuana, with larger amounts of marijuana, or with stronger drugs such as cocaine and heroin, segments of the public were outraged. In 1990 an initiative to outlaw the possession of any amount of marijuana was approved by 54 percent of the voters. However, voters cannot change the constitution by initiative. Therefore, the court's interpretation of the constitution's privacy clause regarding personal use of marijuana still stood. A 2004 ballot initiative to legalize the use and sale of marijuana in any amount by adults was defeated by 56 percent of the vote.

Then, in November 2014 an initiative (Ballot Measure 2) was passed by a 53 to 47 percent margin, and the possession and sale of marijuana was made legal for persons over twenty-one years of age in Alaska. The campaign saw many major state organizations, such as the Alaska Federation of Natives (AFN) and many local governments, opposed to legalization. So apparently Alaska's long battle over the legalization of marijuana is over. However, following the vote, major concerns were expressed about the consequences of legalization by many local governments and other opponents. This will likely influence the substance of laws the legislature enacts to regulate its sale. And in theory, the legislature can amend the initiative at any time and repeal it after two years (Alaska Constitution, Article XI, Section 6). So the politics of marijuana may be ongoing for some years to come.

Abortion Rights

Another Alaska Supreme Court ruling in 1997 held that the state constitution's right to privacy provision prevents the state from interfering with a woman's right to obtain an abortion.[24] In 1992, a newly elected governing board of a private hospital in the City of Palmer adopted a policy to prohibit abortions in their facility, relying on a state law that said neither a person nor hospital would be liable for refusing to participate in an abortion. A lawsuit contested the board's decision, and the plaintiffs were ultimately successful. The court said that the hospital, which was licensed by the state and received substantial amounts of public money, must allow abortions to be performed, and the state law upon which the hospital board relied was unconstitutional.[25]

In 2007, the Alaska Supreme Court ruled that a state law requiring a minor to have the consent of her parents in order to obtain an abortion also violated the constitutional right to privacy.[26] As of early 2016, the Alaska Supreme Court had heard arguments, but had not yet issued a decision, in an appeal brought by Planned Parenthood of the Great Northwest challenging a 2010 voter-approved initiative that requires a physician to notify a parent, guardian, or custodian of a minor prior to performing an abortion. In August 2015 an Anchorage Superior Court judge held unconstitutional on equal protection grounds a state law passed in 2014 that narrowly defined what constituted "medically necessary" for abortions but not for other procedures covered by Medicaid. The state has appealed the ruling.[27]

Same-Sex Marriage

In February 1998 there was a preliminary ruling in a case brought by a homosexual couple against the Alaska Division of Vital Statistics for refusing to issue them a marriage license. In the ruling a superior court judge suggested that the state law defining marriage as a union of people of the opposite sex was an unconstitutional violation of the state constitutional rights to privacy and to equal protection of the laws. Alarmed that the Alaska Supreme Court might eventually agree with this interpretation, the legislature acted swiftly. It proposed a constitutional amendment defining marriage as a union between a man and woman. This amendment, in Article I, Section 25, was placed on the ballot in November 1998. It was overwhelmingly ratified by 68 percent of the voters.

Controversy over same-sex unions flared up again when the Alaska Supreme Court ruled that, despite the amendment, the equal protection clause of Article I, Section 1, required public employers in Alaska to provide same-sex partners with the same health and insurance benefits provided to conventional spouses of public employees. In reaction the legislature considered proposed constitutional amendments to overturn the decision, but the necessary two-thirds majority in each house could not be mustered. However, the legislature did pass a bill that called for an immediate advisory vote on whether such an amendment should be proposed to the voters. At a special election in April 2007, 53 percent of the voters indicated support for having a constitutional amendment placed on a future ballot to prohibit same-sex partner benefits.

But in June 2013 in two decisions the U.S. Supreme Court arguably sanctioned same-sex marriage: (1) by ruling that married same-sex couples were entitled to federal benefits despite prohibitions in the federal Defense of Marriage Act (DOMA); and (2) by declining on jurisdictional grounds to decide a case from California, effectively allowing same-sex marriages to continue being recognized there. These rulings, however, did not affect laws and constitutional provisions banning same-sex marriage in many states around the nation.[28] Following those rulings, a number of federal courts held that state prohibitions against same sex-marriage were unconstitutional. By November 2014, thirty-five states and the District of Columbia allowed same sex-marriages, although a number of judicial rulings were on appeal.[29]

Any doubts about the future of same-sex marriage in Alaska and elsewhere in the nation were removed in June 2015. Plaintiffs from four different states had challenged the constitutionality of state provisions either outlawing same-sex marriages to be performed in that state or refusing to recognize same-sex marriages lawfully performed in other states. In a 5 to 4 decision, the U.S. Supreme Court ruled that such provisions, which would include the one in Alaska's constitution providing that marriage is between a man and a woman, violate the due process and equal protections clauses of the U.S. Constitution.[30]

Subsistence Hunting and Fishing Rights

As one of the major political issues in Alaska in recent years, the subsistence issue is dealt with from several perspectives in this book.[31] Here we consider it as another contemporary controversy involving a provision of the Alaska Constitution.

When Congress enacted the Alaska National Interest Lands Conservation Act (ANILCA) in 1980, it stipulated that subsistence hunting and fishing by "rural residents" be given priority over sport and commercial harvests on federal lands. Although the law used the word "rural" rather than "Native," its clear intent was to protect the interests of traditional Alaska Native villagers who relied heavily on fish and wildlife for subsistence. ANILCA permitted the state to regulate fishing and hunting on federal land only if it honored this subsistence priority for rural residents.

In 1986 the Alaska legislature passed a law that was consistent with ANILCA, and authorized the boards of fish and game to give priority to rural residents for subsistence hunting and fishing in circumstances of resource scarcity. Urban residents who were excluded from subsistence hunts sued, and in 1989 the Alaska Supreme Court ruled that the state subsistence law violated provisions of the Alaska Constitution that prohibit the creation of exclusive and special privileges for the taking of fish and game (Article VIII, Sections 3, 15, and 17). The Court said that granting a priority for subsistence use was lawful, but that using residency as a criterion for determining who could qualify as a subsistence user was not. Without a rural subsistence preference, state law no longer complied with ANILCA, and the federal government took over regulation of subsistence hunting on all federal lands and subsistence fishing on navigable waterways within federal reserves.

Alaska's constitution and ANILCA were in a clear legal and politically intense conflict. One or the other had to give way in order for the state to resume management of fish and game on federal lands. Suits in federal court challenging the legality of the subsistence provision in ANILCA under the U.S. Constitution were unsuccessful.[32] Alaska's congressional delegation said that efforts to persuade Congress to repeal the rural subsistence preference in ANILCA would be hopeless, and refused to press the matter. The only other solution was to amend the Alaska Constitution. The Alaska legislature steadfastly refused to do this, despite, and perhaps because of, the bitter resentment among some vocal segments of the Alaska public against the federal government's usurpation of the state's management of fish and wildlife.

The matter received a great deal of attention, including two special sessions of the legislature called to address it, but there was not enough support for an amendment to bring a proposal to the voters. Federal regulation of subsistence hunting and fishing on federal land continues, to the dismay and indignation of many (mainly urban) Alaskans. Ironically, this policy deadlock undermines a major purpose of Alaska's founders, as it places some authority back in the hands of the federal government.

The Issue of Forming Borough Governments

The state's constitution is at the root of still another political issue: that of forming borough governments. Boroughs are a type of local government analogous to counties in other states, but with enough differences that the convention delegates deliberately gave them another name. The problem is that the system of borough government envisioned by the constitution is not the one that has come to be, and the disparity between the constitutional ideal and the political reality is the source of ongoing conflict and confusion.

The delegates were determined to avoid in Alaska the haphazard development of local government typical of the other states, where there were too many jurisdictions (cities, counties, utility districts, local service districts, and school districts) with independent taxing authority and uncoordinated, overlapping, and competing functions. The delegates thus resolved to allow only two forms of local government—cities and boroughs. In the constitutional design, cities would serve more or less compact urban areas and boroughs the regions surrounding the cities. The constitution called for the entire state to be divided into boroughs, organized and unorganized. Unorganized boroughs were envisioned to be those regions suitable for borough status but that did not yet have the population and financial capacity to exercise the essential powers of borough government (taxation, planning and zoning, and education).

The legislature has never had a taste for creating regional unorganized boroughs. Rather, it has designated the areas outside of organized boroughs as a single Unorganized Borough. Efforts to further the constitutional ideal of a system of regional boroughs are the source of continuing political conflict (see Chapter 18 for a more detailed discussion).

5. CONCLUSION: ALASKA'S CONSTITUTION PAST AND PRESENT, POLITICAL ISSUES, AND PUBLIC POLICIES

Much about Alaska politics is made clearer by understanding the role of the constitution as a vital, ongoing part of the state's political life. Despite the number of issues that have been generated over the years by various provisions in the document, most of the more intractable political problems facing Alaska today are not the result of any major defects in Alaska's "model" constitution. Instead, as will be demonstrated throughout the book, the problems arise from deep-rooted differences among the people, regions, and various interests across the state, perhaps combined with another characteristic of Alaska's politics, that of the state's pragmatic dependent individualistic political culture.

Many of the explanations in this chapter will be useful in understanding issues covered in other chapters, such as Chapter 9 (on the Native community), Chapter 18 (local government), Chapter 19 (the state budget), Chapter 23 (fisheries), Chapter 25 (the

Permanent Fund), and Chapter 30 (on past and present attempts at reform in the state). Furthermore, several past and present issues arising from the actions of the delegates and provisions in the constitution are considered in various chapters. These include: the contemporary consequences of a small legislature and large rural-bush legislative districts, legislative-gubernatorial relations, the operation of the court system, and many issues involving natural resources and the developer-environmentalist conflict that often erupts in the state.

ENDNOTES

[1] The division of labor on this chapter was as follows. Gordon Harrison wrote the bulk of the chapter except the introduction, the first section covering the preliminaries, and the conclusion, which were written by Clive Thomas.

[2] Alaska's constitution can be read online at www.ltgov.state.ak.us/constitution.php. Two books provide an introduction to the constitution and brief commentary on each section: Gordon Harrison, *Alaska's Constitution: A Citizen's Guide*, 5th ed. (Juneau: Alaska Legislative Affairs Agency, 2012), which can be read online at http://w3.akleg.gov/docs/pdf/citizens_guide.pdf; and Gerald A. McBeath, *The Alaska State Constitution: A Reference Guide* (Westport, CT: Greenwood Press, 1997).

[3] *Book of the States*, vol. 39 (Lexington, KY: Council of State Governments, 2007), 80. See also, *A Preliminary Report and Special Final Addendum on the Study Devoted to Reorganization of Territorial Government*, Publication 23–9 (Juneau: Alaska Legislative Council, 1958), 14.

[4] For a comparison of state constitutions, see Thomas R. Dye and Susan MacManus, Chapter 2, "Democracy and Constitutionalism in the States," in *Politics in States and Communities*, 15th ed. (Upper Saddle River, NJ: Pearson Education, Inc., 2014).

[5] Details of the convention can be found in Victor Fischer, *Alaska's Constitutional Convention* (Fairbanks: University of Alaska Press, 1975). Fischer, who wrote the Foreword to this book, was a convention delegate.

[6] Fischer, *Alaska's Constitutional Convention*, 16.

[7] Alabama is a state where constitutional amendments have run amok and benefit an array of special interests from county sheriffs to employees of Mobile County to the cattle industry. See David L. Martin, "Personalities and Factionalism," in *Interest Group Politics in the Southern States*, eds. Ronald J. Hrebenar and Clive S. Thomas (Tuscaloosa: University of Alabama Press, 1992), 252–54.

[8] *Alaska Constitutional Convention Proceedings* (Juneau: Alaska Legislative Council, 1965), 293–94.

[9] As discussed later in this chapter, the length of the legislative session was first changed by a constitutional amendment in 1984 and later by a statutory change adopted by voter initiative.

[10] See Chapter 30, Box 30.5, for the pros and cons of a unicameral legislature.

[11] Article III, Sections 19, 20, 23, and 26, and Article IV, Sections 8 and 10 provide for action to be taken in joint legislative sessions. It is easier to pass a measure by a majority of both chambers meeting together than it is to secure a majority in each chamber separately (see for example, Article X, Section 12).

[12] Alaska Legislative Council, *A Preliminary Report*, 14.

[13] See for example, Council of State Governments, *Reorganizing State Government* (Chicago: 1950).

[14] Council of State Governments, *Book of the States*, 181.

[15] The pros and cons of an elected attorney general for Alaska are considered in Chapter 30, Box 30.4.

[16] See Chapter 17 on the Alaska court system for a review of the various ways that judges are selected and in many cases elected across the states and the intense politics often involved in their selection and retention.

[17] A summary of amendments to the constitution, including rejected proposals, is included in the electronic copy of the constitution available on the lieutenant governor's website, cited in endnote 2 above.

[18] See Gordon S. Harrison, "Alaska's Constitutional 'Literacy Test' and the Question of Voting Discrimination," *Alaska History* 22 (Spring/Fall 2007): 23–38.

[19] Section 15 is commonly referred to as the "spending limit," but incorrectly so, because there is a difference between the appropriation of money by the legislature and the subsequent spending of it by the various agencies of government. Section 15 is intended to limit the appropriation of money.

[20] See Alaska Department of Revenue, Treasury Division, at: www// treasury.dor.alaska.gov/Investments/ConstitutionalBudgetReserve.aspx. For more on the politics of the CBR see Chapter 8, Section 5, on state revenues, and Chapter 19 on the state budget.

[21] Patti Epler, "Alaska Legislature Reconsiders 90-day Session," *Alaska Dispatch*, March 8, 2011.

[22] Legislative redistricting in Alaska is discussed in more detail in Gordon S. Harrison, "The Aftermath of *In Re 2001 Redistricting Cases*: The Need for a New Constitutional Scheme for Legislative Redistricting in Alaska," *Alaska Law Review* XXIII, no. 1 (June 2006): 51–79. For the politics of the reapportionment process, see Chapter 14, Section 3, especially Box 14.3.

[23] *Ravin v. State*, 537 P.2d 494 (Alaska 1975).

[24] In 1973 the U.S. Supreme Court ruled in *Roe v. Wade* that abortions were protected by a fundamental right of privacy founded in the concept of personal liberty expressed in the Fourteenth Amendment to the U.S. Constitution.

[25] *Valley Hospital Association, Inc., v. Mat-Su Coalition for Choice*, 948 P.2d 963 (Alaska 1997).

[26] *State v. Planned Parenthood of Alaska*, 171 P.3d 577 (Alaska 2007).

[27] *Planned Parenthood of the Great Northwest v. State of Alaska*, Alaska Supreme Court, Case No. S15010; and Becky Bohrer, "Alaska judge strikes down law to limit Medicaid funds for abortions," *Alaska Dispatch News*, August 27, 2015.

[28] Adam Liptak, "Supreme Court Bolsters Gay Marriage with Two Major Decisions," *New York Times*, June 28, 2013.

[29] National Conference of State Legislatures, "State Same Sex Marriage Laws Map," retrieved December 30, 2014, from http://www.ncsl.org/research/human-services/same-sex-marriage-laws.aspx.

[30] *Obergefell v. Hodges*, 576 U.S. ___ (2015), 83 USLW 4592 (U.S. 2015).

[31] See Chapter 9, "Alaska Natives and the State's Political Economy," Chapter 10 on the federal government and intergovernmental relations, Box 10.4; and parts of Chapters 21, 22, 23, and 24 on various aspects of Alaska's natural resources policies.

[32] The two most recent defeats came in 2007 and 2014, both from the U.S. Supreme Court. In the first, the Court refused to hear an appeal by a group of Alaska sportsmen of an appellate court ruling denying their claim that ANILCA's subsistence requirement violated the equal protection clause of the U.S. Constitution. The second denied the state's petition in the so-called *Katie John* case extending federal subsistence jurisdiction to navigable waters on federal lands. See Chapter 9 on Alaska Natives, Box 9.4, for a subsistence chronology.

★ CHAPTER 5 ★

Alaska's Political Culture: The Confluence of Individualism, Dependence, and Pragmatism

John P. McIver and Clive S. Thomas

Politics and public policy in Alaska, as in any pluralist democracy, are not primarily shaped by the size of its lawmaking body (legislature or parliament), the authority of its chief executive (governor, president, or prime minister), nor the details of its constitution, though all are important. As elsewhere, politics and public policy in Alaska are shaped primarily by political culture—the values, attitudes, and beliefs of Alaskans as they relate to politics. As a central element of the analysis in this book, indicated by *beliefs* in the book's subtitle, this chapter examines Alaska's political culture as a means for understanding the day-to-day politics and government in the state—the policies that are enacted and those that never make it to the statute books.

Gerald A. McBeath, who conducted research on Alaska's political culture in the 1980s, describes the elements of a political culture as "complex."[1] We agree with this assessment in regard to Alaska's political culture. Even though there has been little systematic research on Alaska's political culture, by combining general academic research with various sources specific to Alaska, it is possible to identify the elements of a contemporary Alaska political culture. In so doing, we provide new perspectives that have valuable practical application for understanding Alaska politics and public policies. Moreover, because the elements of a political culture provide an all-embracing perspective on politics, this chapter offers insights into all twelve characteristics of Alaska politics identified in Chapter 2. But the main characteristic treated here is the political culture of pragmatic dependent individualism.

All states share common influences upon and elements of political culture. Yet, when all of the particular influences and elements within a single state are considered together, the combination produces a unique political culture in each state, including Alaska. This chapter argues that Alaska's political culture melds both conscious and subconscious elements of individualism, as well as dependence and pragmatism. This analysis draws on Thomas Morehouse's concept of dependent individualism, but enhances it by adding the all-important element of pragmatism.[2] Political pragmatism is probably the most significant element of the way that Alaskans think about, deal with, and react to politics and government. The same can be said of the American West generally.

This chapter is divided into two parts. The first deals with political culture in general by exploring the most prominent interpretations of state political culture and describing the ways in which Alaska fits into these interpretations. The second part of the chapter focuses specifically on Alaska. It begins by explaining our approach to identifying the elements of the state's political culture, followed by two sections examining what has shaped the state's political culture and identifying its major elements. The next section considers the influence of political culture on democracy and public policy in Alaska. Then we step back and compare Alaska's political culture with that of other states, particularly Nevada. The conclusion identifies several chapters in the book that expand on several aspects of political culture presented in this chapter.

1. THE CONCEPT OF POLITICAL CULTURE AND RELATED TERMS

The general culture of a group, locality, state, or nation, is literally everything that its inhabitants were not born with. Food, clothes, attitudes toward the roles of the sexes, the family, society, religion, education, work, time, how outsiders are viewed, and so on, are all part of the general culture. Compare, for instance, the contrasting culture of a banker living in New York City with an Alaska Native living in Barrow or women in many Muslim countries with the social, economic, religious, and political barriers they face compared with most women in the Western world. The extensive influence of the cultural environment is such that, if we took two children born on the same day, one in Kansas of American parents and one in Riyadh of Saudi Arabian parents, and the parents swapped the babies, the American would grow up with a Saudi culture and the Saudi with an American value system.

Over time, what shapes a general culture is the relationship between the environment, mainly the physical environment, and the society's basic need for food, water, clothing, and shelter. Desert dwellers in North Africa, for example, developed a different culture regarding clothing, food, and shelter than the peoples of the Arctic. This relationship between physical environment and need also influences political culture. It certainly does so in Alaska.

Political culture is one part of the broader culture of a society.[3] More specifically, a political culture consists of the beliefs (the evaluation of the truth or falsity of ideas or purported facts) and attitudes (the outward expression of a belief or emotion about an idea, fact or person) regarding three elements:

- The range of acceptable behavior by those involved in the political process, including elected and appointed officials, political party personnel, lobbyists, political activists, and so on
- The extent of government operations and power and the limits on them
- How individuals view their relationship to the political and governmental system, including their political efficacy (the perception of the ability, or lack thereof, to affect the actions of government)

Political culture is fundamental to the structure, operation, and policies of all political systems, but as Almond and Verba point out, this is especially true in a democracy.[4] Political culture shapes the actions of the citizens within the political system and toward government, the actions of government, and the reactions to these actions by the governed—the people. In turn, the effect and manifestations of this culture have much to do with what issues arise (and the ones that do not), what policies are pursued and enacted, and the type of democracy—elitist, egalitarian, populist, among others—that is dominant in a nation, state, or locality.

People acquire their political culture through a process of political socialization. This process begins in early childhood and continues throughout life, but it is particularly formative in late adolescence and early adulthood. Political cultural values are transmitted by parents and families, peer groups, schools and colleges, the media, churches, government officials, and candidates for political office, among other socialization agents. Much of this process is subliminal and is acquired as part of everyday life. Consequently, many people are unaware that they have acquired a political culture.

For instance, many students taking their first American government class are surprised to find that they have a political culture. Their subconscious political values can be made conscious by asking questions such as: How should student body presidents get their jobs—by appointment or through election by the student body? Should you have the right to complain to the legislature, even hold a peaceful protest march, if student fees are increased? What right do the police have to break up your march? Clearly, American students (including the Saudi child now attending school in Kansas) have been socialized from an early age with an ingrained belief in participation and election and the right to voice their opinions. Many would fight to defend these rights. In contrast, many citizens in authoritarian countries, including the Kansas child brought up in Saudi Arabia, would have a very different process of political socialization and would acquire a much different political culture. Unless they are members of an elite family, their political culture will likely manifest extreme deference to authority and no right to choose public officials or complain about government decisions, let alone protest in public.

2. VARYING EXPLANATIONS OF POLITICAL CULTURE IN THE AMERICAN STATES AND THEIR APPLICATION TO ALASKA

Citizens of individual states, whether they are New Yorkers, Minnesotans, or Alaskans, see their own states in a unique light. So, while there are common elements to an American political culture, there are also subcultural differences from state to state. In this regard, work by Daniel Elazar is a benchmark to which other scholars refer and react. A review of his work and alternative approaches shows both the value and limitation of political culture as an analytical tool.

Daniel Elazar's Approach

In books and articles spanning four decades, Elazar sought to distinguish common American political subcultures.[5] He identified three of them: *moralistic, individualistic,* and *traditionalistic*. America's national political culture is a synthesis of all three. Although communities in a state may display characteristics of any of them, Elazar argues that each state has distinct tendencies toward one of these subcultures.

Dominance of a particular subculture results from one or more circumstances. One is historical political geography and settlement patterns that began on the East Coast and transferred west as the nation expanded toward the Pacific. Another is the influence of direct immigration from Europe, such as Scandinavians with communal values settling in the upper Midwest. Unique historical circumstances, such as socio-economic and political conditions in the South, are another influence.

The Moralistic Subculture

Originating in New England, a moralistic subculture emphasizes the role of politics as a public activity devoted to advancing the public interest. Here the idea of a "commonwealth" is often a dominant political image. Government intrusion into private activities is not necessary unless the well-being of the community requires it. In practice, however, intervention is expected as government plays a positive role with responsibility for the general welfare of the community—a communal obligation to the commonwealth.

This subculture encourages political participation. Indeed, it is a duty of citizens to participate in the political affairs of the community. Moralistic cultures also place expectations on political leaders. Party and individual loyalties must not overwhelm the critical value of the public good—a commitment to communalism—and there is little tolerance for political corruption. States in the upper Midwest, such as Minnesota and Wisconsin, have major elements of this subculture.

The Individualistic Subculture

Largely a product of the mid-Atlantic states, the individualistic subculture sees politics as a means to an end, with the end defined by personal aspirations rather than community goals. The role of government is variously conceived as limited or as a facilitator, and its intrusions into private affairs should be restricted to activities necessary to encourage private initiative. Elazar notes, however, that earlier notions of laissez faire may not be fully appropriate to contemporary America, in which the role of government as a facilitator of market activities has greatly expanded. Even so, government should minimize its intervention into the marketplace and allow relationships between individuals, groups, and business corporations to define public life. This is the dominant subculture across the fifty states, particularly in the mid-Atlantic, lower Midwest, and Mountain states.

The Traditionalistic Subculture

Traditionalistic subcultures, Elazar argues, are found only "in a society that retains some of the organic characteristics of the pre-industrial social order," and political leaders in such cultures "play conservative and custodial roles."[6] Consequently, these subcultures are elite driven. Traditional values as represented by church and family, and the "correct" relationships between people (based on gender, race, and birth) are more important than government in such societies. Government's minimal role is to maintain these traditions. The Deep South (from before the Confederacy to a hundred years after), exhibited this subculture before the civil rights movement and desegregation of the 1960s. The region continues to exhibit traces of the traditionalistic subculture today.

Where Does Alaska Fit?

Elazar's perspective on Alaska's political culture evolved over the years, with his last assessment made in 1994.[7] He classifies Alaska as dominantly individualistic, buying heavily into the notion that its residents see Alaska as a frontier where individuals can maximize their own welfare without government intervention. But Elazar also sees elements of the other two subcultures present in Alaska.

He sees a strong moralistic strain, though he goes into no detail as to what this might mean.[8] The traditionalistic political culture presumably embraces that of Alaska Natives and its impact on the Alaska political mind-set. By deduction, this traditionalistic subculture is also represented by the increasing number of evangelical Christians in Alaska and their promotion of traditional family values including opposition to abortion and gay marriage.

Intuitively, Elazar's application of his subcultures to Alaska appears plausible, particularly to an outsider. Many Americans still see Alaska as a frontier and its inhabitants as rugged individualists and "just plain different." Yet, while the images persist, recent changes have most likely affected Alaska's political culture.

A Critique of Elazar

Elazar's classifications are impressionistic and based, in large part, on migration patterns. Many scholars have tried to validate his work by using more systematic social science techniques. Some of these attempts have questioned the existence of these subcultures in the various states. So there are concerns about the enduring nature of Elazar's classifications. Other scholars have speculated that the nationalization of politics will slowly eliminate significant state differences. Still other scholars accept this nationalization premise, but also see further population shifts as producing unique elements in evolving local cultures.

That said, Elazar's scheme has often proven predictive of state political differences.[9] It is still widely used in its original form or by incorporating amplifications.

Alternative Perspectives on Political Culture

Scholars have developed several alternative explanations to Elazar's scheme. Here we briefly outline three of them and what they say directly or by implication about Alaska's political culture.

Joel Lieske

Lieske uses census data to classify each county across the nation as representing one of ten or more distinct cultures. He claims his classification system is "more precise" than Elazar's and is one that "takes into account recent demographic changes."[10]

In a 2010 update, Lieske classifies Alaska as predominantly "rurban" with a subordinate "Native American" subculture. The "rurban" subculture (young, highly educated, urban, and professional) applies primarily to the Anchorage, Fairbanks, and Juneau population centers. The Native American (Alaska Native) subculture describes rural-bush Alaska and is related to Elazar's recognition of a traditionalistic subculture in the less populated western and northern regions of the state.[11]

Rodney Hero

In contrast to Elazar and Lieske, Hero speculates that political culture as a significant means of explaining politics may have had its day. In his view, modern politics is dominated not by cultural differences but by racial and ethnic divides. To Hero, social diversity better explains contemporary politics. The influx of minorities, particularly Hispanics, is changing the politics of many Lower 48 states. Today it is not simply majority-minority differences that define the new politics. Diversity within the white ethnic population also influences state politics.

Even though its white ethnic population is relatively homogenous, Hero ranks Alaska among the more majority-minority diverse states, classifying it as a "bifurcated" state. Based upon its minority and white ethnic diversity scores, Alaska looks like those of the Deep South (Georgia, South Carolina, Louisiana, and Mississippi). Yet Hero sees Alaska as distinctive from these states. This results from the nature of the minority groups, particularly Alaska Natives, who are distinct from African Americans, the predominant minority in the Deep South.[12]

Robert Erikson, Gerald Wright, and John McIver

Rather than viewing culture as the accumulation of the beliefs and values of those who populate a region, these authors see culture as the unique contribution of a state's politics over and above mere demographic characteristics of local residents.[13] That is, the melding of the influences upon a particular state's culture produces a unique political culture.

While they do not deal with the culture of Alaska specifically, deductions can be made from their work and applied to Alaska. For instance, many of the sparsely populated western states are more Republican and more conservative than their demographic composition would suggest. Alaska fits a similar profile. But, as we argue, today Alaska's political culture is more complex than this. That is to say, it is more than the sum of its parts.

3. SPECIFIC POLITICAL ATTITUDES AS AN ASPECT OF POLITICAL CULTURE: PARTISANSHIP AND IDEOLOGY

This section examines ideology and attitudes toward partisanship for what they tell us about political culture, politics, and public policy. There is an interesting link between partisanship and ideology in Alaska that we argue plays out in the state's political culture and in practical politics.[14]

The Extent of Partisanship—More Significantly, Nonpartisanship

State partisanship is represented by the distribution of voters who identify with the two major political parties—Democrats and Republicans. Nationally, those identifying themselves as Democrats have outnumbered Republicans since the 1930s, though the gap has narrowed since the early 1980s. While minor political parties play a role in some policy debates, most debates, both nationally and in the states, involve only the major parties.

Alaska entered the Union as predominantly a Democratic state. But its conservative tendencies, even among Democrats, have never been far from the surface, and it has become more and more Republican since the late 1980s. Except in 1964, the state has always voted Republican in presidential elections. Alaska's congressional delegation was Republican from 1980 to 2008. It became entirely Republican again in 2014 when its sole

Democratic Senator was defeated. The legislature has been dominated by Republicans since the early 1990s (though the majority caucuses in both houses have often included some Democrats). From 2002 to 2014, governors were Republicans, and in 2014 a former Republican was elected on an independent ticket

Since the early 2000s, almost 60 percent of those Alaskans who identify with a party are Republicans. Overall, Alaska is slightly more Republican than the nation, with an average of just over 35 percent in Alaska versus 30 percent nationally. By contrast, only about 25 percent of the electorate in Alaska identify as Democrats versus over 35 percent nationally. Together these tendencies make Alaska among the most Republican of states. Our estimates place Alaska ninth among the states—slightly more Republican than South Dakota and Nevada and slightly less so than North Dakota, Arizona, and Montana.[15] As explained below, however, nonpartisanship is also significant in Alaska politics.

Ideological Commitment

Ideological commitment is a measure of the distribution of ideological preferences in a state on a scale from conservative to moderate to liberal. While states vary in their ideological leanings, conservatives outnumber liberals nationally. The Alaska electorate leans to the right of the nation. Less than a quarter of Alaskans identify themselves as liberals—about the same percentage as the national electorate. But Alaska has a slightly higher percentage of conservatives than the nation (about 37 versus 33 percent) and fewer moderates (about 40 percent versus 46 percent nationally). Alaska conservatives outnumber liberals about two to one.

If we compare the ideology of the Alaska electorate to other states, it does not look much different from Nevada, Missouri, Iowa, and Virginia. It is not liberal like Massachusetts, Vermont, or Hawaii, nor does it appear to be as conservative as the Dakotas or some of the states of the Deep South, like Alabama and Mississippi.[16]

Partisanship and Ideology

Delving deeper into the nature and consequences of partisanship and ideology in Alaska reveals some interesting insights that add to an understanding of the state's political culture and its practical politics.

Among similarly conservative states, Alaska has more Democrats. Moreover, conservative Midwestern and border states such as Iowa, Ohio, Missouri, West Virginia, Virginia, and Kentucky have much stronger Republican bases than Alaska. Democrats in Alaska, however, are mainly conservative Democrats; there are few liberal Democrats. This picture fits with the designation of the state at statehood as being Democratic and the increase over the years in registered Republicans. Among Republican states, the ideological preference of Alaska's electorate is most like the southwestern states of Nevada and Arizona.

The partisan and ideological composition of Alaska's electorate is shown in Figure 5.1. Alaska's closest neighbors are Nevada, Arizona, and Montana. Far distant are the liberal Democratic Northeast and the conservative Deep South. Alaska is also distant from the most conservative, most Republican states of Utah and Idaho.

But in Alaska, the extent of nonpartisan identification (independent voters) is as significant politically, in some cases more so, than party identification. Alaska has far above the national average of members of the electorate identifying as independents (over 40 percent compared with about 30 percent nationally). In fact, Alaska is among the five or six least partisan states in the nation. Only the New England states (Maine, Vermont, New Hampshire, Massachusetts, and Rhode Island) share this level of voter independence from the major political parties.

In recent years, this partisan independence has had consequences for political parties in Alaska. More than 50 percent of Alaska's voters do not register with a political party: the figure was 53.8 percent in August 2014.[17] This high figure likely helped nonpartisan candidate Bill Walker win the governorship in 2014 as head of the Alaska First Unity ticket, though a major element in his support were Democrats who fused their efforts with Walker to form the nonpartisan ticket.

One thing that independence from the major parties does not mean, however, is that Alaskans are politically apathetic—not interested or not involved in the political debates of the day. While the common image of the political independent is to be apathetic, uninvolved, and uninterested (at least in comparison to the typical partisan), Alaskans have long had higher than national turnout in elections.[18]

Alaskans also have strong, often intense, ideological commitments. There are fewer moderates in Alaska (about 42 percent) than any state except Mississippi (about 39 percent), not what might be expected in a state filled with political independents. Being an independent voter in Alaska does not mean being a moderate—in fact, quite the contrary. A high percentage of Alaska's independent voters are, in fact, conservatives—higher than any other state. The combination of ideological commitment and the large numbers of independent voters makes Alaska a unique political entity. Figure 5.2 shows how different Alaska is from its forty-nine sister states.

The Implications

Its political preferences suggest that Alaska is not like its nearest neighbors, the so-called Left Coast states of Washington, Oregon, and California (although many Alaska residents come from these states). Alaska is also unlike Hawaii, its fellow latecomer to the Union. The partisan attachments and ideological preferences of Alaska's voters are most like those in the Rocky Mountain states, with a little bit of the Deep South thrown in. All

FIGURE 5.1

Political Ideology and Political Party Identification of State Electorates: Liberals versus Conservatives and Democrats versus Republicans

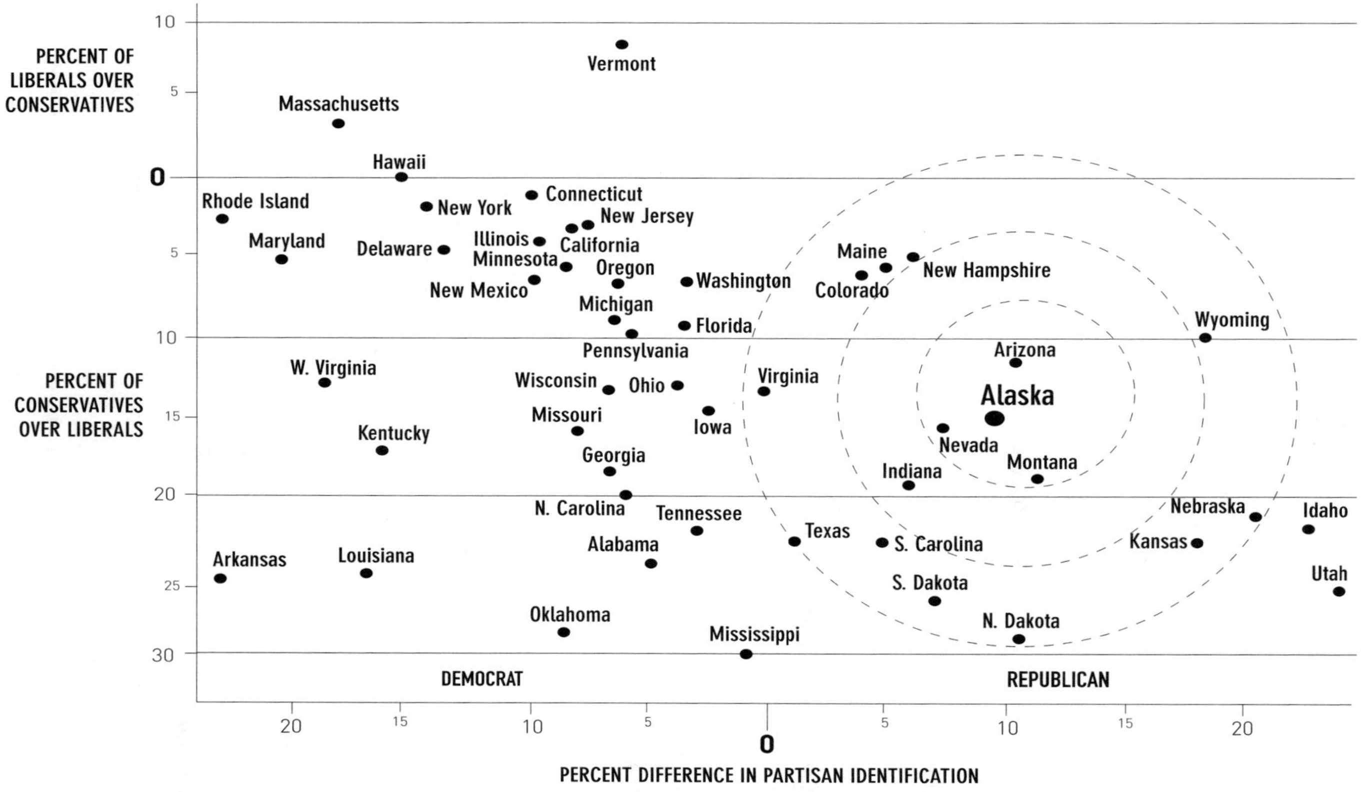

Note: Zero is at the point at which liberals equal conservatives and Democrats equal Republicans.

Source: Developed by the authors by reference to the sources in endnotes 13, 14, and 15.

FIGURE 5.2

The Relationship of Moderate Political Ideology with Political Independence across the Fifty States

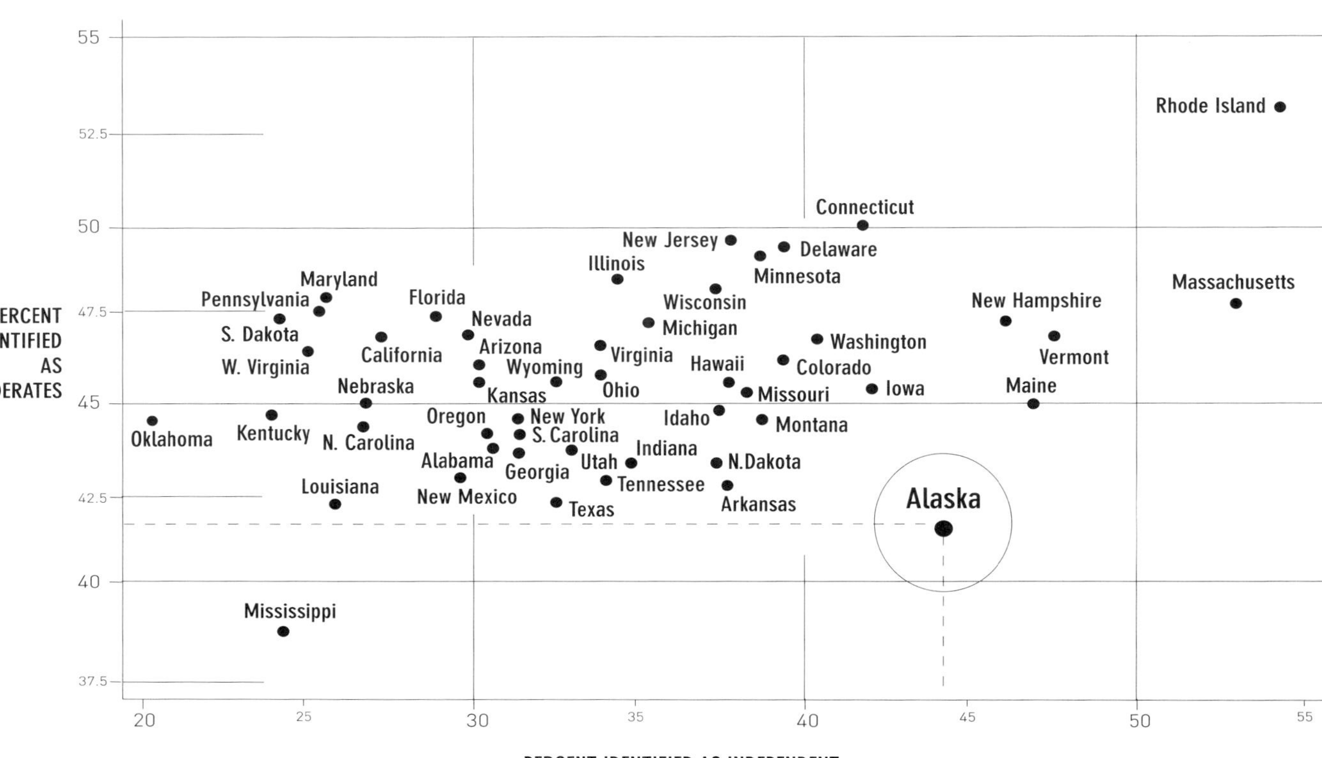

Source: Developed by the authors by reference to the sources in endnotes 13, 14, and 15.

this tends to corroborate the similarities between Alaska's political culture and that of Arizona, Nevada, Montana, Georgia, South Carolina, Louisiana, and Mississippi.

4. UNDERSTANDING ALASKA'S POLITICAL CULTURE: THE CHALLENGES AND A COMPREHENSIVE APPROACH

Our explanation of political culture shows that it is a useful concept for understanding the fundamentals of politics and public policy in the states. At the same time, the research on the concept is inconclusive and the content and development of political culture is complex.

In regard to its complexity, political culture can vary even within the same town or locality as well as across a state. Also, like any human value system, including a political ideology, a political culture can include myths, misconceptions, misinformation, inconsistencies, and contradictions, such as the belief that one's society is the most democratic, the most different, the least understood, or most unfairly treated by outsiders, and so on. Moreover, these beliefs may be subconsciously held, and those who consciously hold them often seek to justify such beliefs in various ways.

That said, a political culture is no less valid or significant politically even when its elements are inconsistent, subconscious, or based on misinformation, political unawareness or ignorance, or denial of existing political realities. With all its complex elements, a political culture is what it is—a psychological construct by the inhabitants of a place that translates into attitudes toward politics and government, government actions, and reactions by the people to these actions. So it is in Alaska.

Furthermore, political cultures are dynamic. Major population changes and an increasing nationalization of the general culture since the 1970s are likely working to produce a kind of nationalization of political culture in the states. And yet, differences among the states persist.

Making Sense of Alaska's Political Culture

How do we make sense of the varying approaches, complexities, and evolving nature of political culture to understand Alaska's political culture and, through it, the state's politics and public policy? In the absence of any systematic research, our approach is to synthesize two sources of information. One source consists of relevant aspects of the various approaches to political culture considered earlier in this chapter. The other source is information specific to Alaska. This includes a combination of previous work on Alaska's political culture, survey research on political topics conducted in the state, newspapers and other media sources, political speeches, and original research on Alaska politics.[19]

5. WHAT HAS SHAPED ALASKA'S POLITICAL CULTURE?

Chapter 2 considered the traditional and contemporary influences that shape politics in Alaska and the West. We now draw upon aspects of these influences as they affect Alaska's political culture, focusing on five influences that have been particularly important: the physical environment, demographic and social factors, the nature of the economy, Alaska's political development, and the patterns of land ownership and management. Then we consider the extent to which Alaska's contemporary political culture reflects Alaska's pioneer experience and Alaska Native culture.

The Physical Environment

Alaska's noncontiguous status with the Lower 48, its remote location, vast size, diverse terrain, and harsh climate, have all influenced the state's political culture. They have fostered regionalism in the state and a feeling of being isolated and "different" from the rest of the country. Given the challenges of the physical environment, along with Alaska's high cost of living, there is also a belief among many Alaskans that government has an obligation to help in overcoming the challenges. This is one of the contradictions of the Alaska mind-set, given antigovernment, particularly anti–federal government, attitudes among many Alaskans.

The nature of the physical environment may also have led, in some quarters, to a sense of communalism and helping one's neighbor. This may likely have fostered a political pragmatism among those separated by ideology, as they wrestled with the public policy issues of building a new state in a remote and challenging environment.

Demographic and Social Factors

What sets Alaska apart from many states, both socially and demographically, are its small population and the make-up of its minority groups. Yet, Alaska is far from being as rural as states like Vermont, North Dakota, and Wyoming.[20] With close to 70 percent of Alaskans living in the largely urban Southcentral region, they share much with other Americans in their lifestyle, attitudes, and beliefs. The rest are concentrated in a few smaller urban areas and in villages in rural-bush Alaska.

So despite the expanse of the state, it has a friends and neighbors atmosphere that has had a major effect on attitudes to politics among the public and public officials. Alaska Natives, at approximately 15 percent of the state's population, have had such a major impact on the state's politics that their role and influence is identified in Chapter 2 as one of the twelve characteristics of Alaska politics. The state has no other large ethnic or racial minorities that appear to have influenced state politics or state political culture.

The Nature of the Economy

Alaska's economy has always been heavily dependent on government (federal, state, and local) as a source of employment and revenue. The part of the private sector providing much of the funds to pay for government has been natural resource extraction. In the early years this was mining, fishing, and timber and more recently oil. Because the prices of Alaska's natural resources are subject to world market forces, the economy has experienced fluctuations and, as a result, state revenues have been chronically unstable.

These realities have had profound and, in some cases, contradictory influences on the state's political culture. Among them are a political dependence on government and resentment toward Outside economic and political forces that affect the value of natural resources. This resentment leads many Alaskans to feel exploited, part of a modern-day colony, and generally victims of Outside interests. In some quarters, there is also a disconnect between economic reality and the potential of the economy. Alaska's potential for economic diversification is extremely limited, and government is the major economic driver. Among many Alaskans, particularly some politicians, these economic realities have fostered a political pragmatism of using government expenditures to help fuel the economy, while paying lip service to fiscal conservatism.

Political Development

The dominant factor in Alaska's political development is that it occurred within the American political tradition of an advanced pluralist democracy. The all-pervasive presence of the national government, past and present, has also had a major influence on the political attitudes of many Alaskans. It led to the move for statehood and has been a subject of controversy ever since. Alaska's political development has also been influenced by other Outside forces. These include multinational companies and national public opinion.

The Pattern of Land Ownership and Land Management

Only about 4 percent of Alaska's land area is in private hands. Like most western states, vast areas are in federal hands, about 55 percent in Alaska's case. Eleven percent is owned by Alaska Native corporations, and about 30 percent is state-owned.[21] Over the years, the state has taken a major role in managing its land and the resources on and under it, which has given rise to the concept of Alaska being an Owner State.

Furthermore, as John Katz noted in Chapter 2 (Box 2.2), the rise of the conservation and environmental movements has challenged the role of public lands as being solely for economic development. In so doing, the movement has complicated the role of the Owner State and produced some ongoing, deeply rooted, and often emotional political conflicts in Alaska.

The Pioneer Experience and Rural and Alaska Native Values

The perception of Alaska that persists among many people outside the state might suggest that Alaskans' attitudes toward government and politics have been influenced by the pioneer and frontier experiences of its early Caucasian settlers. In addition, the well-documented influence that Alaska Natives have had on Alaska politics might suggest that Native values and attitudes have also influenced Alaska's political culture. There is no hard evidence to support either proposition.

Outside the state, the perception of Alaska is a complex mix of reality, myths, and misconceptions. One perception is that Alaska is a wild and wooly place, evidenced by Wyatt Earp finishing his career in the Territory. Here miners and others opened up a territory through rugged individualism, self-help, and tenacity. Its past and present politics are thought to be fast and loose on a par with the traditional American West. This image has been perpetuated by many books, such as Joe McGinnis's *Going to Extremes* and TV shows like *Northern Exposure* and *Sarah Palin's Alaska*.[22] In recent years, Alaska's image of political flamboyance has been reinforced by political scandals, including the indictment of the late U.S. Senator Ted Stevens. Moreover, several scholars have made a case for the influence of the pioneer ethos on Alaska's culture.[23] This includes such traits and characteristics as increased opportunity and the ability to make a difference; a feeling of freedom of all types, including from social and religious strictures; individuality and resistance to authority; resilience in dealing with isolation; and a unique local parlance, including terms like "Outside," "down South" (the Lower 48 states), and the "Owner State."[24]

It is far from clear, however, to what extent this pioneer ethos has and continues to influence the state's political culture. There are several reasons for doubt. First, while intuitively it appears that this pioneer ethos may have had an influence, as with other aspects of Alaska's political culture there is no hard evidence to demonstrate its effect. Second, even if it once did shape political actions, Alaska is a much different place in 2015 than it was in 1959, particularly since the construction of the trans-Alaska pipeline system (TAPS) in the 1970s. Urban Alaska is not that much different from other urban centers in the United States, and few Alaskans today have had anything close to a pioneering experience. At most, they may occasionally venture into the wilderness to hunt and fish. Third, individualism and antigovernment attitudes may be rooted in the pioneer ethos, but they are just as likely (if not more so) to arise from other factors, such as ideology or self-interest.

All four of the scholarly interpretations of state political culture we discussed earlier see the unique social makeup in rural-bush Alaska, and in particular Alaska Natives, as influencing the state's political culture. No doubt this rural-bush and Native value system

BOX 5.1

Ten Significant Elements of Alaska's Political Culture

1. FRIENDS AND NEIGHBORS POLITICS

The small populations in urban House and Senate districts facilitate easy access by citizens to state elected officials. And despite the geographic size of rural-bush districts, their elected officials are well known to constituents and very accessible.

2. A LOW LEVEL OF PARTISANSHIP BUT STRONG IDEOLOGICAL COMMITMENT

Alaska's low level of partisan commitment facilitates bipartisanship despite strong ideological commitments.

3. REGIONALISM AND URBAN VERSUS RURAL-BUSH TENSIONS

In reality, Alaska is five or six states geographically, each with different economies and other distinguishing features. Political loyalties of both the public and elected officials often coalesce around region.

4. MYTHS, MISCONCEPTIONS, CONTRADICTIONS, AND INCONSISTENCIES

These exist in Alaska, whether consciously or subconsciously held. Some of the following elements illustrate these aspects of the political culture.

5. AN AMBIVALENT ATTITUDE TOWARD GOVERNMENT

The strong antigovernment attitude among many Alaskans, particularly regarding the federal government, is coupled with high expectations of government and major demands made upon it.

6. A BELIEF OF BEING DIFFERENT, SOMETIMES MISUNDERSTOOD, OFTEN WITH A FEELING OF BEING BELEAGUERED

The confluence of these feelings produces a variety of reactions, including populism and a feeling that one of the roles of state government is to protect Alaskans from certain Outside forces.

7. DEPENDENT INDIVIDUALISM

Alaskans tend to laud American individualism—self-reliance, private initiative, and minimal interference from government—as keys to personal success. However, the nature of Alaska's economy and other constraints make the realization of this form of individualism unattainable without major aid from, and thus dependence on, government.

8. A PARTICULAR BRAND OF CONSERVATISM

Alaskan conservatism manifests traditional social values, strong family values (at least in some quarters, particularly evangelicals), a major role for the private sector, and fiscal conservatism regarding government spending.

9. RECURRING ELEMENTS OF POPULISM

Populist sentiments are often reactions to Outside economic and political forces, and can translate into support for politicians who act as "defenders" of the state.

10. A STRONG STRAIN OF POLITICAL PRAGMATISM

Several of the previous elements, particularly the strictures on individualism and conservatism and low levels of partisanship, lead to political pragmatism as a major way to deal with issues and solve problems. Here ideology and party affiliation often take a backseat to achieving the political goal at hand.

Source: Developed by the authors from the sources used in this chapter.

does have its effects. But when we delve beyond the generalities and intuition, similar to the influence of the pioneer element, clearly identifying a causal relationship is problematic. In this regard, the following points are useful to bear in mind.

First, a distinction needs to be made between what might be a rural-bush culture and an overall state political culture. It may be that there is a distinct rural-bush political culture, but in the absence of any hard data it is impossible to say. Second, regarding the Native community, differences between the social structures of Indians, Eskimos, and Aleuts suggest that there is no common Native political culture. Third, while influences of Alaska Natives on politics and specific public policies can be identified (such as rural-bush influence in the legislature and on issues like subsistence and Native sovereignty), their particular influence on the state's political culture is much more difficult to determine. This is for similar reasons to those regarding the influence of the pioneer element. Likely, however, and particularly regarding Natives in rural-bush areas, the need to secure basic services, such as sewers and water, education, and affordable energy, has led many Natives and their rural-bush elected officials to manifest a low level of partisanship and emphasize political pragmatism and bipartisanship.

In short, we must be careful not to let intuition or common beliefs that continue to be perpetuated cloud an understanding of Alaska's contemporary political culture and state politics in general. The evidence and arguments regarding the influence of both the pioneer spirit and Native values on Alaska's political culture are too inconclusive.

6. THE MAJOR ELEMENTS OF ALASKA'S POLITICAL CULTURE AND THEIR COMPLEXITY

Box 5.1 synthesizes the analysis in the chapter so far to identify the ten major elements of Alaska's contemporary political culture. The beliefs and values that underlie these elements have helped shape many of the characteristics of Alaska politics identified in Chapter 2. Although these ten elements provide a general overview of the state's political culture, no single element applies to all Alaskans or to all the state's public officials.

Furthermore, political culture can vary across a state, even small states like New Jersey and Connecticut, and certainly across large ones like Alaska. So some qualifying remarks about the framework will be useful.

Complexities, Variations, Exceptions, and Changing Values

The ten elements in Box 5.1 are not placed in any order of importance. They are, however, placed in a sequence that facilitates an understanding of both the integrated nature of all ten (as each factor appears to influence, and is influenced by, one or more of the other factors), and to illustrate the complexities involved in many of the elements. In particular, element 4, "Myths, Misconceptions, Inconsistencies, and Contradictions," aids in understanding elements 5 through 10.

A good case can be made that the most complex element of Alaska's political culture is the ambivalent, often contradictory, attitude toward government. More than the citizens of any other state, Alaskans owe their quality of life to federal and state government spending. State management of the resources of the Owner State has helped enhance their standard of living. And while the federal government has certain intrusive traits in terms of regulation, state government is far less intrusive and, as of 2015, levies no state income tax on individuals and no statewide sales tax. Despite all this, negative attitudes toward government at all levels persist.

To be sure, attitudes toward government vary across the state, as do other elements in the state's political culture. There is a strong strain of pragmatic conservatism in the Mat-Su Valley (north of Anchorage) and pockets of liberalism in Juneau, Anchorage, and Fairbanks. Rural-bush areas are essentially pragmatic, less antigovernment, and more liberal.

Likely, there are also differences in attitudes toward government between Alaska's public officials and the public at large, though again, no survey research is available to verify this. However, judging from research on other states and observations on Alaska, public officials are likely to have a more positive attitude to government and those involved in it, including lobbyists and bureaucrats. Public officials also tend to see the necessity of compromise and pragmatism more than the general public.

Across the nation and in Alaska, the political culture and political attitudes have undergone change over the years. Alaska has become more conservative and has moved more toward Republican values and an increasing fiscal conservatism. A small but strong liberal value system has persisted, however, in part in reaction to a rising national conservative value system. This increasing conservative-liberal divide has produced some intense political cultural clashes in Alaska. At the same time, in 2014, Alaska legalized the use of marijuana through a ballot initiative, one of only four states and the District of Columbia to do so at that time. This is usually considered a liberal, highly progressive policy and adopting the ballot measure obviously took some support by conservatives. This is further evidence of the complexity of Alaska's political culture.

The Essence of Alaska's Political Culture

Given the explanation of the elements of Alaska's political culture and the caveats regarding it, how is its essence best described? Are Elazar's designations of moralistic, individualistic, and traditionalistic appropriate? Is Lieske's "rurban" designation more useful than Hero's view of the majority-minority tensions in a bifurcated state? Is Alaska's

BOX 5.2

Political Corruption, Graft, Kickbacks, and Political Ethics: Issues of Definition, Assessment, and Comparison

What is included within political corruption, graft, kickbacks, and political ethics and the forms they take vary from country to country. It partly depends on political culture. Accordingly, legal definitions of these terms and their stringency of enforcement also vary across countries and often within a country, including the United States.

In the broadest sense, political corruption means the illegal use of public resources for private gain. As generally viewed in the United States and in most states, Chris Edwards explains political corruption as a practice that:

> occurs when legislators and bureaucrats use their discretionary power over budgets, regulations, procurement, and taxation to reward themselves and private interests, while subverting the general welfare. Officials are motivated by bribes, campaign contributions, favorable investment opportunities, promises of jobs for themselves and family members, and other payoffs.[1]

While graft, corruption, and kickbacks are usually included under a generic heading and all involve some form of corruption, graft and kickbacks are slightly different forms of corruption, though the distinction between the three is often murky.

Corruption usually involves some form of direct illegal payment, fraud, or influence peddling. Graft is more subtle and might involve a public official using insider knowledge, for example on the government's intention to privatize a public service or to zone some land, to make money by purchasing part of the service or buying and selling the land. A kickback might be paying off a public official who has steered a contract or other financial benefit to a business by paying that official a percentage of the contract value or some other form of compensation.

Political ethics usually refer to a set of practices, generally enforced by law or regulation and reflecting contemporary morality, governing the appropriate conduct of public officials, particularly those who are elected but often appointed officials. At the U.S. federal level and across the states, it usually includes campaign finance disclosure; disclosure of personal assets; conflict of interest rules, such as those against employing family members (nepotism); and "revolving door" or "sitting out" period provisions, usually for a year after they leave public office, during which public officials cannot accept employment or contracts with organizations that they have made decisions on while in office.

---

[1] Chris Edwards, "Reducing Federal Corruption." *Tax and Budget Bulletin* (Washington, D.C.: The Cato Institute, 2006), Number 34. p. 1.

Source: Developed by the authors.

political culture one that manifests the elements of a unique wilderness, or is it just another "red" (Republican) state? While all these elements may be present, close examination leads to the view that Alaska's political culture is most appropriately described as pragmatic dependent individualism.

This designation captures the individualistic attitude of many Alaskans and the political rhetoric that often supports and reinforces it. At the same time, this designation also embraces the all-pervasive dependence on government and the use of government by citizens and politicians, if sometimes subconscious or not acknowledged, melded by a strong dose of political pragmatism. This combination of political cultural values appears to most reflect the Alaska public's and elected officials' view of politics and the role of government.

Political culture also provides insights into the nature of democracy in Alaska and the types of public policies that get enacted and those that do not. Consideration of the link between political culture and the public policy process will make more sense by first considering the issue of political corruption.

7. IS CORRUPTION AND A LOW LEVEL OF PUBLIC ETHICS PART OF ALASKA'S POLITICAL CULTURE?

Anyone with a cursory familiarity with Alaska politics, particularly during the period 2005–2010, might be surprised that we have not included political corruption and a low level of ethical behavior in politics as one of the major elements of the state's political culture. In this section we address this issue. As Box 5.2 (on the previous page) explains, exactly what constitutes political corruption and political ethics reflects normative values and tends to be viewed differently, not only from country to country, but within the same country over time and in different parts of some countries at the same time.[25]

A Short History of Alaska's Political Scandals

From the late 1970s to the early 1990s, Alaska had several high-profile political scandals and some criminal convictions. The *Anchorage Daily News* (since 2014 the *Alaska Dispatch News*) won a Pulitzer Prize in the mid-1970s for exposing the Teamsters Union's racketeering activities and its connection with Alaska's political elite.[26] Scandals in the 1980s included the conviction and prison sentence for corruption of both a powerful state senator, George Hohman of Bethel, and a powerful lobbyist, Lew Dischner, and his associate, Carl Mathisen.[27] In 1985 the legislature attempted to impeach Governor Bill Sheffield on alleged corruption charges involving a lease on a Fairbanks office building, but the attempt failed. Some political analysts viewed the impeachment as largely politically motivated.[28]

The mid-1990s to the early 2000s was a quiet time for political scandals. However, by the mid-2000s, political corruption scandals in Alaska began to attract national attention, such as a 2007 headline in the *Los Angeles Times* that read, "In Alaska scandals flow like crude," and in reports of good government organizations like Citizens for Responsibility and Ethics in Washington (CREW).[29] These scandals involved criminal convictions, ethics investigations, and much suspect political behavior.[30]

In 2007 the U.S. Department of Justice brought federal bribery and conspiracy charges against legislators, lobbyists, and executives of VECO, an oil field service company. This resulted in several convictions and prison sentences for Bill Allen and Rick Smith of VECO and legislators Pete Kott and Vic Kohring. New trials were eventually ordered for Kott and Kohring and they were allowed to go free based on time served in prison. In 2007 CREW listed all three members of Alaska's congressional delegation as among the twenty-two most corrupt members of Congress. Senator Lisa Murkowski was listed number three, Senator Ted Stevens number four, and Representative Don Young number twenty-two. As part of the VECO investigation, Senator Stevens was convicted of filing false financial disclosure statements a few days before his bid for reelection in November 2008, but in April 2009 these charges were thrown out because of federal prosecutorial misconduct. Also in 2008, Jim Clark, Governor Murkowski's former chief of staff, was found guilty of campaign finance violations, though his conviction was also later overturned. Several other legislators and lobbyists were found guilty of bribery or corruption during these years.

Other actions by Alaska politicians have not helped their image or that of politicians in general. One was the so-called Troopergate affair (a play on the Watergate affair) involving former Governor Sarah Palin. It was claimed that she had pressured the commissioner of the Department of Public Safety to fire her former brother-in-law, a state trooper who had been involved in a nasty divorce from her sister. The ethics complaints against her were dismissed, but the investigations brought into question the independence of the attorney general (who is appointed by the governor) in such investigations. Another unethical situation involved Joe Miller, the official Republican Party candidate for U.S. Senate in the November 2010 election. While he sought to claim the moral high ground in the campaign, one of his opponents, Senator Lisa Murkowski, and the media accused Miller of lying about his reasons for leaving a part-time attorney's job at the Fairbanks North Star Borough and of concealing a conflict of interest violation while he was employed there. It was also alleged that he engaged in conflict of interest activities while a federal magistrate in Fairbanks.

Countering Political Corruption and Promoting Political Ethics

While this history of political scandals does not put Alaska in a class with many countries in Latin America or Africa, where corruption is rampant, a comprehensive study of political corruption in the states between 1976 to 2008 places Alaska at seventh on the list of most corrupt states. The number one corrupt state in the survey was Mississippi, followed by Louisiana, Tennessee, and Illinois, with Oregon, Washington, and Minnesota among the least corrupt states.[31] Other studies, however, have not listed Alaska in the top ten, and the 1976–2008 study does not list New Jersey as among the most corrupt states in the nation, although most other studies do.[32] In fact, the ranking of states on corruption

BOX 5.3

The Alaska Public Offices Commission: Promoting a Culture of Ethical Political Behavior

The Alaska Public Offices Commission (APOC) is a quasi-judicial body that administers four public information laws: campaign finance disclosure, public official financial disclosure (originally called conflict of interest provisions), legislative financial disclosure, and lobby regulations. Of the five commissioners who oversee APOC, two each are nominated by the central committees of the two parties whose candidate for governor received the highest number of votes in the most recent gubernatorial election (this is most often the Republican and Democratic parties). These four nominate the fifth member. The governor appoints all five, and the legislature must confirm the appointments. APOC is placed in the Department of Administration for administrative purposes.

Similar to agencies in other states, the impetus for APOC was the Watergate affair of the early 1970s and ballot initiatives by Alaskans regarding election campaign finance disclosure and public official conflict of interest rules. These initiatives won overwhelming public support and encouraged the legislature to create the Alaska Election Campaign Commission (AECC) in 1974. Then, in 1976, when new lobby regulations were created, their enforcement was assigned to AECC, which was renamed APOC to reflect its expanded mission.

Today, financial disclosure is required of the governor, lieutenant governor, department commissioners and division directors, legislators, judges, municipal officials, and members of state boards and commissions, among other state and local officials. Candidates for elected office must make disclosures of campaign contributions received and expenditures made, and adhere to strict rules of campaign conduct. In addition, APOC's responsibility for registration and monitoring of lobbyists and their employers means that it receives regular reports from them. Almost two thousand public official financial disclosures are received annually and about the same number of lobbyist and lobbyist employer reports. Disclosures are public, and often generate considerable interest in the media and among political activists, candidates, and their opponents.

Failure to meet the filing deadlines and requirements can result in civil penalties. Willful violation of the disclosure law can result in criminal charges. This was the case in 2008 when longtime lobbyist Ashley Reed was charged by APOC with continual failure to submit lobbying reports on time for which he had built-up fines of $30,000. He was found guilty, received a fine, community service, and a short prison sentence that was suspended. In 2014, Democrat Representative Chris Tuck of Anchorage was fined $14,000 for campaign violations.

Despite its official independent status, APOC is not immune from politics and is often in the thick of it. APOC must go through the same budget process as other state agencies, which means that it depends on the very officials it regulates for its budget—in fact, for its very existence. As a result, there is a constant struggle between APOC and legislators. On the one hand, legislators want to uphold the will of their constituents and to promote transparency and ethical behavior. On the other, they do not want to give too much strength and influence to APOC, because many find the disclosures and reporting requirements burdensome and some see them as unduly intrusive or unnecessary.

In 2003, Governor Frank Murkowski sought to abolish APOC. When that failed, he convinced legislators to reduce APOC's statute of limitations and cut funding for its sole investigator. A few years later, when political scandals rocked the state and public awareness was raised, pressure was brought on elected officials for more stringent regulations and for increased funding for APOC. This, in large part, was led by the populist rhetoric of newly elected Governor Sarah Palin and her campaign promise to curb the influence of big money and powerful interests.

There appears to be a strong public consensus, if not always explicitly vocalized, that APOC's mission is critical to promote transparency, accountability, and some level of political equality in Alaska's politics and its public policy process.

Source: Developed by Jeff Berliner and Reuben Yerkes, both former employees of APOC.

lists varies depending on the focus of the study. In this regard, listing Alaska as one of the most corrupt states is likely an inaccurate comparison for the following reasons.

Like all states, Alaska has a regulatory agency, the Alaska Public Offices Commission (APOC), which oversees campaign finance, financial disclosure of the assets of public officials, and lobbying activity. Box 5.3 explains the history, role, and jurisdiction of APOC as well as the politics surrounding it. APOC has existed since the early 1970s and in 2003 it was ranked by the Center for Public Integrity in the top third of such state agencies in comprehensiveness of coverage and stringency of enforcement. No review of these agencies has been conducted since 2003, but if one had been, Alaska would likely rank even higher. This is because since 2003, in response to Governor Frank Murkowski's attempt to loosen public disclosure and following the VECO and other scandals, Alaska has passed more stringent campaign finance and lobby laws.[33] Ironically, considering the ethics complaints filed against her in her last year as governor, Sarah Palin championed ethics reform in her successful 2006 gubernatorial campaign and was able to secure its enactment once in office.

The impetus for these reforms came, in large part, from Alaska citizens by bringing pressure on their representatives. It was a citizen initiative that led the legislature to adopt the 2006 reforms in campaign disclosure. Likely the Alaska public is no more tolerant of corruption than the public of any other state. The defeat of Ted Stevens by Mark Begich in the November 2008 election, following Stevens's conviction, is likely evidence of the public's intolerance of shady political dealings. Joe Miller's defeat in the 2010 U.S. Senate race against the write-in campaign of incumbent Lisa Murkowski may also be evidence of the Alaska public's rejection of perceived disingenuousness in politics.[34] Then in 2015 an initiative petition was filed to place a proposed law on the ballot in 2016 to make it a crime for public officials to be involved in policy decisions that would directly benefit them, their families, or their employees.[35]

Several other factors tend to promote political ethics and work to prevent corruption in Alaska politics. Alaska's judiciary has a national reputation for professionalism and integrity. Judges are nominated and appointed through a more or less independent process and then confirmed by the voters and reconfirmed at intervals (the so-called Missouri Plan). Thus, they are largely insulated from political pressures because they do not have to run for office and raise campaign funds, as candidates do in states like Texas and Ohio. The legislature has its own Committee on Legislative Ethics, which oversees separate ethics rules from those of APOC governing legislators and lobbyists. However, as McBeath and Morehouse commented in the early 1990s and which likely still holds true today, many powerful legislators have been able to thwart enforcement of these rules.[36] Furthermore, Alaska has no history of party machines and the political patronage and corruption that often accompanies them, as in Illinois and New Jersey. Neither does Alaska have an elite tradition, in the form of the traditionalistic political culture of the southern states, where benefits to family often dictate political action.

Alaska's Political Corruption and Ethics: A Balance Sheet

Studies that have attempted to relate levels of corruption with political culture, such as the moralistic subculture being less likely to produce political scandals, have shown mixed results.[37] Even so, on balance it does not appear that corruption and a low level of political ethics is a major aspect of Alaska political culture. Certainly, many corrupt incidents and unethical activities have taken place over the years. But the vast majority of the public and public officials do not condone and, in fact, work to prevent such activities and provide stiff penalties for transgressors. Making an educated assessment based on knowledge of scandals and convictions across the states since the early 1980s, Alaska is probably in the top third of the most corrupt states. It is certainly not on a par with the very "clean" states, such as Nebraska, Vermont, or Washington State. On the other hand, it is not close to the top of the list of corrupt states.

McBeath and Morehouse put it this way: "Alaskans don't condone sleaze but they forgive and forget transgressions."[38] What they could have added is that this is particularly so when a politician has raked in major benefits for his constituents. George Hohman returned to Bethel from prison and became city manager. More recently, despite his 2008 conviction (it was later thrown out but Stevens was never declared not guilty), the Anchorage airport is still named after Ted Stevens and in April 2011 Governor Sean Parnell signed a bill designating the fourth Saturday in July each year as Ted Stevens Day. Stevens was by far Alaska's most effective and powerful politician since statehood, bringing tens of billions of dollars into the state. Continuing to honor him may be an expression of Alaska's pragmatic dependent individualism.

8. THE INTERPLAY BETWEEN ALASKA'S POLITICAL CULTURE, THE NATURE OF ITS DEMOCRACY, AND PUBLIC POLICIES

The extent to which political culture shapes the form of pluralist democracy and the types of public policies adopted is an ongoing question in political science. Nonetheless, existing research enables us to make observations about these links and apply them to Alaska.

Political Culture and the Nature of Alaska Democracy

Both moralistic and traditionalistic cultures suggest a political system in which responsiveness to public preferences for specific public policies is muted. As a result, these cultures produce a form of elitist democracy. The moralistic orientation gives leeway to public officials to put the interests of the "commonwealth" first and thus tend to be less subject to populist type demands. The traditionalistic culture sees democratic institutions as serving the interests of local elites who act to maintain the existing order.

In contrast, individualistic cultures more closely fit the public's expectations of democratic representation, which include populist elements. In individualistic cultures, politics is the politics of the marketplace, and competition between political parties produces policies that are responsive to public demands. Politicians are pragmatic, seeking to retain office by giving the public what it wants. If public preferences tend toward conservative policies, politicians will compete to offer the public conservative policies. If liberal preferences dominate, then the parties will compete over policies at the liberal end of the poltical spectrum. The median (typical) voter will determine the kinds of policies that are actually put forward, debated, and ultimately adopted. This form of democracy appears to be the form operating in Alaska.

The notion of pragmatic dependent individualism reflects the way politicians respond to the demands of Alaskans. Responsive public officials do not always act in the general public good, but on behalf of the median voter. Looked at another way, politics can be rational in giving a majority of voters what they want rather than reflecting a trusteeship orientation toward the general good of all voters. In Alaska, citizens prefer that government does not interfere. At the same time, the majority of residents want government subsidies. This has resulted in Alaska being a state of citizens who expect not simply lower taxes but actual payments from extractive activities, as they do with the Permanent Fund Dividend (PFD), as well as federal government support for a range of services from education to infrastructure.

Political Culture and Public Policy

Some scholars see political culture as having a direct effect on public policy. Elazar suggests that moralistic, individualistic, and traditionalistic cultures should each produce a different mix of public policies. As a consequence, many researchers have included culture as a key predictor of specific policy outcomes. Moralistic states are seen as liberal, traditionalistic ones as conservative, and individualistic states as producing moderate policies.

Other scholars question the direct link between political culture and public policy. Some see culture as doing nothing more than explaining general variations in state and local government policies. Others see national attitudes as more significant than state cultures. In this regard, Wirt notes that "national tides of reform" can sweep across the land with the general will dominating local interests.[39] At the same time, broad reform movements, such as federal welfare reform in the 1990s, usually allow the details in the implementation process to reflect state preferences.

Furthermore, political culture by itself is not always the dominant explanation for many policies. Implementing policies requires resources and, whatever the desire of the public or public officials, without those resources certain policies may be beyond the capacity of the state to enact. State policies for the disabled, for example, depend not only on a willingness to aid those with various types of disabilities, but on the financial means to do so. States populated by wealthy residents, states with higher tax rates, and states like Alaska that are rich in natural resources, have the ability to spend revenue on disabled residents if they so choose. Theoretically at least, Alaska is in this enviable position.

A third approach to the political culture-public policy link is that of Erikson, Wright, and McIver.[40] Rather than consider culture as having a direct impact on public policy, they suggest that culture affects policy by influencing how policies are made. For instance, the sense of obligation to community welfare that exists in moralistic subcultures produces a tendency toward public policy in the public interest even when not explicitly demanded by the general public. In contrast, the traditionalistic subculture is often associated with a conservative predisposition against government action. The individualistic political culture is less predictable because it is the one most responsive to public opinion. To illustrate this we use welfare policy in the states and in Alaska.

Political Culture and Welfare Policy

Moralistic states are thought to devote significantly more resources to welfare benefits for its less fortunate citizens in contrast to traditionalistic states that are less likely to fund such benefits. While individualistic states are less predictable, they are likely to be moderate in their endorsement of and support for welfare. However, because individualistic states are more responsive to their constituencies, welfare policies may reflect the liberal, moderate, or conservative preferences of their electorate. This is borne out by the response of the states to President Clinton's welfare reform of 1996, the Personal Responsibility and Work Opportunity Reconciliation Act.

The emphasis of reform was to change the incentive system for potentially productive individuals through the Temporary Assistance for Needy Families (TANF) program, which cut off federal funds after sixty months. Federal block grants were made available to the states with the states retaining control over many of the rules governing their use. Given the opportunity to define their own variations on the "welfare to workfare" theme, the states did just that. And while each state can supplement the funds distributed by the federal government, few have done so.

The traditionalistic states of the Deep South (Louisiana, Mississippi, Alabama, Georgia, and the Carolinas) exhibited a greater tendency to adopt a five-year lifetime limit on welfare support and restrict beneficiaries to twenty-four consecutive months of state support. In contrast, moralistic states (Minnesota, Wisconsin, Michigan, Maine, and

Vermont) are generally among the most lenient states with respect to TANF restrictions. None is more restrictive than the federal sixty-month standard for lifetime participation, and several do not restrict the number of months a recipient may participate.

The individualistic states are more diverse regarding access to TANF support. Alaska adopted the federal standard, a sixty-month lifetime limit and no periodic (consecutive month) restrictions. Nevada, on the other hand, substantially restricted access to recipients: twenty-four months of consecutive assistance within the lifetime restriction of sixty months. Ohio adopted a slightly less restrictive policy, limiting consecutive participation to thirty-six months. Its neighbor, Indiana, is one of the states least willing to support the TANF program: lifetime participation is limited to twenty-four months.

The Implications

Alaska's liberal application of the Clinton welfare reform further illustrates the complexities of the state's political culture, as many states with such individualistic tendencies are far less liberal in this regard. The analysis also shows the egalitarian, essentially populist, link between the individualistic element in the state's political culture and democratic government, perhaps partly due to friends and neighbors politics and low levels of partisanship. Governments generally respond in states with individualistic cultures with policies reflecting the demands made by citizens. In some states the policies may be broadly more liberal, in others decidedly conservative. In each case, however, it is because public officials act to give citizens what they want, as they generally appear to do in Alaska.

At the same time, we must be careful to avoid a circular argument. Alaska is not individualistic because of its public policies. Alaska's government adopts certain policies because its culture reinforces the notion that citizens matter. Indeed, a caution regarding describing the political culture as pragmatic dependent individualism is that the culture appears defined by particular types of policies when, in fact, policies evolve out of a relationship between citizens and governments. In this regard, it might be best to think of Alaska as individualistic and its policies being the result of dependency, with the two melded by pragmatism. In the absence of any exit polling, it would appear that the individualistic element was in play in legalizing marijuana in 2014, with perhaps a pragmatic element involved, and that Alaska's political culture had evolved over the years given the unwillingness to legalize marijuana in past public votes.

9. ALASKA'S POLITICAL CULTURE COMPARED TO OTHER STATES

Where does Alaska fit as a state regarding its political culture? Comparisons can identify unique aspects of Alaska's political culture that offer insights on aspects of the state's

BOX 5.4

Nevada's Political Culture

The first state to openly embrace gambling and the only state to legalize prostitution (licensed brothels operate in ten rural counties), Nevada seems to exist on the social and political fringe of American politics, reinforced by Hollywood images of Las Vegas glitz, gangsters, and self-made millionaires. The hands-off approach to regulation and government intrusion into the lives of Nevadans is also reflected in the state's limited levels of governmental services and spending, especially for social welfare. Yet, while Nevada's social, economic, and political attributes mark its uniqueness, its development and contemporary political characteristics share much with both the Old and the New West.

Nevada was settled by pioneers and entrepreneurs with an individualistic, antigovernment, western ethos. From early days government was viewed as a part-time activity and service delivery was very limited. To this day the Nevada legislature is still part-time, meeting just 120 days every other year, one of only four states that still hold biennial legislative sessions. In the early years of statehood, mining and railroad lobbyists held far more sway than elected officials in directing public affairs. Other than mineral deposits and some parched land, Nevada had little to offer except its isolation and openness. So it faced a major challenge in its search for economic viability.

With this accepting and morally flexible political culture, the state saw that it could exploit its isolation by tolerating social activities, such as divorce, gambling, prostitution, and even professional prizefighting for economic advantage. The transformation of Nevada's economy, especially the rise of Las Vegas (where 70 percent of the state's population live), was founded on federal dollars for water projects, particularly the construction of Hoover Dam, other infrastructure projects, and military and defense spending. Despite this significant federal contribution, the Sagebrush Rebellion, which swept across the West in the late 1970s, began in Nevada, where federal land comprises 85 percent of the state. This protest movement sought to transfer federal lands to state and private ownership. So, Nevada reflects a common political cultural attitude among western states, particularly in the Mountain West, of an anti–federal government attitude contrasted with the reality of significant federal contributions to its economic development and sustained economic viability.

In 2012 more than 60 percent of employment in the state was either directly or indirectly linked to gaming activities. Tax revenues from gaming produce nearly one-third of the state's general fund revenue. So it is no surprise that gaming is also the most dominant interest group in the state and rarely loses political battles in the legislature. Gaming lobbyists have replaced the power once wielded by mining and railroad interests. In contrast to most western states, however, Nevada has only 12 percent of its workforce employed by all levels of government, one of the lowest in the nation and well below the national average of 18 percent.

Daniel Elazar classified Nevada's political culture as highly individualistic, where government is instituted strictly for utilitarian purposes to meet limited citizen service demands, and where individual liberty is often placed above broader concerns of the social good. Nevada regularly ranks near the bottom of the fifty states in spending on education, health care, child services, and welfare. Given low levels of social welfare spending but simultaneously rather permissive social structures, it is hard to characterize the state as being either liberal or conservative. In fact, the state has a strong strain of libertarianism, with its distinct mix of individual liberty and conservative fiscal views toward government services. In today's Nevada of the New West, the frontier ethos is no longer epitomized by the lone individual conquering the inhospitable land, but by the individual left alone to pursue his or her dreams.

Source: Developed by Eric Herzik, Professor of Political Science, University of Nevada, Reno.

politics and policy. Our approach is first to compare the state with Nevada, which appears to be its sister western state, and then to place Alaska in the broad context of the fifty states.

Nevada: Is It Alaska's Political Culture Sister State?

Because Nevada and Alaska have much in common, both as states of the Old and of the New West, they might be viewed as sister states in their political culture. In Box 5.4 we outline Nevada's evolving political culture.

With all the past and present similarities between the two states, there are certainly some similarities in their political culture. There are also some major differences, four of which are particularly noteworthy.

First, among the individualistic states, when it comes to spending on welfare Alaska is a close second to New York on a per capita basis, whereas Nevada is the lowest ranked state. Second, Alaska is involved in a major way in the management of its state lands and is also second to New York. Nevada, on the other hand, is again the lowest ranked.[41] Third, Nevada appears to be more genuinely antigovernment and more libertarian than Alaska. With one of the lowest percentages of government employment in the nation, Nevada is much less dependent on government.[42] And fourth, as a society Nevada is more open and permissive than Alaska with gambling, legalized prostitution, and related activities geared to economic gain. So even though Nevada and Alaska are close in many aspects of history, economic geography, and politics, the sum of all the influences adds up to a unique political culture in each state.

Where Does Alaska Fit Among the Fifty States?

From comparison with Nevada and from the other analyses in this chapter, it is clear that there is no simple answer to where Alaska fits among the states in regard to its political culture. Alaska shares common traits with many states with individualistic tendencies, such as Nevada and Indiana. But it also shares traits with some moralistic states from the upper Midwest and Northeast on low levels of partisanship, for example, and with some traditionalistic states, like Mississippi and Louisiana, on ideological commitment and conservative social values. Moreover, based on the argument of Erikson, Wright, and McIver, each political culture is unique.

Nevertheless, by combining the academic sources and perspectives considered here, we can identify states with similar political cultures and contrast them with other states. This is best represented by clusters of states (similar to Figures 5.1 and 5.2) rather than placing them on a continuum or scale. Alaska is most similar to states that are individualist, with minor elements of traditional and moralistic subcultures. This places it closest to Nevada, Arizona, Idaho, Montana, Indiana, and Ohio and with some similarities to Pennsylvania, New Jersey, Louisiana, Mississippi, and South Carolina. It is least similar to the states of Minnesota, Wisconsin, Michigan, Hawaii, California, Oregon, and Washington.[43] So, clearly, regional location and date of admission to the Union are not significant factors that have shaped Alaska's political culture.

10. CONCLUSION: HOW USEFUL IS POLITICAL CULTURE AS A MEANS FOR UNDERSTANDING ALASKA POLITICS AND PUBLIC POLICY MAKING?

The concept of political culture is the subject of much debate among scholars regarding its origin, classification, development, and effects on public policy. Moreover, we have seen that Alaska's political culture is more complex and dynamic than it appears to be on the surface. This raises the question of what value, if any, the concept of political culture has as a tool for understanding politics in the states and particularly that in Alaska.

Although political culture provides no definitive answers on what shapes politics and public policy, it does offer many valuable insights and has some predictive value. Evidence strongly suggests that political culture, and the political socialization that shapes it, are the most influential factors in how people do or do not relate to politics and government. Studies on political culture provide valuable perspectives on the differences among the states in their degree of ideology and partisanship, attitudes toward government and government services, and how these and other attitudes likely affect certain public policies.

Alaska's political culture is in essence one of pragmatic dependent individualism. As such, it includes many elements common to other states. But using the argument of Erickson, Wright, and McIver, like all states, Alaska's political culture is unique, and its elements and complexities (including the contradictions and subliminal aspects) tell us much about the way that the public and public officials feel about politics and the way they work to translate these attitudes into public policy. This includes the interplay between weak partisanship but strong ideological commitment, the role of the Owner State, a particular brand of conservatism and populism, and a strong strain of political pragmatism.

As a fundamental influence on the state's public life, most of the chapters in this book consider one or more of the elements of Alaska's political culture as they affect various aspects of Alaska politics or public policy. In many cases the authors go into depth on elements of this culture and its influence. This includes how the complexities of the political culture affect the role of political parties (Chapter 13), campaigns and elections (Chapter 14), the role, structure, and development of local government (Chapter 18), and the state budget process (Chapter 19). It is probably in the attitude to government, particularly the federal and state governments, that Alaska's political culture manifests its major complexities. Chapter 10 looks at these attitudes with respect to the federal government, and Chapter 12 considers the general role and operation of government in Alaska with a focus on state government.

ENDNOTES

[1] Gerald A. McBeath, "Alaska's Political Culture," in *Alaska State Government and Politics*, eds. Gerald A. McBeath and Thomas A. Morehouse (Fairbanks: University of Alaska Press, 1987), 53. See also, "The Alaska Character," in *Alaska Politics and Government*, McBeath and Morehouse (Lincoln: University of Nebraska Press, 1994).

[2] Thomas A. Morehouse, "Alaska's Political and Economic Future" (Lecture Notes and Illustrations), a lecture delivered to the faculty at the University of Alaska, Anchorage, on his retirement, April 28, 1994.

[3] The overview of political culture and political socialization in this section is based on a synthesis of the following sources: Gabriel A. Almond and Sidney Verba, *The Civic Culture: Political Attitudes and Democracy in Five Nations* (Beverly Hills, CA: Sage Publications, 1989, originally published in 1963 by Princeton University Press); Daniel J. Elazar, *American Federalism: A View from the States*, 3rd ed. (New York: Thomas Y. Crowell, 1984); Edward Greenberg, *Political Socialization* (Piscataway, NJ: Aldine Transaction, 2009); James G. Gimpel, J. Celeste Lay, and Jason E. Schuknecht, *Cultivating Democracy: Civic Environments and Political Socialization in America* (Washington, D.C.: Brookings Institution Press, 2003); and Robert S. Erikson, Gerald C. Wright, and John P. McIver, *Statehouse Democracy: Public Opinion and Policy in the American States* (New York: Cambridge University Press, 1993).

[4] Almond and Verba, *The Civic Culture*, Chapter 1, "An Approach to Political Culture."

[5] See particularly, Daniel J. Elazar, *American Federalism* (1984), especially Chapter 5, "The States and the Political Setting"; Elazar, *The American Mosaic* (Boulder, CO: Westview Press, 1994); and Elazar and Joseph Zikmund III, eds., *The Ecology of American Political Culture* (New York: Thomas Y. Crowell, 1975).

[6] Elazar and Zikmund, *The Ecology of American Political Culture*, 23 and 25.

[7] Daniel J. Elazar, "Series Introduction," in McBeath and Morehouse, *Alaska Politics and Government*, xxiii–xxvii.

[8] *Ibid*., xxvii.

[9] For example see, Ira Sharkansky, "Economic Development, Regionalism and State Political Systems," *Midwest Journal of Political Science* 12, no. 1 (1968): 41–61; and his "The Utility of Elazar's Political Culture," *Polity* 2 (Fall 1969): 66–83.

[10] Joel Lieske, "Regional Sub-Cultures of the United States," *Journal of Politics* 55 (1993): 910.

[11] Joel Lieske, "The Changing Political Subcultures of the American States and the Utility of a New Cultural Measure," *Political Research Quarterly* 63, no. 3 (2010): 538–52.

[12] Rodney E. Hero, *Faces of Inequality: Social Diversity in American Politics* (New York: Oxford University Press, 1998).

[13] Robert S. Erikson, John P. McIver, and Gerald C. Wright, Jr., "State Political Culture and Public Opinion," *American Political Science Review* 81, no. 3 (1987): 797–814; Erikson, Wright, and McIver, *Statehouse Democracy*, and "Public Opinion in the States: A Quarter Century of Change and Stability," in *Public Opinion in State Politics*, ed. Jeffrey E. Cohen (Stanford, CA: Stanford University Press, 2007), 229–53.

[14] The assessments in this section are based on preferences of state electorates over time, including Alaska voters, available in national surveys. The data provides a synthesis of partisan and ideological preferences since the early 1990s and a composite of partisanship and ideology preferences

that is more representative than for one or two years only. See the work by Erikson, McIver, and Wright cited in endnote 13 and their "Public Opinion in the States: A Quarter Century of Change and Stability," esp. Appendix: Current Estimates for State Partisanship and Ideology, from CBS/ *New York Times* Polls, 1996–2003.

[15] The 2006 Cooperative Congressional Election Study estimated that Alaska ranked fifth of the most Republican states, see Tom Carsey and Jeff Harden, "New Measures of Partisanship, Ideology and Policy Mood in the American States," *State Politics and Policy Quarterly* 10 (2010): 136–56.

[16] Based on the source and survey in endnote 15, in 2006 Carsey and Harden ranked Alaska as the sixth most conservative state in the nation.

[17] For recent data on party affiliation in Alaska gathered by the Alaska Division of Elections and other sources, see Chapter 13 on political parties, Tables 13.1 and 13.2.

[18] For voter turnout in Alaska, see Chapter 14 on campaigns and elections, especially Section 5 and Table 14.3.

[19] Besides the work by McBeath and Morehouse cited above, sources include surveys conducted by public opinion research firms, particularly Dittman and Associates, an Alaska-based company whose survey results are cited in several chapters in the book. The original research includes more than three hundred interviews of public officials and political observers conducted since 1981 by Clive Thomas.

[20] *Almanac of the 50 States: Basic Data Profiles with Comparative Tables*, 2008 Edition (Woodside, CA: Information Publications, 2008), Tables 11 and 12.

[21] Public Land Ownership by State, retrieved August 15, 2014, from www.nrcm.org/documents/publiclandownership.pdf.

[22] Joe McGinniss, *Going to Extremes: A Search for the Essence of Alaska*, 4th ed. (Kenmore, WA: Epicenter Press, 2010).

[23] Examples of scholarly studies include Lee J. Cuba, *Identity and Community of the Last Frontier* (Philadelphia: Temple University Press, 1987); Susan Kollin, *Nature's State: Imagining Alaska as the Last Frontier* (Chapel Hill: University of North Carolina Press, 2001); and Judith Kleinfeld, "How the Frontier Imagery of the Alaskan North Shapes the People Who Come," *Northern Review* 27 (Fall 2007): 48–55.

[24] See Chapter 1, Box 1.2, for the parlance of Alaska's geography.

[25] This overview of the nature of political corruption draws on Transparency International's website at http://www.transparency.org/ and Chris Edwards, "Reducing Federal Corruption," in *Tax and Budget Bulletin* no. 34 (Washington D.C.: The Cato Institute, 2006).

[26] Richard A. Fineberg, "The Press and Alaska Politics," in McBeath and Morehouse, *Alaska State Government and Politics*, 222–23.

[27] McBeath and Morehouse, *Alaska Politics and Government*, 160–61; and "2 Men Convicted of Alaska Fraud," *New York Times*, May 24, 1989.

[28] Clive S. Thomas, "'*The Thing*' That Shook Alaska: The Events, the Fallout and the Lessons of Alaska's Gubernatorial Impeachment Proceedings," *State Legislatures* 13, no. 2 (February 1987), 22–25.

[29] "In Alaska Scandals Flow Like Crude," *Los Angeles Times*, August 17, 2007; see also, Timothy Egan, "Where the Goods are Odd," *New York Times*, June 14, 2007; and CREW, "The 22 Most Corrupt Members of Congress," 2007, at http://www.citizensforethics.org/.

[30] The overview of corruption in Alaska draws on a range of sources including newspapers, radio and TV coverage, good government websites, such as CREW, the authors' observations, and the involvement as a expert witness in one of the corruption trials by chapter co-author, Clive Thomas.

[31] Cheol Liu and John L. Mikesell, "The Impact of Public Officials' Corruption on the Size and Allocation of State Spending," *Public Administration Review* 74, no. 3 (May/June 2014): 346–59.

[32] See, "Public Corruption in the United States," *Corporate Crime Reporter* (Washington, D.C.: National Press Club, 2004), retrieved July 1, 2012, from http://www.corporatecrimereporter.com/corruptreport.pdf; and "Louisiana Most Corrupt State in the Nation, Mississippi Second, Illinois Sixth, New Jersey Ninth," *Corporate Crime Reporter* (Washington, D.C.: National Press Club, 2007), retrieved July 1, 2012, from http://www.corporatecrimereporter.com/ corrupt100807.htm. See also, B. Marsh, "Illinois is Trying, It Really Is, But the Most Corrupt State is Actually . . . ," *New York Times*, Dec. 13, 2008, retrieved on July 1, 2012, from http://www.nytimes.com/2008/12/14/weekinreview/14marsh.html?_r=3.

[33] Center for Public Integrity at http://projects.publicintegrity.org/hiredguns/nationwide.aspx. However, when it comes to ease of access to records (as opposed to the extent of regulations), APOC gets only an average grade, according to a 2013 study. See, Alexandra Gutierrez, "Alaska Scores Low on Lobbying Transparency," *Alaska News Nightly*, Alaska Public Radio Network (APRN), July 30, 2013.

[34] See Chapter 14 on campaigns and elections, Section 6 for an account of the Miller-Murkowski election.

[35] Zachariah Hughes, "Petition Against Corruption Needs 30,000 Signatures to Make 2016 Ballot," KSKA Radio (Public Radio for Anchorage), December 16, 2014.

[36] McBeath and Morehouse, *Alaska Politics and Government*, 160–62.

[37] See, for example, Michael Johnson, "Corruption and Political Culture in America: An Empirical Perspective," *Publius: The Journal of Federalism* 13 (Winter 1983); and Kenneth J. Meier and Thomas M. Holbrook, "I Seen My Opportunities and I Took 'Em: Political Corruption in the American States," *Journal of Politics* 54, no. 1 (February 1992): 135–55.

[38] McBeath and Morehouse, *Alaska Politics and Government*, 161.

[39] Frederick M. Wirt, "'Soft' Concepts and 'Hard' Data: A Research Review of Elazar's Political Culture," *Publius: The Journal of Federalism* 21 (1991): 1–13.

[40] Erikson, McIver, and Wright, "State Political Culture and Public Opinion"; Erikson, Wright, and McIver, *Statehouse Democracy*; and particularly, Erikson, Wright, and McIver, "Public Opinion in the States: A Quarter Century of Change and Stability."

[41] Public Land Ownership by State, cited in endnote 21.

[42] See Chapter 12, Table 12.1 for comparative state data on government employment.

[43] For further evidence as to Alaska's grouping in this regard, see Tom Rice and Alexander Sumberg "Civic Culture and Government Performance in the American States," *Publius: The Journal of Federalism* 27, no. 1 (1997): 99–114.

★ CHAPTER 6 ★

Alaska's Political Economy: Structure and Power Dynamics

Britteny A. Cioni-Haywood

Because the economy is so important to all residents of a nation, state, or locality, the health (or ill health) of the economy is a major factor in the way people vote in elections for or against those in power. Elected public officials well understand that they will be judged at the next election largely on their success in dealing with economic issues. Furthermore, the economy is the basis for much of the nitty-gritty of politics from debates during political campaigns and elections and the platforms of political parties, to the types of interest groups that lobby government, to debates about budget decisions and raising revenues to fund government. In turn, political decisions can affect the nature of the economy today and in the future, such as those regarding taxation, encouraging Outside investment, the extent of infrastructure, and so on.

Political economy refers to the interplay of the economy with politics, including the way the economy of a particular place affects its political system, the policy process, and policies. Different economies produce different issues and present different policy choices. These differences will be seen in the contrast between Alaska and other states explained in this and the next chapter.

Some view Alaska's economy with unbounded optimism. Others are less sanguine. The following statements by two prominent Alaskans illustrate these differing views: "I describe Alaska today as a diamond, a brilliant star, a state with an outstanding quality of life, a glorious natural environment, and an economy with enormous potential."[1] These are the words of Wally Hickel, twice Alaska governor, and one-time U.S. Secretary of the Interior, who long touted his vision of an Owner State to policy makers and the Alaska public. In contrast, in the words of long-time Alaska economist George Rogers, "the realistic option for policymakers is to come to grips with the limitations of the Alaska economy."[2]

These contrasting perspectives represent two views across a spectrum of the possibilities and potential of the Alaska economy. Some strongly believe that a combination of Alaska's plentiful natural resources and the right government policies are the key to unlocking the state's economic potential. Others view Alaska's economy as unbalanced, precarious, and too reliant on a few basic sectors (natural resources, government, and defense) to ever become anything more. While there is some truth to both views, neither is wholly accurate.

The purpose of this and the next chapter is to explain the realities of the Alaska economy and the choices open to the state. The two chapters show that the nature of Alaska's political economy presents constraints and opportunities as well as some challenging choices to policy makers. This chapter provides an overview of the structure of the Alaska economy and how it affects the power dynamics within the state's policy process. Building on this overview, Chapter 7 considers the significant relationship of the state's economy with other economies in the nation and abroad, and discusses how this relationship affects the economic and political options open to state policy makers.

Together, both chapters provide illustrations of several of the characteristics of Alaska politics identified in Chapter 2. The four most prominent are the significant role of external economic and political forces, the all-pervasive importance of government, aspects of regionalism (in this case differences between urban and rural-bush areas), and the myths and misunderstandings of Alaska's political discourse. Aspects of four other characteristics are also evident: the prominent role of Alaska Natives in state politics, the conflict between economic development and environmentalism, the political culture of pragmatic dependent individualism, and the element of self-proclaimed fiscal conservatism.

This chapter is divided into several sections. The first explains some important economic and related terms used in this chapter and in Chapter 7. Contrasting the myths and misconceptions about Alaska's economy with the realities is the subject of the second section. Sections 3 and 4 provide an overview of Alaska's economy compared with other states and the nation as well as details on Alaska's economy. The prospects for economic development and diversity in Alaska are considered next, followed by an explanation of the elements and power dynamics of Alaska's political economy.[3] The conclusion provides the link to Chapter 7.[4]

1. ESSENTIAL ECONOMIC TERMS

Box 6.1 explains terms specific to this chapter and to Chapter 7. These terms are essential for understanding basic economic theory, the structure of Alaska's economy, and the characteristics of the state's political economy. In addition, two other terms require particular emphasis—basic and support industries.

BOX 6.1

Economic Terms, Concepts, and Acronyms

Business cycle: Long-term, recurring fluctuations in business activity characteristic of diverse market economies. The cycle occurs in the following sequence: growth, prosperity, decline, recession, growth, and so on. The cycle is largely self-correcting. Its effects can be mitigated through government fiscal and monetary policies, as well as prosperous economic sectors that can keep the economy buoyant during recessions.

Comparative advantage: Where one country, region, state, or locality has a cost advantage in producing a good or service over other places. That is, it can produce a product at lower cost and often at higher quality.

Depression: A long-term downturn in economic activity over several years due to major dislocations in a nation's economy, often resulting in widespread business bankruptcies and closures and high unemployment. The Great Depression of the 1930s is an example. See also **recession**, below.

Economic drivers: The most important economic activities, which provide the foundation of an economy by generating the bulk of employment and income.

Economic outputs: Products of an economy and the four main categories of employment. In Alaska, these include the following:

> **Natural resources** are raw materials extracted from the environment, such as oil, fish, minerals, and timber. Since the 1970s, this definition has been broadened to include environmental assets, such as beautiful scenery and wild animals.
>
> **Manufactured products** are made using natural resources and other inputs such as labor, machinery, and energy.
>
> **Services** are economic outputs other than natural resources or goods—such as dental care, education, legal advice, and haircuts.
>
> **Government** produces many economic outputs from services, including education, to goods, such as owning a dairy or through prison industries. The wages and benefits government pays to its employees and the various payments to citizens, such as social security, are also economic outputs. Government spending is often seen as less legitimate than that of the private sector, but it has the same effect economically as that of private spending.

Economies of Scale: Cost savings resulting from producing a product or service on a larger scale or volume. Typically, as a factory, company, or region produces more of something, the cost per unit goes down. The unit cost of producing a book that sells a million copies is lower than one that sells a thousand copies.

Free trade: Where there are no barriers, such as tariffs or import quotas, to trade between countries or regions. Free trade usually results in certain products and services being produced in a location where the cost is lowest. See also, **comparative advantage**.

Gross Domestic Product (GDP): The total value of goods and services produced in a nation, state, or region, usually during a year. GDP is the measure used to compare how much different economies produce, and to calculate how rapidly an economy is growing. It includes labor income (wages, salaries, and other benefits), business taxes (excise, sales, property, and other taxes) and capital income (income earned by individual or joint business entrepreneurs, corporations, and income from capital and depreciation).

Gross Domestic Product Per Capita: The GDP divided by the population to give a per-person average.

Multiplier effect: An increase in economic activity; for example, a business hiring a hundred more workers starts a chain reaction and increases the level of activity in the economy overall, because the new workers buy groceries, gasoline, and clothes, and pay rent. The reverse occurs when workers are laid off. See **reverse multiplier effect**.

Natural resource extraction: Economic activity involving the production of a natural resource. Some types of resource extraction are nonrenewable (petroleum or other mineral production) because the resource is gone once produced. Other types (fish and game or timber) are renewable if properly managed.

Real Gross Domestic Product: The value of all goods and services in a year, adjusted to remove the effects of inflation.

Recession: A short-term downturn in economic activity for a year or two due to national factors or local circumstances, such as the closure of a manufacturing plant. See also, **depression**.

Remote region: A region that is geographically distant from major markets, is relatively sparsely settled, and has high costs due to climate, lack of infrastructure, or other factors. Alaska, northern Canada, northern Russia, and the Australian Outback (interior) are remote regions.

Reverse multiplier effect: A downward spiral of economic activity resulting from cutbacks in employment and/or private sector and government spending. This may cause layoffs leading to an economic **recession** or even a **depression**. See also, **multiplier effect**.

Value added/Value-added product: The increase in value from processing raw materials or goods calculated by the value of the final product less the cost of production. Gasoline is a value-added product made from crude oil, and frozen fish sticks a value-added product made from fish.

Source: Developed by the author.

Basic versus Support Industries

Economists use the term *basic* for industries (broadly defined to mean economic activities, businesses, or sectors of the economy) that sell primarily to markets outside a particular economy, and the term *support* for industries that sell primarily to markets inside the economy. Basic industries bring money into an economy; support industries depend on money circulating within the economy. An example will make this clear.

Suppose an Alaska fisherman earns $1,000 from selling fish to a company in Idaho. If he spends $800 of this income in Alaska on groceries and clothes, that creates an additional $800 of income in Alaska's retail industries. If those working in retailing then spend $600 of that income in Alaska on movies and restaurant meals, that creates $600 more income in Alaska's entertainment and food service industries. Economists call this chain reaction of spending the multiplier effect. As the original *basic* income from fishing circulates through the Alaska economy, it is *multiplied* into additional income in a wide variety of *support* industries.

While both basic and support industries provide jobs and income for Alaskans, basic industries are particularly important as they bring money into the economy from sources outside of it. Each basic Alaska job may be multiplied to create several additional support jobs.

2. MYTHS AND MISCONCEPTIONS VERSUS THE REALITIES OF ALASKA'S ECONOMY

Separating the myths and misconceptions from the realities of the state's economy is important for two reasons. It helps in understanding the development of Alaska's economy, its present condition, and future prospects. It also throws light on the challenges and opportunities open to Alaska's policy makers regarding economic policy.

Myths and Misconceptions

Of the various myths and misconceptions that have developed about Alaska's economy, six are most prominent. One is that Alaska's economic potential is stymied by the federal government because it has a stranglehold on the state through land ownership and regulation. Second, a related contention is that Alaska has boundless economic potential if only Outside forces would not block the state from developing them. These forces include Lower 48 and international environmental interests that oppose, for instance, opening the Arctic National Wildlife Refuge (ANWR) to oil and gas exploration. These first two points were long espoused by Wally Hickel and continue to be reiterated by politicians. For instance, U.S. Senator Lisa Murkowski, in her 2010 address to the Alaska Legislature, blamed the oppression of the federal government, litigation by public interest groups, and the federal court system for the state's inability to deal with its economic problems.[5]

Third, Alaska's geographical location on the crossroads between North America and East Asia gives it major economic potential that needs to be exploited by the right policies. Fourth, Alaska's abundant resources can attract major investments from Outside to provide both employment and revenues for the state. Fifth, if Alaska can work the previous four situations to its advantage, it can diversify its economy and be insulated from national and international economic fluctuation. And sixth, Alaska should become less dependent on government and develop its private sector more.

There is certainly some legitimacy to all these viewpoints, but for the most part they are a combination of wishful thinking, political grandstanding by politicians, misunderstandings and, in some cases, plain ignorance. Each is dealt with in more depth in various chapters in the book.[6] Here we examine the general realities of the Alaska economy. Then, later in the chapter, we go into more detail on the realities of economic diversity and development and what these realities mean for the power relationships within Alaska's political economy.

The Realities of Alaska's Economy

Several realities of Alaska's economy work in combination to limit both economic potential and the political options of policy makers. But the realities also provide some policy opportunities.

Probably the most obvious and fundamental reality is that the Alaska economy is part of a national and international capitalist or free enterprise economic system. Added to this is that within the United States and among most Western countries there is virtually free trade. In this free enterprise system, prices are, more or less, determined by the market through supply and demand. That is, goods and services are produced at the lowest possible cost and sold at the highest price the market will bear.

Within this system, businesses often have little or no control over the prices for their products. Prices are determined by larger market forces. In some cases world markets may set the prices. Moreover, goods will be produced and some services will be provided more efficiently (that is, at a lower cost) in some places than in others. Iowa, Kansas, and Nebraska produce wheat and corn more efficiently than New England, and China produces all sorts of goods cheaper than companies in the United States. These places are said to have a comparative advantage in cost, partly because they can also take advantage of economies of scale (see Box 6.1).

Another significant factor is that the Alaska economy is unbalanced. It is a "two-crop economy" in terms of the basic industries that bring money into the economy—natural resource extraction and federal government spending. There is virtually no agriculture and minimal manufacturing in the state.

The major natural resource industry and economic driver is oil, with minerals, forest products, and fishing also of importance. As to the government's role in the two-crop economy, a distinction needs to be made between the federal government and that of state and local governments. State and local governments are certainly major employers, but they are not basic industries because they do not bring Outside money into the state. The federal government, by contrast, is a major source of funds from Outside, and for this reason it is the other basic industry acting as an economic driver in Alaska.

Statistics regarding the economic importance of oil and the federal government are revealing. Depending on which data source is used and depending on the year, between 75 and 95 percent of the annual own-source revenues of state government come from oil and gas taxes and royalties. Moreover, the Institute of Social and Economic Research (ISER) at the University of Alaska Anchorage has estimated that one in three Alaska jobs depends on oil development and 96,000 jobs are supported by federal government spending. In 2004, for instance, the federal government spent $8.4 billion in Alaska, almost as much as all wages paid by private industry. This rose to $12.6 billion by 2010, almost double the $6.6 billion just ten years earlier, but federal spending was not increasing as rapidly after 2008. Even so, federal spending in Alaska that year was still over 70 percent above the national average at $17,762 per capita versus $10,460. This ranked Alaska number one in per capita federal spending in 2010.[7]

State and local governments are not entirely support industries, however. They can be seen as partly basic industries because so much of the funding that pays for state and local government comes directly from oil taxes and royalties. In effect, the Outside buyers of Alaska's oil pay not only for the employees who operate the oil fields, but also a large share of state and local government employees. Depending on the year, combining federal, state, and local levels, Alaska is always in the top five of the fifty states and often first in the percentage of its workforce employed by government.

Because Alaska has only a few viable industries, government spending is very important because of its multiplier effect on the economy. Through direct payments to individuals, such as federal social security to senior citizens and wages to federal, state, and local employees, money is put in the hands of Alaskans to pay rent and mortgages, buy gas and groceries, and help keep the private sector in Alaska, particularly consumer services, a viable part of the economy. So clearly, a reduction in government spending has a reverse multiplier effect by reducing government payments and employment and the money that could be used for consumer spending.

A third reality of the Alaska economy is the boom-bust cycle. This rollercoaster pattern of economic activity is a result of alternating between a multiplier and a reverse multiplier effect. The boom-bust cycle is, however, different from the normal business cycle. The latter is common to all market economies, but boom-bust cycles are more prevalent in natural resource and defense-based economies such as Alaska. The prices of natural resources are subject to world market forces and other external economic and political influences, such as the actions of the Organization of the Petroleum Exporting Countries (OPEC), of which the United States (and, therefore, Alaska) is not a member. In combination, these economic and political forces result in the volatility of the world prices of natural resources as demand for them fluctuates. Reductions in federal defense spending after wars and budget cutbacks in peacetime also affect the economy. Box 6.2 outlines the history of this cycle in Alaska.

Another reality affecting the Alaska economy is the influence of geography, which affects Alaska's economy in three major ways. First, the harsh climate precludes commercial agriculture of any economic importance in contrast to the situation in most of the other forty-nine states. Second, being both noncontiguous with the rest of the nation and in a remote region, the cost of shipping goods to and from Alaska is high compared with states on a road, rail, or river system. Third, Alaska's sheer size and physical geography have limited the extent of roads and railroads, particularly in rural-bush areas. This makes shipping goods within Alaska expensive, particularly to remote villages.

Geographical location and small population are contributing factors to two more economic realities. Alaska has among the highest labor costs in the nation. High labor

BOX 6.2

Alaska's Boom-and-Bust Cycle History

FROM RUSSIAN RULE TO WORLD WAR II

Even before World War II, Alaska had a long experience with boom-and-bust cycles. The first cycle began under Russian rule as the fur seal and sea otter harvests declined in the mid-nineteenth century. After the United States purchased Alaska in 1867, the economy was primarily one of commercial fishing, hard-rock mining, and fur trading, all of which experienced booms and busts. Building the Alaskan Railroad (1914–1923) and the layoffs once it was completed produced another boom-bust cycle.

WORLD WAR II AND COLD WAR SPENDING

Japan's 1942 invasion of the Aleutians was the beginning of a major military presence in Alaska and produced another boom. The onset of the Cold War in the late 1940s and the construction of detection, interception, and retaliatory systems in Alaska sustained a boom in the construction industry for two decades. The breakup of the Soviet Union in 1991 created a peace dividend for the world but extensively reduced one of Alaska's most important economic sectors—military installations. In 1995 the Federal Base Closure and Realignment Commission announced that the Adak naval base on the Aleutian Islands would close, effectively eliminating Alaska's eighth largest city.

OIL BOOM AND THE 1980s CRASH

In 1968, Atlantic Richfield announced its oil discoveries at Prudhoe Bay on Alaska's North Slope, and in 1969 a consortium was created to construct the trans-Alaska pipeline system (TAPS). When it was being built, average monthly construction employment surpassed the defense construction levels of the 1950s. The first shipment of crude through the pipeline occurred in 1977. The timing for Alaska could not have been better. The Organization of the Petroleum Exporting Countries (OPEC) drove up the world price of crude from $3 a barrel in the early 1970s to a high of $30 in the early 1980s. State revenues increased fourteen-fold from 1972 to 1984 and the size of state government nearly doubled in these years.

However, the bust inevitably reoccurred. Between November 1985 and April 1986 the price of oil fell from $30 per barrel to $10 and dipped even lower for a brief period. As a result, state revenues fell dramatically, layoffs occurred in government and the private sector, real estate values were cut in half, and an estimated 30,000 people left the state.

SINCE THE LATE 1980s

Oil prices rose again as a result of the Gulf War of 1990, but fluctuated for the next fifteen years. Beginning in 2004 they began to rise considerably and reached almost $150 in mid-2008. While the global economic downturn in the summer of 2008 certainly affected Alaska, high oil prices cushioned the state against major cuts and kept government employment fairly stable. Because oil prices remained high and stable at around $100 a barrel from 2010 to mid-2014, employment remained strong. But another bust was on the way. With oil prices dropping to less than $40 a barrel between June 2014 and January 2016, the next bust had arrived.

Source: Developed by the author.

costs plus the fact that most products have to be shipped into the state increase the costs of services and manufacturing. Moreover, high labor costs make producing manufactured goods uneconomical compared with low-cost labor in southern states, such as South Carolina and Alabama, not to mention in China. In addition, because of its small population, Alaska does not have a large enough internal market to take advantage of economies of scale in production of goods or processing raw materials. Even with lower production costs, Alaska would still need to sell its excess manufactured or processed goods elsewhere, but shipping costs would make many of these products uncompetitive.

The Economic and Political Consequences of the Realities

In combination, these realities show why the myths and misconceptions about the Alaska economy are, in fact, distortions of the actual situation. The unbalanced nature of the economy imposes many constraints on the state's policy makers, not just regarding economic issues but on a whole range of other policy choices. At the same time, Alaska's economy, particularly the financial bonanza from oil revenues, has given Alaska politicians many opportunities enjoyed by few other states, and over the years some wise economic policies have been developed. However, many economic policies have resulted from purely political forces, both from within and outside the state, and have not been based on sound economics.

The interaction of economic reality (as well as economic wishful thinking) with political values and political pressures gives Alaska's political economy its particular characteristics. The details of these characteristics, constraints, challenges, and opportunities will make more sense by first comparing Alaska's economy to those of other states and the nation.

3. ALASKA'S ECONOMY COMPARED TO OTHER STATES AND THE NATION

Table 6.1 compares the Alaska economy with five states and the nation in 2009.[8] Although the total figures may change from one year to the next, 2009 is typical of Alaska compared to other states since the early 1980s and is likely to be so for the foreseeable future. The comparison uses general statistics and distribution of types of employment classified by economic outputs. Of particular importance is total and per capita gross domestic product (GDP) by state. GDP by state is the counterpart to national GDP and is the sum of GDP originating in all industries in a state.

The broad category of "primary production" is often replaced with "natural resources" in referring to Alaska's economy. Even though the percentage of those employed in the natural resource sector in Alaska is very low, it is much larger than in most states. In 2008, for example, Alaska's share of employment in natural resource industries was eight times as high as for the United States overall (4.00 compared with 0.5 percent), and the share of Alaska's GDP created by natural resources was more than ten times the fifty-state average (30.3 versus 2.9 percent).[9]

The service sector, everything from health care to education to legal services, is by far the largest employment sector nationally and in all states. It has replaced much of the

TABLE 6.1

Placing Alaska's Economy in Perspective: Comparisons with Selected States and the United States in 2009

	ALASKA	CALIFORNIA	WYOMING	INDIANA	NEW HAMPSHIRE	KANSAS	UNITED STATES
General Statistics							
Total Population	698,473	36,961,664	544,270	6,423,113	1,324,575	2,818,747	307,006,550
Gross Domestic Product, (GDP) $ millions	$41,656	$1,739,674	$32,943	$240,833	$54,454	$114,615	$12,903,778
GDP Per Capita	$59,639	$47,067	$60,527	$37,495	$41,111	$40,662	$42,031
Number of Fortune 500 Companies	0	98	0	15	1	7	500
Type of Employment as a Percentage of Total Persons Employed*							
Primary Production	4.4%	2.3%	9.8%	0.7%	0.4%	1.5%	1.4%
Manufacturing	3.7%	8.5%	3.1%	15.4%	10.7%	11.8%	8.7%
Services	47.7%	59.3%	46.9%	55.4%	62.5%	53.3%	58.7%
Government	30.9%	17.9%	25.0%	16.0%	15.1%	21.1%	18.0%
Other	13.3%	12.0%	15.2%	12.6%	11.3%	12.5%	13.3%

* See Box 6.1, "Economic Outputs," for definitions of types of employment.

Sources: U.S. Bureau of Economic Analysis (2010). Advance 2009 and Revised 1963–2008 GDP-by-State Statistics. Retrieved from http://www.bea.gov/newsreleases/regional/gdp_state/2010/pdf/gsp1110.pdf; U.S. Bureau of Economic Analysis (2010). Full-time and part-time wage and salary employment by NAICS industry (1990-2009). Retrieved from http://www.bea.gov/regional/spi/default.cfm? selTable=SA27N&selSeries=NAICS; U.S. Census Bureau (2010). National and State Population Estimates. Retrieved from http://www.census.gov/popest/states/NST-ann-est.html; Fortune Magazine (2010). Annual Ranking of America's Largest Corporations 2009. Retrieved from http://money.cnn.com/magazines/fortune/fortune500/2009/states/KS.html.

employment in America's declining manufacturing sector. As protection against a downturn in economic activity in a particular sector, the more balanced or diversified a national or state economy is in its distribution among the four sectors—primary production, manufacturing, services, and government—the more stable the economy is likely to be.

The states included in Table 6.1 represent a range of types and sizes of economies. California is the largest by state GDP. It is also one of the most diversified and is home to almost a fifth of the five hundred largest companies in the nation, the so-called Fortune 500 as published in *Fortune* magazine. California accounted for over 13 percent of national GDP in 2009. Indiana (ranked sixteenth with just under 2 percent of national GDP), Kansas (ranked thirty-first with just under 1 percent), and New Hampshire (ranked forty-first with less than one-half of 1 percent) are much smaller when measured by state GDP, but all have more or less balanced economies. Wyoming is one of the smallest (ranked forty-seventh with about one-quarter of 1 percent of national GDP) and is one of the least diversified.

Table 6.1 also shows that Alaska's economy is one of the smallest in the nation, falling midway among the bottom ten of the fifty states. It ranked forty-fifth in state GDP in 2009, and accounted for less than one-third of 1 percent (about one three-hundredth) of the national GDP. Like Wyoming, Alaska has a relatively undiversified economy with a heavy reliance on government employment. Hovering around 30 percent in recent years, Alaska's level of government employment is more than ten percentage points above the national average and one of the highest of all states. Also, like Wyoming, Alaska had no Fortune 500 companies based in the state. Large companies do operate in Alaska but are all based out of state.

From four other perspectives, however, Alaska has done well economically in recent years as compared to other states. First, measured by real gross state domestic product (state GDP adjusted for inflation) the state's economy grew between 2 and 4 percent from 2005–2014. Second, Alaska has long ranked in the top ten states in terms of per capita state GDP, often in the top five. Third, Alaska has reflected the low level of inflation in the nation in recent years and often has an inflation rate below the national average. And fourth, unemployment in Alaska following the economic downturn in 2008 was consistently close to two points below the national average, hovering around 7 to 8 percent in 2010 compared with 9 to 10 percent nationally. Though as the nation recovered, by 2014 it was about at the national average of 6 to 7 percent. This buoyancy in the state's economy following the recession of 2008 was due less to national factors than to some purely Alaska circumstances, particularly the role of oil in the economy.

4. A CLOSER LOOK AT ALASKA'S ECONOMY—IN REALITY, THE STATE'S TWO ECONOMIES

As the researchers at ISER have pointed out, in reality, there are two economies in Alaska, one in urban Alaska and one in rural-bush Alaska.[10] So while the state's economy is similar to that of other states in many ways, it does have some different, even unique aspects. To illustrate these differences, first we explain the particulars of what in effect is Alaska's urban economy and then the features of the rural-bush economy. The development, structure, and types of employment, plus the makeup of the private sector business community, tell much about the uniqueness of the state's economy.

The Development of the Alaska Economy

Today, Alaska's economy is just as dependent upon natural resource extraction and federal government spending as it was in 1959. The characteristics and importance of these two basic industries and major economic drivers have changed considerably, however, and other developments give Alaska's contemporary economy a much different makeup than in 1959.

During its first fifty years of statehood, Alaska's population more than tripled, from about 225,000 in 1959 to over 700,000 in 2010 (and is estimated to be 800,000 by 2020). Many members of the state's expanding workforce found employment in the rapidly growing service sector and in state and local government. Three particular developments helped transform Alaska's economy and its political economy into their present form.

By far the major development was the discovery of oil on the North Slope and the completion in 1977 of the 800-mile-long trans-Alaska pipeline (TAPS) from Prudhoe Bay to the ice-free port of Valdez in Prince William Sound. Since then, oil has far outstripped Alaska's original natural resource industries of mining, fishing, and timber as the foundation of the state's economy, though mining and fishing are still important. Oil revenues made possible the second major development in the Alaska economy, the creation of the Alaska Permanent Fund in 1976, which contained over $52 billion in December 2015. A third important development is the result of the Alaska Native Claims Settlement Act (ANCSA) of 1971. ANCSA established thirteen regional for-profit corporations to manage the land and money given to the Alaska Native community in exchange for extinguishing aboriginal land claims to enable the Alaska pipeline to be built. ANCSA also provided for nonprofit Alaska Native regional and village corporations to be formed to administer federal (and later state) programs for health, housing, and other social services.

Alaska's Contemporary Economy

Alaska's present-day economy is characterized by dominance of the oil industry, a major presence of the federal government, and by an undiversified distribution of employment.

The Oil Industry and the Permanent Fund Dividend

Without oil, Alaska's economy would be half its present size and 300,000 fewer people would live in the state. This is largely because oil revenues provide a giant portion of state expenditures despite the fact that the oil industry has less than 3 percent of total Alaska employment. A study by ISER calculated that in 2006 oil supplied each Alaskan with $13,150 worth of government services and government aid. By comparison, Alaska's economy without oil would look like that of Maine, which in 2006 ranked forty-third in the nation in terms of output per resident. Another way that oil increased the income of Alaskans is by financing the Permanent Fund Dividend (PFD) program. Begun in 1982, this dividend program provides an annual payment made from Permanent Fund earnings to each Alaskan who has been a resident for at least a year. The payments have ranged from just under $400 in the early years to more than $2,000 in recent years and have averaged around $1,200.[11] So with the PFD and totaling up all the other financial benefits in Alaska (higher paychecks, lower taxes, and so on) and even after accounting for higher prices, the average Alaska family has a $50,000 per year advantage over a family in Maine.[12]

PFDs have several effects on the day-to-day operation of the economy, especially in the fall when they are paid. ISER estimates that every $1 million in PFD payments supports 9.5 jobs in the private sector. In 2005, this translated into roughly 5,300 jobs that were supported because of the dividend. Dividends also help to reduce poverty. ISER estimated that without the PFD twice as many Anchorage residents would have been below the federal poverty line in 2000.[13] Plus, the PFD is one of the major sources of cash in rural-bush Alaska.

Dependence on oil revenues is a double-edged financial sword, however. On the one hand, high oil prices—$80 a barrel and higher—produce stability and often the foundation for economic growth in Alaska. High oil prices can also insulate Alaska from national downturns as was the case after the 2008 economic recession. On the other hand, largely because the price of Alaska's natural resources is subject to world market fluctuations and the boom-bust cycle, the state is vulnerable to economic instability. National policies can help reduce instability to some extent, as with President Obama's stimulus package of 2009–2010. Beyond that, and unlike states with more balanced economies, growth and stability in Alaska are more problematic.

Alaska oil production peaked in 1988 at more than two million barrels a day, but declined to hover around 500,000 barrels a day by the end of 2014. This decline is expected to continue as production from Alaska's oldest and largest oil fields, particularly the giant Prudhoe Bay field, declines. The increase in production from newer, smaller oil fields is not sufficient to make up for this decline.[14] When lower production is coupled with lower oil prices as was the case from mid-2014 through early 2016, it has a significant effect on the economy and presents Alaska's policy makers with major challenges.

The Role of the Federal Government

The federal government's impact on the economy is also far greater than the size of Alaska's federal civilian workforce would indicate. Estimated at about 16,400 in 2012, federal employees made up just 4.9 percent of Alaska's total full-time workforce, represented about 7.2 percent of wages, and brought in about a billion dollars to the economy.[15] In addition, the federal government has major military installations (with close to 24,000 personnel located in the state and an estimated additional 6,000 civilian employees). The federal government also makes direct payments to Alaskans, such as Social Security. It also provides grants and other funds to state and local governments and funds a range of programs from highways to the Indian Health Service. This all adds up to the federal government making a major contribution to the Alaska economy.

TABLE 6.2

Alaska Wage and Salary Employment 1990-2012

	TOTAL EMPLOYMENT FOLLOWED BY PERCENTAGE OF TOTAL									
	1990		2000		2005		2009		2012	
Total Employment	269,848	100%	307,475	100%	335,796	100%	351,261	100%	365,281	100%
Primary Production[1]	14,536	5.4	11,514	3.7	11,355	3.4	15,540	4.4	17,259	4.7
Manufacturing[2]	14,024	5.2	11,964	3.9	12,566	3.7	12,867	3.7	13,929	3.8
Services[3]	107,813	40.0	142,054	46.2	161,871	48.2	167,366	47.6	177,605	48.6
Government[4]	99,455	36.9	96,681	31.4	101,327	30.2	108,655	30.9	108,934	29.8
Other[5]	34,020	12.6	45,262	14.7	48,677	14.5	46,833	13.3	47,554	13.0

[1] Primary production: forestry, fishing, and related activities; mining; oil and gas extraction; farm wage and salary employment. (Farm wage and salary employment is the number of hired laborers engaged in the direct production of agricultural commodities, either livestock or crops.)

[2] Manufacturing: fish processing. particularly canning salmon; boat building; food production; wood products; handicrafts and specialty Alaska products, such as jams.

[3] Services: utilities; wholesale trade; retail trade; real estate and rental and leasing; health care and social assistance services; educational services; information; administrative and waste services; accommodations and food services; art, entertainment, and recreation services; professional, scientific, and technical; other services, except public administration.

[4] Government: federal, state, and local government.

[5] Other: construction; transportation and warehousing; finance and insurance; management of companies and enterprises

Source: Bureau of Economic Analysis (2010). Full-time and part-time wage and salary employment by NAICS industry (1990-2009). Retrieved from http://www.bea.gov/regional/spi/default.cfm? selTable=SA27N&selSeries=NAICS; and Bureau of Economic Analysis (2014). Regional Data: GDP and Personal Income. Retrieved from http://www.bea.gov/iTable/iTable.cfm?reqid=70&step=1&isuri=1&acrdn=4#reqid=70&step=1&isuri=1.

The Distribution of Employment

By far the major sectors of employment are government and services. Table 6.2 lists the major employment sectors for five different years between 1990 and 2012.

While the overall number of those employed has steadily risen as the population has increased, the percentage of employment among the major sectors has remained more or less the same.

Figure 6.1 provides another perspective on employment in Alaska. It groups jobs by goods-producing sectors and by services-producing sectors for 2009, which is a typical recent year since the late 1980s, and again, is likely to be similar for some years to come. The retail trade dominates the goods-producing sectors followed by construction, manufacturing, and natural resource extraction. The services-producing sector is led by education and health (health care being a major source of job growth since 2000), followed by leisure and hospitality (in large part dependent on tourism), closely followed by professional and business services.

FIGURE 6.1

Goods and Services Producing Employment in Alaska by Sector in 2009

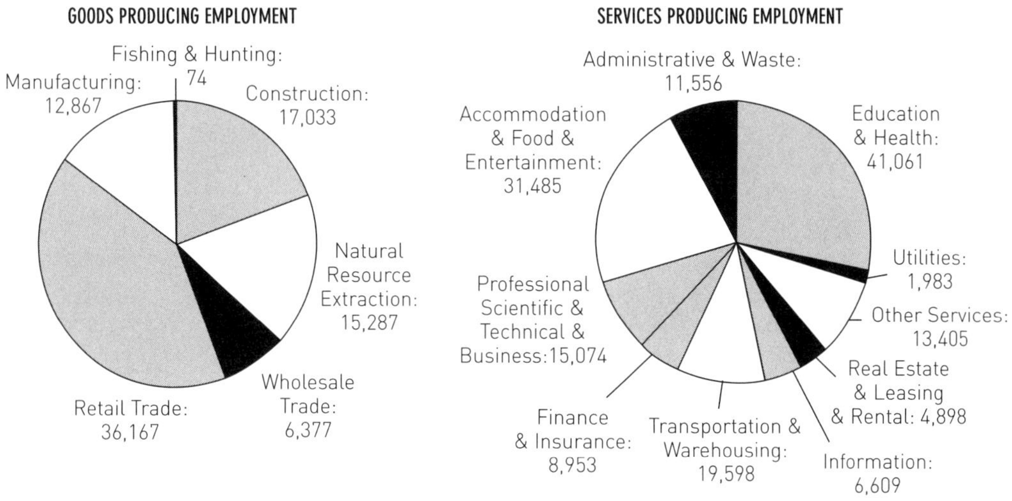

Source: Based on information gathered for Box 6.2; U.S. Bureau of Economic Analysis (2010). Full-time and part-time wage and salary employment by NAICS industry (1990-2009). Retrieved from http://www.bea.gov/regional/spi/default.cfm? selTable=SA27N&selSeries=NAICS.

Regarding the major private employers in the state, as Table 6.3 shows, in 2010 only three of the top ten were based in the state. Six were based in the Lower 48 and one, British Petroleum, in the United Kingdom.[16] When it comes to Alaska-based companies, in 2013 eight out of the top ten were Native corporations. In fact, as Table 6.4 shows, fifteen of the top twenty were Native corporations. As they own about 11 percent of Alaska's land (and the resources both on and below the land), these corporations are the largest private landowners in the state.[17]

The Rural-Bush Economy

The rural-bush economy is Alaska's "other economy"—one quite different from the urban economy and from economies in the rest of the nation. This is because of the remoteness of rural-bush areas, difficulty of access, sparse population, lack of employment opportunities, and minimal private business activity. Even though only about 10 percent of Alaskans live in rural-bush areas, this is where Alaska Natives are concentrated and comprise the majority of residents.[18]

As a consequence, while the rural-bush economy has little activity associated with highly specialized money-based economies, it does incorporate aspects of both traditional Native culture and recent aspects of Native political agreements and settlements like ANCSA. These aspects include the role of for-profit and nonprofit regional and village corporations,

TABLE 6.3

Home Office Locations of Alaska's Ten Largest Employers in 2010

RANK	COMPANY	AVERAGE MONTHLY EMPLOYMENT	BUSINESS ACTIVITY	HOME OFFICE LOCATION
1	Providence Health System	4,000+	Hospital/medical center	United States (non-Alaska)
2	Walmart/Sam's Club	3,000 to 3,249	Grocery/general merchandise	United States (non-Alaska)
3	Carrs/Safeway	2,750 to 2,999	Grocery	United States (non-Alaska)
4	Fred Meyer	2,500 to 2,759	Grocery/general merchandise	United States (non-Alaska)
5	ASRC Energy Services Alaska	2,500 to 2,759	Oil field services	Alaska (Native Corporation)
6	Trident Seafoods	2,250 to 2,499	Seafood processing	United States (non-Alaska)
7	BP Exploration Alaska	2,000 to 2,249	Oil and gas extraction	United Kingdom
8	CH2M HILL	1,750 to 1,999	Oil field services	United States (non-Alaska)
9	NANA Management Services	1,750 to 1,999	Catering/lodging/security	Alaska (Native Corporation)
10	Alaska Native Tribal Health Consortium (ANTHC)	1500 to 1,749	Hospital/medical center	Alaska

Source: Alaska Department of Labor and Workforce Development, "Alaska's 100 Largest Private Sector Employers in 2010," *Alaska Economic Trends* (July 2011), retrieved from http://laborstats.alaska.gov/lgstemp/lgstemp.htm. In 2011, *Alaska Economic Trends* discontinued its 100 largest employer list.

which provide employment and cash income as well as various services, including day care for children, in-home care for the disabled and elderly, and health services.

Table 6.5 (on page 184) provides an overview of the contributions of different activities to the rural-bush economy in 2007, the latest year for which comprehensive estimates are available. By far the largest contributions come from government activities. The federal government dominates the in-flows of cash to rural-bush Alaska in the form of grants, wages to federal employees, and payments to individuals and to federal contractors. Various forms of state government spending come next, with education spending representing the major portion. The cost of providing most services to rural-bush areas is much higher per capita than to urban areas because of access problems, lack of economies of scale, and higher costs of labor and energy. The next largest contributor to the region's economy is the extraction of natural resources, such as oil, minerals, and fish. We have already mentioned the PFD's contribution to the rural-bush economy. Activities based on Native cultural traditions, such as handicrafts, subsistence hunting and fishing, and herding, are also important. The unique nature of the rural-bush economy has produced some interesting political dynamics in Alaska, which are briefly considered later in the chapter.

TABLE 6.4

Top Twenty Alaska-Based Businesses in 2013

2013 RANK	2012 REVENUE $ MILLIONS	COMPANY	2010 RANK	HEAD-QUARTERS	TYPE OF BUSINESS	2012 ALASKA EMPLOYEES
1	$2,628.9	Arctic Slope Regional Corporation	1	Barrow	Native Organization	4,525
2	$1,961.7	Bristol Bay Native Corporation	2	Anchorage	Native Organization	818
3	$1,800.0	NANA Development Corporation	3	Anchorage	Native Organization	5,300
4	$1,100.0	Chenega Corporation	5	Anchorage	Native Organization	520
5	$885.0	Lynden Transport	7	Anchorage	Transportation	740
6	$709.0	Chugach Alaska Corporation	4	Anchorage	Native Organization	586
7	$534.6	Afognak Native Corp./Alutiiq	6	Kodiak	Native Organization	179
8	$404.2	Calista Corporation	16	Anchorage	Native Organization	272
9	$338.2	Doyon, Limited	10	Fairbanks	Native Organization	1,331
10	$338.0	Alaska USA Federal Credit Union	11	Anchorage	Finance	1,357
11	$312.4	Ukpeagvik Inupiat Corporation	9	Barrow	Native Organization	475
12	$311.6	Sealaska	17	Juneau	Native Organization	108
13	$266.9	Chugach Electric Association, Inc	12	Anchorage	Utilities	332
14	$254.3	The Wilson Agency, LLC	15	Anchorage	Finance, Insurance	19
15	$237.8	Cook Inlet Region, Inc.	43	Anchorage	Native Organization	1,189
16	$218.0	Davis Constructors & Engineers, Inc.	23	Anchorage	Construction	150
17	$213.0	Bering Straits Native Corporation	21	Anchorage	Native Organization	551
18	$198.6	Olgoonik Corporation	16	Wainwright	Native Organization	180
19	$190.0	Ahtna, Inc	14	Glennallen	Native Organization	276
20	$187.00	US Travel	20	Anchorage	Tourism	157

Note: 2013 rank is based on 2012 revenue, and 2010 rank on 2009 revenue.

Source: *Alaska Business Monthly* (October 2013), retrieved from http://www.akbizmag.com/Alaska-Business-Monthly/October-2013/Alaska-Business-Monthlys-2013-Top-49ers-Blockbusters-of-Business; and *Alaska Business Monthly* (October 2010), retrieved from http://www.akbizmag.com/Alaska-Business-Monthly/October-2010/Alaska-Business-Monthlys-Top-49ers-Announced/.

5. PROSPECTS FOR ALASKA'S ECONOMIC FUTURE: ECONOMIC DEVELOPMENT AND ECONOMIC DIVERSITY

Economic development is the growth of economic wealth, jobs, or capital equipment (buildings, machinery, and so on) within a political unit, such as a city, state, or nation. Economic diversification occurs when an economy develops across several economic sectors, such as primary production, manufacturing, and services, to provide a balance in employment and wealth. For instance, a state might add to its major industry of motor vehicle production by producing computers, printing books and magazines, and manufacturing cosmetics.

TABLE 6.5

An Overview of Alaska's Rural-Bush Economy

ACTIVITY	ESTIMATED CONTRIBUTION TO RURAL-BUSH ECONOMY
Oil and gas	$10 million in payroll
Zinc mining	$9.2 million in payroll; $16.4 million in additional payments
Other mining	$20 million in production; $94 million in exploration and development
Bottom fishing	$12 million in payroll; $84 million in additional payments
Wild salmon	$20 million in payroll
Recreation and tourism	$50 million in expenditures by visitors
Arts and handicrafts	$10 million in sales
Furs, timber, and agricultural products	$200-400 thousand in reindeer products; fur harvest $1 million
Federal government	$878 million in grants, payments to individuals, agencies, and wages
State government	$250 million*
Permanent Fund Dividend—PFD	$66 million

* Figure is an estimate based on the share of the state population within rural-bush regions.

Source: Scott Goldsmith, "The Remote Rural Economy of Alaska," ISER, University of Alaska Anchorage, April 12, 2007.

While economic development in some places leads to economic diversification, as it has in countries like Germany and the United States and in states like Ohio and Indiana, this is not always the case. Often, development may simply be expansion in an existing sector, such as increasing primary production by extracting more natural resources, like coal or iron ore. The advantage of a diversified economy is that when one sector, such as agriculture, or parts of a sector become depressed, other sectors often remain steady and help the economy maintain some stability. In contrast, the lack of diversification makes an economy vulnerable to fluctuations in the prices of its products.

Alaska's potential for economic diversification is hindered by high costs of labor, construction, and shipping. Labor costs remain higher in Alaska than elsewhere in most occupations. Construction costs are also higher because of higher wage rates, plus the special requirements of the climate, such as more insulation from the cold, protection from the wet climate in Southeast Alaska, and protective building measures in areas vulnerable to earthquakes. Transportation and shipping costs are also higher than in the contiguous forty-eight states and rise as fuel costs increase. For rural-bush Alaska, construction equipment and materials must be transported great distances, increasing costs considerably. The distance from Alaska to major ports in the Lower 48 imposes a cost disadvantage for manufacturers seeking to locate in Alaska.

BOX 6.3

Renewable Energy as a Means of Economic Diversification

Coal, minerals, and especially oil have been important economic sectors in Alaska's economy. With oil production on the North Slope having peaked in January 1988, the legislature focused on the development of a natural gas pipeline. The high cost of energy is beneficial to the state treasury but is a burden on Alaska's smaller communities, which often heat with heating oil or diesel. Alaska also has a vast amount of renewable energy that could be developed and connected to British Columbia's Northwest Transmission Line and sold to British Columbia and the Lower 48 states.

Alaska has the potential to develop hydroelectric, wind, wave, geothermal, and solar power. This would add a new sector and some economic diversification to its economy. Development of many of these energy resources is currently being held back by lack of infrastructure to move it to market. If cheaper sources of electricity could be developed it would help both Alaska residents and businesses. Lower production costs could make Alaska more profitable to existing businesses and encourage others to locate in the state.

Source: Developed by Terry Otness, former assistant to the Director, Tlingit-Haida Central Council, Tribal Energy Program.

There has been some slight diversification in the Alaska economy as more services and retail outlets have opened operations, particularly to support the tourism industry. Alaska also has the opportunity to add renewable energy to its economic sectors as a way to further diversify the economy. This is explained in Box 6.3. Other possibilities for economic diversification are to develop economic sectors that are not reliant on transportation, such as education and information technology.

Economic development in Alaska is more possible than economic diversification. Even here, however, there are economic constraints and some political obstacles. The major economic ones are the state's geography, which limits the economic activities in which Alaska can be competitive, the fact that prices for Alaska's resources are determined by world markets over which the state has virtually no control, that prices for resources affect the profitability of firms operating in the state, and that the state has little control over federal policies that impact it.[19] Nevertheless, from an economic point of view, as Scott Goldsmith has pointed out, given the minimal potential for economic diversification, Alaska should worry less about diversification and focus more on economic development, particularly developing the oil resources on the North Slope.[20]

Alaska's Economic Future

In the future, Alaska's economy will very likely exhibit more of the same—an unbalanced natural resource economy supplemented by government. Oil will continue to be the major driver of the economy, but there is a growing sense of urgency to deal with the decline in oil production that began in 1988. Exploration is taking place on federal land in the National Petroleum Reserve-Alaska (NPR-A) on the North Slope west of Prudhoe Bay and, until the fall of 2015, in the Arctic. Whether or not other fields can be opened, like those in ANWR, and a natural gas pipeline built to compensate for this decline is uncertain, as, of course, are future oil prices as evidenced by the major fall in oil prices beginning in mid-2014.

Despite the 2008 economic downturn, stable and increasing federal spending has contributed to Alaska's twenty years of economic growth and job creation since the mid-1990s. However, mainly for political reasons, it is expected that federal spending will decrease in the future. Given the importance of federal monies to the state, this could be particularly serious for the economy and especially for employment. The question then is whether growth in other sectors or possible increases in state oil revenues will be enough to offset this loss in federal government dollars.

As in the past, economic reality will not always drive state policy in the future. In fact, in dealing with issues of economic development, policy makers will likely subordinate economic reality to political considerations, and economic policy will be the victim of a lack of understanding by some policy makers. Box 6.4 points out two realities of economic development that have often been the subject of misunderstanding or economic and political wishful thinking and will likely continue to be. Box 6.4 also brings into question some of the suggestions in Box 6.3 about renewable energy, even though the suggestions appear to make good sense and may be a smart move politically. It is to this melding of economics, politics, myths, misunderstandings, and wishful thinking that we now turn.

6. THE JUNCTURE OF ECONOMICS AND POLITICS: THE DIMENSIONS OF ALASKA'S POLITICAL ECONOMY

It is the various elements of Alaska's political economy, and not the structure of the economy or its economic realities, that influence public policy. An understanding of the state's political economy is best approached by considering four of its interrelated aspects: a broad description of its economic, political, and administrative characteristics; perspectives on its policy implications; its political cultural dimensions; and its changing power structure. The first three are briefly outlined in this section, the fourth is considered in Section 7.

BOX 6.4

Two Economic Development Realities

TRANSPORTATION INFRASTRUCTURE

One of the arguments often made to encourage economic development is for the government to build transportation infrastructure. While it is true that the lack of infrastructure raises the cost of production, it is not the only relevant cost. Transportation access is no guarantee that development projects would be competitive in world markets. Also, building a road does not make transportation inexpensive. Due to the long distances that must be traveled to many parts of Alaska, the cost of transporting goods would still be high. Infrastructure, such as roads and railroads, is not only expensive to build but also expensive to maintain—even more so in Alaska's harsh climate. Development of transportation infrastructure would have a short-term boom effect during construction, but it might not continue in the long term.

MAKE PUBLIC RESOURCES AVAILABLE

Many Alaskans argue that we should open up the resources under government control to development. Again, there are many potential problems. First, just because resources are available does not mean that it will be profitable to develop them. For instance, development of a natural gas pipeline from the North Slope to the Lower 48 (with perhaps a spur to Southcentral Alaska) has been on-again-off-again in recent years because of fluctuating gas prices and competition from fields in the Lower 48 where a gas pipeline infrastructure already exists. As of late 2015, low natural gas prices put the pipeline to the Lower 48 on hold and favored a line from the North Slope to Southcentral Alaska. Second, if resource prices might be higher in the future than at present it would be more valuable to develop them tomorrow rather than today. Third, sustainable practices must be used with renewable resources so they maintain their future value.

Source: Developed by Gunner Knapp and Clive Thomas.

Economic and Political Characteristics

Alaska's political economy is best described as one that is dependent on natural resources and the federal government and in which state government (including the Owner State) plays a significant role, combined with regional economic and political loyalties.

Alaska's economic dependence translates into considerable federal political influence (though there are other sources of federal power in Alaska), and the real and potential political influence of the oil industry and, to a lesser extent, mining and fishing interests. These economic forces do not have free reign, however. This is because state ownership and management of a third of Alaska's land, which includes the major oil deposits, provides a political counterweight, particularly to natural resource industries. Plus, state expenditures on state employment and services, and local government aid of various types, create a political power base for a range of government-related interests from public employees to local governments to school boards. Regional affiliations of both the public and of elected officials also affect the juncture of economics and politics and attitudes toward governmental economic policies.

To place Alaska's political economy in perspective, we can briefly compare it to Nevada and New York State. Nevada, with a population four times that of Alaska's, has an economy dominated by the gaming and the hospitality industry and by Las Vegas where 70 percent of the state's population lives. Government is much less activist than in Alaska, and there is no equivalent to the Owner State, despite large state land holdings. Service industry and education unions and ranching interests exert some countervailing power, but the gaming and hospitality industry is a dominant political force.[21]

In contrast, there is no one dominant political force in New York State's political economy. With close to twenty million people (nearly thirty times that of Alaska's population), all but 10 percent of whom live in urban areas, New York has one of the most diversified economies in the nation and is home to one in ten Fortune 500 companies. A complex regionalism characterizes the state, with New York City often pitted against "upstate" interests and the needs of the suburbs of the state's many large cities. Added to this are strong unions that have succeeded in promoting economic policies beneficial to their members and an activist government that seeks to improve the economic status of a socio-economically diverse population. There are also elements of social responsibility among segments of the electorate. As a result, power in New York State's political economy is shared by business, labor (both blue and white collar), and the sports and entertainment industries, among others.[22]

Perspectives on the Policy Implications

Here is it instructive to return to the two views of Alaska's economic potential mentioned at the beginning of the chapter, as they tell much about the policy approaches and mind-set of many Alaskan politicians and citizens. George Rogers, an economist by training, emphasized the limitations of the Alaska economy. He argued that although Alaska saw considerable development following statehood, the economy remained very unbalanced and dependent on natural resources. The economy continues to be vulnerable to the boom-bust cycle, and tapping many of Alaska's vast resources is simply not economically viable, despite the desires of politicians and the public. Given these limitations, Rogers saw long-term planning and use of the Permanent Fund and its earnings as Alaska's best economic options.[23]

In contrast, Wally Hickel, one of Alaska's most successful businessmen, had almost boundless entrepreneurial optimism. In his view, Alaska's economy could be whatever Alaskans want it to be, with riches just waiting to be tapped. Over the years, this led

Hickel to be very supportive of Alaska-based projects, such as an all-Alaska gas pipeline from the North Slope to Valdez. During his second term as governor (1990–1994) he even proposed a water line—in effect, a very long hose-pipe—that would take the plentiful water of Alaska to the parched lands of southern California. Rarely did Hickel allow economic reality to get in the way of his ideas and proposals.

Between these two economic policy views, there is a range of positions. Even though most politicians realize the vulnerability of the Alaska economy and the limited options available to affect it, this is not something they readily admit. Moreover, they realize that they have to deliver some economic benefits to their constituents to get reelected, even if the capital project or subsidy they are proposing may not be economically sound.

Like most people around the world, Alaskans do not want to hear negative perspectives on their future. They would much rather believe the promise of Hickel's Alaska or something close to it. So Alaska's political leaders perpetually work to capture the public's ear and imagination with promises and visions of an economically independent and robust state. While this is not feasible, many Alaskans have and will continue to be swayed by the rhetoric of economic development and diversification.

The Political Cultural Dimensions

One explanation of why politicians pursue particular types of economic policies can be traced to the state's political culture. As Chapter 5 points out, Alaska has a complex political culture, melding reality, myths, misconceptions, and contradictions. The dominant political culture appears to be pragmatic dependent individualism. This is manifested in the desire for both private and government jobs and a kind of populist protection of the state's resources from "big Outside interests" like the oil companies, but at the same time wanting less government regulation and spending.

Demands to reduce government spending and its involvement in the economy are often ideologically driven and generally not in the economic interests of most Alaskans. In particular, the state's fiscal conservatism presents Republicans and conservatives with difficult policy choices.

7. SHIFTING POLITICAL POWER RELATIONSHIPS IN ALASKA'S POLITICAL ECONOMY

Many power relationships, particularly in politics, are a function of dependence or need. This is the situation when an individual, group, state, or nation depends on an individual or entity, like a business, for what is essential to their survival or to enhance their status or standard of living. Control or possession of resources—financial, technical, political, and so on—are another of the many elements of political influence.[24] Directly or indirectly, most chapters in this book deal with the power relationships within Alaska's political economy. Here we outline and raise questions about four of the most significant of these relationships.

The Political Economy of Power Relationships in Unbalanced Economies: Where Does Alaska Fit?

One power relationship results from Alaska's unbalanced natural resource extraction economy and the fact that a handful of Outside businesses drive the economy. Examples abound of a powerful business or other economic interests dominating the politics of a place, particularly in developing nations. For example, the United Fruit Company controlled Costa Rica, Nicaragua, and Honduras in the first half of the twentieth century. This kind of economic dominance is not just a phenomenon of developing nations, however. Most economies go through this stage as they grow. For many years, for instance, Montana was controlled by the Anaconda Copper Company, and many states by railroad interests. As a state, Wyoming was in many ways a creation of the Union Pacific Railroad. Often this unequal political power relationship is seen as placing the particular political system in a colonial status to the dominant economic interest.

The issue of whether or not Alaska is a colony of Outside economic forces and other interests was considered in Chapter 1, Box 1.3, which suggests that the issue is considerably more complex than it appears. Certainly, from soon after the Alaska Purchase in 1867 until the late 1960s, Alaska was dominated by a few Outside interests—fishing and canneries, mining and lumber companies. Getting some control over these Outside interests was a major impetus for statehood. Since then, the political power relationships with Outside businesses have changed considerably in favor of the state, largely because Alaska was wise enough to have selected North Slope lands at statehood.

There are still a handful of private businesses that drive Alaska's economy—mainly oil and gas—and they certainly wield considerable influence. They are constrained, however, by the fact that Alaska owns a significant portion of the oil and gas deposits in the state, by state and federal regulations, by increased public participation, and by the rise in the political influence of the environmental movement. Furthermore, the state has enormous financial resources in the form of oil revenues and the Permanent Fund. So with one of the highest standards of living anywhere, Alaska does not begin to resemble a developing nation in its power relationship with Outside economic interests, and thus its "colonial status" is very debatable.

The Federal Government

As one of the state's two basic industries, the federal government has always been, and likely always will be, a major political force in shaping the power relationship in Alaska's political economy. The federal-state power relationship has changed considerably since statehood, however, in favor of the state. Like the state's power relationship with the oil companies, this is a complex one and has many dimensions to it besides the economy. Several chapters in the book deal with the various facets of the federal government's place in Alaska's political economy.[25]

Other Outside Economic and Political Forces

Besides the major Outside business corporations and the federal government, other Outside economic and political forces affect power relationships in Alaska's political economy. As noted earlier, one is the influence of national and international interest groups that may constrain Alaska's economic development. The role of these and other Outside interests in shaping political power dynamics in the state are also dealt with in several chapters.[26]

The Native Community, Alaska's Economy, and Urban and Rural-Bush Power Relationships

The overview of Alaska's economy in this chapter shows the prominence of Native corporations among Alaska-based businesses both in the number of their employees and the amount of money they pump into the state's economy. Compared with Native Americans in other states, even those who receive large revenues from Indian gaming enterprises, this places Alaska Natives in a rare position within the economy of any state and most likely has increased their political influence in Alaska over what it would have been without such an economic base, and will likely continue to do so. While it is clear how this economic base translates into political power in certain local governments like the North Slope Borough (NSB), how it translates statewide and in state policy making is more difficult to determine.

Chapter 15 on interest groups and lobbying shows that, over the years, Alaska Natives have been among the most influential interests in the state. The difficulty, however, is separating the political aspects of this influence, based on their dominant presence in rural-bush Alaska, from their economic base. Chapter 9 on Alaska Natives and the state's political economy tackles this question to some extent. The influence of the Native community is significant but varies from policy area to policy area, issue to issue, and from time to time.

A large element of the urban versus rural-bush power relationship in Alaska relates to the economic and political status of Alaska Natives within the state's political economy. There are, however, more elements to it than the Alaska Native one alone. Close to 60 percent of the state's population and the headquarters of most major businesses are located in Anchorage, and this concentration determines much of the urban versus rural-bush power relationship.

8. CONCLUSION: FROM STRUCTURE AND POLITICAL POWER DYNAMICS TO EXTERNAL ECONOMIC RELATIONS AND ECONOMIC POLICY OPTIONS

The goal of this chapter was to explain the various aspects of Alaska's political economy. Given Alaska's dependence on the Outside economy for its economic health, external influences are important in shaping not only Alaska's political economy but the economic policy options available to the state's public officials. The analysis in Chapter 7 and the information in this chapter provide a foundation for understanding the economic policy constraints and opportunities available to Alaska.

ENDNOTES

[1] Walter J. Hickel, "Crisis in the Commons: The Alaska Solution," Speech to Commonwealth North Forum, Anchorage, April 4, 2002.

[2] George W. Rogers, "The Alaska Economy and Economic Issues: An Historical Overview," in *Alaska Public Policy Issues: Background and Perspectives*, ed. Clive S. Thomas (Juneau, AK: The Denali Press, 1999), 31.

[3] The author acknowledges use of statistics and tables gathered by Gunnar Knapp (author of Chapter 7) and his work, plus work by Scott Goldsmith (author of Chapter 25) and others at the University of Alaska Anchorage, Institute of Social and Economic Research (ISER).

[4] Statistics on various aspects of the Alaska economy differ somewhat depending on which database is consulted—federal, state, or a private source. In some cases, recent data is not available, particularly comparisons with other states. Generally, these differences and shortcomings do not affect the general points made in the chapter about Alaska's economy and its comparison with the nation and other states, as these comparisons have been more or less consistent, particularly since the late 1970s.

[5] U.S. Senator Lisa Murkowski's address to the Alaska Legislature, February 17, 2010; and Dave Donaldson, "Murkowski: Alaska's Place in Nation's Economy," *Alaska News Nightly*, Alaska Public Radio Network (APRN), February 18, 2010.

[6] See, for example, Chapters 10, 11, and 12 on federal influences, Alaska's role in international affairs, and the role of government, respectively.

[7] ISER, "Understanding Alaska: People, Economy, and Resources" (Anchorage: University of Alaska, 2006), 7, available at www.alaskaneconomy.uaa.alaska.edu; and Scott Goldsmith and Eric Larson, "What Does $7.6 Billion in Federal Money Mean to Alaska?" in ISER–UA Research Summary No. 2, Understanding Alaska Series (Anchorage: ISER, 2003), 1 and 9; and "Federal Spending in Alaska," *Alaska Economic Trends* 32, no. 2 (Juneau, AK: Department of Labor and Workforce Development, 2012), 4.

[8] In addition to Table 6.1, data comparing state economies from 2000 onwards is taken from the U.S. Department of Commerce, Bureau of Economic Analysis.

[9] See Chapter 7, Table 7.2 for the importance of oil, mining, and fishing in the Alaska economy compared with other states and the nation.

[10] See Scott Goldsmith, "The Remote Rural Economy of Alaska," Understanding Alaska Series (Anchorage, AK: ISER, 2007); and Gunnar Knapp, "Four Alaska Innovations," a Presentation

to the Board of Directors of the Federal Reserve Bank of San Francisco and its Seattle Branch, Anchorage, July 11, 2007.

[11] See the Alaska Permanent Fund Corporation's website, at http://www.pfd.state.ak.us/DivisionInfo/SummaryApplicationsPayments.

[12] "Alaska without Oil? We'd Sure Be a Different State," *Anchorage Daily News*, July 9, 2009.

[13] ISER, "Understanding Alaska: People, Economy, and Resources," 13.

[14] State of Alaska Department of Revenue, Tax Division, at http://tax.alaska.gov/programs/oil/production/ans.aspx?8/1/2014.

[15] Alyssa Shanks, "Federal Civilian Jobs Bring in $1 Billion per Year to Alaska," *Alaska Journal of Commerce*, October 2013, Issue 1.

[16] There are several methods for determining the largest businesses operating in a state. One ranks companies by number of employees, another by total yearly revenue. The State of Alaska Department of Labor uses the first method. Table 6.3 uses Department of Labor data, based on the average monthly employment. Table 6.4 is based on the *Alaska Business Monthly* (2010) figures, which rank companies based on their yearly revenue.

[17] ISER, "Understanding Alaska: People, Economy, and Resources," 12.

[18] Goldsmith, "The Remote Rural Economy of Alaska," 3.

[19] Gunnar Knapp, "Notes on the Eleven Strategies for Alaskan Economic Development," University of Alaska Anchorage Economics course on the economy of Alaska, February, 2007.

[20] "Alaska without Oil?" *Anchorage Daily News*, July 9, 2009.

[21] Robert P. Morin, "Nevada," in *Political Encyclopedia of U.S. States and Regions*, ed. Donald P. Haider-Markel, vol. 1 (Washington, D.C.: C. Q. Press, 2008), 439–48.

[22] Robert F. Pecorella, Jeffrey M. Stonecash, and Jessica E. Boscarino, "New York," in Haider-Markel, *Political Encyclopedia of U.S. States and Regions*, 97–110.

[23] Rogers, "The Alaska Economy and Economic Issues," 29-31.

[24] For a discussion of the elements and nature of political power, see Chapter 2, Section 7, and Chapter 15, Section 7.

[25] See, in particular, Chapter 9 on the role of Alaska Natives, Chapter 10 on the role of the federal government and intergovernmental relations, Chapter 12 on the role of government in Alaska in general, and the chapters on policy issues in Parts IV and V.

[26] See Chapter 7 on the Outside economy, Chapter 11 on Alaska and the world, Chapter 15 on interest groups, and the policy chapters in Parts IV and V.

⋆ CHAPTER 7 ⋆

Alaska's Political Economy: Outside Forces, Economic Viability, and Public Policy Options

Gunnar Knapp

Almost all of the resources and products produced in Alaska are shipped outside the state—either to other states or to other countries. Similarly, almost all of the products consumed in Alaska come from Outside—either from other states or (directly and indirectly) from other countries. Also, the major businesses operating in the state, some of which are the major sources of state government revenues, are not based in Alaska. Clearly, then, a major aspect of Alaska's economic life, which over the years has been central in shaping the state's political economy, is that it is inextricably bound to, and dependent upon, Outside economic forces. This chapter examines these outside forces, which include the economies in the states across the nation and those in foreign countries.

Alaska's commercial ties to the Outside are responsible for the state's relatively high standard of living, but at the same time they are a limiting factor on how Alaska's economy can be developed. Specifically, these commercial ties affect economic concerns ranging from the financial well-being of state and local government to incentives to encourage businesses to locate in Alaska to promoting Alaska products Outside to hiring Alaskans or out-of-state workers, among many others. As a consequence, many of these economic issues become political issues, sometimes hot-button issues, like increasing or reducing oil and gas taxes, and have been instrumental in shaping Alaska's political economy. The federal government's economic influence is also part of this political economy. This chapter, however, is concerned only with Outside economic forces in the private sector.

In particular, we are concerned about how business affects trade and Alaska's economy and how, in combination, these have affected and continue to affect Alaska's politics and the economic policy options available to Alaska's leaders. The argument presented is that there are two fundamental factors driving and limiting Alaska's economy that affect the economic policy options open to policy makers. These are the remote location of the state and the open economy—that is, the fact that Alaska operates within a global free trade system. Of the characteristics of Alaska politics identified in Chapter 2, this chapter particularly illustrates the influence of external forces, with a focus on economic forces. Other characteristics illustrated are the importance of government, economic development versus environmentalism, some myths of Alaska politics (in this case, they are more misunderstandings), and elements of regionalism and the economic contrasts between urban and rural-bush Alaska.

The chapter is organized as follows. After identifying key terms, we recap the major characteristics of Alaska's economy and explain some essential aspects of the theory of trade. This is followed by considering types and flows of trade in which Alaska is involved. Sections 2 and 3 explain the way that Outside economic links affect the state's economy in general followed by the more specific effects of Alaska's dependence on world resource markets. Then we bring together the analysis in this and Chapter 6 and summarize the constraints and challenges facing Alaska's policy makers and the opportunities that they have in economic policy. The conclusion points out how the explanation of Alaska's political economy can be useful in understanding other chapters and topics in the book.[1]

1. ESSENTIAL TERMS AND CONCEPTS

The information set out in Chapter 6 and the terms and concepts in Box 6.1 are essential prerequisites to understanding this chapter. In addition, we need to explain the use in this chapter of *region* instead of *country* and *Outside trade* instead of *international trade*.

Region versus Country

A *region* is a geographic area that may be part of a *country* (Alaska, for example, can be viewed as a remote region of the United States), a country by itself (Canada), multiple countries (North America), or parts of many countries (the Arctic). In assessing the role of trade in Alaska's economy, it is useful to see Alaska as a region that trades with the rest of the world, including other states in the United States and other countries.

Outside Trade versus International Trade

Trade is the buying and selling of goods and services, usually for money. It is largely the same, whether it takes place between people in the same town, between towns, between states or regions within a country, or between countries. International trade may be affected by barriers, such as tariffs or bans on trading certain goods, but is otherwise very similar to other types of trade.

Furthermore, often overlooked is that much of the world's trade is within countries (internal trade) rather than between countries (external trade). Michigan exports cars to

Florida, and Florida exports oranges to Michigan. The economic effects of trade on state economies are very similar to the economic effects of trade with other countries. Trade between states leads to the same kind of specialization as trade between countries, and makes it difficult or impossible for some states to produce things that other states can produce more efficiently or more cheaply.

Consequently, because the focus of this chapter is the link between the Alaska economy and the rest of the world—the other forty-nine states and other countries—we mainly use the terms *Outside economies* and *Outside trade* as opposed to international trade or international economy. The word "Outside" is a play on Alaska parlance of referring to everything outside the state. There is little difference for Alaska in the economic effects of selling salmon to New York or Japan, buying cars from Michigan or Sweden, receiving tourists from Ohio or Germany, or leasing oil lands to a company based in Houston or London. When we do use the term *international trade* we mean trade between nations.

In this chapter, then, *exports* include all Alaska goods and services purchased by the rest of the world, both within the United States and abroad. Similarly, *imports* include all goods and services purchased by Alaskans that come into the state both from the rest of the United States and from abroad. So trade refers to both exports and imports.

2. A RECAP OF THE MAJOR CHARACTERISTICS OF ALASKA'S ECONOMY AND AN EXPLANATION OF THE STATE'S FREE TRADE STATUS

To set the scene for this chapter, we first present a brief recap of the characteristics of the Alaska economy. Then we identify two key elements to keep in mind when considering Alaska and the Outside economy, followed by some basic economic theory of trade.

Economic Realities, and Two Major Influences Shaping Alaska's Outside Trade

Of the realities of the Alaska economy identified in Chapter 6, the fact that Alaska operates in a capitalist or free enterprise system is fundamental to understanding the internal Alaska economy as well as its economic relations with the Outside. Plus, the lack of barriers in most economies for both internal and foreign trade means that goods and many services will be produced or provided in places where it is most cost-effective, be it in the United States or abroad. In economic terminology such places have a comparative advantage in production.

The second reality is that Alaska is a two-crop economy, oil and government. Other significant realities are the boom-bust cycle, the influence of geography, the high cost of production in Alaska, and the state's small internal market. All these realities will be apparent as we look at Alaska's relations with the Outside economy.

Two particular economic realities are important to the argument here. One is Alaska's remoteness from the rest of the United States, the world's population centers, and major trade routes, as well as the state's physical size. Remoteness and size increase transportation costs, affect access within the state, particularly to rural-bush areas, and generally increase production costs. The second reality is free trade. This has both pros and cons for the state.

Closed versus Open Economies: External and Internal Economic Relations

The terms *closed* and *open* refer to the extent to which there are restrictions on trade, investment, and migration between an economy and the rest of the world. A fully closed economy has no economic interactions with the rest of the world. A fully open economy has no restrictions on such interactions. Free trade refers to the degree of openness of the economy involving the removal of restrictions between countries to make it easier to export and import goods and services.

Trade and investment restrictions are laws, taxes, or other regulations imposed by governments that make trade with other regions more difficult or expensive or that limit investment and the movement of labor between regions. These include tariffs (special taxes imposed on imports), quotas (limits on how much of a product may be imported or exported or on foreign labor allowed into a country), banning importing or exporting particular kinds of products, and restrictions on foreign ownership in particular industries. Governments typically impose trade and investment restrictions to help domestic industries compete with imports, and to limit foreign control over particular industries or the economy as a whole.

As a result of the Commerce Clause of the U.S. Constitution and federal laws, internal trade among the states within the United States is almost completely free. The economic effects of trade on state economies are very similar to the economic effects of trade with other countries: subject to the same kind of specialization, making it difficult or impossible for some states to produce items that other states can produce more cheaply. Few Americans today argue about free trade between the states, although this was a contentious issue in the early history of the nation. In fact, most Americans (including Alaskans) forget how overwhelmingly dependent their own state is on free trade with other states, even though they vigorously debate the merits of free trade with other countries.

The Characteristics of a Closed Economy

A closed economy must be fully self-sufficient. It must produce everything it consumes. It must grow its own food and manufacture its own clothing, tools, medicines, and anything else it needs. So from an economic perspective, closed economies face five kinds of challenges.

First, they may lack certain types of resources. If they do not have iron ore, wood, or oil, they will not be able to make or use products that depend upon these resources. Second, closed economies may have unfavorable conditions for producing some kinds of goods and services. If the climate is cold or dry or the soil is poor, it may be difficult to grow food. If the country has mostly unskilled workers, it may be difficult to produce outputs that require skilled labor, such as watches or software. Third, it may be difficult to achieve economies of scale in production. A society that produces only for its own use may not be able to produce many things at an efficient scale. Fourth, all investment must come from inside the region. Investment—such as building roads and bridges, drilling oil wells, developing mines, and building factories and office buildings—is what drives growth in an economy's productive capacity. In a closed economy, the rate of investment and growth is limited by the capacity of the region to generate savings that can be invested in the economy. Fifth, all labor in a closed economy must come from within the country. The number of workers can grow only as rapidly as the population grows. Skilled workers must be educated within the country. In combination, these five challenges affect a country's standard of living and prospects for economic growth.

While there are no completely closed or open economies, communist North Korea has one of the world's most closed economies. In contrast, Western countries have very open economies.

Effects of Opening an Economy to External Trade, Investment, and Migration

Economic interactions between regions have not only been major topics of research and theorizing by economists, but also perennial political issues, particularly the issue of trade. In terms of economic theory, opening an economy distributes economic resources most efficiently between an economy like Alaska's and the Outside economy. Its particular effects on trade, investment, and migration (particularly on labor), are set out in Box 7.1.

Alaska as Part of the Free Trade System

Alaska has always been heavily dependent on international resource markets and Outside labor and investment. This dependence imposes limits on Alaskans' ability to control their own economy and increases political tensions as politicians offer varying solutions on how to deal with these limitations. Statehood and an equal political status in the American Union did not end these challenges, because they derive fundamentally from Alaska's remoteness and openness.

Alaska's contemporary economy is inextricably linked to the Outside global free trade system for two reasons. First, Alaska is subject to the free trade rules that operate internally within the United States. Second, as a state in the Union, it is subject to all the external trade rules enacted and negotiated by the federal government. Free trade, investment,

BOX 7.1

Effects on an Economy of Free Trade, Investment, and Migration

GENERAL EFFECTS

Free trade allows a country to import resources that it needs but does not have. It can export products that it is good at producing (has a comparative advantage), and import products it is not good at producing. By specializing in what it is best at, a country reduces costs by realizing economies of scale. For all these reasons, most economists argue that countries benefit by trading internationally, since open economies are able to enjoy a higher standard of living.

Despite these potential benefits, critics argue that trade harms those who face competition from imports. They contend that free trade makes countries less self-sufficient and more vulnerable to changes in production by other countries, and, therefore, more politically dependent on those countries. Free trade also makes an economy more vulnerable to Outside economic forces that may affect the prices of what the region exports and imports.

EFFECTS ON MIGRATION: POSITIVES AND NEGATIVES

POSITIVES	NEGATIVES
Free trade allows an economy to grow rapidly to take advantage of new economic opportunities, as the labor force can expand more rapidly than allowed by "natural growth" of the population (births minus deaths). Skilled labor can be imported to do specialized jobs that locals are not able to do. The opportunity to migrate from a region may also benefit residents if economic opportunities within their own region are limited. Those who stay face less competition for jobs, and pressures on government funds for payments like unemployment benefits will decrease.	In-migration may result in people taking jobs away from residents. Migrants may send much of their income to people living outside the region. By increasing the supply of labor, migrants may depress wages. If migration into the region causes rapid population growth, it may also lead to demand for expensive new public services, such as education and health care. Migration may also have complex social and political effects, such as changing the character of the population. This could lead to tensions between newcomers and long-time residents, and shift the political balance of power to newcomers with a different vision of what kind of society the region should have.

EFFECTS ON INVESTMENT: POSITIVES AND NEGATIVES

POSITIVES	NEGATIVES
If a region is opened to "free investment," the economy can grow more rapidly. Investment from outside can pay for new roads, bridges, oil wells, factories, and office buildings that drive economic growth. If there are attractive economic opportunities in the region—such as opening a gold mine or building big-box stores like Costco or Home Depot—investors from outside will seek to take advantage of them. There are relatively few restrictions on investment flows between the United States and other countries.	A downside to "free investment" is that it can work both ways. Residents of the region may seek to invest in more attractive economic opportunities outside—potentially leading to less rather than more investment within the region. Other downsides include reduced local control of the region's economy, and the flow of investment profits to investors based outside. Also, as with free trade, free investment may benefit some groups within a region and harm others.

Source: Developed by the author with assistance from Kristina Klimovich.

and migration affect Alaska as they do any country, state, or region. However, free trade affects Alaska in particular ways because of the nature of its economy. As to the broad effects of free trade on Alaska, there are four consequences.

The first is stiff competition within the free enterprise system. Alaska must compete to sell its products and to attract business, investment, and labor to the state. Second, this competition means that, in reality, Alaska does not have the potential in trade, particularly in international trade, that many believe is just waiting to be unlocked with the right policy and fewer government restrictions. Third, Alaska is very vulnerable to world market prices for its natural resources, particularly for oil. Fourth, the fact that Alaska's economy is very much a creature of Outside economic forces presents Alaska policy makers with more challenges than opportunities.

3. ALASKA'S TRADE WITH THE OUTSIDE ECONOMY: SELECTED STATISTICS AND SOME COMPARISONS WITH OTHER STATES

Turning to the specifics of Alaska trade with the Outside, this section considers three aspects of that trade: Alaska's international exports, the "hidden" exports of visitors to the Last Frontier, and investment flows to and from Alaska.

Alaska's Exports and Its International Trade

What are the end-markets for Alaska's exports as we define them in this chapter? Surprisingly, this is not an easy question to answer. Although the federal government collects data on trade with foreign countries, it does not collect data on trade between states, which would allow us to measure directly "exports" from Alaska to other states.

What we can say is that Alaska's most valuable and most well-known export, oil, is almost entirely shipped by tanker to refineries on the U.S. west coast. Between 2000 and 2009, typical years since the late 1980s, 26 to 43 percent of the value of Alaska mineral production was exported to foreign countries.[2] Of the wide variety of seafood produced in Alaska, such as halibut and canned pink salmon, most is shipped to markets in the other forty-nine states.

Figures 7.1 and 7.2 provide an overview of Alaska's exports to foreign countries. The bar graph in Figure 7.1 shows that the state's overall exports increased steadily over the sixteen years from 1996 to 2012, with a slight dip following the recession of 2008–2010. According to the table below the graph, in 2010 on a per capita basis Alaska ranks high among the fifty states at number five, though in total dollars and the percentage of U.S. exports overall, the state ranks near the bottom and on a par with other smaller states. As in many national comparisons, California dwarfs most states.

FIGURE 7.1

Alaska Exports 1996–2012 Compared to Selected States in 2010

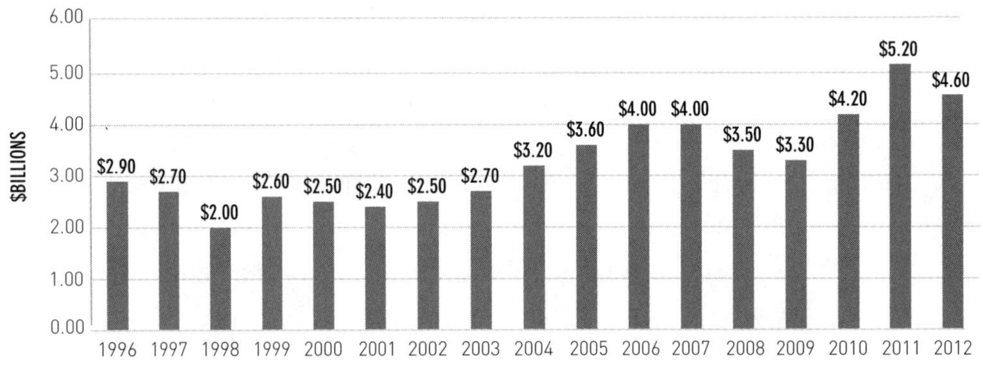

	ALASKA	WYOMING	NEBRASKA	CALIFORNIA	NEW HAMPSHIRE	UNITED STATES
Total export value in $billions	$4.2 — 25*	$1.0 — 50	$5.8 — 35	$143.3 — 2	$4.4 — 41	$1,278.1
Export value per capita	$5,846 — 5	$1,744 — 45	$3,178 — 30	$3,846 — 17	$3,318 — 27	$4,140
Percent of U.S. total	0.3 — 42	0.1 — 50	0.5 — 35	11.2 — 2	0.3 — 41	100

* The second number in each category for each state is its ranking among the fifty states and Washington, D.C.

Sources: For the graph: Alaska Office of International Trade, *2013 Export Update*, retrieved from http://www.gov.state.ak.us/trade/pdf/AlaskaExportCharts2009.pdf; U.S. Census Bureau, *Foreign Trade Statistics: U.S. Trade in Goods by State, Based on Origin of Movement, by NAICS-Based Product: 2010*, retrieved from http://www.census.gov/foreign-trade/statistics/state/origin_movement/index.html#2010.

For the table: U.S. Census Bureau, *Foreign Trade Statistics: U. S. Trade in Goods by State, Based on Origin of Movement, by NAICS-Based Product: 2010*, retrieved from http://www.census.gov/foreign-trade/statistics/state/origin_movement/index.html#2010.

Figure 7.2 provides a snapshot of the types and destinations of Alaska foreign trade in 2011. The pie chart on the left shows that the state's international exports reflect the dominance of natural resource extraction in the economy. The percentage share of the individual types of natural resource exports has stayed fairly constant since the early 2000s.[3] About half of all Alaska's foreign exports are seafood and seafood products. This percentage has also been consistent since around 2000. These products include salmon roe, pollock roe, herring roe, surimi and sablefish (mostly exported to Japan), and canned sockeye salmon (mostly exported to the United Kingdom and other European markets).[4] Another quarter to a third or so of exports, depending on the year, is zinc. In fact, Alaska's most valuable mineral export is zinc ore shipped from the Red Dog Mine in Northwest Alaska to a smelter in Japan. Ten percent of exports are energy, including coal, liquefied natural gas and refined petroleum products. The pie chart on the right shows that China is Alaska's best customer, a status previously held for many years by Japan. Alaska's

FIGURE 7.2

Alaska Exports by Product, Value, Percentage, and Country of Destination in 2011

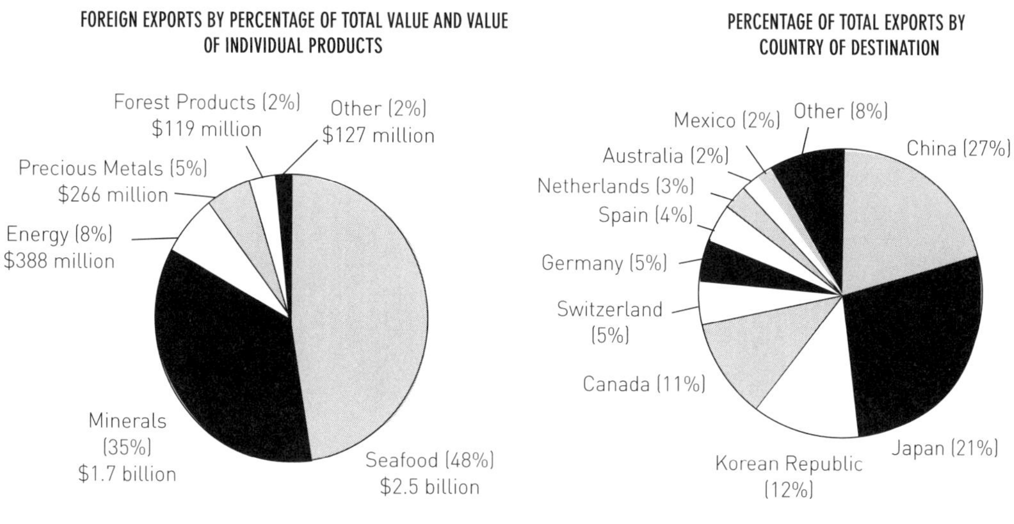

Source: *2011 Export Update*. State of Alaska, Office of the Governor. Retrieved from http://gov.alaska.gov/parnell_media/resources_files/alaskaexportcharts2011.pdf (URL removed when Parnell left office in December 2014).

trade with China increased five-fold in the ten years from 2004 to 2013 and is taking an ever-increasing share of the state's exports. The Far East accounts for 60 percent of Alaska's exports, just over ten percent goes to Canada and most of the rest to Western Europe, with some going to Mexico.

Alaska's Hidden Exports—Visitors to the Last Frontier

The data above does not show the full importance of foreign markets to Alaska's economy because it shows only exports of resources and manufactured products. It does not show the value of services sold in Alaska to foreign buyers. In terms of overall U.S. exports, in typical years since 2000, natural resource and manufactured products accounted for only about 70 percent of total U.S. exports. Services accounted for the remaining 30 percent. Examples of services include fares paid by foreign passengers on U.S. airlines and cruise ships and sales by U.S. engineering and consulting firms in foreign countries. Data are not available on the value of these "hidden" Alaska exports. However, two kinds of nonresource exports are clearly important and growing. Tourism and airport services have become more important Alaska "hidden" exports because increasing numbers of people from abroad and around the United States use Alaska airports, particularly the Ted Stevens International Airport in Anchorage.

FIGURE 7.3

Summer Visitors to Alaska 1989–2012

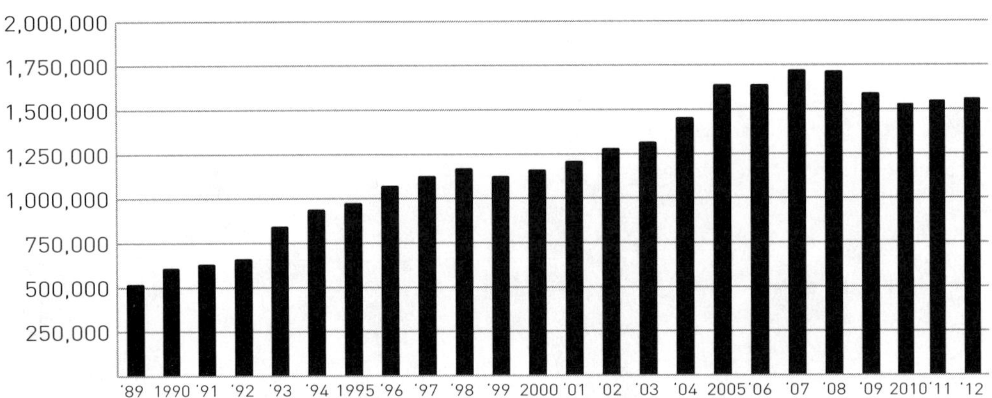

Note: No data is available for 2000, so an average of 1989–2005 was taken.

Source: Alaska Office of Tourism and Development, *Alaska Visitor Statistics Program VI Interim Visitor Volume Report*, Summer 2012, retrieved from http://commerce.alaska.gov/dnn/Portals/6/pub/TourismResearch/AVSP/AVSP_VI_2012_Summer.pdf; State of Alaska Department of Commerce, Community and Economic Development, *Alaska Visitor Arrivals and Profile Summer 2001*, retrieved from http://www.dced.state.ak.us/ded/dev/toubus/pub/AVSPSummerArrival111402.pdf; State of Alaska Department of Commerce, Division of Tourism, *Alaska Visitor Statistics Program: Alaska Visitor Arrivals Summer 1993*, retrieved from http://www.dced.state.ak.us/ded/dev/toubus/pub/AVSP_III_Summer_Arrivals_1993.pdf.

Tourists are an important source of export income for Alaska. As Figure 7.3 shows, the number of tourists coming to the state has increased steadily over the years, but with a dip following the recession of 2008–2010.[5] The vast majority of people visiting Alaska are from the other forty-nine states. In a typical year these visitors account for about 75 percent or so of all tourists, with about 8 percent coming from Canada and around 15 percent from other countries, mainly Western Europe and Japan. In 2008–2010 tourists spent an estimated $1.3 to $1.5 billion in Alaska, providing many summer jobs and having an important multiplier effect on the economy.[6] Plus, the state now imposes a head tax on cruise ship visitors, who represent close to 50 percent of the tourists who reach the state each year. The head tax provides state and local governments with additional funds to offset costs incurred for such facilities as docks. But the tax has been controversial, as noted later in this chapter.

Investment Flows to and from Alaska

Over the years, most of the large-scale investment in Alaska's economy has been by corporations based outside Alaska. This has been true not only for resource-producing industries, such as oil, seafood, and mining, but also for service industries such as transportation and trade. Given the openness of Alaska's economy, and the vastly greater capital resources available to non-Alaska–based companies, it is not surprising that they have dominated Alaska investment.

As Alaska's economy grows and Alaska residents and Alaska-based companies acquire capital, this historical pattern is gradually changing, and the share of Alaska-based investment is increasing. Particularly important has been the emergence of Alaska Native corporations, which have invested heavily in Alaska's economy. However, even "home-grown" companies started by Alaskans do not necessarily remain Alaskan-owned. Two examples are the Carr-Gottstein grocery chain, which was acquired by Safeway in 1999 (now owned by the Albertsons grocery chain), and the National Bank of Alaska, acquired by Wells Fargo Corporation in 2000.

Data are not available on the extent of Outside investment in Alaska's economy. For example, it is not easy to trace the ownership of large corporations that may have thousands of shareholders. However, one indicator of the scale of Outside investment is the location of the home offices of the largest companies operating in Alaska, as measured by the employment. As explained in Chapter 6, most of the largest companies are located out of state.[7] This is particularly the case with Alaska's resource industries. The three oil companies that control Alaska's North Slope oil and gas leases—BP Exploration Alaska, Exxon, and ConocoPhillips—are based in the United Kingdom and Texas. Most of the large fish-processing companies are based in Seattle or Japan, and most of the large mining companies are based in Canada.

Although American-owned companies account for the largest share of internal investment, foreign-owned companies also play a major role in Alaska's economy and are among the largest in the state. The most important by far is London-based British Petroleum (BP), the operator of the giant Prudhoe Bay oil field. Japanese-owned companies such as Unisea, Peter Pan Seafoods, Westward Seafoods, and North Pacific Processors, are among the largest seafood processors in Alaska. Canadian-owned companies like Teck Cominco, Kinross, Northern Dynasty, Freegold Ventures, Nova Gold, and Placer Dome dominate Alaska's mining industry.

Table 7.1 shows total foreign direct investment (FDI–the value of businesses owned in full or in part by foreign-based companies) in Alaska compared with selected states for 2007, likely a fairly typical year since 2000. It shows that Alaska ranked eighth among the fifty states in FDI in terms of total value and first in FDI per capita.[8] Alaska was at the national average in terms of employment by U.S. affiliates of foreign firms. But because of the small size of its economy, Alaska accounted for only a tiny percentage of national FDI.[9]

The lack of restrictions on investment flows between Alaska and other regions means not only that non-Alaskans can invest in Alaska, but also that Alaskans can invest Outside. Like other Americans, most Alaskans tend to invest personal savings and pension funds

TABLE 7.1

Foreign Direct Investment (FDI) in Alaska in 2007: Selected Indicators and Comparisons with Other States

	ALASKA	WYOMING	NEBRASKA*	CALIFORNIA	NEW HAMPSHIRE	UNITED STATES
FDI in $millions	$34.3 — 8**	$ 11.5 — 23	$ 2.4 — N/A	$ 110.2 — 2***	$ 5.1 — 35	$ 1,283
FDI per capita	$ 50,346 — 1	$ 21,983 — 36	$ 1,377 — N/A	$ 3,042 — 25	$ 3,896 — 17	$ 4,254
Percentage employment by U.S. affiliates of foreign firms	4.8%	4.6%	2.9%	4.6%	6.6%	4.7%
FDI as percentage of U.S. GDP	0.2%	0.08%	0.02%	0.8%	0.04%	9.1%

Note: FDI is gross value of U.S. affiliates of foreign companies. A U.S. majority-owned affiliate is a U.S. business in which a foreign entity has a voting interest greater than 50 percent. The data on total employment, used to calculate percentage of employment by U.S. affiliates in the states, equals employment in private industries less employment of private households. Therefore, percentage of employment by U.S. affiliates of foreign companies shows what percentage of private employment belongs to businesses directly or indirectly controlled by a foreign entity with voting interests of more than 50 percent.

* 2006 data was used for Nebraska.
** The second number in total FDI and per capita FDI is the state's ranking among the fifty states in those categories.
*** The number one ranked state was Texas.

Sources: The U.S. Census Bureau, *The 2011 Statistical Abstract of the United States*, Tables 12, 1265, retrieved from http://www.census.gov/compendia/statab/2011/2011edition.html; The U.S. Census Bureau, *The 2010 Statistical Abstract of the United States*, Tables 12, 1265, retrieved from http://www.census.gov/compendia/statab/2010/2010edition.html; and U.S. Bureau of Economic Analysis. *National Income and Product Accounts*, Table 1.1.5, retrieved from http://www.bea.gov/national/nipaweb/Index.asp.

in stocks and bonds that best meet their personal investment objectives, without consideration for whether they are investing in Alaska. In particular, Alaska Native corporations, seeking the highest rates of return for their shareholders, have invested heavily in non-Alaska companies. Most significantly, Alaska's $50 billion Permanent Fund is invested almost entirely outside Alaska.

4. THE EFFECTS OF OUTSIDE ECONOMIC FORCES ON ALASKA'S ECONOMY

Trade affects what kinds of economic activities are profitable for private sector businesses in Alaska. Trade also affects the scale of government, because state and local governments depend on revenues raised from private businesses. Given its open economy, for Alaska to be profitable, the costs of producing a product and transporting it to market cannot be significantly higher than those of competing producers from other states or countries. Otherwise, Outside producers will supply goods and services for prices with which Alaska private businesses cannot compete. The extent to which private businesses in remote regions like Alaska can be competitive varies, depending on the type of economic output and the end market.

To be sure, Alaska has some products that have their own unique market, such as Alaska salmon and halibut and, of course, its scenery, wildlife, fishing, hunting, and the general outdoor experience. People may be willing to pay a premium for these Alaskan experiences, but there is a limit. Similar experiences are available in the Rockies, the Alps, the Andes, and elsewhere, and at some point people will not be willing to pay the premium to enjoy them in Alaska. Other than these few products, competition is the major determining factor regarding the success of Alaska's private businesses.

Implications of Trade for Alaska Resource Production

Historically, the only type of economic output that private sector companies in remote regions like Alaska have been able to produce competitively for export on a significant scale has been natural resources. This is because remote regions have many of the natural resources that other regions need but do not have, or have already used up—such as oil, minerals, fish, and timber.

Alaska's most important resource industries are oil, mining, and seafood.[10] In 2009, the most recent year for which comprehensive comparison data on all three industries are available, Alaska ranked second among the states (after Texas) in crude oil production, sixth in the value of mining production, and first in the value of fishery landings. Even though by 2013 Alaska had dropped to fourth in oil production (behind Texas, North Dakota, and California), it was still ranked number one in fisheries landings and among the top states in mineral production. Expressed in per capita terms, Alaska's production of these resources is much higher than in any other state.

Although seafood and mining are important to Alaska's economy, the value of oil production dwarfs them. In 2005, for example, before the rise in oil prices after 2006, oil amounted to more than $26,000 per Alaskan, compared with less than $4,300 for mining and $2,000 for fish. In 2008, when oil reached close to $150 per barrel, this per capita figure reached close to $40,000 for each Alaskan compared with about $3,600 for mining and $1,900 for fish. From 2010 to 2014, as oil hovered around $100, even with lower oil production, the per capita amount was over $30,000 per Alaskan with that of minerals and fish similar to the past. Oil's significance to Alaska's economy is particularly important in its contribution to state revenues. Since the late 1970s, taxes and royalties paid by Alaska's oil industry have accounted for between 70 and 95 percent of the state's own-source revenues, depending on the year.[11]

The fact that Alaska is a major producer of some natural resources does not mean it can be competitive in producing all of its natural resources. It can only be competitive in a particular resource when the costs of production and transportation to end markets are less than world market prices. For instance, there are huge coal resources in northern and northwestern Alaska, and large forest resources in Interior Alaska. But the costs of exploiting and transporting them to markets have always been too high to develop them profitably and competitively. Other regions produce these resources more cheaply.

This economic reality helps dispel another misconception about the Alaska economy. Alaska's resources may be extensive, but they do not, as many believe, constitute actual wealth that could be tapped if only the right government policy were developed to exploit them or restrictions on their use were lifted. Only when the market prices are right do these resources have the potential for their wealth to be unlocked.

Implications of Trade for Manufacturing in Alaska

It is difficult for remote regions with open economies like Alaska's to be competitive in producing manufactured goods, either for export markets or for their internal markets. Most of the world can get most kinds of manufactured products and services—from cars and computers to fashion design and economic consulting—more cheaply from places other than Alaska. Plus, because of the openness of Alaska's economy, very few consumer goods are manufactured in the state, even for sale in Alaska. Almost everything Alaskans buy is imported from somewhere else. You can see this by going into almost any store in Alaska. There may be a few products that are made in Alaska, such as smoked salmon and wild berry jams, but the grocery stores, department store racks, and car lots are full of products from all over the world, with an increasing share of them from foreign countries, particularly China.

Residents and politicians in remote regions like Alaska often argue that they can improve the local economy by making value-added products made from resources produced within their region. This includes Governor Bill Walker, who mentioned this during his 2014 election campaign as one of three main ways to diversify Alaska's economy.[12] So, for instance, because Alaska produces fish it should be able to produce fish sticks, thereby adding value to the fish and deriving more economic value from them. However, just because a region is able to produce natural resources does not mean that it can compete successfully in producing value-added products made from those resources. Producing and transporting a natural resource are only two of the costs of a value-added product. Other costs may include, for example, labor and packaging. It is usually cheaper

BOX 7.2

Alaska and Value-Adding in International Trade

A problem with value-adding in a high-cost economy is that it is also often "cost-adding," which can end up actually reducing the income received by the resource producers.

Suppose an Alaska Native corporation wants to cut down trees in Alaska to produce logs that will be sawed into boards and sold as boards in Japan at a price of $100 a board. Say it costs $25 a board to saw the logs into boards in Japan but $40 to produce a board in Alaska because of the higher cost of labor, and $15 to ship either logs or boards to Japan. The income received by the Native corporation is the price of the boards in Japan minus the costs of sawing and transportation. The chart below shows that the Native corporation will receive more for its logs by shipping them as logs rather than having them sawed first into boards by an Alaskan company.

	Without value-adding	With value-adding
Price of boards in Japan	**$100**	**$100**
Cost of sawing boards in Japan to be paid by the Native corporation	$25	
Cost of sawing boards in Alaska to be paid by the Native corporation		$40
Cost of shipping logs or boards to Japan	$15	$15
Total profit earned by Native corporation	**$60**	**$45**

Sawing the logs into boards in Alaska would certainly increase their value, but the ultimate purchaser of the boards will still pay only $100 for each board. As a result, the Native corporation gets $15 less profit because "value-adding" does not just add value, it also adds to their costs. This is why raw material producers, such as oil companies and fishermen, are often less enthusiastic about value-adding than are politicians.

Source: Developed by the author.

to produce value-added products by shipping natural resources to other regions where labor, packaging, and distribution to customers are cheaper, than to ship packaging materials to a remote region, pay higher labor costs, and then distribute the products from the remote region to multiple end markets. Box 7.2 provides a hypothetical example of the problem of value-adding by turning logs into boards.

Not only is it difficult for Alaska private sector companies to compete profitably in manufacturing products for exports, it is also difficult for Alaska companies to compete in manufacturing products for consumption in Alaska. Manufacturing costs are so much lower in other areas that this is more than enough to offset the relatively low cost of bulk transportation to Alaska. And, ironically, declining transportation costs between Alaska and other states and countries, and improved reliability of transportation links, make it harder for Alaska's manufacturers to compete in the Alaska market with imports from other states and countries. For many years, Alaska had a small dairy industry in the Matanuska Valley, producing raw milk and selling it to the Matanuska Maid company for processing into various dairy products for Alaska markets. Then, as transportation costs between Washington State and Alaska declined, it became more and more difficult for Alaska's small dairy industry to compete with dairy products imported from Washington, where costs are lower due to a milder climate, lower feed costs, and economies of scale. In 2007, Matanuska Maid closed, leaving the few remaining dairy farmers no place to sell their milk.

For these reasons, manufacturing represents a much smaller share of Alaska's economy than for the United States as a whole or for most other states.[13] About half of Alaska's entire manufacturing industry consists of primary fish processing—mostly canning and freezing fish—which is necessary before fish, a highly perishable product, can be shipped to most markets.[14]

Implications of Trade for Alaska's Service Industries

In contrast to manufactured and natural resources products, many kinds of services are difficult to trade between regions. Most services have to be provided where they are consumed. Alaskans cannot get a haircut from someone in Seattle or make a doctor's visit in Portland unless they travel there. But the reverse is also true. Someone in Kansas or Europe cannot easily buy snow-plowing or accounting services from someone in Alaska.

For these reasons, businesses in remote open regions like Alaska have been competitive in providing services for their own markets. Even the remote places in Alaska have at least a few businesses providing services to the local market, such as restaurants and grocery stores. Alaska's urban centers have a full array of services comparable to other parts of America, ranging from law firms to auto body shops to big box stores. Services account for about half of all Alaska employment.[15]

In the past, some kinds of services, such as cancer treatment, were too expensive to provide in Alaska, so Alaskans had to travel to other states for these services. However, as Alaska's population and economy have grown, economies of scale have made it possible for more and more services to be produced competitively in Alaska, such as specialized health and engineering services.

Implications of Trade for Alaska Governments

Trade also affects the size and scope of government, because state and local governments depend on revenues raised from taxes on private businesses. This is even more important in Alaska, where, as of 2015, there is no state sales tax and income taxes are imposed only on corporations, not on individuals. So taxes paid by the major businesses operating in the state very much determine the size of government and the services it can provide.

It has been primarily Alaska's oil bonanza and the taxes paid by the oil companies that made the expansion in state and local government employment and services possible for a decade following completion of the trans-Alaska pipeline (TAPS) in 1977. Alaska's state and local government spending has a major multiplier effect on the state's economy. Thus, any long-term change in oil revenues, such as a downturn in oil prices or the Alaska pipeline closing down, will have devastating effects on the state's economy.

The Effects of Migration on Alaska's Economy

Historically, there have been few restrictions on migration between Alaska and other states. In periods of economic opportunity, migration provided the labor necessary to enable Alaska's economy to grow rapidly. In periods of economic decline, migration allowed workers to leave Alaska, keeping unemployment rates lower than they would otherwise have been. The significance of migration for Alaska's population can be seen by comparing natural population growth (births minus deaths) with net migration since World War II, as set out in Figure 7.4. There were three periods in which net in-migration significantly exceeded natural growth: the post–World War II, Cold War military buildup, the mid-1970s construction of the Alaska pipeline, and the early 1980s economic boom driven by state spending. There were two periods when net out-migration exceeded natural growth, resulting in a decline in Alaska's population: the brief recession of the late 1970s following completion of the pipeline and the much deeper recession following the collapse of oil prices in 1986. Interestingly, following the worldwide recession of 2008–2010, Alaska's economy was buoyed by high oil prices and did not feel the recession as severely as the rest of the nation. So there was no net out-migration from the state. In fact, as Figure 7.4 shows, in 2009–2010, Alaska had a boost in in-migration, likely the result of many people coming for jobs.

FIGURE 7.4

Changes in Alaska's Population: Net Migration and Natural Growth, 1946–2013

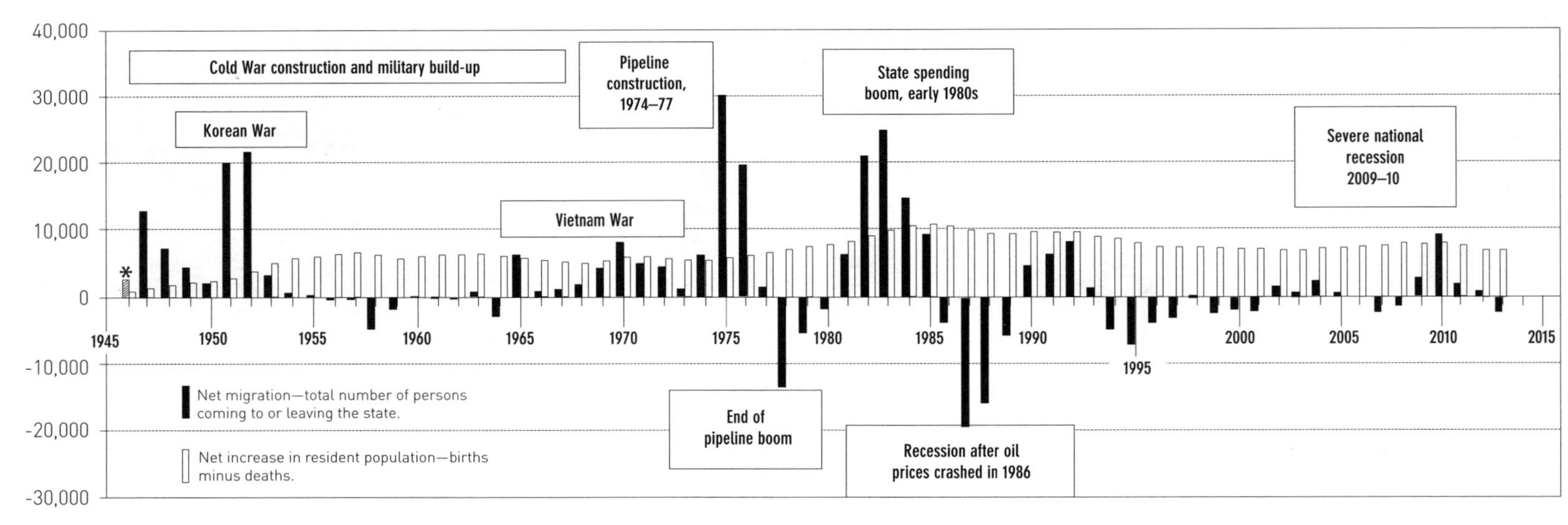

No migration data is available for 1946.

Source: Gunnar Knapp, *An Introduction to the Economy of Alaska* (Anchorage: Institute of Social and Economic Research (ISER), University of Alaska Anchorage, February 2012), p. 7, and updated for 2011–13 based on data from the Alaska Department of Labor and Workforce Development, Research and Analysis, Demographics Unit, at: http://laborstats.alaska.gov/pop/popest.htm#.

Migration includes not only long-term migrants (people who move to or from Alaska), but also short-term migrants (people who live Outside but work in Alaska, or vice versa). In 2012, of Alaska's total workforce of 418,779, 84,496 were nonresidents who made up 20.4 percent of the workers and 14.8 percent of total wages.[16] The percentage of nonresident workers has risen only slightly since the late 1980s from 17.3 percent in 1988. The share of nonresident workers is particularly high in industries such as food processing (mainly fish processing), fishing, logging, and tourism-related enterprises, such as scenic and sightseeing transportation (whale watching and helicopter tours, for example), as Figure 7.5 shows.

Alaska would be very different without free long-term and short-term migration. Without it Alaska's economy could not have grown as rapidly during the gold rush, the Cold War, and other periods, and it would have taken far longer to build TAPS. In addition, without the opportunity to hire skilled workers from outside Alaska, highly technical economic developments ranging from oil exploration to communications systems would have occurred much more slowly or not at all. With no opportunity to hire nonresidents willing to work for relatively low wages, much of Alaska's seafood processing industry would not be profitable—and Alaska's unemployment rates would be much higher.

In fact, the right of Alaska employers, whether Alaska-based or out-of-state, to hire workers from the other forty-nine states is guaranteed by the U.S. Constitution. In a 1978 U.S. Supreme Court ruling in *Hicklin v. Orbeck*, the Court struck down an Alaska statute that effectively required companies engaged in pipeline construction and oil and gas production on state land to give hiring preference to qualified Alaska residents.[17] Here is yet another example of the effect of free trade (in this case the right to hire) between Alaska and the other states resulting from the free internal market in the United States and which increases competition between Alaska's and Outside economic forces. Nevertheless, many Alaskans and their politicians still argue for local hire by bringing pressure to bear on employers, particularly large companies locating in the state, such as big-box stores like Costco and Home Depot. The local hire issue has been a continuing aspect of Alaska economic policy.

5. THE CONSEQUENCES OF ALASKA'S DEPENDENCE ON WORLD RESOURCE MARKETS

Alaska has benefited tremendously from its natural extraction industries. Yet, the state's heavy dependence on natural resources saddles it with endemic and chronic problems, as is the case for all natural resource–dependent economies.

The root of these problems is that the prices of these resources are determined by world markets and not by Alaska. Most natural resource economies do not produce

FIGURE 7.5

Non-Resident Employment in Alaska: Percentage of Total Employment in Major Private Industries in 2009 and in the Fishing Industry, 2001-09

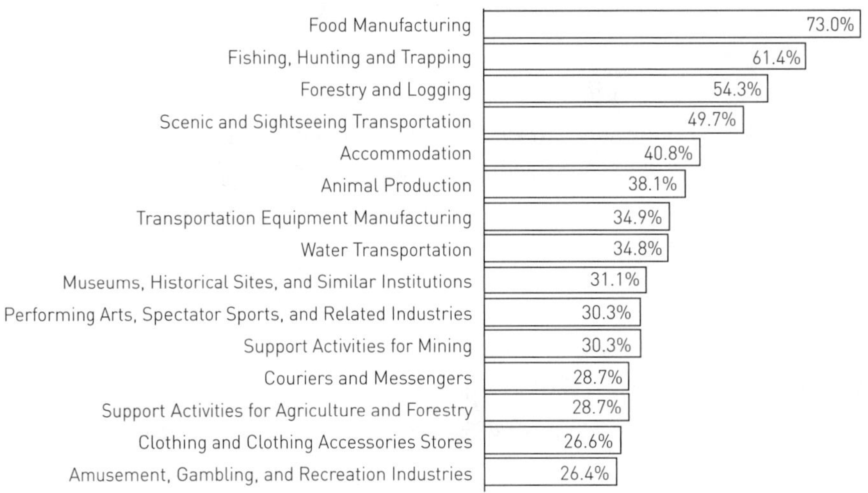

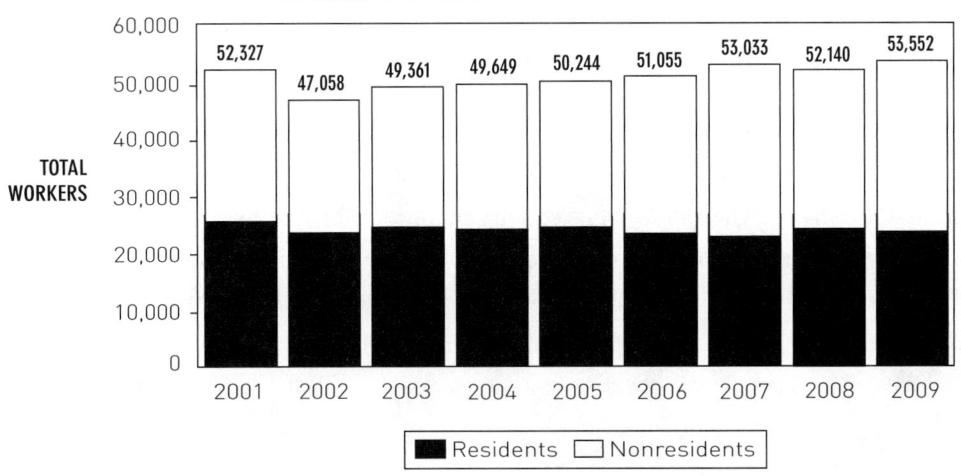

Sources: *Nonresidents Working in Alaska 2009* (Juneau, AK: Alaska Department of Labor and Workforce Development, 2009), p. 3; and "Employment in Alaska's Seafood Industry," *Alaska Economic Trends*, Vol. 30 (11), Alaska Department of Labor, November 2010.

enough of the world's supply of a resource to have even minimal impact on its price. The world price for natural resources depends on the simple free enterprise principle of supply and demand. On the supply side, other economies compete with Alaska, from Saudi Arabian oil producers to Norwegian salmon farmers. In addition, the world demand for Alaska resources depends on factors such as the health of national, regional, and world economies and the exchange rates between the U.S. dollar and foreign currencies, which affect what foreign buyers are willing to pay in dollars for U.S. resources. For all these reasons, natural resource–dependent economies have long been subject to the boom-and-bust cycle as a result of the volatility of the prices of those resources.

Figure 7.6 and Table 7.2 illustrate the problems of natural resource dependence for Alaska. Figure 7.6 shows the volatility of the world price of Alaska's major natural resource products—oil, minerals, and seafood—for various periods since the late 1970s. Table 7.2 shows Alaska's share of U.S. production and world production of four specific resources for 2005 and the latest data on each for 2011–2013. Clearly, the state's share of world market production is very small for all of these resources. Thus changes in levels of production in Alaska do not affect world prices. In contrast, changes in the price of resources such as zinc, lead, gold, silver, salmon, halibut, and especially oil, do affect Alaska's economy, particularly those places and sectors dependent upon them. Major changes in the price of oil can have a far-reaching and, as noted earlier, even a devastating effect on Alaska's economy. Added to this is the declining production of oil in Alaska, down almost 45 percent between 2005 and 2013 (Table 7.2). So the combination of declining production and lower oil prices will spell double financial disaster for Alaska.

Just as oil prices are beyond Alaska's power to control, economic activities around the globe also affect the prices of other Alaska natural resources. Economic growth in China, for example, has driven up zinc prices, benefiting the Native corporation shareholders in Northwest Alaska. By contrast, salmon farming in Norway, Chile, Scotland, and Canada has expanded the world supply of salmon, thereby reducing both the price and Alaska's share of the world salmon market. The decline in salmon prices and market share led to an economic crisis in the salmon industry, the closure of many salmon processing plants, a sharp decline in the value of salmon fishing permits, and a reduction in participation in Alaska salmon fisheries.[18]

A final example of the problems with the global determination of the price of Alaska's natural resources is provided by the long history of the desire to build a natural gas pipeline from the North Slope to the Lower 48 with maybe a spur line to Southcentral Alaska. Accordingly, in 2007, when natural gas prices were high, the state passed the Alaska Gas Inducement Act (AGIA). But soon after, new sources of natural gas from North Dakota

FIGURE 7.6

World and U.S. Prices of Selected Alaska Natural Resources During Extended Periods

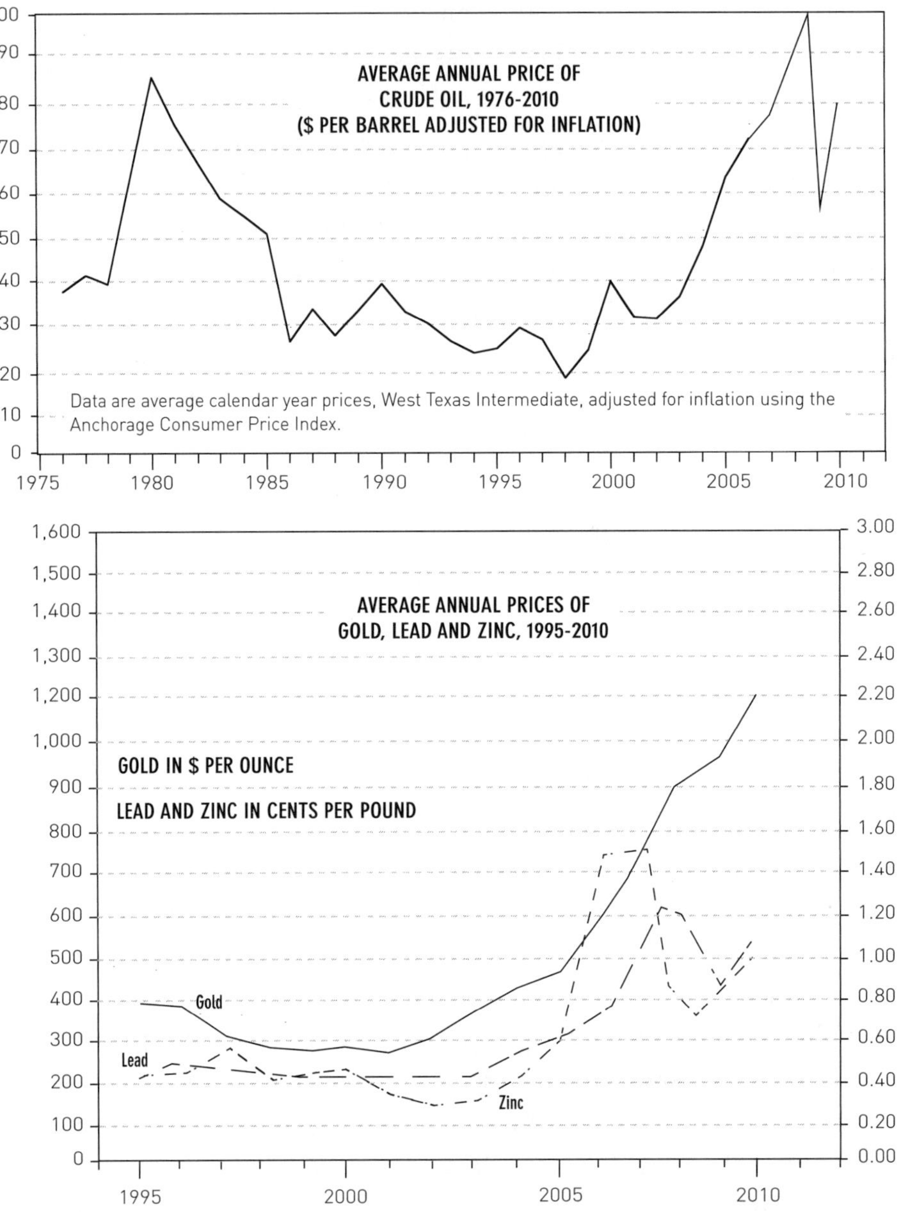

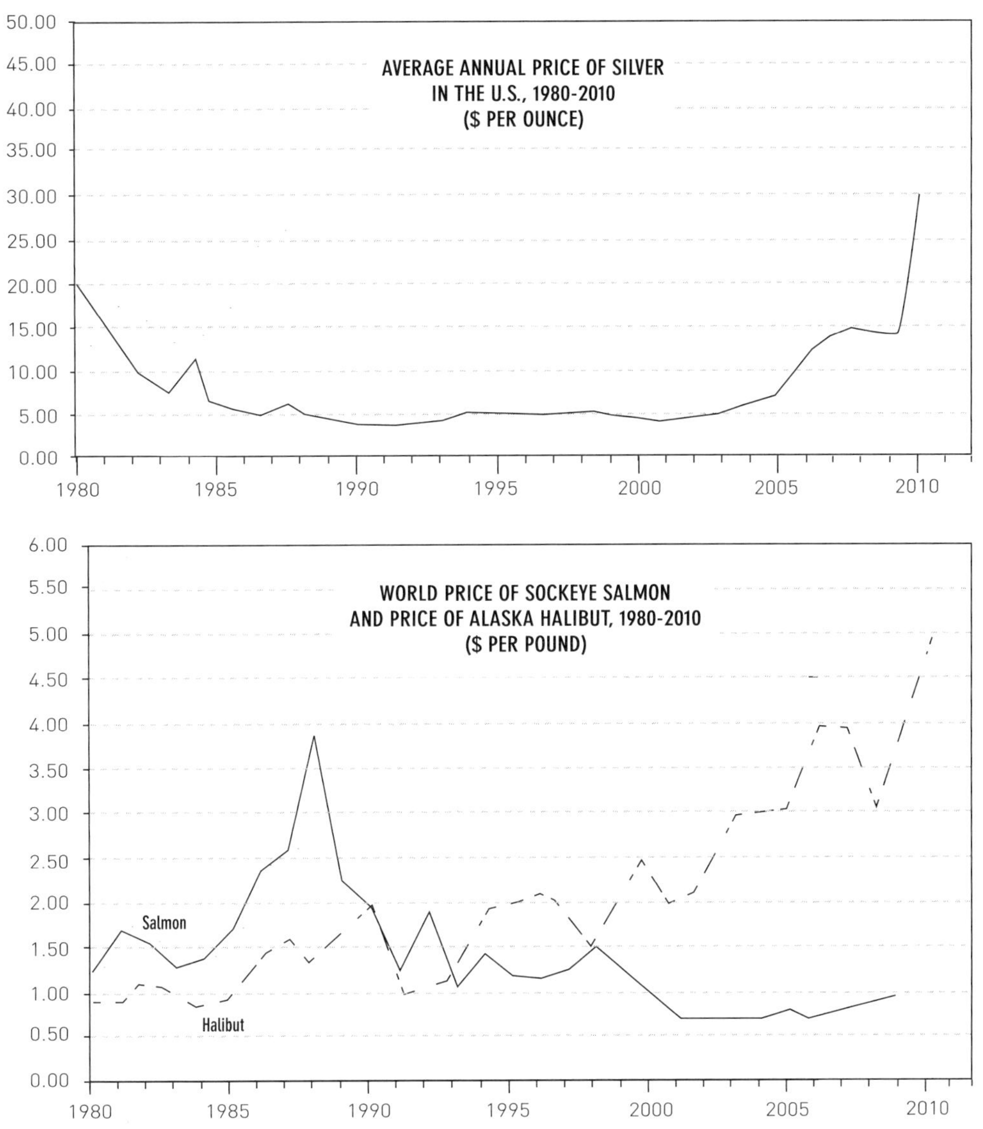

Sources: Oil prices: Alaska Department of Revenue, Tax Division. www.tax.state.ak.us; U.S. Energy Administration: www.eia.doe.gov; Gold, Lead, Zinc, and Silver prices: U.S. Geological Survey Historical Statistics for Mineral and Material Commodities in the United States, and the Alaska Department of Natural Resources: Silver statistics, retrieved from http://minerals.usgs.gov/ds/2005/140/silver.pdf; Salmon prices: Alaska data from Alaska Commercial Fisheries Entry Commission; other data from the Food and Agricultural Organization of the United Nations (FAO), FAO Fishstat+ database. Average Salmon prices are adjusted for inflation and expressed in 2009 $/lb; Halibut ex-vessel prices: for 1980–83, Mark Hermann and Keith Criddle, "An Econometric Model for the Pacific Halibut Fishery," *Marine Resource Economics*, Vol. 21 (2006), 134; and for 1984–2010, Alaska Department of Fish and Game, Division of Commercial Fisheries, COAR Buying Database, 6/3/2011.

TABLE 7.2

Share of U.S. and World Production of Four Major Alaska Commodities in 2005 Compared with 2011–2013*

								ALASKA'S SHARE OF PRODUCTION			
		ALASKA		UNITED STATES		WORLD		UNITED STATES		WORLD	
Commodity	**Units**	**2011–13**	**2005**	**2011–13**	**2005**	**2011–13**	**2005**	**2011–13**	**2005**	**2011–13**	**2005**
Crude oil	Millions of barrels per day (b/d)	0.515	0.936	7.44	5.83	90.45	81.08	6.9%	16.1%	0.5%	1.2%
Gold	1,000s of metric tons	26.1	16	230	256	2,500	2,470	11.0%	6.3%	1.0%	0.7%
Zinc ore	1,000s of metric tons	647	684	748	748	13,130	9,930	86.0%	91.4%	5.0%	6.9%
Wild fish, all species	Millions of metric tons	2.40	2.45	6.31	4.30	91.30	93.22	38.0%	57.1%	3.0%	2.6%

* Figures for oil are for 2013, for gold are estimates for 2011, and for zinc and fish for 2012.

Sources:

For 2005:

Alaska Department of Revenue: Tax Division, *Revenues Sources Book, Fall 2007.*
British Petroleum. *BP Statistical Review of World Energy*, June 2006, www.bp.com/statisticalreview.
D.J. Szumigala and R.A. Hughes, *Alaska's Mineral Industry 2006*, Alaska Division of Geological & Geophysical Surveys, Special Report 61.
U.S. Geological Survey, *2005 Minerals Yearbook, Gold* (March 2007), http://minerals.usgs.gov/minerals/pubs/commodity/gold/gold_myb05.pdf.
U.S. Geological Survey, *2006 Minerals Yearbook, Zinc* (February 2008), http://minerals.usgs.gov/minerals/pubs/commodity/zinc/myb1-2006-zinc.pdf.
National Marine Fisheries Service, *Fisheries of the United States*, 2006.

For 2011–2013

U.S. Energy Information Administration, *Global Petroleum and Other Liquids* (2013) http://www.eia.gov/forecasts/steo/report/global_oil.cfm.
U.S. Energy Information Administration, *Crude Oil Production* (2013) http://www.eia.gov/dnav/pet/pet_crd_crpdn_adc_mbblpd_a.htm.
Alaska Department of Natural Resources, *Alaska's Mineral Industry 2012*, Special Report 68: Estimated Mineral Production in Alaska, http://137.229.113.30/webpubs/dggs/sr/text/sr068.pdf.
U.S. Department of the Interior/U.S. Geological Survey, Mineral Commodity Summaries (2013), http://minerals.usgs.gov/minerals/pubs/mcs/2013/mcs2013.pdf.
All the World's Gold (2014), http://www.numbersleuth.org/worlds-gold/.
International Lead and Zinc Study Group, *Lead and Zinc Statistics* (2014), http://www.ilzsg.org/static/statistics.aspx?from=1.
Fisheries and Aquaculture Department, FAO Global Capture Production database, Summary Information (2014), ftp://ftp.fao.org/FI/STAT/Overviews/CaptureStatistics2012.pdf.
NOAA, National Marine Fisheries Service Office of Science and Technology, "Fisheries in the US" (2012), http://www.st.nmfs.noaa.gov/Assets/commercial/fus/fus12/FUS2012.pdf.

and other states were developed much nearer the market for the gas, and the increased supply caused prices to fall. So by 2014 the plan for a pipeline to the Lower 48 was shelved in favor of the Alaska Stand Alone Pipeline (ASAP)—from the North Slope to Southcentral Alaska (with a spur to Fairbanks) for local consumption and liquefied natural gas exports, mainly to East Asia.[19]

However, the situation became more complicated after the election of independent candidate Bill Walker to the governorship in November 2014, beating Sean Parnell who had championed ASAP, a narrow-diameter pipeline. Walker favors a larger diameter line, and the issue got bogged down in a political stand-off in the 2015 legislative session between Walker and the Republican majority who favored the narrower diameter line. By the end of 2015, however, the two opposing sides had come closer to an agreement. Even so, in a situation of low oil prices and fewer state funds to help construct the gas line, it is doubtful if it will be built anytime soon.

In contrast, when oil, gold, and silver prices are high, they provide an economic cushion for Alaska's economy. But no one can predict how long these prices will hold. They can drop considerably in a short period, as the price of oil dropped 70 percent from over $100 a barrel for close to six years to less than $30 between July 2014 and February 2016. There is little, if anything, Alaska's politicians can do to affect prices of natural resources in any significant way.

6. ALASKA'S POLITICAL ECONOMY: CONSTRAINTS AND CHALLENGES, OPPORTUNITIES, PUBLIC PRESSURES, AND POLICY APPROACHES

In this and the previous chapter several references have been made to the constraints and challenges that the realities of economic circumstances present to Alaska's policy makers. We have also alluded to the opportunities that certain aspects of the economy offer. This section focuses on the characteristics of the Alaska economy as they affect the decisions of policy makers. First, we look at the various policy tools available to Alaska's policy makers to affect the state's economy. Then we turn to the policy challenges from an economist's perspective, followed by the political dimension.

The State's Authority to Adopt Policies Affecting Alaska's Economy

Like any state, Alaska policy makers have the ability to affect the economy and its development over both the long and the short term, though such actions can have both positive and negative effects.

One way for the state to affect the economy is to ban or restrict certain kinds of economic activities. An example is the Alaska legislature's ban on salmon farming, passed in 1990. While this ban protected those fishing for wild salmon, it arguably prevented what might have become a large-scale industry from developing. Another way to affect economic activity is to impose taxes on those coming to do business in Alaska. However, Alaska's policy makers are constrained in the extent to which they can regulate and tax economic activities in the state because investors have the option of not investing in Alaska or shutting down their Alaska operations if the cost of doing business is too high.

Finding the proper balance between too much and too little taxation and regulation is an economic and political conundrum for all governments, including Alaska's. Businesses, supported by conservative politicians such as former Governor Parnell, argue for lower taxes as a business incentive. Accordingly, in 2010 Governor Parnell was instrumental in reducing the head tax on cruise ship passengers imposed a few years earlier. Then in 2011 he proposed lowering oil and gas taxes, reversing an increase enacted a few years earlier at the urging of Governor Palin. In the absence of hard economic data on the effect of taxes on investment and development, the debate inevitably became a political and ideological one. Parnell's tax reduction legislation was defeated by the legislature in 2012. However, a new more conservative legislature passed the measure in 2013. The legislation was challenged in an August 2014 referendum in which the voters upheld the legislation.[20]

The state can also have an effect on the economy through environmental regulations to protect the natural "Alaska experience" of the tourism sector of the economy. It can establish workplace regulations, such as attempting to promote local hire of Alaskans, though, as explained earlier, that kind of effort may run afoul of federal laws. In addition, state government can actively promote:

- Investment in transportation, communications, energy, and other utility infrastructure to lower costs of doing business in Alaska.
- Adoption of policies to reduce political risks of doing business in Alaska, including clear business and environmental regulations, and a state fiscal policy that reduces the risk of future large tax increases on businesses if or when oil revenues decline.
- Adoption of clear and stable policies for the management of Alaska resources in order to provide opportunities for resource industries to gain access to a stable, long-term resource supply.
- Support of generic marketing for industries such as seafood and tourism in order to help develop an "Alaska brand."
- Training programs to provide a supply of skilled labor for firms locating in Alaska.
- Improving the quality of life, through investments in public safety, schools, universities, parks, sports facilities, and other ways to make Alaska a place where employees want to live and work.

Alaska's status as an Owner State gives policy makers, at least in theory, some flexibility that they would not otherwise have, given the unbalanced structure of the economy. All opportunities that the Owner State affords policy makers regarding use, management, and regulation over land, fish and game, and other resources are significant in terms of aiding the economy. Nothing comes close, however, to the economic opportunities presented by Alaska's oil bonanza.

Dependence on the export of natural resources leaves Alaska vulnerable to wide swings in natural resource prices driven by global economic forces. Nonetheless, the massive oil revenues that have flowed into state coffers afford Alaska's policy makers enormous economic freedom if they choose to exercise it. These revenues have given policy makers the opportunity to promote economic stability and help even out the inevitable periodic boom-bust cycles. Dealing with booms and busts was an original purpose for establishing the Permanent Fund in 1976.

Moreover, if state investments were judicious—not used for projects that were clearly not viable economically—state revenues accruing from oil could be used to promote the long-term economic growth and health of the state's economy. With the right planning and policies, the state's revenue resources are such that Alaska could even weather national and international economic downturns. Because oil prices continued to be high during the economic downturn of 2008–2010, Alaska did not face the major budget cuts that most states did. In fact, in fiscal year 2010 the state accrued a $12 billion surplus, more than the amount of the state budget that year. During that same period, the Permanent Fund contained close to $40 billion, four times the annual state budget. Plus, the state has other "savings" accounts, such as the Constitutional Budget Reserve (CBR), which stood at $5 billion at the time of the $12 billion surplus, and by June 2015 had grown to over $10 billion and the Permanent Fund to over $52 billion.

So, from an economic theory perspective, Alaska's policy makers have the means to promote both stability and growth. There are, however, a number of constraints and challenges, both from the economist's perspective and from the political realities that affect any kind of policy choices, including economic ones.

The Economist's Perspective: Constraints and Challenges

Because of the openness of Alaska's economy, the limiting factor that inhibits private industries from developing is not investment capital, but external competition from both other states and other countries. Given this competition, Alaska's high cost of labor and production, climate, size, and remoteness, coupled with high transportation costs to and from the state and within it, severely limit the efforts of policy makers to restructure the economy. These limitations virtually preclude agriculture and allow for only minimal manufacturing, thus making economic diversification economically infeasible.

So, when state policy makers attempt to create new industries by investing public funds, the chances are that they are investing in industries that private investors have already considered to be non-competitive. It is unlikely that policy makers or bureaucrats will have better information or insights about the economic viability of projects or industries than private investors. Furthermore, among the biggest factors affecting Alaska's economy—for good and for bad—are decisions made by companies based outside of Alaska. Decisions made in corporate board rooms in Seattle, Houston, Tokyo, and London may lead to billions of dollars of investment in oil or mine development, providing well-paying jobs for hundreds or thousands of Alaskans. Or such decisions may lead to the abrupt closure of fish processing plants upon which Alaska fishermen and communities have depended for decades. In September 2014, for example, less than a month after voter approval of Governor Parnell's oil tax reductions, BP announced a plan to lay off 475 oil workers, which took the governor by surprise.[21] Clearly, the influence of Alaska policy makers on such decisions is minimal compared to the influence of global economic considerations of cost, markets, competition, profitability, and risk.

The realities of the Alaska economy also mean that the state does not have the potential in trade, particularly in international trade, that many believe is possible simply by adopting the right policy or repealing what is viewed as a particularly onerous regulation or restriction. Attempts by Alaska's government to develop new markets, such as trade missions by public officials to foreign countries, are unlikely to have much effect on demand for Alaska products. Serious business people are in constant search of economic opportunities. Where there are real opportunities to do business with Alaska, they are likely to discover them much more quickly than Alaska policy makers.

The economic reality is that Alaska is stuck with a natural resource–extraction economy. Additional development in this sector is certainly possible, but the state will still be vulnerable to the world prices of the natural resources it develops. Even if Alaska were an independent nation, free to develop its resources without "interference" from the federal government, world markets and the free enterprise system would impose many constraints, as countries like Zambia (dependent on copper) are reminded from time to time.

In combination, all these constraints help explain an apparent paradox in Alaska policy making, one not well understood by many citizens or by some politicians. This paradox is that even though the State of Alaska owns a third of Alaska's lands, has management control over its salmon and herring fisheries, and has enjoyed very high state revenues and accumulated enormous wealth, state policy makers have been relatively unsuccessful in their attempts to directly influence the structure of the economy by promoting new industries.

Not all the challenges and constraints faced by Alaska's policy makers on economic issues are the result of economic realities, however. Many result from politics and the elements of Alaska's political economy.

The Political Dimension

It is the interplay of politics with economics that not only helps to define the political economy of a state but also influences the approach to economic issues. The influence of politics on economic choices is not necessarily a bad thing. Through political choices, societies, including Alaska's, often place other factors above economic efficiency, including the greater public good and the needs of the less well-off. In other circumstances, politics may benefit narrow economic interests, to the economic detriment of the state as a whole. Here, we explain the effects that politics can have on economic policy in Alaska in three ways: political cultural and ideological influences, Outside political forces, and the perspective of public officials. Then we present a balance sheet of the intertwining of politics and economics in Alaska.

The Political Cultural Dimension

The approach to economic issues by public officials depends to a large extent on the political values of the environment in which they operate. As Chapter 5 on political culture points out, this environment in Alaska manifests a culture of pragmatic dependent individualism and a strong strain of self-proclaimed fiscal conservatism.

Political individualism and fiscal conservatism have worked to restrict policy makers from pursuing innovative solutions, including fiscal planning, to deal with the consequences of the unbalanced economy. Even the innovative Permanent Fund, originally established as a savings account to help even-out state revenues in years of revenue shortfalls, has, at least until late 2015, been off limits for that purpose primarily because of the Permanent Fund Dividend (PFD). The amount of the yearly payout is determined by the size of the fund's recent earnings, which in turn is largely a function of the total size of the fund. Thus, the clear message that voters send to policy makers is, "Don't mess with the Permanent Fund or you won't get my vote." This may change to some extent, however, due to low oil prices beginning in 2014.

Another consequence of individualism and fiscal conservatism is Alaska's low level of state taxes on individuals. The state income tax on individuals was abolished in 1980 as oil revenues began to increase dramatically, and, also as of 2015, there is no statewide sales tax (though several local communities have sales taxes). Lack of such taxes further reduces the choices of policy makers in dealing with revenue shortfalls. It also leads to what might be called the "Alaska Disconnect." In most states, there is a direct connection between the amount of taxes individual voters pay and the level of governmental services they receive. That is not the case in Alaska. Also, economic development creates new jobs that require additional governmental services, such as schools and public safety. In most states new arrivals help pay the costs of those increased services through taxes. In Alaska, economic development creates an increase in demand for public services, but not the funding to provide them. Since the late 1970s the only sector that has paid its own way is oil.[22]

Yet, as Chapter 5 also points out, the political cultural traits of individualism and fiscal conservatism are laden with pragmatism. What this means is that fiscal conservatism is subject to "modification" when it comes to personal interest. Local communities and individuals want to protect the government spending coming their way, but often oppose funding or want to cut programs for other districts, seeing them as "wasteful." This perspective is often reflected in the attitudes and actions of public officials, especially elected ones.

Outside Political Forces

The Outside economic influences of the free enterprise system on the Alaska economy often translate into political forces. In addition, there are Outside government and political forces that can translate into political influence on Alaska's economy.

Private political influences include major oil, mining, fishing, cruise lines, airlines (particularly Alaska Airlines), and some retail companies, such as Safeway and Walmart. The natural resource companies, in particular, have a permanent political presence through lobbying by their own employees and by hiring contract lobbyists, and most of them are major contributors to political campaigns. Their concerns are to keep taxes low, combat what they consider to be irksome regulations, and generally foster a positive business atmosphere in the state. The political economy of Alaska has been very much influenced by the political activities of the oil companies based on their major contribution to state coffers. The companies certainly do not "run" Alaska politics—far from it. But they do have a major influence in the state and on the economic policy decisions of state policy makers and apparently on the majority of Alaska voters too, judging by the approval of Governor Parnell's oil tax cut in the August 2014 referendum.[23]

The political effects of Alaska's other basic industry, the federal government, are extensive. Alaska's major dependence on federal funds plus the federal government's land ownership and regulatory authority in the state make the federal government perhaps the major political force in Alaska. Some of the most publicized effects of federal control have been the prohibition on oil development in the Arctic National Wildlife Refuge (ANWR) and restrictions on logging in wilderness areas of the Tongass and Chugach national forests. Besides the issue of local hire, federal constitutional protections on economic migration among the states constrains Alaska policy makers in other ways, such as the length of residency required to receive a PFD. This dependence on, and the constraints of, the federal government are also central elements of Alaska's political economy and a never-ending source of conflict between Alaska and Washington, D.C., as related in Chapter 10.

The Perspective and Approach of Public Officials

Public officials, particularly elected ones, are in a difficult position politically in regard to the economy. On the one hand, as the economy is a major concern to most of their constituents, public officials must be seen as proactive in promoting the health of the economy and providing benefits to their districts (and the entire state in the governor's case). On the other hand, their options are limited by Alaska's economic realities and further by the political cultural trait of fiscal conservatism, an anti-tax attitude, and the influence of Outside political forces.

Elected officials are reluctant to admit that they cannot do anything major to enhance Alaska's economy. Each one deals with this situation differently, depending on their personal beliefs, party affiliation, political ambitions, their constituents' attitudes, and their level of knowledge. However, we can make some general observations about how elected officials in Alaska deal with economic issues. Their proactive stance produces a range of suggestions from the illusionary to the practical. Three of these politically motivated approaches are particularly significant.

One we can call the "blame game" or the "if only" syndrome, which in many cases involves exploiting the myths of Alaska's political rhetoric and are not really proposals at all. The blame gamers and "if only" adherents cite what they believe is the oppressive nature of federal regulations, along with environmental interests and too much state government bureaucracy. If only these could be reduced or eliminated, they claim, Alaska's economic future would be assured forever. This is related, in part, to the belief that, under the right circumstances, economic diversification is very possible.

A second approach is more constructive, even if sometimes not economically viable. Under this approach, subsidies for business activities are pursued, such as agriculture and processing agricultural products. As explained earlier, this often ends in major losses to the state, though it may temporarily benefit a politician and his or her constituents. More economically viable is to subsidize the start-up costs of certain businesses, as was done with the Red Dog Mine near Kotzebue in the mid-1980s. Other economic policy ideas proposed in the past are clearly unfeasible or unwise, but may serve the needs of a politician who wants to appear proactive. One proposal was to collect abandoned cars and other metal items in bush communities and bring them into Anchorage to melt down into steel. Another was using Permanent Fund principal as well as earnings for economic development.

A third perspective of elected officials is one of pragmatic dependent individualism. This perspective represents the major practical approach of Alaska policy makers to economic problems, issues, and concerns. It enables them to finesse their difficulty of taking action in the face of major constraints. There are three aspects to this approach.

First, in some form or another, legislators have to secure some tangible economic benefits for their districts in order to be seen as effective and ensure reelection. This is particularly the case with rural-bush legislators who are often judged in a major way by their ability to secure capital project money for school buildings, fire halls, airstrips, and so on. And if they can bring state jobs to their districts, this is also advantageous. Even urban legislators need to secure such budget funds for their districts.

Second, dependance on government means that politicians realize that government money is essential to their districts. So they want to protect funding and programs for their constituents. However, particularly in the case of conservatives, attitudes of fiscal conservatism push them to advocate reducing government spending and, in some cases, transfer functions and services to the private sector. They may be pressured to do both by their constituents. This contradiction has to be reconciled.

Democrats are generally less subject to this contradiction. But many Democrats still represent districts in which fiscal conservatism and opposition to personal taxes and using Permanent Fund earnings for anything other than PFDs are strong public sentiments. Republicans and conservative Democrats tend to reconcile this contradiction by ignoring it, arguing for special needs, justifying their district's projects, and, if not always directly, distinguishing the value of these projects from other less worthy projects in other districts that should be cut as part of needed government cost savings.

As noted in Chapter 3 on policy making, district and regional needs and politicians' own interests often trump ideology or statewide interests. And if local, personal, and statewide benefits can all be obtained, so much the better for any politician. In most cases, however, as in securing money for a local road, dock, harbor, or airport facility, the fact of whether or not this project fits into an overall state transportation plan is of little or no significance to a politician. What is important is that it brings in money and jobs to the district and a facility that people will associate with them when election time rolls around.

Third, given the realities of the economic and political constraints faced by politicians on economic issues, they reconcile dependence and individualism (defined as their and their constituents' interests) through political pragmatism. In the end, they and their constituents want jobs, good local facilities, and a good standard of living, and these needs usually outweigh ideology, particularly fiscal conservatism.

A Balance Sheet: Mixed Consequences for Alaska's Economic Policies Over the Years

Politics usually dominates economic reality. This dominance in Alaska has had mixed results in enhancing the state's economy overall. There have been downsides but also wise decisions and foresight on the part of politicians, the latter aided by Alaska's oil bonanza.

Once oil revenues began flowing to the state, state lawmakers made perhaps the most important and far-reaching economic policy decision since statehood—they created the Permanent Fund. Perhaps the second most important decision was to require that the fund's principal be invested conservatively and to resist the political pressures to invest in a host of economically unviable Alaska projects. The fund and its earnings provide an economic and political cushion for the state and its policy makers in providing spending and policy options that would not otherwise exist.

More of a mixed economic blessing was the establishment of the PFD in 1980. Certainly, the yearly dividends provide a major boost to the economy and are a major source of cash in rural-bush areas. Not surprisingly, this free money program is wildly popular and it has come to be viewed as a right by most Alaskans. But this attitude effectively puts the use of Fund earnings off limits politically for its originally intended purpose of supplementing state funds when oil revenues fall, and thus has limited economic policy options available to Alaska's lawmakers. But, again, necessity may change this situation due to low oil prices for an eighteen-month period through early 2016 and likely beyond.

Additionally, the elusive pursuit of economic diversification, subsidizing uneconomic Alaska projects, and blaming the federal and state governments for whatever economic woes the state faces, are all examples of political realities trumping realistic economic possibilities. If these attitudes were confined to political rhetoric there would be little harm done. Sometimes, however, they get translated into public policies, such as the state's past subsidies for agricultural and agribusiness ventures.

Economically misconceived or politically motivated projects will likely exist as long as politics does. Where a course of action is politically expedient, economic reality and facts will be subordinated to political necessity. As in the past, Alaska's politicians will not want to admit that they have little control over the way that the state's economy is structured. Thus, we can expect more of the same and a mixed future in terms of both wise and not so wise decisions on economic policy.

7. CONCLUSION: UNDERSTANDING ALASKA POLITICS THROUGH ITS POLITICAL ECONOMY

While it is not the only way to acquire insights into Alaska politics, the political economy approach does provide a valuable perspective on the nature of political discourse in the state, both past and present. This includes helping to explain why and how some issues are dealt with while others are not considered at all. The political economy approach is particularly useful when combined with other approaches to Alaska politics, such as the policy cycle (or policy process) approach or the realist approach (emphasizing personalities and power relationships).

Several chapters that follow are written from a political economy perspective or can be approached with this perspective in mind. This is particularly the case with Chapters 21 through 24 on land, the environment, fisheries, and oil. These chapters all address issues and policies generated by Alaska's Owner State and in turn affect the operation of the Owner State. The political economy perspective is also helpful in approaching Chapter 9 on the role of Alaska Natives, Chapter 18 on local government, Chapter 19 on the state budget process, and Chapter 28 on transportation. And the political economy perspective is especially useful in understanding the nature and continuing debate about state revenues, the subject of the next chapter.

ENDNOTES

[1] This chapter draws in part on Gunnar Knapp, *An Introduction to the Economy of Alaska*, Institute of Social and Economic Research (ISER), University of Alaska Anchorage, February, 2012. The chapter also draws on a variety of sources for information and statistics on Alaska's relations with the Outside economy. In many cases, up-to-date information and figures are not available and, for some aspects of Outside trade, a synthesis of several sources is necessary to draw inferences and conclusions. However, the goal of the chapter is not to provide a specific current picture but a general context to identify trends in Alaska as a state, and place it in comparison with other states.

[2] D. J. Szumigala, L. A. Harbo, and R. A. Hughes, *Alaska's Mineral Industry 2009*, Special Report (Juneau: Alaska Department of Natural Resources, Division of Geological and Geophysical Services, 2010), 64.

[3] Statistics on Alaska exports, in addition to those in the tables and figures, combine sources from the State of Alaska Office of International Trade, at http://www.gov.state.ak.us/trade/, and the World Trade Center-Alaska (WTC-AK) at http://www.wtcak.org/.

[4] Estimates are based on discussions by the author with Alaska seafood producers and comparisons of U.S. export data with Alaska production data.

[5] Data used here are from the State of Alaska. Other sources, such as the Alaska Travel Industry Association, have slightly different totals. The difference is largely due to how the figures are calculated. Some are calculated by fall/winter, others by summer, others by the calendar year.

[6] This estimate is based on a McDowell Group report, *Economic Impacts of Alaska's Visitor Industry: 2012–13 Update* (Juneau: Alaska Department of Commerce, Community, and Economic Development, Division of Economic Development, 2014), 2. It takes the total spending by all visitors to Alaska, which includes 400,000 people in addition to summer tourists for a total of two million visitors, and makes an estimate of tourist spending based on the total spent by all visitors of just under $2 billion. The figures include only money spent in Alaska and not on fares or other costs to travel to and from the state.

[7] See Chapter 6, Table 6.3.

[8] Foreign Direct Investment (FDI) is a component of a country's national financial accounts. FDI includes investment of foreign assets in domestic structures, equipment, and organizations, but not in the stock market. FDI is considered more useful to a country than those in the equity of its

companies because equity investments are potentially "hot money," which can leave at the first sign of trouble. In contrast, FDI is durable and long term whether or not things go well economically.

[9] Obtaining accurate data on FDI and other national and state statistics since 2007 is difficult because one of the major sources of information, the *Statistical Abstract of the United States*, published by the U.S. Census Bureau, was discontinued effective October 2011 due to federal cost-saving measures.

[10] Information on the recent significance of oil, minerals, and fish to Alaska and in comparison with the nation is a synthesis of the following sources, retrieved on September 21, 2014: U.S. Energy Information Administration, at http://www.eia.gov/dnav/pet/pet_crd_crpdn_adc_mbblpd_a.htm; U.S. Geological Survey, *U.S. Nonfuel Mineral Production Increases for Third Straight Year*, at http://www.usgs.gov/newsroom/article.asp?ID=3506#.VDBJIfmzGDo; U.S. Census Bureau, *The 2011 Statistical Abstract: Forestry, Fishing, and Mining: Petroleum Industry, Natural Gas*, Table 901: Value of Domestic Nonfuel Mineral Production by State, at http://www.census.gov/compendia/statab/cats/forestry_fishing_and_mining/petroleum_industry_natural_gas.html; and National Marine Fisheries Service Office of Science and Technology, *Annual Commercial Landing Statistics*; National Marine Fisheries Service, at http://www.st.nmfs.noaa.gov/pls/webpls/mf_lndngs_grp.data_in.

[11] This is a percentage of the state's own-source revenues, the amount it raises by its own efforts, and does not include federal funds. See Chapter 8, on state revenues, Figure 8.4.

[12] *Alaska Dispatch News*, "Bill Walker Answers Questions about the Issues in the 2014 Election for Alaska Governor," October 11, 2014. The other two policies that candidate Walker identified were a gas pipeline and development of the Arctic.

[13] See Chapter 6, Table 6.1.

[14] Bureau of Economic Analysis, U.S. Department of Commerce, *Gross Domestic Product (GDP) by State and Metropolitan Area*, at http://www.bea.gov/regional/index.htm#gsp.

[15] See, Chapter 6, Tables 6.1 and 6.2.

[16] Recent and historical figures on resident and nonresident employment are from the Alaska Department of Labor and Workforce Development, Research and Analysis Unit, at http://labor.alaska.gov/research/reshire/reshire.htm.

[17] *Hicklin v. Orbeck*, 437 U.S. 518 (1978).

[18] Gunnar Knapp, Cathy Roheim, and James L. Anderson, *The Great Salmon Run: Competition Between Wild and Farmed Salmon* (Washington, D.C.: TRAFFIC North America and World Wildlife Fund, 2007).

[19] See Chapter 24, on oil and gas, Box 24.2, for a consideration of the economics and politics of an Alaska natural gas pipeline.

[20] See Chapter 14, on campaigns and elections, Sections 3, 4, and 5 for details on the referendum, and Chapter 16, on legislative-executive relations, Box 16.9, for an account of the initial stage of the politics involved in the Parnell oil tax reduction proposal.

[21] Alex DeMarban, "BP to Reduce Alaska Workforce by 475 by Early Next Year," *Alaska Dispatch News*, September 15, 2014.

[22] Institute of Social and Economic Research (ISER), "The Alaska Disconnect," in *The Alaska Citizen's Guide to the Budget*, April 2003, See also, Chapter 8 on state revenues for discussion of the economics and politics of the income tax, state sales tax, and other tax issues.

[23] See Chapter 24 on oil and gas issues and policy, Section 7, for perspectives on the political influence of the oil industry in Alaska.

★ CHAPTER 8 ★

Alaska's State Revenues: Economic Reality Colliding with Political Pressures

Jason Turo, M. Wayne Marr, and Clive S. Thomas

The most significant challenge that Alaska's policy makers will face in the decades to come is that of dealing with unstable state revenues.[1] This challenge has three elements to it: chronically unstable oil prices, declining oil production, and uncertainty regarding federal aid to state and local governments. Given that over 90 percent of Alaska's state revenues, which averaged around $12 billion a year between fiscal years (FY) 2012 and 2015, comes from oil revenues and federal funds, this is a particularly major challenge. In this regard consider the following two news headlines:

- "State applies drastic cuts to oil price forecast, reflecting world market" (*Alaska Dispatch News*, December 6, 2014). The article went on to say that the revenue deficit for FY 2015 could be $3.5 billion, about 30 percent of the proposed state budget.
- "Federal spending in Alaska has leveled off, report says" (*Anchorage Daily News*, May 20, 2012). While this refers to all federal spending in Alaska, the increasingly conservative complexion of Congress could affect funds coming directly to the states. And lower state revenues mean less money available to provide the matching funds required by the federal government as a condition of some federal funding, especially in the areas of Medicaid and transportation.[2]

And it is all too likely that Alaskans might be reading the following news bulletin from CNN on their smartphones as soon as ten years from now:

- "Earlier today the Trans-Alaska Pipeline shut down for good, as Alaska's North Slope oil production finally came to an end, along with the massive tax revenues Alaska previously received from the oil industry. The state faces economic disaster."

Many might respond that these are not really problems given the vast oil and gas reserves in the Arctic National Wildlife Refuge (ANWR) and the National Petroleum Reserve–Alaska (NPR-A) in the state's far north, which are just waiting to be tapped, and given the state's $52 billion savings account (the Alaska Permanent Fund), which is four or five times the size of recent state budgets. Plus, the state can look to new taxes—perhaps by enacting a statewide sales tax or reimposing the state income tax on individuals that was repealed in 1980. Indeed, these are all ways of dealing with Alaska's budget gap, often called a fiscal gap (the difference in a fiscal year between state revenues and planned state spending). The problem, however, is that politics gets in the way.

The experience since the 1980s shows that politically Alaska is unwilling to move toward balanced revenue streams despite economic reality and the pitfalls of unstable revenues. Even the Alaska Permanent Fund, created largely to supplement state revenues when they are low, has, at least until December 2015, been politically off-limits as a budget supplement. Accordingly, this chapter explains how politics affects Alaska's state revenues and how economic realities have been subordinated to political decisions. The argument made here has also been made for many years by some policy makers and Alaskans: the state cannot count on federal funds for a bailout to pick up the slack when oil production reaches an unsustainable level or oil prices stay low for a long time. Alaska needs to plan for a new economic reality, and planning and implementation cannot be done overnight. Thought must be given now to approaches to meet major revenue shortfalls in the future.

In explaining how politics dominates economics, three characteristics of Alaska politics are clearly evident: (1) the significant role of external economic and political forces, (2) fiscal conservatism, and (3) the political culture of both pragmatic dependent individualism and populism.

This chapter begins with an explanation of key revenue terms. Then Sections 2, 3, and 4 compare Alaska's state revenue sources with other states, provide an overview of how Alaska got to its present dependence on oil revenues and federal funds, and offer an explanation of the problems this dependence brings. Sections 5 and 6 review approaches to dealing with the revenue problem, first in terms of revenue sources and planning and then specific policy options. In Section 7 we look at the way politics has dominated revenue planning and policy. Section 8 sums up the main points of the chapter from a political economy perspective.

1. KEY REVENUE TERMS AND CONCEPTS

Box 8.1 explains the key terms specific to the discussion of revenues in this chapter. Of particular importance is the distinction that the Alaska Department of Revenue makes

BOX 8.1

Revenue Terms

Earmark: Sometimes called pork-barrel legislation or riders on a bill, a one-time item in a budget for a specific purpose, such as building a harbor or fire station.

General purpose unrestricted revenue: Money that the state government can spend the way it wants to, subject to appropriation by the legislature.

General revenue: Money governments raise through taxation and other sources, which may be used for any purpose authorized by law.

Government revenue/revenues: Income from all sources, including taxation, **user fees** (see below), money from other governments (intergovernmental transfers), and in some cases revenue from government-owned industries or services, such as utilities and prison industries.

Own-source state revenue: State revenue acquired by a method determined by its government, such as through a state income tax, and contrasted with funds received through intergovernmental transfers, particularly from the federal government.

Restricted revenue: Revenue directed for a specific purpose by the state constitution, federal or state laws, or by financial obligations; for example, highway revenues from toll roads to be spent on road improvements.

Selective tax: A fee on items such as alcohol, tobacco, and gambling.

User fees: A charge for the use of public services or facilities, such as to camp in a state park or travel on a state ferry.

Source: Developed by the authors.

between restricted revenue and general purpose unrestricted revenue, usually referred to simply as unrestricted revenue.

Unrestricted revenues or general purpose revenues are the major source for state budget spending and are used as a planning guide by budget makers. Higher general revenues allow for flexible spending on roads, schools, public health, and other public services. The Department of Revenue separates general revenues into four major subcategories based on the source of the revenue: (1) oil revenues; (2) federal funds; (3) investment income; and (4) "other," which includes non-oil corporate, income, and other taxes. The "other" category also includes fees charged for services, fines, and forfeitures; licenses and permits; non-oil rents and royalties; and other revenue sources.[3] In FY 2014, for example, the state received total revenues of $17.2 billion, of which $5.7 billion came from oil, $2.5 billion from federal funds, $8.1 billion in investments, and $1 billion in other revenues. This was the first year that investments outstripped oil revenues as Alaska's major source of state funds. However, most of these investment funds, $6.9 billion, were restricted funds from Permanent Fund earnings. So oil is still the major source of Alaska's unrestricted state funds.[4]

In fact, since the late 1970s a yearly average of well over 80 percent, and occasionally as high as 95 percent, of the state's own-source general revenue has come from oil production taxes, royalties, settlements, rents, and bonuses. Most oil revenue is unrestricted and goes into the state's main operating account (the general fund) for general spending purposes.

2. ALASKA'S STATE REVENUES COMPARED WITH OTHER STATES

Across the fifty states there are two basic principles that govern the stability, efficiency, and general health of revenue systems. One is the interdependence between agencies and levels of government. The other is the diversity of revenue sources. Cooperation among state agencies dealing with revenues, the legislature and governor, and local governments can enhance the effectiveness of a government's revenue system. The principles of interdependence, however, are beyond the scope of this chapter. Our focus is on the second principle—the need for diversified revenue sources. Lack of diversity can and often does pose serious problems for a state's budget. This has certainly been the case for Alaska.

What, then, are the sources of state revenues across the states, and how does Alaska compare nationwide? This can be viewed from two perspectives. One is general overall state revenues, which include direct payments from the federal government, known as intergovernmental transfers. The other perspective is own-source revenue (see Box 8.1).

Overall State Revenues and Revenue per Person

There are two major ways to compare overall state revenues across the states. One is by total numbers and percentages of state and federal funds in a state budget. The other, more informative, way in terms of potential citizen benefits from state spending, is revenue per capita.

The Total Amount of State Revenues and Federal Funds

Table 8.1 compares Alaska's overall state revenues in 2012 with those of several states. 2012 is a more or less typical year for comparison since the late 1970s, although the percentage of federal funds in Alaska's state budget was slightly lower that year than in most other years. Between 2001 and 2012 Alaska received an average of just under 25 percent of its total expenditures from the federal government, ranging from $2 to $3 billion per year.[5] This percentage is among the lowest of any state. Alaska regularly ranks in the bottom five states in this regard. In 2012, for instance, at 19 percent it ranked forty-eighth. But in terms of federal funds per capita, Alaska regularly ranks in the top five. Moreover, other than the District of Columbia, Alaska ranked number one, with $3,146 per capita in stimulus federal monies received between 2009 and 2011 to help deal with the 2008

TABLE 8.1

Comparing Alaska's State Revenue with Selected States: Revenues for Fiscal Year 2012

STATE	TOTAL STATE REVENUE INCLUDING FEDERAL FUNDS (IN $ BILLIONS)	TOTAL FEDERAL FUNDS IN STATE BUDGET (IN $ BILLIONS)	FEDERAL REVENUE AS PERCENTAGE OF TOTAL STATE REVENUES	REVENUE PER CAPITA AND NATIONAL RANKING		POPULATION IN MILLIONS
Alaska	**$15.050**	**$2.860**	**19**	**$20,576**	**1**	**0.731**
California	250.882	54.145	22	6,595	16	38.041
Florida	82.823	22.850	28	4,287	49	19.317
Kansas	16.144	4.061	25	5,594	33	2.885
Louisiana	26.942	11.136	41	5,855	31	4.401
Michigan	64.021	17.849	28	6,478	18	9.883
New Mexico	15.195	5.171	34	6,496	12	2.085
New York	179.604	48.698	27	9,177	5	19.570
Texas	137.723	37.310	27	5,285	39	26.059
Wyoming	6.845	2.213	32	11,876	3	0.576
United States*	**$1,912,253,172**	**$514,181,193**	**27% average**	**$6,092**		**313,914,000**

* These rankings exclude Washington, D.C., from the original source.

Source: Data compiled by the authors from U.S. Census Bureau, "Annual Estimates of the Resident Population for the United States, Regions, States, and Puerto Rico: April 1, 2010 to July 1, 2012," at https://www.census.gov/popest/data/state/totals/2012/; and U.S. Census Bureau, "2012 Annual Survey of State Government Finances," at http://factfinder2.census.gov/faces/tableservices/jsf/pages/productview.xhtml?src=bkmk.

recession and its aftermath.[6] But other than the one-time stimulus funds, federal transfers do little to increase flexibility in state spending since they are normally restricted funds (that is, required to be spent on certain programs or projects, mainly Medicaid and transportation). One form of federal funds that does have somewhat more flexibility is the federal earmark. These are funds "earmarked" for specific Alaska projects, and placed in the federal budget by Alaska's congressional delegation. For many years Alaska led the nation on earmarks, although they have declined since 2009.

Total State Revenue Per Capita

As to revenues per capita, Figure 8.1 illustrates the amount in dollars for the same ten states in Table 8.1 for both 2006 and 2012 (the 2012 column for each state is the dollar amount from Table 8.1 in the form of a graph). The comparison across a six-year period shows the consistent relationship between Alaska and other states, which has also been similar since the early 1980s.

FIGURE 8.1

Combined State and Federal Revenue Per Capita: Alaska Compared with Selected States for Fiscal Years 2006 and 2012

(With National Ranking for Each Year)

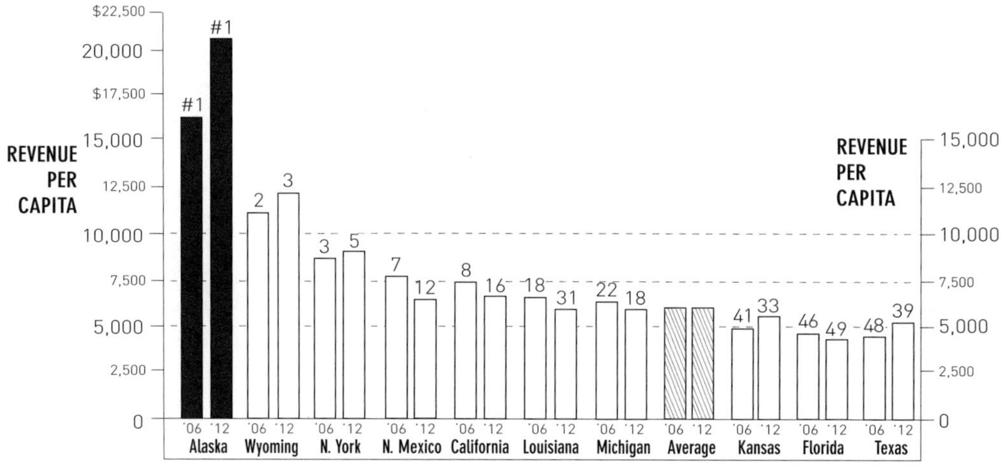

Source: Created by the authors using data from the U.S. Census Bureau, State and Local Government Finance, Historical Data, "2006 Annual Survey of State Government Finances," at http://www.census.gov/govs/estimate/historical_data_2006.html, and Population Estimates, "Annual Estimates of the Resident Population for the United States, Regions, States, and Puerto Rico," at http://www.census.gov/popest/states/NST-ann-est2008.html; U.S. Census Bureau, "Annual Estimates of the Resident Population for the United States, Regions, States, and Puerto Rico: April 1, 2010 to July 1, 2012," at https://www.census.gov/popest/data/state/totals/2012/; and U.S. Census Bureau, State Government Finances, "2012 Annual Survey of State Government Finances," at http://factfinder2.census.gov/faces/tableservices/jsf/pages/productview.xhtml?src=bkmk.

Clearly, Alaska far outstrips any state in per capita revenues, being 2.5 and 3.5 times the national average in 2006 and 2012 respectively.

Alaska had close to 60 percent more revenue per capita in both 2006 and 2012 than Wyoming, the number two state, and almost four times that of Texas. Even accounting for higher costs in Alaska, the state has been in an enviable position on a per person revenue basis.

Own-Source State Revenues and Alaska's Financial Vulnerability

Alaska's total revenues and its enviable per capita position are far from secured for the future. Much of this vulnerability is associated with Alaska's own-source state revenues. It is own-source revenues that determine the self-reliance of a state's fiscal system and its ability to prepare for future changes that may affect its revenue picture.

By using the same group of selected states, Table 8.2 shows the general picture of diversified revenue sources of several states in 2008. Then, in Figure 8.2 the average fifty-state per capita own-source revenue picture excluding the "Other" category is compared with

TABLE 8.2

Own-Source State Tax Revenues: Alaska Compared to the Fifty-State Average and Selected States in Fiscal Year 2008

(All Totals in $ Millions)

NATION AND STATES	TOTAL TAXES	INDIVIDUAL INCOME TAX		CORPORATE INCOME TAX		GENERAL SALES		SELECTIVE SALES		LICENSE TAXES		OTHER TAXES	
Fifty-State Average		5,567	36%	1,015	6%	4,820	31%	2,350	15%	991	6%	889	6%
Alaska	**8,425**	**0**	**0%**	**982**	**12%**	**0**	**0%**	**280**	**3%**	**143**	**2%**	**7,021**	**83%**
California	117,362	55,746	47%	11,849	10%	31,973	27%	7,835	7%	7,642	7%	2,317	2%
Florida	35,850	0	0%	2,209	6%	21,518	60%	7,779	22%	1,875	5%	2,469	7%
Kansas	7,160	2,945	41%	528	7%	2,265	32%	826	12%	304	4%	292	4%
Louisiana	11,004	3,170	29%	703	6%	3,459	31%	2,080	19%	499	5%	1,093	10%
Michigan	24,782	7,181	29%	1,778	7%	8,226	33%	3,695	15%	1,354	5%	2,548	10%
New Mexico	5,646	1,214	21%	355	6%	1,950	35%	714	13%	258	5%	1,157	20%
New York	65,371	36,564	56%	5,038	8%	11,295	17%	8,855	14%	1,356	2%	2,263	3%
Texas	44,676	0	0%	0	0%	21,669	49%	11,696	26%	7,174	16%	4,137	9%
Wyoming	2,405	0	0%	0	0%	981	41%	135	6%	121	5%	1,168	49%

Note: These rankings exclude Washington, D.C.

Source: Data compiled by the authors from U.S. Census Bureau, "2008 Annual Survey of State Government Finances," at http://www.census.gov/govs/estimate/.

FIGURE 8.2

Alaska's Own-Source State Tax Revenues Per Capita Excluding the "Other" Category Compared to the Fifty-State Average

(Based on Tax Revenue for Fiscal Year 2012)

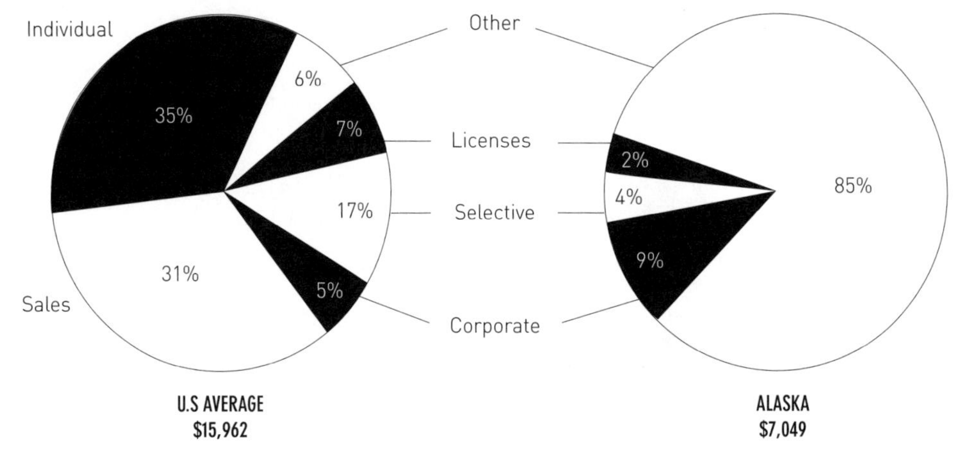

Note: These percentages exclude Washington, D.C.

Source: Created by the authors using data compiled from U.S. Census Bureau, "Fiscal Year 2012: Annual Survey of State Government Finances," at http://factfinder2.census.gov/faces/tableservices/jsf/pages/productview.xhtml?src=bkmk.

that of Alaska for 2012. Excluding the "Other" category facilitates comparison between Alaska's sources of revenue other than oil with sources for the fifty states overall minus their "Other" category. Again, the percentage distribution in 2008 and 2012 are very consistent, as they were for the previous thirty years or so. Whether judging by the sample of ten states or the fifty states overall, Alaska clearly lacks diversity and, in fact, has the most unbalanced state revenue system in the nation because of the nature of its own-source revenues. Wyoming also has unbalanced state revenues, but does not come close to Alaska.

Balanced and diversified revenue sources across the states primarily include an individual state income tax, a statewide sales tax, and corporate income tax. The majority of states receive significant contributions to their general fund from these three tax streams. In contrast, at least up to 2015, Alaska had no individual income tax or a statewide sales tax. In fact, as most Alaskans receive a Permanent Fund Dividend (PFD) each year, Alaska's state taxes on individuals are actually negative. A standing comment among newcomers to the state is that "Alaska is terrific. It actually pays me to live here." Oil taxes, classified by the U.S. Census Bureau into "Other Tax" revenue, have closed the gap left by no individual income tax and no state sales tax revenues and account for Alaska's lack of diversity and unbalanced revenue picture.

In the rest of this chapter we explain why Alaska has foregone individual state income and sales taxes as significant sources of state revenue and why they may need to be implemented, not only to provide balance to the state's revenue stream, but as a supplement if oil production continues its significant decline, particularly if oil prices remain as low as they were from summer 2014 through early 2016. This explanation will make more sense by first reviewing a little history about Alaska's state revenues.

3. A SHORT HISTORY OF ALASKA'S OWN-SOURCE STATE REVENUES

When Alaska became a state in 1959, state government revenue streams were not much different from most other states. Before oil became the dominant state revenue source, Alaska received taxes from many sources, including alcohol, motor fuel, corporate and individual income, business licenses, fisheries, inheritance, and school taxes. The largest source of state revenue for the first twenty years of statehood was the individual income tax, an item, at least as of 2015, that most politicians and candidates running for office opposed or avoided discussing. In two graphs, Figure 8.3A and Figure 8.3B show, the history of Alaska's revenue sources. Two graphs are needed because it is difficult to visually represent the increase in oil revenues on one graph and compare them with other state sources after the late 1970s. The two graphs in Figure 8.3 are one way of expressing how oil revenues have dwarfed all other own-source state funds since that time.

The individual income tax, known as a stabilizing tax because of its relatively predictable levels of revenue, provided about 20 percent of unrestricted revenue supplying the treasury with a total of $459 million through 1975.[7] As the first graph in Figure 8.3A shows, individual income tax revenue rose significantly during the time workers flooded into the state for the construction of the trans-Alaska pipeline system (TAPS) and other oil industry–related jobs. As a consequence, individual income tax revenue vastly outstripped corporate income tax until the individual income tax was eliminated beginning with the 1981 tax year. Significant revenue from oil not only allowed the state to abolish its largest revenue source within twenty-one years of statehood, but also provided the means to eliminate the school, inheritance, and some business license taxes. Even though it is far easier for a candidate for political office to campaign on cutting taxes on individuals and raising taxes on "entities" such as corporations, corporate income tax (as of FY 2014 the state's third-largest own-source unrestricted revenue) is limited by the number and financial strength of corporations doing business in Alaska. Excluding corporate income tax on the oil industry, corporate income tax on all other businesses has never brought in as much revenue as the individual income tax did at its high point.

FIGURE 8.3

Alaska's Own-Source State Revenue and Tax History, 1959–2014

FIGURE 8.3A
OIL REVENUE COMPARED TO PERSONAL INCOME TAX AND CORPORATE TAX, 1959-2014

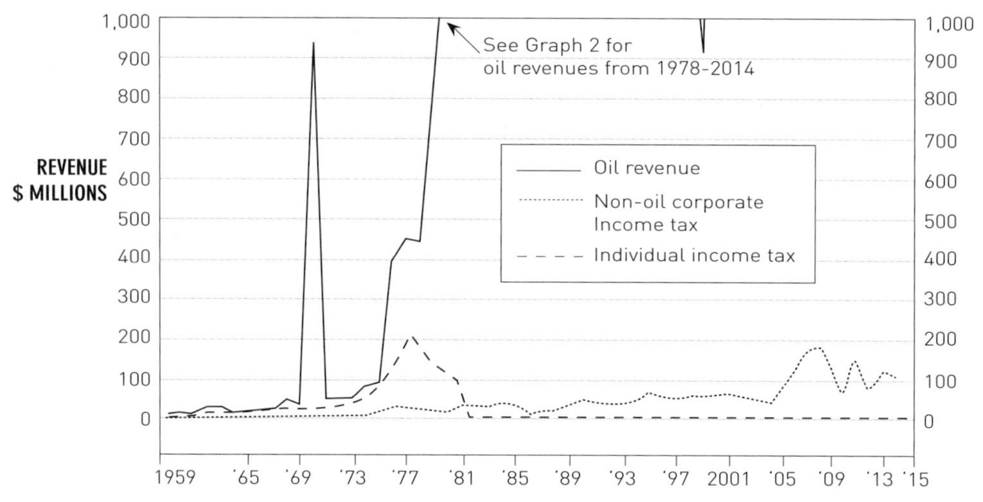

FIGURE 8.3B
OIL REVENUE, 1977-2014

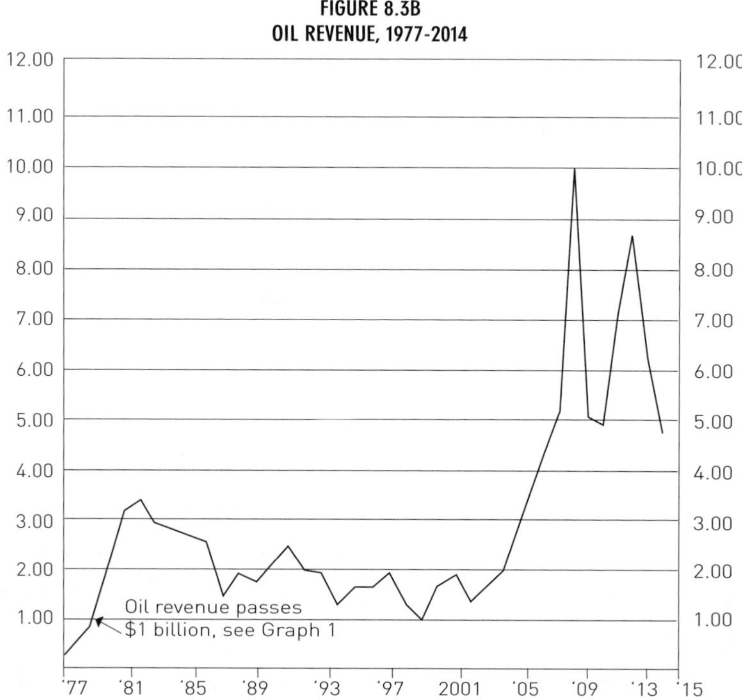

Note: In these graphs, oil revenue is composed of (1) petroleum corporate income tax, (2) production tax, (3) petroleum property tax, and (4) petroleum rents and royalties.

Source: Developed by the authors using data prepared by the Alaska Department of Revenue, Tax Division, *Revenue Sources Book* for fall each year from 2008–14," at http://www.tax.alaska.gov/programs/sourcebook/index.aspx.

FIGURE 8.4

Oil Income as a Percentage of Alaska's Own-Source Unrestricted Revenues, 1959–2014

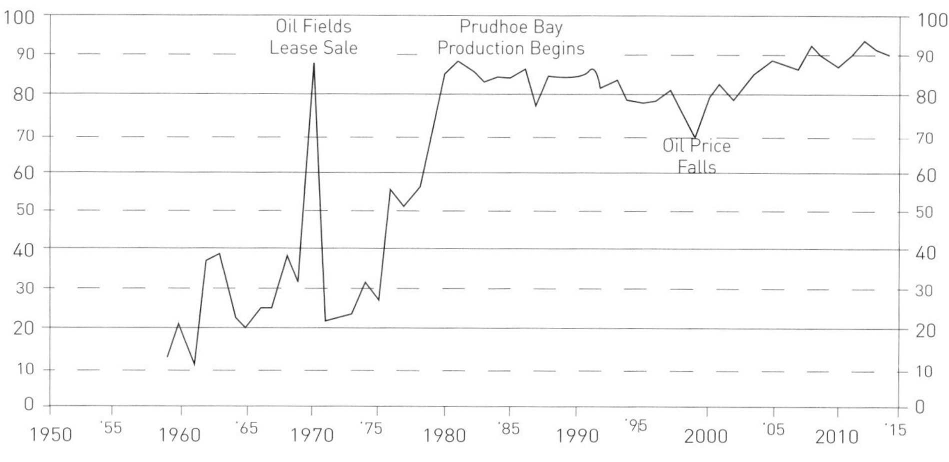

Source: Developed by the authors using data prepared by the Alaska Department of Revenue, Tax Division, *Revenue Sources Book* for fall each year from 2008–14, at http://www.tax.alaska.gov/programs/sourcebook/index.aspx.

The politics surrounding the elimination of the individual income tax were complex, and are referred to briefly later in the chapter. In essence, though, it was made possible by the massive revenues that flooded into the state general fund in the late 1970s following TAPS coming online in 1977. As Figure 8.4 shows, for most years since 1980, Alaska has received over 80 percent of its unrestricted revenue from various types of oil taxes and royalties. In fact, from FY 2005 through FY 2014, state oil income averaged a staggering 89 percent of total unrestricted revenues, and for some of these years was over 90 percent of unrestricted revenues.[8]

So the state's own-source revenues are dominated by oil, a nonrenewable resource that is not sustainable and that will not last forever. In fact, it may run out by 2027, and the hypothetical CNN headline at the beginning of this chapter may become a reality. Given this state of affairs, what has been and what can be done? Before addressing those questions, we first examine the current problems of Alaska's government revenues.

4. THE PROBLEM OF DEPENDENCE ON OIL REVENUES AND FEDERAL FUNDS

Since the late 1970s, Alaska's total state revenues have consisted of its own-source revenues (predominantly from oil taxes and royalties) and federal funds. Here we explain why oil revenues are an undependable source of state income and why undependability will continue in the future. We also explain why federal funds may be far less reliable in the years to come than they have been in the past.

Oil Revenues

The major problem with oil revenues as a source of state funds is their inherent instability. The state's revenue picture for many years has been feast or famine, depending on the price of a barrel of oil, and with no way of accurately predicting the price in the short or long term. There are also problems of declining production, political and economic problems with developing new oil and gas reserves, and issues concerning the age of TAPS and its suitability for the types of oil that may be produced in the future.

Fluctuations in the Price of a Barrel of Oil

The price of oil is determined globally and Alaska has no control over its price. Since the early 1980s oil prices have ranged from a low of under $10 a barrel in 1986 to close to $150 in mid-2008. Many factors go into determining the world market price, particularly demand, which is largely determined by the strength or weakness of the U.S. and world economies. In fact, the Alaska Department of Revenue cites economic health (or lack of it) as the most common reason for the fluctuation in oil prices.[9] World oil demand is expected to continue increasing from 85 million barrels per day in 2006 to approximately 117 million barrels per day in 2030.[10] Supply is also a major factor. Overproduction or news of a major new oil supply coming on tap may reduce the price, but an interruption in supply from a major oil-producing country like Venezuela or Nigeria may increase it. Other factors that affect oil prices are the political conditions in oil-producing countries, the actions of the Organization of the Petroleum Exporting Countries (OPEC), of which the United States (and therefore Alaska) is not a member, refinery capacity, commodity trading, and currency fluctuations.

The increase in oil prices from 2005 to mid-2014 was attributable to several factors, including political instability in major oil-producing countries, lower supplies of oil, and increased demand, especially among emerging economies such as India and China. But some or all of the conditions listed above can change rapidly and unexpectedly. As a result, prices can plummet as they did in 1986 and again beginning in the second half of 2014. In two graphs, Figure 8.5A and Figure 8.5B illustrate both the major fluctuations in the daily oil price (called the spot price by those who trade in oil) over a twenty-eight-year period (1987-2014), and the changes that can occur in just one year, 2008.

Problems in Forecasting Future Oil Revenues

In 2008 the Alaska legislature amended the Executive Budget Act to require the governor to provide an annual estimate or forecast of state revenues and expenditures for the

FIGURE 8.5

Daily Oil Spot Price: Fiscal Years 1987–2014 and Calendar Year 2008

(In Dollars per Barrel)

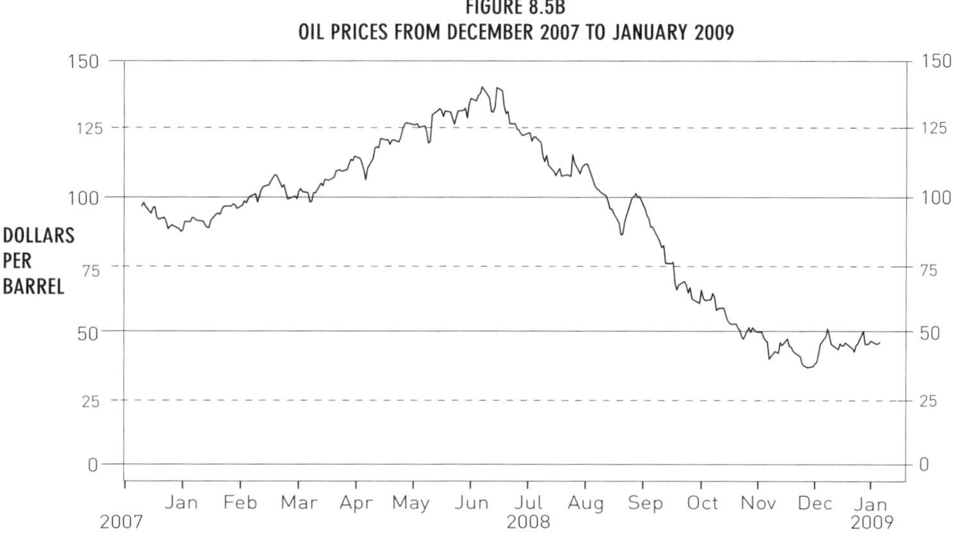

Source: Compiled by the authors using data from the U.S. Energy Information Administration, Independent Statistics and Analysis, "Daily Europe Brent Spot Price (Dollars per Barrel)," at http://www.eia.gov/dnav/pet/hist/LeafHandler.ashx?n=PET&s=RBRTE&f=A.

following ten years. This estimate does not include alternative or possible new revenue sources, such as a state sales tax or an individual state income tax; it only includes existing sources of revenue. Obviously, a major part of this forecast involves estimating short- and long-term oil prices. However, for the reasons associated with fluctuating oil prices, estimating revenues ten years ahead is problematic.

Yet, many public officials are reluctant to admit the difficulty of making long-range plans based on estimated future oil prices. When they are unsure about the future, many officials nonetheless try to paint a positive picture. For example, in a 2008 interview with Commissioner of Revenue Patrick Galvin, when oil was close to $150 a barrel, he was very upbeat and saw the major problem facing Alaska as what to do with the financial surplus that was flooding in daily to the state's general fund. At the same time he admitted that a year earlier he was concerned about major revenue shortfalls because of oil prices at that time and their likely future downward direction. Galvin explained, however, that generally the state's oil price estimates are on the conservative side and based on an average per barrel price in the $80 range through 2016.[11] This may well have been a good range to use given the price of oil from 2006 to mid-2014. But it was an overestimate for the second half of 2014, all of 2015 and into 2016, when oil dropped under $30 a barrel at one point. And what will happen in 2017 and beyond? Judging by past experience, no one knows, though many make a living out of such forecasting (or perhaps more accurately, such "guessing").

Declining Production, the Technology of TAPS, and Problems of Developing Further Reserves

TAPS has seen a dramatic decrease in oil flow since its greatest throughput of 2,145,297 barrels a day on January 14, 1988. According to the Alaska Department of Revenue, this had dropped to around 525,000 barrels a day by the end of 2014, only 26 percent of the maximum throughput in 1988. During FY 2010 alone oil production on the North Slope declined 7 percent from the previous year.[12] Nationwide, between 2003 and 2010 Alaska's decline in oil production was the highest of all the oil-producing states at around 30 percent.[13]

When the volume flowing through TAPS dwindles to approximately 300,000 barrels per day, the pumps will not be able to operate, and the pipeline will be forced to shut down.[14] As Figure 8.6 shows, the smaller fields under development, and those evaluated for future development, will not be sufficient to replace the rapid decline in current production of North Slope crude.

TAPS could very well shut down before all the easily accessible and low-viscous oil is extracted. To avoid a shutdown of TAPS, major oil fields such as those in ANWR or NPR-A need to be tapped, but the federal government controls these vast areas and, so far, has not allowed oil development in ANWR, though some exploration and development

FIGURE 8.6

Oil Field Production Levels on Alaska's North Slope: Oil Extracted Between FY 2000–2010 and Forecasted Production Levels from 2011–2020

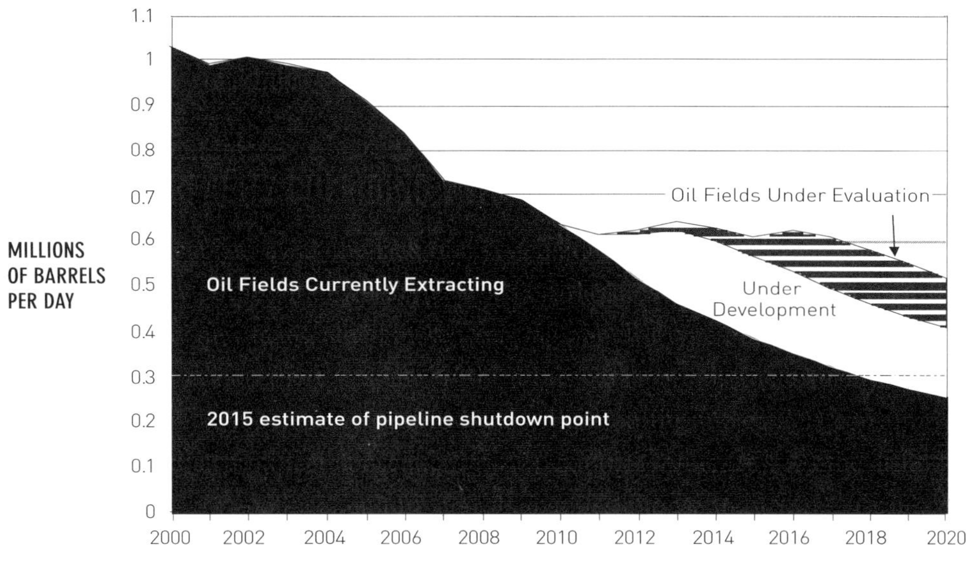

Source: Figure modified by the authors, collected from the State of Alaska Department of Revenue, Tax Division, *Revenue Sources Book, Fall 2010* Figure 4-9, page 40. http://www.tax.alaska.gov/programs/documentviewer/viewer.aspx?2136f.

has occurred in NPR-A. One potential problem, even if oil is eventually tapped from these two areas, is that the federal government has indicated that it might want a 90/10 split in revenues (that is, 90 percent to the federal government and 10 percent to Alaska), in contrast to the present 50/50 split for oil produced on federal land in Alaska. A 90/10 split would seriously reduce the state's revenue from ANWR and NPR-A.

Substantial amounts of more viscous crude oil have been found in the vicinity of TAPS, but the pipeline was not designed to transport this kind of oil. It is possible that the oil industry might decide there is enough of this new oil to make it worthwhile to restructure TAPS to carry it. But such a restructure would likely require a long shutdown, resulting in a major loss of revenue to the state.

Reducing oil company taxes, as Governor Parnell did in 2013 with his More Alaska Production Act (MAPA), may encourage the oil industry to explore and develop more oil fields and "stop the drop" in oil production, as Parnell repeated in the 2014 gubernatorial campaign. But using tax incentives to increase production is far from certain, and there is wide disagreement about its effectiveness. Figures released by the Alaska Department of Revenue in December 2014 showed that while production in FY 2014 was about the same as FY 2013 (at 531,000 barrels a day), it will drop from FY 2015 onward to an estimated 455,000 by 2024 if all present exploration and development occurs. But if exploration and development is not forthcoming, or does not result in increased oil output, production could be as low as 315,000 barrels a day, dangerously close to the level when TAPS would need to shut down.[15] Furthermore, when oil prices are low, companies have less incentive to expand their operations, and oil prices will inevitably fluctuate over the next decade. There is also the possibility of state revenue from a natural gas pipeline from the North Slope to Southcentral Alaska, with some being exported as liquefied natural gas to East Asia. But this has been talked about for decades, and even though the planning has moved forward since 2008 and was a major issue in the 2014 governor's race (and a pet project of the victor, Governor Bill Walker), whether or not it will be built in the foreseeable future is very uncertain.[16]

In contrast to the difficulty of predicting future oil prices, provable reserves can be estimated reasonably well with the latest scientific tools. At the current declining rate of production, an estimate of when TAPS will have to close is anywhere from ten to twenty years. However, some energy analysts have estimated forty additional years of production from Alaska's oil fields. This assumes that Congress allows more drilling on federal lands, that more oil is recovered from wells than originally estimated because of improved extraction technology, perhaps that TAPS is technically restructured for new types of crude, and that TAPS spur lines will be built to access the new oil.

The Consequences

Regardless of whether the ten-year or the forty-year estimate is the accurate one, it is clear that Alaska's heavy dependence on oil taxes and royalties for the bulk of its own-source revenues is, to say the least, problematic. This is particularly so because the health of the state budget is closely linked to the price of oil, as Figure 8.7 shows. When oil prices are high, the budget outlook is healthy and so is the Alaska economy. As Alaska's economy is highly dependent on state and local government employment and the consumer spending that this makes possible, along with the economic multiplier effect, low oil prices, or a lengthy shutdown of the pipeline, would have serious consequences for Alaska's economy. A permanent TAPS closure would be economically devastating. It would cause extensive unemployment, a major drop in real estate values, mass migration from the state, and a plummeting of the standard of living of Alaskans.[17]

The rise in oil prices beginning in 2007 and the U.S. dependence on foreign oil combined to create a political and economic climate to increase domestic oil production. Most of that development did not take place in Alaska but in states with oil shale deposits such as North Dakota. Then, the freefall of oil prices in late 2014, and continuing through 2016, put a worldwide damper on oil development. But even if oil prices go back to $100 or

FIGURE 8.7

Annual Oil Prices in Relation to Alaska's Unrestricted Revenue: For Fiscal Years 1987–2014

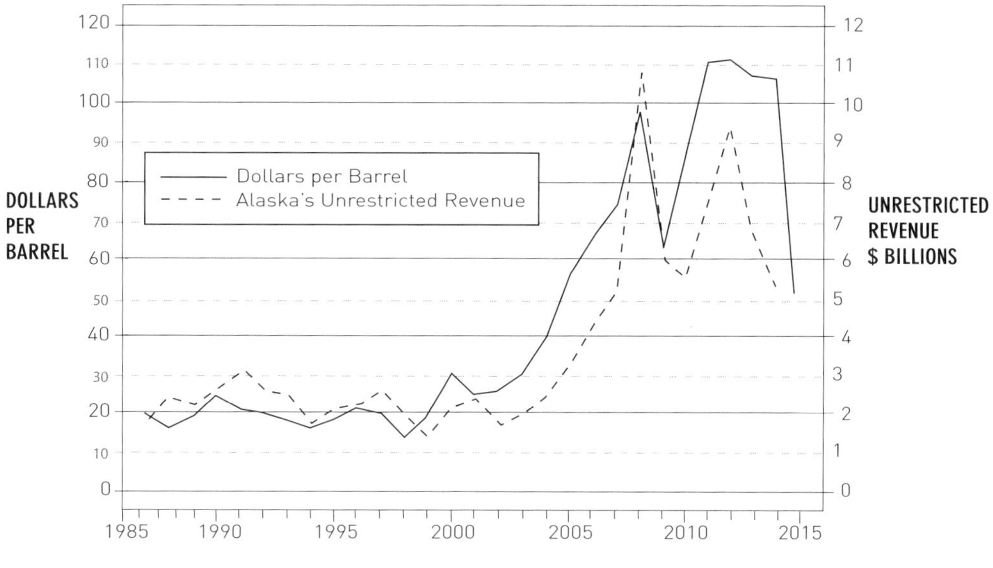

Source: Created by the authors using data from Alaska Department of Revenue, Tax Division, *Revenue Sources Book, Fall 2008*, "Fifty Years of Revenue," Figure 3-7, at http://www.tax.alaska.gov/programs/documentviewer/ viewer.aspx?1531f; and for the years 2009–14, from Alaska Department of Revenue, "Revenue Sourcebook" for fall of each year, at http://www.tax.alaska.gov/programs/sourcebook/index.aspx.

more a barrel (as they were for the five years up until the summer of 2014), new Alaska oil fields are developed both on- and offshore, and TAPS is upgraded to accommodate the transportation of that new oil, Alaska's revenue problems will not disappear.

For one thing, future oil revenues will still be subject to the world price of oil, so revenue volatility will remain a serious problem. It is also possible that some alternative energy source will be developed that would further reduce the demand for oil and cause a drop in prices. So if the past is any indication of the future, which it has proven to be time and time again regarding oil price fluctuations, Alaska will be continually subjected to unstable oil revenue with all the ramifications that accompany it. Clearly, something needs to be done to increase revenue stability. This is especially so because federal funds, the other major source of state general revenues, may also continue to decrease in the near future.

Federal Funds and Alaska's Political Influence: An Uncertain Future

In the early years after statehood, over 50 percent of Alaska's state revenues came from federal funds because of the state's lack of a revenue source. By the early 1970s, however,

FIGURE 8.8

Congressional Earmarks Per Capita: Alaska Compared with Selected States

(With National Average and Ranking in Dollars Per Capita)

FISCAL YEAR 2009

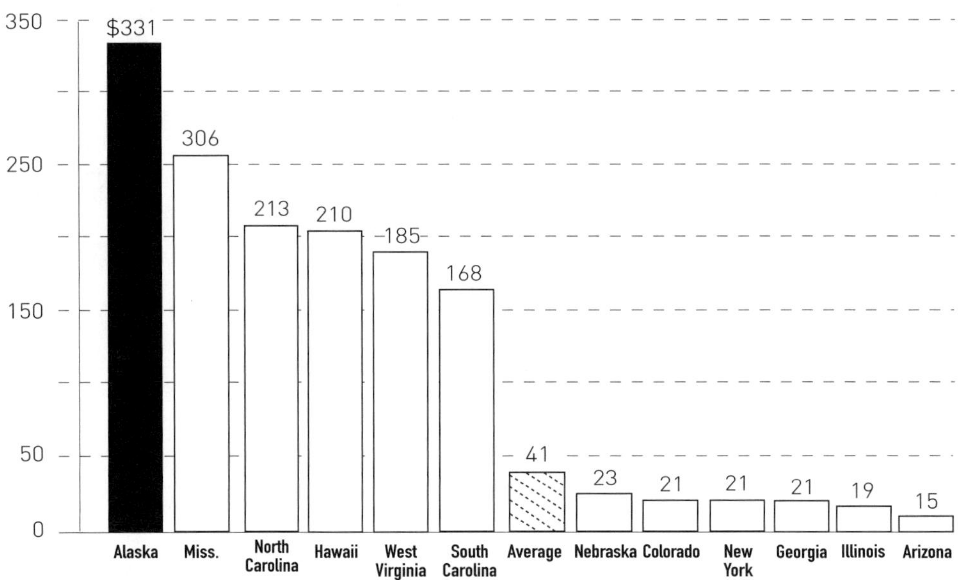

FISCAL YEAR 2010

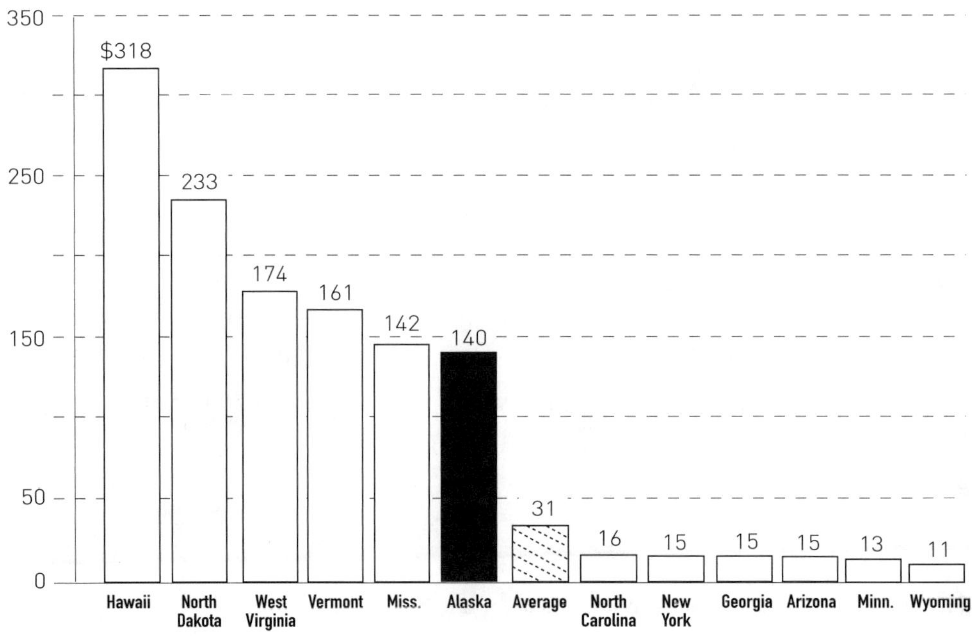

Source: Created by the authors using data collected from Taxpayers for Common Sense, State Earmark Numbers, Ordered by Earmarks Per Capita, "BigKahuna2009" and "BigKahuna2010," at http://taxpayer.net/earmarks.php.

this figure had dropped to the present range of 20 to 30 percent, depending on the year, how flush the state was, and how much it spent of its own-source revenues.[18] The bulk of federal money coming directly to the state is restricted revenue, tied to programs like Medicaid and transportation projects. Many of these funds require a state general fund match of money. If a match is not forthcoming, the state does not get the federal funds. In addition, for a long time the state received money from federal earmarks. A key issue for Alaska's future revenue picture is the trend regarding federal funds coming to the state.

While the trend in federal funds to the states has been one of a gradual increase since the 1960s, for several reasons this trend is likely to be reversed or at best flattened out in the near future and perhaps in the long term. First, the general mood in the nation and in Washington, D.C., is to curb government spending and decrease the role of government. This conservative fiscal policy, which became particularly evident with the rise of the Tea Party Republicans in the federal elections of November 2010, means that some of the programs for which Alaska has been receiving direct federal funds may be reduced or even eliminated. Second, earmarks, which have been of considerable importance to Alaska's overall budget, have declined and since 2011 have been banned in the U.S. Senate.

The Situation with Federal Earmarks

Power drives politics in Washington, D.C., just as it does in Juneau. The more power a state's congressional delegation has in terms of seniority and positions on key committees, especially when their party is in the majority, the more likely is a state to get additional funds. That is, in addition to the direct payments to individuals and money received by the state based upon federal formula programs, which all states receive, a state may get funds obtained by its congressional delegation that are "earmarked" for specific projects or purposes. Some of these funds go directly to communities or businesses, others go directly to the state depending on their purpose and the politics involved. It is an accounting nightmare to determine the exact amount of earmarks in any one year that come to the state directly, but usually about half of all earmarks come directly to the state general fund.[19] So any changes in earmarks can affect the state budget.

Prior to 2009, Alaska's congressional delegation, particularly the late U.S. Senator Ted Stevens, were masters at securing earmarks or "bringing home the bacon," as it is often expressed. Besides military, defense, and other federal employment, earmarks have played an important role in Alaska's revenues in the form of infrastructure development (the state Department of Transportation has received major earmark funds), municipal improvements, research grants to the University of Alaska system, and other projects. Figure 8.8 shows that in 2009 Alaska ranked first in per capita earmarks, about 60 percent above the national average. This was just under 5 percent of federal funds received by the state and about 2 percent of total state revenues.

The days of major earmark money for Alaska may be over, however. The defeat of Senator Stevens in the November 2008 election is one reason. With him went much of Alaska's political influence in Washington, D.C., evidenced by the precipitous drop in earmarks in 2010, illustrated in Figure 8.8. In terms of comparing Alaska's success in obtaining earmarks in 2008 and 2009 when Mark Begich replaced Stevens, Alaska secured $456.9 million in earmarks during Stevens's last year in office, dwarfing the amount brought in 2009 at only $53.6 million—just 12 percent of the 2008 total.[20]

Another reason for the decline in earmarks is the negative reputation that they have gained in recent years. Interestingly, an Alaska project was the focus of a controversy over earmarks that erupted in the run-up to the 2008 presidential election. The project was a proposed bridge to connect the City of Ketchikan to Gravina Island, where Ketchikan's airport is located. This project was dubbed the "Bridge to Nowhere" by some in Congress, and the term was echoed loudly and frequently in the media. During the presidential campaign, Republican candidate John McCain favored the total elimination of earmarks, and his running mate Sarah Palin joined him in his disdain for this type of funding in general and the "Bridge to Nowhere" in particular. Earmarks were becoming increasingly and widely disfavored.[21]

Then the Tea Party movement elected a number of new Republican members to Congress in 2010. Even though earmarks constitute only about 1 percent of the federal budget, members of Congress's Tea Party caucus saw them as epitomizing abuse of power and one of the many things wrong with Washington, D.C. So in early 2011 they were able to get the Senate Appropriations Chair, Hawaiian Senator Daniel Inouye, to agree to place a ban on earmarks in spending bills. Ironically, together with Stevens, Inouye was one of the most successful senators at securing earmarks. Not surprisingly, Alaska's two U.S. Senators, Mark Begich and Lisa Murkowski, voted against the ban.[22] Despite efforts by both of Alaska's U.S. senators and others in the Senate to lift the ban on earmarks, it had not been lifted as of early 2016.

The Shifting and Uncertain Future Influence of Alaska's Congressional Delegation

With Senator Stevens no longer around and increased polarization in Congress since the 2008 presidential election, the influence of Alaska's congressional delegation over the next twenty years or so is uncertain, particularly in their ability to secure federal funds, including those to be included in the state budget. The 2014 midterm election, which returned a Republican majority in the U.S. Senate, placed Senator Murkowski in a leadership position. Representative Don Young had already been part of the House leadership since the 2010 election. This will be advantageous for Alaska. On the other hand, the defeat of Democratic Senator Begich by Republican Dan Sullivan in November 2014 means that Alaska has a freshman senator with little influence even though he is in the majority.

Moreover, an entirely Republican delegation could hurt Alaska if the Senate or the House or both goes to the Democrats in the 2016 election, given the major ideological fractures in Congress. Added to this, Don Young turned eighty-two in 2015. Should he leave the House for whatever reason, he will be replaced by a junior representative, adding to the uncertainty of Alaska's influence in Washington, D.C., in the years to come.

5. DEALING WITH ALASKA'S UNSTABLE STATE REVENUES: ALTERNATIVE REVENUES AND THE IDEA OF A FISCAL PLAN

In a December 2010 interview with the Associated Press, former Department of Revenue Commissioner Pat Galvin was sanguine about Alaska's financial health, seeing it as the best ever.[23] This was certainly true at the time. As history shows, however, this health could be fleeting or it may be more long term. No one knows. As it turned out, the good years of high oil prices, averaging over $100 a barrel, lasted until the summer of 2014 and then took a plunge to under $28 in January 2016. So the obvious step is to plan for the future and have a way of ensuring revenue stability. Few Alaskans would argue with the need for and desirability of future stability. Yet, when we move beyond generalities and get into the details of how this might be achieved there is no consensus. In the rest of this chapter we examine the possible approaches that have been suggested and some that have been tried for dealing with Alaska's unstable revenues and the political thicket in which these approaches often become entangled. This section identifies the range of possible revenue sources available to fill a so-called fiscal gap and looks at the idea of a financial plan. The next section considers the pros and cons of various policy options, followed by a section discussing the politics of dealing with fiscal gaps.

Major Sources of Revenue for Dealing with Financial Instability

When the state's income is tied to a revenue source that can drop 77 percent in five months, as Alaska experienced with oil prices in 2008, and was the case between 2014 and 2016, there is clearly a need to base the state's income, or at least a major part of it, on a less volatile revenue source. The state can, of course, cut back its expenditures to deal, at least in part, with this fiscal gap, and this is certainly an available option. This is an approach advocated by many Alaskans and public officials to deal with the $3.5 billion deficit Alaska was facing in FY 2015, 2016 and 2017.[24] But there is only so much that can be cut without undermining the basic functions of government, providing essential services, and ultimately adversely affecting the state's economy. So budget cuts are not part of what is considered here. Our concern is with possible stable revenue sources. Two major options and one minor one are open to the state. The major ones are to save money in high income years for the inevitable financial rainy day and increase or impose new taxes that are more stable than oil revenues. A minor option is to increase existing user fees and impose other new fees and taxes.

Saving for Financial Rainy Days

Emergency savings accounts are useful tools to provide backup funds when current revenue is not enough to fund needed expenditures. Alaska's public officials first implemented this idea in the mid-1970s when it became clear that major revenues from oil production would flow into the general fund over the next several years, and the memory of minimal state revenues in the early years of statehood was still fresh in their minds. The belief in the need to save a portion of Alaska's revenues from nonrenewable resources, such as oil, was one of the reasons for establishing the Alaska Permanent Fund. Similar concerns to save present excess revenues to deal with future revenue shortfalls prompted the establishment in 1990 of the Constitutional Budget Reserve Fund, usually referred to as the Constitutional Budget Reserve, or CBR. In January 2016 the Permanent Fund was around $50 billion, about five times the total FY 2015 state budget and about six times the state's own-source unrestricted revenues. Also in 2015, the CBR ranged from $9 billion to $11 billion. There is also a smaller State Budget Reserve Fund (SBR).

Using the Earnings from the Permanent Fund

As a major aspect of Alaska's political economy, the Permanent Fund and the PFD are covered from different perspectives in several chapters in the book.[25] In this chapter we are concerned with the fund only as a revenue source. The fund was established in 1976. Then, in 1980, lawmakers voted to pay residents a dividend—the PFD—from a portion of the fund's earnings. Since the first payment in 1982 these yearly dividends have gone up and down, ranging from a low of $331 in 1984 to a high of $2,072 in 2015.

Given its original purpose, its present size, and the only source that can fill large, multibillion-dollar, fiscal gaps on a long-term basis, Permanent Fund earnings are the most logical source to provide the revenue and budgetary stability that Alaska seeks. Since the mid-1980s, there have been several proposals for using fund earnings to aid in stabilizing state revenues. These proposals were often part of an overall fiscal plan or program and involved using a combination of fund earnings, reinstating the individual income tax, and enacting a state sales tax. The approach of adopting a comprehensive fiscal plan is considered later in this section, and the policy options for closing fiscal gaps using Permanent Fund earnings and taxes are dealt with later in this chapter.

The CBR

In the mid-1980s oil prices took a major tumble. At the same time the state expected to receive considerable revenues from pending settlements with the oil companies over disputed income and production taxes as well as other new monies from oil and mineral payments. The CBR was created as the result of a combination of three factors.[26] One was the need to constrain state spending because of the downturn in oil prices in the late 1980s. Second, many Alaskans wanted to prevent these settlement revenues from going into the general fund, where they might be subjected to the free spending of the late 1970s and early 1980s. Third, since Permanent Fund earnings were no longer viewed as a means to fund revenue shortfalls, another account was needed to take its place. Because of the constitutional prohibition against dedicated funds, it took a constitutional amendment to establish the CBR.

The CBR amendment (Article IX, Finance and Taxation, Section 17) states that the major purpose of the CBR is to fund revenue shortfalls. Theoretically, appropriations from the CBR are limited to the amount necessary to cover the shortfall from the previous year's appropriation. When revenues rise the fund must be repaid. However, as most of the large disputes between the state and the oil companies have now been settled, little in additional dedicated revenue is expected to go into the CBR in the future. So, although the CBR will receive some settlement funds, they are not likely to be substantial.

As a result, growth of the CBR will come primarily from its investment earnings. In theory, the CBR should grow over time because the state is required to use general fund money to repay it when oil prices are high and revenues exceed expenditures. The theory may be sound, but practice may lead to other eventualities. Because of falling oil production, the general fund has not kept pace with expenditures for most years since the inception of the CBR, though high oil prices from 2008 to the fall of 2014 enabled the CBR to be replenished. A long-term drop in oil prices could virtually drain it again. Also, maneuvering within the legislature may also undermine the ability of the CBR to be a predictable source of state revenues.

The Statutory Budget Reserve Fund

If the CBR is a less than reliable long-term source of revenue to plug budget gaps, the SBR is even less reliable and predictable. The SBR is a savings fund managed by the Department of Revenue in its own separate account and consists of appropriations of excess money received by the state. While it is easier for the legislature to make appropriations from the SBR than the CBR, it is much smaller than the CBR and has less potential to grow. For example, on July 31, 2015, while the CBR contained $10.13 billion the SBR contained only $1.66 billion, but it was as high as $4.8 billion just nine months earlier in November 2014. The SBR could be used to help plug budget shortfalls on a short-term basis. But in circumstances like those of FY 2015, FY 2016 and FY 2017 with close to $4 billion budget deficits, it could soon be drained dry and of uncertain future value.

Increasing Existing Taxes and Imposing New Ones

Increasing existing taxes, which means mainly increasing taxes on the oil and gas industry and other natural resource producers, has its advocates but also its opponents. The oil companies no doubt earn a lot of money from their Alaska operations, and with high oil prices from 2006 to the fall of 2014, they have made record profits worldwide. So it is likely that they could afford to pay more tax. Governor Palin and the legislature worked together to increase production taxes on the companies in 2007. Others, among them Governor Sean Parnell, who worked to roll back oil taxes after his election in 2010, argue that increased taxes may discourage the oil industry from future exploration and development in Alaska. After suffering defeat on his legislative proposal in 2012, Parnell was able to get it passed in 2013. It was upheld by the voters in an August 2014 referendum, with the oil companies spending record amounts in the election. The debate over oil taxes is ongoing, highly contentious and, as discussed in Chapter 16, it caused political gridlock between the governor and legislature in 2011–2012.[27]

Other than increasing oil taxes, the major options for increasing tax revenues are to re-establish the state individual income tax and impose a statewide sales tax. Most states have both types of taxes, which form a major portion of their own-source revenues.[28] For Alaska, income and sales taxes would provide predictable yearly income and could be part of a package of alternative revenue sources.[29]

Reimposing a State Individual Income Tax

Interestingly, of the seven states with no state income tax, three (Alaska, Texas, and Wyoming) are major oil producers. Certainly in Alaska, and to some extent in Texas and Wyoming, oil revenues have been sufficient by themselves to fund state government, making an income tax less necessary. In fact, in times of national or global economic downturns, oil-rich states can be insulated from such downturns, as long as oil prices remain high. This was the case in all three states following the major economic recession of 2008–2010. However, the volatility of oil prices can seriously affect state revenues, especially in states with less diversified economies like Wyoming and Alaska. A state income tax offers a more stable and adaptable revenue source. Several states raised their personal income tax rates because of the effects that the 2008–2010 recession and its aftermath have had on their state budgets. For example, in January 2011, Illinois increased its individual income tax rate from 3 to 5 percent in order to help deal with the state's $15 billion deficit.

In hindsight, an interesting question is why Alaska eliminated such a significant and stable revenue source as the individual income tax. It was, in fact, part of a compromise that Governor Jay Hammond had to make with legislators in order to obtain enactment of the PFD program that he had proposed. Simply reducing the tax rate to zero, but leaving the tax on the books, might have made it easier politically to resuscitate.

If the individual income tax were reinstated, what level of funds would it bring into the state's general fund? This is not an easy question to answer given the lack of recent data. But we can provide the following broad estimate based on the assumption that the reinstated tax would be levied along the lines of the previous system and calculated as a percentage of an individual's federal taxes. This is the method used by most states, though some, like Oregon, have their own system for calculating individual income tax, separate from federal taxes.

According to the *Alaska Revenue Sources Book* for fall 2002, in 1977 the individual income tax raised $210.4 million. As a percentage of federal taxable income (with tax brackets from 3.5 percent of incomes up to $8,000 to 14.5 percent on incomes more than $300,000), the Alaska Department of Revenue estimated that if the individual income tax were still in place (and the tax schedule adjusted for inflation), this tax would have brought in $660 million in 2002.[30] Using this as a baseline, and taking into account the increase in population in Alaska based on the 2014 census estimates, the increase in family and median individual income, the updated rate of federal taxes, we estimate that, after adjusting for inflation, a state income tax would have raised between $975 million and $1.3 billion in 2014.

Although an income tax is a stable revenue source, even at the high estimate of $1.3 billion, it would bring in only a small fraction of what oil revenues have produced over the years and particularly since 2005. Depending on the price of oil, revenues from an individual income tax would have ranged from 10 to 20 percent of oil revenues and between 8 and 18 percent of the state's unrestricted revenues between 2010 and 2015.

Imposing a Statewide Sales Tax

As of 2015, of the forty-five states that had a state sales tax, rates ranged from 2.9 percent in Colorado to 7.5 percent in California.[31] In addition, local districts, cities, and counties in some states add their own sales tax. This makes the highest total cumulative sales tax almost 10 percent, with Tennessee the highest at 9.45 percent, and the highest in the West being Washington State at 8.88 percent. Across the nation, statewide sales taxes average 32.3 percent of general fund own-source state revenue. Each state has its own combinations of taxable items and rates at which they are taxed. Several states exempt or have lower rates for certain items, like prescription drugs, and some exempt groceries. Some states also exempt or have lower tax rates for certain organizations, like charities, and for certain individuals, such as senior citizens and the disabled.

While there is no statewide sales tax in Alaska, many local governments levy a local sales tax. It is estimated that about a third of Alaskans pay some form of sales tax. Close to one hundred communities have a municipal sales tax, with the lowest rate in 2015 at 1 percent in White Mountain and the highest in Homer at 7.5 percent. In 2012, the last year for which comprehensive figures are available, Alaska communities with sales taxes received approximately $208 million in revenue. This was about $800 per resident for communities with a sales tax. Using this figure to project what the revenue would be for the entire state if there were a statewide sales tax ($800 times the 2015 population of about 735,000), the amount would have been around $600 million. So in 2015, depending on the percentage statewide sales tax rate, we estimate that the state would have received between $650 and $800 million from a statewide sales tax.

More specifically, Table 8.3 shows the contribution that a statewide sales tax would make to state revenues at various tax rates. As the table shows, even at a relatively high rate of 8 percent and no exemptions, the total revenues would be about $880 million, a small amount compared with the revenue from oil. At a more realistic rate, a sales tax would likely have brought in about 8 to 10 percent of Alaska's unrestricted revenues in 2015.

Increasing Existing Fees and Other Possible Income

The state could increase user fees, such as those for camping in state parks, or establish new ones, such as toll roads, as many states have done. It could also increase license fees for drivers and business operations, among others. The state could increase the head tax currently imposed on tour ship passengers. But this was a controversial measure when adopted by the voters in 2006, as it was seen as discouraging tour ship companies from coming to the state, and the legislature reduced the tax in 2010. Plus, under federal law, use of the revenue from the tax is limited to providing benefits or services to cruise ships and their passengers, thus reducing the flexibility of its use as a source of general revenues. Alaska could also establish a state lottery as exists in forty-three states. This is unlikely, however, given fairly widespread opposition to most forms of gambling in Alaska, whether run by government or the private sector. While increased fees and state-run gambling are possible sources of increased revenue that could form part of a package to even out the state's unstable income, they would be only a minimal part, likely less than 2 percent, of Alaska's 2015 own-source revenues.

The Contribution of New Revenue Sources

If we add up the possible new revenue streams of an income tax, sales tax, and increased user fees and other charges we get the following range of revenue. In the period FY 2010–2015 this would have brought in between $1.5 and $2 billion per year, or around an average of 25 percent of the state's unrestricted revenue during those years, depending on the rates at which these taxes, fees, and other charges were levied. While this is only a quarter or less of unrestricted revenue in these years, it is nevertheless a fairly stable and predictable amount. It would, for instance, have cushioned by half the $3.5 to $4 billion revenue shortfall and budget deficit the state experienced in FY 2016 due to falling oil prices.

TABLE 8.3

Estimated Revenue from an Alaska State Sales Tax

The table shows the estimated revenue from an Alaska statewide sales tax with no exemptions and with estimated average exemptions for various tax rates from 1 to 8 percent.

TAX RATE	ESTIMATED REVENUE IN $ MILLIONS, WITH NO EXEMPTIONS	PER CAPITA REVENUE	ESTIMATED REVENUE IN $ MILLIONS, WITH EXEMPTIONS	PER CAPITA REVENUE
1%	110	$173.70	75	$118.40
2%	220	$347.40	150	$236.90
3%	330	$521.10	225	$355.30
4%	440	$694.80	300	$473.70
5%	550	$868.60	375	$592.10
6%	660	$1,042.10	450	$710.60
7%	770	$1,215.80	525	$828.90
8%	880	$1,389.50	600	$947.40

Source: Developed by the authors from Alaska Department of Revenue, Tax Division, *Revenue Sources Book, Fall 2002*, at http://www.tax.alaska.gov//programs/documentviewer/viewer.aspx?831f; U.S. Census Bureau, *Annual Estimates of the Resident Population for the United States, Regions, States, and Puerto Rico: April 1, 2000 to July 1, 2009*, at http://www.census.gov/popest/states/NST-ann-est.html. In part, based on the Alaska Department of Revenue and Office of Management and Budget revenue estimates from 1 percent statewide sales tax in 2002 of $150 million a year for every 1 percent of an Alaska statewide sales tax on retail goods and services, assuming no exemptions, and $115 million a year for a 1 percent statewide sales tax if foods, shelter, and medical goods and services were exempted.

The Idea of a Financial Plan for Alaska

Most people would agree that a responsible individual, family, or business would develop a financial plan to take care of a possible future rainy day. In the case of government, consistent and predictable income allows for higher quality services (partly because they are not interrupted or reduced in times of low revenues), stabilized employment, and aid in recession proofing. In general, more stable revenues will protect the high standard of living Alaskans have come to expect. Stable revenues for the state are possible if the right policy choices are made.

The word *plan* can mean different things to different people. This has certainly been the case in Alaska, where the word *plan* has been linked to the terms *short term* and *long term* and often is politically charged because of what it may imply regarding use of existing and potential revenues. Generally, the term *plan* is associated with a long-range fiscal plan to plug the fiscal gap that is almost certain to occur when revenues are not sufficient to cover necessary expenditures.

Alaska economist Gregg Erickson has observed that financial plans generally consist of one or more of the revenue sources considered here, including use of Permanent

Fund earnings, reinstating the individual income tax, imposing a statewide sales tax, and increasing user fees and other revenues.[32] Such plans also often include creating special funds or endowments for essential services, such as education (promoted by Governor Steve Cowper in the late 1980s), and reducing or phasing out certain services and benefits that were made possible only by the high oil revenues in the late 1970s and early 1980s, such as municipal revenue sharing. Some also advocate replacing Alaska's present annual budget system with a biennial budget as part of a fiscal plan.[33]

Since the oil crash of the mid-1980s, there have been several plans proposed by elected state officials, organizations like the Alaska Municipal League (AML), and by various task forces. For obvious reasons, the interest in fiscal plans increases when oil prices are low, as was the case in the late 1990s and early 2000s. A joint House and Senate legislative task force at the time adopted the following as its vision statement: "Alaska will provide quality, cost effective public services funded by a system of revenues that is reliable, fair and diverse."[34] Few can disagree with such a vision. To date, however, no plan has been officially adopted to turn that vision into reality. Part of the reason for this failure is the inability, at least as of 2015, of policy makers to discuss, let alone agree on, the use of Permanent Fund earnings or on instituting new taxes.

6. CLOSING THE FISCAL GAP: THE PROS AND CONS OF COMBINING NEW TAXES WITH PERMANENT FUND EARNINGS

So far we have identified several separate revenue sources that might assist the state in working toward a more stable level of income. What is needed beyond this is an overall policy that will accomplish three things: (1) increase state government's capacity to deal with the demands placed upon it (in this case increase its fiscal capacity), (2) ensure a degree of equity in its implementation, and (3) create a direct link between the citizens and the cost of their government. A policy that combines Permanent Fund earnings with new taxes will accomplish all of these and is the most viable policy from an economic and social justice perspective. However, from a political perspective, enacting this policy faces several obstacles.

In terms of enhancing state governmental fiscal capacity, besides providing more predictable state spending on employment and services, some combination of new taxes and use of the Permanent Fund earnings would reduce (though not eliminate) the yearly financial jitters among public officials about oil price forecasts, even in the short term. Major downturns in oil prices would not have the devastating effect on government spending and the overall state economy that they have had in the past and will undoubtedly have in the future.

FIGURE 8.9

Comparing State Income Tax Burden per $1,000 of Income: Maximum Individual State Tax Rates for Selected States in 2010

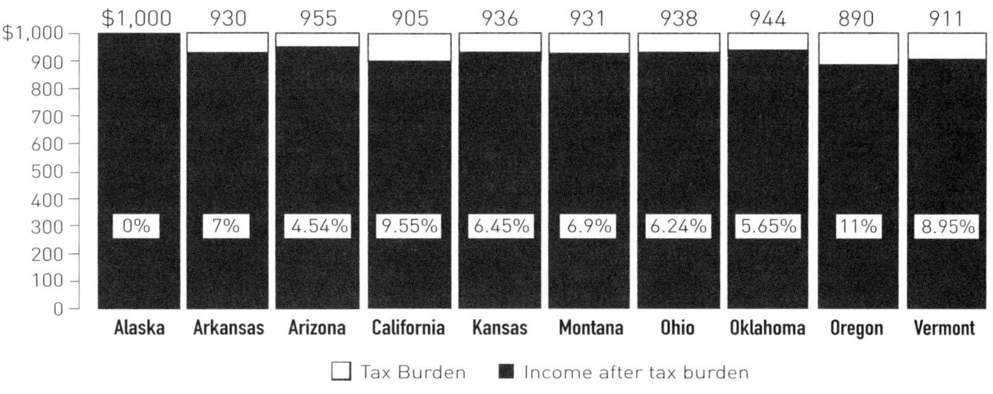

Source: Created by the authors using state tax rates from Thomson Reuters Tax and Accounting, "Checkpoint," at *https://checkpoint.riag.com*.

In considering the pros and cons of various sources and ways of dealing with a fiscal gap, one factor to consider is fairness and equity regarding the ability of people to pay a tax, the percentage of income they pay in taxes (their so-called tax burden), and their relative dependence on a benefit that they might be required to forego, such as a PFD. Equity is important to many policy makers, particularly to most Democrats.

The Pros and Cons of State Income and Sales Taxes

Besides providing a predictable, if relatively small, revenue source for state government, state individual income and sales taxes would more directly link the contributions of Alaskans to the cost of government. As of 2015, individual Alaskans pay no statewide taxes and, in fact, get money back from the state each year through the PFD. Individual Alaskans are not affected financially by increases in state spending because their taxes do not increase as government services increase. Establishing a direct financial connection between citizens and the cost of state services might increase the level of informed judgments about public policy alternatives. Moreover, an income tax is a progressive tax. That is, the tax rate increases as income goes up. So a person's total tax bill is based on his or her ability to pay. As a result, it is less onerous to the poor who may pay no income taxes at all. Thus, an income tax satisfies an economic equity criterion.

The tax burden of a state income tax on any one individual will depend mainly on their income and deductions. Generally, the amount of income tax would be small relative to their total income and a small fraction of their federal tax liability. An approximate amount of the maximum state tax liability of Alaskans at different percentages of income if the state adopted an independent tax levying system not linked to an individual's federal taxes is provided in Figure 8.9 (on the previous page). This sets out the state tax burden in selected states. Even though this calculation does not account for deductions that would likely apply, it is still a small amount, even in a high income tax state like Oregon. And given that Alaska would most likely link its tax to a percentage of each person's federal taxes, the actual amount paid by Alaskans would be perhaps half of each amount listed in the graph for the other states.

In contrast to an income tax, a state sales tax would be regressive—it would take a larger percentage of smaller incomes than from larger ones. So it would not meet the equity criteria. Certain items (such as food) could be exempted in order to provide some relief to lower income households, but that would reduce the overall revenue from the tax. A particular equity issue with a sales tax is the high cost of living in rural-bush areas compared with urban Alaska. Since sales taxes are based on the cost of a service or consumable item, a statewide sales tax would place a proportionately higher tax burden on rural-bush residents who are least likely to be able to shoulder it.

To put Alaska's overall tax burden in perspective, it has the lowest state and local tax burden of all fifty states and just above the average burden in federal taxes.[35] In 2011 the per capita Alaska state and local tax burden was 7 percent. By comparison, the national average was 9.8 percent, with the state of New York having the highest of the fifty states at 12.6 percent. In 1977 Alaska's per capita state and local tax burden, which included a state individual income tax, was 12.8 percent. By 1990 this had dropped to under 7 percent and has stayed around this level ever since. In regard to federal individual income taxes, in 2011, the average U.S. federal income tax burden per capita was $7,918, with Alaskans paying $6,697. The highest was Washington, D.C., at $12,811 and the lowest West Virginia at $3,502. Combining state, local, and federal taxes, and adding in the yearly PFD, since the early 1980s, individual Alaskans have been among the lowest taxed citizens in the nation.

The Pros and Cons of Cutting the PFD and Using Permanent Fund Earnings

Some have proposed reducing the PFD and using all or a portion of that money to pay for general government services. Those who prefer this approach see it as a way to avoid reimposing the individual income tax. In their view, the individual income tax creates a disincentive to work and unfairly puts the burden for paying for government on workers. Additionally, many think it is illogical to collect an income tax from individuals at the same time the state is distributing a dividend to them.

Opponents of reducing the dividend but who support an income tax to pay the cost of government present a number of arguments. First, with an income tax, citizens are asked to contribute to government and thereby have a real stake in the size of government and the types of services provided. Using Permanent Fund earnings does not provide this citizen-government connection. Second, the impact of reducing the PFD would fall entirely on Alaskans, whereas an income tax would also be paid by nonresident workers. Third, the state individual income tax is deductible from federal income tax, effectively reducing the cost to Alaskans of funding government.

Fourth, reducing the PFD would likely increase income inequality. PFD payments to all Alaskans have been a major factor in Alaska's status as having one of the most equitable income distributions among all fifty states. Alaska is, in fact, one of the few states in which income inequity has decreased since the 1970s.[36] If PFD payments are reduced in order to use those funds for government services, the result would be regressive, because it would take proportionately more from the poor than from the wealthy. Moreover, limiting or eliminating the PFD would have significant economic consequences for rural-bush residents for whom it represents a major source of cash.

Fifth, because of distrust of politicians and government, there is a fear among segments of the Alaska public that using Permanent Fund earnings for revenue shortfalls might open the door to the fund's use for other purposes, which might result in a shift from the current conservative investment of the principal to pork-barrel type investments in legislators' pet projects, resulting perhaps in the destruction of the fund. In fact, part of the reason behind the PFD was to raise the public's awareness of the fund and thereby create a constituency for prudent management and investment of the fund's principal.

Some Policy Options

In a July 2008 interview with Karen Rehfeld, Director of the Alaska Office of Management and Budget, she indicated that the state had no plans to tap Permanent Fund earnings nor did she foresee any new taxes being imposed.[37] In the seven ensuing years with Republican Governors Sarah Palin and Sean Parnell, the position of the administration did not change. In fact, in his unsuccessful reelection bid in 2014, Parnell ruled out any new taxes as did his major opponent and the victor, nonpartisan Bill Walker.[38] And despite the $3.5 billion budget shortfall the state faced in FY 2015, Walker did not mention taxes in his first State of the Budget speech to the legislature in January 2015.

What this meant was that other than some extensive budget cuts in the 2015 legislative session, there was no plan to deal with future state revenue problems despite the major fall in oil prices following the summer of 2014. Soon after his election, Governor Walker announced his plan to take money from the CBR to fill the major deficit for FY 2016. But by the fall of 2015 oil prices had not rebounded. In fact, they had dropped to the low $30s a barrel. So, of necessity, Walker reconsidered his campaign promise. In December 2015 he proposed *The Sustainable Alaska Plan*, a fiscal plan to ensure financial

BOX 8.2

Proposals for Dealing with Unstable State Revenues Involving Some Use of the Permanent Fund Earnings

CAPPING THE PFD

Since the establishment of the PFD, several politicians and concerned citizens have proposed putting a cap on its payment. The PFD would be capped at $1,000 a year (or some other amount) and the rest would be available for general state expenditures. If the principal of the Permanent Fund increased over time, this could make a substantial contribution to state coffers. For instance, if the 2014 payment had been capped at $1,000, over $558 million would have been available for state spending. This would have provided between 15 and 20 percent of the state's budget deficit in FY 2015.

PERCENT-OF-MARKET-VALUE—POMV

The POMV plan would stabilize Permanent Fund payouts to 5 percent of the current market value of the fund and divide this percentage each year between PFDs and state government spending. The 5 percent figure is the target rate of return on the fund after inflation. Limiting spending to 5 percent of market value would protect the principal of the fund and allow it to increase. POMV would increase state revenue capacity by creating a consistent and sustainable revenue source.

The proposed change has several other attractive features. First, it would protect the option of an annual payout from the fund, both for PFDs and for other state expenditures. Under current policy, statutory net income—from which the annual appropriations for the PFD and inflation proofing are taken—could be negative. Second, POMV provides complete and automatic inflation proofing of the fund. Under current policy there may not be sufficient funds from statutory net income and unreserved balances to make the fund fully inflation proof. Third, the plan would stabilize the annual payout that is currently subject to dramatic year-to-year fluctuations due to short-term market conditions and portfolio management decisions. Fourth, it would prevent overspending in years when the fund's earnings are high. Finally, it would make the payout method compatible with the fund's diversified investment strategy that seeks to maximize long-term earnings.

The POMV proposal has the support of the fund trustees, but its implementation will require a constitutional amendment. Opponents fear that the change in the method of determining annual spending from the fund could jeopardize the PFD since the dividend formula, which is based on statutory net income, would need to be revised.

THE CREMO PLAN

This approach was developed in 1989 by Roger Cremo, an Anchorage attorney. In place of the Permanent Fund it would establish a "Perpetual Fund" into which all state petroleum revenues would be deposited and retained in perpetuity. A fixed percentage of the value of the fund would be withdrawn each year for any purpose agreed upon by the legislature, including paying part of the cost of running state government and paying a PFD.

The plan would be coupled with the reenactment of the state personal income tax. PFDs would be higher than under the present plan, though a large portion of them would be progressively taxed back to the state, but no one would be taxed more than their PFD amount. This proposal meets the fairness concerns about using Permanent Fund earnings so that lower income Alaskans would not be penalized by a reduced PFD or an income tax. Although it failed in the legislature, Cremo's proposal was championed by Governor Jay Hammond and remains an option.

THE HUDSON PLAN

In 2002, at the height of concern over budget deficits, several members of the Alaska House of Representatives, led by Bill Hudson of Juneau, worked to pass several bills that would combine state use of Permanent Fund earnings with an income tax. The bills passed the House but died in the Senate. These proposals attempted to combine equity in receiving a PFD with capacity to pay state income tax. They encountered strong ideological resistance from many Alaskans who opposed any kind of income tax. No additional legislation was proposed when oil prices began to recover a few years later.

Source: Developed by the authors with reference to works by Scott Goldsmith of the University of Alaska Anchorage Institute of Social and Economic Research (ISER).

stability for the state by separating state revenues from the vicissitudes of oil prices. This involved a proposal to restructure the Permanent Fund and impose an income tax as well as reduce the PFD.[39]

Whether it is Walker's plan or some other one, if oil prices remain low, ultimately a proposal to combine an individual income tax with use of Permanent Fund earnings, with possibly a reduction in the PFD, will emerge, and perhaps enactment of a statewide sales tax as well. Exactly what form that plan will be is anyone's guess. Box 8.2 explains some of the major proposals that have been suggested over the years that combine taxes and Permanent Fund earnings for helping to deal with a fiscal gap. As an example, and based on the calculations given for 2015, if an income and sales tax and higher user fees had been in place and half, or just under $600 million, of the amount paid out in PFDs had been used, that year the state would have received between $2 and $2.5 billion in additional revenues, or about 25 to 30 percent of its unrestricted revenues. So even though this does not come close to replacing oil, it would at least help to create a more stable revenue stream for the state and would cushion major future downturns in state revenue and budget deficits.

For our purposes, a more immediate question is why no plan is yet in place to deal with declining revenues despite the general consensus that for years Alaskans and their politicians have known that a revenue crisis could be just around the corner. The short answer is that politics has gotten in the way of revenue reality. Insights into revenue politics help explain this lack of action on revenues and also tell us a great deal about Alaska politics and policy making.

7. ECONOMIC REALITY COLLIDING WITH POLITICAL PRESSURES

It is easy to explain away the lack of a systematic approach to Alaska's pending revenue problems by putting it down to the greed of Alaskans who do not want their PFDs reduced or to pay new taxes, aided by self-serving populist type politicians who want to be reelected. No doubt, there is some truth in this explanation. The actuality, however, is more complex. Five perspectives throw more light on the subject: (1) constitutional provisions and their political consequences, (2) external influences, (3) the attitude of Alaskans to taxes, (4) political culture and its manifestations, and (5) the fiscal conservative element. Because all five are interrelated, they need to be considered together to understand the subordination of economic reality to political pressures.

Constitutional Circumstances and Their Political Consequences

One characteristic of Alaska politics is the strong contending branches of state government, particularly the legislature and executive. Both branches have major power bases. When that characteristic is combined with those of regionalism, weak political parties, and bipartisanship, the result is often lack of consensus on major issues, as Chapter 16 on the legislative-executive relationship explains.

Another major circumstance is the way that the CBR has been used politically, to some extent undermining its primary role as a supplement to budget shortfalls. The problem stems largely from the provision in the constitutional amendment establishing it that allows funds from the CBR to be spent "for any public purpose upon an affirmative vote of three-fourths of each house of the legislature." This has meant that the CBR has been used for purposes other than budget shortfalls.

Gathering votes to use the funds from the CBR has meant that the minority in both houses must be wooed for support on the vote. These majority-minority negotiations have often subordinated the purpose of the CBR to other political motives and goals. Some have viewed this political wooing as nothing more than "buying" votes from the minority and "wasting money." Democratic minorities generally have voted to spend CBR funds in exchange for the Republican majority's agreement to include funds in the budget for programs the Democrats favor, particularly for education and social services. In the past, even though the Republicans were parties to these budget negotiations, they still accused the Democrats of increasing spending. Dipping into the CBR with state budgets running at a deficit for many years, by 2007 the "debt" to the CBR (the amount that should have been repaid to it) was approximately $5 billion. The CBR was not repaid until the high oil price year of 2008. So despite the fact that the CBR may not be a major revenue source in the future, what contribution it could make to more balanced state revenues may be undermined by politics.

Yet another political reality concerns likely political roadblocks to a statewide sales tax. For many local governments in Alaska, sales taxes provide a significant source of their revenue. Establishing a statewide sales tax could affect local sales of some goods and services and local residents might well press for reduced local sales tax rates. Thus, there would likely be opposition among some local governments to such a tax. Local governments wield considerable political influence in Alaska, and their opposition could be a major obstacle for statewide sales tax proponents to overcome.

External Influences

The political rhetoric of Alaska politics frequently uses external forces, particularly the federal government, American public opinion, and the environmental movement, as whipping boys for constraining Alaska's economic development. For the most part this rhetoric is just that and nothing more. However, there is much truth to the contention by Alaskans and their politicians that external forces have a huge influence when it comes

BOX 8.3

Reconsidering Alaska's Aversion to Paying Taxes

Regarding the reputed tax aversion of Alaskans compared to other Americans, it is worth reviewing the history of statewide tax-cut measures in the United States. Between 1977 and 1980, eighteen states enacted statutory or constitutional limits on taxing or spending even in the face of significant documented losses of desired public services. This trend has continued and the stirring of new tax revolts is constantly in evidence. In Alaska, a statewide property tax cut proposition, modeled on the original California "Proposition 13" of 1978, was put on the ballot in 2000. The proposition was soundly defeated by nearly a 3 to 1 margin and no new "tax revolt" initiatives have surfaced.

It is certainly true that Alaskans have not rushed to adopt new taxes. However, such antipathy to taxes is a long-honored American trait, rather than one that is purely Alaskan. Suspicion of any changes in the status quo is very human. It is most likely that Alaskans act much like other Americans when faced with challenges to the provision of public services, if not better. So Alaskans' aversion to both government and taxation is very debatable.

Source: Developed by Kevin Ritchie, former Director, Alaska Municipal League and author of Chapter 18.

to oil development. Since the mid-1970s, all governors, Republicans, Democrats, and independent Bill Walker, have favored opening ANWR, as have the major construction trade unions and about 70 percent of the Alaska public.[40] Mainly because of external influences, however, ANWR remains closed to oil and gas exploration, though the federal government has allowed some development in the NPR-A.[41] Also, many constraints have been placed on offshore oil drilling due to environmental concerns and actions by the federal Environmental Protection Agency (EPA), including concerns about polar bears.[42] For instance, what Alaska's congressional delegation saw as a triple blow to oil development by the federal government came in January 2015 when President Obama proposed making most of ANWR a national preserve, limiting road access in the NPR-A as well as oil development in the Arctic. However, in August 2015, the federal government approved Shell Oil's application to drill for oil and gas in the Chukchi Sea in the Arctic, though the company abandoned its efforts indefinitely one month later.[43]

If Alaska is to develop its oil and gas reserves to fill its pending revenue gap and to keep TAPS working at sustainable flows, a way must be found to deal with these external political pressures. But no solution appears in sight, especially under a Democratic president. Even Republican presidents have not been able to overcome the opposition to opening ANWR, which requires congressional approval. Yet even if ANWR is opened, the NPR-A produced substantial output, extensive oil development occurred in the Arctic, and a natural gas pipeline built, it would only kick the political can down the road for ten or twenty years and would not solve the problem of oil and gas as an unstable revenue source for Alaska.

The Attitude of Alaskans to Taxes

Conventional wisdom says that Alaskans have a deep-rooted anti-tax culture and a strong aversion to any new taxes. To be sure, evidence shows that politicians who support or propose taxes face political death at the hands of the electorate. This was the case, for instance, in 1986 when Democrat Bruce Botelho, later state attorney general and mayor of Juneau, ran against Republican Bill Hudson for a state house seat in Juneau. This was a time when oil revenues had plummeted. Hudson wanted to deal with the fiscal problem by relying on pending oil tax settlements, while Botelho advocated reinstating the individual income tax. This position likely cost Botelho the election. In 1988, Representative Mark Boyer, a Democrat from Fairbanks, almost lost his seat for advocating reinstating the income tax. As a result, such proposals are rarely made by politicians, especially when oil revenues are high.[44]

Yet, the situation appears to be more complex than a simple and broad aversion to taxes by Alaskans and many of their politicians. Kevin Ritchie, long-time local government administrator and former director of the Alaska Municipal League, presents a counterargument to the assumed Alaska anti-tax attitude in Box 8.3 (on the previous page). His argument is supported, in part, by the pragmatic nature of Alaska's political culture.

Political Culture and Its Practical Manifestations

In Chapter 5 and throughout the book, Alaska's political culture is described as one of pragmatic dependent individualism. Alaska's particular brand of individualism is one that reflects what the median voter wants. In other words, it is a sort of consensus, majority rule as reflected in the collective decisions of politicians acting in Juneau. Sometimes this collective action moves left of center, as with Alaska's relatively generous Medicaid and other welfare payments and the inability of conservatives to reenact the death penalty. Sometimes it moves to the right of center, as with mandatory prison terms for certain crimes and with the lowering of oil taxes in 2013, confirmed by the voters in 2014.

From a practical perspective what this boils down to is that, even though many Alaskans, and an increasing number over the years, favor the reinstatement of an individual income tax or the enactment of a statewide sales tax, the nature of its representational system as of 2015 has not led to such policies.[45] In a less populist state with a more communitarian (or moralistic) political culture, where more liberal elite–elected officials would have more influence, as in Vermont and Massachusetts, tax legislation would most likely have been enacted years ago.

The Fiscal Conservative Element

Of all the reasons for the state's failure to act and plan for impending state revenue shortfalls, the Alaska political characteristic of fiscal conservatism is likely the major reason for politics getting in the way of economic reality. Fiscal conservatism is certainly a significant aspect of Alaska's political culture. But that is also true of most states, and as Kevin Ritchie points out, not wanting to pay taxes is an "honored trait" in the United States. Most states, however, have no choice but to moderate their fiscal conservatism, or they have a political culture that is accepting of state taxes as a major funding source. In contrast, what might be termed the "luxury" of Alaska being able to indulge in fiscal conservatism is made possible by several conditions, but most of all the existence of massive oil revenues and the Permanent Fund.

Some, like Alaskan economist Gregg Erickson, argue that when dire financial necessity hits, Alaskans will draw on the fund or be willing to reduce or eliminate the PFD. But when oil revenues are high Alaskans do not see the need for either new taxes or a financial plan.[46] The history of oil prices helps perpetuate this stance. Oil prices can plummet, as in 1986 and late 2014, and put Alaska in the financial doldrums. But they can also rebound tremendously, and the state once again is awash in money. Thus, fiscal conservatives can say, "We don't need taxes because oil prices will rise again soon." And when oil prices are low and the Alaska economy is struggling, fiscal conservatism is reinforced by the argument that people do not have the money to pay taxes. The major budget crisis that the state faced in late 2015, however, will likely lead to a reconsideration of this argument and Erickson's prognosis may become a reality.

The charged political rhetoric of financial planning, and its perceived implications for Alaskans' PFD checks, helps reinforce these fiscal conservative tendencies. Moreover, many fiscal conservatives would argue that if the state can run on oil revenues for another decade, a natural gas pipeline may be built, providing another significant revenue source. Plus, in another decade or two, the Permanent Fund may increase to the point where investment returns can replace natural resource revenues and make state taxes unnecessary forever. Thus, as of 2015, none of the traditional methods of stabilizing Alaska's revenues has been a viable political option.

As most politicians' thoughts and actions are shaped by the two- or four-year election cycle, and as they have seen what happens to those who support taxes or a fiscal plan, most shy away from the issue. And because one legislature and governor cannot bind the next set of elected officials who may have a different political dynamic and ideological complexion, any plan put in place by one legislature and administration can be changed or abandoned by the next.

The Upshot

The political system and the institutions of government in the United States and in Alaska are weighted in favor of the political status quo. The five factors just considered, in combination, make Alaska's inability to plan for what may be a very rainy financial day is a classic case of the status quo winning the day. In the introduction to this chapter we argued that it is important for Alaska to plan or at least take some steps to meet the challenges of this inevitable rainy day. Whether or not a proactive policy for the future is a good idea or a bad one, the political reality is that it will take a long-term collapse of oil prices, such as occurred in 2014 through early 2016, to bring about a reconsideration of the subordination of economic reality to political considerations. And even if steps are taken to deal with a major budget crisis, the political response is likely to be an ad hoc, incremental approach rather than a comprehensive financial plan as proposed by Governor Walker.

A good argument can be made that there is no such thing as an actual fiscal gap in Alaska but rather a situation in which the gap could be fixed but the political system is geared to conduct business as usual. The danger, of course, as was the case from mid-2014 through early 2016, is that state revenues will be on the verge of collapse. But each state must respond to its particular circumstances, and Alaskans, like everyone else, have choices they can make.

8. CONCLUSION: THE POLITICAL ECONOMY OF ALASKA'S STATE REVENUES

An appropriate way to sum up Alaska's state revenue reality is to view it from a political economy perspective. We have seen that there is an inseparable relationship between economics and politics regarding the state's chronic revenue problems. Five points are particularly insightful.

First, three characteristics of Alaska politics clearly shape the political economy of Alaska's state revenues: (1) external economic and political forces, particularly the internationally determined price of oil and various federal government pressures, mean that under the present funding system, Alaska has little control over the amount of state revenues it receives; (2) fiscal conservatism has been a major factor in stymieing reinstatement of the individual income tax and establishing a statewide sales tax; and (3) some people are willing to pay more taxes, but fiscal conservatism combined with a political culture of both pragmatic dependent individualism and populism have, at least through 2015, worked to reinforce the political status quo regarding state revenues.

Second, given the level of state services that Alaskans have come to expect, most of which are made possible by oil revenues, these revenues cannot be replaced with the mix of sources common in most states, namely a combination of a state income tax and a sales tax supplemented by other taxes. So, without the revenue from oil production to fill state coffers, Alaskans will have to make some hard decisions regarding state revenue and state services. This will inevitably involve some use of Permanent Fund earnings for general state services and a rethinking of the continued payment of PFDs at least at present levels.

Third, for a variety of reasons, as of late 2015 the problems associated with budget shortfalls have been subordinated to political considerations that avoid addressing the issue directly even though many proposals have been put on the table to provide for this eventuality. Much of the inability to deal with the problem is a result of the populist nature of Alaska's political culture and the eyes of politicians on the next election. But it is also a result of the fluctuation in oil prices that leads to the belief among many Alaskans and politicians that the level of urgency is lower than the doomsayers claim. As of early 2016, however, there appears to be some sense of urgency to deal with budgetary issues—the day of Alaska's financial reckoning may have come.

The fourth element of the political economy of state revenues is that with no plan and no large stable revenues in place, it is not clear how Alaska policy makers will deal with a fiscal crisis. Likely they will lurch from crisis to crisis, providing ad hoc solutions when necessity requires it. This is certainly not a textbook, or even a very rational, approach to this potentially devastating situation of plummeting revenues. But it is a political approach that is common in many areas of public policy in Alaska and elsewhere.

The fifth element is that uncertain state revenues lead to uncertainty about the amounts available to spend each year. This uncertainty, in turn, leads to ad hoc policy solutions, usually drastic cuts in years with budget shortfalls as in FY 2015, 2016, and 2017, coupled with an absence of long-range planning and the dominance of politics in the process. Chapter 19 on the budget explains this in detail, and several of the policy chapters, particularly those on education, social services, and transportation, identify budgetary problems that stem from unstable state revenues.

ENDNOTES

[1] The authors thank Karen Rehfeld, former director of the Alaska Office of Management and Budget, and Patrick Galvin, former commissioner of the Alaska Department of Revenue, for their insights in developing this chapter.

[2] There are several types of federal funds that come to the states. Total federal funds include direct payments to individuals (not routed through the state government), such as Social Security, federal pensions, and so on; payments to state governments for programs, for example for special education; payments to local governments for such items as airport improvements; and earmarks from Congress. Many data sources do not distinguish between these various types of federal funds, which can lead to erroneous conclusions regarding state dependence on the federal government. This chapter is concerned mainly with federal aid to state budgets, and not with direct payments to individuals. The latter are covered in Chapter 10 on intergovernmental relations and Chapter 12 on the role of government.

[3] *Revenue Sources Book, Spring 2014* (Juneau: State of Alaska Department of Revenue, Tax Division), 2.

[4] Pat Forgey, "Alaska Money Managers Top Oil Industry in State Revenues," *Alaska Dispatch News*, December 11, 2014. See also, Alaska Department of Revenue, *Revenue Sources Book, Fall 2014* at http://revenue.state.ak.us/Portals/5/Docs/PressReleases/RSB%20Fall%202014%20highres%20page.pdf.

[5] See various editions of the State of Alaska Department of Revenue, Tax Division, *Revenue Sources Book*.

[6] The Tax Foundation, "Federal Aid as a Percentage of State General Revenue, FY 2012," at http://www.taxfoundation.org/sites/taxfoundation.org/files/docs/Federal%20Aid%20as%20a%20Percentage%20of%20State%20Revenue.png; and State Budget Solutions, at http://www.statebudgetsolutions.org/publications/detail/increased-federal-aid-to-states-is-a-long-term-trend; and on stimulus funds, at http://www.recovery.gov/Transparency/RecipientReportedData/Pages/StateTotalsByAgency.aspx.

[7] Alaska Department of Revenue, Tax Division, *Revenue Sources Book, Fall 2008*, 24.

[8] The most conventional approach for calculating petroleum revenues and the method used by the Alaska Department of Revenue includes four sources: (1) petroleum corporate income tax, (2) petroleum production tax, (3) petroleum property tax, and (4) petroleum rents and royalties. While the first three are petroleum revenues that come from taxes, the fourth is nontax revenue. Petroleum rents and royalties are composed of net oil and gas royalties, net bonuses, rents and interest, and special petroleum settlements. The sum of these four sources yields total unrestricted petroleum revenue. It is this calculation that most analysts use, including us, in estimating the percentage of own-source state funds that come from oil revenues. Clearly, the percentage is lower if any of these four, particularly rents and royalties and settlements, is excluded. See Alaska Department of Revenue, Tax Division, *Revenue Sources Book, Fall 2008*, at http://www.tax.alaska.gov/programs/documentviewer/viewer.aspx?1531f.

[9] State of Alaska Department of Revenue, Tax Division, *Revenue Sources Book, Fall 2009*, 31, at http://www.tax.alaska.gov/programs/ documentviewer/viewer.aspx?1845f.

[10] State of Alaska Department of Commerce and Economic Development, *Alaska Economic Performance Report 2006*, 19. Retrieved, June 12, 2011, at: https://www.commerce.alaska.gov/web/Portals/6/pub/2006_Performance_Report_web.pdf.

[11] Interview with Patrick Galvin, June 23, 2008, by Anthony Nakazawa and Clive Thomas.

[12] State of Alaska Department of Revenue, Tax Division, at http://tax.alaska.gov/programs/oil/production/ans.aspx?8/1/2014; and Patrick Galvin, Commissioner, Alaska Department of Revenue "Letter to Governor Sean Parnell," *Revenue Sources Book, Fall 2010*, at http://www.tax.alaska.gov/programs/documentviewer/viewer.aspx?2136f.

[13] Material submitted by ConocoPhillips Alaska to the Alaska House Finance Committee, March 23, 2011, and based on data from the U.S. Energy Administration.

[14] Arctic National Wildlife Refuge, *Arctic Power: Ten Years to TAPS Shutdown?—America's Rejected Oil*, at http://www.anwr.org/Headlines/10-Years-to-TAPS-Shutdown-America's-Rejected-Oil.php.

[15] Dermot Cole, "State Revenue Report Predicts Declining Oil Production to 2024," *Alaska Dispatch News*, December 11, 2014. See also, Alaska Department of Revenue, *Revenue Sources Book, Fall 2014*.

[16] For the politics of oil taxes and the ongoing issue of a gas pipeline see Chapter 24 on oil and gas, Sections 4 and 6.

[17] "Alaska without Oil? We'd Sure Be a Different State," *Anchorage Daily News*, July 9, 2009. See also, Chapter 7 for a fuller treatment of the economic importance of oil to Alaska.

[18] See Chapter 19, Table 19.3, for the relationship between state and federal funds since statehood; and for the period 2001–2012, Bob Williams and Joe Luppino-Esposito, "Increased Federal Aid to States in a Long-term Trend," State Budget Solutions, March 26, 2014, retrieved December 1, 2014, at http://www.statebudgetsolutions.org/publications/detail/increased-federal-aid-to-states-is-a-long-term-trend.

[19] Estimates in this section were developed by the authors from Scott Goldsmith, Institute of Social and Economic Research (ISER), "How Vulnerable Is Alaska's Economy to Reduced Federal Spending?" July 2, 2008, at http://www.iser.uaa.alaska.edu/Publications/webnote/ Federal_Spending2008.pdf; State of Alaska Department of Revenue, Tax Division, *Revenue Sources Book, Fall 2010,* 60, at http://www.tax.alaska.gov/programs/documentviewer/viewer.aspx?2136f; Taxpayers for Common Sense, *FY 2010 Earmark Analysis: Apples-to-Apples Increase in Earmark Totals*, at http://www.gov-exec.com/pdfs/ 041210rb1.pdf; and discussions by Clive Thomas with staff at the Alaska Office of Management and Budget and the Legislative Finance Division.

[20] Taxpayers for Common Sense, *FY 2010 Earmark Analysis*, 5.

[21] For a case study of the politics of the Ketchikan bridge project, see Chapter 28 on transportation, Section 7.

[22] Carl Hulse, "Senate Won't Allow Earmarks in Spending Bills," *New York Times* [*The Caucus: the Political and Government of the Times*], February 1, 2011; and Patti Epler, "Murkowski Wants Alaska Prepared for 'World without Earmarks,'" *Alaska Dispatch*, February 24, 2011.

[23] "Alaska in Strongest Financial Position Ever, Official Says," *Anchorage Daily News*, December 4, 2010.

[34] Governor Bill Walker, State of the Budget address to the Alaska Legislature, January 22, 2015, at http://gov.alaska.gov/Walker/press-room/full-press-release.html?pr=7061.

[25] For a comprehensive review of the origin and development of the fund and the PFD, the broad range of issues the fund affects and its comparison with other government-owned sovereign wealth funds, see Chapter 25. The constitutional foundations are treated in Chapter 4, Section 3.

[26] The overview of the legal and political aspects of the CBR presented in this chapter draws on Gordon Harrison, *Alaska's Constitution; A Citizen's Guide*, 5th ed. (Juneau: Alaska Legislative Affairs Agency, 2012), 162–64; "Constitutional Budget Reserve Draw $474 Million," in *The Alaska Citizen's Guide to the Budget* (Anchorage: Institute of Social and Economic Research, 2002), Section 1.2.2; and interviews by Clive Thomas with State Senator John Coghill and former Representative Harry Crawford, February 10, 2010, and Dave Donaldson, Alaska Public Radio Network (APRN) reporter, February 26, 2013. For information on the SBR, see the Alaska Department of Revenue website, at: http://treasury.dor.alaska.gov/Investments/StatutoryBudgetReserveFund.aspx; and Alaska Statutes, AS 37.05.540.

[27] See Chapter 16, Box 16.9.

[28] Forty-three states have a state income tax and forty-five have a statewide sales tax. Besides Alaska, the states with no state income tax are Florida, Nevada, South Dakota, Texas, Washington, and Wyoming. New Hampshire and Tennessee collect income taxes only on dividend and interest income. Alaska, Delaware, Montana, New Hampshire, and Oregon have no statewide sales tax.

[29] Because of the difficulty of obtaining information from the State of Alaska on the estimated revenues, particularly current estimates, for a personal income tax and a statewide sales tax, the data in this section draws partly on outdated estimates from the state, research by the University of Alaska's Institute of Social and Economic Research, and other sources.

[30] State of Alaska Department of Revenue, Tax Division, Revenue Sources: Revenues and Historical Data (Spring 2002), 45; and Scott Goldsmith, "Federal Spending and Revenues in Alaska," November 20, 2003, at http://www.iser.uaa.alaska.edu/Publications/federalspendingak.pdf.

[31] Information on sales taxes across the nation and in Alaska is taken from the Tax Foundation's statistics for 2014, retrieved January 21, 2015, at http://taxfoundation.org/article/state-and-local-sales-tax-rates-2014; and U.S. Census Bureau, 2012 Census of Governments: Finance, at http://thedataweb.rm.census.gov/TheDataWeb_HotReport2/stateandlocalfinance/stateandlocalfinance.hrml?YEAR4=2012&STATE=3.

[32] Commentary by Gregg Erickson, on *Alaska Week*, February 16, 2001.

[33] For the pros and cons of a biennial budget, see Chapter 30, Box 30.7.

[34] *Fiscal Policy Caucus: Facts and Findings for a Long-Range Fiscal Plan for Alaska* (Juneau: Alaska State Legislature, 2001), 2.

[35] Rankings are based on data from The Tax Foundation, *Annual State-Local Tax Burden Ranking FY 2011*, at http://taxfoundation.org/article/annual-state-local-tax-burden-ranking-fy-2011; *State and Local Tax Burdens: All Years, One State, 1977–2011*, at http://taxfoundation.org/article/state-and-local-tax-burdens-all-years-one-state-1977-2011; and The Northeast-Midwest Institute, at http://www.nemw.org/images/taxburd.pdf. See also, Chapter 12, on the role of government, especially Table 12.2, for comparative tax burdens by selected states.

[36] Economic Policy Institute, Center on Budget and Policy Priorities, *Alaska: Income Inequality Among Families in Alaska has Decreased Since the 1970s*, at http://www.cbpp.org/1-18-00sfp-ak.pdf.

[37] Interview by Clive Thomas with Karen Rehfeld, July 11, 2008.

[38] *Alaska Dispatch News*, "Sean Parnell Answers Questions about the Issues in the 2014 Election for Alaska Governor," October 11, 2014; and *Alaska Dispatch News*, "Bill Walker Answers Questions about the Issues in the 2014 Elecxtion for Alaska Governor," October 11, 2014.

[39] Governor Bill Walker, State of the Budget speech, January 22, 2015, at http://gov.alaska.gov/Walker/press-room/full-press-release.html?pr=7061; and *The New Sustainable Alaska Plan*, Office of of the Governor, December 9, 2015.

[40] See Chapter 20 on the media and public opinion, Figure 20.1.

[41] Erika Balstad and Margaret Talev, "Obama to Ease Way on Drilling in NPR-A," *Anchorage Daily News*, May 11, 2011.

[42] Richard Mauer, "Shell Again Delays Exploratory Drilling off Alaska's Arctic Coast," *Anchorage Daily News*, February 4, 2011; and Patti Epler, "Polar Bears Aren't Endangered, Federal Government Says," *Alaska Dispatch*, December 22, 2010.

[43] Liz Ruskin, "Murkowski Says Obama Plans 3 Gut Punches to Alaska Economy this Week," *Alaska News Nightly*, Alaska Public Radio Network (APRN), January 26, 2015; and Alexandra Gutierrez, "Invoices, Invitations, Litigation, and Even Succession: Walker Says All Responses Possible to Arctic Drilling Decision," *Alaska News Nightly*, APRN, January 27, 2015; Coral Davenport, "Shell Wins Final Approval for Arctic Oil and Gas Drilling," *New York Times*, August 17, 2015; and Clifford Klauss and Stanley Reed, "Shell Exits Arctic as Slump in Oil Prices Forces Industry to Retrench," *New York Times*, September 28, 2015.

[44] Interview by Clive Thomas with Bruce Botelho, June 23, 2011, and with Mark Boyer, January 27, 1989.

[45] See Dittman Research and Communications, *Alaska Permanent Fund Program Timeline of Public Opinion, 1976–2004*, presented to the Permanent Fund Task Force at Commonwealth North May 23, 2007. These public opinion polls included attitudes to increasing existing taxes and paying new ones. The results are included in Chapter 25 on the Permanent Fund, Table 25.4.

[46] Erickson on *Alaska Week*, broadcast February 16, 2001.

⋆ CHAPTER 9 ⋆

Alaska Natives and the State's Political Economy: Changing Power Relationships

Thomas F. Thornton and Emil Notti
with Mary Sattler and George Owletuck

Pick up a book on the politics of a state where Native Americans are a large minority, such as Oklahoma, South Dakota, New Mexico, or Arizona, and it soon becomes clear that indigenous people have played only a minor role in their states' politics. This contrasts sharply with Alaska, where Alaska Natives have had a major influence on state politics. So much so that, as explained in Chapter 2, the role of Natives is one of the major characteristics of Alaska's politics. Plus, Alaska Natives have had a significant influence on the nature of the state's political economy—the interaction of economic and political factors in shaping public policy. More specifically, and as argued in Chapter 5, while the extent to which Alaska Natives have influenced the state's political culture is unclear, the Native community has certainly had many, and in some cases major, impacts on public policy. The foundation for this influence is largely the special status of Alaska Natives compared to most Native Americans across the nation.

The major purpose of this chapter is to explain the place of Alaska Natives in Alaska's political economy and particularly their changing power relationships in state politics and policy making. The approach has two interrelated elements. One is to evaluate the successes, problems, and prospects related to the quest to secure self-determination, the guiding principle of political action for Native Americans in all states. Self-determination is the "need to be able to determine our own future," as Emil Notti expressed it in 1969 when Alaska Natives and their allies were pressing for a just land claims settlement.[1] The other approach uses a political ecology perspective. *Political ecology* is a term used by anthropologists to describe the relationship between humans and their physical environment. In this chapter the political ecology approach emphasizes the development and dynamics of Alaska Native political institutions, leadership, and power in relation to valued lands and resources that have been subject to increasing competition and regulation from non-Native interests and governments. The Alaska Native story is one of hard-fought successes and of continuing struggle and possibilities.

Besides the prominent role of Natives in state politics, five other characteristics of Alaska politics stand out in the analysis that follows. Two closely related ones are the all-pervasive importance of government—federal, state and local, and intergovernmental relations (IGR)—and the significant role of external political forces, especially the federal government, which is given responsibility for dealing with "the Indian Tribes" in Article I, Section 8, Clause 3 of the U.S. Constitution. The other three characteristics are the political culture of pragmatic dependent individualism, economic development versus conservation/environmentalism, and regionalism, including conflicts between urban and rural-bush areas.

The chapter begins by explaining some key terms and providing essential background. Then we explain the circumstances leading to the special status of Alaska Natives. This is followed by an overview of the challenges of maintaining and advancing self-determination in the contemporary Alaska and national political environment. The next two sections deal with Native economic and political institutions and the prospects for building a sustainable Alaska Native economy. Then the role of Natives in Alaska politics is considered, followed by an explanation of the subsistence issue as a microcosm of the role of Natives in state and federal politics. The conclusion addresses the changing role of Alaska Natives in Alaska's political economy.

1. KEY TERMS AND ESSENTIAL BACKGROUND

Because of their unique status as indigenous peoples and "dependent nations" under the U.S. Constitution and federal Indian law, Native Americans, including Alaska Natives, have a specialized terminology that defines their relations with federal and state governments. Several of these specialized terms are briefly defined in this book's glossary, but some are explained in more detail here because they are used in more specialized ways in this chapter. Other terms particular to this chapter are also explained in this section.

Tribes and the Indian Reorganization Act of 1934 and 1936

Broadly defined, a *tribe* is a social group based on kinship and customs that existed before the development of nation-states. The tribe was the primary socio-economic and political organization (usually divided into kin groups and clans) of the indigenous population of Alaska for thousands of years before Europeans came to the region. It continued to be so after the Alaska Purchase by the United States in 1867, and in various forms it continues to the present.

Since 1867, federal law has gradually formalized the relationship of the U.S. government with Alaska's indigenous population, including that of the tribe. The first landmark legislation was the Indian Reorganization Act (IRA) of 1934. This law clarified the status of all Native Americans by establishing rules for recognizing tribes, strengthening tribal government, aiding tribal business activities, tribal control over lands, and tribal eligibility to receive federal aid. The 1936 amendment, reflecting the situation in Alaska, allowed groups of Natives associated with a place to petition for tribal incorporation and recognition. The majority of the current 229 federally recognized tribes in Alaska were incorporated under these provisions. Formally recognized tribes are those that appear on the U.S. Department of Interior's list that are eligible to receive services from the federal Bureau of Indian Affairs (BIA).

Tribes may be represented by either a traditional or an IRA council. Traditional councils (sometimes referred to as tribal councils) were formed through custom and necessity by particular tribes. While not formally organized under U.S. law (as are IRA councils), traditional councils may still be recognized under federal and state law and perform certain local government and service delivery functions.

Alaska Natives: Meaning, Ambiguities, and Clarifications

The federal government has dealt with Native Americans in the Lower 48 on a tribe by tribe basis. In contrast, the federal government has chosen to deal with Alaska's indigenous people collectively instead of separately as tribes. The role of Alaska Natives in the state's political economy has been significantly influenced by their collective status and by the Alaska Native Claims Settlement Act (ANCSA) of 1971. While the term *Alaska Natives* has a formal legal meaning, its use in regard to understanding the role of Natives in the state's political economy needs clarification.

Formally, an Alaska Native is a member of an aboriginal Eskimo (Inupiaq, Yupik/Cupik), Aleut (Unangan, Alutiiq), or Indian (Athabaskan, Haida, Tlingit, Tsimshian, Eyak) group enrolled in a federally recognized Alaska tribe or village, or in an ANCSA corporation. Tribes may determine their own membership, but most have followed the federal "blood quantum" formula, wherein *Native* means a U.S. citizen who is one-fourth or more of Eskimo, Aleut, or Indian blood, or any combination thereof.

To the casual observer, however, this collective term—*Alaska Natives*—can be misleading for three main reasons. First, the term embraces three diverse groups—Indians, Eskimos, and Aleuts. Each group has its own subdivisions and there is a range of social, economic, and political cultural systems across the groups, including several different types of Native governments. This cultural diversity can manifest itself in various ways in the political scene within the Native community and in relation to the non-Native community. Second, for purposes of simplifying things, the media, many Alaskans, and those from outside the state often refer to Alaska Natives as if they have one common, unified interest. This is rarely the case. While the Native community can unite politically around some causes, it is often divided, particularly on issues of economic development.

Third, the Alaska Native population is approximately 105,000, or about 1 in 7 of Alaska's estimated total population of 735,000 in 2013. The Native population is divided fairly evenly in residency between rural-bush Alaska, where just over half live, and urban Alaska.[2] Natives living in urban areas often become acculturated to urban and majority cultural values, which can result in political attitudes that diverge from rural-bush Native perspectives. As discussed in various places in this chapter, the complexity and diversity of Alaska Native cultures, values, and varying needs and perspectives, make political unity and effective political action an ongoing challenge.

Sovereignty, Indian Country, and Self-Determination

For Native Americans in general and Alaska Natives in particular, the concepts of *sovereignty*, *Indian Country*, and *self-determination* are interrelated. The *sovereignty* of Indian nations is defined by the unique relationship that exists between the federal government and tribes as set out in the U.S. Constitution and in various treaties, statutes, executive orders, and court decisions. When the governmental authority of Indian tribes was challenged in the 1830s, in a series of cases involving the Cherokee nation, U.S. Supreme Court Chief Justice John Marshall articulated the fundamental principle of tribal sovereignty that has guided federal Indian law ever since. The principle, however, involves a strange mix of independence and dependence under which tribes possess the status of dependent nations and have inherent powers of self-government, while Congress retains plenary power over tribes and "can assist or destroy an Indian tribe as it sees fit."[3]

Legally, the term *Indian Country* refers to lands within the boundaries of an Indian reservation or other land set aside by the federal government in trust for the use, benefit, or occupancy of Native Americans. The status of Indian Country is important for the exercise of tribal sovereignty in criminal and civil matters.

As noted earlier, *self-determination* has been the guiding principle of both Alaska Native and American Indian groups to chart their own political, economic, and cultural destinies. Self-determination has been increasingly embraced by the U.S. government since the 1960s, after the failure of its assimilation and termination policies of the nineteenth and early-to-mid-twentieth centuries. Assimilation sought first to "civilize" Natives by stripping them of their language, culture, and communal forms of governance, and later to "terminate" the federal trust relationship to tribes. The Indian Self-Determination and Education Assistance Act of 1975 codifies the principle of self-determination in law, charting a variety of means for tribes to exercise greater control over governmental programs.

The Alaska Native Claims Settlement Act (ANCSA) of 1971

No event in the past several hundred years has had more impact on the socioeconomic, cultural, and political development of the Alaska Native community than has ANCSA. Indeed, it is one of the major events that shaped the development of Alaska's political economy in general. Accordingly, ANCSA is referred to in several chapters of this book. Here we outline ANCSA's major provisions and consequences as a foundation for much of the analysis in this chapter.

ANCSA became federal law on December 18, 1971. Congress passed the law to settle Alaska Native claims against the federal government after decades of lawsuits, hearings, and political negotiations. The major political catalyst in settling these claims was the discovery of oil on the North Slope. Some of the land needed to build the pipeline from Prudhoe Bay to Valdez in Prince William Sound was the subject of Alaska Native land claims. ANCSA extinguished aboriginal land, hunting, and fishing rights in exchange for approximately 44 million acres of land (11 percent of the state) and $962.5 million in compensation. ANCSA also created twelve for-profit Native regional corporations, shown in Map 9.1. Later a thirteenth was created, receiving money but no land, based in Seattle for Alaska Natives living outside of the state. ANCSA also established more than 220 for-profit village corporations. These regional and village corporations were to manage the lands and money from the settlement.

From both a self-determination and political ecology perspective, ANCSA did much to advance the Alaska Native cause. There was a downside, however. The pros and cons notwithstanding, ANCSA and its effects still dominate the Alaska Native political economy.

Alaska Native Politics

The term *Alaska Native politics* (usually referred to simply as *Native politics*) is used to denote two major types of political activities involving the Native community. One is the internal politics of the community involving Native governments, such as tribal councils, and Native corporation boards of directors, and organizations like the Alaska Federation of Natives (AFN). The other, broader and less precise use of the term denotes the interaction of Native governments, organizations, and individuals with non-Native governments and organizations, particularly local governments, the state government, the federal government, and, in some cases, international organizations and interests. Technically, this is more accurately described as Native political relations with non-Native governments and organizations, but often still comes under the rubric of *Native politics*.

Because of the legal collective status of Alaska Natives, individual Alaska Natives, their governments, Native organizations, and elected and appointed officials need to

MAP 9.1

For-Profit Alaska Native Regional Corporations

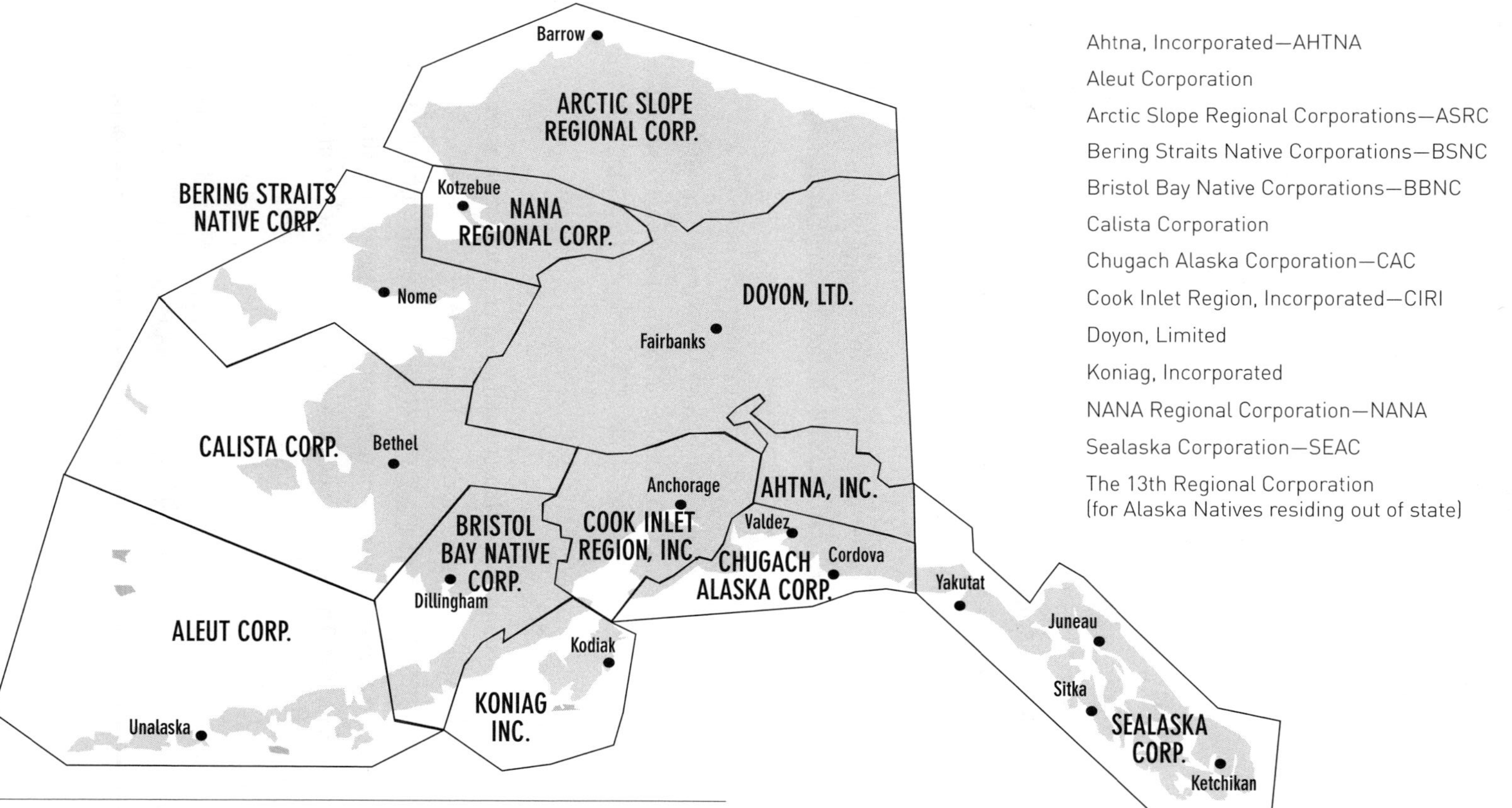

Source: Developed by the authors.

interact with all three levels of government in order to pursue their political and policy agendas. So, one characteristic of Alaska Native politics is involvement in intergovernmental relations (IGR). In fact, together with transportation and social services interests, Alaska Native interests of all types are among the most involved in IGR and its politics.

2. A UNIQUE STATUS: ALASKA NATIVES AND THE EVOLUTION OF NATIVE AMERICAN RELATIONS IN THE UNITED STATES

The contemporary economic and political status of the Alaska Native community is the product of a unique history compared with Native Americans in the rest of the nation. Much of this unique history, their contemporary political power base, and the challenges they face are the result of their special collective status. This is largely a product of the relatively late colonization of Alaska by non-Natives compared with other parts of the nation.

From Russian Colonization to Alaska Statehood

Alaska Natives were the last indigenous people to be colonized and eventually absorbed into the United States. Residing on "the last frontier," they remained relatively undisturbed until the late nineteenth century, when fishing and mining interests brought significant colonization to the region. Before this there had been significant trade in furs, especially sea otters, in the Russian period (1800–1867), but apart from the Russian settlements in Sitka and Kodiak, Alaska Natives maintained their political autonomy and control over the land. In fact, the Russians were dependent upon Natives for both trade and provisions. As a result, the Russians interacted with them on relatively egalitarian terms (with the exception of some Aleuts, who were enslaved).

Geographic conditions, namely remoteness, the harsh climate, and the unsuitability of much of Alaska for agricultural development, also discouraged non-Native migration, settlement, and land confiscation within the region. Even in the early twentieth century there were Interior Alaska Native communities that had scarcely seen a white person, and Alaska Natives remained a majority of the Territory's population until World War II, despite the depopulating effects of epidemic diseases, such as measles and smallpox.

By the time the United States acquired Alaska from Russia in 1867, Congress had already ceased making treaties with Indian tribes. The 1867 Treaty of Cession with Russia recognized that "uncivilized Native tribes [are] to be subject to such laws and regulations as the United States may from time to time adopt in regards to aboriginal tribes of that country." However, Congress chose to deal with Alaska Natives collectively rather than as separate tribes. This is reflected in the Alaska Organic Act of 1884, which provides that Alaska Natives "shall not be disturbed in the possession of any lands actually in their use or occupation or now claimed by them."

This language is reminiscent of the federal government's 1787 Northwest Ordinance, which sought to protect Indians from non-Natives encroaching on their lands on the old western frontier. Congress, however, was derelict in enforcing the provisions to protect the land of Lower 48 Native Americans, who gradually lost control over the bulk of their lands. The period between the Russian presence and Alaska statehood, particularly after the Territory was established in 1912, also saw increasing threats to Alaska Native lands that set the scene for post-statehood land claims politics.

Despite being classified differently by the federal government, the experience of Alaska Natives in the hundred years after the Alaska Purchase was all too similar to Native Americans in the Lower 48. Like other indigenous and ethnic minorities, they faced Jim Crow–style discrimination until the mid-twentieth century. Missionaries and governments viewed Natives as "savages," forcibly segregating them and seeking to "civilize" them through ethnocide—the destruction of their language and culture, including their indigenous forms of self-governance. Citizenship was not granted as a right until 1924, and racist signs such as "No Dogs or Indians Allowed," could be found in non-Native-owned businesses up until the Alaska Territorial legislature enacted antidiscrimination legislation in 1945.[4]

Box 9.1 traces the political development of the Alaska Native community from the early years of the U.S. purchase of Alaska though the early twenty-first century. By the time aboriginal claims were settled in 1971, Alaska Natives and the federal government had had the benefit of hindsight in assessing the strengths and weaknesses of Lower 48 Indian reservations, economic programs, and governance, and presumably could avoid what many viewed as mistakes.

From Statehood to the Present

Statehood in 1959 put the fledgling state in direct competition with Alaska's tribes when the state moved to select more than 100 million acres of land for transfer from the federal government as part of the Statehood Act. Competing claims eventually led to the institution of a "land freeze" by the Secretary of the Interior until Native claims were resolved.[5] Together with the federal government's collective treatment of Alaska's indigenous population, the passage of ANCSA is one of the twin foundations of the unique status of Alaska Natives among Native American groups. This unique status has had both advantages and disadvantages for advancing the self-determination of Alaska Natives.

The Potential Benefits of a Unique Status

ANCSA was intended to bring Alaska Natives into the economic mainstream of America through a kind of self-determination that the reservation system and trust payments had failed to provide Native Americans in the Lower 48. In comparing the resolution

BOX 9.1

Milestones in the Development of Alaska Native Political Institutions

1884—FIRST ORGANIC ACT
A provision of this act regarding the collective status and land protections for Alaska Natives became an important legal basis for Native land claims.

1906—ALASKAN NATIVE ALLOTMENT ACT
Established the first opportunity for individual Natives to acquire title to land. It is a slow and convoluted process, however.

1912—ALASKA NATIVE BROTHERHOOD (ANB)
Followed by the Alaska Native Sisterhood (ANS) in 1915. ANB was founded in Sitka by a group of Presbyterian Natives. This movement was the first to organize Alaska Natives across geographic and cultural lines. In the early years, the ANB mission emphasized acculturation with the majority white culture as a path to equality. In the 1920s, ANB became increasingly political, launching successful campaigns for voting rights and the first land claims suit against the federal government. This claim eventually yielded a $7.5 million settlement for the Tlingit and Haida in 1968. Today ANB/ANS camps operate in communities throughout Southeast Alaska and elsewhere.

1924—FIRST ALASKA NATIVE LEGISLATOR, AND U.S. CITIZENSHIP ACT
William L. Paul (a Tlingit) was the first Native elected to the Territorial Legislature. The U.S. Citizenship Act extended citizenship to all Native Americans, including Alaska Natives. Previously, their only path to citizenship was for a judge to certify their "civilized" status by affidavits from non-Natives, plus evidence of their adoption of white customs.

1926—ALASKA NATIVE TOWN-SITE ACT
Permitted homesteading of lands in the vicinity of Native villages by Natives and non-Natives.

1934—INDIAN REORGANIZATION ACT (IRA)
A partial repudiation of the federal assimilation policies toward Native Americans, it enabled limited Native self-governance at the village level. Sixty-six Alaska Native villages and two regional entities organized as governments under the act.

1936—COMPOSITE INDIAN REORGANIZATION ACT
Allowed the Secretary of the Interior to designate lands used or occupied by Natives (lands to which they had aboriginal title) as reservations.

1943—U.S. SECRETARY OF THE INTERIOR PROPOSES THE FIRST RESERVATION UNDER THE IRA
Covered nearly 1.5 million acres around the Athabaskan community of Venetie in northeast Alaska, plus another one hundred proposed reservations, which would encompass nearly half of the Territory of Alaska. Non-Native Alaska leaders were alarmed by the proposals, and lobbied successfully to prevent the withdrawals.

1945—ANTIDISCRIMINATION LAW PASSED BY THE ALASKA TERRITORIAL LEGISLATURE
Outlawed segregation and other discriminatory practices against Natives. In a famous exchange, a senator asked, "Who are these people barely out of savagery, who want to associate with whites, with 5,000 years of recorded history behind us." Tlingit leader Elizabeth Peratrovich, part of an ANB/ANS delegation attending the floor debate, responded, "I would not have expected that I, who am barely out of savagery, would have to remind the gentlemen with 5,000 years of recorded civilization behind them of our Bill of Rights." Her testimony helped carry the vote.

1958—ALASKA STATEHOOD ACT
Congress approved 103 million acres of land for the state, but disclaimed any state right to Native lands.

1961—INUPIAT PAITOT (THE PEOPLE'S HERITAGE)
First regional Alaska Native political organization founded since the ANB/ANS.

1962—*TUNDRA TIMES*
Inupiaq leader Howard Rock established the first statewide Native newspaper to advocate for Native issues.

1966—ALASKA FEDERATION OF NATIVES (AFN)
Founded to advocate for a just settlement of land claims in the face of competing state land selections and proposed industrial developments. Athabaskan leader Emil Notti was the first AFN president.

1968—*ALASKA NATIVES AND THEIR LAND*
Federal Field Committee report published, which asserted the validity and urgency of Alaska Native land claims and resource needs.

1971—ALASKA NATIVE CLAIMS SETTLEMENT ACT (ANCSA)
A far-reaching development for Alaska Natives. See explanation earlier in the chapter.

1986—8(a) AND NOL (NET OPERATING LOSS) LEGISLATION
Federal legislation that allowed Alaska Native corporations, including both ANCSA corporations and tribal entities, to participate in the Small Business Administration's 8(a) program, offering "special procurement advantages" to remedy barriers to Native economic development created by past government policies. The 1986 Tax Reform Act permitted ANCSA corporations to sell net operating losses to profitable companies, which the latter use to reduce their taxes through write-offs, funneling a portion of the tax savings back to Native corporations. The NOL program is no longer in operation, but 8(a) provisions remain significant for Native tribes and corporations, though attempts to repeal the provision have been made in Congress.

1993—FEDERAL RECOGNITION OF 229 ALASKA TRIBES
Provided for expanded sovereignty for IRA village governments and other tribal entities.

1994—*REPORT ON STATUS OF ALASKA NATIVES*
First major study since the 1968 Federal Field Committee report analyzed the status of Natives. The report found considerable material improvements, but also major disparities with whites in social and economic conditions.

1998—U.S. SUPREME COURT DECISION IN *ALASKA v. NATIVE VILLAGE OF VENETIE TRIBAL GOVERNMENT*
Ruled that Indian Country does not exist in Alaska because of the ANCSA settlement.

1998—DENALI COMMISSION ESTABLISHED
An independent federal agency focusing on developing the economy of rural-bush Alaska and delivering federal services as efficiently as possible.

2000—RECOGNITION OF ALASKA NATIVE TRIBES BY GOVERNOR KNOWLES
The governor sought to strengthen partnerships through the "New Millennium" project.

2004—SECOND REPORT ON *STATUS OF ALASKA NATIVES*
Found that Natives possessed more jobs, higher incomes, better living conditions, education, and health care than ever; but they remained several times more likely than other Alaskans to drop out of school and to be poor or out of work. The Native population continued to grow, becoming younger (with 44 percent age nineteen and under) and increasingly living in urban areas.

Source: Developed by the authors.

of Alaska Native rights to those of Lower 48 Indians, ANCSA has been described as a mixture of self-determination and "termination" policies designed to reduce dependency on federal programs while opening Native lands for general development.[6]

With the financial and land resources that ANCSA provided and by virtue of their population, Alaska Natives have had more potential to be major players in state politics than other Native Americans. Today, despite the loss of 90 percent of their lands, Alaska Natives still control more than 44 million acres, a larger land base than all Lower 48 Indian groups combined. Nearly 15 percent of Alaskans define themselves as Natives, the highest percentage of Native American of any state in the nation, followed by Oklahoma and New Mexico at about 11 percent each.[7] Alaska also possesses the largest number of federally recognized tribal governments, 229 in all, more than 40 percent of the U.S. total of 561.

These assets, along with the economic influence of ANCSA corporations and the coordinated political action and lobbying of the AFN, make Alaska Natives a potent and multidimensional political force. And, as explained later, in many ways the Alaska Native community has been an effective political force, particularly in state politics. Added to the influence of the ANCSA corporations and AFN are the twelve regional nonprofit corporations, some of which were developed prior to ANCSA. For example, the Central Council of Tlingit and Haida Indian Tribes of Alaska and the Tanana Chiefs Conference were active in the pre-ANCSA struggle for lands, resources, and services for their regional constituents. The territory of each of the twelve nonprofit regional corporations can be seen in Map 9.2. Today the regional nonprofits complement the for-profit corporations by providing health, social, and other basic services. Some are recognized as tribal governments, and most advocate politically at the local, state, federal, and international levels.

Problems Presented by a Unique Status

The special status of Alaska Natives has also worked to undermine the advancement of their cause compared to Native Americans in the Lower 48. Some of the problems result from ANCSA provisions. Foremost among these is that the lack of Indian Country in Alaska limits Alaska Native tribal self-determination compared to tribes in the Lower 48. Critics see this limitation as a fundamental weakness in the structure of Alaska Native governance.[8] The reasons and consequences of this criticism are as follows.

In 1998, in *Alaska v. Native Village of Venetie Tribal Government*, the U.S. Supreme Court confirmed that ANCSA extinguished Indian Country and aboriginal rights and vested all Alaska Native lands in ANCSA corporations rather than in tribes. As a result, the Court ruled that Alaska tribes do not possess the classical sovereign powers of self-rule that come with jurisdiction over territory, such as the authority to tax, regulate, and police.[9] Tribal councils and courts in Alaska do have legal jurisdiction over certain matters, such as that under the Indian Child Welfare Act of 1978. But this tribal jurisdiction sometimes leads to conflicts with the state and state law, and the State of Alaska has consistently opposed the exercise of general tribal sovereignty. Friction between state and tribal sovereignty is common throughout the United States, but it is especially strong in Alaska, due in part to the youth of the state. Clearly, the lack of territorial sovereignty, accompanied by limited jurisdictional sovereignty, places Alaska Natives in an ambivalent and murky area in terms of their sovereign rights and status.[10]

Other problems with ANCSA include the fact that, in a sense, it imposed an alien economic culture on Alaska Natives through the corporate model of the free enterprise system, thereby intertwining the often incompatible principles of the profit motive with attempts by Alaska Natives to preserve a communal and subsistence-based culture. This has had several consequences.

MAP 9.2

Nonprofit Alaska Native Regional Associations

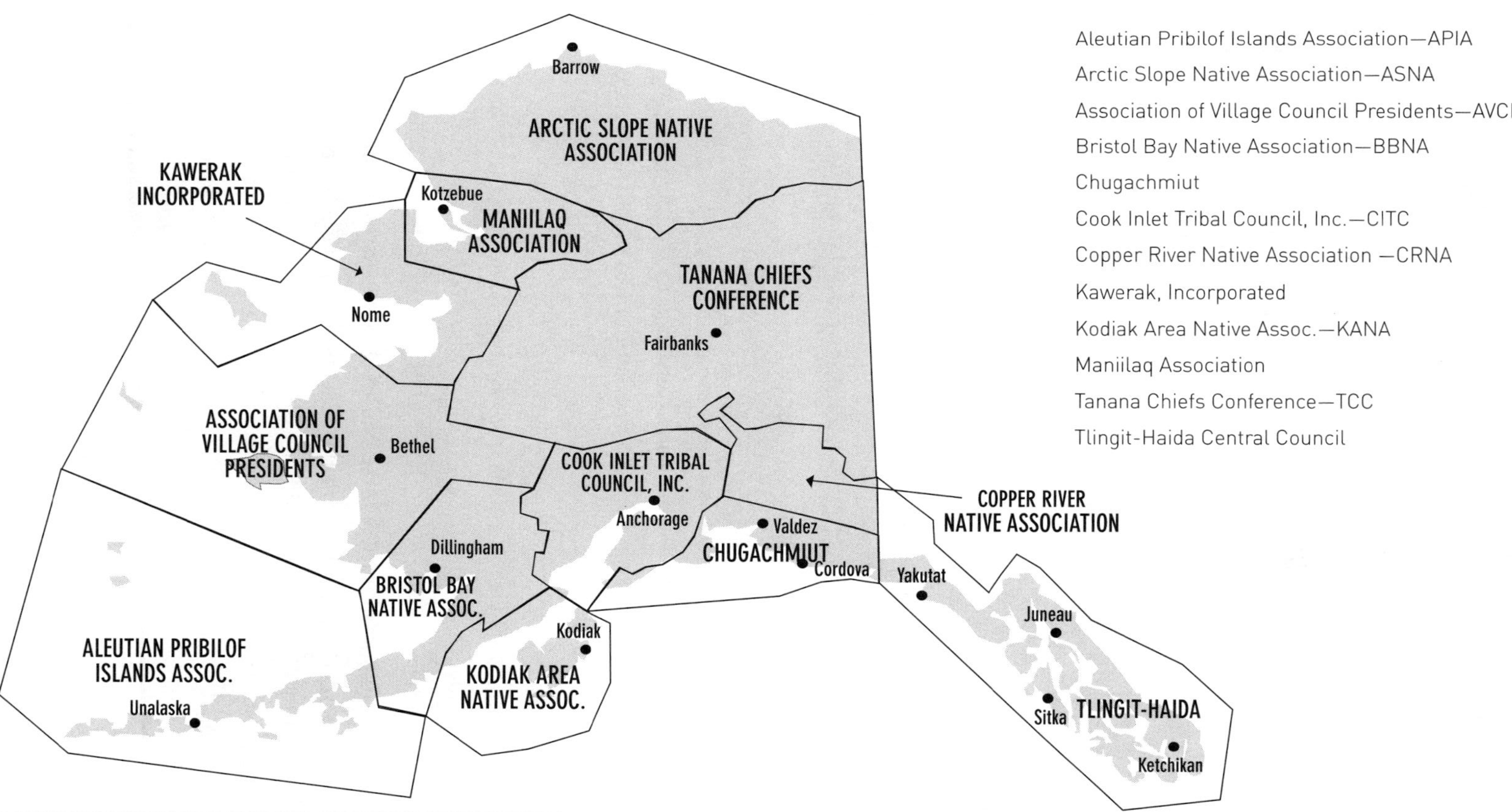

Source: Developed by the authors.

First, given the lack of business experience of many Alaska Natives, it is not surprising that many for-profit regional corporations had serious financial problems in the twenty years following ANCSA. Congress took a number of measures to assist them, including adoption of legislation allowing Native corporations to sell their net operating losses to non-Native corporations throughout the country. Second, ANCSA caused rifts within the Native community between the so-called Brooks Brothers Natives, the corporate officers and leaders, and the rank and file, as well as between those born before December 18, 1971, who received dividends from the corporations and the "afterborns" who did not.[11] Third, ANCSA generally put the survival of many aspects of Native culture under great stress and threat. Furthermore, some observers see ANCSA's results in terms of making major improvements in the economic status of Natives as mixed. Despite the nearly billion-dollar settlement and annual dividends for some, Alaska Natives in general remain at the bottom of the economic ladder in Alaska, are more likely to be unemployed, and suffer from various other personal and social problems.

Other Historical and Contemporary Constraints on Native Self-Determination

Besides the problems brought by ANCSA, there are other factors that have inhibited self-determination for Alaska Natives. One is the "common use" clause in Article VIII, Section 3, of Alaska's constitution, which provides that fish, wildlife, and waters are reserved "to the people for common use." Those hostile to Native rights often cite this clause as the basis for opposing any collective rights or sovereignty for Alaska Natives.[12] A second is the inevitable internal dissension and lack of political coordination and unity in the Native community itself. This results largely from its diverse cultures. The situation is exacerbated by the many Native organizations, several of which have overlapping authority.

A third factor affecting self-determination involves the relationship between Natives and non-Native governments and other organizations. The special "collective" status of Alaska Natives, the fact that many live where they always have and were not removed to reservations, plus the provisions of ANCSA, have resulted in a different experience for Alaska's Native community. Unlike Native Americans living on Lower 48 reservations, who deal almost exclusively with the federal government to secure their political goals, Alaska Natives must deal with federal, state, and local governments to advance their interests and safeguard foundational aspects of their cultures, such as aboriginal languages and subsistence rights. Of necessity, this leads to a complex set of IGR, in which Alaska Natives must work creatively within and between multifarious institutions and spheres of influence to advance their political, economic, and cultural interests. While this complex IGR provides alternative avenues to achieve certain goals, it also often requires more financial and other resources and a more delicate political balancing act. This is because there are more elements to a particular political strategy that can go wrong.

Two other potential constraints on Natives achieving enhanced self-determination are the related ones of urban versus rural-bush conflict and demographics. Conflict between urban and rural areas is common in most states due to differences in their respective economies and needs, and often their political attitudes. In Alaska this conflict is compounded by major racial and cultural differences. Issues like subsistence and Native rights and the high cost of delivering services to remote regions tend to create resentment in the minds of some urban legislators and their constituents, who believe they are subsidizing rural-bush areas. This conflict between urban and rural-bush areas is dealt with in several chapters in the book, and we will not expand on it much here other than to relate it to the changing demographics in the state.[13]

From comprising a majority of Alaska's residents in Territorial days and an estimated one-third at statehood, the Native percentage of the population dropped to about 14 percent in 1980 and has remained fairly stable since. Natives are also declining in their share of the rural-bush population as more Natives move to urban areas to seek increased opportunities.[14] This means that the political influence of Alaska Natives is being gradually reduced as more power shifts to urban Alaska, especially Anchorage. Thus, urban areas have an increasing upper hand in opposing rural-bush, if not explicitly Native, policy goals. Each legislative reapportionment since statehood has decreased the influence of rural-bush areas.

Until the 2013 U.S. Supreme Court decision in *Shelby County v. Holder*, the federal Voting Rights Act of 1965 provided significant protection for ensuring Native representation. Prior to the *Shelby* decision, Alaska (along with fifteen other states) was required to obtain pre-approval of its reapportionment plans from the U.S. Justice Department to ensure that the plans did not adversely affect racial minorities in their exercise of the franchise. The Court's decision in *Shelby* effectively gutted the preclearance requirement in the Voting Rights Act until such time as Congress enacts a new and updated formula for determining what factors will trigger the requirement. Most political observers believe this is highly unlikely.[15]

Lower 48 Native American versus Alaska Native Self-Determination and Contemporary and Future Political Paths

All Native Americans still struggle to catch up with non-Natives in their levels of education, employment, income, and health. From what has been said above, the balance sheet is mixed in comparing the success and possible future potential between Lower 48 Native Americans and Alaska Natives in advancing these and other aspects of their welfare and in achieving and enhancing self-determination. While self-governance is increasing among American Indian tribes, in Alaska it remains distinctly limited, largely because the lack of Indian Country diminishes the possibilities for territorial sovereignty.

The special status of Alaska Natives has, in many ways, led them on a different political path to achieve their goals from their counterparts in the Lower 48. For instance, Lower 48 Native Americans residing on reservations have little need to be involved in state politics, other than in some specific situations, such as the Indian Gaming Regulatory Act of 1990, which allows Native American tribes to operate casinos on "Indian lands" under agreements that must be negotiated with their respective state governments. Native Americans are also a small minority in all other states. Thus, they have minimal influence at the state level with consequent minimal coverage of them in most books on state politics. In contrast, Alaska Natives, with their lack of sovereign status, overlapping jurisdictions between Native and state-authorized local governments, and state legislative districts with large Native populations, must be intimately involved with state government and its politics. This involvement is essential to their IGR political strategies.

So, the path of Native Alaskans in securing and enhancing their self-determination, which embraces their role in the state's political ecology, has largely been set, and this is the path that they must pursue in contemporary and future Alaska and at the national level. This path is characterized by innovative, collaborative, and multifaceted solutions pursued by Alaska's tribes, Native corporations, and other entities to further improve the status of Alaska Natives.[16] Their success today and in the future depends on their ability to put together all the pieces in this political power puzzle. Evaluating the reasons for their successes and problems in this power relationship within Alaska's present and future political economy is the subject of the rest of the chapter.

3. ADVOCATING FOR AND SECURING NATIVE POLITICAL GOALS: THE PURSUIT OF SELF-DETERMINATION IN A COMPLEX POLITICAL ECONOMY

When AFN came together for its first convention in 1966, there was one major issue on the table: negotiating a just settlement to aboriginal land claims. Currently, AFN's members include 178 villages (both federally recognized tribes and village corporations), thirteen regional Native corporations, and twelve regional nonprofit and tribal consortiums that contract to run federal and state programs. AFN is governed by a thirty-seven-member board, which is elected by its membership at the annual convention held each October. Consequently, today AFN's objectives are considerably broader than they were in 1966, as reflected in their present mission statement and objectives:

> Alaska Native people began as members of full sovereign nations and continue to enjoy a unique political relationship with the federal

> government. We will survive and prosper as distinct ethnic and cultural groups and will participate fully as members of the overall society. The mission of AFN is to enhance and promote the cultural, economic and political voice of the entire Alaska Native Community. AFN's major goals are to:
>
> - Advocate for Alaska Native people, their governments and organizations, with respect to federal, state and local laws;
> - Foster and encourage preservation of Alaska Native cultures;
> - Promote understanding of the economic needs for Alaska Natives and encourage development consistent with those needs;
> - Protect, retain and enhance all lands owned by Alaska Natives and their organizations; and
> - Promote and advocate for programs and systems which instill pride and confidence in individual Alaska Natives.[17]

At its annual fall conventions, AFN holds dozens of informational sessions and considers numerous resolutions to address the wide range of issues that concern its members. These range from the most local of problems (for instance, funding for village public safety and infrastructure) to state and federal issues (such as subsistence fish and wildlife management) to international issues (for example, sustainable development amid globalization). In the realm of economics, the 2007 AFN convention featured an "Alaska Marketplace" competition to showcase a new model of small-scale development "based not only on the vast resources of Alaska's land, but on the rich cultural and local knowledge possessed by Alaska's people." This included a special interactive panel "bridging Alaska, South America and the Far East" featuring renowned Peruvian economist Hernando DeSoto and other leaders as part of an AFN initiative to "foster economic growth with an emphasis on innovation and shared prosperity."[18] Other events included an Elders and Youth Conference, a Leadership Forum, and a series of performances, known as Quyana, showcasing Alaska Native cultural traditions. This holistic program reflects the diversity and complexity of the status and needs of Alaska Natives in the twenty-first century.

To effectively address priorities such as improving economic well-being, education, health, safety, infrastructure, and cultural pride through self-determination, Native socioeconomic and political institutions must cooperate at a variety of levels. In particular, they must work politically with an array of governments within and outside the Native community in a nexus of IGR as well as deal with many nongovernmental organizations (NGOs) and private sector entities. The scope and priorities of Alaska Native political institutions vary considerably, however, making coordination and efficiency a challenge.

The coordination problem results from the way the Native political landscape has developed since the Russian colonization, and particularly since the Alaska Purchase. The landscape is the product of ad hoc institutional developments in response to particular stresses and state initiatives, such as discrimination, Indian reorganization, land claims, and so on. In contrast to traditional forms of hunter-gatherer politics, which were intimately linked to social structure and the practices of daily life, the modern political landscape is fragmented and bureaucratized. Authority and institutions develop from laws, court decisions, and the exigencies of dealing with non-Native governments, more than from cultural traditions. Moreover, state and federal orientations toward Natives and their tribal governments have differed considerably, further complicating IGR, particularly on key issues, such as tribal recognition, subsistence, and sustainable economic development.

Compounding the potential political weakness resulting from conflicting governmental and ad hoc policies is the fact that Native needs are as diverse as the community's varied cultural and physical geography. This diversity can and often does lead to divisions within Native ranks and variations of political power internally and in relation to the outside world, particularly the political world. At the regional level, for instance, Alaska's Native corporations hold a disproportionate amount of power because of their land and wealth, and their objectives are not always in tune with villages seeking to chart their own destinies. At the state level, Native villages, even those with formal tribal recognition from the federal government, do not always have the political muscle to influence public policy in an increasingly urban-oriented state legislature. At the national level, the sovereignty of tribal governance is severely constrained by the lack of Indian Country, and there are differing views among Native groups as to how best to deal with the sovereignty issue. Finally, at the international level, the latter part of the twentieth century saw the rise of international indigenous governmental organizations, such as the Inuit Circumpolar Conference (ICC) and the Alaska Eskimo Whaling Commission (AEWC).[19] These organizations, however, have only recently begun to exercise their authority within the emerging global regime of resource rights and environmental regulations.

The complexities of the internal and external political environment in which Alaska Natives operate raises several important questions: (1) to what extent has and does this complex environment affect the Native community's role and influence in state politics, (2) what factors undermine this influence, and (3) how might the Native community increase its role and influence? Looked at another way, the ANCSA settlement gave the Native community a major role in Alaska's economy and potentially a powerful place within the state's political economy, but the extent to which that has been achieved is not clear. We offer perspectives on these questions by looking at internal politics in the Native community, the question of a viable Alaska Native economy, the role of Alaska Natives in state politics, and the major issue of subsistence.

4. INTERNAL POLITICS: THE EFFECTS OF INSTITUTIONAL PROLIFERATION AND FRAGMENTATION OF GOVERNANCE

One obvious feature of the Alaska Native political landscape is the sheer plethora of socio-political institutions. Table 9.1 illustrates the structure of these political institutions on the local, regional, state, national, and international levels. In many cases, Alaska Natives have added new layers to their existing socio-political organization to deal with new challenges, often without eliminating or refashioning existing layers.

This evolutionary proliferation of political institutions has contributed to redundancy, inefficiency, and even competition at some levels of Native government. For example, at the village level, ANCSA corporations and nonprofits may compete with tribal governments for grants and services contracts. Similarly, representative tribal governments and Native corporations (many shareholders of which may live outside the village) might hold very different views on resource management, such as whether to emphasize subsistence uses or resource development. From a political ecology perspective, it is easy to see how such a crowded institutional environment can create fragmentation, inefficiency, and factionalism, all of which undermine effective political action. At the same time, the rich diversity of Alaska Native political institutions creates many opportunities for political participation, civic engagement, and leadership development. All this, plus vested interests of those who currently run the institutions, are reasons the old layers of the political organization are not easily shed.

The complex segmentation of Alaska Native institutions can make holistic goals especially hard to achieve. At base, the strength of Native institutions lies in their various assets, including their financial capital, and human, socio-cultural, and natural resources. With the exception of ANCSA corporations, which possess considerable financial capital and natural resources, most other Native institutions possess little capital beyond human and socio-cultural resources, and are thus often dependent on federal or state funds to carry out projects from year to year. This means that these institutions must continually respond to the priorities and initiatives of the state and other funding sources in order to survive. Ironically, this results in Native institutions becoming more dependent on, and isomorphic with, bureaucratic state and federal governments, and disconnected from their more holistic goals of self-determination.

The Alaska Native Health Board provides an example of this disconnection. While the board's mission statement stresses holism, "Promoting the spiritual, physical, mental, social, cultural well-being and pride of Alaska Natives," its programs reflect the segmented health initiatives of the bureaucratized state, such as HIV/AIDS prevention, solid waste management, and alcohol and tobacco control.[20] Subsistence uses of wild foods, which most Natives would identify as basic to spiritual, physical, mental, social, and cultural

TABLE 9.1

Native Political Organizations

LEVEL OF ORGANIZATION	NATIVE INSTITUTION	SOCIO-POLITICAL FUNCTIONS	TOTAL UNITS
Community	Kin groups	Subsistence production, exchange, and more	1,000 plus
Village	IRA governments and tribal councils ANCSA village corporations Nonprofits (e.g., Alaska Native Brotherhood (ANB)/Alaska Native Sisterhood (ANS)	Tribal governance, services and contracts Land management and development Heritage conservation, services, fraternity, civic development	500 plus
Regional	Native associations and councils (e.g., Association of Village Council Presidents—AVCP) ANCSA regional for profit corporations Regional nonprofits (e.g., Kawerak, Inc.)	Regional representation in state and federal spheres; administration and delivery of services Land and resource management and development Heritage conservation, health services, etc.	30 plus
State	Representative organizations (e.g., Alaska Federation of Natives—AFN; Alaska Inter-Tribal Council) Consortia (e.g., Alaska Native Tribal Health Consortium)	Political coordination, advocacy support Services coordination, delivery	10 plus
National/ International	Representative ethnic organizations (e.g., Inuit Circumpolar Council—ICC) Indigenous political organizations (e.g., National Congress of the American Indian—NCAI; United Nations Indigenous Peoples Forum—UNIPF) Other nongovernmental organizations—NGOs (e.g., Native American Rights Fund)	Facilitate transnational ethnic interaction; advocate for ethnic group interests	10 plus

Source: Developed by the authors.

health, are not listed, because they are not conceptualized as a health "program" by the federal or state governments.

Overcoming this kind of segmentation and achieving a more holistic vision of Native well-being requires strategic partnerships and infrastructural investment, such as the collaboration of the Alaska Native Tribal Health Consortium and the Southcentral Foundation (a nonprofit incorporated under the Cook Inlet regional ANCSA corporation) with the U.S. Department of Health and Human Services to construct and manage the Alaska Native Medical Center in Anchorage. This is one of the largest and most culturally sensitive facilities of its kind in the country.

Proposals to Regionalize Native Social-Political Institutions

Regionalization represents another approach to overcoming problems of institutional proliferation, coordination, and lack of financial capital. Indeed, the diversity of Alaska Native cultures is a function of the ecological diversity of the state's geographic regions. This regionalization is reflected in the political ecology of pre- and post-ANCSA Native institutions, and in ANCSA's regional boundaries, which reflect the state's Native cultural geography. One virtue of regionalization is that it allows Natives to organize at a more efficient level for developing infrastructure and services and to take advantage of economies of scale. Regional Native health corporations, for instance, have found this an effective way to administer health services while remaining responsive to diverse local and cultural needs.

Could regionalization strengthen other forms of Native governance? The answer depends on how much authority regional governing units have and how well they communicate with existing governmental units, including the state government. When U.S. Senator Ted Stevens proposed a top-down scheme to regionalize federal funding for village housing assistance in 2003, many local tribes opposed it as an attack on their sovereignty and self-determination because tribal control would be diminished.

On the other hand, bottom-up schemes for regionalization have proven very practical. Among the most effective was the decision of Inupiaq Eskimo communities to form the 90,000-square-mile North Slope Borough (NSB), incorporated in 1972, to enable them to regulate and tax industrial oil development in the region. Although incorporated under the state local government system, as opposed to a sovereign tribal entity, since Inupiats dominated the NSB's population, borough organization gave them significant authority and access to billions of dollars of revenue generated by the oil industry.[21]

More radical proposals to strengthen Alaska Native sovereignty through regionalization are now being discussed among Native leaders. Willie Kasayulie, a Yup'ik leader from Akiachak, is a leading proponent of a movement to create regional tribal governments. As he explains:

> Regional tribal governments would allow Native villages to retain their governmental authority on the local level while exerting tribal governmental authority in the place of state governmental authority through already existing regional organizational structures. Regional tribal governments would replace nonprofit organizations by consolidating the administrative services of regional Native nonprofit organizations. And, in doing so, regional tribal governments would allow us to exert our governmental authority not only over our own villages but also over those interests that extend beyond the borders of our own villages.[22]

Such a scheme, if it achieved genuine consolidation rather than merely adding another layer of government, could enhance Alaska Native authority and self-determination and reduce intragovernmental competition and inefficiencies. However, these regional governments would still lack the financial and natural resources possessed by Alaska Native for-profit corporations and potentially could compete or clash with them over political and economic goals.

There is an even more radical possibility of regionalization. What if local and regional tribal governments had been the beneficiaries of the ANCSA settlement, rather than Alaska Native corporations? In fact, such a model was proposed by the Arctic Slope Native Association but rejected by the federal government. Undoubtedly, this scheme would have enhanced Alaska Native sovereignty, self-determination, and practical governance while also avoiding some of ANCSA's conflicts and "time bombs" (such as the alienability of stock and other assets).[23] At the village level, two Native communities, Venetie and Arctic Village, actually pursued this model by dissolving their ANCSA village corporations and turning the lands over to the tribal governments in the hope that they could then exercise full tribal sovereignty over these lands as Indian Country. However, when Venetie attempted to exercise tribal sovereignty by levying a tax on a local contractor, its authority to do so was opposed vigorously by the state, and the resulting litigation ultimately led to the 1998 U.S. Supreme Court's decision in the *Venetie* case, holding that Indian Country in Alaska had been extinguished by ANCSA.

Potential Consequences for Alaska Native Political Power

The proliferation of Native political institutions, spawned by the need for various IGR activities with multiple levels of government, renders Alaska Native politics complex to the point of being Byzantine at times.[24] The unfortunate consequences of this complexity often lead to divisions and lack of coordination and sometimes many voices on an issue that can undermine Native political effectiveness in dealing with local, state, and the federal governments. At least at the state level, this was of less concern in the years following

ANCSA when Alaska Natives had a major influence in state politics. But this influence has waned and power is increasingly shifting to urban Alaska (see Box 9.3 below). So there is a pressing need for action to streamline this internal institutional complexity.

5. THE PLACE AND INFLUENCE OF NATIVES IN ALASKA STATE POLITICS

Like their relations with federal and local governments, Alaska Natives' relations with the State of Alaska have been marked by positive and negative developments for the Native community. Moreover, changes in power relationships have affected the community's ability to advance self-determination. Generally speaking, the state has been a major stumbling block for Alaska Natives in achieving many of their political goals. On the other hand, the skill of many Native politicians has made the Native community one to be reckoned with, and their leaders have secured a variety of benefits for rural-bush Alaska.

The Emergence of a Statewide Native Perspective and Rocky Relations with the State

Before the land claims movement of the mid-1960s, Alaska Native politics was largely local, focusing on the village with some regional perspectives. With the formation of AFN, these local and regional politics developed into a loose statewide coalition. An Alaska Native viewpoint emerged on a range of issues, although the diversity within the Native community meant that Native opinion was divided on some issues. On other issues, such as subsistence and to a lesser extent sovereignty, a broad consensus developed. Both issues conflicted with the perspective of many established non-Native state leaders.

The State of Alaska's consistent hostility to changes in governance that might enhance Native sovereignty remains a flash point. The state has mostly viewed Native sovereignty through a zero-sum lens: it sees any increase in Native authority as diminishing state sovereignty. Similarly, from a political ecology perspective, the state holds that the more authority it has over lands and resources, the greater the overall benefit it can achieve for state residents. This is why the state opposed a generous land settlement in the initial ANCSA negotiations until it was convinced that Natives (ultimately assisted by the federal government's land freeze) were not going to yield and that state-sponsored development of the Prudhoe Bay oil fields could not proceed without a land settlement. At the same time, the state successfully insisted that ANCSA eliminate all existing Native reserves created under the Indian Reorganization Act (save for Annette Island, in Southeast Alaska, established prior to the IRA and excluded from ANCSA), which might threaten state sovereignty over those lands. Natives felt state hostility to their self-determination in other ways too, such as attempts to impose English as the state's official language (while Native languages, backbones of their cultures, became increasingly endangered) and the state's reluctance to formally recognize tribes.

By the late 1990s, as the state's non-Native and urban majorities continued to increase and state revenues began to decline, relations between Alaska Natives and the state reached a "crisis point," according to a state Commission on Rural Governance and Empowerment.[25] Writing in the *Anchorage Daily News* in May 1999, Byron Mallott, a prominent Tlingit Native leader from Yakutat and a commission member, declared: "It's not a good time to be an Alaskan Native," noting a "cacophony of negatives and meanness emanating largely from the legislature but echoed in many places."[26]

Mallott's singling out of the state legislature is significant. It was here that Alaska Native priorities seemed to be most consistently ignored or undermined. Beyond demographic shifts and revenue and sovereignty concerns, two other major factors have reinforced this trend. Limited Alaska Native representation within the state political system, coupled with shifting state priorities favoring urban communities, have created a real division between rural-bush and urban regions.

In his second term as governor (1998–2002), Tony Knowles sought to heal the divide through a "Millennium Agreement" by which the state formally recognized tribes as "alive and well in the new millennium, just as they have been for the untold millennia past," and "partners" in the state's future. For this Knowles received recognition from the National Congress of American Indians in 2001 and AFN's Denali Award, the highest award given to a non-Native. He also supported establishment of the Alaska Inter-Tribal Council to improve IGR and address rural-bush Native needs, such as policing and justice, health and education, economic development and infrastructure, and other pressing concerns. But progress on these and other long-standing issues, particularly subsistence, has been limited, due to recalcitrance on the part of the legislature. In response, tribes have sought to strengthen partnerships with the federal government to fill voids left by the state's hostility, withdrawal, and inaction.

An important victory was achieved by the Native community in 2014, however, when the legislature enacted a law that added twenty indigenous languages to a 1998 voter initiative making English the official language of Alaska. The 2014 law was largely symbolic, however, because English remained the only language required in most official documents and meetings. Nevertheless, as State Senator Donny Olson, a Native from Northwest Alaska put it: "This is a small way to say, 'Hey, things haven't always been good in the past, but here's one way we are showing we respect the languages of Alaska's indigenous people.'"[27] Then, in September 2014, the Alaska Division of Elections was ordered by the federal courts to comply with the Voting Rights Act and provide more extensive written translations of election materials in two Native languages, Yup'ik and Gwich'in.[28] The issue surrounding Native language use in Alaska has been ongoing and filled with emotion and conflict, as related in Box 9.2.

Another important victory came with the election of Byron Mallott as lieutenant governor in 2014. The winner of the Democratic primary for governor, but unlikely to beat Governor Sean Parnell in the general election, Mallott and the Democrats joined forces with independent Bill Walker to form the Alaska First Unity ticket. While lieutenant governors usually play a minimal role in administrations (dealing mainly with elections and state regulations), the fact that Walker owed much of his victory to Democratic voters may mean that Mallott will play an important policy role that can aid both Alaska Natives and the state in general. Walker promised that Mallott would play such a role, but it will be interesting to see how this plays out after the euphoria of election victory has faded and the two disagree over some policy issues.[29]

Native Politicians in State Politics: The Necessity of a Bipartisan and Pragmatic Approach

Before the ANCSA settlement, very few Alaska Natives were elected to state office. In the 1970s, however, many Native leaders who had cut their political teeth in the ANCSA negotiations were involved in state politics either as elected officials or through organizations like AFN and Native corporations.

These included Emil Notti, Roger Lang, Nels Anderson, John Sackett, Frank Ferugson, and Al Adams, some of whom rank among Alaska's most accomplished politicians regardless of race. Even with the election of several Native legislators in the 1970s, Alaska Natives were then, and remain today, underrepresented relative to their numbers in the population. This minority status and the pressing needs of rural-bush Alaska have shaped the way that Native politicians (and non-Native politicians representing rural-bush areas) have operated politically. The Alaska Native approach to politics has long been marked by pragmatism and bipartisanship. The essence of this approach is explained in Box 9.2 by Mary Sattler (formerly Mary Nelson), a Native leader and a Democrat, who represented Bethel in the Alaska House from 1999 to 2009.

In the late 1970s and early 1980s, the minority status of Alaska Natives was mitigated by a surplus of state revenue from the state's oil bonanza. As former Representative Nelson mentions in Box 9.2, the cause of the Native community was also aided by the rise of a successful bush caucus, comprised of rural-bush Native and non-Native legislators. One member of the bush caucus in the 1980s and early 1990s was former Senator John Sackett, a Republican. In an interview set out in Box 9.3, he explains the origins and power base of the caucus and speculates on its decline in influence. Even though they are almost a generation apart in their legislative experiences, it is interesting to note the similarities in the perspective and political approach of former Representative Nelson and Senator Sackett. They both identify the minority, somewhat beleaguered, political status of Alaska Natives and rural-bush residents, and the need to build coalitions across

BOX 9.2

Being a Bush Alaska Native Legislator: A Personal Perspective by Former Representative Mary Nelson

When the public thinks about the legislature, many imagine a confrontational or combative environment. While the legislative process has its combative moments, the most successful legislators work hard to build consensus around issues and funding priorities. Consensus is naturally found among lawmakers with similar interests, geographical locations, constituent groups, and issue concerns.

Close to three-fourths of the sixty members of the legislature come from the "Railbelt," the urban communities from Fairbanks to south of the Anchorage area. The rest of Alaska—rural-bush areas, where Natives are in the majority, and Southeast Alaska—make up the other quarter of the population. With continued growth in urban centers and diminished strength in numbers, rural-bush legislators have long sought ways to work strategically for our districts' needs.

Politically, bush legislators must create "buy-ins" from their urban colleagues—ways to help them with their needs—to obtain improvements needed to ensure an adequate standard of living in their communities by securing basic life, health, safety, and infrastructure needs. An effective way to create buy-ins is to engage in political bridge-building in the legislative and executive branches. Rural-bush legislators are all aware of the risk of offending colleagues or the governor, who has veto power, so we work hard at being diplomatic, learning about the needs of our colleagues' districts, and seeking ways to get things done in a nonconfrontational way. This helps underpin our need to secure capital improvement projects, which are often our top priority.

Rural-bush legislators also have a rich history of supporting each other, often within the bush caucus. Regardless of party affiliation and despite ethnic and geographic differences across the state, rural-bush lawmakers almost always speak with a unified voice. Lowering the cost of energy, building and maintaining schools, water and sewage treatment projects, airports, and roads, are common priorities for rural-bush lawmakers, although the solutions are often very different across the state.

In addition to capital projects, regardless of party, members of the bush caucus work together to see that rural-bush needs are addressed within the operating budget. In the 1980s, for instance, Senator John Sackett and Representative Johne Binkley, Republicans from Interior and western Alaska, worked with Senator Frank Ferguson and Representative Al Adams, Democrats from Kotzebue, to advance rural-bush needs.

Bipartisan action has been orchestrated by rural-bush lawmakers on several occasions. In 1981 Representative Al Adams led the House "coup" that installed a coalition of members of both parties. More recently, in 2007, Senator Lyman Hoffman put together a bipartisan working group with urban and rural-bush senators in key positions.

While all legislators have the same job title, those from rural-bush districts have a very different job description. Beyond working to improve the standard of living through capital projects, rural-bush legislators work to explain our differences and in some cases must defend them.

During the 1990s there was legislation introduced (modeled after laws in Lower 48 states) to enact English as the official state language. The model legislation was geared to reducing the costs of translating government meetings and documents for immigrant languages. In Alaska, however, the predominant non-English languages are Alaska Native languages, not immigrant languages. The bill made it illegal to speak any language but English in meetings of state agencies. This was a threat in western Alaska because many people who sit on fish and game advisory boards and on school boards are more comfortable conducting business in their Native languages. The bill struck a very personal chord because educating children and maintaining subsistence rights are critical issues for rural-bush residents, and their ability to testify to these issues from the heart is key.

Rural and Native lawmakers were able to defeat the bill with the help of sympathetic urban lawmakers. But the law was eventually passed through initiative, financed with predominantly Lower 48 contributions. In 2007, the Alaska Supreme Court struck down as unconstitutional the provision that required English in all government actions. The revised law allowed government communication in any language for any purpose, as long as English versions and documents are kept. The 2014 law, making twenty Alaska Native languages official state languages, secures these rights more fully for the Native community, as did the federal court direction to the State of Alaska to provide more extensive written translations of election materials.

Source: Developed by Mary Sattler, formely Mary Nelson.

party lines and be flexible and pragmatic. In short, being Native for them trumps all other factors, particularly party affiliation and political ideology.

One bright spot in the current Alaska Native political power arena is the statewide influence of AFN. As Chapter 15 on interest groups shows, AFN has been consistently one of the most effective big players in state politics since the late 1970s.[30] However, much of AFN's influence in state politics depends on having influential Native members in the legislature and officials in the executive branch. Yet as noted earlier, the decline in state revenues and rise in non-Native urban populations (especially in greater Anchorage) saw a shift in priorities in favor of an increasingly powerful urban majority. And as Senator Sackett relates, the bush caucus has lost a lot of its political influence. Plus, legislative reapportionment will continue to reduce Native representation in the future. Native political power within the state's political economy, then, is on the wane, and it is hard to see how this trend might be reversed. This may further undermine the quest for Native self-determination as the Native community moves to rely more on the federal government for protection against declining influence in the state. In essence, this is what has happened in the case of subsistence.

6. SUBSISTENCE: A MICROCOSM OF ALASKA NATIVE POLITICS AND OF NATIVES IN STATE AND FEDERAL POLITICS

No issue in Alaska politics since statehood has been as divisive and politically intractable as subsistence. It hits a raw and often emotional political nerve in many political constituencies and has political ramifications beyond hunting and fishing rights. These include economic development, environmental protection, and land use. Because subsistence is so central an issue in the state, its many facets are covered in several places in the book.[31]

BOX 9.3

The Bush Caucus: An Interview with Former Senator John Sackett

Former Republican Senator John Sackett, an Athabaskan Indian from Galena, was one of the founders and leading members of the bush caucus, a coalition of rural-bush lawmakers who work for the betterment of rural-bush communities. It was particularly influential during the late 1970s and 1980s. The following is a 2008 interview with Sackett by George Owletuck.

G.O. Why did the bush caucus develop and why was it important?

J.S. There was a desperate need for basic services that was not being met, in many cases overlooked by urban legislators who outnumbered rural-bush legislators.

G.O. Who were the major players in the caucus?

J.S. Myself, Senator Frank Ferguson, Representative Nels Anderson, and later Representative Al Adams who eventually moved to the senate.

G.O. What were the caucus's major accomplishments?

J.S. Among them were: the Permanent Fund, power cost equalization for rural-bush areas, and fiscal appropriations to meet basic needs, such as water and sewer, transportation (like airports and local roads, etc.), rural-bush housing, schools (capital projects as well as yearly funding for education), and anything that affected statewide Alaska. We were a group that had to be reckoned with to get our block of votes.

G.O. What led to the decline in the power of the caucus?

J.S. That's a tough question as there are so many reasons for it, some to do with the gradual power shift to urban Alaska, the relative decline in the number of Natives in rural-bush areas, some of the old bush caucus members leaving the legislature and others getting elected. Personally, I think it's a lot to do with a power void in state government in general these days. The recently formed bipartisan working group in the state Senate may change that, though it's hard to know how long this group will last.

The best way to answer the question specifically is to tell you what I think gave me and other members of the bush caucus the influence that we had. From this you can deduce which of these factors might be lacking in the last ten years or so.

To be effective and successful, first you must have the respect of your colleagues, as they give you the power. Then, you have to have a very strong desire to want to help your constituency, such that you are willing to repress all personal benefits for the good of the whole (which in my case were both constituents and rural-bush residents). You had to be in the majority, whether directly or through a coalition regardless of political parties. Frank (a Democrat) and I (a Republican) were rarely in the minority. Out of eighteen years in the Legislature I was in the minority for a total of two weeks. Then, you had to be on the Senate or House Finance Committees, as 90 percent of all legislation gets referred to Finance, and in most cases the most important questions are financial. Or you could be in other positions of leadership, such as President of the Senate or Speaker of the House. I was respected for my knowledge of the state budget and all fiscal matters. After ten years I was elected as Chairman of Senate Finance for four years. I then served as Co-Chair of Finance for another four years.

Further, to be effective, you must know how to trade, how to compromise, possess a statewide as well as a district point of view, and understand strategy. Many times we would tack on amendments to general legislation to include something for rural-bush areas so that they would be part of any legislation going through to passage (such as revenue sharing for villages, as well as first or second class cities).

Source: Developed by George Owletuck, President of Angall'kut, Inc.

Here we trace the development and current status of the subsistence issue using a political ecology perspective.

The subsistence issue is, in many ways, emblematic of the dynamics of Alaska Native politics at the state, federal, and local levels and thus a quintessential example of the crucial importance of Native community involvement in IGR. In particular, subsidence manifests the cleavages that exist between Alaska Native and non-Native priorities, rural-bush versus urban constituencies, and federal and state governing authorities, plus the issue has local political ramifications. Box 9.4 provides a brief chronology of subsistence policy.

In analyzing the development of subsistence policy, the first thing to recognize is that there is not one level of authority, but three. The first is the indigenous self-management regime in which Natives recognize the authority of their own institutions to regulate customary and traditional uses of wild resources. Traditional subsistence use is basic to Alaska Native self-determination and has existed since time immemorial. Native "customary and traditional uses" are recognized under ANILCA and other federal subsistence regulations and law (see *Bobby v. Alaska*, 1999). The second major subsistence regime is the federal government, which managed all fish and wildlife prior to Alaska statehood and retains authority to provide for Native subsistence through ANCSA, ANILCA, and laws such as the Marine Mammal Protection Act. State constitutional authority and regulations comprise the third subsistence regime. Historically, the state has largely ignored the traditional Native regime and has been hostile to federal attempts to impose Native subsistence on the state. In fact, dissatisfaction with federal management of fish and wildlife resources was a major impetus for Alaska statehood.

Many non-Natives, including some involved in the enactment of ANCSA, have mistakenly assumed that, as Alaska Natives modernized and accommodated themselves to the more "developed" dominant culture, their subsistence needs would decline. This assumption is based, intentionally or not, on the belief that only the most "primitive" or economically "undeveloped" Natives need a subsistence preference. From an Alaska Native perspective, this belief reflects a total misunderstanding because, in their view, subsistence needs do not rise and fall according to a progressive scale of economic or social development. Rather, subsistence is a foundation of Alaska Native culture, and the land is the ultimate source of well-being. This precept explains why high levels of participation in subsistence production, distribution (involving upwards of 90 percent of households in many Native communities), and consumption (as high as two to three pounds of wild foods per day, per person in Native villages) have persisted, despite rising incomes and standards of living. Many Native wage earners use their new economic wealth to complement and bolster their investments in the subsistence economy.[32]

ANCSA extinguished aboriginal hunting and fishing rights, and these rights were only partially restored via the rural preference in ANILCA. Thus was the subsistence foundation

BOX 9.4

Subsistence Chronology

PRE-CONTACT WITH EUROPEANS TO THE PRESENT
Alaska Native customary and traditional rules, practices, and institutions regulated subsistence activities under "self-management" regimes. This continues today at varying levels, despite the imposition of state and federal regimes.

1960—BARROW "DUCK-IN"
To protest the arrest of hunters for shooting ducks out of season, 138 Barrow Eskimos presented themselves, with ducks in hand, to federal officials for arrest. As perhaps the first major act of Alaska Native civil disobedience, the "Duck-In" showed the will of Natives to protect customary and traditional use of wildlife. It eventually led to changes in regulation and enforcement.

1971—ALASKA NATIVE CLAIMS SETTLEMENT ACT (ANCSA)
Extinguished aboriginal hunting and fishing rights but called on the U.S. Secretary of the Interior and the State of Alaska "to take any action necessary to protect the subsistence needs of the Natives."

1972—MARINE MAMMAL PROTECTION ACT
Reversed federal policy of paying bounties to kill certain marine mammals in favor of a hunting ban, due to conservation concerns. Alaska Native villages' historical dependence on certain species succeeded in obtaining an exemption from the hunting ban for subsistence needs.

1977—ALASKA ESKIMO WHALING COMMISSION (AEWC)
Founded in response to a ban on bowhead whale hunting by the International Whaling Commission (IWC). The AEWC succeeded in modifying the ban to allow subsistence hunts under a co-management regime.

1978—STATE SUBSISTENCE LAW
Gives subsistence priority over other consumptive uses of fish and wildlife, but the law establishes no preferences for any group.

1980—ALASKA NATIONAL INTEREST LANDS CONSERVATION ACT (ANILCA)
Federal law provides *priority* for subsistence hunting and fishing over other consumptive uses (Title VIII), and an allocation *preference* for rural residents. Subsistence is defined as "customary and traditional uses by rural Alaska residents of wild, renewable resources for direct personal or family consumption."

1986—STATE SUBSISTENCE LAW REVISED
A rural preference was added to the 1978 state law, but the state defined rural not only on the basis of population but also on economic characteristics. This definition was found to be inconsistent with ANILCA by a federal court in 1988 (*Kenaitze Indian Tribe v. Alaska*).

1989—*BOBBY v. ALASKA* BOLSTERS NATIVE CUSTOMARY AND TRADITIONAL USE REGIMES
A federal court sided with Natives of Lime Village near Bethel, holding that the state must adapt regulations to the realities of local subsistence economies, including that Alaska Native hunters take animals for many uses on the basis of need. State regulations on methods, seasonality, and bag limits cannot arbitrarily prevent subsistence users from satisfying customary and traditional needs.

1989—*McDOWELL v. COLLINSWORTH* NULLIFIES STATE RURAL PREFERENCE
The Alaska Supreme Court rules that the 1986 State Subsistence Law is unconstitutional (under the state constitution) because its rural preference constitutes a "special privilege."

1990—DUAL MANAGEMENT COMMENCES
With the state out of compliance with ANILCA's rural preference, and as a result of *McDowell* and efforts to amend the Alaska Constitution having failed, the federal government takes over management of subsistence on federal lands. The state retains management authority over state lands and waters.

1990–2000—STATE STAGNATION, FEDERAL EXPANSION:
Various initiatives by state politicians to amend Alaska's constitution and subsistence laws to restore state compliance with ANILCA and control over subsistence management fail. The federal government creates a Federal Subsistence Board (FSB) and regional council system to manage subsistence.

1995—*KATIE JOHN* DECISION EXTENDS FEDERAL MANAGEMENT TO FISHERIES
Natives, led by Athabaskan elder Katie John, sues the FSB to enforce subsistence priority access to salmon on the Copper River, near Cordova, where her family fishes. The federal court sides with her and extends FSB jurisdiction to navigable waters on federal lands. The state delays the federal fisheries takeover until October 1999.

2001—MEMORANDUM OF UNDERSTANDING BETWEEN STATE AND FEDERAL GOVERNMENT
Improves coordination of subsistence management.

2003—FEDERAL GOVERNMENT ESTABLISHES ALASKA NATIVE SUBSISTENCE REGULATIONS FOR HALIBUT
The regulations implemented a subsistence halibut fishery for qualified individuals who are residents of 117 rural communities or members of 123 Alaska Native tribes with traditional uses of halibut. The regime is a hybrid of rural, Native, and individualized approaches to subsistence management.

2007—U.S. SUPREME COURT REFUSES TO HEAR AN APPEAL BY A GROUP OF ALASKA SPORTSMEN
The case involved an appellate court ruling that denied their claims that the ANILCA subsistence requirement violated the equal protection clause of the U.S. Constitution.

2013—STATE OF ALASKA FILES PETITION TO OVERTURN *KATIE JOHN* DECISION
The case was filed as *Alaska v. Jewell* (Sally Jewell, Secretary of the U.S. Department of the Interior).

2014—AFN HOLDS SUBSISTENCE RETREAT
Included Native and non-Native leaders from across the state, to plan a way forward in light of the *Alaska v. Jewell* petition.

2014—U.S. SUPREME COURT DENIES THE STATE'S *KATIE JOHN* PETITION
But as of 2016 the basic subsistence issue between the state and federal government and the state and Native community was still unresolved.

Source: Developed by the authors.

of Native culture undercut, and relations to their land were reoriented toward development. As Inupiaq leader Willie Hensley put it, this was not the goal of Alaska Natives:

> Basically, we did not fight for the land because it represented capital, or because it represented money, or because it represented business opportunities. We fought for the land because it represents the spirit of our people. It represents your tribes and it represents your ancestors and it represents that intimate knowledge of the land that your people grew up on for ten thousand years. And when we fought for the land we were fighting for survival as people with an identity—people with a culture.[33]

ANILCA recognized the importance of subsistence to the "cultural existence" of Alaska Natives, but the state vigorously fought establishing any "special rights" for Natives that might infringe on its constitution or its management authority over resources.

The resulting compromise in ANILCA, which created a "rural" preference rather than a "Native" one, caused as many problems as it solved. In fact, many Natives view it as an abrogation of ANCSA's implicit promise to provide for Native subsistence needs. As public policy, ANILCA's rural compromise was also shortsighted because population forecasts in 1980 (when ANILCA was passed) clearly showed the non-Native population increasing vis-à-vis Natives in rural-bush as well as in urban areas. This trend has continued, subjecting Natives to further competition from non-Natives in rural-bush areas. In addition, it cuts out the increasing majority of Natives who dwell in urban areas, or in growing rural-bush communities subject to reclassification as urban.

The main exception to this trend of erosion of subsistence rights has been that of marine mammals, including whales, walruses, and seals. Here federal management authority is greater than the state's, and competition from non-Natives, who generally do not consume marine mammals, is lower. As a consequence, Alaska Native priority and self-regulation in marine mammal hunting has had federal support, which limits or outlaws non-Native hunting (see details in Box 9.4). But marine mammals face other threats to their populations, such as climate change, which may further limit Native subsistence in favor of species conservation. In fisheries, recent federal subsistence regulations governing halibut, a major fish resource for which Natives and non-Natives compete, allow for participation based on Native status.

For subsistence to remain a solid foundation in Alaska Native life, similar protections will likely need to be extended to other critical species, including salmon and ungulates such as moose, reindeer, and caribou. But here a more contentious political ecology prevails because of powerful commercial and recreational interests (such as the Outdoor Council, an influential Alaska sports lobby, with a mainly non-Native membership) and the state's ideology, which resists a permanent subsistence priority based on ethnicity or geography, even as it permits exceptions in some fisheries and hunts (such as for ceremonies).

By whatever means, as Aleut leader Trefon Angasan states: "The Native people of Alaska must have their subsistence lifestyle protected permanently. It is the nucleus of our cultures." What is more, the financial value of subsistence products, leaving aside the many health, social, and cultural values of subsistence, is estimated at $200-400 million a year. As the Barrow "Duck-in" of 1960 (described in Box 9.4) demonstrated, Alaska Natives will go so far as to engage in civil disobedience to maintain self-determination over their subsistence life-ways. With the state's repeated failures to provide meaningful safeguards to subsistence rights, Natives are increasingly seeking permanent solutions through federal management, cooperative regimes, and even national and international organizations that recognize subsistence as a fundamental indigenous right.[34]

7. CAN A SUSTAINABLE ALASKA NATIVE ECONOMY BE DEVELOPED THAT DOES NOT UNDERMINE NATIVE CULTURE?

In explaining the structure of the Alaska economy, Chapter 6 refers to the rural-bush economy (which, in effect, is a Native economy) as Alaska's "other economy." This is an apt description, because this economy is different from both the urban Alaska economy and the commercial-industrial economy of most other states across the nation. If, as Alaska Natives insist, the Native economy, with its major interrelated cultural and economic elements of subsistence, is to co-exist with the commercial-industrial economy rather than be replaced by it, then its development must prove compatible and sustainable.

It continues to be debatable whether it is possible to build a sustainable economic future for Alaska Natives based on a corporate business model of development. The debate is complicated in that for most Alaska Natives the goal is not simply economic growth for its own sake, but using economic growth to preserve culture. By contrast, the vast majority of businesses in urban Alaska and the industrial-commercial economy in general have a single purpose—to make money—and thus their decisions can be made purely on an economic cost-benefit basis. Not so with many Native corporations.

The question of developing a sustainable Native economy compatible with Alaska's industrial-commercial economy is, of course, part of a much broader question. To what extent can and should Native culture be preserved and, if so, what parts? This is a fundamental question and challenge faced by all indigenous cultures beset first by an alien colonizing culture and, more recently, by the less direct but inexorable socio-economic and political forces that the dominant culture brings to bear on a minority population.

The economic development versus cultural preservation issue is another area of disagreement among Alaska Natives. It was a contentious subject during the ANCSA negotiations and is one reason for divisions in the Native community today. A particular disagreement over development involves subsistence because development will likely affect different Native groups in different ways. Take, for instance, the environmental politics and political ecology surrounding large-scale development of oil drilling in the Alaska National Wildlife Refuge (ANWR) versus the Arctic coastal plain. North Slope Inupiaq Eskimos, dependent on marine mammals for subsistence, tend to favor inland development of oil fields like ANWR but oppose offshore drilling that might threaten critical marine mammal supplies. Others, like the interior Gwich'in Athabaskans in places like Arctic Village, are dependent on caribou and vehemently oppose inland development of ANWR, the territory of which is a caribou calving ground.

Western-World Business Culture and Economic Development versus Maintaining Alaska Native Culture

ANCSA imposed a western-world—majority culture—view of the corporate business model as well as property and land use on the Native community. Adjusting to the concept of private property was not difficult, although individual ownership of material goods was not a major aspect of the culture. Land was a different matter. Most western, non-Native cultures emphasize the value of private ownership and use of land, sometimes at the cost of the public interest. By contrast, communal "ownership" and use of land and its various flora and fauna was the major view in Native culture. The forty-four million acres awarded to the Native community by ANCSA were to be privately owned by regional and village corporations. This kind of ownership was difficult for many Natives to adjust to, as has been the increasing regulation restricting the use of land.

In this regard, some critics, like Canadian jurist Thomas Berger, view ANCSA as just another divisive tool of assimilation, like the General Allotment Act of 1887, which abrogated traditional communal ownership and prerogatives over lands and resources in favor of a Western model of land exploitation. Writes Berger, "At each stage the United States wanted its Native population to adopt the current paradigm of progress: in 1887 it was farming, in the 1950s it was factory work, in 1971 it was business."[35] Chief Gary Harrison of Chickaloon puts it more bluntly: "The Alaska Native Claims Settlement Act split family, government, religion, land, resources, fishing and hunting, and children from the Original Peoples. That is Thievery and Genocide."[36] The divisions created between shareholders and 1971 "afterborns," landholding and "landless" communities, and those Natives who have been employed or enriched by ANCSA corporations and those who have not, remain sources of political tension.

Others, including prominent Native corporation leaders, view the business corporation model as the most promising vehicle of self-determination in building sustainable futures. Carl Marrs, a leader in the financially successful ANCSA-spawned Cook Inlet Regional Corporation of greater Anchorage, conveys this view in reporting the results of a 2001 survey of ANCSA corporation performance:

> Native corporations provide jobs, revenue and commitment to the Alaskan economy. Some key highlights for the 43 corporations surveyed include:
>
> - Revenue of \$2.9 billion and assets of \$2.9 billion
> - \$52.1 million in dividends and \$434 million in payroll (within Alaska)
> - Statewide employment of 13,062
> - Alaska Native employment of 3,122
> - \$9.3 million donated to charitable organizations and \$4.1 million distributed for scholarships to 2,821 recipients. ANCSA has become the biggest minority success story of the nation.[37]

Other statistics are less impressive. For example, the twelve in-state regional corporations lost nearly 80 percent of their original cash endowment, almost \$400 million in the first twenty years of ANCSA, though by 2012 their performance had improved considerably and many shareholders were receiving dividends.[38] Much of this improvement is the result of investments outside of Alaska by the corporations. Similarly, the promise of local Alaska Native employment has not been fully realized. While fifteen or so Native corporations are routinely among the largest businesses and top twenty employers in the state, others employ few or no full-time workers.[39] Moreover, as Marrs's statistics show, only 30 percent of ANCSA corporation employees are Alaska Natives. Especially in rural-bush areas, where infrastructure and training is limited and operating costs are high, reducing Native unemployment (or underemployment beyond subsistence) remains a daunting challenge.[40]

ANCSA corporations are one among many evolving tools and institutions that may serve to build sustainable livelihoods in the twenty-first century for the Native community. The corporations' poor performance in the early years—often the result of inexperience and mismanagement—has been improved, as overall investment strategies and opportunities (such as through the federal 8(a) program explained in Box 9.1) have become more diversified and corporate missions more holistic and culturally attuned. This diversity, opportunity, and holism, combined with their rootedness in Alaska lands and revenue sharing, have positioned Native corporations to become major forces in achieving sustainable development beyond the classic boom-and-bust, extraction economy that has always characterized Alaska.

At the same time, some Native leaders, such as Byron Mallott, recognize these challenges. As Mallott wrote, they "have a deep sense of hollowness . . . about ANCSA as a vision very much unfulfilled. . . . It isn't the hollowness of despair; it's the hollowness of anxiety—whether we have it in us to really achieve what the elders and the village people and the leaders felt we could achieve." This means going beyond what Mallott characterizes as the "state's mantra [of] economic development" toward conserving the land "for future generations for reasons that far outstrip the economic use."[41]

Though constrained by their business structure, ANCSA corporations are gradually moving toward becoming total cultural institutions. This is reflected in their mission statements, nearly all of which pay homage not just to profits but to cultural and communal well-being, and increasingly by their actions. June McAtee, a Yup'ik leader of Calista regional corporation, exemplifies this perspective in discussing Calista's approach to developing the Donlin Mine in Southwest Alaska:

> Calista does not look at mineral resource development as an end in itself, but as a driver that helps its communities develop broader-based economies and its shareholders develop work experience that can open doors. Resource development is needed to grow economically healthy

> communities where people with a wide-range of skills and services are in demand. Calista's goal is to have its shareholders participate increasingly as active producers of goods and services and less as passive consumers of this society's products and receivers of its services.[42]

Even in its developmental stage, the Donlin Mine achieved a local Native employment rate as high as 90 percent. It remains to be seen if this project will become a model of economic self-determination. Clearly, however, it is considerably more oriented toward sustainability in its scale, environmental footprint, and attention to local hire and community needs than traditional large-scale natural resource developments, such as the Trans-Alaska pipeline (TAPS) built in the mid-1970s. Greater recognition among ANCSA corporate leaders of local Alaska Native environmental, cultural, and economic diversity, among other needs, is a key step towards reshaping ANCSA corporations as distinctly Native institutions, and in realizing healthy, sustainable communities.[43]

Like the Alaska economy in general, the Native rural-bush economy will never be self-sustaining given the economic realities explained in Chapter 6. For some time to come, federal, state, and local governments will be the major sources of employment and income, and organizations like the federally established but intergovernmentally run Denali Commission to aid in economic development will continue to be important aspects of the "other economy." But regional and village Native corporations, both for-profit and nonprofit, are playing an increasing role in Alaska's political economy and are doing an acceptable job of combining economic return with cultural preservation. No one will ever know for certain, but compared with the experience of most Native Americans in the Lower 48, measured by both economic and cultural criteria, Alaska Natives are probably better off than if ANCSA had not been enacted.

8. CONCLUSION: THE CHANGING ROLE OF THE NATIVE COMMUNITY IN ALASKA'S POLITICAL ECONOMY

The political development of Alaska's Native community has undergone a major evolution since the 1867 Alaska Purchase and particularly so since statehood. This development manifests a major contradiction, however. On the one hand, historical circumstances and the ANCSA settlement have provided a foundation for Alaska Natives to advance their self-determination. Unlike other Native American people, Alaska Natives have developed significant political power at the state level and in various facets of IGR. On the other hand, the absence of Indian Country seriously limits the enhancement of self-determination. This results in a parallel status of increased economic and political resources but continued dependence on the federal and state governments.

Alaska's political economy would look very different if the status of Alaska Natives were similar to that of Native Americans on reservations in the Lower 48. This is particularly evidenced in the dynamics of the political ecology of IGR involving the Native community. Consequently, changes in the socio-economic and political status of Alaska Natives change the nature of the state's political economy. In this regard, the differences between Natives and non-Natives are far less today than they were at statehood, particularly Natives who live in urban Alaska.

Nevertheless, as Gunnar Knapp has pointed out, the major socio-economic and political division in Alaska today is still the difference between Natives and non-Natives.[44] It is one of the major realities of Alaska politics that shape the public policy debate, more so than differences among non-Natives or between long-time residents of the state and recent arrivals, and it is often more important than party affiliation and ideology. How this Native/non-Native division develops in the future (whether it narrows, becomes more pronounced, or remains static) will very much affect Alaska's political economy. The extent to which Alaska Natives might be able to influence this political relationship in the future is addressed in Chapter 30 on future developments and choices in Alaska.[45]

From a broader perspective, as Byron Mallott suggests in a new vision of self-determination:

> Let's look to the year 2050 with a vision of healthy communities, a rural Alaska that is alive and vibrant. We have to put our emphasis on economic development out there. Our children have to have access to quality education that is responsive socially and culturally. In the year 2050, our vision must be that we live with self-esteem and pride because Alaska society and its social policy respects who we are. In the future, we must be recognized not as separate, but as being different and therefore making the whole of Alaska richer by our being here.[46]

ENDNOTES

[1] Emil Notti, President of the Alaska Federation of Natives October 1969 address to a congressional committee on the land claims settlement, at: http://www.alaskool.org/projects/ancsa/testimony/ancsa_hearings/e_notti_s.html.

[2] U.S. Census, "State & Local QuickFacts," retrieved October 12, 2014, at http://quickfacts.census.gov/qfd/states/02000.html.

[3] This status is described in the U.S. Supreme Court case, *Worcester v. Georgia* (1832), excerpted in David H. Getches, *et al.*, *Federal Indian Law: Cases and Materials*, 3rd ed. (St. Paul, MN: West Publishing, 1993), 139–49; see also, Fae Korsmo, "Native Sovereignty: An Insoluble Issue?," in *Alaska Public Policy Issues: Background and Perspectives*, ed. Clive S. Thomas (Juneau, AK: Denali Press, 1999), 263–74.

[4] Donald Craig Mitchell, *Sold American: The Story of Alaska Natives and Their Land, 1867–1959* (Fairbanks: University of Alaska Press, 2003), 332–33.

[5] Fred Paul, *Then Fight for It!* (Victoria, B.C.: Trafford, 2003), 145–48. See also, Donald Craig Mitchell, *Take My Land, Take My Life: The Story of Congress's Historic Settlement of Alaska Native Land Claims, 1960–1971* (Fairbanks: University of Alaska Press, 2001).

[6] Gerald A. McBeath and Thomas A. Morehouse, *Alaska Politics and Government* (Lincoln: University of Nebraska Press, 1994), 112.

[7] U.S. Census, "State & Local QuickFacts."

[8] See, for example, Willie Kasayulie, "Sovereignty in Alaska," in, *The State of Native Nations: Conditions Under U.S. Policies of Self-Determination*, The Harvard Project on American Economic Development (New York: Oxford University Press, 2008), 335–38.

[9] See *Alaska v. Native Village of Venetie Tribal Government*, 522 U.S. 520 (1998).

[10] For more on Native land rights and the legal status of Alaska Native sovereignty vis-à-vis other Native American groups, see David S. Case and David A. Voluck, *Alaska Natives and American Laws*, rev. ed. (Fairbanks: University of Alaska Press, 2002); Stephen L. Pevar, *The Rights of American Indians and their Tribes* (Carbondale: Southern Illinois University Press, 2002); Korsmo, "Alaska Native Sovereignty"; and Douglas K. Mertz, "A Primer on Alaska Native Sovereignty" (1991), at http://www.alaska.net/~dkmertz/natlaw.htm.

[11] As originally enacted, ANCSA provided that shares of stock in the for-profit corporations would be held only by Alaska Natives born before December 18, 1971. In 1992 Congress adopted amendments that, among other things, allow ANCSA corporations to issue shares of stock to these so-called afterborns. By the end of 2014, however, few corporations had adopted a plan to do so, though some, including Calista Corporation in Southwest Alaska, considered it.

[12] See Gordon Harrison, *Alaska's Constitution: A Citizen's Guide,* 5th ed. (Juneau: Alaska Legislative Affairs Agency, 2012), esp. Article VIII, Sec. 3 (fish and game reserved for the people for common use), Article VIII, Sec. 15 (no exclusive right of fishery . . . shall be created), Article VIII, Sec. 17 (regulations shall apply equally to all persons similarly situated).

[13] See particularly Chapter 6 on the structure of the state's economy, Chapter 18 on local government, Chapter 19 on the state budget, and Chapter 26 on education policy.

[14] Alaska Department of Labor and Workforce Development, Pop stats, 2010 Census, PL 94-171 Redistricting Data, at http://live.laborstats.alaska.gov/cen/redistr.cfm, and Urban and Rural Classification for Alaska, at http://labor.alaska.gov/research/census/urbrur.htm; U.S. Census, "Profile of General Demographic Characteristics: 2000," Table DP-1, at http://censtats.census.gov/data/AK/04002.pdf; U.S. Census, "Alaska: General Population Characteristics," (1990), at http://www.census.gov/prod/cen1990/cp1/cp-1-3.pdf; and U.S. Census, "Alaska: Characteristics of the Population," Table 1 (1980), at http://www2.census.gov/prod2/decennial/documents/1980a_akABCD-01.pdf.

[15] *Shelby County v. Holder*, 557 U.S. 193 (2013). For details on reapportionment, see Chapter 4 (Section 3) on the state constitution and Chapter 14 (Section 3) on campaigns and elections.

[16] See Scott Goldsmith, Jane Angvik, Lance Howe, Alexandra Hill, and Linda Leask, *The Status of Alaska Natives Report 2004* (Anchorage: University of Alaska, Institute of Social and Economic Research, ISER, 2004).

[17] Alaska Federation of Natives, at http://www.nativefederation.org/about/index.php.

[18] Julie Kitka, "Welcome Letter," Alaska Market Place Event Guide, Fairbanks, October 24, 2007, 3.

[19] For the development and role of the AEWC and its relationship with the International Whaling Commission, see Chapter 11 on Alaska and the world, Box 11.3.

[20] Alaska Native Health Board, at www.anhb.org.

[21] The oil companies tried unsuccessfully to dilute Inupiat dominance over borough politics by attempting to register their non-Native seasonal workers as voters.

[22] Kasayulie, "Sovereignty in Alaska," 338.

[23] See, Thomas Berger, *Village Journey: The Report of the Alaska Native Review Commission* (New York: Hill & Wong, 1985), and Paul, *Then Fight for It!*, 198, for more on this perspective. As originally enacted, ANCSA put a twenty-year moratorium on sales (alienation) of ANCSA stock in order to prevent loss of Native assets and potential "looting" of ANCSA corporations. Some viewed this moratorium as a "time bomb," and ANCSA was later amended to permanently restrict sales of stock and other assets.

[24] For an analysis of the Tlingit case of such proliferation, see Thomas F. Thornton, "From Clan to Kwáan to Corporation: The Evolution of Tlingit Political Organization," *Wicazo Sa Review* 17, no. 3 (2001): 167–94. See also, Carl E. Shepro, "Rural-Bush Local Government: Towards a More Appropriate System?" in Thomas, *Alaska Public Policy Issues.*

[25] State of Alaska Commission on Rural Governance and Empowerment, Report, issued May 1999.

[26] Quoted in Stephen Haycox, *Frigid Embrace: Politics, Economics, and Environment in Alaska* (Corvallis: Oregon State University Press, 2002), 156.

[27] Zachariah Bryan, "Native Languages Made Official," *The Tundra Drums*, April 24, 2014.

[28] Richard Mauer, "Judge Orders State to Add Language Help for Voters in Alaska Villages," *Alaska Dispatch News*, September 24, 2014.

[29] Pat Forgey, "Byron Mallott's Job: Be a New Kind of Lieutenant Governor," *Alaska Dispatch News*, December 22, 2014.

[30] See Chapter 15, Table 15.4.

[31] See for example, Chapter 4 on the state constitution, Chapter 6 on the structure of the state's economy, and Chapters 21, 22, 23, and 24 on issues regarding the Owner State.

[32] See, Robert J. Wolfe and Robert J. Walker. "Subsistence Economies in Alaska: Productivity, Geography, and Development Impacts," *Arctic Anthropology* 24 no. 2 (1987): 56–81. See also, Thomas F. Thornton, "Subsistence in Northern Communities: Lessons from Alaska," *The Northern Review* 23 (Summer 2001): 82–102. With declines in rural-bush incomes, the subsistence economy has become even more critical; see *The State of Native Nations: Conditions Under U.S. Policies of Self-Determination*, The Harvard Project on American Economic Development (New York: Oxford University Press, 2008), 326-27.

[33] Quoted in Alexandra J. McClanahan, *Alaska Native Corporations: Sakuuktugut, "We are Working Incredibly Hard"* (Anchorage: The CIRI Foundation, 2006), 15.

[34] Trefon Angasan, "Subsistence Is What Connects You to the Seasons and the Land," in McClanahan, *Alaska Native Corporations*, 15.

[35] Thomas R. Berger, *The Long and Terrible Shadow* (Seattle: University of Washington Press, 1991), 104–105; and his "Alaska Natives and Aboriginal Peoples around the World," report presented at the Tanana Chiefs Conference, Fairbanks, Alaska, March 13, 1984, 10.

[36] Chief Gary Harrison, "Then Came the Land Claims," in McClanahan, *Alaska Native Corporations*, 137.

[37] Carl Marrs, "Harnessing Business Endeavors to Achieve Alaska Native Goals," in McClanahan, *Alaska Native Corporations*, 147–48.

[38] See Steve Colt, "Alaskan Natives and the 'New Harpoon': Economic Performance of the ANCSA Regional Corporations" (Anchorage: Institute of Social and Economic Research), at: http://www.iser.uaa.alaska.edu/Publications/colt_newharpoon2.pdf, 2001); and Tim Bradner, "Alaska Natives help put state on path to prosperity," *Alaska Dispatch*, October 19, 2013.

[39] See Chapter 6 on the Alaska economy, Tables 6.3 and 6.4, for the ranking of Native corporations in Alaska's business community.

[40] Another problem with the corporations has been a lack of accountability. Congress initially decided to exempt Native corporations from many of the rules and oversight structures governing publicly traded stock companies under the U.S. Securities and Exchange Commission. This was in part because ANCSA corporation stock could not be freely traded for twenty years. However, this exemption was later extended indefinitely beyond 1991, with the result being a collective lack of oversight, and unfortunate cases of corruption and mismanagement, which have angered shareholders and other investors. Without more extensive ethics training, transparency, and independent monitoring, it is too easy for ANCSA corporate leaders to abuse their power at the expense of their shareholders.

[41] Byron I. Mallott, "Unfinished Business: The Alaska Native Claims Settlement Act," at http://litsite.alaska.edu/aktraditions/business.html.

[42] June McAtee, "Mining Development: Like 'Building a City,'" *Alaska Business Monthly* (November, 2006), 63.

[43] Thomas F. Thornton, "Alaska Native Corporations and Subsistence: Paradoxical Forces in the Construction of Sustainable Communities," in *Sustainability and Communities of Place*, ed. Carl Maida (Oxford: Berghahn Books, 2007), 60.

[44] Gunnar Knapp, "Four Alaska Innovations," A Presentation to the Board of Directors of the Federal Reserve Bank of San Francisco and Its Seattle Branch, Anchorage, July 11, 2007.

[45] See Chapter 30, Box 30.2.

[46] Mallott, "Unfinished Business."

★ CHAPTER 10 ★

Federal Influences and Intergovernmental Relations: Constraints, Conflicts, and Benefits

Clive S. Thomas and Michael L. Boyer

Much of what Alaska's state government does, and much of what it is unable to do, are influenced by other governments, particularly the federal government. Local governments across the state, as well as Alaska Native governments, also play a role. Consequently, the character of Alaska politics, the political issues that arise, and the day-to-day operations of state government are, in significant ways, a product of these ongoing relations with other governments. Issues such as the opening of the Arctic National Wildlife Refuge (ANWR) for oil and gas development, subsistence hunting and fishing rights, commercial and sports fishing, the funding and delivery of K–12 education, aspects of health and welfare, economic development, and transportation policies, among many others, involve some form of intergovernmental relations (IGR). In this chapter we delve into the formal structures and the political aspects of IGR as they affect Alaska.

Because of its central importance to Alaska politics and government, aspects of IGR are dealt with in other places in the book. Chapter 9 deals with federal-state-local government–Native government interactions primarily as they affect the Native community; Chapter 18 focuses on state-local IGR; and the policy chapters in Parts IV and V deal with IGR from their particular policy perspectives. This chapter provides a foundation for these later chapters by explaining the basics of IGR, describing its formal structure, emphasizing its political aspects, and examining the role of the federal government as it relates to Alaska, both legally and politically. Throughout the chapter we acknowledge that the federal-state relationship places some constraints on Alaska and its policy makers and certainly involves them in many conflicts. But we also assert that the state-federal relationship provides major benefits to Alaska and to the vast majority of its citizens, even though many of these benefits may not be readily apparent, fully understood, or appreciated.

The chapter begins with an explanation of IGR and how it relates to federalism. Next we consider the structure of Alaska's current IGR system and what has shaped it, followed by an overview of the development of Alaska's IGR. We then look at perspectives on the Alaska-federal relationship from Alaskan, federal, and holistic viewpoints. Next we consider the day-to-day politics of IGR, followed by a discussion of Alaska's IGR compared with that in other states. The conclusion offers a balance sheet of the constraints, conflicts, and benefits involved in Alaska's IGR, particularly as it relates to the federal government.[1]

1. THE BASICS OF FEDERALISM AND INTERGOVERNMENTAL RELATIONS

We begin by explaining IGR and federalism and identifying their similarities and differences. This section also includes observations on the evolving nature of federalism over the years, raises the question of whether there is one "correct" interpretation of federalism, as some people argue, and offers observations on the problems with viewing the federal government as a governmental, administrative, and political monolith.

Comparing Federalism and IGR: A Legal and Constitutional Relationship versus Day-to-Day Interactions

When the American Founding Fathers met in Philadelphia in the summer of 1787 to revise the previously adopted Articles of Confederation, one of their challenges was to give more authority to the national government while continuing to allow the states extensive control over their own affairs. Although they did not purposely intend to create a new form of government, the solution they devised was, in fact, a new form and one of America's contributions to governance. They initially called this new form a "confederal" system because they saw it as a variation of the system under the Articles of Confederation, but it soon became known as *federalism*.

In a federal system, legal sovereignty—the ultimate power to make laws and thus public policies—is divided between the national government (often referred to as the federal government) and several constituent governments, those that together comprise the nation as a whole (usually referred to as states or provinces). Theoretically, each level of government has its own sphere of authority. Federal systems, such as those in the United States, Australia, and Germany, are contrasted with unitary political systems in which legal sovereignty is held by the central government, as in France, Norway, and New Zealand.

The formal provisions of federalism are typically set out in a national constitution and generally do not include provisions for local government. This is the case in the U.S. Constitution. As a result, each state determines the form of local government and the authority these governments will exercise. Local governments are, however, part of IGR.

Since 1787 the constitutional-legal relationships that form American federalism have led to many political consequences. These legal and political developments shaped not only federal-state relations, but also the relations of the states with other governments, including local governments and the governments of other states.[2] Besides the states and the federal government, according to the U.S. Census Bureau, there were 89,004 local governments of various types across the nation in 2012.[3] There are also interstate compacts and regional governmental arrangements as well as organizations bringing together the states and local governments for a variety of purposes. For this reason, the most informative way to view federal-state relations is as part of the comprehensive and dynamic perspective of intergovernmental relations. IGR embraces both the legal and political ongoing relationships of various levels and types of governments. The day-to-day interactions of a state government like Alaska's may include those with other states, local governments, Native governments, unofficially with foreign governments, as well as with the federal government. Plus, the federal government has direct relations with Alaska's local and Native governments that do not involve state government.

While IGR is based primarily on legal relationships and involves much intergovernmental cooperation, it also produces many conflicts. The origin and development of these conflicts have much to do with the political development of federalism.

The Legal and Political Odyssey of American Federalism

The relationship between the federal government and the states, particularly regarding legal jurisdiction, has been a source of continuing and often heated debate since 1787. This is because conflict between the national and constituent governments is inherent in a federal system. The root of the conflict and the continual debate regarding federalism lies in a combination of factors. One is that the general way the federal-state relationship is set out in the U.S. Constitution (mainly in Article 1, Section 8, and in the Tenth Amendment) makes the relationship subject to various legal interpretations. A second is the varying views of the role of government among segments of American society. A third factor is that, particularly in the twentieth century, there was a substantial increase in federal authority resulting from wars, economic crises (like the New Deal response to the Great Depression in the 1930s), the promotion of civil and minority rights, as well as programs to enhance economic and personal welfare (such as Social Security and Medicare for senior citizens, and Medicaid for those with low incomes), and environmental protection, among other increases in federal authority. The upshot of this combination of developments has been increased conflict between the federal government and the states.

Is There One Definitive and "Correct" Federal-State Relationship?

A repeated theme of Republican Dan Sullivan's successful bid to unseat Alaska's Democratic U.S. Senator Mark Begich in the November 2014 election was that there was far too much "federal overreach" in Alaska. This buzz phrase has become the rallying cry of those who oppose what they see as increasing and unwarranted federal interference in the business of the states. Concern about federal overreach is an important part of the Tea Party movement that emerged across the country after the 2008 elections, and is shared by many right-wing Republicans and some libertarians. This overreach is considered so serious by many Alaska politicians that in 2015 the Republican-dominated state senate passed a resolution to establish a committee to look into this issue as they perceived it. The resolution also requested the governor to set up a working group to consider establishing a permanent state office or authority to protect state sovereignty.

Many supporters of this perspective argue that America should return to the original intentions of the Founding Fathers regarding the Constitution in general, and federalism in particular. This contention assumes that the founders' intentions regarding federalism can be precisely determined. Yet it is very unclear, indeed very much in dispute, exactly what America's founders envisioned. They even disagreed among themselves, as epitomized in the classic clash between Alexander Hamilton and Thomas Jefferson. Hamilton favored the prominence of the national government and Jefferson that of the states, though Jefferson became rather Hamiltonian in his views after he became president. Historians and others have written thousands of pages about this dispute over the "correct" interpretation of the Constitution with no generally accepted definitive conclusion.

Even if the founders' intentions could be definitively determined, it is worth contemplating the following question: Would the federal-state relationship of 1787 in a country of fewer than four million people (about 20 percent of whom were slaves or indentured servants) and with only thirteen states, be appropriate today, well over two hundred years later, in a country of nearly 320 million people and fifty states in a vastly changed world, where nuclear weapons have replaced muskets, multinational corporations have supplanted the single merchant, and minority groups of all types are more or less fully enfranchised?

The debate about the "correct" federal-state relationship raises many questions, but none of them can be answered definitively. The often heated clashes of values and ideology regarding what is the proper role of government are largely the result of differences between what various people, groups, and interests see as their own respective economic, legal, and political gains and losses from various forms of federal-state relations.

From a practical perspective, at any one time political power determines the relationship. Who is in power in Washington, D.C., including the political complexion of the U.S. Supreme Court, is a major determining factor. Plus, the enormous financial resources of the federal government and the importance of federal funds and intergovernmental transfers to all fifty states give the federal government major political leverage in the relationship. These dynamics give rise to the politics of fiscal federalism—broadly defined as the politics surrounding federal intergovernmental transfer payments.

To put things in perspective, over the years both federal and state authority has increased considerably from the laissez faire days of nineteenth century America to the proactive governments following the New Deal. Relatively, however, federal authority has increased more than that of the states. This increase has intensified the conflict in federal-state relations and has directly and indirectly affected the broader nexus of IGR. This has certainly been the case in Alaska.

The Federal Government Is Not a Governmental and Political Monolith

A final introductory point that is useful to bear in mind is that, like Alaska state government, and indeed all levels of governments in a democracy, the federal government is not a political, governmental, and administrative monolith united in its actions and policies—far from it. This is not the impression one might get from many Alaskans and their politicians who often refer to "the federal government" (whether in praise or in criticism) as if it spoke with one voice.

A much more realistic and accurate understanding of Alaska-federal relations is gained by realizing that, while on occasion the federal government can act in a united and forceful fashion, it is often divided within itself. The many departments, agencies, and divisions within the federal government are often in conflict among themselves over policies. One department, agency, or elected or appointed federal official may favor a policy while others oppose it. A state that wants to succeed in reaping benefits from the federal government realizes this and exploits these divisions to its advantage whenever possible.

2. ALASKA'S CONTEMPORARY IGR: INFLUENCES ON THE SYSTEM

Turning to the specifics of Alaska's IGR system, the following six factors have been particularly important in determining both its formal structure and its political interactions: (1) constitutional and legal provisions, (2) a pervasive federal presence, (3) other external political and economic forces, (4) the fusion of elements of Alaska political culture with aspects of its political rhetoric, (5) Alaska's revenue bonanza, and (6) the role of Alaska Natives.

Federal and State Constitutional and Legal Provisions

Of particular note in the U.S. Constitution is the so-called Supremacy Clause contained in Article VI, Section 2. This provides that the constitution, statutes, and treaties of the U.S. government are the "supreme law of the land." So long as the federal provisions are within the authority of the federal government to adopt, they will take precedence over state laws that are in conflict with them.

Also noteworthy, for purposes of IGR, is Article I, Section 8, which gives the federal government sole authority to deal with "Indian Tribes." Section 10 of that article prohibits the states from making treaties with foreign countries but allows them to make compacts with other states with approval of Congress. Article IV, Section 1, provides that each state shall give "full faith and credit" to the laws and judicial proceedings of other states, and Section 2 of that article, the Privileges and Immunities Clause, requires each state to treat citizens of other states on an equal basis with its own residents.

The most important provision of the Alaska Constitution regarding IGR is Article X, which establishes Alaska's local government system. Alaska statutes set out provisions for local government in Title 29.

Judicial interpretations of these constitutional provisions have also shaped Alaska's IGR. A notable decision affecting the state's relationship with Alaska Natives was the U.S. Supreme Court decision in *Alaska v. Native Village of Venetie Tribal Government*, which denied the existence of Indian Country in Alaska and Native sovereignty over land.[4] Similarly, the Alaska Supreme Court has determined in several cases whether a state statute takes precedence over a local ordinance. Federal and state statutes also fill in the details of these constitutional provisions. Several federal laws affect federal-Alaska Native and state-Native relations.

A Pervasive Federal Presence

Federal influence in shaping Alaska's IGR is based on four major factors. First, the federal government is a major landholder, with about 55 percent under its ownership, and it controls what happens on this land in terms of activities and development.[5] Second, the federal government is a major regulator of a range of activities from rules relating to environmental protection to those regarding access to government buildings by the disabled. Third, federal relations with Alaska Natives have a major effect on Alaska's IGR system.

Fourth, federal influence on IGR also comes from its major economic impact. As Chapter 6 on the Alaska economy explains, part of this comes from its presence as an employer in the state. The federal government's role in fiscal federalism is also significant. As Chapter 8 explains in the context of state revenues, the federal government is a major source of state general funds. Some federal monies also go directly to local governments, to Native governments, and to nonprofit organizations.

Other External Political and Economic Forces

Besides the federal government, other external forces influence the politics of Alaska's IGR. American public opinion, often manifested through the national media and national interest groups (particularly environmental groups like the Sierra Club), shapes national policy, which often places constraints on Alaska's use of resources. Federal designation of the Arctic National Wildlife Refuge (ANWR) as off limits to oil development is an example of a federal policy spurred by national public opinion. Such constraints limit state revenues, as well as sometimes limiting state and local government policy, particularly regarding economic development. This situation exacerbates state-federal conflicts.

More indirectly, the decisions of multinational companies—particularly those in oil and mining—to operate in Alaska and the extent to which they wish to operate, plus the world price of natural resources, over which Alaska has no control, crucially affect state revenues and thus the all-important element of funding for the IGR system. Colonialism may no longer exist as it relates to Alaska, but the financial dependence of Alaska on external capital and business decisions made in capitals far away means that its political options, and thus the effectiveness of its IGR system, are not always determined in Alaska or even in the United States.

The Fusion of Elements of Alaska Political Culture with Aspects of Its Political Rhetoric

As noted in Chapter 5, Alaska's political culture is complex. It manifests elements of communalism and traditionalism, but mainly individualism, often expressed in fiscal conservatism and sometimes in libertarianism. These attitudes exist within the reality of a political economy long shaped by economic dependence on out-of-state businesses and on federal and state government. This clash between values and reality has been reconciled, to some degree, by a strong strain of political pragmatism. In this regard, Alaska reflects the political cultural paradox common in many western states, which touts individualism and self-help while, out of necessity, living off the largesse of government.[6] Hence, Chapter 5 describes Alaska's political culture as manifesting pragmatic dependent individualism.

Among some Alaskans and some Alaska politicians, dependence and the constraints that often accompany it generate a populist perception of Alaskans as underdogs (in some cases even victims), particularly regarding the federal government and national and international forces. Some other Alaskans are either unaware of the paradox between dependence and individualism, or they simply deny any need for government or any dependence on it. In combination, these feelings often result in a political rhetoric that manifests these myths and contradictions and is sometimes translated into political action and policy. Examples of the fusion of elements of these traits of culture and political rhetoric and their effect on Alaska's IGR are considered later in this chapter.

Alaska's Revenue Bonanza

The unprecedented state revenues from oil and gas production in the ten years following the opening of the trans-Alaska pipeline system (TAPS) in 1977 enabled the state government to bankroll local governments in significant amounts, including funding for numerous capital projects and providing much of their operating funds. This high level of funding was not directed just to rural-bush governments. Urban governments also received large sums from the state through direct appropriations and programs such as municipal revenue sharing. As a result, local communities had less need to tax their residents and, in many cases, even reduced property and other taxes. But beginning with the drop in oil revenues in 1986 and continuing with their subsequent fluctuations, the state drastically cut its financial assistance to municipalities. These cuts have significantly affected the politics of state-local IGR.

The Influence of Alaska Natives

The significant role of Alaska Natives in Alaska politics is covered in Chapter 9. Here we summarize their influence on Alaska's IGR.

Historically, the Native influence stems partly from the fact that agriculture is not possible on the bulk of Alaska lands. Consequently, there was no reason to remove Natives so that white settlers could farm the land, as was the case in many other states. In addition, by the time Alaska was colonized, a period of atonement toward Native Americans was underway in the United States. This explains why the reservation system never took root in Alaska. As a result, many Alaska Natives still live where they have always lived in rural-bush areas.

This means that Alaska's demographics set it apart from the other forty-nine states. While the rural population in all other states is predominantly white and nonindigenous, over half the population of rural-bush Alaska in 2010 were Alaska Natives.[7] About half the state's 250 communities are Native communities. All these Native communities are located in rural-bush areas, and most are entirely Alaska Native in population, including the bulk of the state's 112 second-class cities.

In addition, there is a parallel Native local government system under federal law stemming from the Native community's relationship with the national government, plus a range of for-profit and nonprofit organizations at both the regional and local (village) level that have an impact on Alaska's IGR system. Most important is the right of tribes to adopt constitutions for self-government and to set up corporations under federal law to aid in tribal economic development. The nonprofit Native associations provide many services, particularly various types of social programs, and both the State of Alaska and the federal government interact with these organizations in several ways.

In combination, these factors mean that the Alaska Native community is a significant participant in the state's IGR system.

FIGURE 10.1

Alaska and the Nexus of Intergovernmental Relations

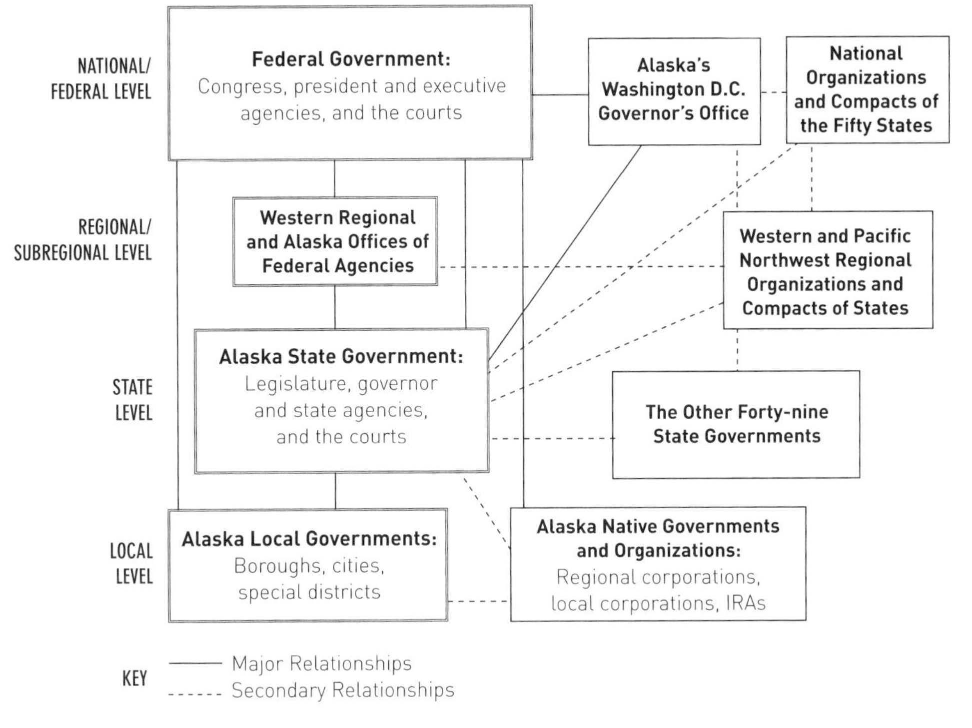

Source: Developed by the authors.

3. ALASKA'S CONTEMPORARY IGR: THE STRUCTURE AND INTERACTIONS OF A MULTIFACETED SYSTEM

The influences just considered produce a particular structure of Alaska's IGR system with some unique features compared with other states. Because of the existence of Alaska Native governments within the state that are not on federal reservations, Alaska has a dual IGR system, one of federal-state-local relations and one of relations of the federal, state, and local governments with Native governments. In particular, it is the relations between the state and its local governments with Native governments that give Alaska's IGR system its dual characteristic.

The nexus of Alaska's current formal interaction with various governments is set out in Figure 10.1. This shows that there are four levels of interaction in Alaska's IGR activities: federal, state, local, and regional. Various aspects of the web of IGR are explained in detail in this chapter and in other chapters.[8] To provide a holistic perspective, however, we supplement Figure 10.1 with a brief explanation of the various levels of Alaska's IGR system in Box 10.1.

BOX 10.1

Types and Levels of Alaska's Intergovernmental Relations (IGR)

FEDERAL, STATE, AND LOCAL GOVERNMENT IGR

Federal-State Relations

These interactions revolve around federal funds flowing into the state; federal agency operations in Alaska, such as the U.S. Forest Service; enforcement of federal regulations, such as air and water quality; and disputes over federal versus state sovereignty and rights, such as over subsistence. Alaska presses its cause with the federal government through its congressional delegation, the governor's office in Washington, D.C., and visits by state officials. Despite the emphasis on conflict, often stressed in the media, and anti-federal rhetoric of many Alaska politicians, the major aspect of federal-state relations is cooperation.

Federal-Local Relations

Since the 1960s, direct IGR between the federal government and Alaska local governments has been increasing. Again, the major connection is funding. For instance, some Community Development Block Grants from the U.S. Department of Housing and Urban Development go directly to local governments, as do some Federal Aviation Administration funds for airports, and Department of Transportation funds for local public transport, such as purchasing new buses. Many local governments, particularly the larger ones, like Anchorage, Fairbanks, and Juneau, lobby for funds and other benefits in Washington, D.C.

State-Local Relations

This relationship also mainly revolves around money, particularly funding of local government services and local capital projects by the state. Local governments are among the most prominent and successful lobbying forces in Juneau aided by their legislators. The state-local IGR relationship is covered extensively in Chapter 18.

Local Government Relations with Other Local Governments

Local governments interact in several ways that, for the most part, involve cooperation. Cities within a borough, such as Homer and Seward within the Kenai Peninsula Borough, work together to share some services and to prevent duplication and unnecessary costs. Adjacent local governments, like the cities of Fairbanks and North Pole within the Fairbanks North Star Borough, also often work together for similar reasons. Local governments interact in a major way through their state organization, the Alaska Municipal League (AML). This interaction occurs through AML's annual conference and other AML programs throughout the year. AML also lobbies on behalf of local government on general issues.

Sometimes, however, local governments differ over issues. This often occurs at AML meetings over policies that benefit some local governments and not others, as in the case of school funding. Also, local governments sometimes conflict over territorial jurisdiction issues. This occurred, for instance, between the Juneau and proposed Petersburg boroughs in 2011 and 2012 regarding annexing land in the Unorganized Borough (the part of the state with no organized local government).

FEDERAL, STATE, LOCAL IGR WITH ALASKA NATIVE GOVERNMENTS AND QUASI-GOVERNMENTS

This aspect of IGR is covered in Chapter 9 on Alaska Natives. In outline the main characteristics are as follows.

Federal-Native Government Relations

The federal government's responsibility for dealing with Indian tribes means that its role is the major aspect of IGR involving Alaska's Native communities. Although the reservation system is minimal in Alaska and the federal government has attempted to reduce its role with Alaska Natives since the Alaska Native Claims Settlement Act (ANCSA) of 1971, the federal government still provides major funding for many Alaska Native programs, including the Indian Health Service. And various Native organizations from the Alaska Federation of Natives (AFN) to regional and village corporations lobby the federal government in Alaska and in Washington, D.C.

State-Native Government Relations

Although the state has never recognized Native sovereignty, it has long worked with Native tribal governments to help fund services, especially where there is no state local government unit. The Alaska Court System and the Department of Public Safety, for instance, have long histories of cooperating with Native governments on legal and law enforcement jurisdictional issues.

Local Government-Native Government IGR

Tribal governments, Native village corporations, and Native regional nonprofit organizations, often overlap geographically with cities incorporated under state law. This is the case, for example, in Bethel in Southwest Alaska and Barrow on the North Slope. For efficiency purposes this necessitates cooperation between Native organizations and local government units, and such cooperation is common.

STATE IGR WITH OTHER STATES AND GOVERNMENTAL ORGANIZATIONS

Alaska State Government Relations with Individual States

Alaska's one-on-one IGR with individual states can occur through the auspices of the federal government or directly. An example of the former is through the North Pacific Fishery Management Council (NPFMC) in dealing with Oregon and Washington State. NPFMC is the federal advisory panel that manages fisheries in the federal Exclusive Economic Zone (EEZ) from three to two hundred miles offshore, whose membership also includes these other two northwestern states. Examples of the second type of interaction include the return of fugitives and arrangements for exempting another state's residents from state sales tax, such as Washington State allows for Alaskans.

Alaska's Membership in State Compacts

These are agreements between the states to facilitate cooperation in areas of policy implementation and other activities that are advantageous to the member states.

Alaska belongs to several compacts. At the national level these include the Driver License Compact, the Interstate Civil Defense and Disaster Compact, and the Multistate Tax Compact. Regionally, Alaska is also a member of several compacts, including the Western Interstate Corrections Compact, the Western Interstate Nuclear Compact, and the Western Regional Higher Education Compact.

Membership in National and Regional Governmental Organizations

Like all states, Alaska, its three branches of government, and various state officials are members of a range of organizations that facilitate the exchange of ideas and often act as an advocacy group with the federal government and sometimes with foreign governments. These organizations include the Council of State Governments (CSG) and its regional office, the Western Council of State Governments, the National and Western Governors Associations (NGA and WGA), the National Conference of State Legislatures (NCSL), the National Center for State Courts (NCSC), and the National Association of State Budget Officers (NASBO).

Source: Developed by the authors.

Alaska's informal interactions with foreign governments are also part of the political aspects of IGR, as is the case in all states. This aspect of Alaska's IGR, however, is not included in Figure 10.1 and Box 10.1 because states cannot have formal diplomatic relations with foreign government such as Canada or Japan. However, the wide-ranging aspects of Alaska's informal interactions with foreign governments both under federal auspices and on its own are considered in Chapter 11 on Alaska and the world.

4. THE EVOLUTION OF THE STRUCTURE AND POLITICS OF ALASKA'S IGR

Even though the United States purchased Alaska from Russia in 1867, Alaska's IGR did not begin in a practical way until the creation of the Territory of Alaska in 1912. This is because from 1867 to 1912 there was no government for the vast region as a whole. Although there were local governments during this period, Alaska was run by various agencies of the federal government. Territorial status brought a Territorial legislature and a nonvoting member of Congress. It also established rules for local government, most notably the prohibition against the establishment of counties. This was the result of the influence of powerful economic interests, especially the fishing and mining companies, who feared the imposition of taxes and other interference by county governments.

The Territorial Period—1912–1959

The federal government was dominant in the IGR relationship during the Territorial period. Dominance was assured by the U.S. president's authority to appoint the governor of the Territory, by the authority of Congress to veto acts of the Territorial legislature, and by the absence of a Territorial judiciary—all courts were federal courts. The fishing and mining industries with major operations in Alaska exerted considerable influence in Congress and worked to prevent the Territorial legislature from having control over the management of fish and game and the management and settlement of Alaska lands.[9] The federal government did contribute to the Territory's development, such as by constructing the Alaska Railroad between 1914 and 1923. However, the Territorial period was marked by a feeling of colonial status on the part of many Alaskans. This feeling ultimately led to the move for statehood.

During the Territorial years, two acts of Congress were particularly important in shaping Territorial-federal relations. Both continue to have important effects on IGR today. One was the Jones Act (formally the Merchant Marine Act) of 1920, which requires that goods shipped between U.S. ports must be transported in U.S.-built vessels with U.S. crews. The higher cost of building a vessel in the United States and the higher wage rates for U.S. crews compared with many other countries increases the cost of transporting goods to and from Alaska. The other act was the Indian Reorganization Act (IRA) of 1934, with particular Alaska provisions added in 1936, which established rules for recognizing tribes, strengthening tribal government, aiding tribal business activities, Native control over lands, and eligibility to receive federal aid.[10]

The expansion of the population as a result of Alaska's strategic importance in World War II fueled the statehood movement. Many Alaskans were frustrated by the constraints on their self-government, their lack of control of Alaska's land and its resources and their inability to combat the powerful Outside interests, primarily those of fishing and mining, which had a huge influence on Alaska's political and economic life at the time. The successful drive for statehood, incorporated in the Alaska Statehood Act signed by President Eisenhower in July 1958, changed Alaska's IGR power relationship with the federal government in Alaska's favor in many ways. The new Alaska Constitution, which played a large part in securing statehood, set the pattern for the state-local IGR relationship.

The First Twenty-Five Years of Statehood

In the formative years of statehood, from 1959 to the mid-1980s, Alaska's IGR developed particular administrative and political characteristics. Together with the Statehood Act, the Alaska Native Claims Settlement Act (ANCSA) of 1971 (and its subsequent amendments), and the Alaska National Interest Lands Conservation Act (ANILCA) of 1980, were landmark events. The latter two marked a major change in federal-state relations in Alaska.

The provisions of ANCSA established for-profit regional corporations and village corporations and helped solidify the regional nonprofit associations, many of which had existed in some form before 1971. ANCSA was particularly instrumental in influencing Alaska's present dual IGR system involving Native governments.[11] ANILCA, which placed more than one hundred million acres of federal lands into national forests, parks, and wildlife refuges, was the manifestation in Alaska of a broader change in federal-state relations. This change was particularly evident in the western states and reflected a power shift in Washington, D.C., with the rise of the environmental movement. As John Katz, for many years the head of the Alaska governor's office in Washington, D.C., comments in Chapter 2, western lands were no longer to be used for economic development alone.[12] There was a strong reaction to this changing use of lands in the West, including in Alaska.[13]

The negotiations on ANILCA and its eventual passage and other actions, such as the U.S. Supreme Court striking down an early version of the Permanent Fund Dividend (PFD) program that gave more money to longer-term residents, together with a general antipathy to federal authority among many Alaskans and politicians, fueled anti-federal sentiment in these years. The state government tried unsuccessfully to block federal legislation to place over a quarter of Alaska's land area off-limits to development. These provisions, found in section 17(d)(2) of ANCSA (often referred to as "d2 lands"), were implemented through ANILCA. An extreme—political fringe—response to these various federal actions, but nevertheless representing a highly publicized manifestation of this federal antipathy, was from the Alaska Independence Party (AIP). The AIP had most of its support in Interior Alaska and at various times advocated Alaskan independence from the United States.

Two mainstream political expressions of concern among Alaskans about federal authority occurred in 1980 and 1982. In 1980 the voters narrowly passed, by 51 to 49 percent, a ballot measure (in this case, an advisory vote) asking the legislature to set up a statehood commission to reconsider Alaska's relationship with the federal government.[14] Then in 1982 the so-called Tundra Rebellion initiative appeared on the ballot. This was Alaska's version of the Sagebrush Rebellion that was sweeping the American West in these years. Alaska's initiative, which passed overwhelmingly by 73 to 27 percent, claimed much of the federal land remaining in the state for Alaska.[15] The statehood commission met and produced a report, but nothing came of it because, like the Tundra Rebellion initiative, it ran afoul of the U.S. Constitution and federal laws.[16] These actions, as with many before and since, were symbolic expressions of the frustration of many Alaskans with federal actions. The federal government largely ignored them, and their effect on federal actions was close to zero.

While many Alaskans and several of their politicians, including members of the state's congressional delegation and Joe Vogler, the leader of the AIP, were soldiers in the battle against the federal government, none was more vocal, tenacious, and combative than Walter J. (Wally) Hickel. He took on this role despite, or perhaps because of, being appointed Secretary of the Interior by Richard Nixon from 1969 until Hickel's resignation in November 1970. From his first term as governor (1966–1969) when he unsuccessfully fought the federal government to get an exemption from the Jones Act for the Wickersham, a foreign-built ferry bought by the Alaska Ferry System, to his fight against the federally-mandated rural preference for subsistence hunting and fishing in his second term (1990–1994), he was a gladiator. It was a David in a battle with Goliath. He nonetheless fought to secure what he considered to be the federal promise to Alaska at statehood.[17] In this case, however, Goliath won.

Hickel's deep belief in federal injustice toward Alaska led him to help establish both Commonwealth North and the Institute of the North, organizations to explore and promote Alaska solutions to problems and his idea of Alaska as an Owner State with its ownership of vast land and resources. In 1990 Commonwealth North published a book with the unambiguous title *Going Up in Flames: The Promises and Pledges of Alaska Statehood Under Attack*.[18] Even as late as 2009, within a year of his death in May 2010, Hickel contributed a piece to the *Anchorage Daily News* headlined, "Feds have Abused Their Compact with Alaska."[19] Even though he used the AIP party label to get elected to a second term as governor in 1990 (after he was defeated in the Republican primary), Hickel never pursued independence. Clearly, he wanted to work out an Alaska solution with the state remaining part of the United States.

Meanwhile, over the twenty-five years following statehood federal funds continued to flow into the state in various forms and in increasing amounts, in large part because of the increasing influence of Alaska's senior U.S. senator, Ted Stevens. And the twenty-fifth anniversary of statehood in 1984 was marked by negotiations to transfer the Alaska Railroad from federal to state ownership. The transfer occurred the following year.

From the Mid-1980s to 2015

The period since the twenty-fifth anniversary of statehood has been marked by three major issue areas in federal-state IGR: the legal and political aspects of federal monies coming to Alaska and the two often related issue areas of federal regulations and land and natural resources management. These issue areas have involved both cooperation and conflict, and most of the specific issues within these areas can be traced to the formative developments in IGR following statehood.

Federal monies coming to Alaska are of various types, including direct payments to individuals in the form of salaries to federal employees and programs like Social Security, payments that go through the state for programs like Medicaid and a host of other services, direct payments to local governments, and funding and payments to Native corporations and other organizations. Whether one type of federal payment is considered by itself or whether total federal funds coming to the state overall are included, Alaska has ranked in the top five, and often as number one, from statehood to the present, among the fifty states in the amount of federal funds received on a per capita basis. Together with oil, the federal government is one of two major economic drivers of the Alaska economy. To put no finer point on it, Alaska is more dependent on federal funds than the vast majority of states, and it would be a much different place without these funds.[20] Even a small reduction can have serious effects on the state's economy. In fact, given the major expansion in programs of all types and the increase in federal funds to help finance them, Alaska was more dependent on federal funds in 2016 than it was at the time of statehood in 1959.

In regard to state-federal relations on particular policies and their administration, as with the majority of aspects of IGR, there has been extensive cooperation, though the state and federal government working in harmony gets little publicity. In part, this state-federal cooperation occurs because many programs, like Medicaid, those for disadvantaged children, as well as many transportation projects, require a state match of federal funds, and the state willingly goes along to receive the major federal contributions. Plus, the federal government protects Alaska's interests in fishing disputes with Canada and Japan and works with it on Arctic issues.

Some issues, however, particularly those regarding developers versus environmentalists (land use, oil and gas and mining development, air quality, protection of endangered species, among others) and involving Alaska Natives (especially subsistence), have been high-profile conflicts. The state won a major victory in the federal courts in the *Venetie* case, which denied the existence of "Indian Country" for most of Alaska and which was not received positively by many segments of the Native population. Perhaps the two major issues in recent years that produced the most antagonism between many Alaskans and the federal government have been failure to open ANWR to oil and gas exploration and failure to resolve the subsistence issue.[21]

Other Developments in IGR since Statehood

Since statehood, there have been other developments in Alaska's IGR besides that with the federal government. Three are particularly noteworthy.

State-local relations have been affected by the slow development of the local government system as envisaged by Alaska's founders (see Chapter 18) and by the oil bonanza. Much of the state is still not organized into local governments, and the state has provided much of the funding for many local governments, though this funding has been considerably reduced since the crash in oil prices in 1986. The second is state relations with other states through the development of one-on-one relationships and state compacts and cooperation with other states through federal auspices like the North Pacific Fisheries Management Council. The third development is state-Native government and local government–Native government relations. Besides the *Venetie* case, these relations have primarily been shaped by ANCSA, the battle over subsistence, and the changing influence of Native politicians that reached its high point in the 1980s and early 1990s.

5. PERSPECTIVES ON THE ALASKA-FEDERAL RELATIONSHIP

While much media coverage of the Alaska federal-state relationship is balanced, and not all politicians vocalize anti-federal sentiments, over the years there has been more emphasis on what we might call the Hickel anti-federal sentiment than on the benefits the federal government provides to Alaska. As former Governor Knowles aptly put it regarding Alaska politicians: "You'll never lose a vote by beating up on the feds."[22] In this section we offer three perspectives on the Alaska-federal relationship. The first is from Alaskans; the second comes from Washington, D.C., and the rest of the nation; and the third is a realistic and practical perspective.

Alaska Perspectives

Some Alaskans very likely understand little or simply do not care about the role of the federal government in their state. This is probably because the federal government does not appear to affect them directly or because they avoid politics and those involved in it. Of those Alaskans and their politicians who are concerned or closely affected by state-federal IGR, the views run the gamut from the former AIP position of seeking Alaska independence to those who see a very positive and indispensable role for Washington, D.C. These attitudes result from a complex set of factors, including ideology and political culture, perceived economic and political gains and losses, particular events, and, in the case of state executive officials, current administration policy. Here we identify five perspectives, but emphasize that they are not mutually exclusive. Different organizations, groups, constituencies, and individuals may, at various times, express one or more perspectives.

First, there are some Alaskans who believe they have suffered from past federal policies and some who see federal actions as detrimental to them today. The point is not whether their concerns are justified. What is important is that they believe them to be so. It is not difficult to show that federal actions have been detrimental to them, at least in some way. These groups may not be totally anti-federal, but simply have what they see as legitimate concerns—concerns that are not so different from those that fueled the drive for statehood. More specifically, for many years and in some quarters today, Alaska Natives have seen themselves suffering at federal hands. For instance, Julie Kitka, president of the Alaska Federation of Natives at various times, characterized the historical role of the federal government as a "take it or leave it type approach or it has been that the federal policy makers make the decisions and the communities are just the recipients."[23] Another group with such concerns is made up of those who want to develop the state, such as the late Governor Hickel, but are constrained by the federal government and who believe they may have fewer employment and other economic opportunities because of it.

Some of this feeling likely comes from the nature of the three broad types of public policies that the federal government develops and administers. These are explained in Chapter 3 as distributive, redistributive, and regulatory policies. Distributive policies, many of which are entitlement programs, such as Social Security and Medicare, raise little ire and are generally favorably viewed by Alaskans. Not so with the other two types of policies. Redistributive policies, like those related to giving rural residents (in reality Native Alaskans) priority over fish and game in times of shortage, irk many Alaskans, as do the many regulatory policies regarding the use of land and environmental protection.

The second perspective is shown by actions taken by the State of Alaska, as represented by the governor and his or her administration. One role that Alaska governors have taken on is that of "Defender of Alaska" against hostile Outside interests, and the federal government is often seen as being one of them. Consequently, over the years the state has taken the federal government to task, and sometimes even to court, on a range of issues, including the opening of ANWR, the Endangered Species Act, subsistence hunting and fishing, and jurisdiction over Little Diomede Island in the Bering Strait. Sometimes state actions are driven by technical and nonpartisan concerns, as with state Senator Bill Wielechowski's "Real ID" bill to prevent implementation of a federal I.D. system in Alaska (see Chapter 3, Box 3.5). At other times partisanship and ideology appear to be the primary motivators, as in Governor Palin's rejection of federal stimulus funds in 2009 and Governor Parnell's opposition to the Obama health care plan following its enactment in 2010.

The third perspective relates to an aspect of Alaska's political culture that is common among many Alaskans—an attitude toward Washington, D.C., that ranges from skepticism to negativism to downright hostility. In recent years "federal overreach" has become a catchphrase for those sharing this perspective. Sometimes this perspective has a rational basis, such as genuine disagreement with the federal government over a particular animal being placed on the endangered species list or restrictions on logging in the Tongass National Forest. But the claim of federal overreach can also be riddled with contradictions and emotions. Many Alaskans who share this perspective, and often the most vocal among them, have limited or selective knowledge on the issue at hand or are simply misinformed about the role of the federal government as it relates to the issue. The past AIP platform urging Alaska to secede from the Union is an extreme example.

A fourth perspective is that of Alaska's politicians. Since politicians often reflect the views of their constituents, it is not surprising that many politicians also have, or at least express, a negative attitude toward the federal government. Even though these politicians may realize the value of the federal government, they see political hay to be made out of federal bashing. Over the years, federal bashing has come from a wide range of politicians from both political parties, including the state's congressional delegation as well as governors, state legislators, and local government officials. The contradiction in this anti-federal attitude among both the public and their politicians is epitomized in the headline of an opinion piece by Julia O'Malley in the *Anchorage Daily News*: "Feds we loath you, please send money."[24] This sentiment, described in Chapter 2 as the western political paradox, is a common feature of attitudes in the American West, particularly in the Mountain states. In Alaska, at least, this attitude is not confined to the federal government. It is part of Alaska's populist side and extends to just about any Outside group—the Seattle fishing industry, big oil, national environmental groups, among other forces. Whether in fact or fiction, these groups are seen as having an undue influence on Alaska's affairs and as holding a different set of values from the people who live in "the great land."[25]

The fifth perspective is that of those who see the value of federal action in Alaska because they personally benefit economically or politically, or they see the broader benefits to Alaska and its citizens. Those who hold this perspective overall may also, on occasion, take action because of what they see as intrusive or uninformed federal policies or for other reasons, such as the case of Senator Wielechowski and his legislation barring the expenditure of state funds to implement the federal Real ID law, even though his actions generally have indicated that he sees the value of the federal government. Those who hold this generally positive perspective range from federal employees to many segments of the Native community to those who want to put some controls on development in the state, particularly the Alaska environmental community. The strength of environmentalists in Alaska comes largely from federal laws and actions and from public support in the rest of the nation and around the world, though there are certainly active, if relatively small, environmental groups within Alaska.

The Perspective from Washington, D.C., and the Nation

As in the case of Alaska's view of the federal government, there is no one perspective on Alaska from Washington, D.C., or among the states, organizations, and constituencies in the rest of the nation. These perspectives are diverse and vary from time to time on particular issues and in response to the positions taken by Alaska's state government and its political constituencies. Nevertheless, there are several reasons why Alaska's perspectives on issues and policies often meet with resistance from Outside forces.

First, the federal government, its branches, and myriad agencies, is the government for the entire nation and its territories. The national government has an obligation to uphold the U.S. Constitution and federal laws and to enforce those laws. Consequently, theoretically and in practice, it has to take a broad view in policy making and not just champion the cause of one state. This broad view produces potential clashes with the states. For example, possession and sale of marijuana is illegal under federal law, yet as of 2015 Colorado, Washington State, Oregon and Alaska have state laws making possession and sale legal in their states. At the same time, for a host of programs, from Medicaid to road construction, the federal government allows the states, including Alaska, the flexibility to fine tune the way they deliver these programs. It is certainly true that the federal government has made mistakes in applying laws and regulations to Alaska and that there will always be insensitive and inflexible federal government officials. However, the charge that the federal government "does not understand Alaska" and that the state is a "victim" of federal shortcomings, is much less accurate than many anti-federal elements in Alaska might believe.

A second Outside perspective, often at odds with prevalent Alaska perspectives, has to do with the view that surrounds Alaska in the minds of many Americans—that of the Last Frontier. From this perspective, Alaska is a special, even somewhat exotic and mystical, place that many would like to visit some day. Much of this mystique results from an idealized view of Alaska, but nevertheless it often translates into federal policies that many Alaskans find objectionable, in part because they simply disagree with them and in part because they undermine Alaskans' control over their own state. These external attitudes tend to favor the preservation of the state's natural resources, such as the outcry over the systematic killing of wolves during 1993–1994 under the second Hickel administration, and the long and unsuccessful fight to open ANWR. However, as a major landholder and with control over most of the oceans surrounding the state and with national policies to protect endangered species, the federal government is asserting its rights as reflected in American public opinion expressed through Congress and federal laws. In the end, it all boils down to politics and power.

Politics and power are at the root of the third Outside perspective relating to the Alaska-federal relationship and federal-state IGR. Federal-state relations across the nation are not static but constantly evolve and will continue to do so. This is largely because of public pressures and needs that are spearheaded by the President and Congress and usually affirmed by the federal courts. In particular, from the late 1960s onward, changes in the federal-state relationship were the case with the rise of federal policies regarding environmental conservation and protection, which has particularly affected Alaska. Consequently, from both a legal and a political perspective, there is no way that the federal government can be held to fulfill what many, including the late Governor Hickel, see as "the promise of Alaska statehood" dating back to 1959. The national government—much like Alaska—was itself on the receiving end of inexorable forces at that time, which swept across the nation as America developed into a post-industrial society and became concerned about not just economic benefits, but also quality of life issues and other values. So, in effect, those like Hickel who see the federal government as betraying the promise of statehood (though exactly what that promise was is subject to dispute) are caught in a time warp—politically frozen in a bygone age of Alaska-federal relations.

The fourth and fifth Outside perspectives are closely related: those of Alaska's financial relationship with Washington, D.C., and how this influences the perceptions about Alaska among some politicians, journalists, and groups and individuals in the rest of the nation. The fourth perspective, which is a clearly demonstrable fact, is that Alaska, its citizens, and their lifestyle are heavily subsidized by the rest of the nation. Journalist Charles Homans sums up this reality well in the title of a 2007 article, "State of Dependence: Ted Stevens's Alaska Problem—and Ours," and in his observation that, "Simply put, Alaska has made a habit of transferring its operating costs to the federal government . . . . a drain that looks especially bad in light of the state's fiscal reality."[26] The gist of Homans's article is that, in large part, the political skill of Senator Stevens got Alaska much more than its fair share of federal monies. These funds have not come out of thin air, but indirectly from other states whose citizens pay more into the federal treasury than they get back. Certainly, many less well-off states, like Mississippi and Louisiana, receive more federal funds than they pay to Washington, D.C. But Alaska is not a poor state, with its $52 billion Permanent Fund and, as of 2015, no state individual income tax and no statewide sales tax. Put bluntly, this means that until Senator Stevens's defeat in 2008, Alaska's advantageous political position in Congress enabled it to use other states' money while Alaskans were unwilling to dip into their own pockets and reserves to help themselves.

The fifth perspective—one of annoyance and resentment toward Alaska by many in Congress and of ridicule in the media—is a direct result of the huge amounts of earmarked federal funds that came Alaska's way, largely through Senator Stevens's efforts. Given the reality of Alaska's dependence and political influence, this perspective is understandable.

And it is not surprising that moves were successful in ending congressional earmarks, at which Senator Stevens was a master. Nor is it surprising that there are sometimes articles in the national press mocking Alaska's annual payout of the PFD, the so-called "Bridge to Nowhere" (linking Ketchikan with its island airport and which in 2008 became the media poster child for the evils of congressional earmarks), and derision of earlier calls by the AIP for Alaskan independence. Concerned about Alaska's image in the rest of the nation, then Governor Frank Murkowski suggested hiring a public relations firm to counter the image that Alaska has acquired as a freeloaders' paradise.[27]

A Holistic, Practical, Give-and-Take Perspective

The Alaskan, the federal, and the national public's views on Alaska-federal relations all have their merits, and the actions based upon them may have some influence on the relationship as it operates day-to-day. But at its core, the relationship is shaped by political power. As a result of the federal government's constitutional and statutory authority, its tremendous financial resources, and Alaska's dependence on federal funds, the federal government has the upper hand in its relations with Alaska. So, Alaska's success in dealing with the federal government depends on recognizing this superior position, on the skill of Alaskan politicians working in Washington, D.C., and on the ongoing give and take in the relationship.

Box 10.2 provides a holistic, give-and-take perspective on Alaska's relationship with the federal government by former Governor Tony Knowles. Four additional points help to supplement this perspective. First, as mentioned before, the federal government is not a monolith and should not be considered as such. Second, as with all states, major funding for programs such as Medicaid, transportation facilities, and some aspects of child welfare and education, come from the federal government, and the states must comply with federal rules and often match federal funds to receive these needed revenues.

Third, despite the restrictions on these and other monies, the federal government has long taken into consideration variations in state populations, geography, levels of economic well-being, and so on in allocating funds, and it often allows for state input and variations in programs. Washington, D.C., has become more "state friendly" in this regard as the result of political pressures since the 1960s. Alaska has benefited considerably from such federal formulas and variations.

Fourth, much of the negative attitude Alaskans have toward the federal government stems from frustration at Alaska's inability to control its own affairs. This frustration was the major push behind statehood in the 1950s and continues to be prevalent today. Ironically, however, Alaska's major dependence on federal funds undermines that independence. But, as Charles Homans points out, this is actually a dependence of choice, the choice to seek major federal funds and thus be bound by federal rules.[28] Furthermore, sometimes ideology as opposed to economics or pragmatism undermines Alaska's control of its own affairs. As Governor Knowles points out in Box 10.2, this occurred over failure to deal with the subsistence issue. Another example is Governor Parnell's July 2012 decision not to set up a health care insurance exchange under the Affordable Care Act (commonly known as Obamacare) for those who need to buy health insurance, but to let the federal government run it instead.

6. THE POLITICS OF CONTEMPORARY FEDERAL RELATIONS WITH ALASKA GOVERNMENTS

While the legal context of Alaska-federal IGR is set by the U.S. Constitution, various legal and regulatory provisions, and their interpretation by the federal courts, the relationship on a day-to-day basis is determined by administrative relationships, politics, and power. Here we briefly examine this practical operation of Alaska-federal IGR, particularly the role of federal and state bureaucrats, the governor, the governor's office in Washington, D.C., and Alaska's congressional delegation.

By far the major aspect of Alaska-federal IGR is low-key, behind-the-scenes interactions between federal, state, and local government officials dealing with the myriad of policies and procedures that involve cooperation between the national and Alaska governments. This involves many diverse activities, including the transfer of funds for programs like Denali KidCare and contact between officials from the federal and state departments of transportation on various projects for roads, the Alaska Railroad, airports, and harbors. It also involves various federal agencies, such as the Bureau of Indian Affairs and the Indian Health Service, dealing with Native governments and Native corporations. Occasionally, high-level federal officials, such as the secretaries and deputy secretaries of departments like Interior and Homeland Security, visit Alaska to meet with state and local officials and with various Alaska constituencies on issues ranging from improving security at Alaska airports to oil drilling on federal land and in the Arctic.

There is no single attitude toward the federal government in Alaska and no broad agreement among its citizens or its politicians on what policies to pursue in Washington, D.C. However, at any one time, Alaska's governor pursues a more or less defined set of policies in close cooperation with the three members of Alaska's congressional delegation. Besides being in regular contact with the three members of the delegation, the governor is kept informed about federal issues by the state's Washington, D.C., office. This office acts as a coordinating body for Alaska state government, such as facilitating visits by state legislators and commissioners and as an information resource. John Katz, who headed this office for thirty years and served seven governors, explains the role of the office and

BOX 10.2

Alaska and the Federal Government—Past, Present, and Future: A Perspective by Former Governor Tony Knowles

The legacy of the heavy-handed federal actions of territorial days, buoyed by the more recent controversial decisions such as d2 lands withdrawals under ANILCA, ANWR's lack of development, and Tongass Forest management, continue to make the federal government an Alaska punching bag. As a result, many Alaskans relate to the anti-federal rhetoric of some state politicians, including Alaska's congressional delegation. And every governor, regardless of party affiliation, has taken the federal government to court, challenging both the administration of various laws and their substance.

Yet, history provides a different perspective. Rather than an extractive and dictatorial absentee landlord, as viewed by conventional wisdom, over the years congressional and presidential actions can be viewed as responsive to Alaska's and America's needs. In the Alaska Statehood Act, Congress addressed future jobs and economic development for a state that had no economic base by providing 103 million acres of land of the state's choosing. The state guaranteed its fiscal future by choosing, among other lands, the acreage on the Arctic North Slope that included the future Prudhoe Bay oil and gas discovery, the largest in American history.

Then, both ANCSA of 1971 and ANILCA of 1980 can be considered major benefits to Alaska and its people. In ANCSA, after two hundred years of broken promises and failed programs for its indigenous peoples, Congress took a new course in addressing social justice. Then ANILCA set the scene for conserving Alaska's natural beauty and environment.

One provision in ANILCA, Title 8, guaranteed an essential part of Alaska Native interests not included in the ANCSA bill. This grants a preference for subsistence hunting and fishing for "rural residents." As long as the state enforced this preference, Title 8 retained state management of all fish and game regulations on federal and state lands as well as private lands. Unwillingness by the state to provide for this preference would turn fish and game management on federal land over to the federal government. By making the differentiation a geographical preference rather than a racial preference, ANILCA avoided imposing different rules for different families in a village, thereby pitting neighbor against neighbor.

Yet, intense legal and political controversy ensued. A group of hunting advocates from the Alaska Outdoor Council led the fight against any preference for access to hunting and fishing. Their cause was bolstered by two developments. The first was an Alaska Supreme Court ruling declaring unconstitutional the state's attempt to comply with ANILCA's rural preference requirement because it failed to provide equal access to state resources as required by the Alaska Constitution. The second was the Hickel administration's challenge to the authority of the federal government to implement such a rural preference.

It was my contention that there was no legal argument that prohibited the U.S. Secretary of the Interior from drawing up regulations implementing a national law. So when I took office in 1994 I dropped the lawsuit that the Hickel administration had begun. I realized that the only way out of the situation was to amend the Alaska Constitution to bring it in line with the federal preference requirement. However, despite overwhelming public support by all polls conducted and strong Alaska Native organizational support, the issue has been narrowly defeated in the legislature on several occasions and has not appeared on the ballot. The consequence was that the state lost the right to manage wildlife on federal lands, including subsistence.

Today, besides the ongoing issue of subsistence there are several other important issues that require good relations between the state and federal governments. While these issues are national in scope, some have a particular Alaska element. The military is particularly important to Alaska, and the state's geographical advantage for global deployment of rapid response military forces insures a continued strong military presence in Alaska. As the state with the largest per capita number of veterans, health care for veterans is of special significance to an aging Vietnam-era veteran population as well as the surge of new veterans from the Iraq and Afghanistan wars needing health care support. More broadly, health care through the Indian Health Service, Medicare to a rapidly aging population, and the national obligation to the uninsured and underinsured require a state-federal partnership that is essential to a many Alaskans.

The consequences of global climate change affect Alaska, America's only Arctic state, to a far greater degree than any other state. The repercussions to the environment, wildlife, fisheries, subsistence foods, and coastal development require close, cooperative relations between state and federal agencies for coping with and mitigating climate change.

Looking at the big picture of the state-federal relationship, there has to be give and take in a federal system like ours. There is a stark inconsistency between taking major federal benefits and not wanting federal restrictions. An anti-federal attitude taken too far can be disadvantageous to the state and even undermine its long-cherished desires. For instance, having subsistence under the co-management of federal and state systems is not in the best interest of the resource or the people affected. Ironically, it means that a major goal behind statehood, for Alaska to exert more control over its own resources, has been partly relinquished because of the inability of Alaskans to come to a political solution to this problem. There continues to be an overwhelming effect on Alaska's future because of federal management decisions on federal lands and waters. The careful protection and utilization of these resources require a collaborative approach by state and federal governments.

Good science, sound management, and a cooperative relationship are the hallmarks of a federal-state relationship that may be bad political theater but provide good government. So however convenient and politically advantageous scapegoating and federal bashing may be, the relationship with the federal government will be far more successful for Alaska with engagement rather than estrangement.

Source: Developed by Clive Thomas and Anthony Nakazawa; based on an interview with former Governor Tony Knowles, March 8, 2009.

assesses its successes and disappointments in Box 10.3. Since Katz's retirement in 2013, however, the office has undergone major changes. The ban on congressional earmarks in 2011 reduced the office's workload as, until then, much time was spent on providing support for Alaska's congressional delegation to secure these special appropriations. Then, as a result of the downturn in oil prices in 2014 and beyond, in 2015 the office was reduced from five to two staff and the director's job went unfilled. This, according to Governor Walker, would save the state about $400,000 a year.[29] In both the short and long term, however, this reduction in staffing could hurt Alaska given its major dependence on federal funds.

Much of the success of the governor's policy goals, both high and low profile, in relation to the federal government depends on Alaska's congressional delegation. With only three members of Congress (out of 535—100 in the Senate and 435 in the House of

BOX 10.3

The Governor's Washington, D.C., Office: Its Role, Successes, and Disappointments

Around forty states and U.S. territories have offices in Washington, D.C. Their functions differ depending upon gubernatorial mandates, issues, and budgets. These offices also range in size and function. Some engage in significant policy analysis and advocacy while others simply exchange information between state capitals and D.C.

Alaska's office was established by Governor Bill Egan in 1972. It usually has a complement of six staff members: a director, three associate directors who work in specific issue areas, and two support staff. When needed, additional technical assistance and lobbying are provided by private D.C. firms. The principal functions of the office are to:

- Identify and monitor issues affecting Alaska that arise in Congress and federal agencies in D.C.
- Analyze and help formulate state policy on these issues
- Advocate policy in various federal forums

The office is also the state's primary contact with the Alaska congressional delegation and works closely with the National Governors Association, the Western Governors Association, and other organizations that have an interest in issues affecting Alaska.

At any one time the office is dealing with more than one hundred issues. About 60 percent involve legislation in Congress; the rest are matters pending before federal agencies and administrative tribunals. Considerable time is spent on Alaska-specific natural resource and environmental matters. Other Alaska issues involve health, jobs and families, education, transportation, appropriations, and international affairs.

Many state-federal concerns can be resolved with the D.C. office playing a minimal role. However, when an issue concerns federal legislation, significant administrative policy, or a matter that cannot be settled elsewhere, the D.C. office becomes more heavily involved.

Recent successes in D.C. have included

- Legislation to facilitate the construction of a natural gas pipeline
- Appropriating funds to address the social, health, and economic needs of Alaskans
- Legislation accelerating the conveyance of lands under the Alaska Statehood Act and the Alaska Native Claims Settlement Act
- Reauthorization of the Magnuson-Stevens Fishery Conservation and Management Act, which governs federal management to the two hundred–mile limit
- Reauthorization of federal surface transportation legislation that provides funding for highways, ferries, and bridges
- Federal approval of a military base realignment plan that maintains essential operations at Eielson Air Force Base near Fairbanks

Perhaps Alaska's biggest disappointment is Congress's continuing unwillingness to approve oil development in ANWR. Another problem is the inability by Alaska and other western public land states to obtain reform of the Endangered Species Act including an increased role for states and making it easier to de-list a recovered species.

Alaska's maintenance of a governor's office in D.C. remains important. This is particularly the case given the significant presence in and impact of the federal government on the state. States with no D.C. office cite the reasons of operational expense and say that representation is the job of their congressional delegations. In fact, the expense is minimal considering the more effective advocacy that occurs, the successes of most D.C. offices, and the savings in travel costs incurred by state officials. Further, it is not the role of governors' Washington offices to duplicate the functions of their congressional delegations. It is to facilitate state decision-making on federal issues, explain policy positions, and enhance understanding between governors and state congressional delegations.

Source: Developed by John W. Katz, former Director of State-Federal Relations and Special Counsel to the Governor.

Representatives), on the surface it appears that Alaska has little chance of major successes given the need for 218 votes for passage of legislation in the House and 51 in the Senate. Success in Washington, D.C., however, depends less on the number of a state's seats in Congress and more on the power of the state's delegation, which is usually a function of what leadership positions, if any, they hold. In this regard, few members of Congress in U.S. history equaled the influence of the late Senator Ted Stevens, a Republican. With his political skill, ability to work across party lines with Democrats, and the powerful committees he chaired, Alaska was able to get far more funds per capita than many states with much larger congressional delegations.

Stevens, who served for forty years until his defeat by Democrat Mark Begich in 2008, was aided for many years by Republican Representative Don Young, who was first elected to Congress in 1972, and by Republican Senator Frank Murkowski, who served from 1981 to 2002. The seniority of the Alaska delegation enabled them to secure funds for Alaska, including five times the average earmarks of the average state. No one more than Stevens himself realized that it was long-standing relationships and political power that ultimately determined Alaska's success in IGR with the federal government.

Since Stevens's defeat, Alaska's power in Congress has waned considerably and will likely take several years to recover.[30] Congressman Young turned eighty-two in 2015, and as of 2015 Alaska had one U.S. senator, Lisa Murkowski, in a leadership position, and a new face, Dan Sullivan, who triumphed over Mark Begich in November 2014. The waning of Alaska's influence is evidenced by the major drop in earmarked funds coming to the state in the fiscal year after Stevens's defeat.[31] Some of this decline can be attributed to the ban on earmarks adopted following the 2010 elections. Even though there have since been several moves to remove the ban on earmarks, the prohibition was still in place in late 2015. The ban has taken its toll on Alaska's share of federal funding.[32] A good example of an IGR organization that thrived under Stevens's term in office, but which has suffered major cuts since his departure, is the Denali Commission described in Box 10.4 (on page 340). Regardless of party affiliation, Alaska's congressional delegation has consistently recognized that working across party lines and using a pragmatic, as opposed to an ideological approach are the key to Alaska exerting what power it has in dealing with the federal government. While Alaska's three members of Congress were in the Republican majority in 2016, if the Democrats win back one or both houses of Congress in 2016, the lack of a Democrat in the delegation could hurt Alaska.

7. ALASKA'S IGR SYSTEM IN COMPARATIVE PERSPECTIVE

In comparison to other states, there are both similarities and differences in Alaska's IGR, depending on the level and specifics of the interaction concerned. We look first at the general elements of IGR throughout the fifty states and then those of Alaska's that distinguish it, in varying degrees, from other states.

At the general level, the constitutional, statutory, and political aspects of Alaska's IGR are very similar to those of other states. As in all states, Alaska's IGR involves interaction between and among the federal government, Alaska state government, and local governments. Like the other forty-nine states, Alaska also has relations with other states individually, through regional and national compacts, and through organizations such as the Council of State Governments and associations for state officials. In addition, whether it is Kansas, Maryland, Oregon, Alaska, or any other state, much of the politics of IGR concerns money and funding issues, particularly intergovernmental transfers between the federal government and state governments, the federal government and local governments, and the states and their local governments. Moreover, there are constitutional and jurisdictional issues that arise among the three levels of government. A recent example is over President Obama's health care legislation of 2010, which many states, including Alaska, opposed in part because they saw it as encroaching on their authority.

On a day-to-day basis, however, it is the fiscal aspects of IGR that determine the dynamics of the power relationship between the federal government and the states as well as between states and their local governments. In particular, the tremendous financial resources that the federal government commands give it the upper hand most of the time in the IGR power dynamic. Moreover, in Alaska, as in all states, IGR is essentially a political power relationship. However, the dynamics of the relationship vary from state to state and from time to time, as new developments occur, particularly major federal programs such as the New Deal programs of the 1930s, the Great Society programs of the 1960s, and the health care legislation of 2010. Overall, however, virtually all states have become increasingly dependent on federal funds as a result of these expanded national programs, as Figure 10.2 illustrates.[33]

Some key contrasts between Alaska's IGR and other states give a unique character to the power dynamics in Alaska's relations with its local governments and the federal government. The genesis of these contrasts is the confluence of Alaska's late admission to the Union, the state's oil bonanza, and its physical geography. These elements have worked to produce three particular contrasts between Alaska's IGR and those in other states. One is the dual IGR system consisting of the relationships among the federal, state, and local governments on the one hand and the relationships of those levels of government with various Alaska Native governments and organizations on the other. The second contrast stems from Alaska's geography, which has contributed to the unusual situation that over 60 percent of Alaska has no organized local government and is theoretically under the jurisdiction of the state legislature. The third contrast is that much of the funding of rural-bush local government (especially for education) and some funding of urban government

BOX 10.4

The Denali Commission: A New Direction in IGR and Alaska's Power Decline in Washington, D.C.

Modeled after the Appalachia Regional Commission created in 1966 under the leadership of Senator Robert Byrd of West Virginia, the Denali Commission is an independent federal agency focusing on developing the economy of rural-bush Alaska. The commission was created by Congress in 1998 largely through the efforts of Alaska's Senator Ted Stevens, then chair of the appropriations committee.

The goals of the commission are to deliver federal government services in the most cost-effective manner by reducing administrative and overhead costs and to provide job training and other economic development services in rural-bush areas, particularly in distressed communities (many with unemployment exceeding 50 percent). However, due to its declining budget, the commission's role in promoting rural-bush development has been reduced to promoting village-based bulk fuel facilities and supporting village energy conservation measures.

Governed by seven commissioners representing the federal and state governments, the university, municipalities, Alaska Natives, and the private sector (labor and contractors), the two key features of the commission are as follows:

- Through its membership, the commission attempts to create a true IGR partnership that is controlled largely at the state level.
- Each commission member represents statewide interests, so there are no structural regional conflicts.

Since its inception the commission has worked with various state and federal agencies providing more than $1 billion for basic infrastructure needs in rural-bush Alaska, numbering some two thousand projects. Currently, the commission's budget is less than $10 million a year. In its peak year of 2006 its funding topped $150 million. To try to maintain its former level of service, the commission is aggressively pursuing alternative funding. The needs in rural-bush areas remain extensive.

Undoubtedly, the defeat of Senator Ted Stevens in November 2008 impacted the funding for the commission. Other causes of reduced funding include President Obama's spending cuts in Alaska, including those to health care construction overseen by the commission. Beginning in late 2012, the commission became embroiled in a controversy regarding alleged mismanagement and financial irregularities. This involved calls by federal investigators to abolish the commission. However, Alaska's three-member congressional delegation sought an investigation to get to the root of the allegation and together with the commission's members fought hard to save the commission.

Then, in August 2015, the commission got a major boost in responsibility and funding from President Obama's visit to Alaska, which focused largely on climate change. The president announced that the commission will be the lead agency in a three-year project to look at the environmentally threatened communities in Alaska and to decide whether they need relocating or not. So the commission's continued existence is assured through 2019 and most likely beyond.

Source: Developed by Krag Johnsen, former Denali Commission staffer, Kevin Ritchie, author of Chapter 18, and Anthony Nakazawa.

(especially for capital projects) comes from the state. This rural-bush funding is, in part, because of the lack of any tax base in rural-bush areas, but mainly because of Alaska's oil bonanza since the late 1970s.

From a political perspective, these special circumstances mean that the IGR power dynamic has elements in Alaska not found in IGR politics of most states. Of particular

FIGURE 10.2

Tracking State Dependence on Federal Funds

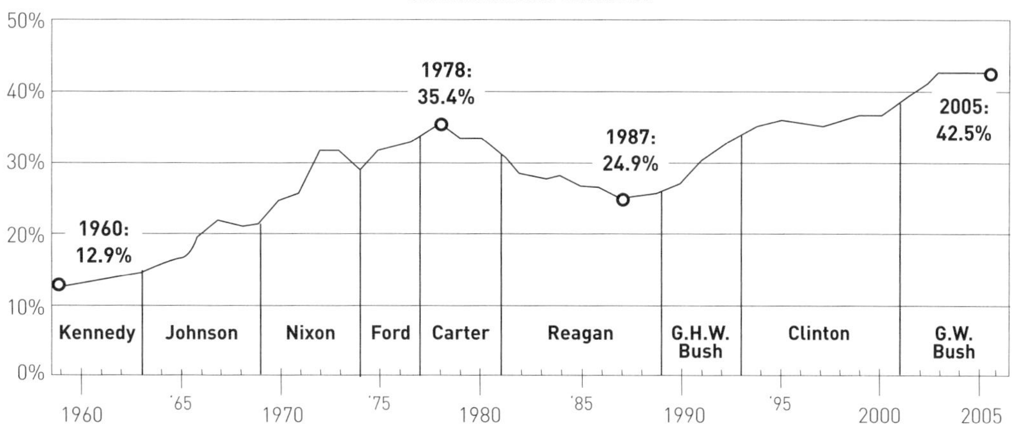

The state dependency rate is a measure of how dependent states are on federal funds. Among recent presidential administrations, only the Reagan administration saw a significant decrease in the rate.

Source: Calculations based on U.S. Department of Health and Human Services, Centers for Medicare and Medicaid Services, National Health Expenditures by Type of Service and Source of Funds, Calendar Years 1960–2006, at http://www.cm.hhs.gov/NationalHealthExpendData/downloads/nhe2006.zip; and U.S. Department of Commerce, Bureau of Economic Analysis, National Income and Product Accounts Tables, Table 3.3, at http://bea.gov/national/nipaweb/SelectTable.asp?Selected=N#S3.

note is the political dimension in Alaska resulting from the dual IGR system and the existence of Native governments. This dual IGR system includes the particularly thorny political issues of Native sovereignty and subsistence. The number of Alaska Natives in rural-bush areas means they are able to elect Native legislators and others who push Native issues, which also affects the state-local IGR relationship in Alaska. To some extent the federal Indian Gaming Regulatory Act of 1990, allowing tribes to set up casinos, has increased Native American-state IGR in states like Idaho, New Mexico, and Oregon, but not in Alaska. This is primarily because Alaska has virtually no "Indian Lands," which is a prerequisite to the establishment of Native casinos under federal law.[34]

There is no data available to make comparisons between Alaska and other states regarding the funding relationships between the states and their local governments. However, because of the dependence of many Alaska local governments on state funding, it is likely that Alaska's municipalities lobby state government more intensely than local governments in other states. The dependence of many local Alaska economies on state employment and capital budget funds contributes to the general dependence of Alaska local governments on state government with consequent effects on the state-local political power dynamic.

8. CONCLUSION: THE BALANCE SHEET OF CONSTRAINTS, CONFLICTS, AND BENEFITS AND THE PERSISTENCE OF POLITICAL RHETORIC

IGR is clearly an important and integral part of Alaska government, politics, and policy making. This is the case with all aspects of IGR: state government's involvement with its local governments, Native governments, other states, and interactions with the federal government and with foreign governments. The most significant relationship with other governments, however, is Alaska's relationship with the federal government. The major significance of this relationship since the Alaska Purchase of 1867, and particularly since statehood, brings into sharp relief several characteristics of Alaska politics—the significant role of external economic and political forces, the all-pervasive importance of government, and the political culture of pragmatic dependent individualism often coupled with the myths and contradictions of Alaska's political discourse. Alaska's dual IGR system illustrates the Alaska political characteristic of the prominent role of Alaska Natives.

The effect of the Alaska-federal relationship on the state and the various segments of its population is not a simple one and certainly not all negative, as some vocal Alaskans believe. The various attitudes toward the federal government among Alaskans and their elected and appointed officials are shaped by the level of knowledge of the role of the federal government and a complex set of values, including views on the role of government and perception of the degree to which various segments of Alaska society benefit or lose as a result of federal actions. These attitudes range across a spectrum from negative to positive and various combinations in between. For the state and its inhabitants as a whole, however, the positive definitely outweighs the negative. Not only is Alaska's standard of living higher because of federal monies flowing to the state, but the state receives more funds per capita than almost any other state. This means, in effect, that many of the other forty-nine states are subsidizing Alaska.

This is not to say that many of the conflicts in which Alaska's state government and its citizens find themselves with the federal government are not justified—sometimes "federal overreach" is real. It is also true that many Alaskans and the state are constrained to their detriment by actions or inactions of the federal government. Even so, it is important to bear two points in mind. First, as in all IGR and in politics in general, Alaska's relationship with the federal government is a political trade-off, in which both sides have legal and political obligations and no side gets all it wants. Second, like Alaska's state government, the federal government is not a monolith. Its three branches, particularly its executive branch agencies, are often at odds with each other. One branch or agency may well favor a policy that benefits a certain segment in Alaska while another branch or agency may disagree. So it is both inaccurate and unjustifiable to brand the federal government at large with all actions considered detrimental to the state and its citizens.

Yet many Alaskans and their politicians are not concerned with such distinctions, often for ideological reasons but sometimes because they do not understand the role of the federal government or do not want to acknowledge it because, as Tony Knowles explains in Box 10.2, federal bashing makes for good politics in many circles in Alaska. So federal bashing is likely to continue to be part of Alaska's political rhetoric for some time to come. This can be more or less harmless when it stays at the level of rhetoric. When rhetoric is combined with ideology, however, the combination can work to deny Alaska control of its affairs by ceding responsibilities to the federal government. That not only goes counter to the intentions of Alaska's founders, it can also be detrimental to Alaskans in general. This could be particularly detrimental to the state in the post–Ted Stevens era in which Alaska does not have the political influence it once had in Washington, D.C.

ENDNOTES

[1] This chapter draws, in part, on Clive S. Thomas, "Intergovernmental Relations in Alaska: Development, Dynamics and Lessons," *The Northern Review* [Special Issue on Central-Local Relations in the North], no. 23 (Summer, 2001): 17–37.

[2] David, C. Nice and Patricia Fredericksen, *The Politics of Intergovernmental Relations*, 2nd ed. (Chicago: Nelson-Hall Publishers, 1995), 2.

[3] U.S. Census Bureau, *Newsroom Archives,* August 30, 2012, at: www.census.gov/newsroom/releases/archives/governments/cb12-161.html.

[4] *Alaska v. Native Village of Venetie Tribal Government*, 522 U.S. 520 (1998).

[5] Public Land Ownership by State, at www.nrcm.org/documents/publiclandownership.pdf.

[6] Clive S. Thomas, ed., *Politics and Public Policy in the Contemporary American West* (Albuquerque: University of New Mexico Press, 1991), 15.

[7] U.S. Census Bureau, *2010 Census: PL 94-171 Redistricting Data,* at http://live.laborstats.alaska.gov/cen/redistr.cfm, and *Urban and Rural Classification for Alaska*, at http://labor.alaska.gov/research/census/urbrur.htm.

[8] In particular, Chapter 9 on the Native political economy considers the formal aspects of federalism and IGR regarding Native governments. Federal-state IGR politics is also considered in Chapter 18 on local government, including some reference to relations with Native governments as well as state-local IGR.

[9] Gerald A. McBeath and Thomas A. Morehouse, *Alaska Politics and Government* (Lincoln: University of Nebraska Press, 1994), 42.

[10] The Indian Reorganization Act and its application to Alaska are discussed more fully in Section 1 of Chapter 9 on Alaska Natives.

[11] See also Chapter 9 for details on the provisions of ANCSA and its pros and cons.

[12] See Box 2.3 in Chapter 2.

[13] For attitudes in the western states toward the federal government in these years, see Richard H. Foster, "The Federal Government and the West," in, Thomas, *Politics and Public Policy in the Contemporary American West.*

[14] Alaska Statehood commission advisory vote, at http://ballotpedia.org/wiki/index.php/Alaska_Statehood_Commission_Advisory_Vote_%281980%29.

[15] See the provisions of the initiative at http://ballotpedia.org/wiki/index.php/Alaska_State_Ownership_of_Federal_Land_Initiative_%281982%29.

[16] Alaska Statehood Commission, *More Perfect Union: A Preliminary Report* (Juneau, AK: 1982); Foster, "The Federal Government and the West," 83; and McBeath and Morehouse, *Alaska Politics and Government*, 87.

[17] On the Wickersham, see editorial, *Anchorage Daily Times*, January 29, 1972.

[18] Malcolm B. Roberts, ed., *Going Up in Flames: The Promises and Pledges of Alaska Statehood Under Attack* (Anchorage: Alaska Pacific University Press, for Commonwealth North, 1990). For a review of the book see *Journal of the West* 31, no. 2 (April 1992): 116.

[19] Walter J. Hickel, "Feds have Abused Their Compact with Alaska," *Anchorage Daily News*, January 3, 2009.

[20] See Chapter 6 on the Alaska economy and Chapter 8 on state revenues, esp. Table 8.1, Chapter 12 on the role of government, Table 12.1, and Scott Goldsmith and Eric Larson, "Federal Spending and Revenues in Alaska" (Anchorage: Institute of Social and Economic Research , ISER, University of Alaska, 2003).

[21] A fuller analysis of the place of IGR in several development and resources issues is provided in Chapters 21 through 24.

[22] Interview with former Governor Tony Knowles, by Clive Thomas and Anthony Nakazawa, June 2, 2008.

[23] Julie Kitka, Presentation to Commonwealth North on April 20, 1999.

[24] Julia O'Malley, "Feds We Loath You, Please Send Money," *Anchorage Daily News*, January 22, 2010.

[25] Interview with former Governor Tony Knowles.

[26] Charles Homans, "State of Dependence: Ted Stevens's Alaska Problem—and Ours," *The Washington Monthly*, November 2007, 13.

[27] *Ibid.*, 17.

[28] *Ibid.*, 15.

[29] Liz Ruskin, "Walker's appointee for top DC job? No one," *Alaska News Nightly*, Alaska Public Radio Network (APRN), November 12, 2015.

[30] See Chapter 30, Box 30.1, for a perspective on what Stevens's defeat and death may mean for Alaska's economic and political future.

[31] See Chapter 8 on state revenues, Figure 8.8, for a comparison of congressional earmarks for Alaska in 2009 and 2010.

[32] Carl Hulse, "Senate Won't Allow Earmarks in Spending Bills," *New York Times* [*The Caucus: the Political and Government of the Times*], February 1, 2011; Patti Epler, "Murkowski Wants Alaska Prepared for 'World without Earmarks,'" *Alaska Dispatch*, February 24, 2011; Peter Granitz, "Congress may Lift So-called Earmark Ban Next Year," *Alaska News Nightly* (APRN), August 21, 2012.

[33] Figure 10.2 goes only to 2005 and not to 2015. This is for two reasons. First, there is a time lag with such data that is often as long as four years. More importantly, the stimulus package money that came to the states in 2009 and 2010 as a result of the major national and international economic

downturn in 2008 and beyond was an aberration and distorts the general trend. Thus, we end the comparison at 2005. However, judging by the close to fifty years covered by the figure, this upward trend in state dependence on federal funds is likely to continue regardless of the rhetoric of national budget cuts and one- or two-year aberrations in funding.

[34] G. Larry Mayes and William Taggart, "Intergovernmental Relations and Native American Gaming: A Case Study on the Emergence of a New Intergovernmental Participant," *The American Review of Public Administration*, 35, no. 1 (2005): 74–93.

⋆ CHAPTER 11 ⋆

Alaska and the World: The Achievements, Potential, and Limits of Public Policy and Private Initiatives

Douglas K. Barry

Since statehood, Alaska's state and local governments and their citizens have engaged in a range of international activities. Past and present, most of these interactions, especially by state government, have been conducted with an eye to generating economic benefits. Alaska's international activities, however, have not always been motivated purely by economic gain. There have been other motivations that have provided benefits to Alaskans.

This chapter looks at the broad range of Alaska's interactions with the world as an aspect of state public policy, explores the motives for this engagement, and, as the title of the chapter indicates, assesses the successes, the potential, and the limits of this interaction. This is a much broader focus than that of Chapter 7, which concentrates specifically on Alaska's interactions with the world as they relate to the economy. Here we deal with aspects of external economic activity not covered in Chapter 7, such as the role of international trade offices and economic relations with Canada.

The engagement of Alaska state government and its citizens with the international community is wide-ranging. It embraces everything from the economic activities covered in Chapter 7, to a delegation of Alaska legislators and businesspeople visiting one of the state's major trading partners, to university faculty collaborating with their counterparts in other Arctic countries on research, to the private and personal travel and dealings of individual public officials and citizens. In this chapter we narrow the focus of international interactions by covering those most significant to the state politically, economically, socially, and culturally.

The first section of the chapter outlines the various types of international relations in which Alaska and its citizens have been involved. Next is a short history of this involvement since statehood. Then we present four diverse case studies. In combination, the historical overview and the case studies enable us to identify the characteristics of Alaska's international interactions and explain and assess the mixed record of state government in this policy area. The conclusion shows how Alaska's international policy record is a good example of the contrast between the ideal and the practicalities of politics.

1. THE RANGE OF PUBLIC INTERNATIONAL INTERACTIONS OF THE STATES

The role of the states in the international sphere is another dimension of their intergovernmental relations (IGR). However, the nature of American federalism places limitations on state relations with foreign governments. The legal basis for these limitations is found in Article I, Section 10, of the U.S. Constitution: "No state shall enter into any Treaty, Alliance or Confederation . . ." Under U.S. Supreme Court interpretations of the Constitution, states are also prohibited from entering into treaties, having other official agreements, and having formal diplomatic relations with foreign governments. The Constitution places these matters solely with the federal government.

Clearly, however, on certain issues the states have an interest in decisions made by foreign governments, including treaties or other agreements that the national government makes with a foreign country that may directly affect them. Moreover, all fifty states have a direct economic interest in foreign commerce to the extent it benefits their own economies. Given the needs of state and local governments as well as other organizations to deal with foreign governments, they utilize the various permissible forms of international relations not prohibited by federal law. Box 11.1 outlines the various types of state interaction with foreign governments. Alaska's interactions reflect this pattern of state-international relationships, with some differences attributable to the unique nature of the state, its inhabitants, and its geographical location.

2. PUBLIC POLICIES AND PRIVATE INITIATIVES: A SHORT HISTORY OF ALASKA'S INTERNATIONAL ACTIVITIES

As former Alaska Lieutenant Governor Fran Ulmer explained:

> Due to our economy (based on natural resources and exports, dependent upon foreign markets, investors, and so on) it has always been more important for us to understand and communicate with other countries than is the case with most states. For this reason, Alaska was at the forefront of establishing overseas trade offices and sending trade delegations abroad.[1]

BOX 11.1

Types of International Relations of the Fifty States and Alaska with Foreign Governments

The interactions of the fifty states and their local governments with foreign governments fall into six major categories: (1) ongoing contacts, (2) state-sponsored programs, (3) local government-to-local government contacts, (4) intergovernmental organizational contacts; (5) international NGO (nongovernmental organization) interactions, and (6) private nonprofit contacts.

1. ONGOING INDIRECT AND DIRECT INTERNATIONAL INTERACTIONS OF THE STATES

These interactions are probably more important in their economic and political impact than the other five types of contacts combined. Thus, they are the most important international concern to state policy makers. These interactions are of two major types: relations through the federal government involving treaties and international agreements, and promotion of international commerce by individual states.

Treaties and Agreements Affecting Individual States

When a treaty or agreement is being negotiated or amended, the federal government usually consults the states affected, either through their congressional delegations or their governors or both. Affected states are also often represented on international councils or commissions that affect them directly. An Alaska example is the Pacific Flyway Council. This is a consortium of western states, including Alaska, plus Canada and Mexico, that advises the U.S. Fish and Wildlife Service (USFWS) in establishing annual migratory bird hunting regulations.

The Promotion of International Commerce by Individual States

All states and their policy makers, from those with giant economies like California's to small ones such as Vermont and Alaska, are interested in promoting international trade with their state. By encouraging such trade, the vast majority of state policy makers are mainly concerned with a one-way process. That is, each state wants to sell its goods and services abroad and encourage foreign investment in the state—activities that broaden the state's economic base or increase its revenues. Two-way trade, which includes foreign imports purchased and consumed by their state's citizens, is less desirable economically. Alaska is no different in encouraging one-way trade.

To promote international economic activity, states set up trade offices or missions in various countries, especially the larger economies of East Asia, Western Europe, Canada, and Latin America. Plus, delegations of state officials, often headed by the governor or the head of the state department of commerce or trade, visit countries with major economies to boost or encourage trade with their state. International commerce is promoted by Alaska's Office of International Trade, which is part of the Office of the Governor, as well as by the Alaska Department of Commerce, Community, and Economic Development.

2. STATE FUNDED AND SPONSORED INTERNATIONAL PROGRAMS

States often fund various types of international interactions, including aiding nonprofit organizations to help promote trade, aiding state delegation's participation in nongovernmental international organizations, and university programs. Alaska, for instance, helps organizations like the Alaska Travel Industry Association promote international travel to Alaska.

3. LOCAL GOVERNMENT-TO-LOCAL GOVERNMENT INTERACTIONS

Local governments often interact with local governments in other countries due to close proximity and mutual concerns, as with Detroit, Michigan's special relationship with its close neighbor Windsor, Ontario. Local governments often set up a sister city arrangement to promote public official and citizen exchanges, including educational opportunities. In Alaska, for example, Juneau in Southeast Alaska and Whitehorse in Canada's Yukon Territory have had a long history of interactions.

4. INTERGOVERNMENTAL ORGANIZATION INTERACTIONS

Intergovernmental organizations bring together state, provincial, regional, and local governments, often under the auspices of their national governments, to address problems of mutual interest or concern. For instance, California and many of its local governments near the Mexican border cooperate on such concerns as waste management and tourism promotion. Particular to Alaska, the state has input into the activities of the Arctic Council, an intergovernmental organization that addresses issues faced by Arctic countries and their indigenous peoples.

5. INTERNATIONAL NONGOVERNMENTAL INTERACTIONS

International nongovernmental organizations (NGOs), of which particular groups in a state or state affiliates are members, work to promote international interactions. These include exchanging information on issues, educational programs, and an advocacy role with their home governments and international organizations like the United Nations. An Alaska example is the Inuit Circumpolar Council-Alaska (ICC-AK), a member of the Inuit Circumpolar Council (ICC). The ICC promotes the interests of some 155,000 Inuit of the United States, Canada, Greenland, and Russia.

6. PRIVATE NONPROFIT ORGANIZATIONS PROMOTING STATE-FOREIGN GOVERNMENT INTERACTIONS

Private nonprofits are focused mostly on promoting international trade, but some focus on other issues. Examples in Alaska include the World Trade Center Alaska (WTCAK), which provides international trade and business services to members and community partners across the state. In contrast, the Institute of the North focuses on Arctic issues, but is not confined to promoting Alaska's economic benefits.

Source: Developed by the author.

Ulmer's reference here is to Alaska's international dealings for economic purposes. Indeed, as previously noted, the economic motive has been the dominant one for such interactions and policy development. Nevertheless, reflecting the range of international activities in Box 11.1, Alaska has engaged in a broad range of contacts over the years involving both the public and private sectors.

Interactions through the Federal Government

The federal government included Alaska in international issues and policies even before it became a state. Most notable is the International Halibut Commission (IHC), which dates back to 1923. The commission regulates catch limits and deals with other issues regarding halibut off Canadian and U.S. shores. The IHC has three representatives from each country. At least one (and often two) of the U.S. delegates reside in Alaska. In the 1940s Alaska's territorial government was involved in the planning of the Alaska Highway, much of which runs through Canada. Since statehood, the federal government has either involved Alaska or protected the state in a range of international concerns, including fisheries issues (particularly conflicts with Canada and Japan over their boats entering Alaska waters to fish), Arctic issues, and aid to Alaska Natives through organizations such as the International Whaling Commission (IWC).

Alaskans might rightly argue that some federal government actions adversely affect their state. They have little to complain about, however, regarding international representation by the national government. For much of the period of statehood this positive relationship was aided by the influence of the late Senator Ted Stevens.

The State's Direct International Activities

As Box 11.1 points out, most of Alaska state government's international activities have been to boost its exports and investment in Alaska, either directly or through support to organizations that aid this goal. The two major direct vehicles used by the state have been sending delegations on trade missions to individual countries and setting up trade offices. For the first thirty years following statehood, Alaska established several trade offices in East Asia staffed by state employees. In recent years, however, as international business relationships, particularly between U.S. and Asia-based companies, have matured, so has trade representation. Like many states in the nation, Alaska has moved toward a contract trade representation system rather than using state employees. Trade representatives assist Alaska businesses by making in-country contacts, collecting general or specific market information, and distributing information from Alaska state agencies to interested organizations in each of their countries as appropriate. The representatives also organize Alaska participation in various trade shows.

As of late 2015, Alaska had three contracted overseas trade offices. These were in Japan (Tokyo), Taiwan (Taipei), and China (Beijing), each of which originally had a trade office staffed by state employees. The state established its first overseas trade office in 1965 in Tokyo, the first state to establish an office there. Alaska was also the first to establish a trade office in South Korea (Seoul) in 1986, though currently there is no trade representation in Seoul. Trade representation in Taiwan began in the late 1980s, before a formal trade office was established there in the early 1990s. A trade office was set up in Beijing in 2002.[2]

Over the years, besides general state activity, individual state agencies have worked to promote various Alaska products. Particularly notable is the Alaska Seafood Marketing Institute (ASMI). Since 1987 it has participated in federal export assistance programs, currently the Market Access Program administered by the U.S. Department of Agriculture's Foreign Agricultural Service. In 2015 ASMI had trade representatives throughout Europe (one each for Central and Western, Northern, Southern, and Eastern Europe), in Japan, China, and Brazil. ASMI's international promotional activities, however, are not limited to those areas.

In addition, Alaska has sent trade missions to a number of countries and hosted many missions in Alaska, including the first trade mission to China by Governor Jay Hammond in 1979. Since 2000, at least two or three outbound trade missions headed by a state official have occurred each year. And the State of Alaska receives ten to thirty international delegations in any given year. Some are trade related while others are government-to-government exchanges.[3]

The Development of Other Interactions and the Mixed Role of State Government Involvement and Support

Particularly since the early 1980s, the state and its local governments have worked with and through other organizations to promote international commerce and other international activities. In fact, much of Alaska's international activity has been initiated and maintained by nonprofit organizations. Generally, state support for international interactions has been mixed, waxing or waning depending on a confluence of circumstances.

The Role of Alaska Local Governments

The international activities of local governments have mainly been through sister city programs. Even in these programs, however, commercial interests often exist just below the surface of the programs' stated goals.[4] The level of local government activities, both economic and noneconomic, tends to fluctuate from time to time depending on particular events.

Besides cities in East Asia, several major Alaska cities established relationships with cities in the Russian Far East (RFE) in the early 1990s after the fall of the Soviet Union in 1990. The enthusiasm and interactions began to wane, however, when expectations of major gains to Alaska were not realized and for other reasons explained in Section 6.

University of Alaska Involvement

The fluctuating levels of state support for international programs can be seen in the state's interactions with various organizations over the past three decades regarding both potential economic gains and other involvement. Two examples from the University of Alaska Anchorage (UAA) illustrate this point.

One was the now defunct American Russian Center (ARC), which existed between 1992 and 2007. The other was the now also defunct Alaska Center for International Business (ACIB). ACIB was established at UAA in the mid 1980s by the Alaska Legislature with a push from Governor Steve Cowper. He lobbied hard for funding, including a $2 million endowment. But the state later withdrew its support in hard economic times. The center taught university courses, conducted teachers' institutes, supported faculty research, and generated millions of dollars in federal grants for programs in the RFE.

International Intergovernmental Organizations, Nongovernmental Organizations (NGOs), and Nonprofits

Several other organizations, ranging from public to nonprofit and private entities, have been particularly important in promoting international interactions. Sometimes these organizations have been utilized or aided financially by the state, and sometimes they act independently.

One of these organizations was mentioned in Box 11.1, the private nonprofit World Trade Center Alaska (WTCAK), established in 1987.[5] Its function is primarily economic, with a mission to assist Alaskans to successfully compete for trade and investment in the global marketplace. WTCAK is involved in activities all over the world. The organization has several sources of funding, including the state, the U.S. Department of Commerce, and private company memberships. WTCAK is the official representative of the U.S. Department of Commerce in Alaska.

Other groups and organizations have a combined economic and noneconomic role and tend to focus their activities on the northern regions and the Arctic. Two of them promote interactions of segments of Alaska's Native population with other indigenous peoples and also act as advocacy groups. One, also mentioned in Box 11.1, is the Inuit Circumpolar Council (ICC, formerly the Inuit Circumpolar Conference), founded in 1977 by the Alaska Inuit leader Eben Hopson. The ICC is an alliance among the Inuit peoples of the Arctic that includes Russia, Alaska (ICC-AK), Canada, and Greenland. ICC works to promote Inuit rights and interests on an international level, with a particular focus on strengthening cultural practices and values through environmental protection, sustainable marine mammal, wildlife, and fisheries policies, and economic and social development.[6] The other organization, the Alaska Eskimo Whaling Commission (AEWC), is considered in a case study in Section 4.

Four other organizations deal more broadly with northern and Arctic issues. Three of them were established in the 1990s.[7] The first to be set up was the Northern Forum, formed in 1991 with major input and personal funding from Governor Hickel. Headquartered in Anchorage until the end of 2013, the Forum is a nonprofit international organization composed of subnational and regional governments from Canada, China, Iceland, Japan, Norway, Russia, and South Korea. The United States was represented until 2011, when the State of Alaska pulled out. This precipitated the closure of the Anchorage office and relocation of the headquarters to Yakutsk in the RFE, though many Alaskans still participate in the organization. The forum seeks to strengthen connections among all Northerners, particularly decision makers, and to share ideas about common problems related to issues such as remoteness, sustainable development, and the interface of the public and private sectors. Membership is available to regional and subregional governments, municipalities (where there is no regional entity), businesses, nonprofits, and NGOs. The forum sponsors conferences and other events in member nations. The organization also partners with the United Nations, the Arctic Council, and the Forum of Global Associations of Regions (FOGAR), among others.

The second organization is the Arctic Council, established in 1996 with eight member countries (Canada, Denmark, Finland, Iceland, Norway, Russia, Sweden, and the United States), and headquartered in Tromsø, Norway. The council provides a means for cooperation, coordination, and interaction among Arctic countries, with the involvement of the Arctic indigenous communities and other inhabitants on common issues. It is particularly concerned with issues of sustainable development and environmental protection and has conducted studies on several topics, including climate change, oil and gas, and Arctic shipping.

The third organization is the Institute of the North, established in 1994, also by Governor Hickel acting in a personal capacity. It became a nonprofit organization in 2003. Based in Anchorage, the Institute is mainly concerned with issues relating to use of commonly owned public resources and their use in northern regions, and sharing Alaska's experience on these issues. Within this mission the organization focuses on infrastructure and resource development issues. It works with state, national, and international policy makers as well as public, private, academic, and indigenous organizations. The Institute holds several conferences and speaker presentations each year and often partners with the state. An example of such a partnership occurred in the summer of 2011 when the Institute organized a visit to Norway for the state, including several legislators, to study how that country handles its extensive oil revenues.

The fourth organization was formed more recently. It is the Arctic Circle, set up in 2013 by two cofounders, President Ólafur Grímsson of Iceland and *Alaska Dispatch* (now the *Alaska Dispatch News*) publisher Alice Rogoff. The organization works to promote discussion among political and business leaders, environmental experts, scientists, indigenous representatives, and other international interested parties to address climate change issues.

In its short history, the Arctic Circle has held three assemblies (2013, 2014, and 2015) attended by more than 1,800 people and has received considerable media attention. One reason for the media interest in its fall 2014 meeting in Reykjavik, Iceland, was the attendance of the newly appointed U.S. Special Representative to the Arctic, Coast Guard Admiral Robert J. Papp, Jr. He leads the U.S. delegation to the Arctic Council and has been a major force in the body as the United States acts as chair for the group in 2015–2017. Although the State of Alaska is not officially associated with the Arctic Circle, many Alaskans, including Alaska Native leaders, ICC-AK members, several Alaska state and local public officials, and members of organizations with interest in the Arctic, have attended the assemblies.

From the General to Specifics: Four Case Studies

These, then, have been the major developments, interactions, and organizations involved in Alaska's contact with the world since statehood. Next we present four case studies that reflect the broad range of Alaska's international activities and that also help identify the characteristics of this involvement past and present, as well as explain and evaluate state government's mixed involvement in this policy area. Three of the examples are ongoing: the state's relations with its neighbor Canada, the role of the AEWC, and Alaska's involvement in the Arctic and circumpolar north. The fourth case study, the spate of interest in Alaska-Russian Far East relations in the 1990s and early 2000s, is no longer a major part of Alaska's international activities, but has important lessons to offer.

3. ALASKA AND CANADA

Most Alaskans are barely aware of their Canadian neighbor and the important ways in which Canada affects the state diplomatically, politically, culturally, and particularly economically.[8] Map 11.1 shows the geographical connection between Alaska and western Canada.

Alaska's economic relations with Canada are very important and have been increasing in importance in recent years. Table 11.1 sets out the contribution of Canada to the Alaska economy in 2008 as well as the significant contribution of Canadian mining activity to the state since the early 1980s. In 2013 Canada was the fourth-largest market for Alaska products (behind China, South Korea, and Japan). By that same year, the value of Alaska's exports to Canada had almost doubled, from $370 million in 2008 to $604 million. The number of Canadian visitors to Alaska had almost tripled to over 326,000 by 2013, and the amount of money they spent had almost doubled, to $164 million. Moreover, in 2011 Canada was the second-largest source of direct investment in Alaska. The Canadians are earnest and long term about their investments in Alaska. For a while the Canadians had a consulate in Anchorage (2007–2012), but cuts in the national budget forced its closure.

Of particular note is the Canadian contribution to Alaska's natural resource extraction industries, including oil and gas, but particularly mining, as Table 11.1 indicates. Canadian companies provide high-paying jobs in mining. In 2013, for instance, Canadian mining companies employed 1,700 Alaskans who earned an average of $87,000 a year. Many communities in Alaska depend heavily on these investments, including Kotzebue with the Red Dog Mine, one of the world's largest producers of zinc. The Fort Knox mine near Fairbanks also contributes to that city's economy. Canadian companies partner with Alaska Native for-profit regional corporations in several ways, including mining. The impact of Canada on Alaska's economy will almost certainly be as great if not more so in the foreseeable future.

MAP 11.1

Alaska and Western Canada

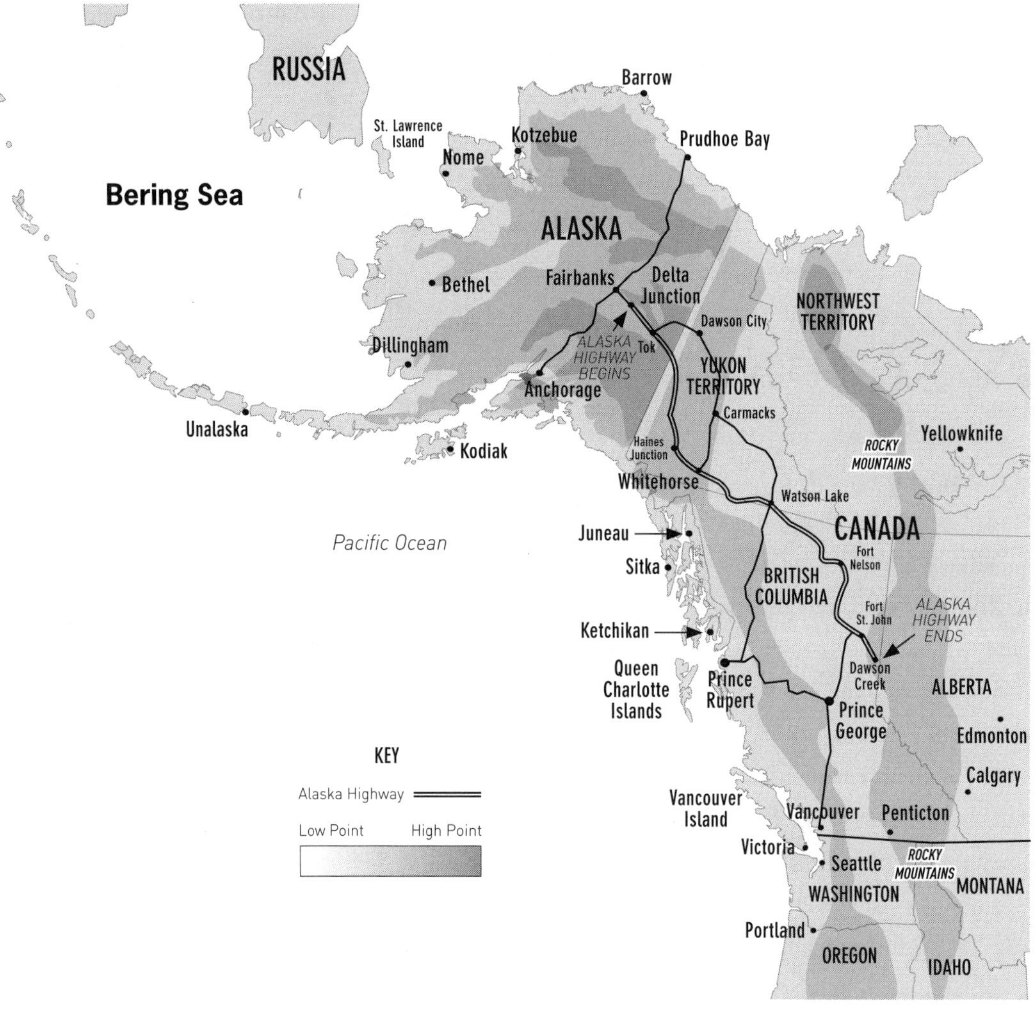

Source: Developed by the author.

For the most part, Alaska Canadian relations are amicable, but there have been conflicts over the years. These include a 2014–15 political spat that got international media coverage. The spat was over using U.S.-made steel to do renovations on the Prince Rupert ferry terminal, which is on British Columbian (BC) soil and which Alaska leases from BC as part of the Alaska Marine Highway System. The "Buy America" provision of U.S. federal law required the use of American steel and American workers on the renovation project. This infuriated Canadian contractors. Governor Walker could have waived the "Buy

TABLE 11.1

Canada's Economic Impact on Alaska

GENERAL STATISTICS FOR 2008	
Total Canada-related trade value	$1.2 billion
Alaska's exports to Canada	$370 million
Alaska's imports from Canada	$441 million
Total Alaska employment and payroll attributable to Canadian economic activity in Alaska	8,500 jobs, $430 million in payroll
Number of Canadian visitors to Alaska and their spending	116,000 who spent about $91 million
Number of cruise visitors to Canada and Alaska in 2008	1,033,000
MINING ACTIVITY IN 2008 AND OVER THE PREVIOUS 30 YEARS	
Number of Canadian mining companies operating in Alaska in 2008	38 companies
Amount these 38 companies spent on exploration in Alaska in 2008	$163 million
Amount the 38 companies spent on development in Alaska in 2008	$304 million
Alaska's exports by Canadian mining companies in 2008 (minus their mineral commodity exports to Canada)	$398 million
Canada's approximate share of total mining industry exploration and development expenditures, 1981-2008	70%
Total investment in mining exploration and development by Canadian companies, 1981-2008	$3.9 billion

Source: McDowell Group Inc. (2009), "Canada's Impact on Alaska," prepared for the Consulate of Canada in Anchorage, http://www.canadainternational.gc.ca/anchorage/offices-bureaux/canada_alaska.aspx?lang=eng.

America" provision, but declined to do so. The dispute was ongoing as of 2016.[9] Another ongoing dispute is over many BC mining developments across the border from Southeast Alaska and their possible damaging effects on salmon-spawning rivers that flow across the border into Alaska. This could drastically affect the fishing industry in the region as well as the subsistence lifestyle of Alaska Natives. These concerns are similar to those regarding the Pebble and Donlin Creek Mines in Southwest Alaska, also being developed by Canadian companies, which are also a source of conflict because of potential harm to the salmon harvest. The cross-border mining versus salmon disputes between BC and Alaska have a long history, as former Alaska Governor Tony Knowles points out in Box 11.2.[10] Knowles looks at the mix of cooperative and antagonistic diplomatic, political, and cultural relationships between Alaska and Canada. He emphasizes, however, that there are many reasons for Alaska to maintain good relations with its neighbor.

Given the importance of Canada to Alaska's economy and its many cultural ties, one might expect some consistent and ongoing policy to sustain and enhance Alaska-Canada relations, perhaps through state funding of university and other programs. Like many of

BOX 11.2

Alaska-Canadian Relations: A Perspective by Former Alaska Governor Tony Knowles

The geographical boundaries of Canada and Alaska defy logic. Western Canada and Alaska should be one country, and there would be no panhandle sliver of Alaska territory land-locking much of western Canada from the Pacific Ocean. Regardless of borders, the cultural, ecological, and economic similarities and the many common interests of Alaska and western Canada make a compelling case for cooperation.

This common-sense attitude, however, did not help when I was informed by my Chief of Staff by satellite phone while traveling on the Yukon River, that Canadian fishermen, with the tacit support of the British Columbia (BC) government, had hijacked an Alaska State ferry in protest against the actions of Alaska fishermen. Fortunately, calmer heads prevailed between Alaska and federal Canadian leaders. The vessel was freed without harm to property or the startled local and tourist passengers.

Later Alaska won a victory in Canadian courts on the hijacking and reached a settlement with the BC government for damages. Another positive outcome of this incident was that a long neglected and abandoned fishing treaty was negotiated between the U.S. federal government, states in the Pacific Northwest, American Northwest Indian tribes, and the Canadian federal government. For the first time, the treaty allowed harvesting only sustainable yields to insure proper conservation and future fish returns.

This was not the only modern Alaska-Canadian friction. In Southwest Alaska, a decades-long stalemate festered concerning the Yukon River Salmon Treaty. Migrating over two thousand miles to spawning grounds in Canada, Yukon chinook (or king salmon) and the Yukon chum salmon are the major subsistence foods for indigenous people of Alaska and Canada. Fair distribution of the catch, while ensuring the necessary escapement for biological sustainability, is a complex and emotional issue. A precipitous drop in salmon runs in the mid and late 1990s added to the tension. Fortunately, common goals and common cultural practices, mutual understanding, and enlightened leadership in the region brought about a fair and enduring agreement.

Another Alaska-Canadian link is the porcupine caribou herd which migrates thousand of miles yearly from the calving grounds on the North Slope coastal plain in Northeast Alaska to the interior Yukon in Canada. The caribou are the major food source for many villages of Athabascan Indians in Alaska and First Nation tribes in the Yukon. Not surprisingly, Alaska and Canadian Indian tribes are fierce protectors of the calving grounds in Alaska and, therefore, strongly against the proposed oil field exploration in the heart of that area, the coastal plain of the Arctic National Wildlife Refuge (ANWR). This opposition has been one of many reasons why ANWR remains closed to development.

Sustainable resource development has been a source of controversy in other areas. The Taku River in Southeast Alaska is the spawning ground of the five species of Pacific salmon. Canadian and Alaska subsistence, commercial, and sport fisheries depend on this productive fishery. Yet, the development of the Tulsequah Chief Mine at the headwaters of the river in Canada poses a serious threat to the continued health of this fishery as do several other proposed mines in the area. Despite protests by the state of Alaska from 1996 to 2002, asking that this be reviewed by the International Joint Commission established by the Border Waters Treaty Act of 1909, the issues surrounding mining development remain a continuing dispute.

Two other alliances between Canada and Alaska are examples of successful collaboration. One is the Inuit Circumpolar Conference (ICC). The second alliance is the effective, science-driven, sustainable fishery of the International Pacific Halibut Commission (IHC). With major Alaska participation, the IHC has a stellar record in stock assessment and basic halibut biology. It establishes the maximum harvest level based upon extensive field research. There has been agreement that the protection of the species is the first priority of the Commission's action and there has been an unbroken record of protection, agreement, and cooperation.

Relationships between closely connected regions are never static. A recently emerged issue of particular consequence is managing global climate change in the Arctic where the effects are significantly more profound than any place on the globe. Another issue is the possibility of one day building an Alaska gas pipeline that may go through Canada. Continuing the collaborative approach by Alaska and Canada to strategic policy development and implementation is essential for future success of both places.

Source: Developed by Clive Thomas and Anthony Nakazawa based on an interview with former Governor Tony Knowles, March 8, 2009.

Alaska's other international endeavors, however, the Canadian relationship is sustained by personal interest and event-driven opportunity or crisis, often combined with serendipity. But there are some exceptions. The University of Alaska Anchorage (UAA), for example, has had a Canadian Studies program for some years that is partly funded by the Canadian government. The program provides a scholarly basis for studying the Alaska-Canadian relationship and produces students with a grasp of its complexity and its prospects. In 2004 the Elizabeth Tower Endowment for Canadian Studies was created, offering hope that local and even national philanthropy plus more state support would provide for the kind of engagement Alaska needs with the cultures, politics, and economies that share its part of the world.

4. THE INTERNATIONAL WHALING COMMISSION

This case involves a segment of the Alaska Native community and the federal government, aided by the State of Alaska, to win a major victory for subsistence rights in an international forum. The International Whaling Commission (IWC) has the authority to allocate the number of whales taken in any given year throughout the world for any purpose. The concern of the North Slope Inupiaq people was to first get a seat on the IWC and then obtain a quota of bowhead whales to meet their subsistence needs. Box 11.3 explains the development of the IWC and the Alaska Eskimo Whaling Commission (AWEC) and the politics involved in getting this quota approved. It shows, in part, that despite the federal government having the exclusive authority to negotiate and implement the agreement, it has allowed the AEWC and the State of Alaska a major role in the process.

This case study is an excellent example of how a segment of Alaska's population, under the right political circumstances, with political coordination and skillful leadership, can succeed in the tough political arena of international politics. The Alaska delegation bargained with big political powerhouses like Japan, Iceland, and Norway and the other commission members. Not only did they obtain their own quota, they also obtained one for the powerless Native people of the Russian Far East, who relate culturally to the Alaska Inupiaq people but had no seat at the table.

Scott Smullen, a spokesperson for NOAA (the National Oceanic and Atmospheric Administration, which worked with the U.S. Department of State to get Alaska Natives their seat), explained that it was persistence and detailed knowledge of whale behavior that won the day and secured the quotas. Smullen said that representatives at IWC meetings tried many strategies, including intimidation, to get the Alaskans to accept a lesser deal, but they held firm.[11]

As to the overall role played by Alaska Natives in the conservation of this and other marine species, the U.S. Deputy Commissioner for the IWC, Douglas DeMaster, had this to say:

> Prior to the direct involvement of Alaska Native subsistence hunters in the research and management of bowhead whales off Alaska, serious mistakes were made regarding their estimation of abundance and the importance of meat from bowheads to the communities involved with subsistence whaling. Since the co-management agreement was negotiated, there have been no such mistakes and access to the animals by subsistence hunters has continued without substantial problems, as has cooperative life history-related research on landed whales. . . . This program is considered one of the most successful of its kind, and has been copied by many other Native and federal resource co-management organizations for other species including seal, walrus, polar bears, and belugas.[12]

In short, Alaska Natives' participation in the IWC has contributed scientific knowledge and practical experience to an international organization whose membership touches every important body of water in which marine mammals live.

5. THE ARCTIC AND CIRCUMPOLAR NORTH

Since 2010 there has been a flurry of activity and suggestions on how to take advantage of Alaska's Arctic location. For instance, in his address to the Alaska State Legislature in March 2012, then U.S. Senator Mark Begich was full of optimism about Alaska's future role in the Arctic:

> What we have is an enormous potential for us as a state. The question is, are we going to grab it and are we going to move it forward? . . . Nowhere do we enjoy new opportunities more than with Alaska's Arctic resources, oil and gas, minerals, fisheries, tourism, transportation, the list goes on and on.[13]

Then, Bill Walker, on the campaign trail a month before being elected Alaska's governor in November 2014, gave the following response as one of three major ways he intended to grow the Alaska economy: "Build up the role of Alaska as the nation's Arctic state, with responsible resource development, shipping centers, and a strong Coast Guard presence." After winning the election, within his first few days in office, Walker appointed an Arctic advisor to his staff.[14]

Many Alaskans share Begich's and Walker's enthusiasm for the Arctic as a new potential source of economic development in Alaska's constant search for broadening the base of its economy. These include U.S. Senator Lisa Murkowski, former lieutenant governor Mead Treadwell, State Senator Bert Stedman of Sitka, who sees the potential employment in the Ketchikan shipyard for building infrastructure for offshore drilling in the Arctic,

BOX 11.3

The International Whaling Commission and Alaska Public Policy

The first International Whaling Commission (IWC) annual meeting scheduled in Alaska was held in Anchorage in May 2007 and was attended by representatives of the Alaska Eskimo Whaling Commission (AWEC). Alaska Governor Sarah Palin addressed the gathering: "We know that successful management is all about achieving balance, and the Alaska Eskimo Whaling Commission is a model of co-management . . ."

Established in 1946, the IWC worked in the 1970s to regulate and ban Alaska Natives' subsistence harvest of bowhead whales. Tension over how the IWC researched and managed the whale populations in the Bering Sea led several Alaska Native communities to form the Alaska Eskimo Whaling Commission (AWEC) in 1977. Because of its international role, formal authority to deal with the IWC is placed with the federal government. However, federal management authority has been largely delegated to the AEWC by a cooperative agreement between the U.S. Department of Commerce, the U.S. National Oceanic and Atmospheric Administration (NOAA), and AEWC. In addition, even though the State of Alaska has no formal authority to regulate subsistence whaling, politically the state has had a significant impact on the policy.

IWC's purpose is to maintain conservation of whale stocks by limiting the number, size, and species of whales harvested, and to determine areas for sanctuaries and seasons for harvesting different species of whales. It is aided by a scientific committee that presents research findings to the commission and makes recommendations. IWC membership, currently at seventy-six members, is open to any nation that adheres to the guidelines of the convention, with each member country having one commissioner.

AEWC's major roles are to advocate politically for the whaling rights of Alaska Native communities, assist in research and management of the resource, and promote education and outreach to the general public about subsistence whaling. Ten whaling communities, including Gambell, Savoonga, and Barrow, have registered whaling captains and crews who are members of the AEWC.

In the late 1990s, politics within the IWC over Japanese commercial whaling resulted in failure of a subsistence quota for Alaska and Russian Natives being approved. Faced with a legal ban on whaling, Alaska Natives turned to their congressional delegation and governor. Through strenuous efforts by U.S. Senator Frank Murkowski and Governor Tony Knowles, political action was successful, and a quota was established for Inupiaq hunters by the IWC.

In February 2011, the AEWC passed a resolution asking the Alaska congressional delegation to introduce subsistence whaling legislation to protect against a possible quota denial from the IWC in 2012. Vice president of the AEWC, George Ahmaogak, said, "It's getting harder and harder to work with the International Whaling Commission." However, due to some intense lobbying, in their July 2012 meeting the IWC renewed the catch limits set in 2007 through the year 2018.

Source: Developed by Daniel Monteith, Associate Professor of Anthropology, University of Alaska Southeast in Juneau, and Clive S. Thomas.

the state legislature, which set up an Arctic Policy Commission (APC) in 2012, and Alice Rogoff.[15] This optimism may or may not be justified. The operative word as of 2015 is *potential* and not *realized* gains. An assessment of the potential of Alaska's involvement in the Arctic requires looking at how much Alaska can be directly involved in Arctic affairs of various types and at the state's role in the region in recent years.

As the only state in the nation located partly in the Arctic, Alaska shares similar benefits and challenges with other Arctic regions and nations. So, Alaska has much to gain from consultation and collaboration with other affected regions and nations to ensure the needs of their peoples are met. There are also opportunities for economic gain from the state's Arctic location.[16] Like most aspects of Alaska's international interactions, its activities in this region are conducted through various levels of government (federal, state, local, and intergovernmental), as well as quasi-governments, and nonprofit and for-profit organizations. Moreover, as in other areas of Alaska's relations with the world, different levels of government cooperate with each other and with other organizations.

Alaska's Arctic Involvement through the Federal Government

What complicates the relations and the role of the state and other organizations in international Arctic relations is that the United States as a nation has a major interest in dealing with Arctic countries. As an expert on Arctic policy, Lawson Brigham has observed that, "Globalization, climate change, and geopolitics converge in this already challenging region."[17] The coming to the fore of these and other issues has meant that Arctic politics as a part of international relations has increased in importance since the mid-1980s.

The U.S. federal government has certainly recognized the Arctic's military and national security significance, as evidenced by two statements and two actions. One statement to this effect was made by former U.S. Secretary of Defense Chuck Hagel at the International Security Forum in Halifax, Nova Scotia, in November 2013. The need for a U.S. military presence in the Arctic was reinforced in a second statement, this time by Hagel's successor, Ashton Carter. Carter's statement came in response to a question from Alaska's newly elected U.S. Senator Dan Sullivan during a Senate Armed Services Committee hearing on March 4, 2015.[18] The two actions were the appointment of Admiral Robert Papp as U.S. Special Representative to the Arctic by U.S. Secretary of State John Kerry and President Obama's establishment of an "Arctic Steering Committee" to guide federal policy and coordinate with state, local, and Native governments, research and academic institutions, and nonprofit organizations.[19]

There are various perspectives on the major motives of Arctic nations for their increased interest in the region. These range from those who see the region as having mostly military and territorial significance to those who view it primarily as having economic recourse potential.[20] Regardless of motives, Alaska's interests are inevitably going to be subordinated to those of the federal government.

When possible, the federal government does include Alaska and Alaskans in activities affecting the region. Admiral Papp visited Alaska soon after his appointment to get input from Alaskans on U.S. Arctic policy. Another recent example involves former Lieutenant

Governor and University of Alaska Anchorage (UAA) Chancellor Fran Ulmer. In 2011 President Obama appointed her to a three-year term as chair of the U.S. Arctic Research Commission (USARC). As chair, Ulmer's role is to advance federal Arctic research in coordination with the State of Alaska and international partners. USARC's current goals include expanding a federal emphasis on Arctic Ocean and climate research, improving efforts to prevent and respond to oil spills in ice-covered waters, and strengthening research in Arctic human health and indigenous languages and cultures. Then, in July 2014, Ulmer was also appointed as Advisor for Arctic Science and Policy to the U.S. Secretary of State. In this role she will work with Admiral Papp while the United States acts as chair of the Arctic Council from 2015 to 2017.[21]

Direct Involvement of Alaska

The direct involvement of the state and state-based nonprofit and for-profit organizations in Arctic affairs, as for most international interactions, is primarily motivated by the promise of economic benefit. This was clearly in the forefront of former Senator Begich's mind when he said "the federal government is beginning to recognize its part in developing the Arctic."[22] To this end, the state, particularly the executive branch, tends to support, directly or indirectly, policies that promote development and is lukewarm to policies that might impede it, such as conservation. Hence, the likely reason for withdrawing from the Northern Forum in 2011 was because the forum favored sustained development—a balancing between developing the Arctic and preserving its ecological and cultural uniqueness. And although the Institute of the North has a mission broader than economic development, it is certainly high on the institute's agenda and at the top of the list for the WTCAK. For instance, the two organizations teamed up to put on a conference in Anchorage in May 2012 titled "Arctic Ambitions: Commercial Development of the Arctic."[23]

There are, however, broader interests than the purely economic ones regarding the Arctic for many Alaskans. This is the case with the Arctic Policy Commission (APC) set up by the legislature, which submitted its report in February 2015. Its twenty-six members included ten legislators and experts throughout the state. One of the most important aspects of the commission's charge is to suggest ways to influence federal Arctic policy so that the needs of Alaskans come first. This includes economic development, the environment, living conditions in the Arctic, and other concerns that have been expressed by Alaska residents as the commission held hearings across the state. All of these matters were very much reflected in the commission's recommendations.[24]

Other involvement of Alaskans that is not purely economic includes the Arctic Imperative Summit, instituted by Alice Rogoff in Anchorage in 2012 to discuss and raise awareness of Arctic issues, particularly climate change.[25] Other activities include those of the Alaska Eskimo Whaling Commission, the Alaska affiliate of the Inuit Circumpolar Council, and the U.S. Arctic Research Commission. The University of Alaska has also worked to promote a broad range of activities and knowledge of the Arctic and circumpolar north. The Arctic Research Consortium of the United States (ARCUS), based at the University of Alaska Fairbanks (UAF), was formed in 1988 as a nonprofit member consortium of educational and scientific institutions having a substantial commitment to Arctic research. There is also a Northern Studies program at UAF that offers a doctorate. And in January 2012 Fran Ulmer was appointed as Resident Scholar on Arctic Research at UAA to help facilitate and offer consultation on teaching, research, public service, and entrepreneurial endeavors.

In addition, many Alaskans (as well as national and international interest groups) are concerned about the environmental costs of Arctic development and its effects on Alaska Native culture and lifestyle. These concerns were raised at the fall 2014 meeting of the Arctic Circle assembly, largely in response to the speech by Admiral Papp. Many Native and non-Native Alaskans do not see U.S. Arctic policy as taking their living needs, including protecting their food sources, into consideration. The co-chairs of the Alaska legislature's APC (Senator Lesil McGuire and Representative Bob Herron) wrote an open letter to Admiral Papp expressing these concerns.[26]

Lack of a Policy Consensus and Constraints on Reaping Major Benefits

These diverse political pressures both within Alaska and from Outside have meant that there is no consensus among Alaskans on Arctic policy. This lack of consensus is despite the APC report and legislation introduced in the Alaska legislature in 2015 to try to create a coordinated Alaska Arctic policy. Alaska's Arctic policy fragmentation is, in part, due to federal actions often trumping state actions on the Arctic. The federal government did so with economic development, one of the major recommendations of the APC when in early 2015 the Obama administration proposed more extensive limits on oil development in the Arctic National Wildlife Refuge (ANWR) and in the Chukchi Sea off the northwest coast of Alaska. Then, in his much publicized visit to Alaska in the late summer of 2015, President Obama focused on Alaska and the Arctic as the poster region for the effects of climate change. He visited receding glaciers and eroding communities to emphasize the need to develop clean energy. Less than a month earlier, however, he had approved Shell's final permit to conduct deep sea drilling for oil in the Chukchi Sea.[27] This sent a decidedly mixed message to Alaskans about development.

As with federal actions in other policy areas, federal action or inaction on the Arctic contributes to Alaska's policy fragmentation and lack of consensus on the Arctic because not all Alaskans are affected in the same way by national Arctic policy. For instance, an international agreement to limit oil and gas development in the region may upset developers in Alaska but please environmentalists. This reflects the Alaska political characteristic of the conflict between developers and environmentalists. Moreover, as federal political agendas change or need to be modified in the Arctic because of national or international pressures and developments, these federal actions will sometimes stymie and sometimes aid the state's efforts to reap major benefits from economic activity in the region.

Besides lack of consensus and the constraints imposed by the federal government, perhaps the most significant factor inhibiting Alaska from reaping a financial bonanza from the Arctic on a long-term predictable basis is the existence of major economic constraints.

The major activity envisioned in the Arctic by many Alaskans is oil and gas development. This, however, is fraught with logistical and economic hazards as well as opposition from environmentalists. The difficulty of drilling in the Arctic is illustrated by the problems that Shell Oil faced. By September 2015 the company had spent close to a decade and $8 billion on exploration with very little to show for it. Undaunted by major protests from Greenpeace and other environmental groups and buoyed by approval from the Obama administration, Shell started drilling in the summer of 2015. By the late summer, however, they decided to indefinitely suspend their Arctic exploration due to lack of a substantial oil and gas find. This was a major blow for those who see the Arctic as producing increased revenues for Alaska. These supporters had their optimism further undermined within a few weeks of Shell's announcement when the U.S. Corps of Engineers decided to halt development of a deep-water port at Nome and the U.S. Department of the Interior placed a two-year moratorium on lease sales in the Arctic due to lack of oil industry interest.[28] With all these setbacks, it will be at least a decade or two before Arctic oil produces any revenue, and maybe much longer.

Moreover, given the fluctuation of world oil prices, continued development of oil and gas in the Arctic and the state's anticipated revenue from it are uncertain and thus do not add any kind of long-term stability to the Alaska economy. Fluctuating oil prices inhibit Alaska's Arctic policy in another way. Even with the best of intentions, low oil prices, as were the case in late 2014 and on into 2016, mean that Alaska has less to spend on developing the Arctic through its own efforts. This was the major constraint on implementing the APC's recommendations in the spring of 2015.

As to a market for Alaska products, the population of the circumpolar north (excluding Canada with which significant trade has a long history, as explained earlier) is around fifty million, depending on how the region is defined. While this is not insignificant, the state and other organizations may be better served by focusing on larger markets like China, Japan, and Western Europe.

All this leads to the conclusion that Begich, Treadwell, and Walker, among many others, may be overly optimistic and their political rhetoric more in the realm of wishful thinking. It remains to be seen whether Governor Walker or future governors can build a hitherto elusive consensus on the Arctic among Alaskans. To be sure, business activity with the Arctic region can help the state economically, but it is no panacea—far from it. It is just one small piece in a large puzzle of dealing with the short- and long-term challenges faced by Alaska's economy. At the same time, there is certainly much to be gained by cultural, academic, and other interactions with the region that may result in increased economic benefits, among other things.

6. ALASKA AND THE RUSSIAN FAR EAST IN THE POST-SOVIET ERA

Alaska's connection with Russia has a long history, with over a century of Russian control before the Alaska Purchase by the United States in 1867. Place names, the Russian Orthodox religion, and ancestral ties of Native peoples across the Bering Strait, are reminders of that past. As a result, until World War II there was moderate interchange between Alaska and Russia, particularly the Russian Far East (RFE), a vast region stretching from Vladivostok in the south to Anadyr two thousand miles to the north. After 1945, with the onset of the Cold War, a sort of ice curtain descended between Alaska and the Soviet Union. During the Cold War (the late 1940s to the late 1980s) most travel was banned and, other than a few scientific exchanges, contact was minimal. Then, in the mid-1980s, Russian President Mikhail Gorbachev's political reforms of *perestroika* (restructuring of the Soviet political and economic system) and *glasnost* (openness to international contacts) eventually led to the collapse of the Soviet Union during 1989–90 and the opening of borders in 1992. As a result, relations between Alaska and the RFE burgeoned for a time.

For more than a decade thousands of Russians and Alaskans flew back and forth between Alaska and the RFE, taking advantage of newly established commercial airline routes by Alaska Airlines and Russia's national airline Aeroflot, as well as charter flights. Map 11.2 shows the air routes established between Alaska and the nearest RFE cities to take advantage of the perceived potential of burgeoning Alaska-RFE relations. The perceived potential was such that, for a time, businesses in Nome accepted Russian rubles. One early symbolic moment of the thaw in U.S.-Russian relations was an Aeroflot airliner landing at Anchorage International Airport. Out jumped smiling government officials, a dance troupe, and a rock band from Siberia.

Yet, by the mid-2000s, this had all petered out. The flurry of activity that took place, however, raises several questions: Who were the Alaska participants involved and what

MAP 11.2

The Alaska-Russian Far East Connection in the 1990s and Early 2000s

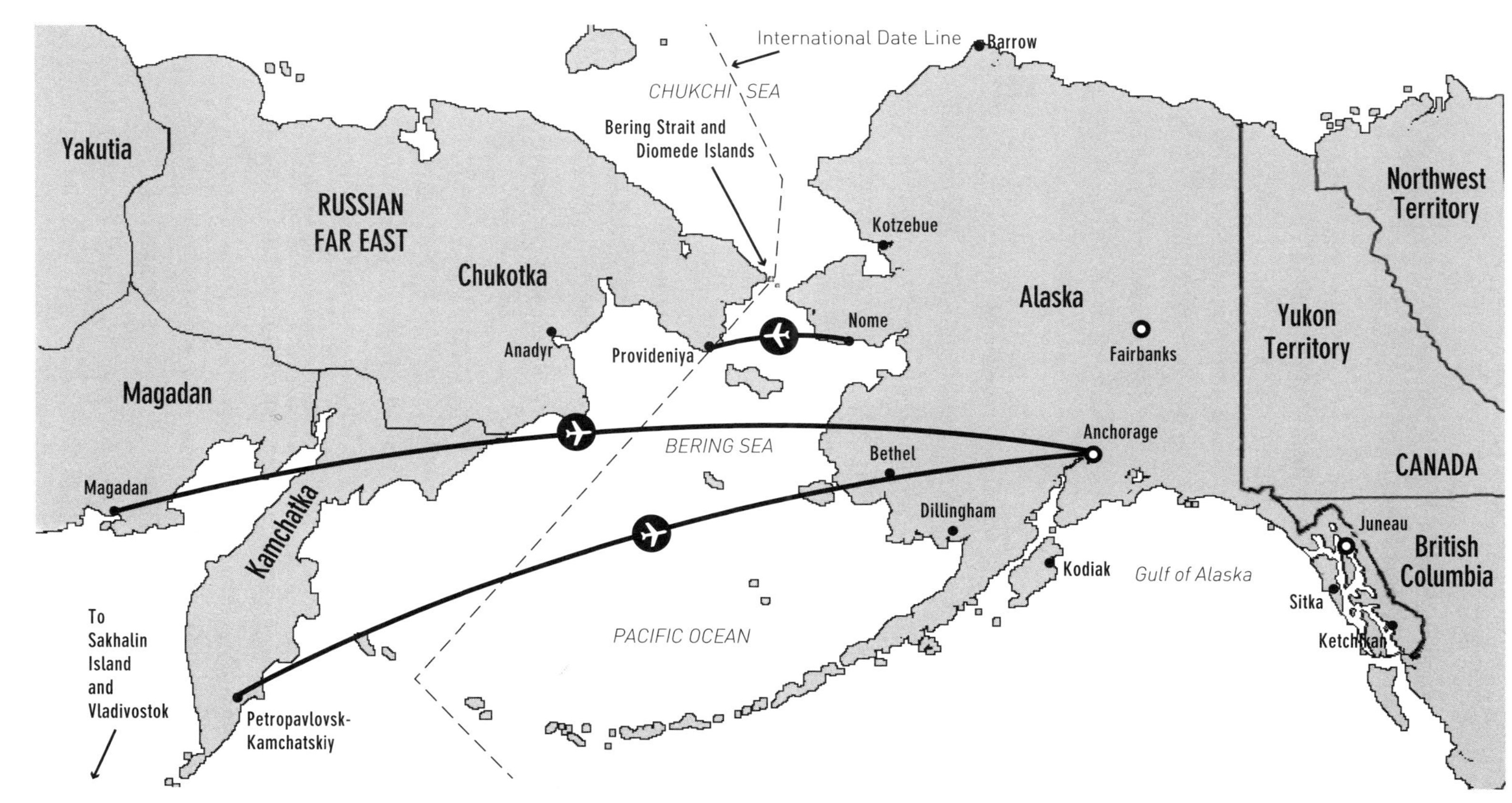

Source: Developed by Kristina Klimovich.

motivated the rush to embrace the RFE? What did the interactions accomplish? And why did the activity decline and what is left today?

The Motivations and Roles of the Major Alaska Participants

Alaska's investigation of the prospects for trade and research cooperation with the RFE began before *perestroika* and *glasnost* reached their peak in the early 1990s. In particular, a delegation from UAA's Institute of Social and Economic Research (ISER) and the Alaska Center for Independent Business (ACIB) visited Russia in 1989 and wrote a positive report on the potential of promoting Alaska-RFE relations of all types.[29]

Various groups in Alaska and the RFE had strong motivation to develop immediate contacts. Alaska businesspeople, Alaska government policy makers, University of Alaska officials, and Alaska Natives had a particular interest.

Alaska Businesspeople

Alaska businesspeople expressed considerable interest in the RFE, believing that it was full of natural resources and had a population that craved Western consumer culture after decades of Soviet deprivation. In the spirit of the moment, potential complications (such as receiving compensation for their efforts) were largely ignored. The first official delegation from Alaska was organized by the Alaska State Chamber of Commerce and was greeted enthusiastically by local RFE officials wherever it went. In addition, excitement grew in Alaska as oil projects off Sakhalin Island were announced.

Typical of the early Alaska businessperson was Doug Drum, owner of Indian Valley Meats, near Anchorage. The poor state of meat processing throughout the RFE suggested there was demand for his services and investment. He was a regular on flights to places like Magadan and Khabarovsk and was featured on Yakutsk television (in the Province of Yakutia) demonstrating how to turn slabs of frozen reindeer into elegantly trimmed and presented fillets.

Alaska State and Local Government Policy Makers

State public officials saw economic advantages to pursuing a relationship with the RFE and an opportunity to diversify Alaska's unbalanced economy. Local government officials saw exchange possibilities and some financial benefits. Yet, Alaska state officials played a mostly ceremonial role in the development of the Alaska-RFE relationship. Some specialized staff was added for a time to the Department of Commerce, mostly to facilitate business contacts. The Alaska-Sakhalin Working Group was chaired by Alaska's governor and his Russian counterpart, though the actual work was done mainly by appointees who met occasionally to develop plans and listen to presentations. Alaska legislators also played a modest role with some brief exchanges with their counterparts in the RFE. The state did facilitate exchanges by allowing Russian students from a city with an Alaska sister city relationship to pay in-state tuition at the University of Alaska (UA), which made studying in Alaska affordable for them.

At the local level, there was a flurry of exchanges stemming largely from sister city relationships. And, in the early 1990s, the Mayor of Anchorage had a coordinator for Russian affairs who also served as the honorary consul of the Russian Federation.

The University of Alaska—Mainly UAA

Academics saw educational, training, and research opportunities in this new era of relations with the RFE. One of the chief architects promoting these Alaska-RFE relations was Victor Fischer, director of the Soviet Studies program at UAA in the late 1980s and early 1990s. Fischer arranged student and faculty exchanges between UA and Russian universities, particularly the International University of Magadan. Fischer and a UA regent were named regents to the Magadan institution.

Along with another UAA professor, John Choon Kim (one of the moving forces behind the Alaska Center for International Business), Fischer established the American Russian Center (ARC). In addition to generating small business training programs, ARC started a program for RFE university students to study in Alaska. Dual degree programs were set up with several Russian universities so that students could get both a Russian and an American degree in four to six years. At the height of the exchanges Alaska had more Russian students than any other state in the nation.[30]

Overall, the state invested very little money in developing and sustaining the RFE-UAA relationship. After failing to get a $200,000 startup grant from the state, Fischer and Choon Kim turned to federal funding. Mainly through the U.S. Agency for International Development (USAID) and the U.S. Information Agency (USIA), the federal contribution was more than $26 million during a thirteen-year period to facilitate exchanges and development in the RFE. All the money passed through the university. U.S. Senator Ted Stevens included riders on USAID appropriations that required them to spend money in the RFE. A major part of this money went to the ARC.[31]

There were other related programs at UAA. One organized fisheries conferences, bringing Pacific nations, including Russia, to the table to discuss regional issues such as over-fishing and protecting marine mammals. Another brought academics together to study governments at the state and municipal levels, working together to deal with cross-regional issues such as trade flows, business opportunities, and environmental degradation.

Alaska Natives

Alaska Natives had two major motives for contact with the RFE. One was economic benefit. Native corporations got involved in the oil industry in the RFE and in other business ventures, and often worked with the WTCAK.

Another motive was reestablishing cultural contacts with indigenous groups in the RFE. After 1946 the Soviet Union declared the entire RFE a border zone where foreigners were not admitted, and even the locals could no longer communicate with each other across the Bering Strait. With the thawing of the so-called ice curtain in the late 1980s and the reopening of air traffic between Alaska and places like Khabarovsk and Vladivostok, the Russian Ministry of Foreign Affairs and the U.S. State Department considered reestablishing an agreement that had been in place until World War II, which enabled Native peoples in Russia and Alaska to visit each other without visas. The agreement between the two countries came into force in 1990.

Accomplishments

The major accomplishment of Alaska's RFE experience was that Alaska, together with other states, helped open up relations with Russia. This exposed the RFE to Alaskans and other Americans, and Russians to the outside world in a way that had not been possible before. This included Russian exposure to the pros and cons of Western democracy and capitalism. According to the ARC's former executive director, Russ Howell, the reaction of many Russians who came to participate in UAA's training programs was a combination of euphoria and disbelief, especially when entering supermarkets and department stores.[32]

As to specific achievements, it is probably too early to judge the success of the exchanges and small business development, or of any of the goals that were anticipated for assistance programs. Nonetheless, we can offer observations that suggest the programs did achieve a measure of success. Data compiled by the ARC shows that more than half of small business development in the oil-producing area of Sakhalin Island involved graduates of ARC's programs. The number in Khabarovsk, which has a much larger population, was 20 percent. In Magadan it was 80 percent, although many of the entrepreneurs eventually abandoned the city because of challenging economic circumstances. Again, according to Russ Howell, many of the Sakhalin small enterprises have been sold to larger businesses based in Moscow, leaving the still youthful sellers with capital to start new endeavors.[33] And a smaller hardcore group of Alaska businesspeople, some associated with Native corporations, did find ways to make money, mostly in the energy sector, and remain busy there. Doug Drum found modest success early on training Russian reindeer herders in meat preparation, packaging, and retailing at his headquarters in Alaska.

Over the fifteen years that ARC operated, the university trained more than sixty thousand residents of the RFE in business principles including accounting, marketing, and management.[34] The training was done on both sides of the Bering Strait by UA faculty and in so doing enhanced the intercultural knowledge of the faculty involved. In addition, the university helped establish several nongovernmental organizations. These are still rare in Russia, but they were virtually nonexistent before the Alaska-RFE interactions. Plus, an

ARC program helped develop a women's center in Magadan that included a program to combat domestic violence. An effective Alaska program to counter domestic violence in Kotzebue was successfully modified and set up in Anadyr, the capital of Chukotka, which included a telephone hotline. The program worked and instances of abuse declined.

Environmental activism by NGOs was also introduced to the RFE by Alaskans. A major effort that has been underway for years is the Beringia Park project, which consists of a national park that includes land in both Northwest Alaska and the northern region of the RFE.

One of the major social benefits that resulted from the Alaska-RFE interchange accrued to the indigenous peoples on both sides of the Bering Strait. The visa-free travel agreement between the United States and Russia of 1990 is still in force but includes only parts of western Alaska and applies only to Native peoples with Bureau of Indian Affairs registration.[35] In addition, Alaska Native expertise was an important resource for the University of Alaska Anchorage programs in areas such as social services, as described earlier, and in reviving skills such as small boat building, which had been lost during the communist period.

Declining Interactions

A major blow to Alaska-RFE interactions came with the collapse of the ruble in 1996. Businesses in Nome stopped accepting rubles, and those who held them lost considerable sums of money. Businesspeople like Doug Drum saw their investments and prospects of making a profit disappear. He and many others pulled out. And even before the ruble crisis, Drum and others had encountered Russian bureaucracy, corruption, and other obstacles. Since he first came to power in 1999, Vladimir Putin has not been particularly supportive of interactions such as that of Alaska and the RFE. The situation has deteriorated further since U.S.-Russian relations soured following the Russian takeover of Crimea and its involvement with pro-Russian forces in eastern Ukraine in 2014. Those in the oil sector who thought they had picked a solid winner received a blow when a major American oil company working on the Sakhalin oil project was replaced by one owned by the Dutch, which preferred Dutch engineers over U.S. ones, including those from Alaska. Then when USAID funds for Russia projects declined precipitously, so did the possibilities for continuing ARC's programs. State of Alaska funds were also reduced. It is unclear why the state did not play a bigger role, especially in funding cultural and educational exchanges in addition to commercial intelligence gathering that offered potential for eventual return on investment. Section 7 below offers some possible explanations.

As a result of this confluence of circumstances, the Alaska-RFE interchange began a decline in the mid-1990s and petered out by 2008.

With considerably reduced business, Alaska Airlines and Aeroflot ended operations to the RFE. Reeve Air Alaska, which operated charter flights to the Russian Far East, went bankrupt because of hyper-competition in the U.S. airline industry. Sister city relationships withered, and other robust exchange programs ground to a halt. Though Russian university students still come to Alaska, Russian authorities revoked Magadan's international status, and the Russian parliament passed a law making it illegal to have a foreigner on the governing board of a Russian university. Professor Fischer and his Fairbanks colleague were fired.

Funding for ACIB was terminated by the legislature in 1997. This was ostensibly because of a ten-year sunset provision in the enabling legislation and because Senator Drue Pearce believed the university could maintain the programs by using staff from other academic programs. UAA struggled to leverage the RFE expertise that some of its staff had developed and to maintain its work in the region, but the ACIB program was eventually discontinued. ARC closed its doors, and the staff was let go. The fisheries program moved to Alaska Pacific University but has never been the same as in its heyday at UAA.

The Current Status of Alaska-RFE Interactions and Future Prospects

Of the millions spent on enhancing RFE relations and the fervent activity that occurred for fifteen years, few tangible benefits are evident today. Certainly, there is still some economic activity by Alaskans in the RFE, including the oil industry. Recently Doug Drum helped design and install a walrus meat canning plant in the Province of Chukotka, and in the summer of 2012 charter flights were instituted between Petropavlovsk-Kamchatskiy and Anchorage. The indigenous people from both sides of the Bering Strait maintain contact. Some Russian students take advantage of coming to UA campuses but few Alaskan students go to the RFE, and little remains on the UAA campus of the high hopes of the interchange envisioned by Victor Fischer.[36] Overall, Alaska-RFE interactions are just a shadow of what they once were.

As relationships continue, even in the absence of government funding, it is possible to envision Native groups partnering to offer tourism opportunities and other kinds of joint ventures in the RFE. Such possibilities must be tempered by the reality that RFE indigenous people are still mired in shocking poverty as a result of decades of mistreatment by central and local governments.

7. THE GENERAL CHARACTERISTICS OF ALASKA INTERACTIONS WITH THE WORLD AND EXPLAINING AND EVALUATING STATE GOVERNMENT'S POLICY APPROACH

The four case studies just considered offer insights into the general characteristics of Alaska's international interactions, particularly regarding state government policy toward the world. In combination, the studies demonstrate the potential and limitations of Alaska's international ventures. There are several major aspects of these ventures, which we outline first and then show how they aid in explaining and evaluating the state's policy role.

The General Aspects

External forces, be these foreign governments, world currency markets, or multinational corporations, very much affect the success or failure of Alaska's international interactions. Alaska state government and its citizens have very little control over these external circumstances. This is particularly the case in the economic sphere, as Chapter 7 on the Outside economy explains.

Also, although Alaska's relations with the world go far beyond the purely economic and the pursuit of financial benefits, it is the economic factor that is by far the major impetus. Consequently, the major emphasis of state policies and expenditures is to promote economic benefits from international commerce. Continued financial gain by Alaskans or gains by Outside businesses and organizations active in Alaska will sustain or expand state international interactions; reduced financial benefits or the inability to cover costs will reduce or end such interactions. The economic factor is the major driver in the Canadian case study, that of the Arctic, and to a large extent the Alaska-RFE flurry of activity, and plays a part in the subsistence lifestyle in the Alaska Eskimo Whaling Commission case.

Yet another aspect is the way state government prioritizes its international involvement. Unless the state can see a major economic benefit, it will become only minimally involved, and what support it does provide will often be reduced or eliminated in times of shortfalls in state revenues or when the state no longer sees any benefit from continued funding. In other words, as policy priorities go, international interactions, even the economic ones, have a low priority with state government and state spending. This kind of prioritization most likely explains why the state's involvement in international interactions has fluctuated so much over the years and the decidedly mixed results of those interactions that the state has chosen to pursue.

Because of the state's often minimal interest or commitment, much of the drive and enthusiasm to establish and maintain international interactions has come from other entities. These include interest groups and for-profit and nonprofit organizations, though the state often partners with various Outside organizations, including those in the private sector.

Whether the impetus for an international program or activity is public or private, grassroots or governmental, one key factor is the leadership of a single person or small group. These are essentially policy entrepreneurs, in this case international policy entrepreneurs, such as governors Hickel, Cowper, and Knowles, Eben Hopson, Victor Fischer, John Choon Kim, Russ Howell, and Alice Rogoff. Without the involvement of these individuals, who triggered or sustained forums, institutes, exchange programs, causes, and courses of study, Alaska's knowledge of and engagement with the world would be very different from what it has been.

Alaska is not unique in the importance of the individual international policy entrepreneur. What is different is that Alaska's small population limits the number of these entrepreneurs. In addition, it is difficult for Alaska to attract and retain out-of-state international entrepreneurs. This contrasts with other states with larger, more stable populations, and whose institutions for training and employing such entrepreneurs are more extensive, developed, and better supported.

Finally, these policy entrepreneurs, as well as other champions of promoting Alaska's international activities, sometimes manifest more idealism and wishful thinking than realism. This manifestation takes many forms but, in essence, holds that because of Alaska's location on the Pacific Rim at the crossroads of North America and Asia, the state has a rosy future in international commerce and a major contribution to make to the rest of the world. This is epitomized in the exuberance of Governor Hickel's belief that Alaska stands at a pivotal place where ideas and connections matter—across the state and on a global scale. This view has been reinforced by the prediction by some that the twenty-first century will be the Asian century. This has fostered the belief that the state can take advantage of Asian and other international relations if only the right policies are put in place. In particular, the Arctic and Alaska-RFE case studies illustrate the continuing belief that somehow the state's geographic location *should* result in some major economic gain and help solve the long and elusive search for diversity or at least stabilize Alaska's economy.

There is certainly some political mileage to be made out of this belief, as Governor Walker experienced in his 2014 election campaign. But it is often wishful thinking that shows a lack of economic understanding and in some circumstances is little more than political rhetoric. Nevertheless, it is a factor that has often shaped Alaska's public policies, as have other aspects of unrealistic thinking and political rhetoric.

Explaining and Evaluating State Government's International Policy

Why is state government's record a mixed one in international policy, and what have been the consequences for the state and its citizens?

In a nutshell, the state's mixed record in international policy is a combination of four factors: budgetary priorities and shortfalls, the two- and four-year election cycle, difficulty in assessing the benefits of state support, and the lack of an organized and effective international lobby in Juneau.

As a government, the State of Alaska's first priority is to provide services, particularly K–12 and higher education, social services, law enforcement and corrections, and transportation and infrastructure. In total these services regularly account for 70 percent of the state operating budget and most of the capital budget in years when there is money for capital projects. Thus there is little money left for other policy areas.[37] This situation has been compounded over the years by unstable state revenues due to the volatility of the state's major income from oil taxes. In years of revenue shortfalls even major services may be cut, so there is certainly no room for what many consider nonessential services and programs.

Then there is the election-cycle psychology of elected officials in state government and their need to demonstrate that they have delivered concrete economic and service benefits to their constituents or the state during their time in office (two years for some, four years for others). For most citizens, Alaska's international interactions are not well understood and are rarely on their political radar screens. Consequently, most legislators do not place a high priority on Alaska's various relations with the world and see international programs as the first to cut in tight budget years. In fact, few legislators are concerned with world relations even in good budget times. Governors and their administrations certainly have an ongoing interest in this policy area, but it is rarely a top priority. The funds there are available for international relations go mainly to promoting commerce.

Another factor undermining funding for international activities, even those to promote commerce, is the issue of costs versus benefits. It is difficult, if not impossible, to determine exactly what the economic return is on trade offices or contracts with consultants and other activities to promote international commerce, let alone the return on supporting university and other programs for international interactions. This is in contrast to the tangible economic and political benefits accruing to politicians when operating and capital project funds go directly to a district or political constituency. There are less tangible ways to assess the benefits of international policy, such as simply counting the number of Alaskans taking courses in international activities or involved in internships or the number of Russians trained in the Alaska-RFE programs. But in the minds of many hard-nosed politicians trying to deal with budget problems, these kinds of assessments carry little political weight, and some see little to be gained by spending Alaska dollars on training Russians.

In combination, these first three factors partly account for the absence of major coordinated interest group activity and lobbying to promote Alaska's relations with the world. Without a major lobby to get issues and ideas on the policy agenda and see them through the lawmaking process, a coordinated international policy has not emerged. Certainly, there are lobbying efforts by individual organizations, like the State Chamber of Commerce, promoting aspects of international trade, and lobbying by several nonprofits. Generally, however, a coordinated effort has been hampered by the wide range of interests in this area of activity and the sometimes intense conflicts, such as the contention between development and environmentalism.

All this adds up to Alaska's state government's international policy being a low priority, ad hoc in nature, and driven by pragmatism, expediency, and short-term decisions, with ebbs and flows of interest in part depending on available funds. Surges of enthusiasm and budget appropriations are often followed by cutbacks and reductions. International policies are rarely major aspects of political party programs or legislative caucus agendas. As a result, much of the initiative in international policy falls to policy entrepreneurs and to private and nonprofit organizations, sometimes in cooperation with state government.

The Consequences for Alaska's Citizens

Have Alaska and its citizens lost economic and other benefits because of this ad hoc, pragmatic record of state government? The truth is that, as with many policies, it is impossible to determine in any definitive way. We can, however, make some observations.

Regarding the loss of economic and financial benefits, the evidence and economic theory leads to the conclusion that these losses have not been major. In regard to the RFE, Andrew Crow, who runs UA's Cooperative Development Program (which is involved with promoting Alaska's international commerce and related activities), does not see that declining state interest and the diminished presence of Alaska entrepreneurs in the region have meant major lost opportunities.[38] In a free enterprise system the market and investors will naturally move capital where there are profits. This phenomenon has been the major determinant of Alaska's international activity. Since state policy can only marginally affect markets, arguably there is little the state can do to promote Alaskans' interests in the international arena, and there seems to be minimal economic opportunity in today's RFE. In contrast, it is the market that sparked the recent surge in oil and gas exploration in Alaska's Arctic waters—activity that would have occurred regardless of the state pushing for more activity. Nevertheless, state promotion of commerce can aid international commerce in some instances.

In terms of a wider vision, Alaska is dependent on the international economy and will certainly be affected by Arctic and other northern regional issues. Thus, the long-term consequences of the state's mixed record in the international sphere may be detrimental to the state. Alaska would benefit from more emphasis on education and training on international economics and international relations in general to train future generations of business people, particularly policy entrepreneurs, to meet the changing needs of a global economy. This would also produce more policy makers with an awareness of the significance of Alaska's relations with the world.

Certainly, private and nonprofit organizations have made and will continue to make a contribution. But state government is in a position, with its major financial resources, to lead this effort by funding and perhaps establishing long-term programs at the university and financing other international activities. Given that Alaska has two major resources to sustain its present and future lifestyle, natural resources and human resources, education is the major way to tap the human resource to benefit all Alaskans. This would be the ideal international policy approach. But given what we have said here and the realities of Alaska politics, this approach is probably not likely to be pursued by state policy makers. It is even less likely in times of low oil prices as occurred from mid-2014 through early 2016 and during future oil price downturns.

8. CONCLUSION: THE IDEAL VERSUS THE PRACTICAL REALITY

Viewed in a broader context, Alaska's experience in international relations provides four insights about state public policy. One is that Alaska's international policy has been predominantly distributive and so is less controversial and conflict ridden than either redistributive or regulatory policies (though, of course, the federal government engages in some regulatory policy on fisheries and other international issues that affect Alaska citizens).[39] Perhaps the major reason that Alaska's international activities are less conflict ridden is that they are not on the political radar of most state politicians because of low importance to their constituents, plus there is no major lobby pushing these issues. A second insight is that this is a policy area where the state and nonprofit and private organizations have worked together to develop and implement policy in various ways. In fact, together with policies and program delivery in social services, international policy development and implementation is one of the two major areas of state policy where such collaboration occurs. Third, as is also the case with social services, it has often been the policy entrepreneurs who have worked to push a cause, establish a policy, and ensure its implementation.[40]

The fourth insight is the contrast between what some may consider an ideal policy prescription and the political realities that shape that policy. From an ideal perspective, especially given Alaska's dependence on exports and attracting investments from the other forty-nine states and from abroad, one would expect a high priority to be placed on promoting these economic interactions by state policy makers as well as educational and other programs that expose Alaska's future private and public leaders as well as nonprofit leaders to the international economic, political, and social environment. Practical politics dictates otherwise, however, even if the political rhetoric of some Alaska public figures sometimes touts the major prospects of increased international involvement. This falls into the realm of one of the myths of Alaska politics and one of its political characteristics, identified in Chapter 2.

What shapes this political reality most, however, is the combined Alaska political characteristics of external forces both economic and political, fiscal conservatism, and in many instances the developer-environmentalist clash. While external circumstances and developments, including the actions of the federal government, can present opportunities, they often impose constraints, such as a change of leadership in a country like Russia, an international recession, or a fall in the price of oil. Fiscal conservatism, the uncertainty of state revenues, and environmental concerns about development of Alaska's resources, including the Arctic, also play a role. Thus, the practical reality of Alaska's international policies wins out over the ideal. Judging by this historical pattern, there is little likelihood that this situation will change any time soon.

ENDNOTES

[1] Interview with Fran Ulmer by Clive Thomas, June 10, 2010.

[2] For a consideration of the role of state trade offices and trade missions, see Andrew J. Cassey, "State Trade Missions," Department of Economics, University of Minnesota, December 2007; and his "The Location of States' Overseas Offices," School of Economic Sciences, Washington State University, October 2008.

[3] Email communication from Patricia Eckert, Trade Specialists, Office of the Governor to Anthony Nakazawa, October 4, 2011.

[4] Douglas K. Barry, *U.S.-Japan Sister City Programs: A Survey* (New York: U.S.-Japan Foundation, 1995), 12.

[5] Information on WTCAK was provided by Alex Salov and by reference to the organization's website at: http://www.wtcak.org/.

[6] See http://www.iccalaska.org/.

[7] Information on the four organizations is taken from interviews and written communications with staff of the organizations and the following websites: Northern Forum at http://www.northernforum.org/; Arctic Council at http://arctic-council.org/; Institute of the North at http://www.institutenorth.org/; and Arctic Circle at http://arcticcircle.org/mission.

[8] The statistics on the impact of Canada on the Alaska economy is a synthesis of the following sources: State of Alaska, Office of the Governor, 2009 Export Update, at http://www.gov.state.ak.us/trade/pdf/AlaskaExportCharts2009.pdf; International Trade Administration, August 2014, "Alaska Exports, Job, and Foreign Investment," at http://www.trade.gov/mas/ian/statereports/states/ak.pdf; and Government of Canada, *Canada and the United States: 2014*, at http://www.can-am.gc.ca/business-affaires/fact_sheets-fiches_documentaires/ak.aspx?lang=eng.

[9] *The Economist*, "My Way or the Highway," January 25, 2015, 30–31.

[10] For fuller details on the cross-border disputes between British Columbia mining interests and Southeast Alaska salmon and conservation interests, see Chapter 22 on environmental politics, Section 5. For the issues on the Pebble and Donlin Mines, see Chapter 21 on natural resources and land issues, Box 21.4.

[11] Author interview with Scott Smullen, NOAA, July 10, 2008.

[12] Personal correspondence to the author from Douglas DeMaster, NOAA, July 20, 2008.

[13] Rosemarie Alexander, "Begich Says Arctic Development in Alaska's Future," KTOO Radio News, *Morning Edition*, March 5, 2012.

[14] *Alaska Dispatch News*, "Bill Walker Answers Question about the Issues in the 2014 Election for Alaska Governor," October 11, 2014; and Alex DeMarban, "Gov. Walker Names Former Running Mate Fleener as Arctic Advisor," *Alaska Dispatch News*, December 4, 2014.

[15] Ed Schoenfeld, "Stedman: Projects Could Help Region's Economy," CoastAlaska News, KTOO Public Radio, May 2, 2012; Alaska Arctic Policy Commission, at http://www.akarctic.com/about-the-commission/; and Casey Kelly, "Could Western Alaska Become the Next Panama Canal?" KTOO News, April 11, 2013.

[16] A dated but still useful overview of the geography of the Arctic from an Alaska perspective is Terence Armstrong, George W. Rogers, and Graham Rowley, *The Circumpolar North: A Political and Economic Geography of the Arctic and Sub-Arctic* (London: Methuen & Co., Ltd. 1978).

[17] Lawson W. Brigham, "The Fast-Changing Maritime Arctic," *Proceedings*, U.S. Naval Institute, Annapolis, Maryland, May 2010, 54.

[18] U.S. Department of Defense, Secretary of Defense Speech, November 22, 2013, at http://www.defense.gov/speeches/speech.aspx?speechid=1821 and U.S. Department of State, Press Release, July 16, 2014, at http://www.state.gov/secretary/remarks/2014/07/229317.htm; and Liz Ruskin, "Secretary of Defense Affirms Need for Arctic Emphasis," *Alaska News Nightly*, APRN (Alaska Public Radio Network). March 4, 2015.

[19] Yereth Rosen, "Obama Issues Executive Order to Better Coordinate Arctic Policy," *Alaska Dispatch News*, January 21, 2015.

[20] A recent report by a think tank sees the military problems as being of major significance in the Arctic, see Rob Huebert, *et. al.*, *Climate Change and International Security: The Arctic as a Bellwether* (Arlington, VA: Center for Climate and Energy Solutions, 2012). In contrast, two other experts see it as resource-based and downplay the military motive. See Roger Howard, *Arctic Gold Rush: The New Race for Tomorrow's Natural Resources* (London: Continuum, 2009); and a chapter and three articles by Lawson W. Brigham, Distinguished Professor of Geography and Arctic Policy at the University of Alaska Fairbanks: "Globalisation and Challenges for the Maritime Arctic," in *The World Ocean in Globalisation*, ed. Davor Vidas and Peter Johan Schei (Leiden/Boston: Martinus Nijhoff Publishers/Brill, 2011), 305–20; "Think Again, the Arctic," *Foreign Policy* (September/October 2010): 70–74; and "Thinking About the Arctic's Future: Scenarios for 2040," *The Futurist* (September/October, 2007): 27–34.

[21] "Fran Ulmer Appointed Chair of the U.S. Arctic Research Commission," at http://www.arcus.org/witness-the-arctic/2011/2/article/1652.

[22] Alexander, "Begich Says Arctic Development in Alaska's Future."

[23] See http://www.institutenorth.org

[24] Carl Restino, "Arctic Policy Commission Hears State, World Concerns," *The Arctics Sounder*, May 15, 2014; and Molly Dischner, "Arctic Policy Commission Submits Report," *Juneau Empire*, February 1, 2015.

[25] http://www.arcus.org/events/arctic-calendar/6238.

[26] Craig Medred, "At Arctic Circle Assembly, as in Arctic, a Delicate Balancing Act," *Alaska Dispatch News*, October 31, 2014; and "10 Takeaways from the Arctic Circle Assembly," *Alaska Dispatch News*, Nov. 3, 2014.

[27] Yereth Rosen, "Feds allow Shell to drill in Chukchi," *The Arctics Sounder*, August 20, 2015; and Julie Hirschfeld Davis, "Obama's Alaska Visit Puts Climate, Not Energy, in Forefront, *New York Times*, August 31, 2015.

[28] Alex DeMarban and Yereth Rosen, "Shell Says It Plans to Drill in Alaska's Arctic in 2015," *Alaska Dispatch News*, January 29, 2015; John Ryan, "Greenpeace Activists Protest Shell Oil's Plan to Drill in the Arctic Ocean," *All Things Considered* (NPR—National Public Radio), July 29, 2015; Erica Martinson, "Shell Calls off Plans to Drill in Arctic," *The Arctic Sounder*, October 1, 2015; Kirk Johnson, "Exuberance and Disappointment at Shell's About-Face in the Arctic," *New York Times*, September 28, 2015; Erica Martinson "Interior Department cancels lease sales in Alaska's Arctic waters, citing low interest," *Alaska Dispatch News*, October 16, 2015; and Alex DeMarban, "Work toward deep-water port in Alaska Arctic on hold, Army Corps says," *Alaska Dispatch News*, October 26, 2015. See also, Alex DeMarban, "Will Off-shore Oil Development in Alaska's Arctic Make State Rich? Don't Count on It," *Alaska Dispatch*, July 1, 2012;

[29] Gunnar Knapp, *et al.*, "Alaska Far-East Trade and Research Cooperation: Preliminary Trip Report" (Anchorage: University of Alaska Anchorage, Institute of Social and Economic Research, and the Alaska Center for International Business, August 1989).

[30] Interview by the author with Victor Fischer, former director of Soviet Studies and senior advisor to the ARC, August 18, 2008.

[31] The author was also involved in creating the ARC, in writing the USAID grant proposal, and recruiting the first executive director, Charles B. Neff.

[32] Author interview with Russ Howell, September 1, 2008.

[33] *Ibid.*

[34] *Ibid.*

[35] Information on the vicissitudes of the U.S. and Alaska-Russian RFE visa programs, particularly the program involving indigenous Alaskans and Russians, was provided to Clive Thomas in an interview and written correspondence in June 2013 by Natalie Novik, formerly of the Northern Forum.

[36] Email correspondence from Andrew Crow, University of Alaska Cooperative Development Program, to Anthony Nakazawa, September 30, 2011.

[37] See Chapter 19 on the state budget, Figure 19.2.

[38] Correspondence from Andrew Crow, September 30, 2011.

[39] See Chapter 3, Section 1 on the state policy-making process for an explanation of distributive, redistributive, and regulatory policy.

[40] See Chapter 27 on social services, Sections 1 and 5.

★ CHAPTER 12 ★

The Role and Operation of Government in Alaska: Myths, Practicalities, and the Owner State

Clive S. Thomas with Anthony T. Nakazawa

In the Foreword to this book, Victor Fischer, writes:

> Although federal dominance over many policy issues waned with statehood, government—federal, state, and local—remains a major player in Alaska as employer, as landowner, as regulator, and as a funding source for education, health, social programs, and transportation.

In effect, Fischer is saying that dependence on government, both past and present, is not only a constant reality, but a dominant factor in Alaska's politics. Yet, as Chapter 5 on political culture points out, there is a strong antigovernment attitude among many Alaskans. Evidence of this was support across the state for the antigovernment, essentially Tea Party, program of Republican Joe Miller in his unsuccessful bid for the U.S. Senate in November 2010. At the same time, like many Americans, including residents of the western states, Alaskans often have good reasons to be concerned about the role, organization, and operation of their state and local governments, as well as the federal government and the way it affects Alaska.

Given the major significance of government in Alaska's economic, social, and political life, this chapter considers the role of government and how it is perceived by Alaskans. The chapter brings together several aspects of government's role and provides a link between the place of government in politics and policy making considered in earlier chapters and the analysis of institutions, policies, and political power presented in the rest of the book. As the subtitle of the chapter indicates, this explanation involves separating the myths and misunderstandings about government from the realities. It also considers the unique role of Alaska as an Owner State with extensive resources on and under the land and in the sea.

While the chapter does consider the role of, and attitudes to, all levels of government, the major concern is the role and performance of Alaska's state government, as opposed to federal and local governments (the federal government's role and citizens' attitudes to it are considered in Chapter 10 and those related to local government in Chapter 18). In a generic sense, however, there are many similarities in the role and operation of all three levels of government. So at various points in the chapter the analysis applies to all three levels. Plus, even though each level has a different function, the public often does not, or cannot, distinguish between the three levels, and often lumps them together generically as "the government." This generic attitude often has implications for the way elected state officials approach the role and operation of government in making policy.

The chapter begins by identifying some attitudes that Americans and Alaskans express about government. The next section focuses on the specifics of the role of government in Alaska compared with other states, including Alaska as an Owner State. Then we examine the debate about the role and operation of government to help separate the myths and misunderstandings from the realities. This is followed by considering the approaches to and problems involved in efforts to increase government efficiency in Alaska. The next section offers explanations for the attitudes of many Alaskans toward government, how these attitudes can affect policy decisions, and how politicians deal with the potential pitfalls of such attitudes. The conclusion shows how the chapter's perspective on government relates to several other chapters in the book.

1. PERSPECTIVES ON THE ATTITUDES OF AMERICANS AND ALASKANS TO GOVERNMENT

The attitudes of Americans and Alaskans to government are a complex and intricate mix of positive and negative attitudes, inconsistencies, and some contradictions.[1] For instance, Americans tend to be skeptical of government in general but, not surprisingly, have favorable attitudes toward the programs that benefit them. National surveys reveal that confidence in government and positive attitudes toward it have declined since the 1960s. However, in times of economic prosperity, as in the 1990s and early 2000s, government receives a more favorable rating. Moreover, surveys that focus on particular aspects of government may affect responses to general questions about government, depending on whether or not the respondents favor or oppose that aspect of government's role or service.

One perennial issue is what government's role should be in society: what functions should it perform and what programs should it operate beyond the necessary ones of law and order and, in the case of national governments, protection from foreign attack and invasion. Another issue is how well government performs certain tasks. Yet another is how much people trust government, including their attitudes toward politicians and politics in general.

This chapter focuses on two sets of attitudes toward government. One concerns the proper size of government and the scope of its activities. The other focuses on how well government performs its functions. In this regard, we can reasonably deduce a number of things from surveys, scholarly research, media reports, and the pronouncements of those holding political office and running for office. Even though virtually all Americans and Alaskans accept the necessity of government for providing certain services, such as public safety and education, people often express concerns about the way government operates. Some people want government to provide a wide array of services, while others want it to stay out of certain activities altogether. Some negative attitudes that Americans express about government are that it is:

- too bureaucratic and more concerned about rules than people;
- bloated in size and needs to be reduced;
- very inefficient and should be run more like a business;
- too intrusive, meddling in the lives of individuals and the operations of businesses and stifling initiative by too much regulation; and
- geared to benefit special interests at the expense of the ordinary citizen.

Specific to Alaska state government, many programs and functions were expanded and new ones added in the late 1970s and early 1980s when oil revenues allowed the state budget to grow significantly. With increased revenues and spending came increased state and local government employment, all of which was funded by state dollars. But with the major crash of oil prices in 1986 and periodic downturns since then, there has been a continuing demand by many Alaskans that state programs and services should be delivered more efficiently, cut back, or eliminated.

In light of the past and present roles of the state and the uncertain revenue picture, views on the size and efficiency of Alaska's state government vary from believing it is very wasteful and could do a much better job to believing that it is actually very efficient and well organized. This divergence of viewpoints is exemplified by two surveys of elected and appointed local government officials conducted in the mid-1990s, but which are still likely reflective of the attitudes of many Alaskans.[2] Some of those surveyed believed that state government was inefficient for a number of reasons, including:

- Wages and benefits for state employees are far above the private sector
- Duplication of effort: too many public employees do the same thing
- Utilization of inefficient and costly methods

On the other hand, some respondents felt that state government was efficiently run and doing a good job (though there were fewer such comments than those citing inefficiency). The most common favorable comment was that state government is "doing more with less," which was likely a reflection of the successive rounds of state budget downsizing throughout the 1990s. Most enlightening about these surveys was the wide range of opinions from the respondents, since all of them were directly involved in local government.

Also, many Alaskans express a strong antipathy toward the federal government. This antipathy stems in part from federal land use regulations and environmental controls that restrict development of natural resources in Alaska. In other cases, it is simply the result of general antigovernment attitudes, and sometimes it is expressed in extreme forms. During a demonstration in 2009 against the legislature's override of Governor Palin's veto of federal stimulus funds, one woman was quoted as asking, "When can we believe anything we ever get from the federal government?"[3]

In a nutshell, the attitude of many Alaskans, including many politicians, toward government is a variation on what was identified in Chapter 2 as the western political paradox: a contradiction between the myth of individualism and the reality of dependence on government. As in many western states, in Alaska this paradox goes hand in hand with political pragmatism.

2. THE ROLE OF GOVERNMENT IN ALASKA COMPARED WITH OTHER STATES

All state governments, including Alaska's, perform many roles, including arbiter of the conflicting demands of its citizens, policy maker, law enforcer, regulator of the actions and behavior of citizens and various organizations (including business and government itself), service provider (particularly education, health and welfare, and transportation), and negotiator with the federal government on behalf of its citizens. The particular way and extent to which each state performs these roles are influenced by many factors, particularly the political culture and ideology of its citizenry, the state's resources, the political orientation of those in power at any one time, mandated federal requirements, and contemporary national socio-economic and political values. Consequently, as pointed out in Chapter 5 on political culture, government tends to be less extensive in the southern states but more extensive in the Northeast and upper Midwest.

The ways and extent to which Alaska's state government goes about fulfilling these roles compared to other states (or not fulfilling them, as the case may be) are covered throughout the book in the various chapters on specific aspects of Alaska politics, government, and policy areas, and in Chapter 29, which assesses the performance of Alaska's state government over the years. There are, however, four roles of Alaska's state government that either set it apart from most other states or that have a particular emphasis in

Alaska. These roles tell us much about the place that Alaska state government holds in the lives of its citizens. The government acts as (1) an economic lifeline, (2) an Owner State, (3) the manager of state resources, and (4) defender against Outside interests.

Government, Particularly State Government, as an Economic Lifeline

All state governments are important to their states' economies in various ways, particularly in the mountain West, where state economies are much less diversified than in many eastern and midwestern states. A good case can be made, however, that no state government is more important to its economy and the survival of many of its communities than is Alaska's.

Many criteria can be used to assess the importance of government to a state, locality, or nation's economy. Two of the most significant are (1) how much people rely upon government (federal, state, and local) for employment and the money that public employment pumps into the state's economy and (2) how much citizens receive in direct and

TABLE 12.1

Government Employment and Per Capita Government Spending: Alaska Compared to the Nation and Selected States in 2006

THE NATION AND SELECTED STATES	PERCENTAGE OF TOTAL STATE WORKFORCE EMPLOYED IN GOVERNMENT	PER CAPITA GOVERNMENT SPENDING			
		TOTAL (ALL LEVELS)	FEDERAL	STATE	LOCAL GOVERNMENT
National Averages	**17%**	**$8,308**	**$8,058**	**$97**	**$153**
Alaska	30	14,537	13,805	485	247
Hawaii	27	10,768	10,495	137	136
California	15	7,284	6,964	121	199
Wyoming	24	10,503	10,039	160	304
Minnesota	14	6,436	6,175	94	167
Louisiana	19	16,507	16,262	103	142
Nevada	12	6,174	5,851	112	211
Mississippi	21	14,708	14,516	55	137
New York	16	8,202	7,922	126	154
Massachusetts	13	9,105	8,889	101	115
Maine	16	8,588	8,308	136	144
Kansas	20	8,030	7,787	96	147

Source: Developed by the authors from the 2007 Employment and Earnings, Bureau of Labor Statistics, at http://www.bls.gov, and the 2006 Survey of State and Local Government Finances, the 2007 Census of Government Employment; and the Consolidated Federal Funds Report for Fiscal Year 2006, U.S. Census Bureau, at http://www.census.gov.

indirect benefits from the state. Using these two indicators, Table 12.1 places Alaska in comparison with nine states and the nation overall in 2006. This is a typical year since the late 1970s and before the disruptions of the recession of 2008–2010, which distorted comparisons because of emergency measures taken by many states.

Then, and since 2006, close to 30 percent of Alaska's workforce has been employed by government compared with a national average of 17 percent. Overall Alaska ranked third in per capita government expenditures in 2006 (behind Louisiana and Mississippi) and received 70 percent above the national average of federal per capita expenditures. Alaska ranked third in federal per capita spending and first in both state and local per capita spending.[4]

Alaska's state government is particularly significant to the state's economic health in two other ways, given the unbalanced nature of the economy and the minimal employment opportunities in rural-bush areas. First, it is a major force in stimulating economic activity and development through the state capital budget and in providing financial incentives for businesses, especially natural resources companies, to set up operations in the state and through agencies like the Alaska Seafood Marketing Institute (ASMI). Second, state government in Alaska is much more involved than most other states in funding local government, and it performs many services provided by local governments in other states, particularly K–12 education in rural-bush areas. In many rural-bush communities the state, through the school system, is often the major employer and, together with the yearly Permanent Fund Dividend (PFD), is the major source of cash income in rural-bush Alaska.

The Owner State

According to Fran Ulmer, former mayor of Juneau, state legislator, lieutenant governor, and Democratic Party nominee for governor in 2002, if there is one aspect of Alaska government that sets it apart from other states it is that Alaska is an Owner State.[5] Associated with Governor Walter J. (Wally) Hickel (1966–1969 and 1990–1994), the idea behind the Owner State is that Alaska owns extensive land and natural resources, presenting the state with unique policy opportunities not available to other states.[6] As Hickel wrote in 2002:

> The Alaskan people, through our state government, won ownership of much of our land and our natural resources. Using neither classic capitalism nor socialism, we have developed a new way to prosperity, based on common ownership and rooted in constitutional democracy. Since then, after more than forty years of striving, stumbling, and regaining our balance, falling flat and standing tall, this new way is now a remarkable success.[7]

As Governor Hickel noted, the Owner State presents Alaska with many opportunities not enjoyed by other states. At the same time, it has also presented state officials, both elected and appointed, with particular challenges and constraints regarding the role of government. Two particular roles of Alaska state government—resource manager and defender against Outside interests—illustrate this.

Manager of State Resources

All states, of course, must manage state revenues and state programs of all types. They also have other assets, such as state parks, that need to be managed. However, because it is an Owner State, Alaska's state government probably has a more extensive managerial role than most, if not all, of the other forty-nine states. This includes managing the Alaska Permanent Fund of nearly $50 billion (as of February 2016), managing and conserving a wide range of state resources (primarily through the departments of Natural Resources, Fish and Game, and Environmental Conservation), and acting as an arbiter in allocating access to and use of state resources, such as through the Alaska Commercial Fisheries Entry Commission, set up to prevent the depletion of the state's fisheries.

It would be one thing if this managerial function could be evaluated by using cost-benefit analyses or scientific and other objective criteria, along the lines of business practices. But the state's managerial function is subject, in large part, to politics and all its related pressures. This produces some constraints and challenges for those managing the Owner State, as we will see in considering the debate about the role and performance of government in the next section.

Defender against Outside Interests

A major force behind the movement for Alaska statehood was the desire of many Alaskans to control their own affairs and protect themselves from Outside interests. These interests included the mining and fishing industries, which many believed were exploiting the state, and the federal government, often seen as not understanding Alaska or not treating it fairly and administering it badly. A feeling of being beleaguered and in some cases feeling victimized by Outside forces still exists among many Alaskans even into the mid-2010s. In its extreme form this feeling is expressed as Alaska being a colony of the Lower 48 states and Outside economic forces. However, as pointed out in Chapter 1 (see Box 1.3), this belief is difficult to justify given its high standard of living, the size of the Permanent Fund, and the political choices Alaska has made.

Nevertheless, today the state is subject to the influence of many Outside forces, particularly large multinational corporations in the oil, gas, mining, fishing, and tourist industries; the federal government; and national and international interest groups (particularly regarding environmental protection), among others. In this situation, the state government acts as a protector of Alaska's interests, perhaps more so than in other states, as few have the same degree of Outside pressure with which to cope. Alaska's state government fulfills its role of defender against Outside pressures by regulating business activity, having a major state presence in Washington, D.C., to put forward Alaska's case, filing court challenges to many decisions of the federal government, and a variety of other ways.

This "defender" role of state government has a strain of populism about it, calling forth the image of a beleaguered, underdog Alaska defending itself against powerful and potentially exploitative interests.

The Practicality: A Crucial and Special Role of Government at a Relatively Low Cost to Alaskans

The state and federal governments are clearly crucial to Alaska's economy, and "dependence" is not too strong a word to describe the economic importance of government to the state and its citizens. The Owner State, with its extensive managerial function, also requires a central role for state government in maintaining and advancing the well-being of Alaskans. And the state's role as "protector from Outside interests" is important to most Alaskans at some time or another—conservatives, liberals, and libertarians alike.

Moreover, the major benefits received from state government come at a very low cost to individual Alaskans, who, as of late 2015, pay no state income tax or statewide sales tax (though many local governments have a local sales tax). They also receive major benefits from federal dollars directed toward Alaska, plus a PFD check each year since 1982, which averaged around $1,230 for each qualified adult and child between 1982 and 2015. Table 12.2 compares Alaska's per capita income, overall tax burden, and cost of living with a range of other states and the nation overall for 2011, the most recent year for which comprehensive data is available.

The table shows that Alaska is one of the two least taxed states in the nation, and since 1980 has consistently been among the five least taxed. And while it has a high cost of living, Alaska's is far from the highest in the nation. In terms of the purchasing power of its residents, Alaska ranks among the top ten states. Also, as John Katz points out in Chapter 2, urban Alaska (where 70 percent of Alaskans live) is becoming more and more like urban America everywhere. So the argument used by many Alaskans that government subsidies and low taxes are justified because of the "hardships of living in Alaska" holds little water, at least for urban Alaska. By contrast, in rural-bush areas, incomes and the standard of living are lower and poverty rates higher, though subsistence hunting and fishing supplements cash income.

Despite the crucial importance of the many benefits they receive from state government at a relatively low cost, many Alaskans persist in having a negative attitude toward government. These Alaskans criticize government's performance, want to reduce its role, size, and budget, and support elected officials and candidates who share their views. Many elected officials hold similar attitudes.

TABLE 12.2

Per Capita Income, State and Local Tax Burden, and Cost of Living in 2011: Alaska Compared to the Nation and Selected States

THE NATION AND SELECTED STATES	PER CAPITA INCOME AND NATIONAL RANK		PER CAPITA STATE AND LOCAL TAX BURDEN	PERCENT OF INCOME PAID IN STATE AND LOCAL TAXES AND NATIONAL RANK		COST OF LIVING AND NATIONAL RANKINGS (BASED ON RPPs)[1]	
	$ AMOUNT	RANK				RPPs	RANK
National Averages	**$42,473**	**N/A**	**$4,217**	**9.8%**	**N/A**	**100%**	**N/A**
Alaska	47,354	9	3,319	7.0	49	105.9	8
Hawaii	44,255	18	4,259	9.6	20	116.8	1
California	45,254	16	5,136	11.4	4	113.4	4
Wyoming	50,805	7	3,500	6.9	50	96.9	24
Minnesota	45,552	15	4,858	10.7	6	97.1	23
Tennessee	36,525	38	2,777	7.6	45	90.3	23
Florida	40,296	27	3,699	9.2	31	99.2	18
Mississippi	31,067	51	2,620	8.4	40	86.9	49
New Jersey	54,422	3	6,675	12.3	2	114.1	3
Massachusetts	54,321	4	5,586	10.3	11	108.1	7
Maine	37,701	33	3,836	10.2	14	97.5	22
Kansas	40,913	25	3,849	9.4	26	90.0	38

[1] There are several ways to compare cost of living between cities, metropolitan areas, regions, and states. The method used here is Regional Price Parities (RPPs). These are indexes that measure price level differences (food, apparel, recreation, medical care, transportation, etc.) between places for one time period that take into account different levels of purchasing power based on variations in prices between places.

Source: The Tax Foundation, 2014, "Annual State-Local Tax Burden Ranking FY 2011," http://taxfoundation.org/article/annual-state-local-tax-burden-ranking-fy-2011.

As pointed out in Chapter 5 on political culture, in the absence of survey research it is difficult to know with any degree of certainty why this attitude persists, though later in this chapter we offer some likely explanations. Much of the debate about government in Alaska involves political rhetoric and symbolism, particularly statements and imagery used by some politicians and Alaskans that do not always jibe with their actions. As a foundation to more fully understanding the attitudes of Alaskans to government and their consequences, it is useful to first critically examine the general debate surrounding the role and performance of government.

3. DELVING INTO THE DEBATE ABOUT THE ROLE AND PERFORMANCE OF GOVERNMENT: SOME KEY TERMS AND CONCEPTS

People have debated what role government should play in society for thousands of years, and the debate will continue for thousands to come. An illustration was the debate among the eighteen members of President Obama's debt-reduction commission, which issued its report in December 2010. Before it could decide on how to reduce the national debt over the next decade, the commission had to decide on what the role of government should and should not be, who should pay for government and its benefits, and how benefits should be distributed.[8] Like many debates on the subject, the commission's discussions were very contentious because there is no definitive answer to what government's role should be despite what some politicians, fervent partisans, and political gurus might claim. As the scope of government's role is largely based on values and not on facts, these values are also key elements in shaping politics. The value-based perspectives are those around which most political parties form and, directly or indirectly, are the root of many political debates and policy choices.

Many Alaskans, like many Americans, believe that state government is inefficient and wasteful. The problem is that there are no simple criteria for assessing governmental efficiency and thus no definitive way to determine whether Alaskans' or Americans' perceptions are justified. It is also impossible to assess definitively whether the government has a beneficial or negative effect on Alaska, as its actions affect individual Alaskans in many and different ways. Yet, even though there are no definitive answers, the following observations are worth considering as they provide a balanced perspective on the role and performance of government in Alaska.

Government Is Not Just Another Form of Business

When Bill Sheffield, a very successful businessman, ran successfully for governor of Alaska in 1982, one of his major campaign themes was, "we ought to run state government more like a business."[9] Here Sheffield was reflecting a long tradition in American politics, reinforced by the Progressive Movement at the beginning of the twentieth century, and a belief among many Americans, including some Alaskans, that government would be more efficient if it were run like a business. Sheffield made a valiant effort at the beginning of his governorship to put his campaign theme into practice. Eventually he came to realize, however, that government was in many ways not like a business at all.[10] This is because there are major differences between private sector businesses and government. Three are particularly important.

The Purpose of Business versus the Purpose of Government

The fundamental purpose of business is subject to little dispute. It is to make a profit for its owners and ensure financial stability. In contrast, there is no such readily agreed upon purpose of government, mainly because what each person thinks government should do is a reflection of that person's views on a host of issues relating to the role of government, including:

- What should be life's priorities (for example, does one put one's self and family first or put society first or some combination of the two)?
- What constitutes a just or fair society, and how can such a society best be achieved?
- What obligations does society have to its members, if any, beyond the basic ones of maintaining law and order and defending against foreign invasion?

Because the answers to these questions involve value judgments, people disagree about the role of government based upon their ideological orientation. Across the Western world, conservatives tend to favor a less prominent role for government and liberals favor a more extensive role, partly to aid in promoting equality. In the United States and in Alaska, however, this situation is more complex because of the prevalence of political pragmatism. This often results in a disconnect between the political rhetoric and symbolism of some groups, particularly conservatives but also liberals, and their practical actions.

Business versus Government Budgets

A budget for a private sector business is first and foremost a reflection of what it takes to get the job done. If a product or service is not needed or can no longer be produced at competitive prices, the consequences can be swift and definite. Examples in Alaska in the 1990s include the closures of *The Anchorage Times* and the Sitka and Ketchikan pulp mills. In the economic downturn of 2008–2010 many Alaska businesses also closed their doors for lack of revenue. In contrast, a government budget reflects much more than a business budget. First, a government budget is in part a reflection of what it takes to get the job done, but first and foremost it is a political document. It reflects compromises resulting from political demands from a host of individuals, interest groups, and other governments. Thus, budgetary flexibility and responsiveness are terms that take on an entirely different meaning in the public arena than in the private sector. Rightly or wrongly, "value for money" in government may often be subordinated to political considerations as explained in Box 12.2 below and in Chapter 19 on the state budget.

The Integrated Purpose of the Divisions of a Business versus the Varying Functions of the Branches of Government

Businesses may be organized into several divisions—production, sales, marketing, personnel, and so on—with all of them working toward the same goal of maximizing the profits and long-term financial health of the company. The situation is far more complex in government. Within the overall goals of representation and providing services, each branch of government has a different purpose or combination of purposes.

The legislature's main goals are representation, deliberation, conflict resolution, lawmaking, and oversight of the executive. The necessity of maximizing public participation in these processes is not always conducive to the most efficient use of time and other resources in the legislative branch. The executive branch is mainly involved with delivering services. These are wide-ranging, however, from proprietary-type operations such as a government-owned telephone utility to providing disaster relief after an earthquake. Moreover, government often provides essential services, such as local transit and environmental protection, which the private sector cannot or will not provide because it cannot make a profit from them. Consequently, some executive branch services are more subject to criteria of efficiency than others. And while some types of governmental services are candidates for privatization (transferring to the private sector), services that require subsidies clearly are not. The third branch of government, the judiciary, is more concerned with ensuring fairness in the process than with a swift, low-cost administration of justice.

Thus, government is far from a monolithic structure with an integrated role like business. The consequences for government efficiency will become clearer by first comparing the relationship of efficiency and effectiveness in business and government.

Efficiency and Effectiveness: Not Always a Simple Relationship in Government

In the business world, *efficiency* (getting the maximum output for the minimum expenditure of resources) is closely related to *effectiveness* (achieving a stated goal) because the two are subject to the same criterion—the extent to which the company achieves its overriding purpose of making a profit and increasing financial stability and, perhaps, growth. In government there is often no such simple criterion for judging both efficiency and effectiveness simultaneously.

One reason is that minimizing the cost of providing a service in government may well reduce its effectiveness and even totally undermine it. For example, a city could have a very low-cost police force—very efficient in its use of resources—that is not very effective in controlling crime. A legislator could cut costs tremendously by using a form letter or e-mail to answer all inquiries on one subject, but people would likely feel they were not being effectively represented by that legislator. And the state health department could have a very low-cost program for preventing venereal diseases that is not well publicized and so not effective in reducing these diseases.

Second, political pressures can result in reduced efficiency. This is the case, for instance, with the multi-campuses of many state universities, including the University of Alaska system. It is not a cost-efficient way to run a higher educational system, with its duplication of programs and administrative structures. One or two main campuses would be much more cost-effective. But politically, people demand regional campuses, and politicians fight to establish and maintain them. In other words, what is politically effective and what is economically efficient may often diverge, and sometimes diverge widely. Third, government often acts in response to crises such as war, natural disasters, and economic emergencies, such as industrial plant closings, and the cost of responding is less important than the need for swift action.

With these and many other governmental services, there may be no criteria for meaningfully measuring efficiency and effectiveness other than unrealistically comparing per capita costs with other states, looking at the growth of expenditures over time, or using people's subjective perceptions of effectiveness and efficiency. Further reasons for the divergence between efficiency and effectiveness in government lie in the nature of democracy.

The "Inefficiencies" of Democracy

Contrary to what some people might believe or assume, overall efficiency is *not* the primary goal of a democratic system of government. Its primary goals are to maximize public participation in the decisions about what government does and does not do and to exercise control over government. Theoretically at least, the most efficient form of government to maximize resource use and promote efficiency would be a well-run dictatorship. In this regard, a business is a form of "dictatorship," with management determining almost all decisions about what will be produced and how.

Unlike the divisions within a business, which must be effectively integrated to make the business successful, in a democracy one reason for separating the functions of government between the three branches is to allow one to check the other to prevent precipitous or draconian actions. Given these goals of government, efficiency is much more difficult both to define and achieve. Moreover, in some cases efficiency may not even be a relevant criterion for judging governmental performance. This was the case when the state responded to the closure of pulp mills in Southeast Alaska in the 1990s, and in 2007 to closure of the Agrium fertilizer plant in Nikiski on the Kenai Peninsula. The state's primary goal was to get financial and other help rapidly to the hundreds of people who lost their jobs, including finding them alternative employment in or outside the area. Here, cost was of necessity subordinated to effectiveness.[11]

What makes the situation even more complex in democracies is the effect of wide public participation in the political system. Public officials, both elected and appointed, must bow to political pressures and respond to the needs of some people who may place a low priority on efficiency or have no concern with it at all. This is compounded at the federal level and in many states, including Alaska, in instances where top executive officials are appointed on the basis of political patronage rather than their managerial skills.

So while the American governmental system and that of the fifty states was not purposely designed to work inefficiently, its goals and structure nonetheless produce inefficiencies in aspects of its operation.

The Varying Effects of Government and Its Agencies

Furthermore, government and its agencies have varying effects, sometimes quite contrasting ones, on different segments of society and on particular individuals. So it is misleading to view the role of "the government" as impacting everyone in the nation, a state, or locality in the same way.

One reason for these varying impacts is that governments and their varying agencies are not monolithic. Not only do the three branches of government have differing roles that may lead to conflict and lack of coordination among or within them, there are also differences of purpose among government agencies, particularly in the executive branch, and those purposes may often be in conflict. The classic case in Alaska is between the three so-called resource departments: the Department of Natural Resources (DNR), which is charged with developing the state's resources; the Department of Environmental Conservation (DEC), which is charged with protecting the environment; and the Department of Fish and Game (ADF&G), which regulates the habitats and taking of fish and game. DNR, for example, might wish to lease state land for a certain development, but ADF&G might view that development as harmful to fish habitats.

Also, government policies affect different groups differently. For example, when the minimum wage was raised nationally in July 2009, it benefited the low paid worker but put a financial strain on many small businesses in the midst of an economic downturn. Similarly, a federal policy restricting development of a mine in Alaska, such as the controversial Pebble Mine in Southwest Alaska, will annoy those who support development or see themselves as benefiting from the employment it would provide, but it will please those in the state who oppose development for various reasons and want to protect the environment.

Governmental, Political, and Policy Capacity

The concepts of governmental, political, and policy capacity and how they relate to each other are explained in Chapter 3 on the policy process.[12] Concerns about the role and performance of government and the difficulty of solutions to address them, particularly the problem of relating efficiency to effectiveness, is further illustrated by comparing these three aspects of capacity as they operate in the public sphere with that of the capacity of a business in the private sector.

In business the capacity of a firm is determined primarily by the decisions of management to expand or contract to meet changes in the demand for its products or services. The labor force, plant, and equipment will be expanded or contracted to fit with these decisions. If demand outstrips the capacity of the firm to meet it, it will be unable to fulfill its orders and it will lose sales. Conversely, if its capacity outstrips demand, it will need to cut back its capacity or else it will not be competitive. Thus, in business efficiency, effectiveness and capacity are closely related.

Again, the relationship is far less clear in government and with respect to governmental capacity, which consists of the human, material, and technical resources available to perform its day-to-day operations. Because government is not an integrated and coordinated operation in the way that businesses must be, government can be given responsibilities but not the resources—the capacity—to perform them, thus undermining its efficiency and its effectiveness. Public pressures are such that there may be demand for more services, but fewer resources available to provide them. Legislatures sometimes charge the executive branch with responsibilities without providing the resources to perform them. These so-called unfunded mandates are not just a phenomenon of the federal-state relationship. They are evidenced in the state-local relationship too, and within levels of government. Again, the problem is partly a result of the difficulty of determining the correct amount of resources needed to provide a service. Much depends on the perceived quality and adequacy of the service, and this perception will vary from person to person, from time to time, and from government to government.

Besides governmental capacity, there is also political and policy capacity. Technically, political capacity relates to the broad political system and policy capacity to the policy-making process, but they are similar enough that they can be treated together. Together they constitute the extent to which the political system (particularly political parties and interest groups) and the institutions of government (mainly the legislature and executive) are structured or capable of dealing with the issues facing the society. In other words, are they sufficiently organized and do they wield enough power to deal with problems or do they lack capacity and therefore allow problems to go unresolved? This element of political or policy capacity (or lack of it) is not of concern to business—human, material, and technical resources are all that count in determining capacity. Unlike government, business cannot put off dealing with problems for long and survive.

A Complex but Not a Hopeless Situation

It should be clear by now that assessing the role of government, its performance in terms of efficiency and effectiveness, and what are and are not its negative and positive impacts is fraught with problems. So, making any meaningful assessment as to whether Alaska state government *overall* is at an optimal level of size and efficiency is very difficult. This does not mean that the situation is hopeless and that we should abandon all attempts to improve the efficiency and effectiveness of state government. There are ways to assess and improve certain aspects of governmental performance.

4. THE SEARCH FOR GOVERNMENTAL EFFICIENCY: APPROACHES AND PROBLEMS IN ALASKA AND IN OTHER STATES

In the search for approaches to achieving efficient government, it is best not to think of government as one vast single unit, but as a number of departments and agencies administering a variety of programs and services to the public. In fact, when most people complain about the lack of efficiency in government, they are usually referring to the provision of services by the departments of the executive branch rather than the legislature or the court system (though since the 2010 election there has been much focus on political gridlock in the U.S. Congress). Given the public's focus on the executive branch as well as the chapter's space limitations, this section focuses on ways to assess and improve the efficiency and effectiveness of the executive branch. First we look at ways to measure performance and then ways to improve government operations.

Measuring Efficiency and Effectiveness: No Easy or One Best Method

Indicators or measures of efficiency and effectiveness in state government often include a comparison of wages or compensation levels relative to other levels of government in Alaska, relative to state governments in other states, or between government and the private sector. Another indicator may be the number of public employees per capita or per budget dollar performing a certain service or function (for example, the number of state troopers per 1,000 residents). Yet another indicator is progress toward a stated goal or objective, such as the number of student loan applications processed or the number of job applications evaluated, and so on. Many of these criteria are crude at best. Therefore, in recent years the focus has been on measurable results and progress toward objectives. The key is to focus on results or outcomes or benefits to citizens and not just on inputs, such as the size of the budget, per capita spending, or the number of state employees.

Reinventing Government

Since the early 1990s there has been a discussion about "reinvention" or rethinking how government is run at all levels. The best-selling book *Reinventing Government*, by David Osborne and Ted Gaebler, did much to focus the discussion on increasing government efficiency and to assess progress toward this goal and the problems of measuring progress.[13]

A step in this direction is for governments to start conducting performance evaluations of the tasks it performs and the services it provides. But, as Osborne and Gaebler point out, measuring results is difficult.[14] They found that it takes years to develop adequate measures. Plus, there is the danger that too many measures may be developed, making it impossible for agencies to know which measures to emphasize. Also, periodic elections change the composition and thus the goals of the legislature, the executive, the local city council, or the borough assembly.

Other difficulties with indicators, as pointed out by a National Conference of State Legislatures (NCSL) report, may make the development and application of performance measures for each governmental program or service inappropriate or almost impossible for a variety of other reasons. These include the fact that significant portions of state operating budgets can only be marginally altered, if at all, because entitlements and mandates mean that services must continue in some capacity and the cost covered regardless of performance. In addition, demand for government services tends to grow independently of performance, especially in a declining economy. A state's ability to define and use performance as a functional measure is also restricted somewhat by sharing funding and regulation of certain programs with the federal government. The flexibility to set performance standards in such cases may be preempted by federal regulations. The Medicaid program, which provides health care for low income individuals, is a good example.[15]

Attempts to Promote Governmental Efficiency and Effectiveness

What approaches have been tried to promote governmental efficiency and effectiveness? Box 12.1 outlines six approaches, three from Alaska and three from other states. All the examples come from the surge of activity to improve the performance of government that took place in the 1990s. They do not include all budget and efficiency reforms that have been considered in the past or attempted in state capitals around the nation. They do, however, reflect the range of improvements and reforms that states, including Alaska, seek in an effort to bring greater accountability to the execution of their budgets and to offer lawmakers information that they can use to defend difficult spending choices. The diversity of the six examples is evidence that there is no single or simple approach to achieving efficiency and effectiveness in government. The approaches in other states, in

BOX 12.1

Strategies for Increasing Government Efficiency: Approaches in Florida, Minnesota, Texas, and Alaska

FLORIDA, MINNESOTA, AND TEXAS

Florida: Taxation and Budget Reforms

The Florida constitution requires that every ten years a tax and budget reform commission be created to conduct an investigation and issue a report. The commission independently evaluates state tax and spending policy and procedure. It is empowered to implement reforms by placing constitutional amendments before voters if, in the commission's assessment, the state fails to act upon its recommendations.

Minnesota: Measuring Performance

In the mid-1990s Minnesota state officials sought citizen input to formulate broad policy statements with related performance indicators and interim targets. The objective was to hold government accountable by regularly measuring its progress toward statewide goals and to focus government resources on efforts with the greatest potential to deliver cost-effective results.

Texas: Performance Audits

The approach in Texas to balancing its budget focused on finding innovative and more cost-effective means to conduct government. To accomplish this, the legislature authorized a statewide performance audit in 1991. Teams of state agency and private sector specialists set out to examine state government organization, management, and policies governing state operations.

ALASKA

The Task Force on Governmental Roles

A task force on governmental roles was established in 1991 by the legislature at the request of the Alaska Municipal League (AML) to examine the role of government in providing services at the federal, state, and local levels. The task force, which included prominent public and private sector members, conducted in-depth discussions regarding government roles and responsibilities.

Among its twenty-six recommendations were (1) the level of government that mandates a program or public service should fund it; (2) the state is obligated to provide for basic health, education, and public protection services for all citizens; and (3) all existing programs provided by the state to local governments, individuals, special classes of citizens, or businesses need to be reexamined to see if they are still needed.

Governor Hickel's Organizational Efficiency Task Force

During Wally Hickel's campaign for governor in 1990 he called for an efficiency review of state government. Once elected, he charged his department heads with reviewing their respective operations. Then, during the fiscal year (FY) 1992, the Hickel Organizational Efficiency Task Force worked with budget and policy analysts in the Office of Management and Budget, reviewing budgets, policies, statutes, regulations, and other documents. Task force members also interviewed and consulted with executives, managers, administrators, and other staff in all fifteen departments of the executive branch, as well as legislators with oversight responsibilities for specific departments.

Two major goals of the project were to promote professional management as a key to greater government efficiency and to encourage increased teamwork among state government employees, both inside state government and with other stakeholders or clients, including private nonprofit corporations, contractors, local governments, and the public. The emphasis on teamwork was centered on the principle of "matrix management and organization." Under this principle, team leaders and members were to be identified according to function and expertise and "work together" to accomplish their mission.

The State Long Range Financial Planning Commission Report

The Long Range Financial Planning Commission was appointed jointly by the Legislature and Governor Tony Knowles in March 1995 to recommend a long range plan for Alaska state government finances. The commission developed a financial plan for bringing Alaska state spending in line with anticipated state revenues.

Governor Knowles's budget for FY 1997 attempted to be consistent with the commission's report by including recommendations to streamline government operations, institute various user fees, and reduce the state's operating budget. Of particular note in the Executive Budget Summary for Fiscal Year 1997 were key performance measures—including various inputs, such as costs, and outputs, such as service delivery measures—to assess progress toward each respective department's stated mission and goals.

Source: Developed by the authors from sources in endnotes 16 and 17.

Box 12.1, are taken from the NCSL report referred to above.[16] The Alaska examples are drawn from the charges given to particular task forces and from their reports.[17]

The results in Florida, Minnesota, and Texas were mixed, but the approaches do illustrate a range of available options. Moreover, in all three states, the efforts were driven by political necessity, which affected both the nature of the task and the results. In essence, the Florida and Texas approaches were driven by fiscal conservatism and in Minnesota by a demand for popular participation following a wave of concern about government programs and spending.

The Alaska Experience and General Observations on the Size and Efficiency of State Government

Like the experiences in other states, all three efforts in Alaska outlined in Box 12.1 had their merits and produced some positive results. Not least of these was accountability, which is a key principle of democracy. All three efforts focused government officials (elected and appointed), the public, and the press on what government is doing, how well it is performing, and what, if any, improvements were needed.

Yet, none of the three approaches provided a political silver bullet, largely because government is different from a business and because politics often gets in the way. The AML-requested study raises questions as to what are "adequate services" and about unfunded mandates, in which the level of government that establishes a program may view needed funding levels quite differently from the level charged with implementing it. Regarding the Hickel task force, the concept of "matrix management" has merit, but with limited time and resources and with the absence of a workable accountability and feedback system, the idea met with limited success. In the case of the Long Range Fiscal Planning Report and similar efforts in Alaska, it was applied with varying success during the Knowles administration. But "long term" usually means until the next gubernatorial election. One administration's policies are not binding on the next. Governor Murkowski (2002–2006), who followed Governor Knowles, had his own approach. Moreover, fiscal planning in Alaska, as in most states, is a much more urgent issue in times of declining revenues than in good years. Even the conservative Governor Murkowski abandoned attempts to cut and curb spending when oil prices, and thus state revenues, began to increase markedly in the second half of his term in office.

The three reports found a number of state service functions that were candidates for privatization or contracting out (outsourcing), such as facilities maintenance in certain circumstances and locations, and services such as issuing drivers' licenses and vehicle registrations.[18] Another area of discussion involved the duplication of programs and service functions by state government. In the late 1990s, it was the argument of duplication in state economic development programs that former Alaska State Representative Vic Kohring (a Republican from Wasilla) used to bring about the merger of the Department of Community and Regional Affairs and the Department of Commerce and Economic Development to form the Department of Commerce, Community, and Economic Development (DCCED).

Whether this merger was justified on efficiency grounds or was a political move involving ongoing urban versus rural-bush conflicts is open to question. What can be said is that what often appears to be duplication may not be duplication at all. And, in fact, economic development is an example. Of the more than one hundred state, federal, nonprofit, and tribal programs listed in the *Economic Development Resource Guide 2009*, many, including a host of government programs, serve different clients, such as urban and rural, small business, youth, former prisoners, and so on, or involve agency cooperation in serving the same clients.[19] For instance, DCCED is the state's lead agency in providing support for the statewide network of regional economic development entities known as Alaska Regional Development Organizations, while the Alaska Department of Labor and Workforce Development lists among its core services, "to support Alaska hire and economic development," often with an emphasis on individual Alaskans.[20]

Moreover, politics inevitably influences crucial policy areas, including economic development. Some programs involve subsidies reflecting political support and rewards to certain interests by politicians. Thus, it is often impossible to say precisely what is and is not duplication and to judge efficiency of service delivery given the political nature of some programs.

Can Alaska state government be made more efficient either through some combination of reorganization of government operations, privatization, outsourcing, or elimination of certain functions to reduce spending to a sustainable level and still accomplish the necessary functions of government? As was the case across the states, past processes that looked at Alaska's governmental efficiency focused on the number of staff or level of funding. To be effective, however, future implementation of any efficiency recommendations will need to be more oriented toward looking at indicators and various performance measures, such as number of people served, response time, indicators measuring changed behavior, and so on. However, as Osborne and Gaebler point out, this will be difficult. Government produces endless numbers and statistics, but for the most part the emphasis is on inputs (how many people are served, what service was provided) and not on outcomes—on results.[21]

5. EXPLAINING THE ALASKA PERSPECTIVE ON THE ROLE OF GOVERNMENT AND ITS PRACTICAL POLITICAL CONSEQUENCES

Having explored the issue of the role and operation of government in Alaska from several perspectives, we can ask why many Alaskans have a negative attitude to government and what are or might be its political consequences. First, we must emphasize that, as with Americans overall, not all Alaskans have a negative attitude to government, and even those who do probably see some benefit to government. But there are enough Alaskans who hold negative feelings to make the role and operation of government a political issue and to make politicians sit up and take notice.

Explaining the Negative Attitude

Even though there is virtually no survey research on the attitude of Alaskans to government's role and operation, from various sources, including communications to members of the legislative and executive branches of government, election campaign meetings and literature, the statements of politicians, letters to the editor, among other sources, we can piece together a plausible explanation for this attitude. Five factors appear to come into play.

One, of course, is that many Alaskans have a strong individualistic and independent streak and find government restrictions to be intrusive and overbearing. However, as Table 12.2 shows, there is no justification for claiming that Alaska governments (state or local) impose an overbearing level of taxes. A second factor is that the federal government does put restrictions on the use of resources, such as preventing the opening of the Arctic National Wildlife Refuge (ANWR) to drilling for oil and gas, which many Alaskans (including all governors since 1982) view as obstructing Alaska's development. Negativism in that context may be justifiable, though not to some Alaska environmentalists. A third factor is that government is, indeed, often less than efficient in its delivery of services, whether for good reasons not well understood or owing simply to incompetence. For many citizens, standing in a long line to renew their driver's licenses may be their only contact with government, and they may translate that experience into a negative attitude towards government in general.

A fourth reason is ideology. In particular, libertarians, who support maximizing individual freedom and the role of the private sector, want very minimal government. This view has had its successes in Alaska where, over the years, about 5 percent of Alaskans have seen themselves as libertarians as measured by party registrations and voting. These Alaskans are mainly located in the northern and southern Railbelt. Other strong and consistent conservatives also oppose government on principle and want to end many of what they see as negative practices, such as those who supported Joe Miller for U.S. Senate in 2010. One plank in his platform was to end earmarks (special appropriations for projects in the state secured by the Alaska congressional delegation).

Fifth, a lot of the antigovernment attitude of Alaskans results from myths, misunderstanding, denial, and sometimes ignorance. Many in the state, like those in the nation, want to see Alaska as the free, independent, and idyllic place portrayed in the fall 2010 and spring 2011 television show, *Sarah Palin's Alaska*. Few people are aware of the tremendous dependence of the economy on state government, or that close to 90 percent of the funds used to build most of the roads Alaskans drive on are federal funds. In the end, people will believe what they want to believe, even in the face of facts. This is Alaska's version of the western political paradox, juxtaposing dependence on government and antigovernment attitudes expressed through political rhetoric and symbolism.

Potential Economic and Political Consequences of the Public's and Politicians' Attitudes to Government

As a result of a combination of public demands and the agendas of elected officials, the negative attitudes to government and the perceived need to reform its operations result in policy proposals and sometimes action by government. Over the years, a number of solutions to these perceived problems have been forthcoming from the extreme one of the Alaska Independence Party, which at one time sought Alaska's secession from the United States, to various task forces to deal with government operations (as explained earlier), to cutting the budget in times of reduced state revenues as well as in times of high revenues. Given Alaska's heavy dependence on government and the absence of any clear approach to ensuring government efficiency and effectiveness, what might the consequences of addressing these perceived problems of government be? This question is considered with respect to three areas: the role of the federal government, cutting state government, and working to increase government efficiency.

The Role of the Federal Government

Chapter 10 deals extensively with the pros and cons of the federal government's role in Alaska. Table 12.1 shows just how much money flows from federal coffers to the state. In addition, over the years, Alaska has received major amounts of funding through federal earmarks and federal employment in Alaska, both civilian and military. These federal funds also add to the economy, especially in Anchorage. And as indicated earlier, much of Alaska's infrastructure is federally funded. Thus, if the state were to refuse to accept federal funds or Congress significantly reduced the level of federal funds coming to Alaska, it could have dire economic consequences and affect state services and the lifestyle of many Alaskans.

Cutting State Government

Political rhetoric aside, regarding economic development and diversification, the economic reality is that Alaska is and will remain a two-crop economy—oil and government. So the practicality is that oil is the major source of revenue and oil revenue fuels government spending, particularly state government employment, plus major subsidies to rural-bush Alaska. While tinkering with small budget cuts may be politically advantageous for certain politicians, major cuts could be economically disastrous for the state and politically unwise for many elected officials.

Furthermore, many of the decisions made now will have major consequences in the future for Alaska and its economy. Not least of these is that, with such dependence on government, reducing its size can have serious negative effects on the private sector. The purchasing power of government employees is enormous, and when it is reduced, there are fewer people buying fewer goods and services from local businesses. For evidence of this phenomenon, we only have to recall the downturn in the Alaska economy following the 1986 crash in oil prices and its effect on the private sector, including real estate values.

Working to Increase Government Efficiency

Improvements can certainly be made in the operational efficiency of Alaska state government. However, when politics are injected into the quest for efficiency and effectiveness, the situation becomes more complex and the results difficult, if not impossible, to assess in a meaningful way. Box 12.2 provides an overview of some of these problems and the unintended consequences of the clash between very laudable public policies.

Box 12.2 also alludes to the fact that reducing the state budget by cutting particular programs faces major political obstacles. People may want to cut the budget and increase governmental efficiency as a general principle, but the devil is in the details. No one wants *their* program cut—it is always someone else's program that is wasteful and that should be reduced in size or eliminated. Thus, elected officials are pressured to protect the programs and budget allocations of benefit to their constituents and supporters. The cumulative effect of these pressures is often to increase programs and budget allocations, not to reduce them.

A Political and Policy Course of Pragmatic Dependent Individualism

Alaska's politicians face the dual realities of difficulty in determining the efficiency of state service delivery and the high cost of providing services in the state, particularly in rural-bush areas. However, even if they fully understood these problems (which is often not the case), a large segment of the Alaska public would continue to press politicians to reduce the size of state government. Moreover, these citizens will most likely insist on serious budget cutting before accepting increased taxes or use of Permanent Fund earnings to fund state government. So Alaska politicians are caught in a political bind. They are pressured to cut government and increase its efficiency, but most of them realize how essential government is to the state's economy.

Alaska's congressional delegation and most of its elected state officials pursue a course of pragmatic dependent individualism in dealing with the problem. Many, mostly Republicans, but some Democrats, use anti-federal and anti–big government and

BOX 12.2

Efficiency and Effectiveness versus Government Transparency, Costs, and Political Constituencies

In 2006, one of the issues that helped Sarah Palin get elected as governor was her insistence on ethics and transparency in government. In this regard, she reflected a national trend for more open and accountable government following many ethics violations and other scandals in Washington, D.C., and several states over the previous decade.

However, promoting such a politically popular and laudable goal is not as simple as it may appear. Efficiency and effectiveness in Alaska state government is impacted by the following constraints:

Transparency: The state's procurement code requires an open and competitive process for securing goods or services over a certain cost and requires that contracts be awarded to the lowest bidder. Often better prices and better quality products and services may be available by direct negotiation and sole-source contracts. But maintaining public trust in the open process apparently has a greater value than potential efficiencies or cost savings.

Keeping costs low: It may be more cost-effective in the long run to build a good quality government building that will cost less to maintain over the years of its life. But public pressure to cut government costs may not make this politically feasible.

Political constituencies: Every single program and service provided by the state has a constituency. These include the employees hired to run the program, the citizens who benefit from it, and the politician who sponsored the implementation or expansion of the program. Efforts to create efficiency must respond to each of these constituencies. And unless fiscal constraints require a shrinking of the budget, these constituencies are rarely willing to give up or reduce their programs.

Measurable outcomes: State programs generally do not have results that are easily quantifiable or measurable. There is no "bottom line" balancing of costs and benefits, or profits, as in the private sector. It is, therefore, not obvious (or often even measurable) whether a program is operating inefficiently.

For all these reasons, while efficiency in government has long been a highly prized political goal at the state level in Alaska, it has been more rhetoric than reality in policy making and the operation of government.

Source: Developed by Rick Barrier, former Executive Director, Commonwealth North, and Anthony Nakazawa.

budget-cutting rhetoric, but in many cases this is lip service for political consumption by some of their constituents. Even as they use the rhetoric, they work simultaneously to get as big a share of the budget as they can and to protect programs benefiting their constituents and supporters. Seasoned politicians know that what endears them to most of their constituents and supporters is creating and expanding programs and benefits, not cutting them. Budgetary issues wax and wane in their importance to the public, largely determined by economic conditions, and politicians generally want to pursue high-profile issues. As a result, budgetary concerns and those relating to governmental operations tend to be dealt with on an ad hoc basis rather than a sustained long-term policy approach. Three situations clearly demonstrate this pragmatic approach, even among conservatives.

First, at the federal level, Senator Ted Stevens was a master at securing earmarks and other funds for Alaska. And despite the anti-earmark sentiment across the nation and in Congress in the fall of 2010, all three of Alaska's delegation (two of whom were Republicans) opposed the banning of earmarks. The ban was eventually imposed, and since then they have all worked to get it lifted.[22] All three realize how important earmarks are to Alaska and the adverse consequences of the ban. The consideration of earmarks in Chapter 8 on state revenues makes this very clear.

Second, at the state level, Republican-led legislatures are no less apt to be spenders than Democrats. They clearly realize how important state funds are to the state and particularly to their constituents. Thus, rather than institute overall spending reductions, they tend to shift the same number of total dollars away from social programs and more to aid the private sector. Also, as in the rest of the country, right-wing conservatives have tended to turn to government to establish and ensure the enforcement of cherished values, such as anti-gay rights and anti-abortion. And third, even Republican governors tend to abandon budget cutting and moves for government efficiency when hard economic times turn good, when their reelection looms, or when they realize that their goals are economically or politically unrealistic. We indicated earlier how Governor Murkowski did so after oil prices took an upswing in the second part of his term (2002–2006), and how Governor Hickel during his second term (1990–1994) abandoned his promise to cut the state budget 5 percent a year after being in office for two years. All three situations are examples of recognizing dependence while touting independence and individualism, and dealing with the contradiction in a pragmatic way.

Certainly, there are elected officials in Alaska who genuinely want to put into practice their beliefs about reducing the size of government and its budget while increasing government efficiency. But they are few and far between. Many who run for office on such a platform soon modify it once they are elected. It is one thing to campaign on these issues but quite another to attempt to put them into practice, given Alaska's dependence on government and the culture of incumbents in both Juneau and Washington, D.C. If Joe Miller had been elected from Alaska to the U.S. Senate in 2010, it would have been interesting to see the extent to which he pursued the anti-earmark and other antigovernment, essentially Tea Party, platform of his campaign. Would he have stuck to his ideology and allowed it to trump the interests of Alaskans and perhaps his own self-interest in being reelected?

6. CONCLUSION: MYTHS, PRACTICALITIES, AND THE OWNER STATE

To return to Victor Fischer's quote at the beginning of the chapter, it is clear how extremely important government is to Alaska, especially in the economic sphere. It continues to be as important to the state today as it was at statehood in 1959. In fact, dependence is perhaps the best word to describe the importance of government to the present and future lifestyle of Alaskans. The role of state government includes that of the Owner State, which adds a dimension to the role of government that is not present in most states. It is ironic, then, that this crucial role of government exists in a state where antigovernment sentiments are often expressed. Consequently, there are continual attempts to reduce government's size and demands by the public and elected officials to increase the efficiency and effectiveness of government.

The role of government and the Alaska version of the western political paradox that exists in the minds of many in the state illustrate several of the characteristics of Alaska politics identified in Chapter 2. The four most obvious are the all-pervasive importance of government, the myths and contradictions of Alaska's political rhetoric, a political culture of pragmatic dependent individualism, and a strong strain of fiscal conservatism. Successful Alaska politicians, consciously or subconsciously, are able to walk the fine political line between the reality of Alaskans' dependence on government and their demands regarding the role and performance of government.

Members of the public often ask and suggest: "If we can put a man on the moon, why can't we figure out how to make government more efficient and run it more like a business?" And one of the common themes presented in political campaigns in Alaska, particularly by those who are seeking election for the first time and who are not familiar with the complexities of government, is the need to reform what government does, to cut waste, and to make government more efficient. Most successful office seekers, however, come to realize that the debate about the role of government and increasing its efficiency is much more complex than it appears from the campaign trail and from the outside looking in. This is because, unlike putting a man on the moon or running a business, where there are objective and scientific criteria that can be used to measure achievement, determining the role and efficiency of government is primarily based on value judgments about which people have disagreed in the past and no doubt always will. This does not mean that the situation is hopeless and that efforts to adjust the role and promote the efficiency of government should not be made, as these are important for the development and accountability of the government in a democracy like Alaska. It is simply to say that there are no easy, quick, or foolproof solutions, and we should be very skeptical of those who claim there are or who package their ideology or values as "indisputable facts" when it comes to the role and performance of government.

The subject matter of this chapter provides a foundation for approaching many of the chapters that follow because of the political and value-laden nature of government's activities and the policies it develops. For instance, familiarity with the role of government aids in understanding the makeup of the state budget (Chapter 19), Alaska's local government system and the policy issues (Chapter 18), why Alaska has a Permanent Fund (Chapter 25), the way resources are managed (Chapters 21, 22, 23, and 24), and education, social services, and transportation policies (Chapters 26, 27, and 28). This chapter also provides essential information needed to assess the overall performance of Alaska state government past and present (Chapter 29), and the nature of many current and future issues and possible ways to deal with them (Chapter 30).

ENDNOTES

[1] There is no statewide survey research directly focusing on the attitudes of Alaskans toward government. Information has to be gleaned from surveys on related topics, such as public views on the need for government ethics reform, and so on.

The attitudes of Americans toward government outlined in this section and throughout the chapter are based on three surveys of attitudes across a forty-year period. These are: "Survey on Americans' Attitudes Toward Government," National Public Radio/Kaiser Family Foundation/Kennedy School of Government (Menlo Park, CA, and Washington, D.C., 2000); "How Americans View Government: Deconstructing Distrust" (Washington, D.C.: The Pew Research Center for the People & the Press, 1998); and an updated version of the previous source, "Public Trust in Government, 1958–2013" released in October 2013. For a general perspective on the attitude of Americans to government, see John R. Hibbing and Elizabeth Theiss-Morse, *Stealth Democracy: Americans' Beliefs About How Government Should Work* (New York: Cambridge University Press, 2002).

[2] This information is taken from a questionnaire distributed by the authors at the October 1995 Alaska Municipal League meeting in Valdez; and at the February 1996 Alaska Municipal Clerks Institute held in Juneau.

[3] *Alaska News Nightly*, Alaska Public Radio Network (APRN), August 10, 2009.

[4] Data sources differ on the rankings of Alaska in government employment and amount of federal dollars received, usually because of differing methodologies. Most, however, have placed Alaska in the top five in both cases since the late 1970s. And these slight differences do not negate the major fact that Alaska is very dependent on government of all types.

[5] Interview by Clive Thomas with former Lieutenant Governor Fran Ulmer, April 4, 2008.

[6] See, Walter J. Hickel, *Crisis in the Commons: The Alaska Solution* (Oakland, CA: Institute of Governmental Studies for the Institute of the North and Alaska Pacific University, 2002), especially, "Part Three: The Owner State."

[7] Hickel, *Crisis in the Commons*, 3.

[8] Jackie Calmes, "As Final Debt Plan is Released, Signs That the Fight Is Just Beginning," *New York Times*, December 1, 2010.

[9] Interview by the authors with former governor Bill Sheffield (a Democrat who served from 1982–1986), May 12, 2008.

[10] *Ibid.*

[11] Interview by Anthony Nakazawa with George Laurito, former Job Training Partnership Act Liaison with the U.S. Department of Labor for the Alaska Department of Community and Regional Affairs, December 22, 2010.

[12] See Chapter 3, Section 1.

[13] David Osborne and Ted Gaebler, *Reinventing Government: How the Entrepreneurial Spirit is Transforming the Public Sector* (Reading, MA: Addison-Wesley Publishing Company, 1992). See particularly, "Appendix B: The Art of Performance Measurement," 350–59.

[14] *Ibid.*, 349.

[15] *The Performance Budget Revisited*, National Conference of State Legislatures, Denver, Colorado, February 1994, 4.

[16] *Ibid.*, 9–16.

[17] Office of Management and Budget and the Alaska Municipal League, *Final Report: Task Force on Governmental Roles*, (1992), 5–14; Office of the Governor, Office of Management and Budget, *Governor Hickel's Organizational Efficiency Task Force: Summary Report*, July 1992; *The State Long Range Financial Planning Commission Report*, State of Alaska, November 1995; and Office of the Governor, Office of Management and Budget, *Executive Budget Summary for Fiscal Year 1997*.

[18] A variant of this approach is "in-sourcing" where groups of state employees can offer their own solutions to reduce costs in programs that may otherwise be contracted out/out-sourced, *State Long Range Financial Planning Commission Report*, 4.

[19] Alaska Department of Commerce, Community, and Economic Development, Division of Community and Regional Affairs, *Economic Development Resource Guide, October 2009* at http://commerce.state.ak.us/dnn/Portals/4/pub/EDRG2009.pdf.

[20] State of Alaska, Department of Labor and Workforce Development, *Key Performance Indicators*, at https://omb.alaska.gov/html/performance/program-indicators.html?p=77.

[21] As Osborne and Gaebler illustrate, result-oriented examples range from states that tie vocational education funding to job placement rates to the way governments fund highway construction by specifying the number of years the highway is expected to last and hold the contractor accountable if it fails, *Reinventing Government*, 141–42.

[22] David M. Herrszenhorn, "Senate Defeats Earmark Ban," *New York Times*, November 30, 2010; and Liz Ruskin, "Earmarks: Congress Mulls Return of Practice that Enriched Alaska," *Alaska News Nightly* (APRN), May 15, 2014.

★ PART III ★

Developing and Implementing Public Policy: The Interaction of Beliefs, Institutions, Personalities, and Power

About Part III

Building on Parts I and II, the eight chapters in this part of the book explain in depth the various components of the policy process set out in Chapter 3. It does so by considering the interactions of institutions, organizations, processes, values and beliefs, personalities, and power structures that shape what government does or does not do in Alaska. Each chapter highlights several of the characteristics of Alaska politics identified in Chapter 2 and provides several illustrations of how they affect day-to-day politics.

The quality and extent of democracy in a country like the United States or a state like Alaska depend on the effectiveness of the link between the public and their public officials, particularly elected public officials. The more effective this link, the more citizens can convey their wishes to public officials and make them accountable for their actions, and the better public officials can convey their message to the public.

There are four major methods of political participation that facilitate this link: political parties, campaigns and elections, interest groups, and the media and public opinion. The first three are covered in Chapters 13, 14, and 15, respectively. These chapters explore the political organizations and processes that directly affect the makeup, ideological orientation, and power dynamics of Alaska's major policy making institutions—the legislature and the executive. The role of the media and public opinion is covered last in Chapter 20 because its role is more easily understood after examining the other topics in this part of the book.

Chapters 13 and 14 on political parties and on elections and campaigns, besides explaining their structures and processes, illustrate such characteristics of Alaska politics as friends and neighbors politics, weak political parties, relatively strong interest groups, and a predilection for bipartisanship in some circumstances, as well as pragmatic dependent individualism. These two chapters also illustrate the dual aspects of low partisanship but strong ideology explored in Chapter 5 on political culture. Chapter 15, on interest groups, while recognizing their influence and potential for undermining democracy, argues that interest groups and lobbyists do not dominate Alaska politics.

In most books on state politics, the legislature, governor, and state agencies are considered in two or three separate chapters. However, legislative-executive interaction is so crucial and interconnected in the policy making process that to get an accurate picture of their political dynamics it is best to consider them together. This is done in Chapter 16. Even though the governor has the constitutional upper hand in this relationship, the chapter illustrates Alaska's political characteristic of strong contending branches, sometimes leading to political stalemate, often to bipartisanship, but generally to accommodation between the branches.

Chapter 17 covers the third of the three contending branches of Alaska state government—the judiciary, often referred to as the court system. This branch is less subject to the pressures of democracy, and especially populist demands, but is not completely divorced from politics. In fact, the courts, particularly the Alaska Supreme Court, have made decisions that have been as significant as any policy decisions made by the legislative and executive branches of state government.

All state governments have a close relationship with their local governments both administratively and politically, as local governments administer many state services, particularly education. In turn local governments lobby the state for funds and other benefits. Chapter 18 examines the role of local government and local-state relations. Besides explaining Alaska's unique local government system, the chapter considers the extent to which the system is a partner with the state and how it enhances or inhibits state government's ability to deal with pressing issues.

Because virtually every state policy costs money, the state budget is central to policy making. The process by which this state spending plan is put together is covered in Chapter 19. As the chapter explains, when we strip away the billions of dollars, the graphs and pie charts, and the rationale for and against including certain items, the budget is essentially a political document, and creating it is an exercise in power brokering.

Finally, Chapter 20 examines the role of the media and public opinion. Both are often seen as important influences on policy making in a democracy as well as a check on corruption by government and powerful private interests. The extent to which this view is accurate in practice is an aspect of what the chapter covers. Dealing with these questions is part of a broader question of how much influence the media and public opinion have on politics and policy in Alaska. They authors conclude that the answer is much more complex than we may have been led to believe.

⋆ CHAPTER 13 ⋆

The Role of Political Parties: Weak Organizations, Strong Caucuses, Intermittent Bipartisanship

Laura C. Savatgy and Clive S. Thomas

The roles of political parties, elections and campaigns, and interest groups are very much interrelated in shaping politics, government, and public policy in Alaska and in other democracies. This chapter focuses primarily on political parties, but we give some consideration to the relationship between political parties and interest groups, which are collectively known as *political organizations*.

The main argument presented here on political parties is that Alaska parties are weak statewide and often are not very cohesive. As organizations, their effect on public policy is limited, but they are nonetheless very important through party caucuses in the legislature. In addition, the fluidity and weakness of parties often leads to bipartisanship, or in the case of Alaska's 2014 gubernatorial race, a type of nonpartisanship.

Six of the characteristics of Alaska politics identified in Chapter 2 help explain the status and role of Alaska political parties. Two are particularly significant: weak political parties versus strong interest groups and influential legislative party caucuses often coupled with bipartisanship. The other four are a political culture of pragmatic dependent individualism, friends and neighbors politics, regionalism, and the prominent role of Alaska Natives in state politics.

In the first section of the chapter we briefly define the terms *political party* and *interest group* and then go into more detail about the various facets of a party and the concept of the strength of parties. This is followed by an overview of the major parties that operate throughout the states, including Alaska. Next we examine the role and present status of political parties in the states in general to provide a comparative context in which to place Alaska's experience with parties. The rest of the chapter examines the role of parties in the Alaska public policy-making process, including the important relationship of parties and interest groups, the role of ideology and partisanship, bipartisanship, and the role of the parties in government.[1]

Because the role of political parties in a state is very much influenced by its political culture, it is useful to have read Chapter 5 on political culture before reading this chapter.

1. SOME PRELIMINARIES ABOUT POLITICAL PARTIES AND INTEREST GROUPS AS MAJOR VEHICLES OF POLITICAL PARTICIPATION

Even though many Americans, especially Alaskans, are skeptical of the political benefits of political parties and interest groups, both are indispensable to democracy in the United States and throughout the Western world. Parties and groups are both major means of political participation because they link the public with public officials and policy making. This is not only the case at election time, but also between elections. In addition, the interrelationship between parties and groups, or lack thereof, has important influences on politics, government, and policy making.

Here we briefly define *political party* and *interest group* and go into detail on the five elements that constitute a political party to set the scene for explaining the role of parties, particularly those in Alaska.

Political Party and Interest Group Defined

A *political party* is a group of individuals who share a broad vision as to the direction that society should take and how government should or should not be used to promote this vision. To achieve its goals a party runs candidates in elections with the intent of winning formal control of government in order to implement its programs and facilitates compromise and governance in society as a whole and in government in particular.

However, to talk of a political party as some monolithic entity is misleading and can cause confusion. Parties should be viewed as political organizations with five elements. We explain each element after briefly defining the term *interest group*.

In Chapter 15 we go into detail about interest groups. For present purposes we use a short definition. An *interest group* is an association of individuals or organizations or a public or private entity that attempts to influence government policy in its favor.

Unlike political parties, interest groups do not want to take formal control of government, though some groups do work toward putting individuals in office who favor their political goals (or work to defeat those who oppose these goals). Sometimes they set up political action committees (PACs) to fund such efforts. The role of interest groups in elections is covered in Chapter 14 on campaigns and elections.

Five Elements of Political Parties

Viewing American parties as loose-knit organizations consisting of five elements is much more enlightening than seeing them as monolithic entities. These elements are: (1) an identifiable party within the electorate (known in political science as a "mass" party); (2) a formal organization; (3) a core of members deeply involved in the organization, known as party activists; (4) factions within the organization; and (5) participation in state governance by individuals identifying or affiliated with the party.

1. The Party of the Electorate

The broadest element of a political party consists of a segment of the electorate in a nation, state, or locality that identifies or is affiliated with the party and may vote for its candidates. Many members of the electorate may or may not be politically savvy or officially a member of the party. In Alaska, people who are strong party identifiers are generally registered to vote as Democrats, Republicans, or with some other officially recognized third party like the Alaska Independence Party (AIP).

2. The Official Party Organization

The formal and official organization of a party is set out in the party constitution. The two major parties and some third parties have national, state, and local party organizations. In addition, the two major parties and some third parties have affiliate organizations such as Young Democrats and Republican women's groups. In some cases, a person can join a party by paying a membership fee, but most states require no fee. Those identifying with a party when they register to vote may or may not be formal members of that party.

Party organizations at both the national and state levels raise funds for the party and for promoting the party at election times as well as working to get out the vote. They also develop the official party platform, which is often put together at their annual or biennial party convention. Closely associated with the official party are party activists and volunteers. Public officials elected under the name of the party may also be associated with the party organization and may follow its platform and ideology. Many elected officials using the party's name, however, may not. This is particularly the case in Alaska.

3. Party Activists

Party activists are the people who work for the party, usually as volunteers. They attend meetings of national, state, or local party organizations and work on political campaigns. They usually have strong opinions on the policies that the party should pursue and are generally very committed to the goals of the party. They form a very small percentage of party adherents, but because of their activism they have influence out of all proportion to their numbers in shaping the platform and image of the party.

4. Party Factions

As broad coalitions of interests, parties are umbrella organizations, a sort of political tent for many interest groups who share the same or similar values and the same or similar positions on many issues. But because of differences on specific issues, most parties have factions within their ranks in the form of minority opinions on various subjects and issues. In effect, a faction is a "party within a party."

The Democrats include a broad range of interests, as do the Republicans. The latter, for instance, include right-wing perspectives against abortion and gay rights (including organizations like Focus on the Family and the Moral Majority) through moderate to left-wing Republicans who favor many social programs but may be against too much regulation of business.

There is often major conflict among party factions. This conflict not only affects the official party platform, which may end up being a compromise between various factions. It can also affect how the party operates in government, even to the point of undermining the party's effectiveness.

5. The Party or Parties in Government: Legislature and Executive and Legislative Caucuses

Broadly defined, the party in government (or parties, if the legislature has different majority parties in the two houses, or if the legislature and executive are of different parties) is made up of individuals elected and appointed to government positions in the legislature and the executive under the banner of a particular party. At both the federal and state levels in the United States, the parties in government are predominantly Democrats or Republicans. There are varying degrees of cohesiveness between the legislative and executive in terms of party and its official platform. In both houses of the legislature (with the exception of Nebraska, which is both unicameral and officially nonpartisan) there is usually a majority and a minority caucus (or like-minded group). These caucuses are usually based on party affiliation, either Democrat or Republican, but sometimes a bipartisan coalition. It is the majority caucus in each house that runs the day-to-day business of their respective chambers.

Regarding ideology and partisanship, there is often a difference between the official platform of a political party and the positions taken by the party caucuses, especially the majority caucus. A legislator who uses a major party label to get elected but is, to varying degrees, at variance with the official position of the party, is often called a RINO (Republican in Name Only) or DINO (Democrat in Name Only). In Alaska the relationship between the parties in government, particularly the majority caucuses in the two houses of the legislature, and party platforms and the beliefs of party activists, is tenuous and often nonexistent. In fact, perhaps as many as 40 percent of Alaska legislators are RINOs and DINOs.

Strong versus Weak Political Parties

Political parties can be viewed on a continuum or spectrum from strong to moderate to weak. A strong party is one that can (1) determine who its candidates will be, (2) enforce voting discipline on those elected, and (3) impose sanctions against recalcitrant elected members. Strong parties have considerable influence over the policy agenda and over public policy making, partly because they control the access of interests and interest groups to the policy making process. The weaker the party, the less it controls its agenda, public policy outcomes, and activities of interest groups. As this chapter progresses we will see the explanatory value of this strong-moderate-weak party classification as it relates to the five elements of political parties and particularly the all-important party-interest group relationship.

2. PARTY SYSTEMS IN THE STATES AND ALASKA'S POLITICAL PARTIES

Moving to the specifics of state parties in Alaska and other states, an examination of types of party systems, party competition, and party affiliation will help place Alaska's party system in perspective and provide information for understanding the role of Alaska's parties in the policy process. More specifically, it will tell us which of the five elements of Alaska's parties considered earlier plays the most important policy-making role.

Party Systems, Party Identification, and Party Competition in the States

The Major Parties and Third Parties

As at the national level, the vast majority of states have a two-party system dominated by the Republican Party and the Democratic Party. Besides these, all states have third parties of various types and levels of operation. For instance, most states have a Green Party and a Libertarian Party. The former, which grew out of the environmental movement, favors restructuring government to increase citizen participation; the latter wants to reduce the role of government to a minimum. In Minnesota, a third party, the Reform Party, won the governorship in 1998 in the person of former wrestler Jesse Ventura.[2]

Generally, however, third parties do not do well in state politics. They are often inhibited by state laws requiring, for example, a minimum percentage of votes in the previous election cast by voters for the party in order for it to qualify for official party status in future elections, or to have a certain percentage of voters registered as identifying with the party. In addition, wide and deeply embedded support for, or at least identification with, the two major parties makes it difficult for third parties to gain widespread support. Thus, third parties generally lack the support necessary to get legislators and executive officials elected. And because they cannot get anyone elected, few voters take them seriously.

Party Identification

Across each of the fifty states, depending on the year, affiliations with the two major parties account for between 45 and 90 percent of total registered voters. Table 13.1 shows the percentage of registered voters identifying themselves with a major party, a third party, or no party in ten selected states in 2008. This is a fairly typical year since the early 1990s. States are listed in order of the percentage of voters who identify with the two major parties. The figures are instructive in placing Alaska's party affiliations, or lack thereof, in comparative perspective, which will be explained later.

Party Systems and Party Competition

Unlike the national level, where the two parties are very competitive, as reflected in party competition in Congress, some states are dominated by one party, some lean toward one party, while still others are competitive. Party competition affects the balance of power in state politics and the way the legislature operates.

TABLE 13.1

Political Party Affiliation in Ten Diverse States in 2008

(Listed in Order of Percentage of Combined Major Party Affiliation)

STATE	DEMOCRATS	REPUBLICANS	TOTAL FOR THE MAJOR PARTIES	TOTAL FOR OTHER PARTIES	UNAFFILIATED*
Oklahoma	49%	40%	89%	11%	0%
Pennsylvania	51%	38%	89%	6%	5%
Wyoming	26%	60%	86%	3%	11%
Nebraska	34%	49%	83%	1%	16%
New Mexico	50%	33%	83%	1%	16%
Nevada	45%	37%	82%	1%	17%
Louisiana	52%	25%	77%	22%	1%
California	44%	31%	74%	5%	20%
Massachusetts	37%	12%	49%	1%	50%
Alaska	**15%**	**25%**	**40%**	**7%**	**53%**

* Includes unaffiliated, nonpartisan, and those who decline to state any response.

Source: Developed by the authors from Nebraska, as of October 2008, www.sos.ne.gov/elec/2008/index.html; Pennsylvania, as of November 2008, www.dos.state.pa.us/elections/cwp/view.asp?a=1310&q=446974&electionsNav=|; Oklahoma, as of January 2009, www.ok.gov/~elections/; Wyoming, as of January 2009, soswy.state.wy.us/Elections/VRMonthlyStats.aspx; New Mexico, as of January 2009, www.sos.state.nm.us/AVRSINDX.html; Nevada, as of January 2009, sos.state.nv.us/elections/voter-reg/2009/0109maint.asp; Louisiana, as of February 2009, www.sos.louisiana.gov/tabid/155/Default.aspx; California, as of October 2008, www.sos.ca.gov/elections/ror/ror-pages/15day-presgen-08/ror-102008.htm; Massachusetts, as of October 2008, www.sec.state.ma.us/ele/eleidx.htm; and Alaska, as of July 7, 2008, www.elections.alaska.gov/statistics/regbyprty7-7-08.html#state.

According to the Ranney Index of State Party Competition for 2007–2011, Idaho and Utah are dominated by the Republicans, and Democrats are on the endangered species list in these states. In contrast, Massachusetts, Arkansas, and West Virginia are Democratic Party–leaning states, and California, Michigan, Oregon, and Washington are two-party competitive states. Since 2000 or so, this index has listed Alaska as a Republican-leaning state.[3] The role of party competition and its consequences for public policy are discussed in detail later in the chapter.

Party Affiliation and Political Parties in Alaska

Party Affiliation

Table 13.2 shows the percentage of Alaskans who declared affiliation with a political party or party group as of September 2015. To become a recognized party in Alaska, a group must either (1) field a candidate for governor and receive at least 3 percent of the total votes cast in the preceding general election or (2) have registered voters identified with that party equal to at least 3 percent of the total votes cast for governor. In years when there is no race for governor, the 3 percent figure may be based on the U.S. Senate race or, if there is no U.S. Senate election, the race for the U.S. House. A recognized political party remains a party unless its designated candidate fails to receive at least 3 percent of the votes cast or the number of registered voters identifying with that party drops below this required percentage. In that case, it becomes a political group.[4]

As Table 13.2 illustrates, compared with other states (see Table 13.1), Alaska has very low party identification. In fact, in September 2015, over 54 percent of the voting public did not identify with any party. Some 37 percent of all voters registered as undeclared, which means they did not wish to declare an affiliation with a party, and over 17 percent registered as nonpartisan, indicating that they did not support the policies or interests of any political party.[5] This fifty plus percentage has remained fairly constant since the 1970s and is very similar to the figure in Table 13.1. This low level of party identification has major implications for the role of Alaska's political parties in policy making.

The Two Major Parties

Like all states, the two major parties in Alaska are the Republicans and the Democrats, both of which are affiliated with their national parties. Both exhibit the five elements of a political party identified in the previous section.

In terms of party organization, each has a similar structure. The Alaska Democratic Party is formally structured with party leaders who make up the Executive Committee, members from each of the state's electoral districts who make up the Central Committee, Democratic legislators, and members of Democratic groups and clubs. Many organizations associate with the party, including the House Democratic Campaign Committee,

TABLE 13.2

Identification of the Alaska Electorate with Political Parties and Political Groups

(As of September 3, 2015)

		RECOGNIZED POLITICAL PARTIES						POLITICAL GROUPS			
TOTALS	**OVERALL**	**A**	**D**	**L**	**R**	**N**	**U**	**G**	**C**	**V**	**T**
Statewide Totals in Numbers (441 Precincts)	506,543	16,012	69,378	7,409	134,542	88,517	187,633	1,720	246	1,082	4
Percentage Totals (Rounded)	100	3.2%	13.7%	1.5%	26.6%	17.5%	37.0%	0.3%	0.049%	0.214%	0.001%

Political Parties

A – Alaskan Independence Party
D – Alaska Democratic Party
L – Alaska Libertarian Party
R – Alaska Republican Party

Political Groups

G – Green Party of Alaska
V – Veterans Party of Alaska
C – Alaska Constitution Party
T – Twelve Visions Party

Other

N – Nonpartisan (no party affiliation)
U – Undeclared (no party declared)

Source: State of Alaska, Division of Elections, as of September 3, 2015, at http://www.elections.alaska.gov/statistics/vi_vrs_stats_party_2015.09.03.htm.

the Senate Democratic Campaign Committee, Anchorage Democrats, and the Young Democrats. The Alaska Republican Party has a similar organizational structure. Some of the groups associated with the Party include the National Federation of Republican Women (with affiliates throughout the state), Midnight Sun Republican Women, and the Young Republicans National Federation. For both parties there is some form of organization at the precinct level, though organization tends to be minimal in rural-bush Alaska.[6]

Each party holds a biennial convention and draws up a party platform. Participation in developing the party platform includes the activists and some ideological factions. As a consequence, the party platform is often more ideologically consistent than the pragmatic perspective of the members of the electorate.

Third Parties and Party Groups in Alaska

Alaska also has third parties. Most prominent have been the Alaska Independence Party (AIP) and the Libertarian Party. Another party that has alternated between political party and political group status, depending on its electoral support, is the Green Party. A Moderate Republican Party was active for the twenty-five years following its establishment in 1986. It was the creation of political activist and anti-corruption crusader Ray Metcalfe, but ceased to exist by 2012. Box 13.1 provides an overview of two third parties and two party groups in Alaska. Most third parties and party groups have minimal organizational structure. The AIP likely has the most extensive organization of the third parties and party groups.[7]

Like their counterparts in national politics and in other states, Alaska's third parties operate at the fringes. Very few third-party candidates have been elected to the Alaska legislature. A total of three Libertarians (Dick Randolph, Ken Fanning, and Andre Marrou) served at various times between 1971 and 1988, but no third-party candidate has been elected since 1988. A non-affiliated candidate, Dan Ortiz, was elected to the House in 2014. Although Walter Hickel was elected governor on the AIP ticket in 1990, this was, in essence, a political maneuver to secure his election. Prior to that campaign, he was a lifelong Republican and had served as governor from 1966 to 1969 as a Republican before being appointed as U.S. Secretary of the Interior by Republican President Richard Nixon.

In the 2014 race for governor a unique circumstance occurred in Alaska party politics. After the August primary the Democrats and their candidate Byron Mallott and independent candidate Bill Walker combined their campaigns to form the Alaska First Unity ticket, a nonpartisan or "no-party" ticket as they often referred to it. The ticket won a narrow victory with Walker as governor and Mallott as lieutenant governor.

BOX 13.1

Two Alaska Third Parties and Two Party Groups

THIRD PARTIES

The Alaska Libertarian Party—ALP

The Libertarian Party has been active in Alaska since the late 1960s. Between 1971 and 1988 three members of the party served various terms in the legislature. Between 1986 and 1999, however, the party lost recognized political party status due to low voter registration numbers. Since then, it has maintained status as a recognized party, allowing candidates to appear on the Alaska ballot.

Notable planks in the ALP platform are: "the drastic reduction and eventual elimination of all taxes," "the complete separation of education and the state," and the legalization of "nonviolent" crimes such as drug use and prostitution. There is also a national Libertarian Party. It has its own platform, though its general goals of limiting government are consistent with those of the Alaska party.

The Alaska Independence Party—AIP

The AIP has been active since the 1970s, but was only officially recognized by the state in 1984. Although a small party, it is the third largest in Alaska. It is also the oldest contemporary third party in the United States. Two of the most recognized personalities of the AIP were the late Joe Vogler and two-time governor Wally Hickel (though, as a life-long Republican, he might be called an "IPINO"—Independence Party in Name Only).

While probably the most well-known goal associated with the AIP is the repeal of Alaska statehood and independence from the United States, the current twenty "planks" of the party platform do not specifically state this as a goal. The major themes in the party platform are individual rights and less government interference in commerce and private life.

Since the 1990s the AIP has maintained a significant membership base, but this has not translated into recent success at the polls. The AIP is currently "hoping to shed its image of a fringe party and (again) be considered a viable third party option."

PARTY GROUPS

The Green Party of Alaska

The Green Party of Alaska was founded in 1990 when gubernatorial candidate Jim Sykes earned enough statewide votes to gain official status for the party. This was the first time the party had been granted official status anywhere in the United States. Since then it has struggled to maintain a significant presence in the state. In 1998, gubernatorial candidate Desa Jacobsson barely captured the required 3 percent of the vote to maintain the party's official status.

Many of the problems the party has encountered in maintaining status as a recognized political party in Alaska likely stem from the unpopularity of the party in general. Conservatives tend to see it as recklessly liberal, while many liberals blame the Greens for causing the Democrats to lose the 2000 presidential election, when Green candidate Ralph Nader arguably took enough votes from Democrat Al Gore to tip the extremely close election in favor of George W. Bush. Combined with a party platform that espouses such principles as reproductive rights, gay rights, environmental justice, and removing the term under God from the pledge of allegiance, it is not difficult to see why the party has foundered in rather conservative Alaska.

Alaska Constitution Party

The Alaska Constitution Party's webpage states, "We exist to uphold the Alaska and U.S.A. Constitutions." It emerged following the 2008 national and state elections and, in essence, is the Alaska expression of the national Tea Party movement that developed in the same period. The party has a conservative, libertarian, and populist orientation. But besides its promotion of a strict construction view of the U.S. and Alaska Constitutions, it is antigovernment and favors lowering taxes and cutting the federal deficit.

The party filed an application to be recognized as a political party in early 2012. On considering the application, the Division of Elections gave the party the status of a "political group" and began tracking its number of registered voters.

Source: Developed by the authors from interviews and from the relevant third party and party group websites, the Division of Elections website, and Matthew Coppock, "On Vogler, an Independent Alaskan," *Juneau Empire*, March 14, 2008. Website addresses can be found in endnotes 4 and 7 of this chapter.

3. THE ROLE AND STATUS OF POLITICAL PARTIES IN STATE POLITICS COMPARED WITH ALASKA

Two contemporary overviews of the role and status of political parties in state politics offer contrasting assessments. Holbrook and La Raja argue that "political parties permeate every aspect of state governments, and political scientists have long stressed their crucial role." By contrast, Bowman and Kearney comment that, when talking about American political parties, including those in the states, the words often used are: "decline, decay and demise."[8] In actual fact, both statements are accurate in that parties are all-pervasive in state politics, but they have also gone through rough political seas since the 1970s.

To place the role and status of Alaska's parties in state politics and policy making, here we explain: (1) the general role that parties play in the social and political life of a democracy, (2) party nominations and endorsements, (3) party competition in elections and in the legislature, (4) two perspectives on the specific political purpose of parties in facilitating government and public policy making, and (5) the changing roles and significance of political parties as political organizations in the states.

The General Social and Political Role of Parties in Democracies and in the States

As Holbrook and La Raja state, there is no doubt that political parties permeate every aspect of state governments and are here to stay for a long time to come, despite recent trends. Like national politics, state politics is essentially partisan politics, and this is reflected in the political cultural values of Americans despite their often antagonistic attitude toward parties. Box 13.2 explains the broad range of functions that parties can and often do perform in state politics. In Alaska, many of these functions are less significant for society, politics, and government than they are in many other states.

Party Nominations and Party Endorsements

One element of party strength is the extent to which the party is able to control who runs for office (officially appointing or nominating individuals as party candidates) and to officially endorse particular candidates running under the party label. By controlling nominations and endorsements, the party ensures that only those subscribing to its ideology and the party platform will be on the ballot.

As a part of the Progressive Movement, the growth of the direct primary system early in the twentieth century turned the nomination of candidates over to the voters. Some of the stronger political party organizations, in states like New York, Connecticut, and Rhode Island, were able to delay adoption of direct primary laws for many years. In such states strong party organizations adopted procedures enabling them to endorse the candidates they preferred before the primaries in an effort to control, or at least influence, the

BOX 13.2

The Role of Political Parties in the States

Outlined below are six roles that political parties can perform. Acquiring political power (role number 5) is likely dominant in all political systems with active parties. The extent to which each of the other roles is performed varies from state to state, depending on the importance of parties to the state concerned. Overall, these functions are more extensively performed in traditionally strong party states in the Northeast and upper Midwest and less so in the South and West, including Alaska.

1. AGENTS OF POLITICAL SOCIALIZATION AND POLITICAL CULTURE

Parties contribute toward citizens' developing their political culture through political socialization by parents, family, peers, church, and so on. Most people take on the political values of their parents (though about one-third reject them in their teen years). Parties provide alternative perspectives on the role of government and how various issues in society should be approached.

2. AGGREGATING, MOBILIZING, AND FOCUSING THE BELIEFS AND INTERESTS OF LARGE NUMBERS OF CITIZENS

Parties provide a vehicle for bringing together, focusing, and channeling the like-minded interests of large numbers of people ranging from tens of thousands in Alaska to tens of millions in the United States overall. The fact that conservatives, liberals, and moderates can associate or align with a particular political party and support it in its attempt to win control of government provides a structure and focus to the political system that would be lacking without parties.

3. PROVIDING CHOICES ON POLICY DIRECTION AT ELECTIONS

By nominating and endorsing candidates and offering a party platform, parties provide the electorate with a set of political and policy choices at elections and help to make sense of what would otherwise be a bewildering set of choices if parties did not exist and all candidates were nonpartisan or independent. And the more competitive the parties, the more meaningful the choices will be. However, some states have little party competition, and some parties are less concerned with promoting an ideology or value system and more with securing control of government.

4. ORGANIZING GOVERNMENT AND OFFERING ALTERNATIVE PUBLIC POLICIES

Government in all democracies, including the U.S. federal government and all the states (except Nebraska), is party government, though sometimes

nominating process. Even today states with strong parties are most likely to have pre-primary endorsing procedures, which is one reason why they are strong party states. As of 2016, party leaders and officeholders in twenty-two states are able to exert influence over party nominations. They make pre-primary endorsements to increase party control over party nominations or to guide the primary voters in choosing a party-endorsed candidate.[9]

The courts have weighed in on the issue of nominations and endorsements, sometimes promoting party strength and at other times undermining it. For example, in 1989 in *Eu vs. San Francisco Democratic Committee*, the U.S. Supreme Court ruled that it is party coalition government. The party that wins the most seats in the legislature (the majority party caucus) and wins the executive, controls and runs government. The minority party or parties—the political opposition—also facilitates government by providing policy alternatives and by taking the majority to task for their actions.

As noted, however, there is often a major disconnect in the American states between the party platform and party ideology, particularly that of party activists, and the policies that the governing party pursues.

5. ADVANCING THE AMBITIONS OF POLITICIANS THROUGH ACQUIRING, EXERCISING, AND RETAINING POLITICAL POWER

Whatever their ambitions in politics, be these self-serving, to help those who elected them, or a combination of both, politicians cannot do anything without power. The organizational structure and, in many cases, the ideological bases of parties offer politicians a vehicle for obtaining power.

Parties promote the power of politicians by providing a political identification that voters recognize and may support. In a pluralist democratic system that places a premium on numbers—be this a majority or minority in government—this recognition encourages elected officials to combine with other like-minded elected officials. In particular, if their party is in power, it gives members of the majority a degree of influence over public policy.

In contrast, those who run as independents have no such identification or structure to use to promote their power. They will be politically powerless unless they join one or more of the parties in some form of coalition.

6. ENHANCING THE CAPACITY TO HOLD PUBLIC OFFICIALS ACCOUNTABLE TO THE PUBLIC AND THE ELECTORATE

Besides the role of the minority party to hold the governing party accountable to the public, the organization of politics and policy making along party lines provides the public with a focus to hold government accountable. The actions of government, whether positive or negative in the eyes of voters, can be attributed to the party in power and that party will be judged in the next election.

In the United States it is not as clear-cut as this in practice and certainly not as clear-cut as in most parliamentary systems, where one party controls and dominates both the legislative and executive functions of government. In contrast, in the United States and its states, there is often less connection between party ideology and the governing party because government is often divided, with opposing parties controlling the legislature and executive and sometimes with opposing parties controlling each house of the legislature. Consequently, responsibility is often hard to pin on one party. This is compounded by party coalitions, both formal and ad hoc, and by bipartisanship.

Source: Developed by the authors from sources in endnote 1 of this chapter.

California law could not prohibit parties from officially endorsing or opposing candidates running in a primary election and could not prohibit candidates running in a primary election from claiming that they were officially endorsed by their parties.[10] The constitutional basis for the ruling was the right of association. By contrast, in October 2008, the U.S. Ninth Circuit Court of Appeals held that political parties do not have the right to control which party members can run under the party label in Alaska's primary election. In essence, the court ruled that any voter registered as a member of a political party could seek that party's nomination.[11]

Party Competition in Elections and in State Legislatures

Although all states have some party competition, its degree varies from very competitive to one-party leaning and, mainly in the case of Idaho and Utah, one-party dominant states. States with more variables in their socio-economic and political makeup (population, racial and ethnic diversity and culture, strong party identification, and so on) are more likely to have competitive elections and policy making in government.

Party electoral competition and competition in policy making generates voter interest and higher voter turnout. Increased voter interest and turnout are the result of increased voter choices. Moreover, the greater the party competition the more likely the state is to produce moderate policies. If a state is overwhelmingly Republican (legislature and governorship both controlled by the Republicans) the party faces limited competition and likely will be more conservative in its policy making, as in Idaho and Utah.

Two Models of Party Operations in State Politics

The Responsible Political Party Model

This perspective or model holds that parties should be ideologically consistent and present to the voting public clearly distinct principled policies. Based on this, voters will decide on a candidate according to the extent to which their political beliefs are aligned with the platform, policies, and politics of the candidate's party.

The Functional Party Model

This model sees a party as a loosely organized group with the purpose of electing candidates with a given label with the major political goal "to wield political power."[12] Unlike Western Europe and most of the world's democracies, in the United States the functional party model is most often the one of choice by political parties at the national, state, and local levels.

A Combination of the Two Party Models in Reality

Given the intricate combination of ideology, partisanship, and political pragmatism, in reality it is not an either/or choice between the responsible and functional party models. All states combine the two to some degree. The exact combination will depend mainly on the extent of ideology and partisanship in a state and this, in turn, will affect the types of public policies that a state enacts. For reasons explained more fully below, states in the Northeast and upper Midwest exhibit less of the functional party model than many western states, including Alaska.

The Changing Roles of State Political Parties

From the beginning of the twentieth century until the 1960s, political parties played a major role in politics and in the day-to-day operations of government at the national level and in many states, particularly in the Northeast and upper Midwest. They not only controlled the policy agenda and the passage of many public policies, but, through political patronage, they also controlled many jobs in government—only loyal party supporters got government jobs. But since World War II, the development of merit appointment systems for civil servants, the passage of campaign finance and conflict of interest laws, and an increase in the independence and nonpartisan nature of the electorate have undermined parties. Also important has been the rise of a more sophisticated political public who see interest groups, with their narrower focus, as more effective agents than political parties in achieving policy goals.

As a result, by the early 1980s, political parties, particularly in the states, appeared to be in major decline in setting policy agendas, as coordinators of policy, and as mainstream representatives of state electorates in regard to their official party organizations, platforms, and party activists, though, again, this varied from state to state. Parties, particularly the two major ones, have adapted to some extent and will not disappear. This is because, regardless of their degree of ideological consistency or functional capacity, parties are essential for the exercise of democratic governance.[13] In addition, as explained in Box 13.2, parties provide some structure and consistency to politics, political debate, and particularly the organization of government.

4. COMPARING THE ROLE OF PARTIES IN PUBLIC POLICY MAKING IN ALASKA AND OTHER STATES

Further insights into the role of parties in Alaska politics in general and in the public policy process in particular can be gained by placing Alaska in context with other states in regard to party-group relations, ideology, partisanship, and bipartisanship.

The Political Party-Interest Group Connection and Its Significance to Alaska Politics and Policy Making

Differences between Parties and Interest Groups

Besides the major distinction that parties work to take formal control of government while interest groups do not, there are three other major differences between parties and interest groups.

First, parties are very broad in their focus and goals because they have a vision for the entire society, and this requires them to have a policy position on all issues within their political jurisdiction. Interest groups, on the other hand, are usually much narrower organizations focusing on promoting the cause of specific groups like schoolteachers, cruise ship companies, or victims of crime. Second, and a related point, parties are broad coalitions of various interests. For example, the Democratic Party embraces many labor groups, environmentalists, and various other liberal causes, which can produce major internal conflicts over party goals and policy in government. Similarly, the Republican Party embraces a broad range of interests including business groups, right-to-life supporters, those who want to get tough on crime, and various other right-of-center and conservative interest groups. So the party also embraces many party factions and, in particular, produces conflicts between moderate and right-wing members and organizations. In contrast, the narrow focus of most interest groups gives them the potential of a much higher degree of internal cohesion.

Third, whereas parties are first and foremost political organizations, most interest groups are not. Getting involved in politics is only one aspect, and often a minor aspect, of the role of many interest groups. Most have other functions, such as providing information to members about activities or training opportunities in their field of interest, such as when the Alaska Municipal League provides training sessions for city managers. Many interest groups may go years without being involved in politics if there are no issues that affect them in the public policy arena.

Despite these differences, the extent of the connection, or lack thereof, between parties and interest groups is central to shaping public policy in virtually all political systems but particularly in democracies, including Alaska.

The Party-Interest Group Connection

Moving to a more in-depth analysis of the party-group connection and setting aside for the moment the nonpolitical roles of interest groups, we can look at this relationship in terms of the degree of closeness between certain parties and groups and also the power relationship between them. These two aspects of the party-group relationship fundamentally affect the power distribution in a state, what gets on the policy agenda, which policies get enacted, and which ones do not.[14]

The Closeness of the Party-Group Relationship

Box 13.3 sets out the five major models that show the relationships between parties and interest groups in the American states. Three comments on these models will be instructive. First, the vast majority of interest groups do not associate with any political party (Box 13.3, model 5). Second, despite this, the major interest group forces in state politics, businesses of all types, labor (both traditional unions and professional groups such as schoolteachers), utilities, health care groups, agriculture, and so on, do tend to gravitate toward either the Democrats or Republicans. It is the association between parties and major interest groups (or the lack of such an association) that is a major factor in shaping each state's particular character as a political system.

Third, regarding Alaska, in terms of political connections, realizing that noninvolvement likely accounts for most group activity, model 3 (One-Party Leaning/Neutral

BOX 13.3

Five Major Models of Political Party-Interest Group Relations in the American States

1. PARTISAN MODEL

The partisan model describes a situation in which there is a strong partisan connection between a political party and an interest group. The connection may be based on ideology, but it can also be based upon historical circumstances that go beyond ideology. The relationship of many labor organizations, both individual unions and state affiliates of the AFL-CIO, with the Democratic Party is an example.

2. IDEOLOGICAL MODEL

This model describes groups that have a strong ideological attachment to a party because of a similarity in political or social and economic philosophy. Or it may be that the group's goal orientation—reaction, status quo, reform—veers it toward one particular party. This is often the case with business, particularly pro-development groups, and the Republican Party.

3. ONE-PARTY LEANING/NEUTRAL INVOLVEMENT MODEL

A group may have leanings to one party—because of ideology, history, or other circumstances—but the group often remains neutral in its association with parties for one or more reasons. This is likely because it sees maintaining outward neutrality as the best way to achieve its policy goals, because its membership is divided in terms of partisanship, or because of the fluid nature of the electoral process, among other reasons. Often, the substance of its demands on the political system (especially if these are technical, administrative or regulatory in nature) does not make party connections necessary or desirable. This is the case with many professional groups.

4. PRAGMATIC MODEL

In this model the group has no partisan and perhaps only a weak, if any, ideological attachment to any particular party. Thus, it is willing to work with any party, whether that party is in or out of power, to help promote its goals. There is a large percentage of such groups in state political systems, especially states with weak political parties. Some groups are also bound by their constitutions or other organizational provisions to be nonpartisan.

5. NONINVOLVEMENT MODEL

Noninvolvement is a situation in which a group or organization may feel that its goals are best achieved outside of the regular party system. It may occasionally work with parties or vie for their attention in certain circumstances. But for a variety of reasons—lack of understanding of the political process, choice, and so on—it has little, if any, relationship with parties. Noninvolvement may also describe a group whose goals and philosophy are such that it finds it difficult, if not impossible, to gain access to a party.

This category is by far the largest of the five identified here in terms of the number of groups operating in the American states and especially if a broad definition of "organized interest" is used to include government and its agencies involved in lobbying. Therefore, lack of interaction or minimal interaction with parties rather than close ties and an ongoing relationship with them is likely the norm in the United States, at both the state and national levels.

Source: Developed by the authors by drawing on analysis in Thomas, *Political Parties and Interest Groups*, cited in endnote 14, especially Chapters 1 and 15.

Involvement) and model 4 (the Pragmatic Model) are most evident. For instance, the oil companies and other businesses tend to lean toward the Republicans and labor and environmentalists toward the Democrats. But all groups are essentially pragmatic in their approach to parties because in some cases, neither Democrats nor Republicans control the outcome of an issue. The reason that models 3 and 4 are most relevant to the Alaska case will become clearer after we explain the second key aspect of this party-group relationship.

The Political Party-Interest Group Power Relationship

Several scholars have noted and examined the power relationship between parties and interest groups in the states.[15] In essence, they argue that there is an inverse relationship between the power of political parties and interest groups. This can be viewed on a power spectrum: at one end, when parties are strong, interest groups will be weak; at the other end, when parties are weak, interest groups will be strong. However, Hrebenar's and Thomas's thirty-year study of interest groups in the states shows that this relationship is not simply an inverse one. They show that it is certainly the case that when parties are weak interest groups will be strong, but strong parties do not necessarily mean weak interest groups. Those groups associated with strong parties may, in fact, be very influential and in some cases may be driving the party's agenda.[16]

The major way that strong parties affect interest groups is in group strategy and tactics. When parties are strong they control the policy agenda, and even strong groups have to work through them or their leaders to get things done. This also means that certain groups will more likely align closely with one party or the other. So this constrains group options regarding strategies and tactics and can be particularly detrimental when the party they align with is out of power. In contrast, in weaker or less strong party states, interest groups have greater political flexibility and may play a more visible, and in many cases, more influential role in politics.

The weakness of parties at the state and federal level in the United States, relative to parliamentary systems and the resulting greater political flexibility of interest groups have increased the fragmentation of policy making in the states. Power is more fragmented among various interests and less concentrated in one place—the party. Political parties have less control over the policy agenda, and certain groups have the ability to affect the content of that agenda. Groups have more options and avenues of access—including election campaign activity, lobbying, playing off the legislature against the administration, and using client groups—than they would have if parties were strong. Interest groups also often have more effect than parties on what gets enacted in the states, though, as Chapter 15 on interest groups shows, this varies from state to state.

Further Implications for Alaska Politics and Policy Making

The party-group relationship in Alaska is essentially one-party leaning or pragmatic on the part of interest groups. As a result, lobbyists tend not to be as overtly partisan—Democrat or Republican—as they are in Washington, D.C., and in some states with stronger parties like New Jersey and New York. The relative weakness of Alaska's parties results in many interest groups not dealing through parties to address their policy needs. Another is that interest groups overall, and particularly the big players, have considerable influence over the public policy process. However, as Chapter 15 argues, groups are not as dominant in Alaska politics as they are in some states like Nevada and Florida.

Political Ideology, Partisanship, Bipartisanship, and Public Policy

Political ideology and partisanship are often closely related, so we consider them together.

Understanding Political Ideology and Partisanship

Party ideology generally has Republicans following a conservative platform—favoring traditional socio-economic values and gradual change—and Democrats following a more liberal course of action involving the use of government to promote change. The two party platforms usually have opposing perspectives on issues such as taxes, abortion, immigration, the death penalty, same-sex marriage, and health care to name but a few. In contemporary America, the political parameters of both parties have expanded to include a broad set of political beliefs. Thus, for example, a person can be a liberal Republican or a conservative Democrat.

Partisanship can be viewed from the perspective of the individual voter or from that of the state as a whole. An individual's attachment to a particular political party is determined when the individual declares affiliation with that party when registering to vote.[17] Individuals sometimes change their party affiliation, depending on political or economic change, socio-psychological factors, or personal or family beliefs. Unlike Europeans, who tend to be strongly partisan and stick with one party for most of their lives, Americans are much less partisan. Just because someone lives in a "red state" (one that is mainly Republican) or a "blue state" (mainly Democratic) does not mean that he or she will align themselves exclusively with the platform of one party or the other. They may pick and choose between them. Furthermore, many Americans see themselves as nonpartisans or independents, especially in the western states and, as we have noted, particularly in Alaska.

Political ideologies and partisanship do not always correlate from state to state. States that are more ideologically conservative are not necessarily more Republican in their party identification. Similarly, states that are more ideologically liberal are not necessarily more Democratic. In states that have closed primaries (or in Alaska's case, a modified closed primary) as opposed to open primaries, individuals may have an incentive to identify and register with one party in order to participate in the primary election process. But they may not necessarily subscribe to that party's platform or value system in its entirety.[18]

This does not mean that partisanship and political ideology play no role in state party activity and in policy making. Both do, but in more complex ways than might be assumed.

Ideology, Partisanship, and Public Policy

So how do ideology and partisanship relate to public policy in the states? Six related points are particularly instructive.

First, the less partisan the electorate, the more variation there is in the type of candidates voters choose, likely selecting from both parties and not blindly following an ideology. Second, because of the various factions within the major parties, even a fairly partisan state may choose a combination of elected officials who represent a broad spectrum of ideologies. Third, and as a consequence of the first two, there is often a gap between the official party platform and the general makeup of the party in government in terms of its political orientation. This is because it is not the party that determines the makeup of the Republicans and Democrats in a legislature but the electorate. So, fourth, most state's policies will reflect "the median ideological preferences of the state's citizens."[19] Fifth, elected state officials often develop and enact policies that help their reelection as opposed to reflecting their political ideology. Sixth, and as a consequence of the first five points, the dominant political ideology does not necessarily dictate policy in most states.[20] As we will see below, this is often the case in Alaska.

Bipartisanship

In countries with strong party organizations founded on strong ideologies, as in much of Europe and to a lesser extent in Washington, D.C., and some strong party states in the Northeast and Midwest, bipartisan relationships occur only occasionally and on an ad hoc basis. In contrast, a combination of weak party organizations, party factionalism, loose nomination procedures (often focusing on candidate personalities), low levels of partisanship among the electorate, and a middle-of-the-road political ideology, gives policy makers more political leeway to operate. This enables them to be pragmatic in their policy making, including pursuing bipartisan arrangements.

These arrangements can be of various types and stem from a number of circumstances. In a legislature, bipartisanship can range from an ad hoc basis, say on one particular bill, to various bipartisan caucuses based upon an issue like health care, to members of one party (usually from the minority) joining another (usually the majority) for a legislative session, to a full-blown multiparty coalition. The major impetus for bipartisanship is usually the desire by legislators to increase their influence in order to get things done to benefit their constituents. This is the major motive for minority members working with the majority in various informal and formal ways. Other motives include like-mindedness on an issue or policy area regardless of party, such as economic development, and geographical affinity, which means legislators working together across party lines in the interests of their city or region of the state.

As President Obama discovered in his first few months in office in 2009, bipartisanship will not occur just because someone thinks it is a good idea or because it is "best" for the country or the state. There must be a direct political benefit in it, in most cases something to be gained or lost by not participating in cross-party relationships. Such quid pro quos are often present in western states, particularly in Alaska.

A high-profile example of this in Alaska was the Walker-Mallott Alaska First Unity ticket in the 2014 governor's race. The coalition was necessary to beat incumbent Sean Parnell because neither candidate would likely have won by himself. To both sides, a nonpartisan merger (effectively a bipartisan ticket since Walker was a registered Republican until the fusion of the tickets) was preferable to seeing Parnell reelected. Moreover, with low party identification they hoped that many independents and nonpartisan voters would join Democrats to bring the ticket victory, which is precisely what happened. A recent example of bipartisanship in the Alaska legislature was the Bipartisan Working Group (BWG) in the State Senate from 2007 to 2012, which we briefly explain in the next section.

5. ALASKA'S PARTIES IN GOVERNMENT AND PUBLIC POLICY MAKING

On a day-to-day basis, particularly when the legislature is in session, it is the parties in government that are the most important aspect of the party in influencing public policy. In this section we explain the characteristics and the scope of political influence over policy making by the parties in control of government in the state. First we deal with the executive and then the legislature.

The Executive Party in Alaska: Past and Present

Of the eleven individuals who have been governors of Alaska, six (Wally Hickel, Keith Miller, Jay Hammond, Frank Murkowski, Sarah Palin, and Sean Parnell) were elected as Republicans and four (Bill Egan, Bill Sheffield, Steve Cowper, and Tony Knowles) as Democrats. When elected the second time, Hickel won as an Alaska Independence Party candidate, but in effect he was a Republican. Walker won as an independent/nonaffiliated candidate, although he had a record as a moderate to conservative Republican.

As the candidates for governor and lieutenant governor run as a party pair (or nonaffiliated in the case of Walker and Mallott) and as the governor has extensive appointive authority, the executive branch has the potential to be highly partisan. This has not usually been the case, however. Certainly some governors, like Murkowski, have been more Republican and conservative than others, but this does not always translate into party orthodoxy. Often the governor and lieutenant governor do not see eye to eye (as was the case with Murkowski and Loren Leman) and most administrations have had commissioners from both parties and some who were largely independent or nonpartisan. Governors and legislative majorities from the same party also often do not agree on issues, as was clearly evidenced toward the end of the Palin administration in late 2008 until her resignation in July 2009.

As Chapter 14 on elections shows, candidates for statewide office in Alaska are elected as much on personality as party and often more on the former. Their election also depends on the various groups that support them, their political track record (if they have one), and their ability to put together a statewide coalition. To assemble a winning coalition, they have to reflect the median ideological preferences of voters. So even if they have liberal or conservative leanings, once in office governors and their administrations tend to be pragmatic rather than dogmatic. Most, more or less, reflect the right-of-center Alaska perspective and policies that involve pragmatic conservatism or pragmatic liberalism, often working simultaneously on such potentially conflicting issues as development and environmentalism. Parties and the state party platforms are often trumped by pragmatism, and bipartisanship, in various forms, frequently marks executive actions and policy making.

Alaska's Legislative Parties and Caucuses

Personality, pragmatic conservatism and pragmatic liberalism, the influence of various interests and interest groups, a range of political perspectives with majority and minority parties, and bipartisanship temper, and in some cases fetter, the operation of parties in the Alaska legislature, just as they do with the party in power in the executive branch. Yet party does have an important, if limited, role to play in the legislative process. Key to understanding the role of parties is their relationship to the majority and minority caucuses.

Like all state legislatures other than Nebraska's, the Alaska legislature is organized by majority and minority caucuses in each house. Other issue-oriented caucuses are also usually formed, though they are not part of the formal organization. In Alaska, membership in the majority and minority caucuses is usually identical to party affiliation, but often caucuses include members of the other party. For example, for over a decade, the Republican majority caucuses that ran the Alaska House of Representatives included a Democrat, the late Richard Foster of Nome, and from time to time other Democrats, particularly from rural-bush areas. When the Democrats in the House were in the majority, which they have not been since the 1994 elections, their caucuses rarely included non-Democrats.

A similar situation has existed in recent years in the Alaska Senate, with the Republicans forming the majority caucus until 2007. That year, in the First Session of the Twenty-Fifth Legislature, six of eleven Republicans joined with the nine Democrats to form a Bipartisan Working Group (BWG). This was specifically *not* called a caucus by its members and was thus less formalized than the House majority caucus. The election of November 2012 brought an end to the BWG. A Republican majority caucus took over the Senate, with two Democrats joining them. One, Senator Olson from Northwest Alaska, did so to ensure benefits for rural-bush communities and his district. The other, Senator Dennis Egan of Juneau, did so to protect his district in the face of reduced representation in the legislature for Southeast Alaska as a result of the 2012 reapportionment of the legislature.[21] Following the 2014 election, however, Egan and Olson were not invited to join the senate majority, with Senator Lyman Hoffman of Bethel the only Democrat in that caucus. In February 2016, however, Olson did join the majority caucus giving it 16 members.

Republican House majority caucuses are most often built around enforcing two rules: that members will follow the majority's position on the state budget and that members obey the rulings of the speaker. On occasion there is other legislation on which the caucus will have a position. But the caucus does not and could not enforce compliance on a wide range of policies, such as those related to regional issues (like taking a stance on the capital move) or abortion or gay rights. Trying to impose strictures on the various factions within the caucus would tear it apart for reasons we explain briefly below (and explained more fully in Chapter 14 on campaigns and elections). In regard to the responsible versus the functional party model considered earlier in this chapter, since statehood the House has combined both, but has tended toward the responsible model.

The BWG in the Senate was a much looser arrangement and likely was put together because former Senator Lyda Green wanted to be senate president, but not all senate Republicans supported her. Senate Democrats had been out in the political cold for so long that they wanted at least some power and influence and were willing to support a Republican for senate president in order to be able to wield some political influence. The BWG controlled the senate agenda and agreed on some common issues, such as certain aspects of the operating budget and allocations of capital budget funds, but avoided policy positions on virtually everything else. The Alaska Senate has had experience with bipartisan coalitions before. In the Sixteenth Legislature (1989–1990), there was a bipartisan coalition with only one Republican, Jack Coghill of Nenana, as the lone minority member, and in the following legislature (1990–1992) a super majority of twenty and no minority.[22] Over the years, the Senate has also combined the responsible and functional party models, but in contrast to the House, it has veered more toward the functional model.

It is, then, the majority caucus in each house, and not strictly speaking the party, that is the driving force in organizing and running the legislature and that has the most influence over the budget and some other policies. As we have seen, though, there is usually a close correlation between the members of the legislature from a particular party and majority and minority caucus membership. Outside of these minimal strictures of discipline imposed on members by joining the caucus, legislators are more or less free to take positions on issues that do not reflect the official platform of the state party. This often involves bipartisan activities on bills and policy making. Thus, there are varying levels of adherence to party affiliation in the Alaska legislature.

Lack of strict adherence to party affiliation and platforms does not, for a number of reasons, mean that legislators do not represent the Alaska electorate. First, the high level of party competition in many legislative districts for many years and the moderate competition in others, plus party competition in the legislature, has led to middle-of-the-road to right-leaning ideological preferences by Alaska voters. Second, Alaska's friends and neighbors politics often leads voters to subordinate party to personality. Third, with their very low party affiliation, Alaska voters, particularly in general elections, may be concerned more with the policy positions of a candidate than his or her party. These first three circumstances most probably produce the fourth factor. That is, the legislature veers toward the functional, more pragmatic party model that tends to reflect the broad range of Alaska opinions in achieving political ends.

A good argument can be made, then, that many of those who are elected to the legislature are more representative of their constituents than if they followed a party line blindly, a line that is put together by a group of party activists. Thus, the various majority and minority caucuses, often with bipartisan elements and the freedom of members to engage in bipartisan activity of all types in policy making, have probably resulted in more representative, if somewhat more populist, legislatures over the years than would have been the case if they had been more controlled by political party discipline.

6. CONCLUSION: THE PLACE OF POLITICAL PARTIES IN ALASKA'S PUBLIC POLICY-MAKING PROCESS

It can be misleading to assume that the labels of the two major parties in Alaska, Republicans and Democrats, mean what they do in Washington, D.C., and in many other states. To be sure, as elsewhere, Alaska's parties play a similar role in regard to elections (see Chapter 14), in organizing government, and in working to affect public policy. Some particular circumstances in Alaska, however, work to make the role of parties less extensive than in most states but still a force in government. Six characteristics of Alaska politics help explain these differences.

These characteristics are weak political parties versus strong interest groups; influential legislative party caucuses often coupled with bipartisanship; a political culture of pragmatic dependent individualism; friends and neighbors politics; regionalism; and the prominent role of Alaska Natives in state politics. In combination these characteristics can produce wide-ranging support for what may seem to be ideologically inconsistent policies. Thus, Alaska parties are considerably restricted as political organizations in many aspects of Alaska's political life. Even the party in government (particularly in the House and Senate) cannot enforce too much discipline without ending up with a revolt on its hands.

The friends and neighbors element of Alaska politics often elevates personality over party. Region often trumps party allegiance, and Alaska Natives and their legislators, particularly those from rural-bush areas, are less concerned about party and more with securing basic services and infrastructure to better their constituents' lives. The political culture of pragmatic dependent individualism means that conservatives and liberals, both voters and their politicians, reconcile individualism with their dependence on government through pragmatism. Nevertheless, while traditional parties in Alaska are relatively weak, the parties in government do function fairly effectively and are largely representative of those who elect them.

ENDNOTES

[1] This chapter draws on information about political parties across the states from: Thomas M. Holbrook and Raymond J. La Raja, "Parties and Elections," in *Politics in the American States; A Comparative Analysis*, eds. Virginia Gray, Russell L. Hanson, and Thad Kousser, 10th ed. (Washington, D.C.: Congressional Quarterly Press, 2013); Todd Donovan, Christopher Z. Mooney, and Daniel A. Smith, "Political Parties," in *State and Local Politics: Institutions and Reform* (Belmont, CA: Wadsworth Cenage Learning, 2009); and Ann O'M. Bowman and Richard C. Kearney, *State and Local Government*, 7th ed. (Boston: Houghton-Mifflin, 2008). The chapter also draws on over a hundred interviews with Alaska legislators, other public officials, and party leaders and members conducted since 1981 by co-author Clive Thomas.

[2] See the On-Line Directory of Political Parties at http://www.politics1.com/parties.htm.

[3] Holbrook and La Raja, "Parties and Elections," 87–89.

[4] For details on qualifying as a political party in Alaska, see Alaska Division of Elections at http://www.elections.alaska.gov/pi_rp.php.

[5] Alaska Division of Elections, *Registrar Handbook*, rev. ed., June 20, 2013, at http://www.elections.alaska.gov/doc/forms/B06.pdf.

[6] See the following websites for details on party organization: Alaska Democratic Party at http://www.alaskademocrats.org/ and Alaska Republican Party at http://www.alaskarepublicans.com/.

[7] See the Independence Party website at http://www.akip.org/. See also the following websites: ALP http://www.alaskalibertarian.com/; Moderate Republican Party http://citizens4ethics.com/

category/cfeg/; Green Party http://www.alaska.greens.org/; and Constitution Party http://groups.yahoo.com/group/AlaskaCP/.

[8] Holbrook and La Raja, "Parties and Elections," 63; and Bowman and Kearney, *State and Local Government*, 105.

[9] Sarah M. Morehouse and Malcolm E. Jewell, *State Politics, Parties and Policy* (Latham, MD: Rowman and Littlefield, 2003), 55; and their "The Future of Political Parties in the States," *Book of the States*, Volume 37 (Lexington, KY: The Council of State Governments, 2005), 334.

[10] Donovan, Mooney, and Smith, *State and Local Politics*, 139.

[11] Sherrie Okamato, "Ninth Circuit Upholds Alaska Law Governing Primaries," *Metropolitan News-Enterprise*, October 7, 2008.

[12] Donovan, Mooney and Smith, *State and Local Politics*, 133–34.

[13] *Ibid.*, 134.

[14] For a general consideration of the party-interest group relationship, see Clive S. Thomas, ed., *Political Parties and Interest Groups: Shaping Democratic Governance* (Boulder, CO: Lynne Rienner, 2001), esp. Chapters 1 and 5 on the relationship in general and on the United States respectively.

[15] See, Belle Zeller, *American State Legislatures*, 2nd ed. (New York: Thomas Y. Crowell, 1954), 190–93; Harmon L. Zeigler and Hendrik van Dalen, "Interest Groups in the States," in *Politics in the American States: A Comparative Analysis*, eds. Herbert Jacob and Kenneth N. Vines, 3rd ed. (Boston: Little, Brown and Company, 1976), 94–95; and Sarah McCally Morehouse, *State Politics, Parties and Policy* (New York: Holt, Rinehart and Winston, 1981), 116–18 and 127.

[16] Clive S. Thomas and Ronald J. Hrebenar, "Interest Groups in the States," in *Politics in the American States: A Comparative Analysis*, eds. Virginia Gray, Russell L. Hanson and Herbert Jacob, 7th ed. (Washington, D.C.: C.Q. Press, 1999), 119–21.

[17] Donavan, Mooney, and Smith, *State and Local Politics*, 142–43.

[18] For an explanation of the various types of primaries see the Glossary at the end of the book and Chapter 14 on campaigns and elections, Section 1.

[19] Donavan, Mooney, and Smith, *State and Local Politics*, 142.

[20] For a more in-depth examination of the relationship between political culture and political ideology and ideology and public policy in the states overall and in Alaska, see Chapter 5 on political culture, esp. Sections 6 and 8.

[21] Mark D. Miller, "Egan Joins New Senate Majority," *Juneau Empire*, November 11, 2012. For information on the politics of the reapportionment process in the past and in 2012 see Chapter 14 on campaigns and elections, Section 2.

[22] Gerald A. McBeath and Thomas A. Morehouse, *Alaska Politics and Government* (Lincoln: University of Nebraska Press, 1994), 149.

⋆ CHAPTER 14 ⋆

Campaigns and Elections: The Interaction of Weak Partisanship, Ideology, Personality, and Pragmatism

Carl E. Shepro, Kristina Klimovich, and Clive S. Thomas

Voting in elections is the major way that most Americans and Alaskans participate in politics and government. This chapter covers Alaska's elections and the campaigns that precede them.

The chapter presents four perspectives on Alaska's election process. First, it shows what campaigns and elections tell us about the link between Alaskans and their public officials, whether it is primarily ideological, pragmatic, personal, or a combination of these and other elements. Second, we show the interrelationship between the election process and the other four vehicles of political participation—political parties, interest groups, the media, and public opinion. Third, the chapter explains how the electoral process translates into public policy. And fourth, we explore what campaigns and elections tell us about Alaska politics in general.

The fact that Alaska's campaigns and elections reflect several of the characteristics of Alaska politics set out in Chapter 2 provides insight into our analysis. In particular, campaigns and elections illustrate the characteristics of pragmatic dependent individualism, fiscal conservatism, friends and neighbors politics, the prominent role of Alaska Natives in state politics, conflicts between urban and rural-bush areas, weak political parties, and strong interest groups. The argument presented here, and encapsulated in the chapter's subtitle, is that the interaction of weak partisanship, particular ideological stances, personality, and pragmatism gives Alaska's campaigns and elections their character and help explain the four perspectives listed above.

The first section of the chapter outlines the types of elections and campaigns in Alaska and their legal framework. This is followed by a section that considers the factors that influence Alaska's elections and campaigns. Next comes a consideration of different types of campaigns followed by Section 4 on campaign finance. Section 5 looks at elections, including voter turnout, patterns in Alaska elections since statehood, and who gets elected and why. After that we present two case studies. One is the 2010 U.S. Senate race between incumbent Lisa Murkowski and major challenger Joe Miller. The other is the 2014 gubernatorial race between Sean Parnell and Bill Walker. The key question of the link, or lack thereof, between elections and Alaska public policy is the subject of Section 7. The conclusion, in part, points to the important role that elections play in influencing other aspects of Alaska politics and government.

Before moving to the substance of the chapter, three points are important to make. First, while we list the various types of elections in Alaska in Section 1—federal, state, and local—the rest of the chapter focuses mainly on state elections for the legislature and governorship, with some treatment of ballot propositions, elections for Congress, and the presidency. Because of their nonpartisan nature and the fact that they are covered in other chapters, we do not cover judicial retention elections (covered in Chapter 17) or local elections (covered in overview in Chapter 18). Second, as in any democracy, campaigns and elections in Alaska are very much influenced by the state's constitutional framework, its political culture, and the party system. For this reason, we recommend reading Chapters 4, 5, and 13 on these subjects before reading this chapter. And third, unlike many chapters in the book, there is no separate section comparing Alaska to other states. Many comparisons are made throughout the chapter, however, as we address various aspects of Alaska's campaigns and elections.[1]

1. TYPES OF CAMPAIGNS AND ELECTIONS, THE RIGHT TO VOTE, AND THEIR LEGAL FRAMEWORK

As in the other forty-nine states, campaigns and elections in Alaska include those for federal, state, and local offices and, as in many states, ballot propositions—the initiative, referendum, and recall.[2]

The Alaska Constitution deals with suffrage and elections in Article V. Other articles of the constitution detail the minimum age and residency requirements for particular offices (for example, the governor in Article III and state legislators in Article II). Box 14.1 provides an overview of the types of elections in Alaska.

Article V of the State Constitution sets out general provisions for qualification and disqualification to vote, methods of voting, and so on. Article V, Section 1, states that any citizen of the United States who is at least eighteen years old and meets state residency requirements may register to vote. Section 1 goes on to provide that a voter must have

BOX 14.1

Types of Elections in Alaska

LOCAL GOVERNMENT OR MUNICIPAL ELECTIONS

Local elections are held for municipal offices such as mayor, city council, borough assembly, and school board members. Unlike state and federal elections, municipal elections are nonpartisan. Candidates stand as individuals with no identified political party affiliation. Local governments can also hold ballot proposition elections using the initiative, referendum, and recall.

Municipal elections are subject to the same statutory requirements as elections for state and federal offices regarding reports of contributions and candidate registration. However, a municipality can exempt itself from these requirements (outlined in title 15 of Alaska Statutes) by either ordinance or initiative election (AS 15.13.010(a)(2)). See Chapter 18 for more details.

STATE ELECTIONS

State elections fall into four categories: (1) for the state legislature (representatives and senators); (2) for governor and lieutenant governor; (3) ballot propositions, including the initiative, referendum, and recall; and (4) the retention of judges. Like all states, Alaska uses a primary election system to choose party candidates to run in the general election for the legislature, governor, and lieutenant governor. Alaska's primary is held the fourth Tuesday in August of even-numbered years. The general election is held on the first Tuesday after the first Monday in November, also in even-numbered years. Representatives serve two-year terms, senators four-year terms, and governors and lieutenant governors four-year terms. Gubernatorial elections in Alaska take place in even-numbered years when there is no race for president. So in the presidential election year of 2012 there was no race for governor in Alaska.

Article II, Section 2, of Alaska's constitution outlines minimum qualifications for serving in the legislature. A candidate must be a resident of Alaska for a minimum of three years and a resident of the district that he or she seeks to represent for a minimum of one year. Candidates for state Senate and House must be at least twenty-five and twenty-one years of age respectively. Those seeking the governorship or lieutenant governorship must have been a state resident for a minimum of seven years, and be at least thirty years old (Article III, Section 2).

Provisions for ballot propositions (so-called direct democracy) are set out in Article XI of the State Constitution and Alaska Statutes (AS) 15.45. Restrictions are placed on the use of the initiative. It cannot be used to propose constitutional amendments, to make appropriations, or to change rules of judicial procedure. The legislature can cause a pending initiative to be removed from the ballot by passing a substantially similar measure before the election is held. Ballot propositions can appear on the primary or the general election ballot, depending on when the they were certified.

Rules regarding the appointment and retention of judges are contained in Article IV of the constitution. Like many states, Alaska uses a gubernatorial appointment process, with a politically neutral body (the Judicial Council) screening candidates, combined with statewide retention elections at intervals specific to a judge's position. For example, Supreme Court justices stand for retention every ten years and superior court judges every six years (Article IV, Section 6). See Chapter 17 for details.

FEDERAL ELECTIONS

Federal elections in Alaska, as in all states, include voting for the state's congressional delegation and for president. As the federal constitution does not provide for the initiative, referendum, or recall, and as federal judges are appointed by the president (with major input from the state's two senators), there are no federal elections regarding these matters.

As do all states, Alaska has two U.S. senators who serve six-year terms. But its small population means that it has only one member of the U.S. House of Representatives, who serves a two-year term. Compare this with California's fifty-three, North Carolina's thirteen, and Oregon's five representatives. The State Division of Elections, which comes under the lieutenant governor's office, administers federal elections, with congressional primary elections being held on the same day as those for state elected offices.

Source: Developed by Reuben Yerkes, former employee of the Alaska Public Offices Commission (APOC).

been a resident of the voting district in which they wish to vote for a minimum of thirty days, unless otherwise prescribed by law.

However, many Alaska Republican politicians have supported a national movement, originating around 2010 in several Republican-dominated state legislatures, to pass so-called voter-ID laws. These are intended to tighten up and restrict voting rights, including absentee, same-day registration, and mail-in balloting. The purported reason given is to prevent voter fraud, but the likely real reason is to gain political advantage and to exclude poorer voters and those from minority groups who usually vote for Democrats.[3] Such a bill, House Bill 3, was introduced in the Alaska Legislature in 2013, but did not pass.[4] Laws restricting voter registration and other aspects of the election process could have serious effects in undermining voter participation and on democracy across the nation, including in Alaska. For this reason, in mid-2013 the U.S. Department of Justice began to file suits against states that have enacted such laws.[5]

Alaska's Primary Election System and Presidential Caucuses

While not unique, two features of Alaska elections that contrast with most states are its primary election system and its system for nominating its U.S. presidential candidates. Thirty-seven states use a primary election system to determine the presidential candidates for whom the delegates to each party's national convention will caste votes. The other thirteen states use a caucus system. Iowa is probably the most well-known state using the caucus system, as it is one of the earliest in the election cycle and has become something of a bellwether for determining who will ultimately be nominated. Seven of the thirteen states using the caucus system are in the West—Alaska, Colorado, Hawaii, Idaho, Nevada, Washington, and Wyoming.

The lack of a primary election system in these states is not what one would expect given their history of populism, progressivism, and direct voter involvement. In Alaska, from time to time, there are suggestions to reform the caucus system, but its reform appears to be of little concern to most Alaskans.[6] Box 14.2 explains Alaska's presidential caucus system.

Like California and Washington State, until the late 1990s Alaska had a *blanket primary* election system for legislative and statewide elections. In this system, candidates from all parties appeared on the same primary ballot, although party designations were listed for each candidate.[7] Any voter, Democrat, Republican, Libertarian, Alaska Independence Party (AIP), or independent, could vote for any candidate of any party. As a result, political parties had little control over who became their candidates in the general election, and this in turn resulted in those officials, particularly legislators, having a high degree of independence from their parties. Moreover, voters supporting one party could vote for weak candidates from the other parties in an effort to help their own party's candidates.

BOX 14.2

Alaska's Presidential Caucus and Nomination System

In Alaska, as in other caucus states, the process of nominating candidates for president and choosing delegates to the national party conventions is run by the political parties, not by the state. In addition, only those affiliated with a particular party may vote in that party's presidential caucus. Alaska, Iowa, Kansas, Maine, Nevada, and Wyoming all have closed caucus primaries. Presidential caucuses in Alaska are held at the state legislative district level for both parties.

THE DEMOCRATIC PRESIDENTIAL CAUCUS SYSTEM

Two types of delegates are sent to the Democratic National Convention. One type includes pledged delegates. The other type are unpledged or "super-delegates" who attend the convention by virtue of their position within the party or because they are current or former elected office holders. Unlike pledged delegates, who are expected to cast their vote based on the state party's preference for president, super-delegates can vote the way they choose.

During Democratic caucus meetings, there is open discussion and campaigning. Pledged delegates are awarded to the presidential candidates based on their percentage of supporters. The national Democratic Party's formula for determining the number of delegates from each state to attend the national convention combines a state's percentage of the total national Democratic popular vote with its share of the electoral vote in the three preceding presidential elections. For the 2012 election, Alaska sent twenty-four delegates to the Democratic National Convention out of a total of 5,552. By contrast, California sent 669 and Indiana 105. Individual pledged delegates to the national convention are chosen at the party's state convention.

THE REPUBLICAN PRESIDENTIAL CAUCUS SYSTEM

Republican district conventions throughout Alaska choose delegates to the state convention. At the state convention, the district delegates elect Alaska's delegates to the Republican National Convention. For this National Convention each state selects ten delegates, plus three delegates for every member it has in the U.S. House of Representatives. With one House member, Alaska gets ten delegates under the first provision and three by the latter. States are given additional delegates if a majority of their popular votes was cast for the Republican candidate for president in the previous election and if they elected Republicans to the U.S. House, U.S. Senate, or the office of governor. By this formula, in 2012 Alaska sent twenty-seven delegates to the Convention out of 2,286 in total. California sent 172 and Indiana forty-six. Delegates are expected to vote for nominees based on the preferences for each candidate determined at the party's district caucuses.

Source: Developed by Reuben Yerkes.

There are two other types of primaries. One is the *closed primary*, in which only those actually registered as a member of a particular party can vote for candidates of that party. The other is the *open primary*, in which any registered voter can ask for any party's primary ballot, but can receive only one party's ballot. In other words, voters are confined to voting only for candidates of the party whose ballot they request.

After 1994, when Alaska's Republicans gained electoral strength, they began to work toward having a closed primary. A series of court challenges, in particular the U.S. Supreme Court decision in *California Democratic Party v. Jones* (2000), led to Alaska passing a law in 2001 that established a modified closed primary.[8] Under this system, those registered as partisan (such as Democrats or Republicans) are given their party's primary ballot. All those registered as undeclared or nonpartisan must choose a ballot of one party or the other. For a party concerned about the ideological commitment and party loyalty of their candidates once elected, this system tends to give the party more control than under an open or blanket primary system. This generally increases party cohesiveness in the legislature.

Establishing Official Candidate Status

A candidate for state or municipal office must first file a "Letter of Intent" with the Alaska Public Offices Commission (APOC).[9] This allows the candidate to begin receiving campaign contributions. Until this letter is filed, candidates may not make campaign-related expenditures, such as media advertising or expenses related to fundraisers. A municipal candidate can file an exemption statement with APOC if they do not intend to raise more than $5,000 in contributions. This exempts them from having to file ongoing financial reports with APOC throughout the campaign.

Next, candidates must file a "Declaration of Candidacy." Candidates for state office file this form with the Alaska Division of Elections. Municipal candidates file the declaration with their municipal clerk's offices. The "Declaration of Candidacy" gets the candidate's name on the ballot. Thus, even if a candidate files a Letter of Intent with APOC and raises campaign funds, his or her name will not appear on the ballot unless a Declaration of Candidacy has been filed.

2. FACTORS INFLUENCING ALASKA'S CAMPAIGNS AND ELECTIONS: AN OVERVIEW

In this section we explore the general influences on Alaska's elections as opposed to specific issues or specific elections. Besides the constitutional and legal provisions, ten influences are of particular importance in shaping the election environment and the election process. They are (1) historical factors, (2) various aspects of geography, (3) the role of political parties, (4) political ideology, (5) the significance of issues, (6) personality and the friends and neighbors factor, (7) incumbency and the competitiveness of the race, (8) the role of the media, (9) campaign finance, and (10) the redistricting process. Some of these elements have been explained in detail in previous chapters and so can be covered briefly. Others need a fuller explanation.

1. Historical Factors

One important historical influence is that in writing the constitution, Alaska's founders were influenced both by the Progressive Movement, with its emphasis on efficient government, and by the evident inefficiencies from too much populism in state constitutions. For this reason, the founders chose a streamlined, unified executive with only the governor and lieutenant governor being elected statewide and as a pair on the same ticket in the general election. This is in contrast to the plural executive in many states, like California and Washington State, where many top executive officials are elected and all of them appear separately on the ballot.

2. Geographical Influences

Physical, political, social, and economic geography have important effects on campaigns and elections. The vast size of Alaska means that statewide elections can be expensive, particularly if the candidate chooses to visit rural-bush communities as well as urban centers.

The vastness of the state also means that many rural-bush legislative districts are large, some larger than most states in the nation, but have small populations, which presents challenges for candidates in reaching many voters. For instance, for several years before 2012, Senator Al Kookesh of Angoon in Southeast Alaska represented Senate District C, the largest legislative district in the United States and almost the size of Texas. His district stretched nearly 1,200 miles, from the southern tip of Southeast Alaska to the borders of the North Slope Borough in the north and almost to the Bering Sea in the west.[10]

The redistricting of the legislature in 2012, subsequently modified in 2013 (see Box 14.3 on pages 450–451), eliminated that district. But as can be seen from Map 14.1, which shows Alaska's twenty Senate districts (designated by letters A through T) and forty House districts (designated by numbers 1 to 40) after the 2013 redistricting plan was approved, rural-bush Senate districts are still very large. Moreover, because each Senate district contains two House districts, this means that rural-bush House districts are also large. For instance, Senate District T, which covers the North Slope and Northwest Alaska, now the largest state legislative district in the nation, covers approximately 220,000 square miles. It includes House districts 39 (Northwest Alaska) and 40 (mostly the North Slope). In stark contrast to rural-bush districts, most Anchorage and Fairbanks Senate and House districts are quite compact, and candidates can cover a lot of their districts by foot and knock on a high percentage of doors. For example, Senate District J, which covers Mountainview and downtown Anchorage, includes House Districts 19 (Mountainview) and 20 (downtown). Senate District J is about three miles long and wide and each of the House districts is half that size.

Compared with many states, both urban and rural-bush districts in Alaska have small populations and an even smaller number of voting age residents. After the 2010 census, the forty state legislative House districts averaged fewer than 18,000 residents and the twenty Senate districts about 36,000. So even in rural-bush areas, people can get to

MAP 14.1

Alaska Senate and House Districts as of the 2012 Reapportionment

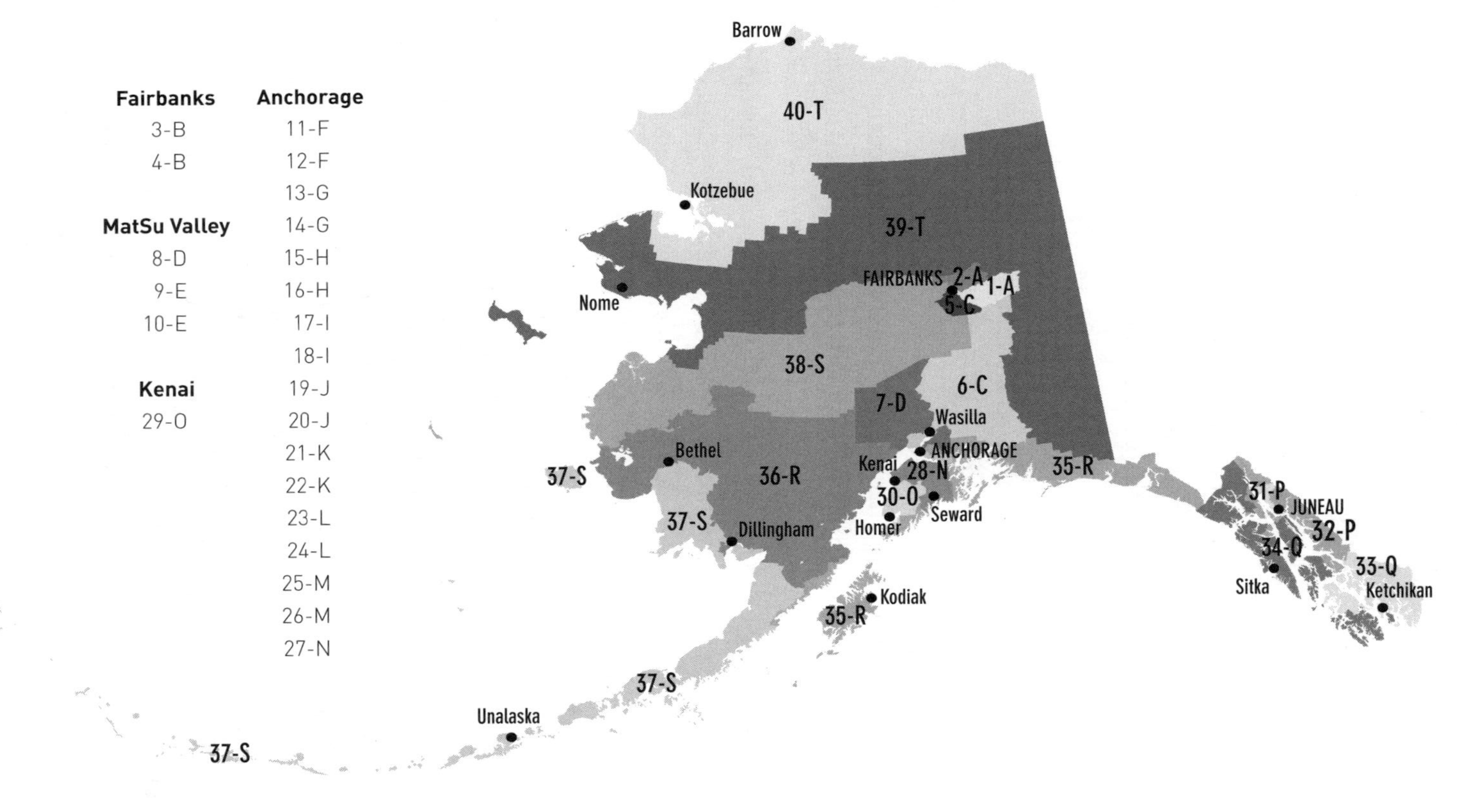

Source: Alaska Department of Labor and Workforce Development, Research and Analysis Section.

know their representatives and senators on a first-name basis, and friends and neighbors politics is a prominent feature. This contributes to Alaska political campaigns being personality focused and less party dominated.

The social, cultural, and religious geography of Alaska also works its influence on campaigns and the outcome of elections. Because over half the residents in rural-bush areas are Alaska Natives, they have elected many Native legislators over the years. In addition, religion, particularly conservative evangelical Christians in the Anchorage area, have been exercising an increasing influence in Alaska politics since the 1990s. These represent another important factor in the outcome of campaigns and elections in the state.

3. The Role of Political Parties

As Chapter 13 points out, party organizations tend to be relatively weak in Alaska. Among the fifty states, Alaska has the highest number of voters not associating with a political party (consistently over 50 percent). This means that both party organizations and party identification play less of a role than they do in states where parties are more established and where party affiliation is stronger, such as in the Northeast and upper Midwestern states. For this reason, many candidates in Alaska downplay party in their bid for election or reelection, particularly in rural-bush areas, but also in some urban areas, especially when the elections are competitive. However, there is a hard core of party activists in Alaska, especially in the three major urban centers of Anchorage, Fairbanks, and Juneau plus the Matanuska-Susitna (Mat-Su) Valley north of Anchorage. These activists are the people most likely to work on campaigns to get their party candidates elected. Moreover, while Alaska's candidates for state offices do not receive major aid from parties in their election efforts, they do receive a higher percentage than in some states.

Nevertheless, the lack of strong party organization, minimal financial resources, and low party identification leave political space for other factors to fill the role that parties perform in other states. Three of the most important of them are political ideology, issues, and personality.

4. The Role of Political Ideology

It should not be assumed that low party identification means a low level of ideological commitment on the part of the Alaska electorate. In other words, although partisanship (support for a party) and political ideology (a value system ranging from conservative to liberal) are often related, an electorate can have strong ideological orientations without association with a party. Alaska is a classic example.

Even though Alaskans do not associate much with parties, they do have strong ideological views, as explained in Chapter 5 on political culture. This is particularly so on the conservative side of the political spectrum, plus there are pockets of liberalism in

Anchorage, Fairbanks, and Juneau, and of libertarianism in Fairbanks and on the Kenai Peninsula. Rural-bush areas are far less ideological than many urban areas, with pragmatism and bipartisanship tending to characterize attitudes to politics. Political pragmatism is also a feature of the electorate in most urban areas, though bipartisanship is less evident. The combination of low party influence and particular ideological orientations affects the way campaigns are conducted, which means focusing on personality, political beliefs, and to some extent political issues.

5. The Significance of Issues

To be sure, issues are important in elections in all democracies. But when we combine the low level of party identification, the significance of ideology, and regional and rural-bush elements in Alaska politics, issues can take on a very significant role in some elections on a par with personality and ideology. Also, elections in some years are, in part, influenced by current issues in a district, in the state, or in the nation.

For example, several Alaska elections have been influenced by proposals to move the capital, particularly in 1982. Other elections have been influenced by what to do about budget shortfalls, whether to reinstate the individual state income tax or change the form of the Permanent Fund Dividend (PFD) program. Many rural-bush state legislative elections are influenced by how successful an incumbent legislator has been in bringing budget money to his or her district. Legislative elections can be influenced by everything from fishing to mining to subsistence issues. Thus, a candidate who finds himself or herself on the wrong side of an issue (or a rural-bush legislator who fails to "bring home the political bacon") may well lose the election.

6. Personality and the Friends and Neighbors Factor

The decline of party affiliation across the nation since the late 1960s has placed increased emphasis on candidates and their personalities. This can be seen in political ads in many states, particularly in the western states, that downplay party and focus on the candidates and their personal qualities. For instance, in his successful 2008 bid for an Alaska U.S. Senate seat, Mark Begich's advertising on radio, TV, and direct mailings virtually never mentioned that he was a Democrat. In so doing he was playing to both sides of the political fence and independent voters. To reinforce this, one of his direct mailings asserted: "Mark Begich—as Independent as Alaska." His unsuccessful bid for reelection in 2014 struck a similar independent theme, emphasizing his personality and what he had accomplished for Alaska. Only on the far right and far left are there strong ties to party in campaigns and voter loyalty in elections in Alaska.

Another factor in elections works to focus on personality and the candidate in Alaska. This is that, as noted earlier, the small population enables a lot of personal contact between candidates and their constituents. This so-called friends and neighbors politics is a feature of urban constituencies as well as those in rural-bush areas. Running into candidates in the post office or local restaurant is commonplace in Alaska, and citizens expect candidates (and their legislators and governor after the election) to give them time to listen to their concerns or perspectives. In rural-bush areas, candidates are often related by blood or have other kinship ties to many people in a community or region. This brings a very personal element to a campaign. Former Representative Mary Nelson explains this in Box 14.5, later in the chapter.

7. Incumbency and the Competitiveness of the Race

Three fundamental elements of a pluralist democracy are (1) encouraging alternative perspectives on solving problems, (2) promoting the general welfare, and (3) preserving the right of the governed to choose those who best represent their particular perspectives to serve in government. So the success of political representation depends, in large part, on a marketplace of political ideas, particularly in a campaign, and competition between two or more candidates. Otherwise, a segment of the population, perhaps a large segment, may have their views ignored, as were African Americans in the southern states from the Civil War to desegregation in the 1960s. When segments of society are excluded, the system may become elitist and even develop authoritarian elements. So how competitive are Alaska's elections? We make some general comments here and also address this important question in several places in the rest of the chapter.

As in all states, an incumbent in Alaska running to retain his or her office has a major advantage. In most elections very few incumbents in Alaska are defeated, though occasionally it does happen, as related later in the chapter. During the 2002 and 2006 elections, 71 and 79 percent of incumbents respectively across the fifty states were reelected. In Alaska during those years, 67 and 82 percent of incumbents respectively were reelected.[11]

In Alaska many legislators get reelected time after time, as did Representative, later Senator, Randy Phillips of Eagle River who served from 1977 to 2002. Senator Lyman Hoffman of Bethel has served since 1987, first in the House and then in the Senate, and Representative Beth Kerttula of Juneau served in the House from 1999 to 2014. Kerttula's father, Jalmar "Jay" Kerttula, served in both the House and the Senate for a total of thirty-four years (1961 through 1994).[12] But no one compares with Don Young, Alaska's single member of the U.S. House of Representatives, with forty-four years in office as of 2016, surpassing the late Ted Stevens who served Alaska in the U.S. Senate for just forty years before his defeat in the election of 2008.

Long tenure as a legislator is partly a function of two factors beyond incumbency itself. First, the incumbent has a clear fundraising advantage, and second, many races, both in Alaska and across the states, lack competitiveness. Across the states, those with a fundraising advantage have an 82 to 84 percent chance of winning. The figure is even higher in Alaska at 84 to 89 percent. For those who have both an incumbency and a fundraising advantage, the figures are 91 to 93 percent across the nation and 90 to 95 percent in Alaska.

As to competitiveness, we need to distinguish between a contested election and a competitive election. Just because an election is contested does not mean it is competitive. A competitive race is usually considered to be one in which the challenger can get at least 40 percent of the vote, while a race is called contested when at least two candidates vie for the office.[13] By this standard fewer than 50 percent of Alaska legislative elections are competitive, with the highest percentage of noncompetitive elections in rural-bush areas. Across the states, an average of 31 percent of all incumbents are not challenged in the primary or general election, and on average 36 percent of all winning incumbents face opposition only in the primary election. The figures are similar in Alaska and likely somewhat higher, particularly in rural-bush areas.

One reform that has affected the competitiveness of elections in many states is term limits, which curtail incumbency and long tenure of office holders. These limits are in place in fifteen states including several in the West, such as Arizona, California, Montana and Nevada.[14] Term limits have never been seriously considered in Alaska for state legislators, but they do exist in several local governments for assembly and council members as well as for mayors, as in Juneau.[15] The Alaska Constitution has always limited the governor to two consecutive terms, but he or she can run again after sitting out a term.

8. The Role of the Media

According to McBeath and Morehouse, Alaska election campaigns caught up with the media age in the 1970s.[16] Since then, the media has played an increasing role in Alaska elections, particularly in statewide races for Congress, the governorship, and ballot propositions. The media also plays a role in many legislative races, especially in the Anchorage metropolitan area, in Fairbanks, and to a lesser extent in Juneau and smaller urban areas. Media expenses, especially for television, radio, and newspaper ads, take an increasing amount of campaign funding in these elections. In two ways, however, the role of the media in elections is different in Alaska than in most states, and the media in Alaska is less likely to affect outcomes.

First, the small size of the state's population enables friends and neighbors politics to operate. Thus, for many Alaska candidates the extensive use of media is not as necessary as it is in large population states like California, Florida, and Texas, or even medium-sized ones like Michigan, Massachusetts, and Minnesota. This is not likely to change in Alaska for many years to come, though as in the rest of the nation, social media—mainly Facebook and Twitter—may well be changing the nature of campaigns in Alaska.

Second, even though the use of social media is also on the rise in rural-bush Alaska, the use of the media in campaigns and elections, particularly for the legislature, in these parts of the state is very different from urban Alaska. There are several reasons for this relative lack of media. For one thing, there are no commercial television stations in the bush. Television is publicly funded through ARCS (Alaska Rural Communication Systems), formerly RATnet (Rural Alaska Television Network). So there is very little use of TV in rural-bush campaigns. Moreover, much of radio in rural-bush communities is also publicly funded, though these radio stations often present candidate forums and call-in shows that allow candidates to publicize their positions. Weekly newspapers are used, such as *The Delta Discovery* and *The Tundra Drums* in the Lower Kuskokwim region and *The Arctic Sounder* on the North Slope. Generally, however, rural-bush campaigns rely less on media and more on personal contacts and direct mailings.[17]

9. Campaign Finance—Money in Elections

Running for election in Alaska, particularly for statewide office, costs a lot of money. With political parties having minimal funds, this means that money has to come from the public, interest groups, or the candidates themselves. The sources of money shape the nature of campaigns as do the regulations about campaign finance—who can and cannot contribute and how much. The financial aspect of getting elected is of such importance that we devote Section 4 of this chapter to the topic.

10. The Redistricting and Reapportionment Process

The terms *reapportionment* and *redistricting* are often used interchangeably, sometimes also with the term *apportionment.* Although all three are linked, they each mean slightly different things. Apportionment is usually used to refer to the original drawing of legislative districts after a state, nation, or local government is established. This was done in Alaska at statehood in 1959. Reapportionment is the reallocation of seats in a legislature due to an increase or decrease in populations in various election districts. Redistricting is redrawing district boundaries to accommodate these geographic population shifts. In everyday speech, however, the three processes are usually referred to simply as reapportionment, though the body appointed every ten years to reapportion Alaska's legislative districts is called the Alaska Redistricting Board.

Chapter 4 on the state constitution explains the constitutional basis for, and developments in, the reapportionment process.[18] In contrast, Box 14.3 focuses on the political elements of the process and why it is so crucial in shaping the election and campaign process and ultimately the public policy process in Alaska.[19]

One of these crucial aspects is the representation of Alaska Natives. But as the box briefly explains, a U.S. Supreme Court decision in June 2013 invalidated an important

BOX 14.3

Alaska's Reapportionment and Redistricting Process: Political Lip Service to Impartiality and Bipartisanship

Article VI of Alaska's constitution, dealing with reapportionment, requires that legislative seats be reapportioned every ten years following each decennial census. The census takes place in years ending with zero, for example 1990, 2000, and 2010. The goal is to have the new plan in effect for the following legislative election, for instance in 1992, 2002, and 2012. Reading the constitution and the information issued by the Alaska Redistricting Board (the five-member body set up to develop the new plan), one could get the impression that this is a impartial and bipartisan process. It certainly is not.

Clearly, in a democracy like the United States or Alaska, where those in the legislature represent geographical districts, the political composition of a district determines the political orientation of the candidate who is elected from that district. If more districts can be drawn in a way that favors a particular political party or political perspective (such as conservative or liberal), the more control that party or perspective will have in shaping public policy. So, because so much is at stake politically, reapportionment is a very contentious process. This has certainly been the case in Alaska.

The highly political nature of reapportionment is evidenced by the fact that, until the 1960s, some states had not reapportioned their legislatures at all. Other states engaged in gerrymandering—drawing district boundaries to favor one party or to disadvantage a particular group—such as African Americans—a practice that was rife in the American South.

Then, in 1962 and 1964 respectively, federal court decisions in *Baker v. Carr* and *Reynolds v. Sims* required states to reapportion their legislatures so that there was more or less equal representation of all citizens—the so-called "one person, one vote" rule. Plus, the Voting Rights Act of 1965 (Section 5), required the U.S. Justice Department to pre-clear (approve) the reapportionment plans of certain states with a record of past discrimination against certain groups. Together with eight other states (mostly southern states), Alaska was required to pre-clear its plan mainly because of an English language requirement in the original constitution (Article V, Section 1) that potentially disadvantaged Alaska Natives. The English provision was removed in 1970, but the pre-clearance requirement remained until 2013. That year the U.S. Supreme Court struck down the pre-clearance requirement in *Shelby County v. Holder*, based on a challenge to the provision brought by Alabama county officials. Pre-clearance was struck down largely because the Court found that the formula used in the Voting Rights Act to determine which states required pre-clearance was seriously outdated.

The population shift from rural-bush Alaska to urban areas has been at the root of contention in several reapportionments, including that of 2012. It is likely to be a continuing issue and may become a stumbling block to reapportionment plans in 2022 and 2032. With the federal pre-clearance provision in doubt unless Congress acts to reinstate it in a form likely to be approved by the U.S. Supreme Court, the lack of pre-clearance could be to the detriment of Alaska Native representation. Even if pre-clearance is not dealt with by Congress, the state will still be obliged to ensure more or less equal representation of all citizens. One solution that has been suggested to protect Alaska Native representation is to expand the number of seats in the state legislature. So far, however, the Alaska electorate has been unwilling to do this, as evidenced by rejection of such a plan in 2010.

Not only does the reapportionment process reflect urban versus rural-bush political tensions in the state, it particularly reflects partisan and ideological divisions. While in theory the redistricting board is, as the state constitution requires (Article VI, Section 8), appointed "without regard to political affiliation," in practice the process has always been highly partisan. The original constitutional provision gave the reapportionment function to the governor. In doing so, Alaska's founders hoped to reduce the intense partisanship that occurs when legislatures conduct the process. But governors usually appointed members of the board from their party or others who favored their perspective.

Under a constitutional amendment adopted in1998 (and pushed by Republicans to prevent Democratic governor Tony Knowles from appointing the board), the five members are chosen as follows: two by the governor and one each by the Speaker of the House, President of the Senate, and chief justice of the Alaska Supreme Court. This appointment system virtually ensures that the board will be dominated by one party or the other depending on the party of the governor, the majorities in the House and Senate, and the party or perspective of the person appointed by the chief justice. For example, the board was dominated by Democrats in 2000–2002, and by Republicans in 2010–2012.

The Alaska Constitution requires that each house district contain approximately the same number of residents and must be reasonably compact. These requirements ensure that gerrymandering in the old sense is not possible. However, domination of the board by one party or the other still means that it is able to draw districts to advantage its party in the final composition of the legislature. The size and shape of these districts often lead to court challenges and concerns from the U.S. Justice Department. The 2012 plan, for example, which was widely believed to have been drawn to destroy the Bipartisan Working Group (BWG) of Republicans and Democrats in the State Senate, was challenged by several cities. Eventually it was approved by the U.S. Justice Department and the Alaska courts, and the challenges were dropped. In the 2012 election the Republicans won large majorities in both houses of the legislature, and the BWG became part of Alaska's political history.

Source: Developed by Reuben Yerkes.

provision of the federal Voting Rights Act of 1965 protecting those rights, which can no longer be implemented unless Congress acts to deal with the Court's concerns. Renewal of the act has been a very divisive issue in Congress. But in September 2015 Senator Lisa Murkowski was the first to break ranks with her Republican colleagues and sign on as a co-sponsor with thirty Democrats to the Voting Rights Advancement Act of 2015.[20] The reform is unlikely to pass, however, until such times as the Democrats again control Congress.

3. CAMPAIGNS—MOST POLITICS IS LOCAL, INVOLVING FRIENDS AND NEIGHBORS

This section first identifies elements common to all campaigns as well as some of the variations in running for office. Then we briefly cover three types of statewide campaigns and finally elaborate on the difference between urban and rural-bush campaigns for the state legislature.[21]

Common Elements and Variations in Alaska Campaigns

Running a political campaign, be it for a seat on a local school board, a city council, borough assembly, the legislature, governor, a ballot proposition, or for Congress, is an exercise in managing resources—campaign staff, volunteers, access to the media, and so on—with the one goal of winning. It involves careful planning and organization and the ability to make adjustments as the campaign progresses. Consequently, many candidates, particularly for legislative and statewide office, set up campaign committees to help plan their bids for election or reelection and to help raise funds. They seek endorsements from major interest groups and prominent individuals, such as present and former governors. And even though money is less a factor in Alaska campaigns than in many states, it is still important. It is important for paying staff, maintaining a website, direct mail flyers, yard signs, paying for surveys of voters, and particularly in statewide elections, for advertising, buying radio and TV time, and paying for travel to campaign across the state. All candidates put a lot of effort into soliciting money through fundraising events in the homes of supporters and at barbeques, by mail solicitations and, these days, through social media, such as Facebook and Twitter, and candidate websites.

Many candidates employ a full-time campaign manager and other full-time or part-time staff, and statewide candidates often have large staffs. Incumbents seeking reelection sometimes use their office staff to run their campaigns, though for legal and ethical reason staffers usually resign their staff positions to run the campaign. Then they are often re-hired as a staffer after the election if the incumbent is successful. Among a multitude of tasks, the day-to-day job of the campaign staff involves developing the promotion for the campaign, organizing volunteers for canvassing on street corners, knocking on doors and putting up yard signs, setting up speaking engagements for the candidate, and filing the APOC reports at the required times. Campaigning for both primary and general elections is a very intense affair, often requiring the candidate and his or her staff to work seven days a week, eighteen or more hours a day. Candidates give many press interviews, attend scores of fundraisers, make hundreds of phone calls, give hundreds of speeches, and shake thousands of hands.

One common element in virtually all Alaska campaigns, including statewide races, is that a politician's success largely depends on the ability to deal with local concerns. This is true in all states, but especially so in Alaska where friends and neighbors politics operate, as explained earlier. This includes less use of the media in many races, the downplaying of party, and the playing up of the personal qualities of the candidate. Friends and neighbors politics may also contribute to the relative lack of dirty politics and negative campaigning among candidates in Alaska elections compared with some other states.

So the variations among Alaska campaigns are due mainly to their scale, with statewide races requiring more funds and fundraising activities, a larger staff, greater use of the media, and considerably more travel by the candidate and senior staff members. Some of the other variations will become clear below.

Three Types of Statewide Campaigns

Campaigns for Congress, governor, and ballot propositions reveal differences in campaigns, partly based on the competitiveness of the race, the issues involved, the groups pro and con, and the funds available for the campaign, among other factors.

Congressional Campaigns

For the first fifteen years of statehood, campaigns for Alaska's three congressional seats were fairly competitive, with Democrats winning in the early years. Then, with the death of Democratic U.S. Senator Robert "Bob" Bartlett in 1968, Republican Governor Hickel appointed Republican Ted Stevens to fill his seat. When Democrat Nick Begich died in a plane crash in 1972, Republican Don Young replaced him in a special election in March 1973.[22] Following the 1980 U.S. Senate race, which elected Frank Murkowski, Alaska's congressional delegation remained solidly Republican for the next twenty-eight years.

In the 1980s and particularly in the 1990s when Stevens, Frank Murkowski, and Young were in leadership positions in Congress, they were able to amass huge campaign war chests, with major out-of-state contributions from national interests who benefited from their leadership positions in Congress. Yet, all three needed to mount only token election campaigns. With a few exceptions, their opponents were weak and could rarely count on help from the national Democratic Party campaign committees who saw supporting such candidates as a waste of money. Young continues to be reelected, is seemingly unbeatable, and is one of the longest-serving members of Congress in the nation's history. Moreover, Stevens and Young particularly exemplified the adage that "all politics is local" by delivering major budget resources to the state.[23] In addition, with their boisterous personalities, both Stevens and Young often campaigned as defending Alaska against Outside interests and particularly the federal government. They took federal money, and lots of it, with one hand and used the other hand to beat on Uncle Sam.

Since 2004, however, races for the U.S. Senate have become more competitive. This included the 2004 Senate race between Republican Lisa Murkowski and Democrat Tony Knowles, the 2008 race between Democrat Mark Begich and Ted Stevens (won by Begich following Stevens's indictment on corruption charges), and the 2010 race, between Republican Joe Miller and the Republican incumbent and write-in candidate Lisa Murkowski, covered in Section 7 below in a case study.[24] The 2014 U.S. Senate race between Mark Begich and Republican challenger Dan Sullivan was also very competitive and won by Sullivan, which once again made Alaska's congressional delegation all Republican.

Gubernatorial Campaigns

Campaigns for governor have generally been competitive in Alaska. Some races have been extremely close and have gone to recounts. This was the case when Republican Jay

Hammond beat Democrat Bill Egan by only 287 votes on a recount with over 90,000 votes cast in 1974, and again in 1994 when Democrat Tony Knowles beat Republican Jim Campbell by only 536 votes on a plurality out of over 210,000 votes cast.[25] Then in the 2002, 2006, and 2010 gubernatorial elections, the Republicans won clear victories. This was followed in 2014 by the electoral oddity of independent Bill Walker defeating incumbent Sean Parnell (also covered as a case study in Section 7 below). Incumbent governors are often challenged in the primary when they seek re-election, but they usually win easily. An exception was Frank Murkowski, who was defeated by Sarah Palin in the August 2006 Republican primary.

Between 1958 and 2014 there were fifteen elections for governor. Of these the Democrats won seven and the Republicans six. The other two were won by candidates who were, in reality, also Republicans. When Walter Hickel, Republican governor from 1966 to 1969, failed to get the Republican nomination in 1990, he ran on the AIP ticket and won, in large part because of major expenditure of his own funds. Then in 2014 Bill Walker, a long time Republican, initially ran as an independent, but after the primary he dropped his Republican registration and merged his campaign with the Democrats to form the Alaska First Unity ticket. Thus, since statehood Democrats and Republicans have more or less shared the governorship equally both in terms of the numbers elected and the years served.

Democrat Bill Sheffield also spent a lot of his own money to get elected when he successfully ran for governor in 1982. This money enabled him to travel to most communities in the state, which is not common in gubernatorial elections due to the cost. Sheffield was also aided by the issue of the capital move. It was on the 1982 ballot as a bond proposition seeking voter approval for a $2.8 billion to cover bondable costs to move the capital to Willow north of Anchorage. Sheffield's support for keeping the capital in Juneau won him a lot of votes outside of Anchorage.

The competitive nature of most gubernatorial campaigns, the need to raise considerable funds, and the grueling travel and speaking schedule, meant that running for governor up until the early 2000s was the most grueling of all Alaska election campaigns. Since the early 2000s, however, U.S. Senate races have become more competitive and consequently increasingly grueling and on a par with gubernatorial races. Box 14.4 relates the experience of Fran Ulmer, the Democratic candidate for governor in 2002. Ulmer lost to Republican Frank Murkowski, who left the U.S. Senate to run for governor.

Ballot Measures—Initiatives, Referenda, and Recalls, including Bond Propositions and Constitutional Amendments

Since statehood, Alaska has made moderate use of ballot measures compared with high user states like California and Oregon. In any election, California and Oregon can have ten or more ballot measures. Alaska, by contrast, may have two or three and rarely four or more.[26] These measures can appear on the primary or general election ballots.[27]

BOX 14.4

Running for Governor in Alaska: Fran Ulmer's Personal Recollections

Can I win? What do my family and friends think? What are the issues that are most important to me and to the electorate? Can I put together the team of volunteers and professionals I'll need? How much money do I need to raise, and can I raise that much? Who else is going to run, and what are their strengths and weaknesses in comparison to mine? Is the timing right for me—professionally, financially, personally, emotionally, physically, politically?

I did that calculation every time I ran for office (once for mayor of Juneau, four times for the legislature, twice for lieutenant governor), and all of those times I made the decision to run and I won.

Running for governor in 2002 seemed right for me on all counts except one: my opponent would probably be a sitting U.S. Senator, Frank Murkowski, who would be able to corral much of the support of the business and political leadership in the state. In spite of these odds, I felt morally compelled to run: I believed I was better prepared to be governor and better able to steer the state on the issues that I felt were the most important ones facing Alaska at that time.

It is never pleasant to ask people for money; but if you believe in what you are doing it is easier. Fundraising for a statewide race is challenging and necessary, unless you can finance your own race, which I could not. Thanks to thousands of donors, many making only small contributions, we raised more than I thought possible. Phone calls to friends and long-time supporters are essential, as well as calls to people you don't know at all. Events for small and large contributors are interspersed with door knocking, debates, press conferences, strategy sessions about radio and TV ads, meetings with advisors, speeches, responding to dozens of questionnaires, and traveling to as many communities as physically possible.

When people who are thinking about running for office come to talk to me, I offer the following advice: Don't run unless you are willing to put your entire self into the race and have fun doing it! I can honestly say I felt that way in every race I ran, including the 2002 gubernatorial campaign.

I sincerely believed I could win if I worked hard enough and talked with enough voters. Every speech, every neighborhood gathering, every door I knocked upon, every letter I wrote, I did believing winning was possible. That belief gave me a constant supply of energy, which is essential because a statewide campaign is an eighteen-month marathon. You eat and sleep and walk and talk the campaign. Fortunately, my family supported me with encouragement and volunteer labor: my son worked on my campaign for six months.

My conviction that I could win began to falter the last week of the campaign when Frank Murkowski's commercials added endorsements from President Bush, Senator Stevens, and Congressman Young, all urging votes for a united Republican team. I remember getting a call from an indignant supporter who said: "You could beat Frank, but it is tough to beat Frank and Don and Ted and George." The neck-and-neck polls between us were switching to a gloomy prediction. I still had lots of events to attend those last few days, rallies and sign-waving and "get out the vote" calls. Fatigue and reality were setting in, but I did not stop until the polls closed.

I woke up the next morning sad about losing and disappointed for my supporters, but certain that I had done my best and very grateful for the remarkable life experience and the generous support from people all over Alaska.

Source: Written by Fran Ulmer.

In Alaska state ballot measures have included initiatives, referenda, bond propositions, and constitutional amendments. Several recall elections against local officials, mainly school board members, have been successful, but no recall election for a statewide official or legislator has ever qualified for placement on the ballot. In the early 2000s these unsuccessful efforts included moves to recall Senator Scott Ogan of the Mat-Su Valley and Senator Ben Stevens of Anchorage. There was also an unsuccessful attempt to recall Governor Hickel and Lieutenant Governor Coghill in the early 1990s.[28]

Campaigning on ballot measures requires a different approach from campaigns for elected office. They usually involve groups forming pro and con to campaign on the issue. This was the case with several of the ballot propositions on the capital move. Many ballot propositions are to approve the state selling bonds to finance construction projects, particularly for transportation infrastructure, and these are rarely controversial and are almost always approved.

Article XI, Sections 1 through 6, of the Alaska Constitution and Alaska Statutes (AS) 15.45 set out the processes for the initiative, referendum, and recall. Of the twenty-four states that have the initiative, Alaska has one of the most stringent processes for qualification.[29] Once a petition for an initiative is approved by the Lieutenant Governor, it requires a number of signatures on the petition of at least ten percent of the votes cast in the last general election and at least seven percent of the votes in thirty or more of the forty house districts in the state.[30] If certified, the initiative appears on the ballot at the next regular primary or general election held after the legislature has had a full session to consider a substantially similar measure.[31] Following the 2012 elections, for example, the number of signatures required was 30,169. Mounting a statewide effort for an initiative where there is opposition to the measure requires considerable funds and a well-organized campaign if the initiative is to stand any chance of, first, being placed on the ballot, and second, receiving voter approval. These legal provisions, the required number of signatures, and efforts by supporters, are similar for getting a referendum on the ballot.

Regarding the first stage, to guard against the disqualification of signatures on the petition, the supporters need to get well in excess of the number of signatures required. Those favoring a change in the law through the initiative or referendum process must first decide whether they have the resources and the likelihood of getting the requisite number of signatures. At the ground level it requires an army of volunteers setting up tables and booths in supermarkets and shopping malls or standing on street corners to gather the requisite number of signatures. One example where more than enough signatures were gathered in a short time was the populist-type referendum to repeal the More Alaska Production Act (MAPA) passed by the legislature in 2013 to reduce oil taxes. In other cases, it takes longer to secure the number of signatures, as was the case with the initiative in 2012 to restore the Alaska Coastal Zone Management Program, which had been allowed to lapse by the legislature.[32] In some cases, those who would like to use the initiative realize that it would be too costly and far from certain that the requisite number of signatures could be gotten. This was the case in 2013 when the legislature rolled back standards regarding wastewater discharges from cruise ships and those opposed to the legislation did not feel they had the resources to get a referendum on the ballot.[33]

As to the second stage, because most initiatives and referenda generate some opposition, the pro forces have to run a major promotional campaign using TV, radio, newspapers, and direct mailings. Even employing all these resources plus social media, it was not enough to secure passage of the Coastal Zone Management initiative in the 2012 August primary, as the opposition mounted a more extensive campaign. The initiative, Measure 2, went down by a wide margin of 62 to 38 percent. The supporters of repealing the MAPA legislation were outspent 18 to 1 by the oil industry and others who supported the tax reduction. This was by far the most expensive ballot measure in Alaska's history with nearly $20 million spent, though the result was less lopsided than the spending might indicate. The MAPA referendum, which appeared on the ballot in the 2014 August primary, was defeated by a 52.7 to 47.3 percent vote.[34] Other campaigns have been more successful, such as the 1996 initiative to ban airborne hunting, mainly of wolf, wolverine, fox and lynx, which passed by 59 to 41 percent.[35]

Comparing Urban and Rural-Bush Campaigns for the Legislature

Geography, cultural differences, and less emphasis on party and ideology make for differences between campaigning in Alaska's largest urban area and the rest of the state. This is particularly the case with rural-bush communities that are largely Alaska Native, but also those with predominantly Caucasian, non-Native populations. Three noteworthy differences are the mode of getting around the districts, more bipartisan cooperation, and the nature of contact with constituents.

While many urban legislators can walk around their districts in a couple of hours, this is not the case in rural-bush Alaska, where districts may be enormous. The easiest way to get around, though an expensive one, is by plane. For instance, Senator Donny Olson flies his own plane to campaign in the huge Senate District T referred to earlier in the chapter, which covers much of Northwest Alaska and the North Slope. In Southeast and Southwest Alaska candidates often use the state ferry system. Former Representative Peggy Wilson of Wrangell used the system to cover her new district during the 2012 election, which included Ketchikan for the first time when the 2010 redistricting expanded the geographic size of her district.[36] In the lower Kuskokwin, the river systems are often used for reaching remote places. Examples of bipartisan campaigning include Alaska Native legislators Senator Al Kookesh, a Democrat, and Representative Bill Thomas of Haines, a Republican, who campaigned together in 2010 to promote the interests of their districts and of rural-bush Alaska. And in the 1980s and early 1990s Sitka Representative Ben Grussendorf, a Democrat, and Senator Dick Eliason, a Republican, worked together in a similar fashion. Major differences in campaigning in urban and rural-bush Alaska are explained by former Representative Mary Nelson in Box 14.5.

4. CAMPAIGN FINANCE: REGULATIONS, SOURCES, AND SPENDING

As in the other forty-nine states and at the national level, campaign finance and the issues related to it affect candidates running for office in Alaska in several ways and, in doing so, shape their campaigns and often the outcomes of elections. In this section our focus is campaign finance regulations, sources of campaign funds, and campaign spending in Alaska compared with other states.

Alaska's Campaign Finance Regulations, Comparisons with Other States and the *Citizens United* Decision

Beginning in the 1960s, the increasing role of money in elections fueled fears throughout the country that elections were being controlled and decided not by voters but by big money interests. These fears led many states to pass laws regulating election campaign spending, especially after the passage of the Federal Elections Campaign Act in 1971, which increased financial disclosure in federal campaigns.[37] Alaska adopted a campaign finance reform law in 1974, establishing APOC to monitor and regulate campaign contributions and spending among other responsibilities.[38] By 1996, Alaska had some of the most progressive campaign finance laws in the nation. These included statutes placing limits on the amount that could be contributed directly to candidates and requiring full disclosure of contributions to and expenditures by all campaigns. Municipal elections are covered by the state requirements unless the municipal assembly or city council votes to exempt the municipality.

Alaska's Campaign Finance Regulation as of 2016

All candidates for state office are subject to the Public Official Financial Disclosure Law. The law requires candidates to file financial disclosure statements listing all business relationships, sources of income, and indebtedness.[39]

There are also several reporting requirements for candidates and campaigns administered and enforced by APOC, covering campaign contributions and expenditures. These include an initial report due on February 15 of the election year (for candidates only), a report due thirty days before the election, and a report due seven days before the election. The law also requires twenty-four-hour reports that must include certain contributions for each twenty-four-hour reporting period starting nine days prior to

BOX 14.5

Running for the Legislature in Bush Alaska: Dealing with Friends, Neighbors, and Family

Running for the legislature in the bush is not only an exercise in friends and neighbors politics, it is also a family affair. A bush campaign for the legislature contrasts with one in urban Alaska in several ways. Much of this is to do with cultural differences given the large Alaska Native population in most rural-bush legislative districts.

While a more combative and aggressive style may be acceptable for urban electoral districts, Native cultures discourage self-aggrandizement and calling attention to oneself. The bush style of working to get elected runs counter to the conventional American campaign process, which relies on self-promotion and glad-handing.

Most people in small towns and villages are interrelated and most candidates are averse to negative campaigning. If you speak ill of a person, you run the risk of offending at least half the town's population, which is sure to be related to that person either by blood or by marriage. Besides this, rural campaigns involve more face-to-face and two-way communication because commercial television and radio is rare, nonexistent, or simply too expensive after paying the high travel costs to campaign from village to village.

In urban Alaska, candidates are taught that spending more than five minutes at a person's door or with a voter is an inefficient use of their time. If you are campaigning in the bush, this is poor advice. Many voters first want to find out who you are, where you and your family are from, and how you might be related to them. Then they may be ready to hear your reasons for running for office. It is never a five-minute encounter. Many villages also rely on "political conduits" or matriarchs and patriarchs to lead in deciding regional representation. These key people must be given a good deal of time and consideration by any candidate from the bush who is serious about being elected to the legislature, or for any office for that matter.

Source: Developed by former State Representative Mary Nelson (now Mary Sattler), a Democrat from Bethel.

the election—detailing all contributions that exceed $250 from any single contributor. If no such contributions have been received a candidate need not file a twenty-four-hour report.[40] Because the purpose of this report is to give the public access to information about a campaign's major contributions during the critical final days before the election, timely reporting is vital. These reports are required to be communicated via fax, e-mail, by hand or voice mail so as to be disseminated to the public rapidly.

A candidate may not accept contributions more than forty-five days after election day, and there are rules regarding the disbursement of campaign funds remaining unspent after election day. For example, a candidate may use such funds to pay expenses reasonably related to the campaign, may donate the funds to a political party or charitable organization, may repay loans from the candidate to the candidate's own campaign, may repay donations to contributors on a pro rata basis, or may transfer a portion of unused campaign contributions to an account for a future election. For legislative candidates whose elections are successful, the funds may be deposited in his or her public office expense account.[41]

Contributions from anonymous sources or those made under a fictitious name are prohibited. Cash contributions are authorized only if the name of the contributor is recorded and the amount does not exceed $100.

Campaign finance records must be kept for a period of six years from the date of the election for which the report was required.[42] The campaign contribution limits and other restrictions and requirements for Alaska state elections as of 2016 are set out in Table 14.1.

Campaign Finance Regulations in Three Other Western States

To place Alaska's campaign finance regulations in perspective, we outline the rules in three other western states. The provisions in these states are fairly typical of the variations in campaign finance regulations across the fifty states.

Washington State: Washington requires candidates to file campaign expenditure and contribution reports only if the total received for that campaign exceeds $5,000. Once that threshold has been reached, reports are required monthly, and more frequently as the election date nears. Washington allows anonymous contributions, as long as their amount does not exceed $300 or 1 percent of total donations, whichever is greater. Within twenty-one days before the general election, aggregate contributions of $1,000 or more received from one source must be reported within forty-eight hours, and no contributor may donate over $50,000 in the aggregate to a candidate for statewide office or over $5,000 in the aggregate to a candidate for any other office or to a political committee.[43]

California: Any campaign that exceeds $1,000 in funds raised or spent is required to report all contributions and expenditures. Candidates are required to file only twice on predetermined dates. Electronic filing is required only if the amount exceeds $50,000. Additionally, any donor who makes contributions totaling $25,000 or more in a calendar year must file all reports electronically in addition to filing paper reports.[44]

Wyoming: All candidates must file campaign finance reports regardless of whether they raise money. All political action committees (PACs—organizations set up by interest groups to raise money for use in elections), ballot committees, and party committees must also file. A person may not contribute more than $1,000 per election to any one candidate or more than $25,000 in total political contributions during the two-year election period. The state does allow small anonymous contributions, but all such contributions must be reported as anonymous. As of 2015, all candidates were required to file electronically. Candidates are required to file four reports during an election year, including

TABLE 14.1

Alaska State Election Campaign Contribution Limits and Restrictions as of 2016

	CONTRIBUTION TO			
CONTRIBUTION FROM	CANDIDATE	GROUP AND NON-GROUP ENTITY	BALLOT GROUP	POLITICAL PARTY
Individuals				
Alaska Residents	$500	$500	Unlimited*	$5,000
Nonresidents	$500 if the candidate has not exceeded the aggregate limit: House $3,000 Senate $5,000 Governor and Lt. Gov. $20,000	$500 if the group has not exceeded the limit of 10% of its total campaign contributions that are allowable from out-of-state	Unlimited*	$5,000 if the party has not exceeded 10 percent of its total campaign contributions that are allowable from out-of-state
Groups				
Based in Alaska	$1,000	$1,000	Unlimited*	$1,000
NOT based in Alaska	Prohibited	$1,000 Must first register with APOC	Unlimited*	$1,000 Must first register with APOC
Political Parties	House $10,000 Senate $15,000 Governor and Lt. Governor $100,000	$1,000	Unlimited*	Unlimited

*Contribution to or payments by a ballot group over specified dollar amounts must be reported to APOC at the time of receipt of the payment.

Source: Alaska Public Offices Commission, "Alaska Campaign Contribution Limits," at http://doa.alaska.gov/apoc/faqs/faq-contribution-limits.html.

a seven-day pre-election report and a ten-day post-election report. Unlike most states, Wyoming does not conduct audits of campaign finance reports.[45]

These three comparisons show that Alaska's regulations are among the most stringent in the nation despite efforts by many politicians and others to loosen the rules. The scandals in the state in 2006 surrounding VECO, when the CEO of this now defunct oil service company was involved in bribing some legislators, helped bring about more stringent laws. This countered attempts by former Governor Frank Murkowski to undermine the role of APOC in this regard.[46] However, a U.S. Supreme Court decision in 2010 may seriously weaken campaign finance provisions across the states, including in Alaska.

The Citizens United *U.S. Supreme Court Decision*

The Supreme Court decision in *Citizens United v. Federal Election Commission* of 2010 was a political bombshell in the politics and administration of campaign finance. Commonly known as *Citizens United*, the decision changed the landscape of politics in the 2010 elections and for many elections to come by removing any limitations on independent expenditures by corporations and labor unions.[47] An independent expenditure is one that advocates the election or defeat of a candidate without the cooperation of, or consultation with, a candidate or his or her agents. The decision did not affect the ban on corporate or labor union contributions directly to individual candidates for federal office.

Independent expenditures in unlimited amounts by individuals and political action committees (PACs) have long been allowed for all campaigns across the nation. This practice was confirmed in the U.S. Supreme Court's 1976 decision in *Buckley v. Valeo.* In this decision the Court ruled that these kinds of expenditures are a form of political expression and restrictions on that right could not be justified under the First Amendment to the U.S. Constitution. The *Citizens United* decision extended this ruling beyond individuals and PACs to include corporations and labor unions. Now corporations and unions, which Congress had previously banned from making any kind of contribution or expenditure for or against individual candidates, are free to make such expenditures so long as the expenditure is "independent," as defined above. Moreover, as a result of the *Citizens United* decision and other federal court rulings, corporations and labor unions are now permitted to make unlimited contributions to PACs that are formed solely to make independent expenditures. These new independent expenditure organizations are called super PACs because of the potentially large and unlimited sums of money that corporations and unions can give to these PACs. With such potentially large contributions, super PACs usually have much larger budgets than most candidates for state office. As a result, many candidates cannot compete financially for air time or any other commercial media.

The *Citizens United* decision affected campaign laws in twenty-four states, including Alaska. In an attempt to restore a degree of transparency to the election process, the

Alaska legislature passed SB 284 in April 2010, which significantly increased campaign finance reporting requirements, including mandatory reporting requirements for independent expenditures.[48]

Toward the end of the 2010 election cycle, the vast majority of the air time available in Alaska had been bought up by large corporations and political groups set up expressly to be independent of any given campaign. Media companies sought to quell the demand by increasing the cost of air time as well as print ads, but this only further exacerbated the problem because the largest budgets were in the hands of the larger corporations and, to a lesser extent, in that of unions. These changes in campaign finance laws, brought about by *Citizens United,* pose the danger that campaign messages in the future will be dominated by corporations with the largest budgets, thus strongly coloring the information that reaches the voting public. By way of example, in 2010, an independent expenditure of $700,747.28 was reported to APOC less than forty-eight hours before the polls opened. In the 2010 elections, however, campaign strategists were only just beginning to grasp the significance of *Citizens United.*

The 2014 election was the first in Alaska with major statewide races under *Citizens United*, a U.S. Senate race and the gubernatorial election. The Begich-Sullivan race was key to the Republicans controlling the U.S. Senate, and the election demonstrated the tremendous resources that super PACs can bring to bear. This was the most expensive race in Alaska history at $60,380,000, and over two-thirds of this ($40,640,000) came from super PACS. Of this, just over $23 million was in support of Begich and just over $17 million for the Sullivan campaign.[49] The amount of super PAC money in the governor's race paled by comparison but was still a large percentage of the total. Of the total cost of the campaign of $4.5 million, about 45 percent came from independent expenditure committees. Two-thirds of those independent expenditures, or $1,305,992.04, went to the incumbent Sean Parnell, with $648,811.72 going to Walker.[50]

Sources of Campaign Funds across the States and in Alaska

In making comparisons between states, particularly in assessing whether Alaska is a high-cost campaign spending state, some cautions are in order. First, comparisons across states are not entirely accurate because states vary in what they require to be reported for both contributions and expenditures. Second, it is important to compare states with similar electoral cycles (gubernatorial and U.S. Senate elections). Third, total amounts of spending are not accurate indicators because they are affected by the size of the population. Larger states may have more expenses for media and mailings even though in some ways they can take advantage of economies of scale with some costs, such as for printing and bulk mailing of advertising flyers.

Nevertheless, we can make some enlightening observations about where Alaska fits in relation to other states not only in sources of campaign funds but also regarding levels of campaign spending. This information helps in making an assessment of the extent to which money is a factor in the outcome of Alaska's elections and thus the extent to which money affects the state's democratic process.

The two major sources of funding campaigns in the states, and to some extent at the federal level, are public sources from state and federal coffers and private sources.

Public Funding

Public funding laws are often referred to as "clean elections provisions," and sometimes as "clean money elections" and "voter owned elections." Over the years twenty-five states have had or still have some form of public financing. As of 2015, fifteen states had such a system, including Arizona, Maine, New Jersey, and New Mexico. However, in all cases, accepting such funding is optional for the candidate.[51] Moreover, public funding has never taken root in the United States the way it has in Western Europe, where there is often compulsory public funding coupled with strict campaign spending limits. In the United States such limits have been largely precluded by the free speech provisions of the U.S. Constitution.[52] Another factor may be that politicians are reluctant to enact public funding because the reelection advantage of incumbents is reduced by about 30 percent when such provisions govern an election. This is in part because incumbents' fundraising options are reduced and that of their opponents increased, as indicated by evidence from Arizona and Maine.[53]

For many years, Alaska had a small-scale form of public financing of state elections. It consisted of allowing contributors to write off a small contribution against their state income tax. But this ended when the state individual income tax was abolished in 1980. Currently, Alaska has no public funding of elections. In fact, in 2008 a public campaign funding ballot measure, Alaska's attempt at establishing a clean elections provision that would be voluntary for candidates, was rejected by 64 percent of voters.

Sources of Private Campaign Funds: Placing Alaska in Perspective

Where do candidates for state and federal office across the states and in Alaska get their money? In regard to elections for state offices, there are four major private sources—individual citizens, interest groups and their PACs, political parties, and the candidate's own funds. Most people are familiar with individuals, parties, and candidates as funding sources. Less familiar to most citizens are PACs.

What are these organizations and what part do they play in contributing to elections in Alaska? Box 14.6 provides examples of PACs operating in the state. Then, the two parts of Figure 14.1 set out contributions for the Alaska legislative elections of 2012.

BOX 14.6

Examples of Alaska Political Action Committees (PACs)

ALASKA BLUE GREEN ALLIANCE PAC

This group unites fourteen of the largest unions and environmental organizations nationwide. The Alaska chapter is part of the nationwide Blue Green Alliance, which has more than fifteen million members and supporters. The group advocates for clean jobs in a number of sectors. Some of its political initiatives include clean energy, transportation, energy efficiency, workers' rights, recycling, and green schools.

ALASKA HOTEL AND LODGING ASSOCIATION PAC

This organization was formed in 1983 and represents 70 percent of the lodging rooms in the state as well as more than twenty-five industry suppliers.

NATIONAL EDUCATIONAL ASSOCIATION (NEA) ALASKA PAC

NEA is one of the largest labor unions in the United States and in Alaska, representing public school teachers and other K–12 employees. Between 2004 and 2012 its PAC contributed $233,711 to Alaska campaigns in 189 separate contributions.

ALASKA MINERS ASSOCIATION PAC—AMAPAC

The Alaska Miners Association is a nonprofit corporation headquartered in Anchorage with branch offices in Fairbanks and Juneau. It advocates for the development and use of Alaska's mineral resources to provide an economic base for the state. AMAPAC supports candidates running for state and federal office who share AMA's political goals of mineral development.

ALASKA RIGHT TO LIFE PAC

The organization is a chapter of a national single-issue political action committee dedicated to supporting candidates for office who will further the goals of the pro-life (anti-abortion) movement.

BP ALASKA EMPLOYEE PAC

This PAC advances the interests of BP employees. It works to further the principles of free enterprise, good government, and a favorable business environment for the energy industry. The PAC contributed $562,250 in campaign contributions between 2004 and 2012 in 128 separate contributions.

ALASKA BUSINESS PAC—ABPAC

ABPAC makes contributions to candidates for federal office, the legislature, governor, lieutenant governor, and ballot propositions that support or advance the role of business and its future in Alaska.

ALASKA CONSERVATION VOTERS FOR CLEAN GOVERNMENT PAC

This is a nonpartisan Alaska-based organization that supports pro-conservation candidates and advocates for conservation policy.

ALASKA HERITAGE PAC

The mission of this PAC is to promote independent and libertarian values in Alaska through education and political action, including the support of like-minded candidates for political office.

ALASKA FIRST PAC

This nonpartisan PAC supports candidates who place Alaska's interests ahead of partisanship. Its philosophy is based on the view that, because Alaska is rich in resources, the state needs leaders who support responsible resource development, education, and job creation. After vetting candidates, the PAC recommends that businesses and individuals contribute to candidates who meet its criteria.

Source: Developed by the authors from the websites and publications of each organization, from information on the Alaska Public Offices Commission website, and from the website of the National Institute for Money in State Politics, at http://www.followthemoney.org/index.phtml.

Figure 14.1A shows contributions by sector and Figure 14.1B contributions by category, with interest groups included under "institutions."[54]

To place Alaska's four major funding sources for state legislative offices in a comparative context, Table 14.2 (on page 468) shows the amount and percentage of these four sources in overall campaign contributions for five other states. This table facilitates comparison with Figure 14.1 for the 2012 election cycle, which looks only at Alaska. The five states include two in the West and one in each of the other three regions of the nation (Midwest, Northeast, and South). One of the five (California) has a large population, and two have populations close to Alaska's (Wyoming and Vermont). The others (Minnesota and Arkansas) have medium-sized populations. This range of states, plus the fact that neither Alaska nor any of the five other states had a gubernatorial election in 2012, makes for some enlightening comparisons.

The funding source pattern that emerges is that in states with large and medium-sized populations, institutions (interest groups and their PACs) are the major source, and the larger the state the larger is their overall percentage as a source of funds. PACs and interest groups are followed by individuals, political parties, and candidates' own funds. The relative percentage rankings for parties and candidates' own funds are reversed in some states, as shown in Table 14.2 for Arkansas. In smaller states, on the other hand, individual contributions tend to comprise the largest percentage, followed by interest groups and their PACs, candidate money, and party funds (see the figures for Vermont in Table 14.2 and for Alaska in Figure 14.1B). Wyoming, however, was an exception in 2012, with a whopping 70 percent coming from candidates themselves, followed by institutions and individuals, with parties having the lowest percentage as in most states. So in this regard, even though parties are often stronger organizationally and politically more important in many states than in Alaska, their percentage of total campaign contributions is not that much different from Alaska's.

As to the specific sources of funds in Alaska, despite major contributions to candidates by labor, education, business, and other interests (Figure 14.1A), individual contributions far outstrip these special interest sources of funds. Moreover, most Alaska candidates do not have a lot of personal money to put into their campaigns. Two notable exceptions were Bill Sheffield, who contributed some $600,000 of his own money to his $2 million campaign to win the governorship in 1982, and Wally Hickel, who spent about $700,000 of his own money in a successful $1 million gubernatorial campaign in 1990.[55]

The prominence of individual contributions as a funding source might lead one to conclude that Alaska candidates once elected are less beholden to interest groups and their lobbyists compared with many other states. This may well be the case, but the situation regarding the influence of money on campaigns and ultimately on public policy is much more complex than this, as we consider later in the chapter.[56]

FIGURE 14.1

Contributions to Alaska 2012 State Election Campaigns

FIGURE 14.1A: BREAKDOWN BY SECTOR

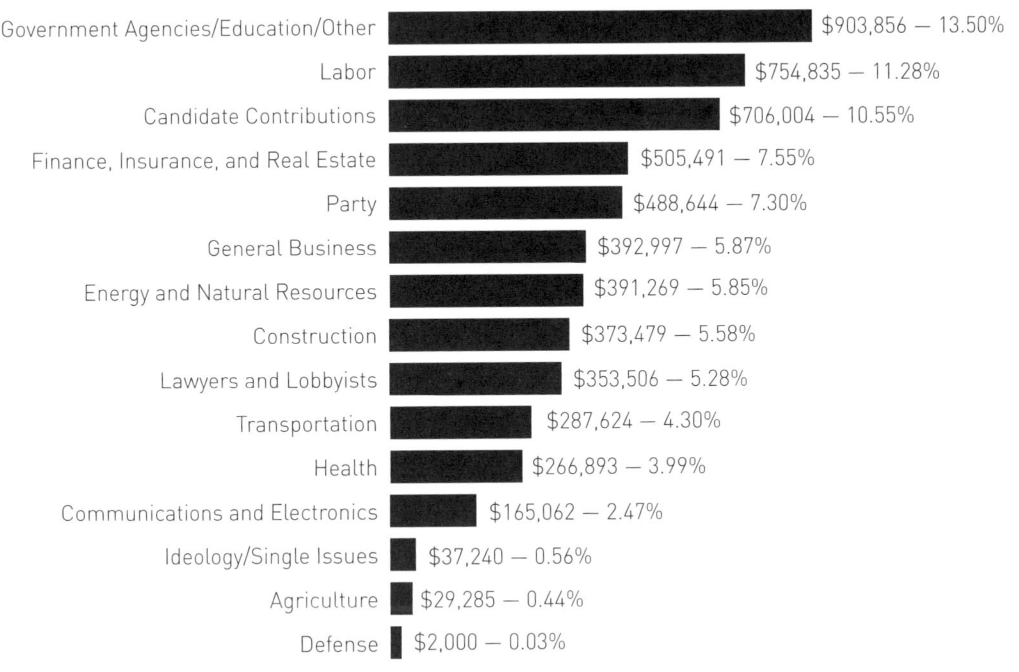

FIGURE 14.1B: BREAKDOWN BY TYPE OF CONTRIBUTOR

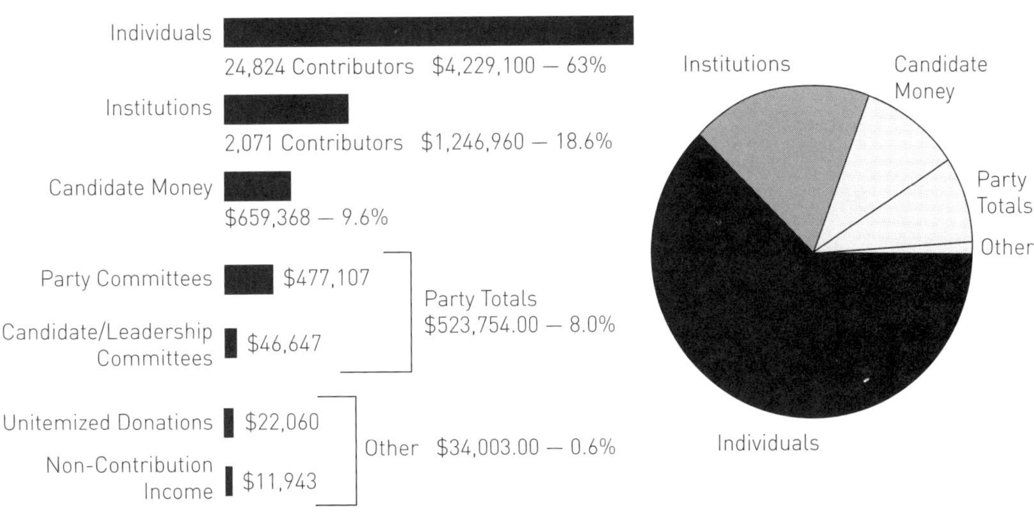

Source: National Institute on Money in State Politics, Follow the Money. Alaska 2012. Contributions. http://www.followthemoney.org/database/StateGlance/state_contributors.phtml?s=AK&y=2012

TABLE 14.2

Campaign Contributions in Five States in the State Elections of 2012: Breakdown by Type of Contribution in Total Dollars and Percent of Total Contributions

TYPE OF CONTRIBUTION	CALIFORNIA		WYOMING		VERMONT		MICHIGAN		ARKANSAS	
Individuals	$184,604,990	28.0	$405,979	11.0	$2,030,857	41.0	$22,227,674	10.2	$5,873,988	28.3
Institutions	$387,111,512	59.0	$470,184	13.0	$977,730	20.0	$181,236,452	84.0	$9,582,140	46.7
All Political Party Funds	$43,709,769	7.0	$247,528	5.9	$182,916	5.0	$10,450,794	4.9	$2,485,819	12.0
Personal Funds of Candidates	$4,428,557	0.7	$2,486,351	70.0	$661,737	13.0	$145,622	0.2	$1,731,070	8.0
Other	$31,287,386	5.3	$5,068	0.1	$1,022,902	21.0	$753,148	0.7	$994,179	5.0
Total	**$651,142,214**		**$3,550,498**		**$4,940,754**		**$214,522,447**		**$20,667,195**	

Source: Follow the Money. 2012. Contributions. Retrieved on Sep. 8th, 2013. http://www.followthemoney.org/database/state_overview.phtml.

Spending on Elections: Where Does Alaska Fit?

How much does it cost to get elected in Alaska to state and federal offices? Is this comparable to or out of line with other states? Are the two all-time record spending elections of over $60 million on the U.S. Senate race in 2014 and the nearly $20 million on Ballot Measure 1 in the 2014 primary election aberrations? To answer these questions we first look at some figures for various types of state and congressional elections.

In the early 1990s, McBeath and Morehouse observed that, on a per voter basis, Alaska elections were among the most expensive in the nation. For instance, at $6 million, Alaska's 1982 elections were the most expensive in the nation on a per vote basis.[57] Alaska election costs still tend to be high whether on the basis of per vote or per capita of state population, but there are wide variations from race to race. Since the early 2000s the expenditures for U.S. House races have generally been lower than other states but higher for U.S. Senate races. Moreover, the patterns of spending on state races have changed in the twenty years or so since McBeath and Morehouse wrote.

Congressional Campaigns Costs

Since the early 1990s, Alaska campaign costs for the U.S. House have tended to be lower than other states. This is largely because Alaska's one U.S. House seat has not been competitive since the late 1980s. The total cost of this race from the mid-1990s to 2014 has ranged between $1 and $2 million, usually nearer the lower figure. Few U.S. House races across the nation cost less than $1 million, and some cost considerably more. Alaska races for the U.S. Senate were also in the $1 million range until 2004 and on a par with other states. Since 2004, these races have become very competitive and much more expensive comparatively. To illustrate the cost of federal elections in Alaska we compare one U.S. House race and three U.S. Senate races for four election years since 2004.[58]

The 2010 U.S. House race in Alaska was a typical year in terms of spending. The total spent was $1,241,454. The incumbent and victor, Republican Don Young, spent $1,001,015, and his challenger, Democrat Harry Crawford, spent about a quarter as much at $240,439. In contrast, the total spending that year in the race for California's House District 1 with close to the same population as Alaska (the state has fifty-three seats in the U.S. House) was $2,027,344, almost two times the amount spent in Alaska's election. Selected races in New Jersey and Michigan ranged between three to ten times higher than Alaska. The race for the single House seat in Wyoming that year cost almost six times that of Alaska, at $7,123,234.

For the U.S. Senate race in 2004, Republican Lisa Murkowski spent $5,702,709 to Democrat Tony Knowles's $5,835,949, for a total of $11,538,658. That year, the U.S. Senate race in Colorado cost $17,568,617 and the one in California $23,372,945. This means the per capita cost in Alaska was five times that of Colorado and twenty-five times that of California. Similar disparities existed in the 2008 race between Republican Ted Stevens and Democrat Mark Begich as well as the 2010 race between Republican Joe Miller, Democrat Scott McAdams, and write-in candidate Lisa Murkowski. In 2008 the $9,837,596 spent in Alaska was six times as much per capita as North Carolina's U.S. Senate race and four times that of Wyoming's. In 2010, at $9,378,448, the total cost of the Alaska race was nine times the per capita cost of the race in California and five times that of New Jersey.

The major comparative disparity, however, came in the 2014 election for the U.S. Senate. Although Alaska's election was only the seventh highest nationwide in total spending at $60 million, with North Carolina's being number one at $113 million, on a per capita basis Alaska's was far higher than any other state. This was over $82 per Alaskan, close to two and a half times the next state, New Hampshire at $36, and over seven times as much per capita as North Carolina at $11.

Gubernatorial Campaigns

Since the early 1980s, the cost of running for governor across the states has increased considerably. The average cost of a campaign more than doubled between that time and 2011. Much of the increase is a result of new campaigning techniques and the increasing cost of media. Another factor is more competitive races in southern states, where Republicans worked to challenge the traditional dominance by the Democrats. To cite some examples, the average cost of a gubernatorial election over these years is $59 million in Texas, $28.7 million in Florida, and $27.2 million in North Carolina.[59] The 2013 election for governor in Virginia cost $54.1 million: $34.4 million spent by the Democratic winning candidate and $19.7 million by the losing Republican.[60]

But all these pale by comparison with the 2010 gubernatorial election in California. At $200 million, this was the costliest election at the state level in U.S. history. The election reflected another recent trend in gubernatorial elections: that of rich candidates increasingly spending their own money in a bid to get elected. In this race Republican candidate, Meg Whitman, a former eBay executive, spent over $140 million of her own funds but still lost to Democrat Jerry Brown, whom she outspent four to one.[61]

Alaska has been much less subject to these trends in the high cost of getting elected to the state's highest office. Following the $2 million spent in the 1982 election, the total cost of gubernatorial campaigns in Alaska has been as low as $2,303,604 for the Frank Murkowski-Fran Ulmer race of 2002 (about $3 million adjusted for inflation to 2014 prices) to $4,010,101 in the 2014 Parnell-Walker race.[62] Adjusted for inflation to 2014 prices, the most expensive race since 1982 was the 1986 race between Arliss Sturgulewski and Steve Cowper, which cost $2,848,500 at the time but would have been about $6 million in 2014 dollars.[63]

Despite these modest increases, on a per capita basis, Alaska's recent gubernatorial elections are on a par with the high-cost states, though considerably lower than the 2010 California election. Yet Alaska has never stood out as a significantly high-cost state, and it is certainly not out of line with states with a similar population. For example, the cost of the gubernatorial election in Vermont in 2010 was $5,866,224 and in Wyoming $3,911,348.

Ballot Propositions

Similar to comparisons of the cost of gubernatorial campaigns, with the exception of Ballot Measure 1 (the MAPA referendum) in 2014, per capita costs of Alaska ballot propositions are on a par with other states. Nonetheless, in several states there are major differences in the intensity of the campaigns, the financial stakes, and often the sources of funding. This is particularly the case in states like California and Washington and, to some extent, in Oregon, all three of which are major users of ballot propositions. In these states, with much larger economies than Alaska's, big money is often spent on propositions involving issues affecting business corporations that may stand to gain or lose billions of dollars if the measure passes or fails. Thus, much money from out-of-state sources is often involved in these ballot measure campaigns.

In contrast, most Alaska ballot measures have involved social issues, like abortion or marijuana use, government operations, or bond obligation propositions. These attract little Outside interest or funds. The propositions that do attract Outside funds are usually those involving environmental issues, such as predator control, as explained in Chapter 22 on the environment.[64] Consequently, for these reasons, raw number cost comparisons alone, be they per vote cast or per capita, do not adequately explain the importance of money in comparing Alaska with other states.

Before 2014, on only a few occasions since statehood has the money spent on a ballot proposition exceeded $1 million, even adjusted for inflation to 2014 prices. By contrast, it can cost up to this much in California just to collect enough signatures to qualify a proposition for the ballot.[65] Many ballot propositions in Alaska, especially those for capital projects bonds, have very little if anything spent on them. Even some controversial issues see spending only in the hundreds of thousands of dollars. One example was Measure 7, an unsuccessful ballot proposition in 1986 to limit abortions, on which $136,981 was spent (about $300,000 in 2014 prices). Another example was Measure 2 in 1998 that resulted in an amendment to the Alaska Constitution requiring the state to recognize only marriages between a man and a woman (thereby prohibiting gay marriages). The total spent on this measure was $571,000 (about $740,000 in 2014 dollars).[66] And few propositions, even very controversial ones, involve as much money as did Measure 7 in 1986, on the personal consumption of fish and game (essentially on the highly emotional issue of subsistence).

At $910,041 (about $2 million adjusted for inflation to 2014 prices), this was the most expensive ballot measure in Alaska history until 2014.

As late as 2010, two highly controversial ballot propositions, Measure 1 to ban government funds being spent on lobbying, and Measure 2, another proposition on abortion, cost just $1,447,333 and $774,763, respectively. In 2014, however, ballot measure costs in Alaska increased significantly. Besides the oil tax referendum at just under $20 million, Ballot Measure 2 to legalize marijuana cost close to $2.5 million, Measure 3 to increase the minimum wage cost $490,000. And Ballot Measure 4 to require legislative approval for mining development in Bristol Bay cost just under $1.2 million. So 2014 can claim three of the four highest spending ballot measures in Alaska since statehood.

It is interesting to compare these with recent ballot measures in California and the State of Washington. In 2010 there were nine propositions on the ballot in California involving a total cost of $147 million, or an average of over $16 million each. Over $25 million was spent on Proposition 26 alone, to require voter approval of new taxes.[67] In 2010 in Washington State, a total of $62,927,357 was spent on six ballot measures (an average of over $10 million each) including "Stop the Food and Beverage Tax Hikes Initiative" to allow liquor sales by private vendors, on which $16 million was spent. With considerable out-of-state spending by large retailers like Costco, the private vendors won. This figure pales, however, compared with the initiative measure on the November 2013 ballot that would have required labeling of foods containing genetically modified organisms (GMOs). Total spending on it was over $26 million, nearly $7 million in favor and $20 million against. Much of the money spent on opposing the initiative came from the food industry located out of state. The large expenditures helped turn early public support for the measure into a defeat.[68]

The Cost of Running for the Legislature

As to the cost of running for the state legislature, the following observations for the 2012 legislative elections compare Alaska with California and Indiana. Despite the fact that 2012 was a legislative election following a reapportionment in Alaska (which often results in more competitive and therefore more expensive races), in terms of average spending per candidate, 2012 was nonetheless a fairly typical year for all three states since the mid-1990s.

In 2012 in Alaska, forty-five senatorial candidates spent a total of $2.7 million (an average of $60,000 each) and 101 house candidates $3.1 million (an average of $30,000 each). In California, fifty-six senate candidates ran and spent $31 million (about $861,000 each), while 272 Assembly candidates campaigned and spent $87 million (about $315,000 each). In Indiana, fifty-five senate candidates spent a total of $5.8 million (an average of $105,000 each), and 245 candidates for the house seats spent $15.4 million (an average of $62,000).[69]

The lowest amount spent by a candidate for an Alaska Senate race in 2012 was $114 (spent by Anchorage Republican Paul Kendall who lost by 36 percentage points to Democrat Johnny Ellis), and the highest $220,129 (by Anchorage Democrat Hollis French, who was in a competitive race and narrowly defeated Republican Bob Bell). In the Alaska State House the low that year was $1,750 (spent by Republican Carl Morgan, who lost by a wide margin to Democrat Bryce Edgmon in District 36 in Southwest Alaska), and the high was $118,489 (by Lance Pruitt, who narrowly defeated incumbent Pete Peterson of Anchorage in a very competitive race). In California, the low and high figures for the Senate were $43,590 and $3,029,267, and for the state Assembly $3,953 and $4,121,680. For Indiana, the equivalent low and high figures were $1,133 and $900,108 for the Senate and $250 and $792,025 for the House.

Taking the many variables among the three states into consideration, the cost of Alaska's legislative races are not out of line. They are slightly less per capita than California and slightly more than in Indiana. The cost of legislative elections in Alaska in 2014 was very similar to the figures for 2012.

Why Are Some Campaign Costs Higher in Alaska?

As we have seen, the cost of Alaska's elections is a mixed bag compared with other states. When they do exceed national averages, why do Alaska's elections cost more and, in the case of U.S. Senate races, much more? More important, does money make a difference in getting elected? Again, it is difficult to give a definitive answer to any of these questions, but we can make the following observations.

In part, the high cost of some of Alaska's elections is the result of generally higher costs in the state for printing direct mailings and yard signs, travel, media ads, hiring staff, and so on. In addition, being a small state there are no economies of scale for some of these expenses—such as cheaper costs per unit for printing a larger number of items—as there are in states with large and medium-sized populations. Clearly, the enormous cost of the 2014 U.S. Senate race in Alaska was due to its national significance in determining control of the U.S. Senate. The high spending on Ballot Measure 1 to maintain lower oil taxes reflected the billions of dollars at stake for some of the world's largest corporations. Other than that, it is hard to account for the high cost in many cases.

We now turn to the more important question of whether money is the major determining factor in getting elected, as many members of the public often believe. In particular, does the highest spender always win, and does campaign money have a detrimental effect on Alaska democracy? These are questions we address near the end of the next section when we consider who gets elected and why.

5. ELECTIONS: VOTER TURNOUT, ELECTORAL PATTERNS SINCE STATEHOOD, AND WHO GETS ELECTED AND WHY?

To what extent do Alaskans exercise their right to vote, who do they elect, and why? This section deals with these questions and concludes with some observations about the connection between the background of elected officials and how this may or may not play out in their actions in office.

Voter Turnout

Much discussion has occurred in the media and among academics since the late 1970s about the decline in voter turnout in American elections. There is particular concern about national elections, where it rarely tops 65 percent, compared with 75 to 80 percent in many parliamentary democracies like Sweden and New Zealand. Political commentators often interpret this relatively low turnout in the United States as a product of a low level of interest of Americans in politics. Comparisons between countries and among the fifty states can be deceiving, however, because some turnout calculations are based on the eligible adult voting population, while others are based upon the total registered voters.[70] Moreover, in some countries, like Australia, Luxemburg, and Uruguay, high turnout is, in part, a product of compulsory voting where citizens are fined if they do not cast ballots. Such a law would likely meet major opposition in the United States and particularly in Alaska. Moreover, even though voting is the major way in which most Americans participate in politics, it is only one form of political participation, which also includes belonging to an interest group and contacting public officials directly.

Most states' election offices, including Alaska's Division of Elections, define turnout as the percent of registered voters who vote in an election. Based on this calculation, Alaskans went to the polls before the early 1980s at a lower rate than the nation overall.[71] Since then, Alaska's turnout has usually been above the national average. For elections held between 2007 and 2010, for instance, Alaska ranked ninth of the fifty states in turnout.[72] In all states turnout varies considerably between primary and general elections, and particularly in presidential election years. And as might be expected, high profile and contentious issues, particularly those contained in ballot propositions, help to raise voter turnout. For instance, the second highest turnout in an Alaska election was nearly 75 percent in the gubernatorial election of 1982. As 1982 was not a presidential election year, most people attribute the unusually high turnout to the inclusion on the ballot of the contentious issue of funding a capital move.

Table 14.3 compares Alaska's voter turnout for president with the nation since 1960, the first election after statehood (the Kennedy-Nixon race), through 2012 (Obama-Romney). The table shows a trend after 1980 of Alaska having an above average turnout.

TABLE 14.3

Presidential Elections Results: The Nation Compared with Alaska, 1960-2012

(Percentage of Turnout and Breakdown of Total Vote)

	PERCENTAGE OF TOTAL VOTE									
	VOTER TURNOUT		DEMOCRAT		REPUBLICAN		INDEPENDENT		OTHER	
YEAR	ALASKA	U.S.	ALASKA	U.S.	ALASKA	U.S.	ALASKA	U.S.	ALASKA	U.S
1960	44.71	63.80	49.06	49.72	50.94	49.55	0.00	0.00	0.00	0.72
1964	43.96	62.80	65.91	61.05	34.09	38.47	0.00	0.00	0.00	0.48
1968	50.02	61.50	42.65	42.72	45.28	43.42	12.07	13.53	0.00	0.33
1972	48.33	56.20	34.62	60.67	58.13	37.52	0.00	0.00	7.25	1.80
1976	53.50	54.80	35.65	50.08	57.90	48.02	0.00	0.91	6.44	0.99
1980	58.70	54.20	26.41	41.01	54.35	50.75	7.04	6.61	12.20	1.62
1984	60.50	55.20	29.87	40.56	66.65	58.77	0.00	0.00	3.48	0.67
1988	47.50	52.80	36.27	45.65	59.59	53.37	0.00	0.00	4.14	0.98
1992	82.96	58.10	30.29	43.01	39.46	37.45	28.43	18.91	1.83	0.64
1996	59.80	51.70	33.27	49.23	50.80	40.72	0.00	0.00	15.92	10.05
2000	68.10	54.20	27.67	48.38	58.62	47.87	0.00	0.00	13.71	3.74
2004	69.10	60.10	35.52	48.27	61.07	50.73	0.00	0.38	3.42*	0.62
2008	67.70	61.60	37.89	52.87	59.42	45.60	1.16	0.56	1.53	0.97
2012	58.90	58.20	40.81	50.93	54.80	47.33	N/A	N/A	4.39	1.74

* Ralph Nader was registered as a Populist in Alaska in 2004.

Source: Turnout and percentages obtained from: Dave Leip's "Atlas of U.S. Presidential Elections," United States Presidential Elections Results, voting age population, retrieved from U.S. Census, "Estimates of the Population of Voting Age by States: November, 1960 to 1976," Table 5; Michael P. McDonald and Samual L. Popkin, "The Myth of the Vanishing Voter." *American Political Science Review*, Vol 95, No. 4 (2001): 963-74; and Michael P. McDonald, "United Stated Election Project. Turnout 1980," (2011), retrieved from http://elections.gmu.edu/voter_turnout.htm; and for 2012 General Election Turnout Rates. http://elections.gmu.edu/Turnout_2012G.html and Alaska Division of Election 2012, http://www.elections.alaska.gov/results/12GENR/data/results.pdf.

What it does not show is turnout in gubernatorial election years because Alaska's races for governor take place in years when there is no presidential election. Turnout in gubernatorial election years has been mixed. It was between 47 and 50 percent in the gubernatorial elections between statehood and 1978. It was well over 60 percent in the 1980s and early 1990s. Since then, however, turnout has not exceeded 57 percent, which it was in the 2014 election.[73] So the trend since the 1980s is for the highest turnout to occur in presidential election years. By far the highest turnout in Alaska political history was in 1992 in the three-way race for president between George H. W. Bush, Bill Clinton, and third-party candidate Ross Perot, when Alaska had the highest turnout in the nation at nearly 83 percent.[74]

As is the case across the other forty-nine states, turnout in Alaska's primary elections, held in August prior to the general election, is considerably lower than in general elections. Over the years the primary turnout rate has ranged from a high of 57.6 percent in 1982 (the fateful capital move ballot year) to a low of 17.2 percent in 2000. Overall, the primary turnout has most often been in the 25 to 40 percent range. For instance, the 2008, 2010, 2012, and 2014 primaries well reflect this range at 40.62, 33.65, 25.34, and 39.02 percent respectively.

As low as these turnout rates may be, they are still higher than most Alaska municipal elections where there are no primaries but only general elections (though sometimes run-offs in mayoral elections). Turnout in these elections ranges from 10 to 40 percent, and most often is between 20 and 30 percent. For example, in 2015 the turnout in the Municipality of Anchorage, home of the largest local government in the state and where one-third of Alaskans live, was under 27.5 percent in the April elections for the Municipal Assembly and 32.5 percent in the May run-off election for mayor. This dropped to 24 percent in the April 2016 Anchorage municipal election.[75] These figures are on a par with many local government elections across the nation.[76]

Explaining Electoral Patterns in Alaska since Statehood

Electoral patterns since statehood, in terms of which party wins a majority in the legislature, the governor's office, and Alaska's congressional seats, and how the state votes for president, show the following. As to federal races, as explained above regarding the congressional delegation, the delegation moved from being predominantly Democrat for the first ten years of statehood to solidly Republican for close to thirty years after 1980 until the election of Democrat Mark Begich in 2008. But in 2014 he was defeated for reelection to give Alaska an all-Republican delegation again. In presidential elections, as Table 14.3 shows, other than 1964 (when Lyndon Johnson ran against Barry Goldwater), the Democratic candidate has never won in Alaska. Since 1972, the Republican presidential candidate has had an average of a fifteen-point margin. Alaska has only three Electoral College votes, which means that Alaskans have little or no impact on the outcome of any presidential election. And with the dominance of Republican votes in presidential elections, Alaska's Democratic voters have even less influence than their fellow Republicans.

Even though Republicans and Democrats have held the governorship for more or less the same number of years since statehood, the Republicans have gained a decided edge since 2002. From statehood through 2010, neither party controlled the office for more than eight years in a row. But Republicans won three consecutive elections in 2002 (Frank Murkowski), 2006 (Sarah Palin), and 2010 (Sean Parnell). And if Bill Walker and Byron

Mallott had not combined their candidacies after the primary in 2014, Parnell would almost certainly have been re-elected. This says much about the failure of the Democrats to field a winning candidate. The last Democrat to be elected governor was Tony Knowles in 1998.

The evolution of party affiliation in the Alaska legislature also shows a movement from Democrats to Republicans. The watershed year was 1994. Until the early 1990s, the Democrats had held a majority in both houses for much of the time since statehood. But since 1994 they have not won a majority of seats in either house. On the surface, and judging by party victories alone, these election results might lead to the conclusion that Alaska is now a Republican state on a par with Idaho and Utah. The results might also indicate that the Republican Party platform drives public policy in the state as the result of elections, particularly since the early 2000s. A more accurate way to describe Alaska's electoral patterns since statehood in electing people to state offices, however, is pragmatism rather than partisanship. Nevertheless, with their poor showing in legislative elections since the mid-1990s and gubernatorial elections since 2002, there are many questions about the viability of the state Democratic Party. In this regard, the 2018 gubernatorial election, and whether the party does or does not field a viable candidate, may well be a pivotal development in the history of the Democratic Party in Alaska.

There is no question that the election patterns have predominantly favored Republicans in federal elections and have moved at the state level to more Republican control of the legislature and the governorship. It is also true that the electorate has generally become more conservative and elected more conservative politicians. However, party is still less important than some other factors in shaping the political orientation and policy positions of many of those elected. Political pragmatism has marked the stance of most of Alaska's legislators, governors, and members of Congress, so much so, that Alaska has had several bipartisan legislative majority caucuses and has had governors who do not fit the usual party mold. This was particularly the case with Bill Walker's election in 2014. Insights into these electoral patterns and their consequences are provided by looking at the type of people who get elected and why, which we consider next, after making some brief comments about the trends in ballot propositions and their funding.

Electoral patterns concerning ballot proposition elections and their funding are less definitive, but we can identify three broad patterns. One is that bond propositions are rarely defeated. Another is that, with the exception of Ballot Measure 1 in 2014 to repeal the oil tax reduction in MAPA, Alaska ballot campaigns have remained relatively low in cost, compared with many other states. Third, little Outside money has come into the state to support or oppose ballot measures. This is largely because Alaska's ballot propositions have rarely involved major economic interests that might have a major stake in the outcome. In this regard the referendum on oil taxes in 2014 was an exception.

What Type of People Get Elected?

Up until the mid-1960s, the demographics of who got elected to state legislatures throughout the United States were predominantly white, middle-class males who were small businessmen, professionals (including many lawyers), and retirees, with some labor and the occasional female and minority members. Governors were almost always white males. This pattern has changed across the states in recent years, particularly in regard to the election of women and minorities to both legislative and executive offices and the level of professionalism of politicians in general. These changes have also been reflected in Alaska elections.

From Statehood to the Early 1990s

McBeath and Morehouse's 1994 study of Alaska politics provides a comparison of who got elected to the legislature in 1967 and those elected in 1987.[77] Their study shows that legislators were predominantly white—54 and 56 of the 60 seats in the legislature, respectively, in each year. The most prominent minority was Alaska Natives. At 16 percent of the population and with fewer than 10 percent of the seats, Natives were underrepresented. Legislators were predominantly male, with only one woman in 1967; but this number had risen to twelve women in 1987. Those women who were elected, even as late as 1987, usually pushed their credentials as Alaskans close to the ideals of the Last Frontier, such as associations with mining, fishing, or possession of a pilot's license. Furthermore, women tended not to focus on purely feminine issues, such as equal pay, improved child care facilities, and parental leave. There were fewer lawyers in the legislature than in most states and more retired teachers and public employees, likely reflecting the state's economy. In terms of average age, this remained fairly stable between 1967 and 1987, with House members just under forty-four and Senate members just under forty-nine years of age, with an average of just over forty-five years for the entire legislature. As is the case in most states, many members of the Senate had moved up from the House. Most legislators listed their occupation as something other than "legislator," even though for most being a legislator was their major occupation.

As in all states, legislators had a level of education well above the average. According to McBeath and Morehouse, most Alaska legislators in 1993 had a college degree, and seventeen had advanced degrees in law, business administration, or education.

From statehood to the early 1990s, there was no discernible pattern regarding the background of governors other than that they were all male. Of the six governors serving during this period, Secretary of State Keith Miller (now the office of Lieutenant Governor) took office after Wally Hickel resigned in 1969 to become President Nixon's Secretary of the Interior. Only one of the six, Bill Egan, was born in the state. Four had served in the legislature before becoming governor (Bill Egan, in the Territorial legislature, and Keith

Miller, Jay Hammond, and Steve Cowper in legislatures after statehood). All sported an image of being a "real Alaskan" in terms of dress and campaign style, though Miller was rather reserved and Cowper liked to portray more of a cowboy persona. Four of the six had business backgrounds, while the other two (Hammond and Cowper) were a fisherman and a lawyer, respectively. None of the six was a diehard party adherent. They all tended to be moderates and were willing to work across party lines.

From the Early 1990s to the Present

As for legislators elected since the early 1990s, many of their characteristics remain similar in terms of age and occupations, though more lawyers have entered the legislature since the early 1990s. Most work at the job of legislating full time even with the reduced legislative session of ninety days. There are, however, an increasing number of legislators who are former legislative staffers. The number of Alaska Natives and other minorities (one African American and one Asian for several years) has fluctuated between five and ten. In this regard, at about 15 percent depending on which legislature is being viewed, Alaska is slightly above the 12 percent that was the average of minority legislators among all states in the late 2000s.[78] As to Alaska legislators' average educational level, it is probably slightly higher today than in 1993.

The major change in the makeup of the Alaska legislature has been in the number of women and their movement into positions of power since the mid-1980s. From around 20 percent of all legislators in the late 1980s, the percentage of women members rose to 25 percent in the 2000s. Again, this places Alaska slightly above the fifty-state average of 23.3 percent for the same period.[79] Since the 1980s, there have been three women elected President of the Senate (Jan Faiks, Drue Pearce, and Lyda Green) and two women have served as Speaker of the House (Ramona Barnes and Gail Phillips). Women have also chaired a number of House and Senate standing committees. And with the election of Sarah Palin in 2006, Alaska elected its first woman governor. Although women serving as legislators since 2000 are less likely to be closely associated with the idea of the Last Frontier than their predecessors, they still need to prove themselves as "real Alaskans." They tend to be professional women (lawyers, a medical administrator, a nurse) or businesswomen. Some rural-bush representatives, too, identify less with the Last Frontier than in earlier years. This departure from the Alaska mystique is part of the nationalization of Alaska and the narrowing gap between the lifestyle of the state and the Lower 48, particularly Anchorage, as John Katz explains in Chapter 2.[80]

Only one of the five governors since 1994, Bill Walker, was born in Alaska. Two, however, Sarah Palin and Sean Parnell, are young enough to have been born after statehood. Tony Knowles was a former mayor of Anchorage and a businessman. Frank Murkowski was nominally a businessman, but because he spent so much time as a U.S. Senator before becoming governor, in reality he was a professional politician. Sarah Palin dabbled in journalism and held local elective and state-appointed office. Sean Parnell was a lawyer who also worked for the oil industry and as a lobbyist, and he served six years in the legislature before being elected as lieutenant governor in 2006 and taking over as governor on Palin's resignation in July 2009. In 2014 Bill Walker, a lawyer with no experience in holding a state elective office, defeated Parnell for the governorship. Knowles was a middle-of-the road Democrat, Murkowski a fiscal conservative, Palin mainly a self-promoter with some fiscally conservative tendencies, Parnell a family values person with strong religious convictions, and Walker a conservative but most of all a pragmatist—he did what he needed to do to get elected in 2014.[81]

Half of Alaska's fourteen lieutenant governors (the position was called Secretary of State until the official title was changed in 1970) between 1959 and 2014 had previously served in the legislature, and one, Red Boucher, served in the legislature after his term as lieutenant governor concluded. Of the fourteen, one was a woman (Fran Ulmer, 1994–2002) and two of Alaska Native ancestry (Loren Leman, 2002–2006, and Byron Mallott, 2014–present). Although several have tried, none has successfully run for governor after being lieutenant governor, including Fran Ulmer in 2002. Two, however, became governor on the resignation of the incumbent governor: Keith Miller and Sean Parnell.

Alaska's Congressional Delegation since Statehood

Finally, we provide some brief comments on Alaska's congressional delegation over the years. Being such a young state and with two members of Congress—Young and Stevens—serving over forty years each, Alaska has had only twelve members of Congress between statehood and 2015, four Representatives and eight Senators. Because being a member of Congress is a full-time job, the former occupations of long-serving members like Stevens, Young, and Frank Murkowski (a lawyer, teacher, and businessman respectively) tell us very little about how their professions may have influenced their actions as politicians. Effectively, because of their longevity in office, they are professional politicians. Most others have a combined business and government service background, including Senators Lisa Murkowski, Mark Begich, and Dan Sullivan. Democrat Mike Gravel, who served in the U.S. Senate from 1969 to 1981, was a not very successful businessman, and Democrat Ernest Gruening, a member of the U.S. Senate from 1959 to 1969, was a journalist who served as Territorial Governor of Alaska from 1939 to 1953.

What Determines Getting Elected? Is Money the Major Factor?

We have alluded to some of the key factors at several points in the chapter that determine who gets elected in Alaska. Having looked at various aspects of the campaign and election processes, we can now address this question more fully. Our approach is to explain why it is not all to do with money as many Alaskans likely believe.

To be sure, money is a major factor in many races, particularly if a challenger to an incumbent hopes to make a race competitive enough to win. In certain circumstances, spending the most money can be the most important deciding factor in a competitive race. For example, spending the most money was likely what gave Lance Pruitt the edge over Pete Peterson in the Anchorage legislative race in 2012 referred to above. Money likely also helped secure victory for write-in candidate Lisa Murkowski, who spent $4,689,683 compared to Republican Joe Miller's $3,357,483, and Democrat Scott McAdams's $1,331,272.[82]

The highest spender does not always win, however. In the gubernatorial elections of 1986 and 1990, Steve Cowper and Wally Hickel won, and both spent less than their opponents.[83] More recently, Bill Walker spent less than Sean Parnell to win in 2014. In U.S. Senate races, Democrat Mark Begich beat Republican Ted Stevens in the 2008 race but spent almost $500,000 less ($4,576,337 to $5,161,259).[84] Begich lost in his bid for reelection in 2014, however, despite spending by him, or on him by super PACs, of about $1 million more than Sullivan in a $60 million race.

Clearly, factors other than money often play into many electoral races in Alaska. With no legislative term limits, very successful or popular incumbents are often not challenged, especially in rural-bush districts, and so they keep getting reelected. But even when they are challenged, like Don Young, their high profile and perceived political successes likely ensure victory even if they do not outspend their opponents. Occasionally, what defeats an incumbent is political complacency, a belief that they are so secure that they do not have to take their challenger seriously, and so they do not mount a serious campaign. This was the case in the 2012 election when Haines Republican Bill Thomas (2005–2012) was defeated by twenty-three-year-old Jonathan Kreiss-Tompkins of Sitka. It was also the case with Lisa Murkowski's defeat in the 2010 U.S. Senate primary by Joe Miller, as explained in the next section. Personality and image also come into play. In 2006, when Sarah Palin ran for governor she was young and vivacious, if short on specifics, compared with Tony Knowles, who was showing his age at twenty-five years her senior and who had a record to defend as a two-term governor. And sometimes there are unusual circumstances that come into play, like the indictment and conviction of Ted Stevens on campaign disclosure charges just before the November 2008 U.S. Senate election. Stevens lost despite outspending Begich.

Another potential influence of money on winning an election is the infusion into campaign war chests of candidates' personal funds. The substantial amounts of their own funds spent by Sheffield and Hickel on their campaigns led McBeath and Morehouse, writing soon after the latter's election in 1990, to predict that it would be hard to get elected as Alaska's governor in the future without being a millionaire.[85] This was a reasonable prediction at the time, but the years since they wrote have shown the situation to be more complex. Sheffield and Hickel were not just millionaires; they were multimillionaires who could afford to spend such money. All five governors since—Knowles, Murkowski, Palin, Parnell, and Walker—were also technically millionaires at the time of running, but only barely in the cases of Palin, Parnell, and Walker. These candidates were like many middle-class Alaskans (and Americans) these days who, when totaling up the value of their homes, retirement accounts, and other savings, are technically millionaires, but not in the class of a Wally Hickel or a Bill Sheffield. None of the five expended much of their own funds on their campaigns, most likely because their assets were not liquid and easily turned into cash like those of Sheffield and Hickel. As we noted earlier, Alaska has not been part of the trend, evidenced in many states, of rich candidates running for governor and spending large amounts of their substantial fortunes in the race. So it would appear that candidates of relatively modest means are not excluded from becoming Alaska's governor.

So overall, money does not appear to be the dominant factor in getting elected in Alaska as it is in some states, particularly the highly populated states. Moreover, up until the 2010s, money does not appear to have seriously undermined Alaska's democratic political system, which remains largely egalitarian in regard to access to public office. What the future holds in the aftermath of decisions like *Citizens United*, however, is difficult to predict.

Whose Interests Do Elected Officials Represent?

It would be wrong to assume that the personal, racial, or gender characteristics of a legislator or governor are major factors shaping their actions and determining what interests they will push the most once in office. Certainly, those elected who are fishermen, union members, small business owners, lawyers, former teachers, Alaska Natives, or women, among many other characteristics, often push the interests of these groups. For example, many Alaska Native legislators (as well as non-Natives) are members of the bush caucus, which works to enhance the interests of rural-bush Alaska, many inhabitants of which are Alaska Natives.

Other elected officials are either neutral about representing elements of their backgrounds or may even be hostile to it. For instance, many heralded Sarah Palin's election as governor and nomination as a U.S. vice-presidential candidate as a victory for women and their role in politics. But Palin never focused on women's issues. Governor Sean Parnell, with his initiative against domestic violence, was much more of an advocate for women. And state Representative, later Senator, Con Bunde (1993–2010), a former University of Alaska faculty member, was often very hostile to the university.

Furthermore, no matter what personal affinity legislators might have with issues affecting Alaska Natives, women, business or other interests, they will have little influence if they are not in positions of power and lack political skill. What is important is being in the majority caucus in the House or Senate or, in some cases, having the ear of the governor and key executive branch personnel. Even though there were only a small number of Alaska Natives in the legislature in the 1980s, some of them—including Frank Ferguson, John Sackett, and Al Adams—were among the most skillful politicians in Alaska history.

6. THE 2010 U.S. SENATE RACE AND THE 2014 GUBERNATORIAL ELECTION

In several ways both the 2010 Alaska U.S. Senate race between incumbent Lisa Murkowski and challenger Joe Miller and the 2014 election for governor between incumbent Sean Parnell and Bill Walker were aberrations in Alaska statewide elections. Nonetheless, they provide some interesting insights into the characteristics of Alaska elections and the mind-set of the electorate.

The 2010 Alaska U.S. Senate Race

The 2010 battle for the U.S. Senate received considerable national attention, not a common occurrence with Alaska elections. The person who won the Republican nomination in the August primary was not incumbent Senator Lisa Murkowski, but Joe Miller, a Fairbanks attorney who had held various legal positions in government.

Miller supported the principles of the Tea Party, with its avowal to return to fundamental constitutional principles that in their view demanded limited federal government with fewer regulations, a balanced federal budget that could be achieved mainly by cutting expenditures, emphasizing personal responsibility, and a return of political power from Washington, D.C., to the states and the people. In fact, the Tea Party officially supported Miller.[86]

Despite warnings that Miller was a serious threat to her seat, Murkowski appeared not to take his challenge seriously and did not mount a major primary campaign effort. As a consequence, Miller won the August Republican Primary with a 2 percent margin. U.S. Senate Republican leaders immediately declared their support for Miller. After some soul searching and with the slogan "Let's Make History," Murkowski announced on September 17 that she would pursue a write-in bid in the general election.[87] This was a long shot. A write-in campaign for the U.S. Senate had only succeeded once before, in a campaign in South Carolina by segregationist Democrat Strom Thurmond in 1953.

The increased scrutiny by the media in the run-up to the November election led to the gradual implosion of the Miller campaign, largely due to ethical issues. Because many perceived him as being arrogant and self-righteous, allegations that surfaced about him were a triple blow. They made him seem not only dishonest, but possibly corrupt and, at times, a very unpleasant person. It came to light that Miller had lied about his reasons for leaving a part-time attorney's job at the Fairbanks North Star Borough (FNSB) and concealed a conflict of interest violation while he was employed at the borough. It was also alleged that he engaged in conflict of interest activities while a federal magistrate in Fairbanks. Questions from the press about these ethical issues revealed the testy relationship Miller had with the Alaska media. Then, at a town hall meeting in mid-October, his security detail handcuffed and detained Tony Hopfinger, the editor of the then online daily newspaper the *Alaska Dispatch*. Hopfinger had asked Miller some direct questions about his alleged misconduct as an attorney with the FNSB.[88]

The general election was a three-way race between Miller, Murkowski, and Democrat Scott McAdams, then Mayor of Sitka. Despite Miller's gaffes, right up until a few days before the election he was expected to win. This was largely because Murkowski had upset many Republicans by mounting a write-in campaign and had failed to win over enough independent voters, though she appeared to have more of them than Miller. As it turned out the election was not even close: Miller lost to Murkowski by over 10,000 votes.[89]

The 2014 Governor's Race

Alaska's 2014 gubernatorial election was unusual in two major ways.[90] It was the first election since statehood in which the Democrats did not field a candidate in the general election, and it was won by a fused Democratic and independent ticket claiming to be nonpartisan, led by a former Republican. Furthermore, the Walker-Mallott campaign was less about substantive issues than about "dumping Parnell," the incumbent Republican governor who had served since 2009.

Coming out of the August primary, Parnell looked like a shoo-in to win reelection. He won 75 percent of the Republican primary vote, more than the total received by all non-Republicans in the gubernatorial primary. Plus, he had won a victory in the defeat of Ballot Measure 1, the attempt to repeal the MAPA legislation to cut oil taxes that he had promoted since 2010. Buoying up Parnell's likely reelection was that the Democratic candidate primary winner, Native leader Byron Mallott, received only 66 percent of the Democratic votes and less than half of Parnell's primary votes. Mallott had run a lackluster campaign, often responding to policy questions with the comment that he was still in the process of working out his positions on the issues. Even Democratic support for him was lukewarm.

Following the primary election, polls showed that Parnell would easily defeat both Mallott and independent candidate Bill Walker. Labor was particularly concerned about a Parnell victory because his lieutenant governor running mate, Anchorage Mayor Dan Sullivan (not to be confused with former state attorney general Dan Sullivan, elected to the U.S. Senate in November 2014), had had major battles as mayor with labor unions. In effect, the Alaska AFL-CIO (American Federation of Labor-Congress of Industrial Organizations), other labor groups, and some prominent Democrats, refused to endorse Mallott unless he merged his candidacy with Walker's. After much soul-searching, the Democratic State Committee overwhelmingly voted to fuse the two tickets and not field a gubernatorial candidate of its own in the election. On September 2, Mallott and Walker joined forces to form the nonpartisan Alaska First Unity ticket. Walker, who had dropped his registration as a Republican, was in the governor's spot, with Mallott running for lieutenant governor.

These were very odd political bedfellows. Other than being the Mayor of Valdez in the late 1970s, Walker had no experience in public office. He had a record of being pro-life and opposing gay marriage. Other than this, and his strong support of the Valdez gas line, very little was known about his position on the issues. Mallott and the Democrats were by and large on the other side of most of the family values issues, but they had thrown in their lot with Walker and given him the top spot on the ticket. Despite Mallott's continued assertions that he firmly believed in Walker and the nonpartisan ticket, clearly the major motive for the fused ticket on the part of the Democrats was to "dump Parnell." Walker, too, realized that he could not beat Parnell on his own. Presumably, the Democrats realized that they needed to give him the top spot because Mallott would not have enough appeal to bring out many Democratic voters—other than the Native community—or win over enough Republicans who were disaffected with Parnell.

Even with all this potential support for the Walker-Mallott ticket, Parnell still had the edge—it was Parnell's election to lose. He ran mainly on his record, particularly cutting the budget (though Walker questioned the statistics on this), promising no new taxes, and the development of the gas pipeline. Walker also promised no new taxes, despite the major fall in oil prices that occurred during the campaign. But he and Parnell clashed over the terminating point and diameter of a gas pipeline. Walker also emphasized the development of the Arctic, value-added industries, and lower energy costs, particularly for rural-bush communities. Plus, he endorsed the expansion of Medicaid under the federal Affordable Care Act, which Parnell had refused to do and which was popular at least among liberals and some moderate voters. What also helped sink Parnell was his poor handling of revelations of sexual abuse and other misconduct in the Alaska National Guard. He and his staff were slow to respond to the revelations, leaving suspicions and an opening for him to be pounded by the media. Whether this was the deciding factor in "dumping Parnell," however, is not clear.[91]

In the end, the First Alaska Unity ticket managed to cobble together enough votes to win the election by a margin of 48 to 46 percent—a difference of 6,000 votes out of 280,000 cast. Three other third party tickets shared the remaining 6 percent of the vote.

The Lessons: An Intricate Confluence of Values

These two elections provide several insights into the character of Alaska elections that reflect the state's political culture and its politics in general. In particular, the elections provide a good illustration of the interaction between campaigns and elections and the four elements of political participation in Alaska: that of parties, interest groups, the media, and public opinion. The lessons are many, but five are probably the most significant.

First and foremost, both elections bring into sharp relief weak party affiliation, bipartisanship, nonpartisanship, and independence among the Alaska electorate. In the case of the Parnell-Walker race, clearly many Democrats were willing to vote for Walker, a nominal independent candidate. In 2010, many of those registered as independents voted for Murkowski, as did many Democrats. It was a hard choice for many Democrats to essentially abandon Scott McAdams at the polls and a bitter pill to write in Lisa Murkowski's name. But many Democrats believed that McAdams had little chance of winning and that Murkowski was the lesser of two Republican evils as between her and Miller.

Second, the Alaska electorate may be generally conservative, but it is a moderate and pragmatic conservatism. In 2010, the Miller Tea Party message was enthusiastically received by right-wing Republicans in the battle against Murkowski for the party's nomination when these diehard supporters turned out for Miller in large numbers in the modified closed primary election. It was a far different story during the general election. Many Alaskans realized that, with the state's dependence on government and particularly federal funds, Miller's government-cutting agenda would hurt the state. In the case of Parnell, his refusal to support Medicaid expansion and his support of tax cuts for the oil industry and other right-wing policies likely brought out enough moderates to help give the edge to Walker, especially as Walker supported Medicaid expansion.

Third, and a related point, is that both elections indicate a link between the Alaska electorate and policy outcomes. Even though Miller's primary victory was achieved with right-wing diehard Republican voters, it was, in part, made possible because Murkowski seemed to be compromising her representation of Alaska in exchange for climbing the Senate Republican leadership ladder. Partly for this reason, she came up short in the August primary. Owing little to the Senate leadership who abandoned her after the primary, and also because she is likely well aware of who saved her political life, she has been more mindful of Alaska interests since 2010. In Parnell's case, his refusal to expand Medicaid and his poor handling of the Alaska National Guard scandal did not help him in the election despite strong support from business groups, including the oil industry.

Fourth is the judgment of the electorate toward candidates who appear to be dishonest or trying to hide something. Alaskans do not seem to vote along straight party lines when a candidate from their party is ethically suspect. Likely most decisive of all in Murkowski's victory, was her perceived honesty in contrast to Miller's demonstrated dishonesty as well as other negative personality traits. As evidenced by the defeat of Ted Stevens in the November 2008 election a few days after being convicted on campaign disclosure charges, Alaska's voters have a sense of ethics and tend to vote against dishonest and disingenuous candidates. Miller fell into this category during the election, and his battles with the press and the thuggery of his bodyguards added to his negative image. While not at the level of Miller's negativism with the public, Parnell's stalling on answering questions, as well as his reluctance to release information on the National Guard scandal, did not help his image. By contrast, Walker conveyed a more positive image with the added asset of being nonpartisan and his claim of "working for all Alaskans."

In this regard, the media and political advertising played a major role. The media kept the pressure on Parnell over the National Guard scandal and eventually exposed extensive wrongdoing. Although Parnell was never implicated directly in the scandal, his handling of it showed poor management on his part. In Miller's case, he brought down the wrath of the press, especially after the handcuffing of Tony Hopfinger, one of their own. In contrast, Murkowski mounted an effective media and public relations campaign. One "Write-in Murkowski" ad sent to households on Halloween, a few days before the election, showed Miller standing in a graveyard made up as a zombie. The ad copy suggested that one of the worst nightmares imaginable for Alaskans would be to see Miller sworn in as a U.S. Senator for the state.

Fifth, as in many states, elections in Alaska are as much lost by the front runner or incumbent as they are won by the challenger. This appears to be the case with both Miller in 2010 and Parnell in 2014. Both looked like winners at the start of the general election campaign. In 2010, Miller had the momentum coming out of the primary and Murkowski had several negatives, including that many Alaskans still had a bitter taste in their mouths from the way she was appointed to the Senate by her father Frank Murkowski in 2003 soon after he was elected governor. Added to this, Murkowski was a lackluster campaigner and not a particularly good speaker. She won the general election against Miller despite failing during the campaign to generate a great deal of enthusiasm among Alaska voters, many of whom voted more against Miller than for Murkowski.

7. ASSESSING THE CONNECTION BETWEEN CAMPAIGNS AND ELECTIONS AND ALASKA PUBLIC POLICIES

A major aspect of political participation in a democracy is that the popular will as expressed through the ballot box should, to some extent, be reflected in the actions of those in elected office. That is, elections should ultimately influence public policy to some degree. So how do campaigns and elections affect public policy in Alaska? The skeptical and cynical voter who is not enamored with politicians, or who reflects the antigovernment sentiments in Alaska's political culture, might respond: "Not at all! Politicians schmooze us during the election and make a bunch of promises, but once elected they do what they want or what their major contributors and the big powerful interests want." While there may be some truth to this in some cases, the situation is more complex in all democracies, including Alaska. In fact, in Alaska there appear to be several identifiable links between elections and public policy outcomes.

The elements of this electoral–public policy link can be briefly explained by drawing on the analysis of the relationship between Alaska's political culture, the state's form of democracy, and the nature of public policies, as explained in Section 8 of Chapter 5 on political culture. That chapter argues that the state's individualistic political culture results in a link between the electorate and policy making—between the outcome of elections and the policies enacted or not enacted—that reflects, more or less, the majority will.

Majority will usually reflects Alaska's politically conservative bent, but this is not always the case. The emphasis on personality as opposed to party in many elections, friends and neighbors politics, bipartisanship, and the relative lack of importance of campaign funds, help account for a degree of liberalism in Alaska's policies. Alaska's lack of a death penalty and its liberal application of the federal welfare reform act of 1996, particularly the provisions for the Temporary Assistance for Needy Families (TANF) program, appear to be evidence of at least some liberal tendencies.

The analysis of the electoral outcomes–public policy link shows the egalitarian, essentially populist, connection between the individualistic element in the state's political culture and democratic government. In short, Alaska's public officials act to give citizens what they want. We are not making a judgment here as to whether such an election–policy link is a good or bad one—we are simply explaining the existence of this political cultural influence.

Some Alaskans on both ends of the political spectrum might wish it to be different. Conservatives might wish that the liberal voice not be heard as much as it is or in some cases not heard at all. And some liberals, for example, who want to deal with likely future state budget crises when oil prices fall or oil runs out, might wish that policy makers were less beholden to the electorate and less fearful of tinkering with the Permanent Fund Dividend program. Nevertheless, the effect of Alaska's political culture on the election–public policy link does seem to serve the majority of Alaskans as opposed to a small segment, as is the case in elitist democracies or those with a traditionalistic political culture, like many in the southern states.

While this political culture explanation has much to offer in terms of explaining Alaska's electoral–policy link, political culture does not tell the whole story. Observers of Alaska politics have long argued that candidates for state offices, regardless of party, are less concerned about the total amount of government spending and more concerned about how best to spend the money that is available to the state. This changed significantly when the Republican Party began to be influenced in the 1990s by the religious or Christian right. Republican legislators who operated on the basis of issues and ideas were replaced by those expected to vote as their caucus decided. Republican legislators who joined Democrats to form coalitions to advance their constituencies were replaced by those who would agree to be accountable to the Republican Party's positions on budgets and other issues. The entrance of the religious right into Alaska politics also brought moral issues to the forefront. The legislative and executive branches began promoting legislation to place limits on abortion, to reduce spending on social programs, and to oppose same-sex marriage and employment benefits to same-sex couples. Since 2012, this has included support of a constitutional amendment to use public funds to support religious schools. These are similar to changes that have occurred in many states.

Moreover, even though the Alaska legislature is sometimes run by coalition majority caucuses, Democrats have most often been a small minority in such coalitions. As a result, liberal voices have not necessarily been heard in terms of policy (though not all Alaska Democrats are liberal by a long chalk). An exception of sorts was the Bipartisan Working Group (BWG) that ran the State Senate from 2007 to 2012. But with some creative redistricting the BWG fell apart after the 2012 election, and the Twenty-Eighth legislature took on a very conservative tone. And with the major fall in oil prices in the latter half of 2014 and into 2016, the Republican-controlled House and Senate set their minds on major budget cuts.

A factor that can counter the general Alaska's electoral–populist policy link is the power of certain political interests and, in some cases, money. Even though money has generally not been a major factor in Alaska elections and not the dominant force it is in many large and medium-sized states, it is still important. This is especially the case when combined with the importance to Alaska of some political interests, such as the oil industry. The oil industry may not be running Alaska, as Chapter 24 on oil and gas argues, but as Chapter 15 on interest groups shows, the industry is a consistently influential force in the state.[92] A similar situation exists with the Outside forces of the environmental movement (buttressed by federal regulations), which are able to thwart the will of most Alaskans to have increased development in the state, including opening the Arctic National Wildlife Refuge (ANWR) to oil and gas development.[93]

8. CONCLUSION: THE INTERACTION OF WEAK PARTISANSHIP, IDEOLOGY, PRAGMATISM, AND PERSONALITY

The introduction to this chapter set out four purposes: (1) to show what campaigns and elections tell us about the nature of the link between Alaskans and their public officials, whether the link is primarily ideological, pragmatic, personal, or a combination of these and other elements; (2) to show the interrelationship between elections and the other four vehicles of political participation; (3) how elections translate into public policy; and (4) what campaigns and elections tell us about Alaska politics in general. We summarize the answers by, in part, using the relevant characteristics of Alaska politics regarding campaigns and elections.

The link between Alaskans and their public officials is an intricate mix of ideology, pragmatism, and personality, with personality being dominant in many elections, especially in rural-bush communities. Ideology has become more important in some elections, particularly in the Anchorage area in recent years, but political pragmatism, in terms of who will serve their interests best, is a major consideration of voters. Here we can see the Alaska political characteristics of individualism, pragmatism, friends and neighbors politics, weak party organizations, and the role of Alaska Natives at work in shaping elections and campaigns.

As to campaigns and elections, the Alaska political characteristics of friends and neighbors politics, pragmatic individualism, weak party organizations but strong interest groups, and the role of Alaska Natives are evident. Organizationally parties are weak, so consequently they play a less extensive role in running for office and getting elected than in most states. Many candidates, especially those in rural-bush areas, play down party and focus more on personality.

Interest groups do play an important role, through campaign contributions, including the use of PACs, candidate endorsements, and, in some cases, providing campaign workers. And in the 2014 gubernatorial race, interest groups were key to bringing about the Walker-Mallott fused ticket. Also, as in most states, conservative forces, such as development interests and the religious right and family values groups, tend to support Republicans, while liberal causes and unions support the Democrats. With the high level of nonpartisanship in Alaska, however, there is no clear divide between support for either party by interest groups. The media generally plays a less important role in Alaska than in many medium-sized and large states because there is less need for it, but it is of increasing importance in Anchorage. Public opinion is best addressed as it relates to the third and fourth purposes of the chapter.

In fact, because of their interrelationship, we can deal together with purpose 3, the link between elections and public policy, and purpose 4, what elections tell us about Alaska politics in general. If we subscribe to the political culture and populist explanation of the link between elections and the policies enacted or not enacted, then there is a clear link. This explanation also shows the influence of public opinion on political outcomes through elections. The electoral–policy link is also evident if we accept the more narrow view of the link based on the influential interest group perspective. Both explanations of the election–policy link plus the role of public opinion illustrate, in various ways, all five characteristics of Alaska politics relevant to elections and campaigns: pragmatic dependent individualism; fiscal conservatism; friends and neighbors politics; the prominent role of Alaska Natives, often leading to conflicts between urban and rural-bush areas in the policy process; and weak political parties versus strong interest groups.

As is the case in most states, studying elections and campaigns in Alaska provides major insights into the nature and substance of state politics in general. This includes the values that drive it, the importance of certain institutions and the lesser significance of others, the distribution of political power, and the important role of personality. And so, the nature of Alaska's elections and their effect on public policy are encapsulated by the chapter's subtitle, "The Interaction of Weak Partisanship, Ideology, Pragmatism, and Personality." This is an intricate relationship that plays out in different ways in different elections and translates into varying effects on public policy. Several of the chapters in the rest of the book, particularly Chapter 16 on legislative-executive relations and those on various state policies in Chapters 21 through 28, provide particular examples of the outcome of campaigns and elections on Alaska politics and policy making.

ENDNOTES

[1] The major sources used for comparisons among the fifty states are: Thomas M. Holbrook and Raymond J. La Raja, "Parties and Elections," in *Politics in the American States: A Comparative Analysis,* eds. Virginia Gray, Russell L. Hanson, and Thad Kousser, 10th ed. (Washington, D.C.: Congressional Quarterly Press, 2013); and Keith E. Hamm and Gary F. Moncrief, "Legislative Politics in the States," in Gray, Hanson and Kousser, *Politics in the American States*. Data on campaign finance was taken mainly from the National Institute for Money in State Politics (hereafter NIMSP), at http://www.followthemoney.org/Institute/index.phtml.

[2] The authors thank Gail Fenumiai, former director, State of Alaska Division of Elections, and her staff for help in tracking down election data and materials from the state election archives.

[3] Jamelle Boule, "Republicans Admit that Voter ID Laws are Aimed at Democratic Voters," *The Daily Beast*, August 28, 2013, at http://www.thedailybeast.com/articles/2013/08/28/republicans-admit-voter-id-laws-are-aimed-at-democratic-voters.html.

[4] Ed Schoenfeld, "Voter ID Bill Still Drawing Opposition," *CoastAlaska News* (KTOO Public Radio, Juneau), April 12, 2013.

[5] Charles Savage, "Justice Department Poised to File Lawsuit Over Voter I.D. Law," *New York Times*, September 30, 2013.

[6] See, for example, Charles Ward, "Keeping Options Open When It Comes to the Electoral College," *Juneau Empire*, February 2, 2012. Particularly enlightening in regard to Alaska public sentiments on this issue are the comments in response to this editorial, at http://juneauempire.com/opinion/2012-02-02/keeping-options-open-when-it-comes-electoral-college.

[7] This overview of the history of Alaska's primary election system draws on Clive S. Thomas, "Alaska," in *Political Encyclopedia of U.S. States and Regions*, ed. Donald P. Haider-Markel, vol. 1 (Washington, D.C.: C. Q. Press, 2008), 356.

[8] "State Has New Primary Election Law," *Election News*, published by the Alaska Division of Elections, vol. 5, no. 1 (July 2001).

[9] This section on establishing official candidate status draws, in part, on the Alaska Public Office Commission's *Candidate Campaign Disclosure Manual* (Juneau, AK: Alaska Public Offices Commission, November 17, 2011), available in pdf format at www.doa.alaska.gov/apoc.

[10] Josh Goodman, "Introducing America's Largest State Legislative District," *Governing*, February 11, 2010.

[11] These and other statistics on incumbency and the competitiveness of legislative seats are taken from, "The Incumbency Advantage," data from the NIMSP, at http://followthemoney.org/press/ReportView.phtml?r=361&ext=5; and Stephen Ansolabehere and James M. Snyder, Jr., "The Incumbency Advantage in U.S. Elections: An Analysis of State and Federal Offices, 1942–2000," unpublished paper, Massachusetts Institute of Technology, 2001, at http://economics.mit.edu/files/1205.

[12] For details on the length of service of all Alaska state legislators between 1959 and 2009, see "The Alaska Legislature Celebrates Fifty Years of Shaping the Last Frontier" (Juneau: Alaska State Legislature, 2009).

[13] Hamm and Moncrief, "Legislative Politics in the States," 173.

[14] The National Council of State Legislatures, "The Term Limited States," at http://www.ncsl.org/legislatures-elections/legisdata/chart-of-term-limits-states.aspx.

[15] However, in 1998 an initiative called the "Alaska Term Limit Pledge" (Measure 7) was narrowly approved by Alaska voters. It allows candidates for all state and federal offices to voluntarily pledge to limit their terms in office, but few candidates have made such a pledge. As term limits cannot be imposed at the federal level without an amendment to the U.S. Constitution, such an unofficial pledge would be the only way to limit the tenure of Alaska's congressional delegation. For the pros and cons of term limits, see Chapter 30, Section 3.

[16] Gerald A. McBeath and Thomas A. Morehouse, *Alaska Politics and Government* (Lincoln: University of Nebraska Press, 1994), 143.

[17] Information on the role of the media in rural-bush campaigns was obtained, in part, through an interview by Clive Thomas on December 22, 2013, with former State Representative Mary Nelson who represented the Bethel region.

[18] See Chapter 4, Section 3.

[19] For an overview of the Alaska reapportionment process following the 2010 census, including the various challenges and revised plans, see Laurel Andrew, "Alaska Redistricting Board Adopts Revised Voting Districts Map," *Alaska Dispatch*, July 14, 2013.

[20] For details on this case and its implications for the nation and for Alaska, see Adam Liptak, "Supreme Court Invalidates Key Parts of the Voting Rights Act," *New York Times*, June 25, 2013; Suzanna Caldwell, "Voting Rights Act: What Does Ruling Mean for Alaskans?" *Alaska Dispatch*, June 25, 2013; Peter Granitz, "Congress Shows No Urgency on Voting Rights Act," *Alaska News Nightly*, Alaska Public Radio Network (APRN), August 14, 2013; and "AFN Commends Senator Murkowski for Co-Sponsoring Key Voting Rights Bill," AFN website, posted September 11, 2015, at http://www.nativefederation.org/afn-commends-senator-murkowski-for-co-sponsoring-key-voting-rights-bill/.

[21] For a consideration of the nature of campaigns and elections in Alaska and how they changed during the first twenty-five years of statehood, see Thomas A. Morehouse, "Alaska's Elections," in *Alaska State Government and Politics*, eds., Gerald A. McBeath and Thomas A. Morehouse (Fairbanks: University of Alaska Press, 1987).

[22] See Morehouse, "Alaska's Elections," Table 5.6, "Winning Candidates for Statewide Office in Alaska, 1958–1984," 124.

[23] See Chapter 8, Figure 8.8, for the extensive earmarks that Alaska's congressional delegation secured until the defeat of Senator Stevens in 2008.

[24] For details on the 2004 Alaska U.S. Senate race, particularly its campaign financing, see Carl E. Shepro and Clive S. Thomas, "The 2004 Alaska U.S. Senate Race," in *Dancing Without Partners: How Candidates, Parties, Interest Groups Interact in the New Campaign Finance Environment*, eds., David B. Magleby, J. Quin Monson, and Kelly D. Paterson (Provo, UT: Brigham Young University, Center for the Study of Elections and Democracy, 2004); and on the Begich-Stevens race, Sean Cockerham, "Begich Topples Stevens in Senate Race," *Anchorage Daily News*, November 19, 2008, and other *Anchorage Daily News* stories of September to December 2008.

[25] See Alaska Division of Elections, results for the 1994 election, at http://www.elections.alaska.gov/results/94GENR/result94.htm#govltg. Results for the Hammond-Egan race were obtained from the Division of Elections archives by division staff.

[26] For information on the ballot process in Alaska and details on all measures since statehood, see Ballotpedia, at http://ballotpedia.org/wiki/index.php/Alaska, and http://ballotpedia.org/wiki/index.php/List_of_Alaska_ballot_measures.

[27] For the constitutional provisions of Alaska's ballot measure process and a discussion of their development, see Gordon Harrison, *Alaska's Constitution: A Citizen's Guide*, 5th ed. (Juneau: Alaska Legislative Affairs Agency, 2012), 179–90.

[28] Alaska Division of Elections, Recall History, obtained from the division's archives.

[29] For the use of the initiative across the states that use it, see Shaun Bowler and Todd Donovan, "The Initiative Process," in Gray, Hanson and Kousser, *Politics in the American States*, 141, Table 5.1.

[30] This provision was itself approved by the voters in 2004 responding to a legislative initiative (Measure 1) which amended the provisions in the state constitution requiring 10 percent of the votes cast in two-thirds of the state's house districts (Article XI, Section 3).

[31] See the Alaska Constitution, Article XI, Section 4, and Alaska Statues (AS) 15.45.190.

[32] Casey Kelly, "Juneau Residents Have Their Say on Coastal Management Initiative," *Morning Edition*, KTOO Juneau, July 27, 2012; and Jeremy Hsleh, "Signature Drive for Oil Tax Cut Winding Down," *Morning Edition*, KTOO Juneau, July 5, 2013.

[33] Alexandra Gutierrez, "Opponents of Wastewater Discharge Bill Pass on Referendum," *Alaska News Nightly* (APRN), May 15, 2013.

[34] An overview of the politics of this initiative which appeared on the ballot as Measure 1, can be found in Chapter 24 on oil and gas, Section 4.

[35] For case studies on this and similar initiatives regarding predator control, see Chapter 22, Box 22.2.

[36] Interview with Representative Wilson by Clive Thomas, August 15, 2012.

[37] For details on the way that federal campaign finance laws developed and their effect on the states, see Thomas R. Dye and Susan A. MacManis, *Politics in States and Communities,* 14th ed. (Upper Saddle River, N.J.: Pearson/Prentice Hall, 2012), 184–86; and Ronald J. Hrebenar and Clive S. Thomas, "The First Amendment and the Regulation of Lobbying," in *Guide to Interest Groups and Lobbying in the United States*, eds., Burdett A. Loomis, Peter L. Francia and Dara Z. Strolovitch (Washington, D.C. Congressional Quarterly Press, 2011), 387–88.

[38] See Chapter 5, Box 5.4, for the development and responsibilities of APOC, including some of the politics surrounding the agency.

[39] Alaska Statutes (AS) 39.50.

[40] AS 15.13.

[41] AS 15.13.116.

[42] AS 15.13.

[43] See Washington Public Disclosure Commission—PDC Contribution Limits, at http://www.pdc.wa.gov/public/contributionlimits.aspx.

[44] See Cal-Access (California's online information on public disclosure) at http://www.cal-access.sos.ca.gov, and Consumer Attorneys of California. 2013, New Filing Requirements for Major Donors, at https://www.caoc.org/index.cfm?pg=MajorDonor.

[45] Wyoming Campaign Finance Information System, at http://www.wycampaignfinance.gov/WYCFWebApplication/GSF_Authentication/Default.aspx.

[46] For details on the VECO scandal, see Chapter 5, Section 7, Chapter 20, Section 2, and Chapter 24, Section 7.

[47] This overview of the substance and likely effects of *Citizens United* draws on John Dunbar, "The Citizens United Decision and Why It Matters," the Center for Public Integrity, November 7, 2012, at http://www.publicintegrity.org/2012/10/18/11527/citizens-united-decision-and-why-it-matters; National Conference of State Legislatures, 2010, "Life After Citizens United", http://www.ncsl.org/legislatures-elections/elections/citizens-united-and-the-states.aspx; Peter Overby, "A Year Later 'Citizens United' Reshapes Politics," *Morning Edition*, National Public Radio (NPR), January 21, 2011; and APOC 2011, "About Campaign Disclosure Law," http://www.doa.alaska.gov/apoc/FAQs/faq297.html.

[48] Alaska State Legislature, 2010, Senate Bill 284, at http://www.legis.state.ak.us/basis/get_bill_text.asp?hsid=SB0284F&session=26.

[49] OpenSecrets, at https://www.opensecrets.org/outsidespending/ summ.php?cycle=2014&disp=-R&pty=A&type=S; Real-Time Federal Campaign Finance, at http://realtime.influenceexplorer.com/race/2014/S/AK/2/; and Liz Ruskin, "What Was Alaska's Senate Race Money Spent On?" *Alaska News Nightly* (APRN), November 14, 2014.

[50] Figures for expenditures in the 2014 governor's race were calculated by Kristina Klimovich from APOC records. APOC does not calculate expenditure totals for candidates. To obtain totals for each individual candidate, disclosed amounts for each candidate have to be added to independent expenditure contributions. Calculations made on April 26, 2015, from data at https://aws.state.ak.us/ApocReports/.

[51] See listing of states with public financing of elections and what is covered in these provisions, at Ballotpedia.org, at http://ballotpedia.org/Public_financing_of_campaigns.

[52] In 2008, the U.S. Supreme Court's decision in *Davis v. Federal Election Commission* suggested that a key part of most Clean Election laws—a provision granting extra money (or "rescue funds") to participating candidates who are being outspent by nonparticipating candidates—is unconstitutional.

[53] "The Incumbency Advantage," National Institute for Money in State Politics (NIMSP) at http://classic.followthemoney.org/press/ReportView.phtml?r=361&ext=5.

[54] For details on the role and activities of a particular PAC, see Chapter 26 on education, Box 26.4, which covers the University of Alaska Anchorage Faculty and Staff Association PAC.

[55] McBeath and Morehouse, *Alaska Politics and Government*, 168–69.

[56] See Chapter 15, Section 8, on money and interest groups in Alaska.

[57] McBeath and Morehouse, *Alaska Politics and Government*, 143 and 168.

[58] Spending on U.S. House and Senate races is taken from OpenSecrets.org. 2010, "Congressional Races," at http://www.opensecrets.org/races/; Open Secrets.org, 2014, "Alaska House Race," at https://www.opensecrets.org/races/summary.php?cycle=2014&id=AK01; and note 50 above for the 2014 U.S. Senate races.

[59] Margaret Ferguson, "Governors and the Executive Branch," in Gray, Hanson, and Kousser, *Politics in the American States*, 212–14.

[60] Trip Gabriel, "Terry McAuliffe, Democrat, is Elected Governor of Virginia in Tight Race," *New York Times*, November 6, 2013.

[61] William M. Welch, "California: Jerry Brown Wins Costliest Race in U.S.," *USA Today*, November 3, 2010.

[62] Figures for spending on Alaska's gubernatorial elections and those in Vermont and Wyoming are taken from: NIMSP, *Follow the Money,* at http://www.followthemoney.org/database/nationalview.phtml?l=0&f=G&y=2010&abbr=0; and from APOC records, including https://webapp.state.ak.us/apoc/choosedatatype.jsp and https://webapp.state.ak.us/apoc/choosedatatype.jsp. Data for 1986 was acquired directly from APOC staff by Clive Thomas, on June 16, 2010. See note 50 above for the source of spending on the 2014 gubernatorial race.

[63] The source used in this chapter for adjusting this and other campaign costs for inflation in Alaska was Inflation Calculator from the U.S. Bureau of Labor Statistics, at http://www.bls.gov/data/inflation_calculator.htm.

[64] See Chapter 22, Box 22.2.

[65] Bowler and Donovan, "The Initiative Process," 142.

[66] Ballot cost information on Alaska for 2014 is taken from the APOC website at http://alaska.gov/akpages/ADMIN/apoc/index.htm; and Ballotpedia; Alaska Marijuana Legalization, Ballot Measure 2 (2014) at http://ballotpedia.org/Alaska_Marijuana_Legalization,_Ballot_Measure_2_%282014%29; Alaska Minimum Wage Increase, Ballot Measure 3 (2014), at http://ballotpedia.org/Alaska_Minimum_Wage_Increase,_Ballot_Measure_3_%282014%29; and Alaska Bristol Bay Mining Ban, Ballot Measure 4 (2014), at http://ballotpedia.org/Alaska_Bristol_Bay_Mining_Ban,_Ballot_Measure_4_%282014%29.

[67] Bowler and Donovan, "The Initiative Process," 142; and NIMSP "Follow the Money," at http://www.followthemoney.org/database/StateGlance/state_ballot_measures.phtml?s=CA&y=2010.

[68] See Washington Public Disclosure Commission, at http://www.pdc.wa.gov/ MvcQuerySyste m/ CommitteeData/contributions?param=U1RP UEZCIDUwNw====&year=2010&type=initiative; and "Committees," Initiatives in 2010," at http://www.pdc.wa.gov/MvcQuerySystem/ CommitteeData/contributions?param=Q0lUSVBPIDExMQ====&year=2010&type=initiative; and Voter's Edge, from Maplight, at http://votersedge.org/washington/ballot-measures/2013/ november/i-522#.UoPodGTk8gU.

[69] Data on the cost of legislative races for 2012 is taken from NIMSP *Follow the Money*. Alaska, at http://www.followthemoney.org/database/state_overview.phtml?s=AK&y=2012; California, at http://www.followthemoney.org/database/state_overview.phtml?s=CA&y=2012, and http://www.followthemoney.org/database/StateGlance/state_candidates.phtml?s=-CA&y=2012&f=H&so=a&p=1#sorttable; Indiana, at http://www.followthemoney.org/database/ state_overview.phtml?s=IN&y=2012.

[70] The three major ways of calculating turnout are: (1) as a percentage of voting-age population or VAP; (2) as a percentage of eligible voters—VEP—which excludes noncitizens, prisoners, and other ineligible groups; and (3) as a percentage of those who are registered to vote. For a discussion on the issues surrounding turnout see, Michael P. McDonald and Samuel L. Popkin, "The Myth of the Vanishing Voter," *American Political Science Review* 95, no. 4 (2001): 963–74.

[71] All election turnout figures for Alaska gubernatorial and primary elections come from various data sets on the Alaska Division of Elections website, particularly at http://www.elections.alaska.gov/ei_return.php; and http://www.elections.alaska.gov/statistics/vi_vrs_stats_history_genr_prior.htm; and from the division's archives.

[72] Holbrook and La Raja, "Parties and Elections," Table 3-6, "Average Rates of Voter Turnout, by Office, 2007–10." This table calculates turnout rates by the VAP and VEP methods and combines them. However, the ranking would be similar based on the calculation of registered voters compared to those who voted.

[73] For gubernatorial elections since 1982 the percentage turnout rates have been: 1982, 74.9; 1986, 62.4; 1990, 65.7; 1994, 64.4; 1998, 52.2; 2002, 50.5; 2006, 51.1; in 2010, 52.2; and in 2014, 56.8.

[74] Some national turnout data sets do not put the 1992 turnout this high, but the archives of the Alaska Division of Elections confirm this figure.

[75] Information provided by the Municipality of Anchorage, Municipal Clerk's Office, April 11, 2016.

[76] Dye and MacManis, *Politics in States and Communities*, 365.

[77] McBeath and Morehouse, *Alaska Politics and Government*, "Who They Are," and Table 9, "Composition of Alaska Legislature, 1967–87," 144–47.

[78] Hamm and Moncrief, "Legislative Politics in the States," Table 6-3, "Measures of Diversity in State Legislatures," 179.

[79] *Ibid.*

[80] See Chapter 2, Box 2.3.

[81] For an overview of the personalities and policies of Alaska's eleven governors to date, see Chapter 16, Section 2.

[82] OpenSecrets.org, *2010 Congressional Races*, at http://www.opensecrets.org/races/election.php?state=AK&cycle=2010.

[83] McBeath and Morehouse, *Alaska Politics and Government*, 169.

[84] OpenSecrets, *2008 Congressional Races*, at http://www.opensecrets.org/races/.

[85] McBeath and Morehouse, *Alaska Politics and Government*, 169.

[86] Joshua Saul, "Tea Party Express Introduces Itself to Alaska," *Alaska Dispatch*, July 19, 2010.

[87] Sean Cockerham and Erika Bolstad, "Murkowski Says, 'Let's Make History,'" *Anchorage Daily News*, September 17, 2010.

[88] Craig Medred, "Miller Guard Says Editor Refused to Leave Private Event," *Alaska Dispatch*, October 17, 2010; and Richard Mauer, "Miller Security Guards Handcuff Editor," *Anchorage Daily News*, October 17, 2010.

[89] Alaska Division of Elections, at http://www.elections.alaska.gov/results/10GENR/data/results.htm.

[90] This account of the 2014 governor's race draws on the following sources: "Walker, Mallott to Join Forces in Governor's Race," *Alaska Dispatch News*, September 1, 2014; "Bill Walker: Why Byron Mallott and I Have Joined Forces on One Ticket," *Alaska Dispatch News*, September 2, 2014: Mike Dingman, "Walker-Mallott Union May Leave Alaska Liberals Out," *Alaska Dispatch News*, Commentary, September 2, 2014; Alexandra Gutierrez, "Walker-Mallott 'Unity Ticket' Faces Legal Challenge," *Alaska News Nightly*, APRN, September 17, 2014; *Alaska Dispatch News*, "Sean Parnell Answers Questions About the Issues in the 2014 Election for Alaska Governor," October 11, 2014; and *Alaska Dispatch News*, "Bill Walker Answers Questions about the Issues in the 2014 Election for Alaska Governor," October 11, 2014. It also draws on interviews and conversations by Clive Thomas with several legislators, staffers, campaign personnel, members of the governor's office, and union personnel in February 2015, all of whom requested anonymity.

[91] For a consideration of the role of the Alaska media in the 2014 general election campaign for governor, see Chapter 20, Section 1.

[92] See Chapter 15, Table 15.4, and Chapter 24, Section 7.

[93] See Chapter 21, Section 8 and Box 21.6, and Chapter 22.

⋆ CHAPTER 15 ⋆

Interest Groups, Lobbying, and Lobbyists, and Their Effects on Democracy in Alaska

Clive S. Thomas and Kristina Klimovich

Few aspects of American and Alaska politics generate a more negative reaction from the public than do interest groups and the lobbyists who represent them. Yet Alaskans join interest groups by the tens of thousands and Americans by the tens of millions. This ambivalence in the minds of Alaskans is well summed up by a 2008 headline in the *Alaska Journal of Commerce*: "Lobbyists: Are they Alaska's heroes or villains?"[1]

Part of the purpose of this chapter is to explore when interest groups and lobbyists are Alaska's heroes and when they are Alaska's villains. Given the generally negative attitude toward them, we approach this issue through three questions that constitute the major themes of the chapter: (1) Do interest groups, lobbying, and lobbyists promote or undermine democracy in Alaska? (2) What are the characteristics of Alaska's group system and how does it operate as part of the public policy process? and (3) How different are interest groups and lobbying activity in Alaska compared with other states and Washington, D.C.? To answer these questions we draw on a wide range of sources. The major source, however, is the Hrebenar-Thomas study of interest group activity in all fifty states conducted over a thirty-year period.[2]

Of the characteristics of Alaska politics identified in Chapter 2, the most obvious one that applies here is weak party organizations in relation to strong interest groups. Other characteristics that are evident are the significant role of external forces, developers versus environmentalists, friends and neighbors politics, and the all-pervasive importance of government, as well as elements of bipartisanship.

The chapter begins by explaining key terms and concepts. This is followed by a consideration of the past and present roles of interest groups as political organizations, which sets the scene for understanding the reasons for the ambivalent attitude toward them and the practical consequences of this ambivalence. The next section deals with the development of state interest group systems and Alaska's system in particular and its contemporary characteristics. The rest of the chapter covers the practical activities of interest groups in Alaska, including sections on strategies and tactics, lobbyists, group power, lobbying and money, and group regulation. The conclusion returns to the question of whether lobbyists are Alaska's heroes or villains, placed in the context of the three major questions posed in the chapter.[3]

1. KEY DEFINITIONS AND EXPLANATIONS

There are several terms used in the academic study and practical day-to-day operation of interest groups that are necessary for understanding the analysis in this chapter. The main ones are explained in this section and others in the appropriate places in the chapter.

Interest Groups and Types of Interests and Lobbies

In Chapter 13, in distinguishing between political parties and interest groups, we gave a short definition of the term *interest group*. Here we explain the term in more detail. There is, however, no generally accepted definition of an *interest group* among scholars.[4] The term is most often defined narrowly to include only those groups required to register under state laws. Yet many groups and organizations engage in lobbying but are not required to register. The most important are those representing the various levels and agencies of government. Most states do not require public agencies at any level of government to register as interest groups (though local governments usually must register if they hire a lobbyist).

To capture the gamut of interest group activity in the states, including Alaska, the following broad definition is most appropriate:

> An *interest group* is an association of individuals or organizations or a public or private institution that, on the basis of one or more shared concerns or values, attempts to influence public policy in its favor.

This definition embraces formal or organized interests, though these are usually referred to simply as interest groups. They have a recognized and usually permanent organization, as opposed to an *interest*, one less formally structured and perhaps less permanent, as explained below. There are three categories of interest groups operating in pluralist democracies including the American states and in Alaska.

1. *Membership groups* are made up of individuals promoting a host of economic, social, and political concerns, such as senior citizens, environmentalists, schoolteachers, students, anti-tax advocates, among many others.

2. *Organizational interest groups* are composed not of individuals but of organizations, such as a state or national association of businesses or trade unions, like the Alaska Oil and Gas Association (AOGA). In effect, they are organizations of organizations.
3. *Institutional interests*, which include various private and public entities, such as businesses, think tanks, universities, state and federal agencies, and local governments. This is the largest category of organized interests operating in state capitals.[5]

The term *lobby* is often used synonymously with *interest* to refer to a collection of groups and organizations of a similar type, such as the education lobby (educational interests) or the business lobby (business interests). As indicated above, however, the term *interest* is often used more specifically to refer to an organized entity, such as a city like Fairbanks or a business like British Petroleum (BP), that may engage in lobbying but is not a formalized interest group of individuals or organizations.

Another useful distinction is that between *insider* and *outsider* groups. Insider groups are those with good access to policy makers and long-standing political relationships, such as business and agricultural groups. Outsider groups are usually new groups, such as those for animal rights, or those advocating less mainstream causes, such as prisoners' rights groups, that have little direct access to policy makers.

Lobbying and Lobbyist

Interests and interest groups operate in the state public policy process by *lobbying*: that is, by conveying their views through a process of advocacy to government officials (elected or appointed officials or both) for the purpose of influencing their decisions. To facilitate this process of political advocacy, a general plan or *strategy* of action is created and specific *tactics* employed to execute it. Groups can use *direct* or *indirect* lobbying strategies and tactics to promote their causes. Direct tactics involve approaching policy makers in person, by phone or email or other ways. Indirect tactics use other means to try to get a point across to policy makers, such as using the media. Insider groups tend to use more direct tactics, while outsider groups may have to use indirect tactics to get the attention of policy makers.

The key link between the group or organization and public officials in this advocacy process is the *lobbyist*, which we can initially define as a person designated by an interest group to facilitate influencing public policy in that group's favor. We will expand on this definition later and also see that there are various types of lobbyists. In line with the definition of interest group above, lobbyists include not only those required to register by law but also those representing nonregistered groups and organizations, particularly government agencies. The outcomes most often sought by interest groups and their lobbyists are those concerning public policies, but they also include outcomes regarding who gets elected and appointed to make those policies in an effort to create relationships conducive to their group's future interests. We go into detail on the various aspects of lobbying, particularly focusing on strategies and tactics, and the role of lobbyists in Section 5 of the chapter.

It is important to point out that lobbying does not take place only in the capitol building. Some studies focus only on the legislature, which is certainly a major target for many groups. But the executive branch has always been lobbied, particularly the governor's office and the bureaucracy where major policy and regulatory decisions are made that affect a host of interests, and this target of lobbying is increasing.[6] Although it is less prominent, lobbying through state and federal courts is also on the rise.

The State Interest Group System

A state interest group system is the array of groups and organizations, both formal and informal, and the lobbyists who represent them, working to affect public policy within a state. The idea of a state interest group system is an abstraction because even though there are relations between groups and lobbyists representing various interests, rarely if ever do all the groups in a political system act in concert to achieve one goal.

However, for analytical purposes, it is the characteristics of the interest group system—its size, development, composition, methods of operating, and so on—in its relationship to the economy, society, and government that are particularly important. To a large extent, this relationship determines such aspects of state politics as the political power structure, what public policies are pursued and which ones are not, and the extent of representation and democracy. So the concept of the group system is useful in helping answer the three main questions of the chapter.

2. INTEREST GROUPS AS POLITICAL ORGANIZATIONS—PAST AND PRESENT

In pluralist democracies like Alaska, interest groups and political parties are the two principal forms of political organizations, and a major vehicle of political participation by linking the governed with their government. Parties, however, are a relatively recent development in political systems. Interests and interest groups have a much longer history. This is because parties are an artificial creation, while interests are a natural consequence of human society. Because interests are natural social and political phenomena, they existed as political forces before formal institutions. Some were a formidable force in promoting their interests, and the influence of interests continues, though today often as formalized interest groups.

The Ubiquity of Interests and Lobbyists in the Power Structure of Political Systems

From the earliest days of civilization, people have naturally banded into groups. Group identity based on location, race, tribe, religion, class, economic status, and later profession and values (such as pro- or anti-slavery) was a major aspect of the dynamics of all societies. As a consequence, societies were structured by various groups and interests. Certain groups, such as the noblemen in the Middle Ages, became major political forces by influencing or, in many cases, controlling government and excluding other groups and interests. This was sometimes to promote their view of life (such as the Catholic Church) or in other cases to secure economic benefits (like the railroads in the mid- and late-nineteenth century).

This long history of groups and interests has meant that lobbyists have also existed for thousands of years, because all groups needed and continue to need someone to push their causes with government. This is the motive for lobbying and why it has always been a central and natural part of human society. It is often said that prostitutes engage in the oldest profession, but lobbyists have been plying their trade at least as long, if not longer. Like interest groups, lobbyists are an indispensable aspect of all political systems, particularly pluralist democracies.

Because interests, and more recently formalized interest groups and their lobbyists, have been so central to the development and power structure of all societies, one way to view political development (the political history) of a society is to identify the groups and interests that have wielded power. Furthermore, today as in the past, group leaders and lobbyists for the most effective groups do not waste their time lobbying public officials or policy makers who cannot advance their causes. So an understanding of the power structure in political systems like those found in the United States can be acquired by identifying the political venues that these effective interests and interest groups lobby, as well as by determining which interests and interest groups are sought out by key policy makers because of their political value to the policy maker. So, by implication, a change in the lobbying patterns of key interests, or a shift in which interests and lobbyists policy makers seek out, indicates a change in the power structure.

At the same time, the history of all societies shows that a major problem with the unchecked power of groups and interests like the railroads or a dominant industry in a town, state, or country, like Seattle fishing interests in Territorial Alaska, is that it will tend to abuse its power for its own benefit. This undermines the potential power of other groups by constraining their political access and representation. Consequently, one of the major reasons for the promotion of pluralist democracy is to even out the balance among various groups by expanding political access and representation. However, the nature and goals of interests, and more recently formalized interest groups, have not changed over time and likely never will.

The Paradox of the Private Goals and the Public Roles of Interest Groups

Unlike political parties, most interest groups are not first and foremost political organizations. Most exist for the economic, personal values, recreational, or other nonpolitical benefit of their members, such as an association of dentists disseminating information about new dental procedures, or a club of model railroad enthusiasts. However, many nonpolitical interest groups become politically active because there is no other way to protect or promote the interests of their members. Agriculture, business, and labor have been lobbying for generations. However, since the 1960s, increasing government involvement in the economy and in society in general has brought a plethora of new groups into the political arena in the U.S., including all fifty states, to protect themselves from or urge increases in government regulation, to secure a piece of the government budget, or to promote some value or belief.

Therefore, while most interest groups have many nonpolitical goals, they have one overriding goal when they become involved in politics—to influence the political process and particularly public policy in their favor. Despite the rhetoric of many groups that their goals are "in the public interest," these goals are often narrow and sometimes very self-serving: gaining a tax break, securing an exemption from a regulation, obtaining a budget appropriation, and so on.

On the other hand, as narrowly focused as some groups may be, their existence and the freedom—the right—to present their case to government is essential to the functioning of pluralist democracy, like that in the United States and Alaska. An essential element of this form of democracy is that it includes a myriad of interests, attitudes, and values, with none of them considered superior to the others. This is in contrast to many authoritarian regimes that tightly control and sometimes ban interest groups and other challenges to government policy, such as the media. Consequently, the First Amendment to the U.S. Constitution guarantees the right to "petition"—in effect to lobby—government, and this is guaranteed in all state constitutions, including Alaska's (Article 1, Section 6).[7] Thus, the essence of pluralist democracy is the competition between numerous interests to affect government policy in their favor. Furthermore, in their public operations, interest groups perform several functions that are essential to the continued functioning of a democratic system. These are set out in Box 15.1.

What is paradoxical about the public roles of interest groups is that the positive aspect of their public roles is purely coincidental. In their private capacity the vast majority of interest groups do not exist to improve the functioning of democracy or the political process. In fact, the reverse is often true. In the rough-and-tumble of hardball interest group politics, many groups work to undermine the access and influence of their opponents. Thus, the positive public role of interest groups is a paradoxical by-product of the sum of their selfish interests.

BOX 15.1

The Public Roles of Interest Groups as Political Organizations

In promoting their private goals, interest groups also perform several indispensable public roles as political organizations. Five are particularly important.

THE AGGREGATION AND REPRESENTATION OF INTERESTS

Together with political parties, interest groups are a major means by which people with similar interests and concerns come together or are aggregated to articulate their views to government. Thus, interest groups are important vehicles of political participation. They act as intermediaries between the governed and the government by representing the views of their members to public officials, especially between elections. Potentially, too, several people who band together are likely to be more successful politically than individuals acting alone.

FACILITATING GOVERNMENT

Groups contribute to the substance of public policy by being major sources of both technical and political information for policy makers. In most instances, groups help to facilitate the process of bargaining and compromise essential to policy making in a pluralist system like Alaska's. Also, in some cases groups aid in the implementation of public policies, as, for example, when the Alaska State Chamber of Commerce disseminates information about a state or federal business loan program.

POLITICAL EDUCATION AND TRAINING

To varying degrees, interest groups educate their members and the public on issues. They also provide opportunities for citizens to learn about the political process and to gain valuable practical experience for seeking public office.

CANDIDATE RECRUITMENT

Groups often recruit candidates to run for public office, both from within and outside their group membership.

CAMPAIGN FINANCE

Increasingly, groups help to finance political campaigns, both candidate elections and, at the state and local level, ballot measure elections (initiative, referendum, and recall). One way they often do this is by setting up a political action committee (PAC).

Source: Developed by the authors.

Moreover, as vehicles of representation—as a link between the governed and the government—interest groups are far from ideal. The major problem is that they do not represent all segments of the population equally. Their bias is toward the better educated, higher income, white, and male segments of the population. Nonwhites, minorities (including women), the less well educated, and lower income segments are underrepresented in the political process by interest groups.[8] As umbrella organizations embracing a host of groups and interests, political parties are far more representative political organizations.

3. THE PRACTICAL CONSEQUENCES OF THE PARADOXICAL ROLE OF INTEREST GROUPS AND LOBBYISTS

A shorthand way to sum up the clash of private goals and public roles of interest groups is as a "triple tension" of their "inevitability, indispensability, and dangers."[9] This clash has resulted in a range of practical consequences for interest groups and the way they are perceived. This, in turn, has shaped public policy toward interest groups and lobbyists and has affected the way they operate in modern societies like Alaska.

The actions of some interests and interest groups, both past and present, have been responsible for imprinting an indelible negative attitude toward group activity and lobbyists on the minds of many Americans and Alaskans.[10] Take, for instance, the case of former Alaska lobbyist Thyes Shaub, who represented timber, banking, tourism, and other business interests. Her daughter came home from school one day to report that when she told her high school class what her mother did, one classmate responded, "What's it like to have a mother who lies for a living?"[11] This student was expressing a common belief among many Americans that lobbyists are villains and not heroes, and by implication, that the role of interest groups and the activity of lobbying are villainous.

To be sure, because the political and financial stakes are often so high in lobbying, some groups and lobbyists are willing to go to any lengths, including illegal ones, to achieve their goals. The well-publicized conviction on bribery charges of Washington, D.C., lobbyist Jack Abramoff is one example. Another is the VECO scandal in Alaska in 2006–2008, in which some lobbyists were involved in bribing legislators to secure an oil tax decrease. Convictions of some lobbyists and legislators were secured, and they served prison terms.[12] More often, this negative attitude toward interest groups and their lobbyists results less from illegal activities than from a powerful interest dominating a state or town.

Consequently, many people refer to interest groups as "special interests," implying that they are at best working for some special privilege and at worst working against the public interest. Also, in the populist tradition of Alaska and the United States, "big and powerful interests" like "big business" are often seen as running the state or the country, with their "wheeler-dealer" lobbyists receiving huge salaries. The media often reinforce these attitudes. The reporting of juicy scandals and the activities of high-paid lobbyists sells newspapers and helps boost TV and radio ratings. These negative public attitudes are hard to change, with nearly two centuries of reinforcement. They are part of most people's political socialization, and the attitudes have become ingrained in the political culture of many Americans and Alaskans.

While the negative image persists, the reality is quite different and likely always was. The vast majority of interest groups and lobbyists work well within the law, and very few lobbyists make huge salaries. Furthermore, many advocacy groups are not very influential, but plod away at working with public officials. The media rarely report such above-board activities and limited successes or show groups and lobbyists in a positive light. All the same, the public does make distinctions between various interests and sees some as more positive than others. Organizations like AARP (formerly the American Association of Retired Persons) are more favorably viewed than political organizations like the American Civil Liberties Union (ACLU).[13]

Moreover, people see the value of joining an interest group to represent their "just cause" and believe in their constitutional right to do so. From this perspective, "special interests" are those of their opponents, those with whom they disagree, or groups and interests they see as too powerful. A term increasingly used these days to identify the "positive" causes is *stakeholders* as opposed to *special interests*.

By contrast, public officials, especially elected officials, most often have a more positive attitude toward interest groups and lobbyists than the general public. This is because they see their value in providing technical information in the area of policy they represent, such as local government or services for the disabled, and providing an efficient way to gauge the views of particular political constituencies. Yet public officials are not blind to the potential negative effects of interest groups and lobbyists. However, unless forced by public opinion, elected officials are not always enthusiastic about regulating interest group and lobbyists' activities.

And so, much of the attitude toward interest groups among the public and public officials is a matter of perception and not always based on reality. Public attitudes are often based on an individual's or group's perception of how they see the personal or public benefit of particular interests or lobbyists. So not surprisingly, the actions of elected and appointed officials are often influenced by public perceptions. For instance, as a presidential candidate, Barack Obama, very much playing to popular sentiment, vowed not to include lobbyists in his administration. After becoming president, however, he appointed many former lobbyists.[14]

One particular consequence of the negative perception of lobbyists is that both public and private organizations try to avoid using the term *lobbyist* and use various euphemisms—in essence, misleading designations. These include legislative liaison, public affairs specialist, policy advocate, government relations coordinator, and political consultant, among others. The University of Alaska, for example, which has a major lobbying presence in both Juneau and Washington, D.C., goes to great lengths to avoid being considered a lobbying entity. One of its former in-house "lobbyists," Pete Kelly, when running for the State Senate in 2012, argued that he had never been a lobbyist and got former university president Mark Hamilton to vouch for it. This was totally disingenuous and complete political subterfuge.[15]

A significant public policy consequence of the dangers of interest groups has been a long history of efforts to regulate them. But as we will see later, there is only so much that regulation can achieve given the nature of political power, the strictures imposed by the national and state constitutions, and the attitudes of many elected officials.

From Background and Theory to the Practicalities of Interest Group Activity in Alaska

Understanding the terminology of interest group activity, and particularly the complexities of the ambivalence toward groups, lobbying, and lobbyists, helps us offer answers to the three questions set out at the beginning of the chapter. These are the way that group activity affects democracy in Alaska, how the Alaska system works within the policy process, and how it compares with other states and with Washington, D.C.

4. UNDERSTANDING STATE INTEREST GROUP SYSTEMS: WHERE DOES ALASKA FIT?

What has determined the characteristics of Alaska's interest group system past and present? In particular, what has shaped the range of groups that operate in Juneau, the lobbying techniques they use, the groups that are influential and the ones that are not, and how powerful is the group system overall? To answer these questions we first explain the factors that shape group systems in democracies in general and then review recent developments across the fifty states' group systems. This comparative approach allows us to assess in what ways Alaska's interest group system, past and present, is similar to and different from those found in other states.

Factors Shaping Interest Group Systems in the Fifty States

Many factors shape democratic interest group systems in general and in the American states in particular. Five are especially important: (1) the level of socio-economic development and diversity; (2) the characteristics of politics and political culture; (3) the structure, policy authority, and level of professionalism of state government; (4) external political influences and intergovernmental relations (IGR); and (5) changes in the policy-making environment.

Level of Socio-Economic and Demographic Development and Diversity

Economic development and diversity refer to the mix of primary production (agriculture, natural resource extraction—minerals, fish, timber, and so on), manufacturing, and services in the economy. Social and demographic diversity involves the range and number of racial and ethnic groups in relation to the majority of the population, the extent of the middle class and professional groups, and the total size of the population.

The greater socio-economic and demographic development and diversity, the more diverse is the range of groups. The larger the population, the more specialized representation and lobbyists become. States like California and Texas have highly specialized interest groups, representing narrow areas such as the agricultural chemical industry, compared with states like Idaho and Alaska with fewer specialized groups and lobbyists.

The Characteristics of Politics and Political Culture

Important factors influenced by the political culture are (1) the types and extent of policies pursued, (2) the party-group relationship and the relative strength or weakness of political parties, (3) what are and what are not acceptable lobbying techniques, and (4) the general context in which interest groups operate and the attitudes toward them, including the extent of group regulation.

As explained in Chapter 13, political party-interest group relations affect avenues of access and influence, group strategies and tactics, and, in the short run, policies pursued and enacted, among other things. A rise in campaign costs puts increased pressure on candidates to raise funds. The more support coming directly to candidates from groups and their political action committees (PACs), the more candidates are beholden to them.

The Structure, Policy Authority, and Level of Professionalism of State Government

Regarding the structure of state government, the more integrated the system (strong parties, strong executive including an appointed cabinet, little or no provision for direct democracy, and so on) the fewer the options available to groups. Conversely, the more the system is fragmented, the greater is the number of access points and available methods of influence. State policy authority will determine which interests will attempt to affect state policy. As the area of policy authority expands, the number and types of groups lobbying will increase.

A high level of professionalism (including state legislators, the bureaucracy, and the governor's staff) makes more varied sources of information available to policy makers. It also creates a higher demand for information by these policy makers, including information from groups and lobbyists. Public disclosure laws increase public information about lobbying activities. This affects the methods and techniques of lobbying, which in turn affects the power of certain groups and lobbyists, though not necessarily group system power.

External Politics and Intergovernmental Relations

The distribution of intergovernmental spending and policy authority refers to the policies exercised and the amount of money spent by state governments versus policies and spending by federal and local governments. Changes in responsibilities between levels of government affect the types of groups that lobby federal, state, and local governments and the intensity of their lobbying efforts. The "nationalization" of issues such as antismoking, term limits, and efforts to enact stiffer penalties for drunk driving have spawned similar groups across the fifty states, increased out-of-state funding for group activity, and generally increased intergovernmental contact by all groups, including traditional interests. This has certainly been the case in Alaska.

Changes in the Short-Term Policy-Making Environment

Changes in party control of government, in either the legislative or executive branch, especially when accompanied by party or caucus control or ideological cohesiveness, can affect the access and effectiveness of certain groups and interests. Spending and policy priorities, which may change as the result of an election or other events, such as a financial crisis, affect policies that state governments emphasize at a particular time.

Government will often give preferential access to groups directly concerned with its areas of policy priority. The extent of this preferential access is related to the degree to which a group is needed by policy makers for policy development and implementation (need and obligation are major sources of group power). Thus, shifts in policy and spending priorities will affect both the access and influence capability of certain groups and the relative power of groups within specific policy areas. Generally, however, certain business groups that are essential to the state's economy have good access as insider groups. Other groups, such as those for the arts, which are less essential to the economy and are not "needed" in the same way by policy makers, will be given less preference in access and likely be less influential in the long run.

The Development of State Interest Group Systems

As with developing political systems in general, most states were dominated by one or a few interests in their early years. For example, Montana was dominated by the Anaconda Copper Company; West Virginia and Kentucky by coal companies; Maine by the "big three" interests of electric power, timber, and the combined lobby of textiles and shoe manufacturing; plus many states were dominated by the railroads. Some states still have a prominent interest, such as the Mormon Church in Utah, the gaming and hospitality industries in Nevada, and agribusiness (processing agricultural products) in Arkansas, the home of Tyson Foods. But for the most part, political power is much more pluralistic as a result of developments since the mid-1960s.

Alaska's Interest Group System up to the Early 1970s

Because interest groups are a central political force in all political systems, the changing role of interests in Alaska's political system overall, and particularly in the policy process, is an enlightening way to view the political history of the Territory and of the State of Alaska. The interest group-political system relationship gets to the root of how power and decision making have been structured and thus the major issues of concern to both those with the power and those with little or no influence.

Like all states, Alaska went through a period when its political economy was dominated by a few powerful forces, particularly the Outside interests of fishing companies based in Seattle and New England, and the timber and mining industries. Consequently, a major motive force behind statehood was to curb the influence of these Outside interests. By 1970, just a decade after statehood, Alaska's interest group system was becoming more pluralistic and, as a consequence, so was the distribution of power and decision making in the political system in general. Insights into how Alaska's interest group system and activity has changed since statehood in 1959 can be acquired by looking at general developments in other states.

Developments in Group Systems across the Fifty States since the 1960s

From the early 1900s until the mid-1960s, group activity mainly involved the so-called traditional interests of business, labor, agriculture, education, and local government. These used mainly direct lobbying tactics, and often only a lobbyist, to achieve their goals. Since then, the number and types of groups operating in the states, the intensity and ways that they lobby, and the money they spend have all seen a major expansion.

The expansion in the number and types of groups, the so-called advocacy explosion, involving more and a wider range of groups lobbying state governments, has paralleled a similar explosion in Washington, D.C. Specifically, this expansion comes from five major sources.

One is that increased government involvement has forced many interests to get involved in politics to either advance or protect their interests. A second reason is that a variety of new groups have entered politics, such as environmentalists, public interest groups, victims' rights groups, and ideological groups, which are often single-issue groups such as anti-abortionists and the Religious Right. More groups became active across state lines when a number of issues, such as drunk driving and antismoking, gathered nationwide momentum. Third, other groups, particularly gaming interests, senior citizens, sportsmen's groups (hunting and fishing and anti-gun control), and Hispanic organizations have expanded their presence in the states. Fourth, the traditional interests have become fragmented in their advocacy strategies as issues became more complex. For example, a trade association or general organization (like a state chamber of commerce) may not serve the specific needs of all of its members. As a result, many businesses and local governments now lobby on their own, even though they remain members of their general state organizations. Fifth, this expansion in membership and the number of groups is also due to advancing political awareness as the nation enters a postindustrial phase of development. Many people have come to realize the benefits of promoting a public policy cause through the focused agenda of an interest group rather than the broad general platform of a political party.[16]

Interests that do not have a presence across all the states tend to be newly formed groups, such as school choice (favoring vouchers or charter schools), children's rights groups, and family values groups, or those representing an interest concentrated in certain states, such as Native Americans, commercial fishing interests, and professional sports franchises. Table 15.1 shows the range of groups that are active today across the states. The table is divided into two sections. One identifies the groups that are continually active because they have issues before state government every year. The second includes groups that are intermittently active and that lobby only when they have an issue to push.

However, it is important not to equate the size of a group, group presence, and increased political activity with power. As we will see below, there is much more to political power than simply being heard by government and having a high political profile through political activity and a large membership.

While differences will probably always exist among the levels of the U.S. interest group system, a nationalization or homogenization of interest group activity is taking place that particularly affects strategy and tactics, group organization, and the professionalism of lobbyists. Furthermore, all states now have some form of lobby regulation.

Alaska's Contemporary Interest Group System: The Range of Groups, IGR Lobbying, and the Political Tone of the Lobbying Environment

Alaska's group system reflects many of the developments across the nation since the 1960s, but with some variations because of the state's particular socio-economic, demographic, and political circumstances. In the rest of this section we look at Alaska's particular range of groups, the aspect of IGR lobbying, and the tone of the day-to-day lobbying environment. Then, in Sections 5 through 9 we consider similarities and differences between Alaska and other states regarding strategies and tactics, lobbyists, group power, money and lobbying, and group regulation.

The Range of Groups Operating in Alaska

The range of interests and interest groups operating in Alaska today can best be understood by comparing them with those operating across the states in general as set out in Table 15.1. Alaska has many of the interests listed in the left-hand column of that table, which identifies organizations and interests operating in more than forty-five states. Alaska has local governments, state agencies, many businesses, traditional labor and professional groups, and public interest and citizen groups. But its dominant natural

TABLE 15.1

Types of Interests and Interest Groups and Their Frequency of Presence across the Fifty States in 2010

1. CONTINUALLY ACTIVE INTERESTS AND INTEREST GROUPS		
PRESENT IN OVER 45 STATES	**PRESENT IN 25–45 STATES**	**PRESENT IN FEWER THAN 25 STATES**
Individual Business Corporations*	Manufacturing Companies	Foreign Businesses. (especially from Japan)
Local Government Units (cities/districts, etc.)	Manufacturers' Associations	Environmental and Disaster Preparedness Entities
State Departments, Boards, and Commissions	Railroads	Animal Rights Groups
Business/Trade Associations**	Agribusiness Corporations	Think Tanks (public/private liberal/conservative)
Utility Companies and Associations (public and private)	Waste Storage/Disposal Companies/Associations	
Banks and Financial Institutions/Associations	Sportsmen's Groups (especially/hunting and fishing)	
Insurance Companies/Associations	Commercial Fishermen	
Public Employee Unions/Associations (state and local)	Aquaculture Groups (farm/pen-raised fish)	
Universities and Colleges (public and private)	Health Care Corporations	
School Teachers' Unions/Associations	Mining Companies	
Local Government Associations (cities/counties/officials, etc.)	Gaming (race tracks/casinos/lotteries)	
Farmers' Organizations/Commodity Associations	Latino Groups	
Traditional Labor Unions	Native American Groups	
Labor Associations (mainly the AFL-CIO)	Pro-Development/Land Use Groups	
Environmentalists	Groups for the Physically and Mentally Disabled	
Tourism Groups/Hospitality Industry	Student Groups	
Oil and Gas Companies/Associations	Taxpayer Groups	
Hospital Associations/Nursing Homes	Children's Rights Groups	
Contractors/Builders/Developers	Gay Rights Groups	
Senior Citizens	Parent-Teacher Associations	
Ad Hoc Issue Coalitions (tort reform, health costs, education, etc.)	Media Associations	
Physicians	Consumer Groups	
Trial Lawyers/State Bar Associations	Veterans' Groups	
Liquor/Wine/Beer Interests	Family Values Groups	
	School Choice Groups (vouchers/charter schools)	

2. INTERMITTENTLY ACTIVE INTERESTS AND INTEREST GROUPS		
PRESENT IN OVER 45 STATES	**PRESENT IN 25–45 STATES**	**PRESENT IN FEWER THAN 25 STATES**
Retailers' Associations	Term Limit/Government Reform Groups	Political Consultants
Real Estate Interests	Moral Majority/Christian Right	Sports Franchises (baseball/basketball/ football/hockey)
Police/Firemen's Associations	Local Community Groups	Hi-Tech Associations
Communication Interests (telecommunications, cable TV, etc.)	Pro- and Anti-Gun Control Groups	Computer Programmers
Nurses	Victims' Rights Groups	
Optometrists		
Dentists		
Truckers		
Women's Groups		
Groups for the Arts		
Pro- and Anti-Abortion Groups		
Mothers Against Drunk Driving (MADD)		
Church Organizations		
African American Groups		
Pro- and Anti-Smoking Interests		
Social Service Groups and Coalitions		
Good Government Groups: (League of Women Voters, Common Cause)		
American Civil Liberties Union		
Various Professional Groups: (accountants, engineers, architects, etc.)		
Federal Agencies		

* An unavoidably broad category. It includes manufacturing and service corporations with the exception of those listed separately, for example, private utilities and oil and gas companies. These and other business corporations were listed separately because of the frequency of their presence across the states.

** Another unavoidably broad category. It includes chambers of commerce as well as specific trade associations, for example, The Tobacco Institute, air carriers, manufacturers' associations, etc.

Source: Compiled by the authors from the 2007 and 2010 updates of the Hrebenar-Thomas study.

BOX 15.2

Examples of Interests and Interest Groups in Alaska

INDIVIDUAL MEMBERSHIP GROUPS

Alaska Bar Association—ABA
With more than four thousand members, represents lawyers to state government on various issues involving qualifications and legal liabilities of lawyers, among other concerns.

Alaska State Employees Association—ASEA
A long-time active lobby in Juneau, which has competed with the Alaska Public Employees Association (APEA) in representing state and local government employees.

Alaska Wildlife Alliance—AWA
Founded by Alaskans in 1978, it is the only Alaska-based organization solely dedicated to the nonconsumptive protection of Alaska's wildlife. It depends on grassroots support and the political activism of its members.

Association for the Education of Young Children-Southeast Alaska—AEYC-SEA
This citizens' group is the local chapter of a state and national organization working to improve funding for, and the quality of, day care and early childhood education. It relies largely on volunteers to advocate to state government.

National Education Association—NEA-Alaska
Represents K–12 employees, mainly schoolteachers, with a long-time active lobby in Juneau.

ORGANIZATIONAL INTEREST GROUPS

Alaska Conservation Alliance—ACA
A statewide coalition of more than forty conservation groups and businesses with a combined membership of more than thirty-eight thousand. ACA believes that a healthy environment and a strong economy go hand in hand.

Alaska Federation of Natives—AFN
Its mission is to enhance and promote the cultural, economic, and political voice of the Alaska Native community. Founded in 1966 to pursue Native land claims, AFN is the largest statewide Native organization. The federation's membership includes 178 villages, thirteen regional Native corporations and twelve regional nonprofit corporations, and tribal consortiums that contract for and run federal and state programs.

Alaska Municipal League—AML
Represents the vast majority of boroughs and cities in the state, advocating on general issues affecting local government such as funding, employee benefits, and so on.

Alaska Oil and Gas Association—AOGA
Has a major presence in Juneau representing major oil and gas companies operating in Alaska.

Association of Alaska School Boards—AASB
Represents Alaska's school boards (including Rural Education Attendance Areas—REAAs) and has a major presence in Juneau.

COMBINED INDIVIDUAL AND ORGANIZATIONAL MEMBERSHIP GROUPS

Alaska Outdoor Council—AOC
An association of individual members and clubs dedicated to the preservation of outdoor pursuits in Alaska—hunting, fishing, trapping, firearms ownership, and public access—and conservation of the habitats upon which AOC members depend. The council is the official state represenative of the National Rifle Association (NRA) and has a major ongoing presence in Juneau.

Alaska State Chamber of Commerce—ASCC
Established before statehood in 1952 as the All Alaska Chamber of Commerce, today it bills itself as "the voice of business" in Alaska. ASCC seeks to promote a positive business environment in the state and has a major lobbying presence in Juneau. Its membership includes individuals, businesses, local chambers of commerce (including chambers from the Seattle area and Canada), as well as other organizations.

United Fisherman of Alaska—UFA
Works to promote and protect the common interests of Alaska's commercial fishing industry. Its members are individuals, businesses, and other fishing organizations. It has a constant presence in Juneau.

INSTITUTIONAL INTERESTS

Alaska Airlines
As a Seattle-based company and the state's major air carrier with a monopoly in many communities, the airline has hired a lobbyist for many years to promote good relations with state government, among other political goals.

Alaska Department of Education and Early Development—DOEED or DOE
With K–12 education accounting for about 25 percent of the state budget, the department works to maintain its budget and deal with various federal and state regulations relating to education. This often includes utilizing its constituent groups such as the PTA and working with other interest groups, including AASB and school administrators.

ConocoPhillips Alaska
Works to protect its interests on its own behalf as well as through membership in AOGA.

North Slope Borough—NSB
Has hired a lobbyist for many years and uses its own staff to promote and protect its interests, particularly in regard to taxing the trans-Alaska pipeline and North Slope oil production facilities for local revenue.

University of Alaska—UA
Includes various interests, such as faculty, students, administrative, and maintenance employees, some of which have their own political representation. As an institutional interest, the UA's statewide office has a continual presence in Juneau, mainly for budget purposes. Plus, its individual campuses lobby on their own, sometimes at cross purposes with the statewide organization.

U.S. Forest Service—USFS
As one of many federal agencies in Alaska (others include the Fish and Wildlife Service [F&WS] and the Environmental Protection Agency [EPA]) the USFS works with state agencies and state elected officials to ensure compliance with federal regulations and to maintain good relations with state public officials.

Source: Developed by the authors from the websites of various organizations and from the Hrebenar-Thomas study.

resource–based economy and its general unsuitability for agriculture mean that it lacks major interests representing manufacturing, agriculture, and agribusiness. Its natural resource interests include oil and gas, mining, timber, and fishing. The special place of Native Americans in the state also means that there are various Alaska Native interests, including Native regional and village corporations and other interests.

Because of these factors, Alaska has one of the least diverse group systems in terms of economic interests, with disproportionate advocacy by government interests (state, local, and federal), out-of-state interests, and a unique role for Native Americans (Alaska Natives), among other differences. Thus, Alaska's group universe is an outlier compared with states like California and New York or even Louisiana or Washington State.[17] Box 15.2 provides a sample of interests and interest groups operating in Alaska. Some of these are common across the states, while others are unique to Alaska or have a major Alaska element to them.

The Intergovernmental Relations-Lobbying Connection

This chapter is primarily concerned with interest groups and lobbying at the state level in Alaska. But lobbying by Alaska interests occurs at all levels of government, as many interests also lobby at the local and federal levels, such as Alaska Natives, fishermen, environmentalists, the university, and schoolteachers. Figure 15.1 shows this interrelationship of lobbying by Alaska interests.

Of particular note over the years has been lobbying by Outside groups at the state and local levels, and often in Washington, D.C., to affect public policies in Alaska. In fact, as we noted in considering the development of Alaska's interest group system, these Outside interests were dominant political forces before statehood and continue to be important forces today. This is particularly the case with the oil and gas lobby and environmentalists (though usually through federal regulations and in Washington, D.C., as opposed to Juneau). Many specific examples of the effect of Outside interests and interest groups on Alaska public policy are included in the policy chapters on natural resources (Chapters 21 through 24) and state services (Chapters 26, 27, and 28).

The Political Tone of the Juneau Lobbying Environment

Tom Stewart, Secretary to the Alaska Constitutional Convention and a life-long Juneau resident, used to tell a story of going to the Territorial Legislature in the present capitol building and seeing a large trash can in a hallway filled with empty liquor bottles. Until the early 1980s, carousing and good old boy activities were common among state legislators, much of it funded by lobbyists. In fact, up until the 1980s a lot of political business was done not in the legislature or state offices, but in the bar of the Baranof Hotel (the Bubble Room) down the hill from the capitol. But things have changed drastically in Juneau, as they have in state capitals across the country.

A major factor in the transformation of the operating environment of interest groups in Alaska, as elsewhere, has been the enactment of laws and regulations dealing with campaign finance, conflict of interest, and lobbying activity. The state agency responsible for the administration and enforcement of these provisions is the Alaska Public Offices Commission (APOC). Agencies across the nation similar to APOC, such as the Public Disclosure Commission in Washington State and the Fair Political Practices Commission in California, have brought increasing public scrutiny to the activities of interest groups and their lobbyists.

The development of APOC and its general authority is explained in Chapter 5 in considering political corruption (see Box 5.4). In regard to their effects on lobbying, the reporting requirements have made the relationships between groups and lobbyists, and the money spent by and on them, considerably more transparent than before. Thus, APOC has made Alaska a much cleaner place politically than it was before the agency was established in the early 1970s. Certainly, the media is important in throwing light on the actions of interest groups and group relations with public officials, but it is APOC that provides reporters with much of the information they use in their news stories.

FIGURE 15.1

Alaska's Intergovernmental Interest Group and Lobbying Activity

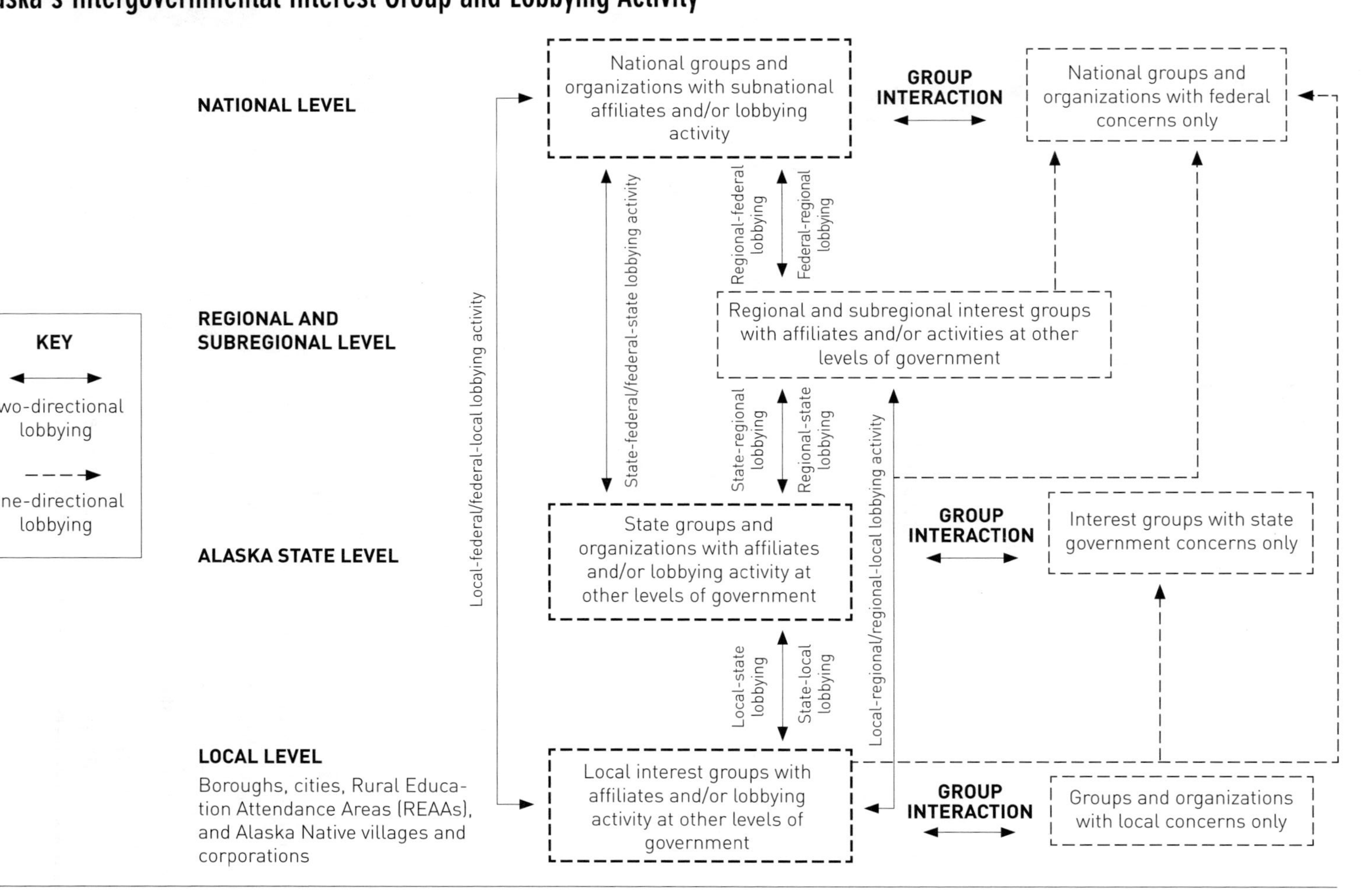

Source: Developed by the authors.

Like similar agencies in other states, APOC has contributed to the general rise in professionalism that has characterized state politics since the early 1970s. One effect of professionalism is the virtual disappearance of the good-old-boy, wheeler-dealer, cigar-chomping, back-slapping lobbyist. This has also meant the virtual disappearance of politicians in state politics who encouraged the activities of the wheeler-dealer lobbyist. In general, interest groups, lobbyists, and politicians are much more concerned about their public image today than ever before, and overall this has had a positive effect on the democratic process in Alaska and in other states.

5. INTEREST GROUP STRATEGIES AND TACTICS IN ALASKA

Those not familiar with the way interest groups go about achieving their goals often hold misconceptions or half truths about group strategies and tactics. One is that lobbying is an underhanded, sleazy, and sometimes corrupt business. A second myth is that lobbying is a complex business, the real nature of which can only be understood by political insiders. Certainly, in some lobbying campaigns the strategies and tactics can be quite involved, and they require much planning, management, and constant refining as political circumstances change. But at bottom there is nothing complicated about lobbying, and there are no secrets about what constitutes lobbying success. Lobbying is a major aspect of what much of this book is about—political power. Lobbying involves organizing political resources to bring pressure to bear, and the more resources a group has and the greater the skill of their lobbyists in using these resources for political purposes, the more successful the group is likely to be.

Another misconception is that there is only one right way to lobby on all issues. While there are essential elements common to all group strategies and tactics, there is no one right or correct way to lobby that should be followed by all groups at all times on all issues. This will become clear as we explain strategies and tactics in more detail. We begin with a fuller examination of some of the concepts we looked at in the introductory section of the chapter.

The Fundamentals of Lobbying: The Basics of Strategies and Tactics

At the most fundamental level, lobbying involves four stages that often overlap in practice:

1. Gaining access to policy makers
2. Building a relationship with them
3. Providing them with information on an issue or cause
4. Influencing their actions

Lobbying campaigns can be one of three types: promotional campaigns, defensive campaigns, and maintenance campaigns. As the term implies, a promotional campaign is used when an organization wants to add a law or regulation to the state's array of public policies. A defensive campaign is when a group or coalition wants to kill a proposed policy. And a maintenance campaign is when the organization has no immediate lobbying goals but wants to maintain good relations with public officials for the time when it may need them for a future issue. As we will see below, each type requires different tactics.

Because insider groups have good access to policy makers and long-standing political relationships in the state, they tend to focus on direct tactics, mainly using one or more lobbyists. But the fact that they often have major financial and other resources means that they can also use indirect tactics if necessary, such as public relations campaigns and contributing to candidates' campaigns. In contrast, many outsider groups have minimal financial and other resources. So although they also use some direct tactics, they are more frequently forced to use various forms of low-cost indirect tactics, including protests and demonstrations, to get the attention of policy makers and influence policy. Most outsider groups, however, work to become insider groups to increase their success. For instance, many environmental groups began as outsider groups in the early 1960s, but some have since become influential insiders.

Strategies and Tactics across the United States: Choices, Time-Honored Methods, and New Techniques

Groups are lobbying more intensively today than ever. They have more regular contact with public officials, use many of the new techniques of lobbying explained below, and have more contact with their counterparts in other states and in Washington, D.C. Box 15.3 sets out the range of direct and indirect tactics available to interest groups. The Hrebenar-Thomas study, and particularly work by political scientists Anthony Nownes and Patricia Freeman, provides insight into the extent to which each tactic is used by lobbyists and the organizations they represent (see Table 15.2 on pages 523-524).[18]

Brief comments on the extent of the use of tactics are included in Box 15.3 and in the next several paragraphs. One important point is that indirect tactics, many of which are so-called new tactics that have been developed and increasingly utilized since the early 1970s, are not a substitute for but a supplement to direct tactics or, as we have noted, are used by outsider groups out of necessity.

Factors Shaping Strategies and Tactics in a Lobbying Campaign

Several factors shape a lobbying campaign. Some are a result of the deliberate choices group leaders make. Others are a consequence of the nature of the issue, the type of group, and how it is perceived. Other factors are a product of the political climate and changing

BOX 15.3

The Range of Lobbying Options: Direct and Indirect Tactics

DIRECT TACTICS

1. Using One or More Lobbyists

This is the most traditional and the most essential of lobbying tactics.

2. Grassroots Lobbying—Using Group Members to Contact Public Officials

Here the group leadership encourages (and ideally coaches) certain group members to contact policy makers directly in support of the group's cause. The widespread use of this is a relatively recent tactic that has been used on a major scale only since the 1960s. When this type of lobbying is completely orchestrated by the group or organization's leaders and lacks spontaneity, it is often called "Astroturf" lobbying—that is, completely manufactured as opposed to natural, spontaneous, grassroots advocacy.

3. Lobbying the Legislature and Executive Branches of Government, including Federal, State, and Local Government Agencies

These have always been and will remain the major targets of policy making and thus the primary targets of direct lobbying.

4. Lobbying through the Courts

Although the courts and the judges who staff them cannot be lobbied directly, as can the legislature or executive, interest groups use the courts to obtain or oppose policy decisions that affect them. While the courts have always been used in this way, their use by interest groups has increased considerably since the early 1950s. Desegregation in the South was given its major boost by the U.S. Supreme Court in the 1954 decision in *Brown v. Board of Education of Topeka*. Since 2010, gay marriage advocates have secured major victories through the courts overturning state bans on gay marriage, and a major victory before the U.S. Supreme Court in 2015.

INDIRECT TACTICS

5. Affiliation with or Support of a Political Party

While very few of the tens of thousands of interest groups across the nation identify with a political party, major and high profile interests like labor, some businesses, many religious groups, and some minority groups either affiliate with or have strong leanings toward one of the two major parties. Such associations can be very advantageous when the group's party is in power but detrimental when it is not. When its party is in power the group may have input into the party's platform, providing an inside track for getting the group's issues before government. In addition, the group has priority access to major policy makers when pressing their issues before government. Certain elements of this tactic could be included under direct tactics.

6. Involvement in Direct Democracy Campaigns

Although there is no constitutional provision at the federal level for direct democracy—the initiative, referendum, and recall—use of these processes is an important tactic of many groups in the states, particularly in the West, especially in California and Oregon, and to a lesser extent in Alaska.

7. Financial Contributions to Help Elect Candidates

With the increasing cost of running campaigns, politicians are always looking for money to fund them. Interest groups realized this very early and have long been major funders (though some are prohibited by law or by their own rules from giving money to candidates). One major source of money is the *political action committee* (PAC)—see Chapter 14, Section 4. Individuals can also contribute to campaigns, and they may do so while making it clear to the candidate the group or groups to which they belong. Group leaders and lobbyists also often suggest to their members the names of candidates to support, as contributions might benefit their organization.

8. Nonfinancial Contribution to Help Elect Candidates

There are many ways that an interest group and its members can help a candidate get elected. These include recruiting candidates from among the group's ranks or from likeminded individuals, giving input into party platforms, providing campaign workers, helping get out the vote, and providing political expertise from the group, among other contributions.

9. Use of the Media, Public Relations, and Advertising Campaigns

This involves groups and interests using newspapers (including editorials and comments on stories), magazines, radio, TV, the Internet, social media, and public relations and advertising campaigns to get a message across to policy makers. Often the motive behind such campaigns is to create a perception that the public strongly supports or strongly opposes the policy concerned.

10. Protests, Boycotts and Demonstrations

While these tactics are used by many groups, they are most often used by outsider groups who do not have access to policy makers but want to attract their attention. Often they are tactics of last resort. Overall, these are the least-focused indirect lobbying tactics and, because of their often confrontational nature, they can easily backfire on a group. But they can also be successful at gaining the attention of the public and policy makers. This was the case with the Civil Rights protests in the 1950s and 1960s and with the Vietnam War protests of the late 1960s and early 1970s.

Source: Developed by the authors.

political circumstances. As we have noted, two major determining factors shaping strategy and tactics are whether the group is an insider or outsider group and whether the campaign is a promotional, defensive, or maintenance lobbying effort.

Because insider groups, particularly traditional interests, such as business, labor, and education, already have major access, they do not have to spend time and resources on this aspect of lobbying. Moreover, while they may use a range of tactics, they tend to focus on direct tactics, mainly using a lobbyist. In contrast, outsider groups are often new groups, usually with minimal resources, that must often gain access through indirect tactics, such as using the media or staging demonstrations.

The U.S. system of government was set up to protect the status quo through the separation of powers. As a result, groups that are engaged in promotional lobbying campaigns have the most challenging task. These groups have to mount major lobbying efforts to garner majority support in the legislature and get support from the governor and any affected state agencies. Such campaigns can involve major resources, particularly money.

In contrast, those who want to prevent action and thus are engaged in a defensive campaign generally have an easier task. To kill a bill or proposal it need only be stopped at one point in the process, say by a sympathetic committee chair or getting the governor to veto it. This "advantage of the defense" helps to explain why business and many other

TABLE 15.2

Lobbying Techniques Used by Lobbyists in Two States: Ohio and West Virginia

	PERCENTAGE OF LOBBYISTS USING THE TECHNIQUE		
TECHNIQUE	OVERALL USE	OHIO	WEST VIRGINIA
1. Meeting personally with state legislators	98	97	99
2. Meeting personally with state legislative staff	97	95	99
3. Helping to draft legislation	91*	86	98
4. Meeting personally with executive agency personnel	90	86	97
5. Meeting personally with the governor's staff	89	84	97
6. Entering into coalitions with other organizations	89	86	96
7. Testifying at legislative committee hearings	88	88	90
8. Submitting written testimony to legislative committees	83	86	78
9. Talking with people from the media	82	79	87
10. Inspiring letter-writing, telephone, or e-mail campaigns to state legislators	78	74	87
11. Submitting written comments on proposed rules/ regulations	77	71	87
12. Making personal monetary contributions to candidates for office	77	74	81
13. Helping to draft regulations, rules, or guidelines	77	73	84
14. Interacting with special liaison offices within the governor's office	72	65	83
15. Issuing press releases	72	69	78
16. Engaging in informal contacts with state legislative staff	67	58	84
17. Engaging in informal contacts (for example, wining, dining) with state legislators	65	57	79
18. Serving on advisory committees and/or boards	65	61	73
19. Meeting personally with the governor	64	50	89
20. Working on campaigns for candidates	62	58	70
21. Inspiring letter-writing, telephone, or e-mail campaigns to the governor	62	58	68
22. Writing op-ed pieces for newspapers	60	54	70
23. Testifying at executive agency hearings	60	54	70
24. Making personal monetary contributions to political parties	54	53	56
25. Engaging in regulatory negotiations	53	49	60
26. Campaigning for or against a state initiative or referendum	51	52	49
27. Doing favors for legislators	50	50	49
28. Holding press conferences	49	44	58

TECHNIQUE	PERCENTAGE OF LOBBYISTS USING THE TECHNIQUE		
	OVERALL USE	OHIO	WEST VIRGINIA
29. Doing favors for legislative staff	46	43	52
30. Engaging in informal contacts with members of the governor's staff	47	39	60
31. Inspiring letter-writing, telephone, or e-mail campaigns to executive agencies	46	42	54
32. Appearing on radio programs	46	43	52
33. Delivering PAC money (that is, money from an organization rather than personal funds) to candidates for office	43	41	47
34. Appearing on television programs	43	38	51
35. Petitioning for a rule making	39	38	43
36. Filing suit or otherwise engaging in litigation	37	34	44
37. Running advertisements in the media	31	23	44
38. Seeking permits from executive agencies	25	21	31
39. Engaging in informal contacts (for example, wining, dining) with the governor	22	7	48
40. Seeking to put a measure on the ballot as an initiative	19	21	15
41. Engaging in protests and/or demonstrations	19	16	25
42. Doing favors for members of the governor's staff	17	12	26
43. Doing favors for executive agency personnel	15	13	19
44. Doing favors for the governor	14	8	25
45. Giving gifts (for example, athletic tickets, books) to state legislators	9	10	7
46. Giving gifts to state legislative staff	8	6	13

* This table is a full reproduction of the table in the source below. However, in a few instances the "Overall Use" (the average of the two state's percentages) of a technique is one percentage point or so different from that listed.

Source: Anthony J. Nownes, Clive S. Thomas, and Ronald J. Hrebenar, "Interest Groups in the States," in *Politics in the American States: A Comparative Analysis*, eds., Virginia Gray and Russell L. Hanson, 9th ed. (Washington, D.C.: Congressional Quarterly Press. 2008), 107–108.

status quo groups who do not want taxes or regulation, among other changes, are more successful than groups, including outsider groups, that want change through the enactment of new policies.

Maintenance campaigns generally require the least amount of resources, but they still require careful planning and constant reassessment as political circumstances change.

Contemporary Strategies and Tactics

Contrary to general belief, a lobbying campaign does not entirely consist of continual direct contact with public officials. Much of the campaign involves such activities as planning and organizing, monitoring what government is doing that might affect the group, and in many cases working to get people who are sympathetic to its cause elected or appointed to office. Table 15.2 makes this clear. The table, by Nownes and Freeman, is the result of surveys of lobbyists in Ohio and West Virginia. While the table covers only two states, the Hrebenar-Thomas study confirms that it is more or less representative of the fifty states.[19]

When it comes to direct tactics, by far the most common and still the most effective group tactic is the use of one or more lobbyists and personal contacts with public officials and their staffs. This is clearly evident in Table 15.2. Since the 1960s, however, changes in interest group activity, particularly the competition between groups for the ear of public officials, have forced groups to supplement the role of the lobbyist with other direct and indirect lobbying tactics. Particularly evident is the increased use of money, the courts, and ad hoc issue coalitions.

Since the mid-1960s, there has been a significant increase in spending by certain interest groups both in their lobbying efforts in state capitals and in campaign contributions by group members, lobbyists, and PACs to state level candidates. PACs, in particular, have become major campaign fund providers in the states.[20] Regardless of the significance of political parties in a state, the money triangle of elected officials, lobbyists, and PACs is very significant.

Because of the role state courts play—like their federal counterparts—in interpreting their respective constitutions, some interest groups have increasingly turned to the courts to achieve their goals. The business community often challenges the constitutionality of regulations in the courts, and groups that cannot get the legislature to act or the administration to enforce mandated functions also often use the courts. This was done in the litigation in the 1980s and 1990s over the Alaska legislature's mishandling of the Mental Health Trust lands. More and more, too, interest groups—business groups, attorneys, and liberal cause groups—are getting involved in the selection and election or retention of judges.

Viewing state lobbying efforts as being conducted by individual groups alone can be misleading. Coalitions of groups and particularly ad hoc issue coalitions are increasingly important. Entering coalitions is the sixth most used lobbying technique according to Table 15.2. To be sure, groups with common long-term goals and a similar philosophy have been natural allies for years—business and professional groups, social issue and public interest groups, for example—and have always used coalitions when it was to their advantage. But today certain issues, such as economic development, health care costs, and education quality, affect a wide range of groups, sometimes cutting across ideological lines and dividing traditional allies. This has produced a new type of coalition—the ad hoc coalition. This usually consists of a number of groups and may last for no more than the life of a legislative session or for the life of an initiative or referendum campaign. The campaign to deal with increasing health care costs is a good example. In many states it has brought together business groups (particularly small business), farm groups, universities, local governments, and social issue and antipoverty groups.

As Table 15.2 indicates, however, even though modern technologies such as computers and television have expanded their options, group strategy and tactics are still very much an art and not a science. The essence of this art is interpersonal communications from an advocacy perspective between group members, leaders, and staff on the one side, and policy makers on the other. In fact, the new techniques and indirect tactics are simply more sophisticated means to increase the effectiveness of group contacts in the policy arena. The success of a lobbying campaign ultimately depends on some form of direct tactics, and this is likely to always be the case.

Explaining the Differences in Strategy and Tactics in Alaska

Virtually all of the strategies and tactics explained here are used in Alaska. And with the increasing nationalization of interest group activity, there is more and more commonality between Alaska and other states in the operation of groups in the policy process. Alaska has been influenced by developments such as the rise of PACs, ad hoc coalitions, and intergovernmental lobbying. The ways in which lobbying strategies and tactics vary in Alaska are largely a result of its small population, which gives rise to friends and neighbors politics, and because of some particular institutional arrangements.

Friends and neighbors politics allows relatively easy access by lobbyists and group members to legislative and executive officials and their staff, and means that there has been less need for the extensive use of many of the new techniques of lobbying. The use of these new techniques is also less necessary because, with its relatively small number of groups, Alaska has not experienced the level of increased and often intense competition among groups—so-called hyperpluralism—that has spawned the use of these new techniques in states like California, New York, and Florida.

Three examples of particular institutional factors that shape strategies and tactics in Alaska are as follows. First, as explained in Chapter 13 on political parties, most major economic groups are not strongly allied with a particular party, as is the case in many states, particularly those in the upper Midwest and Northeast. Second, there are some constraints imposed by Alaska's unified executive, making it difficult for an interest to drive a political wedge between the governor and a department, as can be done in states with plural executives like California and Washington State. And third, Alaska's nonpartisan merit system of appointing and retaining judges reduces the involvement of interest groups in the selection of judges.[21]

6. LOBBYISTS AND THE LOBBYING COMMUNITY IN ALASKA

In all states and in Washington, D.C., even though group members often contact policy makers directly, it is the lobbyist who is the key person linking the group to the public official. This is the case even in the friends and neighbors politics of Alaska. As an essential element, often the major aspect, of a group or organization's strategy and tactics, lobbyists' interactions with public officials are an important part of the dynamics of how personalities affect power relationship in politics. To explain the role of the lobbyists, and to assess whether their role is similar or different in Alaska, we first differentiate between the types of lobbyists, then examine the lobbyist's job and the tools of the trade, and finally look at the Alaska lobbying community.

Five Types of Lobbyists

Most members of the public see all lobbyists as the same and refer to them generically as such. Until recently, this was also how political scientists viewed them. Lobbyists were usually labeled professional or amateur, but this was a hazy distinction. The fifty-state Hrebenar-Thomas study dealt with this haziness by distinguishing five types of lobbyists.

Making a distinction between types of lobbyists is important because different types of lobbyists have different assets and liabilities, and thus are perceived differently by public officials. Such perceptions determine the nature and extent of the lobbyist's power base. In turn, the nature and extent of this power base affects the way a lobbyist approaches his or her job of accessing and influencing public officials. These five types with their major attributes are set out in Box 15.4.

The Job and Role of the Lobbyist

Earlier we defined a lobbyist as a person designated by an interest group to facilitate influencing public policy in that group's favor. Expanding on this, besides this essential role of contacting public officials directly, we can identify other tasks that can be part of the lobbyist's job. So a more comprehensive definition is as follows:

> A lobbyist is a person designated by an interest or interest group to facilitate influencing public policy in that group's favor by directly contacting public officials. The lobbyist's job also usually includes: (1) monitoring political and governmental activity; (2) advising on political strategies and tactics; and (3) developing and orchestrating the group's lobbying effort.

BOX 15.4

The Five Types of Lobbyists across the Fifty States: Their Recruitment, Gender, and Approximate Percentage of the State Capital Lobbying Community

1. CONTRACT LOBBYISTS

Contract lobbyists are hired for a fee specifically to lobby. They often represent several clients. Approximately 20 percent represent five or more clients.

Recruitment: Many are former elected or appointed state officials, usually legislators, political appointees, or legislative staffers. Some are former in-house lobbyists. An increasing number are attorneys from capital law firms as well as public relations and media specialists.

Gender: Contract lobbyists are predominantly men, ranging from 75 to 85 percent of the total, higher in less diversified state group systems and in parts of the South and West.

Percentage: Contract lobbyists constitute 15 to 25 percent of the capital lobbying community, higher in diversified state group systems, such as New York and California.

2. IN-HOUSE LOBBYISTS

In-house lobbyists are employees of an association, organization or business who act as lobbyists in the course of their jobs. For some it is one part of their job; for others lobbying is their entire job. So in-house lobbyists represent one client only—their employer.

Recruitment: Most have experience in the profession, business, trade, or other activity that they represent, such as education, health care, or banking. They are less likely than contract lobbyists to have been public officials.

Gender: Approximately 75 percent are men.

Percentage: This category constitutes from 30 to 35 percent of the lobbying community—likely the largest category of lobbyists in almost all state capitals.

3. GOVERNMENT LOBBYISTS AND LEGISLATIVE LIAISONS

Most state agencies, local governments, and federal agencies appoint a person designated as a legislative liaison to monitor relations with the legislature and to represent them there and to state agencies. The title varies considerably from agency to agency and state to state. Like in-house lobbyists, legislative liaisons also represent only one interest.

Recruitment: Legislative liaisons are often career bureaucrats with broad experience in the agency or government unit that they represent. Some are political appointees, and an increasing number are recruited from the ranks of legislative staffers.

Gender: Approximately 25 to 35 percent of legislative liaisons are women, with the higher end of the range in more economically and socially diverse states.

Percentage: It is difficult to estimate the percentage because most states do not require government personnel to register as lobbyists. An estimate for all government lobbyists is 25 to 30 percent, with the higher end of the range in states where state and local government employment is highest, especially in the West.

4. CITIZEN, CAUSE, OR VOLUNTEER LOBBYISTS

This category consists of persons who represent citizens' and community organizations or informal groups, usually on an ad hoc and unpaid basis. They rarely represent more than one interest at a time.

Recruitment: There are too many variations for any pattern of recruitment to be discernible, but most are very committed to their cause.

Gender: The gender breakdown is also difficult to estimate as most citizen lobbyists are not required to register. However, it appears that the majority, and in some states as high as 70 percent, are women.

Percentage: The best available estimate for this category is from 10 to 20 percent of the lobbying community.

5. PRIVATE INDIVIDUAL, "HOBBYIST," OR SELF-STYLED LOBBYISTS

These are people who act on their own behalf and are not designated by any organization as an official representative. They usually lobby for pet projects, direct personal benefits, or against some policy or proposal that they find particularly objectionable.

Recruitment: Other than self-recruitment, there is no common pattern.

Gender: This is difficult to estimate as many are not required, or choose not, to register as lobbyists. Most are probably men, but this will vary from time to time, from state to state, and from issue to issue.

Percentage: This is also difficult to estimate, but is probably less than 5 percent.

Source: Compiled by the authors from the original and the five updates of the Hrebenar-Thomas study.

Depending on the group or organization, the issue, and the political circumstances, more emphasis may be placed on one or more of these aspects of the job than on others. Lobbyists are called upon to make many decisions and to offer various forms of political advice to their clients and organizations.

As we also noted earlier, lobbyists are not only key to the role of interest groups but also to the successful working of the democratic process. Their key role in dealing with public officials is to provide information. Public officials, from legislators to administration officials to members of state boards and commissions, rely heavily on lobbyists for technical information, and often political information (who is for or against a proposal and why, among other things). Because lobbyists are indispensable to democracy, if they did not exist someone would have to invent them. But as we also noted, the tension between the necessity and possible abuses by lobbyists and the interests they represent is a continual challenge for all democracies, including Alaska.

In terms of the way they operate in the policy process, three common public perceptions are that lobbyists tell only one side of the story, often twist the arms of public officials, and spend a lot of time wining and dining them. All three are far less than half truths. A common denominator of all lobbyists—contract, in house, legislative liaison, volunteer, or individual—is that as a foundation of their basic role of providing information, they seek to build a reputation for honesty, trust, and credibility with those they lobby in order to enhance the impact of their message. Lobbyists certainly put a spin on their side of an issue as part of their job of representing their client or organization. But lobbyists' credibility and trust will be destroyed with public officials if they do not alert them to the other side of the story and do not present accurate information. Plus, no one likes to have their arm twisted, to be put in a corner, or to feel intimidated. This is particularly true of politicians who are used to calling the shots and often have big egos. Third, while wining and dining is still a part of some lobbyists' way of doing business, public disclosure laws, restrictions on spending, and increased legislative professionalism have reduced this considerably. Evidence of the decreased importance of wining and dining and giving gifts is that they rank relatively low in the list of lobbying techniques in Table 15.2. This table was constructed in the late 1990s, but if the survey were conducted again today, wining and dining and gift giving would probably rank even lower.

At bottom, being a good lobbyist takes calculated and skillful personal judgment, including who to lobby, when to intervene or withdraw from the lobbying process, and the most appropriate strategies and tactics to use. Also, particularly in small organizations or shoestring operations, the lobbyist's job may be to work to keep harmony within his or her organization. In essence, the job of the lobbyist is a sophisticated form of interpersonal communications in a fluid political environment. So it takes a particular temperament to be a good lobbyist. It takes a person who likes dealing with people, who has patience, who is not easily riled or offended when politicians dismiss them or sometimes lambaste them, who can be pleasantly but firmly persistent, and who has a good sense of political timing, among other personal assets. Consequently, not everyone is suited to be a lobbyist.

Beyond this, focusing on the different types of lobbyists is important to fully appreciate their particular methods of access and influence. For instance, as Box 15.4 shows, although they get the most publicity because of their often high fees, contract lobbyists constitute only about 20 percent of the lobbying community, with in-house lobbyists and legislative liaisons each constituting between 25 and 35 percent, depending on the state. Also, different types of lobbyists have different patterns of recruitment and power bases.

Contract lobbyists are usually hired primarily for their knowledge of the political and governmental system and their close contacts with public officials. Often referred to as "hired guns," contract lobbyists do not necessarily have technical knowledge among their major assets, though some certainly do. What they usually possess is special knowledge of certain parts of the governmental process—for example, the budget or a particular department—and so they may be used by legislators and other officials to assist in the policy-making process. They also often have a great influence on which candidates their clients will support with campaign contributions. Many contract lobbyists also organize fundraisers for candidates and work in other ways to help them get elected or reelected. They usually represent clients with important economic influence, and this fact is not lost on public officials.

On the other hand, the major political asset of many in-house lobbyists is their unequaled knowledge in the area of concern of their organization or business. This is often supplemented by campaign contributions in cash and in kind and their ability to mobilize their membership. Government lobbyists, in contrast, have only one major weapon—information—though they can, and often do, utilize their client groups to their advantage. Volunteer lobbyists usually rely on moral suasion to sell their cause to public officials. They may also provide information not available elsewhere, but they usually lack the status of political insiders or access to big campaign contributions and sophisticated organizations. Self-styled individual lobbyists have the fewest political assets of all, unless they have been major campaign contributors. These differing assets and liabilities affect the way that public officials view these lobbyists, and this in turn will partly determine their power base.

All these developments have contributed to the old back-slapping, wheeler-dealer contract and in-house lobbyist largely passing from the lobbying scene in state capitals, as in the person of an Artie Samish, the legendary lobbyist and political boss of California in the 1940s.[22] Besides the rise of lobby laws and increased transparency, another reason is that today's issues are more complex, and many more lobbying campaigns involve getting legislation passed. The old wheeler-dealer was not much of a technical expert; he was more adept at killing than promoting legislation. However, the most successful lobbyists today are wheeler-dealers under a more sophisticated guise. Like the old wheeler-dealers, they realize the need for a multifaceted approach to establishing and maintaining good relations with public officials. In addition, the modern-day wheeler-dealer is very aware of the increased importance of technical information, the increased professionalism and changing needs of public officials, and the higher public visibility of lobbying. The result is a low-keyed, highly skilled, and effective professional who is a far cry from the old public image of a lobbyist.

Women Lobbyists

Until the early 1970s, very few women were lobbying in state capitals. Today that has changed considerably, and women are making steady advances as professional and volunteer advocates, though these advances vary across the five types of lobbyists, as Box 15.4 shows. Even today there are few women contract lobbyists. So it does look like the good-old-boy element is still working regarding this low percentage of women contract lobbyists.[23]

On the other hand, an increasing number of women fill the ranks of in-house lobbyists and legislative liaisons. Women who are in-house lobbyists, however, are more likely to represent associations and nonprofits than businesses. It is probably in the legislative liaison category that women have made the most advances as political advocates across the nation and in Alaska. The cause or volunteer lobbyist category has likely always been dominated by women, and is today. But much of this information is based on educated guesses because of the lack of statistics on the volunteer category.

Alaska's Lobbying Community

Over the years, Alaska has had its share of colorful and good-old-boy contract and in-house lobbyists, including Lew Dischner, Wes Coyner, Waco Shelley, Bob Manners, and Alex Miller, who went around with an unlit cigar in his mouth. Several contract lobbyists have been around for decades, including Kent Dawson, Kim Hutchinson, Sam Kito, and Ashley Reed. There have also been several woman contract lobbyists, such as Sharon Macklin and Thyes Shaub, and more recently Wendy Chamberlain and Mary Sattler. As in the rest of the states, though, women are more likely to be in-house lobbyists (like Kathy Wasserman of the Alaska Municipal League) or legislative liaisons (like Wendy Redman, who "lobbied" for the University of Alaska for many years).

A practitioner's view on lobbying is provided in Box 15.5 by contract lobbyist Wendy Chamberlain. This practical perspective corroborates the general points from academic

BOX 15.5

Being a Lobbyist: An Inside Perspective on the Image versus the Day-to-Day Realities

When people ask me what I do, my answer often gets the same response: "Oh," followed by silence. If they can overcome their surprise, the next question is frequently, "How did you become a lobbyist?"

No one grows up wanting to be a lobbyist—most of us get into the business by a series of unforeseen circumstances.

As a registered nurse, born and raised in Australia, I knew nothing about American politics. Marriage brought me to the U.S. in the late 1970s, where I took a job working with abused children. After several years, I became frustrated because the system was failing these kids. So I become a champion for their cause and got my first lessons in advocacy, armed with all the passion of a committed volunteer lobbyist. I met with local and state officials and traveled to Juneau several times advocating for tougher child abuse laws. I loved the excitement of the capitol building—it appeared to be "where everything happens."

Soon I moved to Juneau and became a legislative staffer. As I got to know many of the lobbyists on a first-name basis, I also began to see the different lobbying styles, and I knew which lobbyists I trusted and which lobbyists I liked. Then I took a job with Governor Hickel's administration as the legislative liaison for the Department of Commerce. In essence, I lobbied the legislature on department issues, but because of the negative perception of "lobbyist," governments don't use that term. So I got my second major experience as a lobbyist. Then, in 1996, I joined former House Speaker Joe Hayes's government relations firm as a contract lobbyist and eventually established the contract lobbying firm Legislative Consultants.

A lobbyist's effectiveness has little to do with the *type* of lobbyist they are (contract, in-house, volunteer lobbyist, or legislative liaison)—it is about the *kind* of lobbyist they are. There is one indispensable quality needed to make a successful lobbyist—credibility. This very much relates to the fact that the lobbyist's stock in trade is information: information about issues and information on the customer (the legislator). Legislators have to know the information you provide is accurate and that you have given them all the facts. If you are asking for their support, they need to know every side of the issue and be as well-informed as possible. To present this information in the most effective way, it is critical that lobbyists know each legislator well—their lives, families, education, hobbies, likes, dislikes, and most importantly their election districts. A legislator from a commercial fishing district may well be difficult to lobby on some sport fishing issues; a union member will be more inclined to support union issues.

The importance of doing my homework was made clear early in my career. I met with a legislator to lobby for a tort reform bill that reduced court awards and capped attorney fees. As he had three children and worked in real estate, I assumed he'd support my issue. When I began explaining who opposed my issue he put his hand up and said, "no need to explain the opposition, as an attorney, my colleagues and I will be your opposition." It turned out he worked in the legal department of a large real estate firm. Clearly, I had not done my homework.

Every lobbyist's style is different. Some prefer the social aspect of lobbying and do most of their work at dinners or on the golf course. Others come from the "good ol' boy" era and work hard at maintaining close personal relations with legislators. Some lobbyists are rather aggressive, others are quiet and unassuming. No one style guarantees success. In the end it comes down to hard work, knowing your issue, and maintaining your credibility even if it means losing the issue.

Lobbying for a living is a wonderful, intense, and fun job, but like any job it has highs and lows. The hardest thing is losing—I don't think I will ever get used to it. This is particularly hard on issues you feel passionate about and on which you feel you can make a difference, but you still lose. Even legislators who are your very good friends may vote against your issues a majority of the time. You have to learn to leave it at work. I think the best lobbyists have a life outside of politics. From what I've observed, many lobbying corruption scandals in Alaska and elsewhere involve lobbyists who are "politicos" whose lives are obsessed with winning at the game of politics at almost any price.

Source: Written by Wendy Chamberlain, Alaska contract lobbyist and owner of Legislative Consultants.

research outlined earlier about the job of the lobbyist. The box also shows that the lobbyist's role in Alaska is very similar to that in other states. But because of the small population and the lack of economic diversity, the characteristics of Alaska's lobbying community differ in some ways from those in many states.

For instance, unlike Washington, D.C., and large population states, contract lobbyists in Alaska usually have a broad range of clients, from local governments to tourist organizations to mining to oil companies. This is because there is not the diversity of economic interests or a large number of groups to be able to specialize in, for example, local government or insurance lobbying. Alaska's lobbying corps is small compared with many states. The number of registered lobbyists has ranged from 130 to 300 since the early 1980s. Meaningful comparisons between states, however, are not possible as different states have different rules as to who has to register as a lobbyist. California has averaged around 1,200 lobbyists a year, but it requires local governments that lobby to register. Florida, which requires all entities who lobby to register, averages over 2,000 registrations a year. Utah, on the other hand, with similar rules to Alaska, averages between 350 and 400.[24]

So the size of Alaska's lobby corps is not out of proportion with other states, though a more accurate number of those *actually* lobbying in Juneau should include those not required to register as lobbyists—legislative liaisons and other personnel from the various levels of state government departments as well as volunteer lobbyists. While no official figures exist, a rough estimate is to double the official number of lobbyists for Alaska to about 400 each legislative session. Neither are Alaska lobbyists' salaries and fees out of proportion to other states, as we will see in Section 8 on money and Alaska interest groups.

Partly because of the small size of the state and its weak parties, Alaska's contract lobbyists do not openly identify themselves as Democrats or Republicans. This nonpartisanship gives a certain amount of flexibility to certain interest groups and lobbyists in the political environment of Alaska's friends and neighbors politics. This contrasts with Washington, D.C., and states like New Jersey, New York, and Massachusetts. In Alaska, though, as in virtually all states and regardless of partisanship, labor and its lobbyists tend to be less effective when Republicans are in power, and businesses face more challenges when the Democrats control one or more branches of state government. This brings us to the subject of interest group influence in Alaska.

7. THREE PERSPECTIVES ON INTEREST GROUP POWER

A negative attitude toward interest groups often stems from particular notions about interest group power. One such notion is to equate interest groups with dominant political power and the ability to influence politics in a major way and on a continual basis in a country, state, or city. A second is to see lobbying success as all about money—the more an organization has the more powerful it will be. Another perception is to assume that a large membership or the visibility of a group means it has power. Again, there is some truth in all of these beliefs, but they are at best half truths. Many interests that lobby are not major power players, such as those for the arts and the disabled. Moreover, while money is very important, sometimes groups with little or no money, but with other assets, can be successful, and those with major assets may lose. Numbers do not always translate into power, as the decline in labor union influence since the late 1980s attests. And visibility may not result in power, especially if the organization is a fringe group that engages in confrontational politics.

Scholars have found power to be one of the most elusive aspects of interest groups to study.[25] The Hrebenar-Thomas study attempted to deal with these challenges by categorizing interest group power into three types: (1) single group power, (2) overall individual interest power, and (3) group system power.[26] Let us briefly explain each and what they tell us about interest group power in Alaska.

Single Group Power

Single group power is the assessment by a group or coalition of its own power and its ability to achieve its goals as it defines them. The degree of success is an internal evaluation by the group. Some groups can be very successful in achieving their goals but keep a very low profile in a state and not be singled out as powerful by public officials. This might be because the group is only intermittently active, such as an association of nightclub owners working to defeat proposed regulations that would restrict the sale of alcohol on their premises. It could be an ad hoc group coming together on one issue and then disbanding when success is achieved, such as a coalition to defeat a ballot initiative that would limit the hunting of wolves. Or it could be that the group's issue is far from public view and of minor public concern to the public and politicians, such as working with a department to write regulations, as might be the case with chiropractors interested in the occupational licensing process. Rarely are chiropractors seen as among the most effective groups in a state, but they may be among the most successful groups in achieving their limited goals.

No doubt there are numerous groups across the states and in Alaska that are effective by their own assessment. Likely many are involved primarily in the regulatory process and have very low profile public policy concerns. In fact, many groups involved in the regulatory process are very successful because they have captured their area of concern—gained control of policy making—through dependence of bureaucrats on their expertise. The last thing most of these groups want is public attention and to be singled out as an "effective group." However, developing an objective method to assess the relative power of these groups is virtually impossible. This is mainly because such groups are hard to identify, and there are no common criteria for assessing their success other than their own, likely biased, self-assessment. As a result, no assessment of single group power has been conducted, though the factors that constitute this power are identifiable.

Overall Individual Interest Power

Overall individual interest power is the aspect of group power that most fascinates the media and the public, who are less concerned about the minutiae of government and more with high-profile issues and questions such as "who's running the state" or "who's got real political clout." Whereas single group power is assessed internally by each group, overall interest power is based on external assessments of informed observers. It should be pointed out, however, that while it is the high-profile and often "big players" in state politics that are identified as powerful, they do not always win. Some lose as often as they win and may be less influential overall than some low-profile groups not included in the listings.

As the only fifty-state assessment of overall interest power, the Hrebenar-Thomas study has identified developments in this aspect of power over the years including in Alaska. The method of assessment involved a combined quantitative and qualitative approach relying on experts on state politics across the states.

Placing Alaska's Overall Interest Power in Perspective

Tables 15.3 and 15.4 show how Alaska fits today in regard to overall interest power. Table 15.3 is a composite of the Hrebenar-Thomas surveys over the years and shows the most effective groups across the fifty states compared with those in Alaska over the same period. In Table 15.4 the most effective interests in Alaska in the early 1980s are compared with the most effective ones in 2009–2010.

Table 15.3 reveals some noticeable differences between the most effective groups across the fifty states and in Alaska since the early 1980s. Most of these differences reflect the natural resource and government-based economy in Alaska and its lack of agriculture (and agribusiness), manufacturing, and major private businesses, plus the economic and political importance of Alaska Natives. On the other hand, Alaska does reflect the overall political influence of the education, local government, and health care lobbies across the states and that of higher education, environmentalists, and state agencies in general.

Table 15.4 shows that many more groups were listed in Alaska in 2009–2010 as having some level of influence than in the early 1980s. The oil industry and school boards have retained their power over the years, as have individual local governments, particularly the large boroughs. The decline in influence of state employees and K–12 employees

TABLE 15.3

The Most Effective Interests and Interest Groups across the Fifty States and in Alaska from the Early 1980s to 2010

THE FIFTY STATES (Ranking in 2010, followed by rank in early 1980s)		ALASKA	
GROUP 1: CONSISTENTLY THE TWO MOST EFFECTIVE INTERESTS			
1-2	General business organizations (state chambers of commerce, etc.)	**1**	Association of Alaska School Boards (AASB)
2-1	School teachers'/K–12 employees' organizations (NEA—National Education Association, and American Federation of Teachers—AFT)	**2**	Oil industry (Alaska Oil and Gas Association—AOGA; and individual companies)
GROUP 2: CONSISTENTLY AMONG THE TEN MOST EFFECTIVE			
3-6	Utility companies and associations (electric, gas, water, telephone/telecommunications)	**3**	Individual local governments (mainly Anchorage and Fairbanks Boroughs)
4-4	Manufacturers (companies and associations)	**4**	Alaska Department of Education (DOE)
5-17	Hospital/nursing home associations	**5**	Alaska Federation of Natives (AFN)
6-13	Insurance: general and medical (companies and associations)	**6**	Council of Alaska Producers (major metal mining industry)
7-11	Physicians/state medical associations	**7**	Alaska Association of School Administrators (AASA)
8-22	Contractors/builders/developers	**8**	Sports hunting and fishing groups
9-9	General local government organizations (municipal leagues, county organizations, elected officials)	**9**	Alaska Municipal League (AML)
10-8	Lawyers (predominantly trial lawyers, state bar associations)	**10**	National Education Association-Alaska (NEA-Alaska)
GROUP 3: CONSISTENTLY RANKED AMONG THE 11 TO 20 MOST EFFECTIVE INTERESTS			
11-14	Realtors' associations	**11**	State and local government employee unions
12-10	General farm organizations (state Farm Bureaus, etc.)	**12**	Environmentalists
13-3	Bankers' associations	**13**	Communications companies
14-19	Universities and colleges (institutions and employees)	**14**	University of Alaska
15-5	Traditional labor associations (predominantly the American Federation of Labor-Congress of Industrial Organizations—AFL-CIO)	**15**	Associated General Contractors (AGC)
16-15	Individual labor unions (Teamsters, United Auto Workers—UAW, etc.)	**16**	AFL-CIO
17-36	Gaming interests (race tracks/casinos/lotteries)	**17**	Alaska Court System
18-7	Individual banks and financial institutions	**18**	Lawyers
19-29	State agencies	**19**	North Slope Borough
20-23	Environmentalists	**20**	Tourism/hospitality interests

THE FIFTY STATES (Ranking in 2010, followed by rank in early 1980s)		ALASKA	
GROUP 4: RANKED AMONG THE 21-30 EFFECTIVE INTERESTS			
21-16	K-12 education interests (other than teachers/K-12 employees)	**21**	Alaska State Chamber of Commerce (ASCC)
22-18	Agricultural commodity organizations (stock growers, grain growers, etc.)	**22**	National Federation of Independent Business (NFIB)
23-37	Tourism/hospitality interests	**23**	Insurance lobby (mainly medical underwriters)
24-21	Retailers (companies and trade associations)	**24**	Liquor lobby
25-12	State and local government employees (other than teachers/K–12 employees)	**25**	Electric utilities, including rural co-ops
26-35	Sportsmen/hunting and fishing (includes anti-gun control groups)	**26**	Commercial fisherman (esp. United Fisherman of Alaska—UFA)
27-34	Religious interests (churches and Religious Right)	**27**	Hospitals and nursing homes
28-25	Liquor, wine, and beer interests	**28**	Alaska State Medical Association
29-24	Individual cities and towns	**29**	Alaska Women's Lobby
30-37	Pro-life groups	**30**	Various lobbies for children

Source: Developed by the authors from the Hrebenar-Thomas study.

(mainly schoolteachers represented by NEA-Alaska) reflects a national trend of the declining influence of labor (both blue and white collar) likely due to a conservative trend across the nation. The relative decline in Alaska's homegrown environmental movement is likely due to the increased influence of sport fishing and hunting groups (particularly the Outdoor Council) and of natural resource–extraction interests.

What is particularly noteworthy about both tables is the relative stability of the influence of particular interests over time. Despite the major expansion in group activity since the late 1960s, both across the nation and in Alaska, there has been relatively little change in what are considered to be the most effective groups and interests during that time. This fact amplifies the point that increased activity by some groups, the high profile of others, and a large membership does not automatically translate into political power.

Factors Shaping Individual and Overall Group Power

Much of the explanation for this relative stability of group influence and the ineffectiveness of many new interests lies in factors that shape both single group power and overall individual interest power. The Hrebenar-Thomas study identifies twelve of these factors, which are set out in Box 15.6. The two most important factors are how much the government needs a group and the skill of its lobbyists. Also noteworthy is the type of lobbying campaign the group needs to use over the long term. As we noted earlier, those

TABLE 15.4

The Most Influential Interests and Interest Groups in Alaska in the Early 1980s Compared with 2009–10

2009-10	EARLY 1980s
FIRST RANK	
Oil industry (esp. Alaska Oil and Gas Association [AOGA] and individual oil companies, such as British Petroleum and ConocoPhillips Alaska)	Oil industry
Native groups (esp. Alaska Federation of Natives [AFN])	AML and individual municipalities
Council of Alaska Producers (major metal mining industry)	Education lobby (other than teachers/K-12 employees, particularly AASB)
Municipality of Anchorage	State and local government employees (esp., ASEA and APEA)
Fairbanks North Star Borough	NEA-Alaska
Association of Alaska School Boards (AASB)	Environmentalists
Alaska Outdoor Council/Territorial Sportsmen the National Rifle Association (NRA)	
University of Alaska	
SECOND RANK	
National Education Association-Alaska (NEA-Alaska)	Alaska Native groups (esp. AFN)
Alaska Municipal League (AML)	Alascom
American Federation of Labor-Congress of Industrial Organizations (AFL-CIO) and traditional labor unions	Contractors (esp.AGC)
State and local government employees (esp. Alaska State Employees Association [ASEA], Alaska Public Employees Association [APEA])	University of Alaska
Environmentalists (esp. Alaska Environmental Lobby)	AFL-CIO and traditional labor unions
Lawyers (trial lawyers, state bar)	Trial lawyers
Telecommunications lobby (esp. GCI, Alascom and Alaska Telephone Association)	Insurance lobby (esp. medical underwriters)
Liquor lobby (esp. CHARR—Cabaret Hotel and Restaurant Retailers Association).	General business (esp. ASCC)
Contractors (esp. Associated General Contractors {AGC}])	Senior citizens
Electric utilities (including rural co-ops, esp. the Alaska Rural Electric Cooperative Association [ARECA]).	
Insurance lobby (esp. medical underwriters)	
Hospitals and nursing homes	
Alaska State Chamber of Commerce (ASCC)	
National Federation of Independent Business (NFIB)	
Commercial fishermen (esp. United Fisherman of Alaska [UFA])	
Pacific Seafood Processors Association	
Private prison lobby	
Northwest Cruise Ship Association	
Children's lobby	
Alaska Women's Lobby	

Source: Developed by the authors from the Hrebenar-Thomas study.

BOX 15.6

Twelve Factors Determining the Influence of Interest Groups, Group Coalitions, and Lobbyists

1. THE DEGREE TO WHICH PUBLIC OFFICIALS NEED THE GROUP, ORGANIZATION, OR COALITION'S SERVICES AND RESOURCES

The more government needs a group, organization, or coalition the greater its political leverage. This can be in the form of needing support at election time, technical or political information, campaign funds, or support on other issues. For instance, government needs business to keep the economy functioning well, and this need is a major source of business power.

2. LOBBYIST–POLICY MAKER RELATIONS

An important aspect of this, as Wendy Chamberlain points out in Box 15.5, is the trust between lobbyists and policy makers. Building up and solidifying personal contacts, trust, and credibility is often the key to lobbying success. Another aspect is the extent of dependence of public officials on lobbyists and their groups. The more skillful the lobbyist is in creating a state of dependence, the more successful the group is likely to be.

3. WHETHER THE GROUP'S LOBBYING FOCUS IS PRIMARILY DEFENSIVE OR PROMOTIONAL

A group that is trying to stop a policy being adopted has the so-called "advantage of the defense." Business groups, for example, frequently work to prevent the adoption of new regulations beneficial to labor, while environmentalists often attempt to promote new regulatory policies, which is much more difficult to achieve.

4. THE EXTENT AND STRENGTH OF GROUP OPPOSITION

Obviously, the stronger the opposition to a group or its cause the more difficult it will be to achieve its goals. Some groups are natural political enemies, such as environmentalists and developers, and in many cases business and labor. Other interests, such as dentists and those advocating for stricter laws against child abuse, have little opposition.

5. THE LEGITIMACY OF THE GROUP AND ITS DEMANDS—HOW THESE ARE PERCEIVED BY THE PUBLIC AND BY PUBLIC OFFICIALS

A group must be perceived as politically legitimate, but there are degrees of legitimacy and the acceptance of groups and their demands. Groups advocating violence are seen as illegitimate. Others, like doctors and groups advocating against drunk drivers, are given high levels of legitimacy. Still others, like labor unions, are viewed as legitimate, but their demands may sometimes be viewed negatively. And some groups, like those advocating radical and unpopular causes, such as Marxist solutions to socio-economic and political problems in the United Sates, are given low levels of legitimacy in regard to both their goals and tactics.

6. THE POLITICAL, ORGANIZATIONAL AND MANAGERIAL SKILL OF GROUP LEADERS

Lobbying campaigns in any society require organizational and managerial skill—the ability to direct group resources for political purposes—plus knowledge of the political process, particularly its power points. Having group leaders with these skills is an essential element of success.

7. GROUP FINANCIAL RESOURCES

Money by itself does not equate with political power. In order for money to have an effect on policy making, it must be directed at lobbying purposes. At the same time, money is the most liquid of all resources and can be used to hire staff and lobbyists, make campaign contributions, mount media and grassroots campaigns, and so on. Plentiful funds give a group flexibility to use the most effective strategies and tactics.

8. POLITICAL COHESIVENESS OF THE MEMBERSHIP

The more united the group the more likely it is to have its issues dealt with. Public officials are unlikely to take action if they see a group is divided. An essential element of group leadership is ensuring this cohesiveness.

9. SIZE AND GEOGRAPHICAL DISTRIBUTION OF GROUP MEMBERSHIP

Generally, the larger and more geographically distributed the membership of an organization in a governmental jurisdiction is, the more pressure it can bring to bear on more public officials, especially elected officials.

10. POTENTIAL FOR THE GROUP TO ENTER INTO COALITIONS WITH OTHER GROUPS

When a group can join forces with another group or groups, it can potentially overcome its deficiencies with respect to one or more of the previous nine factors.

11. EXTENT OF GROUP AUTONOMY IN POLITICAL STRATEGIZING

While the flexibility to join or leave a coalition can enhance a group's power, belonging to a coalition may mean the group has less control over strategy and tactics. If that happens, its potential for achieving its goals may be compromised, or its goals may not get addressed at all. This is why many businesses and local governments have begun to lobby on their own in recent years, even though they retain membership in their broader trade or local government association.

12. TIMING AND THE POLITICAL CLIMATE

There are times when it is politically propitious to act on an issue and times when it is not. Making judgments on timing is part of the necessary skill set of lobbyists and group leaders. For example, unless a group has a major power base, it is not politically wise to propose major increases in funding for a program in times of declining government revenues or cutbacks in state spending.

Source: Developed by the authors from the original Hrebenar-Thomas study and its five updates.

who want to kill proposals and mount a defensive lobbying campaign have a big advantage in the separation of powers system.

Interest Group System Power

Group system power is the strength of interest groups as a whole in a state in relation to other political organizations and institutions. As indicated earlier, assessing group system power is important because of what it reveals about the relationship and relative power of political institutions in a state and how policy is made. Group system power is determined by a combination of factors. A major one is the relationship between the group system and the strength of political parties as explained in Chapter 13.[27] Stronger parties mean more constrained interest groups. Another factor is the political culture. States that have moralistic (community-regarding) political cultures, such as Maine and Vermont, generally have less powerful group systems than states that have more individualistic cultures, such as Nevada and New Mexico. Other factors include advanced socioeconomic development, a strong executive branch, and competition between groups, particularly in the more economically developed states. These factors increase political pluralism and reduce the likelihood of the domination of a state by one or a few interests.

TABLE 15.5

Regional Classification of the Fifty States by Overall Impact of Interest Groups during 2005–2010

	STATES WHERE THE OVERALL IMPACT OF INTEREST GROUPS IS				
	Dominant	**Dominant/ Complementary**	**Complementary**	**Complementary/ Subordinate**	**Subordinate**
West	+/-/+Hawaii††	- Alaska	Colorado		
	+Nevada*	Arizona	+/-/ -Montana††		
		California	-/+/-Washington†		
		Idaho			
		- New Mexico			
		Oregon			
		-/+Utah†			
		Wyoming			
South	Alabama	Arkansas	North Carolina	-- Kentucky††	
	Florida	Georgia			
		- Louisiana			
		- Mississippi			
		Oklahoma			
		- South Carolina			
		- Tennessee			
		Texas			
		Virginia			
		- West Virginia			
Midwest		+ Illinois	Indiana	- Michigan	
		+ Iowa	Nebraska	Minnesota	
		+ Kansas	North Dakota	- South Dakota	
		+ Missouri	Wisconsin		
		Ohio			

	STATES WHERE THE OVERALL IMPACT OF INTEREST GROUPS IS				
	Dominant	Dominant/ Complementary	Complementary	Complementary/ Subordinate	Subordinate
Northeast		+/+ Delaware††	+/+/+/- Connecticut††	+/-Vermont†	
			Maine		
			+ Maryland		
			Massachusetts		
			New Hampshire		
			New Jersey		
			New York		
			Pennsylvania		
			+ Rhode Island		

* States with a + or – sign have moved once only—up (+) or down (-)—since the original 1985 survey. There are sixteen of these, seven which have moved up and nine down a category.

† Indicates a state that has moved more than once since the first survey but to an adjacent category. There are three of these states. Utah moved twice, from the Dominant/Complementary (DC) to the Complementary (C) category and back again. Washington moved three times, from DC to C, back to DC, and again to the C category. And Vermont moved twice, from the Complementary/Subordinate (CS) to the C category and back again.

†† Identifies states that have moved across three categories since 1985, of which there are five. Hawaii moved from DC to C to the Dominant (D) category. Montana from DC to D to C. Connecticut moved from CS to C to DC and back to C. Delaware from CS to C to DC. And Kentucky moved from DC to CS.

Source: Compiled by the authors from research for the 2007 and 2010 updates of the Hrebenar-Thomas study.

Table 15.5 lists the states by regions according to their level of group system power in the period 2005–2010, with an indication of changes over the duration of the Hrebenar-Thomas study. The five categories in the table are as follows. A "Dominant" system is one in which interest groups, usually one or a few interests, effectively control state politics, as in the early days of most states. At the other end of the scale, a "Subordinate" group system is one consistently subordinated to other aspects of the policy-making process. The absence of any states in this column indicates that groups have not been consistently subordinate in any state since the early 1980s, and likely never in any state. The "Complementary" category is one in which groups are constrained by other governmental and political institutions. The "Dominant/Complementary" and the "Complementary/Subordinate" columns include states whose group systems alternate between the two situations or are in the process of moving from one to the other. The trend since the early 1980s has been for group systems that were once in the dominant or complementary category to move into the dominant/complementary column.

The regions of the nation with the least dominant group systems are the Northeast and the upper Midwest. This is largely because the states in these regions tend to have relatively strong political parties and a strong strain of moralistic political culture. In contrast, and for opposite reasons, most other parts of the nation, especially the South and the West, particularly the Mountain West, have strong, and in some cases, dominant interest group systems.

Placing Alaska's Group System Power in Context

Table 15.5 shows Alaska ranked in the dominant/complementary category that includes twenty-six of the fifty states. Until the late 1980s Alaska was ranked in the dominant column. Its movement to its present category, where it has stayed since the late 1980s, is likely due to the expansion of the number of groups in the state competing for the attention of public officials. It is also likely a product of more open and transparent government and more cohesive legislative caucuses, particularly the Republican caucuses in the legislature. These factors tend to constrain the options of interest groups.

The days of Alaska being dominated by one or a few interests as in Territorial days are likely gone forever. And even though the oil industry is a prominent political force in the state, it is not dominant in the way that the gaming and hospitality industries are in Nevada, largely because of the increased pluralism in Alaska and the fortuitous circumstance that the bulk of Alaska's oil is being pumped from state land.[28]

8. LOBBYING AND MONEY IN ALASKA

While it is true that interests with money do not always win, money and the resources it commands are still important factors in interest group effectiveness, as we saw in considering group power. The consistently successful groups in Alaska and across the states are those with money, and their expenditures have been growing as the competition between interests increases for the attention of public officials. In 2006 the money spent on lobbying across the fifty states topped one billion dollars for the first time. That year more than forty thousand registered lobbyists representing fifty thousand organizations sought to influence the forty thousand laws and \$1.4 trillion in appropriations enacted by state legislatures.[29]

If you pick up a major Alaska newspaper or turn on a radio or TV news show during or just after the legislative session, you will likely read or hear stories with headlines like, "Lobbying the Legislature Is Big Business in Juneau" and "Big Oil Opens Checkbooks to Influence Legislators."[30] But where exactly does Alaska fit in the connection between money and lobbying? We break this general question down into three specific ones: (1) how much money is spent on lobbying in Alaska, (2) how does this compare with other states, and (3) how does it affect Alaska's democracy? Before we get to these questions, however, it is helpful to point out why answering them precisely is much more difficult than it may appear.

Statistical and Assessment Problems

A major reason why it is difficult to make accurate comparative assessments about how money affects Alaska policy making is the lack of consistency from state to state as to how the terms *lobbying* and *lobbyist* are defined. Generally, the state agencies responsible for monitoring spending by lobbyists include only money spent by organizations on direct lobbying of the legislature and executive branches and on lobbyists' fees and salaries. Also excluded are expenditures on elections by groups through PACs (though most states record these); lobbying by group members (if they expend their own funds), as these are hard to track; many expenditures on public relations and media campaigns; and filing briefs in the courts. Moreover, as we have seen, in defining a lobbyist most states exclude those lobbying for state, federal, and local government agencies.

The variations in definitions and record keeping have two consequences for the accuracy of the actual amount of money spent on lobbying in Alaska and across the fifty states. First, the narrow definitions and exclusion of government employees as lobbyists means that the reported figures are much less than the actual amount spent on lobbying, maybe less than half the actual figure. Second, the variations in reporting requirements make comparison among states less than precise.

In addition, to compare total dollar amounts spent on lobbying would tell us very little. In fact, it would be rather meaningless to compare total lobby spending in California, with its more than thirty-five million people and a large number of registered groups, to states with fewer than a million inhabitants, like Alaska and Montana, with a much smaller number of registered groups. For this reason, per capita spending comparisons are more useful, though still not ideal.

Answering the third question of how spending might affect, even undermine, Alaska's democracy, is fraught with difficulties. In particular, the use of different criteria for judging the extent of democracy can lead to different conclusions. As with the problems with statistics, we can nonetheless use criteria that do provide some valuable insights into the answers to all three questions.

Lobby Spending in Alaska

How much is spent on lobbying in Alaska, and who are the big spenders? Like all states, lobby spending in Alaska has increased since the late 1970s, as more and more groups engage in lobbying and the competition with other groups becomes more intense. Figure 15.2 provides a contemporary look at lobby spending in Alaska. Lobby spending over the ten years from 2004 to 2014 is shown in Figure 15.2A, and spending by the top lobbies in the year 2013 is shown in Figure 15.2B.

FIGURE 15.2

Spending on Lobbying in Alaska 2004–2014

FIGURE 15.2A

Total Spent on Lobbying in $ Millions Per Year from 2004–2014

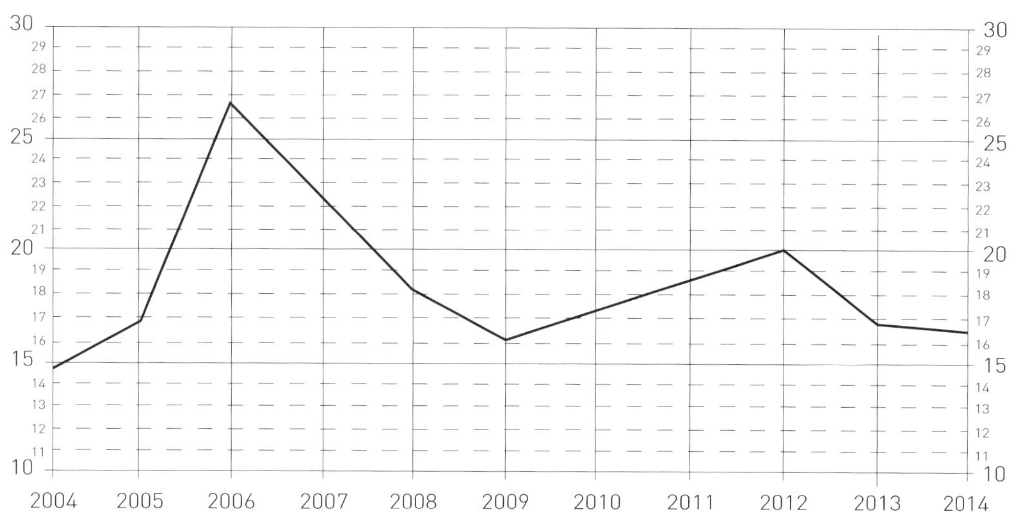

FIGURE 15.2B

Spending in 2013 by Major Interest Group Categories

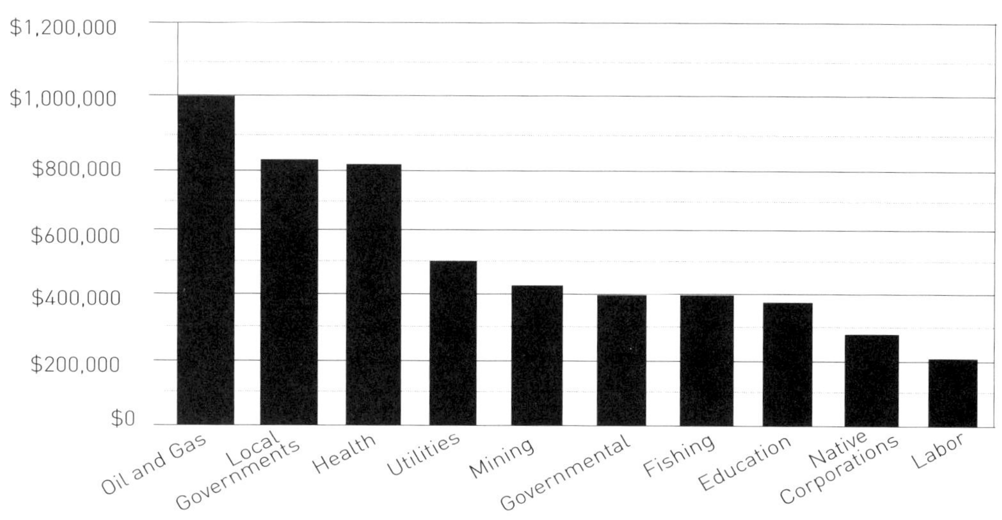

Source: Adapted from a APRN (Alaska Public Radio Network) news story by Alexandra Gutierrez, August 1, 2013; graphics by Josh Edge. Used with permission. Data added by the chapter authors from APOC Online Reports, "Lobbyist Summary for 2013 and 2014," at https://aws.state.ak.us/ApocReports/Lobbying/LobbyistSummary.aspx.

Lobby spending between 2004 and 2014 ranged from just under $15 million to close to $27 million. The variation and the peak in 2006 can be explained, in part, by a push by the oil industry that year for a tax decrease and the subsequent VECO scandal that resulted in increased restrictions on lobby spending and many interests keeping a lower profile for a few years after. In addition, Alaska moved from a 120- to a 90-day legislative session beginning in 2007. The spending trend, however, is likely to be at least stable and most probably upwards and will be considerably higher in years when there are high profile issues before the legislature, especially those involving major interests like the oil industry.

As to spending by individual interests, Figure 15.2B shows that in 2013 the oil industry topped the list with its major successful lobbying effort to secure a reduction in production taxes. Local government and the health care industry were not far behind. In fact, many local governments use their elected and appointed officials to lobby, often in addition to hiring a contract lobbyist. As a result, local governments may outspend the oil industry on lobbying with these so-called hidden expenditures.

To the average Alaskan, this may seem like a lot of money to spend on influencing government unless the interests are getting something in return.[31] And, of course, they do get something in return—there would be little point in spending the money if they did not benefit from it over time. In fact, the cost benefit to the big spenders can often be substantial. Again, we can use the example of oil and local government: the $1 million that the oil industry spent on lobbying in 2013 (and even more in 2011 and 2012) helped secure a tax cut that is estimated to yield them about $1 billion a year. And local governments can benefit tremendously from hiring a lobbyist. For example, in 2013 the City of Unalaska paid contract lobbyist Ray Gillespie about $80,000 to help them secure $6 million for water treatment plants.[32]

Comparisons with Other States

Between the late 1970s and 2010, lobbying per capita expenditures, after adjusting for inflation, more than tripled across the fifty states and increased fivefold in Alaska. We can use more recent per capita spending in four states for comparison and also compare lobbyists' earnings. Looking first at California and Connecticut—two states with diverse group systems—California had a population in 2010 of 35 million, and Connecticut, a much smaller state, about 3.4 million. Alaska's population in 2010 was 710,000. Alaska's per capita spending on lobbying that year was about $26, compared with $8 in California and $11 in Connecticut. Even in 2011, a record year for lobby spending in California at $285 million, Alaska (with total spending at just under $20 million and far from a record year for lobbying spending in the state) still outspent California by over 3 to 1 per capita ($26 to $8).[33] In that same year, in Montana, a western state with a population close to Alaska's at one million, spending on lobbying was $5.70 per Montanan—just about one-fifth of Alaska's spending.[34] And according to Peter Quist, Research Director of the nonpartisan National Institute for Money in State Politics, Wisconsin, with eight times the population of Alaska and a much larger state budget, spends only about one-fifth per resident on lobbyists compared to Alaska.[35]

As to the compensation of contract lobbyists, Alaska is in the top five of the fifty states and has been for several years. Between 2005 and 2015 several lobbyists, including Jerry Mackie, Ashley Reed, Kent Dawson, Bob Evans, and Wendy Chamberlain, were each paid total fees well in excess of $500,000 a year representing multiple clients, with Dawson, Evans, and Chamberlain receiving over $1 million in some years. By comparison, some contract lobbyists in Texas have made well over $1 million a year since the mid-1990s and in recent years some in excess of $2 million.[36] However, at most perhaps 1 or 2 percent of all lobbyists in Alaska and across the states are paid these kinds of fees or earn high salaries. Most in-house lobbyists make in the $50,000 to $150,000 range, as do legislative liaisons. And several contract lobbyists make less than some senior in-house lobbyists working for organizations or businesses.

In regard to spending by individual groups and their PACs, state comparisons for particular groups are not very useful because much depends on whether it is an election year and whether a group has a major issue of concern. And, obviously, interests with major resources, like the oil industry in Alaska, high tech in California, and bankers in Connecticut, have much more flexibility in this regard than many citizen groups that run on a shoestring.

The Implications: Lobbying Spending and Alaska Democracy

Alaska is clearly an outlier in much of its spending on lobbying and lobbyists. Exactly why there is so much spending on these activities compared with other states is not easy to explain. It is likely in part due to the high cost of doing business in Alaska. Kara Mariarty, who is president and CEO of AOGA (the Alaska Oil and Gas Association), and who is also an in-house lobbyist for the organization, points out that there is a lot at stake for oil companies and other natural resources firms operating in Alaska. So it is not surprising that they spend a lot on lobbying.[37]

More important than how much is spent on lobbying is what its effects are on the policy process in Alaska and particularly Alaska's democratic system. Despite what the high spending might lead us to believe, money does not appear to exert undue influence. In fact, money is probably less significant today than it was during Territorial days and the early days of statehood, the occasional lobbying scandal notwithstanding, which involves isolated cases and relatively small sums of money.

Evidence for this less significant role of money overall lies in the less dominant role of the interest group system and of the mixed successes of prominent interests like oil, business, and labor, as explained in the last section on interest group power. This curb on the overall influence of money is true in most other states as reflected in fewer and fewer states being dominated by interest groups. Nevertheless, money and the resources it can command for an interest group have long been a concern among the public and some politicians. It is to this concern, among others, about interest groups that we now turn.

9. CONCERNS ABOUT INTEREST GROUPS AND THEIR REGULATION

In part due to the tension between the positive and negative aspects of the public role of interest groups, there have long been concerns about the role of interest groups in democratic political systems. These concerns are of four major types. First, interest groups are far from ideal in that they do not represent all segments of society equally but are biased toward the better educated, higher income, majority culture (whites in most states), and toward men. Second, those groups that have the most resources, particularly business firms, trade associations, and professional associations, tend to be the most politically successful. Third, extensive resources—including, money, good lobbyists, and favored status with government officials—mean that some groups and organizations exert power out of all proportion to the number of their members or employees. In some instances, a powerful interest can thwart the will of a much larger number of people. And fourth, because the stakes are sometimes so high, a few interest groups and lobbyists may resort to illegal means to achieve their policy goals.

These concerns resulted in the widespread regulation of interest groups and their lobbyists, with Arkansas being the fiftieth state to pass such laws in 1988.[38] In Alaska, as in other states, this regulation has helped transform the lobbying environment. To be effective, lobby laws must be part of a wider set of good governance provisions that apply to elected and, in some cases, appointed officials. The major ones are campaign finance provisions (including public disclosure of, and limitations and prohibitions on, some campaign contributions, and regulation of PACs), financial disclosure and conflict of interest provisions for elected and appointed officials, and governmental ethics laws. Here, however, we focus only on lobby laws. Even within the context of wider provisions for good governance and public disclosure, lobby laws have limitations in terms of what they can achieve. Consequently, understanding the provisions of lobby laws in Alaska will be made easier if we first explain the strengths and weaknesses of such laws.

Assessing State Lobby Laws: Their Strengths, Limitations, and Effects

Across the nation, lobby laws have achieved considerably less than many would have hoped, and this has caused disappointment among many Americans and Alaskans. Part of the explanation is a lack of consensus and understanding about what such laws should and can achieve. Other factors are constitutional tensions and political realities.[39]

Perspectives about the purpose of lobby laws range from the notion that they should even up the political playing field to preventing abuses by powerful interests to informing public officials and the public as to the connections between those lobbying and those being lobbied. Whatever their perceived purposes, experience shows that lobby laws cannot turn hitherto powerless groups into powerful forces, nor reduce the political clout of existing influential groups, which is evident from the section above on group power. No democracy can guarantee equal power of all interests by law or any other means. What can be done, as in Alaska, is to try to prevent potential abuses and to publicize the activities of lobbyists. Some democracies, like those in Western Europe, particularly Sweden, also guarantee the access of some groups to government decision making by providing financial support to engage in political advocacy for groups that represent elements of society that would not otherwise have a place at the table, such as newly arrived immigrants. Such provisions, however, run against the political grain in the United States.

There is, however, a deeply rooted tension involved in regulating interest groups. This tension stems from the right of groups to represent their causes to government, guaranteed by the right to "petition government" in the First Amendment to the U.S. Constitution, set against the potential abuses and questions about the extent to which groups are representationally biased. These abuses and biases may and often do undermine the public interest and democracy and promote the benefit of a single, often a very small, segment of society at the expense of society as a whole.

As a consequence, debates about lobby laws in the states revolve around the extensiveness of regulation and monitoring. However, lobby laws are rarely developed in a systematic and comprehensive way, weighing the pros and cons of various alternatives. History clearly shows that the major impetus for these laws are political scandals that raise public consciousness.[40] As a result, most lobby laws are enacted on an ad hoc basis and often within a highly charged political atmosphere.

Furthermore, evidence suggests that most politicians pay only lip service to the need for new lobby laws or amending existing ones. Most would not deal with the issue unless pressured by their constituents or public opinion in general. After all, incumbents are elected under the present rules and likely benefit from interest group support and by contact with lobbyists. Reform holds the specter of the unknown in the already uncertain world of politics. So legislators' commitment to lobby reform once public concern has peaked is often minimal. Also, agencies that regulate lobbyists are not popular with politicians and their lobbyist friends because in many states, including Alaska, they are also often responsible for administering campaign finance and conflict of interest laws. But perhaps the major reason such agencies and enforcement of the laws are not popular with politicians is that it is not so much the public that makes use of the public disclosure information that is available from these agencies, but the media and candidates running against incumbents. So, the administering agencies are prime targets for being underfunded or even defunded, as Governor Frank Murkowski attempted to do with APOC.[41]

Despite all this, increased regulation does appear to have had a positive effect on the activities of established interests and lobbyists in the states. Restraint in dealings with public officials, greater concern for their group's public image, and increased professionalism of lobbyists, appear to be the three major ones. Lobbyists, especially those representing powerful interests, are less likely to use blatant strong-arm tactics than in the past. As we also noted, regulation and transparency have led to the virtual disappearance of the old wheeler-dealer lobbyist, and interest groups, lobbyists, and politicians are much more concerned about conveying a positive image today than ever before. And while there is pressure in many states to cut funding for lobby monitoring agencies, there is also pressure to make these laws more stringent. For instance, twenty-four states passed disclosure enhancements between 2003 and 2007, and the quality of state lobbying laws are such that forty-seven states are rated higher by the Center for Public Integrity (CPI) than federal lobbying laws.

APOC's Approach to Regulation and Assessing Its Effectiveness

In 1976, during the surge of public disclosure enactments that swept the nation, Alaska made major revisions to its lobby regulations. This law has been revised since, most recently in the 2007–2008 legislature. The law defines a lobbyist in Alaska as anyone who:

> . . . is employed and receives payments, or who contracts for economic consideration, including reimbursement for reasonable travel and living expenses, to communicate directly or through the person's agents with any public official for the purpose of influencing legislation or administrative action for more than 10 hours in any 30-day period in one calendar year; [or] . . . represents oneself as engaging in the influencing of legislative or administrative action as a business, occupation, or profession.[42]

In essence, the Alaska law covers only contract lobbyists as well as in-house lobbyists who work for businesses, associations, and other organizations. It does not cover legislative liaisons or other state and local government personnel or most volunteer lobbyists. In this regard, Alaska's definition of a lobbyist is similar to that in most states.

Those who are included under Alaska's definition of a lobbyist, as well as those who employ them, must comply with the following regulations:

- Register with APOC before engaging in lobbying.
- File regular reports with APOC that are available to the public, with lobbyists filing monthly and employers of lobbyists filing quarterly reports on their activities and expenditures.
- Attend an annual ethics training session.
- Observe restrictions on giving gifts and buying food for public officials.
- While they can contribute to statewide and federal candidates, lobbyists can contribute only to the state legislative candidates in the district in which they reside.

In addition, a legislator cannot work as a lobbyist until one year after leaving the legislature. Penalties are provided for violation of these provisions.[43]

So, as with all states, Alaska's lobby law combines restrictions and prohibitions on lobbyists with public disclosure. Theoretically, this transparency enables any member of the public, the media, or an elected or appointed official to track the relationships between lobbyists and their organizations in the public policy process. But in APOC's case this is not an easy task.

Assessing and Comparing APOC's Effectiveness

In 2003 the CPI ranked Alaska's lobby laws as sixteenth of the fifty states in terms of their stringency and public disclosure provisions. However, the CPI still considered the provisions barely adequate in terms of regulation and providing public information. The reforms in the 2007–2008 legislative session likely put Alaska in the "above adequate" category. The states with the least stringent laws are Pennsylvania, Wyoming, New Hampshire, South Dakota, and Illinois. States with an extensive set of such laws are Washington, Kentucky, South Carolina, Connecticut, and New York.

In a more recent CPI study of the effectiveness of lobby regulation in the fifty states, APOC got a "C" grade, scoring fifty out of one hundred points. This average grade was more the result of lack of easy access to the information that APOC gathers than to a lack of comprehensiveness of its regulations and the stringency of their enforcement, where Alaska still scores higher than most states. Members of the media and the public often encounter problems in acquiring data from the agency.[44] Given the major role of lobby laws in providing transparency and pressure on politicians and lobbyists to act responsibly, better access to APOC data is obviously crucial to the continued success of the agency in achieving the goal of transparency.

Overall, APOC has made a major contribution to the positive climate of lobbying in Alaska. As a consequence, Alaska's politics and government are likely less corrupt, and thus more democratic than before statehood.

The Future of Lobby Regulation

The issue of lobby regulation will be a constantly recurring issue for all states, including Alaska, because the factors that generate concerns about lobbying will always be present. State laws against corrupt lobbyists are no guarantee of eliminating corruption. The vast majority of lobbyists are honest, but because the stakes are often so high there will always be those who will break the law. Not only that, some members of the public and some politicians will always see certain lobbying and related provisions as too loose, while others will see them as too restrictive. Both forces will exert political pressure to change these laws.

Besides these ongoing issues endemic to lobby regulation, three other developments may affect the usefulness of regulation in Alaska. One is that if APOC can get the funds it needs, it can update its online access system and make access to information easier for its citizens. Getting funding for this upgrade, especially in the face of major budget deficits in fiscal years 2015, 2016 and 2017 and likely for some years to come, may take another lobbying scandal or related problem.

The second is the fallout from the *Citizens United v. Federal Election Commission* decision by the U.S. Supreme Court in January 2010, commonly referred to as *Citizens United*. The case struck down the federal provision that prohibited corporations and unions from using their funds to make independent expenditures in support of or in opposition to individual candidates. The ruling also effectively invalidated laws that banned such expenditures in twenty-four states, including Alaska. All these states scrambled in 2010 to amend their laws to comply with the federal decision. To try to counter the effects of the decision, the Alaska legislature passed legislation in April 2010 tightening up campaign finance reporting requirements.[45] Because of the major financial resources business and labor can spend, the *Citizens United* decision has changed the landscape of campaign politics at the national and state levels. All indications are that this decision will put back efforts to even up the political playing field for less well-funded groups and interests in terms of access and influence.

A third development relates to lobbying by government employees. Because most states do not require those working for government to register as lobbyists or to disclose the money that goes into such lobbying, the actual money spent on lobbying activity is not recorded, even though it can be quite substantial given widespread lobbying activities by government employees as part of their official positions. Such spending has become a concern to many citizens, particularly certain conservative and libertarian antigovernment groups and large donors. As a result, there has been a move among these groups to prohibit such spending and lobbying among governments and by private organizations receiving government funds and contracts.[46]

For instance, a measure to promote this goal appeared on the South Dakota ballot in November 2008 but was defeated by a 65 to 35 percent margin. Then, in August 2010 a similar measure appeared on the primary ballot in Alaska but was also defeated by a 61 to 39 percent margin.[47] If passed in any state, such restrictions on lobbying would likely lead to major court challenges under the First Amendment to the U.S. Constitution.

10. CONCLUSION: INTEREST GROUPS, LOBBYING, LOBBYISTS, AND ALASKA'S DEMOCRACY

Drawing on this chapter's treatment of interest groups in general in the American states, and particularly in Alaska, we can answer the three questions we posed at the beginning of the chapter. These are (1) Does interest group activity promote or undermine Alaska's democracy?; (2) What are the characteristics of Alaska's group system, and how does it operate as part of the public policy process?; and (3) How different are interest groups and lobbying activity in Alaska compared with other states and with Washington, D.C.? As the second and third questions throw light on the first we deal with those in combination, weaving in the characteristics of Alaska politics that interest group activity reflect.

In regard to the characteristics of interest groups, their role, their general mode of operation, and potential to abuse their power if unchecked, Alaska's interest group activity is no different from that in other states, in Washington, D.C., or in any other place around the world. Alaska's groups and interests are a major vehicle of political participation, and are a natural consequence of shared interests. Similar types of interests operate in Alaska, using common strategies and tactics, including the services of various types of lobbyists. And the success of groups is determined by how much power (if any) they can bring to bear on the policy process. Moreover, Alaska's group system has gone through similar stages of development—from dominance by a few interests to political pluralism—and reflects other trends in group development across the fifty states and in Washington, D.C., since the early 1960s.

The differences in Alaska's group system and lobbying activity compared with other states, particularly the larger ones in population like California and even medium-sized ones such as Washington State, are due to particular socio-economic, demographic, and political circumstances in Alaska. In particular, the narrowly based natural resource economy, highly dependent on oil and government, and the importance of preserving Alaska as the Last Frontier account for the particular narrow range of interests. Here Alaska's political characteristics of the all-pervasive importance of government, the significant role of external forces, and the tension between developers and environmentalists are particularly evident. The relatively small size of Alaska's population and the fact that the lobbying community is also small and largely nonpartisan, with relatively easy access to policy makers, reflect the state's political characteristics of friends and neighbors politics and elements of bipartisanship.

The most obvious characteristic of Alaska politics that applies here, that of weak party organizations and strong interest groups, provides insights not only into differences between Alaska's group system and that of other states but also into how groups, lobbying, and lobbyists affect Alaska's democracy. Since the late 1980s, Alaska's interest groups overall—that is, its group system—have been categorized as dominant/complementary but not dominant. In this regard, the strength of its group system is similar to that of half the fifty states. Like those other states, it means that Alaska's party-interest group relationship is relatively weak and parties have less control over groups. Thus, groups and their lobbyists have more options in strategies and tactics. However, even though groups are strong in Alaska, no one interest, not even the oil industry, "runs Alaska." Like almost all states today, Alaska has a pluralistic group system, with even the most effective groups sometimes losing their political battles.

This brings us to explain why we argue in this chapter that interest groups, lobbying, and lobbyists are not undermining democracy in Alaska. This situation, however, is not due to the intentions or magnanimity of the groups and interests operating in the system, as our earlier explanation of the clash of their private goals and public roles demonstrated. It is largely due to the development of various constraints and countervailing forces, including an increase in the number of groups and thus increased competition among them; increased professionalism of public officials, group leaders and lobbyists; political ethics, lobby, and campaign finance laws; greater media and public scrutiny of group activity; and increased prosecution of corrupt practices. Another constraining factor is the absence of a powerful oil and gas royalty owners association in Alaska because of state ownership of the vast majority of Alaska's oil fields. This combination of factors, for the most part, prevents any one group or a handful of groups (and thus the group system) from dominating politics and undermining democracy.

Nevertheless, in Alaska, as in all states and democratic political systems, the interest group system is far from egalitarian. The patterns of individual group power that have been more or less constant since the late 1970s are likely to continue in Alaska. Certainly, some outsider groups and those with minimum resources will from time to time score political victories in Juneau. However, it will be those groups and interests with major resources—financial, organizational, and political, mainly through contacts and their access to government—that will exercise influence on a year-to-year basis. This means that, for some time to come, Alaska's interest group system will continue to favor business, the professions, some sectors of labor, and various government agencies. Whether lobbyists are Alaska's heroes or Alaska's villains, then, will depend in large part on one's personal judgment and perspective as to the worthiness of the issues being pursued by the lobbyists.

ENDNOTES

[1] Joe Holbert, "Lobbyists: Are They Alaska's Heroes or Villains?" *Alaska Journal of Commerce*, June 29, 2008.

[2] Organized by Ronald Hrebenar of the University of Utah and Clive Thomas of the University of Alaska in Juneau (now at Washington State University), the Hrebenar-Thomas study was originally conducted in 1984–1985 and updated in 1989, 1994, 1998, 2002, 2007, and for selected states including Alaska in 2010. This study covered a wide range of interest group activity. For an overview of the results, see Clive S. Thomas, Ronald J. Hrebenar, and Anthony J. Nownes, "Interest Group Politics in the States: Four Decades of Developments—the 1960s to the Present," *Book of the States*, vol. 40 (Lexington, KY: The Council of State Governments, 2008): 322–31.

[3] Besides the Hrebenar-Thomas study, other comparative data, particularly on lobbyists and lobby spending, used in this chapter are taken from various sources, mainly state agencies responsible for lobby registration, but also organizations such as the Center for Public Integrity (CPI) and the National Institute on Money in State Politics, both of which are government watchdogs. Because of differences in data collection across the states and by organizations like the CPI, exact comparisons are not always possible. Nevertheless, the data does enable meaningful comparisons to be made between Alaska and other states.

[4] Clive S. Thomas, ed., *Research Guide to U.S. and International Interest Groups* (Westport, CT: Praeger Publishers, 2004), 3–7.

[5] Virginia Gray and David Lowery, "The Institutionalization of State Communities of Organized Interests," *Political Research Quarterly* 54. 2, (2001): 265–284, esp. Fig. 3.

[6] Anthony J. Nownes and Patricia Freeman, "Interest Group Activity in the States," *Journal of Politics* 60 (1998): 96–97.

[7] On First Amendment rights and lobbying, see Ronald J. Hrebenar and Clive S. Thomas, "The First Amendment and the Regulation of Lobbying," in *Guide to Interest Groups and Lobbying in the United States*, eds., Burdett A. Loomis, Peter L. Francia and Dara Z. Strolovitch (Washington, D.C.: Congressional Quarterly Press, 2011).

[8] See Thomas, *Research Guide*, 359–69 for a full explanation of this argument plus a counterargument to this generally accepted theory of the bias of interest group systems.

[9] Mark P. Petracca, *The Politics of Interests: Interest Groups Transformed* (Boulder, CO: Westview Press, 1992), xx.

[10] The attitudes of Americans and Alaskans on interest groups are taken mainly from the Hrebenar-Thomas study and from Robert C. Benedict, "Public Knowledge of and Attitudes Toward Interest Groups and Lobbyists in the United States," in Thomas, *Research Guide*, 135–38.

[11] Martha Bellisle, "Reputation vs. Reality: Lobbying's Top Guns Still Flourishing," *Anchorage Daily News*, January 20, 2001.

[12] On the Abramoff affair and conviction, see Hrebenar and Thomas, "The First Amendment and the Regulation of Lobbying," esp. the insert "Who Is Jack Abramoff, and Why Is He the Most (In) famous Lobbyist Ever?" 386–87; and for an overview of the VECO affair see Chapter 5, Section 7; Chapter 20, Section 1; and Chapter 24, Section 7.

[13] "Survey of 16 Interest Groups in Washington, D.C.," posted December 16, 2007, at http://hotair.com/archives/2007/12/12/poll-among-16-dc-interest-groups-the-least-trusted-is/.

[14] For a consideration of the public's attitude to lobbying and lobbyists, and particularly Barack Obama's position on them, see Conor McGrath, "'They Are Not My People': Barack Obama on Lobbying and Lobbyists," *Journal of Public Affairs* 13, no. 3 (June 2013): 308–28.

[15] Dermot Cole, "This Just In: Pete Kelly Was a Lobbyist in Juneau," *Fairbanks News Miner*, October 19, 2012.

[16] For a fuller account of the expansion in the number of interest groups since the 1960s, see Jeffrey, M. Berry and Clyde Wilcox, *The Interest Group Society*, 5th ed. (New York: Longmans, 2008), Chapter 2, "The Advocacy Explosion."

[17] As a Pacific Northwest state, Washington provides an enlightening comparison with Alaska in many aspects of its interest group system. On the development and current range of groups in Washington State, see Clive S. Thomas and Richard Elgar, "Interest Groups in Washington State: The Political Dynamics of Representation, Influence and Regulation," in *Governing Washington: Politics and Government in the Evergreen State*, eds., Cornell W. Clayton and Nicholas P. Lovrich (Pullman, WA: Washington State University Press, 2011).

[18] Clive S. Thomas and Ronald J. Hrebenar, "Interest Groups in the States," in *Politics in the American States: A Comparative Analysis*, eds., Virginia Gray and Russell L. Hanson, 8th ed. (Washington, D.C.: Congressional Quarterly Press, 2004), 110–12; Anthony J. Nownes, Clive S. Thomas, and Ronald J. Hrebenar, "Interest Groups in the States," in *Politics in the American States: A Comparative Analysis*, eds., Virginia Gray and Russell L. Hanson, 9th ed. (Washington, D.C.: Congressional Quarterly Press, 2008), 107–08; and Nownes and Freeman, "Interest Group Activity in the States," in various places in their article.

[19] As the Nownes and Freeman table was created using data gathered in the late 1990s, it does not include social media—Facebook, Twitter, Linkedin, etc.—as a method of lobbying. No doubt this is becoming increasingly important as it is in many aspects of life. However, as the use of social media is relatively new compared with the other techniques listed, its impact will likely take several years to assess accurately.

[20] For details on the contributions of PACs and interest groups to candidates in the states, see Chapter 14, Section 3, especially Table 14.2.

[21] See Chapter 13, Section 4, and Chapter 17, Section 4.

[22] For an view of the role of a good old boy wheeler-dealer lobbyist, see Arthur H. Samish and Bob Thomas, *The Secret Boss of California: The Life and High Times of Artie Samish* (New York: Crown Publishers, 1971).

[23] Anthony J. Nownes and Patricia Freeman, "Female Lobbyists: Women in the World of 'Good ol' Boys,'" *Journal of Politics* 60 (1998): 1181–1201.

[24] Unless otherwise referenced, statistics on the number of lobbyists, lobbyist salaries, and lobby spending in Alaska and across the states in this section and in Section 9 on lobby spending, are from four sources: the APOC website at http://doa.alaska.gov/apoc/; the CPI website at http://www.publicintegrity.org/; the National Institute on Money in State Politics (NIMSP) website at http://www.followthemoney.org/; and the OpenSecrets website at http://www.opensecrets.org/. The figures

quoted in the chapter are often a composite of statistics from all four websites. It should be noted, however, that most of this material was retrieved in 2013 and 2015, and these organizations regularly update their websites and move some statistics and reports to their archives. If difficulty is still encountered in locating statistics, all four organizations are very responsive to e-mails and phone calls.

[25] See Thomas, *Research Guide*, "Interest Group Power and Influence," 192–96.

[26] Nownes, Thomas, and Hrebenar, "Interest Groups in the States," 115–22.

[27] See Chapter 13, Section 4.

[28] For a consideration of the influence of the oil industry in Alaska, see Chapter 24, Section 7. An assessment of the influence of the local government lobby is presented in Chapter 18, Section 7, and of the education lobby in Chapter 26, Section 4.

[29] Sarah Laskow, "State Lobby Becomes Billion Dollar Business," CPI, Washington, D.C., Press release, December 20, 2006.

[30] Sean Cockerham, "Lobbying the Legislature is Big Business in Juneau," *Anchorage Daily News*, March 26, 2011; and Cockerham, "Big Oil Opens Checkbooks to Influence Legislators," *Anchorage Daily News*, May 31, 2012.

[31] Alexandra Gutierrez, "How Much are Companies Spending Lobbying Juneau?" *Alaska News Nightly*, Alaska Public Radio Network (APRN), July 25, 2013.

[32] Alexandra Gutierrez, "For Alaska Cities, Lobbying Pays," *Alaska News Nightly*, APRN, April 10, 2013.

[33] Patrick McCreevy, "Lobbyists Set Spending Record in Sacramento," *Los Angeles Times*, February 2, 2012.

[34] Charles H. Johnson, "5.7 Million Spent Lobbying Montana Legislature This Session," *Missoulian*, June 6, 2011.

[35] Gutierrez, "How Much Are Companies Spending Lobbying Juneau?"

[36] Texans for Public Justice, "Austin's Oldest Profession: Texas' Top Lobbying Clients and Those Who Serve Them," September 2008, at http://info.tpj.org/reports/austinsoldest07/lobbyists.html.

[37] Gutierrez, "How Much Are Companies Spending Lobbying Juneau?"

[38] For an overview of state lobby laws see, Virginia Gray and Wy Spano, "State and Local Regulation," in Thomas, *Research Guide*, 377–79.

[39] Clive S. Thomas, "Transparency in Public Affairs: Lessons from the Mixed Experience of the United States," in *Challenge and Response: Essays on Public Affairs and Transparency*, eds., Tom Spencer and Conor McGrath, (Brussels: Landmarks Press, 2006), 41.

[40] John M. Broder, "Amid Scandals, States Overhaul Lobbying Laws," *New York Times*, January 24, 2006.

[41] See Chapter 5, Box 5.4, for an overview of the development and authority of APOC and attempts to cut its budget.

[42] Alaska Statutes (AS), 24.45.171(11).

[43] For full details on Alaska's lobby registration requirements, see *Manual of Instructions for Lobbyists and Employers of Lobbyists*, revised December, 2014 (Juneau, AK: Alaska Public Offices Commission, 2014).

[44] Alexandra Gutierrez, "Alaska Scores Low on Lobbying Transparency," *Alaska News Nightly*, APRN, July 30, 2013.

[45] For fuller details on the *Citizens United* case, see Chapter 14 on campaigns and elections, Section 3.

[46] Jason Clemens, *et al.*, *State-Level Lobbying and Taxpayers: How Much Do We Really Know?* (San Francisco, CA: Pacific Research Institute, 2010).

[47] South Dakota Open and Clean Government Act, Initiated Measure 10, 2008, at http://en.wikipedia.org/wiki/South_Dakota_Open_and_Clean_Government_Act; and the Alaska Anti-Corruption Act, Ballot Measure 1, Ballotpedia (a website covering ballot measures in all fifty states) at: http://ballotpedia.org/wiki/index.php/2010_ballot_measures.

★ CHAPTER 16 ★

The Legislature, the Governor, and the Bureaucracy: Conflict, Cooperation, Personalities, and Power

Clive S. Thomas and Dave Donaldson

> I picked up a full glass of water sitting on my desk and threw it across the room at the legislative leaders standing in front of me. I had just explained an initiative to help Alaska, and they asked, "How will this help the Republican majority?" . . . Fortunately, my aim was off. I missed my target, and no one was hurt. The next day, my staff gave me a foam rubber brick for similar dialogues.[1]

Not all legislative-executive relations are as colorful or conflict-ridden (or as potentially dangerous) as this exchange between Governor Hickel and a group of Republican legislators. Despite the occasional conflict, the legislative and executive branches work cooperatively most of the time, though cooperation often comes only after an assessment by each branch of the other's political strength on a particular issue.

No relationship is more important in giving politics its particular characteristics and in shaping public policy than that between the legislature and the executive. In this regard, the characteristics of the relationship at the federal and state levels in the United States contrast with the parliamentary systems of most western democracies, such as those in Canada and Japan. In these systems, the leaders of the executive branch—the prime minister and cabinet members—are drawn from the majority party or majority party coalition in the parliament. As a result, the majority party dominates the policy-making process in most cases. In contrast, in the United States the two branches have separate officials and largely independent power bases. Even though they must work together for government to function, they often can become contending forces producing considerable political conflict. This combination of potential contentiousness and the need for the branches to work together gives American national and state politics and public policy making much of its particular character. So it is in Alaska, where the motives and goals of policy makers play out within their own branches of government and in the interaction between the two branches.

Two chapters in the book have already dealt with aspects of the legislative-executive relationship. Chapter 3 explains the policy process and the psychology of policy makers both in the legislative and executive branches, and Chapter 4 explains the constitutional relationship between the executive and legislature. Other chapters, including those on political parties (Chapter 13), elections and campaigns (Chapter 14), and interest groups (Chapter 15), also provide insights into the motives, goals, and attitudes of state officials. This chapter builds on Chapters 3 and 4 and addresses the dynamics of the legislative-executive relationship in the policy-making process. As we explore this relationship we will see that it is an uneven one, with the advantage going to the executive not only in terms of constitutional authority but often politically as well.

The dynamics within and between the two branches illustrate all twelve of the characteristics of Alaska politics identified in Chapter 2, from self-proclaimed fiscal conservatism to the significant role of Alaska Natives to regionalism to weak parties but strong legislative caucuses. Clearly, though, the characteristic most evident is that of three strong contending branches of state government, sometimes producing a stymied or stalemated policy process. Although we leave the discussion of the role of the judiciary to Chapter 17, the courts often affect the policy process and can trump both the legislature and the executive.

The first section of the chapter provides insights into the contrast between the formal organization and process of the legislature and executive and the political realities of the operations of each branch and their interrelationship. The next two sections look in more detail at the contrast between the formal and practical operations of each branch, first the executive and then the legislature, as a foundation for understanding their relationship. This is followed by a section explaining the factors shaping the dynamics of executive-legislative interaction and then two case studies to illustrate them. The concluding section points to other chapters in the book that illustrate the dynamics of this legislative-executive relationship.[2]

1. AN OVERVIEW OF THE FORMAL ORGANIZATION AND PROCESSES OF THE LEGISLATURE AND EXECUTIVE VERSUS THE PRACTICAL POLITICAL REALITY

To understand the dynamics of the interaction of the legislature and executive it is not necessary to have detailed knowledge of every type of legislative committee or every executive department, board, or commission. For those interested in such details, the

State of Alaska has excellent websites.[3] However, some basic knowledge of the formal organization of the two branches, the lawmaking process, and the terms used in both branches is important for understanding the politics of legislative-executive relations.

Structure of the Executive and Legislative Branches, the Lawmaking Process, and Terminology

The legislature and the executive have their own "government speak" consisting of special and technical terms. The ones needed to understand this chapter are either defined in the glossary at the end of the book or will be explained at appropriate points in this chapter. Budget terminology, which can be particularly daunting to the newcomer, is explained in Chapter 19 on the budget.[4] The formal organization of the legislature and the executive is set out in Figure 16.1. The state judiciary is placed on this chart as a third branch of government, but its organization is explained fully in Chapter 17. Then, in Figure 16.2 the formal lawmaking process is set out in overview, including the roles of both the legislature and the governor. These charts provide a general picture of the two branches and their formal relations. But like the state's websites, these two figures say nothing about political reality or power dynamics and nothing about how public policy actually gets made.

The Political and Power Realities: Dispelling Some Myths and Misconceptions

We begin by considering the legislative-executive relationship from five important perspectives: (1) placing the role of the legislature in context, (2) comparing the formal with the actual process, (3) identifying the power points in the system, (4) discussing the appearance of conflict versus the necessity of consensus, and (5) examining the role of personality and leadership.

The High-Profile of the Legislature versus Other Forces in the Policy Process—Particularly the Governor and the Departments

The high profile of the legislature during the legislative session, and the intense media attention focused on it as it pursues its lawmaking function, may give the impression that the legislature is the determining force in policy making. But as Chapter 3 on the policy process explains, other forces are just as significant, and in some cases more so.

In many ways, the governor and the executive branch are the most important forces in policy making. This is particularly true for the major instrument of government—the state budget. This chapter explains why, in many circumstances, the executive has the political upper hand over the legislature.

The Formal Process versus the Actual Process

The formal authority and structure of the legislative and executive branches are important in that they establish the scope of public officials' authority. However, as related in many

FIGURE 16.1

The Organization of the Legislature and Executive in Alaska

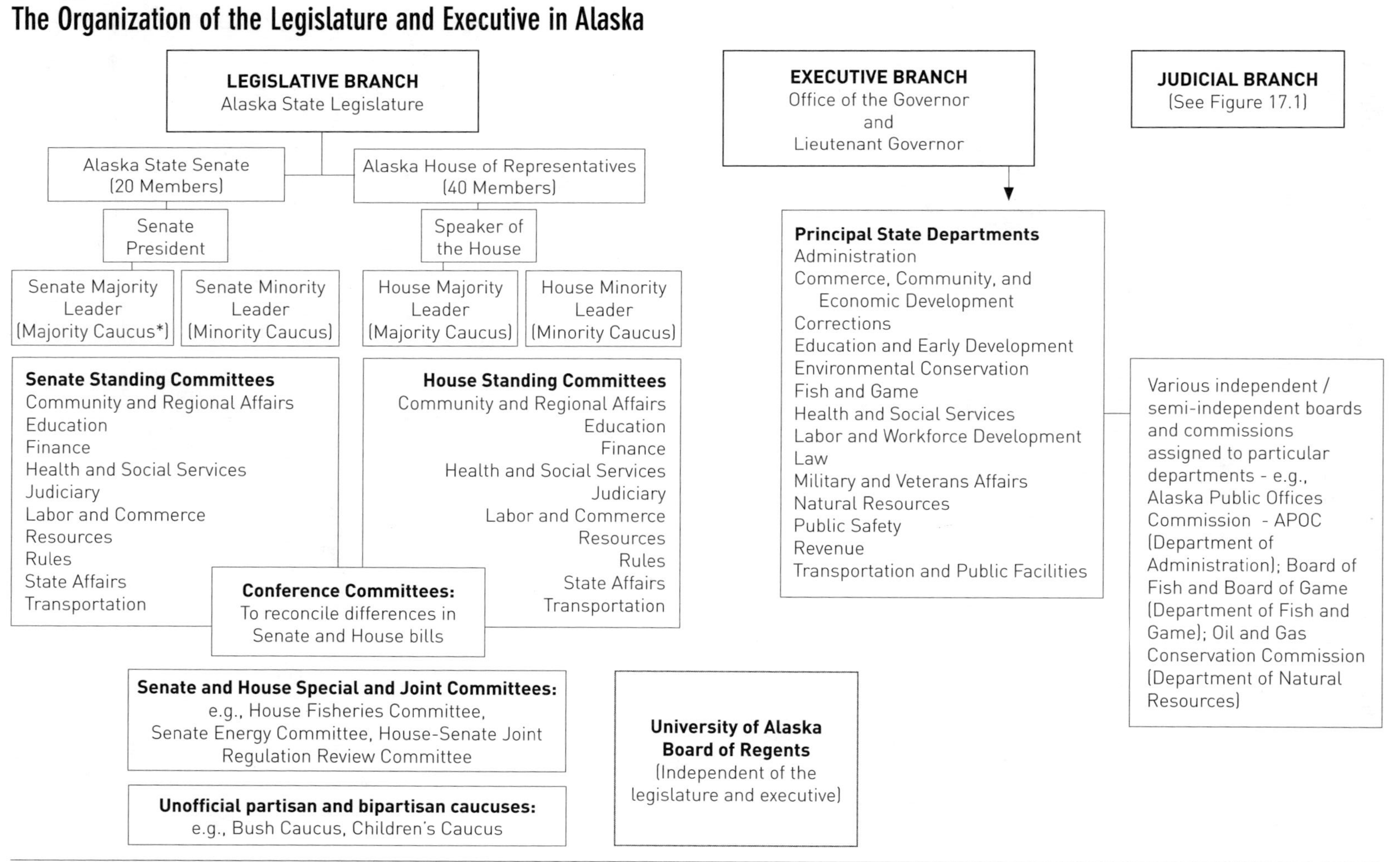

* The Senate bipartisan majority "caucus" between 2008 and 2012 was designated as the Bipartisan Working Group (BWG), and not as a caucus.

Source: Developed by the authors.

FIGURE 16.2
Steps in the Passage of a House Bill

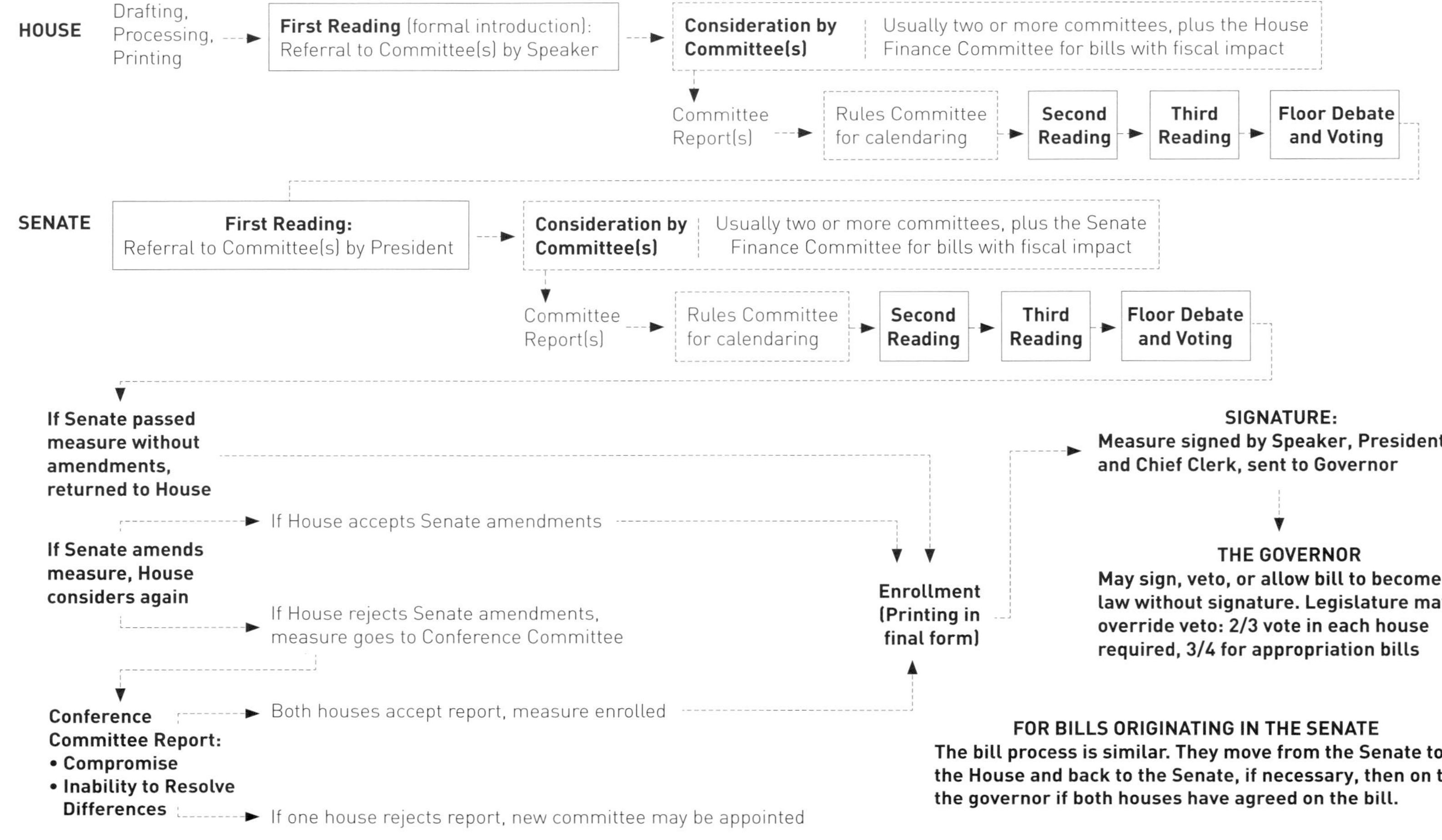

Source: Developed by the authors from various publications of the Legislative Affairs Agency (LAA).

parts of the book, the actual process involves many informal factors, including the power structure within the legislature, personal relationships among policy makers, external influences such as interest groups and constituents, the particular issue at hand, and the political environment at the time. These informal factors operate in various combinations on a day-to-day basis and are often the major influences on the legislative-executive relationship, with the formal and institutional factors forming the backdrop or context of the relationship.

The Power Points of the System

Expanding on the actual as opposed to the formal process, there are certain power points or power bases in the legislative-executive relationship that very much shape the outcome of policy making. Again, we need to look beyond the organizational charts and constitutional processes to understand the actual political reality.

For example, most of us were taught in our high school civics classes that a bill has three readings (as set out in Figure 16.2) and that the committee process is where the pros and cons of the bill are thrashed out, with the most rational arguments ultimately prevailing. That may be the case on occasion. But most of the time bills, and particularly the operating and capital budget bills, must be sanctioned by the majority caucus or a committee chair in order to pass, and the passage of much legislation is highly orchestrated by the leadership. This means that the second and third readings of most bills, as well as the committee process, are often perfunctory and sometimes little more than political window dressing. There are times, however, when an issue is sufficiently controversial that the outcome is uncertain up until the final vote—but this is the exception, not the rule.

This is not to pass judgment on the system as being good or bad, fair or unfair, but simply to point out the reality, as partly explored in Chapter 3. The upshot is that there are certain power points in both the legislature and the executive branches, and it is necessary to know them to understand the process. We identify these power points in the executive and legislature and in the dealings between them in the sections that follow.

The Appearance of Conflict but the Need for Cooperation

When people think about the legislative process and legislative-executive relations, many of them imagine legislators debating in constant confrontations among themselves and envision legislators and governors equally at odds on a host of issues. In many ways this image of confrontation and ongoing disagreement is reinforced by the media in its constant need to attract readers, listeners, and viewers.

While the legislative process does have its combative moments, as do the relations between legislature and governor, the reality is that successful legislators and governors build cooperation and consensus around issues and funding priorities regardless of party or ideological persuasion. Plus, the ability and willingness to arrive at consensus are particularly important in the American separation of powers system, which has a degree of institutionalized contention between the branches built into it. Without such cooperation and consensus, policy deadlock can and often does arise in Washington, D.C., and sometimes in the states, including Alaska. Alaska's policy makers know this full well and most work to promote consensus whenever possible. However, despite valiant efforts, for a variety of reasons, sometimes consensus cannot be achieved.

Personality and Leadership (or Lack of Leadership)

The personalities of politicians—their likes and dislikes, policy preferences, and past experiences, including memories of past political battles—are crucial in shaping public policy making or, in many cases, in blocking new policy proposals. In fact, a good argument can be made that personality is the single most important factor in politics and policy making. This reality is something that makes many people cringe, sometimes in disgust, as they believe that public officials, especially elected ones, should put aside their personal biases in favor of the "public interest." But the reality is that public officials often do not. They act as human beings, like the rest of us.

Given this reality, the interactions among the various personalities in the legislative and executive branches can have a major effect on the nature of legislative-executive relations. In short, different personalities and styles of leadership (or lack of leadership) can affect the balance of power within and between the legislative and executive branches and thus, in effect, change the balance of power in favor of one or the other branch.

2. THE VIEW FROM THE EXECUTIVE BRANCH: THE GOVERNOR, THE GOVERNOR'S OFFICE, AND THE BUREAUCRACY

Alaska's governors have major resources at their disposal both constitutionally and administratively. This usually includes a large personal staff and a bureaucracy that is, theoretically, under their control. That said, some governors are better than others in turning these resources into political power, both within their own branch and particularly in their relations with the legislature. Consequently, it is important to distinguish between the institutional powers (more correctly, the constitutional authority) of Alaska's governors on the one hand and their overall political power on the other. For this reason, we take issue to some extent with the contention of many political practitioners and political scientists that Alaska's governor is the most powerful in the United States.

Institutional Authority of the Governor and Lieutenant Governor

As set out in Article III of the state constitution, which deals with the executive branch, Alaska's governor is elected for a four-year term and can serve two consecutive terms, but then must sit out at least one term before seeking reelection. The constitution gives the governor extensive institutional authority. This includes appointment of all the members of the cabinet (with the technical exception of the commissioners of the departments of education and of fish and game, though in practice governors have at least indirect control of these appointments too) and other top-level executive personnel.

The governor is also given authority to prepare the budget. Plus, the governor has a line-item veto over appropriation bills, which means he or she can either delete or reduce items in appropriation bills enacted by the legislature. This is a power not enjoyed by the U.S. president, though many other state governors have this authority.

Particularly in regard to cabinet appointments, Alaska has a unified executive in contrast to states like California and most other states where a number of senior members of the administration, such as the attorney general and heads of many departments, are elected independently of, and separately from, the governor. Independent election gives these elected officials their own power bases, so they need not (and in many cases do not) follow the governor's agenda. In fact, they may positively benefit from not doing so, especially if they have eyes on the governorship themselves. Overall, the administrative authority of Alaska's governor is ranked in the top five states in the nation, but the governor's overall influence is ranked thirteenth of the fifty states when the political factor is added.[5]

Alaska's governor and lieutenant governor are assured of being from the same political party because they run as a pair on a party ticket—Democrat, Republican, or a third party. The 2014 gubernatorial election was an exception, when a nonpartisan Alaska First Unity ticket was formed after the primary election when the independent candidate Bill Walker and Democratic candidate Byron Mallott merged their campaigns and ran as a team. From a legal perspective, the lieutenant governor deals mainly with state elections and publication of state regulations and is the keeper of the state seal, similar duties to the secretary of state in many states. In fact, until 1970, Alaska had a secretary of state, but that year the name was changed to lieutenant governor. In addition, the constitution (Article III, Section 7) states that the lieutenant governor "shall perform such duties as prescribed by law and may be delegated to him [sic] by the governor."

Generally, however, Alaska's governors have not used the lieutenant governor in any extensive way. This is most likely because of the way the governor and lieutenant governors are elected in Alaska. Even though they run together in the general election, each candidate finds his or her own way to the general election ballot by winning a totally separate primary election (with the exception of 2014 when Mallott agreed to take the lieutenant governor's slot in a deal with Walker). So the governor and lieutenant governor may or may not see eye to eye personally or politically. Governor Knowles and Lieutenant

Governor Fran Ulmer were exceptions. They worked together smoothly, and Ulmer played an important role in the administration. Governor Murkowski and Lieutenant Governor Loren Leman, on the other hand, had less than a positive relationship. Because Walker's election was in large part due to Democratic support, Byron Mallott may play a more significant role as lieutenant governor, but this remains to be seen. A potentially positive step was Walker moving the lieutenant governor's office next to his own office. The lieutenant governor's office has hitherto been located at the other end of the third floor of the capitol building from the governor's office. Whether this move proves to be meaningful or merely symbolic also remains to be seen.

The only past lieutenant governors who have subsequently served as governor are Keith Miller and Sean Parnell, though several have run unsuccessfully for the higher office (including Terry Miller, Stephen McAlpine, and Fran Ulmer). Constitutionally the lieutenant governorship can be a step to the governorship if the governor becomes incapacitated or resigns. This was the case with Keith Miller, who became governor in 1969 when Governor Hickel became President Nixon's Secretary of the Interior, and with Sean Parnell on the resignation of Governor Palin in July 2009. Parnell is the only past lieutenant governor to have been elected as governor, which he was in November 2010.

The Governor's Job: Manager of State Government, Policy Initiator, and Chief State Politician and Representative

Up until the 1960s, state governments throughout the United States did very little to provide services, and most state capitals were sleepy places. Many governors tended to be good old boy politicos, often referred to as "goodtime Charlies" who caroused with legislators and lobbyists.[6] Since the late 1960s, the situation has changed considerably as state governments have expanded their role and the size of state budgets and the number of state employees have expanded fivefold. Public and media scrutiny of state government has also increased markedly. With these changes have come increased responsibility and a greater scrutiny of governors.

Today, all governors, including those in Alaska, perform a range of tasks dictated by demands on state government, many of which by themselves would be more than a full-time job.[7] In the case of Alaska's governor, this entails preparing and managing a state budget of up to $12 billion in high revenue years, a state government of close to twenty thousand employees, and myriad agencies performing a multitude of functions. The governor is also a major source of proposed legislation, both in regard to policies and programs of the various departments and in promoting his or her own agenda. This often involves delivering on electoral promises, such as the ethics reform platform that helped Sarah Palin get elected in 2006 and the natural gas pipeline and expansion of Medicaid that Bill Walker ran on in 2014.

As with all state governors, Alaska's governor is also the state's chief politician and representative. As the most important state official elected statewide, the governor is called upon to rally public support on issues and in times of crisis such as the *Exxon Valdez* oil spill in 1989. The governor also represents the state nationally and internationally, particularly to the federal government. Thus, the governor is the most important state official in intergovernmental relations (IGR). As we have seen in several places in the book, the governor's role regarding federal issues is significant, and for this purpose the governor maintains staff in Washington, D.C.[8]

Gubernatorial Goals, Personality, Style, and Skills

Governors' constitutional authority is one thing, but their actual performance in the way they deal with the legislature may be quite another. It is this aspect of the job that is most important in terms of shaping public policy. Of the eleven governors since statehood, each has had a distinct personality and a particular style, brought different skills to the job, and had his or her sights set on different goals.[9]

Bill Egan (Democrat 1959–1966 and 1970–1974) had to establish Alaska as a state and worked with small budgets in the days before big oil revenues. A small businessman who could remember everyone's name and face, Egan was so personable that it was said that if he backed into a cigarette machine he would jump around and try to shake hands with it. Wally Hickel (Republican 1966–1969 and 1990–1994) was a boisterous, can-do, self-made millionaire in the hotel and investment business with a passionate belief in Alaska's economic potential and a political warrior against the federal government. He faced similar challenges to Egan in his first term but worked to cut government spending in his second term. Keith Miller (Republican 1969–1970) had little time to make any political impact. Jay Hammond (Republican 1974–1982) was a poetry-writing commercial fisherman who had served as mayor of the Bristol Bay Borough and in the legislature. He combined a belief in economic development and environmental protection and served when Alaska's oil bonanza came on tap. Part of his goal as governor was to ensure that these revenues were not squandered, but protected for future generations. His administration oversaw the creation of the Permanent Fund and the Permanent Fund Dividend (PFD). Bill Sheffield (Democrat 1982–1986), also a self-made millionaire businessman in the hotel and hospitality business, had never held elective office before running for governor. One of his major goals on coming into office was to make government run more like a business.

Steve Cowper (Democrat 1986–1990), who purposely cut a Clint Eastwood cowboy image, had served in the legislature, but did not seem too interested in being governor once elected, though he did push an educational endowment for the state that was ultimately unsuccessful. Cowper announced he would not run again fully eighteen months before his term was up. Tony Knowles (Democrat 1994–2002), a successful businessman and former mayor of Anchorage, with a low-keyed, personable style, combined a belief in economic development with the need for social safety nets for the less well off, particularly children. He also had ambitions to run for Congress, and this likely affected his approach to the governorship by alienating as few constituencies as possible.

Frank Murkowski (Republican 2002–2006), a former businessman and state legislator, served in the U.S. Senate from 1980 to 2002. With a stiff, unengaging personality and often displaying arrogance, he came into office with a major agenda, including plans to cut the state budget. His style was very much based on his U.S. Senate experience, and he misjudged the need for good public communications and the fact that neither Democrats nor Republicans walked in political lockstep in the legislature. His unpopularity resulted in his resounding defeat in the 2006 Republican gubernatorial primary, though he was known during his four years in office for always being willing to talk with Alaska Native legislators.

The person who beat Murkowski, Sarah Palin (Republican 2006–2009), the first governor born after statehood, was at one point the most popular Alaska governor of all time. Palin, however, was and remains an enigmatic character—which became clear when she was governor. As an attractive and engaging person and sometimes a good speaker, she had a populist element to her campaign, which was run without the support of the state's Republican Party establishment. She had a vague agenda when elected and appeared to have little interest in the day-to-day operations of government. But she worked with Democrats to adopt a tax increase on the oil industry, spearheaded legislation to establish a new framework for encouraging construction of a natural gas pipeline, and secured ethics reform. After being nominated as U.S. vice presidential candidate in August 2008, however, she seemed to lose whatever interest she had in Alaska policy issues. She resigned unexpectedly in July 2009.[10]

Sean Parnell (Republican 2009–2014), who took over the governorship on Palin's resignation, was elected in his own right in November 2010, but was defeated for reelection in November 2014. A low-keyed and personable former legislator and lawyer by profession, he supported economic development, took issue with many federal decisions regarding Alaska, and launched a program to combat domestic violence. He also pushed a tax cut for the oil companies that failed in 2012 but was eventually passed in 2013.

Bill Walker (2014–present), the only governor besides Egan born in Alaska, is an attorney and former mayor of Valdez who lost to Governor Parnell in the 2010 Republican gubernatorial primary. Walker dropped his Republican registration to fuse his candidacy with Mallott's after the 2014 primary and won by a narrow margin. An engaging person, Walker centered his campaign on building a gas pipeline, value adding to aid the economy, exploiting the potential of the Arctic, and expanding Medicaid under the federal Affordable Care Act. A gas pipeline is an issue that he had long championed. But with oil prices dropping by 70 percent from late 2014 and remaining low into 2016, the building of this pipeline was in doubt. And with state revenues cut by a third as he took office, Walker faced probably the biggest challenge of any governor in Alaska history.

The goals, personality traits, style, and skills of particular governors shape not only their relations with the legislature, but also the tone of their relations with others in the executive branch. To understand the governor's role within the executive branch we next provide an overview of the state bureaucracy and the key members of the governor's personal staff.

The Bureaucracy: State Departments, Boards, and Commissions

Figure 16.1 lists state departments and some examples of boards and commissions. In this section, we describe the key executive branch positions.

Departments

Commissioners are the heads of the various executive departments. Box 16.1 explains their roles. In the commissioner's office are a deputy commissioner and likely a legislative affairs person (legislative liaison) who follows legislation for the department and works with other agencies on policy issues. Under the commissioner's office the departments are divided into divisions, each headed by a director and sometimes a deputy director. For example, the Department of Health and Social Services (DHSS) has several divisions, including Public Assistance and Senior and Disabilities Services. Commissioners and deputy commissioners are political appointees (with the technical exception of the Departments of Education and Fish and Game) and are hired and fired by the governor. Commissioners' appointments, however, are subject to confirmation by the legislature. Legislative liaisons are sometimes political appointees, sometimes permanent employees. Many division directors are long-time state employees, but some are political appointees who come and go when there is a change of administration.

To understand the power structure in a department, as explained in Chapter 1, it is important not to assume that authority and power are identical. The commissioner may, indeed, be the major force in the department as may other political appointees. However, as the late Bill Noll explains in Box 16.1, the permanent staff is there for the long haul and is a formidable force. For this reason, a department's division directors often wield considerable influence, if in a low-keyed way.

Boards and Commissions

Boards and commissions have a chairperson and usually a full-time director or executive director, plus support staff. For example, the Alaska Public Offices Commission

BOX 16.1

The Role of the Commissioner: The Governor's Link with the Departments

A fundamental role of a commissioner is to know and understand the governor's vision for the state and to translate that vision faithfully into those areas that apply to the department. In my case it was the Department of Commerce, Community, and Economic Development, where I worked with five hundred employees.

As political appointees, achieving the governor's goals presents all commissioners with challenges. In dealing with those challenges, different commissioners have different styles, often because they bring different experiences to the job. Some emphasize management, while others are more political in dealing with the legislature, the governor's office, and their colleagues in other departments. I was more of a manager.

Alaska's bureaucracy is staffed by union members. These employees run the day-to-day show of government and operate steadily as administrations and commissioners come and go. So as a commissioner, it is easy to allow the bureaucracy to do whatever it has been doing in the past. To have done that would have been to negate my responsibilities. It was my job to translate the governor's vision in such a way that the bureaucracy would help me execute it and even perhaps agree with that vision. Here the art of leadership and management is critical.

I chose to be proactive, but my leadership experience pushed me away from micromanagement and more toward allocating responsibility and authority. In a meeting of department senior staff, including division directors, I urged focus on just a few key objectives. One was value added for Alaska's fish; another was the establishment of an easier way to form a corporation in Alaska. These were our successes. We also developed an initiative to encourage formation of new boroughs. This was not successful. Achieving that goal will take broader support than we could garner.

Being accountable to the governor, the legislature, and to the public is a big part of a commissioner's job. We had one $50 million federally funded program for revitalization of the salmon industry. To administer this we formed an interdepartmental Fish Cabinet. The money was spread throughout the state and we reported the successful results of the program back to the legislature, to the governor, and to the public.

I was not called to the legislature very much, but I did make the rounds faithfully. Defending the department's budget was part of my role with the legislature. A legislator once asked if the state got its money back when it backed economic development programs like tourism, fishing, or mining and what that return was. In response, I formed a team, and we reported back to the legislature showing a positive return in these areas.

Source: Authored by Bill Noll, former Commissioner of the Department of Commerce, Community, and Economic Development.

(APOC) has a five-member board, a director, and a small staff, some for ensuring compliance with the law, others working as support personnel. Boards and commissions also have someone, sometimes more than one person, who works with the legislature and other agencies on policy issues. This may be the director, a board member or, in the bigger agencies such as the Alaska Permanent Fund Corporation, a person specially designated for the role.

The Governor's Office and Key Staff and Advisors

The governor's office houses the governor's close personal staff, which consists of several dozen individuals, including special assistants for various functions and policy areas. All of these staffers are at-will employees, who can be fired without cause. Most are located on the third floor of the state capitol close to the governor's own office and are distinct from the heads of state departments and boards and their senior political appointed staff. The role of those in the governor's office is to make the governor look good and help implement the governor's policy agenda and other goals. Figure 16.3 sets out a typical organization of the governor's office.

Six of the positions included on Figure 16.3 and one other are particularly important as key advisors to the governor and, in most cases, dealing with the legislature. Three of these positions are dealt with in other chapters. The press secretary, the major spokesperson for the governor, is dealt with in Chapter 20 on the role of the media and public opinion; the director of the Office of Management and Budget (OMB), the person in charge of the governor's budget, is covered in Chapter 19 on the budget process; and the director of state-federal relations is covered in Chapter 10 on the federal government and IGR. The other three positions on the chart are the chief of staff, the legislative director, and until Bill Walker became governor in December of 2014, various special assistants. In addition, although not physically located in the governor's office (and thus not included in Figure 16.3), the attorney general is a key advisor to the governor on legal matters, as explained in Box 16.2.

The Chief of Staff

The governor's chief of staff is his or her right-hand person and usually someone the governor has known and trusted for a long time. Like governors, chiefs of staff vary in their personalities and their operating styles. Some, like Nancy Usera, who authored Box 16.3 on the role of the chief of staff, are low-keyed and work largely behind the scenes. Others, like Governor Knowles's chief of staff, Jim Ayres, are more dominant personalities and power broker types who interact more with legislators.

The Legislative Director

The governor's legislative director deals with the legislature on issues, policies, and legislation of concern to the governor and attempts to maintain harmony between the two branches. For most governors, the legislative director is an important conduit and often a pivotal force in the all-important executive-legislative relationship. Being a liaison between the executive and the legislature, however, makes this job one of the toughest in state government for a variety of reasons, as Box 16.4 points out.

FIGURE 16.3

The Alaska Governor's Office: Typical Organization and Staff Positions

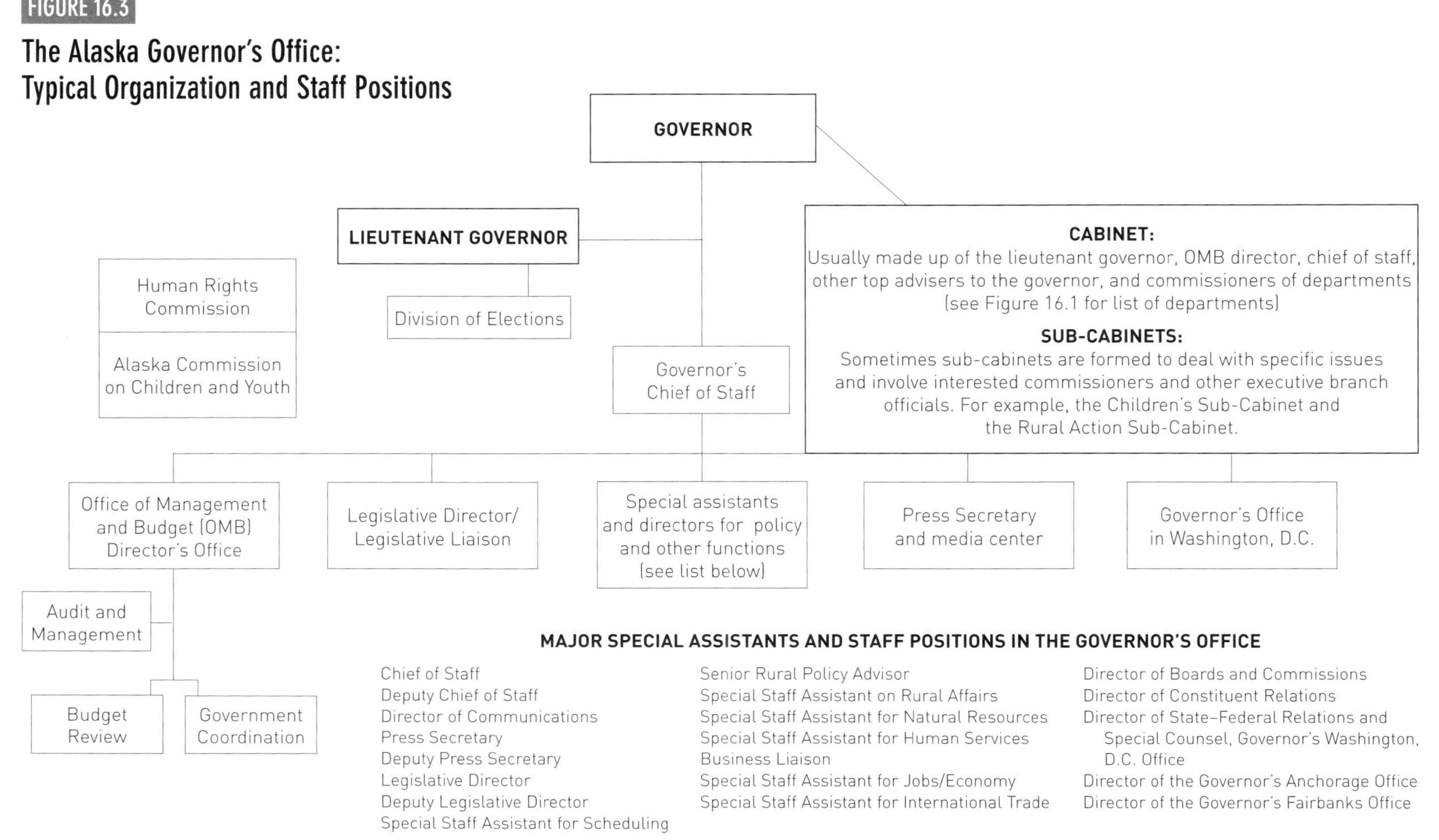

Source: Developed by the authors.

BOX 16.2

The Attorney General: The Administration's Chief Legal Officer

Alaska's attorney general (often referred to as the AG) is the state's chief legal officer. In that role, the AG has a legal function and an advisory role. Plus, as Alaska is one of only a few states where the governor appoints the AG, the AG's advisory role to the governor, sometimes as his or her close confidant, often has a political dynamic to it.

As the state's chief legal officer, the AG performs several functions. These include acting as managing partner of the state's largest law firm (the Alaska Department of Law); advising the governor, most state agencies, and the legislature; arbitrating disputes between departments or between the state and other entities; advocating to the legislature and in the courts on behalf of the Department of Law; issuing opinions; and representing the state in the courts. In addition, the AG supervises all state prosecutors and the prosecution of all state crimes. Only the Delaware AG has this same authority.

Each Alaska AG performs the role differently, reflective of the individual's life experience, personality, and interests; relationship to the governor; and the issues and agendas of the time. Major events can sweep aside all other agendas, for instance the 1964 earthquake or the 1989 *Exxon Valdez* oil spill.

It is the governor's appointment of the AG and the AG's advisory role to the governor that sometimes sparks controversy in Alaska and leads to calls for an elected AG. The pros and cons of whether or not Alaska should have an elected AG is covered in considering possible future reforms in Alaska government in Chapter 30 (Box 30.4). But regarding past and present controversies, we can make the following observations.

Few, if any, Alaska AGs have escaped the accusation that they are beholden to the governor and simply do the governor's bidding, rather than independently protecting the public interest. Usually, this argument arises when there is a major political disagreement with a gubernatorial action that is defended by the AG. Is there any truth to this argument? The institutional practice consistently is that it is the governor who is elected to make policy choices and, so long as they are lawful (whether they are wise or not), the AG will advocate for them. The corollary to this is that the AG must enforce the law when it conflicts with the judgments or decisions of the chief executive.

Fortunately, conflicts within the executive branch over the law rarely reach a crisis point. This is because most governors and their immediate staffs tend to seek legal guidance over proposed policies or involve their respective AG in the formulation of policy from the outset. This opportunity to participate in the behind-the-scenes give-and-take can often alter (or reinforce) the direction of any given policy.

Occasionally, however, irreconcilable differences arise. More than one early departure of an AG was the result of strong disagreement over policy between the AG and the governor or chief of staff. In fact, only a few AGs have served out an entire term, although early departures were not always the result of disagreements. When these disagreements become public, they help fuel the perennial call for an elected AG.

Source: Authored by Bruce Botelho, former Alaska Attorney General.

BOX 16.3

The Governor's Chief of Staff: Political Jack-of-All-Trades

The governor's chief of staff serves in many roles: policy executor, negotiator, arbiter, adviser, protector, gofer, and administrator. Each role changes proportionately depending on the day of the week and the chief's relationship with the governor. What the chief of staff does not do is serve as chief of state—though there have been chiefs who have confused the roles. There is no inherent power in being chief of staff. It is the ability to leverage the perception of power and the ability to get things done through others that determines success or failure. This ability hinges on the political acumen of the chief, how good a relationship he or she has with the governor, and how this is perceived outside the governor's office. Being chief is certainly not a job for people who are easily offended or who need to be liked.

As one of the governor's primary agents in securing the administration's policy agenda, the chief has a role in the four aspects of securing that agenda: implementation of laws; changing administrative rules; selection of the judiciary; and garnering public support. Executing this agenda involves much politics: building alliances; trying to divert or stymie the opposition; and playing all political angles possible. To aid in this, the chief can call upon the governor's legislative director and his or her staff; commissioners of departments, their staffs, and legislative liaisons; the attorney general; and the governor's press secretary.

The chief is also a "doorkeeper," helping prioritize which issues get a share of the governor's personal attention and political capital. Political capital must be used sparingly and be reserved for issues that have the most direct and utmost impact on the governor's primary policy interests. Often this is not easy, because governors want to do good things for their allies and constituents, sometimes at the expense of longer-term policy issues.

Politics in the governor's office is not confined to executive-legislative relations. Some of the greatest challenges the chief faces lie in maintaining compliance or effecting change within the administration. The chief serves as a catalyst for action by giving direction to departments through their commissioners. Soon after appointment some commissioners become biased toward the interests of their departments over those of the governor. Conflicting interests between departments, programs, priorities, and, most importantly, limited financial resources, make the chief's role of broker imperative. This role can create tension between the chief and commissioners, particularly as the chief is often the one who communicates instructions and delivers bad news.

One less obvious road to changing public policy is through the appointment of judges to the state bench, including the prized positions on the Alaska Supreme Court. The nomination and appointment of judges can have long-term impact on policy through the interpretation of laws. Friends and friends of friends weigh in on which candidates will best serve the governor's policy agenda. Besides the governor, the chief is usually a major target of lobbying on behalf of would-be judges.

Public popularity is critical to a governor's success, and the governor's personal staff is integral to image building. The press office, budget director, and director of boards and commissions all play roles that impact public opinion. Their individual decisions can result in unanticipated reactions. The variables are many, and the outcome unpredictable. Damage control when perceptions go sideways is a chief's daily challenge.

Source: Authored by Nancy Usera, Governor Hickel's Chief of Staff in 1994.

BOX 16.4

The Legislative Director: The Major Link between the Governor and the Administration and the Legislature

The governor's legislative director has the general job of coordinating and facilitating the governor's and the administration's legislative agendas, although the director's precise role may vary from governor to governor. In effect, the director is the governor's lobbyist. Their day-to-day duties vary throughout the year and obviously are most hectic, often frantic, during the legislative session.

When a governor comes into office, appointing a legislative director is one of the first and most important decisions. Virtually all those appointed have had experience in the legislature or the administration, and some as lobbyists. For example, Darwin Peterson, Governor Walker's legislative director, had extensive experience as a legislative aide, as did Heather Brakes, Governor Parnell's legislative director, who was also a deputy in the legislative director's office. Jerry Gallagher, one of Governor Palin's legislative directors, had worked as a deputy commissioner and had been a lobbyist. Mike Tibbles in the Murkowski administration had been a legislative aide and Pat Pourchot, one of Governor Knowles's directors, had been a legislator in both houses. Inside knowledge of how the legislative and executive branches work and, as far as possible, of the personalities of legislators and their staff and the locations of political skeletons, is essential to doing the job.

Generally, the director is in charge of two separate, but related, executive agendas. One is the governor's personal agenda, based on his or her campaign promises. The other consists of the administration's priorities in general, including the budget and the executive branch's overall legislative agenda, which includes the needs of departments and agencies regarding new legislation and changes in existing laws. For the governor's personal agenda, the director works closely with the governor. For the administration's overall agenda, the director usually has weekly meetings during the legislative session with department legislative liaisons to plan legislative strategy and again in the fall when the administration's new legislative agenda and budgets are put together. Sometimes strategy involves bills being introduced by the governor, sometimes by friendly legislators.

A good relationship with the governor, department commissioners and legislative liaisons, and individual legislators is essential for success in the job. Many legislative directors have learned that, without good rapport on all three fronts, they become ineffective. Much of the dynamics of these relationships boils down to personality.

Because majority members of the legislature have the most influence on the governor's legislative agenda, legislative directors spend more time contacting them. Generally, the director is given easy and quick access to all legislators. For their part, legislators must trust the director and know that he or she has the ear of the governor. Lawmakers must know that commitments by the director will be honored by the governor. If not, legislators will go around the director to the governor, the chief of staff, or even a special assistant in the governor's office.

Clearly, it is to the governor's advantage to have a good relationship with the legislative director and to allow the director clear and quick access. If not, the governor has to establish relationships with all sixty legislators or, at least, the most influential ones—not an efficient way to do political business. Yet, often things get in the way of a smooth relationship. In the Knowles's administration, the strong personality of the chief of staff often added a complication in that he sometimes dealt directly with legislators without involving the legislative director, thus increasing the potential for mixed messages being communicated to the legislature. Governor Murkowski sometimes blamed his legislative director for mistakes made by others in the administration. As a result, several of his directors resigned. Governor Palin's apparent lack of interest in running government undermined her relationship with her legislative directors.

Dealing with and coordinating the overall administration's agenda is often like herding cats, especially among departments that may have conflicting missions, like the departments of fish and game, natural resources, and environmental conservation. Again, depending on the governor and the personality mix in the governor's office and among commissioners, their deputies, and department legislative liaisons, this relationship can work well or not. In less coordinated administrations, departmental personnel can do end runs around the legislative director to secure their agendas with the legislature with the consequent undermining of the legislative director's credibility. To prevent this, governors and their legislative directors often have strict rules about the protocol of departmental contact with the legislature.

Source: Developed by the authors based upon personal observation and interviews with past legislative directors, governors, legislators, and legislative staff.

Special Assistants for Various Policy Areas

For most gubernatorial administrations, special assistants, such as those for rural affairs, natural resources, and human services, deal with the various policies and legislation within their specific areas of responsibility. Special assistants deal with the departments and other state agencies in these policy areas and may sometimes deal with legislators and legislative staff. However, to set an example of reducing spending because of a major drop in oil prices, Bill Walker left several special assistant positions vacant. Instead, in effect, he used his commissioners as special assistants in various policy areas. He also cut the staff in Alaska's Washington, D.C. office. But he did appoint a special assistant for Arctic issues to fulfill his campaign promise to develop Alaska's role in the region.

Coordinating It All to Work with the Legislature and Succeeding as Governor

Ideally, all these key members of the administration—commissioners and senior departmental personnel, the governor's office staff, and the attorney general—should work as a team to promote the governor's and the administration's agenda in the legislature. This ideal is rarely the case, however. This is partly because of the diverse interests within any administration, partly because of personalities, as the box on the role of the legislative director points out, and partly because of the governor's personal style.

Obviously, conflicts within an administration's team can negatively affect the governor's relationship with the legislature and undermine the administration's agenda. All governors put policies into place to promote agency coordination and for political damage control. For instance, different governors and commissioners have different rules about who in their offices can talk directly to members of the media, to other agency personnel, and to people from the legislature, about an issue.

Clearly, then, a combination of factors determines the governor's relationship with the legislature, and largely shapes his or her success at the job. At root, however, it boils down to two factors: human relationships and acquiring and using power. The success or failure of personal relationships at all levels and between those in the executive and legislative branches go hand in hand with the governor's ability to turn his or her authority into political power.

Successful personal relationships within the executive branch also promote effective teamwork and can make the difference between a hostile legislature and one that wants to help the governor achieve his or her policy goals. Box 16.5 provides perspectives on executive-legislative relations by two Alaska governors. The contrast in personality, styles, and personal reflections conveyed in these recollections reinforces our contention that human dynamics and power are key elements in politics.

3. THE VIEW FROM THE LEGISLATURE: OPERATIONAL AND POLITICAL DYNAMICS, AND ANTICIPATING GUBERNATORIAL ACTION

Several chapters in the book make reference to the legislature in various ways, particularly Chapters 3, 4, 13, 14, and 15 on the policy process, the constitution, political parties, elections and campaigns, and interest groups, respectively. With these various perspectives in mind, the treatment here focuses on the legislature's key organizational aspects and internal dynamics as a policy-making body and its available political resources for dealing with the governor and the administration. The aspects treated are whether the legislature is a citizen or professional body, the four roles of the legislature, its power structure and internal relations, and political fragmentation.

Does Alaska Have a Citizen or a Professional Legislature?

Since the Jacksonian era of the 1830s, when the political elite of the early National period were replaced by the so-called amateur democrat and the power of the "little guy," Americans have had a strong preference for citizen legislators (and politicians in general) and an antipathy toward professional legislators. Among the public, the words "citizen" and "professional" have a variety of meanings. To political scientists, however, the level of professionalism is measured by the size of the legislature, the length of its session, the level of staffing, the pay of legislators, and how legislators view their jobs, including if they list their occupation as "legislator" or as their job outside the legislature, if they have one. Based on these criteria, legislatures range from California's, the most professional, to Oregon's at number twenty-five, to New Hampshire's at number fifty, the latter being the best example of a citizen legislature.[11]

BOX 16.5

Being Governor: Personal Perspectives from Governors Walter Hickel and Bill Sheffield

GOVERNOR HICKEL

I was raised on a Kansas farm, so I think of the governor as the "foreman of the ranch." He doesn't own the ranch but is responsible for getting the best long-term return from the land and the resources for the benefit of the owners—in this case the people of Alaska. In particular, the governor is responsible for the health of the Alaska economy. The governor's job is to make things happen. Proactive leadership requires vision, decisiveness, and toughness. I believe in Alaska and its potential.

Soon after I was elected in 1966, I flew to the North Slope because Atlantic-Richfield had moved an oil rig into place at Prudhoe Bay but hadn't begun drilling. When their head geologist, Harry Jamison, told me that they were leaving the Slope, I blew up:

"Harry, you drill or I will," I threatened.

"You mean you'll drill, Governor?" he asked in shock.

"You're damn right I will," I said. "It's our land and our oil."

Soon after, Harry met with the company's president, Robert O. Anderson, in Los Angeles, and they decided to drill. They found the largest oil reservoir in North America.

Whenever partisanship enters public policy in Alaska it nearly always clashes with what is best for our people, and the governor must rise above it. He must work with the cabinet and the legislature, including across party lines, to decide what resources to develop and what to preserve. With all his constitutional powers and by garnering public support, he's got a lot of equipment to be a great political foreman. This means not only wanting the title of foreman but doing the job of the foreman.

GOVERNOR SHEFFIELD

Even though I'd never held public office before, I thought I knew government—until I got to Juneau. When I got on the inside I learned a whole lot more: about the bureaucracy and the agencies, the budget, the press, and about the legislature and its members.

I thought legislators liked governors, but I found that many hated them because they thought they should have been governor. Very quickly I realized I needed to get to know them, invite them for lunch and to the mansion for receptions, have them up to my office. Once I realized their power base, particularly on the budget, I got to know what they wanted to do for their areas. So after a rough first year, I started to build up some chits with the legislature and was able to accomplish things.

One of my campaign themes was to run the state like a business. The legislature taught me a lesson about that early on, so my line became "it doesn't hurt to know about business." I also campaigned on efficiency and cutting spending—get the budget under control. And we did cut spending; but I learned that cutting the budget was tough as every item in it has some political constituency and they fight to keep their money.

Being governor is an eighteen-hour a day, seven-days-a-week job. Time in the office dealing with my staff, luncheons, speeches, dinners, travel, dealing with the departments constantly, the press, people who wanted to see me, lobbyists, local governments, and particularly legislators. Everyone wanted my time. I rarely met a person who said they didn't vote for me, didn't have a perfect idea, or wasn't the best person for a government job they wanted. Then there was appointing people to various government positions, including judges; hiring staff and commissioners; reaching out to my offices around the state; and dealing with the feds, which I could write a book or two about.

Looking back on it all, I learned a lot about being governor, but four things in particular stand out, three of which are very different from my experiences in business.

First, for every successful businessman there are probably four or five people out to get you because you are successful. Well, as governor, successful or not, there are thousands out to get you! The public, the press, and legislators beating up on you: "You're not doing things fast enough; what about this, you haven't made a decision on these crucial issues; that was an awful decision you made on that, Sheffield." Second, when you are in business you make your own decisions, good or bad, but you make them yourself and you don't have to involve too many people. But as governor, you have to line your horizon up with the things you have to do and involve lots and lots of people and interests. If you don't, you won't get even part of what you want, and compromise is the key, even for the "powerful" Alaska governor. So the third point is that this all takes time, a lot longer than in business, and that took me some getting used to.

Based on these three lessons and the other demands of the job, I came to realize the importance of the governor's office staff and top department appointments, and I recognized the value of loyalty. The late lobbyist, Alex Miller, told me one day: "Sheffield, there are a lot of smart people, but just hire the loyal ones—you can make 'em smart once they're working for you." Well, it was stellar advice, and I didn't always follow it at first and got caught up a couple of times as a result.

Despite an attempt to impeach me by the legislature and being "fired" by the electorate in 1986 when Steve Cowper beat me in the primary, I enjoyed my time as governor tremendously—it's the best job in Alaska. You see the rewards of the job every day, helping people, making Alaska a better place. If I had to do it over again I wouldn't do it much differently, except a little slower, think things through a little better before attacking a problem, and take more time to enjoy it.

Source: Based on interviews by Clive Thomas and Anthony Nakazawa with Governor Bill Sheffield and written material on Governor Walter Hickel provided by Malcolm Roberts.

With forty seats in the House of Representatives and twenty in the Senate, Alaska has the smallest bicameral legislature of all fifty states, with only Nebraska's forty-nine-seat unicameral legislature being smaller. Many Alaskans see their legislature as an amateur or citizen legislature. Although it meets annually, in contrast to some states like Montana and Texas, which meet every two years, Alaska's is certainly not a full-time legislature like California's. Its yearly sessions are short, at only ninety days, and many of its members have other jobs during the interim when the legislature is not in session. But in terms of its staff support, the pay and expenses of its members (which provide a modest but living wage), and other support facilities, Alaska has what is considered a professional or, at least, a semi-professional legislature, and it is ranked eleventh of the fifty states in this regard.[12]

Ironically, the public's preference for a citizen legislature undermines the ability of their representatives to represent them most effectively, especially in dealings with the bureaucracy. Citizen legislators have less time, less information, and fewer resources in general to bring to bear against the major resources of the governor and the bureaucracy. In general, this kind of imbalance translates into more power for the governor and less for the legislature. One approach advocated by many organizations and citizens to promote the legislature as a citizen body is term limits. But term limits may also reduce the effectiveness of the legislature in its political battles with the executive. Certainly, term limits have their advantages, not least in getting rid of burned out legislators. Fifteen states have some form of legislative term limits, including California, Ohio, Maine, and Florida. However, by adopting term limits the legislature loses institutional memory as well as expertise on issues and the policy process. This loss of expertise also means that power shifts to the executive, particularly the bureaucracy, and to lobbyists and interest groups. Term limits can also result in increased influence by unelected long-time legislative staff who know the process far better than most elected legislators.

The relative professionalism of Alaska's legislature, coupled with its lack of term limits, very much benefits that body in its power relations with the governor, the departments, and boards and commissions, though its ninety-day session is problematic, as we will see below.

The Legislature as a Legislative Body: Its Four Major Functions

Legislatures, including the U.S. Congress and the fifty state legislatures, perform four major functions: representation; deliberation; law making; and oversight, including investigations and confirmations of gubernatorial appointments. Here we briefly examine each function, the resources available to perform them, and the extent to which these resources aid the legislature in its relations with the executive. We also briefly explain the legislature's role in impeachment.

Representation

The term representation in the legislative context can mean several things, three of which are of particular significance.

First, to what extent are members of the legislature reflective of the socio-economic and cultural makeup of the state? As Chapter 14 on campaigns and elections points out, the members of Alaska's legislature, like legislators throughout the nation, are more highly educated and better off economically than the average citizen, though Alaska's legislature contains fewer lawyers and businesspeople than most state legislatures. As in all states, women are underrepresented in the Alaska legislature in terms of their numbers in the population. They constituted just 24 percent (four women in the Senate and ten in the House) in the Twenty-Seventh Legislature (2011–2012). The percentage increased in the Twenty-Eighth Legislature (2013–2014) to 27 percent (again with four in the Senate but twelve in the House), and there was another slight increase in the Twenty-Ninth Legislature to 28.5 percent (with five in the Senate and twelve in the House). While minorities, particularly Alaska Natives, have never had the number of legislators that reflect their numbers in the state population, many Alaska Natives have been elected to represent rural-bush districts.

Second, in terms of the citizen-legislator link, the friends and neighbors politics of Alaska means that it is relatively easy to get access to and responses from legislators or their staffs. This says nothing about influence, however. Even if access is open to all, access alone does not translate into influence. At the same time, most legislators and their staffs devote a great deal of time listening to their constituents' problems and attempting to resolve them. For problems that constituents have in their dealings with executive branch agencies, this aspect of the representational function clearly involves the legislative-executive relationship.

Third, is the overall composition of the Alaska legislature reflective of the Alaska population in terms of values and political ideology? If we accept the arguments presented in Chapter 5 and 14 on the state's political culture and campaigns and elections respectively, it does reflect the wishes of the median voter, though there may be significant regional and philosophical deviation.[13]

Deliberation

As a deliberative body the Alaska legislature is not much different from other legislatures in that it is, theoretically, a forum for the open expression of views on issues and proposed laws. To facilitate deliberations, the Alaska legislature holds committee hearings on bills and floor sessions in each house. It also employs its own media people who facilitate coverage by commercial and public media. The often heated debates between the majority and minority in both houses, but particularly in the House of Representatives, is a major aspect of this deliberative function.

Deliberation, however, is often perfunctory in terms of changing the outcome of a proposal that the majority in either house supports, even though the testimony against it may be overwhelming. On other occasions, usually when there is no majority position on a bill or no powerful majority member who wants it, discussion can make a difference. One recent change in the legislative process arguably has constrained the legislature's deliberative process. In 2006 the voters approved an initiative reducing the maximum time for a legislative session from 120 to 90 days, beginning with the 2008 session. There is no question that the 90-day session allows less time for public hearings and debate, and a good argument can be made that the 90-day limit diminishes the oversight, approval, and investigatory roles of the legislature, which are major ways in which it can influence the executive.

Lawmaking

The purposeful division of the lawmaking function by America's founding fathers and by each state's founders is the major reason for the need for each branch to cooperate, but, at the same time, it is the major source of conflict between them. So it is in Alaska. The fact that the governor needs the legislature in order to enact his or her legislative agenda, including the all-important operating and capital budget bills, gives the legislature considerable political leverage. On the other hand, just getting a bill through the

House and Senate is not enough. Legislators who sponsor legislation need to be mindful of the governor's power to veto substantive bills and to reduce or eliminate line items in budget bills. This makes it important to have the governor's support or at least his or her neutrality.

As a consequence, legislators are constantly trying to anticipate what the governor will or will not do in response to their actions on legislation, and they want to know his or her position on various proposals. To assess such intentions, legislators often make inquiries of the governor's legislative director as well as commissioners, department personnel, and legislative liaisons at committee hearings and in private meetings. So, in effect, although the governor is not a member of the legislature, he or she is, in a very real sense, the sixty-first legislator and a major influential force in the legislative process.

As Figure 16.1 indicates, Alaska has a streamlined organization in its legislative committee structure with parallel standing (permanent) committees in both the House and Senate. Again, in theory, this should lead to some efficiency in lawmaking. In practice what determines the way that laws are enacted or blocked depends on politics and the power structure in the legislature, including the anticipated and actual actions of the governor. One factor that may reduce the ability of the legislature to deal with laws and, in particular, to scrutinize the governor's agenda, is the ninety-day session.[14] In this regard, in 2011, then Senate President Gary Stevens commented that the ninety-day session needed revisiting, and several proposals have been introduced in the legislature to extend it, usually up to the 120-day limit contained in the Alaska Constitution.[15] Without a longer legislative session it appears that there will be an increasing number of special legislative sessions after the regular session. Following the 2015 legislative session, for example, three special sessions were held.

Oversight—Investigation and Confirmation

Another important constitutional function of the legislature that gives lawmakers political leverage in their dealings with the governor and executive branch is responsibility for oversight, usually in the exercise of the legislatures investigative and confirmation authority. The investigative function is part of the legislature's lawmaking authority and involves such activities as auditing the budget and conducting performance reviews of departments. In fact, Article IX, Section 14 of the Alaska Constitution requires the legislature to appoint a certified public accountant to conduct these audits. Confirmation authority, involving mainly the governor's appointment of commissioners and members of boards and commissions (but not judges), is a restriction on the governor's authority to have anyone he or she wishes to appoint to an executive position.

Impeachment

While impeachment is rarely used, Alaska's lawmakers do have the authority to impeach elected and appointed state officials, as do the U.S. Congress and the legislatures of all states except Oregon.[16] In recent years successful impeachments were brought in 1988 against Evan Mecham of Arizona and, in 2009, against Rod Blagojevich of Illinois. Both were removed from office. Alaska's impeachment provisions are found in Article II, Section 20, of the constitution. They were used against Governor Bill Sheffield in 1985 for allegedly steering a state lease contract to a political supporter, but these proceedings were not pursued beyond the initial stage in the Senate. There is often a fine line between legal wrongdoing and political disagreements with executive officials, both of which may prompt impeachments. Politics appeared to have been the major motivation in the Sheffield impeachment proceedings.[17]

The Human Element in the Legislature: Organization, Power Structures, Individual Members, and Internal Relations

Legislative operations are certainly affected by the constitutional provisions that govern the legislature. These operations are, however, equally affected by the people who are elected to it and the staff they employ. So in order to understand the workings of the legislature and its relations with the governor, it is important to take the human element into account. Legislatures, like gubernatorial administrations, have defining characteristics and personalities of a type.

Each legislature lasts for two years. For example, the Twenty-Ninth Legislature—the twenty-ninth since statehood—met for its first session in 2015 and for its second session in 2016. Activities tend to be less hectic in the first session, as bills can be carried over to the second session. The second session is usually more frantic because any bill not passed dies at the end of that session. Each legislature has its own character and its own political dynamics. These result from a combination of factors including how the legislature was organized, the personalities of key legislators, the power structure of the body, relations within each house, especially between the majority and minority and between the House and the Senate, and the major issues at hand. All these factors affect the legislature's relationship with the governor.

Organizing the Legislature

Much of the character and the power structure of a legislature is set by the legislative organization that takes place after the November general election, when all House seats and usually half the Senate seats are up for election. Since the 1994 election there has been a clear Republican majority in the House and up to fourteen of twenty seats held by Republicans in the Senate.

Following the election, the members of the majority usually meet in Anchorage and negotiate how an organization will be formed. The aspiring candidates for the top jobs in each house (House Speaker and Senate President) garner support by offering legislators in their party, but sometimes from the other party, leadership positions including key committee chairs and assignments such as membership on the powerful finance and rules committees. One reason many legislative committees have co-chairs is that, in order to put together an organization, a would-be speaker or president needs to offer some inducement to all those necessary to ensure a viable organization that will last throughout the two-year legislature. Usually, within a day or so an organization emerges in each house that will control the business in both houses for the upcoming legislature. This group in each house is referred to as the majority caucus, or the Republican or Democratic majority caucus, depending on which party is dominant. Those who form the minority in each house go through a similar exercise, though, of course, the resulting organization is less important in determining the way the legislature operates.

Very often, Republican house majority caucuses include some rural-bush Democrats. Coalitions have also been common in the Senate. For instance, following the 2006 election, Senator Lyda Green put together a coalition of Republicans and Democrats designated as the Bipartisan Working Group (BWG), which lasted until the election of November 2012 when the Republicans won thirteen seats and with two Democrats formed a solid 15-5 Republican majority caucus. After the key players who helped to put together the majorities in each house have settled the leadership and key committee assignments, other majority members will receive committee assignments, often based upon the interests of their districts or regions or their personal interests. Each committee has a majority of majority caucus members on it to ensure a unified position on legislation coming before the committee, but all committees also include minority members. Sometimes the politics of which minority members get on which committee, particularly in regard to the House and Senate finance committees, is very conflict ridden, as the majority tries to prevent certain minority members from being seated on those committees. Other caucuses of legislators are also formed during each legislature, such as the bush caucus, the children's caucus, and the fish caucus, but they have no operational function in the lawmaking process.

The Power Structure in the Legislature and Major Influences on Its Business

The particular way in which each house is organized following the November general election will obviously determine the power structure in the upcoming legislature and shape the policy agenda of what does and does not get done by that body during the next two years. The power structure also shapes the relationships between the majority and minority in each house, between individual legislators, and between the legislature

BOX 16.6

The Power Structure in the Alaska Legislature

1. MAJOR POLITICAL FORCES ON MOST ACTIONS AND POLICIES

The Majority Caucuses in the House and Senate

Majority caucuses control the legislative calendar and determine what bills will and will not pass. In particular, they control the budget process in the legislature. Members of the majority caucus are expected to support the majority position on the budget, administrative matters, like committee assignments, and sometimes other legislation. Those who do not are usually expelled from the caucus, though this does not happen very often. It did happen, however, in the 2015 legislative session when Republican Representative Lora Reinbold of Eagle River was expelled from the majority house caucus for voting against the budget. The previous expulsion was in 2005.

Key Majority Legislative Leaders

The Speaker of the House and President of the Senate, the majority leaders in both houses (who manage caucus business and enforce its agenda), and key committee chairpersons, particularly of the finance committees, wield major influence. For example, committee chairs can decide which bills to schedule for a hearing in their committees. A decision by the chair not to hear a bill effectively kills it.

2. IMPORTANT FORCES IN CERTAIN CIRCUMSTANCES

The Minority Caucuses in the House and Senate

Minority caucuses can be influential if the majority caucus needs them for a vote requiring more than a simple 50 percent majority (such as overriding a governor's veto) as well as when an issue is not of major concern to the majority caucus, and in certain other circumstances.

Key Minority Leaders and Members

The minority leader in both houses wields influence in certain situations. Other minority members, usually because of their political acumen, personality, or their willingness to cross party lines (often the case with bush legislators), can have influence in particular situations.

Regional Alliances and Caucuses and Policy Issue Caucuses

The bush caucus (bush legislators from both parties) was very influential in the 1980s but is less so today. Regional cross-party caucuses (such as the Southeast and Interior Caucuses) can exert influence on regional issues as long as the majority caucuses give tacit approval. Bipartisan caucuses that are formed to deal with specific policy areas, such as the children's caucus, can also be influential in certain circumstances.

Legislative Aides/Staff

Certain legislative staff members, especially those with long service, are often important participants in policy making. Many staff members move between the executive and legislative branches as administrations change, and these staffers have long institutional memories that are valuable sources of information for policy makers in both branches of government.

Source: Developed by the authors.

and the governor and the administration. Box 16.6 provides an overview of the power structure as it operates in each legislature. The power dynamics in a particular legislature, however, and on a particular issue during a particular legislative session, will depend upon the makeup of the legislature and the individual personalities in both houses.

Legislators as Individuals: A Microcosm of Human Nature

The public tends to think of legislators generically as "legislators," as if they had common mind-sets and were all cut from the same human mold in the way they go about their job as representatives. The reality is much different. Chapter 3 on the policy process considers the motives and goals of legislators and their staffs as participants in the Alaska public policy process, and in Chapter 14, on elections and campaigns, explains the personal and professional background of those who become legislators. Here we make brief remarks about the personalities, and the management, and political styles of legislators.

Each of the sixty offices in the legislature has a different personality that is set largely by the legislator and, to some extent, the staff. Generally very affable and approachable people, legislators run the gamut from the self-effacing to the down-home glad-hander to the aloof, self-important, and arrogant. With everyone trying to get a piece of their time and often paying them deference, it is not surprising that some have big egos. In terms of management style, some allow their staffs a lot of leeway, while others are micromanagers. In regard to political style, some focus on particular policies and are well-informed on them, some to the point of being tedious policy wonks. Others have more of a statewide perspective along with concerns about their districts, while some concentrate their efforts on their own districts and the needs of their constituents. Some legislators are very concerned about the rules and procedures of their legislative body. Others are wheeler-dealer politicos who help broker deals and are more interested in power relationships than the procedures or even the substance of policies.

Exactly what constitutes a good legislator is largely in the eye of the beholder. Many are low profile but serve their constituents well and have no ambitions to rise through the ranks except as may be necessary in order to serve their districts. Others seek out legislative office and leadership positions as a stepping stone to higher state or federal office.

The Internal Relations and Political Dynamics of a Legislature

Besides differences in the personalities and the management and political styles of individual members of a particular legislature, and especially its leadership, the internal relationships also help determine the personality of a particular legislature as a whole. The three key relationships here are those between the House and the Senate, between the majority and minority in each house, and between individual legislators. Insight into these three types of relationships, plus a comment on the importance of the relationship with the governor, are provided in Box 16.7 by former Senate President Lyda Green, a Republican from Wasilla who organized the BWG in the Senate. We can supplement her observations with a few additional comments.

With a membership of forty, the House generally has more spirited debates and is more fluid a body politically than the Senate. Major conflicts between the two houses

BOX 16.7

Being a State Legislator and Senate President

Serving in the Alaska Senate was the greatest learning adventure of my life. It included challenges, victories, losses, near misses, and some very satisfying experiences. There is nothing like seeing your legislation enacted and good results follow. Helping a constituent find a way through the bureaucracy is a close second.

Being a legislator involved in politics and policy making is not much different from many other jobs. It is often driven by the relationships between the people involved, and the Alaska legislature is a prime example. My fourteen years in the Senate taught me that two sets of relationships play a big role in the outcome of the legislative session. First, a natural tension always exists between the legislature and the governor. It's the level of tension that sets the tone for the session. Second, how well the House and Senate get along dictates how smooth the session will be. Personality clashes and differences of opinion between Representatives and Senators can erupt into a bunch of problems and misunderstandings, turning the political art of compromise into a political slugfest and slowing down the process.

Every session brings its own hot issue or issues. For instance, the significant issues in the 2008 session were a gas line, energy needs, and creating savings for the future. In addition, the new ninety-day session, which took effect in 2008, provided a new challenge for legislators.

As to being Senate president, even twelve years in the Senate scarcely prepared me for this new role—it turned out to be another major challenge. I had watched five other people handle this job, but you have to be in the job to understand what it's really like. The role of Senate president is an unusual mix of routine, even mundane responsibilities peppered with challenging political predicaments and decisions. Many tasks are simply part of the process and handled according to tradition. There is even a helpful script for each of the floor sessions. But these formal and mundane aspects might be 10 percent of the job—the bulk and most challenging parts are the politics and the interaction of personalities. The legislative-gubernatorial relationship and the relationship between House and Senate very much shape how easy or difficult the session can be for the Senate president. In particular, this determines decisions on the priorities for the session, the goals for the year, how they will be achieved, and ultimately the successes and failures.

A lot of my day during the session was spent meeting with dozens of special interest groups, nonprofit organizations, elected officials, and individual Alaskans. These meetings provide some of the immense amount of information the Senate president has to take in. Assimilating, categorizing, and sorting it all out is a major effort throughout the year. But whatever you do and however much effort you put in, it seems like a fair number of people are dissatisfied. Plus, it didn't matter how I voted on a bill; as Senate president I was still considered a sponsor of that bill and every other bill in the Senate, and I was held to scrutiny for them all. Journalists and the public want to know the president's opinion on a piece of legislation and that opinion plays a big role in shaping the public's perception of what is going on in Juneau.

When the going gets rough is when legislative leadership steps in. The Speaker of the House and I smoothed over ruffled feathers. We brought lawmakers back together to negotiate compromises and come up with an adjournment plan that would meet most, if not all the goals for the session.

Source: Based on an interview of March 10, 2011, by Clive Thomas with former Senator Lyda Green.

are the exception rather than the rule, but they do occur, as we will see in a case study below. Sometimes these conflicts lead to a political stalemate. For this reason, the idea of a unicameral legislature is suggested from time to time as a way to increase legislative efficiency. But the proposal has never gained much political traction.[18]

Relations between the majority and minority in both houses are usually civil, but may be chilly at times. Minority bills rarely get enacted unless a minority member can get co-sponsors from the majority. Often the minority feels frustrated, and this sometimes spills over into heated debate in committees and in floor sessions. In some years, the majority needs minority votes on an issue, such as drawing money from the Constitutional Budget Reserve for state spending (which requires a three-fourths vote in each house). In those cases, the minority may have more clout on a range of issues. Moreover, the existence of the BWG in the Senate from 2007 to 2012, with many Democrats in positions of power, helped the House minority Democrats politically.

The role of rural-bush legislators can also affect the relations between the majority and minority and, indeed, the entire character of the legislature. This is because these legislators, although usually Democrats, are generally less partisan and are willing to join a majority coalition in order to secure basic benefits for rural-bush areas. In the 1980s, the bush caucus held the balance of power in the legislature in both houses, but the influence of the caucus and of rural-bush legislators has waxed and waned over time. Its influence was reduced further by the 2012 redistricting of the legislature.

A Fragmented Political and Governmental Institution

This overview of the legislature shows that it is not in any way a body that acts in concert or speaks with one voice. With House and Senate majority and minority caucuses, sixty members with varying ideologies, motives, and goals and representing several regions across the state, and often with urban versus rural-bush tensions manifesting themselves, the legislature is a fragmented branch of government in its internal operations and in its political and power relationships. On almost every issue, including overriding gubernatorial vetoes, there are some dissenting voices and votes.

This legislative diversity is, of course, a major aspect of a pluralist democracy in which the legislature represents a broad range of geographical, socio-economic, cultural, and political constituencies in an attempt to reflect the society and to deal with its needs. However, this diversity often undermines the legislature's dealings with the governor. In fact, it is a misnomer to talk of executive-legislative relations. Theoretically, at least, the executive is a united body headed by the governor. The legislature, by contrast, is a collection of group and individual interests, each of which may relate to the executive, and particularly the governor, in different, sometimes diametrically opposed ways.

4. THE LEGISLATIVE-EXECUTIVE POLITICAL, POLICY, AND POWER DYNAMIC

In the introduction to this chapter we argued that the legislative-executive relationship is an uneven one with the advantage going to the executive constitutionally and often politically. Despite this, the legislature is not a deferential body, and things do not always come easy to governors. Part of the reason for the legislature's power base is the so-called advantage of the defense—that is, those who want to maintain the political status quo have it much easier politically as it takes much less effort to stall or kill a bill or proposal than to get it over all the hurdles to passage. This means that both legislators and governors need to build alliances to be successful. Building alliances is crucial but often fraught with difficulties.

Uneven Resources

Governors have major resources and political carrots to offer and sanctions that they can bring to bear in dealing with the legislature. They have full-time staff in their office and in the bureaucracy to conduct research, present material, and plan strategy. Many of these people are specialists in one or more areas of policy. Particularly important is that the administration prepares the annual state budget for the legislature's consideration and enactment. In addition, the governor's signature, or at least his or her neutrality, is needed for any bill to become law. And the governor has a line-item veto that can reduce or eliminate the funding for a legislator's hard fought for program or project. In addition, governors are in a good position to build public support to bring to bear on issues in the legislative-executive tussle.

In contrast, even though the Alaska legislature is one of the best staffed in the nation and with additional resources, such as the Legislative Finance Division to aid with the state budget, legislative staffing is miniscule compared with the executive. The legislature meets for only ninety days a year (with some interim work), many of its members have other jobs, and they and their staff members must cover the gamut of state government activities and policies from economic development to health to environmental issues, to say nothing of maintaining good constituent relations.

Take, for instance, the situation in which a legislator succeeds in getting a piece of legislation enacted, only to find later that the governor and his or her commissioner have implemented the legislation inconsistently with the legislator's original intent. At that point the legislator must introduce a new bill to change direction and do the research necessary to convince others in the legislature that it is worth the time and trouble to "undo the damage." Then, if successful in passing the bill (with agency personnel almost certainly testifying against the bill, well-armed with all kinds of resources and data), the legislator still has to work to avoid a veto.

So, clearly, the legislature cannot give extensive and in-depth attention to most pieces of legislation proposed by the governor, including the budget, and has minimal resources to follow up after executive implementation of a policy. The legislature can certainly cause political heartburn for the governor and the executive departments on their legislation and the budget, but the operating budget proposed by the governor is actually changed very little by the legislature.

To be sure, the legislature can override a gubernatorial veto and can reject gubernatorial appointments, giving the body some political advantage. Neither action is done often, however. It takes a super majority to override a governor's veto (two-thirds on nonappropriation bills and three-fourths on appropriation bills) and getting such a majority is difficult. And generally, the legislature approves gubernatorial appointments. Interestingly, however, Governor Palin suffered defeat in both areas in 2009 when her nominee for attorney general, Wayne Anthony Ross, was not confirmed, and her veto of the use of federal stimulus package money to help boost the economy was overridden.

Legislative-Executive Cooperation and Building Political Alliances

The political key to governors and the administration getting what they wish to enact or kill is building alliances with influential groups and individuals in the legislature. The same is true for the legislature in relation to the executive. Underlying such alliances is always the threat of a governor withholding benefits or using the veto, and lack of cooperation and stalling on the part of the legislature. But cooperation through alliances and a degree of consensus is the major mode of executive-legislative operations.

From the governor's perspective, because of the weakness of parties and the bipartisanship that is often a reality of legislative operations, he or she cannot rely on party loyalty (or in the case of Governor Walker, no affiliated party to appeal to). The governor must build relationships with groups and individuals in the legislature, particularly the majority caucuses in each house, as well as with the minority, depending on the governor's needs and style of operation. In Boxes 16.5 and 16.7 both Governor Sheffield and Senator Green emphasize how important it is to build these relationships.

Different governors have different approaches to building alliances depending on their personal philosophy and style and on political necessity. Governor Hickel had a bipartisan approach, often consulting members of the minority in both houses. The same was true for Governor Palin, at least until her nomination as the Republican vice presidential candidate in August 2008. A bipartisan approach will be useful to Governor Walker as he ran as a nonpartisan. In contrast, Governor Murkowski dealt mainly with the majority. Democrat Tony Knowles, faced with a Republican House and Senate for eight years, focused attention on the majority and individual legislators from both houses to give him the majorities he needed in a generally hostile political environment. Governor Parnell had little luck working with Democrats and was ideologically more oriented to conservative Republicans who gave him several successes when they won control of both houses of the legislature in November 2012.

Looked at from the point of view of the legislature, these relationships and alliances with the governor and various state agencies take many forms. The majority caucus in each house clearly has the strongest political power base to forge an alliance with the governor and key administration staff, such as the governor's chief of staff and the director of the Office of Management and Budget. Cooperation between majorities in both houses and the administration is the key to the successful functioning of state government. The minorities in both houses have fewer opportunities to build alliances. But as noted earlier, there are circumstances that lead governors to seek their support. Legislative committee chairs have a power base to build cooperative relationships with departments and agencies that can be of mutual advantage. And based upon benefit to their constituents or simply their own interest, individual legislators, from both the majority and minority, build relationships and alliances with administrative personnel on a host of issues.

Specific Circumstances, Personality, and Political Acumen

While uneven resources coupled with the need to cooperate and to build alliances generally characterize the legislative-executive relationship, its particular dynamics on a day-to-day basis depend on the specific circumstances surrounding an issue, the personalities involved, and the political acumen brought to bear in the situation.

Legislative-executive relations do not exist in a vacuum. They are subject to all the external pressures and influences of interest groups, media coverage, public opinion, in some cases direct or indirect pressure from the federal government, and so on. This means that the dynamics of the legislative-executive relationship will likely be different at different times even on a similar issue. For instance, on the issue of the stringency and enforcement of campaign finance, lobbying, and ethics laws, Governor Murkowski ran into opposition from the legislature in trying to defund APOC, which administers these laws. In contrast, after the publicity of political scandals, Governor Palin and the legislature worked hand in hand to increase funding for the agency and tighten ethics laws.

Personality can come into play in several ways. Occasionally, a governor and a legislative leader have a personality conflict. This was the case with Governor Sheffield and Senator Jan Faiks in the early 1980s. Powerful legislative leaders or committee chairs can exert tremendous influence on a department for all sorts of reasons, including dislike of its policies or its leadership. In the 1990s Representative Ramona Barnes, a strong and forceful person, exerted great influence on the Department of Corrections from her seat on the House Finance Committee and later as Speaker of the House. During these same years, Republican Senators Robin Taylor and John Torgerson were major influences over the Department of Transportation from their leadership positions.

Finally, some governors and legislators are good politicians, some are mediocre, and some are just not good at politics. By his own admission (see Box 16.5), Governor Sheffield was not good at it when he first came to office, and Governor Murkowski sometimes alienated legislators. Given that he faced Republican legislatures for his two terms, Governor Knowles had some notable achievements. From the legislative side, several Native legislators stand out as good at forging working relationships with the administration even when they are in the minority.

5. TWO CASE STUDIES: A LEGISLATIVE-EXECUTIVE COOPERATIVE SUCCESS AND A POLITICAL STANDOFF

To give concrete meaning to the elements that go into the dynamics of legislative-executive relations, in this section we present two case studies. One, the enactment of Denali KidCare, was a success story. The other, an attempt to lower taxes on the oil industry in 2011, turned into an acrimonious political standoff. While no two situations in the legislative-executive power relationship are identical, there are some common elements that increase the chances of success and others that undermine success or kill cooperation. After providing background on each case, we review their general and specific lessons and implications.

Denali KidCare—Success against the Political Odds

At the end of his first term in office, Democrat Tony Knowles championed an issue that was high on his personal political agenda: a program to provide health care to poor children. Box 16.8 explains the circumstances and politics of what became known as Denali KidCare. It is a good example of how a thoughtful and well-managed gubernatorial strategy can overcome stiff political odds.

House Bill 110: Ineffective Executive-Legislative Relations

One of the stark realities of Alaska's political economy is dependence on oil revenues as both a major driver of economic activity and as the principal source of the state's unrestricted revenues. As a consequence, since big oil money began to flow into the state's general fund in the late 1970s, there has been a debate about taxing the oil industry enough to ensure that Alaska gets its "fair share" of revenues (a vague but commonly used term among politicians) while not discouraging investment in exploration and production by the industry. This debate will continue to be prominent for years to come, as there is no definitive answer. Several ways to tax the oil industry have been tried and modified over the years in attempts to strike the proper balance.[19]

BOX 16.8

A Success Story in Gubernatorial-Legislative Relations: Denali KidCare

In 1997, there was a sudden opportunity for Governor Knowles to achieve one of his primary goals: reduce child abuse and neglect, give kids a healthy start, and prepare them for success in school and life. Congress had just upped the federal percentage of Medicaid coverage for Alaska, freeing up millions of dollars in state funds. Talking on a cell phone from the annual governor's picnic in Anchorage, Knowles made a successful plea to President Clinton not to veto the provision, promising him he would invest the windfall in improving the lives of Alaska's kids. "Smart Start for Alaska's Children" was born, financed by this unexpected federal windfall.

Knowles unveiled the initiative in his November 1997 State of the Child Address. It was a $32 million package of expanded health coverage for children and pregnant women called Denali KidCare, prevention programs to break the cycle of abuse and neglect, and tougher laws and more troopers and child protection workers. He also appointed a "children's cabinet" of various department commissioners.

As the legislature convened in 1998, several Republican legislators opposed Smart Start. It was labeled by one as "dead on arrival." The mantra was that Alaska could not afford these investments. What was not said publicly was that it was a gubernatorial election year, and the Republican majorities in both houses of the legislature were in no mood to approve any of Knowles's proposals. So, five months later, why did most of Smart Start pass? There are three main reasons:

A sustained awareness campaign to highlight the importance of investments in children: The message that resonated with Alaskans was that prevention is cost effective in avoiding future crime and other societal costs. Advocates demonstrated that prenatal and early health care prevent higher medical costs. Good preschool programs improve school success and reduce juvenile crime. Child abuse and violence prevention decrease future criminal behavior. Children's cabinet members carried the message across Alaska for months: child outcomes will improve through smart investments, not broad cuts.

Denali KidCare was and is a great deal: The program was designed in its first year to provide comprehensive health insurance to 11,600 children and 800 pregnant women in families that made too much for Medicaid but not enough to afford insurance. Critics said this was not the government's responsibility, or that there were too many federal strings attached. Yet the proposal—Alaska's version of the federal State Children's Health Insurance Program (S-CHIP)—was very affordable for the state, and Alaska's share would be paid from windfall Medicaid funds and tobacco taxes.

High-profile child abuse cases angered the public and spurred reform: Alaskans had been reading shocking news accounts of child abuse. The coverage was highly critical of the government's child protection system. Knowles decided to focus the public's outrage to strengthen child protection laws and add resources to an overworked system. He told the Anchorage Chamber of Commerce his policy was "zero tolerance for child abuse." In the first half of 1998, the governor and children's cabinet members crisscrossed the state, talking openly about Alaska's high rates of child abuse and neglect and making the link between prevention and better outcomes for children and society.

While it was politically risky to talk about a subject often avoided, the strategy generated an outpouring of support from business leaders, child advocates, police chiefs, educators, and others. By the end of the legislative session, most lawmakers had been persuaded. In May 1998, the bill passed the state House of Representatives with just two votes to spare. A week later, with public support for the program still growing, the state Senate also passed the bill.

Source: Developed by Karen Perdue, who served as the state's Health and Social Services Commissioner from 1994 to 2001. She co-founded and led the children's cabinet.

In 2007, in her first year as governor, Republican Sarah Palin promoted increasing oil and gas taxes based on a principle she called "Alaska's Clear and Equitable Share," or ACES. Then, following his election to a full term as governor in 2010, Republican Sean Parnell proposed cutting oil and gas taxes, essentially reversing Palin's policy. The governor's bill was introduced as House Bill 110, or HB 110 as it was commonly known. The debate over HB 110 (and the political costs that spilled over onto other issues) dominated the Twenty-Seventh Alaska legislative session (2011–2012). The politics involved in this issue, an overview of which is provided in Box 16.9 offers lessons about the problems that can arise in the legislative-executive relationship.

The Lessons and Implications

The Denali KidCare and the HB 110 cases provide several insights into the dynamics of legislative-executive relations. Some of the dynamics are inherent in the separation of powers dictated by the constitution. Others, while not unique to the state, have an Alaska element to them. Still others result from elements common to all political situations. All three sets of dynamics are interrelated.

Separation of Powers: Overcoming the Advantage of the Defense

The institutional authority of both branches is clear in both case studies. In the Denali KidCare case, the governor had the ability to include the program in the budget, the ability to organize his staff and top officials to promote the program, and the resources to mount an effective public relations campaign. The legislature had a Republican majority in both houses that controlled the legislative agenda, and could eliminate the program from the budget bill. The institutional dynamics were slightly different in the case of HB 110 because the Senate was run by the BWG, but circumstances were essentially the same in other respects.

However, the constitutional authority of the two branches is one thing; turning this into power in any one situation is quite another. Governor Knowles was able to overcome the legislature's advantage of the defense and achieve the difficult task of enacting Denali KidCare by executing a well-coordinated public relations campaign. Then he brought public pressure to bear on the Republicans initially opposed to his proposal. Governor Parnell never had the support of the BWG on HB 110, even though he indirectly linked it (and its Senate counterpart, SB 49) to his support for other legislation being promoted by some BWG senators. And though there was a public relations effort in support of HB 110, it lacked the fiscal analysis needed to withstand the opposition's objections.

Alaska Elements

While there are no unique Alaska elements that affected these two cases, there are some factors that came into play because of the political circumstances in the state. One

BOX 16.9

A Standoff in Gubernatorial-Legislative Relations: Governor Parnell's Proposal to Cut Oil Taxes

House Bill 110 (HB 110) to reduce certain oil taxes was introduced on January 18, 2011, the first day of the Twenty-Seventh Legislature. Governor Parnell explained the tax reduction as the way to get more investment directed toward exploration and development in the state's oil fields. It would increase throughput on the trans-Alaska pipeline system from the resulting increase in oil production in the long term. Opponents argued that HB 110 would cut state revenues by $2 billion a year and add to existing oil industry profits. Oil producers agreed that, initially, the state would have less revenue, but they promised the return would be substantial over a twenty-year period.

In the legislature the governor's proposal was supported by the Republican-dominated House majority caucus, led by Speaker Mike Chenault. The four-member Senate minority caucus (all Republicans) also supported the proposal. The oil industry, not surprisingly, strongly favored the bill and gave legislative testimony to that effect. Other business groups in the state, including the Alaska State Chamber of Commerce, the Resource Development Council, and the Alaska Oil and Gas Association, also supported it.

On the other side, Senate leaders in the Bipartisan Working Group (BWG), including Senate President Gary Stevens and Finance Co-Chair Bert Stedman (both Republicans), argued that the time was not right for an oil tax change. They saw the bill as having little chance of passage in the Senate. The Democratic House minority also strongly opposed the bill.

HB 110 passed the House at the end of the first session on March 31 with a 22-16 vote and was referred to the Senate (where a companion bill had been introduced in January—Senate Bill 49 (SB 49). SB 49 was replaced in the second session of the legislature (February 2012) by a newly created Senate tax bill (SB 192) that sponsors hoped would result in a new method for calculating taxes. After nineteen hearings in the Senate Resources Committee and twenty-six hearings in the Senate Finance Committee, the Senate had not gathered enough support for any plan to go to the floor for a vote. A special session of the legislature called by the governor in April proved fruitless.

From the start the tax reduction proposal ran into problems. First, the governor and his staff had not done their political homework: consulting all the various interests in the legislature about the proposal before introducing it. Then, in legislative committee hearings, the administration (principally Revenue Commissioner Bryan Butcher and his staff) could neither convincingly show the inadequacies of the present tax regime nor provide assurances from the oil industry that a new tax would increase exploration, development, or production.

The governor also refused to accept changes to the original bill of January 2011. He presented SB 3001 for the special session, saying it was a new approach and a hybrid of various plans previously discussed. However, lawmakers saw it as basically the same plan as HB 110—pointing out that they had already rejected most of its provisions. The governor continued to call for the original plan's concepts and charged the BWG with "turning its back" on Alaskans.

While some questioned his motives for pushing the legislation, the governor took his case directly to the Alaska public by making speeches promoting the plan. In one publicly released letter he likened the BWG to "a group of hens in the barnyard" and asked finance co-chair Bert Stedman not to "shoot explorers in the head" while they looked for new sources of oil. Parnell urged "all Alaskans to send a clear message to legislators in Juneau that a 'do-nothing' strategy is unacceptable because Alaska's future is at stake."

The Senate was unconvinced by the administration. With his repetition of the arguments and the absence of any outside advisers documenting the administration's case, the governor began to lose support even among his former allies like Anchorage Republican Senator Lesil McGuire, who said his plan was "half-baked." Throughout the Twenty-Seventh Legislature, negotiations resulted in little change from either side's initial position on the issue. The governor continued to talk about his fear of a failure in the state's economy because of declining levels of oil production. Yet, he offered no empirical evidence to link that fear to the ACES tax regime. The Senate majority responded that oil production had been declining for decades—through several tax regimes—with no noticeable change.

While the governor lost this round on his proposed oil tax increase, he lived to fight another political day. The November 2012 election produced large Republican majorities in both houses, and a revised version of the tax cut (the More Alaska Production Act or MAPA) was passed at the end of the first session of the Twenty-Eighth Legislature in April 2013. Almost immediately a citizen campaign was launched and a referendum was placed on the August 2014 primary ballot to repeal the tax cut. It lost by a margin of 53 to 47 percent, so the tax cut still stands.

Source: Developed by the authors with reference to various articles in the *Anchorage Daily News*, the *Alaska Dispatch*, the *Alaska Dispatch News*, and Kristen Nelson, "ACES Angst Continues as House Version of Tax Cut Moves to Floor," *Petroleum News* 16, no. 14 (April 3, 2011).

was the attitude of the public, which often has populist elements to it. A second was friends and neighbors politics. And a third was bipartisanship. Knowles was able to use all three positively to promote Denali KidCare. In contrast, directly and indirectly, Parnell was adversely affected by all three in promoting HB 110.

With the help of his staff, including his press office and commissioners, Knowles was able to garner public support for what was literally a motherhood issue by encouraging concerned members of the public to contact their legislators, and through positive support in the media. In addition, through various means Knowles was able to forge bipartisan support in a legislature that was generally hostile to him and his policy agenda.

Parnell, on the other hand, advocated what opponents perceived as nothing more than a handout to the oil companies. This perception was, in part, grounded in the anti-big business and populist sentiments prevalent in the state and partly because the oil companies had reported record worldwide profits during the previous couple of years. Parnell's support from the oil industry and several business organizations was not enough to overcome public opposition that was shared by a number of BWG members and by the Democrats in the House. The opposition grew when some argued that reducing oil taxes might reduce the state's bond rating.[20] In addition, there was some evidence of political cracks in the House majority's support for HB 110. And so bipartisanship, in this case in the Senate, worked against the governor.

The Fundamentals of Politics: Agendas, Personalities, Political Will, and Acumen, and Political Power

One aspect of these two case studies that is illustrated directly and indirectly is that of political agendas, personalities, political will and acumen, and political power. More often than not these factors make the difference between success and failure for legislators and governors.

In regard to political agendas, in the Denali KidCare case, most Republicans in the legislature wanted to deny Knowles any political success to aid his reelection. Certainly, Knowles wanted Denali KidCare for its social and human value, but he and his staff also realized its election potential, and getting reelected was high on his political agenda. In the case of HB 110, Parnell's motives were not easy to fathom, and there was much speculation about his true motives. The House majority's support for the bill was in tune with the ideological belief that lower taxes always encourage investment by the taxpayer. In the Senate, the BWG's opposition was likely due to a combination of factors, including a belief that there was no need for a reduction in oil taxes, a view to the next election, and the more immediate need to keep the loose and fragile BWG together by not dividing it on a major issue. The general point is that political agendas sometimes drive actions taken on proposed legislation, regardless of the proposal's merits.

Personality, particularly personality conflicts, can also shape the outcome of the legislative-executive political tussle. Personality was not so evident in the battle over Denali KidCare. However, as with all governors, Knowles, his staff, and senior departmental personnel had their detractors in the legislature, and these executive officials for their part had their own personal likes and dislikes regarding legislators. In the HB 110 case, the governor clearly ruffled some political feathers among the leaders of the BWG. As with people in general, it is often hard for some elected officials to separate the personal from the professional.

Political will and political acumen can also make a difference in what legislators and governors accomplish in the contest between the two contending branches. Political will is best described as the strong commitment, tenacity, and persistence that in combination exert pressure within government to accomplish a political goal. Sometimes the political will of one or a few powerful people is enough to carry the day. At other times, it is necessary to galvanize the political will of a large number of people, including those outside government. The political will of a few people in the Murkowski administration ensured that the State of Alaska went from a defined benefit retirement system for newly hired state employees and teachers to a defined contribution system, even though the change was opposed by large groups of Alaskans. In terms of political acumen, some politicians and senior state officials are just better at it than others. Those who have this skill can put together a coalition, convince opponents to join them or to remain neutral, know how and when to compromise, and the right time to bring political pressure to bear. Knowles and his top officials had both the will and the political acumen to get Denali KidCare enacted. Parnell may have had the will, but parts of his administration were only lukewarm toward HB 110, and the governor did not appear to have the political acumen to put it all together.

All these political factors, plus the institutional and bipartisan elements considered in the two cases and, indeed, in all legislative-executive relations (as in all political situations), boil down to the exercise of political power. The side that can amass enough of it to enact something or block it, as the case may be, will succeed, and the other side will lose. Conflict, and the political rhetoric that often accompanies it, is used by one branch as a tool to jockey for power when bargaining with the other branch concerning an issue. In the end, however, cooperation is usually necessary to achieve desired political goals, and it often involves a quid pro quo of some type between the governor and segments of the legislature. Generally, politicians will cooperate when there is mutual political benefit involved (such as funds for their district) or fear of a costly political sanction (like strong opposition at the next election) and not just because they think something is a good idea. In some circumstances, however, cooperation may not be extensive enough to ensure success for legislators or governors.

Clearly, Knowles was able to put all the pieces together in the political power jigsaw to enact Denali KidCare; Parnell had only about half the pieces of the puzzle in the case of HB 110. There are many other examples of the way that power can affect this battle of contending branches. In 1972 Governor Egan put all the pieces together despite widespread opposition in the state and in the legislature to get a constitutional amendment on the ballot to establish limited entry in the fishing industry, an attempt to deal with the problems of too many people fishing with resultant depleting fish stocks and depressed prices. Jay Hammond in 1980 used his large capital budget, and the needs he knew legislators had for a piece of it, to get the Permanent Fund Dividend (PFD) enacted against the will of many legislators. Sometimes governors lose the power struggle, however. This was the case with Governor Knowles's efforts to resolve the subsistence issue and Governor Parnell's failure to get a constitutional amendment on the ballot to allow state funds to go to private and religious schools.

The exercise of political power is an ongoing factor, however, and both governors and legislators live to fight another day. Knowles may have been successful on Denali KidCare, but it may have cost him in future dealings with a legislature not happy about having to acquiesce to him over that issue. And although Parnell suffered defeat on HB 110, he had two more years as governor. And, despite protestations to the contrary by John Torgerson, Chair of the Reapportionment Board appointed in 2012, four of the five members of which were Republican, it is widely believed that a major goal of the board in drawing new legislative district lines was to destroy the BWG in the November 2012 election.[21] It succeeded, and the Republicans took over control of the Senate. The dominantly conservative legislature elected in November 2012 gave Parnell his tax cut less than six months later.

6. LEGISLATIVE-EXECUTIVE RELATIONS IN ALASKA COMPARED WITH OTHER STATES

How do the relations, the conflict and cooperation, between Alaska's legislature and the governor compare to other states? As with the various other state comparisons in the book, there are both similarities and differences. And as has been the approach in other chapters, we can briefly summarize these comparisons by looking at three levels of political and governmental activity.

First, the human interactions of politics and the exercise of political power in the legislative-executive relationship are no different in Alaska from those in other states. That relationship is shaped by the motives, goals, needs, personalities, and political acumen, or lack thereof, of the members of both branches of government as they interact to do the business of government. From this interaction arises a power relationship both within each branch and between the two branches or, more accurately, between individuals and groups in each branch. These relationships will be different on different issues and change as circumstances change. And when the members of each branch change, the power dynamic is likely to change too. This is the case in all fifty states as well as in Washington, D.C.

Second, institutional structures and organizations also make for similarities and differences. All legislatures except Nebraska have an upper and lower house, which can result in conflict at times. All legislatures have a committee structure of standing and special committees and are organized along party lines, with a majority controlling the business of the body (again with the exception of Nebraska, which theoretically is nonpartisan). All governors have a personal staff of specialists to help them perform their various responsibilities, particularly to deal with the legislature, and all governors have some form of veto power over legislation with forty-six having a line item veto like the Alaska governor. In addition, all states have a bureaucracy of various departments and boards and commissions, or their equivalent. Where Alaska varies is in a unified executive and the extensive authority the governor has over the administration, the relatively small size of the legislature, and the high level of legislative staff support and research capability.[22]

Third are political circumstances and issues that, while not all unique to Alaska, when combined with the institutional factors give the legislative-executive relationship certain characteristics not seen in most states. One is bipartisanship, particularly between and among many Alaska Native legislators and governors like Wally Hickel, Sarah Palin, and Bill Walker. Related to this are cross-party majority caucuses, like the Senate BWG. Another characteristic has been the presence of some very divisive issues, such as subsistence and the cost of providing services to rural-bush areas. On the other hand, for most of the period since the late 1970s, Alaska's oil bonanza has made budgetary conflicts between legislatures and governors less intense. At least that was the case down to mid-2014 when oil prices remained high. The situation with low oil prices from mid 2014 into 2016 and most likely beyond may be the political script for a different story.

7. CONCLUSION: CONFLICT, COOPERATION, PERSONALITIES, AND POWER

Turning to the characteristics of Alaska politics most relevant to this chapter, it is clear that the legislature and the executive are, indeed, strongly contending institutions. Within this general political context more specific characteristics come into play. The most important of these are bipartisanship, the significant role of Alaska Natives, regionalism, and friends and neighbors politics. In combination, these characteristics can sometimes tip the political balance against the general rule that the governor has the upper hand constitutionally. Nevertheless, Alaska's governor is still relatively effective, but certainly does not have the dominant role that those considering only the governor's constitutional authority often maintain.

Success from a governor's point of view requires building good relations with key legislators and often working across party lines in the sometimes bipartisan atmosphere of the Alaska legislature. From the point of view of the legislature as a body, there is rarely one criterion of success in its relations with the governor and the administration because of the multifaceted representative role of the body and the varying motives, goals, and needs of its various caucuses, groups, and individual members. For individual legislators, when the governor signs a bill, such as for a tax increase on the oil industry, it will mean success for some and defeat for others.

While contention and conflict are built into the institutional arrangements of the legislative-executive relationship, most policy and other positive results can be achieved only through cooperation. Even so, cooperation is sometimes not easily arrived at and in the end requires one branch or a segment of it bringing political power to bear on the other branch or parts of it. In fact, at bottom, it is the stark reality of political power that, like almost all other political situations, determines the nature of the legislative-executive relationship. Sometimes along the way this is affected by personality and agendas that sidetrack the main issue at hand and result in a policy not being considered on its merits, as Governor Hickel's expression of anger with his water glass (and perhaps the foam rubber brick on later occasions) attests. Generally, however, the power relationship involves giving the governor some benefit in order to get the governor's help for an individual legislator or a caucus. Similarly, the governor has to offer a benefit in order to get support in the legislature.

Within the political dynamics of the legislative-executive relationship the permutations are infinite, and there will be several relationships operating simultaneously. Some of these relationships will be positive, some negative, and some a combination of the two, all operating at once and constantly changing, especially during the legislative session. In addition, the courts, as an influential third branch of government, can affect the legislative-executive relationship in general or on certain issues, as we will see in the next chapter. For the most part, however, the political interplay between the legislature and executive explained in this chapter will help in understanding the formulation and implementation of the various policies considered later in the book. The immediate value of this chapter will become clear in considering the key aspect of state government dealt with jointly by the legislature and the governor—the state budget. This is the subject of Chapter 19.

ENDNOTES

[1] Material in this chapter quoting or referencing the late Governor Walter J. Hickel comes from information gathered on Hickel's experiences facilitated by Malcolm Roberts and submitted in writing on July 8, 2008.

[2] Parts of this chapter draw on Clive S. Thomas, *Dealing Effectively with Alaska State Government: Lobbying the Legislature, the Governor's Office and State Agencies* (Anchorage: University of Alaska Corporate Programs, 2010), esp. Part 3.

[3] See the Further Reading and Research Sources at the end of the book, particularly Section 4, "General Sources on Alaska Politics, Government, and Public Policy," and Section 5, "Governmental Institutions and Processes in Alaska," for various state websites and other factual sources on Alaska's legislature and executive.

[4] See *Handbook on Alaska State Government* (State of Alaska Legislative Affairs Agency, 2004). This contains a glossary of state government terms and can be downloaded from the Alaska State Legislature's publication website at http://w3.legis.state.ak.us/pubs/pubs.php. See also Thomas, *Dealing Effectively with Alaska State Government*, for extensive explanations of state government terminology.

[5] Margaret Ferguson, "Governors and the Executive Branch," in *Politics in the American States: A Comparative Analysis*, eds., Virginia Gray, Russell L. Hanson, and Thad Kousser, 10th ed. (Washington, D.C.: Congressional Quarterly Press, 2013), Tables 7.3, 226, and 7.5, 227.

[6] See Larry Sabato, *Goodbye to Good-Time Charlie: The American Governorship Transformed*, 2nd ed. (Washington, D.C.: Congressional Quarterly Press, 1988).

[7] For a more extensive account of the various roles and jobs of the governor, see Ferguson, "Governors and the Executive Branch,"; and Ray W. Cox III, "Gubernatorial Politics," in *Politics and Public Policy in the Contemporary American West*, ed. Clive S. Thomas (Albuquerque: University of New Mexico Press, 1991), 253–81.

[8] See Chapter 10, Box 10.3, for the role of the governor's special assistant for federal issues.

[9] As of 2016 Alaska had had eleven individuals as governor, Bill Walker being the eleventh. But if Alaska counted its governors like the U.S. counts its presidents, Walker would be the thirteenth governor, because Bill Egan and Walter Hickel each served nonconsecutive terms. But Alaska appears to have no official way of counting governors.

[10] For an assessment of Sarah Palin as a politician and a personality, see Clive S. Thomas, "The Sarah Palin Phenomenon: The Washington-Hollywood-Wall Street Syndrome in American Politics, and More . . ." in *Issues in American Politics*, ed., John W. Dumbrell (London: Routledge/Taylor & Francis, 2013).

[11] Keith E. Hamm and Gary F. Moncrief, "Legislative Politics in the States," in *Politics in the American States*, Gray, Hanson, and Kousser, Table 6.1, 164–65; see pages 163–67 of Hamm and Moncrief's chapter for a fuller discussion of the extent of legislative professionalism across the states.

[12] Hamm and Moncrief, "Legislative Politics in the States," Table 6.1, 164.

[13] See Chapter 5, Section 8, and Chapter 14, Section 7.

[14] For an overview of the history of the length of the legislative session, see Chapter 4 on the state constitution, Section 3.

[15] Report on KTOO FM Juneau, *Morning Edition*, April 1, 2011; and Patti Epler, "Alaska Legislature Reconsiders 90-day Session," *Alaska Dispatch*, March 8, 2011.

[16] Thomas R. Dye and Susan A. McManus, *Politics in States and Communities*, 14th ed. (Upper Saddle River, NJ: Pearson/Prentice Hall, 2012), 247.

[17] Clive S. Thomas, "'The Thing' That Shook Alaska: The Events, the Fallout and the Lessons of Alaska's Gubernatorial Impeachment Proceedings," *State Legislatures* 13, no. 2 (Feb. 1987): 22–25.

[18] For the pros and cons of Alaska moving to a unicameral legislature, see Chapter 30, Box 30.5.

[19] A review of Alaska's tax policy regarding the oil industry is presented in Chapter 24 on oil and gas policy, Section 4.

[20] Sean Cockerham, "Analyst Says Bond Rating at Risk," *Anchorage Daily News*, September 29, 2011.

[21] Casey Kelly, "Democrats Blame Redistricting for Loss of Blue Seats in Legislature," KTOO FM Juneau, *Morning Edition*, January 15, 2013.

[22] For a comparative perspective on the executive-legislative relationship in the states and the role of the legislature, see the following books by Alan Rosenthal, *The Best Job in Politics: Exploring How Governors Succeed as Policy Leaders* (Washington, D.C.: CQ Press 2013); *Governors and Legislatures: Contending Powers* (Washington, D.C.: CQ Press 1990); *Engines of Democracy: Politics & Policymaking in State Legislatures* (Washington, D.C.: CQ Press, 2009); *Heavy Lifting: The Job of the American Legislature* (Washington, D.C.: CQ Press, 2004); and *Legislative Life: People, Process and Performance in the States* (New York: Harper & Row, 1981).

★ CHAPTER 17 ★

The State Courts and Alaska Politics: Independence, Public Accountability, and Political Influence

Michael L. Boyer

The judiciary, or court system as it is often called in Alaska, is established in Article IV of the Alaska Constitution. It is part of the triad of strong and often contending branches of Alaska state government that is identified in Chapter 2 as one of the characteristics of Alaska politics. Yet, unlike the legislature and executive, much of the day-to-day work of the courts, including the Alaska Supreme Court, has nothing to do with politics. Courts spend the vast majority of their time resolving private disputes and enforcing criminal laws.

Sometimes, however, the courts make judgments that have far-reaching political and policy effects, occasionally leading to major conflicts with the legislative and executive branches. Occasional political fallout from judicial decisions is not surprising because courts play an important role in regulating society, defining individual rights, mediating between competing public policy goals, and developing legal rules in areas in which the legislature has not acted. Moreover, decisions of the Alaska Supreme Court are binding legal precedent on matters of state law. Plus, the courts have the power of judicial review to pass judgment on the constitutionality of statutes and executive regulations, and on occasion have invalidated them.

Most fundamental in shaping its inevitable involvement in politics is the fact that, although Alaska's court system strives for independence and impartiality, it is subject to many of the political pressures explained throughout the book. Thus, in some court decisions there is an unavoidable policy outcome. Add to this that the court system must vie for its budget with the two branches upon which it often passes judgment, that its judges must face the electorate periodically, and that the people of Alaska could ultimately restructure the judicial system through one or more constitutional amendments, then the complexity of the courts' role in Alaska government and politics becomes even more obvious.

We begin with an explanation of the chapter's theme: How does the Alaska political and governmental process deal with the tension between the need for judicial independence, public accountability, and the court system's role in politics and public policy making? The following two sections explore the influences that have shaped the Alaska court system and its organization. The next section explains the devices that work to promote independence and impartiality. Then we explore in more detail six aspects of the role of the courts in Alaska politics and policy making.

1. JUDICIAL INDEPENDENCE, IMPARTIALITY, AND THE COURT SYSTEM'S POLITICAL ROLE: AN OVERVIEW

Together with freedom of association and expression, an independent judiciary is one of the hallmarks of a pluralist democracy. In this context "independent" means freedom from control, interference, or influence from the other two branches of government, political parties, interest groups, and any other forces, political or otherwise, in making decisions. The courts need this independence to pass judgment on a host of cases both civil and criminal, to protect the rights of citizens, to enforce the rules of government, and to curb the power of government if it goes beyond its constitutional and statutory authority. Independence is usually achieved by providing for a certain amount of security of tenure for judges.

In theory, at least, independence is bestowed on a judiciary in a democracy so that it can act with impartiality in making judgments and interpreting the law and the constitution. However, laws and constitutional provisions are rarely, if ever, black and white, but are subject to various interpretations. It is interpretation that determines the outcome of many cases coming before the courts for a decision. This ambiguity in the law is the root of the policy-making role of the courts as well as the explanation for much of the political controversy that often surrounds the judiciary.

Alaska's approach to balancing judicial independence with judicial accountability to the public combines two elements: (1) a selection process that is based, theoretically at least, on merit and not the political perspective of the candidates; and (2) periodic reconfirmation of judges by the electorate. This approach is a compromise between the federal system of lifetime tenure and the purely electoral system used in many states. Alaska's system neither eliminates political fallout from court decisions nor completely insulates the courts from political pressures. But compared with many states, it does reduce the intensity of politics surrounding the judiciary.

There are several ways in which the judiciary becomes involved in politics or affects public policy, but five are particularly important. The first two are by far the most significant when it comes to political impact and likely political fallout.

First, the courts interpret the state constitution, interpret and pass judgment on the constitutionality of state laws enacted by the legislature, and interpret regulations adopted by executive departments. Courts are also called upon to decide whether executive officials have acted constitutionally or within the limits of state laws. Laws, regulations, and executive decisions frequently create or affect public policy, and sometimes the policies are major ones. As a result, judicial decisions concerning them may have significant policy implications. A few examples include cases affecting personal privacy, subsistence, Native sovereignty, prisoners' rights, and eligibility for the Permanent Fund Dividend (PFD). Some of these decisions are the result of cases being brought by interest groups on various sides of an issue. Second, although it is a separate branch of government and not simply an agency (in contrast, for example, to the Department of Labor), the court system must still lobby the legislature for its annual operating budget and on other issues that directly affect the judicial system. For example, if the court system needs additional superior court judges in a particular area of the state, it must obtain authorizing legislation. Similarly, salary increases for judges require legislative action, though Article IV, Section 13, of the constitution prohibits the legislature from reducing the salary of sitting judges. Thus, when the judicial branch seeks legislative action, it is itself acting as an interest (a "lobby"), and the court system's administrative director, or his or her representative, sometimes operates in the legislature as a political operative just like any other lobbyist.

Third, while the retention elections that judges must face periodically are rarely controversial, occasionally they do become heated. For example, two chief justices, Jay Rabinowitz in 1988 and Dana Fabe in 2010, received some fairly intense opposition to their reconfirmation, though both secured retention. This opposition shaved ten points or more off of the usual 65 or so percent that judges receive in reconfirmation votes. Fourth, and a related point, there are periodic moves to reform the court system, including the way that judges are selected and retained, and these efforts can also get quite political.

The fifth aspect of the judiciary's role that may have political implications is what can be called judicial administrative activism (related to but not to be confused with *judicial activism,* explained below). Administrative activism is where the court system, particularly the chief justice and administrative director, takes action to make the court system more responsive to Alaska's needs, particularly in rural-bush areas.

The Tension between Independence, Impartiality, and Politics: The Issue of Judicial Activism

When the theory of impartiality meets the reality of the need for courts to interpret the law, tensions inevitably arise. Most judicial interpretations of the law have few political consequences, but others can cause quite a political stir. When courts take an active, often expansive role in interpreting laws and constitutional provisions that have major policy and political consequences, it is often referred to as *judicial activism.* This is a term with many nuances of meaning and can be used in a positive or pejorative way depending on whether a particular judicial decision is viewed positively or negatively.

In essence, judicial activism is the court taking the initiative in making decisions that might normally be seen as the province of legislation, or interpreting the constitution or a law very broadly. Judicial activism is often characterized by a broad construction of the constitution and laws, and can be contrasted with strict construction. Judicial activism is usually associated with courts with liberal leanings and a liberal philosophy in general. Conservatives courts tend toward strict construction and oppose judicial activism. It is often more complicated than that, however, with these various terms being politically loaded and sometimes employed in the rhetoric of opposing ideologies. But there is no doubt that, since statehood, judicial activism has been one element of the Alaska judiciary's decisions.

The fallout from judicial activism, or sometimes when a court simply decides a case that comes before it in an impartial way, can affect the court system's funding, or may produce a movement for judicial reform or opposition to the retention of certain judges. And even though the Alaska judiciary is organized to mitigate its being embroiled in politics, judicial politics is a constant and unavoidable fact of life in the past, present, and future of politics in Alaska.

2. INFLUENCES THAT SHAPED AND CONTINUE TO AFFECT THE STRUCTURE AND ROLES OF ALASKA'S THIRD BRANCH OF GOVERNMENT

Unlike most states, Alaska has a highly centralized and unified state court system. All courts are funded by the state, and ultimate administrative authority over all courts resides in the Alaska Supreme Court. There is no authority for municipalities to establish or administer local courts. Five interrelated influences were particularly important in shaping Alaska's court system and its judicial branch, and some of them continue to influence this third branch of government. These are: (1) the pre- and post-statehood role of the federal government; (2) Alaska's late admission to the Union; (3) the physical, social, and political geography of Alaska; (4) the influence of Alaska Natives; and (5) a strong commitment to individual rights.

The Pre- and Post-Statehood Role of the Federal Government

The Organic Act of 1884 established the structure for Alaska's territorial government and court system. Judges and commissioners of the territorial court system were appointed to four-year terms by the U.S. president and subject to confirmation by the U.S. Senate. This system was fraught with structural and practical problems. Territorial judges were subject to political pressure, such as threats of not being reappointed, and, therefore, were less able to counter powerful interest groups emerging in Alaska, such as mining syndicates and fishing interests. Moreover, the vastness and remoteness of the Territory imposed practical problems for judicial administration. The district court judges were spread across four judicial divisions (Juneau, Nome, Valdez/Anchorage, and Fairbanks), and their resources were largely expended on the most serious crimes. Outside these cities, there was little access to justice, and the system was constantly strained. By the early 1950s, however, with the burgeoning Cold War, federal spending skyrocketed in Alaska. The increased population and accompanying social problems revealed that the judicial system was completely inadequate to handle legal issues in the growing Territory.[1]

Alaska's Late Admission to the Union

Alaska's late admission to the Union had far-reaching effects on its government and politics. This is particularly evident in the court system and its involvement in politics. In particular, the fact that Alaska's founders could draw upon the experiences, both positive and negative, of the other forty-eight states influenced their approach to the organization of the court system. Plus, the dawning and consolidation of the age of atonement toward Native Americans has placed Alaska's state courts in a particular relationship with tribal courts, and the issues regarding Alaska Natives and their political role resulting from Alaska's late admission also affects the court system.

Another factor combines both Alaska's late admission and its newness as a state. When statehood became a reality in 1959, the Alaska courts were faced with a blank slate when it came to many major legal issues. This vacuum of legal authority has allowed Alaska's courts a unique perspective. The Alaska Supreme Court tends to side with the more modern or majority trends unless there is a strong legal or policy reason to do otherwise.

The Physical, Social, and Political Geography of Alaska

Clearly, the physical geography of the state, its sheer size and barriers to transportation, present challenges to the Alaska court system not faced by small states like Vermont and Maryland or even large states that have developed road systems like Texas and Wyoming. These challenges include the cost of providing courts and the most efficient way to organize them in rural-bush areas. Then there are the influences resulting from the social geography of the state and particularly the cultural differences of the Alaska Native population, not only in rural-bush communities but also in urban areas. These factors can influence the court system because of the regional loyalties of politicians, particularly the efforts of rural-bush legislators and others to ensure an equal and culturally sensitive administration of justice in both urban and rural-bush areas.

The Influence of Alaska Natives

Also identified as a characteristic of Alaska politics in Chapter 2 is the influence of Alaska Natives. One of the many facets of this influence has been on the court system. Over the years, this influence includes sensitivity on the part of the court system to providing justice in rural-bush areas and ensuring that the administration of justice is appropriate and sensitive to the effect of sentencing practices on Natives within the criminal justice system. The court system has also been aware of the political influence of rural-bush legislators, many of whom are Alaska Natives, and the effect that they can have on court system budgets and other administrative initiatives.

The influence of the Native community and its issues can be quite complex as they relate to the court system, particularly because of ongoing interactions between tribal courts and the state court system, and jurisdictional disputes between Alaska Native tribes and the state and federal governments on sovereignty issues. These complex interactions often have major political as well as legal consequences. Two particularly thorny issues in this regard have been subsistence and Native sovereignty (for details on these issues, see Chapter 9 on Alaska Natives).

A Strong Commitment to Individual Rights

The protection of individual rights by the Alaska Supreme Court (which has sometimes involved judicial activism) has been a major source of the political controversy surrounding the judiciary. The court is most likely to be at the center of particularly intense political debate resulting from the protection of the individual rights of unpopular groups and politically divisive issues. This can put the court at odds with conservative lawmakers, forcing the state Supreme Court to find creative ways to protect rights while still deferring to reasonable policy goals of the legislature.

Several states have a commitment to the protection of individual rights in their constitutions, including Alaska. However, the Alaska Supreme Court has championed individual rights, such as privacy and religion, as stringently, if not more so, than any state in the nation. For example, nine other states have "privacy" provisions in their constitutions, but only Alaska has a judicial opinion like *Ravin v. State* (1975), holding that personal privacy in the home outweighs the state's interest in prohibiting possession in one's home of small amounts of marijuana intended for personal use.

3. THE ORGANIZATION OF ALASKA'S COURT SYSTEM COMPARED WITH OTHER STATES

State court systems across the United States include a wide variety of structures. Some, like Alaska, have highly unified systems, with the state Supreme Court having administrative supervision of all other appellate courts and all trial courts. Even within a fairly unified system, there may be several specialized trial courts dealing with specific areas of law, such as criminal or family law. And most systems, regardless of the degree of unification, have at least two levels of trial courts with differing levels of jurisdiction. For instance, virtually all states have "superior courts" (sometimes called "courts of general jurisdiction"), which are allowed to hear any kind of case, including civil cases involving any amount of money and criminal cases involving both serious (felony) and less serious (misdemeanor) crimes. Most states also have lower courts with, for example, criminal jurisdiction limited to traffic violations and misdemeanors and civil jurisdiction limited to cases involving small amounts of money. Figure 17.1, comparing the structure of Alaska's court system with those of New York and Wyoming, highlights these contrasts.

The Alaska Supreme Court has total administrative authority over all levels of courts in the state. There are no city courts to contend with or family courts or traffic courts to complicate the administration of justice. Compare this to the organization of the New York system, an example of a more complex, fragmented court structure with many courts dealing with specific and narrow areas of law (as illustrated in Figure 17.1). Alaska and some other western states reflect the modern trend of a unified court system. Some sparsely populated western states have more streamlined court systems because they do not have the population or volume of litigation necessary to justify special courts to handle only probate, traffic, or family matters. New Jersey is an example of an eastern high-population state with a unified system not unlike Alaska's. It was, in fact, New Jersey's court system that Alaska's founders found very appealing in developing the Alaska court system. Wyoming is another example of a unified court system, as Figure 17.1 shows.

Several western states have added levels of courts as needed while maintaining the overall unified organization of their state court systems (see, for example, information on the Alaska Court of Appeals, below). The reliance on fewer courts of specialized jurisdiction in many western states, including Alaska, means that judges must hear all manner of cases, so the judiciary tends to be composed of highly competent generalists rather than specialists in any one area of law. The structure of its court system is another way in which Alaska is like many of its western neighbors.[2]

Box 17.1 explains the types of courts, their jurisdiction, and judicial officials in Alaska. There are some features not present in most states. First, the superior court can act as both a general trial court as well as an appellate court for the district court. Another variation is Alaska's Court of Appeals, established in 1980, which handles only criminal appeals. This court was created as a matter of judicial economy (that is, the allocation of judicial resources and expertise) and to provide the due process right to an appeal without overloading the Alaska Supreme Court. Parties can still appeal an Alaska Court of Appeals

FIGURE 17.1

The Alaska Court System Compared to New York State and Wyoming as of 2015

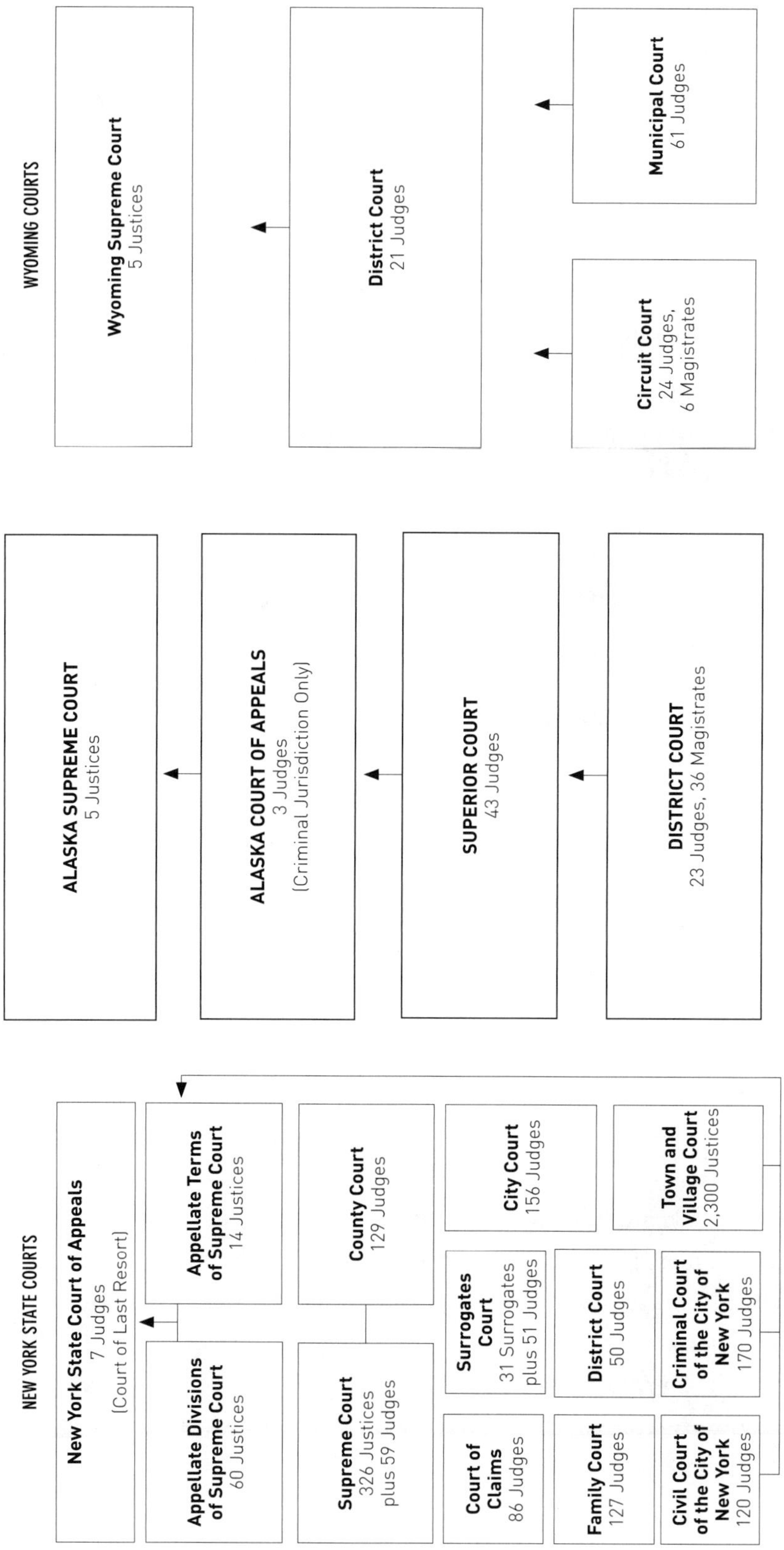

NEW YORK STATE COURTS

New York State Court of Appeals
7 Judges
(Court of Last Resort)

Appellate Divisions of Supreme Court
60 Justices

Appellate Terms of Supreme Court
14 Justices

Supreme Court
326 Justices
plus 59 Judges

County Court
129 Judges

Court of Claims
86 Judges

Surrogates Court
31 Surrogates
plus 51 Judges

City Court
156 Judges

Family Court
127 Judges

District Court
50 Judges

Civil Court of the City of New York
120 Judges

Criminal Court of the City of New York
170 Judges

Town and Village Court
2,300 Justices

ALASKA COURTS

ALASKA SUPREME COURT
5 Justices

ALASKA COURT OF APPEALS
3 Judges
(Criminal Jurisdiction Only)

SUPERIOR COURT
43 Judges

DISTRICT COURT
23 Judges, 36 Magistrates

WYOMING COURTS

Wyoming Supreme Court
5 Justices

District Court
21 Judges

Circuit Court
24 Judges,
6 Magistrates

Municipal Court
61 Judges

Note: New York State uses unique names for some of its courts.

Source: Developed by the author.

BOX 17.1

Alaska's Courts, Judicial Officials, and What They Do

GEOGRAPHICAL ORGANIZATION OF THE COURT SYSTEM

As in Territorial days, Alaska continues to divide the state into four judicial districts. The first judicial district covers Southeast Alaska. The second includes Northwest Alaska and the North Slope. The third covers Southcentral Alaska, the state's major population center, as well as the Bristol Bay region and the Aleutian Chain. And the fourth includes the Interior and Southwest Alaska, including Bethel.

TYPES OF COURTS AND JUDICIAL OFFICIALS

Magistrates

Magistrates are judicial officers of the district court who hear certain district court matters and often work in rural-bush areas where there is no full-time district court judge. They also help with the caseloads in urban areas. Magistrates are appointed by the presiding judges of the four judicial districts. They are not required to be lawyers, nor are they required to stand for retention elections as are all judges. A magistrate's jurisdiction includes small claims cases, solemnizing marriages, domestic violence cases, traffic infractions, arrest warrants, and summonses.

District Courts

The Alaska Constitution provides that the legislature shall establish such lower courts as may be necessary. Accordingly, in 1959, the legislature created a district court for each judicial district. In 2016 the district court had twenty-three judges statewide. District court judges may, for example, hear misdemeanors, first appearances in felony cases, and civil cases valued up to $100,000.

Superior Court

The superior court is the trial court of general jurisdiction. Each of Alaska's four judicial districts has a superior court. In 2016 there were forty-three such judgeships located throughout the state. The superior court has authority to hear all cases, both civil and criminal, properly brought before the state courts, although it does not routinely hear cases that may be brought in the district court. The superior court also hears appeals from the district court and from executive agency administrative adjudications.

Court of Appeals

The court of appeals consists of a chief judge and two associate judges. It has the authority to hear appeals in criminal cases and certain other quasi-criminal cases in which a minor is accused of committing a crime (juvenile delinquency cases), cases in which prisoners are challenging the legality of their confinement (habeas corpus matters), and cases involving probation and parole decisions.

Supreme Court

The Alaska Supreme Court is the highest state court. It hears appeals from lower state courts and also administers the state's judicial system. The court is comprised of the chief justice and four associate justices. All five, by majority vote, select one of their members as chief justice, who holds office for three years. The chief justice may not serve consecutive terms, but can be reelected after sitting out one term. The Court has final state appellate jurisdiction in civil and criminal matters in Alaska. However, certain issues can be appealed to the U.S. Supreme Court—primarily those involving questions of federal statutory or constitutional law.

Source: Developed by the author.

decision to the Alaska Supreme Court, but the Alaska Supreme Court has discretionary authority to hear the case, meaning it can hear the case or decline to do so.

From both an administrative and political point of view, Alaska's unified and centralized court system appears very appropriate for the state's socio-economic and geographical circumstances and has many advantages over a fragmented system. The unified system allows the Alaska Supreme Court, through its administrative director, to organize the system to compensate for the vastness and high costs of administering justice and deal with other—often uniquely Alaskan—judicial issues. This may actually reduce the political involvement in judicial actions as the system anticipates and addresses needs that it can enforce throughout the system. If this were a fragmented system like those found in New York or Arkansas, no such centralized body would exist to develop and administer such statewide legal policy. Moreover, politics are more pervasive in such fragmented systems as various legal jurisdictions vie with one another for state funds.[3]

Native Alaskan Tribal Courts and Councils

Alaska's state court system interacts with Alaska Native tribal courts and village councils across the state. Although the U.S. Supreme Court largely squelched Alaska Native sovereignty in the *Venetie* case in 1998, the fact remains that both formal and informal dispute resolution continues to take place outside the Alaska court system.[4] These tribal courts and councils span both rural-bush and urban areas and cover an array of local issues. Some past and present examples of tribal courts in Alaska include the Sitka Tribal Court, Tanana Chiefs Council, Tlingit and Haida Court, Chevak Tribal Court, Minto Tribal Court, and others throughout the state.[5]

A primary area of jurisdiction for tribal courts involves the Indian Child Welfare Act (ICWA) cases and customary adoptions. Congress passed the ICWA in 1978, prompted by the high number of American Indian and Alaska Native children being removed from their homes by both public and private agencies.[6] Tribal courts or village councils may also handle disputes about public drunkenness, disorderly conduct, and minor juvenile offenses. They also help parties settle small property claims. These courts may impose fines, require community work service and alcohol treatment, or stipulate other conditions. Some tribal courts and village councils are somewhat structured, while others are more informal.

Resolution by tribal courts of minor regulatory offenses benefits both the state (by easing its caseload) and the locality (by providing enforcement). More serious crimes and larger civil claims are still heard in the state court system. Tribal courts rely heavily on cooperation not only with the state's judicial branch but also with executive branch agencies. The success of tribal courts in Alaska largely depends on whether the relationship

BOX 17.2

Bush Justice: An Imprecise Term with Several Meanings

The term *bush justice* is often used in Alaska to refer to judicial and law enforcement activities in rural-bush areas, but mainly in remote Alaska Native villages. However, the term is imprecise and can mean different things to different people. Broadly, it has three different meanings, and often there is overlap among them.

THE STATE COURT SYSTEM'S PERSPECTIVE

The court system tends to view bush justice in terms of the challenges of providing access to state courts in a timely and effective manner across the vast geographical area of rural-bush Alaska. It also involves raising the awareness of judges, magistrates, and other court system personnel to the cultural perspective of Alaska Natives. These challenges have partly been addressed through the initiatives referred to in the text as *judicial administrative activism*.

THE PUBLIC SAFETY PERSPECTIVE

Isolated rural-bush areas accessible only by air or water often wait days before the nearest state trooper can respond to infractions of the law, especially in winter. Thus, village public safety officers (VPSOs) or village councils often fill gaps in law enforcement and dispute resolution. Plus, individuals or groups sometimes resort to self-help, informal community dispute resolution, or other means of enforcement of community norms and values.

THE TRIBAL COURT AND VILLAGE COUNCIL PERSPECTIVE

Some view bush justice as referring to the role of tribal courts and village councils in dispute resolution. Particular areas of their jurisdiction are sanctioned by federal law, as explained in the text regarding the role of tribal courts and councils. To some extent, this perspective is intertwined with the issue of Native sovereignty and the right claimed by many Native groups to pass judgment and enforce those judgments based on the legal sovereignty of Alaska tribes.

Source: Developed by the author.

between state and tribal courts is cooperative or competitive. One issue regarding the state-tribal court relationship is that of comity: state courts are not legally bound to follow tribal court decisions but can do so if they wish.

A term often used in the activities of the court system and law enforcement in rural and particularly bush areas is *bush justice*. But, as Box 17.2 points out, this is a very imprecise term.

4. PROVISIONS FOR INDEPENDENCE, IMPARTIALITY, AND ACCOUNTABILITY: JUDICIAL SELECTION AND RETENTION IN ALASKA AND IN OTHER STATES

In the selection and retention of judges, there is a major distinction between state and federal courts. The U.S. Constitution provides lifetime tenure for U.S. Supreme Court Justices, U.S. Court of Appeals judges, and District Court judges "during good behavior," with no retention elections, though their initial appointments must be confirmed by the U.S. Senate. In contrast, the vast majority of state court judges—some 87 percent—are subject to popular election in some form.[7]

Across the fifty states, the methods of judicial selection and retention run the gamut from never facing voters to contested, partisan elections. These differences are partly an outgrowth of the political culture and the history of each state. Southern states, with their Jacksonian tradition of direct voter accountability, tend to favor a judiciary fully accountable to voters through contested elections. Northeastern states, with judicial systems developed at the time of the birth of the nation, favor appointment and even life tenure, in order to insulate judges from the political atmosphere of a contested election. With their populist and progressive traditions, a number of Midwestern and western states, including Alaska, balance elections and appointments by using a method known as the Missouri Plan, or merit selection system.

The Missouri Plan has two key features. First, the governor appoints a candidate from a list drawn up by a nonpartisan council called a judicial council or judicial commission, among other designations. Use of a judicial commission to assist in gubernatorial appointment is part of a modern trend in use in 34 states and the District of Columbia.[8] Second, there are periodic uncontested retention elections after initial appointment, in which voters are asked to vote "yes" or "no" to the question, "Should Judge X be retained?"[9] The Missouri Plan involves a minimal and sometimes no role for the legislature. The plan considerably reduces the intense partisanship, acrimony and high cost that often accompanies contested judicial elections in many states.[10]

Alaska's Judicial Selection Process

As in most western states, the process of judicial selection and retention in Alaska is a prime example of balancing accountability with the need for judicial independence. History and political culture came very much into play when Alaska's founders developed these aspects of Article IV of the constitution. The Territorial history of strong external economic and political forces and an inadequate judicial system favored creation of an independent judiciary insulated as much as possible from politics. At the same time, there is a strong strain of democracy and populism in Alaska that wants to make officials accountable to voters. Together, these forces help explain the founders' selection of the balanced Missouri Plan.

Alaska's selection of its supreme court justices and other judges is similar to seventeen states in that their appointments are recommended by an independent judicial commission—the Alaska Judicial Council. The governor then appoints the justice or judge from the list forwarded to him or her by the council. The appointee must then stand for retention at the next regular general election. Alaska allows a very limited role for the legislature in determining the composition of its court system. This role includes legislative confirmation of the three members of the Judicial Council who are appointed by the governor, controlling the number of judges in each judicial district, and using the budgetary process to create judicial positions to meet policy goals. However, as explained later, in 2014 there was a move to change the composition of the Judicial Council and the role of the legislature in the confirmation process of members of the council.

Judicial Retention Elections in Alaska

States vary widely in the length of their judicial terms—the years between retention elections. The length of terms in a state is one indication of the state's propensity towards either independence or accountability. Seventeen states, including Alaska, have uncontested retention elections following initial appointment. Of these, seven western states, including Alaska, have uncontested retention elections for general jurisdiction courts.[11]

Alaska bases the frequency of retention elections on the level of court. Supreme Court Justices stand for retention every ten years. Eleven other states have ten-year terms for their highest court, a length surpassed only by six states.[12] Alaska Court of Appeals judges stand every eight years, Superior Court judges every six years, and District Court judges appear on the ballot every four years. Alaska's reluctance to allow contested judicial elections, in theory, shifts the focus from the competing ideologies of candidates to the individual performance of the incumbent. Across the United States, the vast majority of judges who stand for uncontested retention elections are retained. In Alaska, 60 to 70 percent of voters generally choose to retain judges. Only a few have not been retained, usually due to misconduct or performance issues.

Balancing Populism and Judicial Independence: A Look Inside the Alaska Judicial Council and Challenges to Its Nonpartisan Makeup

The key mechanism by which the courts have achieved a balance between populism and independence is through the evaluation and selection criteria employed by the nonpartisan Alaska Judicial Council. The framers saw this body as so crucial to the vitality of the courts that they enshrined it in the state constitution.

Composition of the Judicial Council

The Alaska Constitution Article IV, Section 8, provides that the Judicial Council shall have seven members. Three are lawyers appointed by the Alaska Bar Association and three are non-lawyers appointed by the governor and confirmed by the legislature. The Chief Justice of the Supreme Court is the council's seventh ex officio member and chairperson. The six appointed members sit for staggered six-year terms, are spread geographically throughout the state, and are appointed without regard to political affiliation.

Arguably, the legal profession has the most influence in this nomination process with three lawyers and the Chief Justice, who by law is required to have been a practicing lawyer prior to appointment to the court. However, this influence may not be entirely a bad thing. One of the fundamental concepts underlying the Missouri Plan is that judges should be selected on the basis of merit—that is, the ability to be a good judge—rather than political influence. Law-trained members have more familiarity than laypersons with the subject matter and the candidates. At the same time, it is important to have the balanced views that the three lay members bring to the selection process. Maintaining balance on the council is critical because of its gate-keeping function: the governor may only choose judges from the list forwarded to him or her by the council. While in theory this system should avoid politics entering into the judicial selection process, in practice it has not been without controversy, and there is the potential for partisan politics to become involved.

Avoiding Deadlock: The Council Averts a Potentially Stymied Process

Some past governors have asked the council to provide additional names from which to make a judicial appointment. In August of 2004, however, Governor Murkowski formally rejected the list provided to him by the council. The rejection sparked numerous editorials across the state, mostly in favor of an independent judiciary. Further conflict was averted a month later when the governor made an appointment from the original list. The event is noteworthy as it represents potential for a stymied process. The governor and the Judicial Council could conceivably deadlock in a protracted clash, with the governor refusing to appoint from the list provided, and the Judicial Council refusing to name additional candidates. It is unlikely that the council will ever provide the governor with additional candidates in such a situation.[13] Continued deadlock would probably lead to litigation, and the litigation would be decided in the judicial branch, which would follow the constitution and thus find in favor of the council. Thus there is little incentive for the governor to pursue or sustain this kind of deadlock.

Ensuring Independence and Quality: The Council's Evaluation of Judicial Candidates

The Alaska Judicial Council also makes recommendations regarding the fitness of judges facing retention elections. It scores judges numerically on a range of criteria, and, in rare cases, will recommend to the electorate that a judge not be retained. Some of the criteria the council uses to evaluate existing judges include surveys by attorneys, peace officers, social workers, jurors and court employees; attorney questionnaires; and other records.

A summary of the council's evaluations and recommendations are included in the Official Election Pamphlet published by the Division of Elections in the lieutenant governor's office. The pamphlet contains important information about a judicial candidate's fitness for office. This is particularly valuable because there is a paucity of information available to voters regarding judicial retention elections. This evaluation and recommendation role is another way in which the council plays a prominent role in the merit system in Alaska.

Moves to Reform the Composition of the Judicial Council

Not all Alaskans, however, are happy with the work of the council and particularly the types of candidates it nominates for appointment. Many Alaska conservatives and strongly religious people believe the records of those nominees recommended to the governor and appointed to the bench are too activist and are unhappy with court decisions on abortion and other social issues. They see attorneys as having too much say in the selection of judges. These opponents of the present process have the support of several conservative Republicans in the legislature, including Senator Pete Kelly of Fairbanks. In the 2014 legislative session, Kelly introduced Senate Joint Resolution 21 (SJR 21). The final version of SJR 21 would have increased the number of Judicial Council members to ten by adding three more lay members and also require the legislature to confirm the lawyer appointees, which, as indicated earlier, is not presently the case. The change would require a constitutional amendment first approved by two-thirds of each house of the legislature (fourteen votes in the Senate and twenty-seven in the House) and then approved by the voters.

Jim Miller of Alaska Family Action (a conservative family values organization) said in a blog post supporting the amendment that it, "would fundamentally transform the council from a panel dominated by legal elites into a panel dominated by non-attorney citizens." Opponents of the measure, primarily moderate Republicans and Democrats, argue that it would politicize the appointment of judges.[14] Before their election as governor and lieutenant governor, respectively, in November 2014, both Bill Walker (an attorney by profession) and Byron Mallott, a prominent Alaska Native leader, strongly opposed the amendment. Mallott commented that the amendment would "reshape the judiciary into an ideological rubber stamp of government actions. This is because the governor would choose the six lay members, and the legislature would confirm or reject the attorney members, and political partisanship would inevitably come into play."[15] Although the governor has no role in the constitutional amendment process, Governor Walker's position may help the opponents and supplement the position of the bulk of the state's legal profession who also oppose the amendment. A group of attorneys and concerned citizens, including former Supreme Court Chief Justice Walter "Bud" Carpeneti, have formed Justice Not Politics Alaska, a nonprofit lobby group to fight the amendment.[16]

Even though SJR 21 never came to the Senate floor for a vote in the 2014 session, the issue has probably not gone away. The years to come may see further conflict over this issue.

The Alaska Commission on Judicial Conduct

In all fifty states and at the federal level, judges must follow strict rules of ethical conduct. As the vetting process is so stringent in states like Alaska, judicial misconduct is not widespread. However, every state has an organization to investigate allegations of judicial misconduct. In Alaska this body is the Commission on Judicial Conduct, a body established in Article IV, Section 10, of the Alaska Constitution.

Composed of three judges, three lawyers, and three public members, the commission investigates complaints alleging misconduct by a particular judge. Most complaints are filed by litigants, though some are filed by lawyers who have observed conduct that allegedly violates the ethical rules of conduct for judges. The most typical complaints against judges allege improper courtroom behavior and bias, though any judicial behavior that constitutes a violation of ethical rules may form the basis of a complaint. The commission investigates all complaints that are within its jurisdiction. Its proceedings are kept confidential, although it periodically issues nonconfidential advisory opinions about what a judge may or may not do in a hypothetical situation.

Some complaints, such as those in which a litigant simply disagrees with a legal ruling by the judge, are dismissed immediately without investigation, as the commission does not consider complaints of that nature as being within its jurisdiction. If the commission finds probable cause to believe that a violation of the ethical rules has taken place, it may proceed to a formal hearing. If, after the hearing, the commission finds that a judge has violated the ethical rules, it does not itself impose discipline on the judge. Instead, it makes a recommendation to the Alaska Supreme Court for particular disciplinary action. The Supreme Court has ultimate authority to take disciplinary action, ranging from private or public censure, to suspension, and even to removal from office.

5. THE JUDICIARY AND ALASKA POLITICS AND PUBLIC POLICY

In this section we go into more detail on six aspects of the Alaska court system's political role: (1) the issue of judicial activism; (2) a corollary issue of privacy and individual rights; (3) rural-bush versus urban court facilities and Alaska Native issues; (4) the court system as a lobby; (5) the court system as a target of "lobbying"; and (6) the politics of court reform. In many ways, these six are interrelated. The interrelationship stems from the court system's effect on Alaska politics and public policy and reactions to that influence by the other two branches, by the public, and sometimes by the media.

Opposing Viewpoints: Judicial Independence or Judicial Activism?

The Alaska Supreme Court has engaged in judicial activism in varying degrees since statehood. There are very different perceptions about the validity of this role of the judicial branch among Alaskans.

This was especially apparent when the Alaska legislature and the courts clashed in the late 1990s in cases such as *Bess v. Ulmer* (1999).[17] The case dealt with three highly charged ballot initiatives proposing changes to the Alaska Constitution (restricting marriage to the union of a man and woman, limiting prisoners' constitutional rights, and legislative reapportionment). The Alaska Supreme Court struck down the prisoners' rights initiative and struck a sentence out of the wording of another initiative. Altering the ballot initiative was seen by some as an affront to the democratic process and set the stage for a battle between the will of the people as reflected in the ballot initiatives and the force of law as interpreted by the Supreme Court.

Conservative legislators like Senators Dave Donley, Robin Taylor, and Loren Leman countered with proposed constitutional amendments calling for more frequent retention elections and even judicial appointment directly by the governor without nominations by the Judicial Council.[18] These proposals failed. But, as with the issue of the composition of the Judicial Council considered earlier, competing ideologies about the proper role of the courts in relation to public policy have been a constant in Alaska politics since soon after statehood, and it is likely to continue.

Individual Rights

The expansion of individual rights by the Alaska Supreme Court has also resulted in a clash of ideologies over the proper role of the courts. Chapter 4, on the constitution and its interpretation, pays considerable attention to the hallmark role of the courts, and particularly the Alaska Supreme Court, in defining Alaskans' personal rights, and explains key court decisions.

Other examples of the court's decisions on personal rights include *Mickens v. City of Kodiak* (1982), in which the Alaska Supreme Court held that nude dancing in a bar is a form of free expression protected by freedom of speech, and *Frank v. State* (1979), linking the taking of moose out of season for a funeral potlatch to religious freedom.[19] Then, in the ruling in *Alaska Civil Liberties Union v. State of Alaska* (2005), the Court ruled that the constitution requires the state to provide the same benefits to public employees in a same-sex relationship that it provides to public employees in traditional marriages.[20]

Rural-Bush versus Urban Court Facilities and Alaska Native Issues

The significance of Alaska Native issues remains high among the concerns of the court system, even after the *Venetie* decision. This is for both administrative and political reasons.

Administratively, the Alaska court system has always been cognizant of providing judicial services in rural-bush Alaska that both enhance access and are culturally sensitive. The court system has noted disparities in the access to courts among rural-bush and urban residents. A 1997 report from a Supreme Court advisory committee stated:

> Urban residents have far more access to justice system services than village residents. One-fourth of Alaskans do not live within reasonable reach of many court system services. Rural residents do not receive adequate legal representation in either civil or criminal matters.[21]

The report also catalogued many language and culture problems and provided recommendations to help bridge the urban versus rural-bush divide, as well as the estimated costs to do so. Part of the divide is historical, as the state uses four judicial districts that are a vestige of the Territorial era, so the system is naturally biased toward the population centers of the state. The court system has worked to address these problems through judicial administrative activism. Among other provisions, the court system has ensured that most areas with a significant population have at least some access to a magistrate, that there is cultural sensitivity training for judges and court employees, and, where appropriate, that tribal and village council dispute resolution mechanisms are utilized.

Over the years, these and other provisions by the court system have made many political points with rural-bush and particularly Native legislators. This has been of crucial importance because many Native legislators, such as John Sackett, Frank Fergusson, Al Adams, Lyman Hoffman, and Albert Kookesh, have been in key positions of power and able to influence the court system's budget as well as other issues affecting the courts. The importance of such political points will become clearer in considering the role of the judiciary as a lobby.

Alaska's Court System as a Lobby: Promoting and Protecting Its Interests

Although judges are largely insulated from day-to-day politics, the Alaska court system is a large bureaucracy and has the same needs as any bureaucracy. It needs new buildings, technology, support staff, funds to implement new programs, salary increases,

BOX 17.3

The Administrative Director of the Alaska Court System: A Link to the Executive and Legislative Branches

Section 16 of Article VI of the Alaska Constitution states in part:

> The chief justice of the court system shall be the administrative head of the courts. . . . The chief justice shall, with the approval of the supreme court, appoint an administrative director to serve at the pleasure of the supreme court and to supervise the administrative operations of the judicial system.

The administrative director, then, is a constitutionally mandated official of the judiciary. That person is primarily responsible for the efficient day-to-day administration of the court system and works closely with judges, especially the Supreme Court and particularly the Chief Justice, to develop the goals and priorities of the judiciary.

While individual administrative directors may vary in their approaches, one of their essential roles in implementing court system goals and priorities is a political role—to act as a link to the legislative and executive branches of government. This involves lobbying and developing relationships and reaching agreements with legislators and executive department officials. Part of this role may involve the director acting as a buffer to shield the judiciary from conflicts of interest or the appearance of impropriety.

Since the court system established its budgetary and administrative independence from the executive branch in the mid-1970s, the administrative director, either directly or through a member of the administrative office staff, has been of crucial importance in dealing with public policies that impact the court system. The legislature, in particular, is where the court system must focus its efforts related to budgetary goals and statutory changes.

Different administrative directors may choose to be less politically active personally and may delegate direct contact with the legislature to other administrative office staff. But even though the political styles of administrative directors may differ over time, the court system's role as a lobby is a continual one.

Source: Developed by the author and largely based on a phone interview of February 10, 2010, with Arthur Snowden, former administrative director of the Alaska Court System, 1973–1997.

retirement benefits, and so on. Consequently, even though it is a separate branch of government, the court system, like state agencies, needs to advocate for itself in the budgetary process and weigh in on policy proposals that impact the administration of justice. Responsibility for these duties rests largely with the administrative director of the court system. Box 17.3 explains the director's role.

Until the mid-1970s, Alaska's courts relied on the executive branch to deal with many administrative matters (personnel, facilities, and so on). Therefore, while constitutionally an independent branch of government, the court system's administrative functions were not independent. One major example was the governor's insistence on having a say in the court system's annual budget request before it went to the legislature. This changed with the hiring of a new administrative director, Arthur Snowden, in 1973. Snowden, who served until 1997, worked with the Supreme Court to establish the judiciary as a truly independent branch of government and created an efficient court system administratively. The system also established itself as a credible and effective political force in its relations with the other two branches of government. As a result, the court system secured many benefits for its employees, including a new courthouse for Anchorage, funds for the administration of rural-bush facilities and services, and increased pay and benefits for judges.

The Court System as a Target of Lobbying

There is another aspect of lobbying that often places the court system, particularly the Supreme Court, in the thick of state politics. This is when the courts are the target of lobbying—not in the sense that the courts are being lobbied as courts, but rather the use of the courts by interest groups and other bodies, including the state, to obtain rulings in their favor on an issue directly affecting public policy and in some cases actually making policy. The use of the courts by various interests is on the increase and is often used when the legislature or executive branch will not act on an issue or has not produced a result satisfactory to the interest concerned. Some of these cases involve judicial activism, with the court making a broad policy ruling beyond what the facts of the case might require. In other cases, the courts are passive, and go no further than to resolve disputed facts and legal arguments.

Whether passive or activist, however, the decisions of courts can have far-reaching policy effects and sometime controversial ones. Three of the most prominent Alaska decisions with significant policy implications include the *Molly Hootch* decision in the mid-1970s—with the *Molly Hootch* Consent Decree of 1976—resulting in the establishment of high schools in rural-bush communities.[22] The mental health trust land issue in the 1980s and 1990s was resolved in part by the Alaska Supreme Court's ruling that the state had failed to live up to its trust obligations to set aside state lands to fund mental health programs.[23] And the *Cleary* case, concluded in 2001, dealt with prisoners' rights regarding overcrowded prisons.[24]

Political Issues Regarding Reform of the Judiciary

Even though there are calls from time to time for reforming the judiciary, especially those precipitated by the ideological debate between the activist and strict construction perspectives, none so far has succeeded. The ultimate outcome of calls by Senator Pete

Kelly and others to revamp the Judicial Council is uncertain, as there will likely be future efforts to reform the council. However, there are several factors that make major reform of the Alaska judiciary in the foreseeable future less likely.

First, in many ways, judicial reform in Alaska took place at the Constitutional Convention in Fairbanks in 1955–1956. The founders' efforts to promote judicial independence, impartiality, and public accountability, to minimize judicial involvement in politics, and to ensure efficiency through a unified court system administration, seem to have sat well with the Alaska public and most policy makers. Consequently, there has been no surge of support for judicial reform. In fact, the situation is quite the reverse, as evidenced by the public outcry described above at Governor Murkowski's attempts to inject politics into the judicial selection process in 2004. This included close to two hundred editorials appearing throughout the state defending an independent judiciary.

Furthermore, while the legislature and executive have been touched by several cases of corruption, including prison sentences for public officials, the Alaska judiciary has never been affected in this way. Nationwide, the state's judiciary has a reputation for efficiency and integrity. As a candidate, Governor Walker commented that, "Alaska enjoys the reputation as having the finest state judiciary in the nation."[25]

6. CONCLUSION: INDEPENDENCE, PUBLIC ACCOUNTABILITY, AND POLITICAL INFLUENCE

The theme of this chapter was posed in the form of a question: How does the Alaska political and governmental process deal with the tension between the need for independence, a degree of public accountability, and the court system's role in politics and public policy making?

In an imperfect world, there is certainly no ideal solution to this tension. Yet, Alaska's court system meets this challenge as well as any state judiciary in the United States. Alaska does so by combining centralized judicial administration with merit selection and uncontested retention confirmation of judges, thereby insulating the judiciary from politics as far as possible. And given the inevitability of the court system's involvement in politics, both through court decisions and the bureaucratic needs of the system regarding its budget, among other issues, it appears that this political role has been kept within acceptable bounds. Those opposed to judicial activism would, of course, argue otherwise. However, given the fact that, as of 2016, there have been no successful movements to reform the judiciary since statehood, the balance between independence, accountability, and politics appears to have been advantageous to the development of Alaska as a democratic polity.

ENDNOTES

[1] This overview of the early court system draws on Clause-M Naske, *A History of the Alaska Federal District Court System, 1884–1959, and the Creation of the State Court System* (Prepared Pursuant to RSA 410059 between the Alaska Court System and the Geophysical Institute, University of Alaska Fairbanks, 1985).

[2] For a comparative perspective of the western states see John H. Culver, "Judicial Systems and Public Policy," in *Politics and Public Policy in the Contemporary American West*, ed. Clive S. Thomas (Albuquerque: University of New Mexico Press, 1991). For a fifty-state comparison, see Melinda Gann Hall, "State Courts: Politics and the Judicial Process," in *Politics in the American States: A Comparative Analysis*, eds. Virginia Gray, Russell L. Hanson, and Thad Kousser, 10th ed. (Washington, D.C.: CQ Press, 2013).

[3] Interview with Susan Burke, a former Deputy Administrative Director of the Alaska Court System, February 17, 2014.

[4] In the so-called *Venetie* case, *Alaska v. Native Village of Venetie Tribal Government*, 522 U.S. 520 (1998), the U.S. Supreme Court held that "Indian Country" refers to a limited category of Indian lands (primarily reservation lands) and does not include any of the lands transferred to Alaska Native corporations under the Alaska Native Claims Settlement Act (ANCSA) of 1971. The only designated reservation land in Alaska is Metlakatla in Southeast Alaska. For commentary on the case, see Fae L. Korsmo, "Native Sovereignty: An Insoluble Problem?" in *Public Policy Issues in Alaska: Background and Perspectives*, ed. Clive S. Thomas (Juneau: Denali Press, 1999).

[5] See *A Directory of Disputes Resolution in Alaska Outside Federal and State Courts* (Anchorage, AK: Alaska Judicial Council, March 1999), which lists dozens of tribal courts and village councils.

[6] The stated intent of Congress under the ICWA (25 U.S.C. § 1902) is to "protect the best interests of Indian children and to promote the stability and security of Indian tribes and families." Among other things, the Act adopted minimum standards for the removal of Indian children from their families, allowed the child's tribe and family to intervene in cases that might result in removal of the child, and required placement of the child in circumstances that would allow for continued exposure to Indian and Native cultural values.

[7] Judith L. Maute, "Selecting Justices in State Courts: The Ballot Box or the Backroom," *South Texas Law Review* 41 (2000): 1197–1245.

[8] Ten of these states, however, use the judicial commission only for midterm vacancies. So the nation is roughly split in half on the use of commissions on the one hand and other forms of initial appointments on the other.

[9] Proposed in 1914 by Albert Kales, then research director at the American Judicature Society, this method of selection and retention became known as the Missouri Plan when that state adopted the plan in 1940.

[10] For perspectives on the increasing intensity of political and partisan conflict in contested judicial retention elections, see Clive S. Thomas, Michael L. Boyer, and Ronald J. Hrebenar, "Interest Groups and State Court Elections, 1980–2000: A New Era and Its Challenges," *Judicature: The Journal of the American Judicature Society* 87, no. 3 (November/December, 2003): 135–44, and 149; and Deborah Goldberg, Craig Holman, and Samantha Sanchez, *The New Politics of Judicial Elections* (New York: Brennan Center for Justice, New York University and the National Institute on Money in State Politics, 2002).

[11] Besides Alaska, the other western states are Arizona, California, Colorado, New Mexico, Utah, and Wyoming. The ten non-western states are Florida, Indiana, Iowa, Kansas, Maryland, Missouri, Nebraska, Oklahoma, South Dakota, and Tennessee.

[12] New York has a fourteen-year term and five states have twelve-year terms—California, Delaware, Missouri, Virginia, and West Virginia.

[13] The Judicial Council By-Laws (Article 7, Section 5) state that the Council "will not reconsider the names submitted to the governor after the nominees are submitted unless the disability or death of one or more nominees leaves the governor with less than two names for filling a judicial vacancy."

[14] Richard Mauer, "Amendment of Picking Judges Still Up in Air," *ADN.com*, April 7, 2014.

[15] *Alaska Dispatch News*, "Bill Walker Answers Question about the Issues in the 2014 Election for Alaska Governor," October 11, 2014; and Mauer, "Amendment of Picking Judges Still Up in Air."

[16] Interview by Clive Thomas with Walter "Bud" Carpeneti, November, 12, 2014. See the Justice Not Politics Alaska website at http://www.justicenotpoliticsalaska.org/about.html.

[17] *Bess v. Ulmer*, 985 P2d 979 (Alaska 1999).

[18] Senate Joint Resolution 15 (SJR 15), 1999; and SJR 22, 2001.

[19] *Mickens v. City of Kodiak*, 640 P.2d 818 (Alaska 1982): and *Frank v. State*, 604 P. 2d 1068 (Alaska 1979).

[20] *ACLU v. State*, 122 P.3d 781 (Alaska 2005).

[21] "Report of the Alaska Supreme Court Advisory Committee on Fairness and Access," October 31, 1997.

[22] *Hootch v. State-Operated School System*, 536 P. 2d 793 807 (Alaska 1975).

[23] *State of Alaska v. Weiss*, 706 P.2d 681 (Alaska 1985); *Weiss v. State of Alaska*, 939 P 2d. 380 (Alaska 1997).

[24] *Smith v. Cleary*, 24 P. 3d 1245 (Alaska 2001).

[25] *Alaska Dispatch News*, "Bill Walker Answers Questions."

★ CHAPTER 18 ★

Alaska's Local Government System, Public Policies, and State-Local Power Dynamics

Kevin C. Ritchie

Why is there a chapter about local government in a book on state politics and policy making? There are five good reasons. In various ways, all five involve the relationship between local and state governments in state policy making and throw light on the dynamics of state politics.

First, local governments implement a number of programs that are both enacted and funded by the state. These include K–12 education, health and welfare, and some aspects of transportation and infrastructure facilities. Second, the importance of state and federal government employment to Alaska's economy is discussed in several chapters in the book. But by far the largest government employer in the state is local government. In 2013, for instance, local communities employed an average of 39,195 people monthly (41,450 in December, for example), just under half the combined total of the 82,926 federal, state, and local government workers.[1] This means that in 2013 (and for many years before that), about 13 percent of Alaska's full-time workforce (1 in 8) worked for local government. Third, due in large part to the first two factors, local government is a very influential political force in the state and has a significant impact on many policy decisions of state government. Fourth, Alaska state government is much more involved than those in most other states in funding local government and performs many services provided by local governments in other states. Local government demands for these services, particularly in rural-bush Alaska, translate into some very conflict-ridden policy debates. And fifth, there has been concern in some quarters that the local government system has not developed the way it was intended by the founders of the state. This concern is often intertwined with the issue of state versus local government provision of services. The upshot is that reform of local government has been an ongoing issue in Alaska politics.

Chapter 10 outlines the federal-state-local intergovernmental relationship (IGR) in Alaska. In this chapter we go into more detail about the state-local relationship and provide an understanding of the political and policy importance of local government as it relates to state government. The focus is on the system of local government set out in the Alaska Constitution (mainly in Article X), supplemented by and implemented through state statutes (mainly in Title 29 of Alaska Statutes—AS 29). The chapter does not cover Native governments. They are dealt with, to some extent, in Chapter 9, which focuses on Alaska Natives in state politics, and in Chapter 10 on IGR. However, as a major political force in rural-bush Alaska, the role of Alaska Natives in the development of local government and in the policy and power dynamics of local-state relations is an integral part of our analysis here.

The approach in this chapter is to use the development—more precisely the incomplete development—and present structure of Alaska's local government system as a vehicle for understanding past and present state-local relations, related policy issues, and power dynamics, and to place Alaska's local government system in comparison with other states. Using this approach provides the foundation for the main argument or theme of the chapter, which is that, as in all states, much of the dynamics of state politics and many of the major issues that arise and the policy debates that occur are a product of state-local relations. In other words, ignoring the role of local government, both as an aspect of Alaska's nexus of governments and as a political force, provides an incomplete picture of state politics past and present.

The first section of the chapter explains terminology as it relates to the unique and the so-called model character of Alaska's local government system. Then, Sections 2 through 4 deal with the development and present structure of local government. Section 5 offers an explanation of the stymied development of the local government system and how it affects state politics, government, and policy. Prominent issues and policies that affect the state-local relationship are briefly considered in Section 6. Section 7 builds on references to the state-local power relationship in previous sections and examines the power dynamics of the local government lobby and urban versus rural-bush conflicts as they relate to local government. The conclusion returns to the chapter's theme and the value of understanding the role of local government in Alaska in state politics, IGR, and for making sense of particular policy areas.

1. IMPORTANT TERMS AND CONCEPTS AND THE UNIQUE AND "MODEL" ALASKA LOCAL GOVERNMENT SYSTEM

Throughout the book many chapters argue that Alaska's politics, government, and public policy are not as exceptional as many Alaskans believe them to be. However, the state's local government system really is different from that of any other state.

As a consequence, although Alaska local government shares some common terminology with other systems, such as *city* and *borough*, these and other terms often have a particular meaning in the state. So, it is important not to assume similarities in the use of terms. To avoid confusion, Box 18.1 explains several terms that relate to local government in general and Alaska local government in particular.

In addition, some of the most familiar aspects of other local government systems, such as counties and separate special districts, do not exist in Alaska. The different types and powers of the various local government units may seem complex and a little daunting at first. It is not necessary, however, to understand the details of the powers of all types of local governments. All that is needed is a general familiarity with the types of local jurisdictions and the basics of their authority.

The framers of Alaska's constitution made a well-documented effort to avoid the mistakes and limitations of the constitutions of other states. In so doing, they developed a system of local government that attempted to deal with past problems and meet the challenges of Alaska's physical geography and its socio-economic and political realities. The result, as assessed by Gordon Harrison, is that Article X of the constitution is "a unique and flexible framework for the development of local government institutions in Alaska."[2] And a study written eight years after statehood saw the Alaska borough as a model for other states considering "area wide or metropolitan" government. The study characterized the borough as a "flexible and adaptable tool of government."[3]

In order to more fully appreciate the reasons for this uniqueness and flexibility and to understand why the present local government system has not met the founders' goals, some history is useful.

2. A SHORT HISTORY OF LOCAL GOVERNMENT IN ALASKA BEFORE STATEHOOD

A good case can be made that Alaska has had a history of strong local government. For one thing, reliance on local governments compensated for the minimal government that existed before 1900. Second, this reliance reflected and continues to reflect the general antipathy toward "distant governments," particularly the federal government, but also the territorial, and later the state, government.

Between 1745 and 1900 there was minimal government in Alaska. The Russians provided little effective governance and virtually no protection for Alaska's Native people, whose numbers were decimated during Russian rule. Between 1867 (when the United States purchased Alaska from Russia) and 1884, the U.S. military provided what limited government existed. At various times Alaska was under the jurisdiction of the U.S. Army, the Treasury Department, and the U.S. Navy. In 1884 Alaska became a district, but

BOX 18.1

Alaska Local Government Terms

A *borough* is one of the two forms of municipal government set out in the Alaska Constitution; the other is a *city*. A borough is a regional local government (similar to a county in other states) and may include cities within its borders. Or it may become a *unified municipality*, a single consolidated city-borough government. The governing body of a borough is an *assembly* and that of a city is a *council*.

A city or borough that has adopted a *home rule charter* is called a *home rule municipality*. The home rule provisions of Alaska law give home rule municipalities a great deal of freedom to design their own government. A home rule charter, which must be approved by the electorate, sets out the purpose, powers, and organization of a home rule municipality.

The *mandatory areawide powers* are required statutory responsibilities of boroughs (and organized cities not located in boroughs). These powers are operating a school district and partially funding schools, assessment of local property values and taxation, and land use regulation. Those responsibilities that must be applied throughout the entire borough are referred to as *areawide* responsibilities.

There are two types of boroughs in Alaska. An *organized borough* is a region organized under state law as a local government. Alaska is unique in that a large area of the state does not have any form of municipal government. The entire area of the state located outside organized boroughs is designated as the *Unorganized Borough*, and the state legislature may deliver such services it deems advisable in this area. Most notably the state provides schools in this area but does not levy local government taxes.

Organized boroughs may be of several classes: *unified, first class, second class*, and until they were abolished by the legislature in 1985, *third class* boroughs. The distinction is based upon the authority that they can exercise, including taxing authority. Similarly, cities can be *home rule, first class*, or *second class* in designation and powers.

The *Local Boundary Commission (LBC)* is provided for in the state constitution to maintain reasonable flexibility in municipal boundaries.

There are fifty-four *school districts*, broken into two basic categories: municipal school districts and *Rural Education Attendance Areas (REAAs)*. School districts in municipal areas are operated by boroughs and by first class or home rule cities not located within organized boroughs (those located in the Unorganized Borough). There are nineteen borough school districts and fifteen city school districts, none of which is financially autonomous. Borough and city school districts have an elected board, but they have no authority to raise revenues. Thus they must request an appropriation for schools from the borough assembly or city council.

For school administration in communities in the Unorganized Borough that are not home rule or first class cities, the area is divided into nineteen REAAs. These are funded entirely by the state, but each has a local school board. There are no local taxes imposed for funding school in the REAAs. The Mount Edgecombe High School in Sitka is a special school funded by the state.

Source: Developed by the author.

congressional attention was focused on post–Civil War Reconstruction and Congress had little time to dedicate to Alaska. Consequently, according to Jeanette Nichols, "no squatter could acquire title to land; no creditor could collect debts; no dying could will their possessions; no lovelorn could marry; no murderer could be tried."[4]

Authorization of Municipal Government and Territorial Status

Congress authorized limited municipal governments in 1900. Within a year, Alaska's five largest communities—Juneau, Douglas, Sitka, Skagway (all in Southeast Alaska), and Nome (in Northwest Alaska)—had incorporated. The salmon canning and other large industries opposed local regulation and taxation with some success.[5] The Territorial Act of 1912 prohibited the creation of counties, probably as a concession to natural resource industries that feared local regulation and taxes. Most communities of one thousand or more people had incorporated as cities by statehood in 1959.

The Approach to Local Government at Alaska's Constitutional Convention

The expansion of population in Alaska that occurred during World War II and the early postwar years helped fuel the movement for statehood. This expansion and the issues it raised for burgeoning cities and towns, the widely dispersed population of the Territory, and the desire to strengthen the tradition of strong local government, presented the delegates to Alaska's Constitutional Convention with many challenges. As with their approach to other provisions of the constitution, the founders went about their task regarding local government in a very systematic way. As a latecomer to the Union, Alaska, like Hawaii, developed a constitution that closely follows the model state constitution developed by the National Municipal League, now the National Civic League. In particular, both states incorporated model provisions for local government into their constitutions. Insights into the challenges that Alaska's founders faced are best understood by briefly explaining the organizational problems of local government across the United States that persist, even in the second decade of the twenty-first century.

The Patchwork of Modern Local Governments and Their Jurisdiction

Regarding the development and present status of local government throughout the United States, Bowman and Kearney conclude that:

> American local governments were not planned according to some grand design. Rather, they grew in response to a combination of citizen demand, interest group pressure, and state acquiescence. As a consequence, no rational system of local government exists. What does exist is a collection of autonomous, frequently overlapping jurisdictional units.[6]

Today the average U.S. citizen is simultaneously subject to a half-dozen or more units of local government with taxing or regulatory authority—county, city, school district, transit authority, parks board, waste district, and so on.[7] In addition, some states place limits on local government functions and authority, and there are other problems. For example, in some states municipal boundaries are frozen and cannot be altered to meet changing demographics and current needs. There are also many constitutionally established local elected offices that dilute central authority, including an elected clerk, coroner, sheriff, prosecutor, assessor, and treasurer. In addition, there are archaic structures and procedures, including "local amendments"—legislative provisions that apply only to one or a few designated local governments—as well as court decisions in many states that narrowly construe the powers of local government.[8]

The Goals of the Founders

When Alaska's founders met in Fairbanks in the winter of 1955–1956, U.S. local government was even more of a patchwork than it is today. Given this situation, the goal of the convention's local government committee was to create an efficient and effective system of local government. In order to do so, the committee gave great weight to a report prepared by the Public Administration Service (PAS), a nonprofit organization headquartered in Chicago that provided research and consulting services for governments.[9] The PAS report reviewed trends and problems of local government organization in the United States and elsewhere and recommended the creation of unified regional local governments. This was a goal that local government reformers and specialists had been striving to attain in many states over a period of several generations.[10]

3. THE FOUNDERS' PROVISIONS AND VISION FOR ALASKA LOCAL GOVERNMENT

As they emerged from the Constitutional Convention, the provisions for local government in the Alaska Constitution included several unique and advanced features. Most notable were (1) broad home rule powers, (2) a streamlined system of local jurisdictions, (3) provisions to avoid overlapping jurisdictions, (4) provisions to avoid decentralized administration, and (5) provisions for local public and state legislative participation in developing and changing the system. In addition, the founders envisioned a logical process of stages by which the local government system would develop so that, eventually, the entire state would be covered by some form of local self-government.

Broad Home Rule Provisions

The Alaska Constitution provides broad, liberally construed "home rule" powers for municipalities, including broad taxing authority and legislative powers. This essentially allows local governments to exercise at the local level the same powers available to the legislature. Also, a first-class city or borough can adopt a home rule charter without the approval of the legislature. In addition, Section 1 of Article X states, "A liberal construction shall be given to the powers of local government units." This provision serves as a guide to future legislatures and the courts, ensuring that courts in Alaska would not follow the judicial decisions in other states that have narrowly construed local government powers.[11] From a practical political perspective, these constitutional provisions set the stage for a state-local power relationship that makes local governments in Alaska far less beholden to the legislature than in many states.

A Flexible and Streamlined System of Local Jurisdictions and Its Development

In order to allow flexibility and rationality in the creation of local governments and to provide a means of changing local government boundaries, Section 12 of Article X creates the Local Boundary Commission (LBC). This provision allows for the relatively easy creation of cities or boroughs as well as changes to city or borough boundaries, subject only to a legislative veto.

Article X provides for streamlined organization for local governments, without the myriad local, often overlapping, jurisdictions characteristic of many other states. Article X also allows for cities and unincorporated areas to form organized boroughs, and for overlapping cities and boroughs to consolidate into unified boroughs with relative ease and flexibility. Finally, Article X provides for the creation of multiple unorganized boroughs. The concept of an unorganized borough is a unique Alaska creation to allow for the evolution of local governance in areas that lack the population or economic base to support an organized local government. It was intended to be the first level of local government evolution, during which the borough would be a state operated and funded public service district.[12]

Avoiding Both Overlapping Jurisdictions and Decentralized Administration

Prior to statehood, Alaska, like other states, had special local taxing authorities, mostly school districts and public utility districts. Thus Alaska's founders were well aware of the lack of coordination, and the fragmentation and decentralization that can occur in local government policy making when there are multiple autonomous special districts, many of them with their own budgets and their own elected governing bodies. They were also aware of problems that occur when local jurisdictions are given policy responsibility that is better placed with the state government, particularly responsibility for courts and jails.

Avoiding these problems was partly achieved by provisions in the constitution that minimize the number of special districts and that allow for only one centralized local government budget. Service areas may be created and may provide different levels of service and different tax rates, but the taxing power of the service area may be exercised only by the borough assembly or city council. Whether to allow autonomy and separate taxing authority to school districts was hotly debated during the convention. Ultimately, it was decided to avoid overlapping taxing authority by making school districts financially dependent on boroughs, with school boards setting education policy but seeking funding from their borough or city government. Rural education attendance areas (REAAs) within the Unorganized Borough are funded entirely by the state with a local school board. The founders sought to further centralize municipal authority by providing that only city council and borough assembly members, school board members, and, in some boroughs, the mayor, are elected. As later provided by statute, all are elected on nonpartisan platforms.[13]

Provisions for Local Public and Legislative Participation in Developing and Changing the System

Article X of the constitution and the minutes of the convention make it clear that the founders were very concerned, some might say "possessed," with involving the public in decisions about their local government, its powers, and its development. This is evidenced in the phrase, "to provide for a maximum of local self-government with a minimum of local government units" in Section 1 of Article X. Along with the right of participation went the responsibility and obligation of local communities for developing and running their local governments. The founders also left much of the fleshing out of the local government system to the elected state legislature.[14] There were several reasons for the concern for local participation.

The first reason was political. The constitution promotes unified regional local governments. However, abolishing cities through mandatory consolidation and replacing them with regional boroughs was not politically feasible. Instead, the legal framework was created for cities and boroughs to voluntarily consolidate. A second reason was to accommodate local differences in communities across the state due to the wide variation in socio-economic and geographical circumstances. Only local participation could achieve this. A third reason was to create a sense of personal investment and responsibility among local residents for their local government, a feeling that was absent in many places when Alaska was a federal territory.

The Vision of Local Government Development

Before statehood, cities had been the most consistent and reliable units of government in Alaska. Consequently, the convention delegates were reluctant to reduce the number or power of cities without a vote of the residents of each city. On the other hand, the vast size of the state and its small and widely dispersed population created a huge challenge for providing efficient and affordable local government. Therefore, setting a constitutional goal of developing regional local governments (that is, a network of "unified," or consolidated, boroughs) and leaving its future implementation to be worked out region by region, seemed to make both political and democratic sense.[15]

The constitutionally promoted evolution of local government was, theoretically, to progress as follows.

Stage One

Initially, the legislature would create multiple "unorganized boroughs" in all parts of the state that were deemed unable to sustain an organized borough. These unorganized boroughs would have services provided by the state, but with "maximum local participation and responsibility," presumably to train residents to work together and to manage services regionally. The evolution to an organized borough would take place when there was a reasonably cohesive region that worked together and a sufficient regional economic base or access to other funding to support a borough. The first stage in the evolutionary process might be termed "boroughs in training."

Stage Two

When strong working relationships were established and the regional economy had developed sufficiently, an organized borough would be formed. To facilitate this stage, "Second Class" and "Third Class" boroughs were created as part of the local government evolutionary process. Second class boroughs do not have a local charter but generally have very similar powers and duties to a home rule borough. A second class borough administers education borough-wide, plus other services delivered within "service areas," such as roads or fire services.

The primary difference between a third class borough and an unorganized borough was an elected governing "assembly" for the third class borough, along with the duty to raise local funds through taxes to partially support schools. Under the 1985 revision of the statutes governing local governments, third class boroughs could no longer be formed. As of that time, only one such borough (Haines in 1968) had ever been formed, and Haines abandoned that status in 2002 to become a home rule borough.

Stage Three

The final stage was creating a unified borough. It was hoped that an organized borough with one or more organized cities within its boundaries would see the efficiency of consolidating into one unified local government with a single taxing authority, home rule powers, and a local charter.

From Vision to the Realities of Alaska Politics

This, then, was the vision of Alaska's founders for local government and its relationship to state government. But how has it worked out in practice? The next section examines the contemporary Alaska local government system and explains how and why it differs from the founders' vision. This discussion sets the scene for understanding the nature of local-state relations and particularly the policy and power dynamics of that relationship. In addition, the difference between the vision and reality illustrates several of the characteristics of Alaska politics.

4. ALASKA'S CONTEMPORARY LOCAL GOVERNMENT SYSTEM: THE FOUNDERS' VISION ONLY PARTIALLY REALIZED

At least in theory, today Alaska has a streamlined local government system, with two basic local government units—boroughs and cities—and no major overlaps in jurisdiction. There is, though, a wide gap between the theory and what has developed in practice. An initial indication of this gap is evident by viewing Map 18.1, which shows that close to 60 percent of the state still has no form of local government. This huge area comprises a single Unorganized Borough and is a far cry from the multiple unorganized boroughs throughout the state that the founders envisioned as "boroughs in training." Table 18.1 lists the number and types of boroughs and cities as of 2015, as well as the number of school districts and unincorporated villages, mainly Alaska Native villages.[16]

Grading the Evolution and Present Status of Local Government

In assessing and grading the development and present status of local government in Alaska, we can view it from five perspectives: (1) compared with other states; (2) with regard to Alaska's urban communities; (3) cooperation between communities; (4) Alaska's rural-bush communities; and (5) political support for, and public participation in, the organized statewide local government system.

First, with the exception of Hawaii, which has counties but no cities, Alaska has been much more successful than other states in achieving unified local governments. A list of city-county consolidations compiled by the National Association of Counties showed that of 3,069 U.S. counties in 2005, only 37 had consolidated in the past 200 years—that is, since 1805—and five of them (Anchorage, Juneau, Sitka, Haines, and Yakutat) were in Alaska. With only one-half of 1 percent of the country's regional local governments (that is, boroughs), Alaska has 14 percent of the successful local government consolidations in the United States. The figures in Table 18.1 show that Alaska has just over 200 local government units, including REAAs in the Unorganized Borough. This is close to the 210 in Nevada but in sharp contrast to the 5,031 in Pennsylvania.[17] So we can give Alaska an A– for the practical streamlined characteristics of its local government system.

Second, larger urban communities like Anchorage, Fairbanks, Juneau, Kodiak, Ketchikan, and Sitka have robust local governments with sufficient authority and resources to create and sustain thriving communities. Many smaller cities and boroughs have also become thriving communities. So this aspect deserves at least a B+.

MAP 18.1

Alaska Boroughs and the Unorganized Borough

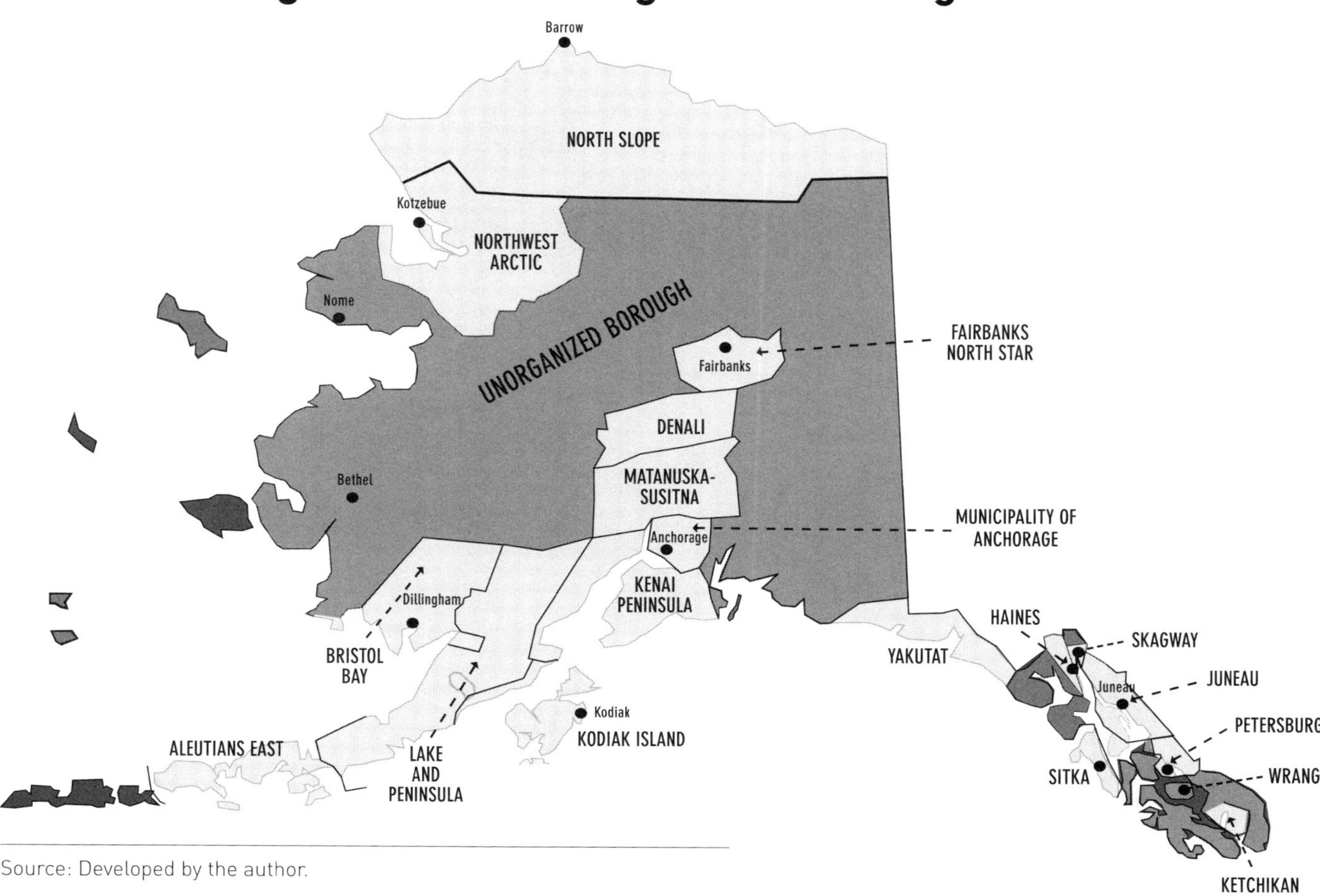

Source: Developed by the author.

TABLE 18.1

Types and Number of Alaska Local Governments
(as of December 2015)

BOROUGHS

Unified Home Rule	4
Home Rule	7
First Class	1
Second Class	7
Total Boroughs	**19**

INCORPORATED CITIES

	WITHIN BOROUGHS	WITHIN THE UNORGANIZED BOROUGH	TOTAL
Home Rule Cities	6	4	10
First Class Cities	7	11	18
Second Class Cities	34	80	114
Total Cities	**47**	**95**	**142**

VILLAGES IN ALASKA 229

SCHOOL DISTRICTS

Within Boroughs	19
Cities within the Unorganized Boroughs	15
Rural Education Attended Areas	19
Total	**53**
Special State School, Mount Edgecombe, in Sitka	1
Total of All School Districts	**54**

Source: Developed by the author.

Third, cities and boroughs sometimes compete and come into conflict, but more often they work together on both local and statewide issues. To illustrate this compatibility, Alaska is the only state that has a consolidated city and borough municipal association, the Alaska Municipal League (AML). Every other state has chosen to keep city and county associations separate. The explanation for the compatibility of cities and boroughs in Alaska may be their very similar duties, structures, and powers. In contrast, cities and counties in the lower forty-eight states often have different governing structures, powers, and service responsibilities. The relative lack of conflict between cities and boroughs benefits Alaska citizens. So here another B+/A– can be awarded.

Fourth, with respect to rural-bush communities, particularly the situation in the Unorganized Borough, the grade is much lower—perhaps a C+ at best, as the concept of multiple unorganized boroughs was never implemented. A single Unorganized Borough emerged instead as a huge and geographically messy catch-all that comprised the area left over from the formation of organized boroughs. Today, the Unorganized Borough covers 57 percent of the land area of Alaska, or approximately 375,000 square miles. Alaska is the only state with an unorganized region without a county or other form of regional government.

One huge statewide, unorganized borough certainly violates the constitutional provisions for determining regional unorganized boroughs because Article X, Section 3, of the constitution states that:

> The entire State shall be divided into boroughs, organized or unorganized. . . . The standards shall include population, geography, economy, transportation, and other factors. Each borough shall embrace an area and population with common interests to the maximum degree possible.

It is difficult to argue that the Unorganized Borough has ever met these standards. Given this situation, there is a concern among some politicians that this huge area of Alaska, albeit a relatively small percentage of the state population, has not voluntarily formed regional governments and, in effect, remains a protectorate of state government.

Fifth, there has been little political support for and participation in an organized statewide local government system. The formation of regional local governments throughout the state, as envisioned by Alaska's founders, has not come to pass. With the exception of local school boards (REAAs) there have been few, if any, formal local participation processes centered on cohesive regions throughout the state that could eventually become boroughs.

Besides the present nineteen organized boroughs, there were nineteen additional "model boroughs" proposed in a study by the LBC in 1992 (revised in 1997) to divide up the single Unorganized Borough according to constitutional principles. The model boroughs have never been adopted by the legislature, though they have guided the LBC in its local government plan for Alaska.[18] Ten voluntarily organized boroughs can hardly be considered a broad citizen endorsement of the borough concept. Plus, of the nineteen current organized boroughs, only three (Sitka, Anchorage, and Juneau) have become official unified boroughs (that is, having consolidated city-county governments).[19]

So, perhaps a C–/D+ is in order for the political support for, and public participation in, an organized statewide local government system. It certainly falls far short of the founders' hopes.

5. EXPLAINING ALASKA'S STYMIED LOCAL GOVERNMENT SYSTEM AND ITS IMPACT ON STATE POLITICS, GOVERNMENT, AND POLICY

Explaining the reasons for the underdevelopment of Alaska's local government system enhances an understanding of the dynamics of the system. It also provides insightful perspectives on Alaska politics and power relationships.

Local Circumstances: Why Boroughs Do and Do Not Form

The major explanation for why the founders' vision for local government has not been realized is both obvious and simple. With the very best of intentions and caught up in the euphoria of their task, idealism, plus the academic advice they received and the ambiance of the University of Alaska campus, perhaps got the better of them. As a result, they underestimated the tendency of Alaskans to prefer self-interest, individualism, and pragmatism over concerns about the general welfare of the community. Alaska's local government history since statehood tends to support this contention. Take, for instance, the reasons some boroughs have formed and, by implication, why others have not.

Table 18.2 shows that nine of the existing nineteen boroughs were "mandated," that is, they were formed as a result of a "shotgun wedding" approach—the Mandatory Borough Act enacted by the legislature in 1963. The other ten boroughs formed voluntarily. The reasons for their voluntary formation provide insight into why other areas within the Unorganized Borough continue to remain unorganized.

The ten voluntarily formed boroughs share one of two incentives.

One is a revenue incentive. A regional government was needed to capture regional tax revenues from oil, mining, tourism, or fishing. For instance, the Denali, Aleutians East, Northwest Arctic, and Lake and Peninsula Boroughs fund their operations without either a local property or general sales tax. Instead, they use one or more of the following targeted revenue measures: raw fish tax, severance tax (mining tax), payments in lieu of taxes under contracts with one or more major local industries, or a tourism sales tax (such as a bed tax). The second incentive is that residents perceive a need for local protection. Creation of a regional government is seen as a defensive measure to protect the area from being subsumed by another borough or from some other state-mandated incorporation process. Fear of being annexed by the adjacent Fairbanks North Star Borough (which has high property taxes) was a significant factor for voter approval of the Denali Borough, which at the time of its creation had no property or general sales tax.

Even where the incentives of revenue and protection from extraterritorial incursions are present, borough formation does not necessarily occur. For example, the proposed Copper River Basin Model Borough, with about three thousand residents, could capture significant new revenue by taxing a portion of the trans-Alaska pipeline and tourism facilities, but its residents have very much opposed borough incorporation.[20]

TABLE 18.2

Types of Boroughs and the Economic Driver behind Their Formation

(Listed in Order of Year of Creation)

BOROUGHS	INCORPORATED	TYPE OF BOROUGH	ECONOMIC DRIVER*
Bristol Bay Borough	1962	2nd Class	Fish
Ketchikan Gateway Borough	1963	2nd Class	Mandated**
Kodiak Island Borough	1963	2nd Class	Mandated
City and Borough of Sitka	1963/1971	Unified Home Rule	Mandated
Municipality of Anchorage	1964/1975	Unified Home Rule	Mandated
Fairbanks North Star Borough	1964	2nd Class	Mandated
Kenai Peninsula	1964	2nd Class	Mandated
Matanuska-Susitna Borough	1964	2nd Class	Mandated
City and Borough of Juneau	1964/1970	Unified Home Rule	Mandated
Haines Borough	1968/2002	Home Rule***	Mandated
North Slope Borough	1972	Home Rule	North Slope Oil
Northwest Arctic Borough	1986	Home Rule	Red Dog Mine
Aleutians East Borough	1987	2nd Class	Fish
Lake and Peninsula Borough	1989	Home Rule	Fish/Tourism
Denali Borough	1990	Home Rule	Tourism/Mining
City and Borough of Yakutat	1992	Home Rule***	Fish/Mining
Municipality of Skagway Borough	2007	1st Class***	Tourism
City and Borough of Wrangell	2008	Unified Home Rule	Land
Petersburg Borough	2013	Home Rule	Land/Economic Development

* Economic drivers were determined from conversations with municipal officials and examining the tax receipts of the boroughs (Alaska Taxable 2008). The formation of a borough allowed for the capture of revenue from regional industries outside of existing cities, except for Skagway, which incorporated primarily to maintain existing revenues.

** The nine boroughs initially incorporated between 1963 and 1968 were legally required to incorporate as a result of the Mandatory Borough Act of 1963.

*** While the Haines Borough, City and Borough of Yakutat, and the Municipality of Skagway Borough are not officially Unified Home Rule boroughs, they each exhibit the characteristics of one, largely because there is only one unified municipality area-wide.

Source: Developed by the author.

There are also several disincentives to the formation of more boroughs that work to discourage existing local governments from seeking additional authority. First, increased responsibilities of local government usually involve levying local taxes or generating other revenues for services that are currently provided by the state. Second, a new municipality must start dealing with potentially thorny issues that are currently handled by the state or other organizations, such as public safety and education. Added to these disincentives is the loss of power by the existing political structures that have developed to fill the public service and leadership void. And there is the potential for conflicts within the proposed regional government resulting from this restructuring of power, among other conflicts that many present public officials and citizens may rather avoid.

State Policy Regarding Local Government

Since statehood, the pragmatic self-interest of local residents, plus the lack of a tax base in most of rural-bush Alaska, have presented state policy makers (both in the legislature and the executive branch) with some difficult choices. They have had to combine paternalistic action with providing incentives to aid the development of local government. More significantly, they have had to fill the funding and service void when local communities cannot or will not provide for themselves. In these and other ways, the state has both aided and impeded the founders' vision of local government.

Paternalistic action included the Mandatory Borough Act of 1963. An example of an incentive is local revenue sharing by state government, begun in the flush oil revenue days of the early 1980s. The creation of the Department of Community and Regional Affairs (DCRA), an agency primarily dealing with rural-bush Alaska, is an example of helping to fill the void over a range of services.

Some of these proactive, beneficial state government policies have also had some unintended consequences and have contributed to the stymied development of local government. In particular, state services provided for free, which would otherwise cost an organized local government a considerable amount to provide for itself, make forming a local government less attractive. The key pressures against voluntary organization include a steady decline of state revenue sharing since the mid-1980s, the increasing cost of schools in boroughs and in first class cities in the Unorganized Borough versus the schools provided for free by the state through REAAs, and the rising cost of employee benefits, especially retirement and health care.

A related consequence of state policy that has probably worked to undermine the voluntary creation of more boroughs is another aspect of paternalism. Again, probably unintentionally, the state has failed to provide for the "maximum local participation and responsibility" of citizens in the one huge Unorganized Borough. In this regard, a 1981 study by DCRA concluded, in essence, that the present system encourages dependence and that inhabitants of the Unorganized Borough are encouraged to be supplicants and clients of state-provided services and largely spectators upon the political life of local government. They are not citizens effectively participating in governance and local policy making. Moreover, this system is not supportive of Native cultures and effectively requires Natives to submerge or abandon traditional cultural values in order to participate in state politics.[21]

In addition, and ironically, the big money days after oil began to flow from Prudhoe Bay in the late 1970s also likely worked to undermine the state's political will to realize the full development of a local government system. In these years the legislature understandably tried to use the state's excess wealth across a range of policy areas to solve many immediate problems rather than develop long-term solutions. During this time, much of the enthusiasm generated by the framers of the Constitution for promoting the evolution of local government faded as well. The political odyssey of the state's local government agency (DCRA), explained in Box 18.2, reflects these changing state attitudes toward local government and the politics and power plays that were involved.[22]

The Upshot: A Political Status Quo

Local circumstances and the intended and unintended consequences of state policy have, in effect, led to a political status quo regarding the development of Alaska's local government system. Part of the explanation lies in the political power relationships in the state. Most elected local government officials in rural-bush Alaska, and those elected to the legislature from the various communities and regions, reflect the strong tendency against forming more extensive and powerful regional governments. Furthermore, rural-bush legislators and their allies have been able to stall attempts by some urban legislators, most notably former Senator Gary Wilken from Fairbanks, to impose regional governments on the Unorganized Borough. So far, no effective attempt since the 1960s has been made to repeat the "shotgun marriage" of the Mandatory Borough Act. Herein lies another example of a political power dynamic revolving around state-local relations that illustrates regionalism and urban versus rural-bush conflict.

There are still no state taxes imposed on residents in the Unorganized Borough, though a number of cities located there have, by their own choosing, imposed a tax load heavier than in some organized boroughs.[23] As time goes on, taxes in an organized borough, or a city in the Unorganized Borough, will continue to increase. In contrast, residents outside of cities in the Unorganized Borough will have no local taxes and will get further accustomed to a tax-free existence.

Alaska's political culture of pragmatic dependent individualism, together with an antitax attitude in many areas and general skepticism of government, helps fuel this tendency against a more comprehensive and integrated local government system. In addition, unless there are incentives of the type explained above regarding tax revenues or jurisdictional protection, the status quo—reinforced by fear of negative consequences resulting from change—is a very powerful force. This makes the decision to form a borough voluntarily more difficult and less likely with the passage of time.

BOX 18.2

The Political Odyssey of Alaska's Local Government Agency

To help ensure development of Alaska's novel system of local government, Alaska's founders mandated the creation of a local government agency in Article X, Section 14, of the constitution. Accordingly, in 1959, the first legislature created a Local Affairs Agency and placed it in the Office of the Governor. To give local government a higher priority in state policy, and to encourage and aid in its lagging development, in 1972 Democratic Governor Egan raised this agency to department level as the Department of Community and Regional Affairs (DCRA). He did this with the support of Democrats in the legislature, particularly those from rural-bush areas, and over the objections of many Republican legislators who were concerned about state spending.

Although DCRA's responsibilities included more than local government, such as day-care assistance, job training, and other forms of economic development, its major role was dealing with local communities. It also provided administrative support for the Local Boundary Commission (LBC). One of DCRA's first accomplishments was playing a major role in the establishment of the North Slope Borough in 1972.

As the department evolved, its functions became focused on rural-bush governments. This was largely because urban communities, especially large boroughs like Anchorage and Fairbanks, had considerable resources and needed little help from DCRA. Consequently, the department never developed a strong political constituency, largely because of lack of urban support but also because other service providers were operating in rural-bush communities, especially Native nonprofit associations. This is in contrast to departments such as Commerce, which had the business community, and the Department of Labor with its constituency of unions and other labor interests.

This combination of circumstances made DCRA politically vulnerable when state revenues plummeted in 1986 and fluctuated in the 1990s. In the late 1990s, a concerted effort led by Representative Vic Kohring (a Republican from Wasilla) was made to merge DCRA with the Department of Commerce and Economic Development. Kohring and others argued that there was duplication between the two departments in the area of economic development. Urban versus rural-bush tensions also played a role in this merger, perhaps a major one, given the long-standing concerns among some urban, particularly Republican, legislators about the costs of providing services to rural-bush areas and the lack of any taxes paid by residents receiving those services. Many Republicans believed that merging the departments would reduce the political advocacy potential of rural-bush communities and might help spur local government reform.

Although there was support for the continued existence of DCRA by some communities such as the City of Bethel, the pro-merger forces had the momentum. And Democratic Governor Knowles, with a Republican House and Senate, chose to fight more important political battles. So, in 1999 the merger occurred and the new agency became the Department of Commerce, Community, and Economic Development (DCCED).

The only agency voice for local government that existed during Governor Murkowski's administration (2002–2006) was located in DCCED's Division of Community Advocacy (DCA). Then, with the election of Sarah Palin as governor in 2006, a recommendation of her transition team regarding DCCED was to reestablish a local government department to give communities, particularly in rural-bush areas, more of a presence in her administration. To what extent this was supported by Governor Palin is unclear. A new department was not created, but DCA was renamed the Division of Community and Regional Affairs (DCRA) with expanded responsibilities for dealing with local governments. The administration of Governor Sean Parnell (2009–2014) left the organizational structures intact. It remains to be seen how Governor Walker, elected in November 2014, will deal with DCRA, given that his election was due, in no small part, to strong support from rural-bush voters and that the Lieutenant Governor, Byron Mallott, is a prominent Alaska Native leader.

Source: Developed by Clive Thomas and Anthony Nakazawa based on sources in endnote 22.

The Consequences for Alaska Politics and Government Operations

Ironically, from a political perspective, the very thing that the founders sought to promote—a high level of citizen participation in the decisions of their local government and its development—is largely responsible for this lack of local government development. Constitutional provisions with more mandated forms of local government, or restrictions on local attempts to block development of local governments, would likely have resulted in a different history of local government development in Alaska. But it is not clear whether that would have been a good thing from either an organizational or democratic perspective. Nor is it clear who would have benefited from such an outcome. We approach the issue by weighing the policy pros and cons of maintaining the status quo.

What are the Cons?

The first con relates to general efficiency in local governments. The traditional argument of the LBC is:

> The absence of organized boroughs throughout Alaska has led to a proliferation of government and quasi-government organizations in the unorganized borough. The reform proposed by the Local Boundary Commission (i.e., more boroughs) would create the foundation to promote greater efficiency and effectiveness in the delivery of services in the area currently encompassing the unorganized borough.[24]

John J. Kirlin, in his 1981 state-funded study of services in the Unorganized Borough, characterized the current structure as follows: "To assert that the present situation is a 'worst case' scenario is not comforting to those seeking to make this system effective, but it may well be accurate."[25]

Another negative aspect of the current situation is the issue of tax equity. Many rural-bush residents do not pay local taxes for public services, especially for education, while urban local taxes are steadily rising. This situation is often seen by urban residents and their legislators as unfair and in need of reform, triggering yet another instance of urban versus rural-bush conflict in the state. For years, a particularly irksome point of contention was the state mandate that boroughs and first class cities must contribute to education while small cities in the Unorganized Borough do not. In November 2014, in a suit filed by the Ketchikan Gateway Borough, this mandate was struck down by an Alaska superior court judge as violating the state constitution's ban on dedicated funds. The state appealed the ruling, and in early 2016 the Alaska Supreme Court reversed the lower court's ruling and upheld the local contribution.[26]

What are the Pros?

One argument favoring the status quo goes as follows. While about 60 percent of the area of the state has no organized boroughs, only 12 percent of the population (just under eighty thousand) lives in the Unorganized Borough. Of those, a significant number live in the ninety-six organized cities in that area. The relatively small number of people residing in the Unorganized Borough does not necessarily argue against multiple borough formation. But the status quo may make more sense when one considers that a large number of people not covered by borough governments are Alaska Natives and there may be more appropriate forms of government for them and their areas, such as tribal governments.

In this regard, Morehouse, McBeath, and Leask suggested in the early 1980s that "two separate systems of local government seem to be emerging—one for urban areas and another for rural areas." The "several hundred" public service providers that have proliferated in the Unorganized Borough may be better for the residents than a traditional borough government. This is because these providers may have access to more sources of state and federal funding, multiple channels of representation and influence, and local organizational alternatives that have more independence from state government than do state-sanctioned municipalities. This may be especially the case to "help protect Native cultural interests from central bureaucratic leveling."[27] As Chapter 12 on the role of government in Alaska points out, expanding the effectiveness of representation and meeting the needs of a political constituency in a democracy (in this case Alaska Natives) often comes at the price of efficiency. Put another way, a government that is able to deliver services at low cost may be viewed as efficient, but it would not necessarily be effective in an area of the state where services are expensive to provide.

Alaska Native corporations, Native nonprofits, regional utility cooperatives, and city-tribal agreements are examples of evolving public service providers that benefit from economies of scale but are less fettered by state laws and strictures. Moreover, as strong service providers, Native nonprofits and Native corporations have proven that they have the resources to be an effective political voice for Native interests. Certainly, boroughs have worked well in some rural-bush areas, such as with the North Slope Borough, to capture natural resource revenue generated outside of cities. But borough governments may not be the only effective tool for governance in rural-bush Alaska.[28]

6. MAJOR CONTEMPORARY LOCAL-STATE POLICY ISSUES

Issues surrounding the underdevelopment of the state's local government system have a political ripple effect on urban communities, particularly in shifting to these urban areas part of the cost of running the Unorganized Borough. However, the issues mainly affect rural-bush communities in their relations with state government. In this section, we briefly identify major contemporary issues that have more general implications for the political and power dynamics of state-local relations.[29]

As in the state-local relationship across the nation, the primary characteristics of this relationship in Alaska are coordination and cooperation. The state and local governments are, for the most part, partners in the provision of many services that benefit Alaskans in both urban and rural-bush areas. However, as with any IGR, conflict also occurs. Across the nation, state-local disputes occur most often when a local government seeks to expand its authority and when local governments want more state aid, but state government wants to provide less, attach strings, ensure value for money, or some combination of these. Because of broad home rule powers for many communities in Alaska, the expanding authority of local government is not a major source of conflict, and in the case of many rural-bush governments, the issue is quite the reverse—a desire not to expand their powers. Like many other parts of the United States, state funding for local governments is a major source of conflict in Alaska, particularly for communities in the Unorganized Borough.

Box 18.3 outlines three aspects of state-local financial relations—state revenue sharing, school funding, and funding of municipal employee pensions—which are ongoing contentious issues. All three issues, result, in part, from the state deciding not to be as generous with its funds as it once was. Although Alaska has significant revenues and reserve funds, the state's strong strain of fiscal conservatism gets in the way of spending on local governments.

7. FURTHER OBSERVATIONS ON THE DYNAMICS OF STATE-LOCAL POWER RELATIONSHIPS

So far we have made several observations about state-local power relationships and how they affect Alaska politics. Examples of these power dynamics have included the home rule authority of local governments which gives them considerable independence from state government, the state's imposition of borough government formation in the early years of statehood, the influence of rural-bush political forces in preventing extension of the borough system throughout the state, and the political odyssey of the state's local government agency. In this section we provide one additional perspective on the power dynamics of the state-local relationship—the role of the local government lobby. We then bring together key points about the nature and consequences of urban versus rural-bush conflict.

BOX 18.3

Three Major Local-State Policy Issues

THE DECLINE OF REVENUE SHARING AND STATE ASSISTANCE

When oil revenues increased in the early 1980s, the legislature greatly expanded its municipal revenue sharing program. This enabled many small rural-bush cities to be established, allowing their residents to share in Alaska's newfound wealth. The program reached a peak in 1984–1985 and has declined almost annually since then.

Likely causes for the legislature being less willing to share state resources with its communities include an emotional response to the excess spending of the early 1980s; the chilling influence of several severe state revenue declines due to fluctuations in oil prices; and a re-emphasis on Alaska's more traditional individualistic nature accompanied by fiscal conservatism and distrust of government.

Local governments have had to absorb much of the declining state support. This includes significant reductions in state funding for both capital and operating expenditures, imposition of charges for previously free state services, lack of funding to inflation-proof education costs, and decreased state aid to fund employee retirement and other benefits.

SCHOOL FUNDING: AN ONGOING SOURCE OF LOCAL-STATE CONFLICT

As with most local governments across the nation, it is difficult to fully understand any Alaska municipality's politics or state-local intergovernmental politics without considering schools. K–12 education is the major service that most local governments provide in Alaska, as elsewhere in the nation, and it takes the largest slice of their budgets.

From soon after statehood, three long-standing issues have defined much of the state-local debate on school funding. One is allocating state education funding "fairly" between urban and rural-bush areas in light of the far higher cost of education in most rural-bush communities. Many rural-bush residents—particularly those in REAAs—feel that they do not receive adequate funding given higher operating costs and because they are totally dependent on reimbursement from the state for school construction and improvements. In contrast, many urban residents cover some school costs from local taxes and sell bonds—a percentage of which are reimbursed by the state—for school construction and improvements. However, due to the severe revenue shortfalls that began in mid-2014, in 2015

The Political Influence of Local Government across the States and of Alaska's Local Government Lobby

Across the fifty states various local government groups and organizations are political forces to be reckoned with by legislators and governors. This is evident by referring to Chapter 15 on interest groups, particularly Table 15.3, which includes local government interests among the most effective groups and organizations across the fifty states in 2010 and since 1980. Prominent interests that have a presence in state capitals are associations of cities and counties, individual local governments, municipal employee unions, as well as local elements of the education lobby, such as school boards, PTAs, and especially schoolteachers. State agencies dealing with local government, such as departments of education/public instruction and economic/community development, are also often part the legislature suspended all reimbursements for five years through 2020. The second, and a closely related issue, is tax equity regarding the lack of local tax support of schools in REAAs. The tax equity issue gained in importance after 1980 when the state repealed the state personal income tax—a tax that all state residents paid. Many urban residents and their legislators feel that they are subsidizing rural-bush schools.

A third issue is that of school effectiveness regarding student performance. Alaska's urban K–12 students are more likely to graduate from high school and score higher on scholastic aptitude tests than their rural-bush counterparts. Again, many urban legislators feel that the direct and extra state funds expended for REAA schools are being borne by their communities and they are not being spent effectively to produce well-educated high school graduates.

PUBLIC EMPLOYEES PENSIONS

The Alaska Public Employee Retirement System (PERS) and the Teachers Retirement System (TRS) present major policy concerns for local governments as well as for the state. The state has long underfunded its retirement obligations, which threatens to adversely affect the state's financial rating in the nation's bond markets. With its significant financial resources, however, Alaska can choose to manage state and local government pension obligations to reduce negative short and long-term impacts on its communities.

Of the approximately 190 employers in Alaska's PERS, the vast majority are cities, boroughs, and school districts. All of Alaska's school districts are in TRS. Because Alaska's constitution (Article XII, Section 7) provides protection for public employee pensions, the legislature is limited in its options for dealing with these increasing costs. So for PERS, the legislature has created "tiers" that do not reduce benefits for existing employees, but reduce them for new employees.

The significant cost increases in PERS and TRS have a major negative impact on municipal finances. A series of one-time annual infusions of cash by the legislature has helped delay the full financial impact of these increases. Then, in the 2014 legislative session, a long-term plan was developed to deal with the funding through 2038. The first step was an infusion of $3 billion made in 2014 ($2 billion into TRS and $1 billion into PERS). The second step involved a deposit of $345 million in 2016 with increasing amounts to be deposited at intervals through 2038. However, while the infusion of cash reduced the debt, some last minute changes in the original plan by the legislature and governor mean that this plan does not assure that long-term pension obligations will be well funded. The final plan as enacted shifts some of the future costs to local governments and future generations of Alaskans. So, as with revenue sharing and K-12 funding. TERS/PERS funding will be an on-going state-local issue and likely very contentious.

Source: Developed by the author.

of this general local government lobby. Because many policies pursued by state government affect local governments in some way, several local government lobbies will usually be in the thick of state policy making on a day-to-day basis year round, but particularly in the legislative session.

The reasons that local governments have political power as interest groups are covered in detail in Chapter 15. In summary, they include the fact that local governments are a major economic force because of their employment and spending and because they are well organized politically and have extensive resources for lobbying. Probably the major basis of the power of local government, however, is that there is usually a close tie between local elected and appointed officials and those elected from the area to the state legislature. This tie takes the form of friends and neighbors political relationships which, depending on the size of the local government, may extend to relationships between members of the state legislature and their local constituents. The link between constituents and state legislators is crucial because constituents can reelect them or vote them out of office. Keeping constituents happy requires, among other things, a well-functioning local government.

All these factors add up to give the various elements of local government access to state government and often considerable influence over its decisions. The trend across the nation since the early 1990s, however, has been a decline in the influence of some elements of this lobby, particularly teachers and other local government employees.

Alaska's Local Government Lobby

Alaska is very similar to other states in the role and influence of its local government lobby. On any one day during the legislative session in Juneau, many of those lobbying legislators and their staffs, the governor's office, and state agencies will be there on behalf of local government. This high degree of local government presence reflects the crucial importance to local government of the issues outlined in the last section—education funding, state assistance to local government, and funding for local government employee and teacher pensions—as well as many others, such as health and social services and transportation.

The reasons for local government influence in Alaska are similar to those in other states. However, as in many western states with small populations and where government is a major employer, two factors are particularly important. One is the importance of local employment to all municipalities, but particularly rural-bush communities. The second is friends and neighbors politics. With the small number of people in each legislative district, and the compactness of most urban districts, state representatives and senators must become very familiar with local officials and with many of their constituents' needs and concerns. The forces of economic need, personal acquaintance, the desire for reelection by legislators, and their wanting to make their community a better place to live, are all important factors that help the local government lobby convince their representatives to support their political goals.

As Box 18.4 indicates, local government and its employees have been among the top political forces in the state since the early 1980s and likely for some time before. One member of the local government lobby, the Association of Alaska School Boards (AASB), has been one of the two consistently influential lobbies in the state overall from 1980-2010 (the other is the oil industry).

Not all groups and organizations in Alaska's local government lobby have been consistently among the top rank of effectiveness over the years, as Box 18.4 shows. In line with national trends, local employees, including members of teachers' unions, have been

BOX 18.4

Alaska's Local Government Lobby

Listed below are the local government interest groups and organizations assessed as among the first rank of influence in the state over the thirty years from 1980 to 2010 based on six surveys conducted during those years. The list also indicates when other local government interest groups were in the second rank of influence or not listed at all. Those in the first rank were assessed as consistently influential over the five years prior to the particular survey, and those in the second rank as rising or declining in influence, or not a major influential force.

ALL SIX SURVEYS

The Association of Alaska School Boards (AASB) was the only local government organization listed in the first rank in all six surveys.

FIVE OUT OF THE SIX SURVEYS

The Municipality of Anchorage and the Fairbanks North Star Borough were listed among the first rank in five surveys (both were in the second rank in 1994).

FOR THREE OF THE SURVEYS

The general education lobby, including the Alaska Association of School Administrators (AASA) and the Alaska Department of Education (DOE), was in the first rank for three of the six surveys. Neither AASA nor the DOE was ranked in any category in 2007. The general education lobby covers all groups involved in education, including AASB and NEA-Alaska.

FOR TWO OF THE SURVEYS

The Alaska Municipal League (AML) was in the first rank in 1984 and 1994.

NEA-Alaska was in the first rank in 1984 and 1994, and in the second rank in the other four surveys.

The North Slope Borough was in the first rank in 1984 and 2010.

State and local government employees, especially the Alaska State Employees Association (ASEA) and Alaska Public Employees Association (APEA), were ranked in the first grouping in 1984 and 1994.

Source: Developed by Clive Thomas from the Hrebenar-Thomas study. See Chapter 15, endnote 2, for details of the study.

less effective since the mid-1990s than before. AML has also declined in effectiveness. The reasons for these declines may reflect national trends toward increasing fiscal conservatism and public calls to cut state budgets. In Alaska, this combination of circumstances was likely exacerbated by the downturn in oil prices in the late 1980s and the ongoing political effects of the downturn as related in the policy issues considered in Box 18.3 in the last section.[30]

Urban versus Rural-Bush Conflict

Various aspects of urban versus rural-bush conflict are dealt with in several places in the book.[31] Not all conflicts between urban and rural-bush areas result from differences between their respective local governments and the issues generated by state-local relations. There are, however, some key elements of urban versus rural-bush conflicts that are the product of state-local political dynamics.

To place things in a comparative context, all states manifest political conflicts between urban and rural areas. These conflicts result from a variety of sources, including different economies (such as industry and services versus agriculture) and differing service needs (for example, public transport is less important in rural areas than in urban ones). Also, conflicts over state budgets and resource allocation and ideology (rural areas are generally more conservative) translate into differing views of the role of government. In addition, state legislatures are dominated by legislators representing urban areas. The major differences between Alaska and other states are the large gap in Alaska between the urban and rural-bush cost of living, the virtual lack of a cash economy other than what is provided by government and Native organizations, and culture and lifestyles, particularly those of Alaska Natives. With few roads, the cost of access to rural-bush communities restricts travel to these places. This lack of access may inhibit urban residents and policy makers from building relationships with rural-bush residents and advancing understanding of rural-bush conditions and concerns.

As in other states, Alaska's legislature is dominated by urban legislators. However, over the years and for a variety of reasons mentioned earlier and explained in various places in the book (see especially Chapters 2, 9, 10, 14, and 15), rural-bush areas have been able to exert influence in the legislature, ranging from having a major influence on it in the 1980s to working to defeat proposals over the past decade or so. Add to this the needs of rural-bush areas versus those of urban areas, particularly Southcentral Alaska, and elements of urban versus rural-bush conflict result.

Also noted earlier was the power of rural-bush interests in keeping the status quo on local government development. Other points of conflict are tax equity between urban and rural-bush areas and the cost of services to rural-bush communities. The urban versus rural-bush school funding issue is a particularly sticky one. Also important has been the failure of state government to fully respond to rural-bush needs such as maintaining programs to offset the rapidly increasing costs of electricity (power cost equalization) and fuel in rural-bush areas. The severe reductions in revenue sharing programs and the general increase in fiscal conservatism among urban legislators have not helped this situation. We saw earlier in Box 18.2 that the state's local government agency was caught in the political crossfire of a combination of many of these factors.

When we consider the nature of the specific issues faced by the state's local governments and state involvement in many of these issues, it would appear that urban versus rural-bush conflict is not likely to go away any time soon. It will continue to be an element of state-local relations and of Alaska politics for some time to come.

8. CONCLUSION: LOCAL GOVERNMENT-STATE GOVERNMENT RELATIONS AND THE DYNAMICS OF ALASKA POLITICS AND PUBLIC POLICY

To return to the theme of this chapter, it should be clear that ignoring the role of local government results in an incomplete picture of state politics past and present. The underdevelopment of Alaska's unique local government system, its contemporary structure, and the ongoing local government-state government relationship provide a fuller understanding of several major state policy issues. In so doing it illustrates several characteristics of Alaska politics and power relationships.

For instance, a full understanding of the issues and policies regarding K–12 education cannot be acquired without knowledge of the structure of local government and the state-local relationship. This chapter, then, provides a good foundation for Chapter 26 on education as well as the chapters dealing with issues of social services and transportation (Chapters 27 and 28), and on land use, environmental, and fisheries issues (Chapters 21, 22, and 23).

More broadly, the local government system and its relations with the state illustrate aspects of pragmatic dependent individualism, friends and neighbors politics, regionalism, the prominent role of Alaska Natives, strong interest groups and fiscal conservatism. Moreover, the juncture of specific state-local policy issues with these characteristics throws light on several key power relationships in state politics including those between urban and rural-bush areas and state legislators, on particular interest groups, and on how the provisions of the Alaska Constitution provide a power base for many local governments and their constituents.

ENDNOTES

[1] Alaska Department of Labor and Workforce Development, at http://laborstats.alaska.gov/qcew/ee11.pdf.

[2] Gordon S. Harrison, *Alaska's Constitution; A Citizen's Guide*, 4th ed. (Juneau: Alaska Legislative Affairs Agency, 2003), 162.

[3] Ronald C. Cease and Jerome R. Saroff, eds., *The Metropolitan Experiment in Alaska: A Study of Borough Government*, Praeger Special Studies in U.S. Economic and Social Development (Westport, CT: Praeger Publishers, 1968), ix. On the Constitutional Convention and the discussion on local government, see Victor Fischer, *Alaska's Constitutional Convention* (Fairbanks: University of Alaska Press, 1975), esp., 116–27.

[4] Jeanette Nichols, *Alaska: A History of its First Half Century Under the Rule of the United States* (Cleveland, OH: Arthur Clark Company, 1924), 40.

[5] Thomas A. Morehouse, Gerald A McBeath, and Linda Leask, *Alaska's Urban and Rural Governments* (Latham, MD: University Press of America, 1984), 13-23.

[6] Ann O'M. Bowman and Richard C. Kearney, *State and Local Government*, 6th ed. (Boston: Houghton Mifflin Company, 2005), 273.

[7] Russell L. Hanson, "Intergovernmental Relations," in *Politics in the American States: A Comparative Analysis*, eds., Virginia Gray, Russell L. Hanson, and Thad Kousser, 10th ed. (Washington, D.C.: C.Q. Press, 2013), 54–56.

[8] Bowman and Kearney, *State and Local Government*, 7th ed. (2008), 61, 63–64 and 278–79; and Harrison, *Alaska's Constitution*, 5th ed. (2012),165–67.

[9] Public Administration Service, "Constitutional Studies, Volume III," prepared on behalf of the Alaska Statehood Committee for the Alaska Constitutional Convention, November 1955 (mimeograph), 60.

[10] Morehouse, McBeath, and Leask, *Alaska's Urban and Rural Governments*, 25–36.

[11] *Ibid.*, 31.

[12] *Ibid.*, 7.

[13] Alaska Statutes (AS) 29.06.320.

[14] Morehouse, McBeath, and Leask, *Alaska's Urban and Rural Governments*, 7 and 35.

[15] Harrison, *Alaska's Constitution: A Citizen's Guide*, 2nd ed., (Anchorage: Institute of Social and Economic Research, University of Alaska, 1986), 86.

[16] For an overview of Alaska's local government system, see Clive S. Thomas, Anthony T. Nakazawa, and Carl E. Shepro, "Alaska," in *Home Rule in America: A Fifty-State Handbook*, eds., Dale Krane, Platon N. Rigos, and Mel Hill (Washington, D.C.: Congressional Quarterly Press, 2000), 33–40.

[17] Bowman and Kearney, *State and Local Government*, 6th ed., 273.

[18] Local Boundary Commission, *Model Borough Boundaries*, revised June 1997. With the creation of the Skagway, Wrangell, and Petersburg Boroughs, this number is now sixteen proposed model boroughs.

[19] However, while not officially categorized by the state as unified boroughs, Haines has also embraced consolidation with its city, and Yakutat and Skagway have no other local governments in their boroughs.

[20] Local Boundary Commission, *Model Borough Boundaries*, revised June 1997.

[21] *Problems and Possibilities for Service Delivery and Government in the Alaska Unorganized Borough* (Juneau, AK: Department of Community and Regional Affairs, Division of Community Planning, 1981), 26–41.

[22] Information on the state's local government agency is based upon Morehouse, McBeath, and Leask, *Alaska's Urban and Rural Governments*, 33 and 41; and interviews by Anthony Nakazawa with Gene Kane, George Laurito, and Jim Sinnett, all formerly with DCRA, December 3, 8, and 9, 2011, and Sig Strandberg, Director of the Local Affairs Agency under Governor Keith Miller (1969–1970), December, 23, 2011.

[23] Alaska Department of Commerce, Community, and Economic Development, Office of the Assessor, *Alaska Taxable Volume XLVII*, January 2008.

[24] Local Boundary Commission, *The Need to Reform State Laws Concerning Borough Incorporation and Annexation* (2001).

[25] *Problems and Possibilities for Service Delivery and Government in the Alaska Unorganized Borough*, 54.

[26] Leila Kheiry, "Superior Court Rules Alaska Education Funding Mandate Unconstitutional," KRBD Radio (Ketchikan Public Radio), November 25, 2014; and *State of Alaska v. Ketchikan Gateway Borough*, Opin. No. 7075 (Alaska Supreme Court, January 8, 2016).

[27] Morehouse, McBeath, and Leask, *Alaska's Urban and Rural Governments*, 233–34.

[28] For a fuller discussion of the effectiveness of state versus Native local government, see Carl E. Shepro, "Rural-Bush Local Government: Towards a More Appropriate System," in *Alaska Public Policy Issues*, ed. Clive S. Thomas (Juneau: Denali Press, 1999).

[29] For a general treatment of the contemporary local-state relationship across the United States, from both an administrative and a policy perspective, see Russell L. Hanson, ed., *Governing Partners: State-Local Relations in the United States* (Boulder, CO: Westview Press, 1998).

[30] For another perspective on the local government lobby, see Alexandra Gutierrez, "For Alaska Cities, Lobbying Pays," *Alaska News Nightly*, Alaska Public Radio Network (APRN), April 10, 2013.

[31] See, for example, Chapter 3 on public policy making, Chapter 9 on Alaska Natives, and Chapter 10 on IGR.

★ CHAPTER 19 ★

Understanding Alaska's State Budget: The Process and Its Political Dynamics

Alison Elgee

A good case can be made that the process and debate regarding creation of the budget and the assessment of its goals are the major activities of government and the ones that most influence politics both long and short term in a nation, state, or community. This is certainly true in Alaska. At the state level the budget process affects such fundamentals as the political power structure, the relationship between the governor and the legislature, what issues get addressed or not and to what extent, and state government's capacity to deal with crises and contingencies, particularly economic ones, now and in the future. The practicality is that it is not policy that drives the budget but the budget that drives policy and the process by which policies are pursued or stymied. This is because the level of available funds determines what policies the government can and cannot pursue for its citizens.

To be sure, there are elements to the budget and the budget process that can be both daunting and baffling. This is true not only for many members of the public. Many public officials, including legislators and governors, do not feel comfortable with the budget and rely on their staff and close associates to help them deal with this central aspect of their jobs. Reduced to its basics, however, the budget and the budget process are not complicated at all. Three simple points help make sense of the budget.

First, like that of an individual, family, or business, a government budget is simply a plan of allocating available funds for specific purposes for a period of time, including identifying the sources and amounts needed to finance the expenditures. In government, this plan is usually for a fiscal year (usually shortened to FY).

Second, a basic understanding of a few key budget terms and concepts and of the chronology of the budget process, its legal foundations, plus the various approaches to writing a budget and assessing whether it achieved its intended goals, is a first step in demystifying the budget document and the way it is compiled. This information also helps make sense of the administrative, and particularly the political, aspects of the budget process.

Third, as a spending plan the budget is not based upon some idealistic view of what is "best" or "right" for Alaska, because it is impossible to define what is "best" and "right" in ways that everyone would agree upon. The budget is, in essence, a political document, and as such it is a policy statement that reflects the politics of the state and particularly the policy goals of those public officials and other influences—such as interest groups and the federal government—who wield power at the time. As political scientists Ann O'M. Bowman and Richard Kearney aptly describe it, the budget document is:

> . . . a political manifesto—the most important one you will find in state and local government. It is a policy statement of what government intends to do (or not do), detailing the amount of the taxpayers' resources that it will dedicate to each program and activity.[1]

This is why the oft-used phrase by politicians that "there isn't enough money" is only a theoretical limitation and often a political subterfuge by those who want to spend money on some items but not others. There is always money, even if it may be limited at times. It is more a matter of how this money will be spent than its limited amount that is of concern in the budget process.

Attempting to make sense of the budget process by explaining its basics and exploring the political element of Alaska's budget form the dual purposes of this chapter, with emphasis on the political dynamics of the process. Specifically, we argue that the budget process is a political exercise to produce a political document. Plus, as the budget is so important to state government, the process by which it is put together is a perfect and perhaps the best illustration of the subtitle of the book—the *Dynamics of Beliefs, Institutions, Personalities, and Power*. Thus, understanding the politics of the budget process is essential to understanding Alaska politics and public policy making. As such, in various ways all twelve of the characteristics of Alaska politics identified in Chapter 2 are relevant to the budget process.

The first section of the chapter provides a primer on the terms, legal requirements, and key administrative and procedural elements of the budget. Then we place the contemporary state budget in context with that of other states, followed by a short history of Alaska's budget. Next, approaches to compiling and evaluating budgets and the methods used in Alaska are explained. Following this we turn to the politics of the budget process. This begins with an overview of the political factors that shape state budgets in general and Alaska's budget in particular, followed by three case studies to illustrate some of the key political factors. The often significant role of the courts in the budget process is considered next. Then we compare Alaska's state budget spending with other states, particular those in the West. Following this is a short section on what can be called the paradox of budget politics—the contradictory pressures to cut state spending and at the same time to expand it. The conclusion summarizes Alaska budget politics from a political economy perspective.

1. A PRIMER FOR UNDERSTANDING THE BUDGET AND THE BUDGET PROCESS

This primer provides the foundation for understanding the budget document, the budget process, and budget politics. It does so by explaining key budget terms, its constitutional and legal foundations, the major public officials involved in the budget, and its annual administrative and political calendar.

Key Budget Terms and Concepts

There are dozens of specialized terms, concepts, and acronyms relating to the budget. In this chapter, however, we need to understand only a few key ones to be able to get a handle on the budget process. Several of these terms and concepts have been used in the book already and are defined in the glossary at the end of the book. For the purposes of this chapter it is useful to explain some key budget terms in more detail.

Fiscal Year (FY) and Dealing with Multiple Budgets

The *fiscal year* (FY) in Alaska is a twelve-month period that begins on July 1 and ends on June 30 (in contrast, the federal government's fiscal year runs from October 1 to September 30). Budget years are designated by the year they end. So the FY 2015 budget is the budget year that started on July 1, 2014, and ended on June 30, 2015.

At any one time the state is dealing with budgets covering three fiscal years. For example, in October 2015, the state was in the process of auditing the funds spent during FY15 (July 1, 2014, through June 30, 2015), spending funds that were budgeted and appropriated for the current FY 2016 (July 1, 2015, through June 30, 2016), and putting together the budget for upcoming FY 2017 (July 1, 2016, through June 30, 2017). The part of the process we will be most concerned about will be putting a budget together for the upcoming fiscal year.

The State's Unrestricted General Fund Account

This is usually referred to as the *general fund* (GF), which is the major state account into which revenues are deposited and expenditures made to finance the operations of state government. The GF is unrestricted in that its funds can be used for any purpose determined by the legislature. This is contrasted with dedicated funds, such as those in relation to the Permanent Fund and some mental health purposes, where revenues from certain sources can be used only for specified purposes.

The Operating Budget and the Capital Budget

The distinction between the annual operating and capital budgets is important, as each budget often involves different politics in the writing and approval process.

The *operating budget* is a plan for the yearly funding of the ongoing operation of state programs and of government in general. The proposed expenditures usually include those with an anticipated life of one year or less, such as employee salaries, supplies, utility bills, janitorial services, aid to schools and communities, and various entitlement programs. Operating fund appropriations are made for one fiscal year and any unexpended or unobligated funds revert (or lapse) to the state's general fund when the authorization expires at the end of the fiscal year.

The *capital budget* is a plan for the expenditure of state funds for one-time projects or one-time purchases of equipment that have a value of over $25,000 and an anticipated life of more than one year. This includes construction of buildings and infrastructure facilities, land purchases, and one-time studies of issues or potential projects. Capital budget appropriations do not lapse if funds remain at the end of a fiscal year. They lapse only if funds remain after the project is completed.

Appropriations and Related Terms

An *appropriation* is a law enacted by the legislature that provides specific statutory authorization to spend money for a stated purpose. Article IX, Section 13, of the Alaska Constitutions provides that appropriations must be enacted before a state agency can spend funds. The governor's proposed operating and capital budgets are normally contained in separate appropriation bills, introduced each January at the request of the governor. Both bills includes specific expenditures on particular goods, services, or projects called *line items*. Most line items are placed in the budgets by the governor, but some are added by legislators as the appropriations bills go through the process of legislative enactment. This is particularly true for the capital appropriations bill.

Often legislation is introduced to establish a program that will require the expenditure of funds to operate. Such legislation must be accompanied by a *fiscal note*, an attachment to the legislation that contains an estimate of the anticipated cost of the proposed legislation. Fiscal notes, as we will briefly explain later, can often generate political conflict.

Sometimes the estimated expenditures for a program or items turn out not to be enough because of unforeseen costs or because the legislature decided to only partially fund the program in the initial budget. Then the agency puts in a *supplemental funding request*, usually referred to simply as a *supplemental*. In some cases the funds allocated in the original budget are not used or needed because of various circumstances. In this case, the funds can be *reappropriated*—that is, reassigned by legislative action to another program or item in the budget bill. Both supplementals and reappropriations require a new appropriation by the legislature, and these can also lead to much political maneuvering.[2]

Because of all these changes to any particular budget from the beginning to the end of its budget cycle, to avoid confusion we need to distinguish three different budget dollar amounts or, more accurately, two full amounts and one partial amount. The first amount is the *governor's submitted budget* as it goes to the legislature at the beginning of a legislative session. The second is the *enacted budget* as signed by the governor after the end of the legislative session and after additions and cuts by the legislature and any gubernatorial vetoes. The third is the final amount of the operating budget actually spent (often referred to as *actuals* by budget people) as determined by the Office of Management and Budget (OMB) when it does the final *budget closeout* following the end of the fiscal year in July and August. This amount includes supplementals, reappropriations, and other changes made when spending budget funds during the fiscal year. This closeout is only partial because it does not include capital monies from the budget that may be spent over several years beyond the fiscal year in which it was authorized.

Constitutional and Legal Authorization

Virtually all state constitutions direct the governor to submit a proposed budget to the legislature, and most do so in the article on the executive.[3] As they were intent on creating a systematic and streamlined approach to the budget and avoiding the problems in other states, Alaska's founders placed the governor's authority and aspects of legislative authority on the budget in Article IX of the constitution, which covers taxation and finance. Section 12 of that article states:

> The governor shall submit to the legislature, at a time fixed by law, a budget for the next fiscal year setting forth all proposed expenditures and anticipated income of all departments, offices and agencies of the State. The governor, at the same time, shall submit a general appropriation bill to authorize the proposed expenditures, and a bill or bills covering recommendations in the budget for new or additional revenues.

The governor must submit a budget to the legislature by December 15 of each year, about a month before the legislative session begins.[4] The governor's responsibility for preparing a budget is elaborated in the Executive Budget Act, which, as amended in 2008, requires a comprehensive, long-range fiscal plan for the state.[5] Section 14 of Article IX of the constitution requires the legislature to appoint an auditor to conduct "post-audits" of state expenditures to determine whether the funds were spent for the purpose intended, including expenditures by executive agencies as well as the judiciary and the University of Alaska.[6]

Four other constitutional provisions are important to note. First, unlike the federal government, which can run a deficit on its yearly budget by engaging in all sorts of maneuvers, Article IX, Section 10, of the Alaska Constitution can be interpreted to require the state to balance its budget each year. It cannot spend more than it receives in revenue, but it is given leeway for a year to receive all funds to cover expenditures. In fact, all states except Vermont have this provision.[7] The political upshot of this for Alaska is that, in years when there are revenue shortfalls, it leads to some hardball and often emotionally laden politics. Over the years, actual and potential deficits have involved the state in a constant search for solutions to its chronic revenue woes.

Second, there is a prohibition against dedicated funds in Article IX, Section 7. The founders included this to prevent special interests from tying up revenues for their particular programs, thereby limiting budget options. It takes a constitutional amendment to dedicate funds, as was done in 1976 to create the Alaska Permanent Fund.

Third, a constitutional amendment intended to limit government spending (Article IX, Section 16) was passed in 1982 and reconfirmed by the voters in 1986. This amendment was a product of Alaska's runaway spending years of the late 1970s and early 1980s. It limits increases in spending to $2.5 billion over the previous year based on a formula of factors that existed at the time in July 1981. This amendment has never kicked in as the increase was set too high to be realistic. But it is an example of Alaskans' concerns about government spending and increasing the state budget.[8]

Finally, Article II, Section 15, of the constitution gives the governor the authority to veto any substantive bill in its entirety, but that section also allows the governor to use the veto power to "strike or reduce items in appropriation bills." As we discuss later in the chapter, this so-called line-item veto authority gives the governor enormous leverage over the legislature in the budget process.

Key Public Officials Involved in Alaska's Budget Process

Because virtually no government function can be performed without money, all legislators and senior members of the executive branch are concerned about the budget and participate in its development in various ways. There are, however, some key individuals in the executive and legislature who are particularly involved with the budget.

To aid in putting together and shepherding the budget through the legislature and to monitor its implementation and evaluate its effectiveness, the governor appoints a director of the OMB who serves at the will of the governor. The OMB is part of the Governor's Office and has a staff of analysts to assist the director. In the legislature, the chairs (often co-chairs) of the House and Senate finance committees and their committee members, some of whom chair subcommittees on aspects of the budget such as transportation and education, are key participants in the budget process and, as a result, are very influential legislators. To aid the legislature with the budget there is the Legislative Finance Division.[9] The division's staff conducts research, fiscal analyses, and budget reviews at the request of the House and Senate finance committees and the Legislative Budget and Audit Committee, which is a permanent interim committee for monitoring the budget, composed of five members of each house.[10]

The Budget Cycle and the Budget Calendar

Those not familiar with state government and its inner workings often think that the only time major decisions are made on the budget is when the legislature is in session. This is largely because the media generally gives much more coverage to the legislature than to the executive branch.

In reality the development and refining of the budget is a year-round process, with the major activities taking place between September and June in the fiscal year. Not only that, as explained earlier, the governor and executive branch, particularly the OMB, have the first and major say in what goes into the budget, not the legislature. Moreover, the legislature often appears to make major changes in the budget, judging from the press coverage. In fact, it changes the budget very little overall, though it may make some deep cuts in particular programs or add funds, particularly appropriations for pet programs and constituent needs.

Because the preparation, formulation, adoption, implementation, and audit of the budget constitute a year-round process, it is best understood as a cycle that repeats itself year after year, with work on budget years overlapping. Figure 19.1 illustrates the typical state annual budget cycle. Alaska has an annual budget cycle, as does the federal government, but some states use a biennial budget approach, such as Oregon and Wyoming. The trend among state governments is to move budgeting to an annual cycle. Forty-four states used biennial budgeting in 1940, but only twenty-one states used a biennial budgeting approach in 2004, and only nineteen states by 2011.[11] Moving to a biennial budget is a possible reform in Alaska, and its pros and cons are considered in Chapter 30, which looks at possible future reforms in the state.[12]

Table 19.1 breaks the budget cycle down into a typical fiscal year calendar. The details of this calendar show the month-by-month involvement in the process by both the executive and legislative branches.

It is clear from this table that until December the legislature has very little influence in putting the budget together, though individual legislators may be working with—or trying to pressure—the governor's office and OMB to get their projects into the budget.[13]

FIGURE 19.1

The Budget Cycle

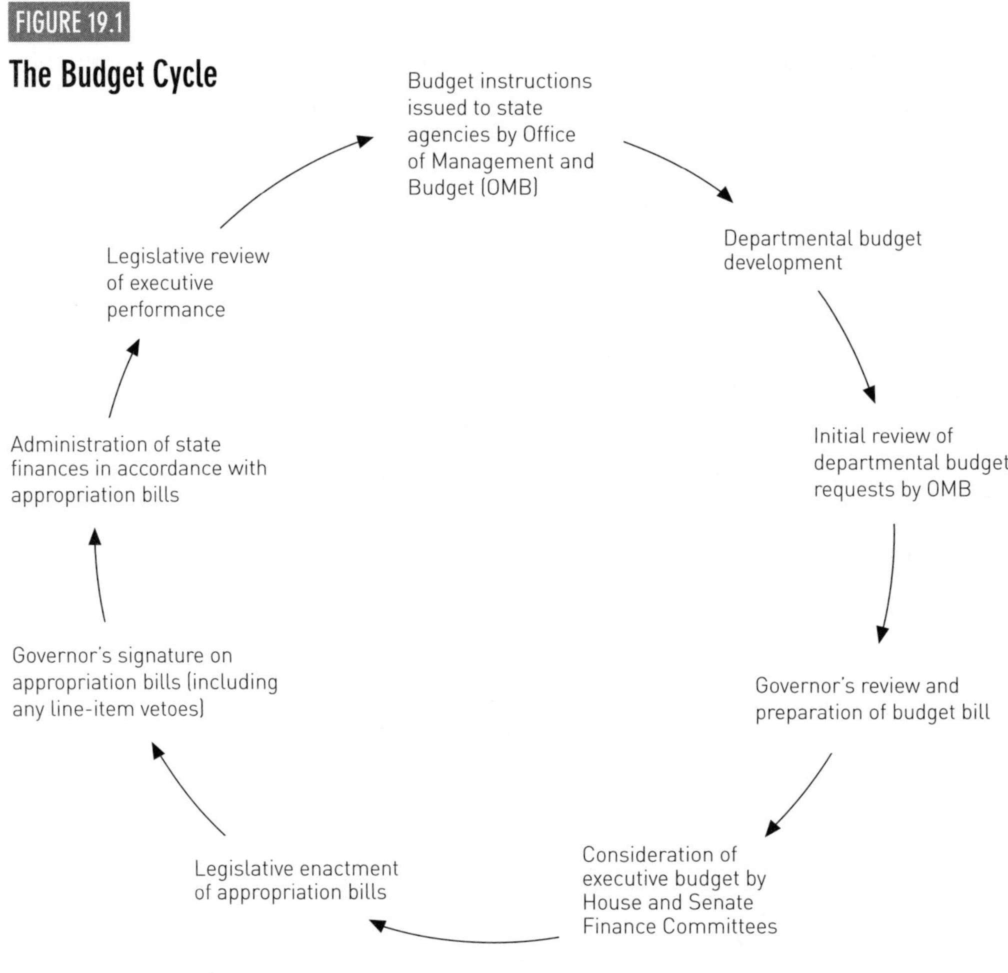

Source: Developed by the author from a publication of the Alaska Office of Management and Budget (OMB).

2. ALASKA'S RECENT STATE BUDGETS: REVENUES AND EXPENDITURES COMPARED WITH OTHER STATES

The Alaska FY 2012 operating and capital appropriation bills signed by Governor Sean Parnell on June 29, 2011, totaled $11.4 billion, of which $9.6 billion was in the operating budget appropriation and $2.8 billion was for capital spending.[14] For our purposes in understanding the state budget and budget politics, the important questions are: where did this money come from in terms of overall revenues, and on what programs and other items was it spent? An enlightening way to do this is to compare Alaska's recent budgets with those of other states. Not only does this place Alaska in a national context, it also helps explain the similarities of the Alaska budget with other states and accounts for the differences and in some cases unique elements.

TABLE 19.1

The Annual Budget Calendar for Preparing and Approving the State Budget

MONTH	EXECUTIVE BRANCH ACTIVITY	LEGISLATIVE BRANCH ACTIVITY
July	1. Record new budget authorization from fiscal year just ended. 2. Begin closeout of past fiscal year.	1. Legislative audit review of prior year's budget activity commences based upon federal audit requirements and legislative priorities. This activity continues throughout the year.
August	1. Closeout past fiscal year. 2. Develop interagency payment rates (e.g., for computer services) for upcoming fiscal year for use in budget preparation.	
September	1. Begin development of budget request for upcoming fiscal year. Identify needs and priorities. 2. OMB budget instructions issued.	1. Legislative Budget and Audit (LB&A, an interim finance committee of the legislature) meets to consider audits and authorization of new federal revenues. LB&A meets as needed throughout the year.
October	1. Agencies negotiate budget requests with OMB/governor. 2. Develop expenditure projections for current year and quantify any prospective supplemental appropriations needed.	
November	1. Complete budget documentation. 2. Fall revenue forecast made public.	
December	1. Public release of governor's proposed budget for upcoming fiscal year.	1. Legislative finance staff begin budget review.
January	1. Appropriation bills prepared and introduced in legislature for governor's proposed budget. 2. Governor usually makes State of the Budget address to legislature. 3. Agency presentations made to legislature. 4. Supplemental requests and budget amendments are prepared for OMB review and approval.	1. Legislative overview analysis and budget details published for use by legislative committees in reviewing the governor's proposals. 2. Legislative subcommittee hearings begin. 3. Veto overrides considered/taken up.
February	1. Supplemental requests introduced in legislature by the 15th legislative day of the session. 2. Budget amendments introduced by 30th legislative day.	1. Legislative subcommittees develop recommendations for action by full finance committees for appropriation levels. 2. Full finance committee review begins.

MONTH	EXECUTIVE BRANCH ACTIVITY	LEGISLATIVE BRANCH ACTIVITY
March	1. Agencies lobby for proposed budget. 2. Agencies and OMB respond to legislative requests for information.	1. Legislative budget development continues. 2. Both House and Senate pass versions of the budget. 3. Conference committee appointed/ meets
April	1. Agencies continue lobbying for proposed budget.	1. Conference committee concludes work on budget and presents it to both bodies for concurrence. 2. All other appropriation measures (e.g., capital, supplemental, reappropriations) approved by legislature.
May	1. Review appropriation bills and recommend final action (veto/reduce/ approve) by governor. 2. Governor takes final action on legislation.	1. Transmit passed budget bills to governor.
June	1. Establish necessary accounting entries to record new budget authorizations. 2. Conclude spending for current fiscal year. 3. Establish encumbrances for outstanding financial obligations.	
During Legislative Interim, May-December	1. The governor may call a special legislative session to deal with specific issues, including budget items.	1. The legislature may call a special session to consider overriding a governor's veto or vetoes, including budget items.

Source: Developed by the author.

General Revenue Sources and General Expenditures

By general revenues we mean all revenues, including from both state and federal sources, and by general expenditures we mean total state spending as opposed to particular service categories like education or corrections (these are considered in a later section). Table 19.2 compares Alaska's revenues and expenditures with ten other states for state fiscal years 2006 and 2012, which are typical years since the early 1980s across the states.[15] The sample of states was chosen from the four major regions of the nation, with four states from the West.

The table shows that Alaska's overall state revenues and expenditures are dwarfed by large states like California and even medium-sized ones like North Carolina. However, when we move to the more meaningful comparison of per capita revenues raised and dollars spent, Alaska consistently ranks first in both categories. Alaska outstrips Wyoming, the second-ranked state in both categories, by from 40 to 50 percent depending on the

TABLE 19.2

Comparing Alaska's State Budget with Selected States: Revenues and Expenditures for Alaska Fiscal Years 2006 and 2012

STATE	TOTAL STATE REVENUES INCLUDING FEDERAL FUNDS IN $ BILLIONS		PER CAPITA REVENUE AND NATIONAL RANKING				FEDERAL FUNDS INCLUDED IN STATE BUDGET IN $ BILLIONS		FEDERAL FUNDS AS PERCENTAGE OF TOTAL STATE REVENUES		TOTAL STATE SPENDING/STATE BUDGET IN $ BILLIONS		SPENDING PER CAPITA AND NATIONAL RANKING			
	2006	2012	2006		2012		2006	2012	2006	2012	2006	2012	2006		2012	
Alaska	**10.8**	**15.0**	**16,011**	**1**	**20,576**	**1**	**2.2**	**2.8**	**19.88**	**19.00**	**8.6**	**11.7**	**12,709**	**1**	**16,035**	**1**
California	263.8	250.8	7,331	8	6,595	16	53.7	54.1	20.35	21.60	225.3	267.1	6,262	10	7,019	16
Georgia	38.2	40.5	4,091	50	4,083	50	11.2	13.8	29.34	34.10	36.2	44.8	3,884	49	4,511	49
Hawaii	9.9	10.6	7,727	6	7,613	8	1.8	2.3	18.61	22.20	8.9	11.6	6,887	6	8,306	8
Illinois	62.5	68.9	4,916	43	5,351	38	13.4	15.6	21.41	22.70	55.7	72.6	6,383	39	5,640	36
Massachusetts	45.5	48.9	7,029	10	7,369	11	8.8	12.9	19.35	26.40	39.1	56.5	6,049	11	8,499	7
North Carolina	45.5	56.5	5,129	39	5,790	32	12.9	15.2	28.38	26.90	40.5	53.6	4,569	34	5,498	38
Oregon	25.7	25.1	7,000	11	6,426	19	4.6	7.8	18.02	31.20	20.1	26.9	5,457	20	6,888	18
Vermont	4.9	6.3	7,873	5	10,141	4	1.3	1.9	26.39	30.00	4.6	5.9	7,467	4	9,519	3
Washington	40.8	40.6	6,408	20	5,896	29	7.7	9.7	18.93	24.00	33.9	45.5	5,322	24	6,597	27
Wyoming	5.8	35.8	11,371	2	11,876	3	2.0	2.2	34.46	32.30	4.0	5.8	7,822	2	10,016	2
U. S. Average	**35.5**	**38.2**	**6,253**	**N/A**	**6,091**	**N/A**	**8.4**	**10.2**	**24.76**	**26.80**	**31.1**	**39.5**	**5,455**	**N/A**	**6,297**	**N/A**

Sources: U.S. Census Bureau, *2012 Annual Survey of State Government Finances*, at http://www.census.gov/govs/state; population estimates from *Annual Estimates of the Resident Population for the United States, Regions, States, and Puerto Rico*: April 1, 2011 to July 1, 2012, at https:/www.census.gov/popest/data/state/totals/2012; U.S. Census Bureau, *2006 Annual Survey of State Government Finances*, at http://www.census.gov/govs/state/; U.S. Census Bureau, *Annual Estimates of the Resident Population for the United States, Regions, States, and Puerto Rico*: April 1, 2000 to July 1, 2009, at http://www.census.gov/popest/states/NST-ann-est.html.

year. Even after taking into account higher costs in Alaska, Alaskans receive more per capita from state spending than citizens of the other forty-nine states, including Hawaii where the cost of living is on a par with Alaska.

Alaska also ranks first in total receipts per capita from the federal government. However, when federal funds are considered solely as a percentage of the state budget, Alaska ranks among the bottom five of the states and was, in fact, number fifty in FY 2012. As part of Alaska's budget, federal funds are usually around 20 to 25 percent, in exceptional years rising to 30 percent.[16] Nevertheless, similar to all states, federal funds are an indispensable part of the state budget. These funds were particularly important in 2009 when the states had major budget shortfalls due to the recession that began in the summer of 2008. Alaska federal receipts accounted for almost 27 percent of the state budget that fiscal year.[17] The percentage figures are not as significant a comparison nationwide as per capita federal receipts, because the percentage of federal funds is largely a function of the amount of state funds expended in any given fiscal year. Alaska's percentages are no doubt distorted, at least in high revenue years, by the very large total amounts of state funds expended.

As to the percentage of funds divided between the operating and capital budgets across the states, as might be expected, this varies largely depending on available revenues. Capital expenditures are by far the smaller of the two parts of Alaska's budget and rarely exceed 20 percent of the total even in high revenue years. But this can drop to close to zero, as has been the case in many states since the economic recession of 2008 and the slow recovery from it. Alaska's capital budgets of close to 25 and 35 percent respectively of the total FY 2012 and 2013 expenditures reflected unusually high state revenues for those years. In contrast, of the $8.5 billion the state spent in FY 2006, only about 10 percent, or close to $1 billion, was spent on capital projects. Yet this was more than in the lean years from 1986 to around 2004 when oil revenues were down, resulting in very low capital budgets, often less than 2 percent of total expenditures. The major drop in oil prices, from over $100 a barrel in June 2014 to less than $30 in early 2016, led Governor Walker to propose some of the leanest capital budgets in years, in the $100 million range, which mainly consisted of outlays needed to match federal funds.[18]

Spending on Specific Programs and Services

Even more revealing information about Alaska's budget and how it compares with other states can be found in seeing what types of programs and services are funded. There are many similarities in this regard but some major differences. To fully appreciate these differences it is useful to look first at the history and politics of Alaska's budget since soon after statehood and then return to the comparison later in the chapter.

3. A SHORT HISTORY OF ALASKA'S STATE BUDGET: INCREASING SIZE AND SHIFTS IN REVENUES AND EXPENDITURES

In providing a historical overview of Alaska's state budget and the politics involved in the budget process, four aspects of budget development are useful to understand: the major increase in per capita expenditures; changing funding sources and budget instability; program additions, expansions, reductions, and eliminations; and the approaches used to develop and evaluate the budget. The first three are covered here, the last one in Section 4.

A Major Increase in Size and in Per Capita Expenditures

Since statehood in 1959, Alaska's state budget has grown considerably in size, particularly when measured by per capita revenues (including federal funds) and per capita expenditures.[19]

Table 19.3 includes two tables showing the development of Alaska's state budget since 1965 (the first year that accurate figures are available), including federal funds that were part of the state budget. Table 19.3A shows this in absolute dollar amounts. Table 19.3B is adjusted for inflation at 2012 prices. In summary, Table 19.3B shows that since 1965, adjusted for inflation, Alaska's state budget has increased approximately tenfold, federal funds have increased fivefold, per capita overall state spending has increased almost fourfold, and federal per capita spending has close to doubled.

What were the sources of funds that enabled this major increase to take place? Four major sources can be identified. First and foremost are oil revenues. Although they fluctuate, they have made overall increases in state spending possible since the early 1970s and particularly since the trans-Alaska pipeline system (TAPS) came on line in 1977. Second is federal spending for various programs, particularly Medicaid and various transportation funds. Third is the increase in Permanent Fund earnings that translate into increased expenditures for the Permanent Fund Dividend (PFD). Fourth is a miscellaneous category of increased user and licensing fees and interest earnings by state agencies that oversee what are essentially lending programs, such as the Alaska Housing Finance Corporation (AHFC).

Funding Sources and Budget Instability

As in all states, Alaska's' state budget funding sources are of two types: federal funds in the form of intergovernmental transfers and the money that the state raises on its own, commonly known as own-source state revenues. Taking these two sources together, over the years Alaska has not been much different from other states, with about 20 to 30 percent of its funding, depending on the year, from federal funds and the rest from own-source state revenues.

TABLE 19.3

Alaska's State Budgets 1965–2014: Total Dollar Amounts and Adjusted for Inflation

TABLE 19.3A: TOTAL DOLLARS

ALASKA STATE BUDGET, 1965–2014: NOT ADJUSTED FOR INFLATION*				
Year	General Revenue in $1,000s	Federal Money in $1,000s	Per Capita Federal Spending	Per Capita General Revenue
1965	178,274	109,570	$413.16	$672.22
1970	1,184,327	103,453	341.90	3,914.06
1980	3,011,400	378,400	941.64	7,493.82
1990	3,500,000	622,581	1,131.88	6,363.14
2000	7,330,352	1,201,549	1,916.55	11,692.42
2010	11,035,812	2,961,501	4,169.77	15,538.34
2012	11,787,600	3,186,700	4,443.73	16,437.37
2014	9,714,200	2,966,900	4,036.00	13,214.00

TABLE 19.3B: DOLLAR AMOUNTS ADJUSTED FOR INFLATION TO 2012 PRICES

ALASKA STATE BUDGET, 1965–2014: ADJUSTED FOR INFLATION 2012				
Year	General Revenue in $ Billions	Federal Money in $ Billions	Per Capita Federal Spending	Per Capita General Revenue
1965	1.21	0.71	$2,950	$4,800
1970	6.84	0.58	1,982	3,914
1980	8.22	1.04	2,571	20,457
1990	6.02	1.07	1,948	10,951
2000	9.57	1.57	2,503	15,273
2010	11.39	3.05	4,301	16,029
2012	11.79	3.19	4,444	16,437
2014	9.71	2.81	3,834	12,555

* Revenue information for 2012 and 2014 was obtained from the Alaska Office of Management and Budget. Other budget data is from the U.S. Census Bureau (see sources below).

Sources: Compiled by Kristina Klimovich from U.S. Census Bureau, *State Government Finances*, at http://www.census.gov/govs/state/; Alaska Office of Management and Budget, *Fiscal 2010 Enacted Budget Less Vetoes*, at http://omb.alaska.gov/ombfiles/12_budget/PDFs/FiscalSummary_6-29-11.pdf; Alaska Department of Labor and Workforce Development, *Alaska Population Projections 2010-2034*, at http://laborstats.alaska.gov/pop/projected/pub/popproj.pdf; U.S. Census Bureau, *State and County Quickfacts*, at http://quickfacts.census.gov/qfd/states/02000.html; and Alaska Office of Management and Budget, *FY 2014 Enacted Budget*, at http://omb.alaska.gov/ombfiles/14_budget/PDFs/2_Enacted_2014_Fiscal_Summary.pdf.

Taking own-source revenues alone, there was a major change in their sources in the 1970s, making Alaska very different from other states. Until the mid-1970s, a major source of Alaska's own-source revenues was a state personal income tax. Since then Alaska's own-source revenues have overwhelmingly depended on oil revenues, as much as 95 percent in some years between 2008 and 2014. This is in sharp contrast to most states which rely on a state personal and corporate income tax and state sales tax for the bulk of their revenues, from 65 to 70 percent in most states.[20]

As the price of oil is determined by world market conditions, over which Alaska has no control, and as this price fluctuates considerably depending on the demand for oil and various economic and political conditions, as a source of revenue oil is very unstable. Thus, as state revenues have fluctuated over the years, so have budget expenditures. Furthermore, predicting these fluctuations is not an easy matter: prices can fall or rise in the course of months or weeks, making budget forecasts difficult. Dealing with budget shortfalls and what to do about them in both the short and long term has, therefore, been a prominent aspect of budget politics in Alaska and, indeed, of Alaska politics in general.

For various reasons, explained in Chapter 8 on state revenues, as of late 2015 no long-term plans have been developed to deal with these chronic fluctuations including the issue of using Permanent Fund earnings to fill budget gaps. But in 1990 the state did establish the Constitutional Budget Reserve (CBR) for helping to fund year-to-year budget shortfalls. As Chapter 8 also explains, and as we will briefly relate below, the CBR has also become part of budget politics.

State Spending: Expansion, Additions, Reductions, Funding Shifts, and Eliminations

While there has been a major overall increase in the state budget since statehood, Alaska's budget spending has seen fluctuations and shifts in emphasis. The 1970s, particularly after large oil revenues became available with TAPS, saw a major expansion in funding for local governments, the university, senior citizens facilities, and the development of new programs, such as subsidized home mortgages and agribusiness projects, including a state dairy.

With the plummeting of oil prices in 1986 and fluctuating prices for the next twenty years, a major rethinking of program spending took place. Several programs were cut considerably or eliminated, such as municipal revenue sharing and the longevity bonus for senior citizens. In some programs, the costs were partly shifted through increased user fees, as with university tuition and pioneer homes (assisted living facilities) for senior citizens. In other cases, infrastructure and building maintenance was deferred, creating a backlog of increased future maintenance costs.

Less affected were programs requiring a general fund match to secure federal monies, such as Medicaid. These programs have taken a larger percentage of the budget over the years. This is also true of PFD spending in the budget. Overall, despite unstable revenues, spending on programs has increased steadily.[21]

4. APPROACHES TO PREPARING, APPROVING, IMPLEMENTING, AND EVALUATING STATE BUDGETS, AND ALASKA'S SPENDING PLAN

Another aspect of the history of the Alaska budget process that has shaped budget politics is the various approaches to developing and evaluating the budget. Just as there are several ways that businesses, families, and individuals can develop and evaluate their budgets, so governments have developed and experimented with several techniques to provide policy makers with the tools needed to make informed decisions about the merits of annual spending proposals. Box 19.1 provides an overview of the major approaches. These approaches are often used in combination for two main reasons. One is that each has its strengths and weaknesses from a procedural and administrative perspective and none is ideal. In part, this is because, as explained in Chapter 12 on the role of government in Alaska, in the absence of a profit yardstick or other ways to assess efficiency and success in government given the broad range of tasks and roles of government, no one method is clearly superior to any other. Second, public officials often inject their personal values and ideology into their approach to the budget. This is because of their previous experiences or deep-rooted beliefs about how government should or should not operate. All of this leads to methods of budget preparation and evaluation being part of the politics of the budget.

Budget Approaches Used in Alaska in the Past

In the 1970s Alaska tried program budgeting. However, the governor found it difficult to pit the various department heads against each other in an effort to prioritize programs within a particular category, so this step was skipped. In addition, legislators were frustrated by a review process that resulted in an inability to hold any specific individual accountable for program performance. Partly for this reason, in 1982 the legislature amended the Executive Budget Act to require the executive branch to prepare budgets by departments.

Management by objectives (MBO) was also used in the 1970s and early 1980s. This budgeting technique was never fully implemented, however. To fully implement MBO required a modification of objectives based upon the legislative appropriation levels authorized for program operations and follow-up performance reporting against those revised objectives. But once the legislature finished the appropriation process, no further action was taken regarding program objectives until the following budget development cycle. The approach was abandoned in the early 1980s as being cumbersome, time-consuming, and irrelevant.

BOX 19.1

Six Major Approaches for Developing and Evaluating State Budgets

INCREMENTAL BUDGETING

In this method the justification of a proposed budget is based mainly on relatively small changes—incremental additions or reductions—to current year outlays. Current outlays are considered the baseline justification for expenditures on that program or item. The incremental approach is contrasted with zero-based budgeting outlined below.

LINE-ITEM BUDGETING

This approach groups proposed expenditures according to type, such as personal services, janitorial services, supplies, travel, and so on. These are listed as lines or objects in the budget document and form the basis of budget analysis, development, and authorization, thus, the term line-item budgeting.

PERFORMANCE-BASED BUDGETING

This is designed to demonstrate the effectiveness of program operations. It requires state agencies to develop missions for each program against which program performance is measured. The measures to determine the success or failure of each program are negotiated between the executive branch agencies and the legislators in charge of budget review and recommendations.

PROGRAM BUDGETING

In this method, all state agency operations are divided into one of several categories: education, public protection, economic development, health, social services, general government, and so on. The merit of the program approach is to group agency programs, regardless of which agency houses the operation, into a category designed to provide a comprehensive review of, and an ability to prioritize, government operations targeted to specific constituent groups and desired outcomes.

MANAGEMENT BY OBJECTIVES—MBO

In many states, including Alaska, MBO was the precursor to performance-based budgeting. The MBO approach involves program managers developing goals (missions) and objectives (annual progress desired) for their programs and identifying a way to measure progress in obtaining those objectives.

ZERO-BASED BUDGETING AND MODIFIED ZERO-BASED BUDGETING

In its pure form, and in contrast to incremental budgeting, state departments and agencies must justify their budgets in their entirety, from a base of zero, without reference to the previous year's budget. Each budget must be reevaluated and approved in its entirely each year or budget cycle. The purpose of this method is to ensure the need for the expenditure and that the funds are being spent as efficiently as possible.

Partly because of the tremendous labor involved by both government agencies and the legislature to administer such a system, zero-based budgeting is usually combined with other approaches. Alternatively, agencies are directed to prioritize spending on certain programs and items based upon the assumption that only a percentage of their budget, say 50 or 75 percent, will be funded.

Source: Developed by the author.

In the mid-1980s, an effort was made to use a modified zero-based budgeting approach. Agencies were directed to prioritize program operations based upon a percentage of funding in an attempt to identify the highest priority activities of the agency. The budget for a program's operation was rebuilt in increments of 5 or 10 percent to the existing level of funding and, finally, additional funds above current year spending authorizations (increments) were identified. Not surprisingly, agencies resisted identifying proposed reductions to program operations. Plus, the arbitrary nature of the funding levels against which the program operations were compared did not lend themselves to discrete program activities that could be reviewed in a manner designed to make budget decisions. As a result, modified zero-based budgeting was abandoned after only one year.

Alaska's Recent Budget Approaches

Even while emphasizing particular budget methods over the years, Alaska has employed a combination of approaches, primarily using incremental and line-item budgeting. As of 2015, overlaying this incremental and line-item approach is a performance-based budgeting system. Adopted in the mid-1990s, this approach is designed to demonstrate the effectiveness of program operations.

Performance-based budgeting has the merit of attempting to quantify program performance. There are, however, some problems with program performance measurement. Frequently there is no frame of reference against which to measure performance. The measures tend to count output, that is, how many widgets are produced over a specified period of time. Without additional information, policy makers reviewing the budget know only whether the goal of producing a certain number of widgets has been met. Consequently, it is quite possible that the state pays twice what any other government operation might pay to produce those widgets.

Plus, performance reporting generally lags two years behind the fiscal year for which a budget is prepared due to the timing of budget preparation and review. Legislators are up for reelection in two-year cycles. New legislators may not have the program history to understand the significance of any change in program performance or be able to put it into a budget context that is meaningful. As a result, while initially there was considerable enthusiasm for this approach, in recent years program performance advocates have dwindled in both the executive branch and in the legislature.

Approaches in Other States

Like Alaska, in other states the lack of one clearly advantageous approach to budgeting and the politics often involved in particular methods, which wax and wane in popularity, have resulted in all states using a variety of approaches. The diversity in the range of approaches is well represented over the years by California and the Pacific Northwest.

California has used a modified form of zero-based, program, and incremental budgeting. Oregon, which has a two-year budget cycle, has also used a modified form of zero-based and performance-based budgeting. Idaho has placed emphasis on program budgeting. In contrast, its neighbor to the west, Washington State, has combined incremental and performance-based budgeting.[22]

5. THE POLITICS OF STATE BUDGETS

Any process that involves politicians will be by its nature political. And because the budget process involves the allocation of monies without which implementation of the vast majority of policies is not feasible, debate and conflict over the budget are often intense, and political maneuvering is extensive. Budget dealings sometimes expose the negative side of politics and politicians as they fight for resources for their constituents and upon which their political futures may depend. Alaska's budget process often exhibits such elements. There are, in fact, several common factors that shape budget politics across the states and in Washington, D.C. We consider these first as the general context in which to understand the specifics of Alaska's budget politics.

Of the many factors that shape budget politics, six are particularly important: (1) the political composition and the internal relations within the legislature and executive branches, (2) the political relations between the two branches, (3) external forces that affect budget decisions, (4) the political force of the status quo, (5) the role of individual legislators, and (6) simultaneous pressures to increase spending and to control and even reduce it.

The first two can be considered together. In Alaska, as in all states, the political composition of the legislature determines attitudes toward the kinds of programs, services, and projects that will be funded. The strength or weakness of party discipline in the legislature and relations between the majority and minority will determine such things as legislative reaction to the governor's budget proposal, legislative dealings with particular executive departments, and the influence of individual legislators over aspects of the budget. Clearly, the governor's political ideology and agenda will affect the administration's budget proposal and how it deals with the legislature. A unified executive, like Alaska's (where the governor controls virtually all cabinet appointments), will give the executive a more united voice on the budget than a plural executive, where several cabinet members are separately elected.

As to the third factor, obviously, much of the budget is affected by external influences, such as interest groups, public opinion and, from time to time, crises such as physical disasters and economic downturns. There is also the external influence of the federal government and occasionally the courts, particularly the state courts. Many programs administered by the states, including Medicaid and other programs for individuals and families in need or at risk in some way, are funded largely by the federal government through transfer payment to the states and require a state match of funds. Now and again, the courts rule on a constitutional issue, as they have on prison overcrowding in several states, requiring those states to provide better correctional facilities. This affects budget outlays, often over several years. Thus, whatever method of budget preparation a state may use—incremental, performance, or modified zero-based budgeting—much of the budget, likely as high as two-thirds, consists of statutory formula funding (such as Medicaid) that cannot be changed, thereby reducing the flexibility of budget decisions by governors and legislators.

Fourth, the governor's proposed budget represents the status quo, which is a major force in budget politics as it is in all legislative politics. Although many members of the public and some public officials may—often in vague terms—see a particular budget as too large and wasteful and in need of trimming, every item in the budget is there because of a legally mandated federal match or because some interest group or political constituency wants it there. What to one person, group, or constituency is a wasteful government program, to another is essential government spending. Consequently, those favoring a program will fight to protect it. And because it is often much harder to effect change in politics than to defend the status quo, this is another reason that making major changes to the budget can be difficult.

Fifth, legislators represent geographical areas, and the pressure on them is to do positive things for their districts, particularly to aid them economically but also to improve services such as education, transportation, and various local government operations. Only after those needs have been addressed do most politicians look beyond their constituency to respond to other needs of the state. So even if they ran for office on a platform of cutting the budget, once in office they may still pursue this goal for the state budget as a whole but not for their own districts. They run on ideas—perhaps even ideals—but govern on political reality. It will not help their reelection if they have reduced state funding to their districts, especially if this has resulted in unemployment or an obvious reduction in state services for their constituents.

So, the sixth point is that a prominent, if not always obvious, aspect of budget politics is an inherent political contradiction, a political paradox, of pressure on public officials to increase spending but at the same time to control and even reduce it. On the one hand, there are the pressures on legislators and governors to deliver the bacon sought by segments of the public, interest groups, and by state and local government agencies that want to maintain or improve their services. On the other, in both bad and good economic times, there is pressure on American governments at all levels to cut budgets or at least hold spending at current levels. This is largely explained by a combination of skepticism about government and its perceived lack of efficiency among the public, and a strong strain of conservatism—particularly of the fiscal variety—and of individualism in the national political culture. Consequently, those who are elected to public office either reflect these values ideologically or come to do so for pragmatic, political survival reasons.

On occasion, particularly during serious revenue shortfalls, the spend-cut paradox is less evident, and it is easier to reach consensus on the need to cut the budget, though exactly what to cut often leads to some very contentious politics. Usually those groups and organizations with less political influence suffer the most from cuts. On other occasions, but rare ones, budgets are cut based on ideology or perhaps necessity, despite the grumblings that may be heard from adversely affected constituents. In most circumstances, however, the paradox leads to much political maneuvering and is most often reconciled through a combination of political pragmatism and political rhetoric. For instance, a particular conservative legislator will justify his or her district's needs on all sorts of grounds while supporting other budget cuts.

Overall, legal requirements, federal funding, and state and legislative district needs lead to pressure to increase budgets or at least not cut them. Thus, those who want to control or cut government spending have an uphill political fight not least because, in the end, it is difficult to make a political career by being a budget cutter in reality as opposed to being one solely in rhetoric.

6. ALASKA'S BUDGET POLITICS: LONG-TERM AND IN PARTICULAR YEARS

All six factors just explained are part of Alaska's budget politics. The particular form they take is largely determined by the state's political economy and its political environment, both in the long term and in any particular budget year and budget cycle. We will look first at the long-term influences and then those that can affect a particular budget.

Long-Term Factors

The specifics of these economic and political factors are reflected in the twelve characteristics of Alaska politics explained in Chapter 2. All twelve provide insights into the nature of Alaska's spending plans, and the role of each characteristic will be seen later in the chapter. Some, however, are particularly prominent, including the three strong contending branches of government, strong legislative caucuses, regionalism, urban versus rural-bush differences, and an interesting mix of fiscal conservatism and political pragmatism, including bipartisanship. In combination with these characteristics, the state's physical, political, and social geography and its unstable revenues provide a comprehensive perspective on Alaska's budget politics.

Three Strong Contending Branches and Strong Legislative Caucuses

Chapter 16 details the continuing tussle between the legislature and executive but also the cooperation that must be present to get policies, and particularly the budget bills, enacted each year. Much of the politics of the budget involves legislative-gubernatorial relations and much of the relationship between the two branches is defined by budget politics. The role of the third of the contending branches, the courts, can also be significant, as explained later in the chapter.

The strong majority caucuses in the House and the Senate, in effect, determine the legislature's response to the governor's budget and have an important influence on some aspects of the final budget signed by the governor. In fact, these majority caucuses are usually centered on presenting a united front on the budget. Thus, insights into the power structure in Alaska politics can also be gained by realizing this fact. In other words, another example of how the budget is at the root of what gets done and not done in Alaska is, in part, determined by these caucuses. The reality is that, given all the constraints on changing the budget explained above, the legislature alters the governor's budget very little overall, although the legislature may affect some programs in a major way.

One reason for the relatively small legislative impact on the governor's proposed budget is the governor's line-item veto power. A legislator may want to have some pet project included in the budget bill. But because the governor can reduce or eliminate that project with the stroke of the veto pen, and because overriding a veto is difficult, the legislator needs the governor's support for the project. Obtaining that support may require the legislator to provide the governor with some political favor in return. And if the legislator is in the minority, he or she probably lacks the power to provide such a favor. Even majority members may find it difficult to obtain the governor's support for an addition to the budget bill. The same is true for a legislator who wants to cut one of the governor's proposed budget expenditures. That legislator will think twice about doing so, knowing that the governor is in a position to veto one or more of the legislator's pet projects or programs that year or in the future.

Geographical Influences on the Budget: Regionalism and Urban versus Rural-Bush Differences

With the weakness of political parties and strong regional loyalties and needs, elected representatives from a region, such as Southeast Alaska or the Interior around Fairbanks, will often work across party lines to get funding in either the operating budget, such as more money for running schools, or the capital budget for their region, such as a new building for the university or for a state agency located in their region.

Besides regional alliances on the budget, there are often separate urban alliances and separate rural-bush alliances. The factor that produces these separate alliances is that with representation based upon population, some districts are fairly homogeneous in their socio-economic and cultural characteristics, while others are quite diverse. Consequently, in urban areas, like the Municipality of Anchorage, elected representatives are often dealing with a compact geographical constituency with common interests. So in urban areas where services, such as various aspects of transportation, are utilized by constituents from several adjacent legislative districts, any particular legislator shares responsibility for meeting the needs of their constituents with several other elected officials from the same urban area.

In contrast, while most rural-bush legislators represent approximately the same number of people, the region they cover is geographically larger than many of the other forty-nine states. A single district may include coastal villages with erosion problems, villages on rivers subject to spring flooding, and a town that serves as a regional hub providing services throughout the area with needs comparable to the more urban and accessible communities in the state. Many of these communities, isolated by lack of access other than by air, require the development of services within the community that could be consolidated to serve many more people in a compact urban district like Anchorage. Each village needs its own schools and infrastructure, such as sewer, water, and electricity, its own airport, and health facilities.

This divergence in constituencies and needs means that generally the priority for rural-bush legislators is addressing capital needs, while urban legislators are more interested in providing operating funding that will support services to constituents while defraying costs to local government taxpayers. Also, rural-bush districts generally cannot take advantage of economies of scale in service delivery as can urban areas. In addition, the costs of getting materials to remote locations and the cost of living in these places considerably increase the cost of delivering state services and of building and maintaining facilities. It can, for example, cost four times as much to educate a child in a rural-bush community than in Anchorage, Fairbanks, or Juneau. These differences in the importance of the operating and capital budgets and the divergence in service delivery costs are two of several tensions that often exist over the budget (and other issues) between urban and rural-bush legislators, addressed in various places in the book.

Some Manifestations of Political Pragmatism: Bipartisanship Activity and Bipartisan Coalitions

Urban and rural-bush interests are, to some extent, also differentiated by party, with rural-bush legislators historically having been mainly Democrats. However, whether for cultural or practical reasons or both, over the years rural-bush legislators have been less ideological and more pragmatic than most urban legislators, regardless of whether the rural-bush legislator is a Democrat or a Republican. Some, like former Representative and Senator Georgiana Lincoln, have changed parties during their political careers. Because securing capital dollars and maintaining operating funds for their districts is so crucial to rural-bush legislators, and because being in the majority provides them a greater chance of securing major funds, this has led to increasing bipartisanship on the part of several rural-bush legislators. In 1981, for example, Democratic Representative Al Adams of Kotzebue led a coup against the Democratic House Speaker Jim Duncan of Juneau, to put a bipartisan group in charge of the House of Representatives that was pledged to benefit rural-bush budget needs.

Since the early 1990s, the state's politics have been increasingly dominated not only by urban legislators but also by Republicans. This has led many rural-bush Democratic legislators to engage in formal bipartisan relationships with Republicans. Some have joined the majority caucuses in the House and Senate to get access to the budget dollars they so desperately seek. A major power boost, particularly in securing budget funds, came with the establishment of the Senate's Bipartisan Working Group (BWG) of Republicans and Democrats following the 2006 election. Several prominent rural-bush legislators, including Senators Lyman Hoffman of Bethel and Donny Olson representing Northwest Alaska, obtained significant influential positions in the BWG. The BWG, however, fell apart when the Republicans won back solid control of the Senate in the 2012 election. Some rural-bush Democrats, however, have joined the majority caucuses in both houses since then, including Hoffman and Olson in the Senate and Representatives Bob Herron of Bethel and Bryce Edgmon of Dillingham in the House, for the very reasons we have just explained.

Because of the central role of the budget, not only does bipartisanship and political pragmatism shape aspects of budget politics, the budget process also shapes Alaska politics in general, as many chapters in the book illustrate. In several places in the rest of this chapter we comment further on bipartisanship and political pragmatism as they relate to the budget.

Economic and State Revenue Instability

As noted in reviewing the history of the Alaska state budget, and as explored extensively in Chapter 8 on state revenues, the dependence of the state's economy on natural resources and the lack of any stable revenue source are at the root of many chronic budget problems. Consequently, concerns about the size of the budget not only face the fiscal conservatism of Alaska's political culture but also produce chronic political jitters among conservatives and liberals alike about how much money will be available to spend. So, at least until late 2015, dealing with potential or actual budget shortfalls has been a continuing aspect of budget politics in Alaska. This has taken the form of continuing, but so far elusive, attempts to address Alaska's long-term budget problems. In years when there have been actual shortfalls, the problem dominates not only the budget debate but state politics in general.

The Politics of Particular Budgets

In some way or another both the general political factors of budget politics considered in the last section as well as the specifics regarding Alaska just reviewed come into play in writing and enacting budget bills. The factors that determine the budget politics of a particular year depend, of course, on political and power relationships at the time (often affected by ego and personality), current issues, recent events, and the extent of oil revenues. Perhaps the three most important factors in any one year are the amount of money available for expenditure, the relationship between the governor and the majority in both houses of the legislature, and the relationship between the majority and minority caucuses, particularly in relatively lean years when it is necessary to tap the Constitutional Budget Reserve Fund—CBR (the CBR is explained in detail in Section 3 of Chapter 4 on the state constitution and in Section 5 of Chapter 8 on state revenues).

If the important relationships are positive and there are ample available funds, budget politics may lack major conflict and political grandstanding. Even fiscal conservatives may be low-keyed as they work to get money for their districts. In such years, there are also likely to be substantial capital budgets, which particularly benefit rural-bush legislators. All three situations were fairly positive during Sarah Palin's two-and-a-half years as governor (2006–2009), for example, and stayed that way for the years Governor Parnell was in office (2009–2014). When state revenues are flush, as they were from 2006 to the summer of 2014, the majority leadership in each house often provides an unofficial allocation of capital budget funds to each legislator, both those in the majority as well as the minority, which each legislator can allocate at his or her discretion. The minority, of course, gets less money to allocate.

However, if one or more of the three conditions outlined earlier are negative, and particularly if oil prices are low, political fireworks and drawn-out political battles can ensue. This was the case for most of the budgets during the Knowles administration between 1994 and 2002. During these years as well as the years following the oil price crash of 1986, there was very little money for a capital budget and thus no "unofficial" discretionary allocations. The major drop in oil prices in the second half of 2014, facing the state with a $3 to $4 billion annual deficit, dominated Governor Walker's first year and a half in office and both sessions of the Twenty-Ninth Legislature (2015-2016), producing some major conflicts and financial soul-searching.

In legislative sessions when there are revenue shortfalls, another dimension that usually enters into budget politics is the issue of taking money from the CBR. Because of the need for a three-fourths majority in each house of the legislature to withdraw money from the CBR, this has usually required support of the minority in both houses (usually the Democrats in the House and, until 2007 and after 2012, in the Senate too). Thus, the majority must woo the minority, and this can change the dynamics of what does and does not get done in the legislative session. It may affect budget allocations in a way that benefits the minority, if only in a small way given the shortage of funds.

Three additional points are worth noting in regard to the day-to-day budget maneuvering in any one year. One is that often a lot of politics accompanies supplemental and reappropriation allocations as individual legislators, particularly majority members, use these processes to send messages to the governor and the executive departments, to gain political leverage or, in the case of reappropriation, to channel the money to their preferred projects. Second, and similarly, politics can also accompany fiscal notes that must be attached to many bills. Those who support the bill will try to minimize the amount of the fiscal note, and those against it will try to jack it up as it goes through the process.

Third, the magnitude of the budget, the fact that much of it is spoken for in federal matching funds and entitlement programs, the minimal time the legislature has in its ninety-day session, and its minimal resources for thoroughly reviewing the budget, mean that the parts of the budget that are examined in depth and the comittee hearings on the budget that are held are very selective. Much of what the legislature chooses to focus on is determined by politics, shaped largely by the majority caucuses in both houses, the chairs of House and Senate finance committees, and the policy goals or pet projects of influential legislators.

7. THREE CASE STUDIES TO ILLUSTRATE ALASKA'S BUDGET POLITICS

To give practical meaning to the various influences on Alaska's budget, we consider three case studies. These demonstrate how different power relationships between and among various individuals and groups of elected officials and various interests and interest groups can affect the budget process.

Rural-Bush Television

Good politicians understand how to develop a strong base of support for budget requests by enlisting the public, state government personnel, legislative leaders, and other top political figures. They know how to generate enthusiasm among these constituencies in a lobbying effort to achieve their desired goals, including their budgetary objectives.[23] One of the masters of coalition building was the late Frank Ferguson, an Alaska Native from Kotzebue.

Ferguson served in the House from 1971–1974 and the Senate from 1975–1986. Given the numerical minority status of rural-bush legislators compared with those representing urban areas, he understood that to meet the needs of rural-bush Alaska, it was absolutely necessary to sell a package of interests that served all of Alaska. He also understood that position was power. While he never served as a finance chair, he was instrumental in securing the powerful finance chairmanship positions for legislative members who shared his rural-bush perspective, including Representative Al Adams, also of Kotzebue, and Senator John Sackett of Ruby. With their concurrence, he brokered deals benefiting rural-bush Alaska by trading favors that the finance chairmen were in a position to fulfill. He also understood the need to properly package appropriation requests to achieve his ultimate goals.

Senator Ferguson was the primary sponsor of an operating and capital project package to provide televised curriculum to schools throughout Alaska. In the early 1980s, educators throughout the nation were exploring the potential of television as a delivery mechanism for coursework. Because rural-bush communities were served by a series of one- and two-teacher schools, teachers could not possibly be experts in all fields. Televised curriculum was promoted as a way to overcome the limitations of teaching in small schools. Senator Ferguson enlisted the state's education community to support the establishment of a system to develop and deliver televised coursework. This included the University of Alaska and many urban school administrators who were sold on the potential of televised coursework to supplement the curriculum that on-site teachers could offer.

Once the education community had endorsed televised learning, Senator Ferguson took the next step. Most of rural-bush Alaska had access to public radio, but there was no television service. To deliver television, a network of earth stations throughout rural-bush Alaska was needed. Ferguson obtained the necessary funds to acquire the earth station infrastructure required. He enlisted the support of the educational community and sponsored the appropriations necessary to establish the statewide infrastructure, both operating and capital. While embracing urban as well as rural-bush schools in his plan was necessary to sell the project and provide the required public purpose for state funding and continuing expenditures, his unspoken agenda was also fulfilled. The same infrastructure enabled rural-bush communities to receive public and commercial television broadcasts for the first time.

The Susitna Dam and Rural-Bush Power Cost Equalization (PCE): A Power Shift in the Politics of the Budget

Energy policy in Alaska has always been fragmented because no single and integrated policy solution has been found to supply reasonably priced energy to all parts of the state. In 1980 only Anchorage, with access to natural gas, enjoyed low-cost energy. It was ironic that the state was realizing huge increases in revenues from oil production while the majority of Alaska continued to pay some of the highest energy prices in the nation. And so a solution was sought to create low-cost energy sources for the state.

In coastal communities, the solution appeared to be a system of hydroelectric plants. A similar solution was endorsed regarding the Interior's energy needs with proposed construction of a dam on the Susitna River, north of Anchorage, and a network of electrical interties to communities on the road system. No solution was immediately apparent to reduce energy costs for rural-bush Alaska. Again, Senator Ferguson, together with other key rural-bush leaders in the legislature, realized that rural-bush Alaska would be left out of the energy solution and the negotiations for state funds because energy-producing infrastructure projects (like hydroelectric dams, power transmission lines, and so forth) were simply not geographically or economically feasible ways to reduce rural-bush energy costs. Rural-bush legislators brainstormed a solution, and they enlisted both the House and Senate finance chairs to support the plan. The answer was a program to subsidize rural-bush electric rates, the power cost equalization (PCE) program. With rural-bush legislators in key leadership positions, the legislature could not ignore these needs, and a subsidy program for rural-bush Alaska became a key component of a larger state energy program.

Statutory law provides the framework for government action, but in most instances money is necessary to carry out the goals of the legislation. This enables policy makers opposed to particular government programs to nullify law without taking on the policy directly simply by failing to fund the program, so-called unfunded mandates.[24] The creation of the PCE program in 1980 provided a subsidy to rural-bush residents that required an annual appropriation. When oil prices collapsed in the mid to late 1980s and difficult decisions were required to establish state spending priorities, continued funding of PCE came under increased scrutiny. Fortunately for rural-bush Alaska, the two House finance co-chairs were from remote rural-bush districts, as was one of the two Senate finance co-chairs. From their positions of power, these leaders were able to negotiate the necessary deals to obtain support for the continued funding of PCE. Rural-bush legislators in key positions continued to protect the fund until 1993 when, following the 1992 election, a major change in legislative leadership occurred that saw increased numbers of urban and Republican legislators. A shift from rural-bush to urban political control over various aspects of the budget process was about to occur.

Studies of the feasibility of the Susitna Dam project conducted in the late 1980s and early 1990s demonstrated that the cost and the potential environmental impacts made it unrealistic. Funding previously set aside for the project was placed in a "Railbelt Energy Fund" while a long-term solution was sought for the Interior. A renegotiation of statewide energy project funding was undertaken in 1993 to terminate some state hydroelectric projects that had been funded over a decade earlier, identify project funding for construction of interties for the Railbelt, and create an endowment fund for PCE. The PCE endowment was intentionally underfunded, putting rural-bush legislators in the position of having to negotiate the necessary additional appropriations every year to fully fund the program. In 1999, and again in 2006, these legislators obtained additional appropriations to the fund in an attempt to properly capitalize the endowment and to provide the annual revenues to fully fund the program. Rural-bush legislators had to commit their support to projects and policies favored by powerful urban legislators in order to obtain the additional funding for PCE.

Funding for PCE was protected under the BWG, which ran the Senate from 2007 to 2012. But with Republican majorities in both houses after the 2012 election and a continued shift of political power to urban Alaska, the future of PCE is in doubt. When the state was flush with oil money, there were plans to revive a Susitna dam project in 2012, but the major drop in oil prices in the fall and winter of 2014–2015 put this on hold and continued low oil prices may well eat into PCE funding as well.[25]

The Alaska Longevity Bonus Program: An Unfunded Mandate

There are many examples of laws passed that have been effectively nullified by the lack of appropriation. One example is the discontinuation of the Alaska Longevity Bonus program established in 1972. The program paid Alaska residents over the age of sixty-five a monthly stipend of $250 to offset the high cost of living. In 2003, Governor Murkowski suggested eliminating funding for the program as part of a package of budget cuts designed to reduce state spending. The legislature chose to ignore his proposed funding cut and appropriated the money necessary to continue the program. The governor vetoed the appropriation for the program, and the legislature failed to override the veto. The bonus continues to be an unfunded mandate. That is, the statutory framework for the bonus remains on the books, but without an appropriation the program is inoperable and, in effect, it has been discontinued.

8. THE THIRD BRANCH IN THE APPROPRIATIONS PROCESS: THE ROLE OF THE COURTS

Some public policy decisions, including some on the budget, do not always meet the intent of the constitution as viewed by certain individuals and organizations. This can be for a variety of reasons, including deadlock between the two branches, failure to include certain citizens or unequal treatment of them in the budget, or a clear disregard for a particular provision in the constitution, among other reasons. When that happens, lawsuits may be brought to challenge the constitutionality of particular policy decisions. The state courts may then become the arbiters of these policies, sometimes providing oversight to ensure compliance with the law. Such court decisions can impact the budget and often in a major way, sometimes for many years.

The Courts, School Funding, and the State Budget

Nowhere is the court's impact on state policy, including the budget, more apparent than in the education arena and particularly regarding rural-bush schools both in terms of student access and funding. The many lawsuits brought regarding this issue were mainly founded on the provision in Article VII, Section 1, of the constitution requiring a "system of public schools open to all children of the State."[26]

In 1972, a lawsuit was filed on behalf of a group of Alaska Native school children who had no secondary schools in their home villages and who were forced to attend regional boarding schools. The plaintiffs in the *Molly Hootch* case, as it was informally called, argued that a school system that forced children to leave family and home to acquire an education was not a system that was open to all children of the state, as required by the Alaska Constitution. Moreover, plaintiffs alleged that the lack of local secondary schools in the villages constituted racial discrimination, as the children primarily affected were Alaska Natives. After much litigation, the state entered into an out-of-court settlement in 1976 that required the state to build and operate K–12 schools in many rural-bush villages (the *Molly Hootch* case is explained in more detail in Section 1 of Chapter 26 on education).

Specific to the budgetary impact of the settlement, the legislature was required to appropriate the necessary funds to enable the state to embark upon a construction program throughout rural-bush Alaska for new schools. Without the court's intervention, and given the state's tight budget at the time, construction of the schools might have occurred over time, perhaps over several decades, but not with the urgency that resulted from the settlement.

Then, in the 1980s, decisions regarding the direct appropriations from the state's general fund for school construction and major maintenance were made based upon a priority system developed by the Department of Education (DOE) that included both rural-bush and urban schools. One of the main criteria for determining priority on the DOE list was the number of students impacted by the project. This put small rural-bush schools at a major disadvantage. The outcome was an appropriation process that resulted in a disproportionate share of state funding going to urban school capital projects versus rural-bush school construction. Again, a lawsuit was filed. The courts found that the system of school construction funding was inequitable. In response, the legislature reluctantly appropriated millions of dollars for a rural-bush school construction and major maintenance package in an attempt to redress the issue.[27]

The *Cleary* and Mental Health Lands Cases

There are many other examples of the impact of court decisions on the state budget. Two of the most noteworthy, in terms of both their high political profiles and their impacts on the budget, have involved prison overcrowding and mental health trust lands. The *Cleary* case was brought by prisoners in 1981 and lasted for several years (see Chapter 27, Box 27.5, for details on the case). Ultimately the state was ordered to deal with the overcrowding problem, which meant considerable costs in building and expanding correctional facilities and arranging for prisoners to be housed out of state. No one has ever calculated the budget impact of this decision, but it likely runs into the tens of billions, and many of these outlays were required in tight budget years. In the mental health lands case, the state had illegally transferred lands given to the Territory by the federal government in trust, and designated to help fund mental health care, for other purposes. The case, which spanned from the late 1970s to the mid-1990s, resulted in the state having to reestablish the trust and pay the trust $200 million.[28]

9. ALASKA'S SPENDING ON SPECIFIC PROGRAMS COMPARED WITH OTHER STATES

Viewed in comparison with the fifty states overall, some of Alaska's specific budget expenditures are similar in regard to broad categories, but some are quite different. Figure 19.2 shows these broad categories and their relative size for the fifty states and for Alaska in 2012, which was more or less a typical year since the mid-1980s. Education (K–12 and postsecondary) and social services (particularly Medicaid) take up the bulk of spending, followed by transportation (mainly highways), and police and corrections. The cost of administering state government (through public employee salaries, building rents and maintenance, and funding state employee retirements, included as part of the "Other" in Figure 19.2) are also significant expenditures.

Although Alaska more or less fits these spending pattern percentages, there are some major differences in service delivery and the costs of that delivery between Alaska and many states. For instance, corrections, public assistance, and higher education spending are more or less similar in Alaska to the fifty states, but spending on K–12 education and Medicaid is much less than the national average, and Alaska spends more than twice as much on transportation as a percentage of its state budget than the national average.

The Distortions of Per Capita National Comparisons

National publications frequently present state spending comparisons on a per capita basis. From this perspective Alaska's budget statistics do not stack up well against other states. There is, however, more to these raw comparisons than simply much higher costs of government in Alaska resulting from inefficiencies as many like to claim.

First, in Alaska the state provides many services directly that are usually provided by local governments in other states. Of particular note is the centralized court system,

FIGURE 19.2

Percentage of Total Budget Expenditures on Major Programs and Services in 2012: Comparing Alaska with the Fifty States

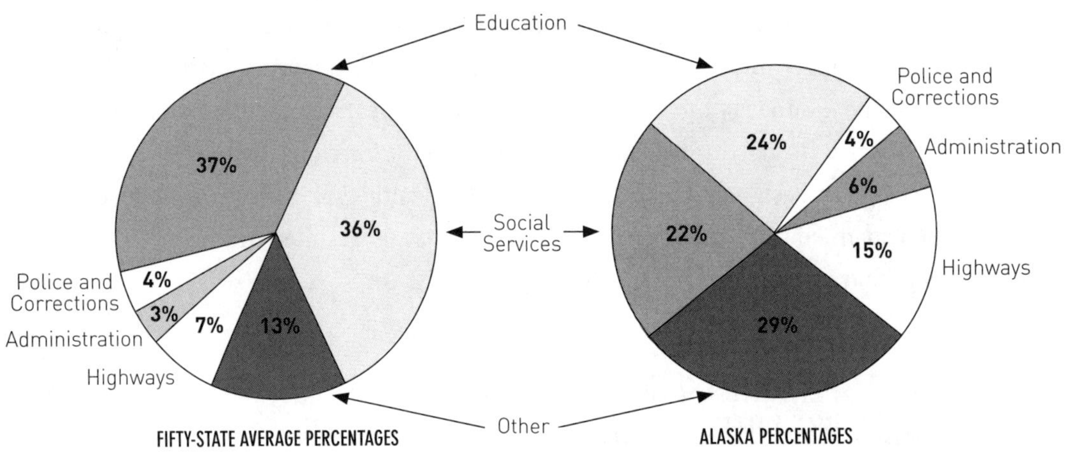

Source: The National Association of State Budget Officers, reports for financial year (FY) 2012. Retrieved from http://www.nasbo.org/sites/default/files/State%20Expenditure%20Report%20%28Fiscal%202011-2013%20 Data%29.pdf.

which is entirely funded by the state. The state directly funds and operates most correctional institutions housing long-term offenders and contracts with local governments to fund community jails. Plus, most of the more urban parts of Alaska provide local policing, but the majority of the state is served either by the Alaska State Troopers, employed directly by the state, or by village public safety officers (VPSOs) funded through state contracts with nonprofit Native organizations. In other states, local governments pay the costs of some courts (such as traffic courts), are the primary funders and providers of police protection, and fund and operate local jails and some prisons.

Second, particular geographical conditions distort costs in Alaska and increase budget outlays relative to other states. One is the overall cost of providing services in rural-bush areas. As explained earlier, this increases the cost of everything from education to health to transportation. The high percentage of total spending on transportation in Alaska is due to several factors. One is the disproportionately high share of federal highway funds received by the state compared to most other states. Another is the need to provide not only surface transportation over great distances but also to maintain a comprehensive system of airports throughout Alaska (generally funded through local government revenues in other states). The marine highway system of ferries and facilities in

Southeast and Southwest Alaska is also a special case affecting the transportation budget. This disproportionate budget outlay for transportation and other contrasting spending on specific services between Alaska and other similar states in the West are set out in Table 19.4 for fiscal years 2003, 2009, and 2012. Using this series of budgets over a ten-year period enables us to detect accurate comparative patterns that might be distorted by a one-year comparison alone.

A third distortion in comparing Alaska spending on specific services results from the large sums paid out yearly for the PFD. Since 2008, and average of $800 million has been necessary to fund the PFD distribution each year, which has averaged about 4 percent of the state budget between FY 2008 and FY 2015. This expenditure increases the total percentage of spending categorized as "Other" (the far right-hand column in Table 19.4) and reduces the overall percentage of the total budget allocated to specific services. This distortion results in a much lower expenditure, percentage-wise, than some of the other western states in areas such as K–12 education when, in fact, Alaska's per student expenditure is equal to or greater than most of the other states. The effect of the distortion also means that Alaska's actual spending on transportation is even higher than Figure 19.2 and Table 19.4 indicate as a percentage of the whole than in the majority of states.

Despite these mitigating circumstances and distortions, the per capita outlays and their unfavorable comparisons with other states often become the focus of many Alaskans and their state politicians. Many who advocate for reduced spending, particularly those from urban areas, point to such statistics, as well as the high cost of delivering services to rural-bush areas, to bolster their argument that state government is too large and spends too much. At least in theory, this is a manifestation of the Alaska political characteristic of fiscal conservatism. It is to the paradox in this fiscal conservatism as it relates to the budget that we now turn.

10. ALASKA'S VERSION OF THE CENTRAL PARADOX OF BUDGET POLITICS

As emphasized several times in this chapter and as related in many places throughout the book, one of the major characteristics of Alaska's budget politics has been regular attempts to cut the budget. To be sure, such budget-cutting pressures exist in all states and in Washington, D.C., but they are particularly chronic in Alaska because of unstable state government income due to its major dependence on fluctuating oil revenues. However, we also noted that across the nation there is a paradox in state spending between the political pressures to cut the budget and to increase, or at least maintain it, for all groups, organizations, and constituencies that have a stake in state spending. A good argument can be made that this is the major characteristic of budget politics. In reality, it means that

TABLE 19.4

Comparing Alaska State Budget Expenditures with Selected Western States by Policy Category for 2003, 2009, and 2012

(As Percentage of Total State Budget)

	K-12 EDUCATION			HIGHER EDUCATION			PUBLIC ASSISTANCE			MEDICAID			CORRECTIONS			TRANSPORTATION			ALL OTHER EXPENDITURES		
State	**2003**	**09**	**12**	**2003**	**09**	**12**	**2003**	**09**	**12**	**2003**	**09**	**12**	**2003**	**09**	**12**	**2003**	**09**	**12**	**2003**	**09**	**12**
Alaska	**15.5**	**10.0**	**13.4**	**9.6**	**7.5**	**9.3**	**1.8**	**0.9**	**1.1**	**12.1**	**7.5**	**11.6**	**3.3**	**2.3**	**3.0**	**19.3**	**14.9**	**16.8**	**38.3**	**57.0**	**44.8**
California	24.0	23.6	19.9	10.8	7.7	7.0	6.2	5.3	3.8	18.5	20.6	21.6	3.4	4.9	5.4	4.5	4.1	6.3	32.6	34.0	36.0
Idaho	26.6	27.4	25.7	8.6	8.2	8.1	0.3	0.3	0.3	19.6	22.8	27.2	4.0	3.6	3.7	12.2	8.9	10.9	28.8	28.8	24.1
Oregon	15.1	15.7	14.0	12.2	9.5	2.5	0.9	0.8	0.7	18.7	14.3	18.2	5.5	3.3	3.9	6.8	6.6	6.7	40.7	49.7	54.1
Washington	23.6	24.6	22.9	17.0	13.3	17.8	4.4	1.2	1.0	22.2	21.4	12.1	3.0	3.4	2.7	6.7	8.0	8.4	23.3	28.0	35.1
U.S. Average	**21.7**	**21.7**	**19.9**	**10.8**	**10.4**	**10.5**	**2.2**	**1.7**	**1.5**	**21.4**	**21.1**	**23.7**	**3.5**	**3.4**	**3.2**	**8.2**	**7.8**	**7.8**	**32.2**	**33.9**	**33.3**

Source: The National Association of State Budget Officers, reports for financial year (FY) 2003, 2009, and 2012. Retrieved from http://www.nasbo.org/sites/default/files/State%20Expenditure%20Report%20%28Fiscal%202C11-2013%20Data%29.pdf.

expanding the budget trumps cutting it, even in states with chronic revenue problems like Alaska. So how has this budget paradox played out in Alaska and why?

In a nutshell, there are six main explanations for the paradox in Alaska. Three are common to all states and three are particularly Alaskan, though not unique. The three common factors are the need to meet federal matching payments, court decisions affecting spending, and the fact that there is no permanent constituency or a coordinated interest for cutting budgets. The particular Alaska factors are: the seductiveness of economic booms, particularly high oil prices; the state government as a major economic driver; and a disconnect between taxes on individuals and state spending. We deal with the Alaska factors first.

The Alaska Factors

In a young state with many infrastructure and service needs, with heavy dependence on natural resource revenues, with state government as a major economic driver, and, as of 2016, with a state bank account of over $50 billion (the Permanent Fund), the pressure to increase spending in Alaska is probably more intense than in older states with developed infrastructure, a more balanced economy, and a much larger private sector.

One element that appears to put pressure on spending is the seductiveness of economic booms. While Alaska goes through highs and lows in revenues, the high years have, at least so far, always returned. And in high years state spending increases considerably, including capital budgets. Rural-bush legislators in particular have a constant need to direct funds to their districts for state services, particularly in education and health, which serve as a major economic driver. But with such an unbalanced economy, urban legislators also realize the need for state spending to fund all sorts of services, from government employment to infrastructure, in order to maintain economic stability in the state.

In addition, with regular oil price booms, $50 billion in the bank, a yearly PFD, no individual income tax or state sales tax as of 2015, and little recognition by the public of the significant role of the federal government in keeping Alaska afloat economically, there is a disconnect among large segments of the public between what government costs and what they are required to pay for it. Thus, a sort of unreality exists about the cost of government. Among many Alaskans this is reinforced by a "here and now" mentality. In particular, those who do not plan to stay in Alaska want their PFD and low taxes as they have little if any long-term commitment to the state.

Common Factors across the States

Earlier we explained how state court decisions across the nation can affect state spending and force the governor and legislature to increase the budget, sometimes with long-term outlays. Over the years, as state populations have increased and will continue to increase, the trend of spending is also upward because of the need of the states to match federal funds for entitlement programs such as Medicaid and various health and education programs. These pressures are largely legal and technical in nature. Probably the major general pressure to increase state budgets, however, is a political one.

To get a policy enacted and sustained over the long run it needs an organized and sustained constituency to promote and protect that policy. However, there is no coordinated, permanent, and long-term interest or constituency for cutting budgets. This is because, while there is a general belief among many Alaskans that budgets are too big or too bloated, everyone wants to maintain their own part of the budget. Although in the short term it may be necessary to cut a budget, in the long run elected state officials, conservatives and liberals alike, feel local pressure to help their constituents, which results in expanded budgets, particularly when revenues are high. Thus, over the long term, despite political rhetoric and fiery stump speeches about budget cutting, there are no cohesive, organized interest groups that can obtain a consensus large enough to secure sustained cutting of the budget.

This paradox is one reason why many Americans and Alaskans have a negative view of politics and politicians. Cutting the budget seems a simple task to the public, but it is far more complicated and difficult for politicians. The naïve candidates who are elected on a budget-cutting platform soon come to realize this and often have to endure the wrath of their constituents for not keeping their promises. Even the Tea Party movement that emerged across the states following the 2008 national elections, with its major focus on cutting government and government spending, has had minimal impact on spending. If history is anything to go by, the Tea Party may peter out as a political force, but its budget-cutting cry will be taken up by other constituencies in the years to come.

The Practical Reality of Alaska's Expanding State Budget

In combination, then, the Alaska factors and the general factors just discussed help explain the paradox of a major element of the state's budget politics—constant calls to cut the budget by the public and politicians alike but the constant pressure to increase spending. In fact, as we saw earlier, this upward trend in state spending in Alaska over the years has been a major one, with a fourfold increase per Alaskan since the mid-1960s.

Three of the characteristics of Alaska politics help explain this paradox: a political culture of pragmatic dependent individualism, a strong strain of self-proclaimed fiscal conservatism, and the myths and contradictions of Alaska political discourse. In the end pragmatism prevails, subordinating calls for fiscal conservatism to personal interest. The paradox is also bound up with the myths of Alaska politics, such as individualism (made possible only by dependence on government), and telling the public what they want to hear during an election ("I'll go down to Juneau and cut government") but governing on the basis of reality ("my district needs funds for economic development and a new school"). As the late Speaker of the U.S. House of Representatives Tip O'Neill so aptly put it: "all politics is local." Elected representatives see their first obligation as addressing the interests and needs of the people who elected them. Even normally fiscally conservative governors realize this. Both Governor Hickel during his second term (1990–1994) and Governor Murkowski (2002–2006) abandoned budget cutting when state revenues improved.

Another good argument can be made that the failure of the state to develop a fiscal plan is the product of the desire, if subconsciously, to continue to expand the budget. In this regard, one group argues that the state has so much money that it does not need a plan that might curtail spending. A related argument by another group is that the motive behind a plan is to control spending and deprive certain groups of needed funds. The populist connection between Alaska voters and their representatives has so far prevailed in this regard.[29]

11. CONCLUSION: THE BUDGET PROCESS AS A REFLECTION OF ALASKA'S POLITICAL ECONOMY

In Alaska, as elsewhere, it is the politics of the budget process that is the key factor to making sense of the state's spending plan at any one time and over time. Because government can do virtually nothing without money and because how much money it has influences what it can and cannot do, how it raises and spends money is the central aspect of governance. Add to this the power relationship between politicians with varying goals and motives and different ideological perspectives on what government should and should not do, and the result for all governments, including Alaska state government, is that the budget process often produces some of the most intense and contentious political battles. This is particularly the case in places like Alaska where the revenue sources for spending are unstable and unpredictable.

For all these reasons, the politics of the budget process reflects the overall politics of a governmental system and the dynamics of its political economy. This is why, to varying degrees, Alaska's budget process manifests all twelve characteristics of Alaska politics identified in Chapter 2 but particularly the role of the three strong contending branches of state government, regionalism and the urban versus rural-bush conflict, fiscal conservatism, and individualism with a strong strain of populism. Moreover, the instability of oil revenues is a major factor shaping Alaska's political economy. Oil revenues are the lion's share of unrestricted funds in the state budget, and state spending is a major driver for the state's economy. As a result, fluctuations in oil prices and revenue shortfalls often dominate political debate in particular years. This revenue instability has also shaped long-term discussions about the budget and what this means for the Alaska economy and the state's quality of life. Thus, one way to view Alaska politics is through the lens of the political economy of the budget process.

Judging by Alaska's budget politics since the mid-1980s, the nature and outcome of this debate are going to be hard to change. Because the budget and state revenues are two sides of the same political coin, changing the nature of short-term budget politics in Alaska requires tackling the instability of oil revenues and developing some stable revenue sources. This will require a major shift, or at least a short term change, in several elements of Alaska's political mindset. These include making political inroads into the state's fiscal conservatism and the nature of electoral politics, tempering populism with proactive political leadership, and overcoming the political seductiveness of oil price booms. It will also require some use of Permanent Fund earnings. But even if some plan to deal with Alaska's unstable revenues and the revenue crisis of 2014-2016 is forthcoming, the paradox of constant calls to cut the budget or hold the line on it while exerting inexorable political pressure to expand it will continue. As a consequence, the development of any long-range budget plan is unlikely.

ENDNOTES

[1] Ann O'M. Bowman and Richard C. Kearney, *State and Local Government*, 7th ed. (Boston: Houghton Mifflin Company, 2008), 202.

[2] For an extensive glossary of budget terms, see the Alaska Office of Management and Budget website, at https://omb.alaska.gov/html/information/budget-terminology.html. Other budget glossaries can be found in: *The Legislative Budget Guide: The Swiss Army Knife of Budget Handbooks* (Juneau, AK: Alaska State Legislature, Legislative Finance Division, 1995), esp. pp. B34–B43; and the Legislative Affairs Agency's *Glossary of Legislative Terms*, at http://w3.legis.state.ak.us/pubs/pubs.php.

[3] Gordon Harrison, *Alaska's Constitution; A Citizen's Guide*, 5th ed. (Juneau: Alaska Legislative Affairs Agency, 2012), 159.

[4] See Alaska Statutes (AS) 37.07.020(a).

[5] Alaska Statutes (AS) 37.07.

[6] See Harrison, *Alaska's Constitution*, 160; and Alaska Statutes (AS) 24.20.270.

[7] Todd Donovan, Christopher Z. Mooney, and Daniel A. Smith, *State and Local Politics: Institutions and Reform* (Belmont, CA: Wadsworth Cengage Learning, 2009), 344.

[8] Harrison, *Alaska's Constitution*, 161.

[9] See Alaska Statutes (AS) 24.20.211-231.

[10] See Alaska Statutes (AS) 24.20.151-209.

[11] Ronald K. Snell, *Annual and Biennial Budgeting: The Experience of State Governments* (Denver: National Council of State Legislatures, October 2004); and the 2011 update of this publication, at http://www.ncsl.org/research/fiscal-policy/state-experiences-with-annual-and-biennial-budgeti.aspx.

[12] See Chapter 30, Box 30.7.

[13] For an in-depth examination of budget processes, see James J. Gosling, *Budgetary Politics in American Governments*, 6th ed. (New York: Routledge 2016); for a succinct overview of budgeting in the states, see Robert C. Lowry, "Fiscal Policy in the American States," in *Politics in the American States: A Comparative Analysis*, eds., Virginia Gray, Russell L. Hanson, and Thad Kousser, 10th ed. (Washington, D.C.: CQ Press, 2013), esp. 328–32; and for a perspective on the legislative-gubernatorial budget relationship, see Alan Rosenthal, *Governors and Legislatures: Contending Powers* (Washington, D.C.: Congressional Quarterly Press, 1990), esp. Chapter 6, "Determining the Budget."

[14] News release, Office of Governor Sean Parnell, June 29, 2011.

[15] Comparative statistics on state budgets lag three to four years behind current year budgets. For this reason comparisons across the states in this and other sections of the chapter are made with figures through 2012, though more recent data for Alaska is available.

[16] "Federal Aid as a Percentage of State General Revenue (Fiscal Year 2012)," The Tax Foundation, at http://taxfoundation.org/blog/federal-aid-percentage-state-general-revenue-fiscal-year-2012; and State Budget Solution, at http://www.statebudgetsolutions.org/publications/detail/increased-federal-aid-to-states-is-a-long-term-trend. See Chapter 8 on state revenues, endnote 2, for an explanation of the various types of federal funds coming to Alaska and the other states. Alaska's ranking among the states as to federal funds received depends on which type of federal funds are considered in the comparison.

[17] See U.S. Census Bureau, "2009 Annual Survey of State Government Finances," at http://www.census.gov/govs/state/.

[18] Alexandra Gutierrez, "Walker Submits Skeletal Capital Budget," *Alaska News Nightly*, Alaska Public Radio Network (APRN), December 16, 2014.

[19] Developing an accurate history of the Alaska budget since statehood is fraught with difficulties. This is mainly because accurate records were not kept in the early years and ways of calculating and presenting the budget (both the operating and the capital budget) have changed on several occasions. However, by combining various federal and state data and other research sources, it is possible to build a picture of the overall budget including federal revenues, and adjust all these figures for inflation.

[20] See Chapter 8, Table 8.1 and Figures 8.1 and 8.3.

[21] Scott Goldsmith, Linda Leask, and Mary Killorin, "Alaska's Budget: Where the Money Came from and Went, 1990–2001," *Fiscal Policy Papers*, no. 13 (Anchorage: University of Alaska, Institute of Social and Economic Research, ISER, 2003).

[22] National Association of State Budget Officers, *Budget Processes in the States* (January 2002); and Snell, *Annual and Biennial Budgeting*.

[23] Thomas R. Dye and Susan A. MacManis, *Politics in States and Communities*, 14th ed. (Upper Saddle River, N.J.: Pearson/Prentice Hall, 2012), 283–84.

[24] James E. Anderson, *Public Policymaking: An Introduction*, 6th ed. (Boston: Houghton Mifflin Company, 2006), 163–64.

[25] "Hydro Project Planners Submit Environmental Plans," Associated Press, December 18, 2012; and Dermot Cole, "New Report Questions Viability of Susitna Dam Project," *Alaska Dispatch News*, December 8, 2014.

[26] See generally, Harrison, *Alaska's Constitution*, 123–25.

[27] *Kasayulie v. State*, 3AN-97-3782 Civ. (Superior Court of Alaska, Sept. 1, 1999). The trial court in this case, in an order granting the plaintiffs' motions for partial summary judgment, ruled that education is a fundamental right under the equal protection provision Alaska's state constitution.

[28] See Chapter 26 on education policy for a discussion of politics and policy implications of rural-bush access and funding of education, and Chapter 27 on social services and corrections for the issues surrounding prison overcrowding and mental health funding.

[29] See Chapter 8 on state revenues, particularly Sections 5 and 7, for details on the reasons why no long-term solution has been found to this chronic budget instability and Chapter 5 on political culture, particularly Sections 6 and 8, for an explanation of Alaska's populist bent.

⋆ CHAPTER 20 ⋆

The Media and Public Opinion in Alaska: How Influential?

Mike Doogan, Laura C. Savatgy, and Clive S. Thomas

The media and public opinion are integral parts of Alaska politics and its policy process. Indeed, it has long been recognized that a free press (in modern terms, a free media) and the free expression of public opinion are indispensable aspects of a democracy. In theory, at least, both the media and public opinion perform several important functions in the public policy-making process. The media links the governed with the government, educates the public on issues, and publicizes the actions of politicians and in so doing acts as a watchdog and a force for political accountability, exposing shady dealings and activities and actions that are not in the public interest. Theoretically, the public's feelings and concerns on issues should guide the policy decisions of public officials in a democratic government. In practice, however, the situation is much less clear-cut than our high-school civics class may have led us to believe.

The problem is that while we can more or less assess the influence of other forces in public policy making, such as the governor and interest groups, it is very difficult to be definitive about the influence of the media and public opinion. In part, the difficulty arises with the press because there are varying perspectives on its role in the policy-making process and also because it is often hard to separate the influence of the media on a policy issue from the influences of other forces. Similar difficulties arise in assessing the influence of public opinion. Its influence on an issue may vary widely depending on political circumstances, and different policy makers may respond to public opinion in different ways, depending on how they view the issue and how it affects them personally and politically. Also, as with the media, there are differing perspectives on what the role of public opinion is and should be in a democracy like Alaska.

Rapid changes that digital media, particularly the Internet and social media, have brought to both the media and public opinion, but especially the newspaper industry, have complicated matters further. An example of this kind of change in Alaska came in early 2014 when the state's major newspaper, the *Anchorage Daily News*, or ADN as it was often known (referred to as the "old ADN" in this chapter), was purchased by the online newspaper the *Alaska Dispatch* and renamed the *Alaska Dispatch News* (referred to here as the "new ADN").

Despite the difficulties in defining their role and determining their influence, there is nonetheless a clear relationship between the media and public opinion. Accordingly, this chapter considers them together and addresses two major questions: How important are the media and public opinion in the Alaska public policy-making process and under what circumstances will either or both be influential? As we address these questions, some of the characteristics of Alaska politics outlined in Chapter 2 will be evident. These include the influence of geography, regionalism and the conflict between urban and rural-bush Alaska, the role of external economic and political forces, and friends and neighbors politics.

The first section of the chapter deals with the media and the second with public opinion. The third section, primarily through two examples, examines the role of the media and public opinion as they can affect policy in combination. The chapter concludes with some observations about the past, present, and future influence of the media and public opinion on the policy-making process.[1] Throughout the chapter we use the terms "media" and "press" more or less interchangeably and frequently use the term "the press" to refer to both print and broadcast news outlets.

1. THE ROLE OF THE MEDIA AND OF JOURNALISTS

In examining the role of the media we first consider its role in a democracy in general and then turn to specifics on the Alaska press. Next, we provide an overview of the Alaska press and details on the Juneau press corps. Finally, we consider press coverage of some recent Alaska policy issues.[2]

The Role of the Media and of Journalists in a Democracy

Much of what the press does in a democracy—for example, presenting human-interest stories, travel tips, and entertainment—has nothing to do with politics. But in regard to its political and public policy role, according to the U.S. Agency for International Development (USAID):

> Access to information is essential to the health of democracy for at least two reasons. First, it ensures that citizens make responsible, informed choices rather than acting out of ignorance or misinformation. Second, information serves a "checking function" by ensuring that elected representatives uphold their oaths of office and carry out the wishes of those who elected them.[3]

So, in theory at least, the press provides information and acts as a watchdog. There are numerous examples of the press performing these tasks in an exemplary fashion. The classic example is exposure of the Watergate scandal during the presidency of Richard Nixon in 1973–1974. Too often, however, the press seems to fall short of these goals, resulting in skepticism about the press and often a strong antipathy toward the media from both politicians and the public. The tension between the theory and the practice is as old as America and a perennial concern across the world's democracies, including Alaska. The gap between the ideal and the practical reality is largely a product of the constraints that the press and journalists face. These constraints will be explained after considering what are probably the two major criticisms of the press and of journalists: lack of accuracy and poor quality.

The Issue of Accuracy

There is likely no politician dead or alive who has not experienced having their statements "misquoted" by the press or who has not questioned the accuracy of a story. Some might even accuse the press of distortions and lies. No less a person than Thomas Jefferson had such concerns.

Jefferson the theorist wrote in 1787, "Were it left to me to decide whether we should have a government without newspapers, or newspapers without a government, I should not hesitate a moment to choose the latter." Twenty years later, after he had had extensive experience in public office, including two terms as president, Jefferson the politician wrote, "The man who never looked into a newspaper is better informed than he who reads them, inasmuch as he who knows nothing is nearer to the truth than he whose mind is filled with half-truths and errors."[4]

Few, if any, journalists or editors purposely misquote a politician or anyone else or intentionally print or broadcast an inaccurate story. But misquotes and inaccuracies occur all the time. And even if the offending media outlet apologizes for the error, the correction will likely appear at the bottom of page 9 in small print or buried somewhere on its website. Once an error has been printed or broadcast, the damage is done, and it is the memory of the original article, not the apology, that lingers.

The Quality Issue

Adlai Stevenson, a prominent U.S. senator from Illinois and the Democratic Party's nominee for president in 1952 and 1956, was speaking for many involved in the political process when he said, "Newspaper editors are men who separate the wheat from the chaff, and then print the chaff."[5] In other words, why does the quality and seriousness of political reporting sometimes appear to be low? For instance, on a day in the mid-1990s when several important bills were up before the Alaska legislature, a legislator got so angry with a lobbyist who was buttonholing him in the hallway that he grabbed the lobbyist by his coat lapels and shook him. That story made the front page of the papers the next day and coverage of the bills ended up on page 3—a clear case of the chaff taking precedence over the wheat.

Reporters and editors do not take important policy issues lightly or seek out sensationalist stories for their front pages and lead stories on radio and television news programs. But a lot of chaff does get printed and broadcast, for reasons that will become clearer from the points below.

Constraints on the Press and on Journalists

Reporters and editors do not work in an ideal world. Like the rest of us, they function under a variety of constraints. These constraints, along with some of their consequences, are as follows.

Limited Time and Limited Page and Air Space. Like everyone else, reporters and editors have limited time. They also have limited space in newspapers or limited time for broadcasting a story. This means they must make choices about which stories to pursue, which ones to write about or broadcast, and how extensive the story should be. Inevitably, some things are reported extensively, while others do not get covered at all.

Reporters' Knowledge Base and Extent of Their Beat. Reporters cannot know everything about everything. Thus, if the job assignment—in the parlance of reporting, the "beat"—is broad, inevitably they will struggle to get a grasp on the many issues that arise throughout their "beat." As a result, there may be a lack of depth in a report and sometimes even inaccuracies and distortions. The Alaska state capital press corps is very small, and, unlike many large political media markets, reporters do not specialize in aspects of government but cover a wide-ranging political and public policy gamut.

A Disconnect Between Reporters and Editors. Reporters submit their stories to their newspaper, radio, or TV station, and the stories are then most often reviewed by an editor. The editor has to fit each story into the paper or broadcast in relation to other stories and features. In this process, the editor may make cuts and changes—sometimes reducing quotes—that may lead to inaccuracies or perceived inaccuracies and distortions of the message of a politician or other person quoted in the story.

The Need to Sell Advertising or Maintain Sponsors. Most newspapers (print or online), radio and TV stations, and, increasingly these days, websites and other electronic media are first and foremost businesses. They must sell advertising or, in the case of public broadcasting, maintain paid memberships from listeners and contributions from corporate and other sponsors. The media in all its forms is under pressure to attract a high number of readers, audiences, and users. This is because advertisers and sponsors look for high numbers when deciding where to place ads or sponsorships and how much they are willing to pay for them. This pressure to raise revenue may lead to compromises in both the quality and depth of reporting and in the content—the mix between news, filler, and human-interest stories. Readers like to be informed and entertained and have their interest piqued when they read a headline or hear the lead-in to a radio or TV story. Such stories increase readership, listeners, and viewers and enhance the chances of securing advertising and sponsorships.

Obviously, the press corps assigned to the government beat wants political information of all types for news stories and various angles on the stories. A major factor in piquing interest in such stories is the human-interest angle, particularly when there is conflict involved. Conflict or disagreement is often the essence of a news story because it makes it more interesting than straight reporting of factual information, though the press also does information reporting. Thus, the story about the legislator grabbing the lobbyist is more likely to be printed or aired in a prominent way than a story about a proposed corporate tax increase, even though the tax may have a much wider potential impact on readers and listeners.

Overall, and ironically, many journalists admit that, for many of the reasons noted here, it is probably their own organizations, the newspaper or radio or TV outlet, that place the most constraints on their reporting and their ability to be both a source of information and a watchdog. The next constraint is also significant, however.

The Journalist–Policy Maker Connection—a Symbiotic Relationship. Perhaps an even greater irony of the job of the political reporter is that, on the one hand they report the actions of public officials to inform the public and to keep a check on government, but, on the other, they need access to and the help of public officials to perform this job. So, there is a mutual dependency, a symbiotic relationship between the political press and public officials, which is both adversarial and interdependent.

Politicians need the press as a major means of communicating with the public. They do not want to alienate the prominent political reporters in the state for fear of bad press or, what is often worse—no press. Reporters need access to politicians for the information needed for their stories, but the story that is actually written based on the information may not be the story the politicians expected or wanted to read. The media also see themselves in a watchdog role and often ignore prepared press releases and ask the questions they think public officials do not want to hear. At the same time, a political reporter needs access to public officials, and the reporter who alienates the governor or major legislative leaders will have serious problems producing good stories.

The Ideal versus the Reality

In combination, the above factors have produced the gap between the ideal role of the press in a democracy and its actual role. By drawing attention to the gap, we are neither defending nor condemning the media. We are simply pointing out why this gap, which often perplexes and sometimes angers both politicians and the public, is the way it is. Jefferson's contradictory views of the media, related above, highlight the complexities of the relationship between the media and those who fashion public policy. This is the reality within which the Alaska press operates.

The Makeup and Ownership of the Alaska Press

The term "press" is generally understood to mean the news gathering and dissemination operations of both newspapers and the broadcast media, including radio and television. Recent developments in radio programming (especially talk shows) and communications technology (specifically web pages, networking sites, blogs, and mass e-mails) challenge that definition. So for the purposes of this discussion, we use the term *traditional* press to mean the former and *polemic press* to mean the latter.

The Composition of the Traditional Press

The traditional Alaska newspaper industry has fluctuated in numbers since the early 1970s, though much depends on how the various types of newspapers are classified.[6] According to the 1985 *Alaska Media Directory*, there were fifty-one newspapers published in Alaska. Then, as now, the publications were divided between general circulation daily and weekly papers and specialty publications: everything from the old ADN and the *Juneau Empire* to the *Alaska Journal of Commerce* to the *Alaska Oil and Gas News* to the *Senior Voice* to three military tabloids. By 1993 this number had grown modestly to fifty-four. In 2012 the *Media Directory* reclassified various print and online newspapers using a more narrow definition. So in January 2015 the directory listed forty-two newspapers.[7]

The modest growth was offset somewhat by the closure in 1992 of the *Anchorage Times*. Once the state's largest newspaper, the *Times* lost a bruising newspaper war to its rival, the *Anchorage Daily News* (the old ADN). The closure of the *Times* reduced Alaska's daily newspapers from eight to seven and reduced the number of people reporting and editing the news by about one hundred. As a consequence, it reduced competition between the state's two major newspapers and the only two with a significant statewide circulation.

The old ADN was established by Alaskan Norman Brown in 1946 as the *Anchorage News*. It changed hands in 1967 when it was purchased by Larry and Kay Fanning and again in 1979 when Kay Fanning, who had run the paper since her husband's death in 1971, sold an 80 percent share in the paper to the McClatchy Company of California. During its existence the old ADN won two Pulitzer prizes for investigative reporting. Then, in the spring of 2014, Alice Rogoff, the major owner and publisher of the online *Alaska Dispatch*, bought the old ADN from McClatchy for $34 million. Rogoff, a very wealthy person from back East, has lived part of the year in Alaska since the early 2000s, and has an extensive background in journalism. The *Dispatch* was established in 2008 by Alaska journalists, Tony Hopfinger and Amanda Coyne, as the closest online version of a traditional newspaper covering Alaska. Though Rogoff bought a majority ownership in 2009, the *Dispatch*'s broad coverage of Alaska continued and the site received thousands of hits a day.[8]

Welcomed in some quarters, the purchase of the old ADN also drew its critics, largely because, like the closure of the *Times* two decades earlier, it appeared to reduce competition.[9] On purchasing the old ADN, Rogoff stated in an interview that the goal of merging the two papers was to "offer a level of coverage never before seen in Alaska history, and to offer it to readers across the state through a variety of mediums."[10] To reflect this new focus, the paper's print and online editions were renamed the *Alaska Dispatch News*, and the two websites were merged. Rogoff has kept many of the old ADN's reporters and hired others from Alaska newspapers and has reporters based in major rural-bush hubs like Barrow.

The handful of newspapers that attempt to cover public policy in Alaska face a daunting task. The size of a newspaper's circulation or the size of a broadcast outlet's audience affects its advertising rates and both affect the financial resources that a newspaper, TV, or radio station can devote to news. As an example, in 2012 the major newspaper in Alaska, the old ADN, with an average daily circulation of 41,684 (down from 63,595 in just five years, since 2007), had far less in the way of resources than the largest newspaper in Washington State (*The Seattle Times*, 221,665), Oregon (*The Oregonian*, 228,599), or California (the *Los Angeles Times*, 641,369).[11]

The old ADN, however, did have at least as high a readership, and in some cases more so, than the largest newspapers of states with similar populations. Take December 2012, for example, when estimates put Alaska between South Dakota and North Dakota in population. The largest newspaper in South Dakota, the Sioux Falls *Argus-Leader*, had an average daily circulation of 31,597, and the largest in North Dakota, the *Fargo Forum*, had 43,563 readers, on average, each day.[12] But the task of covering an area eight times the size of either of those states, much of it without road access, makes the new ADN's task even more expensive and difficult. It is considerably more difficult to provide statewide coverage for the state's second-largest daily, the *Fairbanks Daily News-Miner*, circulation 14,557, and the state's five other, even smaller, print dailies (the *Juneau Empire*, *Ketchikan Daily News*, *Kodiak Daily Mirror*, *Peninsula Clarion*, and the *Sitka Sentinel*).

The growth of television and radio stations in Alaska has been somewhat more extensive than for newspapers. In 1973, according to Richard Fineberg, the *Alaska Blue Book* (a state government publication, since discontinued) listed seven TV stations. Twenty years later, in 1993, the number of TV stations had grown to eighteen (including two religious stations and the Home Shopping Network). Just over twenty years later, as of January 2015, there were twenty-three TV stations (including one religious station). The largest growth, however, has been in radio stations. The twenty-one stations listed by Fineberg as operating in 1973 grew to eighty by 1993 (of which ten were religious stations). The *Media Directory* listed 120 as of January 2015 (including twenty religious stations).[13] But the federal Telecommunications Act of 1996 loosened regulations by allowing ownership of a range of types of media. This reduced competition and in effect lessened requirements for providing news.[14] So the growth in stations has not been matched by an increase in news coverage but in more popular programming.

Ownership of the Traditional Press

The 1979 sale of the old ADN to the California-based McClatchy Company began a trend of replacing local and independent ownership of newspapers and television and radio stations in Alaska with out-of-state individuals and national chains. In 1969, the predecessor of Morris Communications (based in Augusta, Georgia) bought the *Southeast Alaska Empire* (now the *Juneau Empire*). By 2015, only three of the state's seven daily newspapers (the new ADN, the *Ketchikan Daily News*, and the *Sitka Sentinel*) were locally owned. Two of the remaining four were owned by Morris, and two by MediaNews Group of Denver, Colorado (MNG—which merged with 21st Century Media in 2013 to form Digital First Media). It could be argued that the new ADN is not Alaska-owned; but with Rogoff's commitment to Alaska and residence in the state for much of the year, one can make a good case that it is locally owned.

As of 2015, MNG also owned an Anchorage television station. Morris owned six Anchorage radio stations, the maximum allowed in a local jurisdiction under federal law, as well as the weekly *Alaska Star* (covering Chugiak-Eagle River), *Homer News*, and *Capital City Weekly*. Clear Channel Communications, of San Antonio, Texas, also owned six radio stations in Anchorage and four radio stations and one television station in Fairbanks.[15]

Have external corporate influences been detrimental to the breadth or depth of the coverage of politics in Alaska? As Outside ownership increased, many feared that the need to export profits to corporate headquarters would diminish news coverage, although Alice Rogoff's purchase of the old ADN appears to have had the opposite effect. But the effects of corporatization have been masked by the competition from the polemic media on the one hand, and the relaxation of news broadcasting requirements under federal law on the other. This makes it difficult to say just how external corporate ownership has affected the political role of the Alaska press.

The Polemic Press and Computer-Based Online Media

To expand on the meaning of *polemic press*, the term is used here to describe the use of technology to advance a particular point of view, including interpreting events in ways that conform to that point of view. The polemic press is typically subjective rather than objective, and one-sided rather than attempting to provide all sides of an issue. In this regard, its role is almost exactly the opposite of the traditional press. Instead of using facts to shape public policy positions, the polemic press uses public policy positions to shape facts. This activity, called "spin," among other things, combines a fixed opinion with selective reporting to reinforce the beliefs of those who produce and consume the polemic press.

Polemic talk radio has long been a part of the national landscape, at least since the Roman Catholic priest Charles Couglin, called by many "the father of hate radio," began broadcasting in 1926. But talk radio programs were limited and episodic until, in 1988, Rush Limbaugh showed AM radio programmers a way to compete with FM for listeners. Alaska began developing its own radio talkers in 2001, when disc jockey Rick Rydell began his own conservative talk show.[16] Half a dozen years later, no fewer than four talk shows were competing for listeners in the afternoon commuter slot in Anchorage, one of them a liberal host on a station owned by a labor union.

In recent years, the biggest growth in the polemic press has been in computer-based media. The potential of this medium was first demonstrated nationally in 1998, when an e-mail publication called *The Drudge Report* exposed the Monica Lewinsky scandal involving President Clinton, alleging that *Newsweek* was suppressing its own story on the scandal. Almost twenty years later, *The Drudge Report* was one of numerous web pages or blogs dealing with politics, ranging from the electronic version of the *New York Times* to the irreverent, often ribald, blog on Washington politics, *Wonkette*.

Alaska has followed this trend. The traditional Alaska press quickly got into the business of producing web versions of their newspapers, as did radio and TV stations. But Alaska's independent blogs have not achieved either the numbers or the stature of *Drudge* or even *Wonkette*. The closest thing Alaska had to offer was *An Alaskan Abroad*, the blog of former Alaska reporter Robert Dillon, then living in Washington, D.C., but it is no longer in existence. Two widely read blogs on Alaska politics have included amandacoyne.com, by former reporter Amanda Coyne, and Mudflats by Jeanne Devon, a writer for *The Huffington Post*.[17] The site dealing with Alaska politics that likely gets the most hits per month—between 35,000-45,000—is the *Anchorage Daily Planet*. While claiming to report the news in a factual and unbiased way, its website states: "you will find unabashed support of private enterprise and responsible development, the limited role of government in our daily affairs and the idea that Alaskans truly know what is best for Alaska."[18]

The emergence of computer-based media has meant new challenges for the traditional press in Alaska, as in the rest of the nation. The impact on newspapers has been especially severe, as advertisers have followed readers onto the web. Some statistics illustrate the problem. On the first Tuesday in March from 1990-1994, the old ADN averaged ninety-nine pages. For the same day in 2000-2004 it averaged forty-eight pages, and often fewer than forty by 2012.[19]

Finally, Alaska politicians have been quick to seize on computer-based media. As early as 2005, political parties, legislative caucuses, and individual politicians were using web pages, networking sites, blogs, and mass e-mails to communicate with the faithful and, in many cases, raise funds. By 2015, in part a product of Sarah Palin's use of social media in the 2008 presidential election and afterwards, most Alaska politicians could be found on Facebook and Twitter. Needless to say, these computer-based media serve the purposes of those who produce or post items on them rather than any broader goal of even-handed inquiry or presentation of information.

The Juneau Press Corps

Nothing is covered quite so well by the traditional media as national politics. In mid-2014, there were close to fifty newspaper, radio, TV, and online organizations that collectively employed sixty reporters covering only the White House. Because these jobs are highly sought after and often make the reporters household names, there is relatively little turnover. Before she retired in 2014, ABC News Radio's correspondent Ann Compton, was reporting on her seventh U.S. president and CBS-TV News correspondent Bill Plante was reporting on his fifth.

The situation in Washington, D.C., as well as in larger states like California and New York, contrasts sharply with Alaska. No news organizations employ specialized political reporters who limit their coverage to the governor, departments of state government, or the legislature. As might be expected, Alaska is closer to the Mountain states, like Idaho, Montana, and Wyoming, in terms of the relatively small number of reporters based in the state capital.

The Juneau press corps is largest when the legislature is in session, but it is never very large. In recent years, it has consisted of seven traditional press organizations: the Associated Press (AP), the state's three largest general circulation newspapers, two Anchorage television stations, and the state's public radio network. A variety of newsletters also report on various subjects to their subscribers, such as the *Alaska Legislative Digest* and the *Alaska Budget Report* (though in 2015 its future was in doubt).

This coverage has been supplemented by *Gavel to Gavel*, a nonprofit cable television and streaming Internet service providing both live and taped telecasts of the legislature without reporters or commentary. *Gavel to Gavel* is aired live on public television, and the legislature's official Internet home page contains links to streamed Internet broadcasts of *Gavel to Gavel*. It is funded largely by the City and Borough of Juneau and by private corporate sponsors.

In 2012, only three of the traditional press organizations' eight capital reporters had held the same jobs five years earlier. The state's three major newspapers, for example, employed thirteen different capitol reporters from 2004 to 2010 and the AP seven. The turnover is the result of a variety of factors: low pay, better opportunities elsewhere (particularly in state government as communications and press people), and a reluctance to relocate to Juneau for the session, among others.[20] Box 20.1 provides insights on the job of a radio reporter, Dave Donaldson of the Alaska Public Radio Network (APRN). Now retired, he had twenty-two years of experience reporting on Alaska politics which included six governors. His insights also provide a perspective on the role of the press in public policy making, to which we now turn.

How the Media Can Influence Public Policy: Three Case Studies

The traditional press influences public policy mainly by reporting on policy issues and policy makers. The issues it chooses to report help to shape the public policy agenda, and how it reports on those issues often influences the particular actions that policy makers take on the issues. In addition, some traditional press outlets offer commentary on public policy matters. These opinions (called "editorials" when written by the outlet's editorial staff) sometimes influence policy makers in choosing the matters to focus on and shaping policies to deal with those matters.

The traditional press is also supposed to serve a watchdog role, watching for behavior and policies that do not serve the public interest. In Alaska, as elsewhere, the traditional press is sometimes successful in this role and sometimes not. The first two case studies show this contrast. The third is an example of how the press can focus public attention on an issue simply by reporting on the actions of public policy makers.

The VECO Scandal

On August 31, 2006, FBI agents raided the offices of six Alaska state legislators. Their purpose was to collect evidence of bribery and extortion involving legislators. Several areas of malfeasance were being investigated, many involving the activities of Bill Allen, the founder and president of the oilfield services company VECO.

The FBI already had plenty of evidence. It had installed hidden video cameras in the room in the Baranof Hotel in downtown Juneau used by Allen and VECO Vice President Rick Smith for their lobbying activities in the 2006 legislative session. Among the activities filmed by the FBI were handouts of cash to two legislators and making promises to other legislators in return for their support for a tax bill friendly to the oil industry.

BOX 20.1

The Political Reporter-Politician-Citizen Connection: An Insider's Perspective

News comes from watching and listening. That's why my day begins with a slow walk down the halls of the state capitol or with a chain of telephone calls, encouraging conversation and sharing information I've picked up elsewhere. Most of all, I listen to people tell me what is important in their part of the world. After this, I usually have a good idea of what needs to be shared with a wider audience.

Alaskans are personally close to their political leaders. It is easy to talk to an elected official directly at the legislature or in the local grocery store. That intimate relationship makes people comfortable with what politicians tell them. As a political journalist, I try to present the world from a perspective they might not have heard from their neighbors.

However, I'm not an advocate for anybody—I am only a messenger. If I do my job well, neither you nor any public official will know my opinion on the subject because my opinion doesn't matter. I try to make you—the citizen—look beyond yourself and your world with a fresh understanding of an issue or a person or an event. The most I can hope for is to give you the information you need to be the advocate—your own advocate—and to know that, after you'd listened to me, you picked up the phone and told your leaders that I sent you.

A newly arrived legislator once told a group of reporters at the capitol, "You are all monsters," and refused to talk to any of us ever again. He was reflecting a common politicians' view of journalists, paralleling the simplistic view of politicians by the public as corrupt and self-serving. And certainly there are biased journalists—just play with your radio or TV dial or log on to the Internet. This journalist-hating politician gave me an interview two days later because I spent time finding out about him as a person. I convinced him that he would never know from the story I produced whether I disagreed with him or not. I presented his views fairly, and we established a healthy give-and-take for the rest of his time in the legislature.

With this politician and with others I have a symbiotic relationship. I need them to provide the substance of my reporting; they need me to maintain a connection with the public. In truth, though, most reporters never find an elected official that they completely trust, and politicians never lose their fear that reporters will misrepresent them. There is always a line between "me" and "them." If that line is blurred, the relationship rightly becomes suspect.

Do I, and my journalist colleagues, have influence? Do we set the political agenda? Most of the time we don't; but sometimes we can, by highlighting the issue or the concern that the politician doesn't want to acknowledge. Usually, though, our influence is much more modest and the result of education rather than influence. The media and the traditional press corps, as well as Internet bloggers and radio talk shows, have influence only when an audience finds new and fresh information.

All of us, whether we are engineers, fishermen, or artists, want to see the results of our work touch people in some way. A journalist's job is done when, because of this new and fresh information, voters ask difficult questions to candidates, bureaucrats change their policies, or the legislature passes new laws to correct previous mistakes.

With influence, though, comes a horrible risk—being wrong! To a reporter, credibility is everything! If I'm wrong too many times you won't trust me anymore, and I might as well look for a job as a disk jockey.

Source: Developed by Dave Donaldson, former APRN political reporter and co-author of Chapter 16.

Allen and VECO were no strangers to the spotlight. The company's executives had long been major financiers of pro-oil Republican politicians. Those activities were not always legal. At one time, Allen and VECO held the record for the largest fine paid to the Alaska Public Offices Commission (APOC), the state agency that enforces campaign finance laws.[21] VECO had also employed Republican legislators directly.

But Allen had something more than financial resources at his disposal. When the *Anchorage Times* folded in 1992, a particular element of its deal with the *Anchorage Daily News* gave Allen one-half of the *News*'s op-ed page to print his opinions. Billed as an attempt to preserve a conservative editorial stance, the *Voice of the Times* quickly became a platform for Allen's business interests and political allies.

Power and influence apparently were not enough. Allen quickly pleaded guilty to federal charges and agreed to testify for the government against the legislators. By early 2008, two Republican House members had been convicted of charges related to Allen and served prison terms, and Allen and Smith also got prison sentences. The investigation expanded to include U.S. Senator Ted Stevens, who was convicted in October 2008 of filing incomplete financial disclosure forms regarding help he received from Allen in refurbishing his Girdwood home south of Anchorage. However, all charges against Stevens were later dropped due to alleged misconduct by the prosecuting attorneys in his case.[22]

How did Alaska's press corps perform on this scandal? Before the FBI raids, the press was asleep at the switch. A search of the databases of the state's three largest newspapers, targeting key phrases clearly shows this. In 2005, the word "corruption" appeared eighty-one times, almost exclusively in letters to the editor. During the eight months before the raid, "corruption" appeared eighty-three times, again almost exclusively in letters to the editor. In the four months following the raids, when no charges had been filed, it appeared 111 times, in letters to the editor, editorials, and news reports. In 2007, when court documents became available and trials were held—that is, when the reporting became very easy—it appeared 768 times. Searches for Allen's name and the name of one of the lawmakers involved, Pete Kott, showed a similar pattern.

The press, then, followed this story rather than taking the lead. They depended on court documents and testimony rather than expending independent effort. In fact, the press ignored indications of problems, which included Allen sitting in the House gallery passing notes to legislators, a public flare-up on the House floor, and continued suggestions from House and Senate Democrats that something was amiss. The *Anchorage Daily News*, which once won Pulitzer prizes for its investigative reporting, did not even have a reporter at the oil-tax special sessions in 2008, when some of the criminal activity occurred. In this case, the press, as the watchdog of democracy, did not even clear its throat or growl, let alone bark.

Governor Parnell and the Alaska National Guard Sexual Assault Scandal

In early 2014 an issue arose that dogged Governor Parnell's bid for reelection that November. It involved accusations that the leaders of the Alaska National Guard had failed to respond adequately to sexual assault complaints. In contrast to the VECO affair, the media was relentless in its reporting and proactive in its response to this issue.

Concerns surfaced in April 2014 that the governor had taken four years to launch an investigation into allegations against the Guard brought to his attention in 2010 by three Guard chaplains. Parnell's response in 2014—that he had met with the Guard's leadership to discuss the complaint process—was deemed inadequate.[23] So the new ADN and the Alaska Public Radio Network (APRN) requested documents from the governor's office in May and June relating to the allegations, but by September no documents had been provided.

At the beginning of the 2014 general election campaign, there appeared little to stop Parnell's reelection. In the August primary his 80,903 votes surpassed the total votes for all other candidates on the non-Republican ballot. The primary election also delivered a victory to him in the campaign he led to defeat a ballot initiative that would have overturned an oil-tax reduction he had gotten through the legislature in 2013. Added to these strengths, as it emerged from the primary election, his opposition in the general election would be divided between Democrat Byron Mallott and Bill Walker, a Republican running as an independent. Polls at the time indicated that neither Mallott nor Walker would have beaten Parnell.

The campaign, however, began to unravel politically for Parnell on September 2, when Byron Mallott and Bill Walker joined forces to form the nonpartisan Alaska First Unity ticket, with Walker in the governor's spot and Mallott running for lieutenant governor. In addition to the strengthened opposition, the Guard sexual assault scandal reappeared with the revelation that in February 2014 Parnell had called on the federal government to conduct an investigation of the Guard. A scathing report by the Pentagon's Office of Complex Investigations found that Alaska victims of sexual assault did not trust the Guard's leadership enough to protect them. The report also listed other management failures and abuses.

Following release of the report, the Adjutant General resigned, and later that month the highest-ranking civilian within the Guard resigned at the request of the governor.[24] Parnell also announced that the federal National Guard Bureau would provide assistance to the Guard in improving their operation and management practices.

Despite Parnell's action, his staff formally rejected the still pending requests for documents by the new ADN and APRN. Following this rejection, the new ADN published an article recapping all that was known about the subject. The story challenged the governor's decision to withhold the documents, asking, "When did he learn about problems in the guard, and did he respond effectively?"[25]

At a hastily arranged press conference the following morning, Parnell elevated the issue before the public when he claimed the new ADN article was "false and misleading."[26] As a result, questions about the Guard affair arose in election debates and forums. Walker accused Parnell of continuing to withhold information while showing a lack of leadership.[27]

Then, on October 15, *The Anchorage Press* published a previously secret federal report on a federal investigation that gave details, names, and dates of alleged activities that had dampened the morale of Guard members. The report found incidents of sexual assault dating back to 2007 involving "fellow soldiers, new recruits, and civilian women, including high school JROTC cadets." There was no indication in the *Press*'s stories that Parnell had seen this report even though it had been given to state officials in December 2013. But the article echoed earlier stories: "Parnell has refused to release public records showing what he knew about sexual assaults . . . when exactly he knew them, and what, if anything, he did about it."[28]

A further development came when the new ADN and APRN obtained a court order for the documents, which were finally released in a redacted form the Friday before the election. Many of the documents indicated that Parnell had quietly been making attempts to investigate the complaints. The released document also showed that, at the request of the governor's staff, the FBI made several investigations and found no merit to the allegations.[29] The governor had maintained all along that he had been misled by Guard officials.[30]

Many unanswered questions remain about the scandal. But this potentially explosive political issue was poorly handled by the governor and his staff, forcing them on the political defensive instead of taking the political offensive. Because of the governor's unwillingness to release documents about his actions, the public had few hard facts about the issue throughout the campaign. The lack of information likely hurt Parnell with the public, who remembered the major revelations of September and not the released documents a few days before the election. While these documents did not implicate the governor in any wrongdoing, they revealed indecisive, if not weak, leadership, which was surprising given his efforts to combat domestic violence—his "Choose Respect" initiative.

Did the scandal cost Parnell the election, and was the media the decisive factor? No one took any comprehensive exit polls to show whether the issue was the deciding factor. But its prominence right before the election did not help Parnell in his small margin of loss. Of nearly 280,000 votes cast, he lost by only 6,000 to Walker. Certainly, the media had a major role in unearthing this issue and keeping it in the news headlines for most of the campaign. We can only speculate whether Parnell would have won if the media had not been tenacious in their reporting on the scandal, including filing the Freedom of Information request and the subsequent court action.

Governor Frank Murkowski's Jet

Investigative reporting is not the only way the press can affect public policy. Simply by watching events and reporting them to the public, the press helps to shape the policy agenda, not to mention political careers. This is true even in cases that might seem trivial to students of public policy but, because of their simplicity and emblematic value, the events strike a responsive chord with the public. There is no better example of this than the saga of Governor Frank Murkowski's jet.

Murkowski, a long time U.S. senator, was elected governor in 2002. In the months that followed his inauguration, he made a number of unpopular unilateral decisions. Then, in June 2004, the Alaska press reported that his administration was asking the federal government to allow the use of Homeland Security funds to buy an executive jet. Almost immediately the plan began to draw criticism from Murkowski's opponents and the citizenry at large. One letter to the editor complained about a plan by the Murkowski administration to raise the state business license fee, and ended this way, "Is this just another rip-off from the Murkowski administration that now wants its own corporate jet?"[31] Opposition politicians quickly saw the jet as a powerful symbol of elitism, and found or manufactured ways to keep it in front of the public.

Even more so than Parnell's mishandling of the National Guard scandal, the Murkowski administration's handling of the situation belongs in public relations textbooks as an example of how not to do things. When the federal government denied the request for Homeland Security funds, the administration tried to get the legislature to put money in the state budget for the jet. When that failed, it announced it was going to use state money anyway. Along the way, Murkowski and his chief of staff, Jim Clark, feuded with their critics both privately and publicly. The press reported every twist and turn in the saga.

Murkowski eventually got his jet and used it. He continued to defend the purchase of the jet during his 2006 reelection campaign, which reinforced the image of arrogance he had fashioned for himself and contributed to his overwhelming defeat in the August 2006 Republican primary election. When he left office in December 2006, the press gleefully reported that he left Alaska aboard the state jet that had cost him so much. Soon after taking office, Governor Palin sold the jet.

How important was the jet in the grand scheme of things? It cost the state $2.6 million in a year when the state budget was about $5.5 billion. But even relatively small matters can have a large impact when they connect with the public, and the press recognized and catered to that connection.

2. THE ROLE OF PUBLIC OPINION

In examining the role of public opinion and its effect on public policy, we first consider the challenges in defining public opinion and its role in a democracy. Then we move to the ways the public expresses its opinions and the methods of measuring public opinion in general and in Alaska in particular. Next we look at some current political attitudes in Alaska. Finally, we use two case studies to assess the effects of public opinion on Alaska public policy.

The Challenges of Considering the Role of Public Opinion in a Democracy

Many Americans and Alaskans, as well as those living in democracies around the world, believe that what the public thinks or wants should be a major influence—if not *the* major influence—on what government does or does not do. After all, if democracy is "government of the people, for the people and by the people," the public's wishes and opinions should be paramount in the minds of policy makers. In practice, however, the role of public opinion in the policy making process is much more complex.

First, what exactly is public opinion from both a theoretical and practical point of view? From a theoretical perspective it can be defined as a collective grouping of individual attitudes and beliefs. But in practical terms, how can it be assessed and translated into an accurate and comprehensible message for policy makers? Is public opinion valid only if we can determine that more than half of the public or more than half of a particular group supports or opposes an issue? Is it still valid to consider the views of a minority of the group polled if the number of people in the minority is large? Do we count the intensity of the opinions, since some will care about an issue much more than others? And if we do count intensity, how do we measure it and how much weight do we give to it? Should we give increased consideration to those who are more informed on an issue, and if so, how can we determine who are more informed? Do we count the result of an election as an indication of public opinion? Many a successful office seeker claims to have been given a "mandate" following the election, but it is frequently difficult, if not impossible, to determine precisely what message the voters intended to deliver.

Second, what role should and does public opinion play in the actions of elected officials? Elected officials, in theory, carry the public's message into the process of policy making and in developing state laws. But should these policy makers be *delegates* who simply follow whatever a majority of their constituents, or a majority of the people in the state, desire? Or should they be *representatives* using their own informed judgments to make decisions on behalf of their constituents and the citizens of the state on a proposed policy, even if it lacks major public support?

The differences between these perspectives can be illustrated by the following two hypothetical situations. In the first situation, we assume that opinion polls show that 90 percent of Alaskans oppose enactment of a state sales tax. Politicians reflect this public position and do not enact the tax, thereby demonstrating that public opinion matters and has an impact on policy makers' minds. The other hypothetical situation begins similarly, with 90 percent of Alaskans opposing the sales tax, but this time the legislature enacts the tax despite overwhelming opposition. In this case, the lesson is that elected officials do not listen to the public, but act instead on their own political judgment, or perhaps their whims. In actuality the public may not have the knowledge to make these kinds of decisions. In the case of the sales tax, the tax might well have been part of a package of reforms needed to save the state from financial disaster. The delegate versus the representative perspectives are widely debated in politics and policy making, and are addressed in more detail in Chapter 3.[32]

The subject of public opinion in democracies has been studied, polled, surveyed, researched, and theorized. Yet much of the research regarding the message that public opinion sends and its ability to help policy makers is inconclusive and often contradictory. In the rest of this section we try to make sense of these contradictions and offer an assessment of the role of public opinion in Alaska politics.

The Expression and Measurement of Public Opinion: What It Shows and How It is Perceived by Policy Makers

There are several ways in which public opinion can be expressed in a democracy, including in Alaska. These range from systematic measurement of opinion by polling to expressions by individuals, small groups, and organizations through letters, e-mails, social media, and personal meetings with public officials. The main forms of public expression are set out in Table 20.1.[33] Measuring public opinion systematically is most often done by polling, or sample surveys. Theoretically, the quantitative data gathered in surveys reflect opinions on various aspects of government or policy issues. Since the late 1980s there has been a rise in public opinion polling, nationally and at the state and local levels.

This rise is in part a result of the advent of Internet surveys, high-tech voting equipment, and the ability of the media to reach so much of the public. Less systematic forms of public opinion made possible by the Internet include the comments that readers, listeners, and viewers provide to news stories and issue pieces on the websites of newspapers and radio and TV stations. Those commenting tend to be political junkies, those with intense feelings, and those who like to see their names in print. Governors also sometimes use the Internet to gauge statewide public opinion, as Governor Palin did in seeking Alaskans' view on savings priorities set out in Table 20.2 (see page 723). More recently, in early 2015, Governor Walker, through the governor's home page, sought suggestions

TABLE 20.1

Ways of Expressing and Measuring Public Opinion

Method	Description
Opinion Polls	Designed to represent the opinions of a population (local, state, or national) on a specific subject or candidate by asking a small sample of people several questions and then extrapolating the answers to the larger population in the locality, state, or nation.
Voter Exit Polls	Based on questions asked to voters as they leave their voting places.
Surveys	Usually more extensive and broad-ranging than polls. Surveys target a random sample of the population on a candidates or issues by various means of communication, such as by telephone, via the Internet, or in-person interviews.
In-Depth Opinion Studies	These take polls and/or surveys and analyze them in depth qualitatively and/or quantitatively. They may break down responses by geography, age, racial or ethnic group, ideology or political affiliation, etc.
Hotline or Citizen Lines	Telephone connection set up for citizens to contact a public official in person, or that enables them to leave a recorded message.
Public Opinion Messages (POMS)	Alaska's Internet messaging system that enables a citizen to send a fifty-word message to one, several, or all legislators. The system automatically matches the sender with voter registration information that is included in the message received by the legislator.

Source: Developed by Laura Savatgy.

from state employees and the public for cutting the state budget in light of the major drop in oil prices and state revenues. All these sources mean that there is more information available today on what the public thinks about politics and policy issues than ever before.

As to polling organizations, there are two types. Some are independent, such as the Harris and Roper organizations and the National Opinion Research Center (NORC) attached to the University of Chicago. Others conduct public opinion polls at the request of a particular client, which may create bias in the process.

Several problems can arise when measuring public opinion. These include a low response rate, demographic differences in race, ethnicity, education and so on, knowledge differences among those being surveyed, biased opinions, and the fact that "we can never really know how well the interviewed respondents stack up against the general population in terms of their public views, involvement, and behaviors."[34] These problems raise several questions:

- How valuable as political messages are opinion polls and surveys?
- What is being measured?

- Do opinion surveys measure broad general beliefs resulting from the public's values about politics?
- Are they measuring attitudes based upon the support of political parties, of certain interest groups, grass-roots groups, or a particular perspective of the media, policy makers, or others?
- How informed are these opinions?
- How do and should policy makers use this information?

According to Robert Weissberg, polls and surveys are not a measurement of knowledge and information; they are a measurement of "wishes and preferences of respondents."[35]

One positive view of the role and effect of public opinion is that of Barbara Norrander and Clyde Wilcox. They discuss how state public opinion is linked to state and national politics. When groups organize and promote their views, a counter mobilization of other groups opposing these views occurs, which provides a strong public message that can influence policy.[36] In addition, many states go out of their way to solicit citizen input. In Washington State, for instance, there is a twenty-four-hour hotline that the public can use to "enable government and the citizenry to exchange information."[37] This creates a perception of government openness and willingness to listen to the public and their opinions. In terms of a more systematic expression of public opinion, Weissberg believes that preferences can be measured and that, in principle, contemporary polls are fully capable of soliciting precise public preferences.[38]

However, Weissberg also argues that policy makers should not assume that public opinion is a reliable guide to making public policy. Among the problems of taking public opinion at face value is that it can contain or reflect many distortions. These include irrational ignorance, survey groups that are like-minded, overexposure to the media, biased reporting from the polemic press and sometimes the traditional press, public distrust, and polls that are created or designed to persuade the person responding to the poll to a particular point of view—so-called push polls. Weissberg goes on to argue that, despite the number of polls that actually take place these days, "we should not expect to see the day when polling can replace reasoned policy choices by elected representatives of the people."[39] In regard to the Internet and e-mails as vehicles for expressing public opinion, Bowman and Kearney point out that, "as the push towards e-government grows . . . the so called technology have-nots will be left behind."[40] Clearly, as to the influence that public opinion should have on elected officials, Weissberg and, to a certain extent, Bowman and Kearney, see them as representatives and not as delegates.

The Expression and Measuring of Public Opinion in Alaska: Extent, Limits, and Some Contemporary Attitudes

In Alaska, the public has the ability to contact executive branch officials and their legislators through various means, including meeting with them in person. In fact, in the friends and neighbors atmosphere of Alaska politics, it seems that the expression of public opinion to policy makers should be much easier than in a large state like California or even a medium-sized one like Maryland. In many ways this is true, especially considering the various electronic and telecommunications services the state provides to facilitate free and relatively easy ways to contact public officials. There are, however, some constraints and other factors that inhibit the expression of public opinion by individuals, groups, and the Alaska public at large.

Constraints on Alaska Public Opinion

First, the state's geography and the location of the capital city in Juneau may pose problems in expressing public opinion. Travel to Juneau is expensive, especially from Interior villages and Southwest and Northwest Alaska. This inhibits face-to-face contact with public officials throughout the year but particularly during the legislative session. Furthermore, Internet access is not always available in Alaska's vast and remote rural-bush areas, which can cause an "incomplete" Alaska voice to he heard through Internet surveys or legislative hearings that offer teleconferenced testimony only from a handful of cities and towns.

Second, the fact that there are no independent polling firms in the state may also have detrimental effects. As of 2015 there were four major research groups that survey Alaska public opinion: the Dittman Research and Communications Corporation, Ivan Moore Research, the Craciun Group, and the Alaska Public Interest Research Group (AkPIRG). The first three are policy- and public opinion–related organizations focusing on political polling and public policy for private clients. All four, however, use similar types of tools to measure public opinion. Now and again, national independent polling organizations poll Alaskans, mainly in relation to national elections—as in the 2008 presidential election and the 2010 and 2014 U.S. Senate races—but independent polls on Alaskans' attitudes are conducted infrequently and on a narrow range of subjects.

As a result, Alaska policy makers have minimal information on public attitudes and opinions gathered systematically and objectively. Moreover, the public opinions that policy makers do receive may be the product of one or more of the myths surrounding Alaska politics that are addressed in various places in the book. These include: that government is very inefficient and needs to be cut drastically; and that if only the federal government would reduce its involvement in Alaska affairs the state's economic future would be assured. Policy makers may take action on those opinions, however, despite their lack of factual or logical foundation.

Finally, one could argue that the scandals involving Alaska politicians as explained in the VECO case study and related incidents, plus the indictment of former Alaska U.S. Senator Ted Stevens, have decreased public trust. These kinds of scandals can cause people to reject all things political, resulting in a decline in the public's willingness to express opinions on matters of public policy. It can also be argued, however, that lack of trust in government may serve to galvanize the public to express itself in the pursuit of governmental reforms. Chapter 5 on political culture deals with this issue of public trust and political corruption.[41]

Positive Perspectives on the Role of Alaska Public Opinion

As a result of the scandals, there was a reform of the state's lobby law in 2007, and Senator Stevens was defeated in the November 2008 election. This appears to indicate that the public is sending a clear message to policy makers that it does not tolerate corruption and political shenanigans. In the absence of extensive independent polling, however, it is difficult to know for certain.

Another positive aspect of the effect of Alaska public opinion on policy making is a point made in Chapter 5 on political culture, in Chapter 14 on campaigns and elections, and elsewhere in the book. The majority caucuses in each house of the legislature (generally the Republicans in both the House and Senate) do appear to represent the general opinion of Alaskans, as do the policies of the governor in office. And the freedom of legislators to act on many issues, particularly those affecting their regions, also enables them to reflect their constituents' views. So, through the election process, the assessment by legislators of their constituents' needs, and through the organization of the legislature and executive, Alaska government does more or less represent the state, regional, and local opinions of the public.

Finally, despite public skepticism, virtually every public official—and particularly elected officials—in Alaska and throughout the nation, are concerned about what the public thinks about issues and the current political goings-on. Most legislators start their day by looking at newspapers, their e-mails, social media, and being briefed by their staff on communications from their constituents.

Public Attitudes toward Government in Alaska

Box 20.2 presents findings from a sample survey of Alaskans by Dittman Research conducted for the Alaska State Senate in April 2007. The findings reflect general opinions on government and the state's political leaders and attitudes toward moving from a citizen to a professional legislature. The survey responses on political leadership (where 68 percent thought the leadership was generally good) appears to contradict the responses on the issue of ethics in government (where 54 percent saw it as a serious problem). This

BOX 20.2

Alaskans' Attitudes to Government

Question: Overall, what's your impression of Alaska's political leadership in Juneau at the present time, do they seem to be working well together and better than in other years, or not?

Better	Not Better	Not Sure
68%	17%	15%

Question: Currently, Alaska has a "citizens" legislature, which means that most legislators have jobs outside the legislature. Sometimes that employment can lead to a conflict of interest, so some states have moved to a "professional" legislature where legislators are paid more, and then are not allowed to accept outside employment. Would you support or oppose a change from a citizen's legislature to a professional legislature in Alaska?

Opposed This Change	Supported This Change	Responded Unsure
66%	29%	5%

Question: Do you feel a lack of ethics is or is not a serious problem in Alaska's state government these days?

Felt is a Serious Problem	Felt is Not a Serious Problem	Responded Unsure
54%	40%	6%

Source: Developed by Laura Savatgy from information from the Alaskan Public Leadership and Legislative Overview prepared by the Dittman Research Corporation for the Alaska State Senate, April 2007. Reprinted with permission.

survey was taken before the VECO and related scandals were major news stories, and one would expect those scandals to increase public skepticism regarding the ethics of public officials. Clearly, Alaskans also oppose the idea of a professional legislature even though, in effect, the state has such a professional body.[42]

The three survey questions in Box 20.2 do not, of course, purport to assess the impact of public opinion on particular policy issues. The two case studies presented below address the questions of how public opinion affects policy decisions and whether public opinion has an impact on the decisions being made by the Alaska legislature.

The Influence of Majority Public Opinion: Two Contrasting Examples

Fiscal and environmental issues in Alaska are often addressed in public forums. A prominent fiscal issue is the use of Permanent Fund earnings, and an ongoing developer versus environmentalist issue is opening the Arctic National Wildlife Refuge (ANWR).

Use of Permanent Fund Earnings

Before former Governor Palin released her fiscal year 2009 (FY 09) budget, she conducted a survey titled "Voices Across Alaska," which asked questions about investing for Alaska's future, and state savings priorities favored by Alaskans set out in Table 20.2. One of these concerns is the often intensely debated issue of the use of Permanent Fund earnings and the Permanent Fund Dividend (PFD). Interestingly, however, as a subject of public concern, the Permanent Fund is ranked second from the bottom in this survey. This is an example of where government, at least so far, is listening to the public. Public officials are very well aware that Alaskans want their PFD every year and generally do not support policy makers who want to use earnings from the fund for any other purpose. Along the lines of Weissberg's concerns, however, one can raise the question of whether or not government should be listening to the public on this issue as opposed to designing and implementing a long-term fiscal plan that may involve other uses for fund earnings. Public attitudes to the fund and the PFD are dealt with more extensively in Chapter 25 on the Permanent Fund, which includes a table of public opinion on the fund over a twenty-five-year period.[43]

The Arctic National Wildlife Refuge—ANWR

ANWR provides an example of where the majority of Alaska public opinion favors a policy allowing oil and gas exploration and development in the Refuge, the federal government (both the White House and Congress) does not share this opinion, and the American public is almost evenly divided on opening ANWR.[44] In this case, Alaska public opinion has little or no influence over this issue, primarily because ANWR is located on federal land, and national public opinion trumps Alaska opinion. As Figure 20.1 (on page 724) indicates, a majority of Alaskans favor the opening of ANWR. This opinion remained constant for twenty years from 1990 through 2009, the latest year a poll is available, but it is likely that this opinion persists given the consistency of this attitude over time.[45] The debate continues nationally, but so far those opposing opening the Refuge have won out.

This is a classic example of where external forces, in this case the federal government and national interest groups like the environmentalist group the Sierra Club, override public opinion shared by a large majority of Alaskans. This is partly why many Alaskans have an antipathy towards the federal government and other external influences on state policy.

3. THE INTERRELATIONSHIP OF THE MEDIA AND PUBLIC OPINION

So far this chapter has considered the roles of the media and public opinion separately. To be sure, in many cases each operates independently of the other, but they also

TABLE 20.2

Alaskans' Opinions in 2009 on the State's Savings Priorities

SAVING PRIORITIES	FIRST PRIORITY	SECOND PRIORITY	THIRD PRIORITY	FOURTH PRIORITY	FIFTH PRIORITY	SIXTH PRIORITY
The Constitutional Budget Reserve Fund Constitutionally created savings account. Accessing funds in this account requires a 3/4 vote of the Legislature. Payback of more than $5 billion in CBR spending is required by law.	10.9% (1,085)	10.6% (1,056)	12.2% (1,217)	16.4% (1,638)	25.1% (2,504)	24.9% (2,481)
The Permanent Fund The balance of the Permanent Fund is more than $40 billion. The fund was created to provide a means of conserving a portion of the stat's revenue from mineral resources to benefit all generations of Alaskans.	11.2% (1,125)	12.6% (1,258)	13.4% (1,340)	14.4% (1,447)	19.7% (1,975)	28.7% (2,870)
A Public Education Fund This fund allows money to be saved to help meet future needs in our K–12 education system. Last year $1 billion was appropriated to provide early funding.	25.9% (2,625)	24.1% (2,443)	17.7% (1,795)	14.7% (1,488)	10.5% (1,064)	7.2% (731)
The Public Employee and Teacher Retirement Systems—PERS and TERS State and municipal governments and local school districts face an unfunded liability of more than $8 billion due to rising retirement costs. Current state appropriations total more than $450 million a year to pay this debt. Appropriations into the fund can have a significant impact on reducing the ongoing operating costs for the state and free up additional funds for local governments and school districts.	29.7% (3,048)	21.9% (2,249)	15.8% (1,626)	12.4% (1,269)	10.7% (1,100)	9.5% (973)
Energy The House has passed legislation that would create an alternative energy fund. If capitalized, the fund could generate interest to be used to help increase the use of alternative energy and lower the cost of energy for Alaskans.	13.3% (1,362)	16.9% (1,729)	20.4% (2,087)	19.8% (2,026)	15.5% (1,586)	13.9% (1,417)
Transportation and Infrastructure Alaska has enormous transportation infrastructure needs. Maintaining and improving our transportation infrastructure will be an ever-increasing challenge in light of decreasing federal transportation dollars. Alaska's transportation system must be ready to accommodate the construction of a gas pipeline, and getting too far behind on maintaining our roads will become a public safety issue. Funds can be saved specifically to help the state meet future transportation needs.	12.2% (1,238)	15.7% (1,598)	21.0% (2,141)	21.3% (2,164)	16.5% (1,681)	13.3% (1,357)

Source: Adapted by Laura Savatgy from a document obtained from Governor Palin's office, February 10, 2009.

FIGURE 20.1

Alaska Public Opinion on Opening ANWR for Oil and Gas Exploration: Ten Surveys from 1990 to 2009

Question: What is your opinion of oil and gas exploration in the Arctic National Wildlife Refuge, usually referred to as ANWR? Do you feel oil and gas exploration *should* or *should not* be allowed in that area?

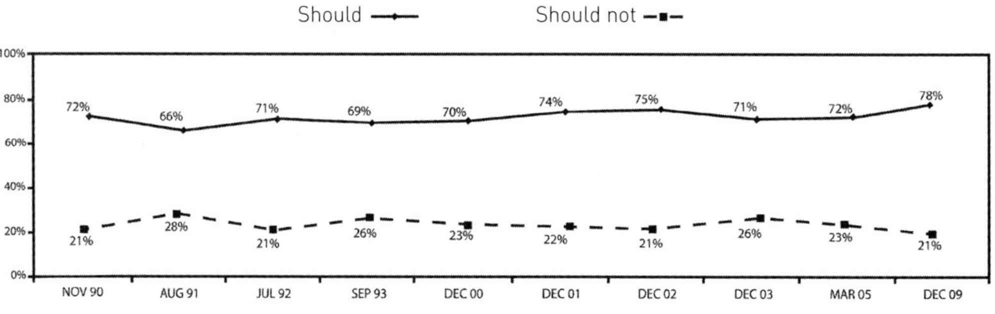

Source: Reprinted with permission from: http://www.dittmanresearch.com/.

interrelate or play off each other from time to time in politics and the public-policy process. Sometimes the media uses public opinion—either formal polls or its own informal assessments of that opinion—to augment its factual coverage of an issue or to perform its watchdog role. Similarly, interest groups or individuals often enlist the press to push their causes, sometimes in concert with legislators or executive officials, to generate public opinion on an issue. In some cases, this press-public opinion interaction is highly orchestrated. At other times it is less organized and may occur in a more ad hoc way.

One example of orchestrated attempts to influence public opinion is when legislators and the executive branch issue press releases. Both the majority and minority caucuses in each house of the legislature have press secretaries to assist in this and other public communications activities, as does the governor. Box 20.3 details an example of the interrelationship of public opinion and the press by explaining the role of the governor's press secretary. The press secretary works to get the word out through the press and by other means to both inform and sometimes influence public opinion regarding the governor's actions and policies.

The media can certainly be very helpful to a group trying to get the word out on its issue. But launching an orchestrated strategy of enlisting the media to promote a cause or issue can also go awry if the group is not careful. There are thousands of stories about neophyte group members who did not understand the role of the media and got burned,

BOX 20.3

The Governor's Press Secretary: An Insider's Perspective

Public communication is critical to the success of any administration, never more so than in today's 24/7 news cycle. To advance any policy goal, Alaska's governor needs to effectively communicate across the broad geographic and political divides that separate the Alaska public.

The person given that assignment is the press secretary: a high-profile yet often thankless job where burnout and turnover is endemic. Having survived eight years in that role in the Knowles administration, let me offer some thoughts about the job, what works, and what doesn't.

First, while the fundamentals of public communications are the same, including being honest, candid, and accessible, working as the governor's press secretary is much more than a run-of-the-mill corporate communications job.

At the highest level of state government, the only problems on your desk are the intractable ones. Issues only reach the governor's office if they can't be solved at a lower level. We had our share: billion-dollar budget deficits thanks to $9-a-barrel oil, natural disasters, parochial in-state disputes, and world affairs that touched our shores.

Add in local politics. During Knowles's terms, the Republican opposition boasted a "veto-proof" majority. To advance any public policy goal, we had to muster overwhelming public support, especially among our opponents' constituents.

Knowles had a communications team that lasted the entire two terms. I don't suggest we did everything right, but here are a few things that were important.

First, respect the media's role as a political watchdog and know how it works. All of us in Knowles's press office had experience as journalists. I worked as a public radio reporter in Dillingham for seventeen years. We understood the media's job and respected their deadlines. Some politicians want to ignore the press or think the press can be easily manipulated. Go ahead, try your best to spin them; tell them "no comment" when you have to, but ignore the media at your peril.

Second, the press secretary must have the confidence of and access to the governor. Press secretaries who do not enjoy such access are doomed to failure.

Third, media planning works best when it is coordinated within the policy development process. Decisions during the Knowles administration were made in a disciplined, four-step process: (1) ensuring internal alignment within the administration; (2) vetting proposed policy with affected constituent groups; (3) consulting with key legislators; and (4) having a media plan. This disciplined approach to policy making served Knowles well in advancing his goals.

Fourth, generate depth within the administration in dealing with the press. Claire Richardson's work on media training for cabinet members and key department personnel was a great strength within the administration so they could handle the press on their own. This relieved the pressure on the governor's office and better served the media.

Finally: Don't let it go to your head. Working in a rarefied atmosphere with political egos and ambitions on the line, scoop-hungry reporters bearing bright TV lights, and a backdrop of glad-handing lobbyists, it's easy to get an inflated sense of self importance. Early in the Knowles administration we were all warned about what was called the "ego virus." It was a good caution.

At bottom, being press secretary is just another high-stress, high-visibility public job. It is best done by remembering that ultimately you are not just serving your governor but the public.

Source: Robert W. (Bob) King served as Press Secretary to Governor Tony Knowles from 1994 to 2002.

with resultant bad feeling toward the press. They thought that they were going to get a straight report on their issue and how important it was, but the reporter found an opposing viewpoint, and the news story may have even been detrimental to the group's cause.

One example of less coordinated but nevertheless significant interactions of the media and public opinion on issues is the corruption scandals centered around VECO considered earlier in the chapter, which helped lead to increased regulation of lobbyists. A second example is the long-standing issue of moving the state capital from Juneau to the Anchorage area. The issue of the capital move was explained in overview in Chapter 2 (see Box 2.4). In Box 20.4 the focus is on the interaction of public opinion and the press in promoting and opposing the move.

4. CONCLUSION: HOW INFLUENTIAL AND WHAT OF THE FUTURE?

In the introduction we asked the question: How important is the media and public opinion in the Alaska public policy-making process, and under what circumstances will either or both be influential? The short answer is that in both cases it depends on many factors, including the nature of the issue, the political environment at the time, and the interrelationship of the press and public opinion. In short, there are no hard and fast rules as to the influence of the two forces on public policy.

So what can be expected in the future regarding the press and public opinion in Alaska politics and policy making?

Regarding the media, the only certainty in Alaska and elsewhere is uncertainty. Rapidly changing technology and reading habits indicate that some forms of the press, particularly hardcopy newspapers, are undergoing major changes, and although they may not disappear, they may be a smaller part of political news sources than at their zenith. The role of the press in politics is also getting blurrier. As traditional outlets decline or fail, they are replaced by more partisan, less professional, and less reliable media outlets. The ideal of an objective, professionally trained press reporting verifiable facts is being replaced by a million strident voices shaping facts to suit their opinions. While the watchdog role of the press may not turn into a lapdog role, it is now possible for people to go through life reading and listening only to views that simply echo their own opinions, without ever having those opinions challenged. In the 1990s few would have predicted the shift to web pages and blogs, so making predictions is fraught with uncertainty.

Public opinion will always have a role in Alaska politics and policy making. But how significant a role it will have is less clear. Elected officials will always consider and posture for the public when re-election is their goal. Plus, the trend in increased polling and the expression of public opinion through traditional means, as well as new technologies, are

BOX 20.4

The Interrelationship of the Press and Public Opinion: A Case Study of the Capital Move Issue

The issue of moving the capital has many elements for a good press story, including controversy, regional loyalties, and economic benefits and losses. And as most Alaskans have an opinion on whether the capital should be moved, public opinion clearly plays a role in the discussion. How has this interplay between the press and public opinion been evident over the years? Has it affected the outcome of the debate?

The press was largely responsible for raising the capital move issue starting in the 1960s when Bob Atwood, publisher of the former *Anchorage Daily Times*, used the paper to advocate moving the capital closer to the population center in Anchorage. Using the *Times* as a pulpit, he subsequently backed two ballot initiatives on the issue.

In recent years though, reporting on the issue is more informational than promotional and tends to reflect regional perspectives. For example, the *Anchorage Daily News* supported holding a legislative special session in Anchorage in June 2007, a stance that differed markedly from that of the *Juneau Empire*. The *Daily News* highlighted the ease of accessibility that was available to all Alaska residents. In contrast, the *Empire* reported the waning crowd of Alaska residents who claimed they need access yet did not remain for even one full day of the Anchorage special session.

Another perspective is that of the *Fairbanks Daily News-Miner* in regard to Governor Palin's unprecedented decision to hold her inauguration in Fairbanks instead of the traditional location of the capital city. The *News-Miner* reflected Fairbanks public opinion affirming support for Juneau as the capital while enjoying the governor's inclusion of Fairbanks as an inaugural venue. Reflecting Southeast Alaska opinion, the *Empire* saw the decision as a snub and certain proof that the governor did not appreciate the current capital location.

These examples illustrate an important aspect of the interrelationship between the press and public opinion on this issue. In particular, press reporting reflects, to a large extent, the opinions of its region and its readership.

Public opinion also manifests itself in various other ways. These include the signatures gathered to support ballot initiatives relating to a possible capital move, the formation of pro- and anti-capital move groups (most notably Juneau's anti-move, city-funded "Alaska Committee"), the public votes on the nine ballot measures that have appeared on the ballot since 1960, legislative action as a result of constituent pressure, and the public polling that occurs on the topic.

Regarding public opinion polling, in 2002 when the most recent ballot initiative to move legislative sessions to the Anchorage area was voted down, Dittman Research found that the majority of Alaskans did want to move the capital. However, the polling question did not take into consideration the cost of the move. Cost disclosure on capital move initiatives was guaranteed in 1994 when Alaska voters approved the Fiscally Responsible Alaskans Needing Knowledge (FRANK) initiative. This initiative has proven to be a strong countermeasure to the capital move. Thus, Dittman's exclusion of cost undermines the validity of this particular poll and highlights the challenge of accurately measuring public opinion.

In the contentious issue of Alaska's capital move, the press and public opinion undoubtedly play an influential role. However, from a scientific perspective it is difficult to say that one has influenced the issue more than the other. Other factors also come into play, such as the economic interest groups, cities, and regions that stand to gain or lose, and the personalities of leading public officials like the governor (Governor Sheffield, 1982–1986, was against the move, and Governor Palin, 2006–2009, favored it). Given the intense nature of the debate over the years and its direct effect on legislators, it is probably most accurate to see the role of the press and public opinion as one interrelated force on this policy issue.

Source: Developed by Ashley Anderson, former University of Alaska Legislative Intern and a social science graduate of the University of Alaska Southeast.

likely to bring increased pressure on public officials to take public opinion into account in decision making.

In a democracy like Alaska's, the debate over whether or not public officials should be delegates or representatives in relation to public opinion will be never-ending. And these officials will continue to claim allegiance to both perspectives, sometimes even playing them off against each other depending on the issue at hand and their particular political perspective and goals.

ENDNOTES

[1] The division of labor on this chapter was as follows. Mike Doogan did most of the work on the press and Laura Savatgy on public opinion. Clive Thomas added other parts, including the purchase of the *Anchorage Daily News* by the *Alaska Dispatch*, one case study, and the interrelationship of the media and public opinion.

[2] For a fuller consideration of the role of both the media and public opinion in a democracy and in American politics in particular, see the Further Reading at the end of this book, Section 6.

[3] U.S. Agency for International Development, *The Role of Media in a Democracy: A Strategic Approach*, at http://www.usaid.gov/policy/ads/200/200sbc.pdf.

[4] Thomas Jefferson to Edward Carrington, Jan. 16, 1787, Papers 11: 48–49, at http://presspubs.uchicago.edu/founders/documents/amendIspeechs8.html, edited by Philip B. Kurland and Ralph Lerner. *The Founders Constitution*, Amendment I (Speech and Press), Document 8, 16 January 1787, Papers 11: 48–49. http://press-pubs.uchicago.edu/founders; and Thomas Jefferson to John Norvell, 1807. ME 11: 225 http://etext.virginia.edu/jefferson/quotations/jeff1600.htm 1995. Eyler Robert Coates, Sr., *Thomas Jefferson on Politics and Government, Quotations from the Writings of Thomas Jefferson*, The University of Virginia, *Jefferson Online Quotations*, at http://etext.virginia.edu/jefferson/quotations/.

[5] Quote by Adlai Stevenson from "Undermining Digg: Special Interest Groups vs. News-ranking Sites," by Stephen Strauss, *CBC News and Analysis*, April 16, 2008, at http://www.cbc.ca/news/viewpoint/vp_strauss/20080416.html.

[6] The authors thank Harry Walker of the *Alaska Media Directory* (published annually in Anchorage by Sally B. Blackford and Harry M. Walker) for his aid in providing a historical overview of the traditional Alaska press and particularly statistics. The publication was disocontinued in 2015.

[7] See the *Alaska Media Directory* for 1985, 1993, and 2015.

[8] *Alaska Dispatch*, information retrieved on March 1, 2011, at http://www.alaskadispatch.com/AboutUs.

[9] See for example, Lori Townsend, "Former ADN Executive Editor Pat Dougherty Speaks on Newspaper's Sale," *Alaska News Nightly*, Alaska Public Radio Network (APRN), May 19, 2014.

[10] Mark Thiessen, "On-line Rival to Buy Anchorage Daily News for $34 Million," *The Seattle Times*, April 8, 2014.

[11] "Newspaper," Alliance for Audited Media, Audit Bureau of Circulations: Total Circulation: February 17, 2013 at http://abcas3.auditedmedia.com/ecirc/newsform.asp and "eCirc," Audit Bureau of Circulations: Schaumburg, Ill.: January 2007 at http://abacs3.accessabc.com/ecirc/index.html.

[12] "Newspaper," Alliance for Audited Media; and "eCirc," Audit Bureau of Circulations.

[13] Richard A. Fineberg, "The Press and Alaska Politics," in *Alaska State Government and Politics*, eds., Gerald A. McBeath and Thomas A. Morehouse (Fairbanks: University of Alaska Press, 1987), 217; and figures provided by Harry Walker from the various edition of the *Alaska Media Directory*.

[14] "The Fallout from the Telecommunications Act of 1996: Unintended Consequences and Lessons Learned," *Common Cause*, May 9, 2005, 3, retrieved October 2, 2015, at/ http/::www.commoncause.org:research-reports:National_050905_Fallout_From_The_Telecommunications_Act_2.pdf.

[15] In recent years the ownership of various forms of media has changed more frequently than in the past. See the 2015 edition of the *Alaska Media Directory* for current ownership of newspapers, radio, and TV stations.

[16] Sheila Toomey, "Radio Heat: Rick Rydell's Brash Style of Entertainment May be Helping Shape Anchorage Politics," *Anchorage Daily News*, April 13, 2003.

[17] Robert Dillon, "An Alaskan Abroad," at http://alaskanabroad.typepad.com/; "Amandacoyne.com: "Inside Alaska Politics . . . So you don't have to be," at Amandacoyne.Com; and "Mudflats: Tiptoeing Through the Muck of Alaskan Politics," at http://www.themudflats.net/. Also, former APRN political reporter, Dave Donaldson, the author of Box 20.1, has over the years occasionally written a political blog that can be found at AKJ3.com.

[18] See the *Anchorage Daily Planet*, at http://www.anchoragedailyplanet.com/.

[19] Mike Doogan reviewed microfilm copies of the newspaper for these statistics.

[20] Mike Doogan gathered the information on the Juneau press corps and on the causes of turnover from interviews with members of the press corps.

[21] Richard Mauer, "Allen to Open a New Chapter in Powerful Alaska Career," *Anchorage Daily News*, November 21, 1989.

[22] This information is summarized from extensive news accounts, especially those by the *Anchorage Daily News* and KTUU television in Anchorage.

[23] "Compass: Governor's inadequate response to Alaska National Guard sexual assault complaints," *Alaska Dispatch News*, June 25, 2014; and Richard Mauer and Jill Burke, "Parnell waited years to take direct action on National Guard misconduct," *Alaska Dispatch News*, October 1, 2014.

[24] Becky Bohrer, Associate Press (AP), "Alaska Guard Adjutant General Resigns Amid Scandal," Military.com, September 5, 2014; and Jill Burke "Military and Veterans Affairs official resigns at Parnell's request," *Alaska Dispatch News*, September 25, 2014.

[25] Mauer and Burke, "Parnell waited years to take direct action on National Guard misconduct."

[26] Alexandra Gutierrez, "Parnell on Defense Over National Guard Response," *Alaska News Nightly*, APRN, October 2, 2014.

[27] "Parnell fires more National Guard leaders; Walker says 'too little, too late,'" KTVA CBS 11 News, Anchorage, October 20, 2014.

[28] David Holthouse, "The Three-Headed Monster," *The Anchorage Press*, October 15, 2014.

[29] Alexandra Gutierrez, "Top Parnell Aide Outlines National Guard Response Timeline," *Alaska News Nightly*, APRN, November 3, 2014.

[30] Gutierrez, "Parnell on Defense Over National Guard Response."

[31] Rosemary R. Wiener, "Is big fee hike another rip-off by the Murkowski administration?" *Anchorage Daily News*, June 22, 2004.

[32] See Chapter 3, Section 3.

[33] Social media, particularly Facebook and Twitter, are increasingly used in politics, particularly to organize people for demonstrations and also as an informal way for both the public and politicians to communicate with one another. However, the role of social media is not yet clear or formalized as a public opinion tool in the United States or in Alaska. Therefore, we have not included it in this chapter.

[34] Carroll J. Glynn, Susan Herbst, Garrett J. O'Keefe, Robert Y. Shapiro, and Mark Lindeman, *Public Opinion*, 2nd ed. (Boulder, CO: Westview Press, 2004), 81.

[35] Robert Weissberg, "Why Policymakers Should Ignore Public Opinion Polls," *Policy Analysis*, no. 402 (May 29, 2001), 1.

[36] Jeffery E. Cohen, *Public Opinion in State Politics* (Stanford, CA: Stanford University Press, 2006), 200.

[37] Ann O'M. Bowman and Richard C. Kearney, *State and Local Government*, 7th ed. (Boston: Houghton-Mifflin, 2008), 99.

[38] Weissberg, "Why Policymakers Should Ignore Public Opinion Polls," 1.

[39] *Ibid.*

[40] Bowman and Kearney, *State and Local Government*, 99.

[41] See Chapter 5, especially Section 7.

[42] Since the late 1970s Alaska's legislature has been consistently ranked among the top quarter of states in terms of staff support and the pay of legislators and is generally considered to be a professional legislature. See, Keith E. Hamm and Gary F. Moncrief, "Legislative Politics in the States," in *Politics in the American States: A Comparative Analysis*, eds., Virginia Gray, Russell L. Hanson, and Thad Kousser, 10th ed. (Washington, D.C.: Congressional Quarterly Press. 2013), Table 6.1, 164–65.

[43] See Chapter 25, Table 25.4.

[44] In a 2011 nationwide Gallop Poll, for example, 49 percent of Americans surveyed supported exploration in ANWR, 45 percent opposed it, and 6 percent had no opinion."Latest GALLUP Shows Majority Support for ANWR," ANWR.org, at http://www.anwr.org/Latest-News/Latest-GALLUP-Shows-Majority-Support-for-ANWR.php.

[45] Polls may have been conducted since 2009 for private organizations but none is available to the public at the time of writing. Dittman Research, the source of the polls in Figure 20.1, no longer makes its surveys available to the public online.

★ PART IV ★

Issues and Policies Generated by the Political Economy of the Owner State

About Part IV

Parts I through III of the book provide perspectives on the *Beliefs, Institutions, Personalities, and Power* that shape Alaska politics and government. These factors determine what policies are enacted and in what form, and which ones get short shrift or never reach the policy agenda. In this part and in Part V of the book we examine the major issues and policies that Alaska politics has generated over the years and that will continue to be at the forefront of state politics for years to come. Part IV deals with natural resources–related issues and policies and Part V with issues and policies regarding major state services.

Each chapter in Part IV has a dual purpose. One is to explain the various aspects of the substance of its particular policy area and place them in comparison with other states. The other purpose is a broader one, in line with one of the major goals of the book—to show how these particular issues and policies shed light on Alaska politics and public policy making. In this regard, all five chapters in Part IV illustrate several characteristics of Alaska politics set out in Chapter 2, offer examples of types of distributive, redistributive, and regulatory policies as explained in Chapter 3, and explore different power dynamics in the making of policies in their particular policy areas.

The image of Alaska in the Lower 48 states is largely of a wilderness, and there is a need felt among many to preserve this Last Frontier for American posterity. This attitude provides a major insight into the politics of the policy areas concerned with natural resources that are considered in this part of the book, all of which are products of Alaska's natural resource political economy. The five chapters in Part IV have three related common elements threading through them. One is that the issues and policies described in the chapters are generated by the political economy of the Owner State, which in turn affects policies toward the Owner State. The second and third elements are that all five chapters involve the Alaska political characteristics of external influences and four of them involve that of the conflict between economic development and environmentalism. The exception is the chapter on the Permanent Fund.

Chapter 21 on natural resources and the Owner State presents an overview of the economic and political realities and policy dynamics of these resources. It explores the range of interests involved in natural resources policy making, the central issues of user conflicts over resources, particularly land, and the complexities of the intergovernmental relations (IGR) involved in this often contentious policy area. User conflicts and whether to develop or not develop Alaska's resources are major aspects of Chapter 22 on the politics of Alaska's environment. Working to resolve conflicts between and among developers, environmentalists, Alaska's Owner State interests, and the national interest, is an ongoing aspect of Alaska's environmental politics.

Besides a spectacular wilderness teeming with wildlife, and these days the image of Sarah Palin's Alaska, three other images of Alaska that come to mind among people outside the state are fish, oil, and the "giveaway" Permanent Fund Dividend (PFD) program. These are the subjects of Chapters 23, 24, and 25 respectively. Among other things, Chapter 23 on fisheries explains the problems of having unregulated access to commercial fisheries, the conflicts among commercial, sports, and subsistence fishing, and the IGR nature of fisheries policy.

Chapter 24 on oil and gas examines the advantages and disadvantages of being an energy producing state and compares Alaska's so-called oil regime—the way it goes about generating and attempting to stabilize revenue given the volatility of the price of oil—with that of other oil regimes around the world. Part IV concludes with Chapter 25 on the Alaska Permanent Fund and the PFD. The chapter explains the state's approach to conserving oil revenues as another aspect of the role of the Owner State. Particularly with regard to the PFD, likely one of the most popular policies ever developed by any government in the United States, this aspect of state public policy manifests several characteristics of Alaska politics, including pragmatic dependent individualism and fiscal conservatism.

★ CHAPTER 21 ★

Natural Resources and the Owner State: Economic and Political Realities and Policy Dynamics

Anthony T. Nakazawa, Robert F. Gorman, George Goldman, and Clive S. Thomas

Most tourists come to Alaska to enjoy its physical beauty and abundant wildlife. Some no doubt leave with an idealized view of Alaskans enjoying their natural resources in the same way. What many visitors probably do not realize is that these resources—the land, the wildlife, including fish and marine mammals, and Alaska's subsurface resources—are the source of some of the most intense, often emotional, political conflicts facing Alaskans, both within the state and in relation to Outside forces. During the years since statehood, disputes over the use of natural resources have been a central element in Alaska politics. Their resolution has required a great deal of time and effort on the part of elected and appointed officials in both Juneau and Washington, D.C.

Explaining the nature of the conflicts over natural resource uses, the resulting politics and policy approaches, the various groups and interests involved, and the political power dynamics among them is one of the two purposes of this chapter. This explanation provides essential background for the rest of the chapters in Part IV as well as for the second purpose of this chapter, which is to explain perspectives on how these conflicts affect land use. The major components of natural resource politics and policy making—land, the environment, fisheries, oil and gas, and, to some extent, the health of the Permanent Fund—are interrelated and, from a practical perspective, it is often difficult to separate them. Nevertheless, many land issues and policies can be treated as separate topics, even though they may affect other aspects of natural resource politics.

As natural resources are central to the state's politics, it is not surprising that all twelve of the characteristics of Alaska politics identified in Chapter 2 are manifested in some way in natural resource politics. Five characteristics, however, will be particularly evident when we apply them to land issues in the second half of this chapter.

The first part of the chapter consists of five sections. The first deals with the general terminology of natural resource politics and includes a natural resources and environmental map of Alaska as well as a timeline of major events in Alaska's natural resource development. Then in Section 2 we consider the major issues in natural resource policy from both a historical and contemporary perspective. Sections 3 and 4 identify the policy participants and the major issues and conflicts involved, and Section 5 provides a brief comparison of natural resource issues in Alaska with those of other states. Section 6 deals specifically with the politics of land use and the complexity of land issues. Section 7 presents three case studies illustrating these complexities. A fourth case study in Section 8 covers the issues surrounding the development of the Arctic National Wildlife Refuge (ANWR). The chapter's conclusion links land issues to the other four natural resource chapters of Part IV.

1. MAJOR TERMS, GEOGRAPHY, AND HISTORICAL TIMELINE

Many of the general terms and concepts used in this chapter relating to natural resources, such as the Alaska National Interest Lands Conservation Act (ANILCA) and the National Petroleum Reserve-Alaska (NPR-A), are explained in the glossary at the end of the book. Other terms specific to particular types of natural resources, such as fish and oil and gas, are explained in the appropriate places in this and the following four chapters that make up Part IV of the book. There are, however, particular terms and federal laws referred to in most of the chapters in Part IV, particularly in this chapter and Chapter 22 on environmental politics, that are not covered in the glossary or that need particular emphasis. These terms are explained in Box 21.1. Map 21.1 shows the locations of current and proposed natural resource developments and other areas of current and historical significance to resource development in Alaska.

The Evolving Meaning of *Natural Resources* and the Developer-Conservationist/ Environmentalist Perspectives

The meaning of the term *natural resources* has evolved over time, and this has very much affected natural resource politics. Traditionally, the term included only the land and what was on or under it, such as timber, oil and gas, coal, gold, and other minerals, plus water and fish and wildlife resources.

Distinguishing between Conservation and Environmentalism

Today the term *natural resources* has a much broader meaning than it once did. To understand this it is useful to explain the difference between the terms *conservation* and *environmentalism*. The two are often used interchangeably, and there are several similarities that revolve around the word *conserve*. Both terms were products of the Progressive era (c. 1900–1920), but there are major differences between them.

BOX 21.1

Key Natural Resources Terms and Laws

SPECIALIZED TERMS LISTED ALPHABETICALLY

Co-management: The joint administration of a policy by two or more governments or quasi-governments, such as the federal and state government in fisheries, and various levels of government and Native organizations in regard to land management.

d2 lands: Shorthand for section 17(d)(2) of the Alaska Native Claims Settlement Act (ANCSA) of 1971 and the lands it directed to be set aside for wilderness areas. It was implemented by the federal government in the Alaska National Interest Lands Conservation Act (ANILCA) of 1980.

Environmental Impact Statement (EIS): A document describing potential environmental effects of a proposed development, required by federal law before a project may proceed. Since 1970, the requirement for an EIS applies to all federal projects and all projects requiring federal permits or receiving federal funding.

Limited entry: A policy adopted in Alaska in 1972 by constitutional amendment limiting the number of people who can fish in various fisheries. The policy is administered by a three-member Limited Entry Commission.

Mental Health Trust Lands: These are lands managed by the Alaska Mental Health Trust Authority to generate revenues to provide services to the mentally disabled. Set up in 1956 in Territorial days, much controversy surrounded the trust in the 1980s and 1990s when a group of citizens, with help from the courts, brought about restoration of these lands after the state had violated the terms of the trust relating to their use.

Predator control: The reducing of natural predation, particularly wolves, on big game animals for the benefit of human consumers. Usually this is done through killing predators in more effective ways than by general hunting and trapping.

Renewable versus non-renewable resources: The former are resources that can be replenished, such as timber reforestation (replanting trees after logging activity) and managing stocks of fish and game to allow them to reproduce. The latter are resources like gold and oil and gas that, once taken from the ground, are gone forever.

Sustainable development: Emphasizes environmental quality as a condition of economic development, so that development does not deprive future generations of the benefits of such quality.

FEDERAL LAWS LISTED CHRONOLOGICALLY

National Environmental Policy Act (NEPA) 1970: Established national policy for protecting the environment, created the Environmental Protection Agency (EPA), and requires EISs for certain projects.

Marine Mammal Protection Act (MMPA), 1972: Reversed federal policy of paying bounties to kill certain marine mammals in favor of a hunting ban, due to conservation concerns. Because of their historical dependence on certain species, Alaska Native villages succeeded in obtaining an exemption from the hunting ban for subsistence needs.

Coastal Zone Management Act (CZMA), 1972: Encourages coastal states to develop coastal zone management plans. The act's goal is to preserve, protect, develop, and, if possible, restore or enhance, the resources of the nation's coastal zone for present and future generations.

Endangered Species Act (ESA), 1973: Designed to identify wildlife species in danger of becoming extinct due to consequences of economic growth and development and provide them with adequate protection.

Magnuson-Stevens Fishery Conservation and Management Act, 1976: Sets up regional councils to manage fisheries in the two-hundred-mile Exclusive Economic Zone (EEZ). Alaska is included in the North Pacific Fishery Management Council (NPFMC).

Sustainable Fisheries Act, 1996: Expanded the authority of regional fisheries councils, including provisions to consider the effects of management decisions on communities, protect essential fish habitats, and reduce bycatch (fish caught incidentally when fishing for another species).

Source: Compiled by the authors.

MAP 21.1

Natural Resources and Environmental Map of Alaska

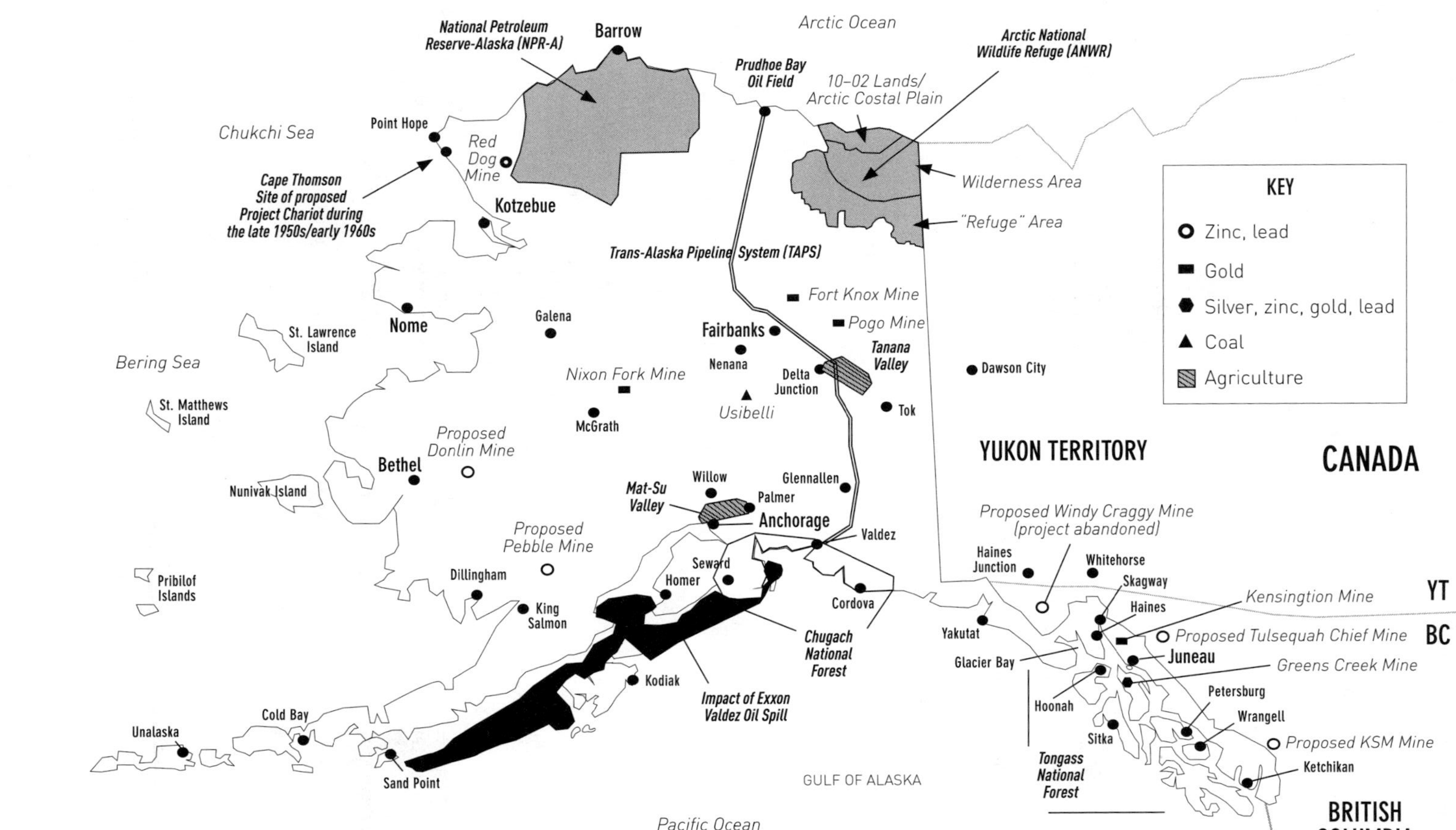

Source: Developed by the authors.

Conservation has its origins in the response to the degradation of the landscape that resulted from deforestation and agricultural settlement. It comes from a rural, agricultural perspective and is founded in a pragmatic view of "wise use"—that humans need to restore and manage the environment in order to sustain the economic benefits that accrue from it. A conservationist plants trees but also cuts them down, restores wildlife habitat but also hunts. Thus conservation is human-centered and can be described as protecting nature for humans. Up until the 1960s, conservationism was the province of individual voluntary efforts as opposed to being mandated and enforced by government.

Environmentalism, on the other hand, is a response to the destruction of the natural environment caused largely by pollution from the industrialization of the landscape and comes from a more urban perspective. It is not grounded in promoting purely human benefit but in advocating the intrinsic value of nature, and is more idealistic than conservation. Environmentalism holds that there is something special about natural things, such as birds, animals, marine life, trees, plants, and their habitats. These, its proponents argue, need to be protected and preserved, not just in the general sense, but with respect to particular species. Thus, environmentalism can be described as protecting nature from humans. An environmentalist might plant trees, but would likely protest against logging them, and would protect wildlife rather than hunt it. Environmentalists see government action as the most effective way to implement their perspective.

These explanations of the conservationist and environmentalist perspectives are simplifications, but they provide the gist of each. In practice, it is best to see the two perspectives along with that of developers as points on a spectrum, as we explain next.

An Expanded Definition of Natural Resources and the Spectrum of Perspectives

The conservationist perspective was the dominant one for the first half of the twentieth century. Then, beginning in the 1960s, environmentalism gradually became the dominant view of the physical environment. As a result, added to the traditional definition of natural resources as physical assets were natural beauty, clean air and water, and wilderness, as these attributes have economic value, as do wind and water power for generating electricity. Plus, many aspects of this broader concept of natural resources, particularly clean air and water, enhance both the economic and noneconomic quality of life for the residents of a particular area.

This contemporary and broad definition of natural resources underlies much of the conflict between developers and environmentalists and thus forms much of the substance of natural resource politics. In essence, the developer-environmentalist conflict involves contending philosophies of how human beings should relate to the natural world. In its basic form the conflict is best understood as a spectrum of values. At one end of the spectrum are uncompromising economic development advocates and at the other end are die-hard environmentalists, with various combinations in between.[1] Conservationists are somewhere in the middle, veering slightly toward the developer end of the spectrum.

The broad category of developers includes, among others, a number of groups and individuals ranging from those who stand to gain economically (such as mining and lumber companies and corporate fishing interests) to conservatives who oppose government regulation on ideological grounds. Generally developers tend to view natural resources in the traditional—pre-1960—sense and as mainly economic assets, as do many conservationists. In contrast, environmentalists, also a broad category, tend to use the contemporary and all-embracing definition of natural resources. Under the broad umbrella of conservationists and environmentalists are those who simply want to conserve resources (as in water and soil conservation) as well as those who want to strike a balance between development and protecting the environment (see the concept of *sustainable development* in Box 21.1) to those who embrace very ideological causes that are less compromising about the use of resources, including wildlife.

As we will see in this chapter and throughout Part IV, even viewing the developer versus conservationist-environmentalist conflict as a spectrum does not tell the whole story of natural resource politics or of the variety of forces lined up on both broad and narrow issues. Political pragmatism often comes into play so that sometimes developers and economic interests embrace the environmental cause and vice versa. The former is the case, for instance, when the tourist industry or oil and mining companies emphasize their commitment to the environment in order to improve their public image. The latter may occur when environmentalists form an ad hoc policy coalition with a development group to achieve a goal such as building a road that will provide access both to an economic development site as well as to parks and recreational facilities.

In other instances, a group may support development in some cases and environmental concerns in others. This is often the case with Alaska Native groups that may, for example, favor development of a mine for local employment while at the same time promoting conservation on other issues such as those related to fish and game to support their subsistence lifestyle.

Box 21.2 is a historical timeline of major natural resource developments in Alaska and includes references to the political conflicts and issues that these developments have generated. But the chronology tells only part of the story of how the political economy of natural resources developed in Alaska. This is because Alaska does not exist in an economic or political vacuum. An enlightening way to view Alaska's natural resource politics, past and present, including land ownership and use, mining, timber, oil and gas, and environmental issues, is to view them as having been shaped simultaneously by the interaction of Outside influences—both national and international—and the political economy of Alaska.

BOX 21.2

Alaska Natural Resource Development: A Political Issue and Public Policy Timeline

1741–1867: Russian control of Alaska and the exploitation of fur-bearing animals.

1867: Purchase of Alaska by the United States from Russia.

1872: Gold discovered near Sitka.

1878: First salmon canneries established at Klawock and Old Sitka in Southeast Alaska.

1880s: Treadwell gold discovery fuels population growth in Juneau.

1891: First oil claims staked in the Cook Inlet area.

1896: Oil discovered at Katalla near Cordova.

1898: Gold discovered on Nome beaches.

1900: Kennecott Mine near Cordova begins producing copper; area population grows quickly.

1906: Peak gold production year in Alaska.

1907: Tongass National Forest in Southeast Alaska created through the efforts of President Theodore Roosevelt.

1912: Alaska granted Territorial status by Congress.

1917: Treadwell Mine closes after tunnel collapse and floods; Juneau population drops.

1920: Federal Mineral Leasing Act opens federal lands to coal, oil, and natural gas exploration and development.

1921: Over four hundred oil exploration permits issued in Alaska.

1922: Texas and Oklahoma oil discoveries flood market, prices crash, Alaska oil exploration stops.

1923: Congress creates National Petroleum Reserve No. 4 (now National Petroleum Reserve-Alaska—NPR-A).

International Pacific Halibut Commission (IPHC) established to regulate the halibut catch in the North Pacific by cooperation between the United States and Canada.

1935: Matanuska Valley Project begins; moved farm families to Alaska from the Midwest and other places.

1938: Copper prices crash; Kennecott Mine closed; area population plummets.

1945: The U.S. government asserts that its Exclusive Economic Zone (EEZ) extends to the continental shelf off its shores, not just the traditional three miles.

1957: Oil discovered at Swanson River on the Kenai Peninsula, marking the start of Cook Inlet oil and gas production.

1958: Alaska Statehood Act provides for transfer of over 100 million acres of land (one-third of Alaska's area) to the State of Alaska.

Project Chariot announced. This was an offshoot of the Atomic Energy Commission's "Atoms for Peace" program. This involved a plan to excavate a harbor on the Chukchi Sea coast of Northwest Alaska using thermonuclear explosives.

1959: Alaska becomes the forty-ninth state.

1963: Congress passes the Clean Air Act. Major amendments made in 1967, 1970, and 1990.

1968: Oil and gas discovered at Prudhoe Bay on the North Slope of Alaska.

1969: Oil lease sale on state lands at Prudhoe Bay brings in $900 million to state coffers.

Project Chariot finally abandoned.

1970: Passage of the National Environmental Policy Act (NEPA—some accounts refer to this as the NEPA of 1969).

Injunction granted against trans-Alaska pipeline system (TAPS) for not following provisions of the new NEPA.

1971: Congress enacts Alaska Native Claims Settlement Act (ANCSA), granting 44 million acres of land and providing $962.5 million in payment to Alaska Natives.

1972: Congress passes Clean Water Act. Major amendments and new legislation come in 1977 and 1987.

Federal passage of the Coastal Zone Management Act (CZMA) and the Marine Mammal Protection Act (MMPA).

Alaska passes a constitutional amendment to limit entry into commercial fisheries.

1973: Congress passes the Endangered Species Act (ESA).

1974: TAPS receives final approval; construction buildup begins.

1976: Creation of the Alaska Permanent Fund by constitutional amendment.

Congress enacts the National Forest Management Act.

Congress passes the Magnuson-Stevens Fishery Conservation and Management Act.

1977: Completion of TAPS from Prudhoe Bay to Valdez.

1978: A two-hundred-mile offshore fishing limit goes into effect.

President Carter withdraws fifty-six million acres of federal lands in Alaska to create seventeen new national monuments.

1979: State of Alaska files suit to halt the withdrawal of these fifty-six million acres.

1980: The Alaska National Interest Lands Conservation Act (ANILCA) enacted by the federal government. A key provision is Title 8, which grants a preference for subsistence hunting and fishing for "rural" residents. Alaska needed to amend its constitution to be in compliance and to continue managing fish and game on federal lands.

1982: First Mental Health Trust Lands lawsuit filed.

The United Nations recognizes a two-hundred-mile EEZ for all nations.

Tundra rebellion vote by Alaska electorate. It claims much of federal land in Alaska as state land.

Mid-1986: Price of oil drops to under $10 a barrel (usual price was around $30) causing major budget crisis, economic downturn, and out-migration from Alaska.

1988: January 14, TAPS reaches its peak production to date of 2,145,297 barrels a day; has slowly decreased in production since.

1989: Worst oil spill to that time in U.S. history occurs in Prince William Sound when the *Exxon Valdez* hits Bligh reef.

1990: With Alaska out of compliance with ANILCA's rural preference because of failure to amend its constitution, the federal government takes over management of fish and game, including subsistence, on federal lands. The state retains management authority over state lands and waters.

Congress passes the Tongass Timber Reform Act (TTRA).

1990–2000: Despite many efforts, Alaska fails to resolve the subsistence issue to comply with ANILCA. This issue remains unresolved today.

1993–94: Major moves to control predators, especially wolves. This becomes a national issue after news footage released of a wolf's paw caught in a trap.

1994: Exxon is found liable for actual and punitive damages in litigation over the 1989 oil spill in Prince William Sound. Years of litigation follow which was not concluded as of 2015.

Final settlement in Mental Health Trust Lands case.

1996: Congress enacts the Sustainable Fisheries Act.

1997: Tongass Land Management Plan (TLMP) issued.

1998: Oil prices drop to $10 a barrel.

2002–14: Various proposals and some changes in taxes on the oil and gas industry.

2002: Congress defeats an amendment to open ANWR to oil and gas development.

2004: Alaska land transfer Acceleration Act intended to accelerate the rate of ANCSA land transfers from the federal Bureau of Land Management (BLM) to ANCSA corporations. But by 2015 clear land title to ANCSA corporations was still not complete.

2. NATURAL RESOURCE ISSUES AND PUBLIC POLICY IN ALASKA: A HISTORICAL AND CONTEMPORARY OVERVIEW

This section provides a brief history of the rise of the environmental movement and its implications for natural resource development throughout the Western world, including the movement's effects on natural resource politics and policy in the United States and in Alaska.

2005–15: Several mining projects, including the Donlin and Pebble Mines, became state and national issues due to environmental concerns.

2006–10: Predator control again becomes a prominent issue in Alaska.

2007: Alaska passes the Alaska Gasline Inducement Act (AGIA) to encourage building of a natural gas pipeline from the North Slope to the Lower 48 states and central and Southcentral Alaska.

2008: Oil reaches nearly $150 a barrel. State projects a $12 billion plus surplus by 2009—twice the annual state budget at that time.

TLMP revised.

2010–12: A surfeit of natural gas through developments in North Dakota and western Canada reduces its price and undermines the economic feasibility of an Alaska gas pipeline to the Lower 48.

2012: Federal government gives the go-ahead for exploration in the NPR-A west of the Prudhoe Bay oil field on the Arctic Ocean.

The Shell Oil Company encounters problems with its equipment and opposition from environmentalists in its plans to drill for oil in the Arctic. No drilling takes place in 2012.

Continuing efforts by the Alaska congressional delegation to open ANWR were unsuccessful.

2013: Shell decides not to drill in the Arctic during 2013.

Public comment on TLMP sought by U.S. Forest Service, as required every five years.

Alaska State Senate passes resolution to encourage the opening of ANWR, Senate Joint Resolution 3 (SJR 3).

2014: Because of falling natural gas prices, AGIA is replaced by a proposed in-state gas pipeline from the North Slope to Southcentral Alaska, the Alaska Stand Alone Pipeline (ASAP).

In the November general election, independent candidate Bill Walker elected governor with an alternative, wider diameter plan for an in-state gas pipeline.

In the second half of the year, oil prices fall from over $100 a barrel to less than $50 a barrel.

2015 The price of oil hovers between $35 and $60 for most of the year. Alaska faces a major revenue and budget crisis.

Continuing discussion about a North Slope to Southcentral Alaska natural gas pipeline. Some agreement reached between the governor and the legislature during a third special session of the legislature in October.

In late summer, President Obama came to Alaska and visits several rural-bush communities to focus on the issue of climate change.

Shell given the go-ahead by the federal government to drill for oil in the Chukchi Sea. But in late September, after eight years of effort and $8 billion spent, it abandons its Arctic drilling operations indefinitely due to lack of sufficient discoveries.

In October the U.S. Department of the Interior announces a two-year moratorium on oil lease sales in the Arctic (specifically the Bering and Chukchi Seas) due to lack of oil company interest. This decision generates major criticism from Governor Walker and the Alaska congressional delegation.

Together, the Shell decision to abandon exploration and the moratorium on lease sales is a major blow to those who see a major part of Alaska's economic and revenue future in Arctic oil development.

2016 January—oil drops to less than $30 a barrel.

Source: Developed by the authors.

Historical Developments in the Environmental Movement

When countries in the Western world (Europe, North America, and several other countries) sought to develop their economies from the late eighteenth century to the mid-twentieth century, their focus was on exploiting their natural resources and those of their colonies to the full. There was little concern for the negative fallout of some practices for the environment, such as dumping chemical waste into rivers and polluting them, and little concern that the resources would eventually run out. Then, in the early 1960s, particularly in advanced industrial countries like the United States, Germany, and Sweden, so-called post-industrial or post-materialist values emerged. With a large middle class that now had a high material standard of living, these countries and their electorates turned part of their political attention to protecting human rights, including those of prisoners, women, and indigenous peoples, and also to the problems of pollution of the planet, the near extinction of many of its animal species, and the problems of depleting natural resources.

These concerns about the planet and its resources gave a boost to the conservation and environmental movements throughout the Western world. The conservation movement began in the late nineteenth century in the United States and in some other countries, and initially it was mainly confined to creating national parks. In some countries, like Germany and Sweden, the environmental movement led to the establishment of political parties known in everyday speech as "green" parties, whose main agenda included environmental issues. Over time, these parties became a political force to be reckoned with. A Green Party was established in the United States and later in Alaska, but it has never been a major political force. On the national level, the Democratic Party and to some extent liberal Republicans have been the champions of a broad range of conservation and environmental policies. These include the Environmental Protection Agency (EPA), established in 1970, and the Endangered Species Act of 1973.

The Consequences: A New Political Era in Alaska

The rise and increasing strength of the environmental movement have had a major effect on politics in general and natural resource politics in particular. This has been the case at both the national level and in the fifty individual states, particularly in Alaska. These effects have been fourfold.

First, the movement injected into politics new and often emotionally charged areas of conflict between those who want to develop resources (or whose livelihoods depend upon their continued development) and those who want to conserve them. This conflict is often vehement and vitriolic because the rise of the environmental movement disrupted, and in some cases destroyed, the economic livelihood and lifestyle of many people and communities, such as those involved in logging and mining. This highly charged atmosphere often results in epithets being thrown at one side by the other, with developers calling environmentalists "greenies," "eco-freaks," and "tree huggers," and environmentalists accusing developers of "raping the land," and "destroying the planet." Sometimes these conflicts even spill over into violent protests, though Alaska has so far not experienced this.[2] The 1960s, then, can be seen as the origin of the developer versus conservationist-environmentalist conflict. As John Katz points out in Chapter 2, Alaska became a state at the end of the era when natural resources were viewed as being for development alone.[3]

By the end of the first decade of statehood, the rules had changed, and thus began one of the major policy conflicts in Alaska's political history.[4]

Second is the fact that the federal government has major responsibility for environmental and natural resource regulation, which produces many head-to-head conflicts with the states over jurisdiction and policy differences. This has certainly been the case with Alaska's relations with the federal government.

Third, the rise of the environmental movement spawned a host of new participants in the policy process, such as environmental and conservation groups of all types. It also galvanized many business and development groups to become more politically active to defend their positions or push alternative policies. This has been the case in Alaska, and many of the major natural resources interests and interest groups are among the most effective in the state, such as the Outdoor Council (hunting and fishing advocates), the Alaska Oil and Gas Association (AOGA), and government agencies, such as the Alaska Department of Fish and Game (ADF&G).[5]

Fourth, the first three developments have broadened the natural resource policy community from those that have a primary interest in natural resources to all sorts of other groups, organizations, businesses, and government agencies that may be affected directly or indirectly by conservation or environmental legislation. For instance, before the 1960s labor unions were rarely affected by issues of conservation and the environment. But EPA regulations and other provisions have affected many segments of the workforce from fishermen to electricians, as these regulations may restrict their employment opportunities and what they can and cannot do on the job. Thus, sometimes unions get involved in issues regarding the environment.

3. ALASKA'S CONTEMPORARY NATURAL RESOURCES POLICY COMMUNITY

Box 21.3 provides a list and a short explanation of the major participants in the natural resource policy community. They are federal, state, and local governments, Alaska Native corporations, tribal governments, and other Native and non-Native interest groups. Some comments on the membership of the community, the interrelationship between them, and the level of involvement of the members, will help set the scene for understanding its political dynamics.

First, while the listing in Box 21.3 is extensive, it is not exhaustive. This is because many policies today, from education to transportation to natural resource policy, are interrelated so that a policy in one area can have far-reaching effects on what may look like a totally unrelated area. To list all of the stakeholders affected by natural resource policy at one time or another would be difficult and not particularly helpful. For this reason, Box 21.3 lists only the major participants.

BOX 21.3

The Natural Resource Public Policy Community: The Political Stakeholders

THE FEDERAL GOVERNMENT

All three branches of the federal government have played a part in dealing with Alaska's natural resource issues and policy development. Presidents have weighed in on ANWR, drilling in the Arctic and climate change. The federal courts have made decisions on land use and interpreted environmental protection laws, and Congress deals with Alaska issues regularly in its natural resources and other committees. On a day-to-day basis the following federal departments and agencies play a key role.

Bureau of Land Management (BLM): Part of the U.S. Department of the Interior (DOI), the BLM manages 260 million acres of federal lands in Alaska not directly controlled by other federal agencies.

Environmental Protection Agency (EPA): A quasi-cabinet level entity created in 1970 and charged with protecting public health and the environment through administration of laws pertaining to land, water, air, and hazardous materials, notably the Clean Air Act of 1963 (substantially amended in 1970) and the Clean Water Act of 1972.

National Marine Fisheries Service (NMFS): An agency of the National Oceanic and Atmospheric Administration (NOAA) in the U.S. Department of Commerce, NMFS is responsible for stewardship and management of living marine resources from three to two hundred miles offshore of U.S. coastlines. It has jurisdiction over fisheries, marine mammals, and endangered species.

National Park Service (NPS): Another DOI agency, NPS manages all national parks, many national monuments, and other properties of historic or conservation significance.

U.S. Coast Guard (USCG): Pursues a broad mission, including protection of marine environments and living marine resources.

U.S. Department of Energy (USDOE): Among many responsibilities, it has within its purview domestic energy production and energy conservation.

U.S. Department of Transportation: Among other duties, it regulates shipment of hazardous materials and houses the Office of Pipeline Safety.

U.S. Fish and Wildlife Service (USFWS): Also part of the DOI, USFWS preserves and manages wildlife on federal lands. The agency has direct responsibility for national wildlife refuges, national fish hatcheries, and some other federal properties.

U.S. Forest Service (USFS): An agency of the U.S. Department of Agriculture that administers national forests and national grasslands by managing timber harvests, regulating commercial activity, promoting recreation, and fighting wildfires.

ALASKA STATE GOVERNMENT

Like the federal government, all three branches of state government are involved with natural resources policy, but the following executive branch agencies are concerned with it on a day-to-day basis.

Alaska Department of Commerce, Community and Economic Development (ADCCED): Because of its major responsibility for economic development, ADCCED often gets involved directly or indirectly in developer versus conservationist-environmental conflicts.

Alaska Department of Environmental Conservation (DEC): Responsible for protecting public health and the environment by controlling pollution of land, water, and air.

Alaska Department of Natural Resources (DNR): Manages Alaska's natural resources, including minerals, petroleum, timber, lands, and waters, to provide both resource development and public use and enjoyment.

Department of Fish and Game (ADF&G): Protects and manages fish, wildlife, and aquatic plant resources for the benefit of human users. It does so according to the sustained yield principle—controlling periodic harvesting of these resources to insure replenishing of the resource.

Division of Governmental Coordination (DGC): An entity within the Office of the Governor that tracks and facilitates multi-agency permitting.

LOCAL GOVERNMENTS

As authorized by the Alaska Constitution and state law, boroughs and some city governments have land planning authority. They can regulate development and environmental health through local ordinances that mirror or enhance federal and state rules.

In addition, the Local Boundary Commission (LBC), a constitutionally mandated state agency, makes decisions on local government boundaries and thus the extent of their land use jurisdiction and control over natural resources.

ALASKA NATIVE CORPORATIONS, GOVERNMENTS, AND INTEREST GROUPS

Among other concerns, natural resources and related issues are of major importance to various Native organizations. Their involvement in the natural resources policy community stems largely from the land settlements in ANCSA and further provisions in ANILCA. The twelve for-profit Native regional corporations have extensive landholdings and subsurface rights on that land. Native village corporations also own land and are also concerned with development and natural resources issues.

Plus, Native interest groups, particularly the Alaska Federation of Natives (AFN), have natural resources issues, including environmental concerns, high on their agendas. Of particular interest to the Alaska Native natural resource policy community is the issue of subsistence.

INTEREST GROUPS: NATIONAL, STATE, LOCAL, AND INTERNATIONAL

A number of local, regional, state, national, and even international interest groups are part of the Alaska natural resource policy community.

Local Interests: These include chambers of commerce concerned about land use and development and environmental restrictions that increase the costs of doing business, city and borough economic development councils, and local branches of environmental groups.

Regional Interests: These include the Southeast Alaska Conservation Council (SEACC) and the Northern Alaska Environmental Center (NAEC), both environmental groups, and the Alaska Eskimo Whaling Commission (AEWC).

State-Level Interest Groups: These constitute one of the largest sectors of Alaska organizations lobbying in Juneau and in Washington, D.C. On the development side these include the Alaska Miners Association (AMA), the Alaska Oil and Gas Association (AOGA), and the Resource Development Council (RDC). On the conservation and environment side are the Alaska Center for the Environment (ACE), the Alaska Wildlife Alliance (AWA), and Trustees for Alaska. Often straddling the developer conservationist fence are United Fisherman of Alaska (UFA), the Alaska Professional Hunters Association (APHA), the Outdoor Council, and various tourism groups, like the Alaska Travel Industry Association (ATIA).

National Interest Groups: These include groups whose primary base of support is outside the state, including the Sierra Club, the Wilderness Society, and the Audubon Society on the side of environmentalism. The American Petroleum Institute (an oil industry trade group), the American Forestry Association, and the American Mining Association support development.

International Interests and Interest Groups: Some of these groups are environmental groups, such as Greenpeace and the World Wildlife Fund (WWF). Others are predominantly economic interests, including multinational corporations headquartered in foreign countries, such as Japan's seafood processors, British Petroleum, and Canadian mining companies such as Cominco, which runs the Red Dog Mine near Kotzebue.

Source: Developed by the authors.

Second, some members of the policy community included in Box 21.3 have natural resource issues and policies as their major concern. These include the EPA and the ADF&G. Others, like the U.S. Coast Guard, the Alaska Department of Commerce, Community and Economic Development, many local governments, Native organizations, and interest groups, have natural resources as only one aspect of their responsibilities and have a direct interest in only a narrow range of such policies. As indicated earlier, though, those with major or partial responsibilities in various areas of natural resource and environmental policy may enter into ad hoc political coalitions with governmental and other organizations not generally considered part of the natural resource policy community. This might be the case, for example, with the Alaska Railroad when it proposes a branch line that might affect protected habitat.

Third, this policy community involves intergovernmental relations (IGR) among federal, state, local and Alaska Native governments, and in some cases international relations too. To be sure, virtually all aspects of state policy have some IGR element, but together with Native issues, social services, and transportation, natural resource issues have a major IGR aspect. This is because of the significant role played by the federal government in natural resource issues. Consequently, lobbying on natural resource and environmental issues is done at least as much in Washington, D.C., as in Juneau. And so federal, state, and local governments, Native organizations, and interest groups must have an IGR operation to compete in this policy community. This is the case from the federal EPA to the ADF&G to Native for-profit corporations to the Alaska Oil and Gas Association to the Alaska Center for the Environment.

4. THE ESSENCE OF NATURAL RESOURCE POLITICS: THE DIMENSIONS OF CONFLICT AND POLITICAL POWER DYNAMICS

Contemporary natural resource politics in Alaska are the result of a confluence of events, developments, circumstances, and varying values and perspectives. These can be grouped into six sets of influences, some of which have been mentioned in the chapter so far: (1) the political rise of the environmental movement, (2) Alaska's economic dependence on natural resources, (3) the view of Alaska from the Outside, (4) the circumstances of the Owner State, (5) varying IGR perspectives, and (6) the nature of natural resource policy making.

The Political Rise of the Environmental Movement

Today, the character of natural resource politics in Alaska reflects, in large part, the rise of the environmental movement nationwide. The expanded definition of natural resources that accompanied the movement's rise has led to an increase in disputes over their use between Alaska developers and Alaska environmentalists. Among the major disputes, which can be very emotional and conflict-ridden, include d2 lands, logging in the Tongass National Forest, predator control, and bans on hunting and fishing for endangered species, among others.

Alaska's Economic Dependence on Natural Resources

No state in the Union is more dependent than Alaska on natural resources, with from 80 to 95 percent of the state's own-source revenues coming from oil and gas activities, depending on the year. With very few other sources of economic activity and state revenues, there is major political emphasis on extracting natural resources and strong opinions about their use, the extent to which they should be developed, and the way and level that natural resource use and extraction should be taxed.

In addition, Alaska's susceptibility to the natural resources boom-bust cycle, evidenced in Box 21.2 with the rise and fall of the price of natural resources like gold, zinc, oil, and salmon, adds a related dimension to natural resource politics. It makes the need for development that much more intense and immediate, given that prices may rise or fall tomorrow or in the next week or month. This in turn ratchets up the conflict by increasing the organized political opposition from the environmental community to counter or control this development.

The View of Alaska from the Outside

If Alaska were an independent country or had no federal land, its conservative political bent and its dependence on natural resources would most likely lead to developers having the upper hand politically. Alaska, however, is not an independent nation and does not live in a political vacuum. Quite the contrary, Alaska has a special place in the American psyche unequaled by any other state because of its natural beauty and its image as the unspoiled Last Frontier.

Alaska's special place in the minds of Americans (and, indeed, people around the world) has come to manifest itself politically since the 1960s through moves by the federal government, environmental groups, the media, public opinion, and other political forces to work to preserve the natural beauty and wildlife of Alaska. Thus, a major Outside force has been added to the political equation of Alaska natural resource politics. The upshot is that developers, both from within the state and from Outside who seek to develop Alaska and extract its natural resources, do not have free rein. There is major political pushback against unbridled development from these in-state and Outside forces.

The Circumstance of the Owner State

The fact that the state government owns about 30 percent of Alaska lands and that almost all oil and gas and many minerals come from state land, has also influenced natural resource politics in Alaska. State ownership means that there is no major private constituency for oil development and, unlike other major oil states like Oklahoma, Texas and Wyoming, no royalty owners' association. Plus, the Alaska Permanent Fund and the Permanent Fund Dividend (PFD) are made possible by oil and gas revenues. However, there is dispute about the role of the Owner State in regard to natural resource policy, and in many ways this role, as envisaged by the originator of the concept, Governor Walter Hickel, is constrained by Outside forces.

Varying IGR Perspectives

For the most part, the three levels of government in Alaska—federal, state, and local, plus various tribal organizations—cooperate in the administration of natural resource policy. This is the case, for instance, with the state and federal governments on fisheries policies of various types, and between various Native organizations and the state and local governments on land use policies, such as access across one another's lands. On other issues, often the high-profile ones, like subsistence, mining permits, oil and gas exploration, and logging, there are often major conflicts between the federal and state governments, which sometimes also involve local governments and Native organizations.

Many of these issues arise out of the inherent conflicts in a federal system as explained in Chapter 10 on IGR. The federal government has particular responsibilities, such as requiring EISs, which often slow down development in the view of the state and some local governments and cause conflict. In addition, because the federal government has control over its landholdings in the state, if the federal policy is not to develop them, such as ANWR, this can also cause conflict when the state wants to benefit from developing resources on those lands. Other conflicts occur among local governments over annexation of lands, such as that between Juneau and the proposed Petersburg Borough during 2010–2012. Then, there are conflicts between various levels of governments and Native organizations over issues such as mining development, timber harvesting, and subsistence.

The Nature of Natural Resource Policy Making

Chapter 3 on policy making in Alaska identifies three basic types of policy: distributive, which distributes money or other benefits to people or organizations; redistributive, which reallocates resources from one group or constituency to another; and regulatory, which restricts or requires certain actions by individuals, groups, or organizations, such as businesses. Distributive policies are not usually conflict-ridden once enacted. In contrast, redistributive and regulatory policies are often very controversial and can generate considerable conflict. Some natural resource policies are distributive, such as the Permanent Fund Dividend (PFD). Most, however, are redistributive or regulatory.

For instance, redistributive policies include the d2 lands legislation, which took federal lands in Alaska that could potentially be used for development and placed them in a protected status; subsistence, which takes the use of fish and game resources in times of shortage out of the hands of the public at large and gives preference to rural residents (in effect, Alaska Natives); and fisheries limited entry, which restricts certain fisheries to permit holders and not to the public at large. While primarily redistributive, these three policies also have regulatory elements. Major regulatory policies include many environmental laws and rules, such as requirements for EISs and protections for endangered species. Redistributive and regulatory policies can deprive certain individuals or groups of resources, restrict their use, increase the cost of doing business, or in other ways limit their actions and often affect their livelihoods. So it is not surprising that these policies are often the source of major conflicts.

The Consequences for Natural Resource Policy Making and Power Dynamics

The confluence of the six circumstances just identified explains much about the nature of policy making and the power dynamic in Alaska's natural resource politics. Several major elements are involved.

First, while cooperation often occurs among various natural resource interests, conflicts between user groups are common. They occur because different users want to use the same resources for different purposes, from various types of development to not using them at all. These conflicts take many forms and involve a wide range of interests. A few examples include the IGR conflicts noted earlier; mining, oil and gas, and timber interests that want to develop land and other resources versus recreational and environmental interests that want to preserve the land and its resources; hunters and sports interests who want to take fish and game versus Native interests and conservationists who want to protect them; fights over predator control among hunters and environmentalists; and the range of issues surrounding subsistence.

Second, these user group conflicts resulting from potential multiple uses of land and other resources are not simply those of developers versus conservationists and environmentalists. Nor are the interests on both sides always united in their actions. As we noted earlier, positions on natural resource policy range from the extreme right to the far left, with many interests in the middle, both developers and environmentalists, realizing that compromise is necessary to move forward. Plus, on some issues a group or organization may be pro-development but pro-conservation on others. Such divisions exist within the Native community over the opening of ANWR and on various mining projects, such as those involving both the Pebble and Donlin Mines in Southwest Alaska. User group conflicts are rarely simple and often involve ad hoc political alliances.

Third, the State of Alaska as an administrative and political entity is far from a united body when it comes to policies on land, natural resources, and the environment. One major source of conflict is the different responsibilities given to the state's three natural resource agencies—ADF&G, DNR, and DEC—as explained in Box 21.3. With different charges and perspectives, partly resulting from representing different user groups, conflicts often occur among these agencies. One classic conflict results from placer mining (working streams and riverbeds to find deposits of gold or other valuable minerals) on state land, with DNR supporting the development of state resources, DEC attempting to protect water quality of the rivers used in the mining operations, and ADF&G concerned about the effects of mining on the fish and game dependent upon these streams and rivers. Other interagency conflicts arise from logging, wolf management, and many forms of economic development. The governor is often called upon to mediate such conflicts.[6]

Fourth, in terms of the dynamics of power within natural resources and environmental policy making, largely because of the supremacy of national law, the federal government exerts major influence. And because it owns so much land in Alaska, the federal government has been able to place limits on human uses of natural resources on its lands as well as manage wildlife resources, such as migratory waterfowl, polar bears, and bowhead whales.

Federal authority and influence put considerable constraints on the state's ability to exploit its natural resources even on or under its own land. This is one reason for the strong anti-federal attitude among many Alaskans that manifests itself in movements like the so-called Tundra Rebellion in the early 1980s. This "rebellion" was a response to ANILCA and claimed that much federal land within Alaska actually belonged to the state. Another high-profile act of protest along these lines occurred in the 2015 legislative session, largely in reaction to the federal government proposing further restrictions on the development of ANWR. The legislature considered a bill to claim most federal land for Alaska.[7] Like most negative reactions to the federal government, the "rebellion" and the 2015 action were largely symbolic and without any plausible legal foundation. In addition, federal dominance renders the viability of the Owner State concept highly questionable in practice. The state may control one-third of Alaska's land and reap major financial benefits from those who extract resources from it, but the state is far from being in control of its own destiny when it comes to natural resource development.

Fifth, natural resource interests, particularly the oil industry but also to a lesser extent mining and commercial fishing, while somewhat constrained by the Owner State and federal authority, are nonetheless significant political forces in natural resource policy making and in state politics in general. As Chapter 15 on interest groups points out, the oil industry has been consistently among the most influential interests in Alaska since statehood, though it has not always been successful in fending off tax increases or environmental regulations.[8] Plus, certain hunting and fishing interests, particularly the Outdoor Council, have also exerted considerable, but by no means dominant, influence.

The prominence of these interests is the consequence of pure power politics. The state needs the oil industry and that gives the industry political leverage. The Outdoor Council has worked skillfully to promote its interests by making campaign contributions, working on campaigns to get its supporters elected, endorsing some candidates, and openly opposing others. In contrast, the Alaska-based environmental community is relatively weak, but that weakness is compensated for by the role of the federal government and by Outside interests and interest groups bringing power to bear in Alaska and at the federal level on behalf of Alaska's homegrown environmental cause.

Finally, with so many user groups, governments, interest groups, and public opinion as part of the political mix, it is obvious that today Alaska's natural resource policy making is pluralistic. This is in sharp contrast to Territorial days when a few fishing and mining interests influenced federal policy and held huge sway over not only natural resource policy, but Territorial politics in general. A good argument can be made that the increased range and types of political forces now involved in Alaska natural resource policy making have tipped the balance away from developers and toward those who want to conserve the state's natural resources. An argument can also be made that this increased political pluralism has reached a state of hyperpluralism where there are so many interests that they cancel each other out, making it hard to move forward and make policy. Even when there are only a few interests involved in an issue, stalemate often occurs in natural resource policy making in Alaska. The subsistence issue is a prime example of a political stalemate.

5. COMPARISONS WITH OTHER STATES

To conclude this overview of the development and contemporary characteristics of natural resource politics and policy issues in Alaska, and before moving to the specifics of land issues, we briefly place Alaska in comparison with other states. As in many other areas of politics, institutions, and policies addressed in this book, there are many commonalities between Alaska's approach to natural resource politics and polices and those of other states, some aspects with a particular Alaska aspect to them, and some unique Alaska elements.

The broader definition of natural resources and the expanded view of their uses resulting from the rise of the environmental movement have affected all states, from Maine to Hawaii. This broader perspective has resulted in increased user group conflicts across the nation. This is largely because all states are affected by federal laws, such as the National Environmental Policy Act (NEPA), with its requirements for EISs, and the Endangered Species Act (ESA). Moreover, coastal states like Alaska are affected by national fisheries legislation and laws protecting marine mammals, among other laws and regulations. As a result of these developments, the federal government has taken an increasingly active role in natural resource and environmental policy across the states and is often the major political power in this area. The increase in federal authority and influence has led to much political pushback by the states and increased antagonism toward the federal government from many state governments and state residents. So Alaska is far from unique in its often negative reaction to federal actions on natural resources and related issues.

There is also a range of ways in which Alaska's natural resource politics and policy issues are similar to other states, but with a particular Alaska element to them. Two examples are illustrative. One concerns user group conflicts. For example, Native Americans are not major players in resource politics in most states, either because they constitute a very small percentage of the population or because they are largely removed from state politics and live on reservations. Not so in Alaska. As a result of Native land ownership conferred under ANCSA and federal laws protecting Native interests like subsistence, Alaska Natives are a major force in natural resource policy and are involved in many user group conflicts at the state, local, and federal levels. The second example is that, while there are many states whose economies are very dependent on natural resource production, such as Montana and Wyoming, Alaska is clearly the most dependent considering its overwhelming dependence on oil production for state revenues and for general economic health. Thus, not only are debates about the various aspects of natural resource policy central to Alaska politics, but they affect many other aspects of state policy and service delivery largely because of the overwhelming dependence of most state services on natural resource revenues.

The unique aspects of Alaska's natural resource and environmental politics and policy result, as might be expected, from the state's location, geography, demographics, and its special place in the minds of most Americans. Some or all of these circumstances were the forces behind the politics surrounding the building of the Alaska pipeline, the passage of ANILCA, the thorny issue of subsistence, and, most recently, moves to build a natural gas pipeline from the North Slope to the Lower 48 states (in 2014 and 2015 focusing more on a gas pipeline from the North Slope to Southcentral Alaska). The factors that shape these unique features of Alaska's natural resource politics most likely result in the state being more subject to Outside forces than any other state.

As in many other aspects of its politics, government, and public policy, Alaska has much in common with states in the American West, and particularly the Mountain states, in regard to natural resource politics and policy.[9] One major reason is that the economies of states like Alaska, Montana, Wyoming, Idaho, and New Mexico are based on natural resource development to a much larger degree than most states in the nation. Thus, these and other western states have similar experiences with the federal government regarding restrictions on logging, protection of endangered species, and the Clean Air and Clean Water Acts. One particularly contentious and long-lasting dispute has been over federal restrictions on logging in southern Oregon and northern California because of the endangered status of the spotted owl.

The main reason Alaska and other western states share common issues and concerns about natural resources policy, however, stems from the fact that the federal government is a large landowner in most western states, including Alaska. The western states rank one through thirteen of the fifty states in regard to the percentage of federal lands within their states. This ranges from 85 percent in Nevada to 20 percent in Hawaii. In ten of the thirteen western states, at least one-third of their land area is in federal hands. Only one other state, New Hampshire, with 13 percent, even reaches double digits in this regard.[10]

Increasing federal restrictions on the use of its lands resulting from the rise of the environmental movement have produced many state-federal and federal-user group conflicts in the western states since the mid-1970s. In many cases this resulted in particularly strong and often vocal anti-federal sentiment. A particularly strong anti-federal movement was the so-called Sagebrush Rebellion in Nevada and other western states in the late 1970s, partly because of restrictions on the use of federal lands for grazing, among other concerns.[11] Alaska's equivalent was the "Tundra Rebellion" of the early 1980s. So, with the exception of agriculture (which is minimal in Alaska but a major economic and political forces in all other western states), the specifics of land policy in Alaska have much in common with other western states. It is to the specifics of land politics and policy in Alaska that we now turn.

6. ALASKA LAND POLICY DECISION MAKING: COMPLEXITIES AND CONFLICTS

It will become evident that five of the twelve characteristics of Alaska politics identified in Chapter 2 are particularly relevant to land issues and policy: economic development versus environmentalism, the significant role of external economic and political forces, the all-pervasive importance of government, the myths and contradictions of Alaska's political discourse, and the prominent role of Alaska Natives in state politics.

In manifesting these characteristics, the development and implementation of natural resource policy are marked by a combination of cooperation, complexity, and conflict. There are, however, three other factors that help explain the complexities and conflicts that accompany Alaska's land policy in particular. These are the pattern of land ownership, fragmented governmental authority in land management, and the concepts of working lands and conservation lands.

The Pattern of Land Ownership

The process of transferring federal lands promised to the state under the Statehood Act and to Alaska Native corporations under ANCSA has been extremely complicated and time-consuming, and the process was not entirely complete even as of 2016. When all transfers have been completed, about 55 percent of Alaska's land area will be federally owned, about 30 percent will be state lands, 11 percent Alaska Native land, and about 4 percent will be in private hands.

This apparently straightforward pattern of land ownership is, in fact, complex and produces conflict for a number of reasons. One is the fragmentation of management considered later in the chapter. Another is that competing interests exist within a single type of ownership. For instance, state lands held in trust by the Alaska Mental Health Trust Authority constitute less than one-third of 1 percent of Alaska's land area (and about 1 percent of state lands), but they have considerable natural resources on them (including the Fort Knox gold mine near Fairbanks), and some are in urban areas. So these lands have become a major focus of Alaska's land and natural resource politics. This occurs, for example, when Mental Health land need to be accessed for exploitation but can only be reached by crossing land owned by other entities or when a local government wants to acquire them for development and the Trust has conditions that the local government is unable or unwilling to meet.[12]

Fragmented Federal, State, Local, and Native Authority in Land Management

In their analysis of land policy in the western states, Fairfax and Cawley noted that besides the changing national agenda brought about by the rise of the environmental movement and user groups conflicts, fragmented federal and state authority is another major cause of the complexity and conflict in land issues, their resolution, and administration.[13] At the federal level, four agencies—the Forest Service, Bureau of Land Management, National Park Service, and the Fish and Wildlife Service—have varying responsibilities for land and natural resource management. This situation is similar to the three government resource agencies in Alaska, as explained earlier. In addition, Native corporations also manage their lands, and local governments, particularly boroughs, have land management responsibilities.

Because of the different charges to the various federal and state agencies involved in land management, there are often clashes among them over policy. At the federal level, for instance, the Forest Service's role of managing forests and the Fish and Wildlife Service's role of protecting habitat sometimes produce conflicts. Local governments and Native governments also sometimes clash over use of adjacent lands. And coordination between levels of government is often wanting.

Working Lands and Conservation Lands

Working lands differ from conservation lands in that the former are managed for the revenues they can produce while the latter are managed (or minimally managed) for noneconomic amenities.[14] Working lands include forests used for timber harvests and non-timber forest products, plus forests managed for large-scale tourism activities. Working lands also include those used for mining and agriculture, among other economic purposes.

The distinction between working and conservation lands is important in understanding land use politics and policy for three reasons. First, the distinction throws light on the changing attitudes toward working lands brought on by the environmental movement and what this means for many policies relating to working lands. The concept of working lands is foreign to many Alaskans today but, until the rise of the environmental movement in the 1960s, virtually all Alaska lands were viewed as working lands. After the Alaska Purchase in 1867, Alaska's political economy was shaped by non-Natives who came to Alaska primarily for commercial fishing, fur trapping, mining, and later agriculture and oil and gas extraction. Today, however, many Americans and some Alaskans consider working lands as a threat to Alaska's conservation lands. A large segment of the modern environmental movement considers all land in Alaska as conservation land and that no land should be working land, except for residences and commercial property.

Second, and a consequence of the first point, conservation lands are not self-supporting for a modern economy. These lands will support subsistence activities but cannot support even the tourism industry except on a very limited basis. So the limitations on use of conservations lands considerably reduce the revenue potential of these lands to the state. Moreover, seeing all lands as conservation lands can have serious consequences for the goals of the environmental movement in Alaska. No development means less transportation and other infrastructure and thus less access for people to enjoy and experience the wilderness. So a political balance between development and conservation must be struck.[15] Third, the manner in which working lands developed in Alaska is one of several reasons that agriculture is not a major economic and political force in the state.

Four Examples of Complexity and Conflict in Alaska Land Policy

The following examples of land policy are not meant to be comprehensive explanations of the issue, but rather short case studies illustrating the complex and conflict-ridden aspects of land policy. The first three examples, large-scale mining, forestry, and agriculture, are grouped together in Section 7 dealing with working lands. The fourth example, ANWR, is presented in a separate section (Section 8), because it is one of the most high-profile Alaska policy issues since the late 1970s and is a classic example of land and natural resource politics and policy.

7. WORKING LANDS: MINING, FORESTRY, AND AGRICULTURE

Since the 1970s some of the most heated debates between developers and conservationists/environmentalists over land use have been those over mining and timber harvesting. Agricultural lands have produced less conflict, but agricultural policy has been fraught with its own complexities and politics.

Large-Scale Mining

Part of the aura surrounding Alaska can be traced to the prospectors who came north a hundred or more years ago in search of gold and riches, and turned towns like Nome and Juneau into thriving communities, at least until the gold ran out. Together with fishing and timber, mining was one of the major economic drivers that helped populate Alaska in its early years under U.S. control, and provided employment and government revenues. Since the 1970s, all three industries have been overshadowed by oil and government as economic drivers. But mining is still a major private sector employer, with about 4 percent of Alaska's workforce (about twelve thousand employees). Mining companies, many based in Canada, have invested billions of dollars in Alaska since the 1960s, and Alaska is a major producer of zinc and other metals. About a third of the state's exports are mining products.[16]

Mining is important to the economy of many Alaska communities, such as Kotzebue, Fairbanks, and Juneau. In particular, mining development offers the possibility of jobs to many rural-bush communities where there are few or no employment opportunities. In 2012, with high prices for most minerals, there were potentially about fifteen large-scale mining operations in the state, each employing or potentially employing at least three hundred people. The emphasis here is on the word *potentially*. Of these fifteen or so operations, only a half dozen or so were producing, including the Kensington Mine near Juneau and the Red Dog Mine near Kotzebue. Others, like the Niblack Mine project on Prince of Wales Island in Southeast Alaska, and the Whistler project, 100 miles west of Anchorage, are in the exploratory stage. Others are bogged down in politics, particularly the Pebble Mine and to a lesser extent the Donlin Mine, largely due to user group conflicts and regulatory requirements.

Before the 1960s, all these mines would have been opened with little or no impediment except for the role of world prices for their products. In considering new mining projects, developers have always had to be sure that world prices were high enough to justify the expense of new projects. But today they also have a field of political and administrative hurdles to clear because of the rise of the environmental movement and increased government regulation. Every mine proposal requires many federal and state permits, including compliance with NEPA and its EIS requirements, the Clean Water Act, and the Clean Air Act, among others. In addition to the EPA, other federal agencies responsible for regulating mining operations and development include the Bureau of Land Management (BLM), the Army Corps of Engineers, the Forest Service, the National Park Service, the Fish and Wildlife Service, and the Bureau of Indian Affairs. The Alaska Departments of Fish and Game and Environmental Conservation also get involved. Then there are the various user groups that support or oppose the projects. So in many cases the stage is set for a natural resource showdown—a sort of civil war pitting businesses, residents, and in many cases Native communities against each other.

The upshot is that it can take years for a mine to overcome political opposition and obtain all the necessary permits, and in some cases it may never open. When the Kensington Mine opened in Southeast Alaska in 2010, for example, it marked the culmination of a twenty-year process. Box 21.4 explains the background and the conflicts surrounding the proposed development of the Pebble and Donlin Creek Mines.[17]

Forest Lands

The complexity and conflict involved in the use of Alaska's forest lands are similar to those of large-scale mining. For generations virtually no one—not the local residents, government officials, or organized interests—questioned the lumber and pulp companies as they clear-cut forests and adversely affected the local environment. Particularly in Southeast Alaska, which contains the nation's largest national forest, the Tongass, many communities were dependent upon the forest industry, with several sawmills and some pulp mills. Again, all this started to change in the 1960s, and today the forestry industry is a shadow of its former self. The Tongass National Forest and the politics surrounding it provide an instructive example of the decline of the industry and the complex conflicts that resulted.[18]

The Tongass covers 80 percent of Southeast Alaska and its seventeen million acres are administered by the U.S. Forest Service (USFS). Although the Tongass was one of the earliest national forests, created in 1907, its immense size, remote location, and transportation difficulties rendered it almost unmanageable until after World War II. Following the war, the USFS, with the strong support of the Territorial administration and the people of Southeast Alaska, pursued efforts to establish a year-round timber industry. By the early 1950s, pulp mills had been built in Ketchikan and Sitka, and the USFS had signed contracts with them guaranteeing fifty years of federal timber. Timber became a major industry in Southeast Alaska.

BOX 21.4

Developing the Pebble Mine and the Donlin Creek Mine: Regulatory Regimes and User Group Conflicts

BACKGROUND

The Pebble Mine, located northeast of Bristol Bay in Southwest Alaska, was initially conceived in the 1980s, but the first feasibility studies were not conducted until 2001. The site contains gold, copper, and molybdenum. According to the Canadian developer, Northern Dynasty Minerals, as of 2015 the project was in the "advanced exploration" stage and has been held up by having to secure more than sixty state and federal permits.

In 2005 NovaGold Resources, another Canadian company, proposed the development of the Donlin Creek Mine north of the village of Crooked Creek on the Kuskokwim River, also in Southwest Alaska. The permitting process for this proposed gold mine has been underway for several years. Like the Pebble Mine, with many federal and state agency permits required, each one with its own timeline, the process will take considerable time.

THE ISSUES

Both mines raise similar environmental concerns, mainly regarding water pollution. A major issue with Donlin's operation is water contamination with mercury that could impact fish and affect the livelihoods of Alaska Natives dependent on salmon as their main food source. However, the Donlin Creek project has not attracted as much media attention as the Pebble Mine. Reasons include Donlin's location in an area populated by subsistence residents and on Alaska Native lands, which require less permitting. In contrast, the Pebble Mine is located on state-owned land. According to its opponents, its development threatens Bristol Bay's world-class salmon fishery. This alone has given Pebble much more statewide and national exposure than Donlin, and even some international attention.

USER GROUPS AND INTERESTS INVOLVED

The Donlin Gold Working Group was created to offer information and to serve as a public forum for those concerned about the proposed mine's impacts. The group consists of individuals as well as nonprofits, such as Trustees for Alaska, Ground Truth Trekking, and the Center for Water Advocacy.

For the next twenty years the timber industry and the USFS were left to run the Tongass without interference. But by the late 1960s concerns over environmental issues, such as the impacts on fish and wildlife of clear-cut logging and road building, were becoming national issues. As a result of congressional passage of NEPA and the National Forest Management Act, the USFS was required to provide for public review of its plans and issue an EIS for forest plans and individual projects, including proposed timber sales. Environmentalists were not satisfied. Believing that the USFS was still too timber oriented, they pursued more protection for the Tongass and won major victories with the creation of the Admiralty Island and Misty Fjords National Monuments.

Generally, however, there has been less opposition to Donlin than to Pebble, and its development is less conflict-ridden.

Several groups oppose Pebble. For instance, the organization Stop Pebble Mine compiled a list of signatories who oppose Bristol Bay ecosystem pollution that included Tiffany & Co., Zales Corporation, and others. There are high-profile environmental interest groups, such as the National Wildlife Federation, the National Parks Conservation Association, and the Pew Environmental Group, that oppose the mine for ecological reasons. And the Natural Resources Defense Council enlisted the support of film star Robert Redford, and Fins and Fluke, an organization protecting beluga whales. On the other side is a nonprofit organization, Truth About Pebble, which supports responsible development, plus the State of Alaska, the Resource Development Council (RDC), and a number of Alaska Native village and tribal groups also in support of the mine project mainly for the jobs it will bring.

The statewide profile of Pebble was significantly heightened in media campaigns by both proponents and opponents of the project. Opponents of future large scale mining were able to get enough signatures to put Proposition 4 on the statewide ballot in November 2014 to require the legislature to approve any mines in the Bristol Bay region in the future. The measure passed overwhelmingly by 2 to 1 (66 to 34 percent). While the anti-mining measure will not affect Pebble's development, this was, in effect, a statewide referendum on the mine.

LIKELY OUTCOMES

Despite a major public relations effort on the part of Pebble and the mine's potential as a major employer, it is a long way from being opened. In fact, it may be too controversial and environmentally sensitive ever to open. The mine suffered major setbacks in 2013–2014. Besides the Proposition 4 vote, major financial supporters pulled out, and the federal Environmental Protection Agency issued a report imposing increased restrictions on the mine. Given all the permits and other regulations it must comply with, even the less controversial Donlin Creek Mine is not expected to open until 2016, even if all goes well. In the meantime, economics may take over for both mines. In 2012 Donlin's developer expressed reservations about the high costs of operating in a remote area. Similar concerns have been voiced by Pebble's developers. Plus, world market prices for minerals and the proverbial boom-bust cycle will affect the decisions on both mines. The longer the delay in their opening the more likely this cycle will work to affect corporate boardroom decisions in Vancouver, BC, regarding the two mines.

Source: Developed by Kristina Klimovich from sources listed in endnote 17.

In 1979 the first Tongass forest management plan was completed, but environmentalists viewed it as more of the same, with timber harvests still being the primary emphasis of the plan. A concerted effort by national environmental groups and grassroots organizations in Alaska led to the passage by Congress of the Tongass Timber Reform Act (TTRA) in 1990. The TTRA imposed new limits on USFS logging, creating areas of special importance where logging was not allowed. The battle over TTRA brought the Tongass into the national environmental arena. These developments soon had a major impact on the management of the Tongass.

In 1993 the Alaska Pulp Company's (APC) Sitka mill closed. The owners claimed that the USFS was not providing enough timber as required by their fifty-year contract.

But environmentalists and some timber industry analysts believed that market forces were to blame for the mill's closure. The USFS responded by voiding APC's contract. Three years later Louisiana Pacific closed its Ketchikan pulp mill due to lack of timber. Environmentalists and some industry analysts again claimed that market forces, not environmental regulations, were the cause of the closure.

After ten years in the making, and at the cost of several million dollars, the USFS released the Tongass Land Management Plan (TLMP) in May 1997.[19] The plan was a management guide for the Tongass for the next decade and more. The TLMP provided for a maximum timber sale quantity of 267 million board feet of timber per year, protected some old growth forests, provided protection for fish and wildlife, and recognized the growing tourist industry. The plan recommended thirty-two rivers for designation as national wild, scenic, or recreational rivers and provided increased protection for caves and karst (a landscape formed by the dissolution of soluble rocks, like limestone).

Despite both the timber industry and environmentalists claiming some victories over various elements of the 1997 TLMP, the Tongass is an ongoing issue and continues to be one of Alaska's most hotly debated natural resource policies. Some pro-logging interests view decisions on the Tongass as potentially destroying their livelihoods, while passionate environmentalists continue to dig in their political heels. As in the past, Alaskans will have only minimal effect on future policy developments regarding the Tongass. The latest version of TLMP was approved in January of 2008. Public comment is invited on the plan every five years to assess the extent to which it is working, with the most recent comment period taking place in 2013. By far the largest number of public comments come from Outside. In 2014 a Tongass Federal Advisory Committee was set up to advise the U.S. Department of the Interior on future Tongass policy. The committee represents various viewpoints from the timber industry to environmentalists to local businesses to tourism interests. In 2015 the committee unanimously agreed to move to the harvesting of second-growth timber.

The State of Alaska also owns extensive forest lands, and there are also privately owned forest lands. Conflicts have occurred as to both, but perhaps because they have not involved the same degree of Outside influences as the Tongass, they have been relatively easier to deal with, and some long-term political solutions have been found. Box 21.5 on the Alaska State Forest Practices Act provides an example.

Alaska Agriculture

The problems of agriculture as a productive aspect of Alaska's working lands are different from those of mining and forestry. Agriculture has been less affected by the rise of the environmental movement, user group conflicts, and regulations like those requiring EISs, though all have affected it in some ways.

BOX 21.5

The Alaska State Forest Practices Act: An Unusual Success Story

By the mid to late 1980s, degradation of salmon streams from logging activity was too much for many commercial fishermen to look the other way. Rural village residents also began to raise similar concerns in their Native corporation shareholder meetings. When fishermen joined with the elders of the Native community, a strong political force emerged calling for better management of Alaska's private and state forests.

In response to this growing criticism and recognizing the need to maintain a timber industry, Governor Steve Cowper (1986–1990) set up a formal process to review the issue. But he didn't just say "let's review it." Instead he set up a consensus-driven process aimed at writing new legislation. If the stakeholders could agree, he would submit legislation with the understanding that it would not be subject to legislative tinkering even from those groups with influential lobbyists. There would be no "end run" around any negotiated agreement. For a first-term governor with no track record on forestry issues, this was a bold move.

Governor Cowper set up a steering committee made up of five representatives of forest owners and operators, five users affected by forest practices (fishing and environmental groups), and three from each of the three affected state resource agencies. With the aid of professional mediators, the steering committee then set about establishing the following principles to guide the negotiations:

- Fairness: a successful outcome must be based on shared risk and incentives for both timber owners and regulators.
- No big hit: a balance was required so that neither fish nor timber should bear an inordinate share of the burden.
- Enforceable: standards and regulations should be understandable and measurable for ease in implementation.
- Professional management: any new system must be built on careful planning and a targeted field effort.

Working groups of biologists and stakeholders, using these principles, set up a series of negotiations on each major aspect of forest practices, from road building to reforestation. Recognizing that streamside protection and water quality issues were at the heart of any meaningful reform to forest practices, the groups dealt with this aspect first. In the end, the stakeholders discovered that the "no big hit" principle was the key to reaching a fair conclusion on streamside buffers.

Once this was agreed, the negotiations on the other aspects of forest practices fell into place. The agreement was drafted as the Alaska State Forest Practices Act and introduced by the governor in 1990. Its first committee of referral was Senate Resources, chaired by State Senator Bettye Fahrenkamp. In wrestling with the unusual notion that the bill was not subject to legislative tinkering, she requested that all members of the steering committee come to her office and collectively declare their "as is" support. Upon hearing the strength of the consensus, she then used her influence to keep the bill fully intact. Passage of the State Forest Practices Act was one of the very few times that a bill made it through both the House and Senate free of amendments.

Thanks to the boldness of Governor Cowper and the commitment of affected stakeholders, Alaska passed one of the best forest laws in the nation for governing activities on private timber land. In 1996, the Board of Forestry convened a team of scientists to review field data to see if the act was working as intended to protect fish, wildlife, and water quality. The review found that the act was performing as intended and that only a few adjustments were necessary.

Source: Authored by Kate Troll, who has spent many years involved in Alaska natural resource politics.

As we have noted, Alaska is the only state in the Union where agriculture was not a major force in its development and is relatively insignificant today, both compared with other states and as a segment of the state's economy. The lack of a major role for agriculture is usually explained by the Alaska climate and the high costs of production compared with other states. This makes Alaska-produced milk, eggs, and poultry more expensive than imports from the Lower 48, even after factoring in the cost of shipping to Alaska. Even so, agriculture could be maximizing the state's working lands more fully than it is today. There are historical, market choice, economic, and political reasons why this is not the case.[20]

The Alaska Agriculture Experiment Station was established in 1898 (originally in Sitka, later with branches in Kodiak, Kenai, Rampart, Fairbanks, Palmer, and Copper Center) primarily to provide fresh produce and meat to miners and fish-processing workers. Alaska's agriculture was developing at a time when other states had already developed transportation and other infrastructure to facilitate the distribution of agricultural products. As Alaska's population grew after World War II, partly because it was easier and cheaper to ship food into Alaska than to produce it locally for distribution within Alaska, the infrastructure never developed in a way to facilitate the economic viability of Alaska's agriculture industry. This remains the case today.

In current commodity markets, Alaska farmers are not competitive in Lower 48 and international markets for two related reasons. One is past reliance on Alaska demand and not taking advantage of economies of scale that would have lowered the cost of production and made Alaska farmers competitive in some Lower 48 markets, particularly in the Pacific Northwest. The other reason is that because of the way federal regulations work, Alaska farmers are not eligible for many of the farm subsidies that other American farmers receive, the very farmers with whom Alaska farmers should be competing for markets.

Moreover, unlike the Lower 48, particularly major agricultural states like those in the Midwest, most farmers in Alaska are part-time or hobby farmers and do not make the majority of their income from farming. Part-time and hobby farmers effectively provide a private subsidy to their individual operations and also have little incentive to expand and take advantage of economies of scale.

Besides individual farmers, the main sources of capital for Alaska agriculture have been the federal and state governments. Government capital has in the past been disbursed with conditions that often proved to be burdensome and provided inappropriate incentives for production and prices. For example, state agriculture programs, in addition to inappropriate infrastructure development such as the Matanuska Maid creamery (now closed), have mainly focused on providing loans for individual farmers to engage in specific activities. These include land clearing, construction of facilities, or production even when producing certain products was not economical. In general, state-supported agriculture projects have been subject to market failure, not because of the inability of Alaska farmers to produce, but because of the lack of an operating commodity marketing system.

Instead of following the example set by successful commodity production subsidy programs in the Lower 48, the state model of development has resulted in a large agricultural asset base, but little production. By depending on subsidies that reward production instead of debt acquisition, Lower 48 farmers have been able to focus on lowering production costs through economies of scale. In the future, state and federal agricultural agencies offering production subsidies to tie Alaska commodity markets to international markets would be one way to aid in increasing the efficiency of Alaska agriculture.

Alaska agriculture will not be a significant economic force in the state unless it takes advantage of economies of scale and expands beyond Alaska's present limited market. However, for reasons explained earlier, it is now too late for Alaska to compete in traditional agricultural markets, such as for grains, meat, and dairy products. So the economies of scale must be in other markets. In this regard, Lower 48 and international niche markets, the concern of many Americans with health and vitality, and the age of Internet marketing may provide new opportunities for those able to seize them.

For instance, a marketing niche exists for the Alaska peony, a popular shrubby plant. It can be harvested in Alaska in July, August, and September when peonies are available nowhere else in the world. Commercial planting of peonies in Alaska began in 2004, and by 2011, approximately ten thousand cut stems from Alaska growers were shipped to Canada, Japan, and locations throughout the United States including Hawaii. The Alaska Peony Growers Association estimates that they will realize 500,000 cuts per year by 2016 and beyond. This equates to $1 to $2 million per year in sales at a conservative estimate of $2 to $4 per stem. Due to Internet marketing, interest in Alaska peonies from worldwide markets continues to be promising.

Alaska farmers are also in a good position to take advantage of increasing consumer consciousness regarding healthier lifestyles and food choices. One that has recently begun to be cultivated is golden root or Arctic root (also known as the Rhodiola rosea) which is reputed to have medicinal qualities that can control mood swings and depression, particularly in women. These Alaska farmers hope to find a niche in the international market for golden root by organizing the first Alaska farmer's cooperative for the plant.

8. THE ARCTIC NATIONAL WILDLIFE REFUGE—ANWR

ANWR has been and remains one of the most high-profile land use issues in Alaska and in the nation. As such, it manifests all the elements of natural resource politics considered in this chapter with a very heavy dose of Outside involvement. Moreover, it can be described as a political marble cake, with various political constituencies working for and against opening the refuge to oil and gas exploration. In terms of the concept of working versus conservation lands, ANWR is currently in conservation status, although many Alaskans and some interests from the Outside would like to turn it into working lands. Box 21.6 provides a review of the background, terminology, and timeline of the issue, which will make the following overview of the various forces involved more understandable.[21]

A Political Marble Cake: Outside and Alaska Interests and Conflicts

Making sense of the complexities of the politics of ANWR is, indeed, a challenge, in large part because of the number of interests involved and the conflicts that often arise among and within them. Here we briefly outline three aspects of this complexity: the Outside influences, those in Alaska, and some internal user group conflicts.

Outside interests involved in the ANWR debate range from the U.S. Congress, the President, and federal agencies to development and environmental groups. Republicans in Congress generally favor opening ANWR, as have Republican presidents, while many Democrats and Democratic administrations have not. When George W. Bush was elected President in 2000 and the Republicans held a majority in both houses of Congress, it looked like ANWR might be opened. However, the terrorist attacks of September 11, 2001, put ANWR and many other policies on the political back burner. The interests favoring development include the Petroleum Institute (the major oil industry trade group) and the oil companies that would stand to gain from developing ANWR. Those opposed include an array of environmental and conservation groups, including the Sierra Club, the Wilderness Society, Friends of the Earth, and Greenpeace.

The state has long favored opening ANWR, including most governors, both Democrat and Republican. Alaska's bipartisan approach to the issue reflects the fact that the majority of Alaskans (around 75 to 80 percent, judging by opinion polls over the years and other indicators) would like at least part of ANWR to be working lands.[22] Leading Alaska's fight to open ANWR over the years has been the state's congressional delegation. From 2009 to early 2015 this also included former Senator Mark Begich, the only Democrat elected to Congress from Alaska since 1974. With Begich's defeat by Republican Dan Sullivan in the November 2014 election, the Alaska delegation was back to three Republicans who will undoubtedly continue to push for opening ANWR.

One of the major issues that the Governor's Office in Washington, D.C., has worked on since the early 1980s in coordination with the Alaska congressional delegation is opening ANWR. John Katz, the former and long-time head of that office, sees the failure to open ANWR as one of the major disappointments of his tenure.[23] And the late Senator

BOX 21.6

The Arctic National Wildlife Refuge: Background, Terminology, and Timeline

The Arctic National Wildlife Refuge (ANWR), which is located largely on federal land but includes some Native corporation lands, lies in the northeast corner of Alaska (see Map 21.1). The Refuge was originally formed in 1960, with 8.9 million acres. In 1980 and 1983 ANWR was added to, for a current size of 19.6 million acres comprising three distinct legal areas of use within its borders.

Even though it is designated as a "refuge," ANWR is not entirely a refuge. Only the southern part, consisting of 9.16 million acres, is officially classified as "refuge." The central eight million acres is designated as "wilderness," and the 1.5 million acres in the northern part are called the "10-02 Area." The uses and definitions of these designations are set out in the Wilderness Act of 1964, and the permissible uses are different for each of the three areas. Under the act, there can be no development of any kind in either the "refuge" or the "wilderness" areas of ANWR, which together comprise over 92 percent of the total area. So to suggest that ANWR's entire area could potentially be opened for oil and gas exploration is inaccurate.

Under current law, development can occur only within the 10-02 Area. The area takes its name from section 10.02 of the Alaska National Interest Lands Conservation Act (ANILCA), which expanded ANWR in 1980. In that section Congress classified the area as neither "refuge" nor "wilderness." It set aside this acreage of the Arctic Coastal Plain specifically for "oil and gas exploration" due to evidence of large hydrocarbon deposits.

The 10-02 Area is further distinguished in that it contains 92,000 acres of private land owned by the Kaktovik Inupiat Corporation of Kaktovik, ANWR's only settlement and population. The subsurface rights of these 92,000 acres are owned by the Arctic Slope Regional Corporation (ASRC), the North Slope's regional Native corporation.

Further specifying the land that can be used within ANWR, Congress limited any development footprint to two thousand acres. So within the 1.5 million acres of 10-02 and within the total 19.6 million acres of ANWR, less than one-half of 1 percent is potentially open to development.

ANWR could produce a million barrels of oil a day, and 150 billion cubic feet of natural gas a year. The 10-02 Area, however, cannot be explored despite its specific oil and gas definition without congressional approval. This approval has not been forthcoming despite high dependence of the U.S. on foreign oil and notwithstanding strong support in Alaska to open the area. Moreover, in a proposal by President Obama and the U.S. Department of the Interior in 2015, all federal land in ANWR would be placed off limits to development, including the 10-02 Area. This, in effect, precludes development in ANWR unless Congress acts to rescind this proposal.

Source: Developed by the authors. See endnote 21 for sources.

Ted Stevens, probably the most influential politician in Alaska history and a powerhouse in Washington, D.C., once complained that he had become "clinically depressed" over his inability to get the coastal plain opened for drilling, even when Congress and the White House were controlled by Republicans.[24]

Republican state legislators tend to favor opening the refuge, while Democrats are less uniformly in support of it. Of all the points of federal-state conflict, ANWR is second to none among Alaska politicians who support its development. Moves by the federal government to limit development, as occurred in early 2015, sent Alaska's congressional delegation into a political rage, with all the familiar epithets of anti-federal political rhetoric. The congressional delegation spoke of “federal overreach,” “a stunning attack on Alaska’s sovereignty,” and “war on Alaska families.” Governor Bill Walker suggested that possible responses might include secession and said he would send a $2 billion invoice to the White House, charging for the loss of potential revenue to the state.[25]

Several Alaska development groups also favor opening ANWR. The effort has been led since the early 1990s by Arctic Power. With a membership of ten thousand and offices in Washington, D.C., it bills itself as a grassroots organization.[26] This may be partly the case, but it also has many large corporate members. Other Alaska development groups, some of which are members of Arctic Power, include the Alaska State Chamber of Commerce (ASCC), the Resource Development Council (RDC), the Alaska Oil and Gas Association (AOGA), and the state affiliate of the AFL-CIO (American Federation of Labor-Congress of Industrial Organizations), largely because of the job opportunities it offers. Most major Alaska environmental groups oppose opening ANWR.

The Alaska Native community generally favors opening ANWR, including the Alaska Federation of Natives (AFN), the Arctic Slope Regional Corporation (ASRC), and Doyon Limited (based in the Interior around Fairbanks). But Natives living within the refuge are mixed in their support. The Gwich’in people continue their opposition to the possibility of oil drilling in ANWR. This is because the Porcupine caribou herd calves on the coastal plain in ANWR, and caribou are traditionally a major part of their diet and culture. Further north, in the village of Kaktovik, there is strong support for oil and gas development.

In 2012, an attempt was made by Congress to open ANWR, in the form of a bill from the House Natural Resources Committee. At that time, the committee was chaired by Alaska’s Congressman Don Young.[27] And over the years, both houses of the Alaska legislature have passed resolutions to promote opening ANWR. In the Twenty-Seventh Legislature (2011–2012), for instance, the House passed a resolution urging Congress to open the coastal plain of ANWR and also passed a bill to authorize an advertising contract to promote its opening.[28] All these efforts failed in large part because of opposition from the Obama administration.

Given the failed attempts in the past, it is difficult to predict what circumstances would have to be present to open ANWR. It is an ongoing political power struggle dominated, as are so many Alaska natural resource policy issues, by Outside forces, particularly the federal government, despite the wishes of the majority of Alaskans. Judging by the opinion polls, however, at least 25 percent of Alaskans oppose opening ANWR.[29]

9. CONCLUSION: LINKING LAND ISSUES WITH OTHER AREAS OF NATURAL RESOURCE POLITICS AND POLICY MAKING

It is often difficult to separate political issues involving land from other natural resource issues and potential solutions. This is certainly the case with those regarding mining, forestry, and oil and gas development, which involve the interrelationship of land and environmental aspects of natural resource policy, and sometimes fisheries policy. Examining specific aspects of land policy, such as we did in the four case studies, illustrates the similarities and differences between land and other aspects of natural resource politics and policy. The brief review of the similarities in this conclusion helps set the scene for Chapters 22, 23, and 24 and to some extent for Chapter 25 on the Permanent Fund.

One similarity among all aspects of natural resource issues is that they each exhibit several characteristics of Alaska politics, including the conflict between development and environmentalism, the effects of both political and economic external forces, and the important role of Alaska Natives. Another characteristic also at play in natural resource politics is the myths and contradictions in Alaska's political discourse, which manifest themselves in several ways, not the least being the idea that Alaska and its citizens, through the concept of the Owner State, are or should be in control of their natural resources.

Cooperation is a major element of natural resource policy making among agencies and user groups. However, like land politics, environmental, fisheries, and oil and gas politics is riddled with user group conflicts in which lack of compromise often stymies the policy process. In all these policy areas, the status quo tips the political power balance against development and, in the case of the Permanent Fund, makes it difficult to change the present system, particularly with regard to the PFD. There is also evidence of increasing Outside influence identified in all five chapters in this part of the book, and this is only likely to increase as the years progress and Alaska becomes more and more part of a globalized world.

On the other hand, there are some issues and policies that are more or less exclusively land issues. These include the federal transfers of lands to the state and the Native community and Mental Health Trust lands. Land issues have their own sets of interests, interest groups, and government agencies and focus on particular political goals. The politics surrounding these land issues tells us a lot about the nature and specifics of Alaska's political economy and its political culture.

The fundamental contemporary question of how to balance economic benefit against environmental cost in Alaska is anything but simple. In general, natural resource politics and public policy manifest a complexity that at first may seem a straightforward case of black and white, right versus wrong. In this process not all Alaskans are "victims" of the federal government, as many would have us believe. In fact, many Alaskans benefit from the present regime of natural resource politics. But this regime results in difficult, complex conflicts, and far more so than many visitors to the state or those steeped in the mystique of Alaska likely realize.

ENDNOTES

[1] James N. Gladden and Dan Austin, "Land, Natural Resource and Environmental Issue: The Political and Policy-Making Context," in *Alaska Public Policy Issues: Background and Perspectives*, ed. Clive S. Thomas (Juneau, AK: Denali Press, 1999), 189.

[2] *Ibid.*, 191.

[3] See Chapter 2, Box 2.3.

[4] For an analysis of the rise of the environmental movement in the United States, see Samuel P. Hays, *Beauty, Health, and Permanence: Environmental Politics in the United States, 1955–1985* (Cambridge, UK: University of Cambridge Press, 1987).

[5] See Chapter 15 on interest groups, Tables 15.3 and 15.4.

[6] Gladden and Austin, "Land, Natural Resource and Environmental Issue," 186.

[7] Alexandra Gutierrez, "House Passes Bill to Seize Federal Lands," *Alaska News Nightly,* Alaska Public Radio Network (APRN), April 7, 2015.

[8] See Chapter 15, Tables 15.3 and 15.4.

[9] See, for example, Sally K. Fairfax and R. McGreggor Cawley, "Land and Natural Resource Policy, I: Development and Current Status," and Cawley and Fairfax, "Land and Natural Resource Policy, II: Key Contemporary Issues," in *Politics and Public Policy in the Contemporary American West*, ed. Clive S. Thomas (Albuquerque: University of New Mexico Press, 1991).

[10] *Almanac of the 50 States: Basic Data Profiles with Comparative Tables*, 2010 edition (Woodside, CA: Information Publications, 2010), Table 2, page 421. See also, *Public Land Ownership by State*, at www.nrcm.org/documents/publiclandownership.pdf.

[11] See Richard H. Foster, "The Federal Government and the West," in Thomas, *Politics and Public Policy in the Contemporary American West*, esp. 78–84.

[12] See Tracy Kalytiak, "Alaska Mental Health Trust: Putting Resources Back into the Community," *Alaska Business Monthly* (April 2012): 36–38.

[13] Fairfax and Cawley, "Land and Natural Resource Policy, I," 426–31.

[14] See the Working Lands Alliance, at www.workinglandsalliance.org.

[15] See Box 21.5 and Chapter 22, Sections 4 and 5 on sustainable development for possible ways for developers and environmentalists to strike a compromise between their competing claims.

[16] See Chapter 6, Table 6.2 and Figure 6.1, Chapter 7, Table 7.2 and Figure 7.2, and Chapter 11, Table 11.1, for various statistics on the contribution of Alaska mining to the Alaska, U.S., and world economies.

[17] The sources for Box 21.4 are *Pebble's Promise* (Anchorage: The Pebble Partnership) a promotional packet sent to Alaskan households in mid-2012; http://www.donlingold.com/about-us; a February 12, 2015 interview by Clive Thomas with Mary Sattler, a former Manager of Community Development and Sustainability for Donlin Gold, LLC; Lisa Demer, "EPA Proposes Strict Limits

on Pebble Mine to Protect Salmon," *Alaska Dispatch News*, July 18, 2014; Liz Ruskin, "Shively Takes Aim at Recent TV Ad," *Alaska News Nightly* (APRN), February 6, 2014; and Liz Ruskin, "Rio Tinto Gives Pebble Stake to Nonprofits," *Alaska News Nightly* (APRN), April 7, 2014.

[18] This review of the history of the Tongass draws, in part, on Michael F. Turek, "Three Case-Studies: The Arctic National Wildlife Refuge, Management of the Tongass National Forest, and Wolf Management," in Thomas, *Alaska Public Policy Issues*," esp. 199–202.

[19] *Tongass National Forest, Land & Resource Management Plan 1997: Final Environmental Impact Statement* (Washington, D.C.: U.S. Department of Agriculture, U.S. Forest Service, 1997).

[20] The authors thank Julie Riley, Professor of Extension Education with the University of Alaska Fairbanks Cooperative Extension Service, for her help in developing this section on Alaska agriculture.

[21] This discussion on ANWR, including the information in Box 21.6, draws, in part, on the following sources: Turek, "Three Case-Studies," 195–99; Juliet Eilperin, "Obama Administration to Propose New Wilderness in Arctic Refuge—Alaska Republicans Declare War," *Washington Post*, January 25, 2015; Richard Mauer, Alex DeMarban and Nathaniel Herz, "Obama Plans to Block Development in Arctic Refuge; Alaska Leaders Irate," *Alaska Dispatch News*, January 25, 2015; the Associated Press, "Lawmakers propose resolution pushing back on refuge proposal," January 30, 2015; *Arctic National Wildlife Refuge (ANWR): A Primer for the 112th Congress* (Washington, D.C.: Congressional Research Service, February 14, 2012); the pro-opening ANWR website of Arctic Power, at http://anwr.org/about/; and the anti-opening ANWR site of the Northern Alaska Environmental Forum, at http://northern.org/programs/arctic/arctic-national-wildlife-refuge/arctic-refuge-101-what-is-201canwr-201d. The authors thank Judy Hargis for her help in summarizing the masses of material on ANWR.

[22] See Chapter 20, Figure 20.1, for public attitudes in Alaska to opening ANWR.

[23] See Chapter 10, Box 10.5.

[24] Mauer, DeMarban, and Herz, "Obama Plans to Block Development in Arctic Refuge."

[25] Alexandra Gutierrez, "Invoices, Invitations, Litigations, and Even Secession: Walker Says All Responses Possible to Arctic Drilling Decision," *Alaska New Nightly* (APRN) January 27, 2015.

[26] See the Arctic Power website, at http://www.anwr.org/. This site includes extensive information about the organization and ANWR, albeit from a development perspective.

[27] U.S. House of Representatives, H.R. 3407; Congressional Research Service, *Arctic National Wildlife Refuge (ANWR): A Primer for the 112th Congress*; and Politico, "ANWR Bill Clears House Natural Resources Committee," at http://www.politico.com/news/stories/0212/72323.html.

[28] Alaska House of Representative Bill 358, at http://www.legis.state.ak.us/basis/get_bill.asp?session=27&bill=HB 358; and House Joint Resolution 9 Endorsing ANWR Leasing, at http://www.legis.state.ak.us/basis/get_bill.asp?session=27&bill=HJR9.

[29] See Chapter 20, Figure 20.1.

★ CHAPTER 22 ★

The Politics of Alaska's Environment: Reconciling Conflicts

Ronald G. Clarke with Clive S. Thomas

On a warm spring evening in Juneau, a visitor wandered out of the nearby woods and toward the emergency entrance of Bartlett Regional Hospital, Southeast Alaska's largest medical center. The visitor triggered the motion detecting automatic doors and ambled inside the lobby. To their credit, the hospital's evening staff did not panic when they saw the yearling black bear. They quickly ushered her safely out, reminded again of one of the constants of life in Alaska: the wilderness is never far away.

It probably never occurred to the staff that the rest of the world is never far away either. In fact, groups, organizations, businesses, governments, and individuals from outside Alaska with a broad range of perspectives take an active interest in environmental affairs on the Last Frontier. They can and do exert enormous influence on events in Alaska, so that, to a large extent, Alaskans do not control their own destiny in environmental matters.

Much of this chapter explores the external influences on environmental politics and policy. We examine trends in Outside influence, consider the extent to which this influence can be reconciled with the needs and goals of Alaskans, and look to the future of Outside control of Alaska issues in this policy area. Much of the background on the politics of natural resources explained in Chapter 21 is essential for understanding this chapter. The first five sections of that chapter (especially Section 1 and Box 21.1) are particularly important in that they explain the major terms used in natural resource and environmental politics. Specialized terms and concepts specific to this chapter are explained here where necessary.

Chapter 21 identifies five characteristics of Alaska politics that shape both land and natural resource politics and influence their policy outcomes. These five apply equally to this chapter. They are developers versus conservationists, today primarily environmentalists; the significant role of external economic and political forces; the all-pervasive importance of government; the myths and contradictions of Alaska political discourse; and the prominent role of Alaska Natives in state politics. These characteristics also throw light on the major theme of this chapter—the extent to which the various interests involved in environmental issues (developers, environmentalists, the state and federal governments, and Alaska Native interests) can or cannot be reconciled now and in the future.

The analysis begins with some specifics to supplement the general explanation of natural resources politics explained in Chapter 21, including the evolution of environmental politics, and makes comparisons with other states. The next section provides an overview of the major landmarks in Alaska environmental politics and policy that help explain its contemporary status. Then there are five case studies, each illustrating an aspect of the evolution of Alaska's environmental politics. Next comes a consideration of the issue of sustainable development, and a possible approach to political compromise in the often highly emotional developer-environmental debate. A consideration of ongoing issues and challenges follows. The conclusion seeks to answer the question that forms the theme of the chapter—whether the competing interests involved in environmental politics can be reconciled.

1. FORCES DRIVING ALASKA'S ENVIRONMENTAL POLITICS: SOME ADDITIONAL OBSERVATIONS

There are some specific developments and perspectives that are useful for fully appreciating contemporary environmental politics and policy in Alaska. In this section we explain some important historical developments from an environmental perspective and offer additional observations and perspectives on Alaska's contemporary environmental politics and policy making. We also explain key differences between Alaska and other states in the environmental policy realm.

Alaska's Early Development and Attitudes toward the Environment

To understand the attitude toward Alaska's physical environment or, more accurately, the disregard for it before the 1950s, take the typical example of Juneau. As the Bartlett hospital staff hustled that black bear through the automatic doors and safely into the night, they probably gave little thought to the terrain outside. Today the hills behind the hospital are thick with woods, but a century ago this area and most of the Juneau landscape had been completely clear cut—with bare areas where woods had once stood before Juneau was settled in the 1880s. In the heyday of gold mining, practically every standing tree was reduced to lumber and put to work supporting the extraction of gold. In the 1890s, the Kensington Gold Mine near Juneau opened without interference from government regulators or environmental activists. It operated for more than thirty years and, with the nearby Jualin prospect, produced over forty thousand ounces of gold.

From soon after the Alaska Purchase in 1867, private interests driven by the profit motive came to Alaska to exploit its natural resources. The wilderness was seen as limitless and endlessly able to absorb whatever damage humans might inflict upon it. During World War II the military undertook numerous projects, from building the Alaska-Canada Highway to establishing outposts in the Aleutian Islands, often with minimal planning and generally with little or no regard for the environment. When it came to wilderness versus war, war won out every time.

In those days, the miners and loggers could not possibly have imagined protestors, lawsuits, Environmental Impact Statements (EISs), or the possibility of distant interest groups working to shut them down. But, as modern day gold mine developers know well, all these are now facts of life. As mentioned in Chapter 21, the reopening of the Kensington Gold Mine illustrates this new era. The process of reopening the mine took nearly twenty years, from the early 1990s to 2010, and involved lawsuits, intense lobbying by its opponents, and many actions by regulatory agencies to ensure proper disposal of the tailings (the waste rock left after removing the metals) from the mine.[1]

Perspectives on Alaska's Contemporary Environmental Politics

The political saga of the Kensington Mine is a classic example of the complexities and conflicts that often accompany development projects in Alaska. These are largely due to modern day concerns with the environment and the contemporary power of the environmental movement. Yet, Kensington is only one of many such high profile conflicts. The fight over opening the Arctic National Wildlife Refuge (ANWR), the National Petroleum Reserve-Alaska (NPR-A), and the Arctic to oil and gas drilling, opening the Pebble and Donlin Mines, issues over predator control, and concerns involving cruise ship wastewater, are other examples among many. Chapter 21 provides perspectives on such conflicts and the politics that generate them in regard to natural resources in general. Here we take this analysis a step further with five observations and perspectives on the specifics of Alaska's contemporary environmental politics. These are: the importance of profit to the developer-environmentalist conflict; the counter forces of laws, regulations, and public opinion; the misnomer of "Alaska environmental policy"; the important role of the courts; and a schizophrenic attitude to Outside influence and development among many Alaskans.

The Importance of Profit to the Developer-Environmentalist Conflict

At root, what generates the developer-environmentalist conflict in Alaska and forms the core factor shaping environmental politics is the continuing quest for profits from exploiting Alaska's natural resources. Money and the prospect of big profits have driven investment in Alaska from fisheries to gold to timber to oil and gas. And the money typically comes from Outside, not from Alaska.[2] Without this Outside economic interest in the state, while the developer-environmentalist debate would still exist, it would likely be less conflict-ridden and probably of a different character.

Before the 1960s and the rise of the environmental movement, the mode of this Outside investment was to maximize short-term gains—to exploit the resources as fast as possible while world prices were high and get out when the resource, most often gold, was exhausted or the market took a downturn or even collapsed. In this regard, Alaska did have the status of a colony exploited for its resources, with little put back into the Territory, and with much hardship left in the wake of the departure of the Outside economic interests. Today, this Outside economic interest in Alaska is bigger than ever, but the activities and free hand of investors and natural resource–extraction industries have been considerably curbed. As a result, today Alaska cannot be considered a colony, at least in regard to resource extraction.[3]

The Counter Forces of Interest Groups, Laws, Regulations, and National and International Public Opinion

As Chapter 21 explains, the rise of environmental groups, their pressure on the federal government to deal with problems of the environment in general and Alaska in particular, and the role of national public opinion have provided an increasingly heavy political counterweight to the profit motive. With the special place of the Last Frontier in the minds of most Americans, many environmentalists began to focus on Alaska for two major and interrelated reasons. First, they sought to preserve Alaska's incredible beauty and wildlife. Second, they saw Alaska as the last chance in America to "do development right." The environmental community, therefore, lobbied to constrain the free hand of companies to exploit Alaska's resources and adversely affect its environment. Thus began the developer-environmentalist debate and the increasingly intense conflict that has become a hallmark of Alaska politics.

This core tension between "getting the resources out" versus the "last chance for getting it right" underlies virtually all discussion of developing public infrastructure, promoting economic stability, and the future of Alaska. Consequently, economics, laws and regulations, and public opinion figure prominently in Alaska environmental political discussions. Not only that, as Chapter 21 also points out, given the major influence that the political counter forces exert and given that the status quo is generally the major force in politics, a good case can be made that the political upper hand in environmental policy in particular, and natural resources policy in general, is now tipped against developers.

"Alaska Environmental Policy": A Misnomer?

In this chapter and in other places in the book, there is reference to "Alaska environmental policy." Based upon what we have said in the chapter so far and particularly regarding Outside influences, a good argument can be made that this term is a misnomer.

In practice Alaska has little control over much of the environmental policy that affects it—a major portion of this policy is, in reality, an aspect of national environmental politics and policy. Consider the following as evidence for this contention.

First, intergovernmental relations (IGR) shape Alaska environmental policy in a major way, and in this particular intergovernmental relationship the federal government has the major influence.[4] This is clear to anyone who picks up a newspaper or watches or listens to the news or goes online almost any month of the year. December of 2012, for example, saw many news stories about environmental issues with major federal involvement. Among many others, these included concerns of Bristol Bay residents about the effects of mining on salmon streams in Southwest Alaska, cleaning up pollution in the NPR-A, issues regarding a proposed access road into Juneau, a proposed dam on the Susitna River, and drilling in the Arctic.[5] In large part, federal involvement comes in the form of federally mandated EISs, the adequacy of which is judged by federal agencies. Alaskans and their state government have very limited control over any of these and a host of other decisions regarding the environment in their state.

Second, national public opinion often carries much more weight in determining what happens in Alaska than either the state government or Alaskans themselves. This was clearly evident, for example, in early December 1994 when the national evening news showed graphic footage of a bungled effort to kill a trapped wolf in Interior Alaska.[6] The reaction was swift and predictable—an outraged American public demanded an end to wolf control in Alaska. This influenced Alaska policy, as we will see later in the chapter.

Third, many environmental concerns, including clean air and water and those regarding birds, mammals, and fish, particularly those that migrate, are not confined within Alaska's borders or territorial waters, but cross national borders or international waters. This is the case with Canada, as we will see below in the case study of the Windy Craggy debate over opening a mine and some more recent transboundary mining issues. As the U.S. Constitution gives the federal government exclusive authority to make agreements with foreign governments, of necessity, the federal government needs to be involved in these cross-national environmental issues.

Fourth, and as noted in Chapter 21, the Outside forces of interest groups, the federal government, and public opinion are the major influences on environmental issues in Alaska. These Outside influences generate much resentment among Alaskans, particularly among developers, even though they may themselves be from Outside. So another good case can be made that much of the antagonism toward the federal government in Alaska is rooted in the fact that the federal government is seen as bolstering the cause of the Outside environmental lobby.

The Important Role of the Courts

More than in most areas of public policy, the courts, both state and federal, have played a major role in shaping environmental policy affecting Alaska. Therefore, in many ways, the courts—together with the President, the governor, federal and state departments, Congress and the Alaska legislature, interest groups, public opinion, and the media—are part of environmental politics in the state, although much of this politics is played out on the national stage. The important role of the courts has been shaped by three factors.

First, new interest groups on the American political scene and those with little access or influence in the executive and legislative branches, as was the case with gay rights and animal rights groups in their formative years, often use the courts as a means to achieve their goals. They do so either to promote their causes or to stop the implementation of policies that are detrimental to them. When the environmental movement was in its infancy it used the courts as part of its political strategy and had some successes, as we will see below with the case studies. Using the courts has remained a major part of the strategy of the movement. Second, many conflicts between developers and environmentalists involve disagreements about the interpretation of environmental laws and regulations, and courts are well suited to resolve these kinds of disputes. Third, when either developers or environmentalists disagree with legislative or executive actions, they often turn to the courts for redress.

Since the early 1960s, almost all high-profile and many less well-known developer-environmentalist conflicts in Alaska have been played out largely in the courts. A prime example is the long-standing debate over logging in the Tongass National Forest in Southeast Alaska, which shows how judges' decisions can have major and lasting impacts on development in Alaska. Virtually every move in the process of designating and executing Tongass timber sales has been accompanied by court challenges and appeals. Federal and state courts can redirect resource extraction projects, completely rewrite environmental rules, and delay or halt development projects. The debates and conflicts over many issues are often drawn out because of the slowness of court action.

A Political Schizophrenic Attitude to Development and a Negative View of Outside Influences among Many Alaskans

Another set of factors shaping the character of environmental politics in Alaska is a complex set of values and attitudes involving the myth of individualism combined with a sort of schizophrenia toward development, plus negative feelings toward Outside influences among many Alaskans. In their most extreme form, the attitudes reflect the view that Outside interests are illegitimate because they infringe on the independence of Alaskans and influence the course of Alaska's development, which Alaskans believe should be their preserve alone. These attitudes manifest themselves in actions like the Tundra Rebellion of 1982, a ballot measure that claimed most federal land as rightfully owned by Alaska. A similar provision was considered by the Republican-dominated Alaska legislature in the 2015 legislative session, in reaction to the January 2015 federal government proposal to further restrict development in ANWR.[7] As explained in Chapter 21, some of this attitude stems from the nature of federal policies regarding development and the environment. Many such policies are regulatory and limit, restrict, prescribe, or prohibit certain development activities. Many Alaskans do not like to be told what to do or how to do it in their own state.

Several chapters in the book explain the reasons why the belief of independence and individualism is a myth and that Alaskans are, in fact, dependent individualists—individualists in spirit perhaps, but not in economic reality. Furthermore, most Alaskans want federal dollars but not federal regulations and controls. Many Alaskans do not realize the irony of dependent individualism, and the reality is that their schizophrenic attitude affects environmental policy.

No one exemplified the Alaska development schizophrenia more than the late Governor Walter Hickel. He was a proponent of both coexisting with nature and pursuing large-scale development projects. Acknowledging a deep respect for the value of wildlife, wild country, and long-standing traditions of subsistence, he was also an unabashed fan of huge development projects, even those that would affect the environment profoundly. A major aspect of his concept of the Owner State is that since Alaska owns the resources, those resources ought to be developed on Alaska's terms. He argued that Outside commercial interests have exploited Alaska's natural wealth at the expense of its citizens, but at the same time urged Alaskans to oppose the efforts of environmentalists who are trying to "lock up" the state and its natural resource wealth.[8]

How exactly does this political schizophrenia, the persistence of myths, and the use of political rhetoric in Alaska affect environmental politics and policy? We can identify three major, interrelated effects.

First, political schizophrenia causes increased conflict of various types both within the state and with Outside forces, often leading to lawsuits and emotional debates that make it harder to compromise on issues. Second, many of Alaska's elected public officials both reflect and reinforce these populist attitudes. Like Governor Hickel, they run the risk of alienating the very people who have the power to make decisions that affect Alaska's environment, particularly in Congress and the federal administration. Of course, this attitude may help some Alaska politicians get elected and reelected. Third, some Alaskans and their politicians are not realistic about the power structure of environmental policy making. Filing lawsuits and making various protests that usually lead nowhere means that Alaska often does not have a seat at the table from the start of an issue and decisions may be made without serious Alaska input. This may work to the disadvantage of some in the state, particularly developers, since a reality of contemporary environmental politics is that the onus is on developers to show the environmental soundness of their projects.

Alaska Compared with Other States

Section 5 in Chapter 21 examines general similarities and differences between Alaska's natural resources politics and that of other states. Many of these comparisons apply to environmental politics specifically. This is especially true of the increased role of the federal government across all fifty states with respect to regulating the environment, user group conflicts, and similarities between Alaska and the western states. This is particularly the case with the Mountain states regarding the prominence of environmental politics and often with very intense conflicts because of the importance of natural resources in their economies, history, and culture.[9]

There are, however, some differences specific to Alaska's environmental politics, policy, and administration that have a particular effect in the state. Some differences are major, such as the place of Alaska—the Last Frontier—in the American psyche, drawing special attention to Alaska from across the nation and around the world, and the particular role of Alaska Natives. Other differences are less prominent but nevertheless add to the political mix of environmental politics in Alaska or when Alaska issues are being considered in Washington, D.C. We briefly look at five of these: (1) incomplete infrastructure, (2) enhanced importance of government spending, (3) the desire for short-term gains, (4) the enhanced role of government agencies, and (5) a less significant role for the Environmental Protection Agency (EPA).

Incomplete Infrastructure

As both a young state and one of enormous size, Alaska is still developing its major infrastructure as evidenced by high per capita spending on capital improvement projects, especially in the form of federal grants to state and local governments. Capital projects frequently result in environmental impacts or are themselves designed to mitigate such impacts, for example, sewage treatment plants, drinking water systems, and fuel storage facilities. In addition, because of poorly developed transportation infrastructure, disadvantageous economics render unaffordable certain aspects of daily life taken for granted in other states. In Alaska, advances such as progressive solid waste disposal and widespread recycling programs are economically out of reach for all but the largest communities.

Enhanced Importance of Government Spending

Incomplete infrastructure is one reason for the enhanced importance of government spending in Alaska. Plus, Alaska's rural-bush cash economy is poorly developed and, in general, there is more reliance on government spending than in other states. With that reliance comes the obligation to abide by the terms of federal and state grants, which frequently include complying with environmental standards. To secure the basic infrastructure that many Lower 48 states have enjoyed for decades, Alaska must follow the rules of federal agencies and other granting authorities. The need to follow government rules does not make Alaska unique, but most other states developed their infrastructures well before modern environmental laws were in place. As a consequence, many Alaskans bristle at the rules other jurisdictions have avoided.

The Desire for Short-Term Gain Is Prevalent

No state has a monopoly on residents whose primary interests start and end with making a profit. But the "here and now" mentality of realizing benefits today and letting tomorrow take care of itself is especially prevalent in Alaska. Its relatively transient population has less of a long-term commitment to the state's future than is common in the Lower 48, including many western states. The resulting absence of long-term planning manifests itself powerfully in Alaska environmental issues. Developers' intent to maximize profits from resource extraction is frequently widely supported by the state's residents, opinion leaders, and elected officials because development usually means more jobs and more tax revenues. Often the only roadblocks to potentially environmentally damaging projects are federal agency regulations or lawsuits filed by interest groups.

The Enhanced Role of Federal and State Government Agencies

The first three factors help explain why there is an enhanced role of federal and state government agencies in environmental politics and policy in Alaska compared with other states. Much of this enhanced role stems from the fact that close to 60 percent of the area of the state remains unincorporated at the local level and is part of the Unorganized Borough.[10]

In environmental matters, this means that the state or the federal government assumes the regulatory roles in affairs more commonly addressed by local authorities in other states. Consequently, local debate over the merits of local projects is frequently overlain with a chafing sense of interference from afar. While not unique across the states, this attitude is common and persistent in Alaska. Even though the citizens in the Unorganized Borough do have the choice to incorporate, they generally do not do so to avoid paying taxes. So, in this regard, their victimization by state and federal interests is of their own choosing.

A Less Significant Role for the Environmental Protection Agency—EPA

In the other forty-nine states, the federal EPA is frequently the lead agency in designing and carrying out national environmental policies. The agency's jurisdiction is especially focused on pollution and toxic waste challenges resulting from long years of human presence coupled with poorly executed or nonexistent waste management programs. As a young state with a large area and a small population, Alaska has not developed toxic dumps and other contaminated sites to the degree of other states. As a result, the EPA assumes a less prominent role in Alaska's environmental matters.[11]

Reconciling Conflicts among Developers, Environmentalists, and the State and Federal Governments: An Initial Assessment

Having covered the factors that shape Alaska environmental politics and policy, we can make an initial assessment of the chapter's theme: the extent to which it is possible to reconcile the conflicts in this policy area. Three observations are clear from what we have said so far.

First, what underlies and drives environmental politics and policy are economics, through decisions to develop resources and make a profit, and government regulation, with, in theory at least, the purpose of balancing economic gain and environmental costs. Both forces are largely Outside forces in the form of oil, mining, and fishing businesses and the federal government. Second, because of Alaska's minimal influence on environmental matters in Washington, D.C., the strong bias of national public opinion against developing Alaska and the tussle of Outside development and environmental interest groups, Alaska and its citizens have little influence on the major policy decisions that affect its environment. There are some issues, however, where the state may have more control, such as matters affecting its lands, forests, and waters, especially if the issue does not reach the national political stage. Third, Alaska does not help itself politically because of its failure, and in some cases refusal, to face political reality. Consequently, Alaska is often viewed in Washington, D.C., as an eccentric and headstrong teenager living in a dream world.

Considering all this, our initial assessment is that development and environmental interests are almost always reconciled in the end, but the state often has little to do with the outcome. Given that the state government and most Alaskans favor development and that in recent years Outside environmental interests have been so successful, it is clear that Alaska is on the receiving end of much environmental policy with very little room to maneuver politically. Of course, the 25 or so percent of Alaskans who oppose development prefer this arrangement. If the state were completely in charge of its own environmental affairs, this 25 percent would have a string of political failures to list.

The case studies and the approaches to dealing with environmental issues now and in the future presented in the rest of the chapter will enable us to make a judgment as to the accuracy of this initial assessment. Where appropriate, the following sections consider the extent to which reconciliation was or was not achieved.

2. THE ORIGINS OF ALASKA'S CONTEMPORARY ENVIRONMENTAL POLITICS AND POLICY: LANDMARK DEVELOPMENTS, LAWS, AND INCIDENTS

Although the wonder and beauty associated with Alaska were apparent to poet-naturalist John Muir when he visited Alaska in 1879, it was not until the coalescing of the environmental movement with television and film media in the 1960s that the Lower 48 became increasingly involved in conflicts and issues associated with Alaska's environment.[12] Chapter 21 covers the rise of the environmental movement as part of Alaska's natural resources history. In this section we focus specifically on several elements that help explain the specifics of contemporary environmental politics and policy in Alaska. This involves briefly explaining the following: (1) four key federal acts specifically affecting Alaska natural resources, (2) general national laws affecting Alaska's environmental politics, and (3) key environmental incidents and developments in Alaska.

Four Key Federal Acts Specifically Affecting Alaska's Natural Resources

The four key federal acts are the Statehood Act of 1958 authorizing statehood in 1959, the Alaska Native Claims Settlement Act (ANCSA) of 1971, the Alaska National Interest Land Claims Act (ANILCA) of 1980, and the Tongass Timber Reform Act (TTRA) of 1990.

At first sight, the Statehood Act and ANCSA might appear to have little relevance to environmental politics and policy. Indeed, their major purposes were not primarily environmental in nature. The primary purpose of the Statehood Act was to authorize statehood, and of ANCSA to forge an agreement to allow building of the trans-Alaska pipeline (TAPS) while providing Alaska Natives with land and money to help preserve their culture. However, the Statehood Act granted 30 percent of Alaska's land area to the state, and ANCSA granted another 11 percent to Native corporations. These major land grants have meant that, as the environmental movement built up steam, any development of these lands would be subject to certain environmental rules and regulations.[13] And so the state and the Native community are inevitably drawn into environmental conflicts—sometimes on the developer side, sometimes on that of environmentalists, and sometimes trying to act as the arbiter.

It is more obvious why ANILCA and TTRA have had environmental political and policy impacts. Because ANCSA delivered so much of Alaska's land into the hands of those who would develop the resources for profit, environmental interests insisted on inserting a provision in Section 17(d)(2) of ANCSA to withdraw eighty million acres of federal land for interim protection. This goal was realized through ANILCA. The law put under protected status over a quarter of Alaska's land area and was a major victory for the national environmental community over vocal Alaska objections. ANILCA signaled the first major realization that Outside interests had major control over Alaska's natural resources policy and that the balance of political power had tipped in favor of those opposing development. ANILCA generated much of the antagonism toward the federal government over environmental policy that many Alaskans feel.

While confined to Southeast Alaska, TTRA brought a similar message to Alaska as ANILCA. A consequence of the federal National Forest Management Act of 1976, TTRA led to major restrictions on the use of the Tongass. TTRA can also be considered a victory for the national environmental community and culminated in the Tongass Land Management Plan (TLMP) of 1997, revised in 2008.[14] It continues to be a work in progress.

General National Laws Affecting Alaska's Environmental Politics

Sections 1 and 2 of Chapter 21, particularly Boxes 21.1 and 21.2, identify the major national laws affecting Alaska's natural resources and how they evolved. Here we identify the major ones that have affected Alaska's environmental politics. First, however, it is worth reiterating a point made in Chapter 21. This is the broadening of the concept of natural resources from the 1950s onward to include not only the land and sea and what was on and under it, but also physical beauty, clean air and water, and the intrinsic value of certain plant and animal life that makes them worth protecting. Added to these was the realization that many natural resources are finite and that when they are gone they are gone forever. It was this broader view that drove the rise of the environmental movement and played a major part in enacting federal laws to protect the environment. Without this broader definition there would be only a shadow of the present environmental movement, and Alaska, for better or for worse, would be a much different place today economically, socially, and politically.

Of the many federal environmental and related laws that apply to all states, we can single out six as being particularly significant for Alaska. These are the Clean Air Act of 1963 and its amendments over the years, the Clean Water Act of 1972 and its amendments, the National Environmental Policy Act (NEPA) of 1970, the Endangered Species Act (ESA) of 1973, the Marine Mammal Protection Act (MMPA) of 1972, and the Sustainable Fisheries Act of 1996.[15]

These six laws have affected the quality of water in Alaska's rivers and around its shores, affected the quality of air in its major cities, placed animals like the polar bear and stellar sea lion on the endangered species list, protected various marine mammals, and regulated ways of avoiding bycatch—catching fish that are not the target species of a particular fishery.

But probably the most far-reaching federal provision is NEPA's requirement of an EIS for most major development projects. The EIS requirement was a precedent-shattering invention, and public discourse on environmental issues has never been the same, as conflicts over the Pebble and Donlin Mines and hydroelectric projects like the proposed Susitna River dam attest. The requirement for an EIS, now a standard feature of the development and environmental landscape, puts the onus on developers to show that their projects are environmentally sound and will continue to be in the future. In Alaska, as elsewhere in the nation, the EIS requirement has definitely tipped the balance of power in developer-environmental conflicts in favor of environmentalists.

Key Incidents and Developments in Alaska

Along with federal and state laws, there have been several developments and incidents that shaped Alaska's environmental politics and policy. In several cases these led to legislation and regulation. Among them are some unsuccessful proposals, such as one to blast a harbor near Point Hope in Northwest Alaska with nuclear bombs and one to dam the Yukon River at Rampart in Interior Alaska, which would have created the largest reservoir in the western hemisphere. There have also been some successful proposals on which developers and environmentalists have come to agreement, most notably the Alaska pipeline and the Red Dog Mine near Kotzebue. There have been fights over predator control, polar bears, global warming, and the major disaster of the *Exxon Valdez* oil spill. Other issues, such as disputes over water and air quality, the disposal of mine tailings, and the environmental effects of taking fish by commercial, sport, and subsistence users, are less spectacular but often no less contentious and sometimes harder to resolve.

The interplay between federal and state laws and these various developments and incidents has worked to transform environmental issues from a minor part of Alaska politics at statehood to a major element in the second decade of the twenty-first century. Three particular developments have characterized this transformation. One is that, as in natural resources politics in general, the transformation has broadened the environmental policy community because of the far-reaching effects and comprehensive nature of federal and state laws. Second, it has ratcheted up the level of conflict between developers and environmentalists and sometimes has produced debates that are so contentious and emotional as to preclude compromise and the ability to move forward politically.

Third, as a consequence of the first two developments, there has been a major increase in the level of sophistication of the political advocacy of both environmental and developer interests and interest groups. National, and to some extent Alaskan, environmental interest groups cut their teeth on early conflicts like Project Chariot and the fight over the Alaska pipeline and honed their strategies and techniques on the d2 lands legislation, *Exxon Valdez*, and predator control, among others. They built on legislative and executive branch lobbying, used the courts and later public relations campaigns, and set up political action committees (PACs) to help get sympathetic supporters elected to office, particularly in Washington, D.C. Developers, too, have increased their advocacy role and adopted similar techniques. Both sides now have major financial resources, and this underlies their political power. The five case studies that follow help illustrate the increasing clash of interest groups, particularly the increasing political sophistication and influence of the environmental community.

3. FIVE CASE STUDIES

To provide concrete examples of the development and contemporary politics of environmental issues as they affect Alaska, this section presents five short case studies. These studies are not necessarily the five most significant environmental issues since statehood, but each provides insights into issues and developments that have generated national attention (in some cases taking the decision out of the hands of Alaskans), major clashes between developers and environmentalists, and aspects of the increasing range of environmental issues in the state.

The first case, Project Chariot, illustrates the early development of the environmental movement and one of the first challenges to unbridled development in Alaska. Next, the Windy Craggy debate illustrates, among other things, international cooperation among governments and the United Nations on an environmental issue, as well as the influence of environmental groups and the political naivety of a developer. The third case, the *Exxon Valdez* oil spill, shows in part how a major environmental disaster can spur government to action, increasing regulations and further tipping the political balance in favor of the environmental community. Predator control, the next case, shows the complexity of the interplay between Alaskans and their policy makers and Outside forces and of the various motives and roles of interest groups. Finally, the case of the polar bear illustrates the conflict that can develop around the 1973 Endangered Species Act and the scientific challenges that can arise regarding environmental issues.

Project Chariot

In 1958, despite a growing call to halt nuclear testing, the U.S. Atomic Energy Commission (AEC) announced "Project Chariot." The plan was to detonate five thermonuclear bombs on the Chukchi Sea coast, south of Point Hope in Northwest Alaska (see Chapter 21, Map 21.1), to blast an enormous, keyhole-shaped crater that would create a deepwater port. Alaska opinion leaders welcomed the project, but the Inupiat Eskimo residents of Point Hope voiced immediate concerns about the effects that radiation would have on the land, the animals, and the fish on which they relied for food. No one could provide an immediate answer. Chariot's proponents conducted an extensive, pre-blast scientific investigation that they hoped would placate the worriers.[16]

From simple beginnings with discussions around kitchen tables, the anti-Chariot movement grew. Point Hope artist Howard Rock joined Fairbanks journalist Tom Snapp to found the *Tundra Times*, Alaska's first statewide Alaska Native newspaper, and Chariot's opponents gained a voice. In the meantime, the fledgling Alaska Conservation Society (ACS), fresh from a successful campaign to create the Arctic National Wildlife Refuge, turned its sights on Project Chariot.

By 1961, the detonation seemed imminent, but opposition was building. Scientists had documented evidence that radioactive contamination of the area could seriously affect the entire web of life in the region. Fallout from previous nuclear tests was already accumulating in Arctic lichens at an alarming rate. Caribou eat lichens, and people eat caribou. Two scientists, Leslie Viereck and William Pruitt, who were directly involved in the pre-Chariot studies, were openly critical of the project. Both were fired from their University of Alaska positions. Prompted by local and ACS activism, national level attention by major newspapers, magazines, and interest groups brought unprecedented scrutiny to Chariot. The AEC placed the project "in abeyance" in 1962. For all practical purposes it was abandoned in 1969.

The Project Chariot experience lent momentum to protests across the nation on a range of other issues. These included government disruption of neighborhoods and environmental destruction resulting from construction of interstate highways in the 1950s and 1960s. The protests led to enactment of NEPA in 1970. So before EISs became part of the environmental landscape as a result of NEPA, Point Hope residents had, in effect, demanded that the government produce an EIS before allowing Project Chariot to proceed.

The Windy Craggy Debate

In May 1988, Canadian mining company Geddes Resources sought approval to develop a large, mainly copper, ore deposit ($8.5 billion in probable and proven reserves) within Windy Craggy Mountain, a 6,200-foot peak in northwest British Columbia (BC). The mountain sits about fifty miles north and east of Alaska's Glacier Bay National Park and Preserve, nestled among important fish and wildlife habitats (see Map 21.1).

Geddes's original proposal included a new seventy-mile road to accommodate an estimated 150 ore trucks a day. When local environmental activists objected, Geddes proposed a 150-mile slurry pipeline to carry a muddy mixture of ore and water to tidewater. Opponents worried about road accidents and pipeline breaks that could pollute the nearby Tatshenshini and Alsek Rivers. These waterways are long-held icons of pristine wilderness and popular destinations for backcountry raft and kayak enthusiasts.

But arousing greatest concern was Geddes's plan to reach the ore by cutting off the top of the mountain, grinding it up, and dumping it in nearby valleys, including the watersheds of the Tatshenshini and the Alsek. This was of particular concern because the ore and overburden (rock and soil removed to get to the ore) would oxidize into acid mine drainage, which can persist for decades and is frequently lethal to fish and other aquatic life.

By 1990, the BC, Canadian federal, and U.S. federal agencies had rejected Geddes's plan as environmentally unacceptable. Alarmed by the plans and buoyed by the governments' initial reaction to them, over fifty environmental groups banded together as Tatshenshini International (TI) to oppose the mine. They launched a public awareness campaign and mounted a multipronged lobbying effort to enlist government support in defeating the proposal.

When Geddes came back the next year with a revised plan, they attempted to avoid a NEPA review. U.S. agencies determined a NEPA review was indeed required, so Geddes postponed U.S. review pending approval of Canadian permits. TI began actively portraying Geddes as trying to circumvent environmental safeguards.

By 1992, at the urging of TI and others, the U.S. Congress had weighed in with resolutions calling for protection of the Alsek and Tatshenshini Rivers and to submit Geddes's proposal to the International Joint Commission as a trans-boundary issue. The group American Rivers designated the Tatshenshini as "the second most endangered stream in America," and the United Nations Educational, Scientific, and Cultural Organization (UNESCO) declared Glacier Bay a World Heritage Site. The BC government summarized outstanding deficiencies of the revised project plan and set a lengthy process to evaluate Geddes's proposal. Economically wounded by the delay, Geddes reduced its labor force.

By 1993, BC had confirmed Geddes's plan as environmentally unacceptable. U.S. leaders declared their willingness to use the Boundary Waters Treaty to block the mine, because of both environmental risk and Geddes's attempts to circumvent NEPA. Geddes said it would relinquish its Windy Craggy prospect for $1 billion. That summer, encouraged by public pressure, BC created the Tatshenshini-Alsek Wilderness Park, closed the region to mining, and compensated Geddes and its parent company Royal Oak Mines with a $76 million package. The following year, UNESCO sealed the deal once and for all by declaring the Kluane-Wrangell-St. Elias-Glacier Bay-Tatshenshini-Alsek park system a World Heritage Site.

Beyond Geddes's political myopia—the company seemed incapable of understanding why the public might be opposed to knocking the top off of a mountain, digging city-sized holes in the ground, and dumping potentially toxic tailings into the watersheds of world-class wilderness rivers—the Windy Craggy debate marked one of the first significant contemporary international collaborations of multiple interest groups and nongovernmental organizations. Environmental interests successfully marshaled public pressure and kept up a constant barrage on the government entities charged with reviewing

Geddes's proposal. They overwhelmed industry efforts to counter their arguments and prevailed in one government decision after another.

While the Windy Craggy project was abandoned, other cross-border mining developer versus environmental disputes are currently in play. We briefly explain them in Section 5, focusing on ongoing challenges, pending issues, and future prospects regarding Alaska's environmental politics and policy.

The *Exxon Valdez* Oil Spill

For many years there was a four-foot-high carving in marble of two sea otters in the lobby of the state capitol building in Juneau. The carving commemorated the worst ecological disaster in Alaska's history—the *Exxon Valdez* oil spill of March 1989. Until 2010 it was also the worst oil spill in U.S. history, when it was surpassed by the British Petroleum (BP) spill in the Gulf of Mexico caused by an explosion on the *Deepwater Horizon* oil drilling platform. Spilling over 170 million gallons of oil over the next several months until it was capped, the BP spill was fifteen times larger than that from the *Exxon Valdez*. Nevertheless, over eleven million gallons of crude oil spilled into Prince William Sound from Exxon's tanker and covered beaches throughout the Sound, on Kodiak Island, and all the way down to the beginning of the Aleutian chain (see Map 21.1 for its full extent). The spill had far-reaching effects on the environment and the affected local communities and prompted both the federal and state governments to adopt measures to ensure effective response to oil spills and to prevent future ones. Box 22.1 provides an overview of the event and its consequences.[17]

The spill was a major disaster and realized the worst fears of some opponents of the pipeline back in the late 1960s and early 1970s. These opponents were concerned not just about leaks or ruptures in the pipeline itself, but about precisely the kind of tanker accident that occurred in March 1989. As Box 22.1 explains, however, the nation and the state did learn from this disaster.

From an environmental policy perspective we can identify three positive governmental responses to the spill. First, and most obviously, both the state and federal governments considerably enhanced the rules and regulations designed to prevent and deal with spills in Alaska as well as elsewhere in the nation. Second, through the monitoring agencies set up by the federal government for the major areas affected by the spill, local participation of various stakeholders in oil spill prevention and related policies were enhanced. Third, the intergovernmental coordination between federal, state, and local governments and other local organizations was improved, initially in dealing with the spill and then toward better spill response and prevention for the future.

Disasters like the *Exxon Valdez* oil spill can sometimes be catalysts for improvements in governmental regulation and oversight that would not have been possible before

BOX 22.1

The *Exxon Valdez* Oil Spill: The Event and its Ecological, Economic, Political, and Policy Consequences

On the morning of March 24, 1989, Alaska, the nation, and the world awoke to the news that an oil tanker, the *Exxon Valdez*, had run aground on Bligh Reef in Prince William Sound after leaving the TAPS terminal in Valdez. Within a few days it was clear that this was a major ecological disaster that would have far-reaching economic, social, and political consequences.

The spill oiled approximately 1,300 miles of shoreline. Some 2,000 sea otters, over 300 harbor seals, and 250,000 seabirds died soon after the event. Nearly three decades later, the local ecosystem is still recovering. Herring fisheries, which were most affected by the spill, have not fully recovered. Moreover, research shows that some of the near-shore wildlife, for instance mussel beds, will take over thirty years to recover from oil contamination. And the National Oceanic and Atmospheric Administration (NOAA) estimates that 1 percent of oil spilled still remains on the beaches and continues to be toxic to wildlife. The human effects included increased alcohol and drug abuse, domestic violence, mental health problems, lost jobs, and destruction of lifestyles.

The *Exxon Valdez* disaster triggered major changes in federal and state policy. The U.S. Congress passed the Oil Pollution Act of 1990 requiring that loaded single hulled tankers be escorted by two tugs in Prince William Sound and banned single hulled tankers from U.S. waters after 2015. The act required improved preparation for oil spills, including better response plans by tanker and facility operators, prepositioned cleanup equipment, oil spill response training for commercial fishermen, establishment of a permanent oil spill response organization, and improvements to the Coast Guard's Vessel Traffic Service System, which tracks oil tankers in the Sound.

At the state level, the legislature addressed numerous spill-related issues in its 1989 and 1990 sessions. A nickel-per-barrel tax was imposed on crude oil produced in Alaska, the money going into a fund to pay state costs in preventing spills, planning state response, and responding to spills of

these disasters. Together with the BP Gulf of Mexico spill, the *Exxon Valdez* disaster has increased skepticism among the American public and many in Alaska regarding development, and oil development in particular. Both spills have had a major impact on oil and gas exploration and, it can be argued, the BP spill is yet another incident that tipped the balance in favor of the environmental community around the nation and in Alaska. In particular, it affected the plans of the Royal Dutch Shell Oil Company since 2011 to drill in the Arctic off of Alaska. Beleaguered by technical problems, anti-development interests, and difficulties in complying with federal regulations, Shell finally began drilling in the summer of 2015. At the end of the summer and after having spent some $8 billion on the drilling project over eight years, the company announced that its test well results were disappointing and that it was giving up its Arctic activities for the "foreseeable future."[18]

oil or other hazardous substances. Requirements for contingency plans were also strengthened. For example, the oil industry must have enough equipment and personnel on hand to clean up an *Exxon Valdez* scale spill within seventy-two hours. The state also increased both civil and criminal penalties for oil spills.

The disaster also triggered a long and complicated legal battle involving Exxon, the federal government, the state, and groups and individuals affected by the spill. By 1994 criminal proceedings against Joe Hazelwood, the captain of the *Exxon Valdez*, and Exxon, as well as civil suits filed by Alaska Natives and by the state and federal governments, were concluded.

However, aspects of a civil suit filed by 32,000 fishermen, businesspeople, and property owners, among others, were still in litigation as of the fall of 2015. In 1994 an Anchorage federal jury awarded $287 million in actual damages and $5 billion in punitive damages. Exxon paid the actual damages but had the punitive damages reduced in a series of appeals. This culminated in a June 2008 U.S. Supreme Court ruling that capped punitive damages at $507.5 million. Accrued interest was expected to bring the total payment to about $1 billion. The ruling provoked widespread outrage by Alaskans ranging from fishermen to Governor Sarah Palin. In August 2008, Exxon and the plaintiffs announced an agreement on payment of about $447 million of the $507.5 million of punitive damages. The company continued, however, to contest in court the remaining $60 million in punitive damages, as well as interest charges on the damages. As of 2015 Exxon also had $130 million of outstanding payments to the state of Alaska and the federal government for long-term effects of the spill.

One outcome of federal and state policy and the lawsuits was the creation of spill restoration and monitoring organizations. At the state level, the Exxon Valdez Trustee Council, made up of federal and state representatives, among other responsibilities, uses settlement funds to help restore the area affected by the spill. And two federally mandated independent, industry-funded, citizen oversight groups, the Prince William Sound and the Cook Inlet Regional Citizens' Advisory Councils, have broad responsibility for monitoring oil spill prevention and response capabilities and related duties.

Source: Authored by Stan Jones, a former reporter whose stories on the spill won national awards and who later worked for Prince William Sound Regional Citizens' Advisory Council. The overview was updated by Kristina Klimovich.

Soon thereafter, the U.S. Interior Department announced that it was cancelling future lease sales in the Arctic and would not extend current leases.[19] Although environmentalists may view all these constraints on the oil industry as very positive, others, who are concerned with Alaska's economic development, see it as detrimental to the long-term interests of the state.

Predator Control: Changing Values, Conflicts, and Complexities

Alaska, with both big game (notably moose and caribou) and large predators (wolves, brown bears, and black bears), is also unique because thousands of Alaskans subsist on wild fish and game. Especially in rural-bush Alaska, where jobs are scarce and costs are high, wild-taken food is often a necessity.

So controlling predators that might feed on this fish and game is logical and, it might seem, a simple public policy to enact. Yet, predator control, particularly involving wolves, has been one of the most contentious and complex issues in the state. In many ways, predator control is a textbook case of the complexities of environmental issues. First we review the evolution of the issue and then its political complexity.

The Evolution of the Attitudes and Public Policy toward Wolves

Perhaps no other animal symbolizes the Euro-American idea of wilderness as does the wolf, and there is a strong movement to protect the species.[20] It was not always this way, however. With the arrival of thousands of gold seekers in Alaska in the 1890s and early years of the twentieth century, indiscriminate killing of wolves became institutionalized, and later the state paid bounties for killing them. By the 1950s the federal government was conducting systematic wolf control, poisoning and shooting them from the air. There is little evidence that these extreme measures had much effect on wolf populations.

When Alaska became a state, the ADF&G, through what was then the Board of Fish and Game, a gubernatorial appointed body to oversee wildlife management, recommended hunting seasons and bag limits for wolves (subsequently, the legislature divided the single Board of Fish and Game into two boards—the Board of Fisheries and the Board of Game). By the late 1960s the state repealed the bounty system, and ADF&G suspended all wolf control programs in the belief that wolf predation on big game had little impact on overall game populations.

A series of severe winters in the late 1960s and early 1970s coincided with high numbers of wolves and excessive harvests of moose and caribou by the ever-growing population of Alaskan hunters. With moose and caribou populations declining and a growing number of vocal hunters demanding more game, ADF&G tried several ways to increase game populations. These included reducing or eliminating hunting seasons—not popular with hunters—and various wildlife habitat improvement projects, but nothing worked. By the late 1970s ADF&G resorted to lethal wolf control efforts. But by this time the image of wolves had changed from vermin requiring elimination to the quintessential symbol of all that is wild and free. Unfortunately, even into the 1980s, the State of Alaska was either unaware of, or politically insensitive to, the symbolic power that the wolf had acquired over most Americans.

A major controversy erupted when ADF&G resumed wolf control programs and supported regulations allowing hunters and trappers to use aircraft to locate wolves, land, and then shoot them. Environmental organizations and animal rights groups reacted by initiating media campaigns and lengthy legal challenges against both ADF&G and hunters and trappers. In 1990 ADF&G brought together a citizens' wolf management planning team of hunters, trappers, and environmentalists, culminating in the development of a Strategic Wolf Management Plan. In 1991 the state adopted the plan, which called for long-term wolf conservation.

This progressive plan did not last long. In 1992 the Board of Game approved a renewed aerial wolf hunt. In response, environmentalists called for a boycott of Alaska. The state's growing tourist industry was dependent upon visitors from Outside, and Alaska stood to lose millions of dollars from a boycott. With pressure from organizations like the Alaska Visitors' Association (at that time the state's tourist industry trade association and lobby), the state backed down, canceling its 1992–1993 aerial wolf hunt. Governor Walter Hickel then called for another wolf summit. In 1994 the legislature passed the "intensive management" law, directing the Board of Game to identify areas where human consumption of big game is a priority. In those areas, the board designated target levels of game populations and annual harvests. If either fell below those targets, ADF&G would take action to reverse the declines. It was in an effort to do this that snares were set for wolves in 1994, and the issue hit the national news with footage of a wolf's paw caught in a snare and the animal trying to gnaw its paw off. Again, major national protests ensued.

The Motives of Pro and Con Predator Control Interests, and the Influence of Outside versus In-State Forces

As a result of this history of wolf and other predator control, the politics surrounding the issue have come to involve a wide range of lobbying tactics. Both Outside and Alaska environmental interest groups employ traditional advocacy tactics such as lobbying the legislative and executive branches, using PACs to help fund political campaigns, and working on elections to get sympathetic candidates elected to office, among other tactics. In addition, these groups sometimes employ confrontational tactics to delay or derail planned actions or activities already under way. In the case of predator control, for example, confrontational efforts included lawsuits, requests for public records, petitions, public advertising campaigns, boycotts like those referred to above, and other actions. Such tactics often undermine active control programs and occupy agencies with administrative minutiae that distract agency personnel from program implementation. Clearly, as indicated by the history of predator control in the 1990s, Outside forces can exert considerable influence.

To be sure, political pressure on the legislature, the Board of Game, and ADF&G also comes from inside Alaska. Four times between 1996 and 2008 Alaska's electorate voted on citizen-sponsored ballot initiatives regarding predator control. With major funding from outside the state, campaigns supporting or opposing these locally instigated initiatives and other wildlife-related issues have spent millions of dollars on publicity in Alaska. In examining two of these four ballot measures, Box 22.2 explains how these propositions often involve complex sets of political alliances and do not always work out to the satisfaction of Outside environmental interests.

Furthermore, emotionally charged solicitations about wolves and bears sent out by interest groups to draw attention to predator control generate thousands of impassioned complaints annually to the State of Alaska and the U.S. federal government. They also attract financial contributions needed to pay staff, monitor changes in laws and regulations, review public records, track ongoing control efforts, orchestrate campaigns to oppose programs, and spread their perspective among the public. Competition for the public's limited dollars and attention is fierce. Thus, environmental interests regularly raise the wildlife equivalent of a revolutionary martyr's bloody shirt to rally their supporters. When another group does likewise, the first finds a bloodier shirt and holds it higher. In the age of electronic communications, such campaigns are widespread and enormous in scope. Opposing predator control is big business.

The ADF&G is caught in the middle of pro and con predator control advocates. The department is quick to point out that their task is to ensure viable populations of all wildlife, predators and prey alike. They profess reliance on scientific data to support their courses of action, and claim intent to maintain sustainable numbers of wolves throughout their range in Alaska. This is quite contrary to common charges by opponents.

Polar Bears, Global Warming, and the Endangered Species Act (ESA)

In the early 2000s, evidence of diminishing sea ice habitat led some scientists and environmental activists to call for the federal government to list the polar bear as threatened under the ESA. The ESA is intended to protect species and the ecosystems upon which they depend. To this end, it dictates some actions and prohibits others to help species recover to desirable population levels, including limiting or prohibiting development and other activities likely to degrade critical habitats. The case of the polar bear provides insights into the political conflicts and complications that an ESA listing can produce.

In 2008, and interestingly under the conservative, generally pro-development, George W. Bush administration, the U.S. Fish and Wildlife Service (USFWS) placed the polar bear on the "threatened" list under ESA. This is one step below the designation of "endangered" under the act. The "threatened" listing was the result of a 2005 petition and litigation filed by three environmental interest groups: the Center for Biological Diversity, the Natural Resources Defense Council, and Greenpeace. The polar bear was the first species added to the Endangered Species List due solely to the threat from global warming.[21]

The listing produced increased scrutiny of the bears' sea ice habitat and placed restrictions on the exploration and development of petroleum resources both on and offshore from Alaska's North Slope, covering 187,000 square miles. A major conflict ensued between the proponents and opponents of the listing. This was a familiar fight, with developers complaining that economic benefits were being threatened by

BOX 22.2

Ballot Measures and Predator Control: The Complexities of Environmental Politics Writ Large

The fallout from the predator control furor in the 1990s resulted, in part, in a 1996 ballot measure to prohibit airborne hunting of wolf, wolverine, fox, and lynx, one in 1998 to prohibit wolf snares, a third in 2004 to prohibit bear baiting, and a fourth in 2008 to prohibit hunting wolf and bear the same day that a hunter was airborne. Here we examine the politics involved in the 1998 and 2004 propositions.

In 1998, a citizens' group placed an initiative on the November general election ballot prohibiting not only the use of snares in trapping wolves, but also possessing, buying, selling, or offering for sale the hide of a wolf taken in a snare. As with previous ballot initiatives regarding Alaska predators, in-state proponents were joined by Outside animal rights and wildlife advocacy groups. They mounted a well-funded and hard-hitting advertising campaign in an attempt to secure voter approval.

Fearing that passage of the measure would unleash a backlash against all hunting and trapping, rural-bush, Native, and subsistence interests in Alaska joined forces with urban hunters and trappers (their sometime opponents on fish and game issues). Their Coalition for the Alaska Way of Life raised over $250,000 (including Outside funds) and focused advertising on the perceived threat to Alaska, especially rural-bush, lifestyles. The initiative failed by 63–37 percent, an overwhelming defeat.

A 2004 ballot measure to criminalize the baiting of bears—a technique used to entice bears for easier hunting—attracted advertisements and expressions of support from concerned citizens, environmental groups, and animal rights organizations. Well-financed and armed with compelling advertisements, Citizens United Against Bear Baiting characterized shooting bears over bait as unsportsmanlike and unfair, a threat to public safety, and an unnecessary management tool. The measure seemed destined to win voter approval.[1]

Once again, an unlikely ad hoc coalition of several disparate hunting and outdoor groups banded together to highlight the importance of hunting to Alaskans. Urban hunters and rural-bush subsistence proponents united to defend what they saw as a common tradition. Their strongest tactic was to portray the ballot measure as an attempt by non-Alaska environmental extremists to dictate how Alaskans should manage their wildlife. The opponents warned that if Outside extremists prevailed, and uneducated voters' opinions replaced the scientific judgment of professional wildlife managers, predator populations would rage out of control.

The sponsors—cast by the opponents as Outsiders—pledged to reject campaign donations from Outside Alaska. But ironically the opponents themselves raised significant campaign funds from Outside donors and outspent the sponsors seven to one. The initiative failed 57–43 percent.

Of the four predator control ballot propositions since 1996, only the 1996 one prohibiting airborne hunting received voter approval, with a margin of 59–41 percent. The fact that the major national publicity regarding the wolf kill (particularly the footage of the wolf's paw caught in the snare), was still fresh in the minds of many Alaskans, may have accounted for the 1996 proposition's success. The 2008 initiative to prohibit same-day airborne hunting failed 55 to 45, a result that was made possible, in part, by portraying the supporters as Outsiders trying to tell Alaskans how to run their affairs. So, at least in regard to predator control, campaigns organized by Outsiders wielded limited influence upon state decision makers and on the Alaska public, despite huge expenditures and legions of upset Americans. Even Alaskans who might agree with national interest group positions on predator control frequently resent Outside money and influence expended on state election issues.

---

[1] Dean E. Murphy, "Bear Baiting as a Way of Life Is on the Ballot," *New York Times*, October 16, 2004.

Source: Developed by the authors.

government regulations inspired by environmentalists and enforced by the federal government. Designating polar bears as threatened did not sit well with developers, particularly the oil industry, with some hunting and fishing groups, or with the State of Alaska.[22] Opponents filed court challenges to the listing.

The trigger for the Endangered Species Act listing of polar bears as threatened was that there was sufficient evidence to conclude that their current worldwide population is likely to become an endangered species throughout all or significant portions of their roaming range within the foreseeable future. The evidence to support the listing had to be demonstrable data rather than predictive models. The evidence presented and on which decisions were made, however, combined present data and predictive models. Given this combination, opponents of the listing argued that curtailing development activities is of dubious benefit to the bears. Proponents of the listing maintained that the action was absolutely necessary. [23]

In June 2008 a federal judge upheld the USFWS decision that polar bears throughout their range should be protected as a "threatened" species under the ESA. The opponents appealed, but the ruling was upheld again by a federal judge in June 2011.[24] The developers and the state did not give up and continued to fight the listing into 2013. Opponents argued that the polar bear was not decreasing in numbers and that the ESA was being used for the wrong reasons—not to protect an endangered animal, but to prevent development of resources from which Alaska would benefit.[25] In February 2013 the U.S. Court of Appeals in Washington, D.C., upheld the June 2011 decision. So the polar bear remains on the "threatened" list and is likely a candidate for the "endangered" list under the act.[26]

The case of the polar bear illustrates some of the scientific issues involved in justifying placing a species on the endangered list, and the problems of data to back up environmental policy in general. Scientists studying polar bears face a difficult dilemma. The more pessimistic of several future climate models predict significant loss of sea ice in this century, which researchers largely agree is almost certain to exert adverse impacts on polar bears and other marine mammals. Intuitively, if polar bears' sea ice habitat diminishes, their numbers will fall. But, as the state argues, actual data show that bear populations are generally robust and stable, and suggest the recent unprecedented retreat of Arctic sea ice has not adversely affected polar bears. Experts are nowhere near agreeing on whether or how to use climate modeling to predict future sea ice/polar bear dynamics. In the midst of such disagreements, politics has more room to play a role. And while there was also scientific data to support the listing of both the Stellar sea lion and the beluga whale, politics had its role to play in those listings too, which the state also opposed.[27]

4. SUSTAINABLE DEVELOPMENT: A SOLUTION FOR ALASKA?

Several of the case studies considered in this chapter, in Chapter 21 on land policy, and in the fisheries and oil and gas chapters to come, document some intense and emotional conflicts between developers and environmentalists. The conflicts often involve long drawn-out litigation, name-calling on both sides, and the expenditure of millions of dollars by each side to achieve their policy goals. Compromise is often hard to achieve. The result is that decisions are often imposed by federal agencies and the courts and are not the result of consensus. Lack of consensus and disgruntled stakeholders on one or both sides just prolong the conflicts.

One approach that has gotten a great deal of press since the early 1980s to try to minimize developer-environmentalist conflict is to apply the concept of *sustainable development*. This approach is an attempt to "do development right" and deal with the tradeoffs between economic benefit and environmental protection so that both sides and society as a whole benefit. Many argue that this approach is the path that the United States and Alaska should take in dealing with the developer-environmentalist clash. We now look at the theory behind sustainable development and its practical application to Alaska.

The Concept of Sustainable Development

Sustainable development is a broad term often used in different ways by economists, sociologists, and political scientists. In the political realm and in regard to public policy, it usually denotes the need to strike a middle course between economic development and maintaining the ecological balance of an area. The concept of sustaining (or maintaining) natural systems (ecosystems) in the face of increasing human pressures from growing populations has been around since the late 1960s. But it was the United Nation, World Commission on Environment and Development (the Brundtland Commission, named after its chairman Gro Harlem Brundtland) that provided the definition of sustainable development commonly used today: "development that meets the needs of the present without compromising the ability of future generations to meet their own needs."[28]

The origin of the term was, therefore, an international one. International conferences, most notably in Rio de Janeiro in 1992, as well as academic analyses, have refined and advanced the term.[29] The literature and writing on sustainable development is voluminous. But central to both the practical and academic concept of sustainable development is that economic growth and market economies are not necessarily in conflict with environmental goals. The concept presupposes a dialogue between developers and environmentalists, in contrast to the violent clashes and protests of the 1960s and 1970s. Even as business interests offer their solutions to protect the environment, sustainable development allows for the incorporation of environmental concerns into the economic system.

Intuitively, sustainable development sounds like the ideal solution to balancing development and environmental protection and maintaining the political and cultural systems and values of various groups and societies. It is an idea upon which a general consensus can be reached and has become a rallying cry for various businesses and environmental groups around the world, particularly in the United States and Western Europe. At first sight it sounds like an approach that could help deal with many of the chronic developer-environmentalist conflicts that Alaska faces. However, it is not as simple as it appears.

The Challenge of Putting Sustainable Development into Practice

There are many examples of practical efforts to achieve sustainable development. For instance, Canada passed a Federal Sustainable Development Act in 2008, with the federal government defining goals and establishing implementation strategies for each goal.[30] Each government agency has a responsibility to work together and integrate environmental concerns in their decision making.

In the United States, Maryland adopted the genuine progress indicator (GPI), which measures economic growth, similar to gross national product, and discounts so-called uneconomic growth.[31] In other words, GPI strives to measure sustainable growth, well-being, and the quality of life. GPI incorporates twenty-six social, economic, and environmental measurements. The concept of sustainability has also been part of some U.S. federal policies. For instance, it was a major aspect of the 1996 revisions to the Magnuson-Stevens Fishery Conservation and Management Act of 1976. The 1996 revision included provisions to reduce bycatch, to consider the effects of management decisions on communities, and to protect fish habitats.

The theory of sustainable development may be laudable, but putting it into practice is problematic. For one thing, there is no clear process for turning the theory into policy, particularly in specific cases. As a concept it is sufficiently vague that it can mean different things to different constituencies and can be used as political subterfuge by some. At the international level, a series of meetings regarding sustainable development, referred to as "Rio + 20," faced mounting criticism for failing to reach a binding agreement in order to tackle imminent environmental issues.[32] Furthermore, criticism arises when companies or rich countries use the concept as mere rhetoric to justify their economic activity. And developing economies, like India and China, see balancing economic development with environmental concerns as putting a drag on their economic growth. Consequently, they pay only lip service to sustainable development or ignore it entirely.

In various ways, most of these shortcomings of sustainable development as a practical tool, particularly the vagueness of the term, undermine its use in Alaska. What may be seen as sustainable development by the developer on a particular project, such as the Pebble Mine, may be viewed as far from sustainable by environmentalists, and vice versa.

So a general consensus on protecting the environment often does not pan out in particular instances. In Alaska this may be intensified by the "get in, get rich, and get out quick" mentality of some developers. These developers may have no long-term interest in the state other than economic benefit, but use the idea of sustainable development as a public relations tool. So in the end the developer-environmentalist conflict over particular issues and projects will boil down to a power relationship and who can exert the most political influence.

5. ONGOING CHALLENGES, PENDING ISSUES, AND FUTURE PROSPECTS

What is the future likely to hold for Alaska's environmental politics and policy? Can we expect more of the same conflicts described in the chapter so far, or will there be new developments that change the direction of this aspect of the state's crucial natural resource issues and how they are dealt with? These, of course, are questions with numerous aspects, and the answers are largely speculative. Nevertheless, they are important questions because environmental issues are taking up an increasing share of Alaska's political energy both within the state and in its relations with the federal government.

By using past and present experiences as a guide we examine six topics that together provide some indication of what the future may hold. These are (1) demand for Alaska's resources and Outside pressures, (2) continuing big development projects, (3) Canadian-Southeast Alaska cross-border disputes, (4) global warming, (5) increasing urbanization, and (6) the continuing search for compromise.

Demand for Alaska's Resources and Outside Pressures

National and global demand for Alaska's energy and other resources will certainly increase in the years ahead. New technologies will enable extraction of previously inaccessible commodities. Increasing demand with rising prices will enable previously uneconomic natural resources to be developed. This means that the state will continue to attract investments from Outside by those who see big profits. On the other side, environmental interest groups are likely to continue to grow in membership and oppose many development schemes, and development interests will continue to fight them. Both will enlist the assistance of large Outside groups and their money. In addition, national and international public opinion will likely grow in importance, largely in the direction of favoring the environment.

Continuing Big Development Projects

It is a safe bet that big development projects will continue to be proposed and that some will actually take place. Future development is likely because of the attractiveness of big profits as well as Alaska's need for employment, infrastructure, and state revenues. In addition, the sheer size of the state often necessitates projects of enormous size, like the 789-mile-long trans-Alaska pipeline (TAPS). Questionable ideas, such as damming the Yukon for hydroelectric power, piping fresh water to California, and covering McKinley Village at Denali National Park with a huge Teflon dome, have all been abandoned, but new plans emerge from creative capitalist minds every day.

Among the major projects underway as of 2016 are the Pebble Mine and the Donlin Mine in Southwest Alaska (see Chapter 21, Map 21.1 and Box 22.4) and talk of a dam and hydroelectric generation on the Susitna River. The Susitna project was initially proposed in the1980s but was abandoned because of lack of funds. The idea was revived around 2010, but lack of funds again put the project on hold as of 2016. One day, however, it is likely to be built and unleash a raft of developer-environmentalist conflicts. But the most ambitious project proposed since the TAPS was developed, though its construction is still uncertain, is that of a natural gas pipeline.

Until 2014 the route favored by state officials was to parallel TAPS for part of its route and transport natural gas to Alaskan, Canadian, and Lower 48 markets. But when natural gas prices fell, the plan shifted to an in-state gas line with a terminus in Southcentral Alaska, with perhaps exports of liquefied natural gas to Japan and other Asian destinations.[33] Once again, the impetus of profit is the most powerful force behind this project, with additional momentum from the prospect of increased state revenues, and alternative, more affordable energy, especially for Fairbanks and the Anchorage area. On one side of the issue, proponents tout jobs and positive economic benefits. On the other are those with land use and environmental impact concerns. In the end, however, it will be the viability of the markets for natural gas and the economics of building the pipeline that will overshadow development and environmental concerns in determining the future of this project.

Cross-Border Disputes: Canadian Mining versus Alaska Salmon

As we saw with the Windy Craggy case study, the proximity of the Canadian province of British Columbia (BC) to Southeast Alaska and its marine life makes mining development in BC of particular concern to Southeast Alaska residents (see Map 21.1). The concern centers on salmon-spawning rivers and their tributaries, particularly the Taku, Stikine, Unuk, and Nass Rivers that are in the watershed of many BC mines and flow across the border into Alaska's Inside Passage waters. According to opponents of the mines, Canadian water-quality standards for rivers and streams are less stringent than U.S. standards, running the risk of river pollution. This could seriously affect both the cash economy of fishing and the subsistence lifestyle of the region's Alaska Natives.[34]

What makes these continuing issues potentially more complex and difficult to solve is that they require agreement between two sovereign nations—the United States and Canada. Sometimes such agreements are possible, as in Windy Craggy, but more often they are less easily resolved. One long drawn out dispute is reopening the Tulsequah Chief Mine just over the border northeast of Juneau and near the Canadian headwaters of the Taku River. This dispute has been ongoing since Governor Tony Knowles's second term in the late 1990s.[35]

As of 2015 there were twenty-one mining projects in northwest British Columbia that were either in operation or in the later stages of exploration. Besides the Tulsequah, these include the Red Chris Mine, the Galore Creek Mine, the Schaft Creek Mine, and the large multimetal Kerr-Sulphurets-Mitchell, or KSM, Mine. Many, including the KSM Mine, are large open-pit developments similar to the proposed Pebble Mine in Southwest Alaska. Like Pebble, the fear is that the mine tailings, which turn very acidic, can pollute the rivers and streams if they are not properly stored. Most open pit mines use a tailings dam. But if not properly constructed these dams can fail, as one did at the Mount Polley Mine in east-central BC in August 2014.

The issue of the effects of BC mining on Southeast Alaska salmon involves a host of interests. On the one side opposing the developments are Southeast communities, like Ketchikan, Petersburg, Sitka, and Wrangell, and the State of Alaska, which in 2015 established a working group on the issue. These governments have been joined by conservation groups, like Rivers Without Borders and Inside Passage Waterkeepers as well as Native groups like the Tlingit-Haida Central Council and the United Tribal Transboundary Mining Work Group. On the other side are the mining companies, like Seabridge Gold of Toronto and Imperial Metals of Vancouver, the BC Ministry of Energy and Mining, and the Canadian federal government. The First Nations people in British Columbia are divided; some view jobs as key, while others see protecting their lifestyle as paramount. The latter group has worked with Southeast Alaska tribal organizations.

The Canadians are willing to put the issue for consideration before the Pacific Northwest Economic Region, a public/private nonprofit for enhancing the quality of life in the region. But mine opponents see this organization as too development oriented. Several communities in Southeast Alaska have appealed to the U.S. federal government to intervene and invoke the arbitration authority of the International Joint Commission established by the Border Waters Treaty Act of 1909 by the United States and Canada. But so far the Canadians have resisted using this body.

Clearly, there is no benefit to Southeast Alaska from BC mining development. There is only the great potential of environmental disasters waiting to happen. But the current pro-development policy of the BC and Canadian federal governments as of 2016 has given the advantage to the Canadian mines. Furthermore, as an international issue it is one over which even the U.S. federal government has little influence. Judging by the past and given the BC and Canadian federal governments' current position, this issue could remain unresolved for decades.

Global Warming or Climate Change

Because Alaska is more susceptible than other states to the effects of global warming, the state is on the front lines of the emerging battles over global warming often referred to as climate change. For this reason, President Obama, the first U.S. president to travel to the Arctic, visited the state in late summer 2015 to, in part, highlight the problem of the consequences of global warming by visiting several places affected by the problem, including Kotzebue.[36]

Much of the state is underlain by permafrost, and northern portions are surrounded seasonally by ocean ice. At high latitudes, even minor temperature changes can trigger widespread thawing, with potentially enormous economic impacts and other disruptions. Thawing can cause subsidence of the ground that supports homes, businesses, and transportation infrastructure. Temperature changes can alter vegetation systems over large areas, with attendant changes in the wildlife communities that rely on them. Retreating sea ice has been cited as a concern for the future health of marine mammal populations. The ramifications of catastrophic climate change are largely conjectural, but potentially devastating.

The likely effect on the polar bear, considered earlier, is just the leading edge of what will surely be a growing concern over the predicted effects of a warmer earth. Climate change will affect debate on new developments, especially extraction of fossil fuels and the climatic impacts of using them. Engineering and economic implications of thawing permafrost are hard to predict. But they could well overwhelm political discussion as Alaskans address the implications of everything from moving coastal communities ahead of rising sea levels and shoring up or rebuilding infrastructure collapsed into thermokarst sinkholes, to responding to changes in economically important salmon runs, and adapting to new biological regimes and the changes in plant and animal life those changes will bring.

Because climate change has such major implications for Alaska, it is listed in Chapter 30 (dealing with Alaska's future challenges and prospects for reform) as one of the major concerns and challenges for the years to come.[37]

The Consequences of Increasing Urbanization

As more and more people move to the state and to Alaska's cities from rural-bush areas, increasing urbanization may affect the political balance of the core of environmental politics—the developer-environmentalist debate. Urbanization has certainly affected the way Alaskans think about fish (or no longer think about them), as Chapter 23 points out. In many ways urbanization is likely to promote the environmentalist cause, with urban Alaskans more likely to share the values of Lower 48 urbanites that call into question the desirability of predator control and mine development, among other forms of development. On the other hand, recreational hunting and fishing interests in Alaska have considerable political influence, and when Alaskans were in a position to adopt or reject a ballot initiative restricting wolf hunting, even urban Alaskans became resentful of too much Outside influence and accordingly voted against the restrictions (see Box 22.2).

The Search for Compromise in the Developer-Environmentalist Debate

It will not be easy to find a satisfactory way for developers and environmentalists in Alaska as well as Outside interests to deal with issues calmly and rationally and replace the pitched battles and often highly emotional conflicts of the past. As we have seen, sustainable development is a worthy general concept, but it is not a practical solution on an issue-by-issue basis. Political power relationships will most likely continue to dominate in this conflict. In some circumstances there may be a way to resolve issues if there is a reason for both sides to buy into a solution. Box 22.3 offers one way of approaching this problem.[38]

From the perspective of Alaska, it might behoove the state government to be less confrontational with Washington, D.C., and come to realize it will probably get more by trying to work with the federal government than against it on major issues. However, as we noted earlier, some politicians will find it easier to get elected and re-elected if they are more confrontational than cooperative. At the same time, environmentalists must also realize that they need to compromise as well and that, in the very extreme, zero development may mean that there will be many fewer humans around to enjoy the pristine environment.

6. CONCLUSION: RECONCILING DEVELOPMENT AND ENVIRONMENTALISM AND STATE AND NATIONAL INTERESTS

In concluding our consideration of Alaska environmental politics and policy, we return to the question in the subtitle of the chapter. Can conflicts between and among developers and environmentalists and state and national interests be reconciled? At the end of Section 1 of this chapter, we concluded that Alaska has little influence over this policy area and so Alaska policy is really just a part of national environmental policy. After considering the case studies, can we still draw the same conclusion? We approach

BOX 22.3

"Eco-nomics": An Approach to Resolving the Developer-Environmentalist Conflict

As the late Alaska Governor Jay Hammond noted, it is not just the nature and size of Alaska's development proposals but also the nature of Alaskans that make Alaska such a battleground for conservation issues. As he observed, the two types of people most inclined to come to the Great Land assure conflict. Along with would-be rustics comes another type of pioneer no less determined to find a different kind of good life—the developer. In an effort to bridge the gap between developers and environmentalists, Hammond often empathized a little with both factions. He often placed a foot in each camp, only to find he had stepped into a campfire.

As a professional natural resource manager engaged in fish politics, I too found myself stepping in many fires. But I have also experienced progress. I learned that instead of looking for trade-offs between environmental and economic values, I accomplished more when I looked for synergy of interests. When I focused on ways to fuse agendas, to translate environmental concerns into economic interests, and vice versa, I gained more political traction.

Connect community planning, economic theory, and ecology 101, and it becomes easier to see that healthy environments and stable economies have a yin-yang relationship in which one supports the other. Stable, healthy ecosystems sustain economic communities. Stable economies foster better environmental practices than unstable, boom-and-bust economies. The renewability of Alaska's natural resources and the long-term viability of its air, water, and land are more readily advanced by a caring society that has long-term growth and stability. And conversely, sustained and controlled growth comes with thoughtful management of renewable resources and healthy ecosystems. In other words, it is not jobs *versus* the environment, but rather jobs *and* the environment. It is about tapping into the synergy of having both sound economies and healthy ecosystems. My shorthand description for this synergy is *eco-nomics*.

And where better to practice eco-nomics than in Alaska? After all, in 1998, economist Steve Colt with the University of Alaska's Institute of Social and Economic Research determined that 84,000 jobs in Alaska are dependent on healthy ecosystems, and likely the number is nearer 100,000 in 2016. Where else in the world do you have four large-scale fisheries leading the way for sustainable fisheries and certified by an international eco-labeling program? Where else do you have one of the first laws regulating cruise ship discharges? Certainly, Alaska represents the place "to do development right."

Along with these advances, we are also seeing a shift in attitudes. For example, in a statewide poll conducted in July of 2006, 79 percent of Alaska's registered voters considered themselves to be either strong or moderate conservationists. These results suggest we are getting closer to Governor Hammond's dream for Alaska that only through an amalgam of economics and environmentalism can Alaska hope to sustain values that make this the place most of us wish to live.

However, value shifts alone will not suffice to address Alaska's most serious challenges—a natural gas pipeline, global warming, and ocean acidification. To face these daunting challenges we must have more eco-nomics merging within our systems of action and change, not less. Economy with Ecology. Markets with Causes. Technology with Knowledge. Conservation with Community. Politics with Vision. Then, and only then, can Alaska become ground zero for solutions. Then, and only then, can we take Governor Hammond's vision for Alaska to the next level for future generations.

Source: Authored by Kate Troll, who has spent many years involved in Alaska natural resource politics.

the answer by viewing it as a product of the characteristics of Alaska politics that influence environmental issues and their resolution.

Two of these characteristics in combination—the influence of external forces and the all-pervasive importance of government, particularly the federal government—mean that when external forces and the federal government share a common interest in the outcome of an issue that the state opposes, there is little hope of reconciling state and national interests. The imposition of federal rules is the almost certain outcome. This is also often the case with issues when American public opinion becomes a major political factor. In these situations, with the overwhelming power of Outside forces, the developer-environmentalist conflict is generally resolved by power, these days often in favor of environmentalists.

In the case of high-profile issues attracting national attention, the state often does not help itself by resorting to another characteristic of Alaska and environmental politics, that of relying on myths and political rhetoric—claiming its rights and filing largely baseless lawsuits that just prolong the conflicts and that are usually decided against the state. On occasion the involvement of Alaska Natives, another characteristic we identified in relation to environmental politics, can make a difference to promote in-state interests, as in the case of predator control. On the other hand, Native involvement can also work to promote the interests of both Outside development and environmental forces, as in the case of some mining projects like the Red Dog Mine near Kotzebue and the opposition by some Native groups to opening ANWR.

In general, reconciliation among the state, developers, and environmentalists is more likely to occur on a negotiated basis and be acceptable to all parties when there is less Outside interest and involvement, such as on the cruise ship waste water legislation in 2001. So this is a qualification of our initial conclusion at the end of Section 1 that Alaska environmental policy is almost identical with national policy toward the state. This means that although the concept of the Owner State has very limited meaning if national forces are deeply involved, Alaska solutions can be found when Alaska is left to itself to resolve an issue.

Given increasing globalization and increasing developer and environmentalist interest in Alaska, it is uncertain how many development issues will remain solely Alaska issues. This may be bad news for many Alaskans, particularly those favoring development. On the other hand, those Alaskans who support the environmental cause may see this as a positive development. As pointed out in this chapter and in Chapter 21, it is Outside influence that gives the environmentalist cause in Alaska a prominence it would not have if it were entirely Alaska based.

What is certain is that the conflicts between pro-development Alaskans, environmentalists, Alaska Natives, and the state and federal governments will continue as long as there are natural resources in the state to fight over. And to an increasing extent, the young bear that wandered into the lobby of Bartlett Regional Hospital will have her fate determined less by the hospital evening staff and more and more by the power politics of the developer-environmentalist struggle.

ENDNOTES

[1] Jack Caldwell, "Kensington Mine, Alaska Opens Officially," *I Think Mining*, September 30, 2010; and Russell Stigall, "Kensington Mine Continues to Grow," *Juneau Empire*, April 12, 2012.

[2] See Chapter 7, especially Section 3, on the Outside economy for the importance of Outside capital to Alaska's economic development.

[3] For a consideration of Alaska as a colony and what this may and may not mean in the past and present, see Chapter 1, Box 1.4.

[4] The dominant political significance of the federal government in IGR is covered in Chapter 10, particularly Sections 2, 3, 4, and 5.

[5] Kelsey Gobroski, "Juneau Access Funding in Gov's Proposed Budget," KTOO, *Morning Edition*, December 24, 2012; Annie Feidt, "State Presses BLM on Legacy Well Issue," *Alaska News Nightly*, Alaska Public Radio Network (APRN), December 11, 2012; four news releases by the Associated Press: "NPS Proposes to Counteract State Hunting Changes," December 11, 2012; "Treadwell Certifies Proposed Initiative on Mining," December 20, 2012; "Hydro Project Planners Submit Environmental Plans," December 18, 2012; and "EPA: No New Timetable for Bristol Bay Report," December 20, 2012. In addition, Lisa Demer, "Tow Lines Attached to Shell Oil Drilling Vessel in Gulf of Alaska," *Anchorage Daily News*, December 31, 2012, was just one of a host of stories in the news in December 2012 regarding Shell's failed attempt to drill in the Arctic because of failing to meet EPA and other regulations.

[6] Michael F. Turek, "Three Case-Studies: The Arctic National Wildlife Refuge, Management of the Tongass National Forest, and Wolf Management," in *Alaska Public Policy Issues: Background and Perspectives*, ed. Clive S. Thomas (Juneau: Denali Press, 1999), 195.

[7] The provisions of the 1982 initiative can be found at http://ballotpedia.org/wiki/index.php/Alaska_State_Ownership_of_Federal_Land_Initiative_%281982%29; and for the 2015 legislative activity, see Alexandra Gutierrez, "House Passes Bill to Seize State Lands," *Alaska News Nightly* (APRN), April 7, 2015.

[8] See Governor Walter J. Hickel, "Who Owns Alaska?" Governor's Weekly Radio Commentary, April 9, 1994; and the following obituary of Hickel which succinctly sums up the conflict between his development and conservation views, Dennis Hevesi, "Walter Hickel, Nixon Interior Secretary Dies at 90," *New York Times*, May 8, 2010.

[9] For a general treatment of environmental politics and policy see, for the national level, Norman J. Vig and Michael E. Kraft, *Environmental Policy: New Directions for the Twenty-First Century*, 8th ed. (Washington, D.C.: CQ Press, 2012), and David M. Konisky and Neal D. Woods. "Environmental Policy," in *Politics in the American States: A Comparative Analysis*, eds. Virginia Gray, Russell L. Hanson, and Thad Kousser, 10th ed. (Washington, D.C.: CQ Press, 2013); and for the Western states, Zachary A. Smith, and John C. Freemuth, eds., *Environmental Politics and Policy in the West*, rev. ed. (Boulder, CO: University Press of Colorado, 2007); and Sheldon Kamieniecki, Matthew A. Cahn, and Eugene R. Goss, "Western Governments and Environmental Policy," in *Politics and Public Policy in the Contemporary American West*, ed. Clive S. Thomas (Albuquerque: University of New Mexico Press, 1991).

[10] See Chapter 18, Sections 4 and 5.

[11] Confusingly, Alaska is a perpetual leader in toxic waste output per capita. This is because of the way the figures are calculated. Spreading waste output across the relatively few Alaska residents results in an apparently incongruously large per capita figure. But calculations on a per acre basis produce a significantly lower figure.

[12] John Muir, *Travels in Alaska: The Trip of 1879, Part I* (Boston and New York: Houghton Mifflin Company, 1915).

[13] For an overview of the politics involved in ANCSA in relation to the building of the trans-Alaska pipeline (TAPS), see Chapter 9 on Alaska Natives and the state's political economy, particularly Section 1.

[14] See Chapter 21, Section 7 for an overview of the development of the Tongass issue.

[15] Although NEPA was enacted in January 1970, it is often referred to as the "National Environmental Policy Act of 1969" as most of the work on the bill was completed in 1969. This accounts for some sources giving the date of the act as 1969.

[16] This section on Project Chariot draws in part on Dan O'Neill, *The Firecracker Boys: H-bombs, Inupiat Eskimos, and the Roots of the Environmental Movement* (New York: St. Martin's Press, 1995). Republished by Basic Books in 2007.

[17] Besides the help of Stan Jones, this section on the *Exxon Valdez* oil spill draws on Natural Resources Defense Council, 2012, "NRDC: Arctic Drilling Invites Environmental Nightmare," at http://www.nrdc.org/media/2012/120626a.asp; The *Daily Green*, 2012, "4 Dirty Secrets of the *Exxon Valdez* Oil Spill," at http://www.thedailygreen.com/environmental-news/latest/exxon-valdez-20-years-47032401#ixzz2DvcoFefV; Faegre Baker Daniels [law firm], 2011, "*Exxon Valdez* Oil Spill Litigation Update," at http://www.faegrebd.com/2881; *Scientific American*, "Environmental Effects of Exxon Valdez Spill Still Being Felt," at http://www.scientificamerican.com/article.cfm?id=environmental-effects-of; Exxon Qualified Settlement Fund, "Litigation History," at http://www.exspill.com/News/LitigationHistory/tabid/1918/Default.aspx; and PEER (Protecting Employees Who Protect Our Environment), "Exxon Valdez Dispute Drags on into 2015 and Perhaps Beyond," November 10, 2014, at: http://www.peer.org/news/news-releases/2014/11/10/exxon-valdez-damages-suit-drags-into-2015-and-perhaps-beyond/.

[18] Richard Harris and Melissa Block, "After Accident, U.S. To Review Shell's Drilling in Arctic Ocean," *All Things Considered*, NPR (National Public Radio), January 13, 2013; and Stephanie Joyce, "Shell Won't Drill in the Arctic This Summer," KUCB-Unalaska (Alaska Public Radio), February 27, 2013; Yereth Rosen, "Shell Had Major Hurdles to Clear before Chukchi Drilling Resumes," *Alaska Dispatch News*, April 4, 2015; and Erica Martinson, "Shell Calls off Plans to Drill in Arctic," *The Arctic Sounder*, October 1, 2015.

[19] Dan Joling, "Interior Department Curbs Future Arctic Offshore Drilling, Associated Press, October 18, 2015, at http://hosted.ap.org/dynamic/stories/U/US_ARCTIC_OFFSHORE_DRILLING?SITE=AP&SECTION=HOME&TEMPLATE=DEFAULT.

[20] Background on the place of the wolf in the American and Alaska psyche draws on Turek, "Three Case-Studies," especially pp. 202–04.

[21] Peter Grantz, "Court Upholds Endangered Species Act Listing for Polar Bears," *Alaska News Nightly* (APRN), March 1, 2013.

[22] Tom Kizzia. "Legal Fray Likely After Ruling on Polar Bear Status," *Anchorage Daily News*, February 4, 2008.

[23] Grantz, Court Upholds Endangered Species Act Listing for Polar Bears."

[24] Lawrence Hurley, "Judge Upholds 'Threatened' Listing for Polar Bear," *New York Times*, Business Day, Energy and Environment Section, June 30, 2011.

[25] "Alaska Officials Pan Endangered Species Law," *Anchorage Daily News*, Wildlife News, online edition, November 15, 2011; and Sean Cockerham, "Alaska Argues to Keep Polar Bears Off 'Threatened' List," *Seattle Times*, November, 19, 2012.

[26] Grantz, "Court Upholds Endangered Species Act Listing for Polar Bears."

[27] "State Petitions to De-List Stellar Sea Lions," Bulletin from the Office of Governor Sean Parnell, September 2, 2010; and Dave Donaldson, "Federal Court Upholds Endangered Listing for Cook Inlet Belugas," *Alaska News Nightly* (APRN), November 21, 2011.

[28] World Commission on Environment and Development, *Our Common Future* (New York: Oxford University Press, 1987), 43.

[29] United Nations Environment Programme, Rio Declaration on Environment and Development, 1992, at http://www.unep.org/ Documents.Multilingual/Default.asp?documentid=78&articleid=1163.

[30] Canadian Federal Sustainable Development Act,, at http://laws-lois.justice.gc.ca/eng/acts/F-8.6/.

[31] Maryland's Genuine Progress Indicator, at http://www.green.maryland.gov/mdgpi/.

[32] Marc McDonald, "U.N. Report from Rio on Environment a 'Suicide Note,'" *New York Times*, June 24, 2012, at http://rendezvous.blogs.nytimes.com/2012/06/24/u-n-report-from-rio-on-environment-a-suicide-note/.

[33] The proposed natural gas pipeline and the politics surrounding it are considered in more detail in Chapter 24 on oil and gas issues, Section 5, esp. Box 24.2.

[34] The information in this section draws primarily on a series of stories during 2014 and 2015 by Ed Schoenfeld of CoastAlaska News, Public Radio for Southeast Alaska, esp., "British Columbia Mining Boom Concerns Unite Tribes across Borders," May 19, 2014; "B.C. Gives KSM Mine Environmental OK," July 30, 2014; "Is the Mine Tailings Dam Failure in B.C. a Warning for Alaska?" August 4, 2014; "Tribal Groups Disagree about B.C. Mining Projects," August 12, 2014; "State Considers B.C. Mines as Promoters Plan Visit," February 26, 2015; and "SE Tribal Council Boosts Anti-mine Campaign," April 16, 2015. Additional information was obtained from Leila Kheiry, "Ketchikan considers International Joint Commission involvement on transboundary mines issue," KRBD, Ketchikan Public Radio for Southern Southeast Alaska, November 24, 2014; the British Columbia Ministry of Energy and Mines, at http://www.empr.gov.bc.ca/mining/Pages/default.aspx; and the Southeast Alaska Conservation Council (SEACC), "Transboundary Streams and Rivers," at: http://seacc.org/mining/transboundary-mines.

[35] See Chapter 11 on Alaska's international activities, Box 11.2.

[36] Alex DeMarban, "Obama touts support for Alaska in visit to Kotzebue," *Alaska Dispatch News*, September 2, 2015; and Erica Martinson, "Obama brings funding, climate change announcements on trip to Kotzebue," *Alaska Dispatch News*, September 2, 2015.

[37] See Chapter 30, Section 2.

[38] See also Kate Troll's explanation of the resolution of the conflicts over Alaska forest lands and fish habitat in Chapter 21, Box 21.5.

★ CHAPTER 23 ★

Fisheries Politics and Policy Making: The Move from General to Restricted Access

Robert W. King

One of Alaska's first U.S. senators, Ernest Gruening, observed that "salmon and Alaska have been as closely intertwined as cotton and the antebellum South."[1] For a generation weaned on Prudhoe Bay oil and Permanent Fund Dividends (PFDs), Alaska's fishing industry may seem as irrelevant as the Old South. But commercial fishing remains a major industry in Alaska and, together with sports and subsistence fishing, carries some political weight. Consequently, fishing is still closely intertwined with the state's politics and public policy making.

This chapter examines the development and contemporary characteristics of Alaska fish politics and policy with a particular focus on the commercial fishery, as this is by far the largest segment of the Alaska fishery, whether measured by value, the weight of the catch, or by employment.[2] Today no public policy issue is more fundamental to Alaska's commercial fishing industry than the simple question: Who gets to fish? To many Alaskans this should not be an issue at all, as the state constitution reserves fish and wildlife for the common use of people and prohibits any "exclusive right or special privilege of fishery."[3] But a growing trend in Alaska and around the world is to limit access to fisheries for the sustainability of the resource and to maximize economic return for participants. This "rationalization" of the fishing industry runs counter not only to the original Alaska Constitution, but also to Alaska's mythic perception of self-reliance and fishermen's self-identity as "Cowboys of the Sea."[4] This raises a key question: How can limited access to a fishery be justified in a democracy that defines fish as a common property resource?

Of the twelve characteristics of Alaska politics identified in Chapter 2, five are evident in this analysis of fish politics. The two most significant are the all-pervasive importance of government and the significant role of external economic and political forces. The prominent role of Alaska Natives in state politics and the conflict between developers and conservationists (more recently environmentalists) are also evident, as are aspects of regionalism. At bottom, though, it is less Alaska's political characteristics and political environment that shape much of fish politics and policy and more the practical economics of fisheries that are common throughout the world. In combination, these five Alaska political characteristics and the reality of fisheries economics undermine the practical application of the Owner State to ownership of and access to fish.

In order to understand this chapter fully, we recommend reading at least the first five sections of Chapter 21 on the general politics and policy making of natural resources. Also, Chapter 7, on the influence of the Outside economy, provides a good foundation for understanding aspects of the economics of Alaska's fisheries.

Fish politics and policy have some elements that are distinct from other policy areas, and they have their own particular terminology, management systems, government agencies, and interest groups involved in working to resolve issues and implement policy. So the chapter begins with some essential background that highlights these distinctive elements. This is followed by an overview of the evolution of the economics and politics of the Alaska fishery and then by a section outlining the nature of the politics and policy community of the contemporary state fishery. Then we turn to the issue of limiting access, first by explaining the problem leading to its necessity and then through four case studies and a brief overview of the experience in other countries. Next we look at the effects of limiting access on the populist democracy that has existed in Alaska past and present and what this might mean for the future. The conclusion links back to the characteristics of state politics and how much they do or do not tell us about Alaska fisheries policy experience since statehood.

1. FISHERIES FOR DUMMIES: THE JARGON AND OPERATION OF THE ALASKA FISHERY AND ITS USER GROUPS

Most current residents of Alaska are far removed from fishing and therefore are not familiar with the basics of this once central part of Alaska economic and political life. In addition, there is an array of terms and jargon that can be confusing even to Alaskans more concerned with fishing. So it is useful to explain some basics to understand the analysis in this chapter. We begin with the term *fisheries* and the categories of fishermen, then explain gear types, management agencies and techniques, the major species harvested (that is, the "catch") in the Alaska fishery, and some other useful terms.

What Are Fisheries and Who Fishes?

Fisheries is a broad term that is often used in imprecise ways. It is sometimes used more specifically to describe one of a wide range of organizations and individuals engaged in catching fish in Alaska's freshwater rivers and lakes and in the salt waters around the 6,600 miles of the state's coastline. In the broadest use, the "Alaska fishery" includes all these activities. The term *fishery* may also be used to mean a geographical area, such as the Bristol Bay fishery in Southwest Alaska; a type of fish caught, such as the herring fishery; and sometimes a fishing gear type, such as the longline fishery. Often the term *fishery* is used to distinguish categories of fishermen and types of fishing activity.

The usual way that the participants in the Alaska fishery are categorized is to divide them into three major groupings: commercial, sport, and subsistence fishing. There is also a fourth category, the personal use fishery, but this is less significant economically and politically and so is dealt with only minimally in this chapter. The three major groupings are based on the three major categories for which the state keeps statistics on the catch, though as we will see, there are problems comparing the three groupings. Even though there is overlap among the three groupings, this categorization is nonetheless useful because it is the basis of much of the politics of the Alaska fishery and the conflicts between user groups.[5]

The *commercial fishery* category embraces everything from one- or two-person operations for catching salmon in Southeast Alaska to Bering Sea factory trawlers, all of which are based out of state, mainly in Seattle. Whatever form it takes, the major motivation behind commercial fishing is an economic one—making a living for the small operator and satisfying a corporation's need for profit in the case of the major factory trawler operations. *Sport fishing* also embraces a broad category, from the recreational angler to the charter boat operators who take out parties of people, mainly tourists, to fish. So, the motives for this category of fishing range from that of a hobby to making a living. In contrast, the motivation behind the *subsistence fishery* is largely culture and individual or family sustenance. Subsistence uses of wild resources, including fish, are defined as noncommercial, customary, and traditional uses for a variety of purposes.[6]

While non-Natives do have the right to engage in subsistence fishing—though this is a subject of dispute given the unresolved issue of subsistence in Alaska—it is the Alaska Native community that is mainly involved in subsistence fishing, both rural-bush and urban Natives.[7] Fish, particularly salmon, form a major part of the Alaska Native diet and, for many Natives, the annual trip to fish camp is a long tradition that combines cultural, social, and economic significance.

In both size of catch and value, the commercial fishery accounts for an estimated 97 percent of the entire Alaska fishery, sport fishing only 2 percent, and subsistence 1 percent. The sport and subsistence fisheries, however, have more influence in Alaska fish politics and in state politics than their relative economic impact compared to the commercial fishery might suggest.

Gear Types, Management Agencies, Management Methods, and Other Useful Terms

There are many ways to catch fish commercially, and some work better for some species than others. There are several government agencies, both state and federal, involved in management of the catch—not just the commercial catch, but also the sport catch, the subsistence catch, and the personal use catch. These agencies have various ways to manage the catch. Box 23.1 provides short explanations of these aspects of the Alaska fishery.

Gear types, agencies, and management techniques all figure in the politics of fisheries, largely due to user group conflicts. One important reality is that fisheries management is about managing fishermen and not fish, a reality that has had a major influence on Alaska fish politics and fisheries policy.

The Catch

The commercial fishing industry in Alaska harvests a range of marine species, from fish such as salmon, herring, cod, and black cod (also known as sable fish) to shellfish (mainly crab but also shrimp) to mollusks (mainly clams). Of these, four species are particularly important to our purpose in this chapter: salmon, halibut, pollock, and crab.

Salmon are widespread across the state with five different species, each known by three or more names that are not important here. They do, however, share an important trait: they are all born in freshwater and spend the rest of their lives, from two to six years, depending on the species, at sea before they return to freshwater to spawn. Salmon are mostly caught in gillnets, setnets, driftnets, or purse seines (see Box 23.1).

Halibut are large flatfish that sometimes weigh hundreds of pounds, live deep on the bottom of the seafloor, sometimes for decades, and migrate considerable distances. Halibut's firm white meat is popular with the finest restaurants and in fish tacos. Halibut are caught with longlines.

Pollock are small whitefish that are very abundant in the Bering Sea and that were long derided as a "trash fish." Pollock now fill a huge market for fish sticks and fish sandwiches at fast food restaurants. They are squeezed into a protein paste called surimi used to make imitation crab and other products. Pollock are caught by the ton in large nets called trawls on catcher boats that deliver to shore-based processors or on larger factory trawlers that process their catch at sea. As Box 23.1 points out, one should be careful not to confuse "trawlers" with the similar sounding "trollers."

Crab are bottom-dwelling shellfish highly prized for their leg meat. Large king crabs dominate the upscale market, while the smaller snow crabs are popular in seafood restaurant chains. Both are caught in large baited pots set along the ocean floor.

BOX 23.1

A Glossary of Fisheries Terms: Fishing Techniques, Fisheries Management Entities, and Management Methods

FISHING TECHNIQUES

Dipnet: A net, shaped like a large cloth bag, on a pole or long handle dipped in the water to catch fish.

Gillnet: A curtain of net extended in front of a run of fish such as salmon that catches them by their gills. They are called **driftnets** when they trail from a boat and **set-nets** when anchored along the shoreline.

Longlines: Strings of baited hooks anchored along the bottom of the ocean and used to catch halibut and black cod.

Pots: Baited metal cages set along the seafloor to catch species such as crab and cod.

Purse seines: Nets that encircle a school of fish and are then "pursed" or closed on the bottom of the net.

Trawls: Large nets dragged through the water in a column or along the sea bottom to catch relatively low-value species such as pollock and rockfish in volumes by the ton.

Trolls: Sometimes confused with the similarly sounding trawls, they are the exact opposite in many respects. **Trollers** drag baited hooks through the water to catch salmon. Slow paced, trollers target high-value species such as king and coho salmon.

FISHERIES MANAGEMENT ENTITIES

Alaska Board of Fisheries (BOF): Also known as the "Fish Board" or "Board of Fish," this seven-member stakeholder group sets fishery regulations and often makes decisions regarding catch allocations.

Alaska Department of Fish and Game (ADF&G): The state agency responsible for managing Alaska fisheries in state waters (to three miles offshore), implementing regulations set by the Board of Fisheries, and conducting scientific research.

Commercial Fisheries Entry Commission (CFEC): Often referred to as the Limited Entry Commission, the three-member body established in 1973 that implements Alaska's **limited entry** law and adjudicates claims about fishing permits.

International Pacific Halibut Commission (IPHC): Created by a 1923 treaty between the United States and Canada, the IPHC sets quotas and other regulations to manage halibut stocks off Alaska, British Columbia, Washington, Oregon, and California. Decisions regarding allocations are left to each respective local jurisdiction. In Alaska this is the **North Pacific Fishery Management Council (NPFMC)**.

National Marine Fisheries Service (NMFS): This federal agency administers fishery management in the Exclusive Economic Zone (EEZ) based on the actions of **NPFMC** and the U.S. Department of Commerce and provides scientific support.

North Pacific Fishery Management Council (NPFMC): The federal advisory panel that manages fisheries in the EEZ from three to two hundred miles offshore. Dominated by Alaskans, the eleven members include representatives from Washington and Oregon. Decisions are subject to ratification by the U.S. Secretary of Commerce.

FISHERIES MANAGEMENT METHODS

Community Development Quotas (CDQs): The allocation of a small portion of the allowable pollock catch among six regional corporations in Bering Sea coastal communities to provide jobs, training, and economic development.

Harvesting cooperatives: An agreement whereby harvesters divide the catch quota among themselves to avoid the **race for fish** but still compete among themselves in the market.

Individual Fishery Quotas (IFQs): Catch allocations for participants who can catch the amount of fish allocated to them whenever they want, rather than being limited to open period allowed by fishery managers. They are also called ITQs (individual transferable quotas), meaning they can be bought and sold, as are IFQs in Alaska.

Individual Processor Quotas (IPQs): An allocation assigned to a seafood processor intended to protect investment in a fishery. IPQs in Alaska are assigned to IFQs, requiring a harvester to deliver its catch to a specific processor.

Limited entry: A limit on the number of participants in a fishery, which by itself does not stop the **race for fish**.

Race for fish: Another way to describe an open-access fishery where an unlimited number of harvesters try to catch as much fish as they can in the shortest time. This is also called an "Olympic" or "derby" fishery.

Rationalization: A frequently used but vague term that often includes some or all of the above fisheries management methods to generically describe fishery management programs. The term can include both the concept of "ration" as in a quota or share of the fish or "rational" in the sense of bringing order to the chaos of fishing. One definition is a fishery management plan that results "in an allocation of labor and capital between fishing and other industries that maximizes the net value of production."[1]

OTHER FISHERIES TERMS

Bottom fish and groundfish: Interchangeable terms for fish, such as halibut, that live on or near the seafloor.

Bycatch: Fish caught that are not the intended target species of the fishery, for example, catching halibut when fishing for cod. Over the years the rules regarding avoiding bycatch, and how to account for and handle it, have become increasingly stringent.

Parallel fishery: A term that in its full extent is complex, but in essence refers to certain fisheries over which both the state and federal government have some jurisdiction or where there is overlapping state and federal authority.

Personal use and subsistence fisheries: Subsistence and personal use fisheries are open to Alaska residents only and allow for the taking of fish for personal use. Both subsistence and personal use fisheries are designated by geographical areas. By far the largest personal use fishery is the Cook Inlet Salmon Dipnet Fishery because of its proximity to Anchorage and nearby towns. In contrast to personal use fishing, there is no subsistence fishing near large urban areas. No license is required for subsistence fishing (though a permit may be needed in certain areas), and fish caught in the subsistence fishery can be bartered and in some cases sold. The personal use fishery allocation is reduced before that of subsistence in times of a shortage of fish.[2]

---

[1] Mark Fina, "Development of Rationalization Programs in the North Pacific Groundfish and Crab Fisheries," National Fishery Law Symposium," University of Washington School of Law (2003), 1.

[2] See the Department of Fish and Game website for details on who is eligible to fish in various fisheries and how the catch may be used, at http://www.adfg.alaska.gov/index.cfm?adfg=residentfishing.matrix.

Source: Developed by the author.

2. THE EVOLVING ECONOMICS AND POLITICS OF ALASKA'S FISHERIES

The restriction of access to various fisheries in Alaska has been the major and most far-reaching policy regarding the state's fishery since statehood. To fully understand this development it is important to place it in the general context of fish politics and policy making in Alaska, past and present. In this section we review the past importance of fish to Alaska and the Alaska psyche, the changing economic and political role of fish, and the current dimensions of fish economics. Section 7 provides an overview of contemporary fish politics in Alaska.

Fish in Alaska's Past and in the Alaska Psyche

Until the 1970s, Alaska's history was largely shaped by fish. Purchase of the territory from Russia was advocated by Seattle cod fishermen who knew the riches along

Alaska's offshore banks. Canned salmon emerged as Alaska's first major industry and for most years during the Territorial period (1912-1959) it generated over 80 percent of the Territory's annual tax revenues. Yet, a chronic problem with fish is that it is undependable as a source of personal income and government revenue. This is because it is subject to the boom-bust cycle, with prices fluctuating widely over time, sometimes in the course of only a year or two.[8] Commercial fishing is very much part of Alaska's volatile natural resources economy, with exports forming the major market and fish prices largely determined by world demand, economic conditions, and competition with other producers across the globe.

Nevertheless, in the past as well as in contemporary Alaska, fish are a factor in the state's self-identity. This may be in part because, as the only state in the Union where agriculture was not a major factor in its economic development, fishing substituted for the pioneering role of agriculture economically, politically, and culturally. Even today large segments of the population identify themselves as sportsmen, anglers, or subsistence users. As explained earlier, fish are an integral part of Alaska Native culture. Others are attracted to the state for its outdoor opportunities of which fish are a large factor. Meanwhile, commercial fishermen view the vast, windswept sea as the last of the free ranges, a myth popularized on television programs like *Alaska King Crab Cowboys* and the Discovery Channel's popular *Deadliest Catch.*

Fish, the Statehood Movement, and Alaska's Constitutional Convention

The statehood movement was driven, in part, by resentment against the absentee owners of salmon fish traps. The delegates to the Constitutional Convention of 1955–1956 exploited this resentment to help secure public approval of the constitution by including a provision outlawing fish traps on the same April 1956 ballot as the public vote on approval of the constitution.[9] This is clear evidence of the dominance of fish in the consciousness of Alaskans throughout the Territory at the time. Consequently, the delegates at the convention spent considerable time on fisheries issues either specifically or as part of their broader discussions on natural resources. Two of their decisions in this regard were particularly significant, as they not only reflected the politics of the time, but have had political ramifications down the years.

First, recognizing the importance of fisheries, the founders defined fish and game as a common property resource. Article VIII, Section 3, of the constitution states, "Wherever occurring in their natural state, fish, wildlife, and waters are reserved to the people for common use." Section 15 goes even further, providing that "no exclusive right or special privilege of fishery shall be created or authorized in the natural waters of the State." Second, the issue of fishery management emerged as one of the major controversies of the convention. The major area of contention was whether to manage Alaska's fish and game through one single commission or two commissions. This question attracted more public comment than any other issue. Fish and game interests lobbied for the constitution to include one board for commercial fishing and another for sport fishing and hunting. The delegates bowed to this pressure to some extent by authorizing the legislature to designate a board, rather than an individual, to be the head of a department.

The Changing Economic and Political Role of Fish

If for generations fish were to Alaska what corn is to Iowa and coal is to West Virginia, this is no longer the case. The years since the late 1960s have seen fisheries moved off the center of both the economic and political stage. Two realities and two developments have been particularly responsible for these changed circumstances.

One of the realities is that when left to its own devices, unlimited fishing inevitably grows to the point that the resource is either over-harvested or the fishery becomes uneconomic, or both. As we will see, this became clear within a decade of statehood, and there was a move to limit access to the fishery, culminating in the limited entry provision being added to the state constitution in 1972. Federal legislation also extended regulation of marine fisheries resources, specifically those occurring within the federal two-hundred-mile Exclusive Economic Zone (EEZ), established in the 1976 Magnuson-Stevens Fishery Conservation and Management Act. This also set up eight regional fisheries management councils, with Alaska under the jurisdiction of the North Pacific Fishery Management Council (NPFMC). Thus, the Alaska fishery became increasingly regulated as a result of mounting pressure on the resource. Issues surrounding regulation had significant economic, social, and cultural consequences and became an important part of fish politics and policy from the mid-1960s onwards.

The second reality was and remains the uncertainty of the market for fish due to the boom-bust cycle and, as a consequence, the instability of employment in the commercial fishing industry. In addition to downturns in the national and international economies, absentee ownership of fish processing plants and competition from other fish producing nations contribute to this instability. For instance, the explosive growth of farmed salmon in Norway, Chile, and elsewhere in the early 1990s sent prices for Alaska wild salmon plummeting. Halibut prices have also fluctuated widely over the past thirty years.[10] And decisions made in Seattle, Tokyo, New York, and London have led to the closure of fish processing plants with consequent hardship to Alaska fishermen and affected communities.

Alaska policy makers have no control over these market forces and can do little to alleviate their economic consequences, other than declare particular localities as disaster areas and eligible for state aid. To some extent, however, regulation can work to even out this chronic economic fish roller coaster. For instance, Alaska banned salmon farming in 1990 in order to protect wild salmon stocks. So the chronic economic problem of the Alaska fishery is one element that shapes fish politics.

As with other natural resource activities in Alaska, one significant development that has affected the Alaska fishery is the rise of the conservation and environmental movements. The effect of the environmental movement increased as it gathered momentum and political influence from the 1960s onward. Federal legislation, such as the Marine Mammal Protection Act of 1972 and the Sustainable Fisheries Act of 1996, forces the commercial fishing fleet to be mindful of catching and otherwise adversely affecting various marine species, such as seals. State environmental regulations also affect the sport fishery, and federal and state regulations put restrictions on the size of the catch of subsistence fishermen. Consequently, conservation and environmental issues also shape the nature of fisheries politics and policy in Alaska.

The second and probably the major development that changed the political and economic role of fish in Alaska is the development of the state's oil and gas reserves. Through its effects on the state's demographics, the state economy, and state revenues from the late 1960s onwards, oil marginalized fisheries politically and economically in less than a decade.

Largely because of oil development, in the twenty years after statehood, Alaska's population almost doubled, from 225,000 to just over 400,000, and had increased to over 735,000 by 2015. The new arrivals took up residence in urban areas, mainly Anchorage and Railbelt cities and towns that in 2010 had about 75 percent of the state's population. Most of these newcomers found employment in government or service industries. Most have little knowledge of commercial fishing. And although many fishermen live in urban parts of Alaska, most commercial fishing activity occurs far from the Railbelt.

Oil also changed the economic status of fish in a major way. Fisheries were overtaken by oil in the late 1970s as the major private sector producer in the state. Today oil dwarfs fisheries in this regard. In 2008–2009, for example, the value of oil production per Alaskan was around $64,500 compared with $1,900 for fish. Mining also outstripped fish for those years, at $3,600 per capita.[11] Moreover, it is now oil that provides between 80 and 90 percent of Alaska's own-source state revenues and not fish.[12]

In combination, demographics and economic factors have meant that most elected and appointed Alaska state officials are from urban Alaska, and thus few politicians have the knowledge, the interest, or the political incentive to make fisheries a top priority. Few now have fisheries as a local issue and, money being the mother's milk of politics, it is the oil industry that gets their attention on taxation and other issues. Consequently, Alaska fisheries issues today take a political backseat.

The Contemporary Economic Role of the Alaska Fishery: A Significant State, National, and International Contribution

Despite oil dwarfing fisheries as a part of the contemporary Alaska economy, fishing and fish processing are still major industries in the state. Not only that, the Alaska fishery makes a major contribution to the national and international supply of fish. An overview of some data since 2005 will make this clear.[13]

If Alaska were a separate country, it would rank as a world leader in fish production. In 2005, for instance, Alaska ranked eighth among seafood producing nations, behind Norway and ahead of the Philippines. That year Alaska accounted for 2.6 percent of world production of all species, over 16 percent of the world production of salmon, and 80 percent of Pacific halibut. These are revealing statistics considering that about three-fourths of the world's close to two hundred countries have fishing industries. Also in 2005, at the national level, Alaska accounted for over 57 percent of all fish production and 95 percent of all salmon put on the market. By 2012, however, because of increased U.S. landings, Alaska's share of the catch had dropped to 38 percent even though Alaska's harvest was about the same as in 2005. Nevertheless, Alaska actually increased its share of world production that year to 3 percent.[14]

The contribution of Alaska fisheries to the contemporary state economy is also significant. Between 2001 and 2009 the industry averaged over fifty thousand employees a year, which made it the largest private employer in the state and second to government employment.[15] Although some of this employment is seasonal and about half of the industry's workers are from out of state, the industry pours significant money into the Alaska economy. Furthermore, the jobs are spread broadly from the largest cities to the remotest village where, for some, fishing is one of the few sources of a cash income. In addition, on average between 2000 and 2014, seafood accounted for just under 50 percent of the value of Alaska's total foreign exports. In 2011, for instance, this was $2.5 billion.[16]

The Economic Contribution of Major Fishery User Groups

Among the four fisheries user groups—commercial, sport, subsistence, and personal use—investments range from a few thousand dollars, or in the cases of subsistence and recreation, a few hundred, to many millions of dollars. Each user group desires access to the Alaska fishery in general and specific fisheries in particular. As we will see in the next section, these varying and diverse claims on the fishery often lead to conflicts among the groups and sometimes conflicts within a particular user group.

As to the specific contribution of each of these user groups to the Alaska economy and the exact contribution of each to the fishing harvest, we can provide some general figures, though exact amounts and percentages are difficult to determine for several reasons. Based upon a composite of sources, Box 23.2 provides figures in this regard for the

BOX 23.2

Estimated Contribution of Commercial, Sport, and Subsistence Fishing to the Alaska Economy and the Problem of Assessing Their Relative Contributions

Statistics on commercial, sport, and particularly subsistence fisheries are incomplete, and vary according to the method of collection and the body doing the analysis. Difficulties also arise in assessing the relative impact of the three fisheries on the Alaska economy. This is because they can be compared in a number of ways, such as by harvest, dollar value, jobs created, or total economic impact by adding in the economic multiplier effect. The following information synthesizes several data sources to provide perspectives on the various economic contributions of the three fisheries from the early 2000s to 2013.

COMMERCIAL AND SPORT FISHERIES BY HARVEST

By volume of harvest, commercial fisheries comprise probably 97 percent of all marine species harvested in Alaska, with sport fishing at 2 percent and subsistence fishing at about 1 percent.

- In 2013, Alaska led all states in volume with landings of 5.8 billion pounds, followed by Louisiana, 1.1 billion; Washington, 557.2 million; Virginia, 381.7 million; and California, 372.2 million.
- That year, Alaska led all states in value of landings with $1.9 billion, followed by Massachusetts, $566.9 million; Maine, $473.9 million; Louisiana, $402.2 million; and Washington State, $371.4 million.
- There are no weight estimates of sport fish harvested; the statistics are in number of fish. In 2013 over 2.9 million were caught. Between 2004 and 2013 the average yearly catch was just under three million fish.

ECONOMIC IMPACT ON THE ALASKA ECONOMY

The Commercial Fishery

- Since 2000, the commercial fishing industry generated over 60,000 jobs per year. However, many of these were seasonal, ranging from one week to several months. On a monthly average-adjusted basis, in 2011 there were 8,061 direct full-time equivalent jobs in Alaska attributed to the fishing industry.
- In 2009 the estimated economic impact of commercial fishing was $4.6 billion (which had a wholesale value of $3 billion).
- Revenues generated by the commercial fishing industry in fiscal year 2012 (July 1, 2011 to June 30, 2012) totaled more than $100 million in state and local taxes. These revenues ranged from fish processing and corporate taxes to fishery resource landing taxes, license fees, and seafood marketing assessments.
- At the end of 2012, Alaska residents held over seven thousand commercial fishing permits and nearly twelve thousand full-year crewmember licenses. Estimated earnings by Alaska-based permit holders was $681 million.

The Sport Fishery

- The sport fishery generates between 11,000 and 14,000 jobs. In 2006, over 290,000 people (residents and nonresidents) engaged in sport fishing, with their total expenditures amounting to $516,749,000.
- Alaska's sport fisheries, as well as many personal use fisheries, are worth more than $500 million annually, with an economic impact of well over a billion dollars.
- Taking into account the economic multiplier effect of the sport fishery in the United States overall, it is estimated that it outstrips the commercial fishery by $8 billion ($500 million in income directly to those employed in fisheries). But in Alaska, despite often contradictory information, the commercial fishery most likely outstrips the sport fishery on almost every statistic.

The Subsistence Fishery

Data on subsistence fisheries is scarce and uneven. According to the 2011 Alaska Subsistence and Personal Use Salmon Fisheries Report:

> Annual harvest assessment programs do not take place for subsistence fisheries. Programs are in place for most salmon fisheries, but few other finfish or shellfish fisheries have annual harvest monitoring programs.

Other data limitations include:

- Not all subsistence fisheries are included in harvest assessment programs.
- Harvest data only includes fisheries classified as subsistence by regulation. There may be other such fisheries that go unrecorded.
- There are inconsistencies among the management areas in how subsistence data is collected and recorded.
- Because not all communities have up to date information, aggregate comparisons are not feasible. For instance, for Adak (in the Aleutians), there is 2008 data, while for Aniak (in Southwest Alaska) only 2005 harvest data is available.

Regarding subsistence fish harvesting:

- On average, the harvest provides about 183 pounds of food per person annually in rural-bush Alaska.
- An estimated 38.3 million pounds of wild foods are harvested annually for subsistence purposes, 55 percent of which is fisheries from finfish and 3 percent from shellfish.
- Total estimated subsistence salmon harvest for 2011, based on annual harvest assessment programs, was 840,858 fish. The range is from around 800,000 to just over a million. It was one million in 2007.
- Harvest information is available by region and in some cases by community on the ADF&G's website.

Source: Developed by Kristina Klimovich. See endnote 17 for data sources.

commercial, sport, and subsistence fisheries.[17] It does not include the personal use fishery, as this accounts for a very small percentage (likely a fraction of 1 percent of the catch by weight and value), and figures on the catch are even more challenging to calculate than for the subsistence harvest. There are, however, some figures relating to fish caught in some regional personal use fisheries kept by ADF&G.[18]

3. THE CURRENT DIMENSIONS OF ALASKA'S FISH POLITICS AND POLICY MAKING: INTERGOVERNMENTAL AND USER-GROUP COOPERATION AND CONFLICT

This section provides an overview of contemporary fish politics, the policy process, and the policy community involved in resolving fisheries issues. As part of Alaska's natural resource politics, the characteristics of contemporary fish politics and policy making share several commonalities with other areas of natural resources outlined in Chapter 21. But as with land, environmental, and oil and gas politics, there are several characteristics and elements specific to fisheries.

The Broadening of Fisheries Politics, Policy Making, and the Policy Community

Much like the politics of land, the environment, and oil and gas, fisheries politics and policy making have become much broader since the 1960s, particularly since the rise of the environmental movement. At statehood and before, the politics of fish was largely confined to issues directly affecting the catching and selling of fish. So the fisheries policy community was confined to those with a financial or recreational interest in fish and the federal and Territorial agencies involved in overseeing fishing. But the rise of the conservation and environmental movements, the emergence of subsistence issues as a result of the 1971 Alaska Native Claims Settlement Act (ANCSA) and the 1980 Alaska National Interest Lands Conservation Act (ANILCA), the role of fisheries and fish processing in economic development, and the boom-bust cycle in fish prices leading to requests for disaster relief, among other factors, changed all this. As a consequence, fish politics and policy and those directly and indirectly affected by it gradually expanded.

Consequently, today the politics surrounding fish not only include who can catch fish, how, when, and where, but also issues regarding the effects of fishing on the environment and the impacts of development, particularly mining, on fishing, primarily salmon streams. Fisheries policy includes, for example, the need to encourage fish processors to locate their plants in Alaska to aid economic development, as well as aid to communities when fish prices plummet, particularly places where fishing is the major economic game in the town or village. In addition, fisheries groups and non-fisheries interests sometimes form ad hoc political coalitions to achieve a goal, such as a local chamber of commerce or an association of general contractors working to help a fish processor secure tax relief to encourage construction of a new fish processing plant.

Obviously, if we included all interests, groups, organizations, businesses, and governments and their agencies that at some time or another are involved in what can broadly be defined as fisheries related issues, the list would be long and serve very little purpose. So to make things manageable and more meaningful, we confine our consideration of fish politics, policy making, and the policy community to those more or less directly involved with catching and marketing fish and regulating fisheries.

The Characteristics of Alaska Fish Policy Making and Implementation and the Makeup of the Policy Community

The policy process and the various groups, organizations, and governments that determine the laws and regulations that affect Alaska's fishermen and the fishing industry in general, are multifaceted. Box 23.3 sets out the makeup of Alaska's contemporary fisheries policy-making community. Some of the federal and state participants in this community have already been explained and are, for the most part, listed in Box 23.3 by name only. Other members of the community are described in the box in more detail.

BOX 23.3

The Alaska Fisheries Policy Making and Implementation Community

THE FEDERAL AND INTERNATIONAL LEVEL

The federal executive, Congress, and judiciary are all involved with making policy that affects Alaska fisheries. In particular, Alaska's congressional delegation has worked to aid Alaska's fishing industry in a variety of ways relating to easing regulations, economic aid, and marketing Alaska fish. On a day-to-day basis the following federal departments and agencies are significant forces in the development of policy and its implementation. This also includes interactions with interstate and international bodies.

National Oceanic and Atmospheric Administration (NOAA): Part of the U.S. Department of Commerce.

National Marine Fisheries Service (NMFS): An agency of NOAA.

Fish and Wildlife Service (USFWS): Part of the Department of the Interior.

Federal Subsistence Board (FSB): Part of USFWS and responsible for regulating subsistence on federal lands and in federal waters..

North Pacific Fishery Management Council (NPFMC)

International Pacific Halibut Commission (IPHC)

U.S. Coast Guard (USCG): Aids in monitoring and enforcing regulations in federal waters.

STATE GOVERNMENT

As with the federal government, all three branches of state government get involved in fisheries policy. The governor usually has a special assistant dealing with natural resources including fisheries. And from time to time there are interdepartmental coordinating bodies set up to deal with fish. For instance, Governor Murkowski set up a Fish Cabinet to administer a $50 million federal grant to revitalize the salmon industry. In the legislature, those from fishing communities often form a Fish Caucus. The courts also effectively create or confirm fisheries policy, as the Alaska Supreme Court has done on limited entry provisions and on subsistence, which includes the subsistence fishery. On a day-to-day basis the major state agencies involved in fisheries policy and administration are:

Alaska Department of Fish and Game (ADF&G)

Alaska Board of Fisheries (BOF)

Commercial Fisheries Entry Commission (CFEC)

Alaska Department of Commerce, Community and Economic Development (ADCCED): Has part of the responsibility for developing the fishing industry and promoting the marketing of Alaska fish.

Alaska Seafood Marketing Institute (ASMI): Charged with promoting the sale of Alaska seafood in the United States and abroad. The institute uses agents to promote Alaska seafood sales in the Lower 48, in Asia, Latin America, and in Europe.

LOCAL GOVERNMENTS

Boroughs, cities, Native villages, and tribal councils that are economically dependent on fish-

It is, however, misleading to think of the policy process as one single process. It is more accurate to view it as several processes that are more or less interrelated. Three points are helpful in understanding the practical functioning of these policy processes as applied to fish policy.

First, depending on the issue and the jurisdiction of a particular level of government, the process can be largely a state one, a federal one, a cooperative effort between the two, or parallel policy making and administration. Obviously, fisheries issues related to waters within state lands or the three-mile offshore limit involve mainly state policy making. Fisheries issues arising in waters on federal lands and outside the three-mile

ing or are affected by fisheries policy are often part of the fisheries policy community. Generally, however, local governments get involved with fisheries policy on particular issues and then may drop out of the community for a while. For instance, in times of low prices for salmon and economic hardship in some communities, local governments may lobby for disaster relief from the state. Also, some Native communities get involved in policy making to protect their subsistence rights against other user groups, particularly those involved in the sport and personal use fisheries.

A WIDE RANGE OF INTEREST GROUPS

There are a host of interests representing commercial, sport, subsistence and personal use fishing, businesses, and other organizations involved in Alaska's fisheries policy-making process. Most are concerned with particular aspects of fisheries policy.

The corporate fishing industry is represented by organizations such as the At-sea Processors Association (formerly the American Factory Trawlers Association), based in Seattle, and the Pacific Seafood Processors Association, representing offshore and onshore processors in Alaska and Washington State. Both organizations lobby mainly in Washington, D.C., and maintain offices there, but sometimes they have state issues such as landing taxes, and so sometimes lobby in Juneau. Commercial fishermen in Alaska have the United Fishermen of Alaska (UFA), an umbrella organization including many affiliate organizations of various gear types and businesses. Most gear types have their own organizations, and there are some regional gear associations. Examples include the Alaska Trollers Association, the Alaska Longline Fishermen's Association, and the Southeast Alaska Seiners Association.

Sport fishermen have several organizations, which more or less divide into two groups: one for recreational fishermen, the other for the charter fleet. Recreational anglers have the Alaska Sport Fishing Association and also regional organizations like the Kenai River Sportfishing Association. In addition, sport fishing is represented by general hunting and fishing organizations like the Outdoor Council. The Alaska Charter Association is the major statewide organization representing the business side of the sport fishery, but there are also local associations like the Homer Charter Association.

Subsistence fishermen do not have a specific association, but their cause is represented and lobbied by several organizations. These include the state's major Native organization, the Alaska Federation of Natives (AFN), which usually has issues regarding subsistence fishing on its annual meeting agenda and pushes the issue with the legislature and Congress. Subsistence fishing interests are also represented by several Native regional and village corporations. The Federal Subsistence Board and the ADF&G enforce subsistence regulations. They also often act as protectors of, and on occasion as, advocates for, subsistence fishing.

Personal use fisheries are less well organized and represented politically than the other three user groups. But some regional fisheries do have organizations, such as the South-Central Central Alaska Dipnetters Association, and the Chitina Dipnetters Association, covering the Copper River and Valdez-Cordova area.

Source: Developed by Clive Thomas and Kristina Klimovich.

limit and those involving other states or Canada, are federal issues. Nonetheless, federal policy making on these issues often involves major input from Alaska, as in the case of the International Pacific Halibut Commission (IPHC). Cooperation frequently exists between the U.S. Coast Guard and Alaska agencies, particularly the ADF&G in monitoring and regulatory activities. An example of parallel policy making and administration is that there are two major governmental bodies overseeing subsistence fishing in Alaska: the Federal Subsistence Board and the ADF&G, which tracks and manages subsistence fishing in state waters.

Second is a corollary of the first point. Much of the policy making and implementation in fisheries involves intergovernmental relations (IGR), particularly between the state and the federal government. There is much interaction between Juneau and Washington, D.C., on fisheries issues. This is particularly the case regarding Alaska's coastal waters but also on issues involving the effects of development, particularly mining, on various fisheries.

Third, like other areas of natural resource policy and its enforcement, most fishery laws are regulatory, though a few are redistributive (see Chapter 3, Section 1, for an explanation of the terms *distributive*, *redistributive*, and *regulatory*). Alaska's adoption of limited entry in 1972 and the limiting of the subsistence catch are examples of regulatory policies that also have redistributive characteristics. Proposals and actions by the North Pacific Fisheries Management Council (NPFMC) to change the allocation of the halibut catch is another example of redistributive policy. As with Alaska land regulations and environmental restrictions on land and resource development, regulatory and redistributive policies in fisheries lead to a variety of conflicts, sometimes intense conflicts, as we will see next.

Contemporary Alaska Fish Politics: Characteristics and Issues

To be sure, if there were not a high degree of cooperation and compromise among the many members of the fisheries policy community, no policy would get made or implemented. There is, in fact, considerable cooperation, as this chapter shows. But politics is largely the product of clashes of values, needs, and interests and, as in other policy areas, it is these conflicts that give fisheries politics its characteristics. The nature of fisheries politics in Alaska is largely the product of three interrelated factors: user group conflicts, interest group–driven politics, and the mixed political influence of the fishing community. We briefly explain each and then ask the question: Where does political power lie in Alaska fisheries politics and policy making?

Conflicts among and within User Groups and Conflicts between Governments

There are ongoing conflicts among the three main user groups—commercial, sport and subsistence fishermen, and occasionally involving personal use fishing groups. Again, these conflicts are largely over who gets to fish, how much fish they can harvest, and where and when. The major conflict between user groups is between commercial and sport fishing. This can be seen in federal policy making where, for example, sport fishermen bemoan having only one representative on the NPFMC compared with three or more commercial representatives. With its major role of allocating access to fish, the Alaska Board of Fisheries is a focal point for dealing with user group conflicts over allocations. Box 23.4 looks at the role of the board and the politics involved.

BOX 23.4

The Composition, Operation, and Politics of the Alaska Board of Fisheries

The Alaska Board of Fisheries, commonly referred to as the Board of Fish (BOF), has seven members appointed by the governor and confirmed by the legislature. In making appointments, the governor tries to represent the regions of the state and the various user groups. Generally, there is one member representing subsistence fishing, three representing commercial fishing, and three noncommercial fishing representatives who may have sympathies with sport fishing. The board's website states that:

> The Board of Fisheries is established under Alaska Statute 16.05.221 for the purposes of the conservation and development of the fisheries resources of the state. The Board of Fisheries has the authority to adopt regulations . . . including: establishing open and closed seasons and areas for taking fish; setting quotas, bag limits, harvest levels and limitations for taking fish; and establishing the methods and means for the taking of fish.[1]

The BOF spends much of its time on allocation decisions, but also on conservation and regulation issues, including types of gear that can be used and opening and closing dates for particular fisheries. The board has a grueling schedule, meeting up to eight times a year for five to ten days at a time, mostly in Anchorage but also in fishing communities around the state, such as Naknek in Southwest Alaska.

The general consensus is that the board reflects the politics of the Alaska fishery in general, which can be summed up as: "These are my fish. I want more of them, and no one else can have them." This applies particularly to the attitude of commercial toward sport fishermen and vice versa. Votes on most issues before the board are 7–0 or 6–1. However, the commercial-sport fishing conflict means that the board is sometimes divided 3–3, which places the subsistence member in the difficult position of having the deciding vote.

The intense effort of user groups to protect their allocation (and evidence of no love lost between user groups) is illustrated by two examples. One was between commercial and sport fishermen over black cod (also called sablefish). For a long time there was no limit on the sport catch of this species, but one was proposed by the board to come within the overall sport fishing allocation. The reaction of many commercial fishermen was that there should be no black cod allocation for sport fishing at all. In part, this reaction was likely because this is a high value fishery, but more likely because of the strong antipathy of commercial towards sport fishermen. There is no rational explanation for the conflict, because the sport black cod catch is miniscule and has virtually no effect on the commercial black cod catch. Moreover, this fish lives two thousand feet or more below the surface and for efficiency has to be taken with a costly electric reel, which most sport fishermen would not purchase.

The other example is a personal use-subsistence user group conflict. This involved the Chitina Dipnet Association, a largely urban, non-Native organization of fishermen who fish on the Copper River near Cordova. As the personal use regulations for catching and disposing of fish are more restrictive than for subsistence, the association applied to the board for a subsistence allocation and was turned down. The association challenged this in the courts. In December 2012 the Alaska Supreme Court upheld the board's decision.

One former board member commented that conflict between user groups, particularly commercial versus sport, and even within each group, is the norm rather than the exception. "Thankfully," he said, "the feds are totally responsible for allocations on halibut and not us, as that's a mess with the conflicts between commercial and sport users over that fishery."

In performing its charge, the board works in coordination with other federal and state agencies involved in fish policy, administration, and enforcement. This interagency coordination and cooperation is usually smooth and positive. For instance, the board coordinates with the state's Limited Entry Commission before the BOF meets, and usually one of the commissioners attends their meetings. There is also usually a representative at BOF meetings from the Federal Subsistence Board, often one from NMFS, and sometimes representatives from other federal agencies involved in fish regulations.

---

[1] http://www.adfg.alaska.gov/index.cfm?adfg=fisheriesboard.main.

Source: Developed by Clive Thomas based on interviews with former board members and personnel from the legislature and the ADF&G, all of whom requested anonymity.

Conflicts within user groups are also common. Disagreement often occurs among commercial gear types—for example, driftnetters and seiners—over one taking more of the catch and thereby depriving the other. Here the state often steps in to close one gear fishery and give the other more access. A common conflict among sport fishermen is that of recreational anglers complaining about the amount of fish the charter fleet takes.

Federal and state government agencies and occasionally local governments also sometimes conflict. This is not always intentional but can result from differences in laws, regulations and policies. But sometimes, as over the subsistence issue, it is the result of the state not taking the required action to comply with federal laws (see Chapter 9, section 6; and Chapter 10, Box 10.2).

Compartmentalized Politics Driven by Special Interests

Another characteristic of fish politics is that it is essentially driven by special interests and, partly as a result, is ad hoc in its approach to policy making. Looked at from another perspective, there is no overall policy approach to fisheries in Alaska even on the part of the state government. This is despite the fact that the fishing industry, and particularly commercial and subsistence fishermen, often suffer from poor harvests. As in many policy areas, part of the reason for the interest-driven nature of fish politics and its lack of coordination is a result of the separation of powers between the executive and the legislature and of the IGR component of fish politics involving state and federal and often local governments. In addition, there are four reasons for interest-driven politics in regard to fisheries.

The first has its origin at the Constitutional Convention. Then, as today, regulating fishing, including who is allowed to fish, was a prominent and very divisive political issue, and the founders gave the responsibility for regulating fishing to the legislature. The first legislature after statehood, partly because its members knew they would offend some fishing constituencies when making such contentious decisions, passed the responsibility off to what was initially established as a combined Board of Fish and Game (in 1975, the legislature divided the board into two, with one having authority over game and one over fish). If the first legislature hoped that giving the regulatory responsibility over fish to a board would take some of the politics out of the decisions, they were clearly wrong. It simply shifted the arena of political conflict over fisheries from the legislature to what would later become the Board of Fisheries (BOF).

Second, as mentioned earlier, legislative interest in fish today is confined to a small group of legislators—mainly those from fishing communities and from districts where subsistence is a major political factor. Today, not only do few urban legislators relate to commercial fishing, they see fishermen as living up to their cowboy reputation of waging vocal and protracted wars over allocations and species, gear types, and regional conflicts. These legislators are understandably wary of stepping into such internecine battles. For instance, if an Anchorage legislator put forward a policy that would allocate more Cook Inlet salmon to recreational users, he or she might gain the support of that user group, but would certainly attract the anger of subsistence and commercial interests.[19] So even if urban legislators had an interest in enacting some overarching fisheries policy, the divisions among fishermen would likely make enactment difficult, if not impossible, to achieve. Thus, urban legislators have multiple reasons to avoid fisheries issues.

Third, the lack of legislative interest is compounded by the rise of oil as a major state revenue source and consequently little need to pay attention to fisheries as it is no longer a major economic driver and revenue source as is oil and gas. Fourth, fisheries have several issues that cut across different fishery user groups and other natural resources user groups, which exacerbates political contentiousness, including subsistence users versus sport fishermen, clashes between fishermen and developers such as mining companies, and rural-urban clashes over the spending of money for economic development and relief payments during poor fish harvests.

The upshot of these four factors is that fisheries policy rarely takes center stage in any legislative session but is confined or compartmentalized to the fish caucus and other interested legislators. On occasion, though, the legislature has special committees on fisheries, as was the case in the House in the Twenty-Ninth Legislature (2015–2016). Major policy decisions are made in bodies like the BOF and in agencies like ADF&G, the Alaska Department of Commerce, and the Alaska Seafood Marketing Institute. The various venues in which fish policies are made often see intense lobbying by various fish interests.

The Mixed Political Influence of the Fishing Community

Whereas the image of commercial fisherman as cowboys of the sea and loner independent types may be an exaggeration, the divisions within the commercial fishing community, and the marginalization of commercial fishing since statehood, mean that the various user groups have varying influence politically at both the state and federal levels. Divisions within the commercial fishing industry outlined above are reflected in their major umbrella organization, United Fishermen of Alaska—UFA. Composed of various gear types and businesses, many of which have competing political goals, UFA is reduced to advocating for general goals that do not offend its many members, such as promoting fish marketing. According to a survey of the most influential interest groups in Alaska between the early 1980s and 2010, UFA was occasionally among the second rank of influential groups but never among the first rank, in contrast to oil, the University of Alaska, and the education lobby.[20] Nonetheless, the commercial fishing industry does exert influence through state and federal fisheries boards and commissions. In addition, the Alaska delegation to Congress has aided the industry on such issues as compensation over the *Exxon Valdez* oil spill and funding for fish processing plants.

On the other hand, elements of the sport fishing lobby, mainly the Outdoor Council, have been seen as very influential.[21] Subsistence fishermen are, of course, protected by federal law and to some extent state law, but the issue of subsistence fishing and hunting in Alaska remains unresolved.

Contemporary Political Power in Fish Politics and Policy Making and the Transformed Role of Alaska's Populist Democratic Fishery

From what we have said in the chapter so far and particularly in this section, we know that the distribution of power in fisheries policy making is a far cry from Territorial days. At that time, as Constitutional Convention delegate Victor Fischer recalled, "Almost absolute control of the salmon resources had been concentrated in the hands of a few large, nonresident canning concerns, and the fishery was managed strictly for their benefit."[22] Today, there is no one center of power in fisheries policy making. It is most accurately described as pluralistic. Depending on the type of fishery and legal jurisdiction, power is shared between federal and state governments including Congress, several federal executive agencies, and Alaska's legislature and executive agencies, particularly the BOF. Local governments too can play a role at times. And while many fisheries interest groups may not be highly influential in state politics overall, they can be a force to be reckoned with in their particular area of concern, especially at the administrative level.

This pluralization of fisheries policy making over the years plus the rise of oil as Alaska's major revenue source has, however, been partly responsible for the dilution of fisheries influence in the state overall and the lack of an integrated policy approach to the many facets of fisheries issues. These developments have also contributed to a shift in the populist nature of fisheries as an element of Alaska's democracy. Freeing the state from Seattle control of the fishery and placing it in the hands of Alaskans was a widespread rallying cry that partly fueled the statehood movement. Today, however, direct benefits from harvesting the bulk of the resource are restricted to a very limited number of Alaskans. More than any other factor what has caused this shift is the nature of the economics of fisheries, the so-called fisherman's problem, and the increased need for fisheries management and regulation.

4. THE FISHERMAN'S PROBLEM AND FISHERIES MANAGEMENT AND REGULATION

While the delegates to Alaska's Constitutional Convention certainly realized the need for some fisheries regulation, likely few of them foresaw how profoundly the world of resource management was about to change. So while in 1956 the founders sought to reclaim Alaska's fisheries resources from Outside corporate interests for the people of

Alaska, their populist goals were only short-lived. This was because of a fundamental problem with unlimited access to fisheries and other natural resources. This phenomenon is neither new nor unique to Alaska.

The Fisherman's Problem

Observing the results of uncontrolled access to British fisheries in the 1930s, Michael Graham coined what he called the "Great Law of Fishing:" fisheries that allow unlimited access become unprofitable.[23] Then, the year before Alaska's Constitutional Convention met, economist H. Scott Gordon put Graham's theory to the test. If the resources of the sea were so great, he asked, why were fishermen often so poor? Part of the reason, he concluded, was that fishermen were gamblers, willing to work for less in hopes of a "lucky catch." But the biggest problem stemmed from the belief that the resources of the sea were considered common property. This meant everyone's property is nobody's property and the fish in the sea are valueless to the fisherman because there is no assurance they will be there tomorrow if they are left behind today.[24]

The result was a race for fish that dissipated the economic rent, or earnings potential, that the resource afforded. Gordon went on to say:

> Common-property natural resources are free goods for the individual and scarce goods for society. Under unregulated private exploitation they can yield no rent; that can be accomplished only by methods which make them private property or public (government) property, in either case subject to a unified directing power.[25]

Gordon's insight was amplified by others, most notably ecologist Garrett Hardin, who saw a threat to the resource itself. He argued:

> The oceans of the world continue to suffer from the survival of the philosophy of the commons. Maritime nations still respond automatically to the shibboleth of the 'freedom of the seas.' Professing to believe in the 'inexhaustible resources of the oceans,' they bring species after species of fish and whales closer to extinction.[26]

This aquatic "tragedy of the commons," is characteristic of fisheries throughout the world and has resulted in various attempts to limit access or "rationalize" fisheries as a way to conserve stocks and sustain the economic viability of a fishery. Gordon's and Hardin's predictions became apparent in Alaska soon after statehood, especially for the salmon fishery. As Governor Bill Egan expressed it:

> Alaska's salmon resources cannot produce a livelihood for an unlimited number of fishermen, nor can they be successfully managed for maximum sustained yield if utilized by an unlimited number of fishermen. . . . The only alternative to the continuing loss of a healthy professional fishery is the stabilization of entry into the fishery at reasonable levels.[27]

The upshot was the limited entry provision added to the Alaska Constitution in 1972.

Highly controversial in its day, limited entry for salmon was just the beginning. As Graham's Great Law of Fishing proved itself true in fisheries for halibut, pollock, and crab, Alaska responded with a variety of management regimes, each building off the other. In addition, there was increasing regulation by the federal government of Alaska's fisheries. Before we go into specifics about this restriction of access, we briefly explain the nature of fisheries management and regulation.

Managing and Regulating the Catch

When we talk about fishery management, we are really talking about managing fishermen, not fish. Multiple factors affect fish populations that are entirely out of our control: climate, water temperature, and predation to name just a few. Fish populations (technically referred to as biomass), change based on short-term swings in availability of feed, long-term cycles of productivity, and commercial harvests.

Under the divided management authority of the state and federal governments, the state manages fisheries in freshwater lakes, streams, and rivers within the state and in marine waters out to three miles. This includes salmon, herring, and other species. Fisheries within the federal EEZ from three to two hundred miles offshore from Alaska are managed by NPFMC, including pollock, cod, and other ground fish, although the state reserves the right to manage these species when they are within state waters. Management authority for crab is shared under a special agreement between the state and federal government. Halibut are managed by the IPHC, which sets catch quotas for each area.

Catch limits are set by assessing biomass and applying an exploitation rate that ensures the sustainability of the resource. For species like salmon, the biomass is determined by in-season observation. Salmon are literally counted as they enter the rivers, and fishing is allowed when enough salmon reach the spawning grounds. For deep dwelling species like halibut, pollock, and crab, the biomass is assessed by surveys. Test boats sample the resource abundance, the data is plugged into mathematical models, and a catch quota is set.

Fishing seasons are set for a variety of reasons, most obviously the availability of the fish, but marketing and conservation objectives also play a part. Roe fisheries are set when the species is about to spawn. Crab fishing is restricted to the rough months of winter to protect the crab during their annual molting stage. Within a season, time and area closures are used to control the amount of harvest. Season openings are set based on the harvesting ability of the fleet: the greater the catching capacity, the shorter the opening. The length of openings can range from months for a species like halibut to days for crab and just hours for salmon. For other species like herring, openings can last only minutes. Area closures are used to limit fishing effort to particular fishing grounds as well as protect critical habitat.

Along with these basic management tools, a variety of other regulations have evolved. Some, like vessel identification and reporting requirements, are purely administrative. Others include attempts to slow the race for fish through limits on vessel size or horsepower. Hampering fishermen's efficiency, however, has proved to be largely ineffective. For every restriction placed on the fleet, the industry invented new ways around it. In Bristol Bay in Southwest Alaska, the use of powerboats was banned by federal regulation until 1951, making it the last major sailboat fishery in the Pacific. Industry circumvented the rule by simply towing their boats.

5. FOUR CASE STUDIES AND EXPERIENCE IN OTHER COUNTRIES

These four case studies—salmon, halibut, pollock, and crab—explain aspects of the politics and policy of restricted access to the fishery at both the state and federal levels. They are especially insightful in illustrating particular examples of the often intense nature of fisheries politics and policy making. The final part of this section shows that Alaska is not alone in having conflicts over restricting the fishery.

Limited Entry for Salmon

Following World War II, even as salmon runs declined, participation in the salmon fishery began to rise. Alaska's growing population and an increase in independent processors after the war contributed to the increase. Many Alaska Natives entered the fishery as a cash supplement to their subsistence economy. The trend accelerated after statehood. Fish traps were notoriously efficient and their elimination required more fishermen, and increasing numbers of people, such as teachers and those in the military, considered by some to be "vacationing" fishermen, were attracted to the seasonal work. Between 1960 and 1970 the overall number of salmon gear licenses issued by the state grew 75 percent, from 5,110 to 8,923, while in the lucrative Bristol Bay fishery, the number of gear licenses more than doubled. [28]

In response to the growing effort, many Alaskans initially wanted to restrict non-resident fishermen, but like other "local hire" provisions, this ran afoul of the U.S.

Constitution. A broader plan was proposed to limit entry of all participants, but that ran squarely against the state constitution's guarantee of a common property resource. In 1972, Alaska lawmakers proposed, and the voters approved, a constitutional amendment to allow limited entry. As amended, Article VIII, Section 15, now provides that the prohibition on exclusive right of fishery "does not restrict the power of the State to limit entry into any fishery for the purposes of resource conservation, to prevent economic distress among fishermen and those dependent upon them for a livelihood . . . ."

Once the amendment was passed by the voters, Governor Egan formed a Limited Entry Study Group that produced draft legislation that was passed with remarkable speed. The act established the Commercial Fisheries Entry Commission, which was authorized to assign permits based on an individual's fishing history. The act also allowed for the transferability of permits, an important point for many Alaska fishermen who wanted to be able to pass along the privilege to their children.[29]

Even so, Alaskans were deeply divided on the idea of transferability. A voter initiative tried to overturn the law but failed. A Bristol Bay fisherman challenged the law in court, arguing that permit transferability, "creates an aristocracy of fishing families who have exclusive and separate emoluments and privileges in the publicly owned resource of free swimming salmon."[30] The case ultimately went to the Alaska Supreme Court, which upheld the transferability provisions but recognized the legal tension between the constitutional amendment and the guarantee of a common property resource. The Court concluded that:

> . . . . to be constitutional, a limited entry system should impinge as little as possible on the open fishery clauses consistent with the constitutional purposes of limited entry, namely prevention of economic distress to fishermen and resource conservation.[31]

Upholding limited entry opened the door to dozens more lawsuits from persons denied permits for a variety of technical reasons. Limited entry became one of Alaska's most litigated laws, with over seventy Alaska Supreme Court decisions as of 2015. With the court's doctrine of minimal impingement, the number of permits slowly began to increase. Limited entry was a limit on access, but not necessarily a reduction in effort. Still, the cap on access proved significant. It prevented an influx of West Coast fishermen whose fishing opportunities closer to home were reduced by court decisions or depressed stocks. Absent limitation, Alaska fishing fleets would also have surged, especially with the attraction of skyrocketing fish prices in the late 1980s.

Permit transferability proved to be a mixed blessing. Permit ownership among local resident fishermen has gradually eroded as permits were sold to nonresidents. And with the added cost of a permit, some of which ran into the hundreds of thousands of dollars, the cost of entering the fishery increased dramatically. In 2005 one young Petersburg fisherman needed $500,000 to obtain the required permits, boat, and gear to enter the salmon fishery, twice what it would have cost him to get a medical degree from Harvard.[32] But having survived court challenges, limited entry was applied to other state-managed fisheries.

Halibut Individual Fishery Quotas

As Alaska's limited entry law worked its way through the courts, halibut managers also saw the need for access limitation. The IPHC used science-based management, and when halibut stocks prospered the fishery inevitably attracted increased interest. As fishing effort rose, seasons were shortened. A familiar pattern emerged.

Fishery managers considered limited entry for halibut in the early 1980s, but the idea ran afoul of the Reagan administration's opposition to government regulation. Reagan approved of privatization, however, and the discussion turned to individual fishery quotas (IFQs). Whereas limited entry set a cap on the number of participants, IFQs went a step further, assigning catch shares among a limited number of individual participants.

While the IFQ idea was being debated, the situation only got worse. As people sensed some form of limitation was pending, more entered the fishery in hopes of being grandfathered in later. As the number of participants grew, openings became even shorter. By the early 1990s, there were some five thousand participants in the Alaska halibut fishery and the season was reduced to a few twenty-four-hour openings a year.

This "derby fishery" had several consequences, almost all of them bad. Fast paced, it was difficult for fishery managers to estimate the catch, and quotas were easily exceeded. Product quality suffered when millions of pounds of halibut were delivered all at once. Instead of being sold fresh, most of the catch had to be frozen, which reduced quality and value while increasing cold storage costs that were ultimately paid by consumers. Even worse, the derby fishery was dangerous. Openings were set in advance and occurred regardless of weather conditions.

With an IFQ, much of this could be avoided. Quota shares could be caught whenever the holder wanted, avoiding bad weather and targeting market opportunities. Canada adopted a quota share system in 1991, and the NPFMC soon followed for offshore Alaska waters. In 1993, the NPFMC adopted an IFQ system that distributed quotas based on fishermen's past participation. When it took effect in 1995, the number of fishermen who received shares was little changed from the derby days but quickly consolidated. By 2005 the number of quota holders had dropped by a third, and the halibut fleet shrank more than 60 percent. But fleet efficiency came with a commensurate loss of crewman jobs.[33]

Halibut IFQs have largely succeeded in their intended goals. The halibut season, once down to mere days, now lasts ten-and-a-half months. The fishery is easier to manage because the pace is slower, and it is safer because fishermen need not fish in bad weather. And because it resulted in more fresh rather than frozen halibut, product quality and prices soared.

But IFQs remained controversial to those who lost jobs and to communities that prospered during the halibut derby. For instance, Pelican, in Southeast Alaska, suffered from the loss of the seasonal influx of derby fishermen. Because IFQs were transferable, questions were raised about quota concentration, especially out of state, and the expense for young people seeking to enter the fishery. The Alliance Against IFQs argued the plan was arbitrary and capricious. Their claim was rejected by the courts, but the opposition was loud enough that in 1996 Congress adopted a moratorium against new IFQ programs until the effects of this management tool could be evaluated.

Processors also felt cut out of the economic benefits of the program. A study found the processing sector suffered a 56 percent loss in revenues compared to pre-IFQ days. In this regard, economists Scott Matulich and Michael Clark argued:

> The IFQ policy design was not a win-win. . . . The harvester-only allocation guaranteed harvesters would benefit from the efficiency gains intended by the rationalization policy. But the quota allocation only to harvesters also assured they would benefit at the expense of processors.[34]

With the commercial fleet consolidated under IFQs, the fastest growing segment in the halibut fishery is sport charter boats. Catering to Alaska's growing tourism industry, the number of charter boats increased 50 percent over the first decade after the introduction of IFQs, and in several years the charter fleet has exceeded guideline harvest levels. In 2008, for instance, the levels were exceeded by as much as one million pounds. Commercial fishermen proposed an IFQ system for charter operators, which they consider a "commercial-sport" industry, but it was bitterly opposed by sport groups as a give-away of a public resource.

Pollock Cooperatives

Once derided as a "trash fish," Bering Sea pollock has grown into the world's largest fishery, producing a harvest of around 1.5 million tons a year from 2002–2014, between a quarter and a half of the nation's entire harvest of seafood depending on the year. Historically, the fishery was conducted by foreign high seas fleets until enactment of the Magnuson-Stevens Act in 1976 which claimed federal jurisdiction over waters out to two hundred miles. Domestic processors flooded into the fishery, which was fully "Americanized" in 1990. It was a massive investment. One shore-based plant was valued at $100 million while factory trawlers, ships over three hundred feet in length, cost $30 million to $40 million each. Despite the huge expenses involved in the fishery, the Americanized effort predictably overcapitalized. Processing capacity was estimated at 150 percent of what was believed needed for the fishery and harvesting capacity grew to 200 percent.[35]

The Americanized pollock industry was divided into two main factions: onshore processors mostly based in Dutch Harbor in Southwest Alaska and factory trawlers that processed their catch at sea. State policy tended to favor shore-based processing to boost local jobs and the local tax base, but at-sea processing offered efficiencies that made harvesting the low-value species economical. For years, Anchorage was the scene of pitched battles between the onshore and offshore sectors during meetings of the NPFMC to set annual allocations. IFQs were considered as a way to resolve the dispute but were barred by the congressional moratorium that followed its use in the halibut fishery. Then, in 1998, a new option became available: harvesting cooperatives.

Off the coast of Washington and Oregon, three companies that fished for Pacific whiting sought federal approval to divide the catch quota among themselves. Limited to catching the fish and not its processing or marketing, proponents argued that harvesting cooperatives would benefit consumers. By ending the race for fish, companies could reduce waste and increase their overall yield from the same amount of fish. When it passed muster with the U.S. Justice Department's antitrust division, participants in the Alaska pollock fishery immediately grasped its implications. A cooperative plan was struck between the onshore and offshore sectors in the fishery, but when NPFMC balked at parts of the plan, both sides took their cases to Washington, D.C.

Legislation on a related fishing issue working its way through Congress became the vehicle for a major rewrite of the pollock fishery. After what even supporters described as a "contentious process of political logrolling and backroom politics," what emerged was a complicated piece of legislation, the American Fisheries Act (AFA) of 1998.[36] The AFA allowed cooperatives for three pollock sectors: the onshore, offshore, and mothership fisheries. Motherships are large at-sea processing vessels that lack any harvesting capacity. AFA named the individual processors and harvesting vessels that could participate, and set catch allocations for each. Cooperatives were quickly formed among the various sectors. The measure allowed for consolidation, and several of the named participants were promptly bought out. The AFA also included many "sideboard" provisions intended to address incidental issues such as protecting other Alaska fisheries from competition from the displaced fleet.

There were critics of the flawed process of the birth of the AFA, including concerns about the adequacy of the sideboard agreements, and those who questioned the award of a quota to processors, some of whom were partly or entirely owned by foreigners. But the opposition was largely muted. The pollock fishery was an industrial-scale fishery that was highly vertically integrated to begin with, with a number of processors owning or controlling the catching of the fish they process.

Significantly, the proposal also included a big payback to the state by expanding the existing Community Development Quota (CDQ) fishery. Created in 1992, the CDQ fishery divided a small portion of the allowable pollock catch among six regional CDQ corporations to provide jobs, training, and economic development in Bering Sea coastal communities. Expanding the CDQ program helped ensure these Bering Sea residents shared in the wealth of the resource.

The AFA has largely been successful in meeting its goals. Ending the "race for fish" allowed industry to boost production of higher value products from pollock and increase the overall recovery rate (the amount of product produced from the same amount of fish) by 20 percent. The slower pace of the fishery has allowed the industry to address conservation issues such as impacts to sea lions and the incidental catch of non-target species, although this so-called bycatch remains a particular concern. Expansion of CDQ fisheries prompted some to speculate that this sector would eventually dominate the Bering Sea, and a CDQ representative has chaired the NPFMC.

Crab Rationalization

The AFA also included a directive for NOAA to look at rationalization of other fisheries, including Bering Sea crab. Exploited by the Japanese as early as 1930, the domestic Alaska crab fishery began to greatly expand after World War II. The king crab catch boomed near Kodiak in the 1960s, and the effort expanded into the Bering Sea. Catches were big, and the money was even bigger. The Bristol Bay king crab catch peaked at 130 million pounds in 1980 when a fleet of 236 crabbers landed $115 million worth of crab in just forty days. King crab stocks soon crashed, but attention turned to the smaller but more abundant snow crab, the catch of which peaked at 329 million pounds worth $163 million in 1991.[37]

The Bering Sea crab fishery also had a not-so-hidden secret. Taking place during the fall and winter months when weather was notoriously bad and icing conditions were severe, the race for Bering Sea crab was the most dangerous job in the nation. Vessels overloaded with crab pots capsized and crewmen were swept overboard. According to the National Institute for Occupational Safety and Health, the Bering Sea crab fishery had a workplace mortality rate of 356 per 100,000, fifty times the national average of 7 per 100,000.[38] The danger was publicized in books such as Spike Walker's *Working on the Edge: Surviving in the World's Most Dangerous Profession* (1991) and *Nights of Ice* (1997), both playing off the mythology of Alaska's commercial fishermen while at the same time helping to make the case for rationalization.[39]

Following the congressional directive and after years of debate, NPFMC devised a Bering Sea crab program that merged elements of all the previous plans. It began with a license limitation program in 2000 that capped the effort. Later, IFQ shares were distributed to vessels and captains, based on their harvesting history. Like the AFA, the crab plan allowed formation of cooperatives and included a $100 million, thirty-year loan to reduce excess harvesting capacity by buying out vessel owners. Crab rationalization then linked IFQs to individual processors. Processor shares—individual processor quotas or IPQs—were considered necessary to protect the companies' capital interests in the remote fishery. Using the experience in the halibut fishery as an example, economist Scott Matulich argued that the redistribution of wealth created by IFQs should benefit both harvesters and processors and that Bering Sea crab processors stood to be severely impacted without some protection.[40]

IPQs prompted a fierce debate that extended from the fish docks in Alaska to Washington, D.C. The U.S. Justice Department's antitrust division urged NOAA to oppose IPQs, arguing that they were a disincentive for processors to innovate. One interagency communication advised:

> While harvester quotas should eliminate the harmful race for fish, processor quotas are not justified by any such beneficial competitive purpose. If the goal of IPQs is to compensate processors for over-capitalization, we urge NOAA to consider more direct solutions, such as a program to buy off excess processor equipment.[41]

Senator John McCain of Arizona also opposed the processor shares:

> For centuries, fishermen have used market forces to negotiate their dockside prices, and this has had the effect of maintaining competition and benefiting consumers. Processor quotas throw an enormous wrench in the free market machinery.[42]

Despite such opposition, crab rationalization was ultimately passed in 2003, as part of an appropriations bill, and included processor quotas for 90 percent of the harvest. Under the final crab plan, 10 percent of the catch was "unblocked," meaning that the harvesters could sell it to whomever they wanted. The provision was intended to protect the fleet's bargaining rights, but many saw it as too little to be effective.

The first year of crab rationalization saw a sharp drop in effort. The fishing fleet shrank from 251 vessels to just 89, and the season lasted 93 days compared to 3.3 days the previous year for a comparable catch. The fishery also became safer. Since crab rationalization, the number of fatalities in the fishery has been sharply reduced, although some credit for that goes to increased Coast Guard outreach and safety inspections.[43]

Critics of the plan remain vocal and have taken their opposition to the newest medium: the Internet and blogs. Much of their anger stems from the perceived loss of a common property resource. "These rights belong to you, the public, and the managers are giving them away for free," said one blogger in the *Anchorage Daily News*. "This is the equivalent to giving away the National forests to the timber industry."[44]

Concerns were also raised about impacts to fishing communities. The sharp reduction in the fleet resulted in a dramatic decline in fishing employment, with a loss of about 900 jobs in the Bristol Bay king crab fishery and about 450 in the Bering Sea snow crab fishery. Marie Lowe and Gunnar Knapp also noted that "rationalization has cut into sales of some businesses which sell to crab boats and crab fishermen—particularly those whose sales depend on the number of boats and people fishing, such as pot storage, welding, marine supplies, hotels, and taxis."[45]

Crab rationalization raised another problem that was not completely unexpected: high-grading. In the first year of the program, fishermen threw back legal-sized crab that had imperfections, such as barnacles on their shells, which made them less desirable on the market. High-grading increases the market value of the catch but results in increased handling mortality of the crab as they are pulled up and then thrown back. Some high-grading was expected with rationalization but not at the level seen in 2005, when 677,000 legal-sized crab were thrown back, up from the previous record of 80,000.[46] To stem the practice, the estimated loss due to handling mortality was subtracted from the following year's catch quota.

Experience in Other Countries

Alaska is not alone in using access limitation programs to manage its fisheries. Most fisheries in Iceland and New Zealand operate under similar rules, called individual transferable quotas (ITQs). Australia, the Netherlands, and Canada also use an IFQ program for major fisheries such as halibut and tuna. Elsewhere in the United States, IFQ systems are in place for mostly minor fisheries such as surf clams, ocean quahogs (hard clams), and South Atlantic wreckfish (a small, bass-like, bottom fish).

These other programs are not without their controversies, for reasons similar to those seen in Alaska. Regarding Iceland, Einar Eythorsson observed:

> Repeated polls among the public have shown that a majority of Icelanders are either skeptical or opposed to the system, and a new, anti-ITQ political party got two MPs [Members of Parliament] in the 1999 elections.

> The critique against the system is in essence aimed at its distributional effects. The initial allocation of ITQs led to a gratis distribution of valuable rights to certain families, and in some cases these families have enjoyed great windfall gains from selling out their shares.[47]

6. ASSESSING THE ALASKA FISHERIES POLICY EXPERIENCE: FROM POPULIST TO BUREAUCRATIC AND SPECIAL INTEREST DEMOCRACY

In the introduction to the chapter we raised a fundamental question about the major issue in Alaska fisheries policy since statehood: How can limited access to a fishery be justified in a democracy that defines fish as a common property resource? This section summarizes the answer and, more importantly, assesses what the consequences have been for Alaska's brand of democracy and what this might mean in the future.

Justification

Limiting access has been justified on two major grounds. One we already know about. This is the need to address the fisherman's problem, slow down the race for fish, and bring some rationalization to the fishery for economic reasons, which include conserving the resource. Together with other regulations, limiting access has brought some economic stability to the fishery and also improved safety.

The second justification has come via the courts and has bolstered the policies to deal with the fisherman's problem. In essence, this is a repudiation of the idea that access to the fishery is a right for all. This shift has occurred since Alaska's founders included the common access provision in the state constitution. For instance, the U.S. Commission on Ocean Policy supported IFQs, but rejected calling them and other such mechanisms a property right, preferring the term *dedicated access privilege* (DAP). The commission explained its preference for the word "privilege" over the word "right" in this way:

> First, it highlights the fact that fishing is a privilege, not a right. Second, it is an umbrella term that includes access privileges assigned to individuals as well as to groups or communities. Finally, it reflects the fact that the dedicated privilege being granted is *access* to the fish, rather than the fish themselves.[48]

The 2006 rewrite of the Magnuson-Stevens Act changed the wording once again, from DAP to the Limited Access Privilege Program (LAPP), but the key word was still "privilege." The act specifically stated that the law "shall not create, or be construed to create, any right, title, or interest in or to any fish before the fish is harvested by the holder," and noted that it was "a permit that can be revoked at any time and without compensation."[49]

Looking at this rationalization of the fishery in the broadest sense, it essentially places the interests of society above those of individuals and above freedom of access. However, as is generally the case with most regulatory policies that are essentially zero-sum situations, not all individuals and businesses have lost in this process of regulation.

Consequences

The consequences of rationalization can be viewed from several perspectives. Three significant ones are the biological, the economic, and particularly the political perspective.

From a biological perspective, the management of Alaska's fisheries is exemplary. According to a 2007 article in *National Geographic*, Alaska is regarded as one of only three regions in the world considered to have well-managed fisheries. The others are Iceland and New Zealand.[50]

The economic consequences have been mixed. On the one hand it has brought some stability and predictability to the commercial industry. Barring the whims of nature and the vicissitudes of world markets, rationalization has produced a more stable living for all segments of the industry, from the largest to the smallest operations. On the other hand, rationalization has had its economic downsides, and critics of access limitation raise legitimate arguments about who wins and who loses from such programs. As we have seen, entering the fishery is prohibitively expensive. What, in effect, has happened regarding Alaska residents in the commercial fishery is that an economic fisheries elite has been created through supply and demand by limiting access to the fishery. As in Iceland, these individuals can make windfall profits by selling their access privileges along with their boats and gear. But what is most rational for business interests may not be in the best interests of fishing communities or the state. Particularly in the crab fishery, there have been job losses in Kodiak, King Cove, and elsewhere, and concerns about whether the 90 percent processor share allows enough bargaining power for fishermen to negotiate prices.

The Political Effects and Consequences for Democracy

Rationalization has resulted in the Alaska commercial fishery being extensively regulated by the state and federal governments. Plus, the sport, subsistence, and personal use fisheries are also highly regulated. And as we have noted, the level of government involvement in fisheries runs deeper than most fishermen realize. Beyond the complicated relationships between state and federal regulatory regimes and their respective fish boards and councils, Alaska is, through the federal government, also actively involved in multilateral agreements with Canada, Japan, and Russia that deal with fish stocks that migrate beyond the two-hundred-mile limit or straddle international borders. The upshot has been that access to virtually all Alaska fisheries is considerably more restricted than at the time of statehood.

It is therefore ironic that fishing—an industry often viewed as the hallmark of freedom and individualism—became one of Alaska's most regulated industries. Rationalization has been a major transformational factor in fisheries, from its outset at statehood as an element of populist democracy to one of special interest and bureaucratic democracy. Fisheries politics and policy have become largely the preserve of those representing commercial, sport, and subsistence user groups and the government agencies that regulate, administer, and enforce fisheries policy.

Furthermore, widespread public participation in, or influence on, Alaska fisheries policy was short lived. The new restricted-access regime was in place just over a decade after control by Seattle, Chicago, and New England-based corporations largely ended with statehood. Today, the apparently high degree of public participation in selection of Alaska Board of Fisheries members and in board activities and decision making creates an illusion of citizen oversight of state fisheries policy. In reality, fishing organizations often promote prominent members of their groups to fill board seats. If the organization has backed the right gubernatorial candidate it can often select the regional representative, or at least prevent the appointment of hostile board members. These appointees then pursue the agenda of their respective support groups.

Regional goals are attained by building coalitions with members representing other areas. The medium of exchange is usually vote trading. For example, in a manifestation of Alaska regionalism, a Southeast Alaska gillnet representative might vote to maintain current fishing patterns in the Aleutian Peninsula in return for support of an altered allocation policy in his or her region.[51]

7. INTO THE FUTURE: MORE OF THE SAME?

The nature of fish politics and policy making in Alaska is not likely to change much in the foreseeable future. The IGR component of policy making and the intense interest-group politics that often occurs will likely become more intense as Alaska's population expands and as regulation increases as a result of increased demands by environmentalists and others concerned about fisheries resources. This will also include conflicts between fishery user groups with other natural resource user groups, as is the case with concerns of salmon fishermen over continued logging in the Tongass National Forest in Southeast Alaska.[52]

In addition, even though Alaska's major fisheries now operate under some form of access limitation, the debate is far from over. All these efforts of access limitation remain in play in one way or another. Nevertheless, some form of limited access is likely to continue in the Alaska fishery, despite the economic pain that it causes some Alaskans.

Economist Francis Christy summed this up when he wrote that the transition to property rights regimes in fisheries (such as Alaska's limited entry and the NPFMC's halibut IFQs) is occurring with a speed that is not fully appreciated. The process is inexorable. He also recognized that the change in fishery policy is associated with high degrees of real pain for the participants, and warned that attempts to alleviate the pain may, unless carefully taken, result in long-term imperfections to the ultimate outcome.[53] In other words, he was warning against populist solutions that might make political but not scientific and management sense.

Limited access holds the promise of addressing not just the economic challenges facing one of Alaska's major industries but also environmental concerns over what has been portrayed elsewhere as a fish crisis. Using rationalized fisheries as a model, an article in the journal *Science* argued that economics and management are not at odds. The authors concluded, "Conservation promotes both larger fish stocks and higher profits."[54] In sharp contrast, another study reported in the same journal projected a worldwide fisheries collapse by the year 2048.[55] A more recent study, however, pointed to the implementation of quota share systems as part of the answer: "Implementation of catch shares halts, and even reverses, the global trend toward widespread collapse and has the potential for greatly altering the future of global fisheries."[56]

Apparently, then, in the future as now, a bureaucratic democracy to temper special interest groups in fisheries policy making is of more benefit to society at large than a populist democratic approach to fisheries. Nevertheless, populist politics may occasionally dominate over economics and rational management, as it has to some extent with the banning of salmon farming in Alaska.

8. CONCLUSION: TO WHAT EXTENT DO THE CHARACTERISTICS OF ALASKA POLITICS EXPLAIN FISHERIES POLITICS AND POLICY SINCE STATEHOOD?

In conclusion, we move from specifics to place Alaska fisheries politics and policy in the broader context of the characteristics of Alaska politics. This final section explores the extent to which these characteristics help explain fisheries politics and policy since statehood.

Of the five characteristics that are particularly relevant to fisheries, the two most significant are the all-pervasive importance of government and the role of external economic and political forces. Both are seen operating in tandem in fisheries politics, with increased regulation and restriction of access by the state and federal governments and by the effects of the Outside economy on the Alaska fishery. Third is the characteristic of the role of Alaska Natives in fisheries politics and policy, particularly regarding subsistence and the development of regulatory fishing regimes, especially for salmon and halibut. Fourth, the developer-environmentalist conflict is also evident and has increased in importance over the years, restricting commercial, sport, subsistence, and personal use fishing user groups alike. And fifth is regionalism, which manifests itself in Board of Fish appointments, alliances between fisheries groups, and the way legislators relate (or do not relate) to fisheries issues.

All that said, over the years, the major influence on Alaska's fisheries political economy has been the "fisherman's problem" and the need to counter the serious ecological, economic, and social consequences of free and open access to the fishery. This problem is common to fisheries throughout the world, and many countries have taken steps to deal with it. In Alaska's case, state and federal regulation precipitated by this reality of fisheries economics is at the root of much of fish politics and policy in Alaska. So in a broad view, Alaska fish politics and policy are largely the product of the development of restricted access played out over the years against the backdrop of Alaska's political economy and its political characteristics.

Given all these influences on, and characteristics of, fish politics and policy, the concept of the Owner State is not as undermined for fisheries as much as it is for other resource development industries such as mining and oil and gas, where the federal government and Outside interest groups and political forces have considerably more influence. However, Alaska is far from in total control of its fishery. Today most Alaskans have either little interest, or a limited chance of being involved, in fisheries at the commercial level. And while the people of Alaska have never actually been in control of their fishery, the necessity of regulation has meant that they have exchanged a populist participation in the fishery for one increasingly under federal and state bureaucratic control.

ENDNOTES

1 Ernest Gruening, *The State of Alaska* (New York: Random House, 1968), 245.

2 Determining the relationship between the commercial, sport, and subsistence fisheries in regard to value, weight, and overall contribution to the Alaska economy is far more difficult than might be assumed and far from definitive. See Box 23.2.

3 Alaska Constitution, Article VIII, Sections 3 and 15.

4 Described as such by *National Geographic* in a 2007 television documentary of the same name: http://channel.nationalgeographic.com/channel/PT/popup/200708011200.html.

5 Neal Gilbertsen, "Fisheries: A Stymied State Government," in *Alaska Public Policy Issues: Background and Perspectives*, ed. Clive S. Thomas (Juneau: Denali Press, 1999), 221–22.

6 See the Alaska Department of Fish and Game website, at http://www.adfg.alaska.gov/index.cfm?adfg=fishingSubsistence.main.

[7] For a review of the long dispute over subsistence hunting and fishing rights and who is and who is not eligible, see Chapter 4, Section 4, Chapter 9, Section 6, and Chapter 10, Box 10.2.

[8] See Chapter 6 on the Alaska economy for an explanation of the boom-bust cycle, particularly Box 6.2.

[9] Gordon Harrison, *Alaska's Constitution; A Citizen's Guide*, 5th ed. (Juneau: Alaska Legislative Affairs Agency, 2012), 131, 207, 208, 213, and 223.

[10] See Chapter 7, Figure 7.6, for a picture of the fluctuation in salmon and halibut prices from 1980 to 2010.

[11] This data comes from Chapter 7, Table 7.2, and its sources, and from sources in endnote 17 below.

[12] See Chapter 8 on state revenues, Figure 8.4.

[13] See endnote 17 below for sources of these statistics.

[14] See Chapter 7, Table 7.2.

[15] See Chapter 7, Figure 7.5.

[16] See Chapter 7, Figure 7.2.

[17] The statistics cited in Box 23.2 are a composite of the following sources from federal and state agencies: Legislative Research Report, December 18, 2003, "Economic Impact of Alaska's Fishing Industry," at http://www.adfg.alaska.gov/index.cfm?adfg=fishingCommercialByFishery.main; NOAA Fisheries, Office of Science & Technologies, "U.S. Commercial Landings: U.S. Domestic Landings, by Region and by State, 2009 and 2010," at http://www.st.nmfs.noaa.gov/st1/fus/fus10/02_commercial2010.pdf; http://www.adfg.alaska.gov/sf/sportfishingsurvey/index.cfm?ADFG=region.results; http://www.st.nmfs.noaa.gov/Assets/commercial/fus/fus13/FUS2013.pdf; http://www.census.gov/prod/2008pubs/fhw06-ak.pdf; and http://www.adfg.alaska.gov/index.cfm?adfg=fishingSubsistence.main; http://www.subsistence.adfg.state.ak.us/techpap/TP346.pdf.

Additional insights on the contribution of the three fisheries can be obtained from: "Subsistence, Commercial & Sport Harvest of Fish and Wildlife Resources in Alaska," Research Request 90.225, Legislative Research Agency, April 13, 1990; and "Economic Impact of Alaska's Fishing Industry," Legislative Research Report, Report Number 04.047, December 18, 2003; Alaska Department of Fish and Game, Sports Fisheries, 2014, at http://www.adfg.alaska.gov/index.cfm?adfg=fishingSport.main; Technical Paper N387, Alaska Subsistence and Personal Use Salmon Fisheries: Annual Report 2011, at http://www.adfg.alaska.gov/techpap/TP387.pdf; Alaska Resource Development Council, 2014, at http://www.akrdc.org/issues/fisheries/overview.html; and Craig Medred, "Turns Out Alaska Sport Fishery Top Commercial in Total Value," *Alaska Dispatch News*, June 30, 2014.

[18] See the ADF&G website, at http://www.adfg.alaska.gov/index.cfm?adfg=PersonalUsebyAreaSouthcentralKenaiSalmon.harvest.

[19] Gilbertsen, "Fisheries: A Stymied State Government," 231.

[20] See Chapter 15 on interest groups, Tables 15.3 and 15.4.

[21] *Ibid.*

[22] Victor Fischer, *Alaska's Constitutional Convention* (Fairbanks: University of Alaska Press, 1975), 132.

[23] Michael Graham, *The Fish Gate* (London: Faber & Faber, 1943), 155.

[24] H. Scott Gordon, "The Economic Theory of a Common Property Resource: The Fishery," *The Journal of Political Economy* 62, no. 2 (1954): 124–42.

[25] Gordon, "The Fishery," 135.

[26] Garrett Hardin, "The Tragedy of the Commons," *Science* 162 (1968): 1254.

[27] *A Limited Entry Program for Alaska's Fisheries*, 1973, the report of the Governor's Study Group on Limited Entry, State of Alaska, 269.

[28] Thomas A. Morehouse and Jack Hession, "Politics and Management: The Problem of Limited Entry," in *Alaska Fisheries Policy* (Anchorage: University of Alaska, Institute of Social, Economic and Government Research, 1972), 305 and 307.

[29] See Alaska Statutes, AS 16.43.

[30] *Ostrosky v. State of Alaska*, Jurisdictional Statement presented to the Supreme Court of the United States, October Term 1983, 13.

[31] While raised in *Ostrosky*, the Supreme Court test appears in *Johns v. Commercial Fisheries Entry Commission*, 758 P.2d 1256, 1266 (Alaska 1988).

[32] Matt Volz, "The Next Wave of Fishing: As Alaska's Fishing Fleet Grays, Newcomers Find the Price of Entry High," *Anchorage Daily News*, December 4, 2005.

[33] NOAA Fisheries, 2007, *Pacific Halibut-Sablefish IFQ Report for 2005*, 21, 30, at http://www.fakr.noaa.gov/ram/rtf05.pdf.

[34] Scott Matulich and Michael Clark, *Efficiency and Equity Choices in Fishery Rationalization Design: An Examination of the North Pacific Halibut and Sablefish Fishery IFQ Policy Impacts on Processors*, Alaska Department of Fish and Game, Regional Information Report RJ02-02 (2002), 25.

[35] Joe Sullivan, "American Fisheries Act Cooperatives," a presentation at the University of Alaska School of Fisheries and Ocean Sciences, Juneau, July 2007.

[36] James E. Wilen and Edward J. Richardson, "The Pollock Conservation Cooperative," a paper prepared for Workshop on Cooperatives in Fisheries Management, Anchorage, Alaska, June 2003.

[37] NPFMC, 2006, *Bering Sea Aleutian Islands Crab Stock Assessment and Fishery Evaluation*, particularly chapter 6.

[38] National Institute for Occupational Safety and Health, *Commercial Fishing Fatalities in Alaska*, 1997, 2.

[39] Spike Walker, *Working on the Edge: Surviving in the World's Most Dangerous Profession: King Crab Fishing on Alaska's High Seas* (New York: St. Martin's Griffin, 1993); and *Nights of Ice: The Story of Disaster and Survival on Alaska's High Seas* (New York: St. Martin's Griffin, 1999).

[40] Scott Matulich, testimony before the U.S. Senate Committee on Commerce, Science and Transportation on the Economic Implications of Seafood Processor Quotas, February 25, 2004, at: at http://commerce.senate.gov/public/index.cfm?FuseAction=Hearings.Testimony&Hearing-_ID=1066&Witness_ID=3007.

[41] R. Hewitt Pate, Deputy Attorney General, U.S. Department of Justice, Antitrust Division, to James R. Walpole, NOAA General Counsel, August 27, 2003, 2.

[42] Statement by Senator John McCain on the Fiscal Year 2004 Omnibus Appropriations Conference Report, January 21, 2004, at http://commerce.senate.gov/public/index.cfm?FuseAction=PressReleases.Detail&PressRelease_id=217248&Month=1&Year=2004.

[43] Mike Lewis, "Under the Needle: In Reality, 'Deadliest Catch' Has Never Been Safer," *Seattle Post-Intelligencer*, October 10, 2007.

[44] *Anchorage Daily News* "Highliner" blog posting on October 21, 2007, by "jgmac" and attributed to Doug Karlberg, at http://community.adn.com/adn/node/112053.

[45] Marie Lowe and Gunnar Knapp, "Economic and Social Impacts of BSAI Crab Rationalization on the Aleutians East Borough Communities of False Pass, King Cove and Akutan" (Anchorage: University of Alaska, Institute of Social and Economic Research, ISER, 2006), at http://www.iser.uaa.alaska.edu/iser/people/knapp/ISER_AEB_Crab_Rationalization_Preliminary_Report_Executive_Summary.pdf.

[46] Margaret Bauman, "Number of Discarded Crab Soars," *Alaska Journal of Commerce*, June 11, 2006, at http://www.alaskajournal.com/stories/061106/hom_20060611016.shtml.

[47] Einar Eythorsson, "A Decade of ITQ-management in Icelandic Fisheries: Consolidation without Consensus," *Marine Policy* 24 (2000), 490.

[48] U.S. Commission on Ocean Policy, *An Ocean Blueprint for the 21st Century* (2004), 289.

[49] U.S. House Resolution (H.R.) 5946, Section 106(b)4.

[50] Fen Montaigne, "Still Waters: The Global Fish Crisis," in *National Geographic* (April 2007), 42.

[51] Gilbertsen, "Fisheries: A Stymied State Government," 230–31.

[52] Peter Grantz, "Southeast Fishermen Lobby for Watershed Protection," *Alaska News Nightly*, Alaska Public Radio Network (APRN), March 13, 2013.

[53] Francis T. Christy, "The Death Rattle of Open Access and the Advent of Property Rights Regimes in Fisheries," *Marine Resource Economics* 11 (1996), 287–304.

[54] R. Q. Grafton, T. Kompas, and R. W. Hilborn, "Economics of Overexploitation Revisited," *Science* 318 (2007): 1601.

[55] Boris Worm *et al.*, "Impacts of Biodiversity Loss on Ocean Ecosystem Services," *Science* 315 (2006), 787.

[56] Christopher Costello *et al.*, "Can Catch Shares Prevent Fisheries Collapse?" *Science* 321 (2008), 1678.

★ CHAPTER 24 ★

Oil and Gas Issues and Policies: The Risks and Rewards of Being an Energy-Producing State

Douglas B. Reynolds

The powerful director of Saudi Arabia's oil ministry in the 1970s, Sheikh Ahmed Zaki Yamani, once said: "The Stone Age did not end for lack of stone, and the Oil Age will end long before the world runs out of oil."[1] As a universally recognized valuable asset for over one hundred years, oil is much more like gold than stone. It can bring enormous wealth and create huge personal fortunes. Hence, it is often referred to as black gold. This is why every oil and gas producing region around the world, whether a state, a country or a municipality, is intensely interested in developing its petroleum resources. Alaska is no exception.

Oil has such a major influence on Alaska's political economy that it is dealt with from various economic and political perspectives throughout the book. In particular, Chapters 6 and 7 on the Alaska economy explain the significance of oil and gas as a basic industry and economic driver, and Chapter 8 details the dependence of Alaska's state and local governments on oil revenues since the late 1970s. Chapters 21 and 22 identify some political conflicts involving the oil industry. Then, Chapter 25 examines the Alaska Permanent Fund and the Permanent Fund Dividend (PFD), which oil revenues make possible. Given the coverage in these other parts of the book, this chapter has two broad purposes that, when combined with this other coverage, provides a comprehensive understanding of the political economy of oil and gas in Alaska.

The first purpose is to describe Alaska's way of dealing with the oil industry (sometimes referred to here as an oil regime) as an Owner State. We then show how Alaska's approach to the political economy of oil differs from that of other regions, states, and countries that are major oil and gas producers. The second purpose of the chapter is to identify some of the prominent issues that Alaska's oil regime produces that are not covered in detail in other parts of the book. This includes presenting some policy options that have been tried in the past to deal with these issues or that may be available in the future.

An understanding of the economics and politics of Alaska as an oil producing state will be made easier by first explaining the language, basic operation, and major elements of the political economy of the oil and gas business. Then we look at the opportunities and challenges facing energy producing economies and the types of oil and gas political economics that have emerged in response and Alaska's Owner State approach. The rest of the chapter deals specifically with issues of the political economy of Alaska as an oil producer, including the vicissitudes of oil prices and taxes, oil development and its ramifications, and the political influence of oil.[2]

1. SOME PRELIMINARIES: THE LANGUAGE AND OPERATION OF THE OIL AND GAS INDUSTRY AND MAJOR ELEMENTS OF ITS POLITICAL ECONOMY

Like all businesses, oil and gas has its own parlance and jargon and aspects of its operation and organization that are particular to the industry. The socio-economic, political, and environmental impact of the industry also means that there is an identifiable political economy of oil and gas. This section provides an overview of the terms commonly used in the industry and the major elements of its political economy. Terms relating to oil industry taxation are explained in Section 4 of this chapter, which deals with oil taxes.

Terms, Acronyms, and Operating Methods

Oil and natural gas, called hydrocarbons, are often found together, which is why the industry is often called the oil and gas industry. Oil extraction, called "oil production" by the industry, is usually measured by a standard forty-two-gallon barrel of crude oil. A typical measurement for oil production is millions of barrels per day (mbd) and for natural gas billions of cubic feet (bcf) per day. The industry is made up of "producers." These are companies that own or lease the right to extract ("produce") oil and gas from the subsurface of a tract of land or property, including the subsurface of offshore marine property and that are actively producing oil and gas from the property. The term *producer* can be confusing, though, because it can also refer to an oil producing region or country.

The industry calls the process of getting oil to market "exploration, development and production," or E and P. Once oil and gas are found, they need infrastructure, such as a pipeline or tanker port, to get them to market. A natural gas technology to super cool natural gas to minus 260 degrees Fahrenheit, turning it into an icy cold liquid called *liquefied natural gas* (LNG), allows the volume of gas to be condensed and shipped economically around the world in LNG tanker ships. Alaska's Cook Inlet LNG facility has been selling Alaskan natural gas to Tokyo, Japan, since the 1970s.

Usually, E and P is given a tax break to induce international oil companies (IOCs, most of which are multinational corporations), also called the "majors," and small oil companies, also called the "independents," to come to Alaska to look for oil.[3] Many countries have state-run oil and gas companies, often called national oil companies (NOCs). These NOCs also work with IOCs using production sharing agreements (PSAs), which are contracts set up to split the oil and gas profits from new developments by a predetermined percentage.

Six Key Elements of the Political Economy of Oil

Of the many elements of the political economy of oil and gas, six are particularly prominent in democratic countries and regularly appear in the news, sometimes front page news, especially in Alaska. All six are interrelated.

First, unlike many businesses in a country, the oil industry is very much influenced, often on a daily basis, by international economic and political forces. In particular, the price of oil is determined not in local but in world markets. Consequently, global changes in demand due to economic downturns, interruptions in supply or political instability in an oil producing region or country, can cause the price to fluctuate considerably, with major consequences for oil producing regions and countries.

For this reason oil producing countries and regions are concerned about the daily price of oil because its price can change markedly, up or down, literally overnight and certainly within the course of a few days. Just as newspapers, radio, and TV report daily prices of hogs and corn in Iowa, so they report daily oil prices in states and countries with oil production. There are two types of oil prices. One is the *spot price*: the price at any one time, and sold for delivery in a month or so. The major spot prices quoted on a daily basis in the United States are for West Texas Intermediate (WTI) crude and Brent crude (an oil field off the northeast coast of Scotland). The other oil price is for *oil futures*: oil to be delivered at an agreed price at some specified future date, such as three or six months.

Second, largely because of the volatility of oil markets, oil is a risky business in which the losses can be great but the profits enormous. The steady rise in the demand for oil in the past century has created some of the largest multinational corporations in the United States and around the world. This is illustrated in Table 24.1, which shows that in 2014 four of the ten largest U.S. corporations and nine of the top twenty in the world were oil companies. Of these, British Petroleum (BP) and ExxonMobil have a major presence in Alaska and Shell was, until September 2015, working to increase its role, particularly in the Arctic. The enormous economic assets of these international corporations give them potentially major political influence to promote their interests. And, indeed, oil

TABLE 24.1

The Size of Major Oil Companies Compared with Other Businesses in 2014: Their Ranking in the U.S. and in the World by Total Revenues

IN THE U.S.			IN THE WORLD		
RANK	NAME	$ U.S. BILLIONS	RANK	NAME	$U.S. BILLIONS
1	Walmart Stores (retail)	$476.6	1	Walmart Stores (USA—retail)	$476.2
*** 2**	**ExxonMobil**	**$407.6**	*** 2**	**Royal Dutch Shell (Netherlands)**	**$459.5**
*** 3**	**Chevron**	**$220.3**	*** 3**	**Sinopec Group (China)**	**$457.2**
4	Berkshire Hathaway (investments)	$182.1	*** 4**	**China National Petroleum**	**$432.0**
5	Apple (technology)	$170.9	*** 5**	**ExxonMobil (USA)**	**$407.6**
*** 6**	**Phillips 66**	**$161.1**	*** 6**	**British Petroleum (UK)**	**$396.2**
7	General Motors—GM (automotive)	$155.4	7	State Grid (China—utilities)	$333.3
8	Ford Motor Company (automotive)	$146.9	8	Volkswagen (Germany—automotive)	$261.5
9	General Electric (technology)	$146.2	9	Toyota Motor (Japan—automotive)	$256.4
*** 10**	**Valero Energy**	**$137.7**	10	Glencore International (Switzerland—mining)	$232.6
11	AT&T (telecommunications)	$128.7	*** 11**	**Total (France)**	**$227.8**
12	CVS Caremark (pharmaceuticals)	$126.7	*** 12**	**Chevron (USA)**	**$220.3**
13	Fannie Mae (financial)	$125.6	13	Samsung Electronics (South Korea—technology)	$208.9
14	United Health Group (health care)	$122.4	14	Berkshire Hathaway (US—investments)	$182.1
15	McKesson (pharmaceuticals)	$122.4	15	Apple (US—technology)	$170.9
16	Verizon (telecommunications)	$120.5	16	AXA (France—insurance)	$165.8
17	Hewlett-Packard (technology)	$112.2	*** 17**	**Gazprom (Russia)**	**$165.0**
18	J.P. Morgan Chase & Co. (banking)	$106.2	18	E.ON (Germany—electrical)	$162.5
19	Costco Wholesale (retail)	$105.1	*** 19**	**Phillips 66 (USA)**	**$161.1**
20	Express Scripts (pharmaceuticals)	$104.6	20	Daimler (Germany—automaker)	$156.6

* Oil companies.

Source: CNN Money, "Fortune 500," February 2015, at http://fortune.com/fortune500/express-scripts-holding-company-20/, and "Global 500," February 2015, at http://fortune.com/global500/.

companies and their trade organizations are influential interest groups and lobbying forces in many countries, states, provinces, and localities across the globe.

These first two elements help in understanding the third and fourth points. The third deals with the complexities of the extent and form of taxing the industry so that oil producing government entities can balance obtaining the maximum amount of revenue without discouraging the industry from continuing to develop oil producing prospects. Looked at from another perspective, this involves the state taking various levels of risk to maximize revenues. Low taxes are less risky because they are less likely to scare away the industry but they bring in less revenue. Higher taxes increase revenue, but they also increase the risk of less oil development. Fourth is the influence that oil and gas exerts on public policy and the potential for corruption. Issues generated by the third and fourth elements are regularly revisited by policy makers. Debates about them have certainly been at the forefront of Alaska politics over the years.

The fifth and sixth elements relate to the environment. The fifth is the potential negative impact that the industry can have on the environment. Partly as a result of that impact, the sixth element is the extensive regulation of the industry. Because of the rise of the environmental movement since the early 1960s in the United States and most Western nations, an oil and gas company cannot drill for oil without first having obtained various government permits. These permits cover a wide range of potential problems from oil spills to threatened extinction of various flora and fauna to subsistence issues for local indigenous peoples. The federal Environmental Protection Agency (EPA) and Fish and Wildlife Service (FWS) and the Alaska Departments of Fish and Game and Environmental Conservation are the agencies that most affect the oil industry regarding environmental concerns.

Not all regulation of the industry is the result of environmental concerns, however. Others relate to safety in operations or maximizing output, among other things. At the federal level an important agency in this regard is the Federal Energy Regulatory Commission (FERC), which regulates pipelines, power lines, and other energy infrastructure. Alaska has the Alaska Oil and Gas Conservation Commission (AOGCC), whose mission is:

> To protect the public interest in exploration and development of Alaska's valuable oil and gas resources through the application of conservation practices designed to ensure greater ultimate recovery and the protection of health, safety, fresh ground waters and the rights of all owners to recover their share of the resource.[4]

Whether or not the industry is overregulated to the point of discouraging E and P is a matter of opinion and may vary from place to place and from time to time around the world and in various parts of the United States. It can also vary from time to time in the same place if an oil producing regime changes its policies regarding the industry. What is not in dispute is that a major ongoing aspect of the political economy of oil are some heated, often very emotional debates between oil companies and developers on the one side and conservationists and the environmental lobby on the other.

2. THE OPPORTUNITIES AND CHALLENGES OF OIL AND GAS ECONOMIES AND THE RANGE OF REGIMES

Alaska has its own unique political and regional characteristics as an energy producer, but it also shares many similarities, both opportunities and challenges, with other oil and gas producing regions worldwide. Here we briefly look at five of them: boom and bust oil prices, keeping oil wealth at home, the issue of economic development, the taxing question, and government-oil industry relations. The way that oil-rich states, regions, or countries approach these elements shapes the characteristics of their oil regimes and thus the political economy of oil in those places.

The Boom-Bust Cycle in Oil Prices and Its Economic and Political Consequences

All oil and gas producing regions face the cyclical booms and busts that result from the volatile worldwide demand for energy and the consequent fluctuation in oil and gas prices. The effect of these fluctuations is less severe on the overall economy in oil producing states or regions like Texas where there is a balanced economy. But the fluctuations can be particularly severe in places like Alaska, which are heavily dependent on natural resources for employment and revenue. For this reason, Alaska has had some of the most severe economic boom-bust cycles of any state or oil region. However, as one astute student of resource industries pointed out, "it is better to have mined and lost, than never to have mined at all."[5] In other words, a boom-bust mineral-based economy is not all bad. As long as many people benefit from it, even if only for a short period, then it is better to have had a boom and a bust, than never to have had a high level of economic activity at all. Nevertheless, the endemic and chronic nature of the volatility of oil prices is a dominant factor in shaping the actions of governments with oil patches. This will become clear in considering the other elements in the rest of this section.

This boom-bust reality is a major reason why several oil and gas producing countries have banded together to protect their interests. The most high profile oil producer group, which is often involved in international politics, is the Organization of the Petroleum Exporting Countries (OPEC) set up in 1960.[6] The major international organization for natural gas is the Gas Exporting Countries Forum established in 2001. Both organizations work to stabilize prices for the benefit of their members. For several reasons, largely political and not directly relevant to this chapter, the United States and thus Alaska are not members of these organizations. Oil and gas consumers are organized to counter OPEC through the International Energy Agency under the auspices of the Organisation for Economic Co-operation and Development (OECD).

Keeping the Gains from Oil Wealth at Home

Oil development and production in most countries is undertaken by international oil companies not based in those countries, and whose shareholders are scattered around the world. Therefore, a concern facing many governments in these countries is how to keep the gains from the exploitation of their oil resources at home to benefit local residents. This is certainly an issue in Alaska, where all the oil companies that operate are based in other states or other countries. Because the resource is finite (it will one day be depleted) and its price is volatile, there is also an added sense of urgency in oil and gas producing countries and regions. They feel the need to develop and secure benefits quickly when prices are high.

One way to keep some of the gains from oil at home and secure long-term benefits after the resource runs out is by creating a state savings account like the Alaska Permanent Fund. These so-called sovereign wealth funds are common in natural resource countries and states. They are dealt with in Chapter 25 on the Permanent Fund. In the short term, however, policies regarding economic development, taxes, and government-oil industry relations are those that can determine how much benefit local residents get from their black gold.

The Issue of Economic Development

Worldwide, one course pursued to keep oil money in an oil producing region and benefit its citizens is to pursue some sort of economic development, like creating high wage jobs in the oil and gas industry itself. This is one tack pursued in Alaska. The problem for Alaska is that as wages and jobs increase, Alaska becomes a magnet for worker immigration from other states. From 2000–2009, for instance, just under 25 percent of oil workers were from out of state.[7] Indeed, many of the two week on, two week off employees on Alaska's North Slope live out of state and commute to and from Alaska. Such immigration reduces jobs for resident Alaskans. By contrast, most Texan oil workers live in Texas near their jobs, although Texas also has some out of state oil workers.

Another and obvious way to use oil money for local benefits is to maximize state revenues. Higher state oil revenues can potentially provide more government services. Many argue, particularly politicians, that a place like Alaska can promote development and diversify the economy by improving or developing infrastructure, such as building roads to isolated villages or frontier regions that have economic development potential. An example is the "roads to resources" policy of Governor Sean Parnell (2009–2014). High tech industrial parks can be built or new industries can be subsidized.

The problem in Alaska, however, as Chapters 6 and 7 on the Alaska economy point out, is that given its remoteness, the cost of transportation to and from the other states is high, as is the cost of production. Consequently, the state is limited in what it can do to promote diversified economic development through oil revenues. In particular, subsidizing uneconomic enterprises will likely be a waste of money, as the state has largely discovered with, for example, agribusiness ventures such as the grain elevator in Valdez, which cost the state $10 million but was never used. In part, several of these economic problems stem from a condition that many countries experience in rapidly developing their natural resources. This condition is termed "the resource curse." Besides an economic aspect, this curse also often has a political dimension. Both dimensions are explained in Box 24.1.

The Taxing Question: Approaches and Their Relationship to a Business-Friendly Operating Environment

If part of the goal of an oil producing government is to keep at home as much of the gains from oil as possible, then the state or nation is faced with the question of how to do this through its taxing authority. There are two basic types of tax regimes and various combinations of them. One type, used by Mexico for many years, is to have high oil taxes and royalties—or high government PSA shares—in order to extract more value from each barrel of oil. The other, which is used by Texas, is to have low taxes and royalties—or low PSA shares—in order to expand production. The two methods represent the dilemma oil producing areas face as to whether it is better to have a bigger slice of a smaller pie or have a smaller slice of a bigger pie. The answer is not always clear.

The low-tax philosophy sees the most value coming from greater investment by the industry resulting in more oil production over the long run, which in turn may increase government revenue, jobs, and investment in the economy in the future. The high-tax philosophy sees the most value as coming from extracting as much revenue as possible from oil as soon as possible. This approach may result in less oil investment and fewer barrels produced, but the government does get a higher share of each barrel of oil. Some oil producing regions take the business friendly approach, while others take the high profit taking approach. Still others choose a middle ground. So viewed in terms of risk: the high-tax route is the most risky but with more immediate revenues; the low-tax route is least risky but with lower short-term revenues and a view to future gains; and the middle course falls somewhere in between in securing revenue and encouraging development.

BOX 24.1

The Resource Curse: Its Economic and Political Dimensions

Several studies have found a negative relationship between the resource wealth of countries and their rate of economic growth. This phenomenon is often called the "resource curse," "the paradox of plenty," or "Dutch disease" because of its effects on the economy of the Netherlands.

In 1959 the vast Groningen natural gas field was discovered just offshore in the northern Netherlands. These reserves were immediately developed to maximize their value and to create economic development. However, this development brought both wealth and major economic problems. Since the natural gas was extremely valuable, Dutch wealth rose, but the net effect was that nonpetroleum Dutch industries became uncompetitive.

The source of the problem is that when a country has a valuable resource, like oil, natural gas, or gold, those around the world who want it must buy the currency of the country where it is produced. High demand for the currency causes its value to rise, sometimes considerably. This makes importing goods cheaper—more foreign currency can be bought with the home currency—but it makes the home country's exports more expensive. Foreign buyers must use more of their own currency to buy the country's products. The resource-rich country also experiences high internal inflation with wages and salaries, and prices in general rising considerably.

Before the Netherlands found natural gas, there were a number of Dutch products, such as shoes and food, made locally. But because of internal inflation the Dutch no longer bought these products. Instead, they bought cheaper foreign equivalent products. Non-oil exports fell due to their high costs of production and Dutch industry declined. Even if the Dutch had pegged its currency—set a fixed exchange rate with other currencies and not let its value be determined by supply and demand market forces—the problem would have persisted with internal high inflation making imported products cheaper.

There are many examples of situations in which countries have suffered from the resource curse. For example, in oil-rich Nigeria per capita income is actually lower today than it was in the late 1970s. Yet some places, like Norway, seem to have avoided the negative consequences of natural resource wealth. Typical symptoms of the resource curse, in addition to those experienced in the Netherlands, include excessive borrowing, insufficient investment, underfunding of education, increased dependence on resource revenues, and negative political consequences, including corruption.

The negative political consequences are mainly due to the massive financial resources at the disposal of the oil companies, particularly the major international producers, and the billions of dollars at stake in exploration and development. These negative consequences are often the result of close and sometimes symbiotic relationships between politicians and oil companies, especially in authoritarian systems, but sometimes in democracies. Oil often creates a few billionaires and a huge majority of poor as in Libya, Venezuela, and several Persian Gulf states. Political corruption through bribes and kickbacks also often occurs as oil companies compete to get leases and favored status in various countries.

The oil industry and politicians in democracies are also sometimes tempted to engage in questionable and illegal activities. Given the large sums involved and the economic benefits to be reaped by a contractor or firm, now and again they are willing to pay politicians to give them favors. This tempts some politicians and leads them to take risks in order to help the industry in exchange for payment in immediate cash or a job in the future.

Later in the chapter we comment on whether or not Alaska politics do or do not manifest the political aspects of the resource curse.

Source: Developed by the author.

Interestingly, there is a clear pattern to how oil and gas producing countries and regions around the world change their taxes over time, and indeed why their fiscal systems are continually in flux. When oil prices are low, most governments in oil producing regions panic because government revenues are down, even if they have high taxes. The government then realizes that the only way to get those oil revenues up again is to give investors tax breaks or attractive lease agreements and PSAs to get existing operators to expand their production and to induce other oil companies to come into their region. And so a business friendly approach often follows a downturn in oil prices.

When oil prices are high an alternative panic sets in. In this situation, governments and citizens wonder why so much of oil production profits are leaving the region and being repatriated to outsiders. Governments enact new taxing systems to take a higher percentage of oil and gas profits. This is the high profit taking approach. The pie for the high profit taking approach may be smaller, but because of high oil prices, the region's slice of the pie may be larger in terms of government revenues.

The volatility of oil prices in world markets makes doing business very risky for the oil companies. This is why high profit potential is needed to induce investments. Moreover, this risky and uncertain economic situation is also why, to the oil industry, a business environment is often shaped more by the political conditions in an oil producing region than by particular decisions made by the government on taxes. It is generally more risky for an oil company to set up operations in an authoritarian system that might become politically unstable and affect industry operations, perhaps leading to nationalization of its assets, than to set up in a stable democracy, even one with a high tax regime.[8]

Profits in the oil industry are generally high because the risk of losing money is high. The profit to risk ratio for oil companies is not out of line compared to other industries, although certainly high oil prices from the mid-2000s to the summer of 2014 understandably caused taxing jurisdictions like Alaska to revisit their taxing policies. The problem with any taxation system is that achieving a perfect tax rate for every oil market contingency is impossible. From a governmental perspective, the ideal situation would be to change the fiscal taxation system whenever oil and gas prices and costs change, and a number of countries actually do just that. However, if governments change oil fiscal systems too often they get a reputation for grabbing oil and gas profits at every turn, and companies will be leery of investing in their region.

For instance, it is questionable whether Russia and Venezuela will continue to have new oil investments after having confiscated or changed agreements on so many oil fields, and a decline in their oil production may result. As long as oil prices are high, it will not matter, but if oil prices fall, as they did considerably in late 2014, Venezuela and Russia may go back to begging for new investment and may give better contracts and tax breaks to get more investment. The oil companies, of course, prefer fiscal certainty in order to invest in projects that take twenty to thirty years to fully implement. If they do not get that certainty, either due to a lack of contracts or a government reputation for changing taxes, they will reduce new investment in that particular region's oil and gas sector.

Government-Oil Industry Relations: Alaska's Owner State versus Other Approaches

Oil regimes are also shaped by the way that the government in a particular oil producing region relates to the industry. First we look at three types of relationships in this regard and then Alaska's approach.

Three Contrasting Approaches

One type of relationship involves a central government authority or directorate with full power over oil and gas policy decisions, working behind closed doors to make deals and expand production, whether or not the oil lands are privately or state owned. This tends to be the government-oil industry relationship in authoritarian countries like many in the Middle East and North Africa. Normally, the decision making entity has a close relationship with the IOC majors resulting in advantageous terms for both. This has the advantage that each oil development project can have its own specific terms to enhance asset value and even maximize government revenues. The disadvantage of such dealings is a lack of transparency and potential for corruption. Lack of transparency can lead to a weaker government position and even to less aggressive investment activity due to a lack of competition.

A second type of relationship is exemplified by Mexico, at least until the major reforms in energy policy in 2013–2014. Until these reforms, the central government owned all oil and gas mineral rights for seventy-six years and received 100 percent of all profits. This was because the government owned Petróleos Mexicanos (Pemex), the Mexican NOC, and because Pemex was the only oil company allowed to operate in Mexico, according to Mexico's constitution and certain laws. So it was almost impossible for the president of Pemex to negotiate PSAs with IOCs, which limited Mexico's ability to attract new exploration and development within its borders. As a result, Mexico was not as aggressive in exploration and development as oil companies in the United States. This is illustrated by contrasting development in the Gulf of Mexico.

On the U.S. side of the Gulf, which is under U.S. federal jurisdiction and has been run with business friendly taxes, there has long been extensive oil and gas exploration with hundreds of companies involved. In contrast, on the Mexican side there is a dearth of oil and gas exploration. Therefore, in recent years the question has been whether Mexico's policies were maximizing its revenues from oil and whether its economy was benefiting more from oil activity relative to the United States. It may have been that Mexico got the most from each barrel of oil—all the profit—but did not provide enough incentives to expand production. As a result, it may not have been producing enough barrels of oil to compensate for the lack of oil exploration and development investment. There were differing opinions on this subject, however. One person who believed that Mexico was not maximizing its oil revenues was Enrique Peña Nieto, who was elected president of Mexico in 2012.

The 2013–2014 reforms allow private firms to work with Pemex in the exploration and drilling of new fields, though the oil and gas are still state owned. Peña Nieto and supporters of energy reform argue that the constitutional overhaul will bring billions of dollars in foreign investments over the next decade and make Mexico aggressive in exploration and development of oil and gas. Opponents, mainly left-wing politicians and interests, contend that the radical changes cede control over Mexico's natural resources without ensuring that they are developed in a sustainable way that benefits the Mexican people.

A third and contrasting approach is that taken by Texas, where land and mineral rights are mostly privately owned. This has been the case since Texas became a state in 1845. In addition, Texas obtained an agreement from the federal government for a three-league (just over ten miles) offshore mineral rights zone. Beyond this limit, all mineral rights are federally owned and run by the Mineral Management Service, which is part of the U.S. Department of the Interior. Private ownership of oil lands results in royalty owners having the political influence to force state politicians to be favorably disposed toward low oil and gas taxes. Private ownership also means that the Texas government is distanced from the oil industry with less likelihood of backroom dealings leading to corruption. This does not mean, of course, that corruption is eliminated or that the political influence of oil is reduced, as we will see later in the chapter.

Alaska's Owner State Approach

A hybrid relationship between the centralized government-oil industry model, such as the one found in Mexico between 1938 and 2014 and the model exemplified by Texas, is Alaska's Owner State approach. Unlike many authoritarian oil producing regions that use the centralized approach, in the constitutional democracy of Alaska, changes in oil taxes are determined by an open policy-making process. However, a degree of centralization is afforded the Owner State approach by Alaska's political institutions and its history.

Because Alaska's constitution puts more authority and potential power in the hands of the governor than in most states, the governor can pursue a given policy more forcefully. In addition, under the terms of the Statehood Act, Alaska was allowed to choose 30 percent of the state's land area. By making smart choices in its selection of North Slope lands as part of its land selections, Alaska became a major oil and gas and mineral rights owner—thus the term Owner State. Over 95 percent of oil in Alaska is pumped from state owned land, in sharp contrast to Texas and most other oil states in the nation. For this reason, there is no association of oil royalty owners in Alaska to pressure the government and politicians in general. This combination of circumstances enabled Wally Hickel and other governors to negotiate favorable settlements of disputes over oil and gas taxes and royalties with the oil companies. Governor Hickel, in particular, aggressively negotiated these settlements, and they produced major income for the state.[9]

Unlike Mexico, Brazil, Ecuador, and several other countries, Alaska will likely never have a state owned and operated oil and gas company. However, unlike Texas, Alaska owns the mineral rights to most of its oil and takes a middle ground. It has a competitive free market like Texas, but like the situation in pre- and post-2014 Mexico, the mineral rights are retained by the state. At least this is true on Alaska state lands that include Prudhoe Bay. Opinions vary on whether Alaska's Owner State approach creates a positive business environment. A 2007 headline in the industry publication *Petroleum News* stated that "Alaska gets poor marks" as an environment to induce oil and gas investment. There was a similar conclusion in a 2013 report by the Fraser Institute, a conservative Canadian think tank.[10] To be sure, Alaska does not have as friendly a business atmosphere for oil as Texas does. On the other hand, even if Alaska's business environment is not as friendly as Texas's or many other oil producing states across the nation, it is friendlier than many places in the Middle East and Latin America. And Alaska has the third largest proven deposits of oil in the United States (after Texas and North Dakota) and in 2013 it was the fourth largest oil producing area in the nation, after Texas, North Dakota, and the Gulf of Mexico.[11] So whatever the economic downsides Alaska presents to the oil companies, these are clearly outweighed by the upsides, which is why the industry continues to operate in Alaska and in many cases works to expand its operations.

From General Opportunities and Challenges to Specific Policies and Experiences in Alaska's Political Economy of Oil

Here, then, are the general opportunities and the challenges of being an energy producer that Alaska shares with other energy producing countries and regions and its general Owner State approach to government-oil industry relations. Like other oil and gas producers, however, Alaska has had to make specific policy choices regarding these opportunities and challenges including reacting to external influences, particularly the volatility of the world oil market. In addition, with only a semi-sovereign status in a federal union, Alaska is not entirely in control of many policies directly affecting its oil patch. In fact, in some cases it has very little control over the outcome of policies that affect its most important natural resource.

Given this combination of challenges and opportunities and external economic and political influences, the choices the state has made have shaped the specific characteristics of the political economy of oil in Alaska. The rest of the chapter considers these specifics. Sections 3 and 4 provide a short history of Alaska's oil and gas development and an explanation of Alaska's oil and gas taxes. Sections 5 and 6 include an overview of the significant ramifications of the development of the political economy of oil in Alaska and the present and future challenges presented by the state's dependence on oil. Then in sections 7 and 8 we make some observations about the influence of oil in Alaska and conclude, in part, by asking how Alaska's socio-economic and political landscape would look without oil.

3. A SHORT HISTORY OF ALASKA'S OIL AND GAS DEVELOPMENT

Alaska's oil and gas development can be divided into four phases: the pre- and early statehood period; the North Slope oil discoveries; the building of the trans-Alaska pipeline system (TAPS) and the early oil bonanza years; and the *Exxon Valdez* oil spill to the present. Aspects of this history and its impact on Alaska's political economy have been covered in several chapters in the book.[12] Here we provide an overview of these developments, focusing on what has not been covered elsewhere. Because of the major importance of external forces on the political economy of oil in Alaska, we make several references to national and international developments in the oil and gas industry.

The Pre- and Early Statehood Period

Because Alaska came late to the nation both as a territory and a state, oil and gas development lagged behind other states. The first oil well in the United States was drilled in Titusville, Pennsylvania, in 1859. Then in 1901, the first big oil find in Texas was found at Spindletop near Beaumont in the southeast corner of the state. By the 1950s, oil and gas was being produced in about half the states, mainly in Texas, the Midwest, and the West.

In Alaska, oil was first discovered in 1896 at Katalla near Cordova five years after the first oil claims had been staked in Cook Inlet. But the first major, commercially viable oil discovery was made on the Swanson River on the Kenai Peninsula near Anchorage in 1957, two years before statehood. This find marked the start of Cook Inlet oil and gas production. Other than Cook Inlet activity in the late 1950s and early 1960s, there was little oil and gas development in the state, and very minor activity compared to east Texas, western Siberia, and the Middle East. The natural gas discovered in Cook Inlet was far from markets (so-called stranded gas) and was not a commercial proposition. However, it was sold to regional utilities, to the Agrarium fertilizer plant and to the Kenai LNG facility that exported it to Japan. The big discoveries were yet to come.

Prior to Alaska's selection of North Slope lands under the Statehood Act, the North Slope was under federal jurisdiction. Federal regulations prohibited any one oil company from owning a large number of oil leases in one place. So North Slope oil exploration and development was not profitable enough for any single leaseholder to expend a lot of effort. This probably delayed the discovery of Prudhoe Bay by at least ten years. Sohio (Standard Oil of Ohio, bought out by BP in 1987) and other major oil companies aggressively advocated that the state acquire the central North Slope region from the federal government as part of the land that Alaska was granted by Congress. After some equivocating, Governor Bill Egan acquired much of this area for Alaska as well as much of the North Slope coastal plain.

The transfer of ownership from the federal government to Alaska produced a change in oil leasing rules. Alaska allowed a single company to own a large number of leases covering a significant area. Companies were now able to reduce some of the risk and incur the high costs of exploration given the major rewards that they could reap. But Egan was slow to institute lease sales after the acquisition since Alaska seemingly had plenty of oil revenue from Cook Inlet and could not effectively administer even those lands. In addition, Alaska Native rights were a concern. But after the 1964 earthquake, extra money was needed to help pay for rebuilding the damaged areas of the state. Egan did engage the state in a few North Slope lease sales, but when these did not result in successful exploration, calls by the oil companies and many Alaskans for more lease sales increased.

The North Slope Oil Discoveries

When Wally Hickel became governor for the first time in 1966, he aggressively sold important swaths of North Slope oil leases that induced greater exploration efforts and the eventual discovery of the Prudhoe Bay oil field. With a first drill in December 1967 and a second one in May 1968, the oil company giant Atlantic-Richfield (ARCO) and silent partner Humble (now Exxon) were the first to find commercial quantities of oil at Prudhoe Bay. But Sohio (now BP) was the big winner of the initial state lease sales since most of ARCO's find was under Sohio's leases.[13] Soon after Prudhoe Bay—the biggest oil field in North America—came the discovery of the nearby Kuparuk and Point Thomson oil and gas fields.

In 1969 the state held a North Slope lease sale, taking in $900 million in one day. This was more than twenty times the total amount of revenue the state had received from oil the previous year. And although the revenue from oil would not reach this level again until TAPS began to operate, Alaska's oil age had begun. The state's political economy was about to undergo a major transformation shaped in many ways by the opportunities and challenges of being an energy producing state. Ironically, however, before a barrel of North Slope oil was pumped, U.S. oil production reached its all time peak in 1970, not to be equaled since, not even with Alaska oil.

Building TAPS and the Early Oil Bonanza Years

Because the Arctic Ocean off the North Slope is frozen for up to nine months of the year, the only efficient way to get the oil out of the North Slope was to build a pipeline the length of Alaska to an ice free port like Valdez in Prince William Sound, close to eight hundred miles in length (see Chapter 21, Map 21.1). Congressional approval of the pipeline became entangled with Native land claims, which were settled in 1971 with the Alaska Native Claims Settlement Act (ANCSA).

Discussion continued about TAPS with opposition from some environmental groups. But as a result of the Arab-Israeli War of September 1973, OPEC declared an oil embargo that sent oil prices soaring. With Congress feeling vulnerable and wanting to produce more domestic oil, it gave final approval for TAPS and the legislation was signed by President Nixon in November 1973. The construction buildup began, and four years later, in June 1977, the first oil arrived in Valdez and Alaska began rolling in oil revenues. However, the good times would end in less than a decade.

In the mid-1980s, oil prices that had been high for almost ten years began to plummet. Even OPEC panicked. The great bust in oil prices—the per barrel price dropped to less than $10 in 1986—led Alaska, like all oil producers at the time, to look for ways to increase revenue. Most oil producer governments around the world became more business friendly in order to increase their production—pursuing a smaller piece of a larger pie. Alaska's production, however, was constrained by the capacity of TAPS and other infrastructure that kept production at less than two million barrels per day. North Slope oil production peaked at 2,145,297 barrels a day on January 14, 1988, and has been declining ever since. In an attempt to deal with its revenue problems, Alaska increased oil taxes and particularly the so-called Economic Limit Factor (see Section 4, below).

During the 1980s, the state was also resolving issues that began with the startup of the pipeline in 1977. One issue was TAPS tariffs. The state went to court with the producers to lower the tariff on the oil pipeline, which had the effect of increasing the wellhead oil price and thereby increasing taxable oil revenues. The court case lasted for years, and was eventually settled out of court in 1985, adding billions to Alaska revenues.

The late 1980s also saw an event that would transform many aspects of Alaska's political economy of oil as well as that of the nation's oil patches in general. This was the *Exxon Valdez* oil spill on March 24, 1989, in Prince William Sound just south of Valdez. Until the BP oil spill in the Gulf of Mexico in April 2010, this was the biggest oil spill and one of the worst environmental disasters in U.S. history.[14]

From *Exxon Valdez* to the Present

The 1990s saw continued low oil prices with another low of $10 a barrel in 1998. Major reasons for the lower prices were a glut of oil due to the collapse of the Soviet Union and the new Russia's entry into selling oil on the world market, as well as increased technology for recovering oil. By 2004, however, partly due to the major expansion of the economies of China and India and before the economic downturn of 2008, there was major growth in the world economy. Oil prices reached almost $150 a barrel in 2008 and WTI and Brent crude prices remained in the $90 to $120 range through the summer of 2014.

Starting in 2000, Alaska's offshore oil and gas regions were expanded greatly with an eightfold increase in the lease sales area. However, these regions are beyond the state's three-mile jurisdiction, so the responsibility for resolving environmental, safety, and taxation issues resides with the U.S. government. But any offshore oil development helps Alaska with jobs, more oil throughput into TAPS, and at least some federal revenue shared with Alaska. Some suggest that in time, Alaska's offshore oil will rival its onshore oil, including Prudhoe Bay. But when these offshore resources might be developed is far from clear as of early 2016.

Despite high oil prices, Alaska state policy makers were presented with many uncertainties and challenges regarding the political economy of oil. Besides the significant drop in oil prices in late 2014, throughout 2015 and into 2016, the major problems were declining production from Prudhoe Bay and the need to develop new oil and gas fields in order to maintain the high revenues to which the state and its citizens had become accustomed. To meet these challenges the state moved on several fronts. These included regular attempts to persuade Congress to open the Arctic National Wildlife Refuge (ANWR) to oil and gas exploration, encouraging offshore oil exploration, moves to develop a natural gas pipeline, and revisions of the oil and gas production taxes. One of these tax revisions was associated with the biggest political corruption scandal in Alaska politics to date.

4. THE POLITICAL ECONOMY OF ALASKA'S OIL AND GAS FISCAL SYSTEM: TYPES OF TAXES, TAX REGIMES, AND THEIR POLITICAL DYNAMICS

The issue of taxing the oil industry—how and how much to tax it and how to adjust the tax system as circumstances change—is one of the central issues in the political economy of oil producing countries and regions. As a consequence, like other oil producers, Alaska's oil tax system has become very complex over the years. This complexity keeps many state and private lawyers busy developing, administering, challenging, and defending the laws and regulations of the taxing regime. It is not necessary, however, to explain in detail the complexities and intricacies of the existing taxing system or of any one tax regime over the years. Our goal here is simply to explain the basics of Alaska's fiscal system for oil and the politics surrounding it.

In Chapter 8 on state revenues, oil taxes were considered in the context of their major contribution to state revenues and the problems of declining production and what this might mean for these revenues. As this issue was well covered in that chapter and in other parts of the book, it is not dealt with in detail in this chapter. But because this issue is a central concern in Alaska politics, we do refer to it and related issues several times. The two aspects of oil taxes that we are most concerned with in this section are an explanation of the types of taxes imposed and the major tax systems used in the state in recent years. We then explain the characteristics of the politics of oil and gas taxes in Alaska.

The Oil Fiscal System and Types of Taxes

The types of taxes explained here are all part of Alaska's oil fiscal system, which is the array of taxes, royalties, PSAs, and all revenues from the oil and gas industry collected by local and state governments. Federal lands have their own separate fiscal system.

Types of Revenues and Taxes

Alaska's fiscal system for oil includes royalties and taxes, particularly production, corporate income, and property taxes. Production taxes are also called severance taxes.

A *royalty* is a payment by an oil producing company to a land owner in exchange for the right to take oil and gas from the land. Royalty payments are often based on a percent of the value of the oil and gas produced. In Alaska the royalty owner is most often the state, though the federal government also owns some oil and gas lands. Theoretically, there could also be private ownership, though this is rare in Alaska. In contrast, in Texas the land owner is most often a private citizen.

A *severance* or *production tax* is a charge for the extraction or severing of oil or natural gas from the ground. The tax can be either a percent of the value of the resource, usually computed at the point of production or "wellhead," or it can be a percent of profits. It is not, however, the same as a corporate income tax.

Corporate income tax is levied on the entire corporation's income attributed to Alaska from all sources and all oil fields after deductions for royalties, severance taxes, and all other costs. In contrast, severance tax is based on the production from each individual oil field in Alaska.

Property tax is paid on infrastructure and property within a political jurisdiction used for exploration and production (E and P) and transportation—primarily pipelines, including TAPS. For example, as of 2016 the state levies a twenty-mill property tax on the value of industry property located within the state (a mill is one thousandth of a currency unit, so twenty mills is equal to 2 percent or 2 cents per dollar of property value). The state also allows municipalities to tax the same property located within their boundaries, with certain limitations. Thus, the North Slope Borough taxes industry property located within the borough (including the portion of TAPS located there). Municipal property taxes can be taken by the oil companies as a credit against the state's twenty mill oil and gas property tax.

Two other concepts used in relation to oil and gas taxes are progressivity and regressivity. A tax is considered to be progressive when the tax rate increases as profits increase. It is considered to be regressive when the tax rate decreases as profits increase.

Since statehood, Alaska has used these taxes in various combinations in an effort to maximize its revenues and to promote other goals.

Why So Many Oil Taxes and Tax Systems?

Many wonder why all these taxes have to be so complicated and why the state has so many different taxes when a simple single percent of production should suffice. Simplicity would help public understanding. There are, however, two related reasons for the complexity.

First, a great deal of guesswork is involved in trying to anticipate how the market will develop in the short and long term and what will encourage the industry to engage in E and P. This lack of certainty has meant constant additions and adjustments to the oil fiscal system and inevitable complexity. Second, Alaska's fiscal system allows the state to maximize its revenues while offering tax breaks to entice more companies to come to Alaska and invest in new oil development. Of necessity this fiscal system involves some complex formulas to cover changes in oil prices and to encourage development. This will become clear in outlining these tax systems.

Types of Production Tax Regimes

Since statehood Alaska has had five different production tax regimes. The first, prior to 1977 and the coming on line of TAPS, was largely geared to the Cook Inlet field and involved a flat severance tax. This system was regressive and brought the state little benefit from the rise in oil prices after 1973. So the system was reformed in 1977 to one based on the value of oil at the wellhead. The other three tax regimes have been based on oil company profits. Each of the five regimes involves some risk for the state but the risk factor varies with different taxes. Knowledge of the fine details of these complex tax regimes is not necessary to understand the basics of each regime. So what follows is a basic explanation of each.

The Production Tax with an Economic Limit Factor

From late 1977 to 2006 the state imposed a production tax based on a percentage of wellhead values, with the percentage determined by the economic limits of each individual oil field. The Economic Limit Factor (ELF) was a uniquely Alaskan tax mechanism, which was designed to take into account the economics of each oil field. The ELF was originally designed to provide Alaska high production tax revenues from highly productive fields such as Prudhoe Bay, but also to help smaller, more marginal oil fields to develop or to continue profitable operations. In 1981 and again in 1989, aspects of the ELF were changed to increase production tax revenues. The 1989 change, though, was hotly debated and may not have happened had the *Exxon Valdez* oil spill not occurred. The spill caused Alaska to reevaluate oil company profits on the theory that if the oil industry was cutting corners on oil transportation safety, it may have been taking advantage of Alaska in other ways.

By the early 2000s, however, the production tax under the ELF formula was losing money for the state, even as oil company profits were soaring. This was partly because the ELF was in several instances a regressive tax because of its flat rate severance tax on many fields. In addition, once a field reached a certain low level of production it was no longer subject to any severance tax. For example, the Kuparuk oil field was getting close to being severance tax free. By the early 2000s, fifteen out of nineteen oil fields on the North Slope paid no production tax at all under the ELF. Plus, there were other problems. Under one provision, it could be applied or not to the frontier boundaries of the massive Prudhoe Bay field, depending on how the governor designated a particular field.

In 2003, a new well at the Prudhoe Bay frontier, the Orion well, fell under the ELF. In 2005 Governor Murkowski took away the ELF designation from Orion, which caused the oil companies to cancel the Orion project. In short, it appeared that the oil companies were using investment decisions to persuade the governor to change tax policy, although costs may have also been a factor for the industry. In any event, a change was clearly needed in oil tax policy.

A New Oil Tax Regime: The Rationale Behind the Transition to the Petroleum Profits Tax

The year 2006 marked a major change in Alaska's oil tax policy. That year the state moved from the production tax based on percentage of wellhead value to a petroleum profits tax (PPT). Sometimes referred to as a profits-based production tax, the PPT was first developed by the Murkowski administration with the aid of tax consultant Pedro Van Meurs.[15]

The goal of the PPT is to create a balance between keeping taxes somewhat low to induce more oil exploration and development while still allowing the state to retain a fair percentage of oil industry profits. On the one hand, the PPT gives tax breaks and credits for oil earnings that are reinvested within the state. On the other, it has a sliding scale tax rate that increases the state's take when oil prices increase, but generally reduces its take should prices fall. Overall, the goal is to increase Alaska's pie slice, though the PPT's sliding scale tax rate increases the state's risk. Alaska's state revenue will be more volatile than in the past, going up and down more sharply as oil prices gyrate. Some may question why the state should take on such risks when oil companies look to be making extremely high profits. Yet, with more risk comes the opportunity for oil revenues to increase over the long term.

The risk factor brings up constitutional issues. The Alaska Constitution (Article VIII, Section 2) specifies that Alaska must maximize the value of its resources to the state, but it does not mention risk. Thus, it could be argued that too much risk exposure would violate this provision of the constitution. Nonetheless, while the PPT increases the state's risk exposure, it also increases the value of the state's natural resources and likely would not be in violation of Article VIII, Section 2. Ultimately, then, it is up to the governor and the legislature to determine the proper balance between risk to the state and the potential for increased revenues.

Between 2006 and 2014 there were three versions of the PPT. In addition to the Murkowski version, there was one developed by the Palin administration in 2007 called Alaska's Clear and Equitable Share (ACES), and one developed by the Parnell administration between 2010 and 2013 called the More Alaska Production Act (MAPA). Each of these had its own profits tax formula and each was the subject of considerable debate in the halls of government, among the public, in the media, and in the oil industry.

The Murkowski PPT and ACES

Governor Murkowski's version of PPT placed a 22.5 percent PPT on the first $40 of oil company net profits and then a rate of 0.25 percent for profits above that. The latter is known as the principle of "progressivity"—taking a higher percentage of higher profits. Net profits means that the oil companies can first deduct production and transportation costs before calculating the tax. So if oil is selling for $80 a barrel and the cost of production and transportation is $35 a barrel, this means they will be taxed on the remaining $45 of profits. So they would pay 22.5 percent of $40 (or $9) and 0.25 percent on the remaining $5 of profits ($1.25 cents), or $10.25 cents of tax per barrel. This PPT legislation also included provisions to encourage exploration and development.

Although the combination of higher prices and the PPT brought in more oil revenue, in 2007 it was not as much as anticipated because the oil industry's expenses were higher than the original projections by the state. Plus, in 2006 a corruption scandal emerged involving the oil service company VECO (see Section 7) in which an attempt was made to bribe legislators to vote for a 20 percent basic PPT tax. The ACES legislation was in part a reaction to the VECO scandal.

ACES maintained the basic structure of the 2006 PPT, but slightly increased some taxes on the industry. It set a basic profit rate of 25 percent and reduced the tax base from $40 to $30 a barrel, plus it also increased the "progressivity" rate on profits over $30 a barrel from 0.25 percent to 4 percent. ACES also provided incentives for exploration and development including some for small producers. With the explosion in oil prices after 2007 and until its replacement by MAPA in 2014, ACES brought in about $9 billion more than would have been the case under the Murkowski PPT and about $19 billion more than under the ELF.

Nevertheless, there was concern in many quarters that ACES would have the effect of discouraging new investment and new oil and gas production, resulting in lower state revenues in the long term. The oil industry particularly disliked ACES because of its high "progressivity" provision. So while Governor Parnell originally supported ACES, after being elected in his own right in 2010 he proposed a revision in the PPT.

The MAPA Tax Reduction in PPT

While both the Murkowski PPT and Palin's ACES reforms involved some politics, they passed relatively quickly and with much less controversy than MAPA. The political saga of the original version of MAPA began in early 2011 and was not concluded until the referendum vote on the tax in the primary election of August 2014. It proved to be one of the most high profile and divisive issues in Alaska politics since statehood.

Governor Parnell's first proposal was introduced in the Twenty-Seventh Legislature in January 2011 as House Bill (HB) 110. It was promoted as an attempt to increase exploration and production to try and deal with Alaska's declining oil production. Accordingly, the proposal rolled back the highest taxes of ACES in order to give more incentives to invest in oil and gas exploration. But as the case study in Chapter 16 on HB 110 explains, poor strategy and strong opposition combined to ensure that the proposal went nowhere in the two years of that legislature.[16]

However, with major Republican victories in the November 2012 election, the proposal was reintroduced in the Twenty-Eighth Legislature and passed at the end of the first session in April 2013.[17] This version, known as MAPA but more commonly as Senate Bill (SB) 21, replaced the 25 percent tax rate of ACES with a 35 percent tax rate but got rid of the "progressivity" provision per dollar as prices rise. To encourage production MAPA gives a $5 per barrel credit on existing oil field production, which is reduced as the price of oil reaches a certain level, but it gives a flat $5 credit per barrel for all new oil development. Like Parnell's 2011 bill, the rationale behind SB 21 is to sacrifice some revenue in the short run to obtain more revenue in the long run by encouraging exploration and production.

Most of the provisions of the bill went into effect on January 1, 2014, and in so doing replaced ACES. But during its passage and afterward, the law generated major opposition with accusations that the law was a massive giveaway to the oil industry. In one demonstration on the capitol steps in Juneau prior to the bill's passage, Anchorage Democratic Senator Johnny Ellis symbolically tore up a check for $5.5 billion from the state to oil giants BP, ConocoPhillips, and ExxonMobil. This was the estimated cost to the state in lost revenues over the first five years of MAPA. The Parnell administration put the losses at much less, though their estimates changed during and after passage of the legislation.[18]

After passage of the bill, opponents of MAPA got a referendum on the August 2014 ballot, Ballot Measure 1, to repeal MAPA and return to the provisions of ACES.[19] It turned out to be the most expensive ballot proposition contest in Alaska history. Those opposed to repeal, including the oil industry, large segments of the business community, and several Native corporations, outspent those favoring repeal, mainly Democrats, various liberal causes, and some unions by $18.5 million to $1 million. The extensive debate on the ballot measure, like the legislative debate on SB 21, involved more rhetoric than facts. The repeal failed by 52.7 to 47.3 percent, a margin of 10,000 votes out of nearly 190,000 cast.[20]

As of 2016 MAPA still stands, and Governor Walker indicated soon after his election in November 2014 that he planned no changes in oil taxes. But with major budget deficits in fiscal years 2015, 2016, 2017 and very likely beyond, due to the 70 percent drop in oil prices from 2016 to early 2016, at the end of his first year in office he proposed reducing the oil industry's close to $1 billion a year tax credits. Furthermore, supporters of MAPA's tax change had not anticipated oil prices dropping so low that the production tax would drop to close to zero. This was the case by early 2016, potentially cutting state oil revenues in half and seriously compounding the state's money woes. This would not have been the case under ACES. So the debate on oil taxes in Alaska continues and the development of a sixth oil tax regime since statehood may well be just around the corner.

The Politics of Alaska Oil Taxes: Populist Policy Making in the Dark

Oil taxes have been a major issue in Alaska on many occasions since the early 1970s for two related reasons. First is Alaska's overwhelming dependence on oil revenues for state spending (accounting for between 75 and 95 percent of all revenues raised by the state depending on the year). The second is the volatility of world oil prices and concerns about declining production, particularly on the North Slope. In some years, most often following sharp price declines as in the mid-1980s, the late 1990s, and in 2014–2016, oil taxation has been the dominant political issue. Often the politics is very intense as with Governor Parnell's oil tax proposal. Over the years, six major characteristics of oil politics and policy making have become evident.

First, because state revenues, and thus oil taxation, are so crucial and central to Alaska's economic well-being, every state elected official has an opinion on whether the existing tax regime is adequate to meet Alaska's present and future needs. In this regard, oil taxes are hot button issues, like those of K–12 education, the Permanent Fund, and the PFD. These are all issues of wide concern to elected officials reflecting their importance to their constituents and these issues can lead to protracted and sometimes emotional and acrimonious debates.

Second, for the reasons explained in Section 2 regarding the dilemmas of taxing the oil industry in a volatile market, like most policy makers in oil producing regions, Alaska's politicians regularly revise the oil tax system. Thus, the system is continually in flux. A major reason for this is that oil market circumstances inevitably change requiring fine tuning of the existing system and sometimes a major overhaul as with the PPT. Another reason for flux is that with declining oil production, policy makers are always working to adjust the tax system to encourage more exploration and production. This, at least as it was stated, was the major rationale behind Governor Parnell's move to lower oil industry taxes.

Third, because of all the uncertainty about future oil markets and prices, making oil tax policy is largely an exercise in political speculation. This is evidenced by the fact that even after drawing on the expert advice of oil consultants, the state's projections of oil prices are constantly revised.

Given this, with few solid facts on which to base future policy and with the stakes so high, politics and ideology inevitably come into play in the final outcomes in a major way. As a general matter, Republicans favor lower taxes and more incentives for the oil industry while Democrats favor higher taxes and are skeptical that more incentives will increase exploration. In reality, the situation is more complex than this, and the Alaska political forces of membership in majority caucuses, bipartisanship, and so on come into play and affect the outcomes of proposals for change. This has been the case with major changes in Alaska's oil tax policy over the years.

Fourth, as in all other aspects of policy making in Alaska and elsewhere, Alaska's oil tax politics are often not just about tax policy. Decisions by some policy makers about oil and gas tax issues may have little to do with their merits, demerits, or likely effects, as speculative as these tax decisions may be. The ambitions of politicians, including seeking reelection, running for higher office, and personality clashes may take precedence over the policy issue at hand. This adds even more fluidity to an already fluid oil taxing policy process. For instance, it is uncertain if Governor Sarah Palin's ACES proposal, as with many of her other policies, was mainly about the soundness of the policy or about her strong desire to constantly secure public approval and popularity.[21] For her, ACES was also likely tied up with the VECO scandal and with her general antipathy toward the oil industry. Interestingly, during her campaign for governor she had favored moving back to a tax similar to the pre-PPT, ELF-based production tax.[22]

Fifth is an interesting political dynamic regarding two types of policies identified in Chapter 3—regulatory and distributive—as they relate to oil tax policy making and how oil revenues are spent. In most states in the nation with oil patches, the major type of policy used in dealing with the oil industry is regulatory policy such as safety and environmental protection. This is certainly the case in Alaska.

Other states also use their oil revenues for state spending and thus engage in various distributive policies, including making payments directly to individuals or organizations. In Texas, for example, oil revenues help fund K–12 and higher education. In most states, however, citizens would probably not be keenly aware of the direct benefit of oil revenues to their daily lives, largely because such revenues do not make up a significant proportion of state revenues. By contrast, in Alaska the existence of the Permanent Fund and the yearly PFD leads to widespread public concern about the use of oil revenues and a sort of populist attitude toward them.

This leads to the sixth and a related point. Because of a combination of Alaska's dependence on the oil industry and its status as an Owner State regarding its oil and gas reserves, the political economy of oil in Alaska produces both influential industry forces and populist politics and often pits these two political forces against each other. This produces an interesting political power dynamic and, compared to most other states with oil patches, to some extent places constraints on the political power of the oil industry in Alaska, as we explore in Section 7.

5. OIL DEVELOPMENT: THE EFFECTS AND THE RESPONSES

The various effects of, and the responses to, oil development have been covered in various chapters in the book. Given this, in this section of the chapter we outline the major effects as part of an integrated explanation of the political economy of oil and refer the reader to the places in the book where a particular effect or response is dealt with in more detail. The four major effects and responses that we identify here are environmental impact and regulation, oil spill response and readiness, intensified conflict in the developer-environmentalist debate, and the transformation of the state's political economy.

Environmental Impact and Regulation

Like mining and the timber industry, oil and gas is subject to a wide range of environmental regulations that have grown in number and extent since the 1960s.[23] Today, before an oil company can begin exploration, it must get a number of permits from the federal and state governments, including those related to the general environmental impact of their project including completing environmental impact statements (EISs) and those relating to more specific environmental issues, such as the possible effect on endangered species.[24] In Alaska, especially on the North Slope, a particular concern is the effect of E and P on the subsistence lifestyle of Alaska Natives.[25]

Regulation of the oil industry and its impacts on the state are always prominent topics reported by Alaska's news media. For example, beginning in 2010, the controversy about Shell Oil drilling in the Arctic was an ongoing issue, at least until Shell suspended Arctic development plans in the fall of 2015. There has also been a continuing battle between the federal government on the one side and the state and the oil companies on the other regarding the extent to which the polar bear is threatened or endangered and how such a designation might limit where exploration for oil can take place.[26] And in April 2013 the

Alaska Supreme Court ruled that the state must consider the long-term effects of oil lease sales regarding how a sale might affect such things as the environment and transportation infrastructure.[27]

Oil Spill Response and Readiness

Governmental regulations concerning the prevention of, and response to, oil spills can be considered part of environmental protection. But oil spill response has been such an important aspect of oil development in Alaska that we deal with it separately. The major event triggering extensive changes in the rules and regulations for oil spills was, of course, the *Exxon Valdez* spill of March 1989. The details of the response to the spill and how it resulted in major changes in federal and state laws are explained in Chapter 22, Box 22.1. The BP spill in the Gulf of Mexico in April 2010 also increased the public's awareness and concerns about potential spills. The resulting increase in public scrutiny will undoubtedly affect future oil development in Alaska.

Today a range of federal, state, and local agencies, including the U.S. Coast Guard, the Environmental Protection Agency (EPA) and the Alaska Department of Environmental Conservation (DEC), are involved in regulating and monitoring spill prevention and response preparedness. State and federal regulations concerning oil spill prevention and response are extensive and clearly have an economic impact on the oil industry. Two citizens' organizations were set up in the 1990 federal oil spill legislation following the *Exxon Valdez* disaster to monitor and provide recommendations concerning oil spill response and prevention—the Prince William Sound and Cook Inlet Regional Citizens' Advisory Councils.

Intensification of the Developer-Environmentalist Conflict

The rise of the environmental movement, incidents like the BP and *Exxon Valdez* oil spills, and concerns about subsistence and endangered species, have combined to produce a major national, international, and to a much lesser extent Alaska political resistance to new oil and gas development and production. These changes mean that Alaska's political economy of oil is much different today from when oil was first discovered at Prudhoe Bay in 1968.

Organizations like the Center for Biological Diversity, Friends of the Earth, the Sierra Club, and Greenpeace are political forces to be reckoned with. Some would argue that they have the upper hand in development issues because they are defending the political status quo in many instances. Put another way, developers are seeking to change the status quo and thus must persuade policy makers to take some affirmative steps to make those changes. In any case, there is an increased intensity in the oil industry-environmentalist debate and, for better or for worse, this intensity adds to the present and future difficulties in developing Alaska oil and gas reserves.

The Transformation of the State's Political Economy

Oil has transformed Alaska's political economy beyond what most Alaskans could have imagined before TAPS was constructed. Oil made possible the Permanent Fund and the PFD as well as a major expansion in government services and economic development, all without a state individual income tax or statewide sales tax. Traditional Alaska industries like fishing and mining, though still important, have been far surpassed by oil as contributors toward Alaska's well-being. In addition, the increased intensity of the developer-environmentalist conflict has changed the nature of Alaska's political economy.

Probably the major effect of oil development, however, is that it has made the state overwhelmingly dependent on the revenues provided by industry development. Alaska has the most unbalanced sources of state revenues of any state, which poses many problems for the future as was brought home clearly in the 70 percent drop in oil price from mid-2014 through early 2016. Of particular concern are declining oil production and the need to find new sources of oil and gas to maintain the state's current level of spending.

6. MAJOR ONGOING ISSUES, CHALLENGES, AND UNCERTAINTIES

All oil producing governments face continuing uncertainty regarding their oil resources and the benefits they receive from them. Alaska shares the same general uncertainties, but also has particular issues, challenges, and uncertainties. Here we briefly review six of them: declining production; the need for new development in general; an Alaska natural gas pipeline; what to do with oil income; world markets, competition, and alternative fuels; and continuing external and internal political pressures.

Declining Production

In April 2014, two months before the thirty-seventh birthday of TAPS, the 17 billionth barrel of oil reached Valdez from Prudhoe Bay.[28] A telling fact about the declining flow through the pipeline is that it had been nearly five years since the 16 billionth barrel arrived in 2009 and it will be at least six and perhaps as long as eight years before the 18 billionth barrel flows down the 789-mile pipeline. Declining production is probably the most immediate issue and challenge facing the state, not just in terms of oil, but regarding Alaska politics in general. The flow through TAPS has been declining since 1988. Figure 24.1 shows the barrels per day that the pipeline has produced, with projections to 2025. Figure 24.1A traces the past and estimated future decline in production and Figure 24.1B shows the decline by major oil fields on the North Slope. Whether the changes to production taxes in the MAPA legislation will slow or even stop the decline of the oil flow, which was the major rationale behind the new tax regime, remains to be seen.

FIGURE 24.1

Alaska Pipeline Production in Millions of Barrels Per Day: Past and Present and Post-2015 Future Estimates

FIGURE 24.1A:
TOTAL NORTH SLOPE PRODUCTION SINCE 1978 WITH FUTURE ESTIMATES

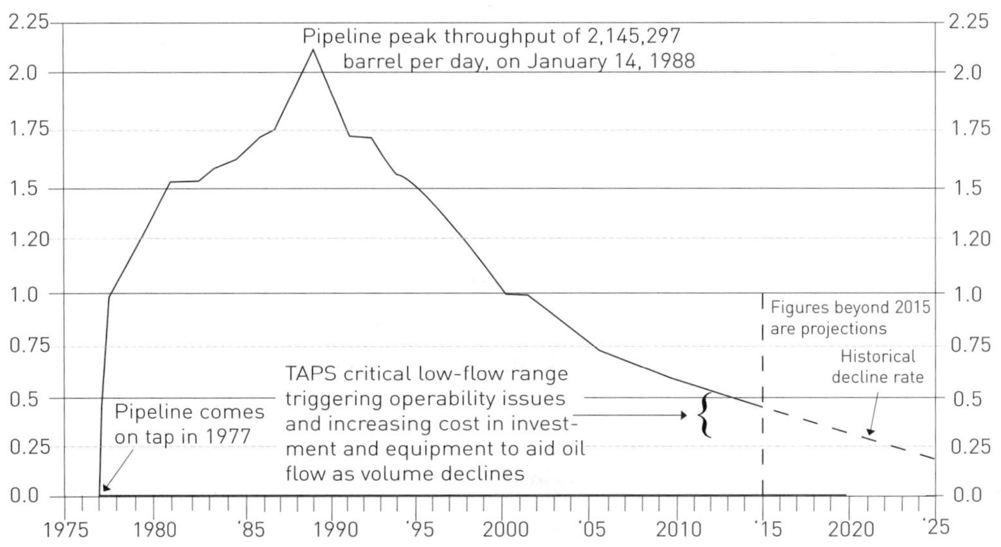

FIGURE 24.1B
NORTH SLOPE PRODUCTION ACTUAL AND ESTIMATED BY OIL FIELD

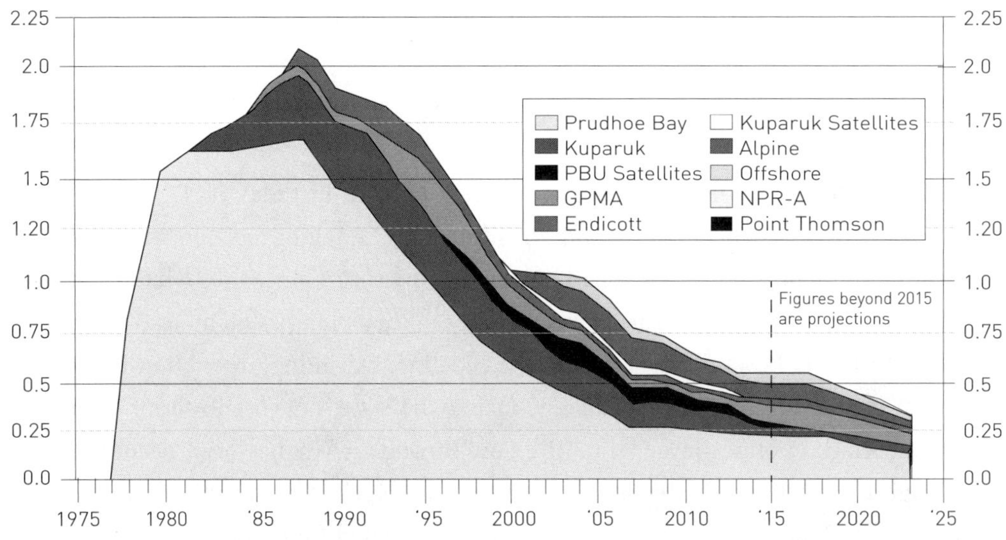

Source: Adapted by the author from Alaska Department of Natural Resources, *Annual Report* TAPS low flow impact study presentation, House Resources, March 9, 2010; Alaska Department of Revenue. *Revenue Sources Book. Fall 2014.* http://www.tax.alaska.gov/programs/documentviewer/viewer.aspx?1124r

It is, however, unlikely to do so without new fields coming on tap. Chapter 8 explains the problems of declining production as they relate to the question of when TAPS might need to be shut down unless new oil is found. This makes the need for new oil and gas development all the more important and pressing.[29]

Sources of New Development

There are several possibilities for increasing Alaska's oil and gas development and production. One that has been around since the 1970s, but not yet realized, is drilling in the Arctic National Wildlife Refuge (ANWR). But as Box 21.6 in Chapter 21 explains, even with widespread support in Alaska for opening ANWR, opposition from the federal government, several environmental groups, and some Alaska Native groups has kept ANWR closed. And the continued closure is despite the fact that both Alaska and the nation would receive economic benefits from ANWR development. One solution to this impasse might be a sort of environmental trade-off. Rather than cutting off all of ANWR development, the federal government could tax ANWR oil and gas production and use that money to help save, for instance, the Florida everglades where there are 100 times as many plants and animals to save as exist in ANWR. Biodiversity in Florida could thereby be enhanced by oil and gas drilling in ANWR. Politics, however, will likely not allow this to be considered, let alone implemented. Proponents of opening ANWR were dealt another setback in January 2015. That month the Obama administration proposed designating more of the Refuge as wilderness, including the coastal plain (or 10.02 area) where many hoped exploration would take place.[30] Thus it will be a long time, if ever, before Alaska will be able to benefit from oil and gas production in ANWR.

Drilling in the federal National Petroleum Reserve-Alaska (NPR-A) is another option. In fact, in 2013 the U.S. Department of the Interior approved a plan for exploration and a pipeline corridor in the NPR-A. In line with this policy, in late 2015 the Department gave ConocoPhillips the go-ahead to drill in the Reserve and the company announced a $900 million construction project that will come on line in 2018 producing 30,000 barrels a day at its peak. Nevertheless, Alaska's congressional delegation did not think the federal 2013 NPR-A plan was extensive enough to meet the state's needs, and despite and probably because of ConocoPhillips's activity, development in the Reserve will continue to be opposed by environmentalists and likely through court challenges.[31] Similar and other problems face offshore oil drilling in the Arctic, including low oil prices.

Many, including former Alaska Lieutenant Governor Meade Treadwell, Governor Walker, and the state's congressional delegation among others, see development of oil and gas reserves in the Arctic as an economic savior for Alaska. And, indeed, for almost a decade up until 2015 Royal Dutch Shell, though strongly beleaguered by the environmental community, did attempt to develop these resources. But in fall 2015, Shell abandoned its efforts because of lack of a substantial find (and because of Shell's action, the Norwegian state oil company, Statoil, which has been involved in Arctic exploration, also pulled out). That fall also saw two other blows that hit those who saw Arctic oil and gas development as a means to help to solve Alaska's revenue problems in the next decade or so. These were a two-year moratorium on oil lease sales by the U.S. Department of the Interior in the Bering and Chukchis Seas for lack of oil industry interest; and the decision by the U.S. Army Corps of Engineers to put on hold work to develop a deep water Arctic port in Nome in Northwest Alaska.[32]

One of the uncertainties with development in ANWR, NPR-A, and offshore oil within federal jurisdiction is how much of a share of federal revenues Alaska would receive. The state currently receives 90 percent of revenues from resources taken from federal lands within Alaska, as set out in the Mineral Leasing Act of 1920. But in discussions of opening ANWR in Congress it has been suggested that the state should get only 50 percent. Alaska's congressional delegation has fought this proposed reduction. Currently, Alaska is not eligible to receive a share of revenues from oil produced from federal waters more than three miles offshore. Such a federal-state oil revenue sharing agreement for federal offshore production is possible, however, since four Gulf coast states forged such an agreement in 2006. Alaska's congressional delegation is also working to deal with this issue.[33]

All this adds up to the fact that Alaska's prospects for developing more oil reserves is far from positive. In fact, it is not at all likely in the short or long run. This is, in part, why many Alaskans and their politicians pin their hopes on a natural gas pipeline.

An Alaska Natural Gas Pipeline?

The idea of building a natural gas pipeline from the North Slope to the Lower 48 states either through Canada or alternatively through an in-state pipeline has been around since the 1970s. However, as Box 24.2 (pages 876-77) explains, building a gas pipeline is a very expensive and risky proposition for several reasons. Like virtually all decisions made by the industry, whether or not to build a gas pipeline comes down to economics and the rate of return the industry can expect on its investment. As Box 24.2 also points out, much uncertainty surrounds building such a pipeline, and even if the decision were made to build it today, it would be at least ten years before it would come on line.

Yet, just like bringing more oil on tap, even if a natural gas pipeline is constructed, it will not solve Alaska's current and future revenue problems. Because the price of natural gas is not determined in Alaska, the state would still be very vulnerable to the boom-bust cycle with its euphoric political highs and increased spending and its panicky, belt-tightening political lows. As Chapters 8, 19 and 25 point out, to alleviate this boom-bust cycle Alaska needs to insulate the state budget from fluctuating oil prices.

What to Do with Oil Revenues?

All oil producing regimes must deal with the question of how best to use the revenues received from oil and gas development. Alaska has answered the question over the years by a combination of using these revenues to fund general government services and infrastructure, building up the Permanent Fund, and using some of the fund's income for payment of PFDs (Chapter 25 explains the decisions and policies surrounding the fund and the PFD).

Except for the Alaska Constitution's requirement that a minimum of 25 percent of oil royalties and lease payments be deposited in the Permanent Fund, the legislature has total discretion to spend oil revenues any way it sees fit. It can continue to use them as it has done in the past or it can make both minor modifications and major changes. Change is not likely to occur, however, when oil prices are high and Alaskans are benefiting from state services and PFD payments. A major crisis, however, like the fall in oil prices in the latter half of 2014 and continuing into 2016 or the shutting down of TAPS could cause a fundamental rethinking of the use of oil revenues, including the earnings from the Permanent Fund.

World Conditions, Competition, and Alternative Fuels

World conditions and the volatility of the price of oil and gas are always an issue affecting Alaska's political economy. What OPEC does or does not do, what happens in Russia, Saudi Arabia, Venezuela, Nigeria, in relations with Iran, and other oil producing regimes, including those in the United States, will affect Alaska's political economy of oil. For instance, most recently, as Box 24.2 points out, the development of oil and gas fields in North Dakota and Alberta has contributed to the fall in the price of natural gas and made an Alaska gas pipeline to the Lower 48 less economically feasible.

A more serious, potentially devastating possibility for Alaska's economy is the development of an alternative source of energy to oil, particularly to gasoline. This seems unlikely and far off today, though as recently as the 1970s the almost universal use of personal computers and cell phones seemed equally unlikely. Electric technology for automobiles and trucks could advance considerably in the years to come, resulting in less demand for oil and sending world prices low enough to dampen the industry's economic incentives for new oil and gas development. Along these lines, in August 2013 the international news magazine *The Economist* ran a lead story and a special report on a projected long-term fall in the demand for oil.[34]

BOX 24.2

The Ongoing Issue of an Alaska Natural Gas Pipeline

When oil was discovered on the North Slope in 1968, natural gas was found with it. However, because the oil was more valuable, only an oil pipeline was built. Many thought a gas pipeline would soon follow.

In the early 1970s a consortium of Lower 48 gas companies proposed a gas pipeline across the Arctic National Wildlife Refuge (ANWR) to Canada's Mackenzie Delta, and then south to Alberta and the continental United States. But the Canadian government eventually ruled against the plan. Another plan was to parallel the oil pipeline through Interior Alaska and then follow the Alaska Highway to Alberta. Substantial work was done and various Canadian and U.S. approvals were granted. Then, deregulation of U.S. natural gas in the early 1980s caused the gas market to be flooded. As a result, gas prices dropped and the project became economically impractical.

The major economic problem of a gas pipeline is that gas is more difficult and expensive to ship than oil. The cost of building a 48-inch pipeline through Alaska and western Canada to Alberta, estimated at between $33 and $42 billion, means the cost of transporting gas is high relative to its market value. Consequently, the project is of modest profitability to the producers and of modest benefit to the state. This is because state revenues, like the producers' profits, are based on the value of the gas at the wellhead on the North Slope, after transportation costs have been deducted from the final sales price.

Major risks with a gas pipeline include possible cost overruns, uncertainties about market prices, and whether the state would increase taxes once the pipeline is built. The North Slope producing companies have been cautious about moving ahead with the project since they bear substantial financial risk. And because the risks are so high, to overcome them and get the project built, federal government help, likely in the form of loan guarantees, will be necessary.

One way to reduce the risks is to ensure a stable natural gas production tax. But because it will take ten years just to plan and build a gas pipeline and another thirty years to get a return, it may not be worthwhile to build such a pipeline unless a tax rate can be guaranteed not to change for forty years.

The state has tried three approaches to promote the project. One, put forward by legislators, was to encourage producers to build the pipeline or pay a large tax on the shut-in gas reserves. Put forward as a ballot proposition in 2002, Alaska voters defeated it. The second, by Governor Murkowski (2002–2006), was a partnership for the state to assume some risks and also own part of the pipeline. The producers liked this approach and the details were being negotiated when Murkowski was defeated for reelection by Sarah Palin in the August 2006 primary election. Governor Palin tried a third approach. The Alaska Gasline Inducement Act (AGIA) of 2007 set out certain state goals on issues such as construction schedules and tariff structures. The idea was to encourage an independent pipeline company to develop the project so the pipeline would not be controlled by the major producing companies, as is the case with the oil pipeline.

TransCanada Corporation stepped forward to undertake the project. The company agreed to the state's goals, and the state provided a $500 million

Continuing External and Internal Political Pressures

Pressures from environmental groups and national public opinion are likely to continue and even increase as more oil development in Alaska is proposed. The recent fight over Shell's proposed offshore drilling in Alaska is a good example. Plus, the issue of global warming will likely bring increased political pressures to use less and less fossil fuels like oil, gas, and coal, all of which Alaska has in large quantities.

grant. Once TransCanada started its initiative, two of the three major producing companies, BP and ConocoPhillips, formed the Denali Pipeline Company to launch their own proposal. ExxonMobil, a third major producer, decided to team with TransCanada.

From a legal perspective, the clash of two Alaska constitutional directives that relate to natural gas pipeline development means that the state is faced with a Catch-22. One directive is found in Article IX, Section 1, which states, "the power of taxation shall never be surrendered. This power shall not be suspended or contracted away." The other is Article VIII, Section 2, which states, "The Legislature shall provide for the utilization, development and conservation of all natural resources belonging to the state, including land and waters, for the maximum benefit of its people." On the one hand, a long-term contract guaranteeing a low tax rate may be necessary to get a gas pipeline built in order to maximize state value and fulfill Article VIII, Section 2, of the constitution. But despite the economic advantages accruing to the state from building a gas pipeline, an agreement that "contracted away" the state's taxing authority would almost certainly violate Article IX, Section 1 of the state constitution.

Changes in U.S. natural gas markets in 2012 and 2013 required major changes in the Alaska gas pipeline plan. The success of domestic shale gas producers in bringing new lower-cost gas to market in great quantities undermined the economic viability of the all-land pipeline route through Canada under AGIA. BP and ConocoPhillips terminated the Denali project and in mid-2012 Governor Parnell persuaded the North Slope producers, BP, ConocoPhillips, and ExxonMobil as well as TransCanada to consider a pipeline across Alaska to a south Alaska port and a large liquefied natural gas plant to export liquefied natural gas (LNG), the so-called Alaska Stand Alone Pipeline (ASAP) project. Its estimated cost is $45 to $65 billion.

The four companies agreed to the plan, the all land pipeline route was tabled, and studies began on the alternative LNG proposal. Nikiski, near Kenai, was selected as a southern terminus and location for the new LNG plant. In 2014 the state and the four companies agreed to pursue the project jointly, with the state taking an equity position, and engineering studies were underway by late that year. If the project stays on schedule, an agreement for advanced engineering would be made in 2016 and a construction decision made in 2018. Construction would require about five years. Shipments of LNG would begin in 2024 or 2025.

The future of this version of the pipeline, however, became less certain during the latter half of 2014 for two reasons. One was Governor Parnell's defeat in his bid for reelection by Bill Walker, a nonpartisan candidate. Walker has long supported a diameter pipeline larger than the one approved for the ASAP project and wanted changes in the partnership formed with industry in order to give the state an increased stake in the project. This included the state buying out TransCanada's share of the investment in the proposed line. This was completed in the fall of 2015 to give the state a 25 percent share in the project. The other reason was a 70 percent fall in oil prices leaving the state with a major budget deficit and less able to fund any pipeline. The oil price tumble also dampened the financial enthusiasm of the private partners, since a decline in oil prices also affects LNG prices. Clearly, many uncertainties and questions remain before the pipeline becomes a reality.

Source: Developed by Tim Bradner, an expert on Alaska oil and gas issues, whose articles on the subject regularly appear in the Alaska press.

In fact, a long-term possibility, but nevertheless a potential major threat to Alaska's reliance on oil revenues to fund government, is international policies toward climate change. For twenty years or more, attempts by the international community to agree on a cooperative approach were unsuccessful until a conference in Paris in late 2015. At that meeting, the United Nations Framework Convention on Climate Change, dubbed the United Nations Conference of the Parties (COP 21), more than 200 countries developed a universal agreement to deal with climate change. In short, they agreed to reduce the use of fossil fuels drastically over the next twenty years or so. If this happens, about 50 percent of the world's oil and 80 percent of its coal, which would otherwise be pumped or mined, would stay in the ground. Clearly, this would have a major effect on Alaska's economy and its revenues.[35]

With the pace of technology in terms of alternative energy sources—including clean fuels such as wind and tidal power and alternative ways to power automobiles—to replace oil, the "Oil Age" could well end with much oil left in the ground. This was part of the message in *The Economist's* predictions on the future of oil.

Again, for better or for worse, the global warming debate will increase the developer-environmentalist conflict and constrain oil and gas development, with likely effects on Alaska's revenues and the nature of its political economy of oil. A good example of the interplay between development and environmentalism on the issue of climate change was epitomized by President Obama's visit to Alaska in the summer of 2015. While his administration had given the go-head for Shell to drill in the Chukchi Sea earlier that year, his visit to Alaska was to focus attention on Alaska's place in the front line of global warming and its effects on the state, particularly its rural-bush and coastal communities.[36]

7. OBSERVATIONS ON THE POLITICAL INFLUENCE OF THE OIL INDUSTRY IN ALASKA AND THE ISSUE OF POLITICAL CORRUPTION AND ETHICS

One of the points mentioned earlier about the political economy of oil around the world is that because the companies have major financial assets in, and their presence is indispensable to, many oil producing regimes, there is potential for the industry to wield great political influence. In considering the politics of oil in Alaska we also mentioned that there is an interesting relationship of oil to the populist politics of the state. In this section we briefly comment on the political influence of oil in Alaska, including the issue of oil and political corruption.

Is the Oil Industry Running Alaska?

Besides polar bears, salmon, snow and freezing cold, Eskimos, spectacular scenery, and most recently Sarah Palin, when many outsiders think of Alaska, they likely think of oil. In many places like Nigeria and the Persian Gulf, as well as states like Louisiana, New Mexico, and Texas, the oil industry has wielded extensive political influence. It would be natural, then, to assume that the oil industry has political influence in Alaska.[37] Moreover, the successful enactment of the MAPA oil tax cut (SB 21) in 2013 and its subsequent validation in the referendum vote in 2014 might bolster such an assumption. And yet the industry has never controlled state politics, if that means getting everything it wants and having most politicians in tow, as the railroads did in many states until World War I and the gaming and hospitality industry is reputed to do in Nevada today. Furthermore, the oil industry is not likely to control Alaska politics in the future for a number of reasons.

It is certainly true that the oil industry is a force to be reckoned with in Alaska, largely because of how dependent the state is on oil revenues and because of the tremendous financial resources the industry can bring to bear to achieve its political goals, as exemplified by MAPA (SB 21). As Chapter 15 on interest groups points out, the oil industry, including the individual companies and the Alaska Oil and Gas Association (AOGA), has been one of the two most consistently influential high profile lobbies in the state (the other being the Association of Alaska School Boards).[38] There are, however, several constraints on the political power of the industry in Alaska that prevent it from being a dominant political force. Four of them are especially important.

First, virtually all oil and gas in Alaska comes from state-owned land. As a result, other than the oil companies and local businesses that have strong economic ties to the industry, there is no private political constituency for oil in Alaska. Unlike states such as Texas, Louisiana, and Oklahoma, there is no oil royalty owners association of private landlords to lobby government alongside the oil industry or on its behalf. Second, the fact that the bulk of state revenues, the Permanent Fund, and particularly the PFD, are dependent on oil revenues, means there is public pressure on politicians not to be too generous to the oil industry when it comes to taxes and other benefits. Third, while it may seem contradictory, given Alaska's dependence on oil for its economic life-blood, there is a strain of populism in Alaska among some groups that translates into an anti-oil company attitude that is not only shared by some politicians but that sometimes resonates through state agencies to affect policy toward the industry. Anti-industry sentiment often follows party divisions and majority caucus lines in the legislature—with Republicans tending to favor the industry and Democrats voicing opposition. This is not always true, however. Opposition, for instance, to the Parnell oil tax cut crossed party and caucus lines and the move to place repeal of the law before the voters was in part a bipartisan effort.

Fourth, as noted elsewhere, the oil industry, like those of mining and timber, has to contend with the influences exerted by external political forces, such as the environmental lobby, U.S. public opinion, and many elements in Congress and federal agencies. To be sure, other energy producing states in the nation are subject to similar pressures. But given its place in the American psyche as the Last Frontier, Alaska has a higher national profile, and incidents like the *Exxon Valdez* oil spill, drilling in the Arctic, and the status of endangered species produce considerable political resistance to the economic and political goals of the industry.

For this combination of reasons the oil companies are not running Alaska, nor have they "captured" their policy area. That is, industry representatives do not always get what they want on oil issues. Sometimes they win and sometimes they lose. For many years, for instance, Alaska had the highest oil and gas taxes in the nation, though that has not been true since the early 2000s. And despite significant industry opposition in the late 1970s, the legislature adopted a separate accounting system for determining oil company income taxable in Alaska. The industry contended that this unfairly increased Alaska's income taxes from oil production activities in the state and filed suit against the state seeking to have the system ruled unconstitutional. Within a few years, the legislature became concerned that the companies' lawsuit might be successful and that the state might have to refund a significant amount of taxes collected under the separate accounting system. Accordingly, the legislature repealed that system and adopted another system more favorable to the industry. We have already noted the resistance of Governor Murkowski to extend tax benefits on the Orion field. More recently, the industry lost the first round in their quest for what eventually became MAPA. They eventually succeeded in getting MAPA enacted, but only after a bruising fight. And although the margin of victory in Ballot Measure 1 in August 2014 was comfortable, it was certainly not overwhelming, especially considering the industry and its allies outspent the opposition 18 to 1.

Despite these constraints on the influence of oil, the high stakes involved in terms of their investments and potential for enormous profit means that there is still temptation for the industry to engage in corruption. Although none of the oil producers was involved, there was a scandal in the recent past involving corrupt practices by VECO, an Alaska oil services company. A look at this scandal is enlightening regarding past and the likelihood of present and future corruption and shady political ethics surrounding the industry in Alaska.

The VECO Corruption Scandal—Alaska's Watergate

The VECO scandal was referred to in considering the general issue of corruption in Alaska politics in Chapter 5 on political culture and in Chapter 20 regarding the role of the media in the affair.[39] Here we consider it as a part of oil and gas politics and a possible result of the political aspects of the resource curse affecting Alaska.

The story of VECO starts with natural gas. Although Alaska has long held over thirty-five trillion cubic feet of natural gas reserves, these reserves are stranded. For reasons explained in considering the gas pipeline above, there have never been the right economic conditions to be able to develop those reserves and get them to market. Governor Murkowski tried to change that. At the beginning of his administration in 2003, natural gas prices were beginning to rise in the United States and the economics of developing North Slope natural gas began to look favorable. So the state began negotiating with the major producers to find a way to develop the reserves. The outcome was a negotiated change in production taxes in the form of a contract between Alaska and the major producers. In particular, the change specified how much production tax oil and gas would be subject to during the life of the natural gas pipeline, about forty-five years. The contract, however, would not be valid without legislative approval.

VECO executives wanted the Murkowski contract to be ratified by the legislature and they wanted a low PPT for North Slope natural gas. VECO had an intense interest in the debate because if the PPT was favorable to the producers and the natural gas pipeline was built, VECO would be the subcontractor for a lot of the work and would make millions or even billions of dollars. One of the ways that VECO's owners affected the outcome was to pay certain key legislators to vote in favor of the contract and a lower PPT for gas, and for those legislators to persuade their colleagues in the legislature to do the same.

In the end, a lower PPT did go through, although not exactly as the Murkowski administration, VECO, and the producers would have liked. But the natural gas contract was shot down. After a major FBI investigation, several of those involved, including two legislators (Pete Kott and Vic Kohring) and two top VECO executives (Bill Allen and Rick Smith), were convicted of bribery and served prison terms.

Other politicians were also tainted. Frank Murkowski, partly due to the ongoing VECO scandal, lost in the 2006 gubernatorial primary to Sarah Palin. Several legislators lost elections in 2006 and some decided not to run, again due to the taint of the VECO affair even though they were not charged with wrongdoing.

How Ethical Is Alaska's Oil and Gas Industry?

The VECO scandal raises several questions as to whether Alaska's oil and gas industry has low political ethics and may even be corrupt, whether Alaska's politicians are corrupt, and whether state politics in general have succumbed to the political consequences of the resource curse. The short answer to all three questions is most probably "no."

First, no major oil company, and none associated with the industry other than VECO, was involved in the corruption scandal. The corruption was mainly the work of two individuals from VECO (Bill Allen and Rick Smith), and there were only a half dozen or so politicians or former politicians convicted or implicated. The vast majority of Alaska legislators and other public officials were not involved. In fact, the incident led to tightening of lobby and conflict of interest laws during the Palin administration. So VECO was an isolated incident fueled by human greed, traits not unique to Alaska. No matter how many political safeguards are put in place, or how much ethics are valued, there will always be some individuals who will work underhandedly for their personal gain or that of their organizations.

Second, with its high political profile, the last thing the oil industry wants is to be tainted with a corruption scandal filling lead media stories for weeks. Such a scandal would likely harm both their short and long term political goals. This is not to say that the oil industry does not play hardball politics to get what they want in Alaska. They put tremendous resources into achieving their political goals, including spending hundreds of thousands of dollars on lobbyists. In fact, the industry is usually the single largest spender as a political interest of any interest group in Alaska. For example, as Figure 15.2B shows in Chapter 15, the oil industry was the highest spender on lobbying in 2013, the year they obtained a tax reduction through passage of the MAPA legislation. All these efforts are up front because political corruption is simply not a policy option for the industry in Alaska or in other states in the nation, as it might be in some authoritarian regimes.

Even if some form of corruption was seen as an option by some elements of the industry, with the exception of the isolated VECO case, they would likely receive a negative reception from the vast majority of public officials in the state and politicians would likely expose the industry's untoward overtures to them. Not only do public officials personally view such behavior as unethical and wrong, public disclosure laws and media scrutiny make it unwise for them to get entangled in shady political dealings with the oil industry or other political interests.[40] As with many other aspects of Alaska politics, political transparency has been an important element in ensuring above-board dealings with the oil industry since soon after it began doing major business in Alaska.[41]

Alaska politicians routinely deal with oil and mineral issues where millions and even billions of dollars are at stake. The state has worked to mitigate the political elements of the resource curse—corruption and funds spent wastefully—by using its oil revenues for public purposes: to fund state government, create the Permanent Fund, and pay a yearly PFD to citizens. Public use of oil revenues increases Alaskans' incentives to be politically active and watch for corruption and untoward activity by public officials.[42]

8. CONCLUSION: ALASKA'S POLITICAL ECONOMY WITH AND WITHOUT OIL AND GAS

One of the purposes of this chapter was to compare Alaska's way of dealing with the oil industry, and the opportunities and challenges it presents, with the political economy of oil in other oil producing regimes. The other purpose was to identify some prominent issues surrounding Alaska's oil production and to explore some of the policies that have been tried in the past or that may be available in the future.

Covering the first purpose showed that Alaska has much in common with the risks and rewards faced by other oil producing regimes, particularly regarding the uncertainly of oil revenues, how to maximize them, and how to benefit from these revenues in the long term. Alaska's solution contrasts with many other oil regimes, including most in the United States. Dealing with the second purpose reveals that Alaska has little control over many of the issues that have arisen and that may arise in the future and thus has little ability to affect those issues in its favor. The issues include the environmental impact of oil and gas development, the need for new development to maintain the state's revenue stream, and the possibility of building a gas pipeline. On balance, however, because of the tremendous economic benefits that oil development has brought, the vast majority of Alaskans and virtually all of its policy makers since the late 1960s would agree that it was better that Alaska drilled than never to have drilled at all.

More light is shed on the two purposes of the chapter by identifying the four characteristics of Alaska politics that are particularly relevant to the state's political economy of oil. Clearly of significance are the influence of external economic and political forces—particularly world markets, the federal government, and environmental interests—and the all-pervasive role of government, particularly in the form of the Owner State. The clash between economic development and environmentalism, as well as elements of the Alaska political culture of pragmatic dependent individualism, also play important roles. The developer-environmentalist clash occurs both in and out of the state—mainly in Washington, D.C.—as it affects Alaska politics and has shaped much of the debate about oil. And it is oil revenues that enable Alaskans to maintain a myth of individualism while at the same time being largely dependent on the government employment and state services that oil makes possible. In less major but nevertheless significant ways, oil has also shaped the role of Alaska Natives in Alaska politics and has affected the influence of interest groups and the dynamics of political power, among other influences.

In regard to the impact of oil on Alaska's political economy, Chapter 6 on the state's present day economy speculates about what Alaska's economy would be like without oil.[43] We conclude this chapter by expanding on that speculation.

First, there would be no $52 billion plus state savings account in the form of the Permanent Fund, no yearly PFD, and thus no discussion about their use to close fiscal gaps and no regular debates about oil taxes. Without oil revenues, the individual income tax would never have been abolished and there would likely be a state sales tax and regular discussions about raising them. With perhaps half the population that Alaska has today, Anchorage and its environs would have a lower concentration of the state's population and thus be a lesser political force in the state. On a related point, there would be no money to move the capital so that would be a moot point and rarely on the political agenda, if at all. While environmental concerns would still exist, there would be fewer of them and the developer-environmentalist conflict would be less intense. The fishing industry would be one of the major generators of taxes and likely be a central part of Alaska politics, instead of being sidelined as it is today by oil. In these and many other ways, Alaska politics would be very different without oil production.

But the clock can never be turned back and the reality is that Alaska does have oil and its politics have been very much shaped by oil and gas development and production. To return to the statement by Sheikh Ahmed Zaki Yamani, quoted at the beginning of the chapter, "the Oil Age will end long before the world runs out of oil." As we have seen in this chapter, and as Chapter 8 on state revenues explains in detail, Alaska's oil age may end in the next twenty to thirty years if TAPS cannot be kept running efficiently, if more oil is not found, or if a profitable gas pipeline cannot be built. Less likely in the near future, but certainly possible in the long run, is the development of a substitute for oil as a major energy source and the effects of international climate change policy. If these developments become a reality, Alaska's political economy will no longer be one dominated by oil and the story of oil in Alaska will begin, "Once up a time . . ."

ENDNOTES

[1] See *The Economist*, October 23, 2003. The quote is from the 1980s. See the full article at: http://www.economist.com/node/2155717.

[2] The author thanks Kristina Klimovich for her aid in updating some statistics in this chapter.

[3] The majors used to be called the "Seven Sisters" which, through a series of mergers, included what are now ExxonMobil, Chevron, British Petroleum (BP), and Shell, as well as Gulf Oil, which has not changed its name. See A. F. Alhajji and David Huettner, "OPEC & Other Commodity Cartels: A Comparison," *Energy Policy* 28, no. 15 (2000): 1151–64.

[4] See the AOGCC website, at http://doa.alaska.gov/ogc/; Sarah Palin is a former AOGCC commissioner.

[5] Based on a quote from Morris A. Copeland, "Fact and Theory in Economics: The Testament of an Institutionalist," in *The Collected Papers of Morris A. Copeland*, ed. Chandler Morse (Ithaca, NY: Cornell University Press, 1958).

[6] As of January 2016, the members of OPEC are Algeria, Angola, Ecuador, Indonesia, Iran, Iraq, Kuwait, Libya, Nigeria, Qatar, Saudi Arabia, the United Arab Emirates (including Dubai), and Venezuela.

[7] See Chapter 7, Figure 7.5 "Non-Resident Employment in Alaska."

[8] Examples of countries that nationalized oil and gas assets or renegotiated PSAs are: in 1972 Iraq nationalized its oil assets; in 1973 Iran replaced all PSAs with service contracts, a de facto nationalization; in 1976 and 1977 respectively Kuwait and Saudi Arabia nationalized all their oil assets; in 1975 Venezuela nationalized all its oil assets, used PSAs to increase oil production in the 1990s, then changed those agreements back to service contracts in the early 2000s; and, in 2006, Bolivia renationalized its oil and gas sector. Today, most countries own all oil and gas assets, but have PSAs with the IOC majors. These agreements often change, however, resulting in de facto nationalizations.

[9] Jerry McBeath, *et al., The Political Economy of Oil in Alaska: Multinationals vs. the State* (Boulder, CO: Lynne Rienner Publishers, 2008), 122.

[10] Kristen Nelson, "Alaska Gets Poor Marks," *Petroleum News* 12, no. 46 (2007); and Liz Ruskin, "Survey Says Alaska Has Poor Business Climate for Oil," *Alaska News Nightly*, Alaska Public Radio Network (APRN), December 3, 2013.

[11] Alexander Kent, "The 10 Most Oil Rich States," *USA Today*, August 3, 2014; and Nick Cunningham. "North Dakota, Texas Top US Oil Output, but Other States are Gaining Steam," *The Christian Science Monitor*, June 30, 2014.

[12] See particularly, Chapter 6, Section 4, Chapter 8 in general, Chapter 19 in general, and Chapter 21, Sections 2, 3, and 4.

[13] ARCO secretly discovered oil on its Prudhoe Bay State No. 1 well. It then offered to drill wells on Sohio's (now BP's) leases for a substantial profit share, but Sohio got suspicious when ARCO offered it so much money for each well. That offer tipped off Sohio that, indeed, ARCO had found oil, so Sohio figured it was sitting on a black gold mine.

[14] See Chapter 22, Box 22.1 for an explanation of the *Exxon Valdez* oil spill and its consequences.

[15] Over the years, the state has used a number of oil and gas tax and economic advisers. They are often paid hundreds of dollars an hour, but are worth it. These experts are internationally renowned and advise governments around the world on what are the best oil and gas tax and contract strategies. Besides Pedro van Meurs, among these experts are Daniel Johnston and the firm Cambridge Energy Research Associates (CERA), now owned by the company IHS Energy.

[16] See Chapter 16, Box 16.9.

[17] Alexandra Gutierrez "Gov. Parnell Rolls Out New Tax Proposal," *Alaska News Nightly* (APRN), January 21, 2013: and Gutierrez, "Legislature Approves Tax Cut for Oil Companies," *Alaska News Nightly* (APRN), April 15, 2013.

[18] Casey Kelly, "Opponents of Proposed Oil Tax-cut Rally on Steps of Capitol, around State," KTOO-FM (Juneau Public Radio), April 4, 2013. From the same source, see also, "Alaska Democrats Debut Their Own Oil Tax Legislation," February 13, 2013.

[19] Information and statistics on Ballot Measure 1 is taken, in part, from the National Institute for Money in State Politics, at http://ballotpedia.org/Alaska_Oil_Tax_Cuts_Veto_Referendum,_Ballot_Measure_1_%28August_2014%29.

[20] More detailed information about the various tax regimes can be obtained from the following sources. For the ELF, the Murkowski PPT, and ACES, see McBeath, *et al.*, *The Political Economy of Oil in Alaska*, Chapter 4, "Petroleum Revenues and Tax Policy," esp. 89–99; and Jim Egan and Joshua Wilson, "Alaska's Oil Investment Tax Structure: Establishing a Competitive Alaska," A Commonwealth North Study Report, Anchorage, March 2011. On the comparison of ACES and MAPA, see Matthew Berman, "Comparing Alaska's Oil Production Taxes: Incentives and Assumptions," University of Alaska Anchorage, Institute of Social and Economic Research (ISER), WEBnotes, August 2014. In addition three popular sources explain the various tax regimes very succinctly: Tim Bradner, "The Evolution of Alaska's Oil Taxes," *Alaska Journal of Commerce*, July 10, 2014; Alex DeMarban, "MAPA or ACES, What's It Going to be Alaska?" *Alaska Dispatch News*, August 14, 2014; and Melissa Griffiths, "The History of Oil Wealth," *Juneau Empire*, August 15, 2014.

[21] On Palin's motives, see the widely held perspectives in Clive S. Thomas, "The Sarah Palin Phenomenon: The Washington-Hollywood-Wall Street Syndrome in American Politics, and More . . ." in *Issues in American Politics: Polarized Politics in the Age of Obama*, ed. John W. Dumbrell (London: Routledge/Taylor and Francis, 2013).

[22] Interview with Matthew Berman, an economics professor at the University of Alaska Anchorage, Institute of Social and Economic Research, by Anthony Nakazawa, May 15, 2012.

[23] See Chapters 21 and 22.

[24] See Chapter 22.

[25] See Chapter 9, on Alaska Natives, Section 6, and Chapter 21, Box 21.6 on ANWR.

[26] See Chapter 22, Section 3.

[27] "Court: AK Must Look at Cumulative Oil, Gas Impacts," Associated Press (AP), April 2, 2013.

[28] The Associated Press—AP, "17th Billionth Barrel of Oil Flows Down Alaska Pipeline," July 21, 2014.

[29] See Chapter 8, Introduction and Section 4.

[30] Sam Sanders, "Obama Proposes New Protections for Arctic National Wildlife Refuge," *Morning Edition*, National Public Radio (NPR), January 25, 2015.

[31] Peter Grantz, "Interior Department Finalizes NPR-A Plan, Creates Pipeline Corridor," *Alaska News Nightly* (APRN), February 25, 2013.

[31] Rachel Waldholz, "Conoco Annonces NPR-A Development on North Slope," *Alaska News Nightly* (APRN), November 18, 2015.

[32] Erica Martinson, "Interior Department cancels lease sales in Alaska's Arctic waters, citing low interest," *Alaska Dispatch News*, October 16, 2015; and Alex DeMarban, "Work toward deep-water port in Alaska Arctic on hold, Army Corps says," *Alaska Dispatch News*, October 26, 2015.

[33] See, Alex DeMarban, "Will Off-shore Oil Development in Alaska's Arctic Make State Rich? Don't Count on It," *Alaska Dispatch*, July 1, 2012; and Peter Grantz, "Begich Introduces Bill Granting State a Share of Offshore Drilling Revenue," *Alaska News Nightly*, (APRN), February 5, 2013.

[34] *The Economist*, August 3, 2013, "The Future of Oil: Yesterday's Fuel," 12, and Briefing, "The Global Oil Industry: Supermajordämmerung," 20–22.

[35] Coal reserves in Alaska are estimated at 170 billion tons but production is a mere two million tons per year; but should COP 21 becomes a reality, much of Alaska's coal may be part of the world's 80 percent of coal that stays in the ground. On the COP 21 conference see, Coral Davenport, "A Climate Accord Based on Global Peer Pressure," *New York Times*, December 14, 2015.

[36] Julie Hirschfeld Davis, "Obama's Alaska Visit Puts Climate, Not Energy, in Forefront," *New York Times*, August 31, 2015; and Erica Martinson, "Obama brings funding, climate change announcements on trip to Kotzebue," *Alaska Dispatch News*, September 2, 2015.

[37] For a listing of the significance of the oil industry in the fifty states in the late 1980s, see Appendix A, "The Most Influential Interests in the Fifty States," in *Politics in the American States: A Comparative Analysis*, eds., Virginia Gray, Herbert Jacob, and Robert B. Albritton (Glenview, IL: Scott Foresman/ Little Brown, 1990). Subsequent updates of this study by Clive Thomas and Ronald Hrebenar, show the continuing influence of the oil industry in many states. See Chapter 15 endnote 2 for a reference to this time-series analysis of interest group power in the states.

[38] See Chapter 15, Table 15.4.

[39] See Chapter 5, Section 7, and Chapter 20, Section 1.

[40] As Chapter 20 points out, however, the press was asleep in the early stages in unearthing the VECO scandal.

[41] For the effects of increased political transparency on interest group activity in general in Alaska, see Chapter 15, Section 11.

[42] For another perspective on the influence of the oil industry in Alaska, see McBeath, *et al.*, *The Political Economy of Oil in Alaska*, Chapter 3.

[43] See Chapter 6, Section 4.

★ CHAPTER 25 ★

The Alaska Permanent Fund and the Permanent Fund Dividend: The Owner State's Experiment in Managing Petroleum Wealth

Scott Goldsmith

A major challenge facing natural resource economies, especially those with nonrenewable oil and gas resources (like Alberta, Iran, Norway, Nigeria, Texas, Venezuela, and Alaska) is how to deal with their wealth. This wealth often accrues in massive amounts in a very short time, perhaps over a decade, but it could be gone in a generation or less. Consequently, this challenge has two related aspects. One is how to manage the immediate wealth accruing daily, which may produce political intoxication in a state or country hitherto poor or financially strapped, as was Alaska before oil. That kind of intoxication carries a high risk of squandering the money. The second aspect is how to use some or all of this wealth for future generations at a time when the oil and gas may be producing much less revenue or has run out entirely.

These two aspects of resource wealth are particularly significant for Alaska. The state's major vehicle for managing its oil wealth for the present and the future is the Alaska Permanent Fund and the related Permanent Fund Dividend (PFD). In January 2016, almost forty years after its creation, the fund's value reached over $50 billion, close to five times the budget the state enacted for fiscal year (FY) 2016. Three months earlier, in October 2015 (on the thirty-third anniversary of the first PFD payment), over 85 percent of Alaskans were qualified to receive a PFD of $2,072. This was the highest payout in the history of the PFD.[1] Not surprisingly, the PFD, made possible by the Permanent Fund, is one of the most, if not *the* most, popular policies ever enacted by the State of Alaska, and likely by any state in the nation.

As the fund and particularly the PFD are such a major aspect of the political economy of Alaska, they are considered in several chapters in the book from a variety of perspectives. In particular, Chapter 4 briefly considers the constitutional foundations of the fund and the PFD, and Chapter 6 examines both the fund and PFD as part of the Alaska economy, particularly that of rural-bush Alaska. Chapter 8 considers the issue of fund earnings and the PFD as sources of supplementary state revenues, and Chapter 19 looks at the place of the fund and PFD in the state budget.[2] This chapter does not repeat these analyses, though reference to some of them (particularly the analyses in Chapter 8) is necessary in achieving our purposes in this chapter.

One of these purposes is to take a holistic look at the fund and PFD, their development and present status, and their future prospects and challenges as a central piece of Alaska public policy. One important aspect is that the fund and PFD operate within Alaska's Owner State, where the state owns much of the oil and gas resources, as opposed to places like Texas where the resources are largely in private hands. Another important aspect is that Alaska's political environment is that of a democracy in which the public has a major influence on public policy. This adds a dimension to decisions about how to manage petroleum wealth that is not a factor in authoritarian regimes like Saudi Arabia and many of its Persian Gulf neighbors. Another purpose of the chapter is to place Alaska in perspective regarding the way it has dealt with its oil revenues compared with other oil producing states and countries.

In presenting this holistic approach, four of the characteristics of Alaska politics set out in Chapter 2 are particularly evident. In order of importance, they are the significant role of external economic and political forces, the all-pervasive importance of government, self-proclaimed fiscal conservatism, and a political culture of pragmatic dependent individualism. As we will see, these characteristics are often intertwined in complex ways.

Since the creation of the fund and the PFD, only minor formal changes have been made in how they operate and serve the citizens of Alaska. However, the major drop in oil prices from mid-2014 through early 2016 and likely beyond, with consequent major budget deficits, may lead to changes. These may include the make up of the fund, use of fund earnings, the way that the PFD is calculated, and the size of the PFD. Possible changes are addressed in the second half of the chapter in the context of the future of the fund and the PFD and the on-going politics that have surrounded possible changes since the inception of the fund and the PFD.

The first part of the chapter (Sections 1 through 6) explains the background of the fund and the PFD. It includes an explanation of the basic character of the Permanent Fund by placing it in context with other sovereign wealth funds (SWFs) and examines the establishment and growth of the fund and the PFD. The second part (Sections 7 through 10) examines the politics and policy effects of the fund and PFD, including the role of Alaska's brand of populist democracy.

1. KEY EXPLANATIONS: THE CONCEPT OF SWFs, THE RESOURCE CURSE, AND THE PERMANENT FUND AS AN ENDOWMENT

Understanding the Permanent Fund and the PFD requires familiarity with several technical terms and concepts. To list all of them here could be overwhelming—especially for those studying the fund for the first time. To complicate matters, since the early 2000s the managers of the fund have changed some of the terms they use to refer to certain accounts and have also altered the way they report information on the fund and what is included under various accounts.[3] To simplify the various terms and changes we take a step-by-step approach by first explaining some general terms in this section and then explaining other, more specific, ones in the appropriate places in the chapter.

In this section we look at the Permanent Fund in a broad perspective by explaining the concept of SWFs and their possible relationship to the phenomenon of the resource curse, and then at the Permanent Fund as an endowment.

Sovereign Wealth Funds

The Alaska Permanent Fund is a sovereign wealth fund (SWF), similar to funds that have been established by a number of countries, most commonly based on petroleum or other mineral wealth to maximize long-term financial returns. Many countries, states, and provinces that have established SWFs (such as Algeria, several in the Persian Gulf, Venezuela, Alberta, and Alaska) have natural resource extraction economies that are heavily dependent on these resources—most often oil—for the health of their economies and for government revenues. Because the resources are nonrenewable, a major reason for setting up an SWF is to provide for revenue when the resource produces less revenue or finally runs out. This is why these funds are sometimes referred to as "rainy day funds." This was a major impetus in creating the Alaska Permanent Fund.

Many SWFs have been in existence for decades, but most have grown dramatically since 2005 because of rising oil prices. In the fall of 2015 the largest of them was held by Norway. At $882 billion, about eighteen times the size of Alaska's Permanent Fund, Norway's fund is well on its way to becoming the first SWF to reach the $1 trillion mark. Other large SWFs include those in Saudi Arabia, China, and Singapore. The growing economic power represented by SWFs has raised concerns among economists and politicians about how the portfolios of these funds will be managed. They could be a destabilizing force in the global economy, and they could also be used for political purposes.

Although the Alaska Permanent Fund is one of the oldest SWFs, it is small by comparison with those mentioned above, but the largest of all U.S. states with SWFs. Nevertheless, given its modest size relative to the U.S. economy and the clarity of its objective to maximize its long-term financial return, the Alaska fund does not represent the same economic and political challenges for the United States as some other SWFs.

SWFs and the Resource Curse

Chapter 24 on oil and gas in Alaska explains the nature of the resource curse (sometimes referred to as Dutch disease) and its consequences in some natural resource dependent countries and regions (see Box 24.1). Here our focus is on how the curse may relate specifically to SWFs and its possible effects on Alaska.

The resource curse has affected many countries, states, and regions. It can cause inflation, inhibit economic diversification, and underfund education and other needed services, among other adverse consequences. In some instances, however, particularly in democracies like Norway, Alaska, and Australia, an SWF can help prevent or alleviate the onset and consequences of the resources curse. Chapter 24 argues that Alaska has not been affected by the political corruption or other consequences often associated with the curse.

Whether Alaska is or will be subject to some or all of the economic effects of the curse is not clear. However, even if not expressed in terms of the resource curse, many Alaska politicians and others have been cognizant of the possible negative effects of the state's petroleum wealth. So, understanding the nature of possible effects of the SWF resource curse throws light on various aspects of the establishment, development, and future of both the fund and the PFD.

The Permanent Fund as an Endowment

One distinction that helps in understanding the establishment, development, the politics, and likely future of the Permanent Fund and the PFD, is the difference between a financial endowment and a trust fund. The distinction is not crystal clear, but there are some major differences between them.

An endowment is a fund invested in various types of assets (stocks, bonds, and so on) dedicated to a special purpose, such as funding education, services for certain disabled persons, or to promote some charitable or cultural cause. In most cases, the principal of an endowment must be preserved, and only the investment earnings of the fund may be spent to further the endowment's purposes. Those who run the endowment, usually a governing board, have a legal obligation to use the earnings from the endowment for the purpose specified.

In contrast, trust funds are often not dedicated to a particular purpose. Thus, the recipient individual, organization, or institution has no obligation to spend the funds in a particular way. In addition, unlike an endowment, a trust can be established in such a way that the principal of the trust fund may be used for the purposes of the trust, and the trust may eventually be liquidated by completely disbursing the funds in the trust to designated beneficiaries. For instance, a trust may be set up for a child by an uncle to earn interest until the child becomes an adult and then the entire trust, including principal and accumulated earnings, is given to the young adult to spend as he or she wishes. Sometimes trusts have specific purposes, such as for the college education of a child. Even so, the money may be disbursed for this purpose and eventually the trust will be liquidated once the person's education is complete.

The Alaska Permanent Fund is best characterized as a financial endowment, the general purpose of which is to generate income for the state, though there was a purposeful vagueness in the language setting up the fund. The use of fund income has changed somewhat over the years, especially with the establishment of the PFD. The politics of the fund and the PFD over the years has, in some ways, made many Alaskans view the fund more as a trust and less as an endowment.

2. ESTABLISHING THE ALASKA PERMANENT FUND: THE IMPETUS AND THE POLITICS

Many Alaskans and people from the Outside now associate the fund mainly with the PFD, even though the PFD was not established until six years after the fund began operations. As a result, it is instructive to outline the original reasons for establishing the fund. First we look at the impetus behind creating the fund and then the politics involved in creating it.

The Impetus Behind Creating the Permanent Fund

When Alaska became a state in 1959, there was concern about how the new state would pay for essential public services. The private economy, dependent primarily on fishing, mining, and forest products, provided a very small tax base. Fortunately, production of oil and gas discovered in Cook Inlet in the mid to late 1950s began to provide a revenue stream just as the federal transitional grants, provided to help the new state get started, expired in the early 1960s. However, the Cook Inlet petroleum tax base was small compared with the needs of the new state, which included not only money to provide current services, but, more importantly, to build the state's infrastructure to develop the economy.

In 1968, oil was discovered on state land on the North Slope, and the subsequent lease sales in 1969 produced what was then an incredible $900 million windfall, seven times the $128 million state general fund budget that year. In the fall of 1969, the question of what to do with that windfall, as well as the anticipated future revenues from oil production, was discussed at a series of citizen conferences in Anchorage, sponsored by the legislature with the help of the Brookings Institution, a think tank in Washington, D.C.

The idea of setting aside some of the current windfall and future revenues in a permanent fund was broached at the conference, but most participants felt that creating such a fund should wait until the start of oil production, which was then expected to be only a couple of years away. The $900 million windfall would instead be used to build what was then an underdeveloped public sector, while avoiding poorly considered economic development schemes.

With that as a short-term plan, the state began to spend the windfall and expand the budget in anticipation of a steady stream of oil revenues once the trans-Alaska pipeline (TAPS) was completed. Between 1969 and 1971 the state general fund budget doubled to $310 million, but pipeline construction was delayed. Long before the pipeline was completed in 1977, the windfall had disappeared, but the state budget continued to increase. The state was able to remain solvent through a short-term fix—a temporary tax on oil reserves in the ground that would be refunded to the oil and gas lease holders as a credit against future taxes on actual oil production.

The source of the new tax base was the oil reservoir at Prudhoe Bay, the largest oil field ever discovered in North America and one of the largest in the world. With recoverable reserves estimated at nine billion barrels, it was easy to visualize the tremendous wealth this good fortune would bring to the state. The likelihood of finding another field of comparable size in Alaska was close to zero, however. So even with intensive development of the petroleum resources on the North Slope, oil production could not be sustained. The giant field would eventually become depleted, and Alaska could, without appropriate planning and investment, become poor again.

It was against this background that the idea of the Alaska Permanent Fund arose. The general perception in retrospect was that the state had wasted the $900 million 1969 lease sale windfall. To avoid a recurrence of that kind of waste, suggestions arose to remove some of the future oil revenues from the hands of the legislature and deposit those revenues in a safe savings account. The fund would create a sustainable flow of revenue that would outlive the production of depleting petroleum assets and be available for the inevitable financial "rainy day." Plus, along the lines of the problems of the resource curse, if not exactly expressed in that way, the notion of setting aside a part of the windfall to prevent the economy from overheating was a major issue at the time.

The Politics of Creating the Fund

The need to save for a rainy day was never unanimously supported, however. Some people felt that with development of new large discoveries, petroleum resources would continue on an upward trajectory after Prudhoe Bay was depleted. Others thought expansion of the petroleum industry would be the catalyst for economic development in other sectors of the economy, and thus there was no need to save for a rainy day that would never come to pass. Still others believed the opportunities provided by statehood would be sufficient for the state to develop a balanced and diversified economy without having to save for the future.

There were also people who felt it was inappropriate for the public sector to have a savings account and that saving was best left to individuals. This view, however, overlooked the problem with purely private savings—the Alaska population is among the most transient in the nation. Future generations of Alaskans would be unlikely to benefit from the private savings of current residents.

The majority of the credit for the establishment of the fund, particularly the PFD, goes to Governor Jay Hammond (1974–1982), who was a major force behind both. Lost in history is that Governor Keith Miller (1969–1970) introduced the first legislation to create a petroleum-based endowment fund in 1970, though it did not pass the legislature. Moreover, when a bill to create a fund in statute passed the legislature in 1975, Hammond vetoed it. He believed that such a fund could not be established by statute without violating the state constitutional prohibition against dedicated funds.[4] He also thought that the bill's proposed contribution rate of 50 percent of royalties was too high.

The Constitutional Amendment Setting up the Permanent Fund

In 1976 Hammond proposed a constitutional amendment to establish the fund. The amendment was adopted by a 2 to 1 margin in a vote of the people that same year. The amendment (added to Article IX on Finance and Taxation, as Section 15) reads:

> At least twenty-five percent of all mineral lease rentals, royalties, royalty sale proceeds, federal mineral revenue sharing payments and bonuses received by the State shall be placed in a permanent fund, the principal of which shall be used only for those income-producing investments specifically designated by law as eligible for permanent fund investment. All income from the permanent fund shall be deposited in the general fund unless otherwise provided by law.

The amendment language was purposely vague, reflecting that opinions differed on why the fund was set up—to get money out of the hands of the legislature or to build for a future after oil—as well as how the fund should be managed.

As the amendment states, and a fact not well understood by many Alaskans and people Outside, only 25 percent of rents and royalties paid to the state from the sale of depleting resources, including minerals, would be deposited in a fund, from which they could not be withdrawn. Because other state petroleum revenues—production, property, and income taxes—were not subject to deposit into the fund, the actual contribution rate from total oil revenues was approximately 10 percent.

The choice of the 25 percent royalty contribution was primarily a political decision rather than a conscious attempt to determine what rate would meet a particular long-term economic or financial goal. The question was how much Alaska could afford to spend out of current revenues without compromising spending in future years. Saving too little and spending too much would benefit the current generation of Alaskans, but would shortchange future generations. Saving too much and spending too little today, by contrast, would shift the benefits from oil wealth unequally to future generations. But determining the right balance depended upon circumstances that could not be determined in advance. This included the total oil production over the life of the fields, the price at which it would be sold, the return on fund investments, the future population, the growth of the nonpetroleum economy, and many other factors.

In fact, as petroleum revenues started to flood into the state treasury in the late 1970s, the legislature increased the contribution requirement to 50 percent for all mineral lease rentals, royalties, royalty sale proceeds, net profit shares, and federal mineral revenue sharing payments on leases issued after December 1, 1979, and 50 percent of all bonuses received on leases issued after February 1, 1980.[5] The huge Prudhoe Bay and Kuparuk fields, however, were not affected by this change.

In times of low oil prices, as from the late 1980s until the early 2000s, state officials were understandably concerned that such a high percentage would result in overly constricting needed state services. Accordingly, in 2003 the legislature reduced the percentage to 25 percent. Additional changes in the deposit formula were enacted in 2008, when oil prices rose again.[6] The percentage will no doubt be changed again from time to time in the future as the result of volatile oil prices, though the 25 percent constitutional minimum will remain in effect (unless a constitutional amendment changes it).

Questions of Management and Types of Investments

The next question was how the fund would be organized and managed. After an interim period of management by the Department of Revenue, the legislature created the Alaska Permanent Fund Corporation (APFC) in 1980, as a vehicle for insulating decision making from politics while retaining accountability. The corporation would be governed by a board of trustees appointed by the governor and would report to the legislature, but would otherwise be independent.

The legislature then turned to the question of the type of investment portfolio the fund should hold. The debate was over whether it should be a development fund or a savings account. A development fund would invest in Alaska projects designed to strengthen and diversify the economy, in anticipation of the decline in oil production. Supporters of this position argued that there were many projects that could help the state's economy grow but could not secure financing from private financial institutions. In their view, the Permanent Fund could be a financing source for such projects and the vehicle to concentrate state efforts to build a more diversified state economy through investments in infrastructure and industrial development. Supporters of using the fund for in-state development also argued that if the fund invested solely in a portfolio of national and international bonds and stocks, it would not be helping the Alaska economy and its benefits would go outside the state.

Proponents of the savings account approach argued that investing in a portfolio of financial assets not directly linked to the Alaska economy would maximize the long-term financial earnings of the fund, and that those earnings would then be available to the state for any purpose needed in the future. A state development fund would, they believed, be driven by political rather than sound economic decisions. Basing investment choices on politics would produce neither a positive financial return for the state nor a strong portfolio of investments. Investing outside the state would diversify the overall economic portfolio of the state—an important consideration for an economy with such a narrow economic base.

After considerable debate, it was determined that it would be most appropriate to create a savings account to be invested in a conservative portfolio of financial assets consisting primarily of bonds, at least at the outset.

Determining Earnings and Some More Fund Terminology

The last decision necessary to start operation of the fund was choosing the method for determining earnings. In explaining the terms relating to operations and earnings, as noted earlier, since the early 2000s the fund managers have changed some terms to refer to certain accounts. To avoid confusion we explain these changes from the previous to the present terms, but use the current terms when explaining the operation of the fund.

Deposits into the fund from the sale of state-owned mineral resources and other sources constitute what was initially called the *fund corpus*, now called the *fund principal* or *nonspendable account*, which cannot be spent. Before 2010 this was called the *reserved account*. The income of the fund, generated by its assets, is deposited in the *earnings reserve* or *earnings reserve account* and is available for spending, or *appropriation*, by the Alaska legislature. Although the earnings reserve may have some cash on hand, the reserve is also largely invested.

In calculating the earnings and the amount of money available to be spent each year, the Alaska Permanent Fund differs from most endowments, which typically draw off a fixed percentage of the value of the portfolio each year—a *percent of market value* (POMV).[7] Because the fund was initially invested in bonds, it was logical when the legislature created the fund to define the earnings available for appropriation by its realized income—the income that actually accrues each year as opposed to a fixed percentage of the fund's value. This realized or actual income is called *statutory net income*. This is the sum of interest and dividends received, plus the *realized capital gains* on the sale of assets in the portfolio. Realized capital gains are the difference between the sale and purchase prices for fund assets sold during the year.[8]

Although the principal of the fund is meant to be permanent, the method of drawing off earnings each year based on statutory net income does not protect the principal from inflation. To deal with this problem, the fund is inflation proofed. This involves an annual appropriation of statutory net income going back into the principal of the fund. The amount added is enough so that the fund's prior year real value (adjusted for inflation) remains unchanged.

Statutory net income is allocated by the legislature both to inflation proofing and to the *dividend fund*, from which annual PFDs are paid to qualified residents. The formula for the amount to be appropriated for the dividend is 21 percent of one-half of the cumulative statutory net income for the preceding five years. This formula, in effect, creates a five-year rolling average of net income in order to smooth out anomalous peaks and valleys in the annual income stream. The appropriation to the PFD account takes precedence over that for inflation proofing. In most years, some fund income remains after these two payments. This remaining income is added to an account, currently known as the *earnings reserve account*, a separate account within the Permanent Fund available for the legislature to appropriate funds from, but which has not yet been designated for a particular purpose. Before 2010 this was often called the *unreserved fund balance*.

Based on the constitutional amendment, the earnings were to be deposited in the state general fund unless otherwise provided by law. In fact, as indicated earlier, some of the earnings have been retained in the earnings reserve account. The rationale is that these earnings may be required to fund a legislative appropriation in a year when net income earned that year is insufficient. This would be the case, for instance, if statutory net income were insufficient to fully fund both the dividend and inflation proofing. This account has been used to inflation proof the fund, and occasionally a portion has been put back into the principal of the fund after a large balance has accumulated. This practice has also insulated these funds from legislative appropriation for any other purpose.

These provisions for management and operation of the fund have made it one of the most successful SWFs, despite its modest size. Hence the fund's creation was arguably one of the most successful as well as popular Alaska policy decisions since statehood. For this reason, changing the role of the fund, and particularly the way the PFD is calculated, has met stiff resistance in the past even in times of major revenue shortfalls. Similar resistance is likely to occur as the state attempts to deal with its budget shortfalls for the years following 2014. However, as these shortfalls have continued, resistance seems to be softening.

3. ESTABLISHING THE PERMANENT FUND DIVIDEND PROGRAM: CONSTRAINTS ON THE OWNER STATE AND POLITICAL AMBIVALENCE

Many factors have contributed to the success of the fund, but arguably it would not have survived and grown without the creation of the Permanent Fund Dividend program. The dividend provides a way for the current generation to benefit directly from a savings account established to benefit future generations of Alaskans, many of whom have not yet been born or have not yet arrived in the state. In the absence of the dividend, which creates a constituency of defenders of the fund, it would have been politically difficult to keep putting money into savings for future generations.

When state government programs expanded in the late 1970s, some Alaskans were concerned that most of the economic benefits would go to special interest groups and that the general population would not receive a fair share. Thus, another impetus for creation of the PFD was to spread a share of the oil wealth as widely and equitably as possible among all Alaskans.

The original PFD proposal, put forward by Governor Hammond in 1980 and passed by the legislature, based the size of the dividend on the number of years a person had been a state resident, to a maximum of twenty-five years. Twenty-five years of residency would entitle them to a maximum of twenty-five "shares." This feature was designed to reward longevity and promote a more stable population in a historically transient state. But newly arrived residents Ron and Penny Zobel challenged the constitutionality of favoring some Alaskans based on how long they had lived in the state, and the plan was declared unconstitutional in 1982 under the equal protection and privileges and immunities clauses of the U.S. Constitution.[9] This is an example of the fact that, although Alaska may be an Owner State, it is still part of a federal system and thus not entirely in charge of its own policies. In response, the legislature established the current program, which makes equal payments from the earnings of the fund to all Alaskans, including children, who have been residents of the state for at least one year. The first payment of $1,000 was made in 1982 from a special appropriation by the legislature.

The PFD program was not initially popular among some politicians, particularly those who favored using fund earnings to build infrastructure for economic development. Others felt that the PFD would be spent frivolously by many Alaskans. A study of the initial dividend payout was conducted to determine whether Alaskans were "wasting" their PFDs, but there was no evidence of a widespread increase in spending on "wine, women, and song."[10] Given the widespread popularity of the PFD today and its strong support by most politicians, it is hard to imagine the tough fight required to get it enacted. A major compromise that Hammond felt he had to make to get the PFD passed was to agree to the abolition of the state personal income tax, a compromise that he later regretted.[11]

4. THE DEVELOPMENT OF THE FUND AND THE PFD

The Permanent Fund and the PFD have both been major economic and political success stories as far as most Alaskans and their politicians are concerned. Let us look briefly at the reason for this success by considering the development of the fund and the PFD.[12]

Development of the Fund

Our treatment of the development of the fund is divided into two parts. First we look at the growth of the fund and its investment policy and then at the reasons for the fund's widely agreed upon success as a way to preserve some of Alaska's petroleum wealth. The success can be summed up in two sets of figures. One is that from its inception until June 30, 2014, a total of $22.3 billion was deposited in the fund, and $21.6 billion has been paid out in PFDs. Thus, the fund's investment policy has enabled it to pay out almost as much as it has taken in from oil revenues and special deposits by the legislature and still have a total principal value of $53 billion as of April 2016. The other set of figures is that, also as of June 30, 2014, the fund has paid out 47 percent of its earnings to current generations, and 53 percent has been saved for future generations.

Growth of the Fund and Its Investment Policy

Tables 25.1A and 25.1B respectively show the accumulation of the fund over the years and its status as of the end of FY 2014.[13] The Alaska Permanent Fund Corporation (APFC) uses some special terms to describe various aspects of the accounting of the fund, many of which are not intuitive. Preceding Tables 25.1A and 25.1B is Table 25.1 which provides an explanation of terms, those used both currently and in the past.

From the inception of the fund in 1977 through 2014 the state received $180 billion in oil revenues. Based on calculations by the author in 2012, at which time the state had received $170 billion in oil revenues, $45 billion (26 percent) had been deposited into the Permanent Fund and other savings accounts (close to $20 billion into the Permanent Fund itself), and $125 billion (74 percent) was spent on government services and programs.[14] The fund produces a large annual stream of earnings. In fact, the statutory net income (rental and interest income, dividends, and any net gains on the sale of assets) has exceeded current oil revenues several times since 2010. However, if inflation had been netted out and the earnings smoothed over time, the annual earnings would have fallen short of current petroleum revenues, particularly between 2008 and 2013, in part because of the global recession of 2008–2010.

Of the fund's total value of $51.2 billion in June 2014 (see Table 25.1B), most of the balance ($45 billion) was in the principal where it is permanently protected by the constitution from being spent. Appropriations from earnings have been primarily for three purposes: payment of the dividend, inflation proofing, and, on occasion, augmentation

TABLE 25.1

Permanent Fund Statistics Past and Present

(Including Explanation of Specialized Terms)

Dedicated state revenues: Mineral royalties and lease revenues deposited into the fund's principal as directed by the constitution and Alaska statutes.

Earnings reserve: Often called the "Assigned Fund Balance" by fund managers (see Table 25.1B), meaning it is the account set aside or dedicated to a particular purpose. This is the part of the fund available—assigned—for appropriations by the legislature. It is realized income earned from the fund's investments. The legislature appropriates funds from this account for dividends, inflation proofing, and for other lawful purposes.

Inflation proofing: Each year an amount is appropriated from the **earnings reserve** to the fund's principal to offset the effects of inflation. This deposit becomes part of the principal of the fund and like all other funds in the principal cannot be spent.

Realized earnings: Designated as "Assigned realized earnings" at the bottom of Table 25.1B. Income from various cash flows, such as stock dividends, bond interest and real estate rental cashflow. These include net profit or loss from the sale of an investment. They are in the form of available liquid cash assets.

Settlement earnings: An appropriation to the principal of the fund from the proceeds of a lawsuit with the oil and gas or related industries.

Special appropriations: Additional monies deposited into the fund principal by the legislature. These are separate from the appropriations required by the constitution or statutes. Special appropriations happen infrequently and at the legislature's discretion.

State revenue deposited: Includes **Dedicated state revenue, Special appropriations, and Settlement earnings.**

Unrealized appreciation or depreciation on invested assets: Gains and losses depending upon the performance of investments.

Unrealized earnings: Current market value of an asset not yet sold minus its original cost. These assets are not in liquid cash form but are value on paper.

Unreserved earnings account: The name of the **earnings reserve (or Assigned fund balance)** until the name was changed in 2010.

TABLE 25.1A

Alaska Permanent Fund Earnings Statistics: From Inception to 2014

	$ BILLIONS
Fund Principal (Nonspendable Account)	**$45.0**
Inflation Proofing	$15.6
State Revenue Deposited	$15.3
Special Appropriations and Settlement Earnings (first deposit made in 1981, the last one in 2003)	$7.0
Net Unrealized Gains	$7.1

TABLE 25.1B

The Alaska Permanent Fund as of June 2014

		$ BILLIONS	
Total Value			**$51.2**
Fund Principal (Nonspendable Account)			
Contributions and Appropriations		$37.9	
Dedicated state revenues	$15.3		
Special appropriations	$6.8		
Inflation proofing	$15.6		
Settlement earnings	$0.2		
Unrealized Appreciation on Invested Assets		$7.1	
Total Fund Principal			**$45.0**
The Earnings Reserve (Assigned Account)			**$6.2**
Assigned realized earnings account	$5.2		
Assigned unrealized appreciation on invested assets	$1.0		

Source: Basewd on the Permanent Fund Corporation's *Annual Financial Report, 2014*, at http://www.apfc.org/_amiReportsArchive/FY2014AnnualReport.pdf. Table developed by the author with assistance from Kristina Klimovich.

of the principal of the fund. About half of total appropriations, $21.6 billion, have been for PFDs which have benefited current Alaskans. The other half, $19.8 billion for inflation proofing and deposits of earnings, will benefit future generations.

The principal of the fund has been built up from four sources. The first consists of the constitutionally mandated contributions of mineral royalties, rents, and bonuses, the vast majority of which are from oil production. As of June 30, 2014, those contributions totaled $15.3 billion. The second source consists of special contributions, which totaled $7.0 billion as of June 30, 2014. These special contributions have been purely discretionary appropriations by the legislature from various sources, including surplus general fund revenues and funds received from the settlement of disputes with the oil companies over oil taxes and royalties. The legislature has also made appropriations from time to time into the principal of the fund from some of its accumulated earnings. The third source is the annual deposit designed to protect the value of the principal against erosion by inflation. The fund trustees realized quite early (during an era of high inflation in the late 1970s and early 1980s) that if all the interest, dividends, and capital gains generated by the fund were taken as income, the real value of the fund would fall over time. To offset inflation, part of the earnings must be poured back into the fund principal. In 1982 the legislature, acting on the recommendation of the fund trustees, directed that an annual appropriation from earnings should go back into the fund principal, sufficient to maintain the purchasing power of the principal from the previous year. From its inception to June 2014, inflation proofing has added $15.6 billion to the principal.[15] The fourth component of the growth of the fund's principal is the unrealized appreciation on assets held in this portion of the fund, amounting to $7.1 billion by the middle of 2014. When those appreciated assets are sold, that $7.1 billion—the difference between their sale price and purchase cost—will be transferred to the earnings reserve.

As explained earlier, the fund also contains an earnings reserve account (technically called the *assigned realized earnings account* and formerly the *unreserved earnings account*), which totaled $6.2 billion in mid-2014 (see Table 25.1B). The earnings reserve account grew by $1.5 billion in the second half of 2014 to stand at $7.7 billion on December 31, 2014. These are funds that have not yet been appropriated by the legislature for a particular purpose. Until money in this account is formally appropriated, the corporation continues to manage it. The balance of the fund calculated at the end of each fiscal year excludes the income set aside to pay the dividend. Consequently, Table 25.1B excludes the $1.2 billion in the dividend account that was distributed as PFDs in the fall of 2014. The amount in this account is not cumulative and simply reflects the funds in it in any one year. Small amounts are also set aside from this account for other appropriations.

The fund has a target rate of return on its portfolio of 5 percent net of inflation, a rate that reflects a relatively conservative investment strategy sometimes called the "prudent investor" rule.[16] This means that:

> The corporation shall exercise the judgment and care under the circumstances then prevailing that an institutional investor of ordinary prudence, discretion and intelligence exercises in the designation and management of large investments entrusted to it.[17]

Over time the legislature, at the suggestion of the trustees, has allowed the fund to expand its portfolio to include other types of assets besides bonds. The trustees believe that maximizing long-term earnings requires investing in equities (stocks) and other assets as well as bonds, even though such a portfolio may be more volatile. Nowadays, a fund fully invested in bonds would be imprudent, as it would not be sufficiently diversified. Moreover, the statutory direction to maximize total returns (while maintaining the principal) means that the fund has to be invested in diversified assets with some income-producing ability.

In 2011, the investment return was 20.6 percent but dropped to –0.1 percent in 2012. In 2013 it was back up to 10.5 percent and to 15.5 percent for 2014.[18] According to APFC, from the mid-1980s until 2014 the average return was 9.2 percent. After adjusting for an average rate of inflation of 2.9 percent over those years, the real return was 6.3 percent, and well over the 5 percent statutory target return rate.[19]

Accounting for the Success of the Fund

By virtually all measures the Permanent Fund has been a successful vehicle for converting a depleting asset—oil—into a permanent financial asset. Eight factors are particularly important in accounting for that success.

First, establishment of the fund recognized the challenge of protecting petroleum wealth by focusing attention on saving for the future. It is like an automatic payroll deduction for a retirement account, compared with taking whatever income might be left over at the end of each month and putting that into savings. Second, the size of the original dedicated revenue stream, 25 percent of rents, royalties, and bonuses, was large enough to make a difference, but not a large enough share of total revenues to generate opposition from legislators and administration officials who were interested in expanding government spending beyond what current revenues would allow. As we saw earlier, this 25 percent has been tinkered with from time to time, sometimes increasing the percentage and sometimes returning to the constitutional minimum of 25 percent. In late 2015, Governor Walker, in response to the major budget deficits, suggested putting all oil revenues into the fund to generate income to cover these major deficits.

Third, good luck also played a role in the fund's success, which has been due in part to a bull—rising—market for investments and high petroleum revenues during much of the fund's existence. For most of the years since the fund was created, with the major exception of the world financial crisis of 2008–2010, there have been bull markets for securities and other investments. This has enabled the fund to increase the value of its assets and post good returns that have increased the size of the principal. It would have been a different story if the markets had been flatter and particularly if there had been declining—bear—markets for significant periods.

Moreover, at least up until 2015, petroleum revenues have been large enough in most years that lawmakers have been able to satisfy constituent demands without tapping into Permanent Fund earnings. Oil revenues enabled the state to create a number of agencies to promote economic development in the state, including the Alaska Renewable Resources Corporation (ARRC), the Alaska Industrial Development and Export Authority (AIDEA), and the Alaska Housing Finance Corporation (AHFC). These agencies diverted attention from the Permanent Fund as a source of funding for economic development, allowing it to be maintained solely as a savings account. The establishment of these agencies was made possible in the early 1980s, just as the fund was starting to grow, because of a period of high oil prices. High revenues also allowed lawmakers to satisfy other constituent demands without tapping Permanent Fund earnings, like eliminating the personal income tax (which was likely not a positive move, see Section 9, below) and expanding state loan programs.

Fourth, the settlement of a number of outstanding disputes over royalties and oil tax payments resulted in increased revenues to the state in the early 1990s that were used to create a separate financial account, the Constitutional Budget Reserve Fund (commonly known as the CBR), the purpose of which was to cover revenue shortfalls when oil prices were low (in high revenue years the "loans" to the general fund are supposed to be repaid to the CBR). The CBR has provided a buffer against the use of fund earnings to cover budget deficits.[20]

Fifth, although the ultimate purpose of the fund was never clearly defined, the decision to manage the portfolio to maximize long-term financial returns gave it a clear focus. By eschewing any discussion of how income should be used, the fund's managers have been free to concentrate on a well-defined objective of maximizing returns, and it has been easy to evaluate its performance against that objective.

Sixth, there was a lingering perception that the state had squandered its original windfall from oil—the $900 million in lease sale bonuses collected in 1969—and that it should not make that mistake again. On several occasions, mainly before 2000, revenues have been sufficient to allow lawmakers to make special appropriations to the fund. This has resulted in $7 billion of extra deposits into the fund corpus (see Table 25.1A, "special appropriations").

Seventh, the APFC has been able to operate independently of the legislative and executive branches of government, particularly in the determination of investments. Being free of political intervention, it is able to perform its duties in a highly professional manner. In this regard, the corporation has been fortunate to have as trustees a group of visionary and responsible custodians of the fund, such as long-time Alaskan banker Elmer Rasmuson, the first board chairman. The fund has also been able to attract a high-quality staff, beginning with the first executive director, Dave Rose, through to the late Michael J. Burns, who was director for twelve years (2003-2015). Several legislators and administration officials also served on the Board of Trustees and helped guide the formation of the fund to help ensure its success.

Finally, the corporation has attempted to be as transparent as possible to the general public as well as the legislature. Board meetings are open to the public and held in communities throughout the state. The corporation publishes a clearly written annual report, produces educational materials for Alaskans, maintains a speakers' bureau, and has a user-friendly and informative website.

Development of the PFD

The major development and effects of the PFD have been in the political realm. This political dimension is considered in Sections 6 through 9. Here we briefly summarize the statistical aspects of the PFD's development.

TABLE 25.2

Permanent Fund Dividend Statistics: Selected Years and Overall Totals for 1982–2014

DIVIDEND YEAR	STATE POPULATION	DIVIDEND APPLICATIONS RECEIVED	PAID	DIVIDEND DOLLAR AMOUNT	AMOUNT DISBURSED
2014	735,601	670,053	631,306	$1884.00	$1,189,289,748.00
2013	736,399	668,362	631,470	$900.00	$568,323,000.00
2012	732,298	673,978	610,633	$878.00	$536,135,774.00
2011	722,190	672,237	615,122	$1,174.00	$722,153,228.00
2010	710,231	663,938	611,522	$1,281.00	$783,359,682.00
2009	692,314	654,462	621,146	$1,305.00	$810,595,530.00
2008	679,720	641,291	610,096	$2,069.00*	$1,262,288,624.00
1998	617,082	581,803	565,256	$1,540.88	$870,991,665.28
1997	609,655	573,057	554,769	$1,296.54	$719,280,199.26
1996	605,212	564,362	546,045	$1,130.68	$617,402,160.60
1995	601,581	563,020	541,842	$990.30	$536,586,132.60
1994	600,622	557,836	534,599	$983.90	$525,991,956.10
1993	596,906	549,066	527,946	$949.46	$501,263,609.16
1985	543,900	525,145	518,479	$404.00	$209,465,516.00
1984	524,000	490,413	481,349	$331.29	$159,466,110.21
1983	499,100	465,567	457,209	$386.15	$176,551,255.35
1982	464,300	484,344	469,741	$1000.00	$469,741,000.00
Overall Totals		**19,283,868**	**18,461,308**	**$37,027.41**	**$21,141,159,036.89**

* The 2008 dividend amount excludes a one-time $1,200 addition of the 2008 Resource Rebate.

Source: Adapted by the author from Alaska Permanent Fund Corporation website, retrieved October 30, 2014, at http://www.pfd.state.ak.us/DivisionInfo/SummaryApplicationsPayments

Using selected years, Table 25.2 provides a picture of the gradual increase in the size of the PFD over the years, the number of applications, and the cumulative total paid out for the dividend. The general increase in the size of the PFD has been due to the good management of the fund, combined with bull markets for securities. Over the years, the dividend has risen steadily in amount with some dips. The dips since 2009 have largely been due to the world economic crisis of 2008–2010 and the major fall in all investment portfolios, including that of the Permanent Fund. Even with the recovery in 2011 and 2012, the PFD was still smaller through 2013 than the five or so years earlier because of the five-year average used to calculate the amount of fund income available for the PFD.

But by 2014, due to high investment returns, the PFD had risen to $1,884, the third highest in its thirty-three-year history, just under $200 short of the $2,069 second highest payout in 2008 and of the record payout of $2072 in 2015.[21] Those Alaskans who received a dividend for the first thirty-four years of the program (through 2015) received an average of just under $1,130 per year. Moreover, because of the high recent earnings of the fund, the dividend is likely to remain at or above the 2015 payout through at least 2020. This assumes that the dividend amount will be based on the five-year rolling average as it was as of 2015, and is not in some way reformed and based on a different method of calcuation.

5. A COMPARATIVE PERSPECTIVE: OTHER SWFs

One measure of the strengths and weaknesses of the Alaska Permanent Fund is to compare it with other SWFs around the world. Comparison is also useful for later in the chapter in looking at the politics and policy aspects of the Alaska fund, particularly possible alternative uses and management.

Table 25.3 lists the top SWFs by value in the United States and around the world as of 2014. The table shows that the Alaska Permanent Fund was ranked twenty-fifth in the world in value. Even so, it was the largest SWF compared with other U.S. states with similar funds. This is true, even though Alaska's fund is far from the oldest of U.S. SWFs (the Texas fund was established in 1854, New Mexico's in 1958, and Wyoming's in 1974). Like Alaska's fund, those of Texas and Wyoming are funded by revenue from commodities—principally oil and gas and other minerals—while New Mexico's is funded by noncommodity sources. The North Dakota fund was not established until 2011, reflecting the fact that large-scale oil and gas development in that state is relatively new. As a consequence, that fund had accumulated under $1 billion as of 2013, but $2.4 billion by June 2014 and $3.1 billion by January 2016.

Not all SWFs are created and managed for the same purpose or purposes as the Alaska Permanent Fund. Comparing two other funds with Alaska's shows the differences behind their creation and how they are operated. The two are those of Norway and the western Canadian province of Alberta. These funds are described in Box 25.1 (on pages 908-09). The Alberta Heritage Fund has been used for much broader purposes than Alaska's, but the Norwegian fund less so. Both funds are potentially subject to more political forces than the Alaska fund. But since Norway is an independent country, a major purpose of the Norwegian fund has been to avoid elements of the resource curse.

Turning to an example of a fund in the United States, the Texas Permanent School Fund's earnings are used to fund K–12 education, while its Permanent University Fund, a much smaller SWF, funds some of the public universities in Texas. The issue of whether or not the Alaska Permanent Fund should be used for other purposes than at present,

TABLE 25.3

Top 25 Sovereign Wealth Funds around the World and Other Selected Funds in 2014

	COUNTRY	FUND NAME	ASSETS IN $US BILLIONS	INCEPTION DATE	MAIN SOURCE OF ASSETS
1	Norway	Government Pension Fund—Global	893.0	1990	Oil
2	Abu Dhabi (United Arab Emirates—UAE)	Abu Dhabi Investment Authority	773.0	1976	Oil
3	Saudi Arabia	SAMA Foreign Holdings	757.2	n/a	Oil
4	China	China Investment Corporation	652.7	2007	Non-Commodity
5	China	SAFE Investment Company	567.98*	1997	Non-Commodity
6	Kuwait	Kuwait Investment Authority	548.0	1953	Oil
7	China—Hong Kong	Hong Kong Monetary Authority Investment Portfolio	400.2	1993	Non-Commodity
8	Singapore	Government of Singapore Investment Corp.	320.0	1981	Non-Commodity
9	Qatar	Qatar Investment Authority	256.0	2005	Oil
10	China	National Social Security Fund	201.6	2000	Non-Commodity
11	Singapore	Temasek Holdings	177.0	1974	Non-Commodity
12	Australia	Australian Future Fund	95.0	2006	Non-Commodity
13	Dubai—UAE	Investment Corporation of Dubai	90.0	2006	Oil
14	Russia	Reserve Fund	88.9	2008	Oil
15	South Korea	Korea Investment Corporation	84.7	2005	Non-Commodity
16	Russia	National Welfare Fund	79.9	2008	Oil
17	Kazakhstan	Samruk-Kazyn JSC	77.5	2008	Non-Commodity
18	Algeria	Revenue Regulation Fund	77.2	2000	Oil and Gas
19	Kazakhstan	Kazkhstan National Fund	77.0	2000	Oil
20	Dubai—UAE	Investment Corporation of Dubai	70.0	2006	Oil
21	Abu Dhabi—UAE	International Petroleum Investment Company	68.4	1984	Oil

	COUNTRY	FUND NAME	ASSETS IN $US BILLIONS	INCEPTION DATE	MAIN SOURCE OF ASSETS
22	Libya	Libyan Investment Authority	66.0	2006	Oil
23	Iran	National Development Fund of Iran	62.0	2011	Oil and Gas
24	Abu Dhabi—UAE	Mubadal Development Company	60.9	2002	Oil
25	**USA—Alaska**	**Alaska Permanent Fund**	**51.7**	**1976**	**Oil**
Other Selected Funds					
26	Malaysia	Khazanah Nasional	41.6	1993	Non-Commodity
28	**USA—Texas**	**Texas Permanent School Fund**	**37.7**	**1854**	**Oil**
29	Azerbaijan	State Oil Fund	37.3	1999	Oil
30	Ireland	National Pensions Reserve Fund	27.4	2001	Non-Commodity
31	France	Strategic Investment Fund	25.5	2008	Non-Commodity
32	New Zealand	New Zealand Superannuation Fund	21.8	2003	Non-Commodity
34	Iraq	Development Fund for Iraq	18.0	2003	Oil
35	Canada	Alberta's Heritage Fund	17.5	1976	Oil and Gas
36	**USA—Texas**	**Permanent University Fund**	**17.2**	**1876**	**Oil and Gas**
38	Chile	Social and Economic Stabilization Fund	15.2	2007	Copper
48	Italy	Italian Strategic Fund	6.0	2011	Non-Commodity
49	**USA—Wyoming**	**Permanent Wyoming Mineral Fund**	**5.6**	**1974**	**Minerals**
55	**USA—Alabama**	**Alabama Trust Fund**	**2.5**	**1985**	**Oil and Gas**
56	**USA—North Dakota**	**North Dakota Legacy Fund**	**2.4**	**2011**	**Oil and Gas**

* Figures available for 2010 only.

Source: Sovereign Wealth Fund Institute, Fund Rankings 2014, "Sovereign Wealth Fund Rankings," at http://www.swfinstitute.org/fund-rankings/. Table modified by Clive Thomas and Kristina Klimovich.

BOX 25.1

The Alberta Heritage Fund and the Norwegian Government Pension Fund-Global

THE ALBERTA HERITAGE FUND

The Alberta Heritage Fund (AHF) was established in 1976, the same year as the Alaska Permanent Fund, but with a very different structure and objective. At its inception the AHF had four broad objectives and thus lacked clarity of purpose. These were (1) to serve as a savings account to offset resource depletion, (2) to reduce the debt load of the province, (3) to improve residents' quality of life, and (4) to strengthen and diversify the economy.

The fund was created by legislative action rather than constitutional amendment with little public debate. Deposits and withdrawals are both controlled by the provincial parliament with no specific guidelines. Because of a parliamentary system operating at the national and provincial level in Canada and strong political party discipline, control of the fund, including investment policy, rests with the cabinet of the government in office. So the direction of the fund from its inception has been in the hands of politicians. Early management decisions undermined the initial success of the fund. For one thing, no long-term target rate of return was set, and the fund had no policy for inflation proofing its principal. In addition, to further its multiple objectives, the fund was divided into five separate management divisions. Alaska's Permanent Fund avoided all of these pitfalls.

The most controversial AHF management divisions invested in projects like parks, hospitals, and irrigation ditches to improve the quality of life of Alberta residents, and as such, it was not expected to earn a financial return. In addition, the division that was charged with economic development invested heavily in corporations owned by the province (called crown corporations). Critics suggested that these investments were motivated by politics rather than sound economics and were sometimes made to subsidize corporations in order to disguise their losses.

For these and other reasons, the AHF lost value during the 1980s and was restructured in the 1990s. Its investment policy now has a narrower focus to maximize its long-term financial return and to generate income for the province's general fund. A form of inflation proofing was also adopted to maintain the value of the fund. However, because the management of the fund remains controlled by the provincial cabinet, there is still concern that it is simply a tool to further the political goals of the party in power. The assets of the AHF in December 2015 were just under $18 billion versus close to $50 billion for Alaska's Permanent Fund. This was just about $4,300 per Albertan compared to almost $70,000 per Alaskan.

THE NORWEGIAN GOVERNMENT PENSION FUND-GLOBAL

Norway actually has two SWFs, collectively called the Government Pension Fund of Norway. The smaller of the two is the Government Pension Fund—Norway (formerly the National Insurance Scheme Fund), established in 1967 and worth about $22.6 billion in the fall of 2015. The other is the Norwegian Government Pension Fund-Global, the world's most valuable SWF. It was worth $882.00 billion in November 2015, or just under $170,800 per Norwegian. It is this larger fund that we focus on here.

Established in 1990 as the Government Pension Fund (the name was changed in 2006), the Global Fund, like the AHF, lacks constitutional protection and is controlled by the government in power rather than an independent board of trustees (which is the case with Norway's other SWF). Parliament allocates to the fund whatever budget surplus remains after paying the cost of government operations and draws from the fund when necessary to cover budget shortfalls.

The fund was created less as a savings account for future generations than as a mechanism to deal with the "absorption problem" of a massive infusion of money. Alaska and Alberta are semi-sovereign governments within a federal system with open borders between their respective states and provinces that allow the free movement of capital and labor. Because Norway is a sovereign nation, when wealth from oil increases domestic demand, it is more difficult to increase domestic supplies of labor and capital without overheating the economy and risking the consequences of the resource curse. The Norwegian solution has been to insulate the economy from an overly rapid expansion by investing much of the new wealth outside the country using the Global Fund. This contrasts with the smaller Norwegian SWF, which is required to invest in domestic companies.

Growth of the budget, monitored to prevent overheating the economy, determines the size of annual deposits and withdrawals from the Global Fund. Deposits and fund earnings grew rapidly between 2005 and 2014, due to high oil prices and because exports of Norwegian oil were surpassed only by those of Saudi Arabia, and the investment policy of the fund sought to maximize the long-term financial return.

The Norwegian structure for managing its petroleum wealth has yet to be put to a significant test. Oil revenues have grown faster than the budget for most of the Global Fund's short life, and the question of whether Norway is saving a sufficient share of current revenues for future generations will not be answered for a long time. But because its borders are closed, Norway has two advantages over Alaska. First, private savings will stay within the country to complement the savings in the Global Fund. Second, the fund does not need to pay a dividend to create a constituency. With a much less transitory population than Alaska's, it is current Norwegian residents who will also be the beneficiaries of savings for the future.

Source: Developed by the author with aid from Kristina Klimovich.

including various specific endowments, is briefly considered in the latter part of Section 8 and particularly in Section 9 of this chapter.

The Practical Realities of the Permanent Fund and the Dividend

We now move to the second part of the chapter and look at the socio-economic, political, and particularly the policy consequences that the fund and the PFD have had in Alaska.[22] Considered first in Section 6 are significant aspects of the fund's effects on Alaska's political economy. This is followed by two sections that look broadly at the effects of democracy on the fund and PFD. Section 7 examines how Alaskans view the fund and its uses, and Section 8 looks at the politics that underlie the transformation of the fund and particularly the PFD. Section 9 discusses future challenges, and the conclusion summarizes the essence of the development and politics of the fund and PFD.

6. THE EFFECTS OF THE FUND AND THE PFD ON ALASKA'S POLITICAL ECONOMY

This section provides an overview of the effects of the fund and the PFD on Alaska's political economy in general—that is, the interrelationship of the fund's and the PFD's economics and politics in Alaska over the years. This provides a foundation for analyzing their particular political and policy consequences and the future choices and challenges facing both politicians and the Alaska public. As the PFD has had a higher political profile than the fund, we look only briefly at the major economic effects of the fund and focus more on those regarding the PFD.

Effects of the Fund

The fund has certainly spread the benefits of oil development across generations of Alaskans. However, as we consider in the sections that follow, exactly how future generations will benefit from the fund is subject to considerable debate. The fund has also acted as an economic stabilizer by taking some of the oil money "off the table" during boom times, thus preventing the legislature from overheating the economy by too much government spending. This may have contributed to the fact that Alaska does not seem to have been subject to the resource curse, though conceivably that might yet occur.

In addition, the fund has taken off the table large amounts of oil revenues that might have been spent on projects that may or may not have been worthwhile. Large amounts of available cash tempt lawmakers to fund pet projects, including nonviable economic development projects, thus wasting the money. Fourth, and certainly the most important consequence of the fund for the vast majority of Alaskans, is that it made the PFD possible and, so far at least, enables its continuation.

Effects of the PFD

The effects of the PFD on Alaska's political economy are more complex and at the same time less clear than the effects of the fund itself. To make the complexity more manageable, we first consider what many argue are the positive actual and potential effects of the PFD, though not all Alaskans and economists see these as advantages. Then we consider some of the major actual and potential disadvantages, though again, whether some of them are negatives is a matter of opinion and hotly disputed by many inside and outside of the state. Finally, we look at some of the unanswered questions regarding the effects of the PFD.

The Pros of the PFD

Perhaps the major positive general effect of the PFD on Alaska's political economy is that it has, as envisioned by Governor Jay Hammond, provided a connection in the minds of citizens with the fund itself and likely works to prevent the fund from being used unwisely and frittered away. In addition, we can divide the pros of the PFD into three parts: its effect on the economy, its effect on individuals and households, and some academic points concerning income equality.

The Effect on the Economy.

When individuals spend their dividends it has a major influence on the Alaska economy, with a multiplier effect increasing economic activity. Studies suggest that several thousand jobs, mostly in trade and services, are attributable to the infusion of income into the economy from the PFD.[23] These jobs create a demand for workers that is met by an increase in migration to Alaska. So both the economy and the population are larger because of the PFD.

The annual dividend represents a substantial infusion of discretionary income into the pockets of Alaskans, and for several reasons, a large portion ends up as increased consumer spending. At first, after the inception of the program, the dividend was viewed as a windfall, which no one could be certain would continue. But after more than thirty years, the annual dividend payment has so far become a predictable event each fall. Households tend to save a large share of a windfall that they do not expect to recur. But if they expect to receive a dividend every year, they are more likely to spend it on current consumption. Second, since the dividend is an equal payment to every Alaskan, a large share of the total goes to lower income households that tend to spend most of their income, including PFDs, on current consumption. Third, although the dividends are subject to federal income tax, only a modest share goes to the federal government. Again, this is because of the equitable distribution of the PFD among both lower and higher income Alaska households. The infusion of over half a million PFDs each year also acts as a stabilizing influence on the economy, especially in times when state expenditures are down due to low oil prices or during downturns in the economy, such as the severe economic recession of 2008–2010.

The timing of dividend distribution also influences how people spend the income. The checks are paid just prior to the Christmas shopping season, a time surely favored by retailers who can and do aggressively compete for sales through advertising campaigns targeted at PFD spending.

The Effect on Individuals and Households.

Because each Alaskan receives the same dividend amount, its effects are felt more strongly in lower income households, particularly those with large families. For this reason, it is particularly important as a part of the income of residents of rural-bush Alaska where cash incomes are lower and households are larger. Take, for instance, the Wade Hampton census area in Southwest Alaska, which includes Bethel and several dozen villages. It had an estimated population in 2012 of 7,809, of which 93 percent were Alaska Natives. As the poorest region in the state, its 2011 per capita income was $11,476. A dividend payment that has ranged between $1,000 and $2,000 to each family member in most years has been a significant component of total cash income in the small communities scattered across this and other rural-bush census areas.[24] For this reason, ending the PFD program or lowering or capping the payout would be regressive—it would hurt poor families more than well-to-do families. In contrast, for higher income households, not only does the dividend represent a smaller share of total income, but the higher federal tax liability on the payment further reduces its importance to them.

Although we would expect most of the PFD to be discretionary income for households and spent similarly, there are some interesting exceptions. First, since Alaskans of all ages get the dividend, a large share goes to children. While there must be many interesting discussions around Alaska dinner tables about what will happen to those dividends, we know little about their outcomes in the aggregate. And to the extent children get to decide, economists have little to go on to predict their behavior. Second, households that are well off are likely to spend more of their income outside the state, or to save a larger share of current income. Third, lower income households are often "liquidity constrained" (unable to borrow or amass the cash necessary to purchase big ticket items). Such households are more likely to use their dividends to purchase large consumer durables like household appliances or snowmobiles that they otherwise would not be able to buy.

Economic Equity.

Regarding lower income individuals and households, there are some economic equity arguments in favor of maintaining the current PFD program. These are arguments often used by proponents of a basic income guarantee, also known as guaranteed minimum income.

First, the dividend distributes the benefits from the production of state-owned resources more equitably than any other possible method of spending the revenues from those resources. Second, advocates of the current PFD program point to a number of economic and social benefits, including the notion of maximizing personal freedom, especially the personal freedom of those of limited means. Thus, the PFD could be viewed as a means of empowering people by providing them with a "grubstake" to begin to build a personal portfolio of assets. Providing individuals with the means to save and invest is a useful strategy to help reduce poverty.

The dividend could also be viewed as a means to level income distribution in the state by raising the income for those at the bottom by a larger percentage than for those at the top. In fact, the gap between rich and poor (between the top 5 percent and the bottom 20 percent) has widened across the nation since the 1970s, but this gap has narrowed in Alaska over the years. Based on 2011 data, Alaska was ranked thirty-seventh of the fifty states in regard to income inequality, with New Mexico ranked at number one with the most unequal income distribution and Iowa at number fifty with the least. Some attribute this trend in Alaska and its ranking to the dividend.[25]

However, neither Alaskans nor their politicians seem to view income equality as a reason to support the continuation of the PFD. The dividend is viewed more as a payment out of the earnings of an asset owned by all residents with no social purpose attached. Moreover, the PFD has never been portrayed as a means of providing Alaskans with a "grubstake," either to build the economy or to help households save for the future. Nevertheless, the policy debate on the PFD will probably become more intense in the years to come, especially given the major revenue shortfalls beginning in 2014. These are arguments that can be used by those favoring the dividend's continuation, as they do make good economic sense.[26]

The Cons of the PFD

From the inception of the PFD program some Alaska politicians and citizens, if a small minority, have had concerns about the effects of giving away public money. As the size of the PFD has grown, concerns about its actual effects and its potential unintended consequences have also grown. The arguments used by those who see the dividend, in part or in whole, as a bad policy choice can be divided into economic and socio-political negatives.

The Economic Negatives.

One of the economic negatives is that the PFD diverts Permanent Fund earnings away from reinvestment that would make the fund larger and better able to sustain the Alaska economy in the future. A second is that money spent on the PFD should be used instead to invest in the infrastructure of the state rather than on consumption of goods and services. Third, many dividends are spent outside of Alaska and do not benefit the state's economy. Fourth, federal income tax takes part of the money paid out as dividends, so the economic stimulus to the economy is less than it would otherwise be if the money were used for public purposes and not subject to income tax. Fifth, it does not make sense for well-to-do Alaskans to receive a handout from state government.

Sixth, the dividend attracts people to Alaska who the state might not welcome, such as the elderly and those not working. To the extent that the PFD increases population, it increases the demand for and cost of housing as well as the demand for public services. Since most public services are paid for with oil revenues, a larger population dilutes that pool of revenues and the size of the dividend per person. The PFD could also increase the Alaska birth rate since it is the equivalent of a subsidy for having a child. And finally, in-migration to the state encouraged by the dividend increases the size of the labor pool and arguably results in lower wage rates. As a result, workers are no better off financially with the PFD—that is, without the dividend, wages would be higher, and perhaps enough to offset the annual value of the PFD.

The Socio-political Negatives.

Some of the downsides of the PFD combine social and political negatives. Others are largely political. In terms of the combined socio-economic effects of the PFD, many believe that the PFD has contributed to building a culture of dependence on government. An entire generation of Alaskans has grown up in an environment where citizens do not pay for public services (as of 2015 Alaska had neither a personal state income tax nor a state sales tax), but instead receive an annual check from the state. Some feel that because Alaskans do not pay for government through broad-based taxes, they are not connected to the process of deciding what public services generate sufficient benefits to warrant funding. And because people are not engaged in the process of collectively deciding how to spend public funds, there is a loss of a sense of community and an emphasis on "me first" individualism. Some also feel that the only aspect of the public sector that many Alaskans are concerned about is the size of their PFD. This is another manifestation of Alaska's political culture of dependent individualism.

The more purely political consequences include the question, if Alaska is giving away money to every citizen, how can the state argue that it needs special financial assistance from the federal government? But probably the major political negative of the PFD is that, because it has become so popular, it is now extremely difficult for the state to use any of the fund's earnings to finance essential government services, especially when oil revenues are down, arguably the main purpose for the fund when it was established. We go into the politics of the PFD and its likely consequences in Sections 7 through 9.

Unanswered Questions about the Effects of the PFD

While there are certain effects of the PFD that we can be fairly certain about, some of its economic effects and its socio-political consequences are not entirely clear. This is due to lack of research.

For instance, the effect of the dividend on the labor market is not clear. The population magnet effect could increase the supply of labor, but the PFD payment might lead some people to drop out of the labor force. In fact, whether or not there is a magnet effect of the PFD attracting people to the state is itself unclear. Although anecdotal evidence suggests this may be true, there are no formal studies linking the dividend to migration.

Moreover, those who think the dividend is a bad idea economically, socially, and politically have very little hard evidence to support their case. Most of the socio-economic arguments are based on value judgments about what society should and should not be in terms of individual versus communal values. In fact, sometimes the negative arguments themselves are extremely value-laden and without empirical evidence to support them, such as those who claim that PFDs are used to buy "bad" things like alcohol and drugs.

On the other hand, as of 2015, there is no doubt that the establishment of the PFD has transformed the perceived purpose of the Permanent Fund. The dividend has subordinated the fund's actual and potential purpose—dealing with fluctuating state revenues—to populist politics. It is to the politics and public policy of the PFD, and particularly how Alaska public opinion has affected its politics, that we turn next.

7. ATTITUDES OF ALASKANS TO POLICIES RELATING TO THE FUND AND THE PFD

If Alaska's political system were authoritarian, like those in China, Iran, and many oil-rich countries in the Persian Gulf, or if it were a developing and limited democracy like those found in Mexico and Nigeria, the general populace would have little say in how the state's petroleum wealth is managed and spent. But Alaska is a democracy with relatively high levels of public participation in politics and policy making and a strong link between the populace and their politicians.

The public has great potential to influence policy makers via the ballot box and has access to them between elections through lobbying by individuals and interest groups. Also, in contrast to authoritarian governments and often some limited democracies, there is a high level of administrative and political transparency in Alaska. This is certainly true regarding the Permanent Fund. The actions of the APFC and public officials regarding most aspects of the fund's management (including the PFD) are open to public view and that of the media. In combination, opportunities to participate in the policy process, enhanced by transparency, add an important actual and potential dimension to the politics and policy regarding the fund and the PFD.

The Alaska public's participation in, and potential influence on, fund policy is bolstered by the fact that Alaskans have a major stake in the PFD as part of their yearly income, even if the vast majority likely have little knowledge of the organization and management of the fund. Consequently, for the various reasons explained in the last section, and perhaps more than almost any other issue in state government, virtually every Alaskan has an opinion on the PFD. In other words, the PFD is a high-profile policy issue, and it has been ever since its enactment. This means that, consciously or subconsciously, the public also has an opinion on the fund and particularly how its earnings should be used.

As a result, in the face of fluctuating oil revenues and often the need to cut the state budget, a large number of Alaskans and the organizations to which they belong are often vocal in expressing their opinions to politicians on the fund and the PFD. These organizations include the Alaska State Chamber of Commerce (ASCC), the Alaska Federation of Natives (AFN), and the Alaska Municipal League (AML). These and other organizations sometimes issue statements and policy positions on the fund and the PFD.

TABLE 25.4

Alaska Public Opinion on the Permanent Fund and State Revenue Options

YEAR	QUESTIONS	RESPONSE
1976:	Permanent Fund (PF) established by constitutional amendment, voter ratio 2 to 1—75,588 to 38,518 votes	
1980:	Legislature approves Permanent Fund Dividend (PFD).	
1983:	How should the PF earnings be used?	Pay cash dividends to Alaskans—35% Fund major construction projects—25% Reinvest in the PF—17% Pay off the state's bonded indebtedness—12% Pay cash grants to local governments—8% Unsure—3%
1985:	Funds allocated to PFDs:	Reduce—38% Leave the same—50% Increase—10% Unsure—2%
1991:	What source of funds should be used to maintain state spending?	Increase oil taxes—28% Reinstate the personal state income tax—23% Enact a statewide sales tax—20% Eliminate the PFD—16% Establish a state property tax—3% Unsure—10%
1997:	Opinion of PF investment strategy:	Extremely/quite good—95% Not too/not good at all—2% Unsure—3%
	Size of the PFD: too big, or not?	Not too big—79% Too big—20% Unsure—1%
1999:	Is the state facing a budget problem that needs to be solved:	Yes—69% No—27% Unsure—4%
	How to balance the state budget?	Reduce spending—39% Raise taxes—18% Use Permanent Fund earnings—21% Combination of first three—18% Unsure—4%
	How to fund the long-term state budget—use some leftover of PF earnings remaining after dividends:	Favor—54% Oppose—46%
	Cap the PFD at $1,500, use earnings above that amount to help pay for government services:	Favor—43% Oppose—56% Not sure/no opinion—1%

YEAR	QUESTIONS	RESPONSE
	Cap PFD at $1,000; use earnings above that amount to help pay for government services:	Favor—36% Oppose—62% Not sure/no opinion—2%
	If new revenues are required, which do you prefer?	State income tax—39% Reduce PFD—36% Neither/unsure—25%
	Do you support or oppose eliminating the PFD if it would solve the state budget crisis without any new taxes?	Support—20% Oppose—78% Neither/unsure—2%
	After paying annual PFDs and inflation proofing the PF, should a portion of PF earnings be used to help balance the state budget?	Yes—35% No—61% Unsure—4%
	Many people believe that Alaska should have a long-range financial plan. However, last September Alaskans voted *against* a proposed long-range financial plan by a margin of 16% in favor, 84% against. In your opinion, what went wrong—why did so many people vote against the plan?	Not a good plan/don't trust government—39% Don't want to lose my PFD—18% Not sure—43%
	Do you feel it's important for the legislature and governor to try again to develop a long-range financial plan for Alaska or should they let things go for a while and see what happens?	Develop a plan—77% Let it go/see what happens—21% Not sure—2%
2000:	Pay each Alaskan a $25,000 cash dividend, cancel the PFD program and use PF investment earnings to help pay for state government programs and services:	Support—36% Oppose—60% Not sure—4%
	Pay a $50,000 cash dividend, cancel the PFD program and use PF investment earning to help pay state government programs and services:	Support—38% Oppose—57% Not sure—5%
2002:	Do you feel that the governor and legislature need to find a solution to Alaska's fiscal gap this year or can it wait until next year?	This year—68% Wait until next year—25% Unsure—7%
	Do you support or oppose a constitutional amendment to limit state spending?	Support—66% Oppose—26% Unsure—8%
2003:	Actions the state should take to balance the budget:	Reduce spending—47% Raise taxes—23% Use earnings from PF—14% A combination of the first three—13% Don't know/unsure—3%
	Are PFDs special entitlements from Alaska's oil and gas resources and not to be considered state spending?	Yes—62% No—36% Not sure—2%
	Do you believe Alaskans are entitled to a PFD when the state has a budget deficit?	Yes—68% No—32%

YEAR	QUESTIONS	RESPONSE
	Have you heard or read anything about a different way to calculate the amount of the annual PFD called Percent of Market Value, or POMV?	Yes—43% No—55% Not sure—2%
	If you answered "yes " based on what you've heard or read, do you basically support or oppose the POMV approach?	Support—41% Oppose—24% Unsure—35%
	Would you support or oppose *increasing* state taxes so Alaska could continue paying a PFD to qualifying state residents?	Support—34% Oppose—56% Unsure—10%
	Do you feel the State of Alaska did or did not make a mistake back in 1982 when it began to pay a PFD?	Mistake—12% Not a mistake—87% Unsure—1%
2004:	Do you support or oppose a state constitutional amendment to limit state spending?	Support—62% Oppose—33% Not sure—5%
	Have you heard or read anything about a possible new way to determine payouts and inflation proofing of the PF called Percent of Market value or POMV for short?	Yes—69% No—26% Not sure—5%
	If you answered "yes" based on what you've heard or read, do you feel like you'd mostly support or oppose the new POMV approach?	Support—44% Oppose—32% Unsure—24%
	Do you support or oppose using a portion of the income from the PF for essential state services, such as education?	Support—60% Oppose—37% Not sure/don't know—3%
	How important do you feel it is for the governor and state legislature to present a plan to voters this year to solve Alaska's budget problem?	Quite/extremely important—93% Not too/not at all important—6% Not sure—1%
	Do you believe the State of Alaska is or is not facing a serious budget problem that needs to be solved?	Is—79% Is not—14% Not sure—7%
	Have you heard or read anything about a possible new way to determine payouts and inflation proofing of the PF called Percent of Market Value, or POMV for short?	Yes—78% No—21% Not sure—1%
	If you answered "yes" based on what you've heard or read, do you feel like you'd mostly support or oppose the new POMV approach?	Support—36% Oppose—38% Unsure—26%
	Do you feel Alaska is or is not at the point where some of the earnings from the PF should be used to help pay for essential stat services?	Is—48% Is Not—46% Not sure—6%

Source: Dittman Research and Communications, "Alaska Permanent Fund Program Timeline of Public Opinion, 1976–2004," presented to the Permanent Fund Task Force at Commonwealth North May 23, 2007. Used with permission and modified by Clive Thomas and Kristina Klimovich.

Over the years, the options and policy choices have centered around how to use, or not use, the fund's earnings and the PFD to deal with the instability of the state budget. This has included the possibility of developing a long-term fiscal plan and trading off the PFD with some taxes. The options are outlined in Sections 8 and 9. To set the scene for understanding the politics surrounding the PFD, Table 25.4 provides a timeline of the opinions of Alaskans on many of these questions and choices. It covers the years 1976 to 2004. No time-series public opinion polls of this type are available after 2004. But given the consistency of opinions over the years, it is most likely that Alaskans have not changed their opinions markedly on these questions and choices.[27] However, as Table 25.4 shows for 1999 and 2004, when there is a budget problem, the public is willing to consider some adjustment to the PFD or new taxes. As we will see in Section 9, a survey in mid-2015 showed a similar public willingness.

8. THE PFD: A POLITICAL SUCCESS STORY OR NOT?

For both Alaskans and those outside the state conversant with the problems of natural resource extraction economies, the Permanent Fund is generally viewed as an all-around successful policy. Many outsiders and some Alaskans question the wisdom of the PFD as a policy choice, however. This view is very much at odds with general Alaska public opinion and the view of many of the state's politicians who see the program as wildly successful. Success as measured by popularity with the public and politicians is one thing. Whether or not these policies are in the short- and long-term interests of the state is another, and perhaps a more important, criterion of success. Here we look at the politics of the PFD by considering the perceived purposes of the fund after the PFD was enacted, the political arguments for continuing or reforming the PDF, what PFD policy tells us about Alaska politics, and the present and future consequences of PFD policy.

How the PFD Transformed the Perception of the Purpose of the Fund: Is It Now Viewed More as a Trust than an Endowment?

In their overview of the Permanent Fund and the PFD, Brown and Thomas point out that the original idea behind the fund was to save in the good times for the financial and budgetary rainy days. They go on to say:

> There was a large consensus among Alaskans for the idea. The ballot box demonstrated that fact unmistakably. But, within a decade, it was the same ballot box and the amorphous (but influential) force of Alaska public opinion that changed the role of the Fund, despite serious budgetary problems in the state.[28]

Clearly, it was the enactment of the dividend program that changed the role of the fund in the eyes of many members of the public in the direction of being a source of the PFD rather than a source of general government funding in lean times. Given that it is paid in the fall, it took on the form of a "Christmas bonus" and a source of income that most Alaskans quickly began to depend upon. Moreover, along the lines of the common human trait that often sees "today's privileges as tomorrow's demands," within a few years of the first payment in 1982 the PFD became seen as a right. Its payment became subordinated to all other uses of the fund, which comes through clearly in Table 25.4.

This fact became very clear to politicians, and they got the strong message that to mess with the dividend could be political suicide. Not only that, Alaska politicians who propose greater protection of the PFD have a sure vote-getter, even more so than beating up on the federal government. One such proposal sponsored by Senate and House Democrats in the 2013 legislative session was to enshrine the formula for calculating the yearly dividend in the state constitution. It did not pass in the 2013–2014 legislature, but was reintroduced in the 2015 session.[29] This essentially populist proposal may be good politics, but it is likely not in the long-term, or even short-term, interests of the state. The state needs the greatest pool and flexibility of revenues for the inevitable financial "rainy days," like the major downturn that began in 2014 and continued into 2016.

To be sure, the purpose of the fund was not changed constitutionally by enactment of the PFD program. The fund was originally and remains, in theory at least, a rainy day fund. But the politics of the PFD has given the fund a sort of parallel purpose—and to many Alaskans a more important one—of ensuring their yearly PFD—their "Christmas bonus." Today most Alaskans are not aware of the original intention of the fund and see the dividend as an entitlement that comes with Alaska residency. The Permanent Fund has become viewed by many residents as the "Permanent *Dividend* Fund" upon which this entitlement program is based.

The Political Arguments for Continuing and for Reforming the PFD

Earlier we looked at what can be considered the positive and negative effects of the PFD as well as other effects that are less clear. In the continuing discussion on the dividend, some of these effects are used to bolster the arguments of the political pros and cons of the dividend, while others are not. In addition, there are other arguments by the pro and con sides.

The Political Pro Arguments

The effects of the PFD that are often invoked in favor of keeping the program in its present form include the following. It provides a connection between citizens and the fund and works to prevent the fund from being used unwisely. It also boosts the Alaska economy and is used for the basic needs of individuals and families—particularly lower income families.

Three additional populist-type arguments often heard in favor of the PFD are that: (1) the fund consists of royalty payments from oil owned by the Owner State, so the earnings rightfully belong to Alaska citizens; (2) individuals can put the earnings to better use than allowing government to decide how to spend the money; and (3) life is tough in Alaska, and people deserve a reward for living in the state. The first two arguments are a matter of personal perspective and values and a case can be made for them. The third argument holds much less political water. As John Katz argues in Chapter 2, the vast majority of Alaskans live in conditions and with a standard of living not much different from the rest of the nation.[30] And while life is certainly difficult in rural-bush areas, those living in similar circumstances in places like northern Canada, Greenland, Lapland, and Siberia receive no such payment or dividend.

Another argument against reforming the dividend goes something like this: The state is rolling in money with its $50 billion savings account, and although doomsayers predict rough financial times ahead, they have not yet set in permanently. Certainly, Alaskans have seen relatively lean times, but the price of oil always rises again and the good times return. Proponents argue that there is no need to get rid of the PFD until it is absolutely necessary, and that day may never come.[31]

The Political Con Arguments

Today, those who want to reform PFD policy rarely use moral arguments (such as that the PFD is spent on "bad" things). Occasionally they use arguments about increasing dependence on government, coupled with the fact that individual Alaskans pay virtually nothing for the services they receive from state government.

Since the early 1980s and ever since the major drop in oil prices in 1986, by far the major argument used to reform present policy regarding the PFD is the unstable nature of state revenues and the need to develop a fiscal plan. Under such a plan, some or all of the earnings currently going to PFD payments would be available to fund government. Interestingly, proponents of this reform rarely argue that using fund earnings only for the PFD and inflation proofing is inconsistent with the original purpose of the fund, which was to provide future funds for government services when oil revenues ran out. But even when that argument is made, as Table 25.4 shows, it makes virtually no political headway among the Alaskan public and consequently among most of their politicians.

Alaska Politics and PFD Politics and Policy: A Familiar Explanation

The explanations for the continuation of the PFD program, and the inability so far of making any political inroads into it, are familiar ones used throughout the book regarding many other aspects of Alaska politics and public policy. However, not all the reasons for lack of reform are purely the product of Alaska-specific politics affecting the PFD and the fund. There are more general reasons facilitated by circumstances in Alaska's political environment. So before identifying specific aspects of Alaska politics as they relate directly to the PFD, we look at these broader political traits.

In the terminology of Chapter 3, the PFD is a distributive policy—one that confers a benefit on all Alaskans. Unlike a redistributive policy, no individuals or groups in Alaska are penalized as a result of the dividend program. At the very basic human level, anyone, whether from Argentina, Arkansas, Australia, or Alaska, would fight to keep a benefit of this type, which Alaskans now view as a right and upon which many have come to depend. The power of the status quo as a dominant force in politics also comes into play. It is much harder to change a policy than to block a change to it, especially in the separation of powers system in the United States and in Alaska.

These general aspects of politics are reinforced and enhanced in Alaska by the following political factors. Virtually all Alaskans receive the PFD and not some small segment of the population, which gives the program a statewide and massive constituency, likely the largest political constituency of any policy in Alaska. Hundreds of thousands of Alaskans acting as a sort of political phalanx against changing the PFD can put tremendous political pressure on politicians. This is evidenced by the fact that, in the search for a way to close the budget gap following the fall in oil prices in late 2014 and into 2016, no major proposal advocated eliminating the PFD, though some did propose reducing its size. For instance, Governor Walker's plan to deal with the major budget deficits proposed reducing PFDs, at least temporarily.[32]

In addition, Alaska's particular political cultural traits, which are translated into public policy, play a role here. As explained in Chapter 5, Alaska politics and policy making combine a form of individualism with a general middle-of-the-road consensus. This combination tends to produce a majoritarian, populist-type democracy and form of policy enactment.[33] By contrast, if Alaska had more of a communal political culture (*moralistic*, in the terminology of Chapter 5), as in some Northeastern states, more movement on reforming the PFD may have occurred. Despite several decades of strong public opposition to changing PFD policy, the severe downturn in oil prices and state revenues starting in the second half of 2014 and continuing at least through early 2016 has caused a sufficiently serious fiscal crisis that public opposition to changes in the PFD program may be diminishing.

The Consequences of Contemporary PFD Politics and Policy

There are several political and policy consequences of the strong public support for the present PFD program and the mortal fear that most politicians have of suggesting any type of reform. The major consequences relate to unsuccessful attempts to deal with the state's revenue and budgetary problems. Related to this is the gradual transformation of the public perception of the purpose of the fund from an endowment to a trust.

Impediments to Dealing with the State's Revenue and Budgetary Problems

As Chapter 8 on state revenues points out, and as we relate in the next section on the future of the fund and the PFD, the only way to deal with Alaska's long-term revenue instability and ensure a predictable income and thus a stable budget is to use some or all of the earnings of the fund. With earnings at a substantial level this would go a long way to insulating state revenues from the boom-bust cycle that is at the root of the state's revenue and budgetary instability. However, the public's support of the PFD and their "hands off the fund's earnings" attitude have prevented the development of a fiscal plan for the inevitable financial rainy day. There is a political irony here. One of the original goals behind establishing the PFD was to give the public an awareness of the use of the fund and prevent politicians from squandering it so that the earnings would be available in rainy financial years. The intention to engage public scrutiny was a resounding success but has had the opposite effect to what was intended. With Alaska's politicians powerless or unwilling thus far to work toward some reform, the situation is an example of an oft-told tale in democracies—the subordination of economic rationality to political reality.[34] Thus, the dividend has, so far at least, become an impediment to using the fund for its original purpose.

In the late 1990s, when the price of oil was low and the CBR was being rapidly drained, Alaskans attempted to engage in a discussion on how to deal with the fiscal gap. In 1997 the Alaska Humanities Forum sponsored a series of town hall meetings to discuss the role of the fund and the dividend in the future of the economy. Although most participants favored the continuation of the fund, there was no consensus about the proper use of fund earnings. Then, in 1999 the state held an advisory vote on a Balanced Budget Plan that included a provision that 5 percent of fund earnings should be allocated to the state general fund each year. The electorate opposed the proposal by an overwhelming 84 to 16 percent. Many policy makers interpreted this result as a referendum against any change in the dividend program and against any use of fund earnings other than for PFDs and inflation proofing.[35]

Furthermore, the political sensitivity surrounding the dividend has extended to the principal of the fund, impeding rational discourse and the implementation of reasonable management improvements. Political fright has thus far prevented a discussion of what to do with fund earnings that are not appropriated for the PFD or inflation proofing. Expenditures from the earnings reserve that could otherwise remain invested and thus increase the value of the fund and the size of future dividends have been characterized by some as a "raid" on the fund.[36] Another example has been the opposition to proposals by fund trustees and others to adopt a POMV approach to determining the amount of annual earnings from the fund that are available for expenditure. This is the method used by most endowments.

From an Endowment to a Trust?

A related but broader question than state fiscal strategy is how political support for the PFD and restrictions on the use of fund earnings have affected the fund's role since the early 1980s, its current role, and perhaps its future long-term role. One result of the PFD's creation is that the fund has taken on some of the characteristics of a trust and is currently no longer viewed by many as a pure endowment.

Many argue that the fund has become an engine for consumption when the state needs to direct more attention toward saving and investment. In this view the fund has operated like a giant trust fund, bestowing benefits on a population with no obligations in return, and concentrating attention on present consumption at the expense of investment to build a strong economy for the future. Not only does this attitude toward the fund restrict the use of present and future earnings to the PFD program, but it could conceivably one day jeopardize the principal of the fund.

Negative Consequences? A Matter of Perspective and Opinion

Many Alaskans would assert that there are no negative consequences of the dividend. Some might reasonably argue that the fund may not have survived without the PFD, though there is no way to know definitively. Many would also argue that even though the state seems unable to develop a financial plan, Alaskans still have a $50 billion plus bank account that provides options for the future.

Moreover, not all Alaskans see the need for a fiscal plan to close the so-called fiscal gap as long as the state enjoys good financial health.[37] Nor do many see a contradiction between the original purpose of the fund and its current perceived purpose. For example, former Governor Hammond argued that when the rainy day arrived, the dividend should continue and the government should close the "fiscal gap" by raising revenues through a broad-based tax.

The endowment versus trust issue is rarely mentioned as such in debates about the uses of fund earnings. But those who see no major negative consequences from the PFD program would likely see no negative consequences if the fund were viewed more like a trust than an endowment. In fact, to many, having the fund used more as a trust is a positive development, giving Alaskans more direct benefits from the assets of Alaska's Owner State.

Interestingly, however, in his "New Alaska Sustainable Plan" put forward in December 2015 to deal with state budget shortfalls, Governor Walker talked of using the fund as an endowment by drawing off an annual amount to place in the state's general fund. Walker also used the term, "sovereign wealth fund" to describe his new plan.[38]

9. FUTURE OPPORTUNITIES, CHALLENGES, AND POLICY CHOICES: AN OVERVIEW

Judging by experience since the 1980s, particularly when oil prices were high, changes in the PFD or use of the Permanent Fund and its earnings appeared unlikely before the revenue crisis that began in 2014. For several years, in fact, it has been inevitable that there would be increasing discussion about the continuation of the PFD in its original form and also about the fund because of the volatility of state revenues. The state needs to address this issue if it is to continue the standard of living, or one close to it, that its citizens have come to expect. The failure of oil prices to recover through early 2016, confronted Governor Walker and the legislature with a major fiscal challenge, necessitating that this discussion take place sooner rather than later. Accordingly, Governor Walker presented his "New Alaska Sustainable Plan" for consideration by Alaskans and their legislators for the legislative session of 2016. Regardless of the political success or failure of the plan, Walker deserves credit for starting a discussion that was long overdue.

In the rest of this section we put aside the politics and provide an overview of opportunities, challenges, and policy choices that the state faces regarding the fund and particularly the PFD. However, our approach is not to look in detail at the various proposals for cutting or trading off the amount of the PFD with certain taxes as covered in Chapter 8. We do, however, list the proposals in brief as part of our holistic coverage of looking at the future of the fund and the PFD. Here we are concerned with more general policy questions. We begin with the fund itself.

The Future of the Fund: Possibilities and Potential Consequences

While the establishment of the fund is written into the state constitution, in the future it could be subject to any number of changes, running the gamut from liquidating the fund to changing its investment policy to revisiting some of its suggested purposes when it was originally created to maintaining the status quo. Some changes could be made by statute, so long as they are not inconsistent with current constitutional provisions relating to the fund. Others would require an amendment to the constitution, such as a proposal to liquidate the principal of the fund. Still other changes might come about unofficially through political pressure, as happened with the de facto transformation of the perceived purpose of the fund resulting from the creation of the PFD. Moreover, changes in the purpose, use, and management of the fund and its earnings could be made independently of the state's fiscal problems and the PFD or with them in mind. Let us briefly consider five possible future developments as the most likely changes: investment policy, using fund earnings to build for the future, the unknown effects of the resource curse, the fund-PFD political connection, and using fund earnings to supplement the state's general fund and state budget.

Fund Investment Policy

Overall the fund has been well managed and its returns high. For many years the fund managers' conservative investment policy led them to invest only in stocks and bonds. In contrast, over the years many SWFs, such as Singapore's, have differed from the Alaska Permanent Fund in purchasing direct stakes in enterprises, in some cases installing their own management team to run the acquisitions. The Singapore SWF owns stakes in semiconductor companies, Universal Studio Theme Parks, Warner Music Group, a Japanese bank, and assorted other companies in Asia and elsewhere. While this strategy has the potential for high returns, if investment managers choose poorly or political risks are not carefully calculated, an SWF can suffer considerably.

The Alaska Permanent Fund now has direct stakes in several private companies. For instance, in the spring of 2012 the fund acquired an 80 percent share in American Homes 4 Rent, a company that buys private homes and rents them. Since then the company has gone public, and the fund's share is 20 percent. Other direct ventures that have been taken on since 2012 include a stake in another American Homes 4 Rent venture, which focuses on higher end homes, and a 30 percent ownership stake in Juno Therapeutics, a cancer research firm.[39]

Expanding into direct investment often requires a different kind of staffing expertise. Singapore boasts that it recruits this expertise from all over the world mostly to work in that city-state, where their knowledge can be captured and used to incubate other investment strategies and spin off businesses, all in the service of the national good. The Alaska Permanent Fund could, for example, take an equity stake in firms that agree to build the proposed gas pipeline. This would serve as an incentive to take the risk and a means for generating revenue in the form of a share of the firms' profits.

Investing in Alaska projects is an age-old and recurring debate that goes back to the creation of the fund. It was, in fact, the issue of an in-state natural gas pipeline that reopened the debate in 2014, the so-called Alaska Stand Alone Pipeline (ASAP). In spring 2014, former Governor Frank Murkowski, in newspaper columns and a letter to fund leaders, urged consideration of the fund investing in the gas line. The idea received a cool response from a consultant and most fund leaders, largely due to the risk and the departure from long-standing policy.[40]

Using Fund Earnings to Build for the Future

Using fund earnings to build for the future could be accomplished in several ways. One way is to return all fund earnings, not only inflation proofing, into the principal of the fund. If the nearly $22 billion of earnings paid out as dividends since 1982 had been reinvested, the fund today would be about two-and-a-half times its present size, likely in the range of $115 to $125 billion. This would be the case because the earning power of those additional contributions would be compounded, and today the state would be in a much stronger financial position. Supporters of this position argue that Alaska would be better off with a larger fund rather than the additional private consumption that results from the PFD program.

A second way would be to use some of the earnings to invest in the Alaska economy. This suggestion has taken the form of a community dividend, where an annual dividend would go to each community in the state. The dividend could be restricted to investing in public infrastructure, or it could be structured to be spent at the discretion of the community. This type of dividend has at least two attractive features. First, it permanently benefits Alaska residents—current and future—rather than dividend recipients, many of whom leave the state. Second, the determination of how this kind of dividend would be spent would build a sense of community.

A third alternative would be to establish programs and procedures that encourage individuals to invest, rather than spend, their dividends. Currently, when dividends are distributed in the fall most attention is focused on how people will spend them. Although there is no guarantee that private investments would benefit the Alaska economy, some would certainly do so.

Given the revenue shortfalls from 2014 at least through mid-2016, and probably beyond, none of these three options to build for the future looks likely to be adopted any time soon. But the return of high oil prices could make them feasible.

The Unknown Effects of the Resource Curse

Any change in the fund's investment policy or the use of its earnings carries risks, and the more speculative the investment, the higher the risk. One risk of increasing investment in the Alaska economy is that it may produce manifestations of the resource curse. As we have noted, whether or not Alaska is or will be subject to the resource curse is as yet unclear.

The Permanent Fund-PFD Political Connection

The alternatives presented above are certainly possibilities for managing the fund in the years ahead, but they are not likely to be adopted unless there is a change in the current de facto purpose of the fund, which seems to be ensuring the yearly PFD. If any reforms are to come at all they will likely affect the relationship between the fund and the PFD. This is because the future challenges and policy choices regarding both the fund and the PFD will be shaped by one stark reality—the state's overwhelming dependence on oil revenues to fund its operations. The dependence on oil and how to deal with the inevitably declining revenues from the resource is the central ongoing question in Alaska state politics. It has long been a conventional wisdom that any changes to the current PFD program and the use of fund earnings will likely come about only if the public and their politicians view the changes as a necessary trade-off between continuing the current PFD program and drastic cuts in state services. In 2015 late, out of necessity, Governor Walker began a discussion about such changes.

Using Fund Earnings to Supplement the State Budget

Over the years there have been several proposals to use fund earning to supplement the state budget, especially when oil prices are low. These include one by the trustees of the fund, one by Anchorage attorney Roger Cremo, and, in 2015, by Governor Walker.

In 2000 the trustees developed a plan that would limit the amount of money that could be drawn from the fund each year to a percentage of market value or POMV. The Cremo plan was similar (see Box 25.2 on page 931). Both would require a constitutional amendment. Governor Walker's "New Alaska Sustainable Plan," which is explained below, would not require a constitutional amendment because it would not limit the withdrawal from the fund like the other two plans.

Whatever final plan emerges, if any, to deal with the chronic shortfalls in state revenues, it needs to insulate state revenues and the state budget from the overwhelming dependence on oil that has been a fact of Alaska life since the late 1970s. The following overview clearly demonstrates this dependence.

The Reality of Oil in Alaska's State Revenues

While Alaska's economy has grown and diversified since the major oil discoveries in the late 1960s, the state has not developed a tax base to replace petroleum revenues. Since 1980 oil revenues have comprised over 80 percent of the state's own-source revenues, and often higher.[41] Table 25.5 provides an overview of Alaska's own-source revenue dependence on oil. The table shows the contribution of oil to Alaska's total state revenues for 2006 and 2012. In 2006 oil prices were in the \$50 to \$55 a barrel range and in 2012 in the \$100 to \$110 a barrel range. Clearly, in both years oil revenues dwarfed all other own-source state revenues, accounting for 81 and 90 percent respectively. All other natural resource industries combined accounted for only 3 percent in 2006 and 1.5 percent in 2012.

Even though the Permanent Fund is likely to increase in value and experience increased earnings, there will be continuing volatility of oil prices, as in the late 1980s through to the early 2000s and again beginning in 2014, and the state will continue to be overwhelmingly dependent on that resource. Added to this is the uncertainty of tapping additional oil and gas resources in the future, such as those in the Arctic National Wildlife Refuge (ANWR), the National Petroleum Reserve Alaska (NPR-A), and the Arctic Ocean, to replace declining production is existing fields, particularly Prudhoe Bay. The clear downward trend in oil production has been masked by fluctuating oil prices and

TABLE 25.5

Alaska's Major Own-Source and Total State Revenues in Fiscal Years 2006 and 2012

ALASKA'S OWN-SOURCE STATE UNRESTRICTED REVENUES

	2006		2012	
Tax Source	**$ Billions**	**Percent**	**$ Billions**	**Percent**
Oil and Gas	4.40	81.00	9.90	90.00
Timber	0.0007	0.01	0.0007	0.006
Tourism*	0.00	0.00	0.02	0.20
Minerals**	0.02	0.37	0.04	0.40
Alcohol and Tobacco	0.099	1.83	0.01	0.10
Fisheries	0.48	0.89	0.09	0.80
Other	0.83	15.41	0.37	7.60
Total Own-Source	**5.4**	**100.00**	**11.00**	**100.00**
Oil	4.4	81.00	9.90	90.00
Non-Oil	1.0	19.00	1.00	10.00

TOTAL STATE REVENUES—RESTRICTED AND UNRESTRICTED

Revenue Source	**Billions**	**Percent**	**Billions**	**Percent**
Own-Source	5.4	50.94	11.00	80.00
Federal	2.0	18.80	2.50	18.00
Investment	3.2	30.18	0.30	2.00
Total Revenue	**10.6**	**100.00**	**13.60**	**100.00**
Oil as Portion of Total State Revenues	**4.40**	**41.50**	**9.90**	**73.70**

* Excludes Alaska State Ferry receipts and cruise ship passenger tax, effective in FY 2008.

** Excludes payment to Alaska Industrial Development and Export Authority (AIDEA) to operate Red Dog Mine terminal near Kotezbue.

Sources: Alaska Department of Revenue, *Revenue Source Book, Fall 2006*, at http://www.tax.alaska.gov//programs/documentviewer/viewer.aspx?839f; Alaska Department of Revenue, Alaska Tax Division, 2012 Annual Report, at: http://www.tax.alaska.gov//programs/documentviewer/viewer.aspx?2788f; and Alaska Department of Revenue, *Revenue Sources Book, Fall 2012*, at http://www.tax.alaska.gov/programs/documentviewer/viewer.aspx?2682f.

has resulted in a less clear downward movement in oil revenues.[42] For about half of years between 1990 and 2014 the state general fund operated in deficits covered by withdrawals from the CBR, which only began to be repaid after the increase in oil prices in 2006. The result of this volatility of oil prices and the downward trend in production is a familiar topic covered in many chapters in the book—the so-called fiscal gap.

A stark reality that stems from this overwhelming dependence on oil revenues is that there is no tax source that can even come close to filling a fiscal gap resulting from a short-term fall in oil prices, or the long-term decline in oil production, either of which would produce chronic revenue shortfalls. The two major tax sources that could help fill the fiscal gap are the personal income tax and a statewide sales tax. But as Chapter 8 points out, although an income tax is a stable revenue source, since 2005 it would only have brought in 10 to 20 percent of the state's own-source revenues and a state sales tax between 8 to 10 percent. Other taxes and fees would account for less than 2 percent.[43]

So in total, all other taxes would provide less than a third of the state's own-source revenues and, more realistically, about one-fifth. This leads to a third stark reality. Given its original purpose, its present size, and the fact that it is the only source that can fill large, multibillion-dollar fiscal gaps in the short run (with some aid from the CBR) and on a long-term basis, Permanent Fund earnings are the most logical source to provide revenue and budgetary stability for Alaska. This use of fund earnings requires, at a minimum, a rethinking of the future of the PFD. For example, the state paid out a total of $1.2 billion in dividends in 2014. Had those funds been redirected to the state's general fund, they would have represented about 20 percent of the state's own-source revenues. This would have been larger than any other revenue source except oil, and about equivalent to the combination of revenue from a statewide sales tax and personal income tax set at realistic rates (that is, a state income tax at 10 percent of federal tax and a 5 percent sales tax). The PFD amount in 2014, combined with income and sales taxes, would have accounted for about 40 to 45 percent of the state's own-source revenues that year—a predictable and stable revenue source. Moreover, the PFD's potential contribution toward the state's own-source revenues is likely to rise as the fund increases in value and thus produces steadily increasing PFD payments.

Changing PFD Payments and Other Reform Proposals

Clearly, then, the most logical policy solution to handling short- and long-term fiscal gaps is to combine some fund earnings with reinstating the individual state income tax, enacting a statewide sales tax, or both. This inevitably raises the question of reforming the dividend program or perhaps eliminating the PFD entirely. Chapter 8 goes into detail about the pros and cons of various ways of closing the fiscal gap. Here we deal specifically with the role of the fund and PFD in this fiscal equation. Box 25.2 outlines

BOX 25.2

Future Public Policy Choices Regarding the Permanent Fund and the Permanent Fund Dividend: An Overview

DIFFERENT WEALTH DISTRIBUTION SYSTEMS

Other than the methods mentioned in the chapter so far, there are many different ways to structure a dividend program by altering the eligibility requirements or the method of payment. One is to tie a dividend program to a particular oil field or other natural resource deposit. Eligibility for such a dividend would be based on Alaska residence at the time of the discovery of the resource. The benefits would then be restricted to people present in the state at that time. Later arrivals would be eligible for dividends from later discoveries, but would not be drawn to the state in order to share in earlier discoveries. This method, however, raises several issues under the equal protection clauses of both the Alaska and U.S. constitutions and the Privileges and Immunities clause of the U.S. Constitution.

CAP THE DIVIDEND

The PFD could be capped at $1,000 (or some other amount). Capping the dividend would make more funds available for general state expenditures.

GIVE A LARGE ONE-TIME PAYOUT AND ABOLISH THE PFD

One suggestion to free the fund from the dividend is to terminate the PDF program by paying every resident one last "super" dividend of something like $25,000 in exchange for redirecting all future fund earnings to pay for government programs. This would create a massive but temporary economic boom and it might trigger elements of the resource curse.

THE CREMO PLAN

Suggested by Anchorage attorney Roger Cremo, this plan would establish a "Perpetual Fund" into which *all* state petroleum revenues, including oil production and income taxes, would be deposited and retained in perpetuity. A fixed percentage of the value of the fund could be withdrawn each year for any purpose agreed upon by the legislature, including paying all or part of the costs of running state government and perhaps also paying a dividend.

PERCENT OF MARKET VALUE—POMV

Like the Cremo plan and the Permanent Fund trustees' plan described earlier in the chapter, this proposal, which is used by most endowments, would allow for annual spending from the Permanent Fund of a particular percentage of the total market value of the fund, averaged over the previous five years. Five percent of total market value is the number most often suggested for the annual payouts. Opponents of this proposal fear that it could jeopardize the dividend, as the PFD formula would need to be revised.

CUT THE DIVIDEND OR REINSTATE THE PERSONAL INCOME TAX?

Opponents of reducing the dividend to pay the cost of government frequently argue that reinstatement of the personal income tax is preferable to reducing the PFD because reinstatement of the income tax would reestablish the link between the costs of government services and those who pay for them.

Those who prefer a reduction of the dividend to personal income taxes point to the disincentive to work created by the tax, the unfairness of putting the burden for paying for government on workers, and the apparent illogic of collecting an income tax at the same time the state is distributing a dividend.

Source: Developed by the author with the aid of Kristina Klimovich.

some of the ways in which reforms might help close the fiscal gap. It is, in fact, very likely that due to the fiscal challenges the state faced following the 2014 fall in oil prices, some form of modification to the PFD will have to take place, though likely not its elimination.

A Necessary and Inevitable Political Decision—Has the Time Come?

Even though there have been no changes on the political horizon over the years regarding the PFD and the use of the fund earnings, the day for such changes will likely come in 2016 or 2017 unless oil prices rebound to at least the $80 a barrel range. Discussions about the use of the fund and the continuation of the dividend, and in what form, will increasingly take center stage in Alaska politics. Such discussions were beginning to be held by both the public and politicians in the second half of 2015. A poll conducted in August 2015 by the Anchorage-based Rasmuson Foundation revealed that many Alaskans prefer new revenue, including use of Permanent Fund earnings, over deep cuts to state services. In fact, the poll showed that the public favored tapping some portion of the Permanent Fund earnings as their first choice, followed by a statewide sales tax, capping the PFD, and reducing oil industry tax credits. A distant fifth choice was reinstating a personal income tax, but even this was preferred over deep cuts by a margin of 2 to 1. Some, however, questioned the methodology and findings of the Rasmuson poll.[44]

Perhaps with the poll in mind, just before the 2016 legislative session, Governor Walker presented his "Alaska Sustainable Plan" to convert the Permanent Fund into what he called an endowment. The purpose was to insulate state revenues (and thus budget expenditures) from fluctuating oil prices. The plan would do so by no longer paying oil revenues into the general fund but depositing them into the Permanent Fund to increase its earnings. And unlike the trustees' plan and the Cremo plan, the Walker proposal would not take a fixed percentage withdrawal from the fund each year. It would take only that necessary to cover state spending. This would reduce the risk of the other two plans that, because they would deposit a fixed percentage of fund earnings in the general fund each year, this could trigger the resource curse by overheating the economy when oil revenues were high. The Walker plan would also change the way the PFD would be calculated. It would be based not on a five year rolling average, as it has been since its inception, but tied to oil prices and based upon 50 percent of oil royalties for the previous year.

Walker's plan also included a modest personal income tax, lower tax breaks for the oil industry and increased business taxes. This raised immediate opposition from some members of the business community and many legislators, particularly Republicans who wanted more budget cuts and opposed taxes. But as Walker pointed out in announcing the plan, "It is a work in progress."[45]

Even before Walker released his plan, a broad coalition of business, labor, Native corporation leaders, as well as former political leaders, including former Governor Tony Knowles, came together to push for the need to deal immediately with the state's budget crisis. The coalition, "Alaska's Future," sees one major solution to dealing with the state's chronic revenue problems now and in the future. This is using Permanent Fund earnings but not imposing increased business or personal taxes. According to the coalition, their surveys show that four out of five Alaskans favor some action to deal with the crisis but public concern about using Permanent Fund earnings is the major impediment to effective action. So "Alaska's Future" has focused its advocacy efforts on changing public attitudes and those of legislators. Some Democrats, however, are skeptical of the coalition's motives given its largely Republican leadership and the absence of taxes, particularly business taxes, in its proposal.[46]

The discussions that began in late 2015 about the state's revenue crisis is one positive effect of the crisis, since the problem is a chronic one. However, if by chance oil prices should rise again, even as late as the fall of 2016, and judging by past experience, most Alaskans and their politicians would breathe a heavy collective sigh of relief and it would be back to business as usual, at least until the next revenue crisis, which will surely come.

As Governor Walker, the "Alaska's Future" coalition, and many Alaskans and their politicians realize, Alaska needs to wean itself off of oil as its predominant revenue source and move to a more stable revenue stream. A policy that combines fund earnings, including some or all of the monies now used for the PFD, with new taxes would be the most viable policy from an economic and social justice perspective. It is also the most likely one to succeed politically. Yet, even with the budgetary crisis of late 2014 and 2015 and likely beyond, it is difficult to predict when and whether Alaska will be successful in making the transition to a sustainable fiscal future after petroleum, and what role the fund and the PFD will play in that transition. Again, judging by past experience, the transition is not likely to be one planned in advance—a programmatic policy—but the result of an ad hoc, incremental, stop-gap policy approach. And, despite opinion polls and broad support from many Alaska's leaders, any change will likely be a tough and steep up hill political battle given the entrenched support for the PFD among the public and the Alaska aversion to paying taxes.

10. CONCLUSION: EXPLAINING THE ESSENCE OF THE DEVELOPMENT AND POLITICS OF THE PERMANENT FUND AND PFD

The Permanent Fund has successfully transformed a large portion of non-sustainable petroleum revenues into a substantial financial asset for Alaska. This has largely been achieved through key decisions made when the fund was established, good management, and a largely bull market during most years of its existence. Alaska's fund compares favorably with other SWFs, such as those of Alberta and Norway. Obviously, the size of the fund puts the state in a much better position in terms of present and future policy options than would have been the case without the fund. On the other hand, the PFD has effectively altered the purpose of the fund, and this constrains both its short- and long-term use as a rainy day fund. How can we explain the essence of these developments and the politics that surround them, past, present, and perhaps into the future?

One useful way is to draw on four characteristics of Alaska politics identified in the chapter's introduction that throw particular light on these developments and politics. More or less in order of importance, these are: the significant role of external economic and political forces, the all-pervasive importance of government, self-proclaimed fiscal conservatism, and a political culture of pragmatic dependent individualism.

The significant role of external economic and political forces can be seen as influencing the fund and PFD in three major ways. First, it is the world economy that determines the price of Alaska's oil, and national and international market conditions that influence the value and returns on fund investments. Second, the volatility oil revenues, combined with the fluctuation in oil prices, and the fact that the fund is the only feasible source to supplement state revenues in the long term, mean that the purpose and use of the fund are likely to be revisited, as they were in 2015 and 2016. Third, the major challenge today, as in the past, is balancing the needs of the current generation of Alaskans with those of future generations.

The all-pervasive importance of government regarding the fund and PFD can be seen in two ways. First, it was the selection of the North Slope lands by the state soon after statehood that made the fund possible. Second, as an Owner State, with virtually all of the oil and gas deposits located on state lands, Alaska has options in terms of managing and securing revenues that it would not have if these deposits were under private lands. The fund is larger because of the existence of the Owner State than it would otherwise likely have been.

In combination, the two characteristics of self-proclaimed fiscal conservatism and a political culture of pragmatic dependent individualism help to explain much of the politics and policy of the fund and the PFD. Their effects are complex and often contradictory, but they appear to manifest themselves in the following ways. To a certain extent fiscal conservatism was at work in the creation of the fund because many saw creation of a savings account as helping to prevent the kind of wasteful spending of oil revenues that many perceived happened with the $900 million lease sale bonuses of 1969. Fiscal conservatism was also at work in the choice not to invest in Alaska economic development projects for fear of major losses. And the creation of the PFD had a major fiscal conservative element in its purpose of protecting the principal of the fund from marauding politicians looking for pork-barrel money and other funds that likely would benefit only a few Alaskans.

A combination of fiscal conservatism and pragmatic dependent individualism, often manifested with elements of populism, has certainly shaped the politics and policy of the fund and the PFD since the 1980s. The overwhelming message to politicians from most Alaskans has been "don't mess with my PFD." This, in turn, has had major consequences for how the earnings of the fund have been used. It has, for example, at least as of 2015, precluded limiting or eliminating the PFD and made it difficult to develop a long-range fiscal plan that would require using at least some Permanent Fund earnings for government services. With low oil prices and a major revenue crisis that began in 2014, this attitude toward the sacrosanct nature of the PFD may be undergoing change. At least the crisis has generated a long overdue discussion on ways to deal with Alaska chronic revenue problems.

Other than the external influences that will have an effect on the future size of the fund and the PFD, it is fiscal conservatism, populist individualism, and political pragmatism that will largely shape policy regarding the fund in the years to come. In addition, the operation of Alaska's SWF in the political environment of a democracy will continue to have advantages, but will also present challenges to the state's politicians. Moreover, the true test of the Alaska Permanent Fund is yet to come and its ultimate success as an institution to manage the petroleum wealth of the state will be determined only after oil revenues have stopped flowing into the state treasury. In fact, the experiment in Alaska's petroleum wealth management is only just beginning.

ENDNOTES

[1] Alaska Permanent Fund Corporation (APFC) website home page, at http://www.apfc.org/home/Content/home/index.cfm; see also, Eric Christopher Adams, "By the Numbers: Alaska Permanent Fund Dividend," *Alaska Dispatch*, September 18, 2012. This article is a treasure trove of facts about the fund and particularly the PFD. See, http://www. alaskadispatch.com/article/numbers-alaska-permanent-fund-dividend.

The 2008 PFD was $2,069, but when sent to Alaskans it included a one time amount of $1,200, called the "resource rebate," as a supplement to offset high energy costs. Thus, the 2015 PDF payment was the highest to that date by $3.

[2] See Chapter 4, Section 3: Chapter 6, Section 4; Chapter 8, Sections 5 and 6; and Chapter 19 at various places.

[3] These changes were required to conform to Generally Accepted Accounting Principles (GAAP). These are the set of common accounting principles, standards, and procedures that companies use to compile their financial statements. Permanent Fund financial reports now use the GAAP system.

[4] See, Article IX, Section 7, of the state constitution. For more details on the constitutional problems surrounding dedicated funds and how the Permanent Fund amendment fits in, see Chapter 4 on the state constitution, Section 3, and Gordon Harrison, *Alaska's Constitution: A Citizen's Guide*, 5th ed. (Juneau: Alaska Legislative Affairs Agency, 2012), 147, 153–54, and 160.

[5] Alaska Statutes, AS 37.13.010(a)(2); see also, *Alaskans on the Future of the Fund*, Alaska State Legislature, Commission on the Future of the Permanent Fund (Juneau: AK: January 31, 1990), 3.

[6] Pat Forgey, "Permanent Fund Deposits to Increase," *Juneau Empire*, October 30, 2008.

[7] Typically the percentage available for spending from most endowments represents the expected long-term real rate of return (after adjusting for inflation) on the portfolio, for example 5 percent.

[8] The fund also reports annual earnings in another way that includes *unrealized gains*—the change in the value of the assets held in the portfolio that have not yet been sold. This is known as *the excess of revenues over expenditures*, and it includes both statutory net income and unrealized gains. The reported annual rate of return on the fund is based on this definition of earnings.

[9] In *Williams v. Zobel*, 619 P. 2d 422 (Alaska 1980) the Alaska Supreme Court upheld the program, but in *Zobel v. Williams*, 72 L.Ed. 2d 672 (1982), the U.S. Supreme Court invalidated it.

[10] Gunnar Knapp, *et al.*, "The Alaska Permanent Fund Dividend Program: Economic Effects and Public Attitudes," Institute of Social and Economic Research (ISER), University of Alaska Anchorage, 1984.

[11] Hammond discusses the Permanent Fund and the PFD program in his autobiography, *Tales of Alaska's Bush Rat Governor* (Fairbanks: Epicenter Press, 1994), see esp. 250–56, 265–66, and 319–21.

[12] The author and editors thank Laura Achee, Director of Communications at the APFC, for her aid in tracking down hard-to-find statistics and other information on the fund. She provided several of the statistics to supplement information from the APFC website, at http://www.apfc.org/_amiReportsArchive/FY2014AnnualReport.pdf.

[13] The way that particular items in the tables are calculated has been modified since 2003. This makes statistical comparisons before and after that date difficult. In particular, until 2003 all unrealized gains and losses were applied to the earnings reserve, but from 2003 onward, all unrealized gains and losses were applied to the principal or reserved portion, and beginning in 2010, these were split proportionally. In 2009, the Alaska Attorney General clarified this proportional split of unrealized gains and losses. See the Permanent Fund's *2012 Annual Report*, at http://www.apfc.org/_amiReportsArchive/FY2012AnnualReport.pdf.

However, these changes do not affect our general explanation in this section or in the chapter in general. They are mentioned for those who wish to pursue research on the fund and the PFD in more depth.

[14] "17 Billionth Barrel of Oil Flows down Alaska Pipeline," Associated Press (AP), July 21, 2014; and Scott Goldsmith, "TAPS at 35: Accounting for the Oil Revenues," Web Note no. 12, July 2012, at http://www.iser.uaa.alaska.edu/Publications/webnote/2012_07_11-WebNote12.pdf.

[15] This method of inflation proofing has been criticized by some people who argue that it puts too much into the principal of the fund to cover inflation. This argument is based, in part, on the fact that a portion of the principal is automatically inflation proofed through increases in unrealized gains held in the principal.

[16] The 5 percent return rate requirement can be found in the APFC *Investment Policy* (May 2014), 5, at http://www.apfc.org/_amiReportsArchive/20140521InvestmentPolicy.pdf.

[17] APFC, *2012 Annual Financial Report*, at http://www.apfc.org/_amiReportsArchive/FY2012AnnualReport.pdf, 33.

[18] APFC, *2012 Annual Financial Report*; "Alaska Permanent Fund Ends Year at $44.9B Value," Associated Press (AP), August 5, 2013; and figures provided by Laura Achee.

[19] Email communication between Laura Achee and Kristina Klimovich, June 18, 2013, and Laura Achee and Clive Thomas, February 5, 2015.

[20] For fuller details on the CBR see Chapter 4, Section 3; Chapter 8, Section 5; and Chapter 19, Sections 2 and 6.

[21] Table 25.2 does not include statistics for the 2015 PFD because, as of the time this book went to press, only the amount of the 2015 dividend was available.

[22] Other useful treatments providing background on the fund and the PFD are: Jerry McBeath, *et al.*, *The Political Economy of Oil in Alaska: Multinationals vs. the State* (Boulder, CO: Lynne Rienner Publishers, 2008), Chapter 7; Gordon S. Harrison, "The Economics and Politics of the Alaska Permanent Fund Dividend Program," in *Alaska Public Policy Issues: Background and Perspectives*, ed. Clive S. Thomas (Juneau: Denali Press, 1999); and William S. Brown and Clive S. Thomas, "The Alaska Permanent Fund: Good Sense or Political Expediency," *Challenge: The Magazine of Economic Affairs* (September/October, 1994): 38–44. A more academic treatment of the fund and particularly the PFD is, Karl Widerquist and Michael W. Howard, eds., *Alaska's Permanent Fund Dividend: Examining its Suitability as a Model* (New York: Palgrave Macmillan, 2012).

[23] Scott Goldsmith and Jeff Wanamaker, "The Economic Impact of the Permanent Fund Dividend," a report prepared for the Alaska Permanent Fund Corporation, Institute of Social and Economic Research (ISER), University of Alaska Anchorage, 1989.

[24] U.S. Census Bureau, *Quick Facts, Wade Hampton Census Area, Alaska*, at http://quickfacts.census.gov/qfd/states/02/02270.html.

[25] Center on Budget and Policy Priorities and Economic Policy Institute, *Pulling Apart: A State by State Analysis of Income Trends, 2012*, at http://www.cbpp.org/files/11-15-12sfp.pdf.

[26] For further consideration of the economic equity arguments, see Scott Goldsmith, "The Alaska Permanent Fund Dividend: An Experiment in Wealth Distribution," in *Promoting Income Security as a Right: Europe and North America*, ed. Guy Standing (London: Anthem Press, 2004).

[27] The Dittman Corporation, which conducted several of the opinion polls listed in the table, no longer allows public access to its data.

[28] Brown and Thomas, "The Alaska Permanent Fund: Good Sense or Political Expediency," 39.

[29] Becky Bohrer (Associated Press), "Lawmaker's Bill Aims to Guard Alaska Permanent Fund Benefit," *Alaska Dispatch News*, January 9, 2015. The proposal did not pass in 2015, but was still alive at the start of the 2016 session.

[30] See Chapter 2, Box 2.3.

[31] See, for example, the argument used by economist Gregg Erickson in Chapter 30, Box 30.8.

[32] Nathaniel Herz, "Walker aims to convert Alaska Permanent Fund to endowment to help fix deficit," *Alaska Dispatch News*, October 28, 2015.

[33] See Chapter 5, Section 8.

[34] Brown and Thomas, "The Alaska Permanent Fund: Good Sense or Political Expediency," 39.

[35] However, because the plan included several provisions, the result cannot be interpreted as a referendum for the dividend in its current form. See Commonwealth North, *At the Crossroads: The Permanent Fund, Alaskans, and Alaska's Future*, A Commonwealth North Study Group Report, Anchorage, Alaska, 2007, 25.

[36] Another interpretation is that using the surplus earning reserve provides a clear trade-off between the benefits of additional public spending against the loss of private benefits from a reduction in the size of the future dividend. However, many people do not see this trade-off as advantageous. They see it as trading the least valuable public expenditure for the most valuable use of the same funds if distributed as a dividend.

[37] See the commentary by Gregg Erickson, Chapter 30, Box 30.8.

[38] Information on the Walker "New Alaska Sustainable Plan" in this chapter is based on the following sources: "New Alaska Sustainable Plan," Office of the Governor, December 9, 2015; "Gov. Bill Walker: Alaska's budget challenge, tightening our belts," Commentary by Gov. Bill Walker, *Alaska Dispatch News*, December 9, 2015; Janet Lee Falsey, "Business groups prepare to reshape details of Walker's budget plan," *Alaska Dispatch News*, December10, 2015; and an interview with Darwin Peterson, Legislative Director for Governor Walker, by Clive Thomas, December 22, 2015.

[39] Information on recent fund investment policy was provided by Laura Achee of APFC in a written communication to Clive Thomas dated December 16, 2014.

[40] Pat Forgey, "Permanent Fund Debated as Source of State Cash for Investment in Gas Export Project," *Alaska Dispatch News*, October 6, 2014.

[41] See Chapter 8 on state revenues, Figure 8.4, for oil as a percentage of Alaska's own-source state revenues from 1959 to 2014.

[42] For a picture of oil production in Alaska over the years and its projected decline, see Chapter 8, Figure 8.6, and Chapter 24, Figure 24.1.

[43] See Chapter 8, Section 6 and Table 8.3, on estimated sales tax revenues.

[44] Alex DeMarban, "Poll: Alaskans prefer new revenue over deep cuts, including tapping Permanent Fund," *Alaska Dispatch News*, August 13, 2015; and commentary by Paul Jenkins, "Rasmuson poll on Alaska revenue 'enhancement' just isn't trustworthy," *Alaska Dispatch News*, August, 29, 2015.

[45] Herz, "Gov. Walker proposes to fix Alaska budget deficit with income tax, Permanent Fund restructuring."

[46] Nathaniel Herz, "Alaska budget-reform coalition adds allies and ramps up Juneau lobbying campaign," *Alaska Dispatch News*, January 23, 2016.

⋆ PART V ⋆

Issues and Policies Regarding State Services Delivery

About Part V

By far the most extensive activity of state governments throughout the United States, including Alaska, is the provision of services. In fact, about 80 percent of Alaska's expenditures go to state services. Of this major outlay, three services account for the bulk of the state budget: education, social services (including corrections), and transportation. These are the subjects of this fifth part of the book.

Each of the chapters in this part of the book has two purposes. The chapters first explain the substance of their particular policy area and then provide insights into what they tell us about Alaska politics and policy making. Two aspects that feature prominently in each chapter are the role of intergovernmental relations (IGR) and the fact that big budget items like education, social services (particularly corrections), and transportation are not just about these policy areas alone, but often involve the politics of economic development. In addition, all three chapters illustrate several of the characteristics of Alaska politics set out in Chapter 2, the various types of distributive, redistributive, and regulatory policies described in Chapter 3, and different power dynamics in the making of policies.

Chapter 26, on K–12 and post-secondary education, examines issues and policies surrounding school funding, equity of access, and service delivery, among other topics. As such it illustrates how the role of Alaska Natives, as well as urban versus rural-bush conflicts, have affected education policy over the years. The chapter also shows that parts of the education lobby, including teachers, school boards, local governments, and the university, are among the major players in Alaska politics. They exert significant political influence not only on educational issues but in state politics in general. This leads to a particular policy and political power dynamic in education in Alaska that contrasts with the power dynamic in both social services and transportation.

Chapter 27 focuses on the politics and policy issues of social services. These include health care, corrections, and interpersonal violence (mainly domestic violence and child abuse). In so doing, the chapter illustrates several characteristics of Alaska politics, particularly those of fiscal conservatism, the influence of Alaska Natives, conflict between urban and rural-bush areas, the significant role of external economic and political forces, particularly the federal government, and aspects of Alaska's political culture. The chapter also illustrates a policy and power dynamic in which, unlike education, there are no big-player interest groups. However, this does not necessarily mean that those segments of the population receiving social services are unrepresented in the day-to-day policy process in Alaska.

The policy and power dynamics in transportation politics are, as explained in Chapter 28, different from those in education and social services. Because of the massive amounts of funds involved in building and maintaining transportation infrastructure, there are many interests involved in this policy area. Not least of these is the federal government, which is a major source of funds and a significant regulator. Moreover, many communities see transportation funds as a source of economic development and so their local legislators push hard to secure such funds. The result is a fragmented policy-making process for transportation that manifests the Alaska political characteristics of pragmatism, regionalism, and the influence of external forces, among others.

★ CHAPTER 26 ★

Education—K–12 and the University: Meeting the Needs of all Alaska Students?

Diane B. Hirshberg, Bernice M. Joseph, Alexandra Hill, and Clive S. Thomas

A common assertion of many members of the public is that some aspects of society should be free of politics. Two of these are sports and eduction. In the case of education, the often-expressed feeling is that "the education of my children is too important to be messed up by politics." Yet, any issue on which people disagree, and have conflicting values or have varying policy approaches to resolving, becomes subject to politics. There are, in fact, a host of disagreements over approaches to education and its administration. These stem from varying values about the very purpose of K–12 and higher education, what should and should not be part of a curriculum, what the best learning environment is, how to judge student performance and success, the working conditions and rights of teachers and faculty, and how educational institutions should be organized.

But probably the major disagreements over education relate to its funding. In most states, K–12 spending is the largest single expenditure in the operating budget, taking between 18 and 30 percent. Postsecondary education takes from 8 to 12 percent. For many years K–12 education ranked first in operating budget expenditures in Alaska, but in the mid-2000s it was pushed into second place by social services spending. Higher education usually ranks fourth in Alaska, behind direct appropriations to the state retirement system, a large portion of which covers K-12 and higher education teachers and faculty.[1] In fiscal year 2013, for instance, 19 percent of the state's operating budget and 5 percent of the capital budget went to K–12 education. The figures for postsecondary education were 11 percent of the operating budget and 6.1 percent of the capital budget.[2] This total of 30 percent of operating funds for education is fairly typical for Alaska over the years. Because of its huge impact on state budgets, education is almost always in the forefront of statewide political and fiscal discussions.

For all these reasons, politics permeates the K–12 education system, from individual schools and school districts to the state and federal levels. Likewise, politics affects all parts of higher education, from the classroom on up to the campus and the statewide system levels. Consequently, education is one of the most contentious of issues in state politics, particularly K–12 education. The 2014 Alaska legislative session, for example, which was dominated by education issues, was one of the most contentious in many years.

This chapter covers the politics and policy of education at both the K–12 and postsecondary (mainly university) levels in Alaska. Because it is such a central aspect of state government, the politics of education in Alaska illustrates virtually all the characteristics of Alaska politics identified in Chapter 2, seven of which are particularly evident. Three in combination—the all-pervasive importance of government, the role of Alaska Natives, and the combined influences of urban versus rural-bush conflict and regionalism—are the most prominent. The other four are strong interest groups, the influence of external forces, fiscal conservatism, and the three strong contending branches of state government. These characteristics help answer the major question of this chapter: Do the public schools and the University of Alaska meet the needs of all Alaska students? As we will see, unfortunately, the short answer is no, whether we are looking at K–12 schooling or postsecondary education.

The chapter covers three aspects of Alaska's educational system. The first, the development, organization, and administration of the K–12 and university systems, is covered in Sections 1 and 2. The second aspect, that of the politics, policy making, and political influence of the education lobby, is covered in Sections 3 and 4. The third aspect, current issues and future prospects, is covered in Sections 5, 6, and 7. The conclusion returns to our contention that politics is the central element in Alaska education policy making.

1. K–12 EDUCATION IN ALASKA: DEVELOPMENT, ORGANIZATION, OPERATION, AND UNIQUE FEATURES

Article VII, Section 1, of the Alaska Constitution states:

> The legislature shall by general law establish and maintain a system of public schools open to all children of the state, and may provide for other public educational institutions. Schools and institutions so established shall be free from sectarian control. No money shall be paid from public funds for the direct benefit of any religious or other private educational institution.

Thus, the constitution places responsibility for providing a public education to all children with the state legislature. The day-to-day administration of K–12 education at the state level is performed by the Alaska Department of Education and Early Development (hereafter DOE). The DOE is headed by a nine-member State Board of Education appointed by the governor and confirmed by the legislature. Board members serve three-year terms and can be reappointed, but they are often asked to resign when a new governor takes office. In theory at least, the board appoints the commissioner of the department who serves at the board's pleasure. But in practice, soon after being elected, the governor chooses who he or she wants and persuades the board to replace the existing commissioner.

The federal government has no direct authority for education. Under the reserved powers clause of the Tenth Amendment to the U.S. Constitution, power over education is reserved to the states. This does not mean, however, that the federal government does not play a role in K–12 education. As we discuss later, since the early 1960s the federal government has, for the most part, increased its role in K–12 education.

The Development of K–12 Education: Issues of Equality and a Political and Administrative Solution

Contrary to the language in the state constitution, for the first seventeen years of statehood, Alaska's education system was anything but open to all. There were two systems of public schooling: one for non-Native and Native children living in urban communities, another for Native students in rural-bush villages. While children in urban areas enjoyed access to state-funded public schools from kindergarten through twelfth grade, most Native students in rural-bush communities attended primary schools operated either by the Bureau of Indian Affairs or the Alaska State Operated Schools (SOS). Native teenagers in many rural-bush areas had no access to high school education in their home communities. They were forced to choose between attending boarding schools run by the state just for Alaska Native high school students or attending high school in an urban area while living with a family other than their own.

In 1972 a lawsuit was filed challenging the constitutionality of the state's secondary school system for rural-bush Alaska Natives. The case, commonly known as the *Molly Hootch* case, was settled in 1976 with a consent decree, under which the state agreed to build local high schools throughout rural-bush Alaska. Well over one hundred schools were constructed over the next fifteen years.[3]

At the same time that the *Molly Hootch* case was being contested, the state was restructuring its system of administration for rural-bush schools. The reforms resulted from the findings of a study of the early 1970s on how the education system could better meet Native educational needs combined with political pressure from Natives and their legislators. Rural-bush schools were placed under Regional Educational Attendance Areas (REAAs). Rural-bush Alaska was divided along regional ethnic and geographic lines into twenty-one autonomous school districts, each with their own locally elected school board members charged with making local policy.

The Contemporary Organization of K–12 Education in Alaska: Unique Features and Alternatives to Public Schools

Following the *Molly Hootch* consent decree and the establishment of REAAs, most Alaska Native boarding schools were closed. Today only Mount Edgecumbe High School in Sitka remains as a state-operated secondary boarding school, mainly for Native students. There are now three types of school districts in Alaska. One type is the borough school district located within organized boroughs, such as the Anchorage School District and the Aleutians East School District. As of 2013, when Petersburg became a borough, there were nineteen borough school districts in Alaska. The second type consists of school districts operated by both home rule and first class cities within the Unorganized Borough, including cities such as Cordova, Valdez, Galena, and Nome. In 2015 there were fifteen city school districts—four in home rule cities and eleven in first class cities. The third type of school district is the REAA. The original twenty-one REAAs, which include the Yukon Flats School District in Northeast Alaska along the Canadian border and the Chatham School District in Southeast Alaska, have been reduced to nineteen. Alaska had a total of fifty-four school districts in 2015, including Mount Edgecombe, which is a separate school district/administrative unit.[4]

While some public schools and districts in Alaska look like those in the Lower 48 states, many, especially in rural-bush communities, look quite different. In fact, there is no "typical" school or school district in Alaska. In the 2013–2014 school year, for example, district student populations ranged from a total of thirteen in the Pelican School District in Southeast Alaska to over 48,200 in the Anchorage School District.[5] There are K–12 schools with enrollments of ten and high schools with over two thousand students.

The geographical diversity of districts in Alaska is unparalleled among the states. While other states have rural schools and districts, they do not include districts that are completely off a road system and few, if any, that are located on islands several hundred miles offshore. For example, the Lake and Peninsula School District, in Southwest Alaska, covers an area the size of West Virginia, but enrolls fewer than four hundred students in K–12 schools scattered across fourteen villages. The Pribolof School District includes two schools with only one hundred or so students on two islands located four hundred miles off the west coast of mainland Alaska. Map 26.1 shows the diversity in geographic size of Alaska's school districts.

Alternatives to K–12 Public School Education

Alaska state law guarantees a tuition-free public education through twelfth grade to all children between the ages of six and twenty. The law also requires that children between the ages of seven and sixteen attend school.[6] However, the law does not require that students attend a public school. Parents may choose to send their children to an independent private or religious school or may home school them.

MAP 26.1

Alaska's School Districts as of 2016

Note: This map shows Alaska's fifty-four school districts as of 2016. Of these nineteen were borough school districts; fifteen were districts in first class or home rule cities located in the Unorganized Borough; and nineteen were Regional Educational Attendance Areas (REAAs) covering the rest of the Unorganized Borough. In addition, Mount Edgecombe, the state high school in Sitka (largely for Native students), is its own school district.

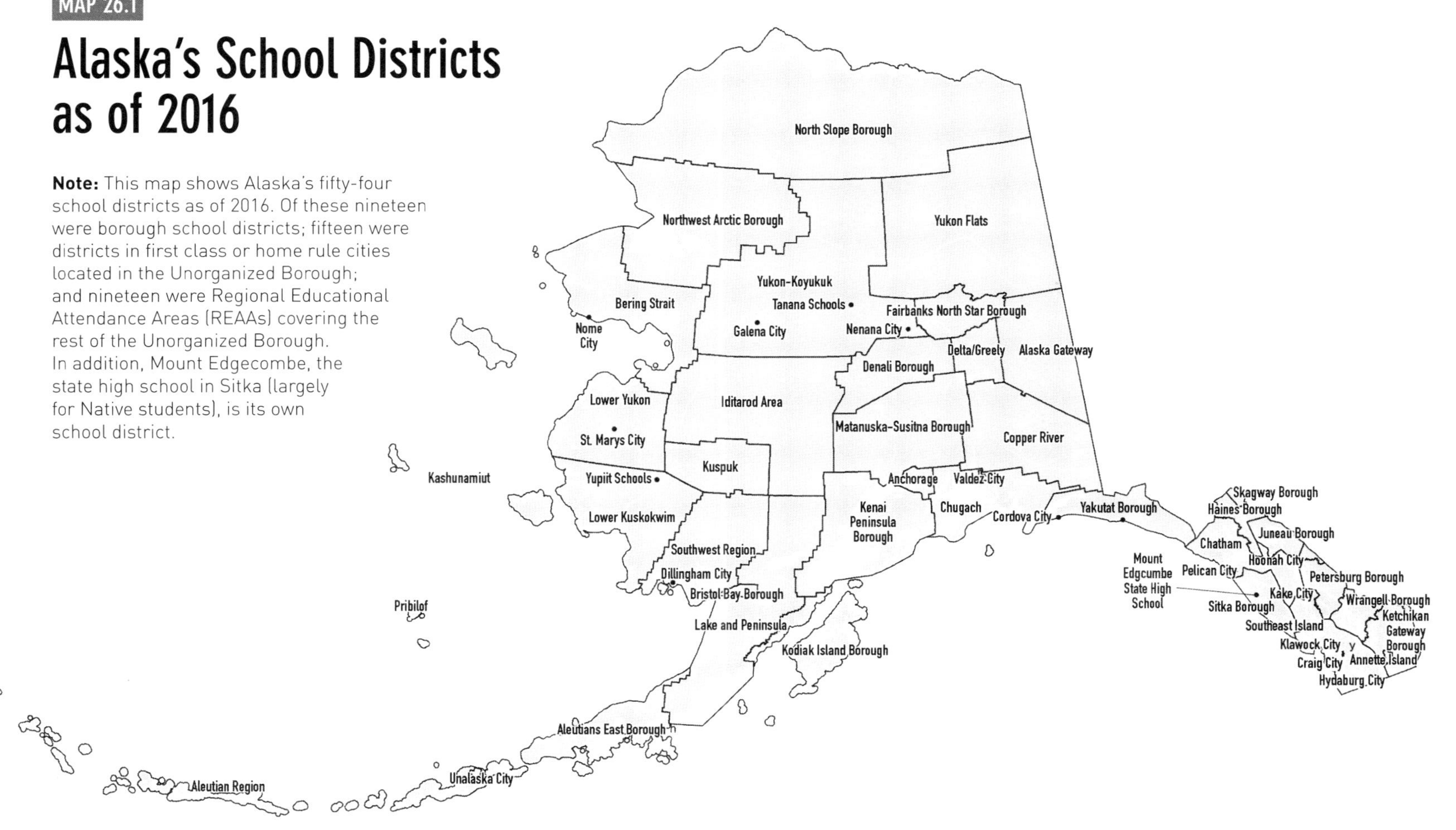

Source: Adapted in 2016 from an Alaska Department of Labor and Workforce Development, Research and Analysis Section 2012 map.

Alaska's regulations regarding home schooling are among the least stringent in the nation. Moreover, Alaska is one of ten states and the District of Columbia where parents who home school do not have to register with either the state or the local school district. Plus, if an Alaska family home schools and chooses not to receive state support, there are no testing or other requirements.[7] Thus, it is hard to estimate the number of home schooled children in Alaska.

A more accurate estimate can be made of pupils attending private schools and charter schools. Private schools are financed entirely from private funds and, theoretically at least, receive no government funds (but see Section 4 below). Private schools are less regulated than charter schools, which are run by parents or local community groups. Charter schools are required to raise some private funds but also receive government funding. These schools gained popularity across the country in the 1990s, including in Alaska.

According to the DOE, in 2015 about five thousand students attended private or charter schools in Alaska.[8] There are some seventy private schools in the state, with about a third of them in Anchorage. Several are religious schools, like the Anchorage Christian School, started by Pastor Jerry Prevo in 1972, the largest private school in the state, with some 650 students.[9] For 2015 the DOE listed twenty-seven charter schools in the state. Again, most are in the Anchorage area, including a Native cultural charter school.[10] The number of private schools in Alaska is larger than in states of similar population. Wyoming, for example, had only forty such schools in 2010 serving about 2,900 students, while at the other end of the scale California had 3,640 that year serving over 623,000 students.[11]

In terms of all K–12 students in Alaska, about 95 percent are in the public school system, which numbered just over 128,500 students in 2015. The 5 percent or so of students who are educated in private and charter schools and at home is about half the national average of 10 percent.[12] In California, for example, the percentage is 11 percent out of a total K–12 enrollment of six million, a student population over eight times that of the entire population of Alaska.[13]

Managing and Funding K–12 Education: The Gradual Ceding of Local Control to the State and Federal Governments and the Reforms of 2015

Particularly since the Progressive reform era of the early 1900s and with a major boost during the 1960s, there has been an increasing degree of both democracy and professionalism in K–12 school management across the nation. All school districts elect a school board, which appoints a superintendent of schools to administer their systems. The superintendent, in turn, hires people to run the financial, personnel, and instructional aspects of the district. Thus, local control and, in most states, local funding have been a hallmark of K–12 education in the United States.

Since the mid-1960s, however, while local administrative professionalism has increased, inroads have been made into the local democratic control of school systems by the state and federal governments. To some extent this has meant increased access and improved educational opportunities for previously underserved student groups, mainly racial minorities, particularly African Americans and Native Americans, including Alaska Natives. And so, whether this erosion of local control was a good or bad development is largely in the eye of the beholder.

Increased Federal and State Funding and Regulations and the Reaction

The shift of power and control from the local to the state and federal levels began with the federal Elementary and Secondary Education Act of 1965 (ESEA), which emphasized equal access to education, established performance standards and accountability, and prohibited a national curriculum. ESEA underwent a major reform in 2001 with the passage of the No Child Left Behind Act (NCLB). The act established new accountability mandates for public schools, including annual testing requirements. NCLB required that all students be academically proficient by 2014. For better or for worse, again depending on one's perspective, NCLB transferred control over certain key aspects of education from local school boards and individual schools to the state and federal governments.

Even though the Tenth Amendment to the U.S. Constitution theoretically leaves education to the states, broad construction and interpretation of the constitution, coupled with the extensive "strings" attached to the receipt of federal funds, have enabled the federal government to become a major political force in state education systems. And while the ESEA of 1965 theoretically prohibited a nationally decreed curriculum, the enumerated powers in Article 1, Section 8, of the U.S. Constitution allow Congress to pass all laws promoting the "general welfare of the United States" and to make all laws that are "necessary and proper" to implement federal authority. These broad powers allowed the federal government to impose criteria that moved in the direction of national standards that the states had to follow.

While it had some positive aspects, largely because of these federally-imposed requirements, NCLB was widely criticized and unpopular with many in the K-12 education community. Efforts were made over a decade to reform it and these efforts eventually paid off. In the fall of 2015 Congress overwhelming approved and President Obama signed the Every Student Succeeds Act (ESSA). This landmark legislation in part reversed over half a century of increasing federal control by returning considerable authority back to the states and school districts. In particular, the act replaced the NCLB legislation of 2001, especially regarding student performance, testing, dealing with under-performing schools and evaluating teachers. School board members and local administrators, state officials and teachers all praised the reforms. Alaska's U.S. Senator Lisa Murkowski, who helped craft ESSA, saw it as getting rid of what, in effect, was a national school board where the federal government dictated to the states. This sentiment was echoed by Norm Wooten, Executive Director of the Association of Alaska School Boards (AASB).[14] As we will relate later in the chapter, however, not everyone was as enthusiastic about ESSA.

Linking receipt of federal funds with adherence to federal standards enables the federal government to impose its education standards on the states. Despite ESSA this is still the situation in many cases. Most states are willing to forgo some local control over standards in exchange for substantial federal funds for local education.

The year 2013 was typical in terms of federal funding sent to Alaska for education. That year, close to 17 percent, just under $243 million, of K–12 funding came from the federal government.[15] To receive this money, the state and school districts had to comply with federal rules and regulations. Many programs, such as those for certain special education students, could not be provided without these federal funds.

The state's influence over local K–12 education policies manifests itself similarly through funding and regulation. DOE had legal authority to enforce NCLB regulations at the local level, and this authority led to some tension between the DOE and school districts. However, Alaska did not go as far as other states, such as California, in adopting statewide regulations to centralize textbook and curriculum decisions. The school governance structure in Alaska delegated responsibility for the daily operation of schools to local school boards, who make policy affecting programs in local schools according to general state laws and regulations.

As in all states, school funding in Alaska is a major political issue and always near the top not only of the education policy agenda but of the state policy agenda overall. Added to this is the much higher cost of providing education in Alaska's rural-bush areas. This, as we will see in Section 4, has led to much political maneuvering in Alaska, which is sometimes emotion-laden and is part of the cluster of issues that produce urban versus rural-bush conflict in the state.

2. HIGHER EDUCATION IN ALASKA: THE HISTORY, ORGANIZATION, AND CHARACTERISTICS OF AN UNDERDEVELOPED SYSTEM

In everyday parlance, the terms *higher education* and *postsecondary education* are often used interchangeably, but there is a difference between them. *Postsecondary education* covers all education beyond high school, including trade and vocational training, such as for plumbers and beauticians, as well as for various university level degree programs, from two-year associate degrees to bachelor's, master's, professional degrees in law and medicine, and doctoral degrees. The term *higher education* (which we refer to in the chapter as "higher ed") is usually confined to university level instruction, which is our major focus in the chapter. All postsecondary institutions in Alaska must register with the Alaska Postsecondary Education Commission.[16]

As with K–12 education, primary responsibility for public higher education is assigned to the states through the reserved powers clause of the Tenth Amendment to the U.S. Constitution. But unlike K–12 education, college attendance is not mandated. A particular characteristic of the higher ed system in Alaska is that by national comparisons it is underdeveloped.

An Underdeveloped Higher Ed System

There are four elements to the underdevelopment of Alaska's higher ed system. First, it is a system dominated by a single institution—the University of Alaska (UA), which is a public institution with three main campuses or major administrative units (MAUs): the University of Alaska Anchorage (UAA), the University of Alaska Fairbanks (UAF), and the University of Alaska Southeast (UAS), with its main campus in Juneau. Second, there are no professional schools, such as medicine or law. Third, the UA system offers few graduate degrees. And fourth, there are minimal athletic programs. The underdevelopment of Alaska's higher ed system is largely a consequence of the youth of the state. But its small population, its size, and its geography also contribute to this underdevelopment. This is because in combination they make the cost of providing higher ed very high.

As to the first element of underdevelopment, in contrast with most states that have a large number of private higher education institutions, Alaska has only a handful of such institutions that operate in competition with the dominant public UA system and a small Alaska Native public institution, Ilisagvik College, in Barrow. The major private school is Alaska Pacific University in Anchorage (APU). Originally established as Alaska Methodist University (AMU) in 1959, it became APU in 1977 after AMU was closed and reorganized.[17] APU is located adjacent to the University of Alaska Anchorage, and the campuses collaborate on grants and events. Most notably, the two campuses share a library, the Consortium Library.

Other private postsecondary institutions include branches of private institutions based in other states, such as Embry Riddle Aeronautical University and Wayland Baptist University, and several other small private religious colleges.

About a quarter of U.S. higher ed students attend private colleges or universities. This figure is less than 2 percent in Alaska, and a good portion of that figure is made up of the four hundred or so students at APU. The relatively minimal role of private higher ed in Alaska (and its consequent absence from the political process in the state) is why we concentrate on public higher ed in this chapter, which effectively means the University of Alaska.

As to the second and third elements of underdevelopment, Alaska has no professional programs and very limited graduate degree offerings. The state is the only one in the nation with no law school.[18] Moreover, together with Idaho and Wyoming, it is one of three states with no medical school. The major reason for the lack of professional schools is cost, but an important contributing factor is that Alaska students who wish to earn degrees in law, pharmaceutical science, and veterinary medicine, among others, can take advantage of the Western Interstate Commission for Higher Education (WICHE) program, which is a consortium of thirteen western states providing reduced tuition to any student who is a resident of one of the participating states. Another program, the Washington, Wyoming, Alaska, Montana, and Idaho (WWAMI) consortium, administered through the University of Washington's School of Medicine, serves as the public medical school for all five states. The program also provides tuition breaks for students residing in any of the participating states.[19]

While UA campuses offer master's programs in such fields as education, public administration, and business, there are very few doctoral degrees offered, and none in the arts and humanities. Those that are offered are mainly in specialized areas such as geophysics and natural resources at UAF, though there is one in psychology (a joint UAA-UAF program) and an interdisciplinary doctoral program in northern studies at UAF. UAS offers no doctoral programs and only a few master's degrees.

The fourth element of Alaska's underdeveloped higher ed system is that, unlike most medium-sized and large universities and colleges in the Lower 48, Alaska has no major intercollegiate sports programs. UAF and UAA have intercollegiate basketball and ice hockey teams but no football, and UAS has had no sports programs of note since the demise of its short-lived basketball program in 1990. Moreover, no private college in Alaska has an intercollegiate sports program. This absence of major sports programs has both positive and negative consequences. On the plus side, it means that the focus of the institutions can be more on academics. On the negative side, athletic programs, particularly successful ones, are very popular with alumni, local businesses, and others in the community and can bring in major private donations to the institution. Private funding will become increasingly important as state and federal aid is likely to be reduced in the years to come.

The Organization and Operation of the UA System Today

Article VII, Section 2, of the state constitution establishes the University of Alaska. Section 3 places university governance with an eleven-member Board of Regents (BOR), appointed by the governor for staggered eight-year terms (except the student member, who serves a two-year term).

The BOR meets at least monthly. It sets general university policy, including approving new programs. The BOR also appoints the university president, who is the chief executive officer of the system and who runs the day-to-day operations of the University of Alaska Statewide System (referred to within the system as "Statewide").[20] The president has a large staff, most of whom are housed in the Butrovich Building on the UAF campus, with some located in Anchorage and some in Juneau during the legislative session.[21]

Like the state court system, the university is a centralized administrative body. Besides the role of the BOR in setting overall policy for the system and appointing the president, centralization is further accomplished by having the president appoint the chancellors (chief administrative officers) of the three MAUs. The chancellors in turn appoint the directors of the community campuses that fall under these MAUs. However, the BOR's legal authority is one thing; the extent to which it turns that authority into power is often quite another, as we will see later in the chapter.

Unlike all other states, since 1987 Alaska has not had a separate community college system, although the three MAUs continue to offer two-year associate degree programs. In terms of student numbers and employees for the UA system as a whole, there were just over 32,000 students taking classes in the spring of 2014. This translated into just over 17,000 full-time equivalent (or FTE) students, which comprises those taking twelve hours a semester or more.[22] In the fall of 2014 the system had the full-time equivalent of 1,440 faculty (which included full- and part-time instructors), 4,528 permanent employees and 3,902 temporary employees (many of whom were students), for a total of 8,430.

By far the largest MAU in terms of students is UAA. In spring 2014 it had over 20,000 students (just over 10,000 FTEs), followed by UAF with just over 10,000 students and 5,000 FTEs, and UAS, a very distant third, with 3,800 students and just over 1,300 FTEs. The community campuses include those in Nome and Kotzebue (which fall under UAF), Matanuska-Susitna (Mat-Su) and Kenai (which fall under UAA), and Sitka and Ketchikan (administered by UAS). Only one publicly funded two-year community college, Prince William Sound Community College in Valdez, operates as a stand-alone community college, although officially it is a community campus of UAA. The economic impact of the university system, as with K–12 education in many places, adds an important dimension to higher ed politics in the state.

By the standards of many public university systems in the nation, the UA system is small. It is on a par with states with small populations like Wyoming and Montana, but pales in comparison even to medium-sized state systems. In 2014 the University of Minnesota had over 56,000 students (about 30,000 FTEs) and 3,500 faculty, Arizona State had 73,000 students (about 40,000 FTEs) and 2,900 faculty, and the University of Washington had 56,000 students (about 30,000 FTEs) and 3,500 faculty.[23] And, as in most states, all three of these states have both a university system (the Universities of Minnesota, Arizona, and Washington) and a state land grant system (Minnesota State,

Arizona State, and Washington State), while Alaska has only a single land grant university—the University of Alaska.

The Development of the University of Alaska System

The first institution of higher education in Alaska was Sheldon Jackson College, a small private college located in Sitka and founded in 1878. It served mainly Native students and for many years maintained a relationship with the Presbyterian Church. The forerunner of the University of Alaska, the Alaska Agricultural College and School of Mines, was established in Fairbanks in 1917 just five years after Alaska became a U.S. Territory. Renamed the University of Alaska in 1935, it did not begin a major expansion until the oil boom years of the 1970s. Anchorage Community College was established in 1954 and the University of Alaska Anchorage (UAA) in 1976. Juneau's community college was established in the 1950s, but Juneau did not get its own university campus, the University of Alaska Juneau (UAJ), until 1980. Community colleges were also established in smaller cities and towns, like Bethel, Kotzebue, Kenai, Ketchikan, Nome, and Sitka. So, as in most states, a university and a community college system existed side by side, but Alaska's community colleges were all administered by the University of Alaska System.

Despite some questionable management practices by the Statewide administrators in the late 1970s, the oil boom kept money flowing into the university and community college systems. As in other aspects of state government, this major expansion came to an abrupt end in 1986 when oil prices dropped below $10 a barrel and state revenues were cut by a third. Beginning in mid-1986 a move was set in process to merge the university and the community college systems. The reason given for the merger was cost savings. Some believed, however, that the merger was merely a convenient excuse to break the community college faculty union, which had become quite strong and many of whose members earned more than university faculty with similar experience and qualifications. At this time the university faculty was not unionized.[24]

The merger went through in 1987 and established the university structure of the three MAUs and the community campuses explained earlier. This structure was challenged in a ballot initiative that appeared on the November 1988 ballot promoted by the Community College Coalition of interested citizens and the community college union, the Alaska Community Colleges Federation of Teachers (ACCFT), which wanted to keep the two systems separate. The proposition was defeated, 55 to 45 percent, largely because of a strong campaign from the university and low state revenues at the time.[25]

Soon afterward, ACCFT initiated legal proceedings when the university gave non-union members a pay raise but not union members. After a long legal battle the union eventually prevailed, the effect of which was to preserve ACCFT as the bargaining unit for those who had been faculty at the former community colleges.[26]

Meanwhile, concerned about several issues, including lack of pay increases, retirement packages, and other working conditions, the university faculty organized in 1996 as United Academics (UnAC), affiliated with the American Association of University Professors and the American Federation of Teachers. The membership ratified their first contract with the University in 1998.[27] As of May 2015, UnAC had 954 members and ACCFT 257. As outlined later in the chapter, the unions affect the dynamics of the university as it relates to state government.

Since the late 1990s, and on a par with many other universities in the nation, Alaska's BOR has appointed three nonacademics as university presidents: Mark Hamilton (1998–2010), Patrick Gamble (2010–2014), and Jim Johnsen (2015 to present). The first two were former generals in the U.S. military, with minimal academic experience. Johnsen, however, has a Ph.D in higher education administration from the University of Pennsylvania, has taught as an adjunct in the UA system, has been in a senior position with the UA Statewide system for twelve years, and has also worked for some large Alaska corporations. Several chancellors have also not been academics. What this represents, as is the case across the nation, is a move to a more corporate style of university management, where academic considerations may take second place to financial and efficiency considerations.

Minority and Culturally Sensitive Postsecondary Education in Alaska

According to the U.S. Census of 2010, about one-third of Alaskans are classed as ethnic and racial minorities. Hispanics and Asians constitute about 5 percent each, African Americans just over 3 percent, with Alaska Natives making up by far the largest minority at about 16 percent.[28] Certainly, Hispanics, Asians, and African Americans in Alaska have special needs, but as most are urban dwellers they tend to be acculturated into the K–12 system and adjust fairly quickly to postsecondary education if they choose to pursue it.

In contrast, many Alaska Natives have adjustment problems in transitioning from K–12 to college. From 1986 to 2007 there were two higher ed institutions in Alaska serving primarily Native students—Sheldon Jackson College and Ilisagvik College. With the closure of Sheldon Jackson in 2007 due to low enrollments and financial problems, this leaves only Ilisagvik.[29] Although not exclusively for Alaska Native students, UAF's College of Rural and Community Development (CRCD), which operates in various rural-bush communities, attempts to meet the special needs of Alaska Natives. In addition, there are other programs, including Native studies programs and those to train teachers for rural-bush areas. We address the question of whether these institutions and programs are successful later in the chapter.

From the Development of K-12 and Higher Ed to Education Politics and Policy

Next we move to the politics and public policy of education in Alaska. In Section 3 we explain the makeup of the policy community and the characteristics and dynamics of the policy process, particularly the politics involved. Section 4 addresses the power of the education lobby in Alaska, followed by a section covering the major current issues facing the K–12 system and higher ed. Next we consider future prospects for Alaska education policy and perspectives on the extent to which Alaska's education system serves all of its students.

3. ALASKA'S EDUCATION POLITICS: THE POLICY COMMUNITY AND THE DYNAMICS OF THE POLICY-MAKING PROCESS

Across the states, state legislatures tend to exercise more power in education politics than governors. In some states, however, governors do take an active role in education policy issues and even stake their careers on this issue, as did Bill Clinton when he was Governor of Arkansas in the 1980s. Since statehood few Alaska governors have made education a major priority, and when they have, K–12 was their focus, not the university. Steve Cowper (1986-1990) tried but failed to establish an education endowment and Tony Knowles (1994-2002) took an active role in proposing school reform initiatives. Neither Governors Murkowski nor Palin was involved beyond budgetary issues. During his tenure, Sean Parnell showed moderate interest at first but came up with a big reform package for K–12 education during the 2014 legislative session.

Parnell's reforms were contained in legislation dubbed the "Governor's Omnibus Education bill" and introduced as House Bill 278 (HB 278), which after enactment Parnell called the Alaska Education Opportunity Act. HB 278 made major changes in K–12 education. These included: increases in the school funding formula, improved funding for charter schools, increased funding for regional residential schools for rural-bush school districts, providing for college credit for certain high school vocational training courses, expansion of science and math programs for middle schools, and expansion of broadband services.[30]

In his first year in office, Governor Walker did not show a major interest in educational issues. His time was consumed by dealing with the major budget deficit, expanding Medicaid, and getting moving on a natural gas pipeline.

Education politics and policy making, however, involve many political forces in addition to the legislature and the governor.

The Education Policy Community

Today education policy can affect a much wider array of interests than just those directly involved in education. This is because of the interrelated nature of modern policy making at the federal and state levels and because major expenditures on education make education an economic driver in the state and in local communities. Thus, the education policy community in Alaska can be viewed from both a broad and a narrow perspective. From a broad perspective, this community can include, at any one time, a wide array of organizations, groups, businesses, and individuals. Some members of this broader community have education as their major policy concern, while others may be affected by certain educational policy decisions but are not primarily concerned with education. Our focus here is on the narrower educational policy community—those institutions, groups, organizations, and individuals who are more or less continually active in the community because their primary concern is education or matters directly relating to it.

Box 26.1 provides an overview of the makeup of the policy community, both K–12 and postsecondary, focusing on the university level. The box first identifies elements of the community that affect both K–12 and higher ed. The box then deals separately with policy community members for K–12 and the university.

The Dynamics of Education Politics and the Policy Process

Because education policy in Alaska is made within the general political and governmental institutional structure of the state, there are no unique characteristics of education policy making as compared with other areas of policy. There are, however, some particular aspects of the politics of the process that are worthy of note. Here we identify six main characteristics and then others that are particular to K–12 or higher ed.

Six General Elements of Education Politics and Policy Making in Alaska

The six general elements are (1) the fact that education politics involves some of the big political interests and interest groups in the state, (2) the dominance of public education, (3) the role of economic development, (4) geographical divisions, (5) intergovernmental relations (IGR), and (6) the redistributive and regulatory nature of education policy making.

Powerful Interest Groups. As in all states, education politics involves some of the most powerful interests in Alaska. As Box 26.1 points out, at the K–12 level they include the National Education Association-Alaska (NEA-Alaska), the Association of Alaska School Boards (AASB), and the DOE. In higher ed the UA system and the individual campuses exercise considerable influence. In fact, a good case can be made that, next to the oil industry, the education lobby (more accurately certain interests within it) is the most significant political force in the state. For this reason, in Section 4 we provide an assessment of the influence of the various elements of Alaska's education lobby compared with other states.

The Dominance of Public Education. The political forces in Alaska education are predominantly public at the K–12 level and particularly so in postsecondary education. This contrasts with the politics of education in most states where there is a major private presence.

BOX 26.1

Alaska's Education Public Policy Community

COMMON ELEMENTS OF THE K–12 AND POST-SECONDARY EDUCATION POLICY COMMUNITIES

State Government

Because education is a major function of Alaska government, all three branches of government are involved in education policy making. It is usually a prominent part of the platforms of candidates running for governor and the legislature, including those seeking reelection. The governor usually has a special assistant in his or her office to deal with education issues. And it is the governor, through the Office of Management and Budget (OMB), who prepares the education budget to which the legislature reacts. Nevertheless, governors do not generally make education issues a high priority in their administrations.

Much of the high-profile politics on education takes place in the legislature. In particular, the majority caucuses have considerable influence on education policy, though the minority caucuses usually also make education policy positions a major part of their role. Each house has an Education Committee (separated from the Health, Education and Social Services Committee in 2008) that considers education issues. But more important are the finance committees in both houses. These usually have separate subcommittees on education and early development and on the University of Alaska. At times, each house also creates special committees on education, as was the case in the Twenty-Eighth Legislature (2013–2014). Generally, both the executive and the legislative branches deal with K–12 and postsecondary ed separately.

The state courts also get involved with education policy from time to time, though as a reactive and not a proactive force. One example of their role includes the *Molly Hootch* case explained in the chapter's discussion of K–12 education. Another is the Optional Retirement Plan (ORP) for some faculty, which the courts directed the university to adequately fund after it had underfunded the program for several years.

The Federal Government

All three branches of the federal government are also part of Alaska's education policy community. On a day-to-day basis the major agency dealing with Alaska is the U.S. Department of Education. While it does have a higher ed division, the bulk of its resources are expended on K–12 education in ways explained in various parts of the chapter. The Alaska Governor's Office in Washington, D.C., often works on K–12 and higher ed issues (see Chapter 10, Box 10.5, regarding this office).

The federal courts rarely deal with specific Alaska education issues. But they affect the state's education policy with decisions regarding such issues as education for the disabled and affirmative action, which apply to all states.

Interests and Interest Groups

As in all areas of public policy, interests and interest groups are very active in all aspects of education policy making. These groups lobby all three levels of government—state, federal, and local. However, K–12 and postsecondary ed have different advocacy groups and organizations representing them.

THE K–12 EDUCATION POLICY COMMUNITY

The Alaska Department of Education and Early Development—DOE

Through the State Board of Education and the Commissioner, the DOE has broad responsibility for K–12 education policy, including teacher certification, state academic content and performance standards, minimum high school graduation requirements, enforcing federal policy, and vocational education. It also administers the state library and museum.

Local School Districts and School Boards

The state's fifty-four school districts and their school boards and senior administrators are major participants in K–12 policy making. Their political advocacy is sometimes done through their major associations (see below) and sometimes by lobbying their legislators and the governor's office directly on local issues. The larger districts, such as Anchorage, Fairbanks, and Juneau, tend to be the most active and influential.

Interest Groups

There are several Alaska interest groups involved directly in K–12 education policy making, but there are two major ones. These are the Association of Alaska School Boards (AASB), mainly representing school boards, and the National Education Association-Alaska (NEA-Alaska), representing schoolteachers and K–12 employees. These organizations are covered more fully in Box 26.3. Other interest groups include the Alaska Council of School Administrators (ACSA), the state and local Parent Teachers Associations (PTAs), the Alaska Association of Independent Schools, and Alaskans for Choice in Education, which supports a school voucher system, explained briefly at the end of the chapter.

THE POSTSECONDARY ED POLICY COMMUNITY

The Board of Regents, Statewide Administration, and University President

While members of the Board of Regents (BOR) do get involved in the Juneau political scene and sometimes lobby in Washington, D.C., the university president is more involved in the public policy advocacy process on a day-to-day basis and is generally the most important political force in the system. He is aided by the chancellors of the three MAUs and the Statewide System public affairs personnel who, in effect, are the university's lobbyists in Juneau and in Washington, D.C.

The Three MAUs and the Community Campuses

The three MAUs and their community campuses are also part of the higher ed public policy process. Theoretically, they are supposed to promote only those issues and the legislative agendas determined by the BOR and the president. The practical reality is often different, however.

Interest Groups

The Alaska higher ed interest group community is much smaller than the K–12 lobby. In particular, unlike states with many universities and colleges, Alaska has no association of universities or colleges. Most of the higher ed lobbying groups are composed of employees or students.

Faculty Unions and Associations

Together, UnAC and ACCFT represent the bulk of university faculty. Both engage in major lobbying activity. In addition, there is a Statewide Faculty Alliance that sometimes lobbies as part of its function. UAA also has an active faculty and staff association with a largely political focus, as explained in Box 26.2.

Other Advocacy Groups: Native Alaskan, Student, and Alumni Interests

The Consortium for Alaska Native Higher Education (CANHE) is a collaborative effort among various higher education entities to create a statewide support structure for development of Native-controlled institutions of higher education.

Each UA campus has a student association, and there is a statewide student organization. These often lobby in Juneau, as does the UAA, UAF, and UAS Alumni Associations.

The Alaska Commission on Postsecondary Education (ACPE)

ACPE's major role is administering student loans and ensuring minimum standards and ethical business practices of public and private postsecondary institutions. Unless it has a major issue to deal with, ACPE is not a major player in the day-to-day politics of Alaska higher ed.

Western Regional Organizations

These include the Western Interstate Commission for Higher Education (WICHE) and the Northwest Accreditation Association, which accredits the University of Alaska. There is also the University of Washington Medical School's program for students from public universities in participating states known as WWAMI. As explained earlier, it includes Washington, Wyoming, Alaska, Montana, and Idaho.

Source: Developed by the authors.

Education and Economic Development. Education policy is not just about educating people. The vast sums of money spent on it mean that education is a very important aspect of the economy for most communities in the state, particularly those in rural-bush areas. As a consequence, and on a par with the huge sums of money going to transportation and corrections, this means that, like these other policy areas, the goal of economic development sometimes trumps best policy practices. In this case, economic development considerations are often entangled with educational goals in policy making. This is one reason why the education policy community often includes a broad range of interests beyond those directly concerned with education. For instance, from time to time construction and development interests and retail and hospitality interests are concerned with education policy decision making.

Education and Political Geography. Political geography plays into educational politics in a big way, as it does in many policy areas in Alaska. This involves both the urban versus rural-bush conflict, mainly in K–12 policy making, as well as regionalism, particularly regarding the university. In fact, other than the long-standing issue of the capital move, conflicts over education politics are perhaps more reflective of the state's geography than any other policy issue.

Intergovernmental Relations (IGR). As in all states, there is a significant IGR component to education policy making, particularly at the K–12 level. Together with health, social services, transportation, and Native issues, the federal government continues to play a major role in shaping K–12 education even after the ESSA reforms. Nonetheless, at least as far as the average Alaskan is concerned, the major intergovernmental relationship on a day-to-day basis is that between the state and school districts, particularly on the issue of funding.

The university is less affected by the state-local policy relationship (though there are elements of this, as we explain below) and more affected by its connection with Washington, D.C., in regard to grant funds for many research projects. These include Sea Grant (for ocean research) and the Geophysical Institute, as well as aid to students with special needs and many other programs.

A Mix of Policy Types. Regarding the three types of policy explained in Chapter 3—distributive, redistributive, and regulatory—education policy is a mix of all three.[31] Distributive policy (from which no group loses) comes in the form of grants and other benefits that schools and campuses receive if they qualify. It is, however, redistributive policy (reallocating benefits from one group to another so that one group gains at the expense of others) and regulatory policy (setting rules and prohibitions that benefit some and disadvantage other groups) that are the source of much conflict in education policy making and that forms the basis for much of education politics.

Redistributive policies include a relatively high percentage of money going to education (both K–12 and the university) from which rural-bush areas benefit. In times of funding problems, redistribution may involve taking monies from one program or a group or subject on the curriculum to benefit another. For instance, it might mean ending music programs to put more money into special education. Regulatory policy pervades K–12 education. It is also a large part of higher ed policy, though it is less visible politically at this level.

Three Specific Elements of K–12 Education Politics

The three major elements of K–12 education politics considered here are the significance of K–12 education to most politicians, the role of the split between urban and rural-bush areas, and the pervasiveness of political ideology.

K–12 Issues Are a High Priority to All Legislators

K–12 issues are likely second only to the Permanent Fund Dividend (PFD) and on a par with economic development and the budget in regard to their importance to legislators. This reflects the significance of K–12 issues to their districts and many of their constituents. This contrasts with issues like commercial fishing, the timber industry, the Alaska Railroad, and even the university, which are of major concern only to segments of the legislature.

K–12 Education and the Urban versus Rural-Bush Split

Over the years, K–12 education has been one of the major manifestations of the urban versus rural-bush split.[32] The major underlying reason is the high cost of providing education in rural-bush areas, as we explain in Section 5. The intensity of the split varies from time to time and from issue to issue, but it is always there. Many in the education community and in Alaska politics in general deny that such a split exists for fear of being accused of racism, since most rural-bush residents are Alaska Natives. But the existence of the split is undeniable. Both representation in the legislature and the nature of the membership and goals of the two major K–12 interest groups—NEA-Alaska and AASB—as explained in Box 26.3 (on pages 969-70), reinforce and contribute to the perpetuation of this split.

Political Ideology Pervades K–12 Education

While there is no watertight division on policy issues between Democrats and liberal policies on the one hand and Republicans and conservative policies on the other, differences based on political ideology do exist. For instance, Democrats, with their focus on equality and communal responsibility, tend to (1) favor a school funding formula that is generous to rural-bush areas, (2) support forward funding for education, (3) oppose school vouchers and aid to private schools, and (4) work to keep the cost of university tuition reasonable. On the other hand, Republicans, with their more fiscally conservative, individualistic, self-help philosophy and their strong support of the free enterprise system, tend to hold contrasting views to Democrats on these issues.

Three Specific Elements of Higher Ed Politics

The three most significant elements of Alaska's higher ed politics are the role of the BOR, the increasing political advocacy role of the university, and the manifestations of regionalism.

The Role of the BOR

The legislature and the governor tend to defer to the BOR on operation of the university. This is evidenced, in part, by the fact that, unlike other state agencies, the legislature gives the UA system a lump sum for its operating budget and lets the Statewide administration allocate it among the campuses. This is in contrast to K–12 education where, even though there is a State Board of Education, the legislature and governor often are involved in issues about performance and quality, curriculum, the qualifications and rights of teachers, and both the operating and capital budgets. Generally, the legislature and the governor are concerned mainly with the total amount of the BOR's budget request. They may sometimes be concerned about particular items in the operating budget, but less for their educational or administrative value than their cost. Most politicians are more concerned with UA's capital budget than its operating budget. And what gets approved or not approved depends more on regional factors, the level of state revenues, and who is in power in Juneau.

The reasons for the insulation of the university from Alaska's politics are likely due to the following. In contrast to K–12, the university takes much less of the state budget, not all legislators have the university as a high priority, and many do not feel comfortable with its issues, its faculty, or its senior administrators. Personality also often comes into it. At least for the first eight years of his tenure as university president, Mark Hamilton had the legislature and some members of the executive in awe of him. The only Commissioner of Education who comes even close to this level of charisma was Marshall Lind in the 1970s and 1980s.

The insulation of the university means that many issues regarding policy are decided internally by the BOR, the president, and the chancellors. This is not true in all states, however. In Idaho, for example, the legislature takes a much more active role in the affairs of higher ed.[33]

The Increasing Political Advocacy Role of the University

The involvement of K–12 education with state governments goes back over a century, with major activity since the 1950s. Not so in higher ed. Until the 1970s the general attitude among many university administrators and academics was to try to insulate themselves from the business of politics, of which many of them were rather disdainful. As the competition for state dollars increased in the 1980s and 1990s, a debate raged as to how much universities should get involved in state and federal politics. Those favoring involvement won out of necessity.[34] As a result, today higher ed has a major presence in state capitals and in Washington, D.C.

The University of Alaska has been very much part of this trend. The statewide system has long had a University Relations Department, which among other things includes a lobbying effort, though the university goes to great pains to deny that it lobbies.[35] The university has had a presence in Juneau with one or two staff working the halls of the legislature and the governor's office. The statewide system also organizes political action to encourage employees to contact their legislators. This includes what, in effect, is a political advocacy webpage where information for use in lobbying on behalf of the university is posted. Moreover, the individual campuses, faculty and staff unions, and campus organizations, including alumni and student organizations, also lobby in Juneau. Sometimes they do this in coordination with the Statewide System, and sometimes on their own.

For many years the university has had a public affairs person—essentially a lobbyist—in Washington, D.C., and has hired a major lobbying firm, Patton Boggs, to push their causes with the federal government. This includes obtaining research grants and funds for students with special needs.[36] In addition, the UA System and some individual campuses belong to a number of the nation's major higher ed associations like the Association of Public & Land-Grant Universities (APLU) and the American Council on Education (ACE), all of which engage in lobbying activities.[37]

The Three MAUs and the Manifestations of Regionalism

While the university is in theory a centralized system run by the BOR and the president, in reality the system reflects the regionalism of the state. This means that each campus often lobbies on its own behalf and sometimes on budget items and other issues not approved by the BOR. Consequently, there is a constant tussle between the campuses and the statewide administration and much internal politics, particularly over budget allocations once the BOR's proposed budget reaches the governor's office and the legislature.

Regionalism within the university is, of course, facilitated by the relationships that the chancellors of the three MAUs and some community campus directors have with legislators from their regions. This is particularly true if their legislators are in positions of power in the majority caucuses. Over the years, these relationships and university operating and capital budget monies have been important to the economic development of various cities and regions. The combined economic and educational concerns have sometimes driven the development of the university. Two examples illustrate this.

The first is UAS. It was largely because of the efforts of Juneau State Senator Bill Ray in the 1970s and 1980s that money was found to construct the buildings necessary to combine the then senior college (offering bachelor's and some master's degrees) and the Juneau community colleges into a university. The academic and financial viability of the newly formed Juneau university was questionable. But to Senator Ray that was of little, if any, concern. Putting up buildings in Juneau served the dual purposes of economic development and helping to keep the capital in Juneau. For his efforts, the campus named a building after him.

The second example is UAA. In 2008 when former Lieutenant Governor Fran Ulmer was chancellor, she was able to secure funding from the legislature for a multimillion -dollar health sciences building and sports center, even though neither of the facilities was in the BOR's budget for UAA. Ulmer's efforts were considerably aided by her long connections with legislators in the Bipartisan Working Group (BWG) in the Senate and friendships in the Republican majority in the House. Ulmer's influence was bolstered by the fact that about 60 percent of all members of the legislature are from Anchorage and its vicinity, and support for the university by Democrats and Republicans alike made good political sense for them. Then, in 2012 and 2013, and after Ulmer's departure as chancellor, funds were secured for a new engineering building, once again without having been approved by the BOR. This time funding was secured by means of a major lobbying effort involving senior personnel in the School of Engineering and a range of support groups. An example of a significant political support group at UAA is provided in Box 26.2.

The success of UAA at doing end-runs around the BOR may be part of the reason that, in 2013, the board decided to do away with separate campus budgets and have one general budget for the entire system. This, of course, will not stop powerful legislators from adding budget items for favored campuses. The BOR may be able to curb the independent role of the campuses, but they cannot eradicate the university–local legislator connection or the deeply ingrained aspect of regionalism in Alaska politics.

Contrasting the K–12 and the University's Political Profiles

Clearly, the factors shaping K–12 politics and issues place it much more in the thick of day-to-day state politics, particularly legislative politics, than the university. This is the result, in large part, of the greater role that redistributive and regulatory policies play in K–12 politics than they play in higher ed. Also, the politics of the university's governance is less public and more internal and is also based less on ideology. As a result, university-state government relations are less conflict-ridden than those between K–12 organizations and the state. Because of this, the role of the university in state politics is more low-keyed than K–12 politics.

BOX 26.2

The University of Alaska Anchorage Faculty and Staff Association: Promoting the Cause of Higher Ed in Anchorage and the State

The University of Alaska Anchorage Faculty and Staff Association (UAAFSA) was established in 1971. It is a voluntary organization working outside the formal structure of the University and supported by membership dues. Its primary purpose is to engage in political activities supporting the development of the University of Alaska Anchorage (UAA) and the University of Alaska (UA) in general. UAAFSA is registered with the Alaska Public Office Commission as a political action committee.

UAAFSA advocates for resources to support the academic mission of the university and to create an innovative educational environment with improved physical facilities, equipment, new construction, and a full contingent of staff and faculty. Weekly breakfast meetings are held away from the university campus, where the ten-member executive committee, representing both staff and faculty, meet with a variety of people having a direct impact on the development and growth of the university's mission. Among those invited are the president of the university, members of the Board of Regents (BOR), the Chancellor of UAA and other university officials, Anchorage area legislators, Municipality of Anchorage officials, UAA student-government representatives, UAA alumni representatives, and others who have a specific interest in university development.

UAAFSA advocates for the annual UA budget drawn up by the BOR and submitted to the governor and legislature. The association sometimes also advocates for other resources it deems important for the university that may not be in the BOR's budget. Each year, before the governor submits his or her budget to the legislature, a postcard campaign is launched in which the 1,900 or so UAA faculty and staff are asked to send a message to the governor urging support of the BOR's budget. Just prior to the opening of the legislative session in January, the association schedules breakfast meetings with key Anchorage area legislators to advocate for UAA priorities. Then, during the legislative session, UAAFSA urges faculty and staff to send letters to their legislators advocating for resources for the university. Some association members fly to Juneau during the session to meet with legislators regarding university funding.

UAAFSA's website provides evaluations of individual Anchorage area legislators.[1] Ratings are assigned based on each legislator's active support for the university's budget request and funding for facilities. Those given the top four-star rating are assessed as active advocates for UAA.

During most election cycles, the association sends a questionnaire to Anchorage area candidates running for the legislature and asks for their comments regarding the university and support of university growth and development. Their responses are posted on the website. In addition, UAAFSA contributes to the campaigns of Anchorage legislators who were ranked as earning three or four stars regarding their record of support for the university.

Among UAAFSA's accomplishments over the years have been participation in securing construction funds for Rasmuson Hall (opened in 2005 and housing the Business and Education schools), the Consortium Library, the Integrated Sciences Building, the Health Sciences Building, and the Seawolf Sports Arena. In 2013, the association advocated for funding for a new School of Engineering building and phase 2 of the Health Sciences facility. Increases in the university budget have occurred each year, allowing the development of many new academic programs, including doctoral degrees. However, the major drop in oil prices in 2014 and 2015 will no doubt adversely affect this trend.

The members of UAAFSA believe that they have made a contribution to the improved academic status of UAA. The 2012 *U.S. News and World Report* College Rankings placed UAA as 58 of 89 among tier 1 Western Region Universities and higher than the other universities in Alaska. Just ten years earlier, UAA was ranked among tier 3 universities.

---

[1] The website is found at http://www.alaska.net/~uaafac/.

Source: Developed by Patrick Cunningham, author of Chapter 27 on social services.

While K–12 education interests and the university may have differences in the level of the profile of their issues, they are both prominent political forces in state politics. We now turn to an assessment of the extent of this influence.

4. EDUCATION AS A POLITICAL FORCE IN ALASKA, PAST AND PRESENT

Evidence clearly demonstrates that the education lobby is one of the most influential across the fifty states and particularly in Alaska, though the fortunes of groups and organizations within the lobby have varied over time. Our assessment is based on the Hrebenar-Thomas time-series study of interest groups in all fifty states.[38]

Some Important Preliminaries on Alaska's Education Lobby

Before looking at the assessment, some comments are in order about the aspects of the education lobby covered here, the divisions within it, and the problems of identifying all influential education groups.

In this section we are concerned with the education lobby as it operates in Alaska state government. So the various federal agencies and national organizations that form part of the broader education lobby in Alaska, across the states, and in Washington, D.C., are not included in our assessment.

It is also important to note that the term "education lobby" can be misleading and may give the misimpression that the members of the lobby are united in their causes and goals—sort of a lobbying monolith. To be sure, there are many issues on which members of the lobby cooperate and pursue common goals. However, as has been mentioned throughout the chapter, there are divisions within the lobby's ranks. Like the business lobby and the environmental lobby, among other policy communities, the education lobby is full of conflicts over policy goals. This is particularly evident between school boards and teachers' unions, university administrations and faculty, and often between the DOE and its client groups. It is these conflicts within the education lobby that contribute to the particular character of education politics across the states and in Alaska.

A third factor in considering the power of the education lobby relates to the limitations of research in identifying all influential groups. The groups that have been identified over the years and in the Hrebenar-Thomas study are the so-called big players—those that have a continual presence year after year in state capitals and thus a high political profile. There are certainly other groups and organizations that are influential by their own assessments, but because these interests are not continually active, do not have a major presence in the state capital, are not big political campaign contributors, or a combination of these and other factors, they are not singled out and identified as influential.[39]

For instance, the state and local parent-teacher associations (PTAs) and the university faculty unions have scored successes by their own assessment, but have rarely been singled out as influential in surveys in Alaska or across the states.

The Influence of Education across the Fifty States

Hrebenar and Thomas listed the top forty most influential interests across the states in their original study and its updates. In each state, interests were listed in each survey as either among the first category of influence or the second category according to how groups were seen by those surveyed. The study shows that since the early 1980s there have been four educational interests and interest groups that have been singled out as influential. These are K–12 employees (mainly the various state chapters of NEA, but also the American Federation of Teachers [AFT] in some states), school board associations (and other education nonemployee groups), state departments of education and public instruction, and university systems.

In terms of overall average rankings across the fifty states, over the thirty years of the study, NEA was consistently one of the two most influential interest groups together with state chambers of commerce. While their rankings varied from state to state, both were seen as most effective or of the second level of effectiveness in over forty-five states, far outstripping all other interests. Over the years, the influence of NEA state chapters has declined, likely as a result of increasing conservatism across the states and a rise in anti-union sentiment among state Republican politicians. By the third survey of the study in 1995, NEA had dropped to second place and remained there through 2010.

The average ranking of school board organizations over the years has been between 16 and 21 out of the top 40. Overall, their influence declined slightly during the thirty years of the study, and they were listed in only twenty or so states as being in the first or second rank of influence. Departments of education and public instruction were grouped with other state agencies and ranked 29 in the early 1980s but 19 by 2010. Education departments were often mentioned by those surveyed as being most influential among the various state departments and agencies. University systems were ranked at 19 in the early 1980s but 14 by 2010. Although not among the major players in state politics, university systems moved from being considered influential in fifteen states to influential in twenty-seven states over the years of the study. This increase in influence is likely because universities became more proactive politically, as explained earlier in the chapter.

Clearly, then, even though its influence has declined over the past thirty years, NEA far outstrips any other education lobbying group in influence across the fifty states, past and present. NEA is followed by university systems, school boards, and departments of education. So how does this nationwide pattern fit with the situation in Alaska?

The Political Influence of Education in Alaska

At least as far as school boards are concerned, and to some extent NEA-Alaska, the Alaska history of interest group influence since the early 1980s contrasts with the fifty states overall. Together with the oil industry, AASB has been consistently ranked as one of the two most influential interests in the state. For the first two Hrebenar-Thomas surveys conducted in the early and late 1980s, NEA-Alaska was ranked as one of the most influential interests, and though its influence declined thereafter, it is still an influential force. The Alaska DOE was mentioned as influential in three of the surveys but not in 2010. This does not mean that it was not an important political force in other years, but likely was not seen by many of the politicians and political observers surveyed as a "lobby" because it is a government agency.

As to the University of Alaska, it has always ranked in the top ten of influential interests in the state and often in the top five. After a shaky political and administrative performance in the 1970s, its credibility increased and with it its political influence, as it followed the national lead of higher ed and put major resources into lobbying. Compared with university systems across the states, the UA system and its campuses are more influential in state politics. In this regard, the UA system is similar to some other western states with less balanced economies and major reliance on government, such as Montana, Utah, and Wyoming.

So where does the education lobby fit overall in relation to other influential interests in Alaska? Over the years it has been one of the top five most influential "big player" lobbies. The others have been the oil industry and other natural resources advocacy groups such as the Council of Alaska Producers (large-scale metal mining), Alaska Native groups, sports hunting and fishing groups like the Outdoor Council, and local governments, including both the Alaska Municipal League and particularly large boroughs like Anchorage, Fairbanks, and the North Slope Borough.

Explaining the Political Influence of Education

Certain elements of the education lobby in Alaska, particularly AASB, NEA-Alaska, and UA are influential for a number of reasons. Initially it is important to note that this influence has less to do with whether particular groups and interests that are part of the education lobby have a "good," "bad," "right," or "wrong" cause, all of which are in the eye of the beholder. Their influence has much more to do with the power base that they can establish and maintain. Chapter 15 on interest groups identifies twelve factors that constitute lobbying influence.[40]

Of these factors, five are particularly important in assessing the influence of the education lobby. One is the extent to which government and politicians need a particular interest group—that is, how dependent on the group they are for getting elected, staying in power, and running state government, among other forms of need. The second is the skill of the lobbyist in building up good relations with policy makers. The third factor is the extent of the geographical distribution of the group's membership in terms of how many legislative districts have members, which gives them a major connection to elected and appointed state officials. Fourth and fifth are the factors of the group's financial resources and the organizational skill and political acumen of group leaders. The influence of education interests becomes apparent when the five factors are combined with the major role of interest groups as sources of information for policy makers, which policy makers need to make informed decisions.

AASB, NEA-Alaska, and the UA system, including its three MAUs, have all five of these assets of interest group power, though to varying degrees. AASB and NEA-Alaska have members in every part of the state and provide a major service—education—that affects Alaskans in a major way and thus the politicians who represent them. Both organizations have skilled lobbyists, professional leaders, and major financial resources to use in lobbying. UA has similar assets, though concentrated in the three major urban areas. But because these urban areas account for nearly 75 percent of the state's population and close to fifty of the state's sixty legislators, the university, like AASB and NEA-Alaska, has easy access to almost all key policy makers, including those in the governor's office and top executive branch officials.

While the DOE also has all five political power assets, its power base is slightly different. Its influence comes largely from its technical expertise, as the major source of data on the state's K–12 system, and as an agent of the federal government enforcing some national standards and its own state standards. The DOE can also mobilize its client groups, such as PTAs and groups for early childhood education, Native education, and others, to lobby for its policies that benefit these groups. And while those from the department who deal with the legislature on an ongoing basis, such as the commissioner and the legislative liaison, are not technically designated as "lobbyists" and do not have to register as such with the Alaska Public Offices Commission (APOC), they are, like those from the university, in fact lobbyists and often very skilled political advocates.

In addition, local governments and the Alaska Municipal League (AML) often lobby on education issues, particularly those of K–12 (in conjunction with AASB, though rarely with NEA–Alaska), because of the importance of education to their missions and education's large percentage of local budgets. Given the overall influence of local government, this adds to the political influence of the education lobby.[41] The dynamics of the AASB-NEA-Alaska relationship and the importance of the local government context in which they operate in addition to the state political environment are covered in Box 26.3.

From Politics and Influence to Policy Issues

Consideration of the major issues of concern to NEA-Alaska and AASB is a reminder that, while the political influence of the education policy community in Alaska is important, the major value of considering its influence is to help understand how these organizations affect particular issues and policy making. So, how do the various elements of education politics manifest themselves on issues and politics? Two common areas in K–12 and higher ed are funding and education for minorities, particularly Alaska Natives. Funding is the major education issue in all states, as it is for most policy areas. But the social and political geography of Alaska as it relates to Alaska Natives, as well as the history of Native K–12 education, means that the funding issue takes on a particular political complexion in Alaska both for K–12 and higher ed.

When we look at standardized assessments and graduation rates at the K–12 level and retention and program completion rates at the University of Alaska, there is clearly a gap in achievement between Native and non-Native students. Many members of other minority groups also fare poorly in Alaska's public school systems, including African American and Hispanic students and those from low-income families. But Alaska Natives have among the highest school dropout rates and the lowest first to second year UA retention rates of any ethnic group. Since Alaska Natives are the largest minority group in the education system, these statistics are troubling.

In addition, the politics surrounding Alaska Native education involve disputes about curriculum and pedagogy, including topics such as the need for bilingual education and heritage language immersion programs as well as including Alaska Native history and culture in Alaska studies courses. In higher ed there are also disputes over the curriculum taught in the UA system as well as the level of support services provided to Native students. These Native education concerns are major issues on the K–12 and higher ed policy agendas in the state today.

In the next section we deal first with K–12 issues, followed by those in higher ed. Then we look at how politics might affect needed reforms in the state's present educational system and possible future policy directions. In particular, we assess whether the state is meeting the educational needs of all Alaskans and if it is likely to in the future. Definitions for some specialized terms needed in our analysis are provided in Box 26.4 (on page 971).

5. ALASKA'S K–12 POLICY ISSUES

In 1999, former Alaska Commissioner of Education Jerry Covey and his colleagues reviewed the major long-standing concerns in K–12 education in Alaska. These included

BOX 26.3

NEA-Alaska and AASB: Two Major Interest Groups in K–12 Education

Two of the most prominent advocates for K-12 education issues are the National Education Association-Alaska (NEA-Alaska) and the Association of Alaska School Boards (AASB).

NEA-Alaska is an affiliate of the national NEA and has local affiliates throughout the state. The association represents more than twelve thousand school employees, including teachers, library media specialists, counselors, psychologists, physical and speech therapists, school secretaries, custodians, classroom aides, cafeteria workers, maintenance workers, and other support professionals. AASB represents the elected boards of fifty-three of Alaska's fifty-four school districts, with about 330 individual board members responsible for students who attend Alaska's public schools. Associate members include school superintendents, advisory school boards, the State Board of Education, the Commissioner of Education, and the Special Education Service Agency, which serves children with autism and their families.

Both NEA-Alaska and AASB have as part of their respective missions to advocate for public education, children, and youth. But each comes to the table with a different slant. According to the NEA-Alaska mission statement, "NEA-Alaska exists to be an advocate for an excellent public education for each child in Alaska and to advance the interests of public school employees." But, from a practical political perspective, NEA-Alaska views this mission through the prism of employee rights, salaries, and benefits. AASB, representing the management side of K-12 education, emphasizes "effective local governance." Its policy lens focuses on protecting the rights of local boards to manage budgets and programs according to community conditions and desires.

Over the years the two groups have worked together on many issues, but their differences in focus often place the two interest groups at odds. For example, they differ widely on performance-based licensure, which allows for alternative routes to teacher certification and requires performance reviews for all teachers. NEA-Alaska and AASB also disagreed on the state's School Performance Incentive Program (SPIP), a short-lived program that existed from 2007 to 2009 and that distributed merit pay increases to school employees in schools where students demonstrated growth in academic achievement. SPIP was not renewed after several problems emerged, including employees at Pearl Creek Elementary School in Fairbanks refusing the bonuses.

Probably the major area of disagreement in recent years concerns changes in the Teacher Retirement System (TRS) enacted in the 2005 legislative session. In effect, the new system shifts the responsibility and risks of funding and maintaining a retirement account from employers to employees hired after the effective date of the changes. As a cost-saving measure for school districts, AASB members generally favor the new system. In contrast, the changes have been vigorously opposed by NEA-Alaska as an impediment to teacher recruitment and retention. Following enactment of the changes, returning to a system similar to the old TRS program has been high on the political agenda of NEA-Alaska and its advocacy efforts.

Another major distinction and a source of potential conflict between the two organizations stems from geography. The bulk—around 70 percent—of NEA-Alaska's members reside in large urban districts: Anchorage, Matanuska-Susitna, Kenai, and Fairbanks, all of which are on the road system. By contrast, 81 percent (forty-three of fifty-three) of Alaska school districts are either off the road system, comprised of small relatively isolated settlements, or both. And so the majority of AASB's 330-plus members represent rural-bush Alaska.

This difference in membership residence can lead to differing priorities, particularly with respect to school funding. While NEA-Alaska advocates for higher levels of state support overall, it is in the interests of the majority of its members to increase funding for the largest school districts serving the greatest number of students and employing the most staff. AASB, on the other hand, must represent the needs of small districts, many of which are losing students. Carl Rose, former Executive Director of AASB, suggests that the shift in political power since the early 1980s to the Railbelt has occasioned "the biggest public policy change in Alaska, affecting all aspects of government, but particularly education." Revisions in the state K–12 funding formula since 2000 bear this out, as they tend to direct state dollars to the more populous school districts. However, NEA-Alaska has long advocated for area cost differentials to ensure rural-bush Alaskans are treated equitably. This is partly motivated by the fact that most of NEA-Alaska's sixty-four local affiliates are in rural-bush Alaska, but also because the organization sees adequate and equitable funding as a cornerstone of its advocacy role in Juneau.

So far, because of the serious need for increased state support for education in all areas of the state, NEA-Alaska and AASB have been able to work together on funding issues. They are also in agreement in opposing an amendment to the Alaska Constitution to allow state funds to go to private and religious schools. However, there may come a time when the urban versus rural-bush split that characterizes so much of Alaska politics will pit these two organizations against each other on one of the primary policy issues facing the state—investment in Alaska's future through education.

Source: Developed by Mary Lou Madden, former administrator at the Alaska Department of Education, Sheldon Jackson Collage, and the University of Alaska Southeast. She had assistance from staff at NEA-Alaska and AASB.

the increasing cost of providing public education, especially in rural-bush areas and the often intense debate that accompanies it, the quality and performance of Alaska's schools, and issues surrounding Native education.[42] With the added factor of accountability, these issues remain at the forefront of policy discussions through the mid-2010s.

State Funding: A Highly Contentious and Ongoing Issue

Funding issues form the core of the politics of virtually all state, local, and federal policy making, and, more often than not, funding drives policy rather than policy driving funding. This is certainly the case with K–12 education.[43] In line with all states there are three sources of funding for K–12 education in Alaska: federal, state, and in some cases local government funds. For a number of reasons, however, Alaska's school funding system looks very different from that of most states in the Lower 48. It is the particular combination of funding sources in Alaska that generates much of the politics not only of school funding but of K–12 education policy in general.

As in most states, except for the complaints about the regulations that come with federal funds, the federal funding aspect of K–12 education generates little political controversy in Alaska. What is at the root of the politics of K–12 education in the state is the particular relationship between the second and third sources of funding—that of state and local monies. This is where a significant difference exists between Alaska and other states.

The Mechanics and Politics of State Funding of K–12 Education

Other than borough school districts, the local funding contribution to K–12 education in Alaska is minimal. With the lack of a tax base in the Unorganized Borough, all

BOX 26.4

Some Specialized Terms Used in K–12 and Higher Education

K–12 EDUCATION

Adequate Yearly Progress (AYP) versus Alaska State Performance Index (ASPI): Both of these sets of standards assess the yearly progress of Alaska school districts and schools, holding them accountable for the proficiency of their students in language arts, math, and other subjects. The AYP standards were developed in response to the federal No Child Left Behind (NCLB) legislation of 2001 and, in essence, gave districts a pass/fail grade. Alaska received a waiver from NCLB in 2013 and replaced AYP with the ASPI standards that are more appropriate to Alaska's unique K–12 circumstances.

Average Daily Membership (ADM): This differs from enrollment in that it uses a twenty-day count in October. The ADM drives the funding that a school receives from the state. (See also, **Base Student Allocation** and **Foundation Formula** below.)

Base Student Allocation (BSA): The base per-student revenue a school district receives from the state. Together with **Average Daily Membership** it is a major element in the **Foundation Formula**. In 2015 the BSA was $5,830 per student. This base is adjusted by several factors to arrive at the actual amount a school district receives.

Common Core: Officially known as the Common Core State Standards Initiative, it is a state initiated and not a federal program. It outlines national benchmarks in English and math that should be achieved at each grade level. The intent is that by graduation from high school each student is prepared to enter higher ed or go into the workforce. Alaska was one of six states that did not adopt the national Common Core. Instead it adopted its own standards. The ESSA reforms of 2015 prohibit the federal government from imposing a common core curriculum on the states.

Dropout rate: This measures the proportion of students who leave school each year without having graduated. This rate is often compared with the **graduation rate.**

Foundation Formula: Established in Alaska Statutes 14.17 (AS 14.17) it includes the formula by which state funds are allocated to school districts. It also sets minimum and maximum local contributions from local governments for school operations. The formula considers six factors: (1) size of schools, (2) geographic cost factor, (3) factor for special needs students, (4) intensive services for certain high cost students, (5) correspondence students in the district, and (6) funds for technical/vocational programs. These adjustments are then multiplied by the **Average Daily Membership** and the **Base Student Allocation** to determine the amount of state funds a school district receives.

Geographic Cost Differential (GCD): The GCD is one of the six factors in the state's school **Foundation Formula** that recognizes that school districts across the state face different costs for similar goods and services, such as energy, transportation, labor, and supplies. These differences produce widely varying costs for operating schools. Anchorage is used as the base for this calculation and assigned a factor of one (1.0). Other districts are then assigned a factor based on their individual cost differential in relation to Anchorage.

Graduation Rate: This tracks the percentage of students who complete high school "on time"—within six years after starting seventh grade.

HIGHER EDUCATION

AlaskaAdvantage Program: A student needs-based grant program administered by the Alaska Commission on Postsecondary Education (ACPE) providing up to $2,000 per year and also granting from $500 to $3,000 for those showing exceptional academic performance and those enrolled in workforce shortage programs. The program also disseminates information about its programs and higher ed opportunities in the state.

Faculty tenure: The awarding of permanent employment to a faculty member (barring illegal or untoward activity on the faculty member's part), usually after a period of six years during which they show a high level of performance as judged by their peers and the university administration. A major rationale behind tenure is the concept of academic freedom: the right to speak, write, and conduct research in the pursuit of knowledge free of the pressures of particular political, religious, or other value systems.

Graduation rate: This measures the percentage of freshmen students who are retained by a university and who graduate within six years.

Persistence: UAF's College of Rural and Community Development (CRCD) finds it more useful and appropriate to use the calculation of persistence rate rather than **retention** or **graduation rates**. Persistence measures students who continue to enroll in classes at any campus and over any period of time, regardless of whether they eventually earn a degree.

Retention rate: The rate at which first time, full-time freshmen are retained to their sophomore year. Retention is one of the best predictors for student success and graduation.

Source: Developed by the authors.

funding for REAAs comes from the state. So this puts the major burden for funding on state government.

Adding to the politics of funding is that there are major differences in what it costs to operate schools in rural-bush versus urban areas of Alaska.

Depending on whose figures are used, rural-bush per pupil costs are estimated to be up to 100 percent higher than those for the Anchorage School District.[44] This is understandable, given that virtually all supplies for rural-bush schools, from food to fuel to instructional materials, must be flown or barged in from afar. Moreover, the average per pupil cost across Alaska is higher than in most states. In 2012, for example, this figure was $18,113 per student, surpassed only by Vermont at $18,882.[45] And Alaska has the largest differential among all fifty states between highest and lowest per pupil spending districts by a significant amount.

As a consequence of these high costs and particularly the major disparity between urban and rural-bush school districts, how funds are distributed across the state has been the source of much contention over the years. State legislators have revisited this topic a number of times since the early 1990s. School districts receive funding from the state based on what is called the Foundation Formula (see Box 26.4 for details). This is rather complex in its calculations, but in essence it is based on student numbers (known as Average Daily Membership, or ADM—see Box 26.4) and the Base Student Allocation, or BSA, the basic dollar amount allocated to each student in the state. As explained in Box 26.4, the BSA is adjusted by six factors to arrive at the amount per student in a particular district. This figure is then multiplied by the ADM, which gives the amount of funding going to each school district. Also, the legislature usually authorizes an additional one-year lump sum appropriation for K–12 education in addition to the basic foundation funding. For example, in FY 2004 this amount was $23.2 million and $25 million in FY 2014.[46]

Of the six elements in the Foundation Formula, the one that causes the most controversy is the Geographic Cost Differential, or GCD (see Box 26.4). It is because of the GCD that considerably more funds per student go to rural-bush schools than urban schools, which annoys many urban Republican legislators. Their annoyance is exacerbated by the fact that student performance in rural-bush schools is generally lower than in urban schools. Republicans and some urban residents also raise the issue of equity. While REAAs contribute nothing to the cost of schools, school districts in organized boroughs are required to contribute to school funding based on a combination of local property tax revenues and the district's "basic need" as determined by the state funding calculation. Boroughs can choose to increase their contribution above this minimum, up to a predetermined maximum.

An Impasse over Reforming the K–12 Funding System

With all these concerns, the Foundation Formula has been considered problematic by many legislators and some boroughs, and there have been many attempts to reform it since it was last rewritten in 1998 and implemented in 1999. Among the many committees and task forces on possible reforms was a Legislative Education Funding Task Force set up in 2007 to look into improving components of the funding formula, primarily the GCD. The task force accepted some recommendations for adjusting the formula made by the Institute of Social and Economic Research (ISER) at the University of Alaska Anchorage.[47] However, the controversy over how this differential should be calculated continues, as does the concern by some municipalities of having to contribute to school funding.

On this latter issue the Ketchikan Gateway Borough filed suit claiming that the municipal contribution was a dedicated fund. Ketchikan won a favorable decision in Alaska Superior Court in 2014. The state appealed the decision to the Alaska Supreme Court, partly because elimination of the local contribution would reduce education funding by some $220 million a year. In early 2016 the Supreme Court overturned the Superior Court ruling.[48] As a result, the municipal contribution to funding education in boroughs and some other jurisdictions remains in place.

Meanwhile, the yearly fight over K–12 funding continues. From 2000 to 2009, K–12 received funding increases that outpaced inflation, but much of that went to pay for the increasing costs of teacher retirement, which is a looming cost for school districts. One of the basic, if not the most important, policy goals advocated by AASB and NEA-Alaska is to ensure full funding of education. This means having the BSA and other funding keep up with inflation. The state has provided its usual additional one-time lump-sum funding each year, but the BSA remained flat at $5,680 from 2011 to 2014, and because of rising costs, school districts had to lay off teachers and district staff. This increased the pressure by school districts on the legislature to increase funding and reform the system.

Partly as a result, in 2013 the State House of Representatives set up yet another committee, the House Sustainable Educational Task Force, to look into the state of education, including school funding. But the composition of the task force was criticized for being, in essence, too biased toward the fiscally conservative position of the House majority caucus and for having no teachers or other education specialists on it. Even then, with a relatively likeminded membership, the task force disagreed over how to deal with funding issues, which is more evidence of the contentiousness and difficulty of this issue. The major message of its report, issued in January 2014, was to cut spending, a recommendation that was clearly not acceptable to many in the K–12 community. Interestingly, though, the committee commissioned a study on the structure and operation of the Foundation

Formula, the results of which were that most school districts were happy with how it worked. The consultants, however, were not charged with considering the adequacy of funding in achieving performance of the school system.[49]

Despite their general proclivity to cut education spending, as part of the Governor's Omnibus Education bill in 2014, the Republican-dominated legislature raised the BSA to $5,830 in 2015, with plans for additional increases in 2016, 2017, and 2018 plus promises of larger amounts of one-time yearly funding. These increases were not acceptable to many Democrats, however, who wanted more extensive forward funding to enable school districts to plan at least two years ahead. Because of the major fall in oil prices in 2014 and their remaining low through early 2016, many of these increases may be only partly funded if at all. The prospect of reducing education funding made for another very contentious legislative session in 2015, with Democrats able to stave off major cuts proposed by Republicans.

So as of early 2016, a plan or consensus on the funding of K–12 education was no closer to being achieved than it was when Covey and his colleagues wrote back in 1999. Many legislators and their constituents think Alaska is spending too much money on schools, while other legislators and their constituents and members of the K–12 education community see the need for much more to be spent. This issue is likely to continue to be contentious as long as rural-bush districts do not provide direct contributions to school funding and costs remain significantly higher in those districts. Hence, this issue will continue to be a major underlying cause of urban versus rural-bush tensions that pervade much of Alaska politics.

K–12 Quality, Performance, and Accountability Issues

Alaska's schools are not succeeding for many students. There are high dropout and low graduation rates and low achievement among many populations in both urban and rural-bush schools. A 2008 report prepared for the Alaska Commission on Postsecondary Education (ACPE) produced some disturbing facts about Alaska's K–12 system from ninth grade onwards in comparison with the other forty-nine states. In 2004 only 62.5 percent of those who entered ninth grade graduated four years later, ranking Alaska eighth from the bottom among the fifty states. Alaska ranked third from the bottom regarding the chance of ninth graders attending college and fourth from the bottom in terms of high school seniors going directly to college.[50] The situation has improved slightly since then. For example, the high school graduation rate was 71.8 percent in the 2012–2013 school year but slightly lower in 2013-2014, at 71.1 percent. In 2014 this was ten percentage points below the national average of around 81 percent and 20 points below Iowa, the top ranked state.[51] Consequently, the quality and performance of many of Alaska's schools are of concern to politicians and citizens alike.

Alaska began a sustained period of state-led school reform in 1991 with the initiation of the Alaska 2000 (AK2K) process, which led to the creation of voluntary state student standards in ten core subject areas. In 1996, Commissioner of Education Shirley Holloway replaced AK2K with the Alaska Quality Schools Initiative, which resulted in mandatory state standards in reading, writing, and math, and the development of benchmark exams to assess student progress toward meeting them. Science standards were added in 2005. A 1997 law mandated that all high school students pass an exit exam in order to receive a graduation diploma.[52]

National concerns about quality and performance were a major force behind the passage of NCLB in 2001 and the rise of the so-called accountability movement. NCLB intensified federal mandates for results-driven education.[53] It was enacted during a time when states were themselves taking action to dictate local curriculum decisions. In essence, this movement was aimed at holding school districts and schools accountable for the money they received by educating students to a certain level of academic achievement or performance, based on standardized testing, mainly objective tests, over a broad range of subjects.

In part, because of the rigidity of both the federal implementation of NCLB and the standardized testing system, in 2009 the Common Core standards were developed through a collaborative process among the states. The Common Core standards focus mainly on English, language arts, and math, making learning more relevant to everyday life by using a more analytical, problem-solving approach and a more open-ended testing system. The NCLB movement affected Alaska, but the state's particular circumstances, especially its geography and cultural makeup, required some major modifications or waivers to enable it to deal with the issues of quality, performance, and accountability.

For instance, the requirement that all teachers be "highly qualified" in the subjects they teach is virtually impossible to meet in small rural-bush schools where one teacher may be responsible for teaching across three or four subjects and grade levels.[54] Nevertheless, the state developed a plan to assess schools and hold them accountable for their performance in meeting NCLB standards. This was the Average Yearly Progress or AYP system. Alaska schools did not do well by this standard. For instance, of the state's fifty-four school districts, only nineteen met the AYP standard in 2009–2010. This fell to twelve in 2010–2011 and to eleven in 2011–2012. As a result, in 2011–2012 a staggering 272 schools across the state were designated as not having met the AYP requirements of NCLB.[55]

While there were numerous critiques of the NCLB before it was largely replaced by ESSA, one of its positive outcomes was the requirement that states make available data on student performance in public schools by various segments of the total student population.

So because of NCLB empirical evidence was available on the differences in achievement for the student population as a whole, compared with Native students, limited English proficient students and low-income students. While the methods and presentation of this data may change somewhat under ESSA, the information will remain available.

New Directions in Quality, Assessment, and Accountability

The poor performance of Alaska's school districts and schools under NCLB, due in part to the state's unique circumstances, led Alaska to seek a waiver from NCLB regulations and replace them with its own set of standards. In total, thirty states received waivers, and Alaska's came in May 2013.[56] Following this waiver the AYP system was replaced with Alaska's own Alaska School Performance Index (ASPI), which is a more flexible system than that under NCLB and AYP, allowing specific areas to be targeted for improvements on a 100-point scale and a rating of one to five stars. In August 2013, 503 schools were rated using the new system and 142 received four or five stars, while 261 got one, two, or three stars.

As to curriculum and performance in particular subjects, Alaska developed its own standards, the Alaska State Standards, and did not adopt the national Common Core. In 2014, DOE Commissioner Michael Hanley stated that the reasons for this were that Alaska wanted to keep control of the standards and to be sure that they fit Alaska's particular needs. But he also admitted that they were not that different from the national Common Core.[57] Like their national counterparts, the Alaska standards curriculum is intended to be more relevant to students' lives, develop more analytical skills, and test students' reasoning and analytical skills as opposed to just their memorization abilities. In addition, as part of the 2014 K–12 reform package, the High School Graduation Qualifying Exam was abolished as it was seen as rigid in its requirements and often students failed even though they had completed all requirements for graduation. The reform allowed the Scholastic Aptitude Test (SAT), American College Testing (ACT), and WorkKeys tests to be used in place of the qualifying exam.

It remains to be seen how schools in the system will be rated based on the new ASPI system and how the new Alaska standards curriculum will aid in improving student performance. Will incremental reform succeed, or is more radical reform needed? Five to ten years should provide some useful answers. However, there is an immediate and troubling statistic in the accountability data: the achievement gap between Alaska Native and non-Native students.

Alaska Native K–12 Educational Issues

In 1999, Covey and his colleagues described a situation in which significant disparities existed in achievement between students in rural-bush and urban schools. Student achievement in general was lower in rural-bush schools, which fueled the on-going debate over whether the state should continue providing an education in rural-bush communities as opposed to a return to a boarding school system.[58] Neither the performance gap nor the political tensions have changed much in the years since Covey's work was published.

Rural-bush school failure is not the only problem affecting Alaska Native students. Native students in urban schools also drop out and fail at far higher rates than many of their non-Native classmates. Efforts to address this challenge have so far fallen flat. Native achievement and graduation rates are far below those of white students. For instance, in the school year 2013–2014, which was fairly typical of recent years, Alaska Natives made up about 24 percent of the school population in grades 7 through 12. That year they had a high school graduation rate of only 55 percent compared with 78.5 percent graduation for white students. That same year 6.4 percent of Alaska Native students dropped out of school, compared with 3 percent of white students. Alaska Native students made up 38 percent of all dropouts in the state.[59]

The root of the problem involves a complex interrelationship of socio-economic and cultural elements and likely others. Dealing with these elements has so far proven elusive. We know that demographics, such as poverty, parent education, and poor health, are linked with student achievement, and that Alaska Native students are far more likely than most non-Native students to come from families with lower incomes and less formal educational attainment. Yet, this in no way means that Native youth are not capable of learning. Rather, it means that educators and education policy makers, together with the aid and advice of Natives and Native leaders, need to find different and better ways to reach these students and to consider reforming some existing practices.

One approach is innovative language and cultural immersion programs. Several of these have been developed around the state, and some are demonstrating great success for their students. For example, students at the Ayaprun Elitnaurvik Yup'ik Immersion School in Bethel have performed better on standardized tests than students from nearby rural-bush schools where the primary language of instruction is English.

Another problem that needs to be tackled is that of high teacher turnover in rural-bush areas. National research demonstrates that high teacher turnover correlates with lower student achievement. Moreover, most of the teachers working in schools in rural-bush Alaska are non-Native and have been trained outside of Alaska. The proportion of Alaska Natives teaching in public schools remains under 5 percent and is declining. Research in Alaska shows that locally trained teachers have lower turnover rates than those who come from Outside. One way to decrease turnover, then, is to increase the number of Alaska Natives teaching in their own communities.[60] Yet there is no large scale initiative aimed at increasing the number of Alaska Native teachers statewide, either within the University of Alaska system or from the Department of Education. The University of Alaska Southeast runs the Preparing Indigenous Teachers for Alaska's Schools initiative (the PITAAS program), but this program produces only a handful of teachers each year.

A more radical approach might be to consider modifying the rural-bush high school system that resulted from the *Molly Hootch* settlement. At the time, the settlement was a great victory for advocates of Alaska Native education reform, and it has had many benefits. But it has also brought some problems. One of these, mentioned earlier, is that with such small enrollments and only one or two teachers in many rural-bush schools, the teachers are not qualified to teach a wide range of subjects and are unable to give students the education they need to get to college or pursue careers. So perhaps some compromise between a village high school system and short periods in regional residential facilities might be one way of improving rural-bush student performance without sacrificing the positive results of the settlement. Such a reform is only one possible approach to dealing with the problems of rural-bush education and would not address Alaska Natives' problems in urban schools. But it is a move worth discussing, as are ways to get the University of Alaska more involved with helping to solve these issues.

Solving the problems of Alaska Native education policy is crucial to the state, so much so that the authors of Chapter 30 have included it as one of the ten most important issues affecting Alaska's future.[61] One development that will likely impact Native K-12 education policy is the passage of ESSA.

Likely Effects of ESSA on Alaska

As a new and untried direction in K-12 education policy, it will take some time, maybe four or five years, before the effects of ESSA can be accurately assessed across the nation and in Alaska. Most schools and their teachers will see little immediate change, as the act will take time to implement. Moreover, while some of the euphoria on the passage of ESSA may be justified, over the long term other elements may need rethinking. Some of these issues may affect Alaska.

In terms of the immediate impact of ESSA on Alaska, because the state received a waiver from some NCLB requirements, ESSA's immediate impact will be minimal. Alaska will continue to administer its own testing system for high school students though the extent of testing will likely decrease. As required by ESSA, however, students in third through eighth grade will still be required to take annual reading and math tests, though the state can decide what weight to give these and other tests. In two areas in particular, school districts and the state will see an immediate benefit from the roll back of federal authority. One is that school districts, with technical assistance from the state, will be responsible for designing ways to improve low performing schools. The other is that responsibility and methods for evaluating the performance of teachers will also devolve to the state and school districts.

The ESSA reforms do, however, raise some issues about rural-bush education and about the special needs of minority students in urban areas. First, it is somewhat ironic that the very districts that are low-performing are expected to develop a successful improvement plan, something they had not been able to do before ESSA. Second, with the major turnover of teachers in rural-bush areas, and with the state and school districts now responsible for teacher evaluation, will this mean less qualified teachers and teachers' aides in rural-bush schools? And third, with less federal control, will minority students and other students with special needs in urban areas have less attention and fewer resources devoted to them than when the federal government imposed regulations and other accountability standards? These and other questions about the impact of ESSA remain to be answered.

6. HIGHER ED POLICY ISSUES IN ALASKA

In 2001, a specialist in higher ed policy, Donald Heller, wrote that affordability, access, and accountability were the key issues facing public higher ed across the states.[62] These three elements remain just as key in Alaska as they do elsewhere in the nation. There is, however, an additional issue in the mid-2010s that was of significance when Heller wrote and is increasingly important today. That is the issue of funding higher ed, which is addressed first in this section. We also consider the issues of quality and the relevance of the UA system to all potential Alaska students, and, as with K–12 education, the particular needs of Alaska Natives.

Funding the UA System

Like all areas of Alaska's state government, the UA system's funding is very much affected by the price of oil and overall state revenues. For a decade or so following the oil price crash of 1986, the university struggled to get adequate funding. While there have been major increases since 2000 that have kept pace with inflation and enrollment increases, these budget increases have not enabled the university to recover fully from the low funding years of the 1990s.

The UA system, however, has fared much better than other state-funded universities across the nation in the years since the international recession of 2008-2010. Many states have made major cuts in their higher ed system budgets, resulting in faculty and staff layoffs and others having to take unpaid leave. By contrast, in the fall of 2013 the major UA faculty union, United Academics, was able to negotiate a favorable contract for the period from 2014 to 2017. Until the fall of 2014 things looked good financially for the university and other agencies in state government. But the problem of low oil prices struck again in 2014 and continued into 2016, necessitating cutbacks in expenditures, including faculty and staff layoffs.

Even if oil prices had remained high and even if they rise again, like other universities across the nation, pressure is mounting in Alaska to at least hold the line on higher ed spending. As costs have risen, the system has experienced increasing tension between keeping tuition affordable and providing all the services and support needed by students. Tuition increased by 10 percent in 2004, another 10 percent in 2005, and 5 percent in both 2006 and 2007. From 2013 to 2014, however, there was only a 2.5 percent tuition increase. According to the UA statewide administration, tuition covers only about 30 percent of the total cost of education, compared to between 50 to 60 percent in other states.[63]

Many ideas regarding funding have been placed on the table. One is to require departments and institutes to seek private funding for their programs from foundations and individuals, including alumni. Another, which joins a trend across the nation, is the establishment at UAF of the Nanook Innovation Corporation to provide opportunities for faculty to develop patents that will generate revenue for the university.[64] How effective this might be remains to be seen. The university will likely face major financial challenges in the years to come.

Accountability

The concept of accountability in higher ed differs from that in K–12 education. There is no federal mandate or statewide testing system for higher ed. Until very recently, accountability at the university level has been concerned with the quality of education provided, which is more generally linked to the accrediting of universities. More recently, the federal government has developed a policy of accountability that provides assessments of postsecondary institutional performance.

The accreditation process is one in which universities and colleges are assessed as to their academic resources, including qualifications of their faculty, and quality of administrative and technical support for delivering higher education. In practice, it is a sort of truth in advertising assessment to ensure that universities are providing the services and program quality they claim to be offering. For campuses in the UA system, this evaluation is conducted by the Northwest Accreditation Association every ten years, with a less extensive assessment every five years. Also, in order to show the quality of their individual programs, many universities seek accreditations for specialty programs, such as public administration, which is accredited by the National Association of Schools of Public Administration.

Recent federal proposals to assess postsecondary performance are driven in large part by an increasing number of undergraduate students relying on federal student loans and also enrolling in for-profit institutions. The percentage of first-time, full-time undergraduate students receiving federal loans increased from 75 to 85 percent in just five years, between the academic years 2006–2007 to 2011–2012. During this time, the largest percentage increase was at four-year private for-profit institutions (from 55 to 91 percent). The percentage of students receiving aid at four-year public institutions increased from 75 to 83 percent, while the percentage of students at four-year private nonprofit institutions had the smallest increase, from 85 to 89 percent.[65]

As a result, the federal government wants to ensure that its student loan programs are getting value for taxpayers' money and to hold institutions of higher ed accountable for providing a quality education. So in 2013 President Obama sought to link performance review with his efforts to make undergraduate education more affordable to lower income students. One aspect of the plan involved the federal government ranking colleges on a sort of "scorecard" based on their performance in graduating students. Based on these rankings, Congress could choose to directly connect federal student aid to college performance. President Obama hoped to put this plan in place by 2018 to ensure that well-performing institutions are also receiving more federal aid and that student loans are more affordable. Overall, the plan aims to encourage transparency among higher ed institutions and ensure that students are able to make more informed choices.[66]

However, the plan, particularly the "scorecard" aspect, did not sit well with many university presidents, particularly those from for-profit institutions but also those from public and private non-profit institutions and their national organizations. As a result of political pressure exerted on the administration against the use of a ranking system, in September 2015, President Obama abandoned the idea of ranking of colleges and universities. The administration did, however, keep the idea of a "scorecard" and developed a website that offers information about tuition, graduation rates, and future salary prospects for graduates.[67] The fact that the President of the United States had to back down on the idea of a ranking system shows the power that the higher ed lobby can exert at the national level.

Barriers to Access: Affordability, Issues of Program Delivery, and Lack of a Higher Ed Culture

According to the "Measuring Up 2008" report card prepared by the National Center for Public Policy and Higher Education in 2008, Alaska is among the states with the fewest college opportunities for young and working age adults, with only Louisiana and Nevada showing worse ratings.[68] Access to higher ed is largely about being able to afford it. But it also includes issues of program delivery and understanding about college—that is, having a higher ed culture.

Affordability

Students are eligible for Alaska student loans and can apply for AlaskaAdvantage grants from the state and Pell grants from the U.S. government. There is also the tax-exempt University of Alaska College Savings Plan that is well advertised. The plan can be used at APU as well as UA and at any out-of-state university. In addition, there is the UA Scholars Program that gives $11,000 grants to Alaska students in the top 10 percent of their graduating classes who come to UA. Since its inception in 1999, over 7,000 students have accepted the scholarship for at least one semester. In fall 2014, the number of new UA Scholars was 429. But this is a very small number, perhaps 1 percent, of those attending the UA system.[69] For Native students there are some funds offered by their Native corporations, such as the $400,000 in scholarships provided in 2013 by the Sealaska Heritage Foundation, based in Southeast Alaska.

In general, the State of Alaska's investment in broad-based aid to students is among the lowest of all states in the nation. Partly as a result of this, Alaska undergraduate students were among the highest borrowers in 2007, with $5,427 more debt per student than the national average.[70] According to the National Center for Public Policy and Higher Education, college costs for students from low- and middle-income families are on average 37 percent of their net income. At that rate, the UA system is not affordable for many Alaska families.[71] And unlike other states, Alaska has no community college system, so there are no low-cost alternatives for a college education. For students choosing private postsecondary education in Alaska, financial options can be even more limited. Thus, while the UA system is striving to increase its academic rigor and become a system of choice for many students, state financial aid issues limit the attractiveness of the system for many, particularly those from low-income families.

Issues of Program Delivery

While students can pursue two-year degrees at all UA campuses, including a number of UA satellite campuses, most of those who want to complete a four-year degree program must move to Fairbanks, Anchorage, or Juneau. Only a few four-year degrees are available via online distance education, and this format is not necessarily the most appropriate for students who do not have experience in the formal higher ed system. For some, the challenges of living far away from home in a large and unfamiliar community are enough to deter them from completing a degree. On top of that, the cost of tuition and supplies is difficult for some to manage, and those costs, together with the cost of living, can make college too expensive for many.

In an attempt to address this problem, the university has made major efforts in distance delivery of various types. Distance delivery is a key component of the programs offered by UAF's College of Rural and Community Development. Much of the success of these programs, however, depends on the extent to which students are prepared for college and particularly for independent learning.

Lack of a Higher Ed Culture

According to the 2008 ACPE report, "Making Alaska More Competitive," referred to above, one of the major barriers to access to a higher education in Alaska is lack of a higher education culture among many Alaskans.[72] There are many students interested in higher ed whose parents do not have first-hand experience with college. These "first generation" students may not know how to apply or register, let alone know some of the techniques for succeeding in college, such as finding study groups, talking with faculty when they are having difficulties, or taking an incomplete or withdrawing from a class when they cannot finish. Rural-bush students face additional challenges, including cultural adjustments and being far from home.

Furthermore, there continues to be ambivalence about higher ed in Alaska. A myth persists in some quarters that people with a high school education (or less) can still make a fortune working on the North Slope oil fields. And some legislators do not understand the role higher ed plays in the economic health and well-being of the state or the need to invest in an adequate postsecondary system. This adds up to less support for student loans and other higher ed funding.

Quality and the Relevance of UA Programs to All Potential Students

By their very nature, universities should strive for academic excellence and the UA system has done so with varying degrees of success across its campuses. One successful effort has been the UA Scholars Program, with well over 80 percent of higher achieving students as of 2014 remaining in the state after graduation.[73] However, there is significant tension between the university's mission as an open access system and wanting to attract high-achieving Alaska students. Many students come to UA campuses lacking sufficient skills to succeed in regular college classes. It is an expensive endeavor to provide these students with remedial courses that do not count toward their associate or bachelor degrees. Yet, providing such remedial courses is an important part of the UA system's core mission.

It may well be that the university did the citizens of the state a major disservice when it abolished the community college system, which could have fulfilled this role as well as other roles, including technical and workforce training. This assumes it could have kept its faculty, staff, and other costs low enough to keep tuition rates at an affordable level. One institution in the state that attempts to serve these needs and at the same time does so within the learning style and needs of Alaska Natives is Ilisagvik College in Barrow. The philosophy behind the college and its program offerings are explained in Box 26.5.

BOX 26.5

A Tribal College in Alaska: A Cultural Sensitivity Approach to Academic and Workplace Success

Ilisagvik College in Barrow began in 1986 as a cooperative effort between the North Slope Borough and the University of Alaska Fairbanks. It was established to serve the residents of the North Slope by offering academic, vocational, and technical education with a strong emphasis on preserving and strengthening the Inupiaq culture, language, values, and traditions.

In 1995 the borough set up the Ilisagvik College Corporation as an independent, public, nonprofit entity governed by a Board of Trustees. Then, in 2007, Ilisagvik became the first federally recognized tribal college in Alaska and the thirty-sixth in the nation. It earned this status by demonstrating a commitment to providing postsecondary education in a learning environment reflective of the culture, traditions, and values of its students.

Through its foundation courses, academic programs, and technical, vocational, and continuing education, Ilisagvik's mission is to provide education in a form and atmosphere to promote student success in college, in their careers, and in their lives in general. To this end, the college makes a greater investment in student services than most postsecondary institutions. There is a major focus on tutoring, building life skills, wellness, and career planning, all intended to help students transition to mainstream institutions. A key aspect of student services is employing a village liaison in each North Slope community. The liaison serves as a contact for students, helping them apply to the college and register for classes. There is also a longer period allowed for students to move through academic programs. In 2009 the average relationship with a student was five years. Students do not get placed on academic probation or have a timeline imposed upon them if they make an effort to complete their courses. Ilisagvik's academic programs include Inupiaq Studies, English, natural sciences, teacher training, and business and information technology. The college awarded fourteen associate degrees in 2015, bringing the total to 172 associate degrees conferred since it opened in 1986.

Foundation education in math, English, and science is a large part of the Ilisagvik curriculum, and its remedial courses are offered and taken with no stigma attached. Courses are also offered in ESL (English as a second language) and toward the GED (General Equivalency Diploma, awarded in lieu of high school graduation). The college facilitates dual high school and higher ed credits and Cooperative Extension classes in secondary schools across the region. In addition, professional development and continuing education are available in the workplace, in the villages, and in student homes through online classes. These offerings are designed to provide learning at a level that enables students to succeed in a place where they are most comfortable and on a schedule that is convenient for them.

The largest number of students, however, is in workforce development, which averages about seven hundred short-term training participants each year. Of particular importance are classes dealing with the needs of the North Slope oil and gas industry. These include courses on allied health, heavy truck maintenance and repair, industrial safety, and associated construction trades, such as Hazwoper certification (hazardous waste protection), CPR/first aid, and other training needed for employment.

Source: Developed by the authors with reference, in part, to the Ilisagvik College website, at http://www.ilisagvik.edu/.

Native Issues in Higher Ed: Retention and Cultural Relevance

As in the K–12 system, Alaska Natives in the higher ed system are among the most at risk of not succeeding.[74] In 2011, the overall system retention rate had reached 75.3 percent. While the system as a whole is improving, Alaska Native students still had the lowest rate of retention of 58.9 percent from their freshman to sophomore year, as well as the lowest rates of degree completion. The ten-year statistics from 2001 to 2011 show a 7 percent increase in retention for Native students. The increase in the retention rate was largely in baccalaureate programs. Nevertheless, Native retention still lags behind that of white students, which reached 77.6 percent in 2011, a slight decline from 78.7 percent in 2010.

Regarding undergraduate degree completions, of those first-time, full-time degree-seeking Alaska Native students who entered in the fall of 2005, only 15 percent finished a degree of some sort (two- or four-year) in four years, and 16.4 percent finished one within six years. The eight-year trend shows a very modest 0.1 percent increase in degree completion in four years among first-time, full-time degree-seeking Alaska Native students. In comparison, 60.4 percent of first-time, full-time, degree-seeking white students who began in the fall of 2005 finished a degree within four years, and 63.3 percent finished one within six years.

Whereas some of the problems with retention of Native students are probably due to cultural adjustment problems, a lot has to do with the failure of the rural-bush school system to adequately prepare them for college. This is where an institution like Ilisagvik College can fill an important void. It can provide cultural sensitivity and give students the academic and other skills needed to transfer to mainstream academic institutions in Alaska and other states.

Although geared to the special needs of all rural-bush residents, UAF's College of Rural and Community Development (CRCD) also attempts to meet the socio-economic and cultural needs of Alaska Natives. It employs several Native faculty, and its assessment system and programs reflect the particular needs and learning styles of the Native community. Rather than using graduation, retention, and dropout rates to judge the level of success of rural-bush student in higher ed, CRCD uses the *persistence* rate of college attendance. Its curriculum also focuses on programs such as rural-bush development and Native studies, subjects that draw on the experience of its students and that are of direct value to them. One such program that has enjoyed considerable success is the Rural Human Services program, details of which are set out in Box 26.6.

The Links between K–12 and Higher Ed

Even though Alaska's K–12 and UA systems have separate administrative structures and their own budgets, our review of the issues facing both systems shows that there are many links between them that affect the quality of life of Alaskans. Not least of these is

BOX 26.6

Rural Human Services: An Innovative University Program to Meet the Needs of Rural and Indigenous Alaskans

The Rural Health Services (RHS) program trains village-based human services providers. It is built on Alaska Native values and incorporates in the program the cultures, traditions, and learning styles of the students. This statewide program is offered by UAF's College of Rural and Community Development (CRCD) and operated from CRCD's Interior-Aleutians Campus.

The training, intended for rural-bush residents who are natural helpers and healers in their communities, is designed to develop skills and credentials in the village's helping profession. This thirty-two-credit certificate program involves elders from around the state, who participate in program design and instruction. The curriculum covers a broad range of community health and human services, such as crisis intervention, suicide prevention, and counseling for grief, substance abuse, mental health, and healing. Individual courses incorporate both Native and Western knowledge.

The RHS program is designed to allow students to work while earning the certificate. Instead of academic prerequisites for admission to the program, applicants must be working for a regional health corporation, delivering village-based human services, or recognized by their community as a natural healer or helper. Students attend short one- to three-week intensive courses in Anchorage, Kotzebue, Bethel, or Fairbanks. Those who complete the program may continue working toward an associate's degree in Applied Science or Human Services, a bachelor of science degree in Social Work, or a bachelor of arts degree in Rural Development or Psychology.

The program has been very successful. As of May 2015, there were 525 RHS graduates working in over 185 rural communities across Alaska. According to RHS Program Manager Ann Hopper, there is a completion rate of 50 percent of those accepted into the program.

Source: Developed by the authors with reference, in part, to the Rural Human Services website, at http://www.uaf.edu/rhs/.

the ability of the K–12 system to prepare students for entry to, and success in, higher ed. Others include the need for the university to train more Native educators, to allow high school students to earn college credits over a broad range of subjects that will also count towards high school graduation. Plus, in the absence of a community college system, the UA system needs to facilitate workplace training, particularly of high school students who do not want to go to a four-year academic institution.

7. INTO THE FUTURE: A PROPOSED EDUCATION POLICY PLAN VERSUS THE LIKELY POLITICAL REALITY

The foregoing consideration of K–12 and higher ed policy issues paints a picture of a very mixed educational system in Alaska in terms of quality and performance and, for higher ed, accessibility. There is somewhat of a parallel between Alaska's system and the American educational system in general as viewed by Linda Darling-Hammond, a Stanford University professor and advocate for reforming the U.S. educational system. She sees the American system as both among the best and the worst in the developed world. It is among the best because it has some of the finest universities, and people with money can get an excellent education in the United States. It is among the worst because of so many poor-performing K–12 school systems, in large part due to poverty and a culture that does not value education.[75] Turning on its head the usual aphorism that education is the way out of poverty, Darling-Hammond argues that without first dealing with poverty, and all that accompanies it, an educational culture will not develop and advances in education will not succeed.

The parallel in Alaska is not identical with Darling-Hammond's national picture in part because she uses inner-city, largely African American and Latino communities in her study. There are, however, many similarities with Alaska. The University of Alaska is far from a world-class university, but it does have some world-class programs in special areas such as geophysics. Alaska also has some well-performing high schools and charter schools. Generally, however, Alaska scores low on virtually every educational indicator. In particular, some Alaska Natives, in many ways Alaska's equivalent to America's inner-city residents, do poorly both in the K–12 and the higher ed systems.

Given this lamentable situation, we now look at the likelihood of the state developing an education policy for dealing with it. Our approach is first to offer a proposed educational policy plan. This plan embraces both K–12 and higher ed because the "The Making Alaska Competitive" report, referred to above, Darling-Hammond's research, and our own observations lead to the conclusion that the two levels of education need to be addressed together in policy planning. Then we assess the likelihood of this plan being adopted in whole or in part. Finally, we briefly identify some other likely future developments in both K–12 and higher ed in Alaska.

A Proposed Education Policy Plan for Alaska

As the incremental approach to dealing with Alaska's education problems has, for the most part, not worked in the past, this plan takes a more extensive systematic approach to reform. The plan has five elements, many of which are interrelated.

Setting up an Alaska Educational Endowment

An educational endowment fund would be a savings account similar to the Permanent Fund but specifically for educational purposes. It could be dipped into when state revenues were down because of low oil prices to ensure a predetermined level of spending to adequately fund education. The creation of an endowment would require a constitutional amendment, as did the Permanent Fund, because of the state constitution's prohibition against dedicated funds. Its revenues could come from a variety of sources including Permanent Fund earnings, oil revenues, other revenues, or even new taxes or user fees. As noted earlier, Governor Steve Cowper (1986–1990) attempted to establish such an endowment but was unsuccessful.

Forward Funding of Education

With forward funding, the governor would propose and the legislature would appropriate funding for education, particularly K–12, for a period of two or more years, preferably up to five years. Funding over more than a single fiscal year enables school districts to make plans to hire teachers and staff, to buy equipment, to ensure that courses will be taught, among other advantages.

Reestablishing the Community College System

The academic mission of a university and the primarily technical and vocational mission of a community college are different in focus and in culture. The community college culture has been largely lost and the community college mission has been more or less ignored since the merger of the two systems in 1987. Not all Alaskans in urban or rural-bush areas need or desire academic postsecondary education. They and the state's economy would benefit from more resources going to a community college system.

The reestablishment of that system would enable the state to more fully meet the needs of a diverse set of learners with widely differing goals. It would also make postsecondary education more affordable for many students and families, assuming it were structured in a way that costs and tuition could be kept low.

A Rural-Bush K–12 Reform Initiative

Clearly, the rural-bush K–12 school system needs improvement. It requires reform on several fronts to provide a quality education to prepare students for college level work, for the workplace, and for life in general. One such reform, as mentioned earlier, might be to combine local rural-bush high school education with one or more stints, perhaps up to a year, at regional residential schools. Another would be to train more Alaska Native teachers and more from local communities with the aid of the university. A third would be to decide upon a long-term geographic cost differential (GCD) so that rural-bush schools can plan and give teachers longer-term contracts.

An Integrated K–16 Education Plan

An integrated plan would view education from kindergarten through graduation with a bachelor's degree, and maybe beyond, by promoting policies to enable the K–12 and university systems to integrate more and get citizens to view them as interconnected.

Specific elements could include:

- Creating a governor's cabinet-level position to promote this integration.
- More formalized DOE and UA statewide coordination.
- A sustained effort to promote a statewide higher educational culture, especially among minority and low-income students. This could be achieved by utilizing the cabinet position described above, DOE, UA's statewide administration, organizations like the State Chamber of Commerce, AASB, and NEA-Alaska as well as increased publicity about the AlaskaAdvantage Program.
- The recruitment and training of more high school and university faculty and administrative staff who are Alaska Natives and who would serve as role models for Native students and help recruit these students in both rural-bush and urban areas.

The Advantages of the Plan

This plan provides a benchmark for assessing the difference between what can be considered a progressive way to deal with improving the quality of education for all Alaskans and the likely political reality of future developments in education policy. In presenting it, we are not claiming that it is an ideal plan, that it would be supported by all educators in the state, or that it is the only possible approach to improving Alaska education overall. There have been many plans over the years. What this plan does is offer a set of approaches to address several of the ongoing, and in some cases apparently insoluble, problems that the state has been grappling with in education, particularly K–12 education, since statehood.

The plan is based on six premises. First, education is perhaps more significant in Alaska than in most states because of the unbalanced nature of the state's economy and the value of education as a foundation for economic development. Second, with a better educated and higher quality workforce, several public benefits will result, including higher productivity and flexibility, higher tax revenues, less dependence on public programs, and lower crime rates. Thus, there would be less government spending on public assistance and criminal justice.[76]

Third, these reforms will increase the quality of life of all Alaskans, but especially those in rural-bush areas, by providing more stability in teacher tenure and also more professionals, such as health workers, substance abuse counselors, among other professionals, who are familiar with the special needs of rural-bush areas. Thus, it would help to alleviate many of the social problems in rural-bush areas. Fourth, despite politicians' protestations to the contrary, the state has a a $50 billion Permanent Fund and can afford to invest in education to reap both short- and long-term benefits for its citizens. Fifth, and in line with our chapter's theme, implementing this plan would go a long way toward enabling Alaska's educational system to meet the needs of all Alaska's students.

Sixth, and perhaps most compelling of all, given the long-standing impasse in dealing with state funding of K–12 education, this plan offers a course of action where none currently exists. In this regard, Representative Tammie Wilson, Co-Chair of the 2013 House Sustainable Educational Task Force, referred to earlier, commented that the biggest issue the task force faced was that Alaska had no statewide direction on what it wanted out of its education system. She went on to say:

> We can look at all the financials we want to, but the bottom line is that we don't have a statewide education plan. That's needed to provide direction to the Legislature. We need to make sure the directions we're taking when it comes to funding are getting us from point A to point B.[77]

Dealing with the Educational Needs of Alaska Native Students

Because Alaska Natives are the major underserved minority in Alaska's educational system, a significant part of this proposed educational plan addresses the needs of Native students both in the K–12 and higher ed systems. To be sure, Alaska Natives make up less than a sixth of the state's population, and many Alaskans, including many politicians, express concern that too much attention is paid to issues surrounding Native education and a disproportionate amount of funding goes toward it. Whether or not such claims are valid is very debatable and in the end boils down to value judgments. What is not in dispute, however, is that the U.S. and Alaska constitutions and court decisions require equal access for minorities in broad areas of economic and social policy, including education.

On the other hand, Alaska Natives are not entirely victims of state policy. Indeed, the Native community, together with the state, must take some responsibility for its present plight regarding the unintended consequences of the *Molly Hootch* settlement. Moreover, the Native community must be a key part of dealing with present educational challenges for a better educational future. For example, if the Native community took the lead in reforming the rural-bush K–12 education system and improving student performance, it could receive political dividends by helping to silence critics who oppose higher GCDs in the K–12 Foundation Formula funding system. Successful initiatives in this regard, however, require a high degree of unity, or at least consensus, within the Native community, and this is often difficult to achieve on many issues. One issue that is often highly contentious among Native groups, particularly in the educational realm, is the tension between maintaining traditional Native culture and fitting into the mainstream majority culture.

The Likelihood of the Adoption of the Plan in Whole or in Part

The plan we have outlined has something for everyone. It would benefit conservatives by saving money on state programs and boosting the economy. Liberals would get a better educational system and more equality of access for all students. Alaska Natives would get long-needed reforms that would benefit young Natives as they face an ever more complex world. And Alaskans in general would have an improved lifestyle because of a strengthened economy. Moreover, the plan is not entirely dependent upon legislative and executive action. Some aspects of the plan require university and private initiatives as well as from the Native community, though key elements do require initiatives and long-term funding commitment from the DOE and the University. So what is the likelihood of such a course of action being adopted by state policy makers? Let us look at the five elements of the plan first.

The toughest political sell of all is probably the educational endowment. Just getting the legislature to support a constitutional amendment to be placed on the ballot would be difficult. For one thing, funding the endowment would divert general fund money that would otherwise be used for other services and programs. It would also be difficult to persuade legislators that education should be a special case as opposed to an endowment for other needed services, such as transportation and disaster relief, both natural and economic. People might worry that funding the endowment would require new taxes, plus many Alaska households are without children. Finally, if Permanent Fund earnings were used to fund the endowment, people would also be concerned about reductions in Alaskans' Permanent Fund Dividend (PFD) checks.

Forward funding has often been suggested, particularly by the Democrats, but has never been seriously considered. This is likely because it ties the hands of future legislatures and governors, especially in light of Alaska's uncertain revenue picture. Plus, given the two- and four-year cycle of legislatures and governors, there is no obligation for succeeding legislatures or governors to be bound by their predecessors.

Reestablishing the community college system is also a political long shot, mainly because of likely opposition from the university, but also probably from the legislature. In the short run, at least, reestablishing the system is likely to increase costs and make increased demands on the statewide budget at a time when the BOR is feeling pressure to reduce spending. A separate community college system would also increase the political fragmentation of postsecondary education and likely intensify the competition for dollars within the UA system. Some legislators might support the idea of community colleges, however, as a benefit to their communities, but many might also oppose it because of the likely increased costs.

Parts of a rural-bush K–12 reform initiative would have some chance of being implemented if, as argued above, the Native community could form a consensus and get behind it. Rural-bush K-12 reforms include aspects of the integrated K–16 education plan, which in several ways is linked to rural-bush educational reforms. The K–16 plan has the advantage that its costs are relatively low and it would likely have public support.

Despite its apparent appeal to a wide range of political perspectives, it is unlikely that much of this proposed plan would be implemented, and certainly not enough of it to bring about a radical change that would move Alaska's education system forward in a major way. The reasons are rooted in the basic nature of Alaska politics that have been identified throughout the book. These include fiscal conservatism, lack of a long-term fiscal plan as of early 2016, even in the face of unstable state revenues, deep-rooted urban versus rural-bush conflict, a jealous guarding of Permanent Fund earnings to ensure PFD payments (again, at least up until early 2016) even in times of low oil prices, and ad hoc and crisis policy making. So, for the foreseeable future, education will have to fight along with all other state services and functions for its yearly allocation of funds.

Other Likely Future Developments in Alaska's Education Policy

An integrated educational policy planning process is not likely to be in the cards politically for Alaska in the foreseeable future. But the increasing shift to the right in Alaska politics (including the rise of the religious right) and the resulting emphasis on reining in government spending may well result in the state serving the needs of even fewer students than it does today. In addition, judging by national trends in both K–12 and higher ed, there are other developments that may eventually work their way to Alaska, particularly in higher ed.

K–12 Education

Undoubtedly, funding of all aspects of K–12 education will continue to be the dominant and most contentious issue and be revisited again and again. A consultant's report issued in July 2015, referred to earlier in the chapter, commissioned as part of Governor Parnell's educational reform package of 2014, saw local school districts as fairly happy with the present system, but the report pointed out several needed reforms. Many Republican legislators had concerns about the methodology and findings of the report, however.[78] Thus, the debate over school funding will continue.

Another funding issue is that of providing funds for teacher retirement which, together with the state employees' retirement system, has become the third-largest yearly expense of state government. This problem was dealt with somewhat in 2014, but a long-term solution still needs to be found.[79] A related issue is NEA-Alaska's attempt to restore the original retirement system to which both the state and the employee contributed, as explained in Box 26.3. NEA-Alaska also opposes both extending the time for teachers to acquire tenure and lowering the standards for teacher qualifications.

A funding issue that has been around for a while and will likely receive increased attention with a conservative legislature is that of school vouchers. This issue has been pushed by the advocacy group Alaskans for Choice in Education.[80] In the 2013 legislative session, hearings were held to consider a constitutional amendment to allow these vouchers to be used by parents to pay for their children to go to private or religious schools. The amendment, which was supported by Governor Parnell, failed to pass the legislature in 2014, but it will no doubt return. This constitutional amendment is a major issue for Alaska's future and is considered in Chapter 30, Section 3. An open question regarding the school choice movement, and particularly aid to religious schools, is which way the U.S. Supreme Court might come down on the issue. It might be that it would find in favor of school choices interests.

A more immediate question is what ESSA might mean for the future relationship between the federal government and the states in K-12 education. A political phalanx of states, interest groups and committed individuals was able through Congress to overwhelm the Obama administration, which favored a different set of reforms to NCLB that would have left more authority with the federal government.[81] Is this roll back of federal authority a one-time success or the beginning of a general pattern that will tip the political balance in favor of more state and local control? It will likely take a decade or so to tell. In the meantime, the federal government retains some mandates and continues to provide major funding, which still gives it significant political influence over K-12 education in all states including Alaska.

Higher Ed

Despite the setback the Obama administration suffered over ranking higher ed institutions according to their performance and value for money for students, the federal presence in post-secondary education is not likely to diminish in the years to come. Under Democratic administrations, though less so under Republican ones, the federal government is likely to move toward rewarding well-performing colleges with more federal aid and penalizing those not performing well. This will likely affect for-profit colleges in particular, many of which are viewed more as money-making machines than educational entities.[82]

A more extensive trend that has been gathering momentum across the nation since the mid-1980s is the reduction in funding that state legislatures provide to higher ed. These reductions likely mean the end of the so-called "golden years" of higher ed, which spanned from the mid-1960s to the early 1980s and which were characterized by low tuition, a large percentage of tenured faculty, and the recognition of all types of education and research as valuable. In fact, this model of higher ed looks to be on the wane for two related reasons. One is the so-called corporatization of higher ed that is taking place. The other is that higher ed was once considered a public good, but is now fast becoming viewed as a private good. Both movements stem from the conservative trend of those elected to state office in recent years, often reflecting the fiscal conservatism of their constituents.

In essence, the corporatization of higher ed is the application of a business model that has been brought about both directly and indirectly by state governments. This involves, among other changes, less public funding, a focus on those programs that have economic value, like business and certain sciences, and the elimination of those that have less immediate applicability for employment, such as the liberal arts and the classics. This also includes a reduction in tenured faculty, which gives university administrators more flexibility in hiring and firing faculty to meet the new focus in the curriculum. The assault on tenure began at the University of Minnesota in 1997, and while it was not successful at that time, inroads into the tenure system are increasing across the nation.

The movement in higher ed from a public to a private good is simply this. In the golden age of higher ed, state government saw it as essential to the entire society to keep tuition low and access as wide as possible. Thus, higher ed was viewed as an important public good like K–12 education. But this attitude has changed because of the increasing costs of higher ed, what is often considered the irrelevance of much of the curriculum, and the increase of fiscal conservatism on the part of policy-makers. Consequently, higher ed is slowly becoming a private good reserved for those who can pay for it.[83]

Corporatization of the university system and the movement of higher ed towards becoming a private good are limiting educational opportunities and access. While Alaska is not at the forefront of these trends, the state may soon be affected by them.

Specific to Alaska, with conservatives in charge of the Alaska legislature, the tradition that the legislature more or less leaves the running of the university to the BOR, the president, and the chancellors, could change if the state keeps funding levels flat or reduces funding for the system, in which case lawmakers could get directly involved in university policy. This could mean the legislature getting involved with the allocation of the operating budget among campuses. In the near future, at least, besides making financially and politically unfeasible the re-establishment of the community college system, the fiscal conservatism of Republicans will likely mean looking for other cost-saving measures. This became an urgent need with the downturn in oil revenues in 2014 and beyond. One proposal that failed was to withdraw Alaska from the WWAMI program, which would have further increased the shortage of physicians in Alaska, particularly in rural-bush areas. The proposal may well resurface, however, if state revenues stay low.[84]

One way to make major savings is to close some satellite campuses and perhaps place UAS, the smallest MAU by far, under UAA or UAF to save its high administrative costs. This would not be a good move for students in remote areas or for those at UAS and would result in a fight for survival. But as we have argued in this chapter, what might be best practice in education policy is often subordinated by public officials to economics, budgets, ideology, and political pragmatism. Perhaps feeling such political pressure, in fall 2015, the university president stated that the rural campuses would be maintained. Nevertheless, in early 2016, facing extensive budget cuts due to a major downturn in state revenues, the BOR announced a plan to restructure the university. Among other things, this included a move to focus the three MAUs on particular areas of study and reduce the major duplication of programs. Despite claims to the contrary, it appears inevitable that major budget cuts will undermine the university's ability to fulfill its mission and serve the needs of all Alaska students who wish to pursue postsecondary education.[85]

8. CONCLUSION: POLITICS AND THE STATE'S ABILITY TO MEET THE EDUCATION NEEDS OF ALL ALASKA STUDENTS

The many concerns, disagreements, and often deep and emotional conflicts over education issues,, particularly K-12 education, make it impossible to eliminate politics from education. The central role of politics obviously does not mean that Alaskans do not receive a K–12 education and, theoretically at least, do not have the opportunity to attend postsecondary schools, particularly the University of Alaska. Nor does it mean that Alaska's education system is unique in being permeated by politics. What it does mean is that almost all aspects of education are subject to political decisions. Moreover, not only are politics central to education decision making, education is central to the role of state government and thus to Alaska politics. As such, education is high on the political agenda of all legislators, many governors, and most local governments. Education also involves some of the most influential interests in the state, including AASB, NEA-Alaska, and the university.

Realizing the role of politics in education, we can return to the question we posed at the beginning of the chapter: Do the public schools and the University of Alaska meet the needs of all students? Our conclusion that neither one is meeting those needs involves the interplay between the characteristics of Alaska politics reflected in education politics, as well as historical, economic, and cultural factors, some of which are not unique to Alaska. Consequently, while the end result is that certain groups, particularly Alaska Natives and lower income Alaskans, are disadvantaged, the situation today is much more complex than simply one of purposeful discrimination based on race or low-income status, though both likely still play a part.

The seven characteristics of Alaska politics that are the most prominent in education policy making are the all-pervasive importance of government, the role of Alaska Natives, conflict between urban and rural-bush areas, strong interest groups, the influence of external forces, fiscal conservatism, and the three strong contending branches of state government. The effects of these characteristics have been mixed, with some advancing and others adversely affecting the needs of students. For instance, the all-pervasive role of government has advanced the needs of many students through such actions as the *Molly Hootch* consent decree and the external influence of the federal government on Alaska education, which has aided minorities and the disabled and has provided funding in many areas. But government actions have also adversely affected some students through fiscal conservatism and the power of urban Alaska in relation to rural-bush areas, particularly since the early 1990s as the political influence of rural-bush areas has declined relative to the Railbelt.

Other factors have also come into play, however. For one, the long-term effects of the *Molly Hootch* settlement have not been uniformly positive. Another factor is the challenge facing all ethnic and racial minority groups in relation to the dominant culture. In Alaska's case it involves disagreements within rural-bush communities about what are the particular needs of students caught between a minority aboriginal culture and the dominant culture of non-Native urban Alaska. Still another is the lack of education culture among lower income groups, a situation that can be changed only over time, especially when it has cultural roots.

Because of the value-based nature of many conflicts in education, particularly on allocations from the annual education budget, the fundamentals underlying education politics are not likely to change much across the states or in Alaska in the years to come. At the same time, particular policy issues, such as how to finance education and the role of public versus private education, may undergo change. Moreover, who gets what, where, when, and how in the rough-and-tumble of day-to-day education politics will most likely depend more on who wields political power than on the merits of an issue, however "merits" may be defined.

The clear message is that for those who want to have their needs met in a more extensive way will have to muster the political influence to do so. These include Alaska Natives, and those who want better access to the higher ed system through lower costs or better grants, such as lower income individuals. Like those who brought about major reforms in K–12 education with the replacement of NCLB with ESSA, ultimately, it takes political influence to achieve policy goals in education as it does in other areas of public policy. The role of politics in education policy may be distasteful to many Alaskans, but politics in education, as elsewhere across the nation, is a fact of life in Alaska.

ENDNOTES

[1] Determining the exact percentage of education spending—both K–12 and higher education—in Alaska and making comparisons with other states is more complicated than it might appear. As explained in Section 9 of Chapter 19 on Alaska's state budget, at the state level percentages can vary with the year for a variety of reasons, and a lower percentage of the budget may not necessarily mean a decrease in spending on education. For this reason, in this chapter we use broad percentages, and specific dollar amounts quoted should be viewed with this caveat in mind.

As Chapter 19 also explains, K–12 spending comparisons between Alaska and other states can be misleading. This is because in Alaska a large percentage of education funding comes from the state (almost 100 percent for rural-bush schools), whereas in most states local governments provide a large portion of school funding.

[2] Office of Management and Budget, *Alaska Enacted Budget 2013*, Fiscal Press Package 2013, at http://omb.alaska.gov/ombfiles/13_budget/PDFs/Press_Packet-5_14_12.pdf.

[3] For an overview of the development of Native education in Alaska see, Carol Barnhardt, "A History of Schooling for Alaska Native People," *Journal of American Indian Education* 40, no. 1 (2001): 1–30; and for an account of the challenges presented in educating students in remote northern regions, including Alaska, Canada, Greenland, and Scandinavia, see Frank Darnell and Anton Hoem, *Taken to Extremes: Education in the Far North* (Oslo: Scandinavian University Press, 1996).

[4] See Chapter 18 on Alaska local government, Table 18.1, from which these numbers are taken.

[5] These and other statistics for Alaska K–12 education are taken from the Department of Education and Early Development (DOE) website at http://education.alaska.gov/stats/, particularly, *Report to the Public*, at http://education.alaska.gov/reportcardtothepublic/.

[6] Alaska Statutes, AS 14.30.010.

[7] DOE at http://www.eed.state.ak.us/faq.html; and Jane Gross, "Lack of Supervision Noted in Deaths of Home-Schooled," *New York Times*, January 12, 2008, Section A, 8.

[8] From the DOE website, "Frequently Asked Questions," at http://education.alaska.gov/faq.html. However, this was the same number given in 2007. It is likely that the private school population has increased over the eight years since then.

[9] See the Anchorage Christian School's website, at http://www.acsedu.org/about-acs/.

[10] See the DOE website at http://education.alaska.gov/Alaskan_Schools/Charter/pdf/ Charter_School_Directory.pdf.

[11] National Center for Education Statistics, at http://nces.ed.gov/programs/digest/d12/tables/dt12_067.asp.

[12] See the Center for Educational Reform website, at http://www.edreform.com/2012/04/K-12-facts/.

[13] National Center for Educational Statistics, at http://nces.ed.gov/programs/digest/d12/tables/dt12_042.asp.

[14] This overview of the increased role of the federal and state governments in K–12 education and other comparisons on K–12 education across the fifty states draws on Michael B. Berkman and Eric Plutzer, "The Politics of Education," in *Politics in the American States: A Comparative Analysis*, eds. Virginia Gray, Russell L. Hanson, and Thad Kousser, 10th ed. (Washington, D.C.: CQ Press, 2013).

Information on the Every Student Succeeds Act (ESSA) is based on Lyndsey Layton, "Senate overwhelmingly passes new education legislation," *Washington Post*, December 9, 2015; and Emma Brown, "How schools would be judged under 'Every Student Succeeds,' the new No Child Left

Behind," *Washington Post*, November 30, 2015. See also Lisa Murkowski, "Sen. Murkowski: Every Student Succeeds Act contains needed reforms good for Alaska," commentary for the *Alaska Dispatch News*, December 11, 2015. The comment by Norm Wooten is from an interview with Clive Thomas, December 12, 2015. This interview also provided much of the information on ESSA's likely effects on Alaska presented in this chapter.

[15] Office of Management and Budget, *Alaska Enacted Budget 2013: Fiscal Press Package*, at http://omb.alaska.gov/ombfiles/13_budget/PDFs/Press_Packet-5_14_12.pdf.

[16] See the Commission's website for a list of postsecondary educational institutions in Alaska, at http://acpe.alaska.gov/EDUCATOR-SCHOOL/Postsecondary_Institutions/Institutional_Authorization/Alaska_Postsecondary_Institutions.aspx.

[17] Interview by the authors with former APU President Doug North, March 19, 2008. See also the APU website, at http://www.alaskapacific.edu/about-apu/.

[18] Alaska does, however, have a law review, *Alaska Law Review*, published in conjunction with Duke University Law School in North Carolina.

[19] See the WICHE and WWAMI websites, at http://www.wiche.edu/ and http://www.uaa.alaska.edu/wwami/akwwamihistory.cfm.

[20] In contrast with most state public university systems, the head of the UA system is not called the chancellor but the president, and the heads of the MAUs are called chancellors, not presidents.

[21] For a short commentary on the constitutional status of the university, see Gordon Harrison, *Alaska's Constitution: A Citizen's Guide*, 5th ed. (Juneau: Alaska Legislative Affairs Agency, 2012), 126–27.

[22] Statistics on the UA statewide system and its campuses are taken from publications and the website of the statewide system, *Spring 2014 Semester Opening Summary*, at http://www.alaska.edu/swbir/ir/publications-reports/unit10/ Spring_2014_Open_Summary.pdf; and *UA in Review 2015*, at http://www.alaska.edu/swbir/ir/ua-in-review/uar2015/UAR-2015_Final.pdf.

[23] See University of Minnesota, Institutional Research, at http://www.oir.umn.edu/static/hrdata/Employee_Head_Counts_2005_2012.pdf; Arizona State University, Institutional Research, at http://uoia.asu.edu/sites/default/files/HC-FTE-SCH/Fall%20HC-FTE-SCH%201970-Present.pdf; and University of Washington, Institutional Research, at http://admit.washington.edu/quickfacts#enrollment.

[24] The authors thank Cyndee West (Business Manager for United Academics) for help in piecing together the history of the UA faculty unions since the early 1980s.

[25] For details on this ballot initiative, see Ballotpedia, *Alaska Higher Education Measure*, at http://ballotpedia.org/Alaska_Higher_Education_Measure_%281988%29.

[26] The case was *University of Alaska v. Alaska Community Colleges Federation of Teachers Local 2404*, No. S-9732. February 21, 2003, at http://caselaw.findlaw.com/ak-supreme-court/1160048.html.

[27] See the ACCFT website, at http://www.uaft2404.org/; and the United Academics site, at http://unitedacademics.net/news/about-us/.

[28] For details on the sources of this information and the Alaska population in general, see Chapter 1, endnote 3.

[29] Scott Jaschik, "Sheldon Jackson Suspends Operations," *Inside Higher Ed* (July 2, 2007), at http://www.insidehighered.com/news/2007/07/02/Sheldon.

[30] Details on the particulars of HB 278 were provided in interviews by Clive Thomas with John Greely of the Association of Alaska School Boards (AASB) during December 2014 and with George Ascott, legislative aide to Representative Chris Tuck (Democrat of Anchorage), also during December 2014.

[31] See Chapter 3, Section 1, especially Box 3.3.

[32] For an explanation of the urban versus rural-bush split, see Chapter 18 on local government, Section 7.

[33] See Clive S., Thomas, Richard H. Foster, and William F. Lunch, "Just Another Special Interest: The Higher Education Lobby in the Pacific Northwest States," a paper presented at the Western Political Science Association, Las Vegas, Nevada, March 2007.

[34] See Michael K. McLendon and James C. Hearn, "Introduction: The Politics of Higher Education," *Educational Policy* 17, no. 3 (January and March 2003): 3–11; William McMillen, *From Campus to Capitol: The Role of Government Relations in Higher Education* (Baltimore: The Johns Hopkins University Press, 2010), Chapters 1 and 2; and Thomas, Foster, and Lunch, "Just Another Special Interest."

[35] For example, when he ran for the State Senate in 2012, Pete Kelly, who worked for several years with the university's main official advocate (read lobbyist), adamantly denied he had ever been a lobbyist and was supported in this by former university president Mark Hamilton. Technically they were right, but their denial was a misrepresentation of the reality. For an account of the disingenuousness of this denial, see Dermot Cole, "This Just In: Pete Kelly Was a Lobbyist in Juneau," *Fairbanks News Miner*, October 19, 2012.

[36] University of Alaska Statewide system bulletin, January 26, 2012, at http://www.alaska.edu/opa/enews/2012/126/.

[37] See the APLU and ACE websites for their role in lobbying, at http://www.aplu.org/page.aspx?pid=249 and http://www.acenet.edu/Pages/default.aspx.

[38] The details of this study are explained in Chapter 15 on interest groups, endnote 2, and Section 7, especially Table 15.3 and Table 15.4. All assessments of interest group influence in Alaska and across the fifty states are taken from these two tables plus Table 4.2, "Ranking of the Forty Most Influential Interests in the Fifty States," in Clive S. Thomas and Ronald J. Hrebenar, "Interest Groups in the States," in *Politics in the American States: A Comparative Analysis*, eds. Virginia Gray, Herbert Jacob, and Robert B. Albritton, 5th ed. (Glenview, IL: Scott, Foresman/Little, Brown, 1990); and Table 4.2 in Anthony J. Nownes, Clive S. Thomas, and Ronald J. Hrebenar, "Interest Groups in the States," in *Politics in the American States: A Comparative Analysis*, eds. Virginia Gray and Russell L. Hanson, 9th ed. (Washington, D.C.: Congressional Quarterly Press, 2008). The 2008 table was updated in 2010 for selected states.

[39] For an explanation of the types of interest group power and the problems of assessment, see Chapter 15, Section 7.

[40] See Chapter 15, Section 7, esp. Box 15.7.

[41] For the influence of the local government lobby and its overlap with the K–12 lobby, see Chapter 18 on local government, Section 7, esp. Box 18.4.

[42] Jerry Covey *et al.*, "Education: Continuing Urban-Rural Tension," in *Alaska Public Policy Issues: Background and Perspectives*, ed. Clive S. Thomas (Juneau: Denali Press 1999).

[43] Information on the mechanics and politics of Alaska school funding draws on Covey, *et al.*, "Education: Continuing Urban-Rural Tension," 113–17; Alaska Department of Education, *Public School Program Funding Overview*, updated September 2014, at https://education.alaska.gov/news/pdf/FundingProgramOverview.pdf; Mary Hakala, "School Funding 101: All You Did and Didn't Want

to Know about School Funding," Great Alaska Schools, April 11, 2014, at GreatAlaskaSchools@gmail.com; and aid from John Greely and George Ascott, see endnote 30.

[44] DOE, *Public School Program Funding Overview*, 4.

[45] Kids Count Data Center: A Project of the Annie E. Casey Foundation, *Educational Expenditures Adjusted for Regional Cost Differences 2012*, at http://datacenter.kidscount.org/data/Tables/5199-per-pupil-educational-expenditures-adjusted-for-regional-cost-differences?loc=1&loct=2#detailed/2/2-52/true/868/any/11678.

[46] Hakala, "School Funding 101."

[47] Joint Legislative Education Funding Task Force, *Report to the Governor and Legislature* (Juneau 2007), 4.

[48] Leila Kheiry, "Superior Court Rules Alaska School Funding Mandate Unconstitutional," KRBD Radio (Public Radio for Ketchikan), November 25, 2014; and Tegan Hanlon, "Alaska Supreme Court rejects challenge to state's education funding formula," *Alaska Dispatch News*, January 8, 2016.

[49] See, Alexandra Gutierrez, "Legislative Task Force to Perform Legislative Review," *Alaska News Nightly*, Alaska Public Radio Network (APRN), August 1, 2013; Becky Bohrer, "Task Force Members Clash on Education Funding," *Anchorage Daily News*, December 31, 2013; Pat Forgey, "Democrats Blast 'Stunningly Underwhelming' Alaska Education Report," *Alaska Dispatch*, January 4, 2014; and Nathaniel Herz, "Legislature's education consultants give good grades to education funding methods," *Alaska Dispatch News*, July 22, 2015. The 2015 report is J. Silverstein, A. Brown and M. Fermantich, *Review of Alaska's School Funding Program*, a report prepared for the Alaska State Legislature (Denver, CO: Augenblick, Palaiich, and Associates, 2015).

[50] Ron Phipps, "Making Alaska More Competitive by Preparing Citizens for College and Career," a report prepared for the Alaska Commission on Postsecondary Education by IHEP (The Institute for Higher Education Policy), Washington, D.C., April 2008, 2.

[51] *Governing: The States and Localities*, High School Graduation Rates by State, at http://www.governing.com/gov-data/high-school-graduation-rates-by-state.html; Emma Brown, "High school graduation rates on the rise in most states," *Washington Post*, October 19, 2015; and Jennifer C. Kerr, "Most states show increase in graduation rates, Alaska not among them," Associated Press, published in the *Juneau Empire*, October 19, 2015.

[52] Alaska Department of Education, *History of Alaska School Reform, 1991–2006*, at http://education.alaska.gov/publications/historyreform.pdf.

[53] The school accountability movement is covered in Kenneth K. Wong and Anna Nicotera, *Successful Schools and Educational Accountability* (Boston: Pearson, 2006).

[54] For more on these challenges, see "Discussion Points on No Child Left Behind," January 2003, at http://www.eed.state.ak.us/nclb/pdf/Ak_Implementation_Challenges.pdf.

[55] Alaska Department of Education, *Assessment Accountability and Student Information*, at http://www.eed.state.ak.us/tls/assessment/accountability.html.

[56] Alexandra Gutierrez, "Alaska Gets Waiver from No Child Left Behind," *Alaska News Nightly*, APRN, May 22, 2013.

[57] Pat Forgey, "Skeptics Keep Up Pressure against Alaska Common Core Education Standards," *Alaska Dispatch*, January 8, 2014.

[58] Covey, *et al.*, "Education: Continuing Urban-Rural Tension," 118–23.

[59] Alaska Department of Education, *Alaska Report Card to the Public, 2013–2014*, at http://www.eed.state.ak.us/reportcard/2013-2014/reportcard2013-14.pdf.

[60] Alexandra Hill and Diane Hirshberg, *Alaska Teacher Supply and Demand, 2005 Update* (Anchorage: UA, Institute of Social and Economic Research, 2006).

[61] See Chapter 30, Box 30.6.

[62] Donald Heller, ed., *The States and Higher Education Policy* (Baltimore: The Johns Hopkins University Press, 2001), Introduction.

[63] University of Alaska Statewide Institutional Research and Budget, *FY14 Approved Operating and Capital Budget Distribution Plans*, at http://www.alaska.edu/files/swbir/FY14_Approved_Operating_Capital_Budget_Distribution_Plans.pdf.

[64] University of Alaska Fairbanks, "Nanook Innovation Corporation Provides Opportunities for Inventors," *Cornerstone* (November 25, 2013), at http://uafcornerstone.net/nanook-innovation-corporation-provides-opportunities-inventors/.

[65] National Center for Educational Statistics, *Fact Sheet*, at https://nces.ed.gov/FastFacts/display.asp?id=31.

[66] The White House, *FACT SHEET on the President's Plan to Make College More Affordable: A Better Bargain for the Middle Class*, at http://www.whitehouse.gov/the-press-office/2013/08/22/fact-sheet-president-s-plan-make-college-more-affordable-better-bargain.

[67] See, Michael Shear, "With Website to Research Colleges, Obama Abandons Ranking System," *New York Times*, November 12, 2015. The administration's website is at https://collegescorecard.ed.gov/

[68] National Center for Public Policy and Higher Education, *Measuring Up 2008: The National Report Card on Higher Education*, at http://measuringup2008.highereducation.org/print/NCPPHEMUNationalRpt.pdf. The Center closed in 2011, but its reports can still be found online.

[69] University of Alaska Scholars Program, *UA Scholar Statistics, Budget and Performance Summary*, at http://www.alaska.edu/scholars/program-overview/stratistics/.

[70] National Center for Public Policy and Higher Education, "Measuring Up 2008."

[71] *Ibid.*

[72] Phipps, "Making Alaska More Competitive."

[73] University of Alaska Scholars Program, *UA Scholar Statistics*.

[74] The following statistics on retention and graduation rates are taken from The University of Alaska Statewide Institutional Research and Budget, *Retention and Graduation FY11 Baccalaureate Retention and Graduation Summary*.

[75] Linda Darling-Hammond, *The Flat World and Education: How America's Commitment to Equity Will Determine Our Future* (New York: Columbia University Teachers College Press, 2010). See also, Suzanne Mettler, *Degrees of Inequality: How the Politics of Higher Education Sabotages the American Dream* (New York: Basic Books, 2014), which argues that the American higher education system is no longer a route to equality but has contributed to solidifying class lines and excluding the poor and some of the lower middle class from obtaining a higher education.

[76] Phipps, "Making Alaska More Competitive," 3–4.

[77] Pat Forgey, "Democrats Blast 'Stunningly Underwhelming' Alaska Education Report."

[78] Nathaniel Herz, "Legislature's Education Consultants Give Good Grades to State Funding Methods," *Alaska Dispatch News*, July 22, 2015.

[79] For details on the 2014 infusion of money into the state's and teachers' retirement systems, see Chapter 18 on local government, Box 18.3.

[80] See their website, at http://akchoice.org/.

[81] Juana Summers, "House And Senate Lawmakers Work to Revise No Child Left Behind Law," *Morning Edition*, National Public Radio (NPR), July 8, 2015.

[82] See, Mettler, *Degrees of Inequality*, for a realistic look at the role of for-profit colleges and for the way that increased costs are limiting access to higher education for poor and minority students.

[83] For more on this movement and other reforms in higher ed, see Louis Menand, *The Marketplace of Ideas: Reform and Resistance in the American University* (New York: W. W. Norton and Company, 2010); Mettler, *Degrees of Inequality*; and Thomas, Foster, and Lunch, "Just Another Special Interest."

[84] Katherine Long, "Alaska may pull out of UW-run WWAMI program, which trains doctors for five states," *The Seattle Times*, March 20, 2015.

[85] Tegan Hanlan, "University of Alaska leaders plan to restructure campuses," *Alaska Dispatch News*, January 27, 2016.

★ CHAPTER 27 ★

Social Services and Corrections: Intergovernmental, Public and Private Policy Making, and Power Dynamics

Patrick M. Cunningham

Social services and corrections issues and policies are perennial items on the policy agenda throughout the United States, including Alaska. This is for two major and related reasons. First, they take a large chunk of national and state budgets. Across the fifty states, social services and corrections combined account for between one-quarter and one-third of the annual operating budget, depending on the state. This places social services on a par with education as one of the two major expenditures of state government. In most states, social services are the number one expenditure. In fact, social services, including corrections, have been the major state expenditures in Alaska since the early 2000s.[1] Second, these issues and policies stir the cauldron of political and ideological conflict. Witness, for instance, the very heated and drawn-out debate in Congress over President Obama's proposal for health care in 2009–2010 and the negative reaction to the law in over half the states.

Social services politics and policy in Alaska involve five aspects. First is the way that these services are delivered. This is an intergovernmental and pluralistic approach involving state, federal, private for-profit, private nonprofit, and Alaska Native agencies and organizations. Second, the general political atmosphere of social services in Alaska is ideologically conservative. Third, in terms of client groups served by social services, there is a particular power dynamic that is distinct from other state services like education and transportation. Because social services client groups, particularly the poor, prisoners, and victims of domestic violence and child abuse, have little political influence, they need a political surrogate or policy entrepreneur to take on their cause. Sometimes someone or a political institution takes up their cause, but often not. Fourth, the first three aspects, in large part, result from a fragmented policy-making process in social services.

Fifth, all four aspects have so far precluded what, from a professional perspective, is the best policy approach to social services. This approach is that health, crime and corrections, and interpersonal violence issues are often interrelated in terms of causes and consequences. Developing effective policies to deal with them requires treating them as an integrated whole and being mindful of the negative effects of legislating in one area only. A holistic approach will see more results in alleviating these problems rather than an ad hoc, fragmented approach of treating each separately.

In terms of the chapter's structure, we first provide some background on social services and their politics in Alaska. Then we examine health policy, followed by consideration of corrections and interpersonal violence policy. Next we provide insights into the past and present role of politics in Alaska as it affects social services and related programs. The conclusion looks at likely future directions in social services policy in light of past patterns and experiences.

1. A SOCIAL SERVICES PRIMER: TERMINOLOGY, PROGRAMS AND THEIR IMPLEMENTATION, AND ALASKA'S SOCIAL SERVICES POLITICAL ENVIRONMENT

Making sense of the wide range of social services and related programs in the United States and in Alaska is challenging. So in this section we provide some essential background.

Terms and Concepts

Underlying the idea of social services programs is the concept of "welfare." In everyday speech, the word *welfare* is used as a generic term for public assistance, as in "they are on welfare." As a policy goal and as used in this chapter, *welfare* refers to the promotion of the well-being of individuals, communities, and society as a whole, in order to ensure security and stability in the physical, emotional, and financial aspects of life. The term *social services* does not usually include all public programs that promote such welfare, however. Education (both K–12 and postsecondary), transportation, retirement systems (such as federal social security paid to qualified senior citizens), unemployment benefits, and corrections, are not usually included in the definition of this term.

Although *social services* has no watertight definition, it is usually confined to programs promoting the well-being of five types of special needs or at-risk individuals and families: (1) those with low incomes that prevent them from affording basic services, such as health care; (2) those with particular needs because of age or physical or mental disability; (3) women and children at risk because of adverse domestic circumstances, such as violence and child abuse; (4) individuals at risk because of alcohol or drug abuse, or an adverse mental condition (often collectively referred to as behavioral health issues);

and (5) youth at risk, which may involve foster care and substance abuse counseling. Our use of *social services* in this chapter embraces these five categories (note, however, that given space limitations we do not cover all five in detail). In many cases, individuals and families fall under two or more of these categories. For instance, poverty and substance abuse can lead to domestic violence. This interconnection is one reason why we argue that policies addressing these problems require integration to be effective.

The term *corrections* in this chapter refers to the range of policies, laws, and regulations that apply to processing individuals convicted of crimes. This includes classifying crimes, understanding the reasons for crime, and sentencing resulting in probation or incarceration. Although corrections policy and administration are not usually included under social services, there is often an overlap between the two. Poverty, domestic violence, child abuse, substance abuse, and mental illness are often associated with crime. Social services programs can be valuable in preventing crime or aiding former inmates to integrate successfully back into society. This is another reason why, ideally and practically, social services and corrections need an integrated policy approach and why we consider them together in this chapter.

Social Services Programs, Their Development and Delivery

The average American and Alaskan may well ask why there are so many social programs, and why so many of them overlap. Why would anyone create such a complex and patchwork system in which several different programs target the same at-risk or needy populations?

The situation is largely the product of two political and governmental circumstances. One is the nature of the American political system, involving federal, state, and local governments, private nonprofit and for-profit organizations, and various combinations of funding and service delivery for programs that often overlap. In fact, the politics, funding, and delivery of social services and related programs provide a textbook case of intergovernmental relations (IGR) as explained in Chapter 10. Second is the incremental nature of policy making in the United States, both at the federal and state levels. Because of the separation of powers system, the power bases in Congress and in state legislatures are pitted against the power centers in the federal and state executive branches, and are sometimes influenced by federal and state court decisions.

In combination, these two factors tend to undermine programmatic public policy making—integrated, streamlined programs—of the type that more or less exist in parliamentary and unitary political systems like Germany, Norway, and the United Kingdom. The upshot is incremental, ad hoc solutions to problems, resulting in complex and patchwork services and programs, with variations from state to state, county to county, and city to city across America.

State and Federal Social Service Programs

From the nation's infancy, states have provided some form of assistance for needy and vulnerable citizens in an attempt to ensure safety and well-being. The laissez-faire philosophy that became dominant soon after the nation's founding resulted in a small financial commitment by government and meager programs. Assistance for the needy came primarily from churches and other religious organizations, charities, private agencies, socially responsible businesses, and family members. Then the Progressive reform era of the early 1900s resulted in changes in political, economic, and social institutions favorably assisting the needy and vulnerable. Workers' compensation insurance to protect those injured on the job, the creation of maternal and child health programs to reduce mother and infant mortality, and widows' pensions became common in many states. Other reforms assisted and protected the working poor.

Those programs proved woefully inadequate, however, when the Great Depression of the 1930s struck and tens of millions of Americans sank into poverty in the absence of an extensive public social safety net. As a consequence, for the first time at the federal level a public commitment was made to aid the needy and the vulnerable. President Franklin D. Roosevelt's New Deal response to protecting the public from another Great Depression resulted in the passing of the Social Security Act of 1935. The intent of the act was to create a safety net for the vulnerable. This was followed by a host of social services programs enacted during the War on Poverty and Great Society period of President Lyndon Johnson's administration (1963–1969). The federal government's role in funding social programs underwent a major expansion, and the states expanded their social services programs considerably. This expansion was a product of increasing awareness and the need to deal with personal and social concerns, such as poverty, domestic violence, child abuse, and substance abuse. These problems had either not been recognized or were ignored until the post–World War II period and the growth of the middle class.

Today, the federal government and all states have a cabinet level agency dealing with social services and related programs. In Alaska, this is the Department of Health and Social Services (DHSS), not to be confused with the federal Department of Health and Human Services (HHS). Most states have a department of corrections, as does Alaska. Thus, since the 1960s, the institutional and political circumstances explained here regarding IGR, incrementalism, and specific factors in individual states, have produced a unique mix of social services programs.[2]

As of 2016, the federal government and the states provided medical and cash assistance to the needy through five major public assistance programs:

1. **Temporary Assistance for Needy Families (TANF):** This originated with President Clinton's "changing welfare as we know it," included in the Personal Responsibility and Work Opportunity Reconciliation Act of 1996.

2. **Supplemental Security Income (SSI):** Administered by the federal Social Security Administration, SSI is cash assistance provided to the blind, poor older adults, and persons with disabilities who meet certain income and health criteria.
3. **Adult Public Assistance:** A state program supplementing SSI that provides cash assistance to needy aged, blind, and disabled Alaskans to help them remain independent.
4. **General Assistance:** Sometimes referred to as **General Relief,** this state program provides cash assistance for low-income adults who do not qualify for any other cash assistance programs.
5. **Medicaid:** A joint federal and state program providing health care coverage to recipients of the eligibility-based programs (TANF and SSI) and low-income families.

Of the five, Medicaid is the major federal transfer payment to the states for health care. It is also one of the major outlays of all states, accounting for about 20 percent of spending.[3] Other social services provided by states include child welfare, senior and disability services, behavioral health, and juvenile and adult criminal justice.

States also contract with private for-profit and nonprofit entities to deliver some social services and often provide grants to these organizations to aid in service provision. These include youth services, services for the disabled, behavioral health, and corrections. Because government resources are limited, contracts with, and grants to, private entities are an efficient way to deliver services. In other cases, contracting out is the result of conservative ideology, which often favors reducing the size of government by transferring functions to the private sector.[4]

Particular Features of Social Services Delivery in Alaska

The delivery of social services in Alaska has some unique features. One is the provision of services to Alaska Natives. Because of the unique relationship between Native Americans and the federal government established in the U.S. Constitution, the federal government is responsible for the delivery of health and social services to Alaska Natives. The federal Indian Health Service (IHS), which is part of HHS, has a major presence in the state. However, particularly since the Alaska Native Claims Settlement Act (ANCSA) of 1971, the federal government has gradually transferred the provision of health and social services to Alaska Native private nonprofit associations.

Another unique Alaska feature is that, even in the larger urban areas, social services provision comes primarily from the state. Similarly, the corrections system is a centralized, unified system. It is entirely a state function—there are no city or locally run prisons, though a number of municipalities operate jails for short-term holding following an arrest or for short jail sentences. Furthermore, although not unique to Alaska, there are an unusually high number of private voluntary organizations providing essential services to such groups as victims of domestic violence, the homeless, disabled, immigrants, and refugees.

The involvement of various levels and agencies of government, the for-profit and nonprofit organizations (including Alaska Native associations), and private volunteer groups, means that a pluralistic mix of private and public services is an overriding feature of social services delivery in Alaska. This mix has both strengths and weaknesses in serving clients and consumers.

Alaska's Political Environment and Social Services Issues and Policies: An Overview

Given the IGR aspect of social services policy making and the major role of federal funding for the most expensive programs, particularly Medicaid, the state is not the only determiner of the types of programs that are developed and how they are delivered. Nevertheless, like all states, Alaska has significant influence in shaping social services and corrections. So what factors determine the political environment of these policy areas in Alaska?

With regard to the ideological differences alluded to earlier, the environment in Alaska is reflective of what exists across the nation. Generally, liberals view social services as essential activities of government to improve the functioning of disadvantaged groups and as an investment in promoting human capital. In contrast, many conservatives view these programs as giving benefits to nonproductive members of society who are a drain on government resources, at the expense of society's productive members. The ideological division that existed over corrections up until very recently is a little different. It consisted of liberals and progressives favoring shorter prison and probationary terms and providing rehabilitation, while conservatives favored longer prison and probationary terms and viewed prison mainly as retribution. Details about recent developments that are tending to blur this division are provided below toward the end of Section 3.

Some social services policies are distributive and give certain groups a defined benefit, such as for the disabled, and do not appear to deprive the rest of society of resources (though they do in reality by increasing taxes). However, many social services policies are redistributive: these clearly use tax dollars from most citizens to provide needed social services to a relatively small number of citizens. Redistributive policies, often lauded by liberals but decried by conservatives, exacerbate ideological divisions and the conflict in social services policy making.

The twelve characteristics of Alaska politics set out in Chapter 2 provide a useful framework for understanding the factors that influence social services and corrections policy in Alaska. All twelve have some effect on these policy areas, but six are especially influential. Two are the all-pervasive importance of government and the significant role of external economic and political forces, including the role and influence of the federal government. Two others are the political culture of pragmatic dependent individualism coupled with a strong strain of self-proclaimed fiscal conservatism. Political pragmatism has been partly responsible for ad hoc "quick fixes" or placating legislation, with little attempt to integrate policies across interrelated needs of social services areas. Consequently, major problems persist.

The other two characteristics are the prominence of Alaska Natives in state politics together with regionalism and conflicts between urban and rural-bush areas. The impact of Alaska's physical, social, and economic geography contributes to conflict between urban and rural-bush areas and poses challenges for the amelioration of social and public safety problems. Public safety issues in particular affect Alaska's Native population, and their health and social welfare system has the potential to be a major force in developing and implementing solutions.

Applying these characteristics and other factors enables us to explore the interrelated issues and Alaska's response to meeting the social services and public safety needs of its population. In this regard we consider two major questions: (1) How has the state's political and governmental system, and particularly its policy process, performed or been lacking in meeting these needs in the past? and (2) Does the state possess the political and governmental capacity to meet the current and likely future challenges in social services and related areas of public need? We return to these questions after looking specifically at issues and responses to concerns about Alaska's present health care system, issues facing the state concerning corrections, and interpersonal violence policies.

2. THE HEALTH CARE SYSTEM IN ALASKA: ONGOING CHALLENGES

To understand the state of health care and the issues of health policy in Alaska it is useful to place it in a national context. So first we provide an overview of the state of health care in the United States in general and some recent history of policy developments.

Characteristics of America's Health Care System and Recent Developments

The United States is the only major industrialized country that does not provide health coverage for all its citizens. In 2011, for instance, 48.6 million Americans or 15.7 percent had no health insurance. This was up from 46 million in 2006.[5] Outside the United States most developed countries use a so-called single-payer system to fund medical care. In this system there is a single insurance account run by the national government but sometimes run by state or provincial governments, as in Canada. Under a single-payer system, universal health care (sometimes referred to as national health care) for an entire population can be financed from a pool to which several parties—employees, employers, and the government—have contributed.

In contrast, funding in the United States is from a combination of public and private sources. The U.S. system has been plagued with problems, notably eroding coverage, with public and private insurance programs paying for less and less, rising costs, and cost shifting from public funding to practitioners and hospitals, and from employers to employees.[6] Strong evidence exists that the American health care system does not perform as well as other industrialized countries, yet spending per capita in the United States on health care far exceeds costs in any other developed country. In 2011, for instance, this was $8,508 per capita, 44 percent higher than the second-ranked country, Norway, at $5,669, and more than double that of the United Kingdom, at $3,405, ranked fifteenth.[7]

A combination of ideological and fiscal concerns has shaped the American health care system. The primary debates are over whether health care should be a right or a privilege, and how the system should be run. Conservatives believe that access is a privilege earned through workforce participation and provided in the private marketplace as part of the capitalist economic system. In their view, government regulation will create inefficiencies, substandard services, and higher prices. Conservatives often derisorily condemn single-payer systems as "socialized medicine." In contrast, liberals view health care as a right that has no place in a market context where decisions are primarily made on an economic basis. Liberals also argue that service should replace the profit motive.

Health Care from the Truman Presidency to the Obama Administration

President Harry S. Truman (1945–1953) was the first president to propose major health care reforms along the lines of comprehensive coverage for all Americans. But in a time of the rise of the Soviet Union and a paranoid fear of the so-called red peril, these proposals met with cries of "socialism" and went nowhere politically. Limited coverage for the elderly occurred with the enactment of Medicare in 1965, and with Medicaid for the needy in the same year. President Jimmy Carter (1977–1981) was sympathetic to universal health care but did not see the time as right for passage.

In 1993, President Bill Clinton introduced the Health Security Act to move health care toward national health insurance for everyone. At the time, opposition from powerful groups, mainly doctors, insurance companies, and the pharmaceutical industry, was overwhelming and killed the legislation. From an incremental policy perspective, the Clinton administration scored a success when Congress enacted the State Children's Health Insurance Program (S-CHIP) in 1997. This created a federal-state partnership to expand health coverage to uninsured children and pregnant women not eligible for Medicaid or not covered by private insurance.

Lack of major health care reforms during the Clinton and George W. Bush years made several states realize that they could not wait for federal action. In 2003 Maine enacted a voluntary subsidized health insurance plan aimed at small business owners and low-income individuals, with a goal of universal coverage by 2009. Massachusetts followed in 2006 with a goal to provide health care to their uninsured residents within three years. Vermont was next in subsidizing health insurance costs for low-income families and individuals. Illinois, Oregon, and Hawaii also made major strides in coverage for their citizens. Then in 2008, presidential candidate Barack Obama ran on a ticket of reforming health care to cover all Americans.

The Patient Protection and Affordable Care Act of 2010

After intense partisan conflict and considerable watering down of the original proposal, President Obama signed this legislation on March 23, 2010. The act is the most significant federal social welfare legislation in half a century and the most extensive health care policy in U.S. history. Opponents of the act dubbed it "Obamacare," and this name has come to be used to describe its provisions by its foes and supporters alike (including occasionally Obama himself). It is also referred to in shorthand as the Affordable Care Act (ACA).

The major intention of ACA is to make health insurance affordable for all Americans by requiring everyone to participate in the system and avoid shifting costs. As a result, the nonpartisan Congressional Budget Office estimates that the number of working-age parents and their children who currently have no health insurance will decline by 32 million and coverage will extend to 94 percent of U.S. residents. The remaining 6 percent are mainly those residents who are undocumented immigrants. Some individuals will receive subsidies to help pay for coverage, and small businesses will receive tax credits to assist with coverage for their employees. Several provisions of the law went into effect following signing of the act. Others were phased in, with the entire act implemented in 2016. Despite the claims by opponents of the ACA, it is far from a "government takeover," because medical insurance remains mostly private.

ACA emphasizes prevention and wellness. Insurance companies will no longer be allowed to exclude a person because of a preexisting condition, to cap coverage annually, or to impose lifetime limits on benefits. People with existing health insurance through employment can expect to see lower costs, improved care, and better protection from arbitrary decisions made by the insurance industry. For the more than forty-five million Americans who receive Medicare, the benefits will include decreases in the cost of medication, expansion of primary care, new assistance for the acutely disabled, and protection from senior citizen abuse. Young adults under the age of twenty-six will benefit by being able to remain on their parents' insurance policies if they have no insurance coverage of their own.

One controversial provision of the act is the requirement that everyone was required to have health insurance by 2015 or pay a tax penalty. To facilitate purchase of coverage by individuals, each state was encouraged to set up a health insurance exchange to enable individuals to purchase state-regulated insurance plans that are approved by the federal government for subsidies. If a state chose not to set up an exchange the federal government would administer the exchange for the state. Over half the states have not set up an exchange, one of which is Alaska. In July 2012, soon after the mandatory purchase provision of ACA had been upheld by the U.S. Supreme Court, Governor Parnell opted out of setting up an exchange for Alaska and left it to the federal government.[8] Opponents got a boost to justify their criticism of ACA when the federal government seriously botched the launching of its health insurance exchange in October 2013. But by early 2014 this problem was largely rectified.

Soon after its enactment, two aspects of the ACA were challenged on constitutional grounds by twenty-seven states (including Alaska) and the National Federation of Independent Business. In June 2012 a narrow 5 to 4 majority of the U.S. Supreme Court upheld the requirement that individuals must purchase insurance. In the same case, seven justices ruled that Congress could not constitutionally coerce states into expanding Medicaid coverage, thus making Medicaid expansion entirely optional by the states. Then, in June 2015 the U.S. Supreme Court decided a second major challenge to ACA. In that case, the challengers argued that certain language in the ACA prohibited giving premium subsidies to people who purchased insurance on the federal exchange rather than a state exchange. The Court, in another 5 to 4 decision, rejected the challenge, reasoning that if subsidies were not available for federal exchange insurance, the private insurance market in federal exchange states would be destabilized. This, the Court went on to argue, was an outcome contrary to one of the key purposes that Congress sought to achieve through the act—the provision of affordable insurance.[9]

Alaska's Recent Health Care Policy History

Alaska's record in recent health policy is mixed regarding meeting the needs of its citizens.[10] This can be seen in three key aspects of health policy: attempts to increase coverage and access, the way that the ACA may affect the state, and behavioral health developments.

Coverage and Access

In 1994 Senator Jim Duncan, a Democrat from Juneau, introduced legislation to create a single-payer health system, which would monitor claims and costs in an effort to establish universal coverage. It drew the opposition of health insurance companies and others invested in maintaining the status quo, and did not move through the conservative-dominated legislature. More successful was Governor Knowles's efforts in 1999 to

BOX 27.1

Anchorage's Project Access Funding Partners

MAJOR DONORS	COMMUNITY PARTNERS
• Alaska Department of Health and Social Services—DHSS	• Alaska Emergency Medicine Associates
• Alaska Mental Health Trust Authority	• Alaska Health Fair
• Denali Commission	• Alaska Primary Care Association
• Municipality of Anchorage	• Anchorage Access to Health Care Coalition
• Premera Blue Cross Blue Shield of Alaska	• Anchorage Neighborhood Health Center
• Providence Health Systems of Alaska	• Carrs/Safeway Pharmacy
• Rasmuson Foundation	• Christian Health Associates
• The Carr Foundation	• Foraker Group
• United Way of Anchorage	• Orthopedic Research Clinic of Alaska
	• The Wilson Agency (employee benefit consultants)

Source: Developed by the author.

establish Alaska's version of the S-CHIP program, called Denali KidCare. The federal government paid 72 cents for every dollar spent for the program, and a grant of $1 million dollars from a major national charitable organization, the Robert Wood Johnson Foundation, facilitated the enrollment of eligible children in the program. This is a good example of a public-private partnership in the provision of social services.[11]

The previous year, at the local level, the Municipality of Anchorage Health and Human Services Commission sponsored a conference on Access to Medical Care for the Underserved. From this meeting the Anchorage Access to Health Care Coalition emerged. The Coalition evolved into Anchorage Project Access, which began operating in December 2005. The project provides free health care to uninsured individuals with income of less than 200 percent of the federal poverty level for Alaska. Over 350 healthcare providers donate their services. Funding comes from state government, private nonprofit foundations, and private for-profit businesses. The project is another good example of how public-private cooperation can work to provide needed social services, and it is significant, given that Anchorage accounts for over 40 percent of the state's population. Box 27.1 lists the major donors and community partners in this program.

In 2007, newly elected Governor Sarah Palin created the Alaska Health Care Strategies Planning Council. The Council defined health care as the prevention, treatment, and management of illness, preserving mental and physical health, and dealing with chemical dependency. It submitted its report in December of that year, recommending to the governor and the legislature ways to effectively provide access to quality health care and to help reduce health care costs for Alaskans. Another recommendation was to set up a permanent body to advise on health matters. This was done in 2010 when the Alaska Health Care Commission (AHCC) was established by the legislature. Its long-term goal is to make Alaskans the healthiest people in the nation, with access to the highest quality, most affordable health care by 2025. But the fall in oil prices necessitating budget cuts in the 2014 legislative session rendered the Commission inoperative.[12]

The legislature elected in 2006 reflected a change of focus, with an increase in elected Democrats and more moderate Republicans. In the Senate, nine Democrats and six Republicans formed the Bipartisan Working Group (BWG). Besides creation of the AHCC, two senate bills were introduced. One was a measure to increase the number of children eligible for Denali KidCare, the other to provide health care coverage for all Alaskans. Only the Denali KidCare bill passed, which was a step toward providing health care to the several thousand children in the state not covered by health insurance.

Alaska and ACA: Some Likely Effects

Based on the 2010 census, in Alaska approximately 17,000 children (9 percent of the total) and 94,000 adults (18 percent) were without health insurance.[13] ACA will expand coverage for these groups. After a slow start in the number of Alaskans signed up by the entity set up to administer the ACA in the state, Enroll Alaska, the numbers began to pick up by early 2015. A 2014 DHSS report showed, however, that about 12,000 Alaskans do not have reliable access to health care, particularly specialty care and mental health services.[14] These are mostly low-income Alaskans, some of whom do not qualify for subsidies under the ACA. But there are other reasons, which stem from problems with Alaska's health care delivery system, particularly an inadequate number of health care providers throughout the state. Moreover, ACA may pose challenges for some providers in the state.

In addition, a 2011 report predicted that by 2019 health care costs would increase 2.3 percent because of ACA.[15] As a result, providers may be inclined to limit their practice to patients who have private insurance with higher payment rates than those allowed under Medicaid and Medicare. Alaska also has a large population (18 percent) who are covered by the Department of Defense, the Veterans Administration, and the Indian Health Service and who are not affected by ACA. Generally, because Alaska has a small, less competitive health care market, a continuation of higher fees and access problems are very likely.

Behavioral Health Developments

A prominent part of Alaska's health care history since statehood has been the fight over funding mental health care. It resulted from the particular circumstances of how mental health was dealt with under the Territory of Alaska and how the federal government chose to transfer the authority and funding to the Territory in 1956. Box 27.2 explains the development and authority of an entity unique to Alaska, the Alaska Mental Health Trust Authority, and its role in funding mental health services. One of the areas in which the authority has gotten involved is funding of mental health programs for young people.

In the early years of statehood, children and young adults with serious mental conditions were usually sent to facilities out of state. In 1985 the state created the Alaska Youth Initiative to provide individualized community-based mental health services for severely emotionally disturbed children who were at risk for institutionalization. In its early years the program was successful in returning to Alaska almost all youths with complex needs who had been placed out of state. But, in 2004, this program was discontinued. Complications in implementation arose from lack of provider training, conflict over coordination at the state level, and difficulty in individualizing programs. The cost of the program in its last year was $2.4 million. In part, these problems and its limited funding undermined the program's ability to keep in-state or bring home the increasing number of children with mental illness. The number of children placed in out-of-state mental health residential facilities grew from 83 in 1998 to 749 by fiscal year 2004. The cost to the state in Medicaid dollars was $38 million.[16] In an attempt to deal with the negative consequences of placing children out of state, in 2005–2006 the Alaska legislature and the Mental Health Trust Authority provided funding to create a "Bring the Children Home" initiative. Box 27.3 explains how the program is funded and what it will take to make it a successful state policy for at risk youth.

Turning to the administration of the state's behavioral health services, in 2003 the Murkowski administration undertook a major reorganization of DHSS. The Division of Alcoholism and Drug Abuse was combined with the Division of Mental Health to form a new Division of Behavioral Health. By focusing upon behavioral health, many people with both mental health and chemical dependency disorders who previously tended not to be identified administratively are now visible as a category needing services. This change did, however, pose challenges for providers who previously specialized in either mental health or substance abuse. The division has offered opportunities for both groups to develop competencies to treat clients with combined diagnoses of mental illness and substance abuse disorders.[17]

The state's major psychiatric facility is the Alaska Psychiatric Institute (API), located in Anchorage. It is run by DHSS. As of 2015, it had eighty beds and averaged about 1,250 admissions a year. API is the only inpatient psychiatric facility in the state.[18] The state is desperately in need of another psychiatric hospital and other mental health facilities.

BOX 27.2

The Alaska Mental Health Trust Authority

Before statehood in 1959, very few mental health services were available in Alaska, and the federal government was responsible for these services. Those requiring hospitalization were sent to Morningside Hospital in Portland, Oregon. Then, in 1956, Congress passed the Alaska Mental Health Enabling Act, transferring responsibility for mental health services from the federal government to the Territory and creating a Mental Health Trust. A million acres of federal lands, which the Territory was to select, were provided as a revenue source to fund a comprehensive mental health program.

After statehood, however, the state government did not honor its trust responsibilities. Beginning in 1978, under pressure from powerful interests, the legislature transferred much of this prime land to individuals and municipalities and created wildlife areas, forests, and state parks. By 1982, only 350,000 of the original million acres remained in the Mental Health Trust. In an effort to redress the misuse of these lands, a lawsuit was filed in the Alaska Superior Court in 1982. It was filed by Alaska resident Vern Weiss, on behalf of his son, who required mental health services not available in the state. This evolved into a class action suit, involving other individuals and the Alaska Mental Health Association. The suit claimed that the state had not fulfilled its obligation as a trustee of the land when it removed federal grant lands from the trust.

In 1985, the Alaska Supreme Court held that the legislation transferring mental health lands out of the Trust violated the obligations placed on the state under the 1956 federal act. The court ordered the trust reconstituted, and the state was ordered to pay fair market value, with interest, for all lands conveyed from the trust. In 1986, the legislature established the Interim Mental Health Trust Commission. What followed was eight years of wrangling over fair market value and what groups should be eligible for funds from the trust, among other conflicts, involving the state, developers, environmentalists, mental health interest groups, and the state Supreme Court as the final arbiter. Eventually the Hickel administration sponsored legislation that constituted the final settlement, approved by the Alaska Supreme Court in 1994. The settlement consisted of the following:

- Creation of the Alaska Mental Health Trust Authority with the right to spend trust income without the approval of the legislature and the authority to provide recommendations to the governor and legislature regarding appropriations from other state revenue sources toward creating Alaska's Integrated Comprehensive Mental Health Program.
- Approximately one million acres of state land would go into the trust. Original trust land would constitute 500,000 acres and the rest would be replacement land.
- The state would give the trust $200 million in cash.
- Four state boards—the Alaska Mental Health Board, the Advisory Board on Alcohol and Drug Abuse, the Governor's Council on Disabilities and Special Education, and the Alaska Commission on Aging—would represent their specific beneficiary groups and make recommendations to the trust.
- The Alaska Mental Health Trust Authority would be managed by an independent Board of Trustees appointed by the governor and confirmed by the legislature.

The Board of Trustees has formed a partnership with the Alaska Permanent Fund Corporation and the Department of Revenue, Treasury Division, to manage the cash assets of the trust, and with the Trust Land Office of the Department of Natural Resources to manage the Trust's land assets. Programs are being developed for the beneficiaries of the trust, including those with mental illness, developmental disabilities, chronic alcoholism, and Alzheimer's disease and related disorders, as well as traumatic head injury resulting in permanent brain damage. The trust has formed additional partnerships with government, Alaska Native tribal groups, private for-profit providers, and nonprofit providers.

Source: Developed by the author with reference, in part, to the Mental Health Lands Trust website at: http://www.mhtrust.org/.

BOX 27.3

The "Bring the Children Home" Initiative

The "Bring the Children Home" initiative is another good example of a public-private health care partnership. Planning grants are provided to private nonprofit, private for-profit, and Alaska Native providers for new residential facilities. Other grants have been awarded to similar groups for developing community-based services. A broad range of stakeholders serving children must be part of the system to make it work. Furthermore, if children are transferred from an out-of-state institution to an in-state facility without available community-based services, the state will replicate the problems of the Department of Corrections, which houses many adults in the state with mental health and substance abuse disorders.

A partnership was developed between the University of Alaska, the Alaska Mental Health Trust Authority, and the Alaska DHSS Division of Behavioral Health to increase the supply of behavioral health workers throughout the state. The state is also working with Alaska Native health corporations to increase their behavioral health services for children. This will benefit the state when Medicaid-eligible Native children receive services from Native corporations, as the federal government pays 100 percent of the cost rather than a percentage when state Medicaid is used.

Source: Developed by the author.

This is, in part, because many crimes are committed by individuals with mental illness, more often than not a condition that is treatable. Most such offenders end up in prison, and many receive no treatment services. As a result, as across the nation, Alaska's prisons have a large number of inmates with behavioral issues. This serves neither the individuals concerned nor the state. Apart from the humanitarian aspect of the problem, it increases costs to the state, as we will see later.

Ongoing Challenges and Problems in Alaska's Health Care Delivery

With the enactment of the ACA, medical insurance coverage of Alaskans may be less of an issue in the future, though this remains to be seen, as coverage has been a continuing concern since statehood. As briefly explained below, early indications are that the ACA poses problems for some Alaskans. Besides coverage, there are other ongoing problems, particularly issues resulting from human and physical geography, costs (including the cost of Medicaid), and provider shortages.

Geographical and Diversity Challenges

Alaska's small population, estimated to be 737,000 in 2015, inhibits taking advantage of economies of scale in many endeavors, including health care. In addition, the ethnic and social diversity of its people spread over hundreds of thousands of square miles, with

TABLE 27.1

How Much Higher are Medical Costs in Alaska?

TYPE OF SERVICE	PERCENT HIGHER THAN U.S. AVERAGE
Visit to a doctor	35
Hospital cost per inpatient day	56
Medical and surgical	27
Prescription drugs	49
Overall costs	**41**

Sources: Ingenix, 2011 National Fee Analyzer; Ingenix Almanac of Hospital Financial Operating Indicators, at www.iser.uaa.alaska.edu/Publications/RevisedHealthcare.pdf.

wide discrepancy in income levels, presents the state with critical challenges in providing medical care. Geography creates problems of access, increases costs, and makes it difficult to recruit health care providers. Some basic health care services are available in rural-bush Alaska, but when the need for specialized services arises, travel to hub rural-bush communities, such as Bethel or Barrow, or one of the three major urban areas in Alaska may be necessary. Some treatments may require traveling out of state for many urban residents as well as rural-bush Alaskans.

Alaska Health Care Costs

Table 27.1 shows that in 2011 overall health care costs in Alaska were 41 percent higher than the national average and as much as 56 percent higher for hospital stays. A research summary published by the University of Alaska Anchorage's Institute of Social and Economic Research (ISER) in August 2011 noted that in 2010 health care spending in Alaska totaled $7.5 billion, or $10,563 per Alaska resident, compared with a national average of $7,960 per person. Health care spending in Alaska tripled from 1990 to 2010, and from 2005 to 2010 it increased 40 percent.[19] In 2012 the average annual growth of health care spending for Alaska was 8.4 percent. Only Nevada had a higher growth rate at 9.2 percent. The U.S. average growth rate was 6.5 percent.[20] Whether or not ACA can help to slow down this steady increase and lower Alaska medical costs overall remains to be seen.

Early indications are that ACA may pose problems for some Alaskans, particularly in obtaining affordable medical insurance. This, however, is less due to the ACA and more to particular circumstances in Alaska. The state's medical insurance market is so small that it cannot take advantage of economies of scale. For this reason there were only two medical insurance providers in the state as of 2015 but one pulled out of the state in 2016, leaving just one carrier. Added to this is the high cost of health care in the state. Together this means that the insurance carriers are forced to charge very high premiums to some Alaskans. The individuals most affected include those who do not qualify for premium subsidies because their income is too high and some who are self-employed. They can pay up to $40,000 a year for premiums for a family of five. Given this, many may take the risk of going uninsured.[21] This is an issue that requires addressing, though short of the state subsidizing the premiums of such individuals, there is likely not much it can do.

Medicaid in Alaska

Medicaid is a federal entitlement program that provides health care primarily to lower-income people who meet certain criteria. It is funded largely by the federal government, but administered by the states. The states must contribute some funds, a so-called federal fund match, in order to receive the federal monies. Even though Alaska provides only a small percentage match, as noted earlier, Medicaid is a major expense, and its increasing costs are of concern to state officials.

Furthermore, funding for the Indian Health Service (IHS) in Alaska has been flat since the early 2000s and is falling behind due to the population growth of Alaska Natives. As a result, many Natives now receive Medicaid. In fact, 45,000 out of the total Alaska Native population of over 120,000 received Medicaid as of 2014. IHS is the primary payer if the recipient receives services in a tribal health facility, at no cost to the state. However, if a recipient uses a non-IHS facility, the state must contribute to the Medicaid payment. Encouraging Alaska Natives to use IHS facilities can save the state between $80 and $100 million a year. An improvement in Alaska tribal health care may be a key to controlling the mounting costs of Alaska's Medicaid program.[22]

It is important for the state to maintain its Medicaid federal match, or many health services for specialized groups will cease. All of the nonprofit mental health clinics and substance abuse agencies, plus agencies serving senior citizens and the developmentally disabled, rely heavily on Medicaid reimbursement. For many nonprofits, close to 80 percent of their income is from Medicaid. A provision of ACA provided full federal funding until 2016 for the states to expand Medicaid, after which the state would be required to pay a 10 percent match. This would cover another estimated 40,000 Alaskans.

In November 2013, Governor Parnell indicated that he would not accept this expansion for Alaska. However, Governor Walker made expanding Medicaid a central part of his 2014 campaign and moved on the issue immediately upon taking office by appointing a Medicaid Expansion Project Director in DHSS. His attempts to work with the conservative Republican legislature to expand Medicaid bogged down during the legislative session of 2015, however. This was partly due to ideological clashes between Walker and legislative leaders as well as a financial challenge in the face of significant budget shortfalls expected for FY 16, FY 17, and most likely beyond. Nevertheless, Walker moved in the summer of 2015 to expand Medicaid by executive action.[23]

Major Health Care Provider Shortages

Health care is an important part of the Alaska workforce. In 2011, for instance, there were 23,740 health care workers, 7.6 percent of the total workforce in the state.[24] Estimates are that the health care industry in Alaska will lead the state's job growth at least until 2020, with about thirteen thousand more jobs to be added to the workforce.[25] While this growth may help somewhat, it is unlikely to overcome the major problems in state provider shortages. Alaska has, in fact, long suffered major shortages in its health care provider workforce.

According to the Alaska Federal Healthcare Partnership, a federal-state voluntary organization to improve access to health care in the state:

> Alaska ranks nearly last in the nation in terms of the number of providers compared to the number of patients. To complicate matters almost all doctors and virtually all specialty care is limited to Anchorage and Fairbanks.[26]

Comprehensive surveys conducted in 2006, 2007, and 2009 confirm this. The figures for the 2009 survey are set out in Table 27.2. The 2007 survey estimated a need for an additional 3,500 providers. As can be seen, the 2009 report showed that this shortage had abated somewhat but was still acute.[27] It is likely that the shortage will continue for the foreseeable future.

In both urban and rural-bush areas in Alaska, one aspect of this shortage is that many providers, particularly doctors, will not accept Medicare patients because the reimbursement they receive is low compared with private insurance. In rural-bush areas, it is difficult to attract trained providers, and those who work in an itinerant capacity often stay a short time and are more costly to employers over the long term. Up to 16 percent of rural-bush physician positions in Alaska were vacant in 2004. In 2006, Alaska had a shortage of 375 physicians.

In response to this shortage, the legislature passed a bill, signed by Governor Palin in March of 2007, doubling the number of Alaska medical students who are provided with support in securing their degrees, provided they return to Alaska and practice medicine for a certain period. This move helped compensate somewhat for a 1995 move by the legislature cutting funding for WAMI (Washington Alaska Montana and Idaho; now WWAMI—Washington, Wyoming, Alaska, Montana, and Idaho), a University of Washington Medical School program that allows students from the participating states to

TABLE 27.2

Alaska's Health Care Provider Shortage

TYPE OF PROVIDER	NUMBER OF VACANCIES	PERCENT VACANCY RATE	AVERAGE VACANCY PERIOD
Physicians	99	10.2	18 months
Registered nurses	322	10.1	Two years
Behavioral health	395	10.1	17 months
Allied health	266	5.5	11 months
Dentists	15	2.6	19 months
Pharmacists	37	8.5	15 months
Therapists (physical, occupational, speech)	53	10 to 28	Two years
Other providers	663		
Total	**1850**		

Source: 2009 Alaska Health Workforce Vacancy Study, Alaska Center for Rural Health, December 2009, at http://www.uaa.alaska.edu/acrh-ahec/projects/upload/2009workforce09.pdf.

receive tuition subsidies from their states. The intent of Alaska's participation in WWAMI is to increase the number of physicians practicing in Alaska. With the downturn in state revenues following the summer of 2014, to save money some Alaska Republicans advocated dropping out of the WWAMI program. This would seriously aggravate Alaska's health provider shortage, especially of doctors. But the program may well be on the revenue chopping block if Alaska's revenues picture does not improve.[28]

Dealing with State Health Issues: The Need for Integration with Corrections and Interpersonal Violence Policies

How should the state tackle these challenges regarding health? Some, such as provider shortages, to the extent that the state has any control over them, are largely health issues. Several other health issues, however, including mental health and substance abuse, which are often associated with crime, require a systematic and integrated policy approach. This is because it is clear from a host of studies that poverty (often accompanied by unemployment or underemployment and low levels of education), crime, interpersonal violence, and certain types of mental illness are interconnected—one condition often leads to one or more of the others.[29]

The need for integration will become clearer in considering two other policy areas in the following sections and the extent to which an integrated approach is or is not taking place. Then, in analyzing and evaluating social services politics and policy in general, we consider the overall contemporary status of the holistic approach and its future prospects.

3. CORRECTIONS: OLD POLICIES, NEW REALITIES, AND PRAGMATIC CHANGES

Prisons, in terms of their economic impact, are one of America's last surviving and thriving industries. However, there is a significant public policy issue in corrections across the United States and in Alaska: a pending budget crisis as the cost of housing the increasing number of inmates has soared and gobbled up more and more of state and federal budgets. Ironically, the cost and the number of inmates have risen despite clear evidence that crime rates have actually fallen since the 1990s, as documented by such organizations as the Sentencing Project.[30] This irony has raised concerns among many politicians and the public and has been the subject of many media stories. For instance, the international news magazine *The Economist* devoted a special report on the situation in July 2013. It is particularly noteworthy that even this conservative publication called for major reforms on both financial and humanitarian grounds.[31]

This section explains the essence of this corrections public policy irony and the attempts to deal with it. Again, it is useful to first place Alaska in a national context. It will also be useful to review Box 27.4, which explains key terms used in corrections and also identifies some problems in obtaining up-to-date and reliable statistics.

Crime and Corrections across the United States Today

The U.S. criminal justice system manifests eight particular characteristics: (1) a high per capita incarceration rate; (2) a disproportionate number of prisoners who are minorities; (3) a major increase in the prison population since the late 1970s, including the mentally ill; (4) high rates of recidivism: (5) prison overcrowding; (6) rapidly increasing costs; (7) using prisoners for prison industries; and (8) a piecemeal, ad hoc policy process driven by politics.[32]

U.S. Incarceration, Imprisonment, Recidivism Statistics and a Warehouse for the Mentally Ill

The United States can be described as the "lock-up capital of the world," incarcerating per capita more inmates than any other country. In 2010, over 7.1 million people across the nation were under correctional supervision of some form (including probation and parole), and 2.4 million of them were in jails and prisons. Table 27.3 (on page 1025) sets out the imprisonment rate for selected states in 2005, 2010, and 2013 and the national incarceration rates for 2005, the last year for which fifty-state statistics are available. There is, however, a national incarceration rate available for 2010 and 2013. At 731 and 716 per 100,000 in 2010 and 2013 respectively, this was the highest in the world as was the rate of 738 in 2005.[33] In 2013, according to the International Center for Prison Studies, the rate for England was 148 per 100,000, for France 98, and Japan 51. The median rate for Southern Europe was 115, and the median rate was 187 for Central and Eastern Europe.[34]

BOX 27.4

Corrections Terms and Some Statistical Issues

IMPRISONMENT RATES VERSUS INCARCERATION RATES

These terms are often used interchangeably but they are different.

According to the U.S. Bureau of Justice Statistics (BJS), the *incarceration rate* counts all those in custody per 100,000 of the population. In contrast, the *imprisonment rate* counts inmates sentenced for one year or more to prison per 100,000.

The two rates are calculated differently. The incarceration rate is more inclusive as it counts all those in custody at any one time whether sentenced or not. Thus, the incarcerated population includes the number of prisoners confined in jail, which may include overnight detentions and persons held in halfway houses, camps, hospitals, and so on. As for the imprisoned population, this number is restricted to sentenced prisoners who are housed in prison facilities under the supervision of state or federal correctional authorities.

Consequently, the incarceration rate is a much higher figure than the imprisonment rate. It was over 70 percent higher nationally in 2005, as Table 27.3 shows, with an incarceration rate of 736 per 100,000 of population compared to an imprisonment rate of 491. However, while the BJS calculates the imprisonment rate every year (usually available after a time lag of about six months), it calculates the incarceration rate only once every five years or at longer intervals. The reasons are the BJS's shortage of staff and funding and the lack of interest in the incarceration rate on the part of the states (and state legislatures), who care more about the imprisonment count than custody count. The latest incarceration count was conducted state by state in 2005, but there are national estimates for 2010.

In this and other aspects of corrections, this chapter uses statistics from the BJS, the Alaska Department of Corrections, and private sources. Minor variations in statistics between sources do not detract from the points regarding the issues the nation, the states, and Alaska currently face and will face in the near future in corrections policy.

PRESUMPTIVE AND MANDATORY PRISON SENTENCES

Presumptive and *mandatory* sentences are related but have slightly different meanings. Both relate to state statutes requiring a certain prison sentence, often based on the recommendations of a state commission set up to review prison sentencing. Under *presumptive* sentencing, the statutes call for either a sentence within a statutory minimum-maximum range or the imposition of a specified sentence for more serious or repeat offenders. For example, some states like California have a "three strikes and you're out" provision that sentences a felon convicted of three crimes to life in prison. Some of the most serious offenses, such as murder, rape, and kidnapping, have *mandatory* minimum sentences which fall outside of presumptive sentencing rules.

Presumptive and mandatory sentencing systems give judges less discretion in sentencing when there are extenuating or other circumstances that might warrant a shorter sentence, perhaps combined with other forms of punishment, such as community service.

THE REHABILITATION VERSUS THE RETRIBUTION-DETERRENCE PRISON MODEL

These are two contrasting approaches for those convicted of crimes. While both perspectives view prison as a punishment, they place different emphases on the role of prisons and the length of sentences.

The rehabilitation model sees a major purpose of prison as helping prisoners deal with the reasons for their crimes and to receive aid to function well in society on release and not return to prison. This includes reasonable living and recreational facilities, services for mental health and other counseling, education opportunities (perhaps learning a trade or other skill), and work-release opportunities. Rehabilitation advocates generally favor shorter sentences, support alternatives to prison for lesser crimes, and oppose the death penalty.

In contrast, those advocating the retribution-deterrence model see prison primarily for punishment and long prison sentences as both a form of retribution for society and a deterrent to committing crimes. Generally, they favor "no frills" living and minimal recreational facilities in prisons and only minimal services to help prisoners function in society once released. Retribution advocates also tend to support longer sentences for repeat offenders, and generally support the death penalty.

RECIDIVISM AND REPEAT OFFENDERS

Recidivism is the tendency to commit one or more additional criminal offenses after being released from jail or prison for a first offense. The recidivism rate is defined as the percentage of those released from prison who are rearrested, reconvicted, or returned to prison within three years. So recidivism rates are technically based on prison releases three years earlier. For example, those for 2015 were based on 2012 releases.

In an attempt to reduce the number of repeat or habitual offenses, both the federal government and the states have enacted what they hoped would be deterrent laws. For instance, Washington State imposes a minimum sentence of ten years imprisonment for a second felony, third misdemeanor, or third petty larceny. In addition, life in prison is imposed for conviction of a third felony, fifth misdemeanor, or a fifth petty larceny.

Various organizations keep statistics on recidivism rates, including the federal and state governments and nonprofit organizations, such as the Pew Charitable Trusts and Released and Restored. The figures for individual states can vary, sometimes widely, depending on the periods under review and which aspects of recidivism are chosen. For political reasons, states often put their recidivism rates in the best possible light.

Source: Developed by the author.

Moreover, the disproportionate number of minorities in U.S. prisons is a long-term and consistent phenomenon.[35] In 2013, non-Hispanic African Americans, at 37 percent, made up the largest portion of male inmates, compared to non-Hispanic whites at 32 percent, Hispanics at 22 percent, and all others at 9 percent. As of December 2013 there were 1,412,745 men and 104,134 women in state and federal prisons, which put the imprisonment rate for men at 904 and 65 for women per 100,000 of population. Furthermore, the rate varied starkly with race and gender. While the imprisonment rate per 100,000 for males was 466 for whites, it was 1,134 for Hispanics and 2,805 for African Americans—over three times the national average. The figures for women were 65 per 100,000, with whites at 51, Hispanics at 66, and African American women at 113—nearly twice the national average for women.

The disproportionate number of imprisoned African Americans becomes even starker when one considers that in 2013 non-Hispanic African Americans accounted for 37 percent of the total prison population, but in that year they made up only 13.2 percent

TABLE 27.3

Imprisonment and Incarceration Rates for 2005, 2010, and 2013

(Totals, Rates per 100,000, and Ranking among the Fifty States)

	INCARCERATION AND IMPRISONMENT RATES FOR 2005				IMPRISONMENT RATES FOR 2010		IMPRISONMENT RATES FOR 2013	
State	Sentenced Inmates	Total Incarcerated	Imprisonment Rate and National Ranking	Incarceration Rate and National Ranking	Sentenced Inmates	Imprisonment Rate and National Ranking	Sentenced Inmates	Imprisonment Rate and National Ranking*
Alaska	**2,781**	**4,678**	**414 - 22**	**705 - 19**	**2,429**	**340 - 34**	**2,682**	**364 - 28**
California	168,982	246,317	466 - 16	682 - 21	164,213	439 - 20	135,981	353 - 31
Kansas	9,068	15,972	330 - 35	582 - 30	9,051	317 - 36	9,506	328 - 34
Louisiana	36,083	51,458	797 - 1	1,138 - 1	39,444	867 - 1	39,298	847 - 1
New York	62,743	92,769	326 - 36	482 - 37	56,461	288 - 39	53,428	271 - 37
Missouri	30,803	41,461	529 - 7	715 - 18	30,614	508 - 9	31,537	521 - 10
Montana	3,509	4,923	373 - 28	526 - 35	3,716	378 - 27	3,642	357 - 29
Texas	159,255	223,195	691 - 2	976 - 3	164,652	648 - 4	160,295	602 - 5
Vermont	1,542	1,975	247 - 43	317 - 47	1,649	265 - 42	1,575	242 - 42
Wyoming	2,047	3,515	400 - 23	690 - 20	2,112	385 - 26	2,310	395 - 21
National Average	**N/A**	**N/A**	**491 - N/A**	**738 - N/A**	**N/A**	**497**	**N/A**	**478**

* This table excludes Nevada, as the Bureau of Justice Statistics provided no 2013 imprisonment data for the state.

Sources: Developed by the author from the U.S. Bureau of Justice Statistics: Prison and Jail Inmates 2005. Retrieved December 29, 2011, at http://bjs.ojp.usdoj.gov/content/pub/pdf/pjim05.pdf; Prisoners in 2010. Retrieved December 21, 2011 at: http://bjs.ojp.usdoj.gov/content/pub/pdf/p10.pdf; and the U.S. Bureau of Justice Statistics, Prison and Jail Inmates and Midyear 2005. Retrieved December 29, 2014 at: http://bjs.ojp.usdoj.gov/content/pub/pdf/pjim05.pdf.

of the U.S. population. African American male and female inmates had higher imprisonment rates across all age groups. Less stark, but still disproportional, was that in 2013 Hispanics (including Latinos and mixed race Hispanics) were 21.9 percent of the total jail and prison population compared with 17.1 percent of the national population.

The United States also has the highest recidivism rates in the Western world. A 2011 report showed that U.S. national recidivism rates have stayed consistent since the late 1990s. They were 45.4 percent from 1999 to 2002, but down slightly at 43.4 percent from 2004 to 2007. In the latter period, Minnesota had the highest rate at 61.2 followed by California with 57.8. Oregon had the lowest at 22.8 followed by Wyoming at 24.8. Alaska, at 50.4 percent, had the sixth highest rate in the nation.[36] The U.S. average contrasts with other countries over the period since 2000. Norway had the lowest recidivism rate of 20 percent, Canada's and Sweden's was 35 percent, and Japan's was just under 39 percent.[37]

Finally, American prisons have become a warehouse for the mentally ill. It is estimated that over half a million mentally ill Americans who are arrested or convicted of crimes are put in prisons or jails each year instead of being placed in psychiatric hospitals. Most cases are treatable, but treatment is rarely available. Consequently, prisons are facing an increasing demand for mental health treatment services.[38]

Explaining It All

How can all this be explained, given falling crime rates?

The major reason for high incarceration rates is most likely the hardening attitude to crime that occurred in the 1970s and worked its way into public policy in several ways. At that time there was rising juvenile and other crime, partly fueled by the rise of the drug culture. For good reason, crime gets the public very agitated, becoming a high-profile issue, and thus a high-priority political issue for many politicians. Elected officials could have approached the problem through continuation of the rehabilitation model that was largely in place at the time. However, conservative ideology took over the criminal justice system, and the rehabilitation approach was replaced with a retribution-deterrence model.

A major foundation and justification for this changing attitude was a 1974 article published by sociologist Robert Martinson titled, "What Works?" The article discredited the idea that rehabilitation of prison inmates is ever possible. In Martinson's words, "with few and isolated exceptions, the rehabilitative efforts that have been reported so far have had no appreciable effect on recidivism."[39]

This idea appealed to both liberals and conservatives for different reasons. To liberals, it pointed out the injustice surrounding indeterminate, lengthy sentencing, and forced treatment. To conservatives, anything that promoted retribution was fine. If nothing worked, then it would be easier to convince an already frightened public that longer sentences and capital punishment were necessary for their safety. So "nothing works" became the slogan of criminal justice policy.

Also from the late 1970s onward, conservatives got the political upper hand in most states, and so the retribution model took deep root. Policies that resulted were the reintroduction of the death penalty in many states, increased sentences (including mandatory sentences for certain crimes), a substantial increase in parole and probation revocations, and a general increase in prison admissions. In this regard, a report from the Sentencing Project stated that since the inception of the War on Drugs, "longer prison terms have fueled the prison population expansion." The report further connected this increase with fewer parole releases and the "three strikes" laws (mandating life in prison on the third offense), which have resulted in 1 in 11 inmates being imprisoned for life.[40] As a consequence, the mission of criminal justice moved from transformative to managerial. This philosophy remains in force to this day, though it may be about to change.

As to an explanation for the high percentage of incarcerated minorities and the high rates of recidivism, space does not permit an in-depth consideration of either. However, the high percentage of minorities in prison is likely due to a combination of poverty (a major incentive for crime), illegal substance abuse and distribution, domestic violence, and racial profiling. High recidivism is more than likely associated with the policy of prison as retribution over rehabilitation. Many inmates are not prepared for life on the outside when they are released. By contrast, Norway's liberal rehabilitation prison philosophy results in low rates of recidivism.

The reasons for using prisons as warehouses for the mentally ill are complex. Money is part of the reason, with more political pressure to fund prisons, education, and transportation than psychiatric hospitals. Another element is less discretion on the part of judges to order mental treatment as opposed to prison, due to mandatory sentencing rules. In addition, conservative control of many state governments since the 1980s has placed less emphasis on treatment and more on punishment.

The Consequences and Some Tentative Policy Approaches

Increased incarceration and tougher treatment of offenders has led to the twin problems of prison overcrowding and skyrocketing corrections budgets across the nation. Both prison overcrowding and increased costs result largely from the phenomenal increase in the U.S. prison population due to the "get tough on crime" movement. This explosion in the prison population was accompanied by skyrocketing state budgets for prisons after 1980. Adjusted for inflation in 2010 prices, these budgets increased from $3 to $16 billion from 1980 to 1994 and had reached $39 billion by 2010, an increase of 1,300 percent in just over thirty years.[41] Many states, including perhaps the most high-profile case of California, are under court orders to reduce prison overcrowding.[42] From two inmates to a cell in the 1970s, many prisons have three or four. Dining rooms and other facilities are stretched to the point of bordering on inhumane treatment, if unintentionally. Part of the overcrowding problem is due to high recidivism rates in the absence of an attempt to rehabilitate many prisoners and using prisons as warehouses for the mentally ill.

Skyrocketing costs and legal problems with overcrowding have set off political alarm bells among the public and have started to soften attitudes favoring long prison sentences. According to the Pew Research Center, in 2012, 48 percent of the public surveyed supported reducing funding for state prisons. The report concluded that, judging by recidivism rates, the present criminal justice system was not working and badly needed reforming.[43] These attitudes have been reinforced by prominent public figures calling for reform. At the 2013 American Bar Association annual conference in San Francisco, for example, both former U.S. Attorney General Eric Holder and former U.S. Senator Hillary Clinton made speeches calling for a serious rethinking of the "get tough on crime" policies of a generation ago.[44] Then in April 2014, the U.S. Justice Department issued details of a plan to consider clemency for thousands of people who are imprisoned on nonviolent drug charges and who had also served at least ten years of their sentences. And in March 2015 a bipartisan group emerged in Congress to reform prison sentences.[45] In line with its new policy, the U.S. Justice Department released 6,000 federal prisoners in October 2015. This was the single largest prisoner release in U.S. history.[46]

At the state level, pressures from the public, as well as budgetary concerns, are forcing conservatives from Florida to California to subordinate ideology to practical considerations and reconsider corrections policy. Two ways that states have tried to offset costs is by using private prisons and prison industries. There are several private prison companies in the United States, such as the Corrections Corporation of America (CCA), which is the largest. Private prisons appeal to many states as a way to deal with overcrowding when they cannot afford or do not wish to build and maintain new prisons. Corporations like CCA have seen their profits mushroom over the past several decades as the prison population has steadily climbed. The use of private prisons aligns with the conservative philosophy of utilizing the free enterprise system as much as possible, though in the long run, it may not reduce corrections costs.[47] Liberals argue that private prisons place profit above the welfare of the prisoners and reduce public accountability, which does not serve the interests of the inmates or society in the long run.

As to prison industries, since the early 1990s, federal and state prisons have partnered with private companies to make, sell, and provide everything from furniture to auto parts to call center services. In 2009, the last year for which comprehensive national figures are available, approximately 100,000 inmates were employed in prison industries, and the annual sales of goods and services reached $2.4 billion.[48] This is a small fraction of the cost of prisons and incarceration facilities, and these facilities will likely never be self-supporting. However, in many cases, working in a prison industry provides inmates with work experience that may help them when they are released and thus reduce recidivism rates.

The fragmented and incremental policy-making process, the dominance of conservative approaches to corrections in recent years, and the power of certain interests, particularly prison guards and economic development interests, means that there is virtually no systematic planning in corrections policy. In addition, little attempt is made to integrate corrections policy with other social services programs, such as those for mental health and interpersonal violence. Political ideology tends to dominate in corrections policy making. As we will see below, it often takes the courts or a policy entrepreneur to defend or push the political cause of inmates.

Crime and Corrections in Alaska: Administration and Variations on National Trends Past and Present

In several ways Alaska's corrections system reflects national trends, though, as might be expected, with particular Alaska elements. Before looking at how these trends play out in the state, we briefly describe the administrative organization of corrections in Alaska. The nature of this organization throws light on many issues that have occurred and the policies developed to deal with them, as well as likely future directions in corrections policy.[49]

Before statehood in 1959, all aspects of criminal justice in Alaska, including corrections, were run by the federal government. For a quarter of a century after statehood, corrections were administered by the DHSS. Then, in 1983, Governor Bill Sheffield created a Department of Corrections (DOC) with its own commissioner and budget. Unlike most states, but similar to Connecticut, Delaware, Hawaii, Rhode Island, and Vermont, Alaska has a unified corrections system with all prison facilities administered by the state but with some local jails for short-term incarcerations.

Crime, Incarceration Rates, and Recidivism in Alaska

In recent years, a rather puzzling picture has emerged as far as crime in Alaska is concerned. According to Table 27.3 (on page 1025), using the imprisonment rate between 2005 and 2013, the crime rate in Alaska decreased from 414 to 364 per 100,000 population and was as low as 340. Also, Alaska's crime rate among the states dropped from 22 to 28 in rank from 2005 to 2013 and was in the bottom third of the states at 34 in 2010. On the other hand, according to Table 27.4, during the same eight-year period, Alaska had by far the highest rate of violent crimes. As in the nation, however, the evidence clearly suggests that since the mid-1980s there has been a decrease in the crime rate in Alaska. Adjusting for population increases, a 2009 research report by the University of Alaska

TABLE 27.4

The Rate of Violent Crimes and Rape in Selected States for 2005, 2010, and 2013

(Number of Crimes per 100,000 of State Population)

	VIOLENT CRIME			RAPE		
State	**2005**	**2010**	**2013**	**2005**	**2010**	**2013**
Alaska	**631.9**	**638.8**	**640.4**	**81.1**	**75.0**	**87.6**
California	526.3	440.6	402.1	26.0	22.4	19.5
Kansas	387.4	369.1	339.9	38.4	45.0	38.9
Louisiana	594.4	549.0	518.5	31.4	27.2	26.9
Missouri	525.4	455.0	433.4	28.0	23.9	26.5
Montana	281.5	272.2	252.9	32.2	32.4	28.3
New York	445.8	392.1	393.7	18.9	14.3	13.1
Texas	529.7	450.3	408.3	37.2	30.3	28.4
Vermont	119.7	130.2	121.1	23.3	21.1	14.5
Wyoming	230.1	195.9	205.1	24.0	29.1	24.7
National Average	**469.2**	**403.6**	**367.9**	**31.7**	**27.5**	**25.1**

* The figures shown in this column for the offense of rape were estimated using the legacy Uniform Crime Reports (UCR) definition of rape.

Source: Developed by the author from the Federal Bureaus of Investigation (FBI UCR), Crime in the United States in 2005, 2010 and 2013, by State, at https://www2.fbi.gov/ucr/05cius/; http://www.fbi.gov/about-us/cjis/ucr/crime-in-the-u.s/2010/crime-in-the-u.s.-2010/tables/10tbl05.xls; and http://www.fbi.gov/about-us/cjis/ucr/crime-in-the-u.s/2013/crime-in-the-u.s.-2013/tables/5tabledatadecpdf/table_5_crime_in_the_united_states_by_state_2013.xls.

estimated this drop to be about 30 percent.[50] Yet, as in the rest of the nation, over these years the number of those incarcerated in Alaska has increased markedly despite the decrease in crime.

The incarceration rate increased 700 percent in the twenty years from 1977 to 1997, while the state population increased just over 50 percent. Twelve years later, in 2009, Alaska was one of the top eight states in per capita prison population.[51] Likely there was an increase in crime because of the mass influx in the mid-1970s of people who arrived to build the oil pipeline. But the major reason for the increase in the prison population was the passage of presumptive sentencing in 1978, which took effect on January 1, 1980.[52] This Alaska "get-tough-on-crime" attitude reflected the national trend. Like that trend, it had ripple effects and consequences that are ongoing.

The total number of Alaska prisoners in the custody of DOC held both inside and outside the state increased from around 600 in 1977 to about 4,300 in 1997, rising to 4,734 in 2011 and 5,013 in 2013.[53] Alarmingly, however, according to the study by the University of Alaska Anchorage (UAA) Justice Center, based on DOC data, the number of inmates is projected to be 10,500 by 2030.[54] As Table 27.3 shows, Alaska's imprisonment rate from 2005 to 2013 was close to that of Wyoming, a state with a similar population and economy. Both states also had similar incarceration rates in 2005. Alaska, with 705 per 100,000, ranked nineteenth in the nation, with Wyoming at 690 ranking number twenty. For reasons explained in Box 27.4, there are no national rankings for incarceration rates since 2005.

Another report by the UAA Justice Center found an interesting contrast between men and women prisoners in Alaska. From 2005 to 2014 a gender shift occurred in the state's prison population. The post-conviction incarceration rate increased by 27.5 percent for women but declined for men by 4.4 percent. Of the approximately 5,100 people in Alaska prisons in 2014, close to 600 were women. The reason for the increase in the female population is unclear, and as of early 2016 the DOC was looking into it.[55]

As noted in Box 27.4, statistics on rates of recidivism vary depending on whether one uses state, federal, or private data sources. We noted earlier that a survey by the Pew Charitable Trusts assessed this at 50.4 percent for Alaska in 2011, putting the state at the sixth highest in the nation.[56] However, the Alaska DOC has long put the recidivism rate much higher. Between 2006 and 2010 the DOC calculated the rate at between 66.03 percent in 2007 and 63.54 percent in 2010. The lower Pew recidivism numbers are disturbing enough, but if the higher DOC's numbers are used, Alaska is ranked in the top two or three states in the nation for recidivism. Consequently, reducing recidivism is a major goal of the Alaska DOC.[57]

The Demographics of Alaska's Inmate Population

Reflecting the national picture, Alaska's inmate population includes a disproportionate number of minorities. But reflecting Alaska's overall demographics, it is not African Americans who are the primary minority in prisons, but Alaska Natives. Nevertheless, African Americans are still the most disproportionately represented in Alaska prisons. In 2013, for example, they composed 9.6 percent of the prison population—over three times their proportion in the state population of 3.9 percent. Next came Alaska Natives at 36.7 percent of the prison population, but composing only 15 percent of the state population. In contrast, while Caucasians made up about 67 percent of the state population, they account for only 46.7 percent of inmates. An even starker contrast is that of a combination of Asians and Hispanics, who made up 6.4 percent of inmates but about 12.4 percent of the Alaska population—an Alaska anomaly compared with the nation at large.[58]

Alaska Prisons as Warehouses for the Mentally Ill and the All-Pervasiveness of Substance Abuse

According to a 2002 report, close to 40 percent of inmates in Alaska have a mental illness. Using data from the DOC, the 2009 report by the University of Alaska estimated a similar figure at 36 percent. Of the latter figure, 6 percent suffered from mental illness alone, while 30 percent suffered from mental illness plus substance abuse problems, and another 60 percent of inmates have substance abuse problems. This is a total of 96 percent with mental illness, substance abuse problems, or both and only 4 percent of inmates with a diagnosis of neither mental illness nor substance abuse.[59]

These statistics provide another compelling reason to integrate social services policy in dealing with crime, mental health, behavioral health (mainly alcohol and drug abuse), and, as we will see later, domestic violence and child abuse policies. However, since 2002 there have been cuts in the state's behavioral health system, particularly under Governor Murkowski (2002–2006). These cuts included eliminating drug treatment programs in thirteen corrections facilities. Only three programs remain, mainly because there is a federally funded match for services provided.

Because of these and other cuts, treatment today primarily involves the use of psychotropic medication and inmate segregation, highlighting the inadequacy of the state's behavioral health system. Substance abuse and behavioral health are major problems in the state and are significant factors affecting crime and incarceration rates.

Crime and Corrections in Alaska: Three Dominant Interrelated Policy Issues

From the late 1970s onward, as in the nation as a whole, many concerns manifested themselves regarding Alaska's correctional system. These included the disproportionate number of minorities imprisoned (particularly Alaska Natives and African Americans), the lack of mental health services available and the minimal attention to rehabilitation (despite the guarantee of the right to rehabilitation in Article I, Section 12, of the Alaska Constitution), prison overcrowding, the need to build more prisons, and increasing costs. Low oil prices after 1986 and Alaska's increasingly conservative legislatures after 1990, combined to produce a reluctance on the part of state government to deal with the racial, mental health, and rehabilitation issues. However, the state could not avoid dealing with the overcrowding issue, the pressure to build more prisons, and the increasing costs, all three of which are interrelated.

Prison Overcrowding and the Out-of-State Prisoner Issue

As in other states, Alaska's prison population mushroomed after 1980 and soon led to overcrowding in Alaska's prisons. This posed some immediate challenges, and the fallout continues to this day. A sentencing commission established by Governor Cowper (1986–1990) and a Criminal Justice Cabinet established by Governor Knowles in 1995, both came to similar conclusions on how to address the issue: (1) reduce sentences, (2) reduce the number of prisoners, (3) develop alternatives to prison, and (4) build more prisons.[60]

In the atmosphere of "get tough on crime" in the 1970s and beyond, and in light of the laws on presumptive and mandatory sentences, the first three recommendations from these two groups were not viable options as far as the legislature was concerned. So the only approach was to build more prisons. In fact, the state was required to expand the capacity of its prisons and make them more humane places for inmates in response to court rulings and ultimately a settlement in *Cleary v. Smith*. The case stemmed from prison overcrowding and is one of the landmark legal decisions in Alaska political history. The details of the *Cleary* case and its legal, political and administrative ramifications are explained in Box 27.5. The overcrowding issue had been building in the late 1970s as the prison population began to increase. As one way to deal with this increase, the state had arranged with the Federal Bureau of Prisons to house some prisoners out of state. For these prisoners, the court's decision was based in part on the premise that the humane action was to bring them home to be nearer to their families.

The Prison Construction, Maintenance, and Operation Issue

The rise in the prison population in the early 1980s, and subsequently the *Cleary* settlement, forced governors and legislatures to embark upon prison construction programs. Partly because of the enormity of the cost of prison construction, maintenance, and operation, these proposals were usually highly controversial and formed a central element in corrections politics that continues to this day. While realizing the need to spend money on prisons, conservative Republicans have generally worked to keep these costs to a minimum. This includes a "no frills" provision in state prisons mandating the bare minimum in cells and recreation facilities. In addition, out of necessity and at the urging of Republicans and some other interests, the state has engaged in partnerships with the private sector for providing prison services of various types and has also explored other possibilities.

One area in which the state has used the private sector is housing its out-of-state prison population. Prior to 1994 it used Federal Bureau of Prisons facilities, but as the populations in these facilities soared and some federal facilities were closed, Alaska had to find additional out-of-state facilities. So that year Alaska's Corrections Commissioner Frank Prewitt signed a contract with CCA (Corrections Corporation of America) to house over two hundred Alaska prisoners at a facility in Arizona. At the end of 2007, approximately 1,060 prisoners were confined in Arizona. In 2009 the contract was transferred to the Cornell Corrections Corporation, and the prisoners were moved to its facility in Hudson, Colorado.[61] As noted below, building Goose Creek prison near Anchorage finally made it possible to bring the 1,000 or so inmates at this facility back to Alaska

BOX 27.5

The *Cleary* Case: Dealing with Overcrowding in Alaska's Prisons

In 1981, a group of inmates in Alaska filed a class-action lawsuit in the Alaska Superior Court, claiming that conditions in Alaska's prisons violated the Eighth Amendment of the U.S. Constitution and Article I, Section 12, of the Alaska Constitution prohibiting cruel and unusual punishment. The suit, *Cleary v. Smith* (commonly known as the *Cleary* case), was named after Michael Cleary, the lead plaintiff in the lawsuit. The suit addressed problems of overcrowding, living conditions, and rehabilitation opportunities in Alaska's prisons. At the time, state courts around the country were showing willingness to review prison conditions, and ten states were under court orders to improve these conditions. There was also the prospect of federal court intervention if Alaska did not respond.

In 1983, a partial settlement agreement was approved by the state Superior Court covering matters such as recreation, the use of phones, clothing, access to law books, and education and counseling services. Part of the agreement required the state to build a maximum security prison to bring home Alaska prisoners housed in federal prisons located in other states. Partly to comply with this requirement, the state built the 486-bed Spring Creek Correctional Center in Seward that opened in 1988.

That year, the state, represented by the Attorney General, and the counsel for the inmates entered into final settlement negotiations over twenty-five issues that were raised by the inmates. After eighteen months and 350 hours of face-to-face negotiations, a final settlement agreement was presented to the Superior Court for approval. The eighty-seven-page document was presented to Superior Court Judge Karen Hunt and distributed to the state's 2,400 inmates for comment. On September 21, 1990, Judge Hunt approved the final settlement agreement (*Cleary* Final Order, 3AN-81-5274 CIV). The settlement was a form of contract and thus legally binding on the state, specifically the Department of Corrections. Inmates could sue for contempt of court to ensure compliance with the settlement.

Specific mandates were included in the settlement. Most significant was the one regarding overcrowding. Population caps were created for each prison. If the state exceeded an emergency population level for thirty days, it would have to inform the court as to how it planned to relieve overcrowding. The court could impose fines if limits were exceeded. In addition to a specified square-feet-per-inmate formula, there were requirements regarding recreation space and other opportunities and rights for prisoners.

The settlement also called for the creation of a separate unit to treat inmates with mental illness and the construction of a women's prison by July 1, 1994. Other sections of the settlement included staffing levels, facility and operational requirements, classification and administrative segregation policies, and the use of discipline and grievance procedures. As well as enforcement, the settlement provided for monitoring and modifications of the provisions. The major changes mandated by the *Cleary* case were consistent with suggested guidelines of the American Correctional Association that accredits correctional facilities. The settlement has substantially reduced the flexibility once afforded to the Department of Corrections.

Source: Developed by the author.

beginning in 2012. One of the last outstanding directives of the *Cleary* settlement was finally realized.

Alaska also considered building private prisons in the state as a means of reducing initial costs to the state, among other reasons for pursuing the private prison route explained earlier. But this was and remains a highly contentious issue. On the one side were some conservative Republican legislators and other public officials hoping to save money, along with private corrections companies and their Alaska agents. On the opposite side were many Democrats, and many residents of the proposed communities where the prisons would be located.[62] Also, state employee unions did not want a private provider running a prison because of the lower wages and benefits that would be paid and the potential long-term threat of the entire correctional system being privatized.

As of 2016, it appeared that prison construction, maintenance, and operation would be performed by public authorities in Alaska for the foreseeable future. The legislature authorized a new 396-bed jail in Anchorage that opened in 2002. Then, as part of regional expansions that also included Bethel, Seward, and Fairbanks, in 2004 the legislature authorized the DOC to develop a contract for a new $330 million prison in the Matanuska-Susitna (Mat-Su) Borough. This venture was a partnership between local government, contractors, and the state in the building and operation of the prison. Box 27.6 examines the politics behind this venture which became known as the Goose Creek prison.[63]

The private prison option may not yet be dead, and it may well be revisited as a result of the major shortfall in state revenues beginning in late 2014 and into 2016 and the major budget cuts that this shortfall required. Governor Walker hinted at this possibility in his State of the State speech in January 2015.[64] So the debate continues.

Prison Costs: Soaring Operating Budgets but Stable Costs per Prisoner

Like all states, Alaska has seen its corrections budget skyrocket since the early 1980s. The most revealing figures are in the operating budget. While the DOC has certainly taken an increased share of the capital budget, this has varied depending on the year. Some of the variation is because municipalities have funded some new construction for prisons, as explained in Box 27.6 on the Goose Creek prison. So tracking DOC's capital budgets does not give an accurate picture of the soaring costs of corrections in the state.

Exact figures for operating budgets are hard to come by before Corrections became a separate department, but a good estimate for 1983 when the DOC was created is $22 million.[65] Adjusted for inflation to 2014 prices this was approximately $50 million. Corrections budgets from 1990 onwards are more readily available.[66] The corrections operating budget had risen to $98.7 million by 1990, to $181.45 million by 2005, and to $333.6 million by 2014. Adjusted for inflation, the 2014 budget was 32 percent higher

BOX 27.6

The Politics of Building the Goose Creek Prison

A common element of including high-cost items in state budgets, like schools, transportation infrastructure, and prisons, is that they often get mired in politics. Building these facilities is not just about educating students or providing the best transportation or corrections system, but often involves a complex combination of forces, including economic development, political payoffs, and political ambitions, as well as the needs expressed by professionals in state and local government regarding these services. So it was with the Goose Creek Correctional Center (GCCC).

The prison, located across Knik Arm northwest of Anchorage near Point Mackenzie in the southwest Mat-Su Borough, is a medium security facility, which began taking in prisoners in 2012. When it operates at full capacity, GCCC will provide 1,536 beds with a staff of up to 350. The final authorization for the prison came in Senate Bill (SB) 65 in 2006 sponsored by Senator Lyda Green of Mat-Su and based on the original authorization adopted in 2004. The prison traveled a very rocky political and financial road from authorization to operation.

From the point of view of corrections professionals in DOC and some politicians, the prison has several purposes. One is to bring home most of the remaining inmates from the private correctional facility in Colorado. A related purpose is to get Alaska out of the private prison business completely even though it will cost several million dollars more each year to house the prisoners in Alaska than in a private out-of-state facility. Another purpose, one pushed particularly by the DOC commissioner at the time, Joe Schmidt, is to gear the prison toward rehabilitation. This is part of the reason the prison was scaled back from a 2,200 bed, maximum security facility to its mostly medium security purpose. The decision occurred after looking at effective methods of reducing recidivism. The prison has a number of programs, including education, substance abuse, job training, mental health, and parenting programs to create behavioral change and provide skills prisoners need to be successful when returning to the community.

From the perspective of the Mat-Su Borough, the prison was primarily an economic development and jobs project. This is where the finances and politics get murky both in the raising of funds and the letting of contracts. SB 65 called for the borough to own the prison (rather than act as a custodian of a state-owned facility) and to lease it to the state for a twenty-five-year term at $17.6 million a year. The bonds used to construct the prison were supposed to be owned by the borough, but instead Mat-Su listed them as held in trust for the State of Alaska. As a result, the original bond offering threatened the state's credit rating.

With a price tag of over $240 million (scaled back from the original $330 million), the prison was of great interest to local contractors. Of the total cost, $225 million went to Nester Construction of Anchorage for designing and building the prison. Rather than run the utilities themselves, the borough hired Valley Utilities, a Wasilla company set up specifically for the purpose by several politically well-connected developers. Other bids for this contract were rejected with little explanation.

Central to the complexities of the financing and the political maneuvering was Senator Green, who held the powerful position of Senate President from 2007 to 2008 following her sponsorship of SB 65. What her motives were in pushing for Mat-Su to own the prison and provide major benefits for local contractors is unclear. Was it a payoff for past political support, a move to aid her reelection, a power play against other politicians and perhaps regions of the state, or a combination of all these? The political waters of the project were further muddied by a major personality conflict between Senator Green and Governor Sarah Palin. Although both left the Alaska political stage by mid-2009, their animosity was an impediment to solving many issues regarding the prison that arose during ensuing legislative discussions.

Other factors that complicated the project included floating the bonds during the financial crisis of 2008, which caused a major increase in interest rates, and the fact that the prison was located far from existing utilities, adding considerably to its cost. These and other details were not worked out in the original bill. Issues like the provision of electric services and wastewater treatment (involving Valley Utilities) were at the forefront of later legislative discussions. In addition, the regional competition for funding of projects that exists in Alaska meant that many legislators from other regions were not supportive of the project.

Source: Developed by the author.

than that of 2005, almost twice that of 1990 and a 600 percent increase since the early 1980s. From taking 2 percent of the total state operating budget in 1990, in 2014 corrections took double that at 4 percent. The peak year was 2005, when it took 5 percent.

This increase in the share of the operating and capital budgets going to corrections has meant less money for other services because the cost of building and operating prisons in Alaska, as elsewhere, is enormously expensive. For instance, the Anchorage jail, which opened in 2002 to house just under four hundred inmates, cost $58 million to build, about the cost of a high school for one thousand students. And in addition to over $17 million a year in lease payments the state makes to the Mat-Su Borough for use of the Goose Creek prison, it will cost the state $50 million a year to run the facility if it operates at full capacity.

Added to this, housing prisoners is not cheap and never has been. In 2012 it cost an average of $49,000 a year to house an Alaska prisoner. That works out to $135 a day, about the cost of a hotel room in Anchorage, Juneau, or Fairbanks outside of the tourist season.[67] This yearly figure is about 70 percent above the national average, as explained earlier, but on a par with many northeastern states (such as Rhode Island at $44,860 and Massachusetts at $43,026) having the lowest imprisonment rates.[68] Alaska's cost per prisoner when factoring in inflation has stayed fairly constant since the early 1980s. In fact, it was probably much lower in 2012 than in 1985, when it was the equivalent of $59,000.[69] It declined considerably from the mid-1990s onward as the "get-tough-on-crime" movement took firm hold. So the increase in the corrections budget over these years is the result of increased numbers of prisoners, not because the state is spending more money per prisoner.

The costs of the "get-tough-on-crime" movement in Alaska did not just affect the DOC's budget, however. It first sent financial ripples and later financial waves across the broader criminal justice state budget. This included the court system needing more judges and support staff, the Department of Public Safety needing more state troopers and related services, the Department of Administration needing more public defenders, and various divisions in DHSS needing more funds to deal with more families and children in need.

Future Corrections Policy in Alaska: A New Philosophy or a New Political Necessity?

In their 1999 evaluation of corrections politics and policy in Alaska, Campbell and Pugh wrote:

> In Alaska . . . policy makers confront the need to build a balanced criminal justice system that is responsive to public protection, the rights of victims, the reformation of the offender and the public's concern about government spending.[70]

This statement paraphrases Article I, Section 12, of the Alaska Constitution, with the added element of spending.[71]

Campbell and Pugh also identified two underlying characteristics of Alaska's corrections policy making. The first is a tension between corrections professionals and politicians, with many of the latter responding to the high-profile emotional issue of crime. In this regard, Campbell and Pugh contend that perhaps no other political issue is the subject of more political rhetoric (reflecting populist demands and playing to the crowd) and political symbolism (appearing to take meaningful action). The second characteristic is that, like so many other policy areas in the state, effective corrections policy is stymied by a fragmented policy-making process.[72] This hinders integration of various aspects of criminal justice policy, which could deal more effectively with many correctional issues, particularly lowering the inmate count.

In combination, the Campbell and Pugh statement and the two characteristics they identified exemplify the challenges that have continued in corrections policy. Since the early 1980s, as in other states, a balance among the concerns of public protection, victims' rights, the reformation of offenders and spending has, for the most part, not been achieved in Alaska. To some extent public protection and victims' rights may have advanced since the 1980s, but little has been done to reform offenders, and the state has lost control of its corrections budget. Overall, the financial and social costs have been enormous in terms of recidivism, untreated mental illness, broken homes, domestic violence, and child abuse.

A New Corrections Philosophy for Alaska?

Rehabilitation is not only the more humane approach to prison inmates, it is also more cost-efficient. Evidence clearly shows that the cost of corrections and other criminal justice programs can be reduced by integrating services to deal with mental health, recidivism, substance abuse, prisoner re-entry into society, and juvenile crime, as well as domestic violence and child abuse. Specific to corrections, a University of Alaska study, referred to above, estimated that by spending $124 million on such preventive, intervention, and treatment programs from 2008 to 2030, the state would save $445 million in costs by 2030, and there would be 10 percent fewer inmates in Alaska prisons than without such programs.[73]

There are, in fact, some glimmers of hope for rehabilitation advocates. One is the development of the Alaska Therapeutic Courts, the first of which was set up in Anchorage in 1998, called the Mental Health Court. These courts are viewed as an alternative to incarceration for those whose primary problem is substance abuse and or mental illness but who are charged with a felony or a misdemeanor.[74]

Moreover, some well-respected and influential voices have called for reform of the Alaska criminal code, particularly the mandatory and presumptive sentencing system, both on humanitarian and financial grounds. One such voice is Walter Carpeneti, former Chief Justice of the Alaska Supreme Court. In his 2012 State of the Judiciary speech to a joint session of the legislature, Carpeneti called for reform of the mandatory sentencing laws on humanitarian, public safety, and financial grounds. He also recommended more cooperation between the legislative and executive branches to address criminal justice reform.[75]

Carpeneti also raised the troublesome issue of the disproportionate percentage of Alaska Natives in Alaska's prisons. He described a pilot program instituted by the court system in the upper Yukon River area to take courts into the villages and involve state, local, and tribal leaders in justice delivery. Carpeneti said that this program has enjoyed some success in reducing crime and repeat offenders and enabled the state's justice system to build community trust and serve rural-bush areas fairly and adequately.

Continuing Political Conservatism but a New Corrections Political Necessity

There is now, and perhaps always has been, a fundamental conflict between the needs and goals of elected politicians on the one hand and that of judges and, to a large extent, corrections professionals on the other. Politicians need to think in two- and four-year horizons to be reelected or to seek higher office, and need to be cognizant of public opinion. Judges and corrections professionals, by contrast, have the luxury of having longer-term professional horizons.

Some elected officials, particularly very conservative Republicans, will not support rehabilitation programs for ideological reasons. Other elected officials may see the long-term value of rehabilitation as one of the solutions to corrections problems. But for their short-term benefit, they are likely to pursue ad hoc solutions and thus perpetuate the conflicts among themselves, professional corrections officials, and the judiciary. Thus, the inter-branch coordination Carpeneti advocated in his State of the Judiciary address is elusive. Two examples illustrate this endemic political problem.

The first is the reductions in the state's behavioral health programs, particularly under Governor Murkowski. These included the elimination of drug treatment programs in thirteen corrections facilities. The second has to do with sex offenses, certainly an emotional issue with the public and seized on by many conservative legislators. However, a 2006 report by the Alaska Judicial Council showed that sex offenders were least likely to commit the same offense again.[76] And yet, during the 2007 legislative session some conservative legislators credited themselves with "keeping Alaskans safe" by increasing the sentences for sex offenders. Governor Murkowski's reductions in behavioral health programs and the legislative actions on sex offenders may have been good politics for those concerned—the first as a way to cut spending and the second as a way to demonstrate being "tough on crime." Both, however, were bad public policy if the long-term goal is to cut the costs of the corrections budget by reducing crime and aiding former inmates to re-enter their communities as productive members of society.

Despite all this, economic necessity appears to be working to overcome ideology and produce some reforms to the corrections system. One reform was the establishment of the Criminal Justice Working Group (CJWG) created by the legislature in 2007. Its members included representatives from the court system, the Departments of Law, Corrections, Public Safety, and DHSS, and the Judicial Council and other agencies. The CJWG defined its two major tasks as reducing both crime and recidivism. One of the projects funded by the CJWG was the Alaska Five-Year Prisoner Reentry Strategic Plan 2011–2016.[77] Legislative committees also began to consider ways to reduce corrections budgets by instituting alternative ways to deal with convicted felons. Legislatures in other conservative states like Texas, Louisiana, Mississippi, and South Carolina have revisited the wisdom of mandatory minimum sentencing.

These developments in Alaska culminated in the landmark Senate Bill 64 (SB 64), an omnibus bill passed in 2014 and sponsored by John Coghill, a conservative Republican from Nenana, near Fairbanks. According to his sponsor's statement, the bill's purpose was to increase public safety, slow prison growth, and cut costs.[78] The bill received broad bipartisan support largely because it had something for both the "get tough on crime" conservatives and the "rehabilitation" liberals. Among its many provisions, the following are the most significant for our purposes in this chapter.

Perhaps most significantly, the law created the Alaska Criminal Justice Commission. The commission is charged with examining the effects of sentencing laws and criminal justice practices and evaluating whether those laws and practices provide for protection of the public, community condemnation of the offender, the rights of victims of crimes, the rights of the accused, the rights of prisoners, restitution to crime victims by offenders, and the principle of reformation. The commission is to make recommendations for improvements in these areas. Members of the commission include present and retired judges, the Commissioners of Public Safety and Corrections, the state Attorney General, a police officer, and representatives of social services agencies. Conspicuously absent, however, is a present or past offender or offenders, whose perspective could be very valuable.[79]

The law also includes tougher penalties for some crimes like abduction, a 24/7 monitoring of sobriety for certain offenders, and reforms in the parole system to bring "swift and certain" punishment to offenders. The law established a program operated by DHSS for reducing recidivism through transitional re-entry programs for those incarcerated and those recently released from prison. The law also includes jail time credit for offenders in court-ordered treatment programs, and increases the amount of property value that makes a crime involving property a felony rather than a misdemeanor. Plus, the law identifies factors that will be considered by the court that may allow imposition of a sentence below the presumptive range.

The clincher to obtain support for the bill from most conservatives was likely the promise of reduced costs (or at least stopping the escalation of costs) and of avoiding having the state build another prison at a cost of $250 million or more. Plus, by 2014 the number of women incarcerated in the state was at an all-time high and, as we saw earlier, had seen a major increase since 2004. By 2014 the Hiland Mountain women's prison near Anchorage was over capacity, and some inmates were being housed in men's facilities.[80] Criminal justice reform, and particularly sentencing reform, could prevent the need to build additional prisons or make other provisions to house offenders.[81] Further extensive reforms to deal with prison costs (partly by alternatives to prison for non-violent offenders), to move towards a rehabilitation approach, and reduce recidivism were made in the 2016 legislature, spearheaded again by Senator Coghill acting as a sort of policy entrepreneur. Corrections reform is a work in progress and the issue will likely be at the forefront of Alaska politics for some time to come.

4. INTERPERSONAL VIOLENCE: DOMESTIC VIOLENCE, SEXUAL ASSAULT, AND CHILD ABUSE

Interpersonal violence is usually subdivided into family, intimate partner, and community violence. In this section we focus on domestic violence, sexual assault, and child abuse. *Violence* is defined as the deliberate use of force to harm another person with the outcome resulting in injury that may be physical or both physical and psychological and result in fatal or nonfatal effects. *Child abuse and neglect* are defined as the perpetration of physical, emotional, or sexual harm or inadequate provision of physical, medical, emotional, or educational care.

The Extent of the Problems and Their Causes

Statistics generated since 2005 show that the extent of substantiated abuse in Alaska (domestic violence, sexual assault, and child abuse) is staggering, particularly against Alaska Natives.[82]

Domestic Violence and Sexual Assault

In the United States, 73 percent of domestic violence victims and 86 percent of spousal abuse victims are women. One in three women will experience domestic violence in her lifetime, and 1.3 million women are victims of domestic violence each year.

Specific to Alaska, in 2005 there were six thousand reported cases of domestic violence, placing the state among the top five in the country. Regarding estimates of violence during their lifetimes, a 2010 study estimated that 58 percent of Alaska women

TABLE 27.5

Victims of Substantiated Child Abuse by Race for Select States in 2012

(Children Under Age 18 by Race, Numbers, and Percentage of Total)

	AFRICAN-AMERICAN		NATIVE AMERICAN/ ALASKA NATIVE		ASIAN		HISPANIC		MULTIPLE RACE		PACIFIC ISLANDER		WHITE		UNKNOWN		TOTAL VICTIMS
Alaska	**75**	**2.6%**	**1,481**	**50.6%**	**19**	**0.60%**	**82**	**2.9%**	**202**	**6.50%**	**37**	**1.3%**	**643**	**22.0%**	**389**	**13.30%**	**2,928**
California	9,458	12.4	481	0.60	1,765	2.80	41,224	54.20	2,586	3.40	219	0.30	17,521	23.00	2,772	3.60	76,026
Kansas	227	12.2	21	1.10	8	0.70	255	13.70	102	5.50	4	0.20	1,243	66.50	8	0.40	1,868
Louisiana	3,984	47.1	29	0.30	21	0.20	192	2.30	136	1.60	3	0.00	3,947	46.70	146	1.70	8,458
Missouri	698	14.9	16	0.30	10	0.30	177	3.80	63	1.30	4	0.10	3,633	77.50	84	1.80	4,685
Montana	13	1.0	248	18.70	2	0.20	78	5.90	52	3.90	5	0.40	865	65.30	61	4.60	1,324
New York	19,620	28.7	253	0.40	1,157	1.70	17,148	25.10	1,469	2.10	25	0.00	22,296	32.60	6,407	9.40	68,375
Texas	10,066	16.1	49	0.10	237	0.40	29,118	46.60	1,974	3.20	54	0.10	19,499	31.20	1,554	2.50	62,551
Vermont	6	0.9	0	0.00	6	0.90	3	0.50	3	0.50	0	0.00	616	94.90	15	2.30	649
Wyoming	19	2.7	8	1.10	4	0.60	96	13.60	8	1.10	0	0.00	534	75.70	36	5.10	705
Percentage of Victims Nationwide	**21.0%**		**1.00%**		**0.80%**		**21.80%**		**4.10%**		**0.20%**		**44%**		**6.90%**		**Not Applicable**
Total Victims Nationwide	**140,079**		**7,770**		**5,587**		**145,559**		**27,174**		**1,208**		**293,667**		**45,880**		**666,924**

Source: The U.S. Department of Health and Human Services, Child Maltreatment 2012, Table 3-7, "Victims by Race and Ethnicity," at http://www.acf.hhs.gov/sites/default/files/cb/cm2012.pdf. Developed by the author.

TABLE 27.6

Substantiated Child Abuse in Alaska by Region and Type of Harm in 2010

(Children under Age 18)

REGION	AREA	MENTAL INJURY	NEGLECT	PHYSICAL ABUSE	SEXUAL ABUSE	TOTAL	PERCENT
Southcentral	Anchorage	1,225	56	146	32	1,459	31.00%
	Kenai Peninsula	293	107	44	12	450	9.67
	Other parts of Southcentral	478	66	10	20	608	13.00
Northern/ Northwest	Fairbanks	425	49	44	19	537	12.00
	Outside Fairbanks	407	205	38	11	661	14.00
Western/ Southwest	Western	368	67	23	21	479	10.29
	Southwest	93	19	23	8	130	3.00
Southeast	Juneau	126	33	20	2	181	3.89
	Rest of Southeast	81	59	10	0	150	3.22
Total	**All**	**3,496**	**661**	**373**	**125**	**4,655**	**100**

Source: Office of Children's Services, Alaska Department of Health and Social Services, *Annual Report: 2010 Allegation and Victim Data*, at http://www.hss.state.ak.us/ocs/Statistics/pdf /Annual_Allgs_10.pdf. Developed by the author from Alaska Department of Health and Social Services.

have experienced intimate partner or sexual violence.[83] And as Table 27.4 (on page 1030) shows, from 2005 to 2013 the rate of rape in Alaska was three times the national average. Moreover, Alaska has the highest rate per capita of men murdering women. Violence against Native women, both domestic and in general, is particularly alarming. According to Greg Marxmiller, who works for SAFE, a domestic violence prevention agency in Dillingham in Southwest Alaska, there is an epidemic of domestic violence in rural-bush Alaska.[84] In addition, Alaska Native women are seven times more likely to be raped and sexually assaulted in Anchorage than non-Native women.[85]

The Demographic Characteristics of Child Abuse and Neglect in Alaska

Child abuse and neglect are not randomly distributed among children in the United States. They are closely associated with poverty, and children of color are overrepresented in the statistics provided by each state. Table 27.5 shows this when Alaska is compared with the nation. Again, the figures are particularly disturbing for Alaska Natives. As the table shows, in 2012 over 50 percent of victims of substantiated child abuse were Natives, but Native children constitute just over 20 percent of the under-18 population in the state. Overall, child sexual assault in Alaska is almost six times the national average. Table 27.6 sets out the number and type of child abuse by region for 2010. The racial distribution of these types of abuse is very likely similar to that set out in Table 27.5.

According to the Child Welfare League of America, from 2000 to 2003, Alaska led the nation in per capita abuse and neglect of children.[86] Since then, maltreatment in Alaska has decreased slightly. The U.S. Department of Health and Human Services 2012 maltreatment report listed Alaska as having the fifth-highest per capita rate of child victims. That year the jurisdictions with the highest rates of child abuse were Washington, D.C., Kentucky, New York State, and Arkansas.[87]

Interrelated Causes and Likely Particular Factors in Alaska

A majority of the victims of interpersonal violence are members of three specific dependent groups—women, children, and elders. Domestic violence and child abuse have interrelated causes, and these feed on each other, often producing a vicious cycle of abuse. Domestic violence is the number one indicator for child abuse, which is fifteen times more likely to occur in households where adult domestic violence is also present. Furthermore, boys who witness domestic violence are twice as likely to abuse their own partners and children when they become adults. In addition, these forms of interpersonal violence and abuse are often associated with substance abuse. In the majority of cases where a child is removed from a family, substance abuse is present. Interpersonal violence is also associated with mental illness.

Another factor is poverty. The poor in America include many people of color, which partly accounts for the fact that interpersonal violence, particularly domestic violence and child abuse, are more prominent in African American, Native American, Latino, and other racial minority communities than among Caucasians, particularly middle-class whites. Specific to Alaska, according to the U.S. Census Bureau, in 2010 there were over 187,000 children in Alaska, representing 26 percent of the total population. Of that total, over 23,773 children under the age of 18 were living below the poverty line—12.9 percent of all children in the state. Many of these children are in Alaska Native households.[88] According to the statistics, they are the most vulnerable to child abuse and their mothers are the most susceptible to domestic violence.

A major factor that likely distinguishes Alaska from other states regarding domestic violence and child abuse, both in terms of physical and social geography, is that it is an isolated state. Close to half of the population has migrated to Alaska from other areas, leaving support systems and extended family behind. The state's remoteness and long winters add to this isolation. Seasonal affective disorder (SAD) and "cabin fever" may increase levels of depression that result in the use of substances as coping mechanisms. Substance abuse is particularly endemic with indigenous people, who often experience stress from cultural disruption, unemployment or underemployment, poverty, and racism. Substance abuse is closely related to the occurrence of interpersonal violence in both urban and rural-bush areas, but particularly so in rural-bush Alaska.

The Response: The Development of a Governmental Legal and Administrative System

Domestic violence and child abuse were two issues that were kept under wraps until the 1960s. Consequently, policies to deal with them lagged behind issues like social security and Medicare for senior citizens. It was not until the early 1970s that a federal legislative response to child abuse began with the 1974 Child Abuse Prevention and Treatment Act. This act has been amended several times and is now the Keeping Children and Families Safe Act of 2003. In 1994, the Violence Against Women Act (VAWA) passed Congress, and it was reauthorized in 2013. It provides funds to encourage states to improve prosecution, law enforcement, and victim services. One issue for Alaska, in contrast to other states, is that because Indian Country does not exist outside of Metlakatla in Southeast Alaska, non-Natives cannot be prosecuted in Native courts for such offenses. This is a major bone of contention among Alaska Natives.[89]

In 1996 the legislature enacted the Alaska Domestic Violence Prevention and Victim Protection Act in response to the federal VAWA. It elaborated on the definition of offenses that constituted domestic violence. Protective order provisions were expanded, prohibiting certain behavior by the abuser, and a central registry of abusers was established. If law enforcement personnel are called, a mandatory arrest must occur. This provides a statewide structure for response to domestic violence. The federal and state legislation were both viewed by advocates as a long time in coming, but as finally moving domestic violence from a family problem to a public issue and mandating a public response.

Alaska uses three major agencies to respond to and deal with domestic violence: the Department of Public Safety (law enforcement), the Office of Children's Services (child protection), and the Council on Domestic Violence and Sexual Assault (CDVSA). The Alaska Office of Children's Services (OCS) is the state agency that responds to child abuse and neglect allegations. It is one of eight divisions in the DHSS. The CDVSA works toward reducing the causes and occurrences and lessening the effects of domestic violence and sexual assault. To promote its goals, the council distributes funds it obtains from both state and federal sources. It administers grants to community-based victim services programs, batterers' intervention programs, and prison-based batterers' programs.

The Response: The Politics—Continuing Issues, Ideology, Budgets, and a Policy Entrepreneur

Victims of domestic violence and child abuse, like prison inmates, wield very little, if any, political influence by themselves. They have very few of the attributes of influential interest groups, such as teachers, the oil industry, and business groups.[90] Not only that, conservatives tend to oppose spending on social programs unless forced to do so by the federal government or the courts (as with corrections), and so social service programs are often underfunded.

In such a political environment it takes a surrogate political force to advocate for dealing with domestic violence and child abuse. Such a surrogate must be in a position of power. However well meaning legislative minority members or others with little political influence might be, their support and good will is not enough. Without influential surrogates, the needs of politically weak groups will remain unmet. Fortunately, domestic violence and child abuse victims did find such a political champion.

Political Developments in Combating Domestic Violence

For many years the Alaska Network on Domestic Violence and Sexual Assault (ANDVSA) has worked to end violence and oppression through social change. It is a nonprofit organization with eighteen programs and two affiliate programs statewide that provide services to victims of domestic violence and sexual assault, offender services, and adult crisis intervention services. It also advocates for increased state services and funding to combat the problem.[91] However, its political efforts and those of other organizations supporting additional funding and an increased policy response to domestic violence got only a tepid political response between 1996 and the passage of the Alaska Domestic Violence Prevention and Victim Protection Act in 2009.

The increase in funding over those years averaged 4 percent and barely outstripped inflation. Services were not available in many areas of the state, often resulting in victims having to leave their communities. Additional funding was necessary for outreach, public education, and prevention programs targeting root causes of domestic violence. Because of rising costs and increased demand, services that reacted to domestic violence anticipated cutting back services or even closing their doors without additional funding. Lack of funding would result in an increase in homelessness of at-risk victims and their children; an inability of victims to leave their community, increasing the likelihood of life threatening situations; and children experiencing domestic violence. These circumstances often result in various types of health problems for the victims and possible entry into child welfare and juvenile justice systems.

Then, in July 2009, Sean Parnell took over as governor on the resignation of Governor Palin. Six months later Parnell launched "Choose Respect," a major initiative to combat domestic violence and child abuse. Until his defeat in the general election of November 2014, those working to combat these types of violence had found in Parnell a surrogate political advocate who could make things happen. The details of the initiative and its various aspects are set out in Box 27.7. The initiative enjoyed many successes, helping to counter some of the previous budgetary and other problems. For instance, service program utilization by victims increased by 34 percent, from 8,550 in fiscal year (FY) 2009 to 11,478 in FY 2011.

BOX 27.7

"Choose Respect": Governor Sean Parnell's Initiative on Domestic Violence

In December 2009, Governor Parnell launched "Choose Respect," a program in which he pledged that Alaska would take every step to stop the epidemic of domestic violence, sexual assault, and child sexual abuse in the state. In the following five years various public policies were adopted and other steps taken to promote prevention and intervention in these aspects of personal violence. The program utilized various state agencies and nonprofits to advance its goals, including the nonprofit Alaska Network on Domestic Violence and Sexual Assault (ANDVSA) and the state's Council on Domestic Violence and Sexual Assault (CDVSA). The program involved increased prevention, law enforcement, and support for survivors of domestic violence.

PREVENTION

The increased involvement of the legislature, state agencies, local governments, and nonprofits in combating the problem included:

- The legislature passing several bills that strengthen laws related to sexual exploitation of children, domestic violence, stalking, and evidence retention.
- Launching the Department of Corrections' Fairbanks Pilot Project for treatment of twenty to sixty domestic violence misdemeanor offenders.
- Training thirty-five teachers from seventeen school districts in "Fourth R," a healthy relationship curriculum.
- The Family Violence Prevention Project, which supports a train-the-trainers initiative and provides technical support on dating violence, adolescent brain development, and substance abuse.
- Adding a Rural Pilot Project in Dillingham and Capacity Grants in Bethel, Kodiak, and Sitka.

Publicity and advocacy campaigns included Choose Respect Marches (eighteen were held in 2010, sixty-four in 2011, and more than 120 in 2012) and a Real Alaskans Choose Respect media campaign, with seventeen radio and television public announcements. Other campaigns included Stand Up Speak Up and Lead On for Peace and Justice!

INCREASED LAW ENFORCEMENT

This included doubling the number of Village Public Safety Officer (VPSO) positions from forty-seven in 2008 to ninety-six in January of 2012, as well as increasing VPSO oversight by adding three support troopers each for Bethel, Fairbanks,, and Kotzebue. Five rural-bush communities also received low-interest loans for VPSO housing. Three positions were added to the Alaska State Trooper cybercrimes unit (as much abuse is now taking place over the Internet) and four additional positions to the Alaska Bureau of Investigation (major crimes and child abuse units). Increased funding was available for sexual assault forensic exams and evidence collection kits and child protection attorneys in Palmer and Kenai.

SUPPORT FOR SURVIVORS

The extent of these services includes:

- ANDVSA pro-bono attorneys donated $826,000 worth of free legal assistance for victims.
- More than seven hundred behavioral health providers received training in trauma-informed services.
- Expanded access to child advocacy centers (CAC) by supporting the new CAC in Kodiak.
- There are 160 Family Wellness Warriors participants in Bristol Bay and the Yukon-Kuskokwim regions.

Source: Developed by the author from Governor Parnell's website. See endnote 92.

CDVSA reports that 93 percent of FY 2011 program participants knew more about enhancing safety and 92 percent knew more about available community resources than before the program began, and ANDVSA pro-bono attorneys donated $826,000 worth of free legal assistance for victims.[92] With Parnell's defeat by Bill Walker in the 2014 gubernatorial election, the future of the program was in doubt. Walker did commit to carrying on the effort in a March 2014 speech.[93] But major budget cuts in the 2014 , 2015 and 2016 legislative sessions reduced his ability to continue the program effectively.

Combating Child Abuse: Dealing with Administrative Dysfunction

From 2009 to 2014, and paralleling developments in combating domestic violence, child abuse prevention also received a boost in financial support and a higher political profile from Governor Parnell's "Choose Respect" initiative. For many years, however, DHSS's Office of Children's Services (OCS) was an agency "under siege" throughout the state because of understaffing, some narrow service delivery philosophies, and some bad press regarding OCS's failure to deal with some particularly egregious child abuse cases.

Studies in 2002 by the Knowles administration and one by the Murkowski administration released in 2007 (after Murkowski left the governorship), found OCS to be overwhelmed, dysfunctional, and hobbled by vague policies. It was riddled with problems including high turnover, inadequate training, troublesome employees, poor communications, and a negative public image.[94] Several state legislative audits identified poor management, high staff turnover, and poor oversight over grants awarded by OCS to private contractors. Over these years, the news media, and particularly the *Anchorage Daily News*, ran several scathing articles on OCS, depicting children as being repeatedly maltreated, families not getting needed help, and children often bouncing from one foster home to another or languishing in foster care with no plan for a permanent home.

Change at OCS has slowly occurred, but other reforms would also help to advance the welfare of children in need. At one time OCS was very insular and cited confidentiality laws as preventing it from being more open and visible to the public. That has since changed in response to legislation providing for more openness. OCS now contracts with numerous private for-profit and nonprofit organizations, including Native organizations, throughout the state and provides funding for a variety of services. OCS could, however, consider further improvements.

For example, state child welfare systems throughout the nation are increasingly entering into partnerships with local communities. They are improving their systems by privatizing parts of it, such as case management, foster care recruitment and training, and by locating child welfare and child protection services in a single building to coordinate efforts working with children and families on a variety of problems. Some states, such as Kansas and Florida, have undergone significant reform, moving large segments of their

BOX 27.8

Alaska CARES (Child Abuse Response and Evaluation Services)

As of 2015 child advocacy centers operated in all fifty states, the District of Columbia, and the Virgin Islands. The federal Victims of Child Abuse Act provides some of the funding for the centers through the National Children's Alliance. The alliance is a nonprofit membership organization working with communities throughout the nation to investigate and respond to severe child abuse. There are now seven such advocacy child centers in Alaska: Fairbanks, Juneau, Wasilla, Nome, Bethel, Dillingham, and CARES—Child Abuse Response and Evaluation Services—in Anchorage.

CARES opened in 1996, and was the first child advocacy center in Alaska. It is a member of the National Children's Alliance, and besides the Alliance it received initial funding from Alaska Area Native Health Service, other nonprofits, and government agencies. Toddlers to eighteen-year-olds who are suspected victims of sexual assault are interviewed and examined by a professional staff. The major emphasis of CARES is to ensure that children are not revictimized during the process of investigation and disposition.

The approach is that of interagency cooperation by involving law enforcement, child protection workers, prosecutors, behavioral health professionals, victim advocates, and health care providers in response to child abuse cases. It also includes the collaboration of federal, state, and municipal governments, along with Alaska Native agencies and private health care professionals. Child advocates are provided by two agencies, Standing Together Against Rape (STAR) and the Alaska Native Justice Center. Major local supporters of Alaska CARES include the Southcentral Foundation (an Alaska Native health care organization), DHSS, and the Children's Hospital (at Providence Hospital in Anchorage), a private nonprofit organization. A number of for-profit businesses in Anchorage also provide financial support.

In August 2007, CARES joined in a collaborative milestone effort to develop a specialized unit, the University Lake Plaza Multidisciplinary Center, to investigate all suspected sexual and physical abuse occurring in the Anchorage area. The center is staffed by investigators of the OCS of DHSS, Alaska State Troopers, the Anchorage Police Department, the Anchorage Sexual Assault Response Team, and CARES. This represents a combined effort of state and municipal governments and private agencies. Similar programs are offered in California, Texas, and Arizona. These services are both reactive and preventive in regard to interpersonal violence.

Source: Developed by the author.

services into the private sector. Arizona, Colorado, and South Dakota are experimenting with privatizing the case management function.[95]

Alaska has yet to move forward on these reforms to any extent. As of 2015, OCS was contracting with private organizations only for adoption and guardianship placement, family preservation, and support services. It also directly provides support services for parent education and training, substance abuse treatment, and mental health counseling. Given the ongoing problems experienced by the agency, further consideration should be given to shifting core child welfare services to private providers. These could include child protection and investigative functions and foster care, as well as transferring case management to the private sector, and giving providers primary decision making authority over day to day management. These measures would provide community investment in the prevention of child abuse and neglect. The case study set out in Box 27.8 is an advocacy effort bringing together government, private nonprofit, and Alaska Native organizations responding to sexual and physical abuse of children in the Municipality of Anchorage. This model could well be emulated throughout the state.

Contradictory Policies: Continued Failure to Attack Root Causes through an Integrated Policy Approach

While the "Choose Respect" initiative was certainly a major advance in attacking the epidemic of domestic violence and child abuse, it nonetheless continued some of the "get tough on crime" policies of the past without addressing some of the root causes of these forms of violence. Again, the initiative ignored the important connection between substance abuse and mental illness that often results in domestic violence and imprisonment. The description of the initiative in Box 27.7 obviously lacks any reference to resources for mental health and substance abuse services. This is another negative aspect of underfunding and program cuts over the past decade in behavioral health programs. Stiffer prison sentences are equally ineffective as a long-term solution to domestic violence.

5. THE POLITICS AND POWER DYNAMICS OF ALASKA SOCIAL SERVICES ISSUES AND POLICIES

Drawing on our consideration of health, corrections, and domestic violence policy, in this section we view social services issues and policy in terms of their politics and power dynamics from six perspectives: (1) the general context of Alaska politics and policy making, (2) political capacity constraints, (3) the influence of political ideology and political culture, (4) the contrasting perspectives of social services professionals and politicians, (5) the influence of social services constituencies, and (6) the role of political pragmatism. The conclusion to the chapter asks whether the future may hold a different direction in social services policy.

The General Nature of Alaska Politics and the Policy-Making Process

Like other policies, social services policy making takes place in the general context of Alaska politics. This includes the values, motives, and goals of elected and appointed officials and the various pressures on them. It also includes the constraints of both the democratic process and the policy process.

For elected officials, the democratic process means standing for election every two or four years, depending on the office held. Consequently, the political and policy horizons of many politicians stretch only as far as their next election. Moreover, there are a multitude of demands on them from a wide range of constituencies, only one of which is social services. These demands must be dealt with in the face of limited resources, particularly available state revenues, as well as the limited time and limited power of each elected official.

A major constraint on achieving an improved social services system is Alaska's fragmented policy-making process, which to a large extent pits the legislature against the executive branch, both of which possess strong power bases. Added to this is the occasional action by the courts affecting policy, like the *Cleary* and Mental Health Trust Lands decisions. But perhaps the major constraint of all is the state budget. Discretionary spending on social services is the last to be added in good financial times and among the first to be cut when revenues fall. We explain the reasons for this below.

In combination, the democratic and policy processes and financial constraints are not conducive to long-term or programmatic policy making. They result in incremental policies and ad hoc, short-term solutions to problems that would often benefit from a long-term, more integrated policy approach. The state's inability, as of 2015, to come up with a long-term fiscal plan or to deal with subsistence issues are prime examples of the results of fragmented policy processes. In social services policy this has, in large part, precluded the integration of health (particularly behavioral health), corrections, and interpersonal violence policies.

IGR and Political and Governmental Capacity Constraints

The IGR aspect of much of social services policy making, particularly the role of the federal government, also limits the state's control in some areas. Many programs, particularly Medicaid, programs for the disabled, and those to combat substance abuse and domestic violence, require the state to provide a match to federal funds in order to receive a major contribution from the federal government. The necessity to secure these and other formula program funds requires the state to comply with the federal rules that go along with the monies. This gives the state less leeway in shaping these programs. In some cases, the state can choose not to accept the funds, as Alaska has done in some instances, but this can often have major political fallout with the electorate. In other cases, as with many provisions of the Affordable Care Act, Alaska has no choice but to comply.

Combining the general characteristics of Alaska politics and policy with the specific elements of IGR shows that Alaska is far from in charge of social policy as it affects its citizens. In other words, and in the language of Chapter 3, the state has limited political and governmental capacity to affect many aspects of this policy area, even though in many policy areas it is a partner with the federal and often local and Native governments. Moreover, as in many other areas of public policy, the state's political and governmental capacity to deal with many problems that generate social services issues is minimal or nonexistent. For instance, Alaska had no control over the major migration to the state in the 1970s to build the Alaska pipeline, which increased demands for health services as well as producing increased crime and other social problems. Furthermore, the state has no ability to prevent a fall in oil prices, the revenues from which are a major aspect of its capacity to fund social services programs, including providing federal matching funds.

This is not to make excuses for the state's inadequate approach to many social services and corrections policies. It is simply to state that some political, institutional, and external forces undermine Alaska's ability to deal with some social policy issues in a fundamental and systematic way. On the other hand, the state does have choices and control in other areas that affect social policy, as the following observations show.

The Influence of Political Ideology and Political Culture

The influence of political ideology and political culture on social policy manifests some predictable divisions but also some more complex political outcomes.

Republican and Democratic partisan affiliation, usually manifested in a conservative-liberal division, affects many areas of social policy. Conservative influence can be seen in making social programs a prime target for cutting in times of tight budgets but also as a matter of ideological principle to reduce the size of government. This perspective is reinforced by a strong sense of individualism and the fact that many social services programs are redistributive policies of which many Republicans and conservatives disapprove. Mandatory sentencing is another manifestation of the conservative "keep Alaska safe" attitude. Democrats and liberals tend to hold opposite views. But as Republicans and conservatives have controlled or had major influence in Alaska policy making since the early 1990s, their ideology and political cultural values have had a considerable impact on social policy.

Ideology in the form of anti-federal sentiments also plays a role from time to time. For instance, as we noted earlier, Governor Parnell's decision not to have Alaska operate its own insurance exchange under the Affordable Care Act and not to accept the additional Medicaid funds was, at root, a product of an ideology that combines fiscal conservatism, anti-federal sentiments, and a stubborn individualism.

Yet political ideology and political culture can work in more moderate ways, and even have a liberal and communal influence. One example is Alaska's lack of a death penalty. As of 2015, Alaska was one of eighteen states and the District of Columbia that does not have a death penalty.[96] But unlike many of these states, such as Illinois and Connecticut, that have only recently abolished or put a moratorium on executions, Alaska abolished its death penalty in 1957, two years before it became a state. Moreover, Alaska did not succumb to the pressures of the movement in the late 1970s and 1980s to reimpose executions, despite the fact that death penalty proposals were introduced in most legislative sessions. In its attitude to the death penalty, then, Alaska has long been among the most liberal states.

Professionals versus Politicians

A complaint frequently voiced by social services professionals is that too often social services policies do not get made on their merits—that is, what is considered the best course for the clients and society and the most efficient use of limited funds. Instead, professional considerations are subordinated to politics. But this is not just the case with social services policy. It is a complaint heard across the gamut of political issues from various professionals and the public alike, including those involved in education, transportation, environmental issues, fisheries, economic development, subsistence, the arts, and even those wanting to improve animal shelters.

Politics often trumps professional expertise and what might be the right policy for those affected by it, which may be good or bad depending on which side of the issue a person stands. But the dominance of politics is a reality and will likely remain so. This inevitable situation stems from a combination of clashes of values, the different motives of those involved in an issue, differing ideologies, disagreements over what is and is not the best course to pursue, and choices about the allocation of funds across the range of demands on state budgets, among other factors.

To many social services professionals, probably the most frustrating aspect of the dominance of political over professional policy solutions is ad hoc short-term policy approaches to the range of social services issues that many argue are best dealt with through long-term solutions that integrate various aspects of health, corrections, and interpersonal violence. It is clear from a host of studies that poverty, crime, interpersonal violence, substance abuse, and often mental illness, are interconnected—one condition often leads to one or more of the others. Ideally, they should all be dealt with together, but for the reasons we have explained, they are not and are not likely to be in the future.

This is not to say that professionals are never listened to, that reforms do not take place, or that client groups never benefit from politics. All three do occur, as we will see in the next two points on social services policy and policy making.

The Influence of Social Services Constituencies: Policy Surrogates and Policy Entrepreneurs

The power dynamic involved in social services policy making contrasts with most other issue areas in state politics. It often involves high-level advocates, surrogates, and what are often called policy entrepreneurs. In the case of social services these policy entrepreneurs are influential elected or appointed public officials who champion the cause of social services groups that otherwise have very little or no political influence.

As Chapter 15 on interest groups points out, there is a bias in interest group representation in favor of the middle and upper classes, the better educated, and the Caucasian and male segments of the population. The poor and various minorities are less well represented by organized interests.[97] Consequently, in most issue areas in American and Alaska politics, such as education, local government, economic development, the environment, and fisheries, among many others, those directly affected by the policy have organized into interest groups that often work hand in hand with public officials, both elected and appointed, to secure policy goals. There are, however, few groups representing client groups in social services, and with the exception of the ad hoc group formed in the 1980s to push for the mental health lands settlement and some groups against domestic violence, few have had any success in the policy process based on their own political advocacy efforts.

There are certainly many provider groups that do have some political clout, like the Alaska Medical Association, the Alaska Dental Association, and the Alaska State Hospital and Nursing Home Association. But these are primarily concerned with the interests of their members and only secondarily, if at all, with social services issues and clienteles. Even when providers do get together to attempt to influence state social services policy on behalf of client groups, they are often not successful. This was the case, for example, when providers urged Governor Parnell to accept the extended Medicaid provisions offered as part of the Affordable Care Act, which he ultimately refused to accept.[98]

However, the absence of or relatively weak client-interest groups does not necessarily mean that social services clients have no political influence. These groups often have both surrogates and some policy entrepreneurs working on their behalf. Major surrogates are federal agencies through their funding of many programs and federal protective regulations, as well as federal and state courts, particularly state courts, through decisions like those in the Mental Health Trust Lands and *Cleary* cases. Examples of policy entrepreneurship include former State Senator Jim Duncan's attempts to get universal health coverage in Alaska, former Corrections Commissioner Joe Schmidt's work on prison reform and recidivism, former Alaska Supreme Court Chief Justice Walter Carpeneti's advocacy for reconsidering mandatory prison sentences, Senator John Coghill's work on comprehensive prison reform, and former Governor Parnell's initiative on domestic violence (although his hard line on offenders undermined the integration of this initiative with criminal justice policy).

This combination of surrogates and entrepreneurs does not give social services clients the political influence of K–12 education, the university, state employees, or the oil industry. It does, however, mean that these client groups' interests are represented to some extent, and sometimes very effectively, even though the political influence of policy entrepreneurs can be fleeting as they retire from office, lose an election, or lose their position in the majority caucus in the legislature. For instance, Governor Parnell's defeat left questions about the "Choose Respect" initiative, though Governor Walker's commitment to its continuation and Native leader Byron Mallott's election as Lieutenant Governor offer Mallott a chance to be a policy entrepreneur in the area of domestic violence and child abuse.[99] Moreover, Governor Walker's appointment of a special advisor on Crime Policy and Prevention could be an indication that he is going to be a policy entrepreneur in the area not only of interpersonal violence but also crime and perhaps might view the two together in developing policy.

6. The Role of Political Pragmatism

Dominant conservative political ideology and inherent political systemic problems, among other factors, shape and often undermine the development and provision of effective and efficient social services in Alaska. However, we should not dismiss the role of political pragmatism in social services politics and policy making. In fact, like many other aspects of Alaska politics (and American politics in general), over the years political pragmatism has been a major force in social services policy. This has had both negative and positive consequences for the client groups served.

On the negative side, political pragmatism often means cutting political deals over social services policies, producing ad hoc "quick fix" solutions to issues unrelated to the wider affected areas of social policy. Often, too, social services policies are a secondary consideration in pragmatic political decisions about economic development or quid pro quos in politics, as was partly the case with the Goose Creek prison. In addition, the relative weakness of the social services lobby on a day-to-day basis means that, from a pragmatic perspective, even Democrats, who generally favor social services programs, may opt to cut back these programs in times of budget shortfalls.

On the other hand, political pragmatism has also had its positive effects. Three examples relate to pragmatism and political conservatism. One is the fact that the conservative general aversion to state spending means that many services have been contracted out. While this sometimes has its downsides, it does mean that the services are being provided and often in a more efficient and cost-effective way than if provided by the state. A second is that pragmatism has sometimes led to bipartisanship on issues and policy making. This was the case, for instance, with various policies on mental health, such as the "Bring the Children Home" initiative, and on some interpersonal violence policies. The third example is that, ironically, the major increase in the cost of prisons in recent years, largely fueled by mandatory sentencing, appears to be forcing a reconsideration of the wisdom of such sentences as well as reconsideration of the effectiveness of retributive prison policies. These cost increases may also result in programs to reduce recidivism and combat domestic violence and child abuse. At least as far as corrections are concerned, actions by Senator Coghill, acting in effect as a policy entrepreneur, are certainly bringing about major changes.

6. CONCLUSION: THE FUTURE OF SOCIAL SERVICES POLITICS AND POLICY: A NEW ERA OR MORE OF THE SAME?

Given the aspects of social services politics and policy considered in this chapter, what can be expected in the future? Most likely we can expect more of the same. It is hard to see any major changes in any of the aspects because they are so deeply rooted in the general nature of the social services policy environment across the nation as well as in Alaska's political culture and political power dynamic.

This likely future situation, however, does not necessarily mean lean times for social services clienteles. The incremental approach to policy making will likely include continued partnering of the state with private agencies in service delivery, and this may well increase. The surrogate and entrepreneurial aspects of representation will also likely continue, though less consistently than interests with direct power relationships with policy makers. And as we have seen, several reforms have been enacted. Whether they are motivated by a genuine commitment to them or political pragmatism, they are now on the books, and others may follow.

What is uncertain, however, is how Alaska's revenue picture will play out in the years to come, which, of course, is not only a crucial factor in continued provision of social services but of all other services in state government. A long-term downturn in state revenues and an unwillingness to develop other revenue streams to supplement the budget would likely affect most social services clients very negatively given their relatively weak position in the state's political power structure. Ironically, though, it may lead to major reforms in the corrections system, as noted earlier.

Taking into account these likely future circumstances, the best approach for social services advocates, both within and outside of government, including social services professionals, is not to lose sight of the ideal of an integrated set of social services policies, but at the same time to be realistic as to what can and cannot be achieved from a practical political perspective. This requires being grounded in the realities of social services politics and policy at the state, federal, and local levels and in effective advocacy techniques. It is also essential that the state, Native tribal groups, and providers work together to develop the best strategies for dealing with social services issues given the realities of the situation. The interests of social services clienteles will be more effectively served only if these two courses of action are pursued and realized.

ENDNOTES

[1] "Where Does the Money Go? Government Spending," in *State and Local Politics: Institutions and Reform*, eds., Todd Donovan, Christopher Z. Mooney, and Daniel A. Smith (Belmont, CA: Wadsworth Cengage Learning, 2009), 342–45, esp. figure 10.5, "Major Government Spending Programs, 2005"; and Office of Management and Budget, *Alaska Enacted Budget 2014*, at http://omb.alaska.gov/ombfiles/14_budget/PDFs/UGF_DGF_OTH_FED_DEPT_Summary.pdf.

[2] See Bruce Jansson, *The Reluctant Welfare State: American Social Welfare Policies: Past, Present and Future*, 5th ed. (Belmont, CA: Brooks/Cole, 2005).

[3] Donovan, Mooney, and Smith, *State and Local Politics*, 342.

[4] A good overview of health and welfare policy across the fifty states and for making comparisons with Alaska is Mark Carl Rom, "State Health and Welfare Programs," in *Politics in the American States: A Comparative Analysis*, eds., Virginia Gray, Russell L. Hanson, and Thad Kousser, 10th ed. (Washington, D.C.: CQ Press, 2013).

[5] The U.S. Census Bureau, *Health Insurance*, at http://www.census.gov/hhes/www/hlthins/data/incpovhlth/2011/highligts.html; and Kaiser Family Foundation, "The Uninsured and Their Access to Health Care," at http://www.kff.org/uninsured/upload/1420_09.pdf.

[6] Stephen Miller, "Increased Health Care Cost Shifting Expected in 2011," Society for Human Resource Management, June, 18, 2010, at http://www.shrm.org/hrdisciplines/benefits/Articles/Pages/CostShifting2011.aspx.

[7] The Organisation for Economic Co-operation and Development (OECD), *Health at a Glance 2013*, Table 7.1.1: Health Expenditures per capita, at http://www.oecd.org/els/health-systems/Health-at-a-Glance-2013.pdf.

[8] Becky Bohrer, "Parnell Says No to State-Run Insurance Exchange," *Anchorage Daily News*, July 17, 2012.

[9] The 2012 case is *NFIB et al. v. Sibelius*, 132 S.Ct. 2566 (2012); see also Adam Liptak, "Supreme Court Upholds Health Care Law, 5-4, in Victory for Obama," *New York Times*, June 28, 2012. The 2015 case is *King v. Burwell*, 135 S.Ct. 2480 (2015).

[10] For an overview of health policy developments in Alaska from statehood to the late 1990s, see James B. Goes, "Health: National Trends in an Alaska Setting," in *Alaska Public Policy Issues: Background and Perspectives*, ed. Clive S. Thomas (Juneau: Denali Press, 1999).

[11] The politics of getting Denali KidCare enacted, and the tussle between the Democratic Knowles administration and the Republican legislature, are explained in Chapter 16, Box 16.8.

[12] The Alaska Health Care Strategies Planning Council, *The Consensus Document: Summary and Recommendations*, December 2007; the AHCC website, at http://dhss.alaska.gov/ahcc/Pages/default.aspx; Annie Feidt, "Budget Cut would Eliminate Health Care Commission," *Alaska News Nightly*, Alaska Public Radio Network (APRN), March 5, 2015; and telephone interview by Clive Thomas with Tara Horton, Special Assistant to the Commissioner of DHSS and former staff person to the Alaska Health Care Strategies Planning Council, March 26, 2015.

[13] Mark Foster and Scott Goldsmith, "Alaska's Health-Care Bill: $7.5 billion and Climbing," UA Research Summary no. 18, August (Anchorage: University of Alaska Anchorage, Institute of Social and Economic Research, 2011).

[14] Annie Feidt, "Report Says 12,000 Alaskans without Reliable Access to Health Care," *Alaska News Nightly* APRN, June 12, 2014.

[15] Mark A. Foster and Associates, Medicare Section, *Estimated Economic Effects of the Patient Protection and Affordable Care Act, As Amended, in Alaska*, May 2011, at http://hss.state.ak.us/healthcommission/meetings/201110/PPACA_AK_estimates201106.pdf.

[16] State of Alaska Department of Health and Social Services, Division of Behavioral Health and the Alaska Mental Health Trust Authority, *Bring the Kids Home Annual Report* (December 2005): 1–30.

[17] For substance abuse policy in Alaska up until the 1990s, see Virginia S. Mulle, "Substance Abuse and Domestic Violence: Consequences of Alaska's Diversity," in Thomas, *Alaska Public Policy Issues.*

[18] For an overview of the mission of API see, Alaska Department of Health and Social Services, Division of Behavioral Health, at http://dhss.alaska.gov/dbh/Pages/api/mission.aspx.

[19] Foster and Goldsmith, "Alaska's Health-Care Bill."

[20] Kaiser Family Foundation, *Health Care Expenditures by State of Residence*, at http://www.statehealthfacts.org/comparemaptable.jsp?typ=2&ind=595&cat=5&sub=143&sortc=1&o=a.

[21] Annie Feidt, "Alaskans weigh options as health insurance rates soar," *Alaska News Nightly*, APRN, October 28, 2015.

[22] Sabra Ayers, "Medicaid Expenses Skyrocket; OUTLOOK: Program's Cost will Rise, but a Report to Lawmakers Offers Ideas on Potential Savings," *Anchorage Daily News,* February 7, 2007; and Kaiser Family Foundation, *Medicaid and CHIP*, at http://www.statehealthfacts.org/comparecat.jsp?cat=4&rgn=1&rgn=3.

[23] Lisa Demer, "Parnell: Alaska Won't Expand Medicaid," *Anchorage Daily News*, November 15, 2013; Tegan Hanlon, "State Creates New Position to Lead Medicaid Expansion in Alaska," *Alaska Dispatch News*, December 20, 2014; and Nathaniel Herz, "Walker Says He'll Use Executive Authority to Expand Medicaid in Alaska," *Alaska Dispatch News*, July 15, 2015.

[24] Kaiser Family Foundation, *Health Care Employment 2012*, at http://www.statehealthfacts.org/comparemaptable.jsp?typ=2&ind=872&cat=8&sub=105&sortc=1&o=a.

[25] Alaska Department of Labor and Workforce Development, *Alaska Economic Trends: Industry and Occupational Forecasts, 2010–2020*, , October 2012, 3–5.

[26] The Alaska Federal Healthcare Partnership, at http://www.afhcp.org/about/alaska-challenges/.

[27] Karleen Jackson, "Report of the Alaska Physician Supply Task Force," Alaska Department of Health and Social Services, August 2006: 1–124; and Beth Landon et al., "Alaska Health Workforce Vacancy Study" (Anchorage: University of Alaska, Alaska Center for Rural Health, 2009).

[28] Katherine Long, "Alaska may pull out of UW-run WWAMI program, which trains doctors for five states," *The Seattle Times*, March 20, 2015.

[29] For a consideration of the advantages of integrating the development of various social services policies, see Fay Hanleybrown, John Kania, and Mark Kramer, "Challenging Change: Making Collective Impact Work," *Stamford Social Innovation Review* (January 2012).

[30] The Sentencing Project, *Reducing Incarceration, Reducing, Crime*, at http://www.sentencingproject.org/doc/Downscaling2.pdf.

[31] See *The Economist*, July 20-26th, 2013, "The Curious Case of the Fall in Crime," 9–10, and various other articles in the issue.

[32] This overview of the politics and administration of corrections across the states draws, in part, on John Wooldredge, "State Corrections Policy," in Gray, Hanson, and Kousser, *Politics in the American States.*

[33] U.S. Bureau of Justice Statistics, *Correctional Populations in the United States, 2010*, at http://bjs.ojp.usdoj.gov/content/pub/pdf/p10.pdf, and *Prisoners in 2013*, at http://www.bjs.gov/content/pub/pdf/p13.pdf.

[34] International Center for Prison Studies, *World Prison Population List*, at http://www.prisonstudies.org/sites/prisonstudies.org/files/resources/downloads/wppl_10.pdf.

[35] The statistics on the racial makeup of the U.S. prison population are from U.S. Bureau of Justice Statistics, at http://www.bjs.gov/content/pub/pdf/p13.pdf; and the U.S. Bureau of the Census, at http://quickfacts.census.gov/qfd/states/00000.html.

[36] The Pew Charitable Trusts, "State Prison Release and Recidivism Rates," in *State of Recidivism: The Revolving Door of American Prisons* (Washington, D.C.: The Pew Charitable Trusts, 2011), 10–11. See also Kevin Johnson, "Study: Prisons Failing to Deter Repeat Criminals in 41 States," *USA Today*, April 13, 2011.

[37] Figures obtained from the nonprofit organization Released and Restored, which works to reduce recidivism, at http://releasedandrestored.org/index.html.

[38] Gary Fields and Erica E. Phillips, "The New Asylums: America's Jails Swell with Mentally Ill," *Wall Street Journal*, September 26, 2013; and "Prisons Are a Very Poor Place to Treat the Mentally Ill," *Wall Street Journal*, October 7, 2013, Letter to the Editor in response to the first article, from Doris M. Fuller, Executive Director, Advocacy Treatment Center, Arlington, Virginia.

[39] Robert Martinson, "What Works," *The Public Interest* 61 (1974): 3–17.

[40] Marc Mauer and David Cole, "Five Myths about Americans in Prison," *Washington Post*, June 17, 2011.

[41] Bureau of Justice Statistics, State Corrections Expenditures, FY 1982–2010, at http://www.bjs.gov/content/pub/pdf/spe96.pdf.

[42] Jennifer Medina, "California Sheds Prisoners but Grapples with Courts," *New York Times*, January 21, 2013.

[43] The Pew Center on States, "Public Opinion on Sentencing and Correction Policy in America," March 2011, at http://www.pewcenteronthestates.org/uploadedFiles/wwwpewcenteronthestatesorg/Initiatives/PSPP/PEW_NationalSurveyResearchPaper_FINAL.pdf.

[44] Charles Savage and Erica Goode, "Two Powerful Signals of a Major Shift on Crime," *New York Times*, August 12, 2013.

[45] Matt Apuzzo, "Justice Dept. Expands Eligibility for Clemency," *New York Times*, April 23, 2014; and Carrie Johnson, "Republicans Join Fight To Reduce Terms for Drug Crimes," *Morning Edition*, National Public Radio (NPR), March 26, 2015.

[46] Sori Horwitz, "Justice Department set to free 6,000 prisoners, largest one-time release," *Washington Post*, October 6, 2015.

[47] Andy Kroll, "This is How Private Prison Companies Make Millions Even When Crime Rates Fall," *Mother Jones*, September 13, 2013, at http://www.motherjones.com/mojo/2013/09/private-prisons-occupancy-quota-cca-crime.

[48] Democratic Leadership Council, 2009, at http://www.dlc.org/ndol_ci.cfm?kaid=108&subid=900003&contentid=255055.

[49] For an examination of corrections in Alaska before 1998, see Charles F. Campbell and John Pugh, "Corrections: Public Pressure, Political Symbolism and Professional Expertise," in Thomas, *Alaska Public Policy Issues*.

[50] Stephanie Martin and Steve Colt, "The Cost of Crime: Could the State Reduce Future Crime and Save Money by Expanding Education and Treatment Programs?" Research Summary No. 71, Institute of Social and Economic Research (ISER), Anchorage, January 2009, Figure 1, "Percentage Change in Alaska Crime Rate."

[51] See Campbell and Pugh, "Corrections," 151–57, esp. Figure 11.1; and "Alaska's Five-Year Prisoner Reentry Strategic Plan, 2011–2016," *Alaska Justice Forum* (Anchorage: University of Alaska Anchorage, UAA Justice Center, Summer/Fall 2011), 2.

[52] For a consideration of the law and its early implications, see Barry Jeffrey Stern, "Presumptive Sentencing in Alaska," *Alaska Law Review* 2 (1985): 226–69.

[53] See Campbell and Pugh, "Corrections," Figure 11.1; and Alaska Department of Corrections, Division of Administrative Services, *Offender Profile 2011*, 7, and the *Offender Profile 2013* at http://www.correct.state.ak.us/admin/docs/2013Profile_Final.pdf.

[54] Martin and Colt, "The Cost of Crime," Figure 8, "Average Number of Alaska Inmates, 1971–2007, and Projected Number, 2008–30."

[55] Jersey Shedlock, "UAA researchers: convicted women in prison increasing, overall population down," *Alaska Dispatch News*, November 2, 2015.

[56] Pew Charitable Trusts, *State of Recidivism: The Revolving Door of American Prisons.*

[57] Office of Management and Budget, Department of Corrections, *Performance Details*, at http://omb.alaska.gov/html/performance/details.html?p=24#td6619.

[58] Alaska Department of Corrections, Division of Administrative Services, *Offender Profile 2013: Counts and Percentages of Offenders in Institutions by Race/Ethnicity*, December 2013, at http://www.correct.state.ak.us/admin/docs/2013Profile_Final.pdf.

[59] Martin and Colt, "The Cost of Crime," Figure 5, "How Many Alaska Inmates Have Substance Abuse or Mental Disorders?"; and *Alaska Justice Forum* 18, no. 4, (Winter 2002).

[60] Campbell and Pugh, "Corrections," 159–60.

[61] Megan Holland, "Alaska Prisoners to Move from Arizona to Colorado," *Anchorage Daily News*, August 10, 2009.

[62] See, for example, two articles in the Kenai area's *Peninsula Clarion*, "Debate Erupts over Talk of Private Prison," December 11, 2000; and "Private Prison Plan Panned, Praised," December 15, 2000.

[63] Box 27.6 is, in part, based on the following sources: Richard Mauer, "Goose Creek Prison Hits Speed Bump," *Anchorage Daily News*, April 16, 2010; Ben Anderson, "Opening Soon: Alaska's $240 Million Goose Greek Prison," *Alaska Dispatch*, June 24, 2012; Lisa Demer, "Goose Creek Prison Almost Ready for Inmates," *Anchorage Daily News*, November 6, 2011; and Zaz Holander, "New Goose Creek Prison Experiences Growing Pains," *Anchorage Daily News*, November 3, 2013.

[64] Governor Bill Walker "State of the Budget" speech, January 22, 2015, at http://gov.alaska.gov/Walker/press-room/full-press-release.html?pr=7061; and Katie Moritz, "In Walker's Budget Proposal, Corrections and Health Take Biggest Hits," *Juneau Empire*, January 25, 2015.

[65] Interview with Charles F. Campbell, former Director of Corrections, by Clive Thomas, October 24, 1998.

[66] The statistics on the DOC operating and capital budgets from 1990 to 2013 draw on the following sources: Alaska Justice Forum, *Alaska Justice System Operating Expenditures*, Winter 2006, vol. 22, no. 4, at http://justice.uaa.alaska.edu/forum/22/4winter2006/c_expenditures.html; and Office of Management and Budget, *Budget Reports 2001–2014*, at https://omb.alaska.gov/html/

budget-report/fy-2014-budget/enacted.html, and at https://omb.alaska.gov/ombfiles/14_budget/14enacted_5-21-13_deptsummary.pdf; State of Alaska Legislature, *Fiscal year 1990: Operating and Capital Budget*, at http://www.legfin.state.ak.us/HDBooks/HouseDistrictBook1989.pdf.

[67] Reba Lean, "Deputy Commissioner Says Alaska Prisons Need More Successes," *Fairbanks Daily News-Miner*, May 18, 2012.

[68] The Pew Research Center, at http://www.pewstates.org/uploadedFiles/PCS_Assets/2007/Public%20Safety%20Public%20Spending.pdf.

[69] Martin and Colt, "The Cost of Crime," Figure 4, "Annual State Cost Per Inmate, 1981–2008."

[70] Campbell and Pugh, "Corrections," 151.

[71] For a short analysis of the criminal administration provisions of the state constitution, see Gordon Harrison, *Alaska's Constitution: A Citizen's Guide*, 5th ed. (Juneau: Alaska Legislative Affairs Agency, 2012), 28–30.

[72] Campbell and Pugh, "Corrections," 151.

[73] Martin and Colt, "The Cost of Crime."

[74] Teresa W. Carns, "Therapeutic Justice in Action: An Evaluation of Three Therapeutic Courts," *Alaska Justice Forum* 22, no. 1 (Winter 2005).

[75] Information on the State of the Judiciary address by Chief Justice Carpeneti is taken from the official transcript, Alaska Court System, State of the Judiciary, February 29, 2012; and Dave Donaldson, "State's Top Judge Advocates for Targeted, Cost Effective Justice," *Alaska News Nightly*, APRN, March 1, 2012.

[76] Alaska Judicial Council, *Criminal Recidivism in Alaska* (Anchorage: Alaska Judicial Council, 2006).

[77] For details on the work of the CJWG, see Teresa White Carns, "Criminal Justice Working Group Update," *Alaska Justice Forum* 26, no. 1, (Spring 2009); and Carpeneti, *State of the Judiciary*, 2012.

[78] Chris Klint, "Omnibus Crime Bill Passes Alaska Legislature," KTUU TV Anchorage, April 22, 2014.

[79] For the perspective of someone who has been incarcerated, see H. Thompson Prentzel III, "Senate Bill 64: a Crime Bill for a Criminal System of Justice," Commentary, *Alaska Dispatch News*, January 25, 2015.

[80] Michelle Theriault Boots, "With More Alaska Women Incarcerated than Ever, Some Moved to Men's Jail," *Alaska Dispatch News*, January 10, 2015.

[81] Jerzy Shedlock, "Corrections officials say reforms will prevent having to reopen prison farm," *Alaska Dispatch News*, November 1, 2015.

[82] Unless separately cited, statistics on these forms of violence and abuse are drawn from those provided by the National Coalition Against Domestic Violence (NCADV), at http://www.ncadv.org/files/Alaska.pdf; and former Alaska Governor Sean Parnell's office, at http://gov.alaska.gov/parnell/priorities/public-safety/choose-respect.html.

[83] "Alaska Victimization Survey: Research on Violence Against Women in Alaska" (Anchorage: University of Alaska Justice Center, 2010).

[84] Lisa Phu, "Participants Voice Hopes and Realities at Domestic Violence Prevention Summit," *Morning Edition*, KTOO—FM Juneau, December 3, 2013.

[85] For an overview of the issue of domestic violence in Alaska and public policy regarding it down to 1999, see Mulle, "Substance Abuse and Domestic Violence."

[86] Child Welfare League of America, *Research and Data*, at http://www.cwla.org/programs/researchdata/default.htm.

[87] U.S. Department of Health and Human Services, *Child Maltreatment 2012*, at http://www.acf.hhs.gov/sites/default/files/cb/cm2012.pdf.

[88] U.S. Census Bureau, "Child Poverty in the United States 2009 and 2010: Selected Race Groups and Hispanic Origin," American Community Survey Briefs, at https://www.census.gov/prod/2011pubs/acsbr10-05.pdf, and U.S. Census Bureau, Quick Facts, at http://www.census.gov/quickfacts/table/AGE275210/02,00.

[89] See Heather Bryant and Dan Peterson, "Alaskans Rally against Domestic Violence and Exclusion from VAWA," *Morning Edition*, KTOO-FM (Juneau Public Radio), March 28, 2013; and for the special status of Alaska Natives, see Chapter 9, Section 2.

[90] See Chapter 15, Box 15.6, for the attributes of interest group power.

[91] See the Alaska Network on Domestic Violence and Sexual Assault (ANDVSA) website, at http://www.andvsa.org/.

[92] Accessed on June 14, 2014, on former Governor Parnell's website, at http://gov.alaska.gov/parnell/priorities/. However, this website was taken down after Parnell's defeat for re-election in November 2014.

[93] Casey Kelly, "Walker Leads Choose Respect Rally as Senators Cut Funding," *Morning Edition*, KTOO-FM (Juneau Public Radio), March 26, 2015.

[94] Alaska Department of Health and Social Services, "Commission on Child Protection Sends Report to Governor," Press Release (2002), at http://www.hss.state.ak.us/press/2002/pr100302child-protection.htm; and Action for Child Protection, Inc., 2007, "An Expert Review of Policy that Regulates Practice and Decision Making During Investigation," Report prepared for the Office of Children's Services, at http://library.alaska.gov/asp/edocs/2007/03/ocn122932739.pdf.

[95] C. Collins-Camargo, "National Needs Assessment and Knowledge Gaps Analysis and Findings," National Quality Improvement Center on the Privatization of Child Welfare Services, 2006, at http://www.uky.edu/SocialWork/qicpcw/documents/QICPCWKnowledgeGapsAnalysisFindings.pdf.

[96] Death Penalty Information Center, 2013, *States With and Without the Death Penalty*, at http://www.deathpenaltyinfo.org/states-and-without-death-penalty.

[97] See Chapter 15, Section 2.

[98] Peter Granitz, "Health Care Providers Push Governor Parnell to Expand Medicaid," *Alaska News Nightly*, APRN, November 27, 2012.

[99] For a call for Mallott to take on such a role, see Elise Patkotak, "Mallott Uniquely Positioned to End Alaska's Acceptance of Violence, Abuse," *Alaska Dispatch News*, December 9, 2014.

★ CHAPTER 28 ★

Transportation and Infrastructure: The Influence of Local and Special Interests in an Intergovernmental Policy-Making Environment

Billy G. Connor, Anthony T. Nakazawa, and Clive S. Thomas

Like most Americans, many Alaskans take for granted their city and state transportation infrastructure (roads, bridges, airports, ferries, and public transit). So construction and maintenance of this infrastructure become high-profile political issues only occasionally—and usually when something goes wrong. Despite this generally low political profile, Alaska, like all states and countries, depends on its transportation system to support its economy and enhance its quality of life.[1]

In fact, adequate funding and wise policy making in transportation are perhaps more crucial in Alaska than in most places. This is because of the state's remoteness from the rest of the United States and the high cost of providing and maintaining transportation facilities and services in the state, given its huge geographical expanse and harsh climate. Developing and maintaining transportation infrastructure and facilities are expensive, taking 5 to 10 percent of the state's operating budget (depending on the year) and the largest single expenditure in the capital budget, often as much as 40 percent of the total. Also, like most states, Alaska's transportation system is driven by local and special interests set in an intergovernmental context rather than by a systematic planning process to develop and implement an integrated statewide transportation system.

In delving deeper into this political reality of transportation politics and policy, several of the characteristics of Alaska politics identified in Chapter 2 become evident. Two are particularly helpful in understanding this often complex policy area: the significant role of external economic and political forces, especially the federal government as a funding source and regulator, and economic development versus environmentalism. Four other characteristics also provide insights: friends and neighbors politics, regionalism and conflicts between urban and rural-bush areas, fiscal conservatism, and a political culture of pragmatic dependent individualism.

The chapter begins by explaining important transportation terms and laws. Then we turn to the expertise of a specialist in Alaska transportation politics and policy to set the scene for the analysis in the chapter.

1. IMPORTANT TERMS, ACRONYMS, AND LAWS

Like all areas of public policy, transportation has its own array of terms and key state and federal laws and regulations that are important to know for understanding its politics and policy making. Box 28.1 explains several terms and entities relevant to transportation issues referred to throughout the chapter. Other technical terms and details, including those about federal and state laws, are explained in the appropriate sections.

2. THE HOPES, REALITIES, AND CHALLENGES OF ALASKA'S TRANSPORTATION SYSTEM: AN OVERVIEW

The politics and policy making associated with transportation can at times be quite complex. At the same time, there are some basic elements that shape transportation politics across the states and in Alaska. The factors shaping Alaska's transportation system and thus its transportation politics and policies can be explained by identifying major developments in the past, describing the current situation, and assessing the likely prospects for the future. This overview is presented in Box 28.2, which represents the perspective of Lois Epstein, a civil engineer and expert on the technical and public policy aspects of Alaska's transportation system, particularly the relationship between transportation development and the environment.[2]

The overview in Box 28.2 provides a basis for the analysis in the chapter, which goes into detail about the developments, challenges, and particular aspects of Alaska's transportation system. The chapter also places Alaska's transportation politics and policy in a national context. We begin in Section 3 by explaining the development of the nation's transportation system contrasted with that of Alaska's. Section 4 then outlines developments that have produced current national transportation politics and policy. These two sections set the scene for understanding the past and contemporary nature of politics and policy making in transportation in Alaska, including funding, current issues, and future challenges and opportunities.[3]

BOX 28.1

Agencies and Terms Regarding Transportation Politics and Policy

Alaska Department of Transportation and Public Facilities (DOT&PF): Referred to in this chapter by the shorter acronym, DOT. This is the agency that is at the forefront of the development and implementation of Alaska's transportation policy. Details on DOT's administrative and political role are provided in Box 28.5.

U.S. Environmental Protection Agency (EPA): Created in 1970 and charged with protecting public health and the environment through administration of laws pertaining to land, water, air, and hazardous materials. The agency requires Environmental Impact Statements (EISs) on many development plans that may impact the environment, including many proposed transportation projects.

Federal Highway Trust Fund (FHTF): The purpose of the fund is to finance federal, state, and local highway construction and maintenance. Its major revenue source is the federal tax on gasoline and diesel fuel and other excise taxes. Congress allocates money from the fund for payment to the states for their highway and other transportation programs. Since the mid-2000s, the FHTF has had serious solvency problems.

Modal, Multimodal, and Intermodal: *Modal* refers to a particular mode, type or form of transportation, such as automobiles, barges, railroads, or aircraft. *Multimodal* refers to systems that use several forms of transportation. *Intermodal* is the linking of different modes, such as rail, road, and water in a transportation system.

State Transportation Plans: Alaska has two plans for transportation development and maintenance. One is required by the federal government, the other by state law. These are separate plans but have some common elements. They are explained in Box 28.5 dealing with DOT.

Transportation Systems versus Transit Systems: The *transportation system* in a nation, state, or locality generally refers to the entirety of modes of transportation—roads, airports, railroads, docks, harbors, ferry systems, and so on. In contrast, *transit systems*, often called mass transit, are usually local systems or connections between nearby cities and consist of bus, light rail, and metro systems, and in some cases, like Puget Sound in Washington State, ferry systems. These are developed mainly to serve commuters and other local resident user groups, in part to relieve road congestion.

User Fees: A charge in the form of a fare, toll payment, or tax collected by a transit company (like a bus line or railroad), a toll road, toll bridge or a government (federal, state or local) to help fund the building and maintenance of transport facilities. For instance, all airline passengers pay a federal tax included in their ticket price to help fund various aspects of airport operations, such as air traffic control and airport development, and to fund maintenance grants to state and local governments.

User Groups: These consist of individuals, businesses, or organizations that use transportation facilities. They include users such as commuters on bus and rail systems and roads; companies that ship goods, like FedEx, Airborne, and United Parcel Service (UPS); air carriers that use airports; and tourism businesses and recreational groups that use various docks and harbors and other transportation facilities. In recent policy moves to multimodalism, *user groups* also include cyclists using dedicated bike lanes and pedestrians and hikers using sidewalks, footpaths, and trails.

Source: Developed by the authors.

BOX 28.2

Alaska's Transportation System and Public Policy from Pre-Statehood to the Twenty-First Century

In the years leading up to and following statehood in 1959, many Alaskans had in mind the development of a state transportation system that looked like those in the Lower 48. But the "spaghetti" pattern of roads they envisioned connecting industrial facilities and communities throughout Alaska was not built for several reasons. These included the large distances between communities; the small population; the challenging terrain; the sensitive environment; and the state's heavy dependence on federal funding to pay for transportation infrastructure.

In some areas in Alaska, roads are the most logical way to connect communities. The state's expansive geography and low population density, however, dictate creative, non-road transportation solutions in other parts of Alaska. For over thirty communities along the coast ferry service makes the most sense. Many communities in the Interior are best connected by boat in summer, snowmobile in winter, and airplane throughout the year.

Alaska became a state at a time when major changes were taking place in the United States. Some of these affected transportation politics and policy, including the development of the interstate highway system; concerns about air pollution, land, and habitat degradation, and, later, greenhouse gases; concerns about road safety; and the problem of America's dependence on foreign oil. As a consequence of these and other developments, the political interests involved in transportation policy making expanded considerably. One element of transportation politics remained constant, however. This is that, because of its economic impact, transportation system development is, in many instances, driven by local and political forces as opposed to statewide and technical concerns. This has involved DOT in an increasingly political situation as it works to develop and implement Alaska's transportation plans.

Money drives all public policies, but funding is particularly significant in transportation politics because of the enormous costs involved in building and maintaining transportation systems, especially in Alaska with its geography and climate. It is, therefore, the level of funding available at any one time that determines the state's transportation priorities. Before statehood but even more so since, the state has relied heavily on federal monies to fund transportation. Due to funding issues with the Federal Highway Trust Fund (FHTF), however, Alaska may receive less federal funding in the future. To preserve even the current level of funding at a time of rising materials and labor costs and increased road and other repair costs due to melting permafrost, Alaska needs to increase state and local funding for transportation. Since there is a state constitutional prohibition on dedicated funds, funding transportation over the long term using state and local dollars will be a political challenge. This challenge will likely make costly, largely nonessential projects—such as the proposed Knik Arm Bridge in Anchorage—very low priorities. Even more important in determining transportation funding are state revenues. When they fall precipitously, as they did beginning in late 2014 and continuing into 2016, the priorities of projects must be reassessed, some put on hold, and others cancelled.

So what might the twenty-first century hold for Alaska's transportation system? As the United States enters an era of the likelihood of declining federal transportation dollars and as greenhouse gas emissions are facing increased scrutiny, Alaskans will need to accept some limits on expansion of their transportation system in order to have sufficient funds to repair and preserve the existing infrastructure. The need for this becomes even more pressing when state revenues fall. On the bright side, the state's abundant renewable resources mean that—eventually—Alaska's transportation system will likely be significantly less greenhouse gas-intensive and cheaper to operate using electricity from renewable fuels than transportation systems in other parts of the country and around the world.

Source: Developed by Lois N. Epstein, a civil engineer and advocate for responsible funding and maintenance of Alaska's existing transportation system. The information was supplemented by Anthony Nakazawa based on interviews with Ms. Epstein.

3. THE DEVELOPMENT OF TRANSPORTATION SYSTEMS AND THEIR PUBLIC POLICY FOCUS: CONTRASTING THE NATION AND THE OTHER STATES WITH ALASKA

Because of Alaska's relatively late development as a territory and state, the transportation systems in the Lower 48 states are much older than Alaska's. There are also other differences in the way Alaska's system has developed, resulting from Alaska's geography, remoteness, climate, economy, political development, and the attitudes of the public and their politicians.

The Nation and the Other States

From the horse and the mule and the wagon traveling on muddy and potholed roads and trails, and ships plying the East Coast in colonial times and the early days of the nation, America's transportation system moved to the steamship, riverboat, and canal barges in the early nineteenth century. Then came the railroad, bringing about rapid change. Just a quarter century after the golden spike was driven at Promontory Point, Utah, in 1869, connecting the first transcontinental railroad, a railroad network had been built across the continental United States.

By the early 1920s, however, the nation's focus on transportation had shifted to roads and highways—a focus that would last for most of the twentieth century.[4] This focus was a result of the invention of the internal combustion engine and the personal convenience of the automobile, a negative attitude to the monopoly of the railroads and their often political heavy-handedness, and the problems of moving troops and materials across America's woefully inadequate roads during World War I. The United States rapidly became an automobile society, and public policy reflected this.

The 1930s saw major federal and state involvement in air transportation and, in several places, continued support of water transport and dock and harbor facilities. The development and funding of the national and state highway systems took priority, however, boosted by the major logistical needs of moving troops and materials during World War II. In the late 1940s and during the 1950s, the reality of the Cold War led to the construction of the National Defense Highway System. Increases in all types of road traffic led President Eisenhower (1953–1961) to support building an interstate highway system, which was authorized in 1956.

Because of the nation's rapidly developing love affair with the automobile and because of increased use of roads by trucks and buses, the 1960s saw creation of the Federal Highway Trust Fund (FHTF) and the Federal Highway Administration (FHWA). The FHTF was set up in 1956 when the interstate highway system was launched. The creation of the FHWA in 1966 embraced the functions of several existing agencies, including the Bureau of Public Roads and the National Highway Safety Bureau, now the National Highway Traffic Safety Administration.

By the late 1950s the federal government had become the major funding source for roads and other transportation facilities such as docks, harbors, and airports, not only for federal roads and facilities but also for those in most states and in many localities. This boom in road building and other transportation facilities, and the enormous sums of money involved, spawned a major national lobby centered on transportation. This lobby also operated in all states, and included the construction industry and those promoting local economic development, as well as highway user groups.

Since the late 1970s three major developments have taken place in national transportation policy and in most states, and another development may well occur. First, in the late 1970s and early 1980s, rail, road, and air transport were deregulated to allow more competition. Second, the rise of the environmental movement in the 1960s and 1970s, concerns about traffic congestion, and America's dependence on oil, among other factors, led the federal government and some states to develop a more multimodal and intermodal transportation policy and to focus spending more in that direction. The third development is the broadening of transportation issues, which is in part a product of the second development. The development on the horizon, always a potential problem, as Lois Epstein mentions in Box 28.2, is the possibility of reductions in federal transportation financial assistance to the states and local governments. As Epstein also mentions, this reduction would be a particularly big problem for Alaska. For the immediate future, at least until 2021, this federal funding issue is less of a problem for all states including Alaska. This is because of the passage in 2015 of the $305 billion Fixing America's Surface Transportation Act, or the FAST Act. We go into detail on FAST later in the chapter.

The Development of Alaska's Transportation System

In the early years of occupation by non-Natives and even today, there are few better examples of the influence of Outside economic and political forces on Alaska politics and policy making than that of transportation. This began with the Russian occupation, which was largely confined to the coasts using boats and ships. From the purchase of Alaska by the U.S. federal government in 1867 until very recently, both federal policy and Outside private interests have been geared to developing Alaska's transportation system for purposes of economic development and profit or for military purposes. Early gold and other mining developments spawned a trail system and the construction of the White Pass Railroad (from Skagway in northern Southeast Alaska to Whitehorse in the Yukon) and the Copper River Railroad (from Cordova on Alaska's south central coast to the Kennecott Mine), both financed by private investors. The discovery of oil on the North Slope in the late 1960s, resulting in construction of the trans-Alaska pipeline system (TAPS) and the Haul Road (Dalton Highway) from Fairbanks to Prudhoe Bay, is the best recent example of the influence of Outside forces on the development of Alaska's transportation system.

The first major road in Alaska was the military wagon road from Valdez on Alaska's southcentral coast to Fort Egbert, near the mining community of Eagle some four hundred miles to the northeast, near the Canadian border. The first part of the road was completed in 1900. This was followed by federal construction of the Alaska Railroad (ARR) between 1914 and 1923. Until the 1940s, however, when Alaska's military significance became apparent, the Territorial transportation system developed slowly.

During World War II the construction of the Alaska Highway, several military airports, and a number of ports made important additions and established the backbone of today's transportation system. In particular, federal investment in airports provided a significant boost to the modern aviation age in the Territory. The opening of the Glenn Highway in 1948 was the symbolic beginning of a true highway system because it connected the transportation systems that had developed around the Alaska Railroad—creating the so-called Railbelt from Seward to Fairbanks—and those that had developed around the Richardson Highway out of Fairbanks to the Canadian border.

At statehood in 1959 all roads under federal jurisdiction were transferred to the state Department of Highways. All other transportation facilities were transferred to the Department of Public Works, which is where the Division of Marine Highways was placed when it was formed in 1961 to run the Alaska Marine Highway System (AMHS). In 1977 the Department of Highways and the Department of Public Works were merged to form the Department of Transportation and Public Facilities (commonly known as DOT). The merger placed an emphasis on multimodalism that is now part of a national trend.

A Minimal Role for Most Local Governments

As in other states where local governments, particularly cities and counties, developed a major role in transportation, today Alaska's two major metropolitan areas, Anchorage and Fairbanks, which combined account for close to two-thirds of the state's population, also take an active role in transportation planning and to a lesser extent funding. Most local governments in Alaska, however, have not developed a major role in transportation planning and funding. There is no formal structure for providing transportation facilities and planning outside of boroughs. Yet, despite this lack of a planning and funding role, almost all local governments are major political forces in the allocation of state transportation funds, particularly capital budget monies.

Historically, several factors combined to work against most local governments taking a major role in transportation planning and funding.

First, in Territorial days the local government system was slow to develop, partly because the formation of counties was prohibited and cities suffered from serious shortages of funds. Second, the highly centralized administration of roads in the Territory by the Federal Bureau of Public Roads worked against the development of a tradition of local participation in transportation policy making. Third, unlike other states, Alaska does not have local governments covering all of its area. In fact, vast areas of the state (the so-called Unorganized Borough) have no local government at all and rely on the state to provide all services, including transportation. In some other areas, residents have chosen a form of local government that has no legal authority to provide transportation services. Fourth, the lack of development of a formal statewide regional government structure (equivalent to counties in other states) with comprehensive planning responsibilities has resulted in a serious shortage of transportation funding at the local level. And fifth, the long-standing weakness and minimal financial resources of rural-bush local governments have not been conducive to their taking a major role in either transportation funding or policy making.[5]

The consequence of this lack of a major policy and funding role for local government is considered in various parts of the rest of the chapter.

Alaska's Contemporary Transportation System—in Reality, "Two Systems"—and the State's Policy Focus and Funding Sources

Map 28.1 shows Alaska's contemporary transportation system. This system is the most underdeveloped in the nation, but at the same time it is a prime example of a multimodal system.

Alaska's Two Transportation Systems

In large part, the underdevelopment of Alaska's transportation system stems from the reality of its being not one but two transportation systems, one often referred to as "on the road" and the other as "off the road."

Although this Alaska parlance is not precise in defining geographical areas, the Railbelt (where over 70 percent of Alaskans live) would be considered "on the road," as would places like Juneau, Sitka, Ketchikan, and other Southeast communities even though there is actually no access to them by road.

In contrast, the "off the road" system in rural-bush Alaska, mainly located in the Unorganized Borough, lacks many of these transportation facilities. Many of these areas are accessible only by air and in some cases also by ocean or river. Residents routinely deal with challenges like dirt roads that have little or no maintenance, unplowed airstrips in the winter, and deteriorating docks on the rivers that are used in the summer to bring food and other goods into the community.

MAP 28.1

Transportation Map of Alaska in Relation to Physical Geography

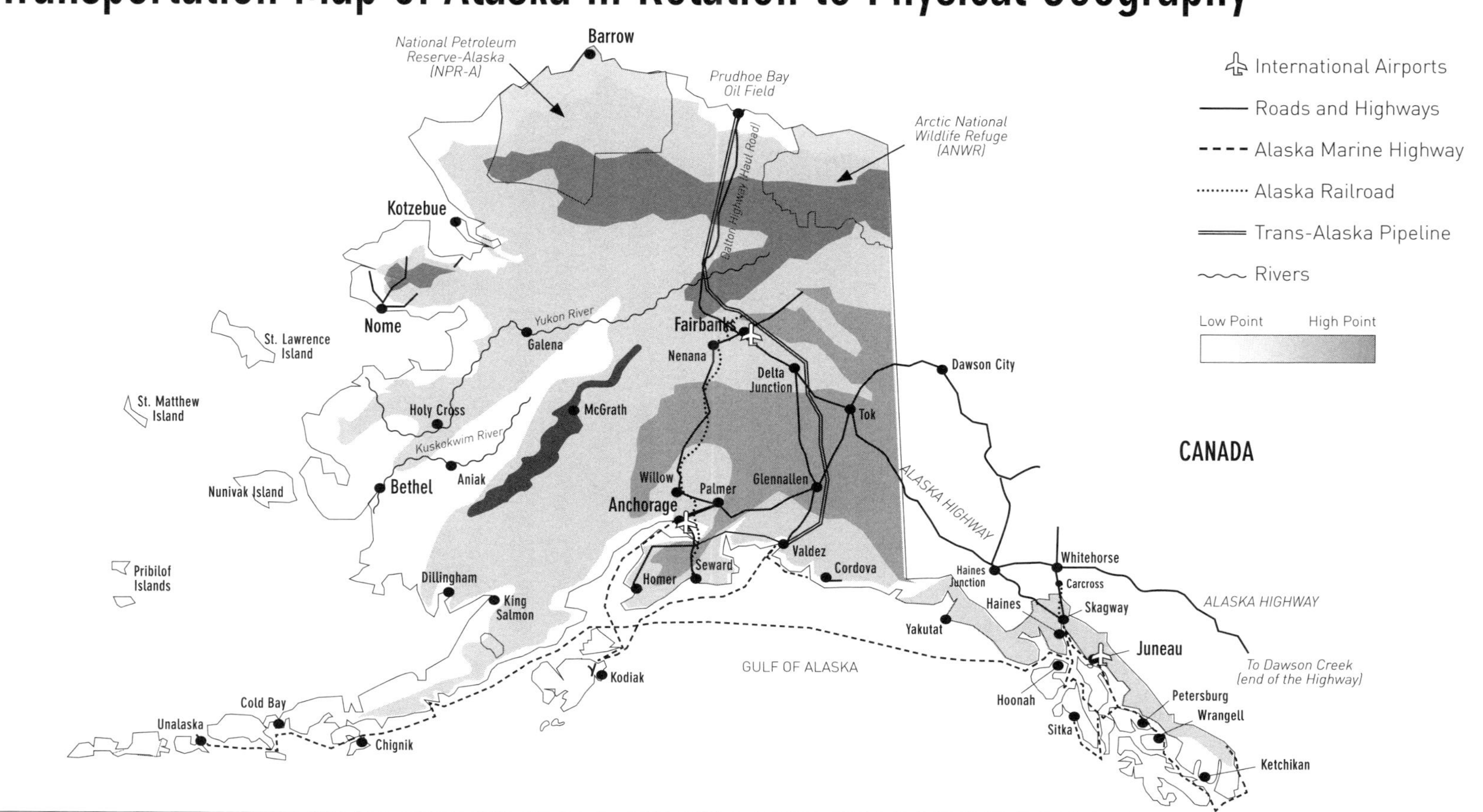

Source: Developed by the authors.

Alaska's contrasting transportation systems provide yet another example of "two Alaskas" existing side by side in one state.[6] The rudimentary nature of the transportation system in rural-bush areas and the demand for better facilities and services, together with the high cost of providing them, is one source of urban versus rural-bush conflict in the state.

A Multimodal System

Decades of federal mandates for funding highway planning, and the encouragement of strong state highway organizations, mean that highway planning in Alaska, as in all states, still receives greater focus than other transportation modes. Nevertheless, Alaska's highway system is still rudimentary. Except for Hawaii, Rhode Island, and Delaware, Alaska has the fewest miles of roads of any state. And although Alaskans own automobiles to a much greater degree than average Americans, Alaskans drive the fewest miles per capita of any state except New York. Despite this, Alaska has a fairly high per capita rate of road deaths.[7]

Despite its underdevelopment, Alaska's transportation system is nonetheless highly multimodal. Transportation systems in all states are multimodal to some extent, but Alaska's is particularly so. This is largely because of geography (making it difficult for one mode to dominate as the highway system does in the Lower 48 states), federal policy, and state and local political pressures, among other factors. Besides roads, Alaska relies on its one railroad as well as airports, docks and harbors, its ferry system, and some mass transit.

The Alaska Railroad (ARR) was run by the federal government from 1923 until purchased by the State of Alaska in 1985. It is a Class II railroad, which means it is medium-sized in terms of track mileage, rolling stock, and amount of business. It is not in the realm of Class I railroads in the Lower 48, like the Union Pacific and Burlington Northern-Santa Fe, but it is not as small as shortline railroads like the twenty-nine such lines operating in Washington State that serve a local area around a town or several adjacent communities. Unlike Lower 48 railroads, however, the ARR is not linked to any other rail system, although Whittier on the Kenai Peninsula connects with Seattle and Prince Rupert in British Columbia through a rail barge system.

While it has only about 470 route-miles and covers only a tiny portion of the state (see Map 28.1), the ARR serves the area with the bulk of the state's population. It carries both freight and passengers and is an important part of Alaska's tourist trade and coal industry. Its charter calls for it to operate as a profit-making business, though it does receive some money from the state and received close to $150 million over the five years of the FAST Act passed in 2015.[8]

Aviation is an important transportation mode in much of the state. Eighty-two percent of Alaska communities are accessible by air. Yet Alaska is unique in the extent to which airports are built and operated, with few exceptions, by state government. In other states, airports are mostly run by local governments (usually counties or special public airport authorities). Here is another example of the minimal role of most Alaska local governments in the delivery and funding of transportation services.

Nevertheless, airports are important local employers in many places. They have a major economic impact that increases yearly. In 2009, through their direct or multiplier effect, they accounted for close to 47,000 jobs in the state and pumped over $3.5 billion into the state's economy. In 2012, five million passengers passed through the Ted Stevens Anchorage International Airport. It was estimated that, as one of the top twenty busiest airports in the nation and the world's major seaplane airport, it accounted for close to fifteen thousand, or one in ten, jobs in the Anchorage metropolitan area. These figures take into consideration the multiplier effect and the airport's role as a major passenger and cargo airport. The importance of air transport to rural-bush communities is shown by the fact that Bethel in Southwest Alaska serves the fifty-five villages in the Lower Kuskokwim and is the second major air cargo airport in the state, not Fairbanks or Juneau, as might be assumed.[9] The often key connection between transportation and the economy, particularly economic development, is considered below in several sections of the chapter.

Likewise, the Alaska Marine Highway System (AMHS) is the main surface transportation for many Alaskans in Southeast and Southwest Alaska. The system serves thirty-five port cities. AMHS is considered a "highway" under federal law and is thus eligible for federal highway funding. Ports and harbors are particularly significant in Alaska's transportation system. They serve many user groups, including commercial needs, such as fishing, barge service, tourism (ranging from cruise ships to charter fishing trips), and the recreational needs of Alaskans. Harbor facilities have most often been constructed by state or federal agencies (like the U.S. Economic Development Administration) and then usually turned over to local governments to collect user fees and run the facilities.

Public mass transit in Alaska consists of the ARR, the AMHS, and some local bus systems, mainly in Anchorage, Fairbanks, and Juneau. The ARR's main user group as a mass transit system is not commuters but tourists. Tourists are also the main users of the ferry system in the summer. In contrast, the primary user groups of local bus systems are commuters and local residents. As of 2016, Alaska had no urban light rail or metro transit system, as do Seattle and Portland and many other U.S. cities.

4. TRANSPORTATION ISSUES AFTER THE 1960s: DEVELOPMENT VERSUS QUALITY OF LIFE CONCERNS

Alaska may not be geographically connected to the Lower 48 states, and is more than three thousand miles from Washington, D.C., but geographical isolation does not translate into political isolation. Just as they did with Alaska's early developments, Outside forces very much shape the state's contemporary transportation politics and policy. So to fully understand Alaska's present transportation politics, it is instructive to look at national transportation policy developments.

Another pertinent point made by Lois Epstein in Box 28.2, is that from the beginning of America's highway era following World War I and particularly from the involvement of the federal government in highway funding, transportation politics and policy have not been solely about transportation. Because of the huge sums of money involved in developing and maintaining transportation infrastructure, transportation policy has always involved political interests in the construction industry, vehicle manufacturers and their retail outlets, energy suppliers, and local governments and their chambers of commerce concerned with economic benefits, among other interests.

However, until the early 1960s those involved in the transportation policy community were primarily concerned about development—developing the transportation system, developing their businesses, or developing their local communities. Little, if any, attention was paid to how the expansion of transportation infrastructure affected the American quality of life in regard to the physical environment, increased traffic congestion, air and noise pollution, and safety issues, among other environmental and social concerns. This began to change in the mid-1960s.

New Elements in Transportation Politics and Policy

Several political forces, but four in particular, developed to change the nature of transportation policy so that by the early 1990s it involved major issues about transportation's impact on the quality of life and, in some cases, major conflicts between developers and those promoting quality-of-life issues.

One of the four developments was the rise of the environmental movement, which gathered momentum in the mid-1960s and became a potent political force nationwide and in many states by the late 1970s. It was, and continues to be, concerned about air pollution caused by vehicle emissions, the destruction of wildlife habitat and wetlands by expanding infrastructure, water pollution by barges and other river transport and ocean-going ships, and noise pollution from trucks and airplanes. Most recently, climate change has become an issue that affects transportation politics and policy. Climate change is caused in large part by the emission of greenhouse gases such as carbon dioxide, which is released when fossil fuels like oil and gasoline are burned. These emissions in turn increase atmospheric temperatures to produce a greenhouse effect.

The second development was road safety and concern about traffic deaths that had reached over 50,000 a year by the 1970s, close to double the number in 1940.[10] The problem of road safety embraced a range of issues. The lack of vehicle safety produced one of the bestselling books of the 1960s, by political activist Ralph Nader. His *Unsafe at Any Speed* exposed automotive safety hazards and helped hasten many improvements in automobile safety.[11] Then, the 1980s saw movements to require crash helmets for motorcyclists, and in that decade and in the 1990s a movement swept across all fifty states to tighten up drunk driving laws led by Mothers Against Drunk Drivers (MADD).

The third major development was the increase in the price of oil caused by the Arab-Israeli War of 1973 and the oil embargo imposed by the Organization of the Petroleum Exporting Countries (OPEC). The embargo increased the price of gasoline to over a dollar a gallon for the first time in U.S. history. This led to efforts to reduce America's dependence on foreign oil in part by reducing consumption of oil and oil-related products. And fourth, the increased use of automobiles and the decline of most intercity passenger rail service by the late 1960s contributed toward major traffic congestion not only in large metropolitan areas like New York, Chicago, and Los Angeles, but also in medium-sized ones like Cincinnati, Omaha, Salt Lake City, and Seattle.

By the mid-1980s, the political forces involved in transportation politics and policy had considerably broadened the membership of the transportation policy community. This in turn produced new directions in policy making and had some important consequences for the dynamics of transportation politics.

The Consequences of the Broadening of Transportation Issues

As the forces seeking change in transportation policy gathered political steam, a series of federal, and in some cases state and local, laws were passed to address these issues.

The environmental movement was able to get laws enacted to take into account the effects of transportation developments on land as well as legislation to reduce vehicle emissions to improve air quality and regulations to protect rivers and oceans from pollution by water transport. To improve vehicle safety, the federal government adopted rules mandating car manufacturers to install seatbelts and air bags, and the states enacted laws on motorcycle safety and stringent laws against drunk driving. To deal with fuel efficiency, the federal government passed a 55-mile-an-hour speed limit in 1974 (raised to 65 in 1987) and required higher fuel efficiency, as did states like California. To deal with traffic congestion and reduce automobile use, many states and communities adopted policies such as bus, taxi, cycle, and "high-occupancy vehicle" lanes, instituted toll charges based on time-of-day use of highways, and developed or expanded mass transit systems.

For twenty years many of these laws and regulations were ad hoc policies to deal with the political demands of the new forces in transportation politics. By the late 1980s, however, two related broad policies were emerging in national transportation policy. One was a move to multimodalism. The second was balancing transportation infrastructure developments with quality of life. These new policy directions were led by the federal government. As a consequence, the national government came to play an even more important role in transportation policy than it had in the 1960s. This, in part, produced a new era of transportation politics.

The Increased Role of the Federal Government

Left to their own devices, most states, particularly those in the South, on the plains, and in the Mountain West, would have been slow to deal with these broadening issues affecting and affected by transportation. And so it took federal agencies like the Environmental Protection Agency (EPA), the Fish and Wildlife Service, and the National Park Service to deal with these new demands on transportation policy. The federal government was also a major force behind increased safety standards and efforts to conserve gasoline, and became a major funding source of transportation development at all levels of government. Of the federal transport legislation passed since the mid-1980s, six acts are particularly significant. An overview of these laws is set out in Box 28.3. A review of this legislation shows the combined emphasis on multimodalism and quality-of-life concerns. Box 28.3 also shows the importance of federal funding, which is considered later in this chapter. Overall, the increased role of the federal government has added to the broadening and complexity of transportation politics and policy.

These new directions in federal (and some states') transportation policy have had mixed success. Americans certainly breathe cleaner air because of improved emission standards. Road safety has improved dramatically.[12] Transportation fuel consumption declined 20 percent between 1980 and 2010.[13] And greater care is taken in land use and protecting wildlife habitats. On the other hand, America's love affair with the automobile continues with great passion even when gasoline is as high as $4 a gallon. For this reason, outside of large cities, the push for multimodalism to get people out of their cars and onto public transport has met with limited success. As a consequence, traffic congestion persists in many cities of all sizes across the nation.

However, the extent of the success or lack thereof of these policies is not of concern to us in this chapter. More important is the political fallout from these federal policies. How these policies, successful or not, were and continue to be viewed as positive or negative by the various members of the transportation policy community is a matter of perspective. This largely reflects the various roles and goals of the members of the transportation community, what benefits they have secured, failed to secure, and hope to attain in the future. The proactive and reactive stances of many members of this policy community reflect three developments in modern national, state, and local transportation policy. These are (1) a broad and diverse policy community, (2) increased political conflict, and (3) increased uncertainty regarding transportation policy outcomes.

BOX 28.3

Six Major Federal Laws Affecting Transportation Politics and Policy across the Nation and in Alaska

THE SURFACE TRANSPORTATION AND UNIFORM RELOCATION ASSISTANCE ACT, 1987

Also called the Federal Highway Aid Act, this is seen as the last authorization for the Interstate Highway System. By 1987 the system was 98 percent complete. The act provided additional funding for construction of the system, for highway safety, and for mass transit. It also authorized an increase in the speed limit from 55 to 65 miles per hour.

THE INTERMODAL SYSTEM TRANSPORTATION EFFICIENCY ACT, 1991 (ISTEA—KNOWN AS ICE TEA)

As the first major piece of legislation in the post-Interstate Highway era, ISTEA marked a major change in the direction of transportation planning and policy. As its title implies, it attempted to promote intermodal (and multimodal) approaches to transportation after sixty years of federal funding dominated by highway development. Its intermodal approach to highway and transit funding included collaborative planning requirements, and giving significant additional powers to metropolitan transport planning entities.

Besides promoting alternative modes to the automobile, the legislation included funding for new activities such as bicycle paths, railroad right of way restoration, and historic preservation. The first trail to be funded under ISTEA was the Cedar Lake Regional Trail in Minneapolis, Minnesota, built in 1995. Thus, the act reflected the growing political pressures of environmentalist, recreational, and tourism forces in transportation policy making.

THE TRANSPORTATION EQUITY ACT FOR THE 21ST CENTURY, 1998 (KNOWN AS TEA-21)

This act was, in effect, a continuation and re-funding of ISTEA and the new direction in transport policy underlying it. TEA-21 provided funding for highways, highway safety, and transit for the years 1998 to 2003. It also provided funding to promote the global competitiveness of metropolitan transportation systems; increased safety, particularly for non-motorized user groups; transportation options for people and freight, including the connectivity of different modes; environmental quality through various policies, including fuel efficiency; and the maintenance and efficiency of existing transportation systems.

THE SAFE, ACCOUNTABLE, FLEXIBLE, EFFICIENT TRANSPORTATION EQUITY ACT: A LEGACY FOR USERS, 2005 (SAFETEA-LU—KNOWN AS GREEN-TEA)

Green-TEA was also a continuation of ISTEA and TEA-21 with a $286 billion appropriation, including many earmarks for particular states and localities across the nation, to fund federal, state, and local transportation systems between 2005 and 2009. As with the two previous acts, it included funds for the Interstate Highway System, transit, highway safety, bicycling and pedestrian facilities, and freight rail operations.

Most significantly, this act made it mandatory for states receiving federal funds (which means all states) to produce a State Transportation Improvement Program (STIP) and update it on an ongoing basis. The STIP is now, in effect, a major transportation planning document in each state, and the subject of much politics.

MOVING AHEAD FOR PROGRESS IN THE 21ST CENTURY ACT, 2012 (MAP-21)

After renewing the funding for Green-TEA several times, Congress passed this new legislation. The two-year authorization of over $105 billion continued both the transportation and funding priorities since the enactment of ISTEA in 1991. The law was enacted amid concerns about the solvency of the Federal Highway Trust Fund (FHTF).

FIXING AMERICA'S SURFACE TRANSPORATION ACT, 2015 (FAST)

The first major highway legislation since SAFETEA-LU in 2005, FAST provides $305 billion in funding to keep the FHTF solvent through 2021. The Act did not raise the federal gas tax of 18.4 cents a gallon to help fund the FHTF, but instead used other funding sources.

The Act also includes funds for other modes of surface transportation, including transit, ferries,, railroads and river transport. And it continues the focus on multimodalism of legislation since the early 1990s.

Source: Developed by the authors.

The Broad and Diverse Modern Transportation Policy Community

There is now a much broader policy community in transportation than in the 1960s. At that time the community included those concerned about transportation as such, particularly the federal government, state departments of transportation, local governments, and user groups like truckers, bus companies, and railroads. It also included economic interests that benefited from new developments, such as construction companies, unions, and state and local chambers of commerce.

Today, most proposals for transportation projects still involve these long-standing interests. But they may also include antidevelopment groups, environmental groups, interests involved in tourism, including ecotourism, and, depending on the project, recreational interests, such as hiking, cycling, boating, and fishing. Most projects also include input from federal agencies like the EPA and perhaps others, again depending on the project, as well as state agencies concerned about economic development, the environment, and fish and wildlife. In fact, today the transportation policy community is one of the broadest and most diverse in the nation. Moreover, like the natural resources policy area, the transportation policy community in each state includes many out-of-state interests and interest groups.

Increased Political Conflict: Developers versus Environmentalists and the States versus the Federal Government

While Americans in general have benefited from more stringent emission standards and safer cars, other developments in transportation policy have been controversial and have generated considerable political conflict. To be sure, there were political conflicts in transportation policy making before the 1960s, particularly between the railroad and trucking industries. However, as the focus was largely on development of the system, there was a much broader consensus on policy among its members than there is today. Two major aspects of contemporary conflicts within the community are between developers and environmentalists and between the federal government and many states.

The developer-environmentalist conflict pits development interests advocating building new or wider roads, constructing new or larger airports, and providing new economic opportunities, against the forces of environmentalism concerned about irrevocable changes to the lifestyle of a community or region, forests, wetland areas or bodies of water, and other social and economic impacts. For instance, the provisions of the 2005 SAFETEA-LU legislation (see Box 28.3) strengthened the environmental and public input requirements. This legislation also pressed transportation agencies to reduce congestion and highway fatalities.

This tension between development and preservation is part of the contemporary politics of public works construction across the nation. It is epitomized by media reports of mothers carrying children and placards to protest the threat of bulldozers and neighborhood disruption, environmentalists and recreation interests protesting against roads through wilderness and wildlife habitat areas, and concerns about building pipelines for oil and gas through unstable geological or environmentally sensitive areas. The annoyance of many in-state development interests at this political opposition is exacerbated by the fact that many of the interests opposing development are from out of state, including many national environmental groups and the federal government.

The political pushback by the states against the actions of the federal government regarding various aspects of transportation policy and related areas has several sources. Four are of particular note and are interrelated. One is the general antipathy that exists in many states, particularly those in the Mountain West and South, toward federal authority in general. Second is a more specific concern by state governments about what is often called "federal overreach" in areas such as imposing speed limits, holding up or undermining needed state transportation developments with the need for Environmental Impact Statements (EISs) and other approvals, and an increasing body of rules and regulations on safety, construction standards, and multimodal provisions. Third, the direction of federal legislation since the early 1980s leads many states and their development interests to see the federal government as favoring the environmental community and being anti-development. The federal government and those favoring new directions in transportation and infrastructure policy counter that they are just seeking balance and are working to promote the general public interest.

Fourth is resentment by many states toward the federal government that stems from the three points just outlined, coupled with state dependence on major federal funds to develop and maintain their transportation systems. This means that, as in other areas of state-federal relations, such as Medicaid, other aspects of health care, and some aspects of corrections, K–12 education, and disaster relief policy, the federal government can use money as a political carrot and stick. So, fiscal federalism (the politics of federal financial support to the states) becomes part of the politics of transportation. The states cannot do without federal transportation funds for financial, political and administrative reasons. Citizens would be up in political arms if roads and other infrastructure fell into disrepair, and a normally low-profile political issue becomes high profile. So states need federal funds to build and maintain this costly infrastructure. But as is often the case in human relationships, dependence breeds resentment. Resentment against the federal political and economic upper hand is often voiced in anti-federal rhetoric and occasionally in refusing federal funds.

Increased Uncertainty Regarding Policy Outcomes

The broadening of the transportation policy community with the varied goals of its members means that today transportation policy is often even less about transportation as such. In addition, the outcomes of policy proposals by state governments are increasingly uncertain. This situation is of concern to many transportation professionals—system planners, road engineers, and academics, among others—who consider this development to be detrimental to America's transportation systems in general and ultimately to the national economy and the lifestyle of Americans.

Today, many groups in the policy community may have little or no concern about a particular policy as it impacts a state, a region, or a city in terms of access to transportation. They are often more concerned about how the policy may affect the welfare of their members regarding jobs, contracts, economic development opportunities, environmental impacts, recreation, and preservation of cultural and historical sites, among other concerns. These issues are increasingly shaping policies and project selection and decisions about the allocation of transportation funds. Moreover, projects are often delayed for years as developers seek the necessary federal and state permits to be able to proceed. An environmental or other challenge to a project can delay it to the point where it may never be completed.

Furthermore, new federal laws enacted since the early 1980s, and the states' need to comply with them, have broadened the range of transportation policies and spread the funds going to transportation over a wider range of projects. For instance, the 1991 ISTEA legislation (see Box 28.3) mandated that new projects called "enhancements" be given a share of the spending pie. These enhancements are often the preferences of environmental and tourist interests. Backed by federal policy, environmental pressures have diverted funding from the construction and rehabilitation of highways to mass transit, vehicle systems powered by alternative sources such as electricity and natural gas, and other means of reducing hydrocarbon use.

We are not arguing that these policies are positive or negative. That is for others to judge. The point is that transportation politics, policy making, and the allocation of funds for infrastructure are very different today than they were before the 1980s. Each state now has to contend with many Outside forces. As a result, since the early twentieth century, what might be considered the best transportation policies, taking into account the big picture of planning for a state or region, continue to be subordinated to political considerations.

From National Trends to Alaska's Transportation Politics and Policy

Alaska's current transportation and infrastructure politics and policy are shaped by the national context of transportation politics and policy. This includes the broadening of both the policy community and the issues involved, combined with the particulars of Alaska's geography, its place in the minds of many Americans as the Last Frontier, its socio-economic and political development, and its present political economy. The rest of the chapter considers various aspects of Alaska's transportation politics and policy.

First, Section 5 explains the contemporary characteristics of Alaska's transportation politics and policy making. Section 6 considers how transportation projects and maintenance are funded in Alaska. Section 7 illustrates Alaska's transportation politics in action through a case study of attempts to fund two bridge projects, and Section 8 looks at current issues in transportation across the fifty states and points out how these affect Alaska. In Section 9 we examine the particulars of Alaska's current issues, some of which are unique, and assess prospects for the future of transportation politics and policy in the state. The conclusion in Section 10 argues that transportation politics and policy making provide a good example of the political economy of intergovernmental relations in Alaska.

5. THE DYNAMICS OF TRANSPORTATION POLITICS AND POLICY MAKING IN CONTEMPORARY ALASKA

Like most areas of public policy, transportation policy can be quite complex in regard to particular issues, and even more so given the developments of transportation politics since the early 1980s. At the fundamental level, however, as is the case in all states, there are six major factors that shape transportation politics in Alaska: (1) the broad range of stakeholders and interests involved; (2) major intergovernmental relations (IGR) role in policy, funding, and implementation; (3) a particular version of the developer-environmentalist debate; (4) a relatively low level of political conflict; (5) the project-driven nature of transportation decision making; and (6) the secondary importance of the overall transportation system in many policy decisions.

A Broad Range of Stakeholders and Interests

As in other states, many interests are involved in current transportation policy making in Alaska. In particular, because environmental groups are so active in Alaska's Last Frontier, more interests likely operate in Alaska than in most states. Box 28.4 sets out the various interests (sometimes called stakeholders) involved in Alaska's transportation policy making. In addition to providing a big picture of the many interests involved, the box also explains their particular reasons for being involved and the perspectives they bring to the table.

The IGR Role in Policy, Funding, and Implementation

Box 28.4 also provides a picture of a major point we have made in the chapter so far, that IGR is a fundamental aspect of Alaska's transportation funding, politics, and policy. For its part, the state is a major developer of projects and an important funding source in some cases. But because the rest of the chapter focuses on many aspects of the IGR role of the state, here we briefly outline the political role of the federal government, Alaska local governments, and the Alaska Native community.

BOX 28.4

Stakeholders and Interest Groups Involved in Alaska Transportation Politics and Policy Making

THE FEDERAL GOVERNMENT

Congress: Appropriates funds from the Federal Highway Trust Fund (FHTF). Until 2011 when they were banned, Alaska's congressional delegation got earmarks added to bills to fund transportation projects in the state.

Federal Highway Administration (FHWA): Traditionally a strong ally with the Alaska Department of Transportation, with a strong highway bias, but trying to distance itself from that image in recent years.

Federal Aviation Administration (FAA): Its relationship to state government in Alaska is mainly through funding and regulation. But because in Alaska the state builds, operates, and maintains nearly all airports, the FAA's policy and operational roles is less prominent than in many states.

Bureau of Indian Affairs (BIA): Is a source of federal funds for constructing village roads. BIA does its own planning and contracting.

Federal Transit Administration (FTA): Provides operating and capital subsidies for public transportation to local governments directly or through the state.

Environmental Protection Agency (EPA), Corps of Engineers (COE), and National Marine Fisheries Service (NMFS): All comment or pass judgment on transportation projects through the Environmental Impact Statement (EIS) and environmental assessment processes.

U.S. Forest Service (USFS), Bureau of Land Management (BLM), and National Park Service (NPS): All are large land managers in Alaska and often are involved in public debate over access and development issues and construction of recreational and visitor facilities.

ALASKA STATE GOVERNMENT

The Legislature: Appropriates all operating and capital monies and specifies funding for particular projects. Legislators generally look upon the allocation of these funds less as a transportation system investment and more as a source of jobs and projects for their districts—bringing home the political bacon.

The Governor: Likely to have more of a statewide perspective than the legislature. He or she includes operating and capital funds for transportation in the annual budgets and appoints the Commissioner of DOT.

Alaska Department of Transportation and Public Facilities (DOT): The major state transportation agency. See Box 28.5 for fuller details about its role and how it is affected by politics.

Other State Agencies Sometimes Involved: The Department of Commerce, Community, and Economic Development (DCCED) is a project advocate when job development requires transportation improvements; the Department of Labor and Workforce Development (DLWFD) when labor regulation or union issues are involved; the Department of Environmental Conservation (DEC) when air or water quality issues are involved; the Department of Fish and Game (ADF&G) when an environmental or habitat study is required; the Alaska Industrial Development and Export Authority (AIDEA) if additional funding is needed for economic development; and the Alaska Railroad (ARR) on occasions when state policy affects its operations or development.

ALASKA LOCAL GOVERNMENTS

With the exception of Anchorage and Fairbanks and some of the larger boroughs having legal authority over transportation, local governments play a minimal role in planning and financing. Local governments are consulted on projects that have a local impact and generally the legislature reflects local views about the allocation of capital spending. Local governments lobby hard to get their share rather than support an allocation or planning process that would apply statewide.

ALASKA AND OUT-OF-STATE INTEREST GROUPS

Alaska Trucking Association (ATA): The ATA has supported higher user fees and taxes only if these revenues would be used for transportation purposes. DOT sees trucks as the major source of load-related damage to state roads.

Alaska Air Carriers Association (AACA): Most of AACA's members are small operators, not national air carriers. The association has fought attempts to impose landing fees at state airports and attempts to raise the aviation fuel tax.

Alaska Municipal League (AML): Concerned with general fund allocations for local government as they affect transportation and public facilities. Like the legislature, local governments have looked after their individual rather than the state's collective needs.

Individual Boroughs, Cities, and Local Chambers of Commerce: Concerned about getting their share of transportation funds.

Contractors/Developers/Builders (especially as represented by the Associated General Contractors—AGC): Work to maintain a high level of capital spending, a significant portion of which flows to their members, particularly through construction contracts.

Labor Groups and Unions: Have an interest in maintaining high levels of spending and in making the rules for capital spending favorable to union contractors. When non-union competition increases, this results in unions lobbying the administration and the legislature to enact rules more favorable to union members.

Environmentalists (such as the Alaska Environmental Lobby and the Wilderness Society): Have risen in influence since the 1970s and, among other activities, frequently monitor and provide comments on EISs, required before many transportation projects can be undertaken. Moreover, because of their increasing influence, environmentalists have become involved in funding allocations for trails, access to historical and heritage sites, and other projects.

The Alaska Transportation Priorities Project: A nonprofit, grant-funded organization that promotes, among other things, maintenance of Alaska's existing transportation infrastructure before embarking on new, costly projects.

Tourism Groups (especially the Alaska Travel Industry Association—ATIA): The industry supports specific transportation projects that expand the number of visitor destinations. A "green tourism" faction within the industry tends to side with environmental groups. An example was the proposal to pave the Alaska Railroad tunnel to Whittier, unsuccessfully opposed by many environmentalists and some sympathetic tourism interests.

Native Corporations and Other Alaska Native Groups: Especially active regarding issues involving Alaska Native lands, heritage sites, and subsistence, among others.

Other Interests Involved on Specific Issues: The State Chamber of Commerce, sportsmen, hunting and fishing groups, and community groups pro and con particular projects.

Source: Based on Table 12.2 in Gerken and Thomas (see endnote 3) and updated by the authors.

The Federal Government

In the transportation IGR nexus, the federal government is a dominant force in funding and regulation. But, other than provisions mandated by federal law, it is a backseat participant in the details of the state's transportation policy making.

Federal funding is particularly crucial in Alaska. The state receives more per capita in this regard, as with many other federal programs, than any other state. Given the high cost of transportation infrastructure and services in Alaska, the state would be a very different place without this funding.

Then there is the federal role of establishing regulations and setting standards. For example, federal transportation funds are tied to air quality, construction standards, safety, speed limits, drunk driving laws, outdoor advertising, among other provisions. One of the key process changes required by ISTEA in 1991 was the need for all agencies with transportation responsibilities in a state to be included in the drafting of the federal plan before it is approved by the Federal Highway Administration (FHWA). In addition, the federal government has its own program of transportation development on federal lands, though it works with state and local governments in developing and implementing these plans.[14]

As with most IGR, the federal government's transportation role in Alaska involves both cooperation and conflict, and the conflict occurs particularly between the state and federal governments. As with other states, the expansion of the issues now embraced under transportation and infrastructure policy has involved federal agencies, such as the EPA, sometimes resulting in stalling or derailing state and local projects. Plus, as we have seen, federal monies usually come with rules and regulations about how the money must be spent. These rules, combined with the fact that transportation is a key factor in state financial dependence on the federal government, often produce resentment on the part of Alaskans and their politicians.

Local Governments

For the reasons explained earlier, most local governments in Alaska play little if any role in transportation planning and funding. Consequently, with the exception of intermodal transportation plans by Anchorage and Fairbanks, the Anchorage Metropolitan Area Transportation Solutions (AMATS), and the Fairbanks Metropolitan Area Transportation Study (FMATS), DOT fills the local government void and makes local transportation decisions on a statewide basis.[15] In addition, lack of local government funds has meant that the state and particularly the federal government have paid the bill for the development and continued maintenance of Alaska's transportation systems. Yet, for a number of reasons, local governments do play a significant role in the allocation of transportation funds through their own lobbying efforts and those of their state and federal elected representative and the organizations to which they belong, such as AML.

Local politics is also involved in transportation decision making in boroughs because of their responsibility for transportation. This authority varies from borough to borough, which can be the root of political conflicts in planning and funding allocations. For example, the Fairbanks North Star Borough (FNSB) gives road authority to local service districts that can be small neighborhood associations. Often, significant jealousies exist between neighboring communities, and often major political conflict results.

Alaska Native Lands and Transportation Politics

As a result of the Alaska Native Claims Settlement Act (ANCSA) of 1971, Native regional and village corporations own 11 percent of Alaska's land area. Many of the state's natural resources are located on or under these lands. This Native land ownership pattern adds a particular dimension to Alaska IGR. The vast majority of Native lands are located in rural-bush areas, but some are located in urban areas like Juneau.

So in building roads and other infrastructure, the state and many local governments must enter into negotiations with various Native corporations and other Native groups. In addition, the Bureau of Indian Affairs provides funds for constructing roads on Native lands. The work for this is planned and contracted out by the federal government, though coordination with the state is often necessary. Thus, depending on the nature of a project and how much Native lands affect state and local plans, the Native community can have significant influence on politics and public policy related to Alaska's roads, ferries, docks, harbors, and airports.

Developers versus Environmentalists, Particularly Outside Influences

The developer-environmentalist conflict is one of the twelve characteristics of Alaska politics identified in Chapter 2. Recent developments in the broadening of transportation policy issues have contributed to the intensity of this debate in Alaska. This is in large part because, besides the often resented role of the federal government by developers, many Americans view Alaska as the Last Frontier and the last pristine wilderness in the nation.

Environmental groups, recreational interests, and American public opinion are all active political forces in Congress and the federal executive branch and affect many aspects of Alaska development, including its transportation system. In fact, as in natural resources policy, Alaska is likely more subject to Outside forces of these types in planning and implementing transportation and infrastructure policy than any other state.

Whether the developer-environmentalist conflict is primarily the product of in-state forces, Outside forces, or both, the situation manifests itself in a series of transportation policy conflicts. These include proposals for connecting Juneau by road to the major population centers in Southcentral Alaska and the Interior, reconstructing the Copper River Highway, and extending the Alaska Railroad, particularly to Northwest Alaska.

A Relatively Low Level of Political Conflict

While the developer-environmentalist conflict produces some intense political fights, political conflict is not the general rule in transportation policy making across the states, including in Alaska. In fact, transportation policy is relatively less contentious than many policy areas, for three related reasons. One is that there is rarely disagreement among politicians about the need for transportation infrastructure development and maintenance. The central issue is how to pay for it, which does lead to some conflicts, but usually not intense or high profile ones.[16] The second and third reasons are that transportation involves mainly distributive policy and it is largely non-ideological except for some environmental issues.

Chapter 3 on public policy makes an important distinction between three types of policy: distributive, redistributive, and regulatory.[17] The second and third types of policy making often lead to major political conflicts between various groups, between government and the groups that see themselves as adversely affected, and between ideological perspectives. Transportation decision making involves all three types of policies, but distributive policies tend to be the most significant in shaping transportation politics and decision making.

To be sure, some transportation policy is redistributive. For example, in the allocation of FHTF monies, some states benefit at the expense of others, as we will see in the next section. Many transportation policies are also regulatory, which is one source of conflict between developers and environmentalists, as explained earlier. But in the overall picture of transportation politics, even redistributive policies are very low profile and so raise very little opposition from politicians, let alone the public. And while regulatory policies are higher profile, they are not the norm in transportation policy and also raise little opposition. So, while some interests do lose something in the transportation policy process, such as when highway funds go to other modes of transportation, on balance most major interests gain something, mainly financial benefits, because of the distributive nature of most transportation policy. Local governments and chambers of commerce get projects that aid economic development, private businesses get multimillion-dollar construction contracts, and environmentalist, recreational, and transit interests get their share of funds.

So a wide range of interests benefits from the distributive policy process of allocating federal transportation funds. Moreover, since most of the costs are borne by the federal government and much decision making in this policy area is highly technical, transportation policy at the state level tends to be non-ideological for the most part. Certainly, some ideology comes into play over the developer-environmentalist clash, and with conservatives who tend to want to cut government spending in general, which might include transportation funding.

It is a combination of these factors that makes transportation politics much less contentious than policy areas like social services and K–12 education in Alaska, two policy areas that involve major elements of redistributive policy making and differences over ideology. The fact that most transportation issues are not conflict-ridden means that most are not in the forefront of the news and so are below the political radar for most citizens.

The Project-Driven Nature of Transportation Decision Making

There are two major ways to approach transportation policy. A *systematic policy process* evaluates transportation needs of the state overall and, ideally, integrates the "on the road" and the "off the road" systems in Alaska. In contrast, a *project-driven policy process* focuses on individual projects promoted by particular interests or constituencies and places little, if any, emphasis on the broader transportation needs of the state. As Box 28.4 illustrates, the governor and DOT are really the only two stakeholders in the policy community with a statewide perspective in planning.

The project-driven nature of transportation policy making in Alaska is based on three fundamental aspects of politics. First, in a real sense, as most politicians find out, all politics is local. Second, politicians feel compelled to deliver tangible benefits to their constituents. And third, pragmatism often dominates on both ends of the political spectrum. While state representatives and senators may understand the need for, and the value of, an integrated statewide transportation plan, the fact that they have supported such a plan, perhaps at the expense of projects for their districts, will not get them votes. What constituents understand and reward their politicians for are benefits like jobs and improved infrastructure of direct benefit to them. Consequently, this is a major political force on politicians. So whether they are Democrats or Republicans, political pragmatism forces them in a local direction and away from a statewide perspective.

However, it is important to make a distinction between rural-bush and urban legislators, particularly those in Anchorage and Fairbanks and their surrounding communities. Those in rural-bush areas feel much more pressure to deliver tangible benefits, as they are the sole representatives or senators in a vast area. So they tend to be much more focused on capital projects because infrastructure of all types is minimal compared to urban Alaska, including transportation facilities. In contrast, legislators representing metropolitan Anchorage and Fairbanks feel less pressure, as transportation development and maintenance usually cover several House and Senate districts. So individual legislators from urban areas cannot be held to account as easily for the failure to secure such projects, though, of course, they may take credit for projects that affect their districts. In addition, Anchorage and Fairbanks legislators represent areas with metropolitan transportation planning authorities (AMATS in Anchorage and FMATS in Fairbanks). This means that it is not just legislators working to secure transportation dollars and projects, and this reduces the political pressure on them further.

Whether or not project-driven decision making is positive or negative depends, to a large extent, on the perceived benefits to those involved. On balance, a project-driven process is of benefit to most legislators and their constituencies and many interest groups. In the long run, however, such a process may have negative consequences for the state as a whole and undermines DOT's ability to plan statewide. Box 28.5 looks at the role of the DOT as it is caught in the politics of this project-driven policy process.

The Often Secondary Importance of Alaska's Transportation System in Many Transportation Policy Decisions

Because transportation politics and policy decision making are not just about transportation, the overall needs of Alaska's statewide system are often subordinated to other political concerns, as is the case in other states. Three factors have largely shaped this outcome: the millions, sometimes tens and even hundreds of millions, of dollars involved in projects; the influence of the environmental movement; and the increased role and broadened transportation agenda of the federal government. Many of Alaska's state and local politicians and the state's congressional delegation often approach transportation issues and the use of funds allocated to transportation and infrastructure less in terms of developing a statewide transportation system and more in ways that promote economic development and employment. Outside interests, particularly the federal government, directly and indirectly, exert pressure upon the state and its politicians, which often diverts the focus of policy making away from purely transportation system considerations.

The upshot is an increasingly complex transportation policy-making process in which the outcomes are often uncertain and the needs of a statewide transportation system take second place. The outcome on any one project will vary, however, depending on the interests involved and their political influence. In addition to examples given in the chapter so far, two other examples of this are found in "A Tale of Two Bridges," in Section 7, below.

Where Does Political Power Lie in Transportation Policy Making in Alaska?

Consideration of the elements just outlined enables us to make some observations on where the influence lies in transportation political decision making in Alaska. In short, there is no single overriding political influence on all issues. Power is fragmented in a pluralistic fashion, with outcomes depending on the nature of the issue, particularly the direct or indirect involvement of the federal government.

Even though the federal government plays only a minor role in the specifics of state transportation policy making and project implementation, it still exercises considerable political influence. As explained in Box 28.5, the central aspect of this influence

BOX 28.5

The Alaska Department of Transportation and the Politics of Project-Driven Decision Making

The DOT's mission is "to provide for the safe movement of people and goods and the delivery of state services." The department is the major source of information, data, and expertise on Alaska's transportation system. It provides many of the services for planning, design, construction, and maintenance, either in-house or through contracts with the private sector or local governments. The DOT's headquarters are in Juneau, with three divisions located across the state that place decision-making responsibility closer to the affected areas. Each regional division has a full complement of design, construction, and maintenance capabilities.

As the major agency involved in the development and implementation of state transportation policy, the DOT is subject to many political pressures both from within, mainly from its regions, and from outside the department. Over the years, this has tended to thwart the development of a statewide political consensus on a transportation plan and has produced ad hoc, project-driven, policy making. One of the DOT's major responsibilities, which often involves it in much politics, is to develop and update two state transportation plans. One is a federal requirement; the other is a state mandated plan.

THE STATEWIDE TRANSPORTATION IMPROVEMENT PROGRAM—STIP

Federal law requires all states to develop a multi-year plan listing all federally funded transportation projects. These include roads, bridges, mass transit, some docks and harbors, and airport facilities, as well as local and regionally significant state-funded projects expected to be built over the life of the STIP. Most states, including Alaska, Oregon, Virginia, New York, and Wisconsin, have four-year STIPs. Others, such as Utah, Missouri, and South Dakota, have five-year plans, while some have six-year STIPs, as do Colorado and South Carolina. Largely because of the requirement that local governments, interested parties, and the public be consulted in developing the plan, it takes about two years to update the STIP. Once adopted by the state and approved by the federal agencies concerned, the STIP becomes part of the governor's capital budget that is submitted to the legislature for appropriation. The legislature may modify the capital budget with the potential for veto by the governor. In most cases, however, the projects put forth by the governor are the ones that are approved by the legislature.

As of 2016, the Code of Federal Regulations requires the STIP to meet eight planning criteria:

1. Support economic vitality
2. Improve safety
3. Increase security
4. Increase accessibility and mobility
5. Promote environment enhancement, energy conservation, quality of life improvements, and consistency
6. Enhance integration and connectivity of transportation
7. Promote system efficiency
8. Emphasize preservation of existing systems.

THE STATE LONG-RANGE TRANSPORTATION PLAN

Since 2002, as provided in Alaska Statute (AS) 44.42.050, the DOT is required to develop and update a long-range statewide transportation plan. Unlike the STIP, the state plan is a policy plan, a strategic vision to address funding issues and not about specific projects. Originally developed in 2003 as a plan through the year 2020, increasing problems faced by Alaska's transportation system led the DOT to update the plan in 2008 with the aid of Anchorage and Seattle consultants. The current plan, *Let's Get Moving 2030*, projects transportation needs out to 2030. This plan underwent minor updates in 2010 and was undergoing a major update as of 2016.

THE POLITICS

Because the STIP reflects the DOT's immediate four-year priorities and is, in effect, the state's short-term project-specific transportation priority plan, it is much more subject to politics than the state's long-range strategic plan. Many legislators and their staff are only vaguely familiar with the long-range state plan, if at all, but they all know about the STIP and especially how it might affect their districts. It is the STIP's list of what is to be built, rebuilt, fixed, or improved, that elicits reaction from the interested stakeholder groups.

Part of the politics involving the STIP stems from the federal requirement that in developing and revising the plan there must be formal input from local governments, other affected interests, and the public. More important in many instances is the informal lobbying by legislators, local governments, and other interests to get favored projects into the STIP and its modifications. Much of this takes place during the summer and fall when the governor's budget is being put together. This is one reason why transportation funding in the governor's budget is not usually changed by the legislature.

Regarding *Let's Get Moving 2030*, both a major administrative and political goal was to explain funding changes and the gap between what people expect and what can be delivered. Implementation of the plan will be guided by its strong recommendations about funding and allocation priorities. Some parts of the plan can be implemented by the DOT. The department's ability to develop transportation projects, however, comes mostly from appropriations. Because of the state constitution's prohibition against dedicated funds, there is no external funding going directly to the department. It has no ability to change the flow of funding directly, which is entirely up to state and federal appropriating bodies. The DOT plan does, however, include recommendations to the legislature regarding the allocation of funds.

Yet, because Alaska's governors and legislators see transportation spending first as providing jobs and economic growth, the implementation of the DOT's mission gets compromised. While the DOT's goals concentrate on statewide improvements, the three DOT regions and their legislators tend to look at the distribution of projects rather than their statewide value and effectiveness. Moreover, while the department's thinking is, in large part, long range—five to twenty years because of the time it takes to plan and implement major changes in transportation infrastructure—state elected officials are focused on a two- or four-year horizon to their next election. The resulting hardball political process produces instability, perceived inequality, and discontent. Over the years, no one—not governors, the DOT, nor legislators—has adhered to a clear long-range plan for transportation. In addition, despite federal requirements, the project-driven process is not conducive to the development of an integrated, statewide transportation policy based on maximum involvement of the affected parties.

Source: Developed by the authors.

is compliance with federal regulations, particularly in the federally mandated Statewide Transportation Improvement Program (STIP). In this regard, the federal government acts as a sort of silent but influential political force in transportation policy.

Alaska's congressional delegation can exert influence in helping to direct transportation dollars toward the state through regular appropriations or earmarks (earmarks have been suspended since 2011, but may return at some point). One famous earmark was over $400 million attached to the 2005 SAFETEA-LU (Green-TEA) transportation legislation for the Gravina Island Bridge in Ketchikan and the Knik Arm Bridge in Anchorage. These funds were later turned down by Governor Palin, as explained in Section 7. Congressman Don Young also got money into this same legislation to aid the construction and maintenance of village roads. Alaska's congressional delegation also works to protect programs such as rural-bush air service when it comes under threat, as it did in February 2011.[18]

As in many other areas of state policy, governors can exert considerable influence on transportation policy if they want to. This is particularly the case when a new governor is elected who wants to change direction from the last administration, in part, by appointing a new team to head the DOT. The governor has the major input into allocation of state funds in the annual transportation budget and can have a significant influence on the STIP prepared by the DOT. Also, the governor works through Alaska's Washington, D.C., office and directly with the state's congressional delegation and federal agencies on transportation issues. What constrains governors' power in transportation, as in other policy areas, is the need to satisfy the interests who helped to elect them and who will perhaps reelect them. Governors are also constrained by the need to work with legislators on non-transportation issues to secure his or her agendas and to address other public concerns.

As part of the executive branch and the major administrative agency dealing with transportation issues, the influence and constraints on DOT are covered in Box 28.5. At root, DOT's power base lies in its technical expertise and its development and modification of the STIP and, to a lesser extent, the long-range state transportation plan. Plus, its planning and administrative authority in most of the state's cities and villages, along with its budget resources, gives it a degree of political influence to counter the pressures on it from legislators and local governments.

Regarding the influence of the legislature and individual legislators, much depends on whether they are in the majority or minority. In good budget years, majority members are more likely to get larger amounts of capital funds for their districts than minority members, plus the governor is likely to need majority members to support his or her agenda and may be more amenable to including their projects in the state budget as originally formulated by the governor. Minority members also get some capital funds, including those for transportation, particularly when oil prices rise, as was the case after 2005 when the state capital budget increased considerably. The House and Senate transportation and finance committees are also influential forces. But when oil prices take a major fall, as they did in the summer of 2014 and into 2016, few, if any, individual legislators get transportation capital dollars for their districts.

Legislators, particularly those from rural-bush areas, are under great pressure from their constituents and local governments to deliver jobs and facilities. In this regard, local governments and their representative organization, the AML, are important political forces in transportation. Plus, through political action committees and campaign contributions, other interests, such as those representing contractors, tourism, and environmentalists, can exert influence on both the governor and legislators.

Some influence is also exerted by the public, though exactly how much depends on the circumstances and the issue. One form of public input is through the ballot measure process. Every few years Alaska voters are asked to approve bond propositions to fund transportation infrastructure, as explained below in Section 6 on funding. As noted in Box 28.5, another aspect of public input is through the STIP and its updates. The DOT must hold public hearings in the various regions of the state that are affected by the plan. For example, in fall 2011 and fall 2013 the DOT held a series of meetings in Southeast Alaska on various aspects of the STIP as it affected that region. These included improvements to Juneau roads, bridges and recreational paths, improvements to the Haines and Klondike Highways because of mining activity, and a new Alaska Class ferry for the AMHS that would serve the region.[19]

While public testimony fills many file drawers and computer disks in DOT offices, much of the input to these plans is less formal and reflects friends and neighbors politics. With Alaska's relatively small population, meetings with trade groups, speeches at chamber of commerce luncheons, conversations with mayors, lobbying by community groups, and political and personal alliances carry great weight in the formulation of each year's transportation policy and spending plans.

6. PAYING FOR IT ALL: HOW TRANSPORTATION IS FUNDED IN ALASKA

Building and maintaining transportation infrastructure in Alaska is enormously expensive, and overall transportation represents the major capital projects funding outlay in all states, including Alaska. Just converting a one-hundred-yard two-lane bridge over the Mendenhall River in Juneau into a four-lane bridge cost $25 million, and resurfacing a few miles of highway or an airport runway can costs tens of millions of dollars.[20]

In most states, transportation revenues and spending are spread among federal, state, and local governments. The state and local portion is usually financed from a combination of user fees, such as fuel taxes (usually at the state level), state vehicle registration fees, and property taxes (usually at the local level). User fees are often set to correlate roughly with the use of the system. Unlike Alaska, a majority of states have some kind of dedication of transportation user fees, sometimes with the allocation of these fees contained in state constitutions, statutes, or executive policies. Twenty-eight states limit the use of highway user fees to highway purposes and an additional eleven states dedicate those fees to all transportation purposes.

All states receive a large portion of their transportation funds from the federal government, but Alaska receives a particularly high percentage in comparison to all other states. In this section we show the staggering amount that comes from the national government, but we also explain the funding role of the state and of local governments.[21]

Federal Funds

Alaska receives federal funds for roads and bridges, airports, docks and harbors, public mass transit, its railroad (ARR), its state ferry system (AMHS) and, since the 1980s, for footpaths and trails and other facilities to promote multimodalism. Some funds, such as for new buses, airports, and paths and trails, go directly to Alaska's local governments, but most go to the state government. Of all this funding, nothing comes close to the amount allocated for highways, which nationwide accounts for between 75 and 80 percent of all federal transportation funding, depending on the state and the year. It is often higher in Alaska. So we focus on this aspect of Alaska's federal transportation funding. Three key questions about this funding system, operated by the FHWA through the FHTF, are (1) how does the funding system work; (2) how much does Alaska get; and (3) how does this compare with other states?

Since the establishment of the FHTF in 1956, Congress has distributed funds from the FHTF through appropriations contained in the various highway acts explained in Box 28.3. The primary sources of funding for the FHTF are federal excise taxes collected from transportation-related activities, particularly on gasoline purchases. In distributing FHTF funds, Congress attempts to assess the needs of states to build, reconstruct, and rehabilitate their federal, state, and local highways. How this money is distributed is an ongoing debate. The more urban and populated states, such as New York, California, and Texas, argue that they should recover all of the taxes their residents pay into the fund. Less populated and more rural states, such as Wyoming, Montana, and Alaska, argue that since the entire nation benefits from their highway systems, the nation should share in the cost of them. Less populated states have a strong power base in Congress, particularly in the U.S. Senate, where each state has an equal number of senators. Because of this power base and other considerations, the formula Congress uses to distribute funds favors these less populated states. As a result, some states, called *donor* states, contribute to the cost of the highway systems of other states. Those receiving more than their residents pay into the FHTF in terms of gasoline taxes are referred to as *recipient* states. However, the FHTF receives revenues other than the federal gasoline tax. For this reason, states receive more in total from the fund than they contribute by way of gasoline taxes. This is illustated in Table 28.1.

Table 28.1 provides a historical overview for Alaska and selected states regarding payments into and receipts from the FHTF since its establishment through 2011. The other states were chosen to provide a representative sample of large and small states and several from the west.

As shown in Table 28.1, Alaska is certainly a recipient state. In fact, no other state has benefited from the FHTF anywhere near as much as Alaska in regard to the ratio of

TABLE 28.1

Payments to and from the Federal Highway Trust Fund: Cumulative Totals, Allocations, and Ratio of Return for Selected States

	1956-2011			2011		
	STATE TO FEDERAL PAYMENTS (IN $1,000s)	ALLOCATION TO THE STATES (IN $1,000s)	RATIO OF STATE PAYMENTS TO ALLOCATIONS	STATE TO FEDERAL PAYMENTS (IN $1,000s)	ALLOCATION TO THE STATES (IN $1,000s)	RATIO OF STATE PAYMENTS TO ALLOCATIONS
Alaska	**1,849,194**	**11,131,681**	**6.02**	**106,296**	**578,327**	**5.44**
Arizona	13,379,585	14,599,495	1.09	638,994	821,774	1.29
California	77,666,797	80,866,560	1.04	3,092,590	3,943,077	1.28
Florida	37,900,560	38,069,876	1.00	1,639,225	1,801,157	1.10
New York	33,893,461	43,788,375	1.29	1,287,537	1,794,701	1.39
Utah	6,113,130	7,998,349	1.31	283,718	357,765	1.26
Wisconsin	14,738,757	15,838,274	1.07	607,684	814,391	1.34
Washington	14,186,873	19,021,742	1.34	594,791	778,149	1.31
West Virginia	5,669,381	11,393,683	2.01	219,453	475,944	2.17
Wyoming	3,519,098	6,166,223	1.75	158,764	289,810	1.83
Totals and Ratio for the Selected States	208,916,836	248,874,258	1.79	8,629,052	11,655,095	1.84
Totals and Ratio for All 50 States	**766,688,905**	**884,755,800**	**1.20**	**31,984,265**	**41,789,074**	**1.30**

Source: U.S. Department of Transportation, Federal Highway Administration, Policy Information, Highway Statistics 2011, *Federal Highway Trust Fund Highway Account Receipts Attributable to the States and Federal-Aid Apportionments and Allocations from the Highway Account: Fiscal Years 2006-2011*, at www.fhwa.dot.gov/policyinformation/statistics/2011/pdf/fe221b.pdf.

payments to allocations. From 1956 to 2011 the state received six times what Alaskans paid in, over twice the ratio of Hawaii, the next highest state, and five times the average for the fifty states. In 2011, for example, Alaska received over four times the fifty-state average and twice that of Montana, the closest state to Alaska that year.

Furthermore, for many years, the influence of Alaska's congressional delegation enabled them to secure substantial earmarks for Alaska transportation projects. For instance, Table 28.2 (note 1) shows that in fiscal year (FY) 2002 Alaska received $415 million in earmarks for such projects and $420 million in FY 2007. The 2011 ban on federal earmarks may, however, hurt Alaska in the future.

State Funds

Unlike many states, Alaska has no major state or local toll roads and minimal user fees. The state does raise some user fees from the passengers, cars, and freight on the AMHS and from concessions and other fees from its ownership of the Anchorage, Fairbanks, and other airports. Because of Alaska's constitutional prohibition against dedication of funds (Article IX, Section 7), all user fees go into the general fund (GF) and are legally available to be appropriated for any purpose, including those having nothing to do with transportation. The legislature, however, often appropriates equivalent sums to the agency that collected the fees to be used for that agency's programs.

The bulk of the state's own-source funds used for transportation comes from the state GF or from bonds that the state sells after receiving voter approval. Some federal funds require a state match in order for the federal funds to be forthcoming. For example, in 2012 the Federal-Aid Highway state match amounted to $42 million, and the Federal-Aid Aviation state match was $12 million.

As with all departments of state government, each year the legislature appropriates funds for the DOT's budget. The budget is presented per project, with a proposed dollar amount associated with each one. Most construction projects are complex undertakings that involve both planning and execution. Contractors, engineering firms, architects, and sometimes legal advisors are hired during the course of a construction project. All these components mean that it is important to allow for uncertainty as there are frequently unanticipated costs on any construction project. Thus, DOT often goes back to the legislature with requests for supplements to its budget (known as "supplementals" in budget jargon).

Table 28.2 sets out the funding sources for Alaska transportation projects from 2001 to 2014, and indicates the percentage of federal and state funds contributed each year. The table shows that the state's contribution has fluctuated from 7 to 26 percent over this period, with federal money ranging from 70 to 85 percent. The amount of state funds devoted to transportation in any one year is largely determined by the world price of oil,

TABLE 28.2

Funding Sources of Alaska Transportation Projects, for FY 2001–2014

(Amounts in $ Millions)

FISCAL YEAR—FY	STATE GENERAL FUNDS	GENERAL FUNDS AS PERCENT OF TOTAL	FEDERAL RECEIPTS[1]	FEDERAL RECEIPTS AS PERCENT OF TOTAL	OTHER STATE FUNDS[2]	TOTAL
FY01	60.327	8	643.291	85	52.513	756.131
FY02	61.448	6	666.186	70	229.810	957.444
FY03	52.766	7	708.440	89	37.063	798.269
FY04	58.762	8	686.498	92	17.132	745.259
FY05	00.750	0	1,101.071	95	60.742	1,162.561
FY06	56.657	6	757.031	87	59.614	873.302
FY07	398.725	26	1,085.319	70	55.941	1,539.985
FY08	182.610	22	600.715	74	31.800	815.125
FY09	84.552	7	904.118	70	307.131	1,295.800
FY10	97.436	11	744.282	81	74.877	916.595
FY11	122.380	12	896.776	88	00.250	1,019.406
FY12	132.532	13	883.085	87	00.250	1,015.867
FY13	287.458	23	692.930	56	254.750	1,235.138
FY14	121.347	13	793.882	85	19.250	934.479

[1] Federal Receipts in FY02 and FY07 include $415 and FY07 $420 million respectively in congressional earmarks. FY09 funds include $285 million for federal ARRA projects (American Recovery and Reinvestment Act), so-called stimulus money.

[2] Other State Funds include General Obligation Bonds issued by the state, for example, in FY09 and FY13 for $271.7 and $254.5 respectively.

Note: To show a breakdown of federal and state funding for transportation, we used data provided by DOT (FY04-FY14) complemented with OMB data for FY01-FY03. This data represents budgeted amounts and does not reflect the dollars actually received or expended by DOT in a given year.

Sources: Alaska Department of Transportation, Annual Budgeted Breakdown, provided by Paul Wehe; and Alaska Office of Management and Budget, Budget Reports FY 2001–2012, Capital Budget, by Department, at https://omb.alaska.gov/.

which constitutes 80 to 90 percent of Alaska state government's own-source revenues depending on the year. When oil prices were low in the early 2000s, the state provided little for transportation spending. In FY 2005, the state budgeted only $750,000, the minimum necessary to provide the federal match for ongoing projects. With the major fall in oil prices in the latter half of 2014 and into 2016, the state also appropriated only the minimum amount required to receive federal funds on ongoing projects. By contrast, in 2006, as oil prices rose, state general fund monies were almost double those of FY 2004, and FY 07 saw a record high state contribution to the DOT's budget.

General Obligation Bonds

The high cost of transportation infrastructure development and maintenance, even after major contributions from the federal government, means that it is difficult to fund the up-front cost of projects and to meet a major federal match from the state GF in any one year, or even over two or three years. This is especially the case when oil prices and thus state revenues are down. For this reason, from the early days of statehood, Alaska has sold general obligation bonds to raise funds needed for some transportation capital projects. Under Article IX, Section 8, of Alaska's constitution, general obligation bonds are limited to capital projects and require prior voter approval through a ballot proposition.[22] Over the years, some bonds have been approved for non-transportation purposes such as University of Alaska buildings, but by far the largest number of general obligation bond propositions put before the voters have been for transportation. There have been more than twenty such propositions since statehood. In the first fifteen years after statehood, several were for the ferry system and for airport construction.

More recently, transportation propositions have been for highways and bridges and the multimodal requirements of new federal laws. Since 2000 these bonds have ranged in amounts from $100 to $200 million. Bonding Proposition A in 2012 was an exception at over $453 million. Rarely do transportation bond propositions face any organized opposition and usually pass by big margins, which is somewhat at odds with the state's fiscally conservative political culture.

The Local Government Contribution

Another source of funds included in the "Other" category in Table 28.2 is from Alaska local governments, although most local governments do not contribute to transportation spending. So the small overall amount in this category, likely between 0.1 and 0.5 percent of total state transportation spending depending on the year, comes mainly from Anchorage and Fairbanks.

Interestingly, however, despite the low participation of local governments, in comparing the ratio of state to local expenditures, Alaska is not at the bottom of the list of the fifty states. In 2004, for example, the year with the latest available figures, the state-to-local expenditure ratio in Alaska was 75 to 25. Comparatively, Alaska ranked more or less in the middle of the fifty states. In Delaware, for instance, the share of state transportation expenditures is over 90 percent (with local share being less than 10 percent). In contrast, in Minnesota, Iowa, Oregon, and Wisconsin the state's share is only 50 percent.[23]

The Big Picture: Unbalanced and Unstable Transportation Funding

Alaska's transportation funding sources are less balanced and less stable than those in any other state. They are unbalanced because, more than any other state, Alaska relies heavily on federal funds with very little local funding. They are also less stable because state revenues available for transportation are largely dependent on the state's income from oil, which can fluctuate widely.

So, as of 2016, federal funding of Alaska's highway construction program continues and likely will do so for many years to come. Moreover, in many other aspects of transportation, particularly airports and mass transit, Alaska is also very dependent upon federal aid. In their treatment of transportation politics in 1999, Gerken and Thomas aptly described this funding situation as "state agency management of a federal endowment."[24] The word "endowment" is appropriate here as these funds are in many ways a "gift" in that other states have long subsidized Alaska's transportation system and continue to do so. This, together with many other federal benefits, both through employment and transfer payments to state and local governments and to Alaska residents, is another example of how the federal government helps enhance the quality of life in the state. Most Alaskans, probably the vast majority, are not aware of the funding facts of transportation and particularly the crucial role of the federal government regarding the roads on which they drive. But as we relate below, even those who are aware of these unbalanced and unstable transportation revenues, have little incentive to reform the system.

7. A TALE OF TWO BRIDGES: THE COMPLEXITIES OF TRANSPORTATION POLITICS

In the introduction to the chapter we noted that transportation issues are usually low profile. Two exceptions are two bridge projects: the Gravina Island Bridge in Ketchikan (population 14,000, located at the southern end of Southeast Alaska) and the Knik Arm Bridge in Anchorage. Both bridges have been highly controversial and have often been referred to by those outside of Alaska as the "bridges to nowhere." The bridges make good case studies not so much because they have been high-profile issues, but because they illustrate virtually all the complexities of transportation politics and policy making explained above.[25]

The Background

The Gravina Access project was designed to enable people to drive to and from the City of Ketchikan and the Ketchikan International Airport on Gravina Island, which at present can be reached only by ferry. It would also promote development on Gravina Island, currently with about seventy-five residents. The bridge had been proposed since the 1970s but began to receive serious consideration only in the early 2000s. U.S. Department of Transportation and Alaska DOT cost estimates for the bridge have been as high as $398 million, of which state and local sources would be responsible for approximately $63 million, or 15 to 20 percent of the project's cost.[26] Federal money would cover the rest.

The Knik Arm crossing would span the Knik Arm portion of Cook Inlet on the northwest side of Anchorage to link it with the southwestern Matanuska-Susitna Valley (Mat-Su). Such a crossing was proposed as early at 1923. The most recent revival is the result of major population increases in the southern Mat-Su. So, ironically, although often dubbed a "bridge to nowhere," it would actually link two major "somewheres" in Alaska—Anchorage and the Mat-Su Valley. Proponents argue that the bridge would reduce by up to an hour the commuting time of Mat-Su residents who work in Anchorage.This would considerably expand the Anchorage commuter belt, saving driving hours, and conserving fuel.

In 2003 the Alaska legislature created the Knik Arm Bridge and Toll Authority (KABATA) to head up the effort to get the bridge built. KABATA has essentially served as the cheerleader for the crossing. KABATA's original plan was to build the bridge using a public-private partnership in which the state would have been under an obligation to repay the costs over a thirty-five-year period after the bridge came into operation. Part of this cost would be offset by revenues from tolls which, it was hoped, would eventually be high enough to help pay for other transportation projects. In December 2010 the FHWA gave the project a green light. Over the years, cost estimates for the bridge have varied widely. In 2009 the state DOT estimated this at $686 million. Some other estimates have been over $1 billion. The FHWA's estimate was $1.5 billion. A December 2014 estimate by a consulting firm hired by KABATA put the cost at $900 million.

The Politics

The politics of the two bridges involve an interplay between the federal and state governments as well as local interests in both locales. The conflict that this interplay has produced is at the root of why the two projects have experienced many political twists and turns. While 750 miles apart and separate projects, the fate of the two bridges has, in part, been linked politically.

Members of the Alaska congressional delegation, particularly Representative Don Young and Senator Ted Stevens, were the bridges' biggest advocates in Congress and helped push for federal funding. As part of the 2005 federal transportation bill, Young secured earmarks of over $200 million for each project. This encountered strong opposition in Congress, with accusations of pork-barrelling for needless projects. Opponents included Senator John McCain of Arizona. As a result, Congress removed the federal earmark for the bridges in 2005 without reducing Alaska's share of transportation funds. Following this, Governor Frank Murkowski vowed to build both bridges and set aside state funding for the required federal match.

In the gubernatorial campaign of 2006, Republican Sarah Palin voiced strong support for both bridges. Then, in her inaugural address, she pledged to pursue a policy of responsible spending and sent a budget to the legislature that rescinded the state's federal match for both bridges. The projects were formally cancelled by Palin in August 2007. The worldwide recession of 2008-2010 put both a financial and political damper on support for both projects at all three levels of government—federal, state and local. But in 2011 some funding for the projects was continued by Congress.

As to the specific politics of the Gravina Bridge, it became a major focus of national attention in the presidential campaign of 2008 after Republican presidential nominee John McCain chose Palin as his vice-presidential running mate. Palin capitalized on Republican concern about wasteful government. In her acceptance speech at the Republican National Convention she declared to thundering applause: "I told the Congress thanks, but no thanks, for that bridge to nowhere." This remark angered many in Ketchikan who saw it as disingenuous in light of Palin's earlier support. Nevertheless, the project received major negative publicity and became a poster child for the many things wrong with Congress and the practice of earmarks. This did not bode well for securing federal funds for the project.

Throughout the ups and downs of the Gravina project, the Alaska DOT largely reflected the changing directions of the governor and legislature. For instance, after Palin's unwillingness to provide the federal match, DOT stated that the bridge was unfeasible. Then, in the summer of 2013 DOT came up with a proposal involving six alternatives for the crossing, including two bridge and four ferry options. There was also a "no action" option. This was likely a way of DOT gradually easing out of the bridge project. Even a year earlier, one of the long-time strong supporters of the project, former Governor Murkowski, argued in a June 2012 article in the *Anchorage Daily News* that it had no chance of being built due to adverse national news coverage. He suggested alternative ways to link Ketchikan with the airport, including an underwater tunnel. By this time, too, Ketchikan leaders had realized that the bridge would likely not be built for lack of funds and bad publicity. Then in October 2015, no doubt influenced by the state's serious budget problems, DOT finally abandoned the bridge project and decided to continue the ferry connection to the airport.[27]

Although there has been some negative national publicity about the Knik Arm Bridge, its politics have been more confined to the state and to local politics in the Anchorage area. The KABATA, along with developers and the Mat-Su members of the legislature, have been the major proponents of the project. Among those opposed are many residents on the Anchorage side whose neighborhood would, in effect, be cut in half by the bridge access road. Others are concerned about major traffic increases on already inadequate roads on the Mat-Su side and increased traffic in downtown Anchorage, thereby undermining efforts to make Anchorage a more pedestrian-friendly place. And some Anchorage businesspeople are concerned that the bridge will hurt the Port of Anchorage and the Municipality of Anchorage by diverting business away from both. In addition, the nonprofit Alaska Transportation Priorities Project has argued that the cost of the bridge would take away money from needed maintenance of existing transportation infrastructure.[28] The media has reflected these concerns, including the *Mat-Su Valley Frontiersman* which was concerned about increased traffic on southwest Mat-Su's inadequate road system. And the *Anchorage Daily News* came out strongly against the project in an April 2009 editorial.[29]

Much of the controversy regarding the project has involved KABATA itself. In 2006 it came under fire for raising the pay of its top staff and producing a short video that cost nearly $60,000 to make and air. KABATA has also had a rocky relationship with AMATS. As the federally recognized Metropolitan Planning Agency for Anchorage, AMATS produces the data that forms the basis of the Metropolitan Transportation Plan adopted for Anchorage out to the year 2035. This data provides the foundation for projected revenues from the toll charged to traffic using the bridge. Revenue from the tolls would provide funds to cover bond costs, the prospect of the project ultimately being self-sufficient financially, and perhaps turning a profit to aid other transportation projects around the state. The revenue data produced by AMATS has been lower than the high predictions of KABATA. As a result, in 2009 AMATS removed the bridge from its short-term plan, pushing it forward to 2018. But in response to a lawsuit from the cities of Wasilla and Houston, AMATS reinstated it in 2010.

Then in April 2013, the Legislative Budget and Audit Committee issued an audit report of KABATA's revenue and traffic predications. This report also assessed the agency's predictions as far too optimistic. The fallout from all this was that in April 2013 the legislature placed KABATA under the direct control of the Alaska Housing Finance Corporation for its bonding authority, though KABATA continues to be a cheerleader for the project.

In 2014, legislation transferred construction of the bridge from KABATA to the DOT but kept the running of the bridge with KABATA. A new financing package was also developed consisting of federal funds and some state funds (mainly revenue bonds and toll revenues). Things looked ready to proceed, and DOT started preparing the Anchorage side of the access road in the summer of 2014. But then oil prices took a major tumble and, soon after his inauguration, Governor Walker put a hold on the project together with five other so-called megaprojects.

The upshot is that the Knik Arm project is in financial and political limbo as of early 2016. Ironically, however, to be completed the bridge requires no additional state GF funds, just the revenue bonds. But from a political perspective Walker had to appear to be pulling back on big spending.

The Insights for Transportation Politics and Policy in Alaska

Of the many insights that this tale of two bridges provides about Alaska transportation politics and policy, five are particularly significant. They are familiar aspects of this chapter so far.

The first is the importance of federal funding. It would be out of the question politically for Alaska to fund the Knik Arm Bridge and to have funded the Gravina Bridge without federal help. Theoretically, Alaska could fund both, perhaps in part through the selling of general obligation bonds as well as using capital funds over several budget years. But the opposition to a bond proposition and general spending would likely be too much to overcome, given the controversial nature of both projects over the years, particularly the Gravina Bridge. It was a political and financial stretch to get the state's 20 percent or so for the federal fund match for the Gravina Bridge, though easier in the case of the Knik Arm project. Second, besides the influence of federal funding, the bad press received by both projects, especially the Gravina Island Bridge, whether justified or not, and the backlash against the ability of the late Senator Ted Stevens and Representative Don Young to get major earmarks, show how Outside forces can affect Alaska transportation projects. These and other Outside forces likely worked to help prevent the Gravina Bridge from ever being built. In this regard, the federal funding problem, egged on by national public opinion and opposition from both environmentalists and those generally opposed to government spending, likely also contributed to the withdrawal of state support for the Ketchikan project and may affect the future of the Knik Arm Bridge

Third, the Knik Arm Bridge is, and the Gravina bridge was, project-driven as opposed to policy-driven in terms of being part of a systematic state transportation plan. Certainly, the DOT more or less supported both projects, but likely they would not have done so and made them such a high priority at various times without political pressures. Stevens and Young got the funding regardless of how these projects might fit into Alaska's transportation priorities because they meant jobs and would promote economic development. The same is true of state legislators from Southeast Alaska and the Mat-Su, who supported the bridges over the years.

The Gravina Bridge offered, and the Knik Arm project still holds, the prospect of major financial gains to developers in both places, but particularly in the Mat-Su Valley and Anchorage. The Knik Arm project also holds the prospects of growth for Southcentral Alaska, as did the Gravina Bridge for Ketchikan, which has gone through rough economic times since the mid-1990s. So, political pragmatism is the fourth factor that affected the prospects of both projects; that is, pragmatism on the part of the various interests affected, including the DOT, and particularly the politicians involved. As sometimes happens in transportation politics, and politics in general, the political pragmatism—in this case political ambition—of one politician, Sarah Palin, worked to complicate the state's political stance on both bridges.

Fifth, as with most modern transportation issues, the case studies illustrate the pluralistic nature of policy making. There were some players involved in the politics of both bridges who were most concerned about developing better transportation facilities. Others were motivated by the promise of local economic development, still others were opposed to the developments for economic, environmental, or other considerations, and some were influenced by political pragmatism or personal economic gain or political benefits. This pluralism continues to be the case given all the players involved in the Knik Arm project. The highly pluralistic character of the politics of these issues and their often negative high political profile in the state and the nation were just two of many factors that dragged out the resolution of these projects for years. Added to this were the international recession that made budgets very tight, a fall in oil prices beginning in the summer of 2014, and an increasingly conservative Congress and state legislature with budget-cutting agendas. As a result, the Gravina Bridge project was abandoned, and much uncertainty continues to surround construction of the Knik Arm Bridge.

8. CURRENT TRANSPORTATION ISSUES ACROSS THE STATES AND IN ALASKA: AN OVERVIEW

Even with the five-year fix to federal transportation funding provided by the 2015 FAST Act, the picture for transportation nationwide does not look rosy, particularly for the long-term. This is mainly due to chronic funding problems.

From 1995 to 2011, despite the importance of the nation's transportation system to sustaining and expanding the economy, the U.S. government spent only 0.6 percent of its gross domestic product (GDP) on transportation infrastructure compared to 1.0 percent and more in Western Europe and as much as 2.0 percent in Japan. Alaska spent only 0.5 percent.[30] The rise of fiscal conservatism across the nation since the 1980s has contributed to the increasing reluctance of states and many local governments to spend money on transportation. This is particularly true in the U.S. Congress, which, on behalf of the federal government, is the major funding source of transportation infrastructure in the nation.[31] Particularly since the 2010 midterm elections, which saw many Tea Party members elected to Congress with their anti-tax and cutting federal spending policies, the atmosphere in Washington, D.C., does not favor spending tax dollars on many programs, including transportation beyond what is absolutely necessary to keep the transportation system functioning and to avert major economic distress.

The consequence is crumbling infrastructure in many places, dramatized by incidents like the collapse of the Skagit River Bridge on Interstate 5 between Seattle and the

Canadian border in May 2013.[32] Amazingly, although several vehicles were thrown into the river, no one was killed, but those involved in the next bridge collapse may not be as lucky. Given these and other problems, President Obama called upon Congress on several occasions to address the need for increased transportation spending.[33]

Regarding specific issues, in this section we focus mainly on the dominant issue of funding, but also look briefly at particular aspects of three other major contemporary concerns: modal issues, transportation efficiency, and the ongoing development versus lifestyle discussion in transportation. Then, in Section 9 we look at how these issues specifically affect Alaska and also consider some issues that are particular to the state.

Based upon what we said earlier, perhaps of equal importance to the issue of funding is the problem of project-driven policy making at the expense of overall statewide transportation planning. So why do we not consider it here? We know that this dominant political modus operandi is deeply ingrained in state politics because it serves the combined needs of politicians, local constituencies, and often major campaign contributors. Furthermore, transportation policy making is often linked to economic development and jobs in a particular legislative district or region of a state. For these reasons, the project-driven approach is unlikely to change in the foreseeable future. Because of its continued inevitability, we do not suggest ways to deal with this fundamental element of transportation politics. Instead, we consider issues that have some chance of being addressed.

Funding Concerns

Funding concerns present transportation officials and policy makers with their greatest challenge across the nation. So what is the problem of transportation funding today and in the future and how might it be solved?

The Problem and Its Causes

In December 2015 after putting off major action on transportation funding for over five years, Congress passed the Fixing America's Surface Transportation Act, or the FAST Act. The Act provides $305 billion to fund highway, bridge, transportation safety, and public transit projects until 2021 but it provides little in the way of dealing with the nation's long-term transportation challenges. So why did Congress take so long to provide this five-year funding for transportation and what are the shortcomings of the Act?[34]

As explained earlier, the major funding source for the nation's highways, and an important funding source for mass transit, is the Federal Highway Trust Fund (FHTF). The major revenue source for the fund has been the federal gasoline tax, which totals about $30 billion a year and has accounted for as much as 85 percent of the money flowing into the FHTF.[35] But since the early 2000s, this has not been enough to keep pace with the demand for funds across the states. Figure 28.1 graphically shows that, until the

FIGURE 28.1

The Federal Highway Trust Fund, 1983–2023: Revenues, Payments, Balances, and Projections

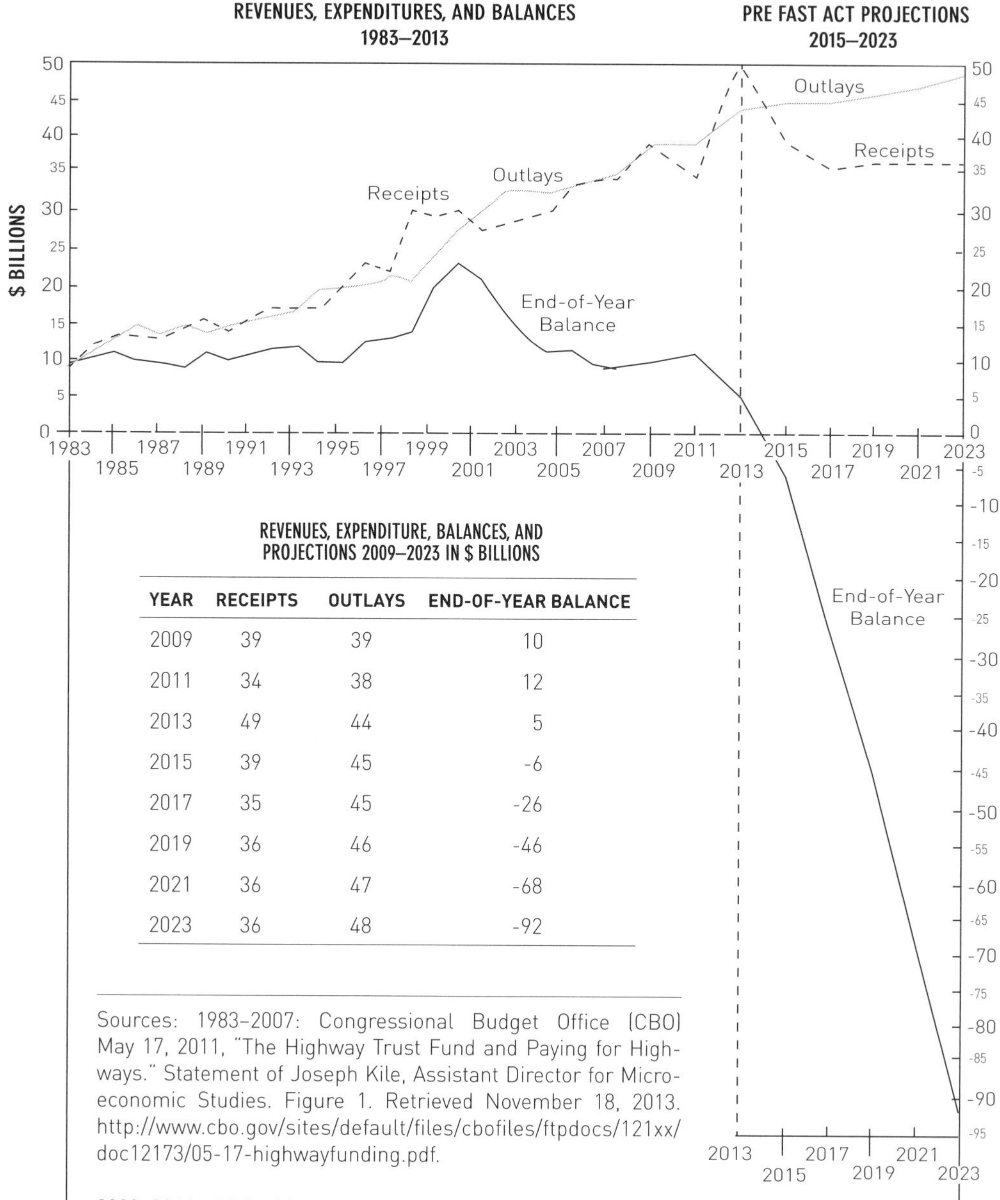

REVENUES, EXPENDITURE, BALANCES, AND PROJECTIONS 2009–2023 IN $ BILLIONS

YEAR	RECEIPTS	OUTLAYS	END-OF-YEAR BALANCE
2009	39	39	10
2011	34	38	12
2013	49	44	5
2015	39	45	-6
2017	35	45	-26
2019	36	46	-46
2021	36	47	-68
2023	36	48	-92

Sources: 1983–2007: Congressional Budget Office (CBO) May 17, 2011, "The Highway Trust Fund and Paying for Highways." Statement of Joseph Kile, Assistant Director for Microeconomic Studies. Figure 1. Retrieved November 18, 2013. http://www.cbo.gov/sites/default/files/cbofiles/ftpdocs/121xx/doc12173/05-17-highwayfunding.pdf.

2009–2011: CBO, 2013, Estimates from the graph, "Statement for the Record Status of the Highway Trust Fund," produced by Sarah Puro, page 5. Retrieved on November 10, 2013. http://www.cbo.gov/sites/default/files/cbofiles/attachments/44093-HighwayTrustFund.pdf.

2013–2023: CBO, 2013. "Statement for the Record Status of the Highway Trust Fund," produced by Sarah Puro, page 4. Retrieved on November 10, 2013. http://www.cbo.gov/sites/default/files/cbofiles/attachments/44093-HighwayTrustFund.pdf.

FAST Act, the FHTF was rapidly running out of money and was threatening to run up major deficits. It went into the red in 2014 and would have reached a staggering $92 billion deficit by 2023. In addition, the Congressional Budget Office (CBO) projected that the transit account alone would have run up a $34 billion deficit by 2023.[36] To deal with deficits between 2008 and 2012, Congress moved $34.5 billion into the FHTF.[37] Congress also passed other stopgap funding to keep the FHTF solvent through the summer of 2015. If the fund had fallen into serious deficit, the resulting reduced payments to the states was estimated to have cost 700,000 jobs across the nation.[38]

Interestingly, little in the negotiations for FAST was said about the issue of the perceived unfairness by the donor states, like California, whose residents pay more in gasoline taxes into the FHTF compared with recipient state residents, like those in Alaska. Alaska certainly benefited from Congress not changing or even tinkering with the FHTF distribution issue. This issue likely became of diminished importance because of the major differences that developed over the sources of the funds needed to cover the five-year cost of the FAST Act. In the end, Congress cobbled together several sources to cover the $305 billion bill, but those sources provide only a temporary fix as we explain below.

There are two significant, though unrelated, developments at the root of the funding shortfall for the FHTF and other transpiration costs.[39] One is that the cost of building and maintaining highways has increased considerably. The other relates to the weakness in the design of the revenue system that funds the FHTF. Together these two factors have reduced the value of the federal gasoline tax by 28 percent relative to 1997 prices, the year that the federal government dedicated the gas tax exclusively for transportation purposes.

There have been considerable increases in the cost of asphalt, machinery, and other construction materials. It is estimated that about 78 percent of the shortfall in gas tax revenues to fully fund the FHTF is due to these increased costs. The other 22 percent of the shortfall is due to increases in fuel efficiency since 1997. So, ironically, the more fuel-efficient gasoline and diesel vehicles are, the less money flows into the federal highway account.

All this could have been avoided if Congress had done a better job of designing the gas tax. The current federal gas tax of 18.4 cents a gallon has not changed since 1993. A well designed variable rate tax structure that rose with inflation and took into account increases in fuel efficiency would have ensured that the FHTF would not go into deficit but would actually realize a surplus every year. This kind of tax structure would have increased revenues by $215 billion over these years (and by $19 billion in 2013 alone) to go toward maintaining and improving America's transportation infrastructure. Moreover, the cost would not have been all that high for the American public. It would have meant a gas tax in 2013 of 29 cents a gallon, just 10.6 cents more than the 18.4 cents that year, and would have cost the average driver only $4.66 more per month.[40] Over the long term the consequences of failing to adopt a rational gas tax structure could be dire.

Approaches for Dealing with the Funding Problem: Immediate and Long Term

Dealing with deficits in the FHTF and attacking the problems of escalating infrastructure cost and how to fund transportation overall are not high-profile political issues of interest to the general public. They are, however, of great concern to federal, state, and local governments. There are various approaches on the part of the federal government and the states that, in combination, could help to solve the problem.

Pressures on the Federal Government

Since the mid-2000s, the federal government has been under great pressure to deal with the shortfall in funding the FHTF, to take steps to provide a long-term solution to FHTF funding, and to develop a long-term plan for funding transportation in general. Avoiding insolvency of the fund required large transfers by Congress in the range of $10 to $20 billion a year.[41] Congress was obliged to do this because, under the provisions of the Deficit Control Act of 1985, the FHTF cannot incur negative balances and has no authority to borrow additional funds. The assumption is that obligations incurred by the fund will be paid in full.

Turning to a long-term solution at the federal level, it is clear that the way the gas tax is calculated and payments distributed needs to be reformed. This might mean reforming the tax to adjust its rates periodically based on inflation and fuel efficiency rates, as explained earlier, and increasing the gas tax rate. The American Association of State Highway and Transportation Officials has suggested a 10 cent per gallon tax increase to maintain the level of needed spending. Others have suggested as much as a 50 cent per gallon increase. Data suggest that in order to fund the nation's highway network at the present level of service will require at least a 25 cent per gallon increase in the tax.[42]

Solutions that the President and Congress have considered to deal with the fund's deficit involve using revenues from corporate tax reform to make the fund solvent. The Obama administration's proposal involves taxing the untaxed foreign earnings that U.S. companies have accumulated overseas. A similar source of revenue was proposed by Senators Boxer (California) and Paul (Kentucky).[43] We have already noted that a long suggested solution of reforming the payment relationship between donor and recipient states regarding the FHTF was not seriously considered in the 2015 FAST Act negotiations.

The FAST Act, the first major transportation legislation since SAFETEA-LU in 2005, missed a major opportunity. Disagreements over how to finance the FHTF in the short term thwarted a long term solution to solvency. In particular, against the advice of the U.S. Chamber of Commerce, the American Automobile Association, truckers and labor unions, Congress refused to raise the gas tax. This would be the solution most likely to secure the FHTF's viability over the period to 2021—the six-year period of the provisions in the FAST legislation. Instead, non-sustainable funding sources were used, including dipping into the nation's strategic petroleum reserve and funds from the Federal Reserve to bridge the gap between what the gas tax brings in and what is needed in the fund. Bringing in about $34 billion a year, the gas tax will cover only about 60 percent of the $305 billion cost of FAST.[44]

Furthermore, what bothered many in Congress and in the executive branch was the failure to raise the gas tax to more or less fully fund the FHTF, which set a bad precedent. It did so by exchanging the certainty of this dedicated source for assuring the solvency of the FHTF with the uncertainty of other ways of financing it. So after the life of FAST, Congress will have to revisit the funding issue. FAST's stop-gap funding measure was referred to by Alaska Senator Lisa Murkowski, who was appointed to the conference committee to reconcile the House and Senate versions of the bill, as "a one-time fix" and that it was time to have a real conversation about funding. She went on to say, "I really think that we need to be looking to making sure that our highway fund is sustainable." Murkowski is well aware that Alaska has the most to lose from funding shortfalls in the FHTF as do the other two members of Alaska's congressional delegation. Probably for this reason, all three members supported an increase in the gas tax. [45]

State Approaches

Of necessity, the states have taken steps to increase revenues and cut costs, in most cases through a multifaceted approach. On the revenue side, one avenue is to raise state and local gas taxes. As of December 2015 the national average for state and local gas taxes was just over 30 cents a gallon, giving an average of about 49 cents per gallon tax across the states when the federal gas tax is added. The Alaska gas tax that year was well below the national average at 8 cents a gallon, for a total of about 27 cents with the federal gas tax added.[46] The elasticity of demand for gas (how price affects demand) is low, which means that increases in price do not appreciably reduce demand. Thus, a gas tax increase could help contribute to transportation revenues, though this may take a political public relations job to fend off anti-tax interests.

Another funding strategy on the part of the states is to increase state user fees and expand them to include additional state services or facilities. Since the early 1980s, there has been increased support across the nation for user fees and applying them to a wider range of transportation uses and situations. Unlike previous generations, many people today are reluctant to pay taxes for anything that does not directly benefit them and find the idea attractive that fees for government services should be paid only by those who use them. Consequently, there is a movement toward toll roads. Furthermore, many who use toll roads argue that they should not be required to pay for the non-toll roads they do not use. An extreme funding proposal from Texas involves imposing tolls to pay for all new transportation facilities.

States are also seeking ways to allocate costs more equitably to the user groups who create the demand and who may increase costs to state and local governments. Oregon, for example, has considered having individuals pay for the number of miles driven rather than traditional gasoline taxes. The Oregon proposal requires each vehicle to pay a different rate based on its impact on the transportation system. The State of Washington has looked at a surcharge based on when a person travels. For example, those who travel during rush hours will pay more than those who travel during off-peak times. Impact fees are being considered on landowners and businesses whose developments impose an incremental impact on the infrastructure and increases construction and maintenance costs. An example is a requirement for developers to pay for signal lights and additional lanes needed for a new shopping center or a new subdivision. In some cases, roadways that benefit only one user may be turned over to the individual to maintain.

Many states, including the Pacific states of California, Oregon, and Washington, are looking for higher contributions from their local governments for funding assistance. And several states and local governments are considering privatization of services, such as contracting out design or maintenance activities.

Modal Issues and Efficiency: A Major Challenge

Highways create the dominant transportation issues in all states for obvious reasons: the high rate of automobile ownership, the importance of highways for freight shipments, taxes levied on users to fund highways, and the impact that the massive amounts of money spent on highway construction and maintenance have on state economies and employment. However, the federal government and some progressive states have attempted to promote multimodalism and have used funding as both a political carrot and stick to encourage it. The right mix of multimodalism can also increase the efficient use of energy because transportation is a major user of energy. Such efficiency can also reduce greenhouse gases and improve the quality of the environment. Many accomplishments have been made in multimodalism and its related advances, but often the progress gets mired in politics.

The biggest stumbling block to major advances in multimodalism is Americans' love affair with their cars. The automobile is certainly the most convenient and personal mode of transport. Consequently, federal, state, and local government policies have had only minimal success in getting people out of their cars and onto public transit systems or even into car pools, let alone on bicycles. Unlike Europeans, many Americans just do not like public transport and will pay high gas prices or penalties for driving in cities at rush hours rather than use public transit where it is available. Given this dominance of the automobile and road transport in general, highway planning in all states, including Alaska, still receives greater focus and takes the lion's share of transportation funds.

Then there are modal rivalries involved in the development of policies and funding decisions because of user interests associated with the different modes. These include land use, environmental, and social concerns. For example, traditional highway development and mass transit have increasingly been in competition with each other for capital and operating funds. This rivalry often plays out in regional planning processes by pitting cities, particularly large ones that are usually proponents of mass transit, against their surrounding suburban communities that are often highway proponents.

Energy used by the transportation sector accounts for 28 percent of all primary energy consumption in the United States.[47] This includes 70 percent of total oil (gasoline, diesel, and jet fuel) consumed in the nation. The sector relies heavily on oil (93 percent of its total energy consumption), with natural gas accounting for 3 percent and renewable energy for 4 percent. As a consequence, the transportation sector is affected by fluctuations in oil prices. So besides saving fuel, increased efficiency will make the U.S. transportation system less susceptible to world oil price fluctuations.

Because of the extensive use of road transport, fuel efficiency is largely dependent on reducing vehicle miles traveled (VMT). In this regard, while past developments are encouraging, future projections are less than positive. On the one hand, fuel consumption declined 20 percent between 1980 and 2010. On the other hand, VMT is expected to increase considerably by 2030 due to the increase in population. In the face of the likely reduced funding for new infrastructure and repair of existing facilities, the growth may overwhelm the nation's highways. Moreover, the American Council for an Energy Efficient Economy notes, "Reducing the rate of VMT growth requires the coordination of transportation and land use planning, which is typically under local or regional jurisdiction."[48]

An important part of local and regional cooperation in reducing the rate of VMT growth is to promote the use of mass transit, which not only cuts down on the use of gasoline but also wear and tear on roads and damage to the environment. For instance, a study conducted in 2007 by ICF International, an energy, technology, transportation infrastructure, and environmental consultancy, shows that mass transit reduces travel by 102.2 billion VMT each year (3.4 percent in 2007). Additionally, direct petroleum savings due to mass transit were estimated at 1.4 billion gallons that year. Moreover, public transport produces less greenhouse gas emissions than do personal vehicles.[49]

The conflicts between different modes of transport, differences of emphasis on modes between central city and suburban areas, Americans' love of their cars, and the prospect of reduced federal funding in the long term, present major obstacles to expanding mass transit. Clearly, then, despite its demonstrated advantages, the move to multimodalism, and with it increased transportation efficiency, faces many challenges.

BOX 28.6

Transportation and Climate Change

No discussion of contemporary transportation policy is complete without understanding the uncertainty of climate change. There are two vantage points: (1) the impact of transportation on climate; and (2) the impact of climate on transportation.

Transportation affects climate in several ways. Large expanses of asphalt and concrete create heat islands. People living near a freeway, airport, or highly developed urban area experience these heat islands. The temperature over a freeway or airport can easily be 20 degrees higher than at an adjacent meadow. Of greater concern is the carbon dioxide emitted into the air by transportation. The Environmental Protection Agency estimates that 28 percent of the carbon dioxide (CO_2) produced in the United States comes from transportation. This figure excludes activities such as fuel production and the manufacture of vehicles.

There are several ways to reduce CO_2 emissions. The most effective is to reduce the number of miles traveled. A second way is to reduce emissions through more fuel-efficient vehicles. Major advances have been made in this regard since 1975, and there are new fuel economy standards through 2025. A third way is to increase the use of public mass transit. This alternative works well in populated areas, but public transit is not cost-effective in rural areas. Added to this is the general aversion of many Americans to public transit even when gas prices soar.

As to the way that climate change impacts America's transportation system and the people who use it, shifts in weather and extreme weather pose the major problems. For example, the Great Lakes remain unfrozen for longer each winter. This causes air masses moving over the lakes to pick up moisture. Once the air mass moves back over land, the moisture falls back to earth in large snowfalls. While these do not cause problems to the infrastructure, they do cause stress and increased inconvenience to commuters and snow removal personnel. Increased hurricanes and heavy rainfall also cause problems.

Alaska has seen increased flooding in the Southcentral region. Each year brings flooding into areas that have no past record of it. If the data is available engineers can design for these extreme events. Unfortunately, climate models are not capable of forecasting these events on a small enough scale to be of value.

Source: Developed by Billy Connor.

Transportation, the Environment, and Climate Change

Modal and efficiency issues currently affect, and will continue to affect, the environment and in several ways continue to pit development against quality-of-life concerns. Of the numerous issues, climate change is one of the most significant and politically charged. In her overview of Alaska's present and future transportation challenges in Box 28.2, Lois Epstein identifies this as a major concern. Box 28.6 examines the basics of the issue as it relates to transportation.

9. THE PARTICULARS OF CONTEMPORARY TRANSPORTATION ISSUES IN ALASKA

All of the transportation issues that affect the fifty states also affect Alaska. Some of them have few, if any, particular Alaska elements. There are other concerns, challenges, and constraints that are specific to Alaska or that have an Alaska twist to them.

Project-driven policy making, for better or for worse, is a reality in Alaska and will be for political generations to come. As a result, we do not suggest ways to get around it, though, as in other states, the STIP, and, in Alaska, the *Let's Get Moving 2030* transportation plan does give Alaska some semblance of statewide transportation planning. We refer to this Alaska plan at several points in this section.

Because highways in Alaska, as in all states, are the mode of transportation that is responsible for the major consumption of energy, particularly fossil fuels, efficiency issues affect Alaska similarly to other states. This is particularly so as much of the policy regarding efforts to increase fuel and other efficiencies in transportation is federally driven. Regarding development versus lifestyle conflicts, these are and will continue to be similar in Alaska to those in other states, though certain issues will attract more national focus than in most states because of Alaska's national status as the Last Frontier. Climate change, for one, has major implications for Alaska geographically, economically, and politically, particularly its effects on the Arctic, including the difficulty of building on thawing permafrost. But the effects of climate change on Alaska's transportation infrastructure are not significantly different from other northern states like Minnesota and Montana and share much in common with all states.

There are, however, three transportation concerns that have special Alaska elements that we consider here. As in all states, the most important is that of funding, now and in the future. Then there is the role of local governments, and access to rural-bush communities.

The Particulars of Alaska Transportation Funding Problems

To maintain its existing quality of life, the safety of its transportation system, and the strength of its economy, Alaska needs to maintain its present level of spending on transportation infrastructure. Adequate transportation investment is necessary as a foundation for Alaska's economy. Businesses will run more efficiently and more money will be kept in the state. Transportation investment is an investment in the future. It is likely, however, that not only will money not be spent on developing the system, there may not be enough money available in the near future to maintain the existing infrastructure.

The potential gap between the money needed and what is available is a product of four major factors. One is the unbalanced nature of Alaska state revenues in general and of transportation funding in particular. The second and third are the rapid increases in the cost of transportation infrastructure and the potential for a leveling off or a reductions in federal capital funding in the years to come. Fourth, and in many ways the most fundamental of all, is the fiscally conservative attitude of many Alaskans and their politicians toward funding transportation and to state spending in general.

Unbalanced General Revenues and Uncertain Funding Sources for Transportation

Five points are important to emphasize here that will amplify and expand on what we have said in the chapter so far.

The first is Alaska's heavy dependence on federal funds for transportation capital investment and maintenance and the changing political circumstances surrounding federal financing. Since the mid-2000s these circumstances have, in some ways, worked to Alaska's disadvantage and may result in a reduction of federal funds in all states, but with some particular Alaska elements, as explained later.

Second is that Alaska makes very little use of user fees as a revenue source, and there is a major absence of toll roads. Over the years Alaska has raised a smaller share of its highway revenues from user fees and tolls than almost any other state. Part of the reason is the aversion of Alaskans to toll roads. But there is also a very practical reason: the ability of any of Alaska's roads to generate sufficient revenue to fund a road is minimal. During the 1990s, for instance, there were two attempts to place a toll on the Dalton Highway (also known as the Haul Road) from the Yukon River Bridge north to Prudhoe Bay in order to cover the highway's maintenance costs. The tolls to make this feasible, however, were higher than anyone was willing to pay, so the idea was dropped.

Third, there is very little contribution from Alaska's local governments to transportation funding and heavy dependence on state funds to supplement federal funding at the local level. Fourth, unlike many other states, there is no revenue stream that is specifically for transportation funding because of the prohibition against dedicated funds in the Alaska Constitution. There have been attempts to establish such a dedicated fund through a constitutional amendment as attempted by former Representative Peggy Wilson (Republican of Wrangell) in 2014 (House Joint Resolution 10), but it failed to pass. It is doubtful that a constitutional amendment, will be passed in the near future to create such a fund. Consequently, transportation will continue to compete with other state services and programs in the annual rough-and-tumble for state budget dollars, as explained in Box 28.5.

Fifth, with no state sales tax or personal income tax as of 2015, there is an overwhelming dependence on oil revenues by state government. Because these revenues fluctuate widely, downturns in oil prices, as occurred in 2014 and into 2016, adversely affect all state spending, including transportation, and reduce the state's ability to meet federal matching funds requirements. This means putting on hold or cancelling transportation projects.

These five circumstances present transportation officials and policy makers with their biggest challenge in Alaska. Overall, however, state officials have little power to change any of these factors. They certainly have no control over federal funds that are directly linked to low federal gasoline and other transportation related excise taxes, and no control over oil prices, which are determined by world markets. Plus, most Alaska local governments are not able to contribute to transportation costs in any meaningful amount. In addition, the state's aversion to imposing additional taxes and long-range fiscal planning is difficult to change.

Increased Costs and Likely Reduced Revenues: Some Additional Points

Like all states, Alaska has seen increasing costs for building and maintaining transportation infrastructure. This, combined with calls in Washington, D.C., to cut the federal budget and the likelihood of less federal transportation funds in the years to come, puts Alaska in a difficult position because of its major dependence on federal funds. It was fortuitous that the ISTEA legislation was negotiated during 1990 when there was a booming American economy; otherwise Alaska could have fared badly. SAFETEA-LU, passed in 2005, continued high levels of federal funding for Alaska primarily because Alaska's congressional delegation held key seats in Congress.[50] Alaska was also fortunate that the formula for allocating funds to states was not changed in the 2015 major re-write of federal transportation policy in the FAST Act.

Even though Alaska continues to be the major recipient state as far as FHTF monies are concerned, the situation regarding federal funds is cause for concern for Alaska for three reasons. All three relate to changes in Alaska's long-serving congressional delegation and their methods of operating.

One is the defeat of Senator Ted Stevens in the fall of 2008. Stevens secured billions of dollars for Alaska, particularly for transportation, often through earmarks. Representative Don Young, who has also aided Alaska in this regard, is still in Congress, but his abilities are undermined to some extent by the second and third points. The second is the banning of earmarks by the U.S. Senate in 2011.[51] Even if this ban were lifted, when Young's tenure in the House ends, with a freshman senator, Dan Sullivan, elected in 2014, and despite Lisa Murkowski's seniority, Alaska will not have the political influence in Congress that it enjoyed for so many years and that was so important to the state's transportation funding.

Third, despite the fact that the FHTF formula for allocating money to the states was not changed in the FAST legislation, Congress may well change the formula at some point in the future. This may occur as early as 2021, when enactment of a new major transportation funding plan will be due. Congress is likely not going to be as generous to Alaska as it was in the past. This leaves Alaska very vulnerable in the medium and long term for the bulk of its transpiration funds. Unless circumstances change in Alaska and it is willing to pay more of its way and be less of a recipient state, not only in transportation but other areas, the image of Alaska as of 2015 as a state that would "rather go broke than pay taxes" may well catch up with it in terms of no longer being supported by largesse from Washington, D.C.[52]

Attitudes toward Taxation, Fiscal Planning, and Transportation Funding

Alaska's relatively low taxes on individuals have been made possible by extensive oil revenues since the late 1970s plus major infusions of federal funds. This, as argued in many places in this book, has led to a political culture of dependent individualism—mainly dependence on the federal and state governments (fueled by oil revenues), which has provided the wherewithal for the myth of individualism. Two major practical manifestations of this dependent individualism have been less need to impose taxes and a lack of long-range fiscal planning, despite the instability of oil revenues and the long-term prospect of less federal funds in the years to come. The result has been ad hoc, incremental, and crisis policy making in reaction to budget shortfalls.

The nature of transportation funding over the years has both reflected and reinforced this attitude of dependent individualism, with the added element of pragmatic fiscal conservatism. As long as there is a generous amount of federal funding the current approach works. Because the status quo is a major force in politics, there is little incentive for Alaskans to develop new politically and financially painful approaches to dealing with transportation funding. The windfall of federal funds reduces pressure to increase state user fees or taxes or make use of toll roads. Alaskans are perfectly happy being a recipient state of federal funds. It is an example of the common human trait of today's privileges being tomorrow's demands. All this helps explain Alaska's very low percentage of GDP contribution of only 0.5 percent of its gross domestic product (GDP) spent on transportation development and maintenance.[53]

This fiscal situation enables Alaska to indulge in the luxury of pragmatic fiscal conservatism. The state may have a general trait of fiscal conservatism, but this does not stop it from accepting huge amounts of federal funds. Despite the rhetoric of budget-cutting, pragmatism is also the modus operandi of most right-wing Republicans, with the possible exception of members of the Tea Party, although its members have so far not been in positions of power in Alaska. So while the legacy of federal funding of Alaska's highways that began before statehood continues, it is a distributive policy welcomed by Alaska and obviously not seen as one of the burdens of federalism. However, because of the low-profile nature of transportation and its funding, many

Alaskans likely have no idea how much money for their roads, airports, buses, and ferries comes from Washington, D.C.

All this, including the low profile nature of the funding issue, has lulled Alaska into a false sense of transportation-funding security. Moreover, as elsewhere, transportation is often taken for granted in Alaska along with an implicit belief that the infrastructure will always be there to get people where they want to go. As a consequence, and as with the state budget in general, Alaskans and their politicians have not developed a long-range fiscal plan in general or for transportation in particular. More than most states, however, Alaska has the wherewithal to develop such a plan. As of 2016, with a $50 billion Permanent Fund and despite low oil prices, Alaska was in much better financial shape than many states.

But present political circumstances suggest that transportation facilities as Alaskans have known them might not be there to the same extent in the future.

Some Possible Options and Courses of Action

Clearly, then, the future of Alaska's transportation system depends on dealing with funding problems. Given the economic and political constraints on funding explained earlier, Alaska does not have many options to deal with this problem, and generally fewer than other states. Nevertheless, the state does have some courses of action it could take.

As in other states, one option is to engage in public-private partnerships to help fund and maintain transportation projects where the private entity receives benefits and the state's costs are reduced. However, there have been only a handful of public-private partnerships in Alaska. The Dalton Highway was constructed by the oil industry and then turned over to the state. The road to the Red Dog Mine (near Kotzebue in Northwest Alaska) was constructed with financial aid from the state. Road access to Whittier was constructed by paving the Alaska Railroad tunnel and was partly financed with revenue from projected future tolls. While other partnerships have been considered, such as before 2014 in building the Knik Arm Bridge, the state has less incentive to join in partnerships with the private sector as long as federal funds are available.

Turning to the approach in the DOT's *Let's Get Moving 2030* plan, a major reason for the plan is to deal with the large gap between what state residents expect from DOT in regard to new transportation facilities and maintenance of existing infrastructure and what the state is able to provide with limited funds.[54] The December 2010 update of the plan concluded that while the gap between needs and revenues has increased since the analysis of 2007, most of the changes, especially the deterioration in asset conditions, were anticipated. The next update of the 2030 plan was scheduled for release in the summer of 2014, but as of early 2016, the update had not been completed.

The 2010 update of the plan attempts to apply three national goals and targets to Alaska: (1) modernize the national highway system; (2) provide demand-driven capacity; and (3) evaluate projects through the use of regional and metropolitan planning organizations. To this end, Alaska's 2030 plan attempts to establish a policy framework for deciding how and where to spend scarce resources in an era of impending federal financial scarcity. The multimodal focus of the plan calls for a major shift in funding policies.

Under the 2030 plan, priorities are established based on system-strategic needs and goals. For example, the infusion of major federal transportation funds reduces pressure to increase state user fees or taxes and increases pressure on the state transportation agency and the legislature to use these capital monies in ways that reduce the need for state maintenance funds. As a consequence, the state may make the repaving of a particular highway a priority not because it will make the greatest improvement to transportation for the most system users, but because its improved condition will require less operating cost after repaving, thereby saving state operating dollars.

In regard to specific funding priorities, the following goals are particularly significant. One is the elimination of low benefit-high cost activities, which likely includes a very low priority given to road access to rural-bush Alaska. Another is transferring the responsibility of local roads to local governments, and letting them levy impact fees. However, like the 2030 plan's goal to have more of a statewide focus and less of a project-driven process, the benefit-cost objective and that of transferring more costs to local governments may well run afoul of politics and simple economic reality. Much of former Governor Parnell's "Roads to Resources" initiative, intended to boost Alaska's economic development, including the road to Ambler mining districts in Northwest Alaska, was politically driven.

Sharing Responsibility for Transportation: An Increased Role for Local Governments?

The question of how responsibility for transportation should be allocated among federal, state, and local agencies in Alaska, as elsewhere, is not only a financial issue. It also involves issues of planning and policy development and of accountability. Participation of local governments promotes responsibility in consideration of cost and benefit and ensures that local needs are taken into consideration, while enabling integrated transportation plans to be developed. In contrast, minimal local government responsibility for operations or funding provides little incentive for smaller Alaska communities to get involved in the transportation policy-making process.

In fact, local governments in Alaska sometimes see clear disincentives to getting involved. In the early 1990s, for example, in conformity with ISTEA, the DOT attempted to develop the Borough Transportation Program as a means to further involve local and regional governments in capital planning. The proposal—to share the capital dollars in return for local planning accountability—was resisted by local governments because they feared that a higher level of responsibility in capital spending decisions for local roads would be tied to future responsibility for maintaining those roads. As a result, DOT's efforts were largely unsuccessful. So with the exception of Anchorage (through AMATS) and Fairbanks (through FMATS), DOT fills the void and makes local transportation decisions on a statewide basis. DOT is limited, however, in its ability to provide the services local areas need without local participation in the planning, financing, and delivery of services.

Then, there are the off-the-road communities with no local government and, therefore, no tax base to pay for transportation infrastructure, and their complete dependence on the state legislature for funding. Without local government, the residents have no voice in decisions concerning road, airport, or dock improvements. But in many cases local citizens choose not to form a local government for fear of taxes and other regulations.

So the inclusion in the 2030 plan of an increased role of local government in both planning and funding is likely wishful thinking. The combination of factors and attitudes just explained and, for the moment, generous federal funding, are likely to mean very little change in the role of local government in Alaska's transportation funding and planning. Local governments, however, will certainly continue to participate in the politics of, and lobbying for, transportation funds.

Increased Access to Rural-Bush Alaska and Lower Transportation Costs?

Because transportation facilities in rural-bush Alaska are very limited and very expensive to build and maintain, two related quality-of-life improvements that are at the top of the political agenda for rural-bush residents and their elected officials are better transportation access and reduced costs of personal travel and shipping of goods. Positive developments in these two areas in the future are unlikely, however. In fact, just maintaining existing services at present costs will be a challenge.

There are three major reasons why rural-bush areas are not likely to see improved road access, such as a road from Fairbanks to Nome and Kotzebue or a road system in Southwestern Alaska. One is the possible decrease in funds available for transportation in general. The second is the criteria of cost-benefit in the DOT's 2030 plan and the plan's emphasis on demand-driven transportation usage to determine spending priorities. By these criteria, rural-bush road access is very low on the priority list. Third, while powerful rural-bush legislators might be able to push some access development, the political influence of rural-bush areas is declining and is gradually being overwhelmed by urban political representation, particularly from Anchorage and its nearby communities.

The costs of traveling in rural-bush areas and getting goods to and from it are also not likely to change in the near future. One reason is the simple and fundamental fact that rural-bush communities represent a small market, and there is little competition among carriers and shippers. Also, with more and more people from rural-bush towns and villages moving to Anchorage and other urban areas, this situation is only likely to get worse. Consequently, Alaska's transportation policy process is hard pressed to reduce rural-bush transportation costs despite constant complaints from rural-bush residents and their politicians. This does not mean that the state, especially through DOT's 2030 plan, fails to recognize the need and importance of rural-bush access. The plan calls for improvements in aviation services, including medevac services, minimum airport lighting, runway length improvements, surface replacement, and snow and ice control.

Perhaps the biggest threat to rural-bush access and keeping transportation costs at their present level are the rumblings in Congress about cutting the subsidy for rural-bush air service mentioned earlier. The U.S. Postal Service provides a subsidy for rural-bush mail delivery that greatly reduces the cost of mail delivery by air to rural-bush communities. Over the years this subsidy has been very generous but its future is very uncertain. Cuts in ferry system service also affect rural-bush communities, and these cuts invariably come when state budget revenues fall as they began to do in a serious way in 2014 and continuing into 2016. For example, the Alaska Marine Highway System took four of its eleven ferries out of service in late 2015.

Three Approaches to Future Transportation Politics and Policy Making

The major issues just discussed add up to a series of constraints on Alaska's transportion policy makers that will continue into the future. Their challenge is how best to address the certainty of increasing costs and an uncertain federal funding future beyond the life of FAST. Perhaps the greatest constraint of all is the uncertainty of oil prices, coupled with the fact that, as of 2015, Alaska had no fiscal plan for its future expenses that takes into account declining revenues and alternative ways to fully or partially fund programs, including transportation.

In these circumstances, what should be the course of action of policy makers in the future? We offer three possible approaches. One approach suggested by Lois Epstein (which is also the approach of the Alaska Transportation Priorities Project—ATPP) is the rational approach. The second is the optimistic perspective, and the third is the realist approach. The three approaches are not mutually exclusive. In fact, future transportation politics and policy will likely include elements of all three, with any particular one being emphasized at any one time depending on who is in power in Washington, D.C., and in Juneau and how much money is available.

Lois Epstein's Approach

In Epstein's view and that of the ATPP, in the twenty-first century Alaska's transportation system must become smarter rather than bigger. Expensive road projects connecting currently unconnected areas must be abandoned as new generations of Alaskans adapt to changed fiscal and environmental realities. Alaska needs to be more self-sufficient in funding transportation if the state has any hope of repairing and preserving its existing infrastructure.

Additionally, as federal and state policies begin addressing greenhouse gas emissions, changes to the state's transportation system will likely be those that reduce fossil fuel consumption. These will include increased emphasis on public transportation in Alaska's urban areas, purchasing fuel-efficient ferries, and using lower carbon fuels for road vehicles, trains, and planes.

The Optimistic Approach

To be sure, Alaska has an unstable revenue source in oil, spends little state money on transportation, and has concerns about federal funding over the long term. But Alaska has faced actual and pending fiscal crises before and has always come through them. Congress has dealt with the FHTF deficit at least through 2021 and will likely do so in the future. Also, Alaska has a $50 billion dollar savings account and can use the earnings from this, if necessary. It is also true that the state has no long-range fiscal plan, but so long as there is federal money flowing into the state, there is little need to develop one.

Those who hold this perspective believe that when Alaska needs money for transportation infrastructure, the Alaska public and its politicians will respond positively as they will to fund other services.

The Realist Approach

This approach combines elements of both the Epstein and the optimistic approaches but adds the political reality of project-driven and ad hoc, fragmented, policy making. It is unlikely that there will be a long-range fiscal plan that includes contingency funding for transportation. Of necessity, the federal STIP will be important, and the updates of the state's *Let's Get Moving 2030* long-range plan will have some impact, but the state is not likely to develop a statewide transportation project plan upon which there is a general consensus. Local political influence on legislators and the connection between transportation infrastructure and economic development will prevent such a consensus. Also, as in the past, with a great deal of politics involved among the legislature, the DOT, sometimes the governor, and interest groups, available funds will determine what projects are funded and which ones are not. The drop in oil prices in 2014 and into 2016 certainly put a serious financial damper on new projects and caused cutbacks to or holds on existing ones.

In other words, the future of policy making in transportation will be similar to policy making in other policy areas in the state.

10. CONCLUSION: THE POLITICAL ECONOMY OF TRANSPORTATION IN ALASKA

Despite all of the politics involved, transportation infrastructure does get built and maintained, and Alaska's transportation system has developed considerably since statehood. But as we have argued, transportation politics and the resulting policies are not just about transportation. As in most policy areas, other factors extraneous to enhancing the state's transportation system have an influence, often a major one, in shaping transportation policy. This has become more the case since the 1970s. Together these factors and developments have produced a particular political economy of transportation in Alaska. Moreover, due to the significance of the federal government and the political role of local governments, this political economy has a major IGR element to it.

Alaska's transportation political economy is driven by local and special interests set in an intergovernmental context, rather than a systematic planning process designed to develop and improve a statewide transportation system. As a consequence, it is a political economy highly dependent on federal funds, one that is project-driven, where local economic development and the desire of legislators to get reelected have so far trumped consensus on a long-range development and funding plan for transportation. Moreover, since the early 1970s it has been a political economy shaped by a highly pluralistic policy community. This community includes the interaction, often a conflict, between those advocating quality-of-life issues and those who want to develop Alaska's economy and its underdeveloped transportation infrastructure.

In this political environment, DOT and to some extent the federal government, through the federally mandated STIP and DOT's required state plan, are the only forces giving Alaska's transportation policy making a semblance of policy coherence, though both plans are subject to national, state, and local politics. As a result, although the transportation policy process tends to be less contentious than most policy areas in the state, the policy making is fragmented and some policy outcomes, particularly controversial ones like the Gravina Island and Knik Arm bridges, are uncertain and can drag on for years. In many ways, however, the political economy of Alaska transportation is not that different from the other 49 states, and the differences that do exist are the result of particular circumstances in Alaska.

Both the nature of Alaska's transportation political economy and its differences from other states can be understood by reference to the six characteristics of Alaska politics that apply to transportation identified in the introduction to this chapter. The first is the significant role of external economic and political forces, especially the federal government as a funding source, and dependence on the world price of oil. This produces a degree of dependence greater than any other state and makes Alaska very vulnerable, again perhaps more than any other state, to reductions in federal funding and fluctuations in oil prices. Other external influences include American public opinion and an environmental movement that often views Alaska as a Last Frontier to be preserved, thus affecting Alaska transportation policy more than such forces do in most other states. The second characteristic is the conflict between economic development and environmentalism, which again takes on special significance because of Alaska's Last Frontier image across the nation and around the world.

The third and fourth characteristics are friends and neighbors politics and regionalism, including conflicts between urban and rural-bush areas. Friends and neighbors politics, in this case the Alaska version of "all politics is local," places great pressure on politicians to deliver local transportation projects, particularly in rural-bush areas. It is this local aspect of politics that undermines, in large part, the development of a real statewide consensus on a long-range transportation plan as opposed to the theoretical consensus represented in the *Let's Get Moving 2030* plan. Regionalism has a similar effect, where regional coalitions of legislators work to get projects funded for their areas, such as new ferries in coastal communities and improved airports and access roads in urban Alaska. As in many other aspects of Alaska politics, these regional political alliances often produce urban versus rural-bush conflict, particularly over the high cost of providing transportation infrastructure and services to rural-bush communities compared with urban Alaska. This conflict is exacerbated when rural-bush communities contribute nothing to help fund these projects. In this regard, Alaska's IGR transportation politics and policy are in contrast to most other states.

Two other characteristics also throw light on Alaska transportation politics and policy and in some ways show the differences between Alaska and other states. These are fiscal conservatism and a political culture of pragmatic dependent individualism. At least through 2015, as in many other areas of Alaska's political economy, the perpetuation of the myth of individualism makes fiscal conservatism possible. Paradoxically, it does so by the political pragmatism represented by subsidies from other states made possible by federal funding transfers. This interrelationship of dependent individualism and fiscal conservatism is deeply ingrained in the Alaska political psyche and is very hard to change.

But perhaps the most significant element of Alaska's politics that affects the political economy of transportation is, at least through early 2016, the state's inability to develop a long-range fiscal plan and to provide a long-term plan for funding major services like education, corrections, health and social services, and transportation. A long-range fiscal plan is particularly important, perhaps more than for most states, because of Alaska's major dependence on federal funds, and Alaska's dependence on such a volatile revenue source as oil. Despite its major financial resources (particularly the Permanent Fund) and inability hitherto to develop such a plan, the political reality is that no plan is likely to be forthcoming without a major economic and financial disaster like the one Alaska appeared to face in 2016. And because transportation is a largely low-profile policy area and most Alaskans take the system for granted most of the time, it is one of the least likely services for the public and politicians to push for a long-range funding plan. In the long run and perhaps in the near future, this funding shortcoming could seriously reduce the quality of life of both rural-bush and urban Alaskans. Even for the 80 percent of Alaskans who live in urban areas, the assumption that there will be a well-maintained highway to take them where they want to go may soon need some rethinking.

ENDNOTES

[1] The chapter authors acknowledge the information provided in several interviews and discussions with Jeff Ottesen of the Alaska Department of Transportation and Public Facilities.

[2] Besides Box 28.2, other statements in this chapter by Lois Epstein are taken from two interviews with her by Anthony Nakazawa and Clive Thomas conducted in June 2008 when she was director of the nonprofit Alaska Transportation Priorities Project and two pamphlets authored by her, *Easy to Start, Impossible to Finish, Recommendations for Action* (Anchorage: The Alaska Transportation Priorities Project, February 2010), and *Easy to Start, Impossible to Finish II, Recommendations for Action* (Anchorage: The Wilderness Society, March 2012).

[3] This chapter draws in part on W. Keith Gerken and Clive S. Thomas, "Transportation: State Agency Management of a Federal Endowment," in *Alaska Public Policy Issues: Background and Perspectives*, ed. Clive S. Thomas (Juneau: Denali Press, 1999). Background on comparisons with other states draws, in part, on Martin Saiz and Susan E. Clarke, "Economic Development and Infrastructure Policy," in *Politics in the American States: A Comparative Analysis*, eds., Virginia Gray, Russell L. Hanson, and Thad Kousser, 10th ed. (Washington, D.C.: Congressional Quarterly Press, 2013).

[4] The background on the development of the U.S. transportation system after 1920 draws on Martin H. Ross, Bruce E. Seely, and Paul F. Barrett, *The Best Transportation System in the World: Railroads, Trucks, Airlines, and American Public Policy in the Twentieth Century* (Columbus: Ohio State University Press, 2006); and Stephen B. Goddard, *Getting There: The Epic Struggle Between Road and Rail in the American Century* (New York: Basic Books, 1994).

[5] For the shortcomings of Alaska local government system, see Chapter 18, particularly Sections 4 and 5.

[6] See Gunnar Knapp, "Four Alaska Innovations," a presentation to the Board of Directors of the Federal Reserve Bank of San Francisco and its Seattle Branch, Anchorage, July 11, 2007.

[7] In 2010, according to the National Highway Traffic Safety Administration, Alaska had 56 deaths or 1.17 per 100 million miles traveled (the figures used to calculate road deaths nationwide and among states). The national average was 1.1 (or a total of 32,885), with California at 0.84 (2,720 deaths), and Wyoming at 1.66 (155 deaths). See National Highway Traffic Safety Administration, *Traffic Safety Facts 2010 Data*, at http://www-nrd.nhtsa.dot.gov/Pubs/811630.pdf.

[8] See the Alaska Railroad website, at http://www.alaskarailroad.com/corporate/; and Erica Martinson, "What Alaska gets out of the new federal transportation bill," *Alaska Dispatch News*, December 4, 2015.

[9] Rosemarie Alexander, "Alaska Airports Are Key Drivers of the State's Economy and an Area for Growth," *Morning Edition*, KTOO-FM (Juneau Public Radio), November 2, 2010; and the Ted Stevens Anchorage International Airport website, at http://dot.alaska.gov/anc/.

[10] National Highway Traffic Safety Administration, *Traffic Safety Facts 2010 Data.*

[11] Ralph Nader, *Unsafe at Any Speed: The Designed-In Dangers of the American Automobile* (New York: Grossman Publishers, 1965).

[12] National Highway Traffic Safety Administration, *Traffic Safety Facts 2010 Data.*

[13] The World Bank, *Road Sector Gasoline Fuel Consumption Per Capita*, at http://data.worldbank.org/indicator/IS.ROD.SGAS.PC?page=6; U.S. Energy Information Administration, *Energy in Brief*, at http://www.eia.gov/energy_in_brief/article/major_energy_sources_and_users.cfm; and U.S. Energy Information Administration, *Motor Vehicle Mileage, Fuel Consumption, and Fuel Economy, Selected Years, 1949–2010*, at www.eia.gov/totalenergy/data/annual/pdf/sec2_25.pdf.

[14] For the details on the most recent federal plan for its lands, see *Alaska Federal Lands Long Range Transportation Plan, Final Report September 2012* (Washington, D.C.: U.S. Department of Transportation, 2012), at http://www.blm.gov/pgdata/etc/medialib/blm/ak/aktest/planning/Transportation_Planning.Par.88739.File.dat/Alaska%20Federal%20Lands%20LRTP.pdf.

[15] See the Anchorage Metropolitan Area Transportation Solutions (AMATS) website, at www.muni.org/departments/ocpd/planning/amats/pages/default.aspx; and the Fairbanks Metropolitan Area Transportation Study (FMATS) website, at http://fmats.us/.

[16] Saiz and Clarke, "Economic Development and Infrastructure Policy," 511.

[17] See Chapter 3, Section 1, esp. Box 3.3.

[18] Rob Stapleton, "Alaska Essential Air Service Tangled in Political Turbulence," *Alaska Dispatch*, February 4, 2011.

[19] Rosemarie Alexander, "Still Time to Comment on STIP," *Morning Edition*, KTOO-FM (Juneau public radio), September 11, 2011; and Rosemarie Alexander, "STIP Comments Due Wednesday," *Morning Edition*, KTOO-FM, October 20, 2013.

[20] See Rosemarie Alexander, "STIP Comments Due Wednesday"; and the Alaska University Transportation Center, University of Alaska Fairbanks, at http://ine.uaf.edu/autc/about/.

[21] Various federal and state statistics as well as private figures, such as those from the private tax watchdog group, the Institute on Taxation and Economic Policy, often calculate transportation receipts and funding in different ways, though usually arriving at similar figures. For instance, the Alaska Office of Management and Budget (OMB) and the Alaska DOT often have different figures for projects. This is due, in part, to OMB being concerned with fiscal years (FY) and the DOT with the cost over the life of a project, which is often several years. However, as our purpose is to provide the basics of funding for understanding the nation's and Alaska's current transportation funding and future challenges, minor differences in statistics do not affect the general points we make.

[22] Information on general obligation bonds is drawn from the Alaska Division of Elections website, at http://www.elections.alaska.gov/ei_return.php; and from "Transportation: Alaska," on the Ballotpedia website, at http://ballotpedia.org/wiki/index.php/Category:Transportation,_Alaska.

[23] *Financing Transportation in the 21st Century*, a report of the Intergovernmental Forum on Transportation Finance, January 2008, at www.napawash.org/wp-content/uploads/2008/08-16.pdf.

[24] Gerken and Thomas, "Transportation: State Agency Management of a Federal Endowment."

[25] Background on both bridge projects and their status as of December 2015 was based, in part, on a synthesis of the following sources: Becky Bohrer, "State Studying Ways to Link Ketchikan, Gravina Island," Associated Press, reprinted in the *Juneau Empire*, July 1, 2013; Pat Forgey, "New Plans Confirm Palin's 2007 Decision to Scrap Ketchikan's 'Bridge to Nowhere,'" *Alaska Dispatch*, August

9, 2013; Jerzy Shedlock and Laura Andrews, "Alaska's 'Bridge to Nowhere' Remains Alive in State Legislature, for Now," *Alaska Dispatch*, April 12, 2013; Richard Mauer, "Knik Arm Bridge Agency to Review Data Behind Projections," *Anchorage Daily News*, June 13, 2013; Associated Press, "State Proceeding with Demolition for Knik Bridge," July 10, 2014; Liz Ruskin, "All Hope for Knik Bridge Rides on Federal Decision," *Alaska News Nightly*, Alaska Public Radio Network (APRN), June 24, 2014; Suzanne Caldwell, "Knik Arm Crossing Rolls Out New Studies, Hopes for Financing," *Alaska Dispatch News,* December 8, 2014; and Nathaniel Herz, "Walker Orders New Spending on Alaska Megaprojects Stopped," *Alaska Dispatch News*, December 27, 2014.

[26] Dan Joling, "New estimate for Ketchikan bridge up 37 percent," Associated Press, published in the *Juneau Empire*, February 2, 2005.

[27] "Ex-governor Has Alternative to 'Bridge to Nowhere': a Tunnel," *Anchorage Daily News*, June 17, 2012; and Pat Forgey, "Alaska 'bridge to nowhere' is no more as state chooses ferry for Ketchikan," *Alaska Dispatch News*, October 22, 2015.

[28] Epstein, "Easy to Start, Impossible to Finish," 2010, and "Easy to Start, Impossible to Finish II," 2012 (the 2012 position paper was written for The Wilderness Society).

[29] Andrew Wellner, "Bridge to Somewhere?" *Mat-Su Valley Frontiersman*, December 21, 2010; and "Our View: No crossing" editorial, *Anchorage Daily News*, April 12, 2009.

[30] OECD (Organisation for Economic Cooperation and Development), *Spending on Transport Infrastructure 1995–2011: Trends, Policies, Data*, at www.internationaltransportforum.org/Pub/pdf/13SpendingTrends.pdf.

[31] Saiz and Clarke, "Economic Development and Infrastructure Policy," 510.

[32] Matt Kreamer and Rick Lund, "Skagit Bridge Collapse: Times Designer and His iPhone Provide First Images," *Seattle Times*, May 24, 2013; and Associated Press, "Collapsed I-5 Skagit Bridge Opens Wednesday," *Seattle Times*, June 18, 2013.

[33] Campbell Robertson, "Obama, Under Health Care Cloud, Hits the Road to Push New Public Works," *New York Times*, November 8, 2013.

[34] Information on the FAST Act draws on the following sources: Keith Laing,, "Dem senator slams 'irresponsible' $305B highway bill," *The Hill*, December 1, 2015; Keith Laing, "Obama signs $305B highway bill," *The Hill*, December 4, 2015; David M. Herszenhorn, "Bipartisan Talks Yield $300 Billion Highway Bill," *New York Times*, December 1, 2015; U.S. Department of Transportation, 2015. "The Fixing America's Surface Transportation Act or "FAST Act"—See more at: https://www.transportation.gov/fastact#sthash.JOk16b20.dpuf; https://www.transportation.gov/fastact; and The Surface Transportation Reauthorization and Reform Act of 2015 at, http://transportation.house.gov/strr-act/.

[35] Institute on Taxation and Economic Policy (ITEP), "A Federal Gas Tax for the Future," at www.itep.org/pdf/fedgastax0913.pdf.

[36] Sarah Puro, the Congressional Budget Office, "Statement for the Record: Status of the Highway Trust Fund," at www.cbo.gov/sites/default/files/cbofiles/attachments/44093-HighwayTrustFund.pdf.

[37] Carol Wolf, "U.S. Highway Trust Fund Faces Insolvency Next Year, CBO Says," *BloombergBusinessweek*, February 1, 2012, at www.businessweek.com/news/2012-02-01/u-s-highway-trust-fund-faces-insolvency-next-year-cbo-says.html.

[38] Brian Naylor, "700,000 Jobs are at Stake if the Highway Trust Fund Goes Broke," *Morning Edition*, National Public Radio (NPR), May 15, 2014.

[39] Information on the problems with the Federal Highway Trust Fund and possible solutions draws in part on ITEP's, "A Federal Gas Tax for the Future."

[40] *Ibid.*, 1.

[41] *Ibid.*

[42] See Intergovernmental Forum on Transportation Finance, "Financing Transportation in the 21st Century: An Intergovernmental Perspective,," January 2008, Washington, D.C., at http://www.ncsl.org/print/standcomm/sctran/NAPAreport0108.pdf.

[43] "Obama Sends Congress $302B Transportation Bill," April 2014, at http://thehill.com/policy/transportation/204675-obama-sends-congress-302b-transportation-bill; "DOT Sends 6-year, $478 Billion Grow America Act to Congress," at www.ttnews.com/articles/basetemplate.aspx?storyid=37822; U.S. Department of Transportation, "GROW AMERICA: An Overview," at www.dot.gov/grow-america/fact-sheets/overview; "Obama's Highway Plan Not Expected to Go Far but Funding Idea Might," at www.joc.com/regulation-policy/transportation-policy/us-transportation-policy/obama%E2%80%99s-highway-spending-plan-not-expected-go-far-funding-proposal-might_20150202.html; and "Boxer-Paul Invest in Transportation Act 2015," at www.boxer.senate.gov/press/related/BoxerPaulWhitePaper012915.pdf.

[44] Ashley Halsey III, "Congress moves a step closer to passing transportation bill," *New York Times*, November 18, 2015; and Infrastructure Report Card, 2015 FAST Act summary part one: The Funding, retrieved on December 9, 2015, at http://www.infrastructurereportcard.org/asce-news/fast-act-summary-part-one-the-funding/.

[45] Erica Martinson, "Murkowski lands key role in transpiration funding fight," *Alaska Dispatch News*, November 15, 2015.

[46] American Petroleum Institute, 2015, "State Motor Fuel Taxes: Notes Summary for Rates Effective 4/01/15," at www.api.org/~/media/files/statistics/state-motor-fuel-excise-tax-update-apr-2015.pdf. In 2015-2016 there was a proposal by Governor Walker to increase the Alaska gas tax from 8 cents to 16 cents a gallon.

[47] Statistics on increased vehicle efficiency and the use of energy by the transportation industry are taken from: The American Council for an Energy Efficient Economy, "Car and Light Truck Fuel Economy," at http://aceee.org/topics/car-and-light-truck-fuel-economy; U.S. Energy Information Administration, *Motor Vehicle Mileage, Fuel Consumption, and Fuel Economy, Selected Years, 1949–2010*, at www.eia.gov/totalenergy/data/annual/pdf/sec2_25.pdf; U.S. Energy Information Administration, *Energy in Brief*, at www.eia.gov/energy_in_brief/article/major_energy_sources_and_users.cfm; and The World Bank, *Road Sector Gasoline Fuel Consumption per Capita*, at http://data.worldbank.org/indicator/IS.ROD.SGAS.PC?page=6.

[48] The American Council for an Energy Efficient Economy, 2013, "Topics: Transportation System Efficiency," at http://aceee.org/topics/transportation-system-efficiency.

[49] ICF International, February 2008, *The Broader Connection between Public Transportation, Energy Conservation and Greenhouse Gas Reduction*, at www.apta.com/resources/reportsandpublications/Documents/land_use.pdf.

[50] Alaska's sole U.S. Representative, Don Young, was a major force in the passage of the SAFETEA-LU legislation and dedicated the bill to his wife Lu.

[51] Carl Hulse, "Senate Won't Allow Earmarks in Spending Bills," *New York Times*, February 1, 2011; and Patti Epler, "Murkowski Wants Alaska Prepared for 'World without Earmarks,'" *Alaska Dispatch*, February 24, 2011.

[52] Ben Casselman, "Alaska would rather go broke than pay taxes," FiveThirtyEight Economics, November 20, 2015, at http://fivethirtyeight.com/features/alaska-would-rather-go-broke-than-pay-taxes/.

[53] OECD, *Spending on Transport Infrastructure 1995–2011*.

[54] The discussion of *Let's Get Moving 2030* draws on the latest version of the plan on the DOT website, at http://www.dot.alaska.gov/stwdplng/areaplans/2030/index.shtml.

★ PART VI ★

Politics, Issues, Policies, and Political Power in Alaska: Past, Present, and Future Perspectives

About Part VI

The two chapters in this final part of the book draw on the information presented in the previous twenty-eight chapters to assess how Alaska's political and governmental system has performed and what its future prospects might be regarding politics, policy, and political power relationships. The chapters are an integrated pair, so more will be gained from Chapter 30 if Chapter 29 is read first.

Chapter 29 assesses the operation and performance of the state's political and policy-making process past and present. It draws several conclusions regarding the strengths and weaknesses of the Alaska political system, utilizing the concepts of political capacity and political development. Then, Chapter 30 looks at the future, including an assessment of the prospects for reform in some key areas of Alaska government and policy. We also speculate about the state's political future and what may and may not develop over the coming decades.

As the focus of these two concluding chapters is reflective, interpretative, and speculative, and less focused on presenting new information, their organizational approach is different from most chapters in the book. This is particularly the case with Chapter 30. The details are explained in the introduction to each chapter.

★ CHAPTER 29 ★

Assessing the Past and Present Performance of Alaska's Political and Governmental System

Clive S. Thomas and Laura C. Savatgy

On January 3, 2009, Alaska celebrated its fiftieth anniversary as a state. This is a short history compared with most states, including many in the American West (Oregon, for example, celebrated its one hundred fiftieth anniversary that same year). The years since statehood have seen major developments, and in many ways Alaska is a much different place today than it was in 1959. Especially relevant for this chapter is that Alaska has undergone various aspects of political development and, presumably, is now much more in control of its own affairs than when it transitioned from a territory to a state.

The purpose of this chapter is to ask the question of how well has Alaska's political, policy-making, and governmental system performed regarding the challenges, problems, and issues that the state has faced since statehood. This raises corollary questions. How has Alaska met its major challenges and dealt with them, if at all? Has it taken advantage of the various opportunities available to it? Has Alaska's model constitution been paralleled by the development of a model governmental system and innovative approaches to politics and policy making, or has it acted in traditional political ways?

This chapter argues that, for the most part, Alaska has not performed as well as it could have, and in many ways has not taken advantage of unique opportunities. As a consequence, many ongoing problems and issues have not been dealt with effectively. We refer to this as the *unfulfilled perspective* in assessing Alaska's political system past and present. There is, however, another perspective on Alaska's political development (or lack thereof) that is referred to as the *pragmatic perspective*, which we also cover. In explaining both perspectives, the twelve characteristics of Alaska politics identified in Chapter 2 will become evident and will enlighten each perspective.

Much of the analysis in this chapter is based on the relationship between political capacity (and the related concepts of policy and governmental capacity) and political development. We begin by explaining this relationship. Then we assess the performance of the Alaska political and governmental systems. Next we devote a section to assessing political leadership in Alaska over the years and another to how the state's political image in the rest of the nation has or has not affected Alaska's political flexibility.[1]

1. THE LINK BETWEEN POLITICAL, POLICY, AND GOVERNMENTAL CAPACITY AND POLITICAL DEVELOPMENT

At various places in the book we have used the concepts of political, policy, and governmental capacity to illustrate various specific relationships between politics, government, and policy making.[2] Here we are concerned with the broader relationship between political capacity and political development as a way to understand the general performance of Alaska's political and governmental systems over the years since statehood.

A Recap on Political, Policy, and Governmental Capacity

While the concepts of political, policy, and governmental capacity are slightly different in what they encompass, there is overlap among them. All three relate to the extent to which a political system (nation, state, city, school district, and so on) is able to meet the demands placed upon it—particularly its success in resolving major issues, policy conflicts, and other problems, and enforcing solutions to them.

More specifically, *political capacity* refers to the effectiveness, or lack thereof, of the political system in general to deal with issues and problems. *Policy capacity* is the effectiveness of the policy process to address particular problems and issues as they arise. And *governmental capacity* refers to the ability of government to effectively run the day-to-day operations of government and to enforce policies embodied in laws and regulations addressing particular problems and issues. In this chapter, we use the term *political capacity* to cover all three elements of capacity and use policy and governmental capacity only when dealing with one of these elements specifically.

Political capacity is a function of the existence of a wide range of resources available to governments, coupled with both the willingness and ability to use them. These resources include:

- The nature and strength of the economy and the government's ability to raise revenue;
- Institutional factors, such as the constitutional and legal relationship of the executive and legislature;
- The strength or weakness of political parties and the extent of the influence of interest groups;

- Political resources, such as public support, political acumen, political leadership, jurisdictional control over a situation, and political power; and
- The technical expertise of elected and appointed officials, as well as physical assets and infrastructure (such as computers, communications systems, and buildings) available to the government for providing various services.

The extent of these elements in combination determines not only the level of a government's political capacity to deal with present demands made upon it, but also its ability to adapt to changing circumstances, crises, and emergencies, and to meet the demands of the future.

The mere existence of these resources does not increase political capacity, however. They have to be mobilized to deal with issues and problems. Some political jurisdictions, like Sweden, are well known for their ability to turn these resources into political capacity and, in turn, into policy and governmental effectiveness. But sometimes these resources cannot be mobilized, either because circumstances constrain or negate their use or because policy makers choose not to deploy them. The result is that political capacity is undermined and government is less effective. This is the case with many African countries, such as Nigeria and Zimbabwe.

Furthermore, the existence of a political issue is one thing. It is quite another whether or not it will be dealt with by government and, if it is, how successfully. However urgent, conflict-ridden, high-profile, or far-reaching a public problem might be, it will be dealt with only to the extent that a society and its government have the political capacity to do so. And, like any organization—a business, a university, a club, and so on—all governments have a limited capacity. In some cases this capacity may be adequate to solve some problems; in other cases it may be woefully inadequate.

Political Development

In the broadest sense, political development is the process by which political systems and their governments in a society grow from relatively simple structures into more complex ones. The political power system of a society is manifested in various characteristics of the political system, such as institutions (lawmaking bodies, executives, political parties, and so on) as well as attitudes and values (as expressed in political culture and political ideology). Over time, political societies have developed from small groupings and tribes to today's complex political systems from democracies like the United States and Norway to authoritarian regimes like Iran and North Korea. Political development is not always linear or positively progressive in terms of increasing political capacity and meeting the needs of its citizens. Some societies experience periods of political decline and decay, while a few suffer terminal political breakdown, like the former Soviet Union.

There are several academic perspectives on political development, including Marxist, political economy, and political sociology. The details of these are not necessary to explain here. Our focus is more general and practical and focuses on the way that political development generally enhances the government's capacity to mobilize and allocate resources, to process policy demands, and to implement and enforce policies that have been enacted. Enhanced capacity, in turn, generally aids in problem solving by adapting to economic, social, and political changes in order to achieve short- and long-term objectives for society. Moreover, as indicated above, political development does not just include institutional adaptation but also changes in attitudes, particularly in political culture.

Because it had been a territory of the United States for many years, Alaska was already at an advanced level of political development when it became a state in 1959. Given this level of development and given its relatively short history as a state, we cannot expect monumental leaps in political development. Change will come, if at all, in the form of small increments. Nevertheless, statehood brought Alaskans more control over their political destiny.

The Link between Political Capacity and Political Development

The close link between political capacity and political development is similar to the link between political socialization and political culture. The political culture of an individual, state, region, or nation is shaped by, and develops through, the processes of political socialization. Likewise, political capacity is largely a product of political development. Events affect political development and the political capacity of a government. That is certainly true for major events such as revolutions and wars, the writing of a new constitution, and major reforms, such as the privatization of government-owned services and industries. But it is also true, though less discernible, for incremental changes like the decline of political parties and the expansion in interest-group activity.

One final point in this review of political capacity and political development is important. Efficiency and effectiveness in politics and government are related but are often far from identical. In Chapter 12 on the role of government, we pointed out that in business, *efficiency* (getting the maximum output for the minimum expenditure of resources) is closely related to *effectiveness* (achieving a stated goal). This is because in a business the two are subject to the same criteria—the extent to which the company achieves its over-riding purpose of making a profit and increasing financial stability and growth. In government there are often no such simple criteria for judging both efficiency and effectiveness simultaneously. There are several reasons for this. The main one is that government does not exist to make a profit but to serve the needs of society. As a result, what may be politically effective in meeting those needs is not always economically efficient.[3]

2. THE ALASKA LIFESTYLE AND THE STATE'S POLITICAL CAPACITY

Looking back over the years since statehood, there is no doubt that, as across the nation, Alaska and its people are much better off on most fronts in the second decade of the twenty-first century than they were in 1959. In 1959, Alaska's economic future was shaky at best. There was no Prudhoe Bay oil bonanza, no Permanent Fund, no Alaska Owner State, and very little state economic aid to Alaskans. Control of Alaska's resources was largely dominated by both the federal government and Outside private businesses. The education system, both K–12 and the university, was rudimentary. Infrastructure was very basic. Alaska Natives were peripheral to state politics, and there was no Alaska Native Claims Settlement Act.

To be sure, some might dispute whether the progress that has taken place has been beneficial. The boom resulting from the building of the trans-Alaska pipeline brought in its wake increased crime and many social problems. The massive expansion in state spending and state programs may have exacerbated economic problems during downturns in the economy and intensified political conflicts when oil prices dropped and money was relatively scarce. And some would argue that the impact of development since statehood on the Native community has not been entirely positive. Nevertheless, those who were in Alaska in 1959, including many Alaska Natives, in most cases likely prefer to live in the Alaska of today, with its enhanced quality of life, than the place they knew at statehood.

The state has certainly made advances in economic strength, infrastructure, education, and social programs, and has much more control over its resources, among many other advances. But the record of its political and governmental system is mixed in terms of its ability to deal with the public policy issues that confront it. To put this another way, the state has experienced considerable political development, and its political capacity has increased in some ways, particularly its technical capacity and to some extent its institutional capacity. But the political elements of that capacity, particularly the ability to reach compromise and to put the state before regional, community, and other special interests, have changed very little. Several chapters in the book have questioned the effectiveness, responsiveness, and adaptability of the state government to deal with the demands made upon it by its citizens. These include economic and fiscal issues, corrections problems, fisheries issues, subsistence, and aspects of Native sovereignty, to name a few. These questions raise concerns about the adequacy of the political and governmental machinery in the state. The lack of political capacity has little to do with individual politicians. Rather, it is the result of institutional factors and certain developments independent of personalities and, for the most part, of specific political philosophies or ideologies.

So while state and local governments have added much to the quality of life of Alaskans since statehood, particularly in the economic sphere, there remain severe constraints on the state's political capacity. The irony, however, is that today Alaska has the potential to exert more political control over its own affairs than ever before.[4] So what is the problem, and is there a solution?

3. THE PROBLEM OF POLITICAL CAPACITY: IN GENERAL AND FOR ALASKA

Alaska is not alone among nations, states, and localities in lacking the capacity to deal with issues that face it. This is a worldwide phenomenon. However, it is particularly a problem with governments in the United States, including state governments, because the institutional structure of government, with its checks and balances, was purposely designed to inhibit close coordination between the branches, particularly control of the legislature by the executive. This separation of powers often inhibits cooperation, in contrast to the integration of executives and legislatures in parliamentary systems. Furthermore, the individualistic, often anti-government, attitudes in the United States give less leeway for government to act on a range of issues, particularly social issues.

Because of a confluence of circumstances, Alaska is lacking political capacity in several ways. The sources of these constraints are both external and internal.

External or Outside Constraints

While some authors elsewhere in the book have argued that external influences on the state do not make Alaska a colony in the traditional sense of the term, they do reduce its political flexibility.[5] There are three major sources of external constraints. First is the importance of the federal government in Alaska and the intergovernmental nature of key and high-profile issues, such as land, natural resources, and environmental policy making. Second, and a related point, Lower 48 interests have influence in Alaska because of its image as the Last Frontier and its abundance of natural resources, particularly oil. Third, Alaska is very much dependent on world economic forces and multinational corporations for the health of its economy, particularly the price of oil, over which it has no control.

The other forty-nine states also have their political capacity limited by external factors, particularly federal authority. And Alaska's power position relative to the federal government is much stronger than it was in the early years of statehood before oil revenues gave the state some financial independence. But with over 55 percent of Alaska's land in federal ownership, federal control over much of the state's fisheries, the state's dependence on federal funds, plus the significance of the Last Frontier image and the natural resource extraction economy, Outside interests limit Alaska's control over its own affairs more than is the case in most states.

Internal Constraints

Added to these Outside influences are several internal constraints. One major limitation is the lack of any strong coordinating influence in state government to develop and implement long-term policies to deal with many of the state's problems. While the governor is strong within the executive branch, the governor does not control the legislature. So with relatively weak political parties, coupled with strong regionalism, stand-offs between the governor and the legislature tend to result in ad hoc, crisis-oriented policy making.

Second, the anti-government, anti-tax attitude of many Alaskans has restricted government from dealing with many problems because of a lack of funds or a lack of willingness by politicians to spend available resources, like Permanent Fund earnings. The focus has been on distributing existing revenues, not on raising revenues or perhaps using Permanent Fund earnings to meet a desirable level of expenditure. In this regard, a major constraint on Alaska's political capacity is one self-imposed by Alaskans themselves. With Permanent Fund earnings and the option to re-impose a state income tax and perhaps enact a statewide sales tax, the state could have many more options. This would go a long way in getting Alaska out from under external influences, particularly the vicissitudes of world oil and other natural resource prices and the state's great dependence on the federal government for funds. Up until 2015, however, Alaskans and their politicians have chosen not to do this, thus undermining their ability to have more control over their own affairs.

Third, there is a rift in the population, often with an undercurrent of resentment, which often pits urban and rural-bush residents against each other. A major source of this resentment is the perception by some urban residents that a disproportionately high amount of state revenues goes to rural-bush areas, especially education funds. Another significant element of this non-Native versus Native conflict results from a clash of cultures, much misunderstanding, a strong belief in certain individual rights such as subsistence, and some racism among non-Natives and Natives alike.

To a large extent these internal constraints on political capacity are a result of Alaska's development and its growing and diversifying population. As McBeath and Morehouse pointed out in the early 1990s, this has brought a version of hyperpluralism—a major increase in the number of competing interests—to Alaska politics.[6] To the extent that there was consensus on issues in the past, it was based partly on the drive for statehood but also, and perhaps mainly, because far fewer interests, including minimal Alaska Native and environmental interests, were involved in the political process. Development interests tended to dominate unchallenged as the new state fought to establish itself. As in the rest of the nation, from the late 1960s onward there was a major expansion in the number and types of interests seeking a voice in Alaska policy making. The Alaska political playing field became crowded. Values, often diametrically opposed ones, clashed, and when these conflicts were combined with institutional fragmentation, the ability of the government to resolve some issues was greatly reduced.

Certainly, to varying degrees other states also manifest these internal problems with political capacity. The paradox is that in Alaska, as well as in other states and at the national level, increased representation and the expansion of democracy has, in many cases, reduced the capacity of government to act and deal with problems. This is because increased competition between groups can sometimes result in deadlock. The situation is particularly acute in Alaska, however, especially with the political limitations on raising revenue and the nature of its urban versus rural-bush conflict. These are two elements of Alaska's uniqueness and development that have had more negative than positive consequences.

Furthermore, the much-touted fact that Alaska has a friends and neighbors political system, where the average citizen has easy access to policy makers, also exacerbates the problem of political capacity even though, in some ways, it enhances representation. This is because, in the absence of strong coordinating influences on government, it takes only a few influential people or one or two powerful interests to defeat a policy proposal.

4. THE RAMIFICATIONS OF CONSTRAINTS ON ALASKA POLITICAL CAPACITY: THE UNFULFILLED PERSPECTIVE

Clearly, some of the constraints on Alaska's political capacity are beyond its control to affect, such as world oil prices. In other cases, such as its relationship with, and dependence on, the federal government and the influence of Lower 48 interest groups, it has very limited political capacity. In others, particularly those related to budgetary and fiscal matters, many social programs, urban versus rural-bush issues, and planning, the state has considerable political capacity.

Nevertheless, the combination of Outside and internal constraints results in an Alaska policy-making process that, for the most part, deals with problems on an ad hoc basis, making it very difficult to plan for future eventualities, and where it takes a major crisis to bring about policy change. In terms of individual policy areas, an external influence like world oil prices places major constraints on predicting future revenues. Regarding the budget, given the internal constraints of anti-tax and anti-government attitudes plus the reluctance so far to consider using Permanent Fund earnings, the state's options to deal with economic crises and revenue shortfalls have been extremely limited. Plus, in some instances, these constraints on political capacity actually undermine or preclude compromise—the essential element of dealing with a political problem. This is the case with the urban versus rural-bush conflict over subsistence and with adequately funding many services in rural-bush areas, although less obvious than the subsistence issue.

To put things in perspective, the argument is not that Alaska's state government is incapable of dealing with many issues. It can and does perform many of its responsibilities, including dealing with some problems with skill and effectiveness, such as reducing the effects of the closing of pulp mills in Southeast Alaska. Moreover, constraints on political capacity are not necessarily all bad for all Alaskans. In fact, as has been noted at many points in the book, for many groups and interests in the state, the inability of state government to deal with many problems is a distinct advantage. These include those who do not want to see a rural preference for subsistence users and those opposed to opening the Arctic National Wildlife Refuge (ANWR) for oil and gas exploration.

On many crucial issues, however, the state's lack of capacity seriously undermines its effectiveness. Part of the state's political capacity problem is the choice on the part of politicians not to act when they could choose to do so. One major decision not to act has been on the issue of fiscal planning and making provision for future revenue shortfalls through taxation and other sources of revenue. This political choice is partly driven by Alaska's populist sentiments and politicians' fear of defeat at the polls. Shying away from such tough and potentially unpopular decisions was easy when Alaska was awash in new oil revenues from Prudhoe Bay. The legislature understandably used its excess wealth to attempt to solve many problems with money rather than negotiating long-term solutions. Once this pattern was established it has been hard to break, even in hard times. So, as noted above, the state has largely foregone the opportunity to increase its political capacity by planning and securing more stable revenue sources. Alaska politicians have so far not taken the opportunity to establish as an aspect of Alaska politics that responsible policy making should take precedence over populist demands.

Other aspects of the lack of political capacity result from deep-rooted conflicts. This situation is growing more acute as the population increases and diversifies and as values change. Two good examples are the state's losing control over fish and game management on federal lands in 1990 because it could not solve the subsistence issue, as well as conflicts over the environment and fisheries policies.[7] The smaller, more homogeneous Alaska population of the past was probably never truly united on any issue, but it was still less conflict-ridden, and thus political consensus and compromise were easier to secure.

Precisely because many aspects of political capacity are beyond the state's control, the unfulfilled perspective argues that Alaska should take full advantage of those aspects where it does have such capacity. With a precarious natural resource economy and so many other factors beyond its control, Alaska needs to use its available resources, particularly its oil wealth, to plan and insulate itself from potential adverse future economic and political developments. It is certainly true that since statehood, something has always turned up to pull Alaska out of a crisis—but this may not be the case in the future.

5. THE RAMIFICATIONS OF CONSTRAINTS ON ALASKA POLITICAL CAPACITY: THE PRAGMATIC PERSPECTIVE

The unfulfilled perspective on the consequences of Alaska's limited political capacity is not the only viewpoint. A contrary one, the pragmatic perspective, sees Alaska's political development and its resulting political capacity as a product of reality. This perspective views the unfulfilled perspective as unrealistic and somewhat idealistic regarding what is politically feasible because it ignores Alaska's deep-rooted political culture. The pragmatists do not see the state's inability to act on many policy issues as negative or as bad public policy, but view it positively. They see inaction as an expression of the democratic will of Alaskans on such issues as the incomplete local government system and public opposition, at least as of early 2016, to using the Permanent Fund earnings to fund government services. This pragmatic view argues that when specific policies are needed to deal with problems, such as serious long-term revenue shortages, the public will press their elected officials to seek a solution to the problem. In the pragmatists' view, there is nothing to be gained from agonizing over these issues in the meantime. In fact, this perspective appears to a good predictor of public attitudes. With revenues down because of the drop in oil prices beginning in the summer of 2014 and showing no signs of recovery almost two years later, a poll conducted in August 2015 indicated that Alaskans would be willing to use some Permanent Fund earnings and consider new taxes rather than make major cuts in state services.[8]

Those who support the pragmatic perspective of doing only what is currently necessary obviously do not address reform on a wide range of issues. This is, in part, because they see reform as being much less necessary than the unfulfilled perspective claims. Moreover, this pragmatic perspective has had the political upper hand in the state, judging by the actions of the politicians whom Alaskans have elected over the years. As argued in Chapter 5 on political culture, this is largely because of Alaska's democratic and populist sentiments underpinned by a political culture of pragmatic dependent individualism.

The Future?

What the future holds for Alaska policy making regarding the interplay of the unfulfilled and pragmatic perspectives on Alaska's political capacity and how this interplay will shape the state's development, and particularly its political development, is open to question. Consideration of this is left to the next and final chapter of the book. Before we get to this future perspective, however, we briefly assess two other aspects of Alaska's political development and political capacity over the years. These are political leadership and Alaska's political image outside the state.

6. ALASKA AND POLITICAL LEADERSHIP—PAST AND PRESENT

As Chapter 1, Box 1.1, points out, leadership is not just equated with charisma and/or high-profile activities. In fact, political leadership is a more complex phenomenon than it appears. Often, effective leadership is far from public view, such as in brokering compromise that is essential to policy making in a democracy like Alaska. One thing about political leadership, however, is clear—the higher the quality of leadership in government, the higher is the government's political capacity and its ability to forge the compromise and consensus needed to achieve political or policy goals.[9]

Alaska has not had a leader of the charismatic quality of a Martin Luther King, Jr., a Ronald Reagan, or a Barack Obama. Her supporters might say that Sarah Palin comes close, but her time as governor was only two-and-a-half years, and since her resignation in 2009 her attention has been much more on national than Alaska issues. Nevertheless, although they may not meet many people's intuitive view of charismatic leadership, Alaska has had its share of leaders over the years, and not all of them are household names.

The late U.S. Senator Ted Stevens was clearly the most enduring political leader in Alaska, even if his personal style did not endear him to many in Alaska and Outside. His long tenure in Washington, D.C., enabled him to steer billions of dollars to Alaska and in so doing increase the state's political capacity. As for governors, Bill Egan, with his minor George Washington role in Alaska, should be singled out. Folksy Governor Jay Hammond, with his promotion of the Permanent Fund, and semi-visionary Walter Hickel, twice governor and U.S. Secretary of the Interior, should also be mentioned, as well as former Lieutenant Governor Fran Ulmer and the late House Speaker Ramona Barnes. All of these men and women brought different qualities of leadership to their elected positions. The Native community has also produced some skillful politicians and leaders, including former Senator John Sackett and the late Senators Frank Ferguson and Al Adams. And as Chapter 17 on the state court system points out, the late Chief Justice Jay Rabinowitz and former Administrative Director Arthur Snowden provided important leadership in developing the state's court system.

These and other Alaska leaders have contributed to enhancing the state's political capacity. Yet however good the leader may be, whether a U.S. Senator, a governor, legislator, or executive branch official, they all encounter constraints. Some of these constraints were identified as characteristics of Alaska politics in Chapter 2, including the strong contending powers of the branches of government, particularly the legislature and the executive, the state's pragmatic dependent individualistic political culture, relatively weak political parties, regionalism, and so on. As many a governor and legislator have discovered, these constraints can often undermine agendas and reduce political capacity. It will take a major and prolonged crisis, or a particularly charismatic and widely supported Alaska leader, to overcome these constraints to enact major reforms in the state.

7. THE OUTSIDE IMAGE OF ALASKA—PAST AND PRESENT

How does the image of Alaska on the Outside affect its political capacity? Three observations are important in this regard: recent national exposure of Alaska politicians and issues, the defeat of U.S. Senator Ted Stevens in November 2008, and Alaska's continuing image as the Last Frontier.

From 2006 through 2010, Alaska was in the national spotlight as never before, at least not since the *Exxon Valdez* oil spill of 1989. This national attention began with the FBI investigations and subsequent imprisonment of several Alaska state legislators, some related to dealings with the former oil service company VECO. Then in 2007, Citizens for Responsibility and Ethics in Washington (CREW), a national good government watchdog, named Alaska's three-member congressional delegation as among the twenty-two most corrupt in Congress. This was followed in 2008 by then-Governor Sarah Palin's nomination as the Republican candidate for U.S. vice president and the conviction of Ted Stevens on corruption charges (which were later dismissed). Next came the national attention that Alaska received in the midterm elections of 2010. With the exception of those across the nation who supported and continue to support Sarah Palin, most of this publicity was negative. It is unlikely, however, that this negative image or particular events of those four years have affected the political capacity of Alaska. This is likely the case, despite negative stories in tabloids, the media's questioning of Sarah Palin's abilities and qualifications for national office, and the exposure of Alaska's U.S. Senate candidate Joe Miller's questionable ethics.[10]

More significant for Alaska's present and future political capacity was the defeat of Ted Stevens after forty years in the U.S. Senate. Whether or not one supported Stevens, there is no doubt that he was one of the most powerful politicians in America and was very successful in securing federal funds for Alaska. His departure has affected Alaska's ability to secure such funds and reduce its financial options. With Stevens no longer around, the undercurrents of resentment at his success, and the often confrontational tactics he used to secure it may well result in a backlash of anti-Alaska attitudes in Congress.[11] Box 30.1 in the next chapter speculates about "Alaska after Ted Stevens."

A more long-term national image of Alaska affecting its political capacity is that of the Last Frontier. This image has politically frustrated those in the state who want more control over developing Alaska's resources. The wild and idyllic image of Alaska in many Americans' minds, and to some extent the reality of this image, has inhibited development on the 55 percent of the state in federal hands—largely through activities by liberal Democrats in Congress, the influential environmental lobby, and the built-in inertia of the federal separation of powers system. Because resource development is crucial to Alaska's short- and long-term economic survival, the Last Frontier image has considerably reduced the state's political capacity. This constraint is not likely to be removed any time soon. Even with both houses of Congress controlled by Republicans after the 2014 midterm elections, with a Democrat in the White House until early 2017 and the possibility of a Democrat after that, the likelihood of major oil and gas and other natural resource development of federal lands is unlikely in the near future.

8. CONCLUSION: FROM PAST AND PRESENT POLITICAL CAPACITY TO LIKELY FUTURE POLITICAL DEVELOPMENTS

In the introduction to this chapter we posed the question of how well has Alaska's political, policy-making, and governmental system performed regarding the challenges—problems and issues—that the state has faced since statehood. We have argued that the answer is a mixed one. In some ways the state has performed well but has generally not taken advantage of some opportunities available to it—particularly those provided by Alaska's status as an Owner State—to develop innovative solutions to problems and, in many instances, the state has acted in a traditional political way. As a consequence, a good argument can be made that, for the most part, Alaska's model constitution has not been paralleled by the development of a model political and governmental system and model approaches to policy making.

Internal constraints within Alaska, as much as those from Outside, undermine its political capacity to deal with many of the problems. Not dealing with these problems could spell disaster for the state. In this regard, an insightful statement made in the late 1970s in an examination of Alaska's development and before the era of the state's oil wealth, still rings true today:

> Perhaps the crucial issue for the state government and people of Alaska is the acceptance of responsibility for its own economic future. Historical precedents for the present Alaska situation are few and far removed. There is little in the past history of the state, and little in the history of other states, to provide guidance for the social choices available to Alaska. . . . In these circumstances it will be easy, though dangerous, for the state to proceed in a business-as-usual fashion and to make policy decisions with long-term implications on the basis of short-term considerations.[12]

Despite many years of oil wealth and the amassing of a $50 billion plus Permanent Fund, Alaska has not seriously confronted this central challenge presented by its unique circumstances. If Alaska met the challenge successfully it could solve many of the state's problems, not least its economic problems.

Given years of largely politics as usual and the current challenges that the state faces, what are some major reforms that the state might consider to increase its political capacity, and what are the prospects of these being enacted? It is to this topic that we turn in the final chapter of the book.

ENDNOTES

[1] Parts of this chapter draw upon Clive S. Thomas and Susan A. Burke, "Alaska Public Policy Issues and Policy-Making Process: Reflections and Prospects," in *Alaska Public Policy Issues: Background and Perspectives*, ed. Clive S. Thomas (Juneau, AK: Denali Press, 1999).

[2] See for example, Section 1 of Chapter 3 on public policy and Section 3 of Chapter 12 on the role of government.

[3] See Chapter 12, Section 3, for a review of this efficiency and effectiveness relationship.

[4] See Gerald A. McBeath and Thomas A. Morehouse, *Alaska Politics and Government* (Lincoln: University of Nebraska Press, 1994), "Conclusion," for an overview of the major advances made in Alaska's political capacity from statehood to the early 1990s. See also David T. Kresge, Thomas A. Morehouse, and George W. Rogers, *Issues in Alaska Development* (Seattle: University of Washington Press, 1977), esp. Chapter 8, "The Future State of Alaska: Prospects and Issues." Although written in 1977, this chapter is relevant today. It explains many of the key advances in the state's political capacity and explores many issues that remain central issues in contemporary Alaska, such as use of oil revenues and Permanent Fund earnings.

[5] See Chapter 1, Box 1.3, for a discussion of whether or not Alaska is a modern-day colony.

[6] McBeath and Morehouse, *Alaska Politics and Government*, 309.

[7] See the chapters in Part IV on natural resources, land, environmental, and fisheries policy for numerous examples of limitations on the state's capacity to solve issues.

[8] Alex DeMarban, "Poll: Alaskans prefer new revenue over deep cuts, including tapping Permanent Fund," *Alaska Dispatch News*, August 13, 2015.

[9] For more information on the concept of leadership and its study, see, Martha L. Cottam, *et al.*, *Political Psychology*, 3rd ed. (New York: Psychology Press, Taylor & Francis Group, 2015), Chapter 5, "The Study of Political Leaders."

[10] For a perspective on Sarah Palin's role in Alaska and American politics, see Clive S. Thomas, "The Sarah Palin Phenomenon: The Washington-Hollywood-Wall Street Syndrome in American Politics, and More . . ." *Issues in American Politics*, ed. John W. Dumbrell (London: Routledge/Taylor & Francis, 2013).

[11] For a perspective on Ted Stevens and the way the nation views Alaska, see Charles Homans, "State of Dependence: Ted Steven's Alaska Problem—and Ours," *The Washington Monthly* (Nov. 2007), 12–17.

[12] Kresge, Morehouse, and Rogers, *Issues in Alaska Development*, 212.

★ CHAPTER 30 ★

Choices and Prospects for Reform: A New Era or More of the Same?

Clive S. Thomas and Anthony T. Nakazawa

This final chapter builds on Chapter 29, which assesses the performance of Alaska's political and governmental system past and present. The approach in this final chapter, however, is more open-ended in two ways.

First, although the chapter has a theme, encapsulated in its title and particularly its subtitle, it does not come to a conclusion on this question—that is left to the reader. The phrase "more of the same" refers to "the unfulfilled perspective," presented in Chapter 29. This perspective is that, in many ways, Alaska's political, governmental, and public policy system has not been able to meet, or has chosen not to deal with, many of the challenges facing the state. Second, the chapter includes a minimum of analysis by the authors. What it does provide is a discussion of the pros and cons of various perspectives on Alaska's political future and possible reforms, leaving readers to draw their own conclusions.

1. ALASKA'S POLITICAL FUTURE AND POSSIBLE REFORMS

Attempts at political reform do not take place in a political vacuum or in some ivory tower. They occur in the contemporary political environment with all that has shaped it from the past and with the present personalities and power structure. Perhaps most importantly, the success of reforms (however "success" may be defined by the reformers) is linked to the choices and prospects for the future and particularly the political future of the state. There are many reasons for this linkage, but three are especially significant.

First, the future prospects for the success of the political system and the reforms that may be proposed depend primarily on the future of Alaska's economy, the relationship with and influence of external forces, and the alignment of political forces in the state. Is it likely that these factors will change in a major way and give Alaska options that it has not had before? Or will they change very little, if at all, straight-jacketing Alaska politically as in the past? Moreover, there is a range of possibilities for Alaska's future from the most positive to the most pessimistic. This range must also be taken into account in assessing the prospects for success.

A second link, related to the first one, is that, although we cannot predict the future and particularly unforeseen events, we can make educated assessments of the likely success of certain reforms. These assessments can be based on what has been feasible in the state's past political development plus its contemporary politics with all its attributes, such as political culture, institutional structures, and power relationships. For example, judging by past and present realities, it is unlikely that regionalism or urban versus rural-bush tensions will disappear for decades to come. But agreement on certain reforms, such as reforming the education system in rural-bush Alaska considered below, may be possible and successful, if enough of a consensus can be reached and continued benefits enjoyed by enough of the stakeholders.

A third link between reform and the future is this: centuries of evidence show that inertia and the status quo are significant forces in political and governmental systems. Inertia will tend to dominate unless a major event precipitates a crisis or a persistent problem that creates an atmosphere for change and perhaps major reform. So the question regarding Alaska is: What kind of event or chronic problem will it take to bring about major reforms in Alaska's political and governmental systems and in its public policies? For example, would this be the federal government drastically cutting its funds to the state? Would a long period of low oil prices, seriously reducing state revenues, as occurred from 2014 into 2016 and likely beyond, bring about such reforms? And if a major event or chronic problem persisted, what sort of reforms might be made?

Bearing in mind these links between reform and the future, readers can decide for themselves on the likelihood of the reforms considered here being adopted and their relative success if they are adopted. Because the political feasibility of these reforms depends upon how the future unfolds, we first consider various perspectives on the future.

2. TEN CHALLENGES, CHOICES, AND PROSPECTS FOR THE FUTURE

Of the numerous aspects of Alaska's political environment that may affect the challenges that Alaska will face and its choices and prospects, here we briefly consider ten that appear most significant. These are (1) population developments, (2) economic health, (3) budgetary issues, (4) issues relating to state and local government institutions, (5) federal-state relations, (6) development versus environmentalism and the issue of climate change, (7) Native issues, (8) urban versus rural-bush conflicts, (9) the extent of external constraints, and (10) the quality of Alaska life, which will very much be affected by a combination of the first nine concerns and issues.

Challenges Presented by Alaska's Diverse and Dynamic Population

As Alaska's population continues to diversify socially and increase in numbers in the twenty-first century, this will present several challenges. The workforce will likely continue to include a large number of transitory nonresidents. In 2012 just over 20 percent of Alaska's total workforce was nonresident, and this percentage has hovered around or just below this figure since 2002. The percentage of nonresident workers in the oil industry was around 30 percent for the first decade of the century. Many North Slope workers, in particular, have permanent residences somewhere else, often spend their money outside the state, and ultimately leave Alaska permanently.[1] The transitory nature of Alaska's workforce is especially visible in the educational system. Teachers rotate in and out of Alaska's schools at a high rate, especially in rural-bush communities.

Other challenges resulting from the state's demographics include dealing with a high incidence of suicide, rape, and violent crimes; unemployment and underemployment, especially in rural-bush Alaska; and addressing the state's low graduation and academic achievement rates for K–12 students, which are among the lowest in the nation. A related challenge is that upwards of 40 percent of Alaska's high school graduates who leave the state for college or jobs do not return.

Another population issue is the increasing movement of Alaska's rural-bush population to urban areas. As energy costs in rural-bush communities increase and various types of support for those communities decrease, people tend to move from villages to larger communities, primarily Anchorage and Southcentral Alaska. This movement can have significant consequences for many villages, especially for K–12 education. As many formula-funded programs are based on student enrollment, when the school-age population drops below a certain number, rural-bush schools may be forced to close. That scenario, in turn, leads to more residents leaving to obtain education for their children. A community's vitality is lost when future village leaders leave to find better employment and educational opportunities in urban Alaska.

In-state population shifts plus in-migration from Outside are also slowly contributing to a political power shift to Anchorage and Southcentral Alaska, increasing the region's political influence in the legislature and in state government in general. This will keep issues like the capital move, conflicts over capital project allocations, and a host of other regional issues in the forefront of Alaska politics for many years to come.

Alaska's Economic Health

As Chapters 6 and 7 argue, Alaska's economy is not going to diversify to any great extent in the foreseeable future. It will remain dependent on natural resource extraction, mainly oil, minerals, and fishing, with some service industries like tourism. This means that employment and the government revenues generated by economic activity will continue to be largely beyond Alaska's control and subject to world commodity prices and federal decisions. And so Alaska's political capacity will also continue to be undermined by economic factors beyond its borders.

State Budget Issues and Alaska's Fiscal Health

The two major interrelated challenges faced by Alaska's policy makers since statehood (and that will remain at the forefront in the next several decades) are dealing with the vicissitudes of the Alaska economy, over which policy makers have little control, and the state budget, over which they have extensive control if they choose to use it. The state budget will continue to depend on oil revenues that can fluctuate widely. Thus, if policy makers fail to take positive action to deal with the 2014 through 2016 downturn in oil prices and the future ones that will inevitably occur, that failure can have far-reaching effects for all aspects of Alaska's economic and social life. How to deal with these revenue shortfalls now and in the future is the major contemporary issue in Alaska politics.

One argument often used by politicians and many members of the public is that "we have to cut back on state spending, as there just isn't the money anymore." This is a specious argument. Despite the 2014-2016 (and likely beyond) downturn in revenues, Alaska still has many more financial options than other states, such as Permanent Fund earnings, to deal with revenue shortfalls. The major political roadblock to exercising these options in Alaska is fiscal conservatism.

A more extensive listing of the range of issues regarding Alaska's economic health and the state budget can be found in Chapter 2, Table 2.1. The reform section below considers various directions policy makers might take in the future regarding Alaska's budgetary and fiscal health.

Issues Relating to State and Local Government Institutions

Over the years, many reforms have been proposed and some enacted to modify the operation of Alaska's state and local government institutions and the processes of government. What reforms in the future might make Alaska's governments more efficient and more representative, and increase its political capacity to deal with the challenges that it will face? At the local government level, as explained in Chapter 18, it appears unlikely that the fully developed system envisioned by Alaska's founders, particularly in rural-bush Alaska, will be achieved because of political pressures against it.

At the state level such reforms as term limits for state legislators, a biennial budget, and even a unicameral legislature may be considered. In fact, because of population development noted earlier, the legislature will be in need of reform in the next few decades. With only forty members of the House and twenty in the Senate, it is harder and harder to provide adequate rural-bush representation and also to represent fairly, in terms of number of seats, the growing urban population.

One way to tackle these problems would be at a constitutional convention. In the reform section below we look at the pros and cons of holding such a convention, and also examine some other possible state government institutional reforms.

Federal-State Relations

As several chapters in the book show, Alaska is dependent on the federal government in many ways. Consequently, many state policies are influenced by the national government. What does the future hold in this state-federal relationship and how might this enhance or constrain Alaska's political capacity? Can anything different be expected other than the past and present relationship?

It is hard to envision that Alaska will by choice become less dependent on the federal government for funds and employment through the military and federal agency presence in the state. The federal government will continue its role as an Alaska landholder and is not likely to relinquish its presence as a regulator of natural resources, including the environment. This, no doubt, will result in continued federal bashing by many Alaska politicians and segments of the public.

An unanswered question is the extent to which the federal government will want to and is politically able to continue to fund Alaska and what the departure of Ted Stevens from the U.S. Senate means for Alaska's long-term ability to secure federal funds. Box 30.1 looks at the future in the absence of Stevens.

Development versus Environmental Values and the Challenge of Climate Change

The conflict between the forces of development and conservation is one that has increased in intensity since statehood as conservationists in their new and enhanced advocacy role as environmentalists have risen in influence. This conflict is likely to be a major issue with many elements to it in the future. This is because it often affects peoples' livelihoods and views of Alaska, resulting in a clash of values in which compromise is difficult. Developers—mainly through resource development of oil, gas, minerals, forest products, and fish—argue that development is necessary for Alaska's economic health. In contrast, the environmental community within and outside the state wants, in varying degrees, to preserve the state's natural beauty and resources that they see threatened by developers. One school of thought, however, argues that development and conservation can both be achieved and both camps accommodated through an approach known as "sustainable development."[2]

BOX 30.1

The Defeat and Death of a Political Titan: Alaska after Ted Stevens

When Ted Stevens died in a small plane crash in Southwest Alaska in August 2010, Alaska and the nation lost an iconic leader.

Stevens graduated from Harvard Law School, practiced law first in Washington, D.C., and later in Fairbanks, and began his U.S. Senate career in 1968, just nine years into Alaska statehood. During his four decades in Washington, D.C., he was known for vigorously fighting any political pressure that might threaten the flow of federal dollars to Alaska. Among provisions that Stevens fought for were the 1971 Alaska Native Claims Settlement Act (ANCSA) and tax exemptions for Native corporations, the 1973 Trans-Alaska Pipeline Authorization Act, the Alaska National Interest Lands Conservation Act (ANILCA), an annual $40 million subsidy for logging in the Tongass National Forest, keeping military bases in Alaska, and billions of dollars for infrastructure in the state. After government employment and oil revenues, the federal funding that Stevens directed toward Alaska was for many years the third-largest source of Alaska state revenues.

In November 2008 his political career ended when he suffered a narrow electoral defeat to Democrat Mark Begich. The defeat was largely the result of Stevens's conviction just one week before the election on seven counts of making false statements in federal financial disclosure forms by not disclosing gifts received from VECO, the former oil service company. The case was dismissed, and charges were dropped six months later because of misconduct by prosecutors. When he left office, Stevens was the longest-serving Republican U.S. Senator in the nation's history. And despite the scandal surrounding the gifts from VECO and his defeat at the polls, the Anchorage International Airport continues to bear his name.

A combination of Stevens's forceful personality and later his seniority translated into political power, and that power benefited the state tremendously. In a December 22, 2008, *New York Times* article, David Kirkpatrick equated Stevens's election defeat to that of the closing of a plant in a company town. It was not just Stevens's loss. It was a major loss for Alaska, which would no longer have the power or the money that Stevens as a modern-day political patron and titan provided. What is this change likely to mean, particularly regarding Alaska's securing of federal funds? Will these dwindle, or will Stevens's legacy be maintained?

Along with Stevens's defeat also came a change in political dynamics in Washington, D.C. In 2008, Democrat Barack Obama was elected president and reelected in 2012. The Senate was controlled by the Democrats during 2008–2014 and the House was in the hands of Democrats until 2010, but the 2014 midterm elections saw Republicans take control of both houses of Congress. Given divided government from 2010 to 2014, Alaska's congressional delegation's successes were mixed. This was partly because of the 2011 Senate ban on earmarks, which was an important part of funding for Alaska under Stevens, and partly because President Obama and Congress cut back on some national programs and held the line on others. But even before the earmark ban Alaska secured fewer funds than in the Stevens years, partly because of Begich's junior status and Lisa Murkowski's not being in the top Senate leadership. Representative Young did regain a leadership position following the 2010 election, but political deadlock set in with a Democratic Senate and President.

In November 2014 former state Attorney General Dan Sullivan beat Begich in his bid for reelection to the U.S. Senate. This meant that Alaska's congressional delegation was once again all Republican with Murkowski and Young in leadership positions, but with Sullivan as a junior senator. It remains to be seen how the delegation does given federal opposition to such moves as opening the Arctic National Wildlife Refuge (ANWR) and holding the line on federal spending.

Also, many people in the Lower 48 view Alaska as too rich to be receiving so much federal funding, particularly since, as of early 2016, the state had no state income tax on individuals, no statewide sales tax, and a Permanent Fund worth $50 billion from which the state pays each Alaskan a yearly dividend.

So for a combination of reasons, some to do with the changing composition and uneven influence of Alaska's congressional delegation and others due to the changing political environment in Washington, D.C., and the nation, Alaska is not likely to get the extensive funds and wield the influence it had in the Stevens years. This influence will take a generation to regain if at all. And so Alaska may never have such national political influence again.

Source: Developed by Laura Savatgy and Clive Thomas.

Development versus Environmental Issues

Development and environmental conflicts are wide-ranging and include issues over oil development in the Arctic National Wildlife Refuge (ANWR), drilling in the National Petroleum Reserve-Alaska (NPR-A), and offshore oil drilling in the Arctic. Development goals will be pitted against environmental concerns regarding oil spills, opening mines such as the controversial Pebble Mine, and the question of the environmental effects of mine tailings disposal on water quality. The clash also includes conflicts between hunting groups and environmentalists on such issues as predator control (particularly killing wolves) and the designation of endangered species. Again, a more complete listing of these issues can be found in Chapter 2, Table 2.1.

In terms of Alaska's political capacity to deal with these issues in the future, the state's options are restricted because many potential development sites are on federal land. The absence of Ted Stevens's influence in Congress may further limit Alaska's options, as related in Box 30.1. In other matters, particularly those involving global problems, the state's political capacity may be even more limited, in some cases virtually zero. One such issue in this regard is climate change.

Climate Change and Global Warming

Climate change, or more precisely global warming, involving gradually increasing temperatures worldwide and the slow melting of the north and south polar ice caps and glaciers, is an issue that has come to the fore since the late 1980s. Increasing international attention has been paid to the issue. For instance, a United Nations Framework Convention on Climate Change (UNFCCC) took place in Lima in December 2014. The event was attended by representatives of more than 200 countries who agreed to commit every country to reducing fossil fuel emissions. Another United Nations Conference of the Parties (COP 21) took place in Paris in late 2015.[3] During the Obama administration (2009-2017), the president brought increased attention to climate change. Moreover, as the chair from 2015 to 2017 of the Arctic Council (a body of eight nations and six international indigenous groups concerned with Arctic issues), the United States is making combating climate change a top priority, especially the reduction of black carbon and methane gas in the circumpolar region.[4]

There is overwhelming scientific evidence that global warming is occurring and slowly advancing each year as ice caps melt, ocean levels rise, and temperatures on land and at sea show yearly increases. The evidence is that this phenomenon is largely human-made and is the result of increasing use of fossil fuels—oil, natural gas, and coal.[5] Yet, many on the right of the political spectrum as well as many developers contest that this is largely a human-caused problem, and many deny that global warming exists at all. Their concern is mainly an economic one because they view reductions in the use of fossil fuels as direct constraints on economic development, particularly the economic development that comes from producing and refining fossil fuels. Some in Alaska subscribe to the climate change denial perspective.

There is clear evidence, however, that no state in the Union is affected more by climate change than is Alaska. With its image as the Last Frontier, its polar bears, grizzlies, wolves, whales, pristine environment, and a Native culture closely tied to the land and ocean, Alaska is a poster child for addressing climate change. As it affects Alaska, climate changes is of great concern to many Alaskans and Americans. Accordingly, when President Obama came to Alaska in the summer of 2015, he made climate change one of the focuses of his visit. He announced grants to study the problem and to prepare for moving communities affected by rising sea levels.[6] The president's visit certainly raised the profile of climate change across the nation and particularly among many Alaskans, both those for and against dealing with the issue.

Global warming has, in fact, been on the political agenda in Alaska for some time, though mainly as a low-profile issue. In 2007 both the legislature and former Governor Palin established investigative bodies to assess its impact on Alaska. Plus, at the University of Alaska Fairbanks, there are now several centers (including the Alaska Center for Climate Assessment and Policy, the Alaska Center for Climate Change, and the Cold Climate Housing Research Center), as well as several programs and grants in progress relating to climate change, sustainability, and related issues. The problem, however, is that while Alaska can, to some degree, assess the impact of climate change, it has little control over and virtually no political capacity to deal with this issue. There are four main reasons for this lack of capacity.

First, climate change is an international problem caused in large part by carbon emissions by large industrial nations and the thinning of the ozone layer protecting the earth from the sun. So, even if Alaska could deal with its own contribution to global warming (which is minimal due to its small population and its lack of industry and agriculture), it would have virtually no effect on global warming. Second, as also noted above, there is great controversy over whether or not global warming is a problem and, if so, its extent and causes and how to deal with the problem. This leaves the door open for disagreements that often fall along ideological or economic development lines. With their major interest in developing the state, as of 2016, all three members of Alaska's congressional delegation were in the climate change denial camp. And after having been the 2008 nominee for vice president, former Governor Palin now advocates the latter perspective in contrast to her concern about the issue when in office. Third, even though there is widespread agreement on its causes, extent, and consequences, politics often gets in the way of concerted world action. Political obstacles resulted in a lack of agreement at the Copenhagen conference on climate change in December 2009, attended by virtually every country in the world and myriad interest groups. Developing countries like China, India, and others tend to oppose restrictions on industrial development that controlling carbon emissions would entail. The COP 21 meeting in Paris in December 2015, however, was somewhat encouraging as it produced an agreement of 195 countries, including China and India, to reduce carbon emissions and spend $100 million annually to help low income countries. There are, however, questions about enforcing the agreement. So, politics may get in the way again as attempts to implement the agreement takes place.[7] Fourth, a combination of the technical nature of the issue and the fact that it is not an immediate problem results in a low level of interest in the issue among the general public. This translates into many public officials giving climate change issues a low policy priority, particularly in the fifty states, including Alaska, where politicians have minimal influence on dealing with global warming.

Alaska Native Issues

Alaska Natives have made significant advances since statehood. Nevertheless, many issues are yet to be resolved and some challenging situations exist, particularly the protection of Native culture and how exactly it relates to the majority culture of the state. Some of these challenges, such as high unemployment, poverty, and social stress (manifested in high rates of alcohol and drug abuse, domestic violence, and suicide), tend to be low-profile issues most of the time, unless a prominent politician, like the governor, draws attention to them and pushes policies to address them. Others are high profile, largely because they involve some aspect of the urban versus rural-bush conflict. These include subsistence hunting and fishing rights, the cost of service delivery to the bush, Native sovereignty, and the quality of Native education. These various issues raise the question of the quality of life to which Natives living in rural-bush communities are entitled.

Ultimately, the future prospects for resolving these issues depend on how much political influence the Native community can muster over the next several decades. Box 30.2 offers some thoughts on this challenge.

Regionalism and Conflict between Urban and Rural-Bush Areas

Throughout the book we have seen how prominent a factor regionalism is in Alaska politics and how is it interrelated in many ways with the political phenomenon of urban versus rural-bush conflict. While these related forces in Alaska politics are largely a product of economic geography, urban versus rural-bush tensions also result from cultural differences, mainly between Alaska Natives and the majority Caucasian culture. In the near future we can expect more of the same in these aspects of Alaska politics.

BOX 30.2

Prospects for the Future Political Power of Alaska Natives

The Alaska Native community succeeded in moving from political obscurity in the years before statehood to playing an important, often decisive, role in Alaska politics and public policy making largely because of its ability to acquire and exercise political power. This power came from a confluence of political circumstances, including the numerical dominance of Natives in most rural-bush communities; the founding of organizations such as the Alaska Federation of Natives (AFN); a combination of a feeling of national atonement toward Native Americans in the 1960s combined with a need to build the trans-Alaska oil pipeline, which together helped to secure enactment of the Alaska Native Claims Settlement Act (ANCSA); the economic base that came from for-profit Native corporations; the Alaska congressional delegation (particularly Ted Stevens) championing the Native cause in Washington, D.C.; and some effective Native leadership. It was this leadership, which was very pragmatic politically, that put all the other factors together and turned them into political effectiveness.

Looking back, Native political influence in the state peaked in the 1980s and has since declined. Why did this decline occur, and what does the future hold for Native political influence?

The late 1980s and the early 1990s saw the departure from politics of a number of Native leaders who had cut their political teeth on ANCSA and then came to be the power brokers in Alaska politics. While new Native leaders have emerged, they must operate in a political environment that is more conservative and in which urban versus rural-bush tensions have intensified. With the movement of many Natives from rural-bush communities to urban communities and with Natives becoming a smaller percentage of the Alaska population, their representation in the legislature is slowly declining. The Native community has also been divided on issues such as the opening of the Arctic National Wildlife Refuge (ANWR). Native success in the federal courts has been mixed, with a major decision on Native sovereignty in the *Venetie* case in 1998 going against them but a favorable decision on subsistence in 2014.

As a consequence, since the early 1990s, the Native community has been unable to secure many policies that would be to its advantage, such as a favorable solution to subsistence issues within the state and sufficient power cost equalization to help defray the high cost of power in the bush. In other cases, inroads have been made into previous gains, such as transportation subsidies to rural-bush areas and many state-supported social programs. And now their most powerful federal advocate, Ted Stevens, is gone. One bright spot in 2014 was the election of Byron Mallott, a prominent Native leader, as lieutenant governor. Even so, none of the circumstances that have made inroads into Native political power in Alaska is likely to change in the near future. In fact, some pressures are likely to increase.

So while the Native community is far from its political obscurity of the old days, it will likely be on the political defensive in the foreseeable future.

Source: Developed by the authors with aid from Miranda Wright, Director Emeritus of the University of Alaska Fairbanks Department of Alaska Native Studies and Rural Development.

It is difficult to see how regional loyalties will disappear or even be abated. The same is true for urban versus rural-bush conflict. In fact, both may intensify and produce increased political conflict. Regional issues like the capital move are not likely to go away, and politicians will no doubt continue to fight for regional economic benefits, such as ensuring the continued existence of the three main regional campuses of the University of

Alaska. In this and other regards, Alaska will, in essence, remain several states—Southeast, Southcentral, the Interior, and various rural-bush regions.

Specific to the urban versus rural-bush conflict, the continuing high cost of providing services to rural-bush areas, coupled with the erosion of Native political power and the unlikelihood of dealing with issues such as subsistence, will draw some hard and fast political lines. This will continue to be manifested in a high degree of emotion regarding who has a right to what in terms of lifestyle and government benefits.

Coping with External Influences

The statehood movement in the 1950s was rooted in the desire of Alaskans to gain more control over their fate—to reduce Outside forces that shaped Alaska's politics and economics and in general adversely affected its quality of life. But the debate did not end when statehood was achieved. As part of a federal Union, Alaska is subject to numerous Outside forces. The debate over local control has been a continuing one and will be for years to come. In essence, this is a debate about how best to maximize Alaska's political capacity. Box 30.3 considers the range of alternatives in this continuing debate and examines their pros and cons.

The Quality of Alaska Life

All nine aspects of Alaska's political environment just considered will affect the quality of life in Alaska in the coming years. They will affect the state's standard of living, educational opportunities, and the extent to which individual Alaskans can make decisions to choose the lifestyle they want. These aspects of Alaska's future will also affect the ability of Alaskans to influence their elected officials on lifestyle issues. This raises three questions. First, what quality of life do Alaskans have a right to expect? Second, to what extent does state government have control over determining the quality of life? And third, can the quality of life be improved for all Alaskans simultaneously?

It is impossible to answer the first question in any definitive way. One of the characteristics of Alaska life often noted is the difference in the quality of life between urban and rural-bush Alaska in terms of employment opportunities, cost of living, education and social services, and the extent of infrastructure. Closing the gap between the quality of life in urban and rural-bush Alaska is, in effect, what most rural-bush legislators view as their primary task. But what is state government's obligation to provide services in remote areas given its cost? This is an issue filled with emotion, as it often involves a cultural clash between Natives and non-Natives.

In terms of Alaskans as a whole, is there some entitlement to a certain quality of life because the state has extensive financial resources? Many would argue that a certain quality of life has to be earned by each individual concerned. For the most part, however,

BOX 30.3

What Is the Best Course for Alaska? The Practical Realities

Most Alaskans would agree that the state would have more control over its affairs if it were less dependent on Outside forces and less subject to their influence. There are several possible avenues that would arguably achieve this goal. Alternatively, Alaskans could choose to maintain the status quo.

Although no longer part of its platform, for many years the Alaska Independence Party (AIP) advocated independence from the United States. The AIP's concerns related to federal control of Alaska's lands and resources and its extensive regulatory regime, which were seen as inhibiting development. But even if Alaska were independent (and could avoid another civil war to achieve it) the state would still be dependent on world market prices for its natural resources. It would also be cut off from substantial federal funds, and business and living costs would probably increase. In fact, independence would certainly reduce both Alaska's political capacity and its quality of life.

In 1990 Wally Hickel failed to get the Republican nomination for governor and nominally ran on the AIP ticket and won, but he never pursued Alaska's independence. The fact is that apart from the 1990 Hickel election the AIP has never received many votes, which can be seen as a rejection of its ideas by Alaskans. Moreover, most state residents likely see themselves as Americans first and Alaskans second.

For much of his career, Hickel advocated "The Alaska Owner State Solution" as a means of gaining more control for Alaska. Hickel's vision included standing up to the federal government in areas where it fetters Alaska's options, such as on opening ANWR; encouraging and perhaps subsidizing Alaska businesses to produce things now imported and diversifying the state's economy in general; having an "Alaskans first" employment policy; and ensuring state control of the use and marketing of its Owner State's resources. Regarding the latter, many prominent Alaskans, including Hickel before his death, support an all-Alaska route for the natural gas pipeline from the North Slope to Alaska tidewater, as opposed to one that reaches the Lower 48 states entirely through a pipeline that goes mainly through Canada.

A third course is for the state to reduce the uncertainty of its revenues and the resulting disruption to the economy by developing a financial plan. This likely would involve increasing taxes and using Permanent Fund earnings for something other than to pay dividends. Several Alaska organizations and prominent politicians have advocated this course.

Neither the Owner State nor the financial plan options have been implemented in any extensive way, probably because they involve financial impact on individual Alaskans. The Owner State option would likely increase the costs of some goods and services and may discourage Outside businesses from investing or operating in Alaska. The financial plan option could adversely affect the state's economy by reducing government spending and reducing the purchasing power of many Alaskans. This is because it would likely involve taking state revenues off the table today for use in the future by measures such as reducing the Permanent Fund Dividend, enacting a statewide sales tax, or reinstating the state income tax on individuals. In effect, a combination of anti-government, anti-tax, and fiscal conservative attitudes, as expressed through the ballot box, has so far resulted in Alaskans choosing the political status quo. They have opted so far for their present quality of life, as opposed to trading this off with the prospect of increasing the state's political capacity.

Source: Developed by the authors with aid from Walter J. Hickel and Malcolm Roberts, who served as Special Assistant to Governor Hickel both when he was Interior Secretary (1969–1970) and Alaska's governor (1990-1994).

improvements in Alaska's quality of life since the late 1970s have been very much a product of heavy state subsidies, the result of a paradox in the state's political culture of marrying pragmatic dependence with individualism—"enhance my quality of life, but stay out of my life." Can Alaskans expect the same quality of life in the future?

The short answer to the question of whether state government can affect the quality of life depends on the state's political capacity to deal with particular issues. In some areas and with some reforms, especially in long-term financial planning, the state could protect and promote its citizens' quality of life. But will Alaskans be willing to pay the price, which might include paying more taxes? The answer to this question and others regarding the quality of life in the years to come will boil down to politics and power relationships.

This brings us to the third question of whether everyone's quality of life can be improved equally. One major problem here is that enhancing one segment of society's quality of life usually involves redistributive or regulatory policies that reduce the quality of life of others, often leading to conflict, and sometimes intense conflict.[8] This is certainly the case with issues such as subsistence and many entitlement programs. The next section considers possible future reforms and identifies some political trade-offs, including some relating to improving the quality of life of some Alaskans and not others.

3. TEN POSSIBLE POLITICAL REFORMS

Of the many possible political reforms that Alaska could pursue in the decades to come, ten are outlined here. They were chosen because they directly relate to the major challenges that the state faces as outlined in the last section, or because they are reforms that have been widely debated in recent years. These ten possible areas of reform are (1) holding a constitutional convention, (2) electing the attorney general, (3) reforming the legislature, (4) term limits for legislators, (5) subsistence, (6) secondary education in rural-bush Alaska, (7) allowing public funds to be used for K–12 private and religious schools, (8) moving to a biennial state budget, (9) use of Permanent Fund earnings, and (10) establishing a long-range fiscal plan.

Holding a Constitutional Convention

The Alaska Constitution requires that the citizens vote every ten years on whether a constitutional convention should be held. These votes are held at general elections in years ending with "2"—2002, 2012, 2022, 2032, and so on. Since statehood, the voters have consistently voted "no" on this question. If a constitutional convention were approved at some time in the future, it could provide the opportunity for assessing Alaska's current situation and discussing desired changes and needs for the future. There are, however, pros and cons to holding a convention.

The 1955–1956 Constitutional Convention was planned to have no lobbyists, special interest groups, or external interests as part of the process in an attempt to provide a broad Alaska public interest perspective among the delegates. If a future convention is called, special interest groups would attend with the intent to promote or protect their interests. This would likely include, among many others, the oil industry, the mining and fishing industries, and Alaska Native interests to promote issues like subsistence, land ownership, and tribal rights. Outside environmental groups who are against any kind of development in Alaska's wilderness areas would also seek a voice. Those who regularly use the legislative process to promote their interests would want to use a constitutional convention in the same way. Currently, the Alaska Constitution is based on the principle that the constitution should lay down only the basic structure for the ways that state government relates to the people. A convention could impact this fundamental character of the constitution and could have detrimental effects on Alaska's future.

The late Thomas B. Stewart, Secretary to the Constitutional Convention, was a strong opponent of calling another convention for all the above reasons.[9] Others, among them former Attorney General John Havelock, support such a convention as a way to deal with some of the problems surrounding reapportionment, campaign finance, and representational problems arising from the size of the legislature.[10]

Electing the Attorney General

In most states, the attorney general (AG) is elected, and Alaska is one of only five states where the governor appoints the AG. Over the years, there have been many calls for Alaska to elect this important state official. The most recent debate was sparked by the so-called Troopergate affair during former Governor Palin's term in office (2006–2009), in which questions were raised about whether an AG independent of the governor might have averted the dismissal of the commissioner of public safety. In Box 30.4, former state Representative Harry Crawford, a strong advocate of an elected AG, and Bruce Botelho, a former AG and supporter of the appointment system, provide perspectives on the issue.

Reforming the State Legislature

Reform of the current structure of the legislature is likely to result from two circumstances. The first is the reduction in rural-bush populations caused by movement from rural-bush areas to urban areas and in-migration from Outside also to urban areas. The most likely reform in this area is to increase the number of election districts. However, given the fact that Alaska voters rejected this reform in 2010, it is unlikely that the legislature will revisit this particular solution any time soon. If diminished rural-bush (that is, Alaska Native) representation becomes a major legal issue, it is possible that the U.S.

BOX 30.4

An Elected Attorney General for Alaska?

Alaska's attorney general (AG) is the top legal official of the state, advisor to government, prosecutor of criminal violations, consumer protector, and watchdog over trade practices, among other important legal duties. The issue of whether or not to elect the AG revolves around the question of who the AG works for, the governor or the citizens of the state.

Alaska has had some experience with an elected AG. The Second Territorial Legislature created the office in 1915, partly to be a counterforce to the federally appointed governor. Yet, with the move to statehood and a governor elected by the people of Alaska and the professed political ambitions of J. Gerald Williams, elected as Territorial AG in 1949, in their minds, Alaska's founders opted for an AG appointed by the governor. Appointing the AG this way was an aspect of their goal to create a streamlined, as opposed to a plural, executive branch like those in California and Idaho. Nevertheless, the issue has been a continuing one in the state.

Those who favor the present system see the AG as working for the governor and that the governor has a right to appoint and remove the AG. The major rationale reflects that of Alaska's founders in an appointed AG aiding in policy coordination and being part of an executive team. An elected AG makes it much more difficult for a governor to utilize executive powers to the full. The situation with the strong contending legislature and its tendency toward fragmented and often stymied policy making is complicated enough. Adding an additional elected officer can be viewed not as reform but as a way to undermine the ability to get things done.

Also, when the AG is elected and independent of the governor, there is a strong chance that the AG will be pursuing political ambitions that may involve running for governor. So he or she has no incentive to be part of a team but has a major reason to work against the governor. As former AG Avrum Gross once put it, appointed AGs are lawyers who have an interest in politics, while elected AGs are politicians who happen to be lawyers. In addition, elected AGs may become beholden to special interests for funds to get elected, and so may be more representative of these interests than the people of the state.

Advocates of an elected AG argue that an appointed AG creates a potential conflict between the rule of law and the will of the governor.

The AG should be beholden only to the people of Alaska and the state's constitution, not an elected governor. Being selected by the governor and serving at the governor's pleasure guarantees a conflict when faced with dilemmas concerning the legality of, or method of implementing, the governor's agenda. Certainly, Alaska has had strong, independent AGs who were not unduly influenced by the governor's political agenda, but were guided by statute, precedent, and the Constitution. On the other hand, there have been AGs who were merely an extension of the governor's will and spent their time conjuring up legal arguments to further the governor's agenda.

To deal with the concerns about political ambition and campaign finance, many of those advocating election of the AG propose the following. The AG could be appointed similarly to how Alaska judges are—that is, nominated by an independent body, appointed by the governor, and then confirmed by a vote of the people. Or if the AG were a purely elected official, the influence of campaign contributions from special interests could be minimized by publicly funding their election campaigns, though that raises First Amendment issues.

Source: Developed by the authors with input from former Representative Harry Crawford and former Attorney General Bruce Botelho.

BOX 30.5

Approaches and Likely Consequences of Reforming the Alaska Legislature

When the time comes for Alaska to reform its legislature, it has two main choices. One is to go to a one-house, unicameral chamber. The other is to keep the bicameral legislature but increase the number of seats in each house.

MOVING TO A UNICAMERAL LEGISLATURE

Although all local government legislative bodies are unicameral, only Nebraska has a unicameral state legislature, which was the product of cost-saving measures in the Depression of the 1930s and the strong personality of George Norris, a major Nebraska politician of the era. In the 1976 general election a majority of Alaska voters indicated in a nonbinding "advisory" vote that they would like to consider a proposal for a unicameral legislature as a constitutional amendment. But the state Senate balked, and no proposal was forthcoming.

A unicameral legislature may save some costs and prevent potential conflicts between the House and Senate. However, entrenched political interests, plus the fact that a single house legislature has been used in only one of the fifty states, means that experimenting with a unicameral legislature makes it a difficult sell in the state. The championing of unicameralism by a well-respected, perhaps charismatic, Alaskan, especially a conservative, could aid its adoption. However, no unicameral advocate of this caliber is currently on the Alaska political horizon.

EXPANDING THE PRESENT LEGISLATURE

Expanding the present bicameral legislature appears to be the only real option. An effort to do so, however, was rejected by the voters in November 2010. Senate Joint Resolution 21 placed before the voters a proposed amendment to the Alaska Constitution that would have increased the number of election districts from forty to forty-four, thereby increasing the number of House members from forty to forty-four and the Senate from twenty to twenty-two.

Proponents of the amendment argued that because each district must have the same number of residents (with only minor variations allowed), increasing the number of election districts would result in districts with smaller populations and smaller physical areas. In addition, because of major population shifts to urban areas, many existing election districts, particularly in rural-bush areas, span huge areas containing highly diverse local economies. This makes it difficult for a legislator to provide meaningful representation to the whole district. Smaller districts, it was argued, would bring people closer to their legislators. And though not part of the proponents' official statements, increasing the number of election districts is generally viewed as one way to improve representation of rural-bush areas.

Opponents argued that increasing the number of representatives and senators would actually reduce the level of representation because, regardless of the total number of legislators, each person would still be represented by only one House member and one Senator. If the number of legislators were increased, however, the representation would be diluted—from 1 out of 40 to 1 out of 44 in the House and from 1 out of 20 to 1 out of 22 in the Senate. The opponents also viewed increasing the size of the legislature as being a huge waste of money for no real benefit. It would have required salaries and benefits for the new legislators and their staffs, additional offices and office equipment in Juneau additional offices in the legislators' home districts, and additional travel costs.

Since the voters resoundingly rejected this proposed amendment, with nearly 60 percent in opposition, it is unlikely that legislators will find the political will any time soon to place a similar amendment before the electorate. If reform comes at all, it may come as a result of some type of federal intervention under the Voting Rights Act. Additionally, the Alaska courts might conceivably mandate reform at some future date, since further population shifts to urban areas may make it increasingly difficult for future reapportionment efforts to comply with Article VI, Section 6, of the Alaska Constitution. This requires that each house district "shall be formed of contiguous and compact territory containing as nearly as practicable a relatively integrated socio-economic area."

Source: Developed by the authors from materials in endnote 11 of this chapter and a July 7, 2011 interview with Gordon S. Harrison, author of Chapter 4 on the state constitution.

Justice Department could force some type of reform under the Voting Rights Act of 1965. Box 30.5 examines the major options for reforming the legislature and the consequences this may have for Alaska's political future.[11]

Term Limits for Alaska Legislators?

Several states, including California, Florida, and Michigan, have adopted term limits for their state legislators. Many local governments, including many in Alaska, have also adopted them. Part of this recent movement across the nation is rooted in the low opinion that many Americans have of politicians and the view that limiting the time an elected official has in office will prevent politicians from amassing too much power. Proponents also believe that infusing the system with new political blood every few years will improve the quality of government.

But there are contrary arguments. Having elections every two years (or four years in the case of state senators) provides voters with the ability to impose a "term limit" based on performance. In addition, when legislators do not have the longevity that provides institutional knowledge, power is ceded to legislative staff, executive personnel, and lobbyists. In other words, there is simply a power shift from elected legislators to hired or appointed staff, coupled with an arguable increase in the influence of lobbyists. So, ironically, term limits may well cause power and policy making to shift to people over whom the public has little or no control.

Resolving the Subsistence Issue

Few issues have been more prominent in state politics since the early 1980s than subsistence. The issue is second to none in terms of the emotions and resulting political deadlock it has created. Alaska Natives hold that as a result of the Alaska Native Claims Settlement Act (ANCSA) and the Alaska National Interest Lands Conservation Act (ANILCA), Congress intended to protect Alaska Native hunting and fishing rights when it referred to a "rural" subsistence preference. Moreover, Natives expected that both the U.S. Secretary of the Interior and the State of Alaska would enforce these provisions. Many feel this expectation has not been fulfilled, particularly by the state. Others, mainly sports hunting and fishing enthusiasts, feel that, in line with the state constitution (Article VIII, Section 3), all Alaskans should have equal access to the state's fish and game resources.

Whether this issue can be resolved is uncertain. Resolution will depend on the power that the Native community and rural-bush Alaska can bring to bear in relation to urban Alaska, with the added uncertainty of the role of the federal government.

Reform of Secondary Education in Rural-Bush Alaska

As Chapter 26 on education policy points out, rural-bush education is a continuing concern in the state. Because this issue, like subsistence, involves the Native community, it is

BOX 30.6

What to Do about Rural-Bush Secondary Education

Alaska's rural-bush secondary education has been a major political issue for decades. Two major approaches have been used, before and after the *Molly Hootch* Consent Decree of 1976. Neither has proven satisfactory. In recent years even Native leaders and large segments of the Native population have come to realize that reform is necessary. By 2010, the system based on a high school built in virtually every village, a product of the *Hootch* decree that replaced the unsatisfactory regional boarding school system, meant that of the 273 schools and programs that issued diplomas statewide, 149 (55 percent) had fewer than ten graduates. This made it difficult to provide quality education in an efficient and cost effective way.

Rural-bush youth need to acquire skills for the twenty-first century, for the continuation of village lifestyles, and for management of the land and natural resources owned by Native corporations. Most Natives and non-Natives agree that the current secondary education system is not presently providing these skills. In addition, the student achievement data in these rural-bush schools is very troubling. Until the Alaska High School Graduation Qualifying Exam (HSGQE) was abolished in 2014, Alaska Natives, many of whom attend small bush high schools, routinely scored significantly below the state average in reading, writing, and math on the exam. Although Native students account for a little more than 20 percent of grades 7–12, year after year they make up close to 40 percent of the total dropouts. Thus, the current system serves neither the students nor the state.

To address this problem, reestablishing state boarding schools has gained momentum since 2000, when a legislative task force concluded that a system of regional learning centers, focusing on different areas—for example, college prep, career and technical education, arts and culture—could better serve Alaskan students. A 2001 survey of one thousand Alaska Native households, conducted for the First Alaskans Foundation, revealed that 65 percent of rural-bush Alaska Native households favored such schools.[1] Then, in 2004, the Alaska State Board of Education passed a resolution "supporting boarding schools in Alaska and calling for a plan of action."[2] And in 2005, the legislature amended the school funding formula to provide state funding for local school districts operating statewide residential education programs. This funding was expanding in the Education Opportunity Act of 2014.

The one existing state-operated boarding school—Mount Edgecumbe in Sitka—has functioned successfully since the mid-1980s. As of 2014, its largely Native student population annually scored above the state average in all areas of the HSGQE. This success suggests that such schools could be operated without the adverse consequences experienced in the past, not least because educational practice has made significant strides since the early days of boarding schools, where total assimilation into the dominant culture was the goal. The larger, more varied student population at a boarding school allows youth to build relationships across regions and statewide. Many leaders of the Alaska land claims movement in the 1960s attended boarding school and had long histories with each other before their involvement in the movement.

A major objection to the reintroduction of state boarding schools is that, while they may be better educationally, they can undermine traditional learning and may repeat the socially destructive aspects of the pre-*Hootch* system. So any new approach to rural-bush secondary education needs to combine several elements, which could include some or all of the following:

- The school year could be adjusted so that students are in their home communities to participate in subsistence and other traditional activities.
- Short-term residential stays. For example, Chugach School District in Prince William Sound sends many students to Anchorage for short, intensive programs in academics, life skills, and career and technical subjects. Bering Straits School District does something similar with the Northwestern Alaska Career and Technical Center.
- The use of technology and/or providing various enrichment programs. The Lower Kuskokwin

School District in Southwest Alaska, for instance, uses highly qualified math and English teachers to deliver instruction to the small high schools in the region via a district-operated video-conferencing system.

Several first-class regional schools will likely be more costly than the current system. There would need to be a long-term commitment by the state to sustain staff and programs over time, not an easy commitment to achieve in a state averse to long-term budgetary planning. And so to secure this commitment requires the advocacy of a broad range of interests, among them Alaska Native and state leaders, local school boards, education associations, parents, and legislators. Plus, reversing the forty-year tradition of local secondary access will test the limits of Alaska's fragmented policy-making process and also exacerbate the urban-rural tensions that color so much of Alaska politics. But without serious rethinking and major reforms, generations of rural-bush high school students will be poorly equipped for the future, with adverse consequences for all Alaskans.

[1] McDowell Group, Inc., *Alaska Native Household Education Survey*, November 2001, Section 4, p. 26.

[2] Alaska State Board of Education, Resolution 01-2005, December 6, 2004.

Source: Developed by Mary Lou Madden, former administrator at the Alaska Department of Education, Sheldon Jackson College, and the University of Alaska Southeast.

often laden with emotion and is one element in urban versus rural-bush political antagonisms. This conflict often clouds clear and rational thinking on the subject. Box 30.6 looks at the pros and cons of reforming the system.

Allowing Public Funds to be Used for K–12 Private and Religious Schools

Another major education issue that surfaced in a serious way in the Twenty-Eighth Legislature (2013–2014) was a proposal to amend the Alaska Constitution to allow state funds to go to private and religious schools. Article VII, Section 1, of the state constitution provides, "No money shall be paid from public funds for the direct benefit of any religious or other private educational institution."[12] This is why it requires a constitutional amendment to allow funds to go to religious and private schools. Accordingly, in 2013 resolutions were introduced into both houses of the legislature to put such an amendment before the voters. However, the resolutions failed to garner the necessary votes to place the amendment on the ballot.

The move to allow public funds for private and religious schools is part of the so-called school-choice movement that has been a prominent issue in K–12 education policy across the states since the early 2000s. It is led by conservatives, particularly right-wing Republicans, who argue that public schools are a monopoly and that parents should be able to send their children to the school of their choice, aided by tax dollars. In Alaska several right-wing Republicans championed the amendment, and former Governor Parnell strongly endorsed it.

Opponents in Alaska include the Democrats in the House and Senate, some moderate Republicans, the National Education Association-Alaska (NEA-Alaska), whose members are school teachers and school employees, and the Association of Alaska School Boards (AASB). Doubts were also expressed by the State Chamber of Commerce (ASCC) and other organizations. Besides violating the fundamental principle of the separation of church and state in the case of religious schools, these opponents see such a constitutional amendment as a drain on the public education system. If adopted, the proposal, in their view, might well turn K-12 public education into a second-class system compared to private and religious schools. As such it would disadvantage the poor to an even greater extent than at present. In the long run, it would increase income and social inequalities by serving the interests of a small elite group. One estimate of the cost of the amendment is that it would siphoning off up to $100 million from the close to $1 billion that goes to Alaska's K–12 schools annually.

Although the proposed amendment died in the 2014 legislature, with the increasing conservative orientation of Alaska's legislature, the issue is likely to be revived and will constitute a high-profile issue in the state for some time to come. However, even if it does eventually pass as an amendment to the state constitution, it is likely to be challenged in the courts.

Moving to a Biennial Budget for the State

Today, some states, including Minnesota, Ohio, Washington, and Wyoming, work on a two-year or biennial budget cycle, as opposed to an annual cycle like Alaska's. Some states, such as Wyoming, devote an entire legislative session to putting together a budget and the other session of the two-year legislature to other business. A biennial budget is an option for Alaska and, together with other reforms (particularly a long-term fiscal plan), could help reduce budgetary uncertainty. The pros and cons of biennial budget versus an annual budget are compared in Box 30.7.

Use of Alaska Permanent Fund Earnings

One of the purposes of the Permanent Fund, to fill shortfalls from fluctuating oil and other revenues, at least as of 2015, has not been politically feasible because many Alaskans believe that their annual Permanent Fund Dividends (PFDs) will be reduced by any use of Permanent Fund earnings other than for dividends. While this is by no means a certain result, until the oil price downturn that began in the summer of 2014, no politician dared suggest such uses of the earnings. One alternative is to cap the PFD at, say, a $1,000 per person per year, and use the rest for state services and expenses. But this proposal, made in 1990 by a special committee to look into uses of the fund, has never been seriously considered.[13] Thus, despite the dip in the amount of the dividend caused by the economic

BOX 30.7

Annual versus Biennial Budgeting

ARGUMENTS FOR ANNUAL BUDGETS

- Increases the attention that legislators and state officials devote to budget analysis and deliberations because budget preparation takes place every year.
- Enhances the legislature's budget oversight capabilities by providing frequent supervision and review of executive branch activities.
- Increases the accuracy of revenue and expenditure estimates and allows more rapid adjustment to changing conditions.
- Gives the legislature greater opportunity to exercise control over federal funds.
- Reduces the need for supplemental appropriations and special sessions of the legislature.

ARGUMENTS FOR BIENNIAL BUDGETING

- Gives the legislature more time for deliberation and debate on non-budget issues and to concentrate on major policy concerns rather than focusing on budget details.
- Gives the legislature more time, especially during non-budget years, to conduct program evaluations and reviews.
- Enhances stability in state agencies with a two-year guarantee of their budgets and provides greater opportunity for long-range planning because less time is spent in budget preparation.
- Reduces budget preparation time and costs, as these are spread over a two-year period.

Source: Developed by Alison Elgee, author of Chapter 19 on the state budget, with some reference to Dennis Prouty, *Annual Versus Biennial Budgeting in the 50 States* (Des Moines: Iowa Legislative Fiscal Bureau, August 8, 1996); and Ronald K. Snell, *Annual and Biennial Budgeting: The Experience of State Governments* (Denver: National Council of State Legislatures, October 2004).

recession of 2008–2010, in the long run the fund will most likely continue to grow—it stood at around $53 billion in April 2016—and Alaskans are likely to receive substantial PFDs each year even if some Permanent Fund earnings go to pay for state services.[14]

Changing the public's attitude toward the use of fund earnings will likely take a serious and extended crisis, though this change may well come about out of necessity as a result of the prolonged downturn in oil prices that stretched from 2014 to early 2016 and that may last much longer. Using fund earnings is the most immediate way for the state to increase its political capacity. Moreover, it is the most flexible tool that Alaska has for dealing with its budgetary problems and one over which it has extensive control.

Financial Planning

Financial planning can mean different things to different people. To some it means keeping down or eliminating spending on services they do not think government should be providing in the first place. In contrast, those who advocate keeping or increasing present levels of spending in Alaska have usually viewed financial planning as creating a plan for five or ten years that provides assured sources of revenue to deal with downturns in state oil revenues and other funds, including possibly federal funds, as political circumstances change. This kind of planning, often referred to as a long-range fiscal or financial plan, will, it is argued, prevent the need to drastically cut government spending because of revenue shortfalls, with all the economic and social disruptions these can cause. As of 2015, however, Alaska has adopted no official financial plan. Instead, the state has taken its chances and lurched from crisis to crisis, and so far something has always turned up to bring it out of the revenue doldrums. One day, however, the state may not bounce back, especially because the state's oil reserves are declining and the world continues to seek to free itself from dependence upon oil. For many, this makes the crafting of a financial plan essential.

As Chapter 8 on state revenues explains, long-range financial plans consist of one or more of the following: use of Permanent Fund earnings; reinstating the state income tax on individuals; a statewide sales tax; creating special funds or endowments for essential services, such as education, as promoted by Governor Cowper in the late 1980s; increasing user fees for various services; and reducing or phasing out certain services and benefits that were products of the high oil revenue years. Some also advocate the use of a biennial budget as part of a fiscal plan.

A financial plan could increase the state's political capacity. Several plans have been proposed, but no plan has been implemented despite support from influential interests like the Alaska Municipal League and various education interests. Part of the reason is Alaska's fiscal conservatism. It is also a product of the Alaska political trait of pragmatic populism that is, in part, represented in Box 30.8, a transcript of a radio commentary broadcast in 2001 by Juneau economist Gregg Erickson. Judging by past experience it certainly appears that Alaskans are averse to long-term planning, and the way that they will deal with a long-term budget crisis is along the lines that Erickson suggests.

4. CONCLUSION: WHAT ARE THE PROSPECTS FOR REFORM?

These, then, are perspectives on Alaska's future and some political, governmental, and policy reforms that might enhance that future. There are, however, trade-offs with many of these reforms in terms of who benefits and who might lose and how the reforms might affect the quality of life of particular segments of Alaska's population.

As indicated at the beginning of this chapter, we take no position on any of these reforms, but leave that assessment to the reader. Given the discussion of the performance of Alaska's political, governmental, and policy systems past and present explored in Chapter 29 and drawing on the analysis in other chapters of the book, how likely are some of these reforms to be enacted? Will some be enacted and not others? What events might make some more likely to be enacted and why?

Put another way, will Alaska's political future usher in a new era, in whole or in part, or will it be more of the same?

BOX 30.8

Long-Range Financial Scam

The governor, the Republicans, the Democrats, the chambers of commerce, the oil companies, they all say we need a long-range financial plan. But what they've been trying to sell us is a long-range scam, and Alaskans have been wise to say no.

The scam is simple: Mr. State Government comes to us and says: "Gee, folks, oil revenue is down, times are tough, and I'm afraid that I might be going broke."

And we reach for our wallets and say:

"Gosh, Mr. State Government, how much do you need? A tax on my income, would that help? How 'bout a piece of my Permanent Fund check? Not enough? Well, what the heck, Mr. State Government, I don't really need to be inflation-proofing my share of the Permanent Fund. Why don't you just take that money, too?"

Why not, indeed.

Never mind that our state government is the richest guy on the block, with more money stashed away than states with forty or fifty times as many people. Never mind that our state government spends more per capita than any other state in the country. Never mind that for over sixteen years now, experts have been claiming that government bankruptcy is just around the corner. And never mind that we already have a long-range financial plan. It's not a perfect plan, but it's simple, and it's been working just fine for over sixteen years. The plan is that we don't reach into our wallets to support state government until state government is really broke.

In the long run, Alaska's oil revenue is declining. When the day comes that Mr. State Government really is broke, Alaska should start paying for its government the way every other state does—with taxes.

Rich Alaskans, of course, don't like the sound of that. They are afraid the state might choose an income tax. And resource industries are afraid they might lose some of the tax breaks they have on oil, and the tax breaks they hope to get on natural gas. So expect a new long-range scam to be hatched in which the promise is made that the cost of government can be painlessly shifted to the Permanent Fund. I predict that the key to this scam will be the elimination of inflation-proofing.

Will the scam be successful? It is hard to say. In September 1999 the people overwhelmingly rejected a less sophisticated plan. Yet in November 2000, the same voters reelected most of the legislators responsible for the rejected long-range plan. In my opinion, it could go either way.

Source: Commentary by Gregg Erickson on *Alaska Week*, broadcast February 16, 2001.

ENDNOTES

[1] Alaska Department of Labor and Workforce Development, Research and Analysis Division, at http://laborstats.alaska.gov/reshire/reshire.htm.

[2] For a perspective on sustainable development, see Chapter 22, Section 4.

[3] See, UNFCCC, 2014. "Lima to Paris," retrieved November 10, 2015, at http://newsroom.unfccc.int/lima/lima-call-for-climate-action-puts-world-on-track-to-paris-2015/; Coral Davenport, "A Climate Accord Based on Global Peer Pressure," *New York Times*, December 14, 2014; and COP 21, "What is COP About?" retrieved November 10, 2015, at http://www.cop21paris.org/about/cop21.

[4] Monica Gokey, "Climate Change progress at Arctic Council's meeting with US chair," *Morning Edition*, KTOO News (Juneau Public Radio), October 25, 2015.

[5] Robert Hannon, "Ice locked in glaciers may substantially contribute to sea level rise," KUAC Radio (Fairbanks Public Radio), November 9, 2015; and Theresa Soley, "Why a local skier is busing around Lower 48 this winter," *Morning Edition*, KTOO News (Juneau Public Radio), November 8, 2015.

[6] Erica Martinson, "Obama brings funding, climate change announcements on trip to Kotzebue," *Alaska Dispatch News*, September 2, 2015; Carey Restino, "Arctic welcomes first sitting president," *The Arctic Sounder*, September 10, 2015; and Julie Hirschfeld Davis, "Obama's Alaska Visit Puts Climate, Not Energy, in Forefront," *New York Times*, August 31, 2015.

[7] For information on COP 21 see: Natural Resources Defense Council, EcoWatch, "12 Key Takeaways from the Paris Climate Talks," December 13, 2015, at http://ecowatch.com/2015/12/13/key-takeaways-cop21/; and Coral Davenport, "A Climate Accord Based on Global Peer Pressure," *New York Times*, December 14, 2015.

[8] For an explanation of distributive, redistributive, and regulatory policies and their effects, see Chapter 3 on the public policy process, Section 1.

[9] Series of interviews with Thomas B. Stewart by Clive Thomas, May–August 2005.

[10] John Havelock, "Constitutional Convention Can Work to Repair Alaska Politics," *Anchorage Daily News*, August 17, 2012.

[11] Material for this section and Box 30.5 was based, in part, on Gordon S. Harrison, "Alaska's Constitutional 'Literacy Test' and the Question of Voting Discrimination," *Alaska History*, vol. 22 (Spring/Fall 2007): 23–38; and John C. Comer, "The Nebraska Nonpartisan Legislature: An Evaluation," *State and Local Government Review* (Sept. 1980): 98–102.

[12] For an overview of the history of this provision in the constitution, see Gordon Harrison, *Alaska's Constitution; A Citizen's Guide*, 5th ed. (Juneau: Alaska Legislative Affairs Agency, 2012), 125–26.

[13] *Alaskans on the Future of the Permanent Fund* (Juneau: Alaska State Legislature, January 1990).

[14] Alaska Office of Management and Budget, at https://omb.alaska.gov/html/performance/details.html?p=150.

GLOSSARY OF TERMS, CONCEPTS, AND ACRONYMS

This glossary includes terms, concepts, and acronyms used at various places in the book. Terms in italics are defined more fully in another part of the glossary.

Ad hoc policy coalition: Two or more groups, organizations, or individuals that form a temporary alliance on a policy issue.

Affirmative action/affirmative action policies: A policy or program intended to counter discrimination against minorities and women, particularly in employment and education.

Alaska Commercial Fisheries Entry Commission: The body that regulates entry into commercial fisheries. See *limited entry* below.

Alaska Highway: The Alaska-Canadian Highway, or the ALCAN. Constructed during World War II to connect the Lower 48 states to Alaska through Canada, a distance of 1,522 miles.

Alaska National Interest Lands Conservation Act (ANILCA) 1980: A federal act that placed 53.7 million acres of Alaska land into the national wildlife refuge system, parts of twenty-five rivers into the national wild and scenic rivers system, 3.3 million acres into national forest lands, and 43.6 million acres into national park land.

Alaska Native Claims Settlement Act (ANCSA) 1971: Federal legislation granting 44 million acres of land and providing $962.5 million to *Alaska Natives.* It also created *Native for-profit coporations* and some *nonprofit regional associations* as well as *Native village corporations.*

Alaska Natives: In local parlance shortened to Natives, refers to Alaska's indigenous population consisting of Indians, Eskimos, and Aleuts. The term does not include all individuals born in Alaska, who are generically collectively known as *native Alaskans*, with a lower case "n."

Alaska Permanent Fund: An Alaska state savings account funded from some oil and gas revenues and created in 1976 mainly to cushion the instability in state revenues.

***Alaska v. Native Village of Venetie Tribal Government* (1998):** See *Venetie* case.

ALCAN: See *Alaska Highway.*

ANCSA: *Alaska Native Claims Settlement Act.*

ANILCA: *Alaska National Interest Lands Conservation Act.*

ANWR: *Arctic National Wildlife Refuge.*

Appropriation: A statutory authorization to spend a specific amount of public money for a stated purpose. Public funds may not be spent without an appropriation made by law.

Arctic National Wildlife Refuge (ANWR): A nineteen-million-acre (30,000 square miles) wildlife refuge on federal land located east of Barrow on the North Slope, rich in oil and gas deposits.

At-large election district: Where a person is elected to represent an entire jurisdiction, such as a city, county, state, or nation, in contrast to a jurisdiction being divided into several election districts.

Attorney general—AG: The chief legal officer of the state, head of the Department of Law, and a member of the governor's cabinet.

Ballot proposition/ballot measure: The generic term for an aspect of *direct democracy*—a *referendum*, *initiative*, or *recall*—in which the electorate vote "yes" or "no" on an item included on a primary or general election ballot, or in a special election.

Bicameral legislature: One with two houses, a lower and an upper chamber. In the United States this is usually a House and a Senate, though the lower house is often referred as an Assembly.

Bipartisan: Cooperative relationships or agreements—sometimes bipartisan coalitions—across political party lines, usually between Republicans and Democrats.

Bipartisan Working Group (BWG): The majority group of sixteen members in the Alaska State Senate from 2007 to 2012 consisting of Republicans and Democrats. This was officially neither a coalition nor a caucus, but in practice it was both.

Blanket primary election: An election in which candidates are chosen for the general election, where all candidates appear on the same list with their party designation, and any voter, regardless of party affiliation, can vote for any candidate. This primary system existed in Alaska until the late 1990s. See also *modified primary election.*

Block grants: See *federal block grants.*

Blue states: Those dominated by the Democrats.

Blue states, red states, and purple states: These refer to whether the state is largely a Democratic state politically (*blue state*), Republican (*red state*), or fairly evenly balanced (*purple state*). This usage of colors (in contradiction to longtime usage in which red meant radical and blue conservative) stems from the use of the terms by the media, especially during and following the 2000 presidential election.

Boom-bust cycle: Where key economic sectors are subject to major changes in activity due to price fluctuations of their products or to changes in government spending.

Borough: A regional local government (resembling a county in other states) that may include cities within its borders. There are two types of boroughs in Alaska: (1) an organized borough, a region organized under state law as a local government; and (2) the *Unorganized Borough.*

Broad construction: Construing or interpreting a constitution broadly by using the concept of *implied powers.* This is usually associated with a liberal political perspective.

Budget: A formal plan of the allocation of financial resources for government expenditure for a fiscal period, including the means of financing the expenditures. State budgets are divided into two parts: the *operating budget* and the *capital budget.*

Bush caucus: A caucus in the Alaska legislature composed of legislators from rural-bush districts. It includes Alaska Natives and non-Natives.

Capital budget: That part of the state budget for funding projects like buildings and infrastructure that may take several years to complete. See also *operating budget.*

Capital projects: Those involving physical assets, such as public buildings, roads, fire halls, and so on, in contrast to services.

Capitalism: An economic system based on the concept of *individualism* and the private ownership of land and capital equipment, where prices are determined more or less by the supply and demand of the marketplace. Often referred to as the free enterprise system.

Caucus/political caucus: A group of people, usually within a larger body, such as a legislature or a political party, which unites to promote a particular policy or interest. See also *majority caucus* and *minority caucus.*

CBR: *Constitutional Budget Reserve.*

Chief of staff: The person in charge of the Office of the Governor or a legislative office and usually the right-hand person for their boss.

City: An incorporated area with a distinct boundary, a degree of self-government, and legal rights.

Colonialism: Where one country, either militarily or economically or a combination of both, dominates another country, or where one part of a country dominates another part of the same country for its own benefit.

Colony: A country or area dominated by another country or area. See *colonialism.*

Co-management: The joint and cooperative management of a resource or provision of a service by more than one level of government (such as land management by the federal and state governments); or a government working with a *nongovernmental organization* (NGO), nonprofit, or for-profit organization to provide a service, such as health services to Alaska Natives.

Commissioner: Usually refers to the head of a principal department of state government, such as the Department of Natural Resources. It can also refer to members of various boards and commissions, such as the Alaska Public Offices Commission.

Communalism: Where individuals, groups, or society emphasize community goals and values and the general interest as opposed to giving primacy to individual goals and *individualism* as a political philosophy.

Conference committee: An ad hoc legislative committee to reconcile differences in a bill passed by both the House and the Senate.

Conservation/conservationist: See *conservation versus environmentalism.*

Conservation versus environmentalism: Conservation is based on a pragmatic view that humans need to restore and manage the environment to sustain the economic benefits that accrue from it. Thus, conservation is human-centered, protecting nature for humans. In contrast, environmentalism is a response to the destruction of the natural environment caused largely by pollution from the industrialization of the landscape and comes from a more urban perspective. It is grounded in a belief in the intrinsic value of nature and that all elements of nature—trees, grasslands, wetlands, various birds, animals, and marine life, etc.—are worth protecting for their own sake.

Conservative/conservatism: Someone who favors conserving the existing state of affairs, usually including traditional social values, a minimal role for government, and a major role for the private sector.

Constitutional Budget Reserve—CBR: Created by constitutional amendment in 1990 and designed to receive settlement payments from the oil industry. It can be tapped when there is a shortfall in annual revenues or for other purposes with a three-fourths vote of each house of the legislature. When revenues rebound the fund must be repaid.

Contracting-out: See *outsource/outsourcing.*

Corruption: See *political corruption.*

d2 Lands: The shorthand term for section 17(d)(2) of the *Alaska Native Claims Settlement Act (ANCSA)* of 1971 and the lands it directed be set aside for national parks, preserves, and other purposes. The provision was implemented by the federal government though the *Alaska National Interest Land Conservation Act (ANILCA)* of 1980.

Dedicated fund: One designated to receive revenue from a specific source that would otherwise go into the *general fund,* and restricted in its use to a specific purpose. The Alaska Permanent Fund receives some dedicated oil and gas revenues.

Dependent individualism/dependent individualist: An apparent contradiction, but the reality that, although many Alaskans see themselves as individualists and "making it on their own," most are either directly or indirectly dependent on government—federal, state, and local.

Direct democracy: The collective term for the *initiative, referendum,* and *recall* provisions or *ballot propositions* placed on a ballot.

Distributive policy: Programs or grants provided by government directly to a group, a particular constituency, or a political jurisdiction that are not the result of competition in the policy process. No group or constituency is denied a benefit—directly loses—as the result of such policies. See also *redistributive* and *regulatory policy.*

Earmarks: A one-time grant included in a budget for a specific purpose, such as building a health clinic. It is similar to *pork-barrel legislation.*

Economic development versus economic diversity: An important distinction for understanding the Alaska economy. The former is possible through tapping existing natural resources. The latter, producing a balanced mix between primary production, manufacturing, and services, is much more difficult to achieve in Alaska, and many would say impossible.

Economic diversity: See *economic development versus economic diversity.*

Economic multiplier: When the infusion of money through wages, grants, government benefits, and so on, has an economic snowball effect on the economy by generating jobs and other spending.

Economies of scale: Cost savings resulting from producing a product or service at a larger scale or volume. This enables the unit price to be lowered to buyers and stimulates economic activity.

Egalitarian/egalitarianism: A belief that all people are more or less equal as human beings and should enjoy equal social, economic, and political rights and more or less equal political treatment and access to the policy-making process. It is contrasted with *elitism*.

Elitism: The belief that some people are superior to others in various ways particularly based on birth, class, race, and level of education. In the context of government it holds that because of their superiority the elite are entitled to particular privileges and that government should be run by the privileged. Elitism is contrasted with *egalitarianism*.

Empirical knowledge: Something that can be definitively measured using *quantitative* and statistical methods. This is contrasted with *normative knowledge*.

Entitlement program: A government program, such as *Medicaid*, student loans, or the *Permanent Fund Dividend (PFD)*, which, if a citizen meets the program's eligibility criteria and applies for the program, they are "entitled" to receive its benefits by right. Entitlement programs form a major predetermined part of the budgets of all states, including Alaska.

Enumerated powers: Those specifically stated in the constitution, such as that of a governor's veto power. See also *implied powers*.

Environmentalism/environmentalist: See *conservation versus environmentalism*.

Faction: A minority group within a larger group with specific interests or beliefs not always in harmony with the larger group.

Federal block grants: Grants to state and local governments for use in general service areas, such as law enforcement and health services, as opposed to specific programs, such as police training or child mental health.

Federal formula program: A program where the federal government provides funds to state government based on a formula regarding population, level of income in the state, etc., in an attempt to even out income and other disparities between states. *Medicaid* is an example.

Federal overreach: An increasingly used catch phrase that has become popular among conservatives to describe what they see as the federal government being too intrusive in the affairs of the states, thus "overreaching" its constitutional authority.

Federal receipts: Funds received by the state from the federal government to support expenditures made for state programs. See also *federal formula program* and *general fund match*.

Federalism: A system of government in which *legal sovereignty* is divided in the national constitution between the national government (often referred to as the federal government) and several constituent governments that together compose the nation (usually referred to as states or provinces). Theoretically, each level of government has its own sphere of authority. Federal systems are contrasted with *unitary political systems*. See also *intergovernmental relations*.

Fiscal conservatism: A general antipathy toward government spending in general and a particular opposition to enactment of new taxes or an increase in existing ones. Fiscal conservatism also often includes opposition to certain social programs and support for *outsourcing* (or privatizing) many of these programs and other government services to the private sector.

Fiscal federalism: A broad concept with several meanings. It is used particularly with respect to federal relations with state and local governments regarding the payment and transfer of federal funds to these governments. Fiscal federalism often involves much political maneuvering.

Fiscal gap/budget gap: The shortfall, in a particular year, between state general fund revenues and expenditures.

Fiscal note: A document itemizing the cost of a piece of legislation attached to a bill proposed by a legislator. Fiscal notes are subject to considerable politics between supporters and opponents of the legislation.

Fiscal policy: That relating to financial matters in general, including the state budget and public revenues from taxation. Such policies are often used to promote full employment, stable prices, and economic growth.

Fiscal year (FY)/budget year: The fiscal year in Alaska runs from July 1 of one year to June 30 of the next. Fiscal years are designated by the year in which they end. Thus, FY 2016 was the fiscal year beginning on July 1, 2015, and ending on June 30, 2016. The federal fiscal year begins on October 1 of each year and ends on September 30 of the following year.

For-profit Native corporation: One that can legally make a profit like any business or corporation, by producing goods and services or through investments. See also *Native corporation* and *Native regional corporation*.

Free enterprise system: See *capitalism*.

GDP: *Gross Domestic Product*.

General election: An election to determine which candidate will represent voters in a state, district, or locality during the next term of office. At the state and local level in Alaska, general elections often include *ballot propositions* and *judicial confirmation and retention elections*.

General fund (GF): The state's primary budget operating account. All revenues and payments are made to or from this fund except those required to be accounted for in another fund, such as a *dedicated fund*.

General fund match: General fund monies that must be appropriated for a specific program, such as bilingual education, to enable the state to receive federal funds for that program.

Gerrymandering: Drawing the boundaries of an electoral district when it is created or redistricted to give an advantage in the election to one group or party and/or undermine the representation and influence of other groups. This includes gerrymandering to reduce the impact of one political party over another as well as of minority groups, such as African Americans and Native Americans.

Globalization: The process by which economic, social, and to some extent political values converge as they are adopted internationally.

Governmental capacity: The resources available to government, mainly human, material, technical, and financial, which can be used to perform its functions on a day-to-day basis. The most important include: implementing policies and programs, dealing with emergencies, and adapting to changing circumstances, particularly economic and financial circumstances. Related to *policy capacity* and *political capacity*.

Great Depression: A major downturn in the world economy in 1929 with effects lasting until the start of World War II in 1941.

Great Society Programs: A series of policies enacted during 1964–1965 under President Lyndon Johnson that promoted civil rights and social programs such as *Medicare* for senior citizens and *Medicaid* for those with low incomes.

Gross Domestic Product—GDP: The total value of goods and services produced in a nation, state, or region, usually during a year.

Home rule: The authority of municipalities to be able to determine their own form of government and exercise wide powers as provided in state law. Home rule limits the interference by the state in local affairs.

Hyperpluralism: Increased competition among forces in the policy process, particularly interest groups, which can stymie policy making.

Ideology: See *political ideology*.

IGR: *Intergovernmental relations*.

Implied powers: Those that can be inferred or deduced from the *enumerated powers* of a constitution, such as the authority of the legislature to establish district offices for members and hire staff.

Incremental policy making: Policy that develops in small, often ad hoc steps as opposed to developing a broad and integrated set of policies (*programmatic policy making*) in a particular policy area, such as the environment.

Indian Country: By federal law, lands encompassed by Indian (Native American) reservations and delineated by boundaries that are under the sovereign jurisdiction of the tribe.

Indian Reorganization Act—IRA: Enacted by Congress in 1934 and fully extended to Alaska in 1936. It clarified the status of Native Americans by establishing rules for recognizing tribes, strengthening tribal government, aiding tribal business activities, control over lands, and eligibility to receive federal aid.

Individualism/individualist: The American version of individualism emphasizes freedom from government control in all aspects of life, especially in the economic sphere, and lauds self-reliance and private initiative, as opposed to government aid, as keys to personal success

Infrastructure: Large-scale public facilities necessary for economic activity and a minimum level standard of living. These include water and power supplies, roads, bridges, harbors, ports, airports, pipelines, and telecommunications systems. Infrastructure also often includes public schools, universities, convention centers, and even sports stadiums.

Inherent powers: Powers that government possesses whether or not they are specifically assigned to it in a constitution. These include the right to maintain law and order and to raise and spend money.

Initiative: A proposed law placed on the ballot by a citizen petition.

Institution: A social, economic, or political organization with an established set of interactions between the members of the organization for achieving a particular goal or goals. Examples include *tribes* and families (to provide sustenance, kinship, and the raising of the young), churches (to facilitate worship), businesses (to produce goods or services), and government bodies (to develop public policies, deliver services, settle disputes between citizens, and provide protection). Large, formal governmental and political institutions, like the U.S. Congress, government departments, and *political parties*, have rules of operation set out in various documents such as constitutions, statutes, regulations, rules of procedure, and by-laws.

Interest group: An association of individuals (such as, a trade union) or organizations (for example, tour ship companies) or a public or private institution (for instance, a government department), that attempts to influence public policy in its favor but does not seek to formally control government as does a *political party*.

Intergovernmental relations—IGR: The day-to-day interaction of governments at the same level, such as states in the Midwest; or at different levels, such as the federal government and Alaska, or Alaska and local governments, or with Native governments.

Intergovernmental transfers: Money transferred from one government to another, such as federal funds paid to state governments, or state government payments to local governments.

IRA: *Indian Reorganization Act.*

IRA council: A village council formed under the *Indian Reorganization Act*, which may perform certain local government and service delivery functions. See also *Native village corporation* and *Native village council.*

Judicial activism: The courts being proactive and making decisions that create public policy. It is similar to *broad construction* and is contrasted with *strict construction.*

Judicial confirmation and retention elections: Elections for confirming the appointment of judges or to confirm their retention in office.

Judicial Council: A body of seven nonpartisan members that recommends judicial appointments to the governor and conducts studies for improvement of the administration of justice.

Judicial review: The authority of the courts to pass judgment on the constitutionality of laws, rules, and actions of the legislative and executive branches of government.

Laissez-faire: A French term meaning "leave it alone," used to describe minimal government interference in the economy and in society in general.

Legal sovereignty: The ultimate power to make laws and thus public policies. In the U.S. Constitution this is divided between the national (federal) government and the states. See also *political sovereignty.*

Legislative committees: These are of various types. See *standing committee, conference committee*, and *special committee.*

Legislative director/liaison: A person appointed by an interest group, business, or government agency (such as the Governor's Office) to organize and coordinate dealings with the legislature and sometimes agencies in the executive branch.

Legislative interim: The part of the year when the legislature is not in session. No laws can be enacted during this time unless the legislature is called into a *special session*.

Legislative liaison: See *lobbyist*.

Legislative supermajority: See *supermajority*.

Liberal/liberalism: Three key elements of political liberalism are promoting equality, enhancing human dignity, and creating a sense of political community through policies that benefit the entire society. Modern-day American liberalism is different from liberalism at the time of the founding of the nation, which saw achieving equality as best secured through minimal (*laissez-faire*) government. Today, liberals favor using government to redistribute resources; protect economic, social, and political well-being of individuals; promote human rights, such as the right to an abortion and gay rights; and to protect the environment against various types of degradation.

Liberal democracy: A democracy similar to those in the United States and Western Europe in which political parties, interest groups, and individuals are free to organize and compete for political power to get policies enacted or blocked, and where there is freedom of expression, including a free press. Often called *pluralist democracy*, it contrasts with democracies, such as the former Soviet Union, with only one party, no political opposition, and strict controls on the media.

Libertarianism: Not to be confused with *liberalism*, it advocates complete freedom of thought and action by the individual unencumbered by the authority and actions of government. Thus, government's role will be very minimal and, as much as possible, its functions performed by private organizations.

Limited entry: A policy adopted in 1972 by constitutional amendment that limits the number of people who can fish in various Alaska fisheries.

Limited Entry Commission: The three-member state body that administers *limited entry* into various fisheries.

Line item: A budget term for a specific expenditure (such as for salaries or for computer services) included in the budget by a state agency, the governor, or the legislature.

Line item veto: A governor's constitutional authority to strike or reduce specific budget items.

Lobbying: The interaction of an individual, group, interest or organization with policy makers, either directly or indirectly, with the goal of influencing current policy or creating a relationship conducive to shaping future policy to the benefit of that individual, group, or interest.

Lobbyist: A person designated by an interest group to facilitate influencing public policy in that group's favor. Lobbyists are of five types: (1) contract lobbyists, who are freelancers and often work for more than one client; (2) in-house lobbyists, who, as part or all of their job, represent their business or organization; (3) legislative liaisons, who represent government agencies; (4) volunteer or cause lobbyists; and (5) individuals who represent themselves or causes in which they are the dominant person.

Longevity Bonus Program: An Alaska state program established in 1972 that paid senior citizens over sixty-five years old $250 a month. Because of state budget problems it began to be phased out in 1994, and no citizens who turned sixty-five after 1996 received a bonus. The program was discontinued in 2003.

Majority caucus: The group in the Alaska House of Representatives or Senate that has the majority of members in that body and runs the chamber. The majority caucus is usually dominated by one party—Republicans or Democrats—but often includes members of another party or is a coalition. See also *Bipartisan Working Group (BWG)*.

Matching funds: See *general fund match*.

Medicaid: A federal program established in 1965 that provides medical care to low-income Americans.

Medicare: Established in 1965, a federal program that provides health care coverage to senior citizens.

Mental health trust lands: Lands given by the federal government to the Territory of Alaska to generate income to fund programs for the mentally disabled. The State of Alaska misappropriated these lands. In the 1980s and 1990s court challenges restored the lands, and $200 million was given to the Mental Health Trust Authority, created to administer the trust.

Minority caucus: The caucus in the minority in the Alaska House or Senate that offers alternative proposals to those presented by the *majority caucus*.

Modified closed primary election: Under this system, those registered as partisan are given their party's primary ballot. All those registered as undeclared or nonpartisan choose a ballot of one party or the other. See also, *primary election* and *blanket primary election*.

***Molly Hootch* Consent Decree:** An agreement (the *Tobeluk v. Lind* consent decree of 1976), between the state and a group of Alaska Native schoolchildren that the state would build high schools in most villages so that students would not have to leave home to attend high school.

Monetary policy: Government policies concerning interest rates and the supply of money designed to influence economic goals, such as full employment, stable prices, exchange rates, and economic growth.

Multinational companies/corporations—MNCs: Companies with operations—production or sales or both—in several countries, such as British Petroleum, Microsoft, and Sony. Sometimes referred to as transnational companies/corporations (TNCs).

Multiplier effect: See *economic multiplier*.

National Petroleum Reserve–Alaska—NPR-A: A federal reserve of twenty-three million acres (36,000 square miles) located on the North Slope west of *ANWR* and rich in oil deposits. Created in 1923 as Naval Petroleum Reserve Number 4, in 1976 it was renamed NPR-A. It is administered by the Bureau of Land Management (BLM), part of the Department of the Interior.

Nationalization/nationalized industries: The taking over of private industries by a government so that the government owns and runs them directly or through a special corporation or other entity. Industries most often run by governments in democratic countries are railroads, utilities, airlines, various aspects of health care, the steel industry, and natural resources extraction. See *privatize*.

Native Alaskan: All those born in Alaska, whatever their race or ethnicity, with the term native usually having a lowercased "n." Not to be confused with *Alaska Natives*.

Native corporations: These are of several types, with membership restricted to certain *Alaska Natives*. These corporations were set up by the *Indian Reorganization Act (IRA)* and the *Alaska Native Claims Settlement Act (ANCSA)*. See also *for-profit Native corporation, IRA council, nonprofit Native regional associations, Native village corporation, Native village councils, traditional tribal council*, and *tribe*.

Native regional corporations: Set up by *ANCSA* (the *Alaska Native Claims Settlement Act*), they are of two types: for-profit regional corporations (twelve in the state and one for nonresidents), which function, more or less, like regular businesses; and twelve *nonprofit Native regional associations*, mainly providing social services.

Native sovereignty: The contention that Alaska Natives are sovereign (completely in control of their own affairs and not subject to any other governmental jurisdictions, such as the U.S. or Alaska governments) within a certain territory, usually Native-owned and controlled lands. See also *Venetie case*.

Native village corporations: Set up under the *Alaska Native Claims Settlement Act (ANCSA)*, they may own land and perform certain local government functions and provide some social services.

Native village councils: These are of two types: *traditional tribal councils* (usually referred to as *tribal councils*) established under tribal customs, and *IRA councils* established by federal law under the *Indian Reorganization Act*. See also, *Native village corporations*.

Natives: Shorthand for *Alaska Natives*.

New Deal: Developed under President Franklin D. Roosevelt in the mid-to-late 1930s, and intended to counter the worst effects of the *Great Depression*. It set up a range of programs, including those to aid industry and agriculture, put people to work, and established *Social Security* for senior citizens.

NGO: *Nongovernmental organization.*

Nongovernmental organization: Those that are not part of government or of the for-profit business sector, and often referred to as the third sector. Some NGOs have a general social purpose that in many cases does not involve them in politics, while other NGOs use political advocacy to promote their cause. Examples include: Doctors Without Borders (largely a non-political group offering medical aid in poor countries and in war zones); and organizations with a major advocacy focus, such as Greenpeace, the international environmental group, and Amnesty International, which works for prisoners' rights and related issues regarding the justice systems around the world.

Nonpartisan elections: Elections where political parties are prohibited from supporting candidates and participating in elections. Local government elections in Alaska are nonpartisan, as are retention elections for judges.

Nonprofit Native regional associations: There are twelve of these. Some existed before the *Alaska Native Claims Settlement Act (ANCSA)* of 1971, while others came into existence at that time or later. They provide social services and programs, such as day care and housing, and were intended to take these services over from the federal government. See *Native regional corporations.*

Normative statement/normative analysis: Related to norms or values as opposed to quantifiable, testable hypotheses and *empirical knowledge.*

NPR-A: See *National Petroleum Reserve–Alaska.*

Office of Management and Budget—OMB: An executive branch office that assists the governor in determining the allocation of state resources, preparing his or her budget, and managing state programs.

OECD: See *Organisation for Economic Co-operation and Development.*

OMB: *Office of Management and Budget.*

OPEC: *Organization of the Petroleum Exporting Countries.*

Operating budget: That part of the state budget authorized for one year only for day-to-day government operations, such as salaries, supplies, and renting buildings. It is contrasted with the *capital budget.*

Ordinance: A law or rule passed by a local government.

Organisation for Economic Co-operation and Development—OECD: An international organization of thirty-four countries established in 1961 to promote economic progress and world trade based on liberal democratic principles.

Organization of the Petroleum Exporting Countries—OPEC: An organization of twelve developing countries, including Saudi Arabia, Iran, and Nigeria, based in Vienna, which works to safeguard the interests of its members with regard to oil production, including the stability of its price. The United States, and thus Alaska, are not members of OPEC.

Outsourcing: A government agency, business, or other organization, placing the performance of a function or service with an outside organization or business, rather than performing it itself.

Owner State: The idea that Alaska is in a unique position in owning extensive land and natural resources that provide the state with major revenue sources and policy opportunities not available to other states.

Own-source state revenue: The funds the state raises through its own taxes and fees. These revenues do not include federal funds.

Parliamentary system: A form of government in which the executive is drawn from the legislature. Most, if not all, members of the cabinet, including the prime minister, must first be elected to the parliament. These systems contrast with the *separation of powers* system used in the United States. But, like the United States, in parliamentary systems that are *liberal democracies*, the judicial branch is separate and independent.

Partisanship: Belonging to, voting for, or favoring the position of one political party over others, such as Republican over Democrat.

Permanent Fund: See *Alaska Permanent Fund.*

Permanent Fund Dividend—PFD: The yearly dividend paid to Alaskans from the earnings of the *Alaska Permanent Fund.*

PFD: *Permanent Fund Dividend.*

Plural executive: Where the top executive officials in a state, including the governor and lieutenant governor, are elected separately by the voters. These officials also include the attorney general and commissioner of education/public instruction, among four or five others. A plural executive can inhibit a governor's ability to coordinate policy and contrasts with a *unified executive.*

Pluralism/pluralist/political pluralism: The natural existence in society and legitimate acceptance of many forces, such as political parties, interest groups, individuals, public bodies (including government agencies), and quasi-public organizations (for example, state-owned enterprises), that compete to get their policies enacted or prevent their opponents' policies being enacted into law or regulation.

Pluralist democracy: Same as *liberal democracy.* See also *pluralism.*

Policy agenda: Sometimes referred to as the political agenda. It is the array of issues being dealt with by government.

Policy capacity: The effectiveness of the *policy process* to address problems and issues brought before government. Related to *governmental capacity* and *policy capacity.*

Policy community: All the groups, organizations, government agencies, members of the public, lobbyists, and elected and appointed officials concerned with an area of policy, such as the environment or transportation. See also *ad hoc policy coalition* and *policy network.*

Policy cycle: Similar to *policy process.*

Policy entrepreneur: An elected or appointed public official or prominent private citizen who champions issues in a policy area, such as educational services for disabled children, which are not high priorities to their party, constituents, or society as a whole. This is contrasted with the promotion of policies by the collective action of parties, legislative caucuses, the executive branch, interest groups, and so on.

Policy environment: Similar to the *political environment.*

Policy evaluation: Reviewing a policy during the stages of its enactment, identifying the political factors that determined its success, and examining whether its intended purpose was achieved once implemented.

Policy network: The various individuals and groups sharing information in a particular policy area, such as K–12 education. It has some similarities to a *policy community.*

Policy process: The series of stages through which a policy proposal goes when being considered. It involves getting it on the *policy agenda,* being considered by government, enactment, implementation and reaction to the policy by groups pro and con. The policy process is often referred to as the *policy cycle* because, once enacted, attempts may be made to modify or reform it. Thus, policies go through a cycle of stages that are repeated as they are reconsidered.

Political action committee—PAC: An organization set up by an interest group to raise and channel money to candidates it wants elected or reelected, to promote a particular issue, or to mount a campaign against a candidate or issue it opposes, including those in the form of *ballot propositions.*

Political agenda: Used interchangeably with *policy agenda.*

Political capacity: The effectiveness, or lack thereof, of the political system in general to muster support within society to form a political consensus to deal with issues and problems that face the society. Related to *governmental capacity* and *policy capacity.*

Political corruption: In the broadest sense, corruption is the illegal use of public resources for private gain. This is the definition used by Transparency International, the world's leading organization working to combat corruption.

Political culture: The values and beliefs about the form and extent of the *political process* (what is and is not acceptable political behavior), government operations, including governmental power and limits on it, and how individuals view their relationship to the system, including the extent of *political efficacy.*

Political development: The development of the institutions, attitudes, and values that form the political power system of a society.

Political economy: The interrelationship of the economy (particularly natural and other resources available or lacking, major businesses, and types of employment) and politics (political beliefs, major conflicts in society and processes for resolving them, and so on) in shaping both the political and economic systems in general, and public policies in particular.

Political efficacy: A feeling or belief that a citizen or organization can affect the actions of government through their involvement in the *political process* by voting, membership in a political party or an interest group, lobbying, political protests, or other action. A successful democratic system requires high perceptions of citizen political efficacy.

Political environment: The numerous socio-economic, religious, historical, geographical, and other factors within which the *political system* and *policy process* operate and that shape the actions of government.

Political ideology: A set of values (often called a political philosophy) from which a person derives his or her attitude and reaction to political events and issues and which guides political conduct. A major question with which political ideologies are concerned is: Should the role of government be minimal, extensive, or a middle course in society and people's lives? Thus, political ideologies range from very left-wing (communist and *socialist*) to moderate value systems (such as *liberalism* and moderate *conservatism*) to right-wing conservative to authoritarian. Political ideology is often contrasted with *political pragmatism*.

Political organizations: The collective term used to describe *political parties* and *interest groups*, which are the two major forms of informal political organizations as opposed to formal constitutional, governmental institutions, such as legislatures, executives, and judiciaries.

Political party: A group with a broad consensus on the direction that society should take and how government should or should not be used to promote its vision. Parties run candidates in elections to win formal control of government and to be able to implement their programs.

Political patronage: The governmental or political appointments or privileges that a politician can give to loyal supporters.

Political pragmatism: Often contrasted with *political ideology* as it de-emphasizes ideology, dogma, and sometimes even cherished principles if these get in the way of achieving a particular political or policy goal. It emphasizes a flexible approach to dealing with political issues and problems. This can involve politicians working across party lines or with opposing groups to form an *ad hoc policy coalition* to deal with a problem.

Political process: The interaction of various elements, including elected and appointed officials, the public, *political parties*, *interest groups*, and *institutions* of governments (including legislatures, governors, and court systems), in an attempt to resolve conflict over issues and produce public policy. The political process involves the *policy process*.

Political rhetoric: Generally used to denote empty talk by politicians, government officials, and the public regarding politics, as in the expression "mere rhetoric," that may include unsubstantiated or distorted facts or opinions. It also often denotes a major difference between what is promised and what is actually achievable in practice.

Political socialization: The process by which people acquire their *political culture*. It begins in early childhood and is transmitted by parents and families, peer groups, schools and colleges, the media, churches, and other socialization agents.

Political sovereignty: The ultimate power to decide on laws and public policies in a society. In *liberal* or *pluralist democracies* political sovereignty lies with the people (technically the electorate) and is separate from *legal sovereignty* (the ultimate power to make laws).

Political symbolism: Generally, a physical symbol or image of speech used to represent a political standpoint or perspective. For example, *red states* in the United States are Republican states and *blue states* Democratic, and many people in the American West talk of themselves as "victims" of federal government power or insensitivity.

Political system: The interconnection of various organizations (such as political parties and interest groups) and institutions (such as a legislature and a governor), as well as individuals, which interact to produce the outcome of public policies. Power is the motive force of the system.

Populism: An amorphous political creed that is largely reactive and often referred to as radical conservatism. It is the product of a segment of society (usually the less well-off, working class, small business-owners and farmers) feeling dispossessed or beleaguered because of major economic or social changes. This was originally expressed in the *populist movement* of the late nineteenth century. Today, elements of populism include overt or covert racism, anti-immigrant, and anti-government attitudes. In essence, populism sees "the people" (as expressed in the "will of the people") as having instincts that provide guidance for the legitimate actions of public officials to remedy existing wrongs. Populist movements are often led by a charismatic politician, who symbolizes popular discontent.

Populist movement: A U.S. movement of the last quarter of the nineteenth century spearheaded by farmers in the South, Midwest, and West. It was a reaction to big business, particularly the monopoly of the railroads, and favored government ownership and/or regulation of big business. See *populism*.

Pork-barrel legislation: An appropriation for funding something that benefits a particular district by "bringing home the pork." As a result the legislator responsible wins favor with local voters. Park-barrel legislation is similar to an *earmark*.

Pragmatism: See *political pragmatism*.

President of the Alaska State Senate: The presiding officer during floor sessions in the Alaska State Senate chamber and the major leader of the Senate majority party or party coalition. Much political bargaining is often involved in the selection of a Senate President.

Primary election: Where candidates of the same political party run against each other to determine the party's candidate in the general election.

Private for-profit organization: A privately-owned business or one with stockholders that provides goods or services to make a profit.

Private nonprofit organizations: An organization, often aided by volunteers, with a board of directors that provides a service to the public but is not based on the profit motive. Usually funded by grants and government or private donations, among other sources. Examples include the American Red Cross, the Salvation Army, and local humane societies.

Privatize: To transfer an enterprise, such as a railroad or utility, from government ownership to private ownership. It is the reverse of *nationalization/nationalized industries.*

Programmatic policy making: The process of creating a comprehensive program as opposed to adding small changes or increments. See also *incremental policy making.*

Progressive tax: A tax, such as a graduated income tax, that increases with income and thus collects a higher proportion of the income of individuals and organizations that have higher incomes. It contrasts with a *regressive tax.*

Progressivism/Progressive Movement: Whereas the *populist movement* was rural and working class, this movement was urban and middle class. The movement spanned the years from 1900 to 1917 and was a reaction against the political corruption and partisanship of the post-Civil War era. It advocated *nonpartisan* and *at-large elections* in local government; the application of business techniques to government; and the appointment of nonpartisan boards and commissions and administrators, such as city managers, based upon their expertise as opposed to their political affiliations. The *initiative*, *referendum*, and *recall* were a product of this movement, with the goal of putting more power over political decisions in the hands of the electorate and out of the reach of party bosses. The success of the goals of progressivism have been mixed.

Purple states: Those evenly balanced politically between Democrats and Republicans. See also *blue states* and *red states.*

Qualitative analysis/research: Based upon the quality or character of something as opposed to its size, number, or other *quantitative* measure.

Quantitative analysis/research: Based on statistics and/or other mathematical approaches. See also *qualitative analysis.*

Quasi-governments: Organizations, businesses, and agencies under the guidance of the government, but largely separate and autonomous from government control. Examples include public universities, government-owned businesses (such as utilities), and organizations to promote trade.

REAA: See *Rural Education Attendance Area.*

Reapportionment and redistricting: Often used synonymously, but there is a difference between them. Reapportionment is the reallocation of seats in a legislature; redistricting is redrawing district boundaries to meet the one-person-one-vote rule established by the federal courts. Reapportionment usually leads to redrawing of legislative districts.

Recall election: The electorate voting to remove an elected official (in some cases an appointed official) from office before their term in office has expired.

Redistributive policy: The reallocation of resources—money, special status or other benefits—from one group to another, such as increasing taxes on the middle class to cover welfare payments for the poor. Redistributive policies often cause major political conflicts.

Red state: One dominated politically by the Republicans. See *blue states* and *purple states.*

Redistricting: See *reapportionment.*

Referendum: Where a governing body, such as a legislature, city council, or borough assembly, submits to the voters proposed laws, constitutional or charter amendments, or bond issues, among other provisions, for acceptance or rejection. It also refers to the process where citizens propose a ballot measure to repeal a recently enacted law.

Regionalism: The feeling of identity with a particular geographical area based upon interest, usually economic but also often ethnic or racial. Regionalism manifests itself in rivalries with other regions in a state or country over factors such as social and political values, public priorities, and the allocation of public funds.

Regressive tax: One that all citizens and/or organizations pay at the same rate regardless of their income level or ability to pay. As a result, the poor pay a greater percentage of their income than the wealthy. Tobacco, gasoline, liquor, and sales taxes, are the most regressive taxes. See also *progressive tax.*

Regulatory policy: Provisions that restrict or control actions by individuals, groups, or organizations, to prevent activities that are deemed to be dangerous, unacceptable, or otherwise protect individuals or society as a whole. Such policies often generate a strong negative reaction from those being regulated.

Restricted revenue: Revenue received by a government that has to be used for a certain purpose, such as funding education or port improvements. It is similar to a *dedicated fund* and contrasts with *unrestricted revenue.*

Revenue sharing: Transfer of funds to another level of government with few strings attached. Once a common form of local government funding by the State of Alaska, it has declined since the mid-1980s.

Rider: A clause added to a bill, usually with little if any relevance to the bill's main subject, to benefit a particular group or constituency of the person adding the rider. When this involves money it is similar to an *earmark.* Riders are prohibited by the Alaska Constitution.

Royalty payments: Money paid to a landlord for the right to take minerals, oil, and gas from their land.

Rural Education Attendance Area—REAA: School districts in the *Unorganized Borough.*

Sales tax: A tax placed on the purchase of goods and services as a percentage (such as 1, 3, 5, or a higher percent) of the total cost. Some states and communities exempt certain purchases, such as essentials, including food and prescription drugs.

Separation of powers: A much misunderstood term. It is often described as three branches of government—legislative, executive, and judicial—with separate officials—where no one member of one branch can be a member of the other—and those branches having separate authority (or power, as used in common speech). The more accurate definition is separate officials sharing power (authority) as all three branches of government exercise various forms of legislative, executive, and judicial powers. The term is often contrasted with a *parliamentary system*.

Severance tax: A charge for the extraction—severing—from the ground of natural resources, such as oil, natural gas, and minerals.

Social Security: A federal retirement and disability program for senior citizens established by the Social Security Act of 1935.

Socialism: When socialism operates in pluralist democracies it emphasizes economic well-being, communal values, and promoting the self-respect and worth of the individual. This often involves public ownership of essential industries and public utilities so that they can be used for the common good. It also includes an extensive social welfare system, including universal health care financed by taxing wealthy individuals and organizations at a progressively higher level.

Sovereign wealth funds—SWF: A government-owned investment fund, such as the Alaska Permanent Fund, invested in the stock market and in other assets. Many SWFs are funded by receipts from natural resource revenues, such as from oil and minerals.

Speaker of the House of Representatives: The presiding officer during floor sessions in the Alaska House of Representatives and the major leader of the House majority party or party coalition. The choice of speaker often involves much political maneuvering.

Special committee: A legislative committee set up for a special purpose, such as on particular aspects of oil and gas. Such committees are often disbanded after the particular task has been accomplished.

Special districts: Sometimes referred to as special purpose districts, these are geographical areas for the delivery of a particular service at the local government level, such as water, electricity, transit, and so on.

Special session: A session of a legislature outside its regular annual or biennial session. In Alaska either the governor or the legislature can call such a session. The topic or topics to be dealt with must be specified, however, and no other business can be conducted outside of that topic or topics.

Standing committee: A permanent committee of the House or Senate that hears bills introduced into the respective houses. They are organized along functional and policy areas, such as education, labor, and so on.

Strict construction: Construing or interpreting the constitution strictly or narrowly by arguing that the only authority of government is that contained in the *enumerated powers*. This is usually associated with a conservative political perspective.

Subsistence: In Alaska this refers to the legal right of rural residents, in effect *Alaska Natives*, to take fish and game and to gather flora (plants, fruits, and berries, among others) for personal consumption, and to have preference in such activities over urban residents in times of shortages of these resources.

Supermajority: The requirement on some subjects and issues that the number of votes for passage or approval be more than 50 percent plus 1. For instance, a proposed constitutional amendment by the Alaska legislature requires a two-thirds majority of each house; and it takes three-fourths of each house to appropriate money from the *Constitutional Budget Reserve—CBR*.

Supplemental budget request: Often called a "supplemental," it is an addition to an existing fiscal year budget for some unforeseen cost.

Sustainable development: Emphasizes environmental quality as a condition of economic development, so that development does not deprive future generations of the benefits of such quality.

TAPS: *Trans-Alaska Pipeline System*.

Tea Party/Tea Party movement: A loose-knit *populist* movement that emerged in 2009 and is *conservative*, in some ways *libertarian*, and anti-government. It favors lowering taxes, cutting the federal deficit, and *strict construction* of the constitution. There is dispute about the origin of its name. Some say it is named after the Boston Tea Party protest of 1773 against the British tax on tea. Others argue that "Tea" is an acronym of *T*axed *E*nough *A*lready.

Traditional tribal councils: Usually shortened to *tribal council,* formed through custom and necessity. While not formally organized under U.S. law (as are *IRA councils*), they may still be recognized under federal and state laws. They perform some local government and service functions. See also *Native village councils.*

Trans-Alaska Pipeline System (TAPS): Built between 1974 and 1977, it runs 789 miles from Prudhoe Bay on the North Slope to the ice-free port of Valdez in Prince William Sound.

Tribal council/government: See *traditional tribal councils, Native village councils,* and *Native village corporations.*

Tribe: A social group based on kinship and customs that existed before the development of nation-states.

Unfunded mandate: One level or part of government, through law or regulation, requiring—mandating—that another level or branch perform a function but providing no funding for it.

Unicameral legislature: A one-house legislature. Nebraska is the only state in the United States with a unicameral legislature.

Unified executive: Where the governor and lieutenant governor are elected directly and are from the same political party, but other top executive officials, particularly heads of state departments, are appointed and can be removed by the governor. It is the opposite of a *plural executive.*

Unitary political system: Where *legal sovereignty* is held entirely by the central government, as in France, Sweden, and New Zealand; it is contrasted with *federalism.*

Unorganized Borough: Often referred to as *the* Unorganized Borough, it is the 60 percent of Alaska with no organized boroughs. But it does contain many cities and villages. Most of its services, particularly education, are provided by the state.

Unrestricted revenue: Money received by a government that goes into the *general fund* and can be used for any purpose designated by law. It contrasts with *restricted revenue* and *dedicated funds.*

***Venetie* case:** A 1998 U.S. Supreme Court decision in *Alaska v. Native Village of Venetie Tribal Government* that held that, outside of a few federal jurisdictions, Indian Country does not exist in Alaska.

Village corporations: See *Native village corporations.*

Village councils: See *Native village councils.*

Watergate Affair: A major scandal of 1972–1974 involving a break-in to the Democratic Party headquarters in the Watergate building in Washington, D.C. It produced a major congressional investigation, resulting in several While House staff going to prison and the resignation of President Richard Nixon in August 1974.

Source: Developed by the editors.

FURTHER READING AND RESEARCH RESOURCES

This listing of resources on Alaska politics, government, and public policy also includes some sources on the states and the nation for making comparisons. The listing is organized into eight sections:

1. Reference and Statistical Sources
2. Politics and Government in States and Regions
3. Alaska's Development, History, and Society
4. General Sources on Alaska Politics, Government, and Public Policy
5. Governmental Institutions and Processes in Alaska
6. Policy Making, Political Institutions, and Influences on Public Policy
7. Alaska Political Issues and Public Policies
8. Biographies, Autobiographies, and Popular Works on Alaska

1. REFERENCE AND STATISTICAL SOURCES

Printed Sources

Almanac of the 50 States: Basic Data Profiles with Comparative Tables, 2010 Edition (Woodside, CA: Information Publications, 2010), and previous editions.

Barone, Michael, *et al.*, *The Almanac of American Politics* (Chicago: University of Chicago Press, 2014).

Gates, Nancy, ed., *The Alaska Almanac: Facts about Alaska*, 35th ed. (Anchorage: Alaska Northwest Books, 2015).

The Book of the States, vol. 47 (Lexington, KY: The Council of State Governments, 2015), and previous volumes.

Websites

Alaska Department of Labor and Workforce Development, at http://labor.alaska.gov/

Dittman Research and Communications Corporation, at http://www.dittmanresearch.com/

Institute of Social and Economic Research, University of Alaska Anchorage, at www.iser.uaa.alaska.edu

National Institute on Money in State Politics, at http://www.followthemoney.org/

U.S. Census Bureau. *State & County Quickfacts*, at http://quickfacts.census.gov/qfd/index.html

U.S. Department of Commerce, Bureau of Economic Analysis, at http://www.bea.gov/index.html

2. POLITICS AND GOVERNMENT IN STATES AND REGIONS

Council of State Governments, at http://www.csg.org/

Donovan, Todd, Daniel A. Smith, Tracy Osborn, and Christopher Z. Mooney, *State and Local Politics: Institutions and Reform*, 4th. ed. (Belmont, CA: Wadsworth Cengage Learning, 2015).

Dye, Thomas R., and Susan A. MacManis, *Politics in States and Communities*, 15th ed. (Upper Saddle River, N.J.: Pearson/Prentice Hall, 2014).

Gray, Virginia, Russell L. Hanson, and Thad Kousser, eds., *Politics in the American States: A Comparative Analysis*, 10th eds. (Washington, D.C.: CQ Press, 2013).

Gray, Virginia, "The Socioeconomic and Political Context of States," in Gray, Hanson, and Kousser, *Politics in the American States*.

The Regions and Selected States

Regions

CSG-West (Western Region of the Council of State Governments), at http://www.csgwest.org/

Danver, Steven. L., ed., *Encyclopedia of Politics of the American West* (Washington, D.C.: CQ Press, 2013).

Haider-Markel, Donald P., ed., *Political Encyclopedia of U.S. States and Regions* (Washington, D.C.: CQ Press, 2008).

Thomas, Clive S., ed., *Politics and Public Policy in the Contemporary American West* (Albuquerque: University of New Mexico Press, 1991).

Selected Western States

Gerston, Larry N., and Terry Christensen, *California Politics and Government: A Practical Approach*, 11th ed. (Belmont, CA: Wadsworth Publishing, 2011).

Daum, Courtney W., Robert J. Duffy, and John A. Straayer, eds., *State of Change: Colorado Politics in the Twenty-First Century* (Boulder: University Press of Colorado, 2011).

Clayton, Cornell, W., and Nicholas P. Lovrich, eds., *Governing Washington* (Pullman: Washington State University Press, 2011).

Pratt, Richard C., and Zachary A. Smith, *Hawai'i Politics and Government: An American State in a Pacific World* (Lincoln: University of Nebraska Press, 2000).

Selected Other States

Conant, James K., *Wisconsin Politics and Government: America's Laboratory of Democracy* (Lincoln: University of Nebraska Press, 2006).

Lamis, Alexander P., and Brian Usher, *Ohio Politics*, 2nd ed., revised and updated (Kent, OH: Kent State University Press, 2007).

Nash, Jere, and Andy Taggart, *Mississippi Politics: The Struggle for Power, 1976–2008*, 2nd ed. (Oxford, MS: University Press of Mississippi, 2009).

Newell, Charldean, David F. Prindle, and James Riddlesperger, *Texas Politics*, 12th ed. (Belmont, CA: Wadsworth Publishing 2012).

Palmer, Kenneth T., G. Thomas Taylor, Jean E. Lavigne, and Marcus A. LiBrizzi, *Maine Politics and Government*, 2nd ed. (Lincoln: University of Nebraska Press, 2009).

Parent, Wayne, *Inside the Carnival: Unmasking Louisiana Politics* (Baton Rouge: Louisiana State University Press, 2006).

Schneier, Edward V., John Brian Murtaugh, and Antoinette Pole, *New York Politics: A Tale of Two States*, 2nd ed. (Armonk, NY: M. E. Sharpe, 2009).

3. ALASKA'S DEVELOPMENT, HISTORY, ECONOMY, AND SOCIETY

Araji, Sharon R., ed. *Society: An Alaskan Perspective* (Dubuque, IA: Kendall/Hunt, 1994),

Cuba, Lee. *Community and Identity on the Alaska Frontier* (Philadelphia: Temple University Press, 1987).

Falk, Marvin W., *Alaska History: An Annotated Bibliography* (Westport, CT: Praeger, 2006).

Gruening, Ernest, *The State of Alaska* (New York: Random House, 1968).

Harrison, Gordon S., *Alaska Public Policy: Current Problems and Issues* (Fairbanks: University of Alaska Institute of Social, Government and Economic Research, 1971).

Haycox, Stephen, *Alaska: An American Colony* (Seattle: University of Washington Press, 2006).

Haycox, Stephen W., and Mary Childers Mangusso, eds. *An Alaska Anthology: Interpreting the Past* (Seattle: University of Washington Press, 1996).

Hickel, Walter J., *Crisis in the Commons: The Alaska Solution* (Oakland, CA: ICG, Institute of Governmental Studies for the Institute of the North and Alaska Pacific University, 2002).

Hunt, William R., *Alaska: A Bicentennial History* (New York: W. W. Norton, 1976).

Kimura, G.W., ed. *Alaska at 50: The Past, Present and Next Fifty Years of Alaska Statehood* (Fairbanks: University of Alaska Press, 2009).

Kleinfeld, Judith, "How the Frontier Imagery of the Alaskan North Shapes the People Who Come," *The Northern Review* 27 (Fall 2007): 38–59.

Kollin, Susan, *Nature's State: Imagining Alaska as the Last Frontier* (Chapel Hill: The University of North Carolina Press, 2001).

Kresge, David T., Thomas A. Morehouse, and George W. Rogers, *Issues in Alaska Development* (Seattle: University of Washington Press, 1977).

Lane, Theodore, ed., *Developing America's Northern Frontier* (Lanham, MD: University Press of America, 1987).

Langdon, Steve J. *The Native People of Alaska*, 4th ed. (Anchorage: Greatland Graphics, 2002).

Lopez, Ana E., *et al. Alaska 50: Celebrating Alaska's 50th Anniversary of Statehood 1959–2009* (Tampa, FL: Faircount Media Group, 2008).

Naske, Claus-M, and Herman E. Slotnick, *Alaska: A History*, 3rd ed. (Norman, OK: University of Oklahoma Press, 2011).

Rogers, George W., *The Future of Alaska: Economic Consequences of Statehood* (Baltimore: The Johns Hopkins University Press, 1962).

———, ed., *Change in Alaska: People, Petroleum, and Politics* (Seattle: University of Washington Press, 1970).

Institute of Social and Economic Research, "Understanding Alaska: People, Economy, and Resources" (Anchorage: University of Alaska, ISER, 2006). On-line report available at www.alaskaneconomy.uaa.alaska.edu.

Whitehead, John S., *Completing the Union: Alaska, Hawai'i, and the Battle for Statehood* (Albuquerque University of New Mexico Press, 2004).

4. GENERAL SOURCES ON ALASKA POLITICS, GOVERNMENT, AND PUBLIC POLICY

McBeath, Gerald A., and Thomas A. Morehouse, *Alaska Politics and Government* (Lincoln: University of Nebraska Press, 1994).

———, eds., *Alaska State Government and Politics* (Fairbanks: University of Alaska Press, 1987).

Thomas, Clive S., ed., *Alaska Public Policy Issues: Background and Perspectives* (Juneau: Denali Press, 1999).

Articles, Chapters in Books, Papers, and Guides

DeArmond, Robert, ed. *Who's Who in Alaska Politics* (Portland, OR: Binford and Mort, 1977).

Handbook on Alaska State Government (State of Alaska Legislative Affairs Agency, 2011). This can be downloaded in pdf format from the Alaska State Legislature's publication website, at http://w3.legis.state.ak.us/pubs/pubs.php.

Haycox, Stephen W., "The View from Above: Alaska and the Great Northwest," in *The Great Northwest: The Search for Regional Identify*, in ed. William G. Robbins (Corvallis: Oregon State University Press, 2001), 145–57.

Knapp, Gunnar, "Four Alaska Innovations," a Presentation to the Board of Directors of the Federal Reserve Bank of San Francisco and its Seattle Branch, Anchorage, July 11, 2007.

Morehouse, Thomas A., "Alaska's Political and Economic Future" (Lecture Notes and Illustrations), a lecture delivered to the faculty at the University of Alaska Anchorage, on his retirement, April 28, 1994.

Thomas, Clive. S., "Alaska," in Haider-Markel, ed., *Political Encyclopedia of U.S. States and Regions*, cited in section 2 above, vol. 1, 353–64.

Thomas, Clive S., "Politics in Alaska: Is It Really Different from Other Places?" in Araji, ed., *Society: An Alaskan Perspective*, cited in section 3 above, 287–97.

Newspapers, Newsletters, Policy Institutes, Blogs, and Websites

Besides print editions, the state's major newspaper, *The Alaska Dispatch News* (http://www.adn.com), as well as the *Fairbanks News Miner*, the *Juneau Empire*, and other local and regional papers, such as *The Bristol Bay Times* and *The Arctic Sounder*, are all online. The weekly *Anchorage Press* also covers politics in both the Anchorage area and statewide.

Major state organizations, like the PTA (Parent Teachers' Association) and the Association of Alaska School Boards (AASB) have newsletters that often go into depth on issues. Some organizations restrict circulation of these to members but sometimes they will send them to other interested parties. There are also subscription newsletters and other publications, such as the *Alaska Legislative Digest* (www.alaskareports.org/).

There are also a number of so-called policy institutes in Alaska that can be useful sources of political and policy information, though many have a particular political or economic slant. The most objective is the Institute of Social and Economic Research (ISER) at the University of Alaska Anchorage (www.iser.uaa.alaska.edu). Others include: the Alaska Policy Forum (www.alaskapolicyforum.org), with a conservative bias;

Commonwealth North (www.commonwealthnorth) with a general Alaska polity focus; and the Institute of the North (http://www.institutenorth.org) dealing with Arctic as well as other issues.

There are also a number of blogs on the Web on Alaska politics. Some have been around for several years. Others come and go with little notice. They are mostly free but vary widely in quality, reliability and how current they are. They also tend to be somewhat general and sometimes ideologically biased. As of January 2016 the major ones included: The Mudflats (http://www.themudflats.net); Alaska Politics and Elections (http://ape-online.org/); Alaska Commons (http://www.alaskacommons.com): and Inside Alaska Politics (http://insidealaskapolitics.com).

The State of Alaska's general website is at http://www.state.ak.us/. Websites for the three branches, departments, and agencies of government are provided in the next section.

5. GOVERNMENTAL INSTITUTIONS AND PROCESSES

This section includes the constitution, the three branches of government, local government, intergovernmental relations and federalism, and the budget process and state finances.

The Constitution

Alaska's constitution can be read online, at www.ltgov.state.ak.us/constitution.php.

Fischer, Victor, *Alaska's Constitutional Convention* (Fairbanks: University of Alaska Press, 1975),

Harrison, Gordon S., *Alaska's Constitution: A Citizen's Guide*, 5th ed. (Juneau: Alaska Legislative Affairs Agency, 2012).

———, "Alaska's Constitutional 'Literacy Test' and the Question of Voting Discrimination," *Alaska History*, 22 (Spring/Fall 2007): 23–38.

Havelock, John, *Let's Get it Right: Why We Need an Alaska Constitutional Convention* (Anchorage, AK: Todd Communications, 2012).

McBeath, Gerald A., *The Alaska State Constitution: A Reference Guide* (Westport, CT: Greenwood Press, 1997).

Tarr, G. Alan. *Understanding State Constitutions* (Princeton, NJ: Princeton University Press, 2000).

The Legislature

Alaska Legislature website, at http://w3.legis.state.ak.us/index.php.

Legislative Affairs Agency (LAA) general website, at http://w3.legis.state.ak.us/laa/laa.php.

Hamm, Keith E., and Gary F. Moncrief, "Legislative Politics in the States," in Gray, Hanson, and Kousser, *Politics in the American States*, cited in Section 2 above.

National Council of State Legislatures (NCSL), at http://www.ncsl.org.

Rosenthal, Alan, *Engines of Democracy: Politics & Policymaking in State Legislatures* (Washington, D.C.: CQ Press, 2009).

Ross, Jonathan S., "A New Answer for an Old Question: Should Alaska Once Again Consider a Unicameral Legislature?" *Alaska Law Review*, XXVII, no. 2 (December 2010): 257–96.

Squire, Peverill, and Gary Moncrief, *State Legislatures Today: Politics Under the Domes* (New York: Longman/Pearson, 2010).

Wright, Ralph W., *Inside the Statehouse: Lessons from the Speaker* (Washington, D.C.: CQ Press, 2005).

The Governor and the Executive Branch

Governor's Office general website, at http://www.gov.state.ak.us/.

Lieutenant Governor, at http://ltgov.state.ak.us/.

List of Departments, at http://www.state.ak.us/local/akdir1.shtml.

Ferguson, Margaret, "Governors and the Executive Branch," in Gray, Hanson, and Kousser, *Politics in the American States*, cited in Section 2 above.

National Governors Association (NGA), at http://www.nga.org.

Rosenthal, Alan, *The Best Job in Politics: Exploring How Governors Succeed as Policy Leaders* (Washington, D.C.: CQ Press 2013).

______, *Governors and Legislatures: Contending Powers* (Washington, D.C.: Congressional Quarterly Press 1990).

Thomas, Clive S. "'The Thing' That Shook Alaska: The Events, the Fallout and the Lessons of Alaska's Gubernatorial Impeachment Proceedings," *State Legislatures* 13, no. 2 (February 1987): 22–25.

Western Governors Association (WGA), at http://www.westgov.org/.

The Judiciary and the Courts

Alaska Court System General Website, at http://www.state.ak.us/courts/.

American Judicature Society (AJS), at http://www.ajs.org/.

Hall, Melinda Gann, "State Courts: Politics and the Judicial Process," in Gray, Hanson, and Kousser, *Politics in the American States*, cited in Section 2 above.

National Center for State Courts (NCSC), at http://www.ncsc.org/.

Thomas, Clive S., Michael L. Boyer, and Ronald J. Hrebenar, "Interest Groups and State Court Elections, 1980–2000: A New Era and Its Challenges," *Judicature: The Journal of the American Judicature Society* 87, no. 3 (November-December, 2003): 135–44, and 149.

Local Government

Cease, Ronald C., and Jerome R. Saroff, *The Metropolitan Experience in Alaska: A Study of Borough Government* (New York: Praeger, 1968).

Christensen, Terry, *Local Politics: A Practical Guide to Governing at the Grassroots*, 2nd ed. (Armonk, NY: M. E. Sharpe, 2006).

Fischer, Victor, *Issues of Regional Government in Alaska* (Fairbanks: Institute of Social, Economic and Government Research, University of Alaska, 1974).

Morehouse, Thomas A., and Victor Fischer, "Borough Government in Alaska: A Study of State-Local Relations," ISEGR Report no. 29 (Anchorage: Institute of Social, Economic and Government Research, 1971).

Morehouse, Thomas A., Gerald A. McBeath, and Linda Leask, *Alaska's Urban and Rural Governments* (Lanham, MD: University Press of America, 1984).

Thomas, Clive S., Anthony T. Nakazawa, and Carl E. Shepro, "Alaska," in *Home Rule in America: A Fifty-State Handbook*, eds. Dale Krane, Platon N. Rigos, and Mel Hill (Washington, D.C.: Congressional Quarterly Press, 2000), 33–40.

Intergovernmental Relations and Federalism

Alaska Statehood Commission, *More Perfect Union: A Preliminary Report* (Juneau, AK: 1982).

Elazar, Daniel J., *American Federalism: A View from the States*, 3rd ed. (New York: Harper and Row, 1984).

Hanson, Russell L., "Intergovernmental Relations," in Gray, Hanson, and Kousser, *Politics in the American States*, cited in Section 2 above.

Hanson, Russell L., ed., *Governing Partners: State-Local Relations in the United States* (Boulder, CO: Westview Press, 1998).

Homans, Charles, "State of Dependence: Ted Stevens's Alaska Problem—and Ours," *The Washington Monthly* (Nov. 2007), 12–17.

Roberts, Malcolm B., ed., *Going Up in Flames: The Promises and Pledges of Alaska Statehood Under Attack* (Anchorage: Alaska Pacific University Press, for Commonwealth North, 1990).

Stephens, R. Ross, and Nelson Wikstrom, *American Intergovernmental Relations: A Fragmented Federal Polity* (New York: Oxford University Press, 2006).

Thomas, Clive S., "Intergovernmental Relations in Alaska: Development, Dynamics and Lessons." *The Northern Review*, no. 23 (Summer 2001): 17–37.

The Budget and State Revenues

Alaska Department of Revenue, at http://www.revenue.state.ak.us.

Alaska Legislative Budget Handbook: For Legislators and Legislative Staff (Juneau: Alaska Legislature, Division of Legislative Finance, 2014), at http://www.legfin.akleg.gov/Other/SwissArmyKnife14.pdf.

Alaska Office of Management and Budget, at www.gov.state.ak.us/omb.

Budgeting 101 (Alaska Office of Management and Budget, 2005/06).

Commonwealth North, "The State's Operating Budget: Critical Crossroads, Choices and Opportunities" A Commonwealth Study Report (Anchorage: Commonwealth North, 2015).

Goldsmith, Scott, Linda Leask, and Mary Killorin, "Alaska's Budget: Where the Money Came from and Went, 1990–2001," Fiscal Policy Papers (Anchorage: University of Alaska Anchorage, ISER), no. 13, May 2003.

Gosling, James J. *Budgetary Politics in American Governments*, Sixth Edition (New York: Routledge, 2016).

Institute of Social and Economic Research (ISER), "The Alaska Disconnect," *The Alaska Citizen's Guide to the Budget, Budget FAQs* (Anchorage: University of Alaska Anchorage, ISER, April 2003).

Legislative Budget Guide: The Swiss Army Knife of Budget Handbooks (Juneau: Alaska State Legislature, Legislative Finance Division, 2006).

Lowry, Robert C., "Fiscal Policy in the American States," in Gray, Hanson, and Kousser, *Politics in the American States*, cited in Section 2 above.

Rubin, Irene S., *The Politics of Public Budgeting: Getting and Spending, Borrowing and Balancing*, 5th ed. (Washington, D.C.: CQ Press, 2005).

The Tax Foundation, at http://taxfoundation.org/.

6. POLICY MAKING, POLITICAL INSTITUTIONS, AND INFLUENCES ON PUBLIC POLICY

The Policy Making Process: Academic Overviews and Practical Perspectives

Birkland, Thomas A. *An Introduction to the Policy Process: Theories, Concepts and Models of Public Policy Making*, 4th. ed. (New York: Routledge 2016).

Clark, Tim W., *The Policy Process: A Practical Guide for Natural Resource Professionals* (New Haven, CT: Yale University Press, 2002).

Eshbaugh-Soha, Matthew, and Kenneth J. Meier, "Economic and Social Regulation," in *Politics in the American States: A Comparative Analysis*, eds. Virginia Gray and Russell L. Hanson 9th. ed. (Washington, D.C.: CQ Press, 2008).

Kraft, Michael E., and Scott R. Furlong, *Public Policy: Politics, Analysis and Alternatives*, 4th ed. (Washington, D.C.: CQ Press, 2012).

Heymann, Philip B., *Living the Policy Process* (New York: Oxford University Press, 2008).

Rushefski, Mark E., *Public Policy in the United States*, 5th ed. (Armonk, New York: M. E. Sharpe, 2013).

Political Parties, Elections and Campaigns

Alaska Division of Elections, at http://www.elections.alaska.gov/index.php.

Alaska Public Offices Commission (APOC), at http://www.state.ak.us/apoc/

Bowler, Shaun, and Todd Donovan, "The Initiative Process," in Gray, Hanson, and Kousser, *Politics in the American States*, cited in Section 2 above.

Burbank, Matthew J., Ronald J. Hrebenar, and Robert C. Benedict, *Parties, Interest Groups and Political Campaigns* (Boulder, CO: Paradigm Publishers, 2008).

Cronin, Thomas E., *Direct Democracy: The Politics of Initiative, Referendum and Recall* (Cambridge, MA: Harvard University Press, 1999),

Harrison, Gordon S., "The Aftermath of *In Re 2001* Redistricting Cases: The Need for a New Constitutional Scheme for Legislative Redistricting in Alaska," *Alaska Law Review*, XXIII, no. 1 (June 2006): 51–79.

Holbrook, Thomas M., and Raymond J. La Raja, "Parties and Elections," in Gray, Hanson, and Kousser, *Politics in the American States*, cited in Section 2 above.

Maisel, L. Sandy, and Mark D. Brewer, *Parties and Elections in America: The Electoral Process*, 6th ed. (Latham, MD: Rowman & Littlefield, 2012).

Moncrief, Gary, ed., *Reapportionment and Redistricting in the West* (Latham, MD: Lexington Books, 2011).

Wilson, James Q., *Political Organizations* (Princeton, NJ: Princeton University Press, 1995).

Interest Groups and Lobbying

Berry, Jeffrey, M., and Clyde Wilcox, *The Interest Group Society*, 5th ed. (New York: Longmans, 2008).

Hrebenar, Ronald J., and Bryson B. Morgan, *Lobbying in America* (Santa Barbara, CA: ABC-Clio, 2009).

Kaiser, Robert G., *Too Damn Much Money: The Triumph of Lobbyists and the Erosion of American Government* (New York: Alfred A. Knopf, 2009).

Lobbying, PACs, and Campaign Finance: 50 State Handbook (Minneapolis, MN: West Publishing and the State Capital Group, 2014).

Nownes, Anthony J., Clive S. Thomas, and Ronald J. Hrebenar, "Interest Groups in the States," in *Politics in the American States: A Comparative Analysis*, eds. Virginia Gray and Russell L. Hanson, 9th ed. (Washington, D.C.: CQ Press, 2008).

Rosenthal, Alan, *The Third House: Lobbyists and Lobbying in the States*, 2nd ed. (Washington, D.C.: CQ Press, 2001).

Thomas, Clive S. "Transparency in Public Affairs: Lessons from the Mixed Experience of the United States," in *Challenge & Response: Essays on Public Affairs & Transparency*, eds. Tom Spencer and Conor McGrath (Brussels: Landmarks Press, 2006), 41–48.

______. *Dealing Effectively with Alaska State Government: Lobbying the Legislature, Governor's Office and State Agencies* (Anchorage, University of Alaska Corporate Programs, 2010).

______. "Lobbying in the United States: An Overview for Students, Scholars and Practitioners," in *The Handbook of Public Affairs*, ed. Phil Harris and Craig Fleisher (London: Sage Publications, 2005).

Thomas, Clive S., and Richard Elgar, "Interest Groups in Washington State: The Political Dynamics of Representation, Influence and Regulation," in *Governing Washington: Politics and Government in the Evergreen State*, eds. Clayton and Lovrich, cited in Section 2 above.

The Media and Public Opinion

Alaska Media Directory (Anchorage: Published by Sally B. Blackford and Henry M. Walker, 2015).

Berinsky, Adam J., *Silent Voices: Public Opinion and Political Participation in America* (Princeton, NJ: Princeton University Press, 2004).

Cohen, Jeffery E., ed., *Public Opinion in State Politics* (Stanford, CA: Stanford University Press, 2006).

Carocci, Vincent P., *A Capitol Journey: Reflections on the Press, Politics, and the Making of Public Policy in Pennsylvania* (University Park, PA: Penn State University Press, 2005).

Erikson, Robert S., Gerald C. Wright, and John P. McIver, *Statehouse Democracy: Public Opinion and Policy in the American States* (New York: Cambridge University Press, 1993).

Fineberg, Richard A., "The Press and Alaska Politics," in McBeath and Morehouse, *Alaska State Government and Politics*, cited in Section 4 above, 222–23.

Glynn, Carroll J., *et al.*, *Public Opinion*, 3rd ed. (Boulder, CO: Westview Press, 2015),

Graber, Doris A., *Media Power and American Politics*, 5th ed. (Washington, D.C.: CQ Press, 2009).

Norrander, Barbara, and Clyde Wilcox, eds., *Understanding Public Opinion*, 3rd ed. (Washington, D.C.: CQ Press, 2009).

Political Culture and Political Socialization, Political Ideology, and Issues of Corruption and Political Ethics

Political Culture, Political Socialization, and Political Ideology

Berry, William D., *et al.*, "The Measurement and Stability of State Citizen Ideology." *State Politics and Policy Quarterly* 7 (2007): 111–32.

Carsey, Tom, and Jeff Harden "New Measures of Partisanship, Ideology and Policy Mood in the American States," *State Politics and Policy Quarterly* 10 (2010): 136–56.

Cottam, Martha L., *et al.*, *Political Psychology*, 3rd ed. (New York: Psychology Press, Taylor & Francis Group, 2015).

Elazar, Daniel J., "The States and the Political Setting," in *American Federalism*, cited in Section 5 above.

Ellis, Richard J., *American Political Cultures* (New York: Oxford University Press, 1993).

Gimpel, James G., J. Celeste Lay, and Jason E. Schuknecht, *Cultivating Democracy: Civic Environments and Political Socialization in America* (Washington, D.C.: The Brookings Institution Press, 2003).

Greenberg, Edward, ed., *Political Socialization* (**Piscataway, NJ**: Aldine Transaction, 2009).

McBeath, Gerald A., "Alaska's Political Culture," in McBeath and Morehouse, *Alaska State Government and Politics*, cited in Section 4 above.

Issues of Corruption and Political Ethics

Center for Public Integrity (CPI), at http://projects.publicintegrity.org/.

Council on Governmental Ethics Laws, at www.cogel.org.

Genovese, Michael A., and Victoria A. Farrar-Myers, eds., *Corruption in American Politics* (Amherst, NY: Cambria Press, 2010).

Meier, Kenneth J., and Thomas M. Holbrook, "I Seen My Opportunities and I Took 'Em: Political Corruption in the American States," *The Journal of Politics* 54, no. 1 (February 1992):135-55.

Rosenthal, Alan. *Drawing the Line: Legislative Ethics in the States* (Lincoln: University of Nebraska Press, 1996).

Sabato, Larry J., and Glenn R. Simpson, *Dirty Little Secrets: The Persistence of Corruption in American Politics* (New York: Times Books, 1996).

Thomas, Clive S., "Interest Group Regulation Across the United States: Rationale, Development and Consequences," *Parliamentary Affairs* 51, no. 4 (October 1998): 500–15.

7. ALASKA POLITICAL ISSUES AND PUBLIC POLICIES WITH COMPARATIVE SOURCES

Economic, Budgetary and Revenue Issues and Policies

Alaska Department of Commerce, Community and Economic Development, at http://ww.commerce.state.ak.us/

Alaska Department of Labor, *Alaska Economic Trends*, published monthly.

Alaska State Legislature, Fiscal Policy Caucus, *Facts and Findings for a Long-Range Fiscal Plan for Alaska* (Juneau: December 1, 2001).

Brown, William S., and Clive S. Thomas, "Diversifying the Alaskan Economy: Political, Social and Economic Constraints," *Journal of Economic Issues* XXX, no. 2 (June 1996): 599–607.

Cornwall, Peter G., and Gerald A. McBeath, eds., *Alaska's Rural Development* (Boulder, CO: Westview Press, 1982).

Goldsmith, Scott "The Alaska Economic Database: Charting Four Decades of Change," ISER working paper 00.1 (Anchorage: University of Alaska ISER, February 2, 2000).

______. "The Remote Rural Economy of Alaska," Understanding Alaska Series (Anchorage: University of Alaska, ISER, April 12, 2007).

Goldsmith, Scott, and Eric Larson. "What Does $7.6 Billion in Federal Money Mean to Alaska?" Understanding Alaska Series, Research Summary No.2 (Anchorage: University of Alaska, ISER, November, 2003).

Rogers, George W. "The Alaska Economy and Economic Issues: An Historical Overview," in Thomas, *Alaska Public Policy Issues*, cited in Section 4 above.

International Trade and International Relations, the Arctic and the Circumpolar North

Armstrong, Terence, George W. Rogers, and Graham Rowley, *The Circumpolar North: A Political and Economic Geography of the Arctic and Sub-Arctic* (London: Methuen & Co., Ltd., 1978).

Barry, Douglas K., "Small Business Development in Russia," *Japan and Russia in Northeast Asia: Partners in the 21st Century,* eds. Vladimir I. Ivanov and Karla S. Smith (Westport, CT: Praeger, 1999), 45–54.

Brigham, Lawson W. "Globalisation and Challenges for the Maritime Arctic," in *The World Ocean in Globalisation,* eds. Davor Vidas and Peter Johan Schei (Leiden/Boston: Martinus Nijhoff Publishers/Brill, 2011).

Byers, Michael, *Who Owns the Arctic: Understanding Sovereignty Disputes in the North* (Vancouver, B.C.: Douglas and McIntyre, 2010).

Cassey, Andrew J., "State Trade Missions," Department of Economics, University of Minnesota, December 2007.

Heininen, Lassi, and Chris Southcott, eds., *Globalization and the Circumpolar North* (Fairbanks: University of Alaska Press, 2010).

Howard, Roger, *Arctic Gold Rush: The New Race for Tomorrow's Natural Resources* (London: Continuum, 2009).

Huebert, Rob, *et. al., Climate Change and International Security: The Arctic as a Bellwether* (Arlington, VA: Center for Climate and Energy Solutions, May 2012).

Knapp, Gunnar, *et al.*, "Alaska Far-East Trade and Research Cooperation: Primary Trip Report" (Anchorage: University of Alaska, ISER, and the Alaska Center for International Business, August 1989).

Young, Oran R., *Arctic Politics: Conflict and Cooperation in the Circumpolar North* (Hanover, NH: University Press of New England, 1992).

The Alaska Permanent Fund

Adams, Eric Christopher, "By the Numbers: Alaska Permanent Fund Dividend," *Alaska Dispatch*, September 18, 2012, at http://www.alaskadispatch.com/article/numbers-alaska-permanent-fund-dividend.

Alaska State Legislature, Commission on the Future of the Permanent Fund, *Alaskans on the Future of the Fund* (Juneau, AK: January 31, 1990).

Permanent Fund Corporation website, at http://www.apfc.org/home/Content/home/index.cfm.

Brown, William S., and Clive S. Thomas, "The Alaska Permanent Fund: Good Sense or Political Expediency," *Challenge: The Magazine of Economic Affairs* (September/October, 1994): 38–44.

Commonwealth North, "At the Crossroads: The Permanent Fund, Alaskans, and Alaska's Future," A Commonwealth North Study Report (Anchorage, AK: 2007).

Goldsmith, Scott, "From Oil to Assets: Managing Alaska's New Wealth," ISER Fiscal Policy Papers, no. 10, University of Alaska Anchorage, June 1998.

______, "The Alaska Permanent Fund Dividend: An Experiment in Wealth Distribution," in *Promoting Income Security as a Right: Europe and North America*, ed. Guy Standing (London: Anthem Press, 2004).

______ "TAPS at 35: Accounting for the Oil Revenues," Web Note No. 12, July 2012, at http://www.iser.uaa.alaska.edu/Publications/webnote/2012_07_11-WebNote12.pdf.

Harrison, Gordon, S. "The Economics and Politics of the Alaska Permanent Fund Dividend Program," in, Thomas, *Alaska Public Policy Issues*, cited in Section 4 above.

Rose, David A., *Saving for the Future: My Life and the Alaska Permanent Fund* (Kenmore, WA: Epicenter Press, 2008).

Warrack, Allan A., and Russell R Keddie. "Natural Resource Trust Funds: A Comparison of Alberta and Alaska Resource Funds," Western Centre for Economic Research, Information Bulletin No. 72, School of Business, University of Alberta, Edmonton, Alberta, September 2002.

Widerquist, Karl, and Michael W. Howard, eds., *Alaska's Permanent Fund Dividend: Examining Its Suitability as a Model* (New York: Palgrave Macmillan, 2012).

Land and Natural Resources Issues and Policies: General Treatments

Alaska Department of Fish and Game, at http://www.adfg.alaska.gov/index.cfm?adfg=home.main.

Alaska Department of Natural Resources, at http://dnr.alaska.gov/.

Busenberg, George J., *Oil and Wilderness in Alaska: Resources, Environmental Protection, and National Policy Dynamics* (Washington, D.C.: Georgetown University Press, 2013).

Cooley, Richard A. *Alaska: A Challenge in Conservation* (Madison, WI: University of Wisconsin Press, 1966).

Hardin, Garrett, "The Tragedy of the Commons," *Science* 162 (1968): 1243–48.

Hardin, Garrett, with John Baden, *Managing the Commons* (New York: W.H. Freeman, 1977).

Haycox, Stephen, *Frigid Embrace: Politics, Economics and Environment in Alaska* (Corvallis: Oregon State University Press, 2002).

Morehouse, Thomas A., *Alaska Resources Development: Issues of the 1980s* (Boulder, CO: Westview Press, 1984).

Robinson, James A., Ragnar Torvik, and Thierry Verdier, "Political Foundations of the Resource Curse," *Journal of Development Economics* 79 (2006): 447–68.

Troll, Kate, *Eco-nomics and Eagles: A People's Guide to Economic Development and the Environment* (Anchorage: Published by the Author, 2002).

Weeden, Robert B., *Alaska: Promises to Keep* (Boston: Houghton Mifflin, 1978).

Mining and Forestry

Durbin, Kathie, *Tongass: Pulp Politics and the Fight for the Alaska Rainforest* (Corvallis: Oregon State University Press, 2005).

North of 60 Mining News [covers Alaska and western Canada, published in Anchorage], at http://www.miningnewsnorth.com/index.shtml.

Szumigala, D. J., L. A. Harbo, and R. A. Hughes, *Alaska's Mineral Industry 2009,* Special Report (Juneau: Alaska Department of Natural Resources, Division of Geological and Geophysical Services, 2010).

Tangen, J. P. *d(2) Part 2: A Report to the People of Alaska on the Land Promises Made in ANILCA, 20 Years Later . . .* (Anchorage: Alaska Miners Association, 2000).

Environmental Issues and Policies

Alaska Department of Environmental Conservation, at http://www.dec.state.ak.us/.

Alaska State Legislature, *Final Commission Report: Alaska Climate Impact Assessment Commission,* Juneau, Alaska, March 17, 2008, at http://www.housemajority.org/coms/cli/cli_finalreport_20080301.pdf.

Allin, Craig W., *The Politics of Wilderness Preservation* (Fairbanks: University of Alaska Press, 2008).

Kaye, Roger, *The Great Wilderness: The Challenge to Establish the Arctic National Wildlife Refuge* (Fairbanks: University of Alaska Press, 2006).

Konisky, David M., and Neal D. Woods. "Environmental Policy," in Gray, Hanson, and Kousser, *Politics in the American States,* cited in Section 2 above.

McMonagle, Robert J., *Caribou and Conoco: Rethinking Environmental Politics in Alaska's ANWR and Beyond* (Lexington, MA: Lexington Books, 2009).

Nash, Roderick, *Wilderness and the American Mind,* 3rd ed. (New Haven: Yale University Press, 1982).

O'Neill, Dan, *The Firecracker Boys: H-bombs, Inupiat Eskimos, and the Roots of the Environmental Movement* (New York: St. Martin's Press, 1995).

Ross, Ken, *Environmental Conflict in Alaska* (Boulder: University Press of Colorado, 2001).

______ *Pioneering Conservation in Alaska* (Boulder: University Press of Colorado, 2006).

Vig, Norman J., and Michael E. Kraft, *Environmental Policy: New Directions for the Twenty-First Century,* 8th ed. (Washington, D.C.: CQ Press, 2012).

Oil and Gas

Alaska Natural Gas Development Authority, "The all-Alaska LNG Project: A Report to the People," Juneau, September 2004.

Alhajji, A. F., and David Huettner, "OPEC & Other Commodity Cartels: A Comparison," *Energy Policy,* vol. 28, no. 15 (2000): 1151–64.

Coates, Peter A. *The Trans-Alaska Pipeline Controversy: Technology, Conservation, and the Environment* (Fairbanks: University of Alaska Press, 1994).

Coll, Steve, *Private Empire: ExxonMobil and American Power* (New York: Penguin, 2012).

Goodstein, David, *Out of Gas: The End of the Age of Oil* (New York: W.W. Norton, 2005).

Karl, Terry Lynn, *The Paradox of Plenty: Oil Booms and Petro-States* (Berkeley: University of California Press, 1997).

McBeath, Jerry, Matthew Berman, Jonathan Rosenberg, and Mary Ehrlander, *The Political Economy of Oil in Alaska: Multinationals vs. the State* (Boulder, CO: Lynne Rienner Publishers, 2008).

Parfomak, Paul W., *The Alaska Natural Gas Pipeline: Background, Status and Issues for Congress* (Washington, D.C.: Congressional Research Service, June 9, 2011).

Petroleum News [covers Alaska and northern and western Canada, published in Anchorage], at http://www.petroleumnews.com/.

Reynolds, Douglas B., *Alaska and North Slope Natural Gas: Development Issues and U.S. and Canadian Implications* (Fairbanks: AlaskaChena Associates, 2003).

Standlea, David M., *Oil, Globalization, and the War for the Arctic Refuge* (Albany: State University of New York Press, 2006).

The Economist, "The Future of Oil: Yesterday's Fuel," p. 12, and "Briefing, 'The Global Oil Industry: Supermajordämmerung,'" August 3, 2013, 20–22.

Fisheries Economics and Politics

Alaska Department of Fish and Game, *Sustaining Alaska's Fisheries: Fifty Years of Statehood* (Juneau: State of Alaska Department of Fish and Game, 2009).

Christy, Francis T., "The Death Rattle of Open Access and the Advent of Property Rights Regimes in Fisheries," *Marine Resource Economics*, vol. 11 (1996): 287–304.

Cooley, Richard A., *Politics and Conservation: The Decline of the Alaska Salmon* (New York: Harper & Row, 1963).

Gordon, H. Scott, "The Economic Theory of a Common Property Resource: The Fishery," *The Journal of Political Economy*, vol. 62, no. 2 (1954): 124–42.

Graham, Michael, *The Fish Gate* (London: Faber & Faber, 1943).

Gray, Tim, ed., *The Politics of Fishing* (New York: St. Martin's Press, 1998).

Knapp, Gunnar, Cathy Roheim, and James L. Anderson, *The Great Salmon Run: Competition Between Wild and Farmed Salmon* (Washington, D.C.: TRAFFIC North America and World Wildlife Fund, 2007).

Mundt, J. Carl, ed. *Limited Entry into the Commercial Fisheries* (Seattle: University of Washington Institute for Marine Studies, 1974).

NOAA [National Oceanic and Atmopheric Administration], *Fisheries of the United States, 2013: A Statisiical Snapshot of 2013 Fish Landings* (Washington, D.C. NOAA Fisheris, U.S. Department of Commerce, 2014).

Tussing, Arlon, Thomas A. Morehouse, and James D. Babb, *Alaska Fisheries Policy* (Fairbanks: University of Alaska, ISER, 1972).

Native American and Alaska Native Issues and Perspectives

Alaska Native Issues in General

Berger, Thomas R., *The Long and Terrible Shadow* (Seattle: University of Washington Press, 1991).

Goldsmith, Scott, *et al.*, *The Status of Alaska Natives Report 2004* (Anchorage: University of Alaska, ISER, 2004).

Harvard Project on American Economic Development, *The State of Native Nations: Conditions Under U.S. Policies of Self-Determination*, (New York: Oxford University Press, 2008).

Roderick, Libby, eds., *Alaska Native Cultures and Issues: Responses to Frequently Asked Questions*, revised 2nd ed. (Fairbanks: University of Alaska Press, 2010).

Pevar, Stephen L., *The Rights of American Indians and their Tribes* (Carbondale: Southern Illinois University Press, 2002).

Williams, Maria Shaa Tláa, ed., *The Alaska Native Reader: History, Culture, Politics* (Durham, NC: Duke University Press, 2009).

Self-Determination, Self-Government, and Native Land Claims

Arnold, Robert D., *Alaska Native Land Claims* (Anchorage: Alaska Native Foundation, 1976).

Berger, Thomas R. *Village Journey: The Report of the Alaska Native Review Commission* (New York: Hill and Wang, 1985).

Buchanan, Travis B., "One Company, Two Worlds: The Case for Alaska Native Corporations," *Alaska Law Review* XXVII, no. 2 (December 2010): 297–340.

Case, David, and David Voluck, *Alaska Natives and American Laws*, 2nd ed. (Fairbanks: University of Alaska Press, 2002).

Daley, Patrick, and Beverly A. James, *Cultural Politics and the Mass Media: Alaska Native Voices* (Urbana: University of Illinois Press, 2004).

Kasayulie, Willie, "Sovereignty in Alaska," in *The State of Native Nations: Conditions Under U.S. Policies of Self-Determination*, The Harvard Project on American Economic Development (New York: Oxford University Press, 2008).

Liebner, Kristine Michelle, *The Political Process Model: A Case Study of the Alaskan Native Land Rights Movement, 1959–1971* (Pittsburgh, PA: Duquesne University, 2006).

Mitchell, Donald Craig, *Sold American: The Story of Alaska Natives and Their Land, 1867–1959* (Fairbanks: University of Alaska Press, 2003).

______, *Take My Land, Take My Life: The Story of Congress's Historic Settlement of Alaska Native Land Claims, 1960–1971* (Fairbanks: University of Alaska Press, 2001).

Morehouse, Thomas A., "Rebuilding the Political Economies of Alaska Native Villages," ISER Occasional Papers, no. 21 (Anchorage: University of Alaska, 1989).

______, *The Dual Political Status of Alaska Natives under U.S. Policy* (Anchorage: University of Alaska, ISER, 1992).

Skopek, Tracy A., Rich Engstrom, and Kenneth Hansen, "All That Glitters: The Rise of American Indian Tribes in State Political Behavior," *American Indian Culture & Research Journal*, 29, no. 4 (December 2005): 45–58.

Zellen, Barry Scott, *Breaking the Ice: From Land Claims to Tribal Sovereignty in the Arctic* (Lanham, MD: Lexington Books, 2008).

Subsistence Hunting, Fishing, and Gathering

Case, David S., "Subsistence and Self-Determination: Can Alaska Natives Have a More 'Effective Voice?'" *University of Colorado Law Review* 60, no. 4 (1992): 1009–35.

Cultural Survival Quarterly, Special Issue on Subsistence in Alaska, vol. 22, no. 3 (Fall 1998).

McGee, Jack B., "Subsistence Hunting and Fishing in Alaska: Does ANILCA's Rural Subsistence Priority Really Conflict with the Alaska Constitution? *Alaska Law Review* XXVII, no. 2 (December 2010): 221–55.

Thornton, Thomas F., "Subsistence in Northern Communities: Lessons from Alaska," *The Northern Review* 23 (Summer 2001): 82–102.

_____, Alaska Native Corporations and Subsistence: Paradoxical Forces in the Construction of Sustainable Communities," in *Sustainability and Communities of Place*, ed. Carl Maida (New York: Berghahn Books, 2007).

Wolfe, Robert J. "Subsistence and Politics in Alaska," in *Politics and Environment in Alaska*, ed. Alexander B. Dolitsky (Juneau: Alaska-Siberia Research Center, 1993).

Wolfe, Robert J., and Robert J. Walker. "Subsistence Economies in Alaska: Productivity, Geography, and Development Impacts," *Arctic Anthropology* 24, no. 2 (1987): 56–81.

Issues and Policies of State Services Delivery

K–12 Education

"A Failed Effort," *Fairbanks Daily News Miner*, A Six Part Series on Rural Education (January 1996).

Alaska Department of Education and Early Development, at http://www.eed.state.ak.us/.

Barnhardt, Carol, "A History of Schooling for Alaska Native People," *Journal of American Indian Education* 40, no. 1. (2001): 1–30.

Berkman, Michael B., and Eric Plutzer, "The Politics of Education," in Gray, Hanson, and Kousser, *Politics in the American States*, cited in Section 2 above.

Darling-Hammond, Linda, *The Flat World and Education: How America's Commitment to Equity Will Determine Our Future* (New York: Columbia University Teachers College Press, 2010).

McBeath, Jerry, and Maria Elena Reyes, "Testing, Testing, Testing: Rural and Urban Responses to Alaska's High-Stakes Assessment Regime," *The Northern Review*, no. 28 (Winter 2008): 207–29.

Wirt, Frederick M., and Michael W. Kirst, *The Political Dynamics of American Education* (Richmond, CA: McCutchan Publishing Corp., 2005).

Higher Education

Bever, Celia, "The Way Things Work: University Lobbying," *The Chicago Maroon*, December 4, 2012.

Cook, Constance Ewing, *Lobbying for Higher Education: How Colleges and Universities Influence Federal Policy* (Nashville: Vanderbilt University Press, 1998).

Hamilton, Mark, "The University at 50: Past, Present and Future," in G.W. Kimura, *Alaska at 50,* cited in Section 3 above.

Lowry, Robert C., and Alisa Hicklin Fryar, "The Politics of Higher Education," in Gray, Hanson, and Kousser, *Politics in the American States*, cited in Section 2 above.

Menand, Louis, *The Marketplace of Ideas: Reform and Resistance in the American University* (New York: W. W. Norton and Company, 2010).

Mettler, Suzanne, *Degrees of Inequality: How the Politics of Higher Education Sabotages the American Dream* (New York: Basic Books, 2014).

Phipps, Ron, "Making Alaska More Competitive by Preparing Citizens for College and Career," A Report Prepared for the Alaska Commission on Post Secondary Education (Washington, D.C.: The Institute for Higher Education Policy, April 2008).

Post Secondary Educational Opportunity at: http://www.postsecondary.org/ A liberal think tank that publishes useful data on higher ed.

University of Alaska system website: http://www.alaska.edu.

Social Services: General Works

Alaska Department of Health and Social Services, at http://dhss.alaska.gov/Pages/default.aspx.

Hanleybrown, Fay, John Kania, and Mark Kramer, "Challenging Change: Making Collective Impact Work," *Standford Social Innovation Review*, 2012.

Karger, Howard, and David Stoesz, *American Social Welfare Policy: A Pluralistic Approach*, 7th ed. (New York: Pearson, 2013).

Rom, Mark Carl, "State Health and Welfare Programs," in Gray, Hanson, and Kousser, *Politics in the American States*, cited in Section 2 above.

Health Care, Sustance Abuse, and Child Abuse

Alaska Advisory Board on Alcoholism and Drug Abuse, at http://dhss.alaska.gov/abada/Pages/default.aspx.

Alaska Council on Domestic Violence and Sexual Assault, at http://dps.alaska.gov/cdvsa/.

Dixon, Mim, and Yvette Roubideaux, *Promises to Keep: Public Health Policy for American Indians and Alaska Natives in the 21st Century* (Washington, D.C: American Public Health Association, 2001).

Foster, Mark A., and Scott Goldsmith, "Alaska's Health-Care Bill: $7.5 Billion and Climbing," UA Research Summary no. 18 (Anchorage: University of Alaska, ISER: August 2011).

Foster, Mark A., and Associates, Medicare section, *Estimated Economic Effects of the Patient Protection and Affordable Care Act, As Amended, in Alaska*, May 2011, at http://hss.state.ak.us/healthcommission/meetings/201110/PPACA_AK_estimates201106.pdf.

Guterman, Neil B., "Advancing Prevention Research on Child Abuse, Youth Violence, and Domestic Violence: Emerging Strategies and Issues," *Journal of Interpersonal Violence* 19 (March 2004): 299–321.

Kaiser Family Foundation, *Health Care Costs: A Primer—Key Information on Health Care Costs and their Impact* (Menlo Park, CA: Kaiser Family Foundation, August 2007), at http://www.kff.org/insurance/upload/7670.pdf.

National Coalition Against Domestic Violence, at http://www.ncadv.org/files/Alaska.pdf.

Crime and Corrections

Alaska Department of Corrections, at http://www.correct.state.ak.us/.

Alaska Judicial Council, *Recidivism in Alaska's Felony Therapeutic Courts* (Anchorage, 2007).

Alexander, Michelle, *The New Jim Crow: Mass Incarceration in the Age of Colorblindness* (New York: The New Press, 2010).

Henrichson, Christian, and Ruth Dalaney, *The Price of Prisons: What Incarceration Costs Taxpayers* (New York: The Vera Institute of Justice, Center on Sentencing and Corrections, January, 2012, updated July 2012).

Martin, Stephanie, and Steve Colt, "The Cost of Crime: Could the State Reduce Future Crime and Save Money by Expanding Education and Treatment Programs?" Research Summary No. 71 (Anchorage: University of Alaska, ISER, January 2009).

Wooldredge, John, "State Corrections Policy," in *Politics in the American States*, Gray, Hanson, and Kousser, cited in Section 2 above.

Transportation and Infrastructure

Alaska Department of Transportation and Public Facilities, at http://www.dot.alaska.gov/.

Alaska Department of Transportation and Public Facilities, *Let's Get Moving 2030: Alaska Statewide Long-Range Transportation Policy Plan Update* (Juneau, February 2008), at http://www.dot.alaska.gov/stwdplng/areaplans/2030/assets/SWLRTPPfinal022908.pdf; and *Alaska Statewide Long-Range Transportation Plan Data Refresh* (Juneau, December 1, 2010) at http://www.dot.state.ak.us/stwdplng/areaplans/2030/assets/LGM2030datarefreshfinal12-10.pdf.

Alaska University Transportation Center (AUTC), at http://ine.uaf.edu/autc/about/. AUTC is one of ten National Transportation Centers funded by the U.S. Department of Transportation. It seeks to improve transportation in cold regions through research, education, and outreach.

Epstein, Lois N., *Easy to Start, Impossible to Finish, Recommendations for Action* (Anchorage: The Alaska Transportation Priorities Project, February 2010).

______, *Easy to Start, Impossible to Finish II, Recommendations for Action* (Anchorage: The Wilderness Society, March 2012).

ICF International, *The Broader Connection between Public Transportation, Energy Conservation and Greenhouse Gas Reduction* (February 2008) at http://www.apta.com/resources/reportsandpublications/Documents/land_use.pdf.

Institute on Taxation and Economic Policy (ITEP), "A Federal Gas Tax for the Future." (Washington, D.C.: ITEP, 2013), at http://www.itep.org/pdf/fedgastax0913.pdf.

The National Academy of Public Administration, *Financing Transportation in the 21st Century: An Intergovernmental Perspective,* A Report of the Intergovernmental Forum on Transportation Finance (Washington, D.C., January 2008), at http://www.napawash.org/wp-content/uploads/2008/08-16.pdf.

Ross, Martin H., Bruce E. Seely, and Paul F. Barrett, *The Best Transportation System in the World: Railroads, Trucks, Airlines, and American Public Policy in the Twentieth Century* (Columbus: Ohio State University Press, 2006).

Saiz, Martin, and Susan E. Clarke, "Economic Development and Infrastructure Policy," in Gray, Hanson, and Kousser, *Politics in the American States,* cited in Section 2 above.

U.S. Department of Transportation, *Alaska Federal Lands Long Range Transportation Plan, Final Report* (September 2012), at http://www.blm.gov/pgdata/etc/medialib/blm/ak/aktest/planning/Transportation_Planning.Par.88739.File.dat/Alaska%20Federal%20Lands%20LRTP.pdf.

Government Performance and Efficiency in Service Delivery

Daniels, Mark R., *Terminating Public Programs: An American Political Paradox* (Armonk, NY: M. E. Sharpe, 1997).

Diiulio, John J., Jr., ed. *Deregulating the Public Service: Can Government Be Improved?* (Washington, D.C.: The Brookings Institution, 1993).

Hibbing, John R., and Elizabeth Theiss-Morse, *Stealth Democracy: Americans' Beliefs About How Government Should Work* (New York: Cambridge University Press, 2002).

Light, Paul Charles, *The Tides of Reform: Making Government Work, 1945–1995* (New Haven: Yale University Press, 1997).

National Public Radio/Kaiser Family Foundation/Kennedy School of Government, "Survey on Americans' Attitudes Toward Government" (Menlo Park, CA, and Washington, D.C., 2000).

Osborne, David, and Ted Gaebler, *Reinventing Government: How the Entrepreneurial Spirit is Transforming the Public Sector* (Reading, MA: Addison-Wesley Publishing Company, 1992).

Pew Research Center for the People and the Press, "How Americans View Government: Deconstructing Distrust" (Washington, D.C.: 1998), updated as "Public Trust in Government, 1958–2013," (October, 2013).

Task Force on Governmental Roles, *Final Report* (Juneau, AK: Office of the Governor, Office of Management and Budget, and Alaska Municipal League, July 1992).

8. BIOGRAPHIES, AUTOBIOGRAPHIES, AND POPULAR WORKS ON ALASKA

Banerjee, Subhankar, *Arctic Voices: Resistance at the Tipping Point* (New York: Seven Stories Press, 2012).

Borneman, Walter E., *Alaska: Saga of a Bold Land* (New York: HaperCollins/Perennial Books, 2003).

Coyne, Amanda, and Tony Hopfinger, *Crude Awakening: Money, Mavericks, and Mayhem in Alaska* (New York: Nation Books, Perseus Book Group, 2011).

Fischer, Victor, with Charles Wohlforth, *To Russia with Love: An Alaskan's Journey* (Fairbanks: University of Alaska Press, 2012).

Hammond, Jay S., *Tales of Alaska's Bush Rat Governor: The Extraordinary Biography of Jay Hammond, Wilderness Guide and Reluctant Politician* (Seattle, WA: Epicenter Press, 1994).

Hanrahan, John, and Peter Gruenstein, *Lost Frontier: The Marketing of Alaska* (New York: W.W. Norton, 1977).

Johnson, Kaylene, *Sarah: How a Hockey Mom Turned Alaska's Political Establishment Upside Down* (Fairbanks, AK: Epicenter Press, 2008).

Krakauer, Jon, *Into the Wild* (New York: Anchor Books, 1996).

McGinniss, Joe, *Going to Extremes: A Search for the Essence of Alaska*, 4th ed. (Kenmore, WA: Epicenter Press, 2010).

McPhee, John, *Coming Into the Country* (New York: Farrar, Straus & Giroux, 1991).

Naske, Claus-M., *Bob Bartlett of Alaska: A Life in Politics* (Fairbanks: University of Alaska Press, 1979).

______, *Ernest Gruening: Alaska's Greatest Governor* (Fairbanks: University of Alaska Press, 2004).

Palin, Sarah, *Going Rogue: An American Life* (New York: HarperCollins, 2009).

Roberts, Malcolm B., *The Wit and Wisdom of Wally Hickel* (Anchorage, AK: Searchers Press, 1994).

Roderick, Jack, *Crude Dreams: A Personal History of Oil and Politics in Alaska* (Kenmore, WA: Epicenter Press, 1997).

Thomas, Clive S. "The Sarah Palin Phenomenon: The Washington-Hollywood-Wall Street Syndrome in American Politics, and More . . ." in *Issues in American Politics: Polarized Politics in the Age of Obama*, ed. John W. Dumbrell (London: Routledge/Taylor & Francis, 2013).

ABOUT THE EDITOR AND THE CONTRIBUTORS

ABBREVIATIONS

ISER: University of Alaska Anchorage, Institute of Social and Economic Research
UAA: University of Alaska Anchorage
UAF: University of Alaska Fairbanks
UAS: University of Alaska Southeast

THE EDITOR

Clive S. Thomas who holds a Ph.D from the LSE (London School of Economic and Political Science) taught political science at UAS in Juneau from 1981 to 2011. In 1988 he established the Alaska Universities Legislative Internship Program, which he ran for twenty-five years. He is now a Senior Fellow at the Thomas S. Foley Institute for Public Policy and Public Service at Washington State University and a Visiting Professor at the University of São Paulo in Brazil.

His publications include ten books and more than sixty chapters in books and articles on U.S. state politics, including Alaska politics, and political parties and interest groups. He has received several grants and research awards, including four Fulbright Scholarships. In addition, he provides commentary on Alaska politics for TV, radio, and newspapers, and has served as a volunteer lobbyist. Through his consulting firm APAS (Alaska Political Advocacy Strategies), he teaches workshops on lobbying in Alaska, across the United States, in Western and Eastern Europe, and in Latin America and advises businesses, groups, and organizations on various aspects of lobbying and lobby regulation.

CHAPTER AUTHORS AND COAUTHORS

Douglas K. Barry, Ed.D (Columbia University), is a political consultant and a former senior international trade specialist with the U.S. Commercial Service, Department of Commerce, Washington, D.C. He has served abroad in Thailand, Hong Kong, and Singapore. Among his publications is *A Basic Guide to Exporting* (editor, 2008). From 1976 to 1997 he was a professor and administrator at UAA.

Michael L. Boyer graduated from UAS magna cum laude, received his JD from the University of Oregon in 2000, and is Associate Professor of Law Sciences at UAS. His work has appeared in *Judicature*, the *Erasmus Journal of Law and Economics*, the *USC Interdisciplinary Law Journal*, and in books on law and public policy.

Britteny A. Cioni-Haywood holds an MSc in Natural Resource Economics from the University of Arkansas and is a Ph.D candidate at Colorado State University, with specializations in environmental and gender economics, and economic development. From 2006 to 2010 she taught economics at UAS. She is now a senior administrator for the Alaska Department of Commerce, Community & Economic Development.

Ronald G. Clarke, who holds a BS in Fish and Wildlife Management (1977) and an MS in Zoology (1987), retired in 2009 as Assistant Director, Wildlife Conservation Division, Alaska Department of Fish & Game. He was Special Assistant to Alaska Governors Steve Cowper and Tony Knowles, and worked as an aide in the Alaska legislature. He now consults for Ron Clarke & Associates and works for the Alaska legislature.

Billy G. Connor, P.E. (Professional Engineer), is Director of the UAF Transportation Center. His experience includes thirty-two years with the Alaska Department of Transportation and Public Facilities, including twenty years as the department's Statewide Research Manager.

Patrick M. Cunningham holds a Ph.D in Social Work and is Associate Professor, School of Social Work, at UAA where he teaches courses in social welfare policy. On sabbatical leave in 2008 he worked in the Alaska legislature. Earlier, he was a faculty member in the Department of Psychiatry, Wake Forest University Medical School, in North Carolina.

Dave Donaldson was a reporter for the Alaska Public Radio Network (APRN) in Juneau from 1991 until 2012, during which time he covered twenty-two regular legislative sessions and five governors. He has a degree in Journalism from Georgia State University in Atlanta and was working for a commercial radio network in North Carolina before coming to Alaska.

Mike Doogan is a third-generation Alaskan who served in the Alaska Legislature from 2007 to 2013. He is a Pulitzer prize-winning journalist and award-winning author of fiction and nonfiction works about Alaska.

Alison M. Elgee has a BS in Business Finance, from the University of Idaho. She is a former Assistant Commissioner for the Department of Health and Social Services in charge of Finance and Management Services. Her extensive state budget experience includes being the Director of the Office of Management and Budget (OMB) for Governor Steve Cowper, 1988–1990.

George Goldman, who received his MS from the Massachusetts Institute of Technology, is a retired economist with the University of California Berkeley, Cooperative Extension

Service. His research includes public land use policy and economic analysis of communities and regions in individual western states and comparatively across the American West.

Scott Goldsmith earned his Ph.D in economics from the University of Wisconsin. He is a Professor Emeritus of Economics with ISER at UAA. He worked at ISER from 1975 to 2012. Among his major research interests are regional economics, Alaska fiscal policy, and energy demand.

Robert F. Gorman, MS Washington State University, is a Professor Emeritus with the UAF Cooperative Extension Service and past Chair, Extension Natural Resources and Rural Development Program. He has served as president of the Farm Foundation's National Public Policy Education Committee.

Gordon S. Harrison, Ph.D, is retired and lives in Juneau. He is a former Executive Director of the Alaska Redistricting Board, Director of the Alaska Legislative Research Agency, Associate Director of the Alaska Office of Management and Budget, and Associate Professor of Political Science at UAF.

Alexandra "Lexi" Hill is a Research Associate at ISER with twenty-five years of experience in public policy research including education policy issues and grant evaluation. She has a master's degree in Public Affairs from Princeton University, an MS in Business Administration from Boston University, and a BS in Engineering Science from Dartmouth College.

Diane B. Hirshberg is the Director, Center for Alaska Education Policy Research and Professor of Education Policy at UAA's ISER. Her research interests include education policy, Alaska Native education, and school improvement initiatives. She received her BA from the University of California–Berkeley, an MPA from Columbia University, and a Ph.D in Education from the University of California–Los Angeles.

Bernice M. Joseph, who passed away in January 2014, was Vice Chancellor for Rural, Community, and Native Education at UAF. In this post she oversaw eight academic units plus the state Cooperative Extension Service, the Center for Distance Education, the Department of Alaska Native and Rural Development, and other services. She earned her BA in 1989 and MBA in 1998 from UAF.

Robert W. "Bob" King reported on fishery issues as news director of public radio station KDLG in Dillingham for seventeen years before being hired as Press Secretary for Governor Tony Knowles. Since then, he has provided media and related services for clients including the Marine Conservation Alliance and the Alaska Trollers Association, and worked in Washington D.C. as Legislative Assistant on fishery and related issues for former U.S. Senator Mark Begich. He returned to live in Juneau in 2015.

Kristina Klimovich has a Master's degree in International Affairs from the New School University in New York City and a Bachelor's degree in Social Sciences from UAS. She has extensive experience as a graduate research assistant in political science as well as broad experience working for non-profit advocacy, research, and aid organizations. Kristina spent three years promoting sustainability in commercial real estate with a national non-profit advocate, PACE*Now*. Currently she lives in the Netherlands pursing a career in financing sustainability development projects.

Gunnar Knapp, Ph.D in Economics from Yale University, is a former Director and a Professor Emeritus of Economics at UAA's ISER. Since 1981, he has been engaged in research on the Alaska economy, particularly markets for and the management of Alaska resources.

M. Wayne Marr, Ph.D Texas Tech University, is a former Professor of Finance at UAF. He is now a Professor at Meta Business School. and a director at SEED CX, a financial trading company, as well as CEO of the Finance Economics Associaiton. He has authored over forty academic articles. Before his appointment at UAF he taught at Virginia Tech, Tulane University, and Clemson University, and worked at Computer Sciences Corporation and other firms.

John P. McIver, Ph.D, Indiana University, is a Senior Lecturer in Government at the University of Texas at Austin, and previously taught at the universities of Colorado, Houston, and New Mexico. He has co-authored two books, and authored or co-authored numerous articles in academic journals. From 1994 to 1996 he directed the Political Science Program at the National Science Foundation.

Anthony T. "Tony" Nakazawa, Ph.D, University of California-Berkeley, is Professor of Economics, UAF Cooperative Extension Service, and was Extension Director from 1997 to 2007. He has served as Director of the Alaska Division of Community and Rural Development, on the Alaska Local Boundary Commission, and the Alaska Board of Agriculture and Conservation.

Emil Notti is an Alaska Native leader who was the first president of the Alaska Federation of Natives (AFN). He graduated from Northrop University in California in aeronautical and electrical engineering. His public service includes several senior positions in state government, most recently as Commissioner of the Department of Commerce, Community, and Economic Development for Governor Sean Parnell.

Douglas B. Reynolds, Ph.D in economics, University of New Mexico, is professor of oil and energy economics at UAF. He has worked on oil and energy issues in Kazakhstan, Norway, Mexico, Russia, Poland, France, and Alaska. His publications include many academic articles and two books on energy. He also works as a consultant.

Kevin C. Ritchie is a past municipal manager of Juneau and retired in 2006 as Executive Director of the Alaska Municipal League and a member of the Federal Denali Commission. He received his MPA from UAS in 2003 and has been an adjunct professor in that program.

Mary Sattler is a Yup'ik Eskimo who grew up in three small villages on the Kuskokwim River. As Mary Nelson, she served in the Alaska State Legislature from 1999 to 2009 as a Representative for Bethel and the surrounding villages. She has worked as Community Relations Manager for the Donlin Creek Mine Project and is currently a contract lobbyist.

Laura C. "Lola" Savatgy, who received her MPA from UAS, has held analyst positions for the State of Alaska, at the Pentagon in Washington, D.C., and is currently Chief of Performance Improvement, U.S. Department of Veterans Affairs in California. She has also been a legislative intern in the Alaska legislature and co-authored articles on interest groups.

Carl E. Shepro is a Professor Emeritus of Political Science at UAA. He specialized in American government, Alaska state and local, including Alaska Native, government, and politics. His publications include articles and chapters on Alaska politics and Alaska Native government. From 2005 to 2011 he was President of United Academics, one of the two University of Alaska faculty unions. He now works as a consultant.

Thomas F. Thornton, Ph.D, University of Washington in Anthropology, taught at UAS from 1992 to 2000. Currently he is Senior Research Fellow at the University of Oxford Environmental Change Institute, where he directs the graduate program in environmental change and management. He has conducted research and published on Alaska Native issues since 1989, including, *Being and Place Among the Tlingit* (University of Washington Press, 2008).

Jason E. Turo holds bachelor's and master's degrees in Finance from UAF. His research interests include entrepreneurial development, capital markets, and fiscal policy. While at Wells Fargo in Alaska he was recognized as their top banker. Currently, he is a Research Consultant with Thomson Reuters in Ann Arbor, Michigan.

Fran Ulmer is the Chair of the U.S. Arctic Research Commission, Advisor for Arctic Science and Policy to the U.S. Secretary of State, and served on the Presidential Commission on the *Deep Water Horizon* Oil Spill. Previously, she was Governor Hammond's legislative assistant and Director of Policy Development and Planning, Juneau's Mayor (1983–1985), State Representative (1986–1994), Lieutenant Governor (1994–2002), a fellow at the Institute of Politics at Harvard (2003), a Distinguished Visiting Professor of Public Policy at UAA (2004), Director of ISER (2005–2007), and Chancellor of UAA from 2007 to 2011.

OTHER CONTRIBUTORS

Ashley E. Anderson has a social science degree from UAS. Of Tlingit and Aleut descent, she has conducted policy research for the First Alaskans Institute and worked as an aide to former Senator Kookesh in the Alaska state legislature.

George Ascott has a BA from UAS, and is currently an aide to Representative Chris Tuck of Anchorage. He has worked for Governor Tony Knowles and other legislators, and managed political campaigns.

Rick Barrier is a former Executive Director of Commonwealth North. He has also worked for the Alaska Court System. His BSc is from Yale University and his MBA from Stanford University.

Jeff Berliner, BA in philosophy, University of California–Berkeley, is a retired Alaska Public Offices Commission (APOC) investigator. He worked for many years as a journalist, including as an investigative reporter.

Bruce Botelho served four terms as Mayor of Juneau and was Alaska's Attorney General for two governors. His BA and JD are from Willamette University (Salem, Oregon), and his ZP (Germanistik) is from Ruprecht Karl University (Heidelberg, Germany).

Tim Bradner is editor of the *Alaska Economic Report* and natural resources writer for the *Alaska Journal of Commerce*. He has a bachelor's degree from Vermont College and received an MPA from the Kennedy School of Government at Harvard University in1985.

Wendy Chamberlain is one of Alaska's top contract lobbyists and owns the firm Legislative Consultants. A registered nurse born and raised in Australia, her participation in Alaska politics began as an advocate for abused children. She has worked as a legislative liaison and held other positions in state government.

Harry Crawford, a Louisiana ironworker and union activist, represented east Anchorage in the Alaska House of Representatives from 2001 to 2011. He pursued a populist agenda of direct government and maximizing public benefits from Alaska's resources and particularly developing renewable energy capabilities.

Lois N. Epstein, P.E. (Professional Engineer) has a master's degree from Stanford University in civil engineering. She has over twenty-five years of public policy expertise. A former Director of the Alaska Transportation Priorities Project, she is now the Arctic Program Director for The Wilderness Society and a member of the Offshore Energy Safety Advisory Committee for the U.S. Department of the Interior.

Gregg Erickson is an economic consultant and journalist who wrote a syndicated monthly column for the former *Anchorage Daily News*. He frequently testifies as an economic expert in state and federal courts.

Victor Fischer is Director Emeritus of ISER, and was a delegate to the Alaska Constitutional Convention in 1955–1956. He also served in the Alaska Territorial Legislature and in the Alaska State Senate.

Lyda Green represented the Matanuska-Susitna Valley in the Alaska Senate from 1995–2009. She was the Co-Chair of Senate Finance for four years before ending her tenure as the Senate President.

Judy Hargis is a community development consultant who worked for Alaska state government for many years. This including the Alaska Department of Commerce, Community, and Economic Development, and the Local Boundary Commission.

Eric B. Herzik is a Professor of Political Science at the University of Nevada in Reno and has been department chair on several occasions. He has published extensively on state politics, including two edited books and multiple articles on Nevada politics.

Walter J. Hickel, who died in 2010, served twice as Governor of Alaska and was U.S. Secretary of the Interior under President Nixon. In 1995, he established the Institute of the North.

Krag Johnsen is the Vice President for Revenue for the Alaska Wireless Network. Previously he was Director of Rural Broadband Development at GCI Communications and Chief Operating Officer for the Denali Commission.

Stan Jones, a former journalist, retired in 2013 as Director of External Affairs for the Prince William Sound Regional Citizens' Advisory Council. In 2009 the council published an oral history of the 1989 *Exxon Valdez* oil spill that he co-wrote.

John W. Katz, who holds BA and JD degrees, ran the Governor's Office in Washington, D.C., for eight gubernatorial administrations before retiring in 2012. He has held other top-level positions, including Alaska Commissioner of Natural Resources. In 1994, he received an honorary degree from the University of Alaska.

Tony Knowles was a two-term governor of Alaska (1994–2002) and previously a two-term mayor of Anchorage. In 2010 he was appointed to the National Park System Advisory Board by the Secretary of the Interior.

Mary Lou Madden, Ph.D in economics from American University, has been involved with education in Alaska since 1972, for the Alaska Department of Education and as Dean of Faculty at UAS. She now runs her own educational consulting firm.

Daniel Monteith is Associate Professor of Anthropology and former Chair of the Social Science Department at UAS. He is a member of the Board of Directors of the Alaska Anthropology Association.

Bill Noll, who died in 2011, was a former Mayor of Seward, and served under Governor Murkowski as Commissioner of the Department of Commerce, Community and Economic Development. Earlier he served under Governor Hickel as Deputy Commissioner for International Trade.

Jeffery C. Ottesen is the Division Director for planning activities with the Alaska Department of Transportation and Public Facilities. He received his BS from Washington State University and MS from the University of Massachusetts.

Terry Otness has worked as assistant to Tlingit-Haida Central Council's Tribal Energy Director, as a legislative aide, and is an exponent for a Southeast Alaska-Canadian transportation and energy corridor. He is currently pursuing a postsecondary degree.

George Owletuck, MA in rural development, is President of Angall'kut, Inc., a business development enterprise. His prior experience includes UAF Assistant Professor of Alaska Native Studies, work in the office of Senator Ted Stevens, and as a University of Alaska legislative intern.

Karen Perdue served as President and CEO of the Alaska State Hospital and Nursing Home Association (2010–2014). Previously she was Associate Vice President for the University of Alaska Statewide System, and Alaska Commissioner of Health and Social Services, 1994–2001. As Commissioner she co-founded and led the Children's Cabinet.

Julie Riley is a Professor of Extension Education with the UAF Cooperative Extension Service. She received her BS in 1977 and MS in 1980 from the University of Wisconsin-Madison.

Malcolm B. Roberts, Senior Fellow at the Institute of the North, served as Special Assistant to Governor Hickel both when he was Interior Secretary (1969–1970) and Alaska's governor (1990–1994).

Bill Sheffield, one of Alaska's most successful businessmen, was governor of Alaska from 1982 to 1986. Since then he has been President of the Alaska Railroad and Director of the Port of Anchorage, and is engaged in many other public activities.

Arthur Snowden, who holds a BA and JD, was the Director of the Alaska State Court System from 1973 to 1997. Before that he ran the courts in Montgomery County, Maryland, and taught political science.

Kate Troll is former Executive Director of both the Alaska Conservation Alliance and the Southeast Alaska Seiners Association. She helped negotiate the State Forest Practices Act of 1990 and was subsequently appointed to the State of Alaska Board of Forestry. In the 1980s she served on the Ketchikan Gateway Borough and was elected to the City and Borough of Juneau Assembly in 2013.

Nancy Bear Usera served in Alaska cabinet positions and in 1994 as Chief of Staff for Governor Hickel. Previously she provided government relations and policy development for state and national trade associations, primarily in Washington, D.C. She was Senior Vice President for Corporate Development at Alaska USA Federal Credit Union and served as Employee Relations Director for the Municipality of Anchorage until her retirement in 2011.

Bill Wielechowski, BS, JD from Seton Hall University in New Jersey, is a State Senator serving northeast Anchorage. He has served on numerous community organizations in Anchorage and is a practicing attorney.

Miranda Hildebrand Wright, BA, MA in cultural anthropology from UAF, is a retired Associate Professor and Director Emeritus of the UAF Department of Alaska Native Studies and Rural Development. She has served as Chair of Doyon, Limited, and is a current Doyon board member.

Reuben Yerkes has a bachelor's degree in International Relations and Economics from Bethany College in West Virginia. He has worked for a lobbyist, the governor's legislative liaison office, the Alaska Public Offices Commission (APOC), for the city attorney in Sitka in Southeast Alaska, and is currently working for the U.S. State Department.

Michael Young, has a BA in Government from UAS, and has worked in the Alaska legislature as an intern and a staffer and for the Alaska Ferry System as a manager. He is now an educator with the Juneau School District.

INDEX

B

E

M

N

O